MW01008341

LAW AND ECONOMICS: PRIVATE AND PUBLIC

MAXWELL L. STEARNS
VENABLE, BAETJER & HOWARD PROFESSOR OF LAW
UNIVERSITY OF MARYLAND FRANCIS KING CAREY SCHOOL OF LAW

TODD J. ZYWICKI
FOUNDATION PROFESSOR OF LAW
ANTONIN SCALIA LAW SCHOOL, GEORGE MASON UNIVERSITY

THOMAS J. MICELI
PROFESSOR
UNIVERSITY OF CONNECTICUT

Foreword by *TOM ULEN*

444 Cedar Street, Suite 700
St. Paul, MN 55101
1-877-888-1330

Printed in the United States of America

ISBN: 978-1-62810-215-4

To Vered, Shira, Keren and Eric

MS

To Claire

TZ

To Ana Maria, Tommy and Nick

TM

Foreword

Thomas S. Ulen[1]

It is an honor and, more than that, a pleasure to introduce this important volume. Professors Stearns, Zywicki, and Miceli, are prolific and important legal and economic scholars. Their various articles and previous books have been on a wide variety of legal topics and were principally addressed to the academic profession, where they received an enthusiastic reception. What they have done in this volume is different from their previous work and addresses different audiences. This work is a significant addition to the literature that began in the 1970s linking economics and the law. So, in order to show this work's importance, let me place it in the context of that now-large intellectual development.

When law and economics began,[2] and for its first 30 years or so, its novelty was to use economics to analyze legal doctrines in the core areas of law—property, contract, tort, civil and criminal procedure, and the like. Theretofore, economics and law had commingled only in the areas of antitrust or competition law, governmental regulation of natural monopoly, and the computation of damages.

Using economics—specifically, the tools of microeconomic theory—to look at those areas that had never been previously touched, by outside academic disciplines (save, perhaps, philosophy) was both intriguing and unsettling to the rest of the legal academy. The intriguing part was that rational choice theory (the default economic theory of behavior) seemed to suggest some new insights into how the law might guide behavior. For example, the notion of efficient breach—that there might be circumstances in which it might be better than performing the contractual promise for the breacher not to perform but to compensate the innocent party for failing to perform (thereby making her no worse off than if performance had occurred)—allowed important new ways of thinking about contract remedies, including liquidated damages. And in tort law, the law-and-economics focus on the ability of the exposure to tort liability to induce social-cost-minimizing precaution shifted the analytical emphasis from *ex post* fairness to *ex ante* efficiency. It also demonstrated that tort liability and safety regulation are related (both as complements and, possibly, substitutes)—a fact that opened a fruitful new area of comparative analysis (one, incidentally, in which there is still much work to be done).

The unsettling aspects of law and economics were, first, that it introduced another normative goal for law (namely, efficiency), necessitating law's finding the right balance

---

[1] Swanlund Chair Emeritus, University of Illinois at Urbana-Champaign; Professor of Law Emeritus, University of Illinois College of Law; Faculty Fellow, Texas A&M University Institute for Advanced Studies, and Distinguished Visiting Professor, Texas A&M School of Law, 2016–2018.

[2] The beginning of law and economics is frequently dated from the publication of Ronald A Coase, *The Problem of Social Cost*, 3 J. L. ECON. 1 (1960). There is some arbitrariness to this dating. No single person or small group of persons typically begins an intellectual revolution. It is usually a much more collaborative and cumulative matter, as was famously argued in THOMAS KUHN, THE STRUCTURE OF SCIENTIFIC REVOLUTIONS (3d ed. 1996). So, one might better say that the modern use of economics to analyze core legal concepts began in the early 1960s.

between justice and efficiency and, second, that it required law students, professors, and practitioners (including judges) to learn the rudiments (or more) of economics.

Those promises and tensions have been—to a degree but incompletely—fulfilled and resolved over the course of the last 40 years. Law and economics has become a prominent tool in the analytical kit of nearly every North American law student and, increasingly, in the kits of students, professors, and practitioners around the world.

One important measure of this prominence is that there seems no particular need for law students to take a separate course in law and economics in order to become familiar with the field as might have been the case 20 or 30 years ago. But the success of the field has led to law-and-economics' concepts becoming central concepts taught as part of the core areas of the law. For instance, many casebooks in contract law use the notion of efficient breach of contract as an organizing concept; property courses introduce the Coase theorem; tort courses discuss Judge Calabresi's notion of the social-cost-minimizing level of care and the economic analysis of the differences between various tort liability standards; legal process courses frequently discuss the economic analysis of the relative costs of suit versus settlement; and criminal law courses introduce Gary Becker's pathbreaking analysis of crime and punishment.[3]

It is worth noting that in the 40+ years in which law and economics has been around, the basics have been elaborated, applied to novel situations, cases and controversies, and public policy issues, and new tools developed and disseminated. The field has had a far more dramatic impact in the legal academy than in departments of economics. It is also important to note that the two most important recent developments in law and economics (behavioral law and economics and empirical legal studies) have occurred almost wholly within the legal academy and among law professors. I think that that intellectual maturation of the field is a further testament to what a marvelously important and interesting field law and economics is.

Law and Economics: Public and Private is superb tour of all of these developments in the field. This volume shows why, despite the infusion of underlying concepts into the general law school curriculum, that there remains a tremendous value in having a course (or more than one) that assembles the related insights from Law and Economics, broadly defined, as a means of identifying integrative patterns within and across disciplines of private and public law. Among the many charms of the book (to which I shall turn) is the fact that the cases discussed and the applications to which the authors apply the tools are fresh, interesting, and timely.

But there are two further aspects of this book that I loudly applaud and commend: first, the authors' description of law and economics as a set of tools for analyzing the law and not a set of results; and second, what they call their "trans-methodological" perspective. Let me say a word about each of these aspects.

I mentioned above that when law and economics first appeared, it excited both interest and disquiet. A portion of that disquiet was due to the already-noted apparent clash between efficiency and justice as legal norms. Another portion arose from the view that law and economics had, its academic credentials notwithstanding, a thinly veiled

[3] Gary S Becker, *Crime and Punishment: An Economic Analysis*, 76 J. POL. ECON. 169 (1968).

political agenda—to argue for market-based policies and less regulation of the market. For example, some scholars suggested that the Coase theorem said more than that when transactions costs are low, bargaining can lead to an efficient outcome, regardless of the law. Some insisted that the theorem also said that our world is a world of low transaction costs and that, therefore, we should look to bargaining, rather than the law, to solve social problems.[4] This is nonsense, almost a willful misreading of the theorem. This is not the place to unpack the Coase theorem in order to discover precisely what it might mean. There is a vast literature that does just that.

Rather, the point of this example is that one of the tensions with which those professing law and economics had to deal was this view that there was a political agenda in law and economics. I am not sure why it happened that this view slowly withered throughout the 1980s and 1990s, but it seems to me that it did. That critical view seemed to be replaced with the view of the authors of *Law and Economics: Private and Public*—namely, that economics (and other social and behavioral disciplines) provides a set of tools for framing hypotheses about the law. Hypotheses, to state the obvious, are not true because they are plausible or precise or pleasing. They become "true" only when they have survived a careful confrontation with data well-suited to testing whether the hypotheses are much, much more likely to be true than not.[5] And then there must be professional scrutiny of the work contending that statistical inquiry demonstrates that any given hypothesis has been confirmed or refuted, retesting of the hypothesis with different data, and reexamination of the hypothesis in light of evolving understandings of the causal relationships of the underlying variables. This is hard, time-consuming work. And even when a learned profession like the law has reached a consensus on the veracity of any given hypothesis, it is almost as certain as the fact that night follows day that the profession's understanding of the hypothesized relationship will change over time. It will typically become richer, more subtle, and a better predictor of events in the real world.

That is precisely the view of the intellectual work of the law that Professors Stearns, Zywicki, and Miceli exhibit in this work.

The second aspect of the book that I heartily commend is its "trans-methodological" perspective. As I mentioned above, when law and economics began, its only significant tool was microeconomic theory. Matters have evolved over the past 40 years so that law and economics, broadly conceived, has added additional economic tools as well as tools from contiguous disciplines such as psychology. The authors are familiar and proficient with microeconomic theory tools. But to their great credit, they are also masters of some additional tools from economics that have not figured in the law-and-economics literature as much as they ought to have done, such tools as Austrian economics, social choice theory, interest group theory, and game theory. In addition, SZM have also brought behavioral findings from psychology (which, as they note, has just figured in the 2017 Nobel Prize in Economic Sciences being awarded to Professor Richard Thaler) and, empirical evidence and techniques to bear on their topics. All of these disciplines are

---

[4] Although many have been taught the Coase theorem in this manner, it is not what the Coase theorem said.

[5] The prevailing standard for statistical significance is that the results of careful statistical inquiry are 95 percent likely to have been generated by the process hypothesized. Alternatively, there is only a 5 percent chance that the results could have been generated by chance.

relevant to the study of law, and I am thrilled to see the authors marshal them, as needed, to explain various issues in the law.

Let me take just two examples of this innovative use of many methodologies. First, many law-and-economics professors will think themselves, like me, to be familiar with public choice theory. Many, or most, will think that public choice theory is principally useful for investigating legislative matters, in which various interest groups—some well-organized, some not organized at all—jockey for attention and influence on legislators. But most will not believe that public choice has much to say about the common law areas.

Second, many law-and-economics professors, again like me, will associate social choice theory only with the bracing predictions of the Arrow Impossibility Theorem. They will know that that theorem says remarkable things about the inability of social choice mechanisms to achieve coherence in public policy. They may recognize that social choice may have something to say about judicial behavior en banc and possibly about administrative law. But, again, most will not believe that social choice theory has much to say about the common law areas and only a little to say about public law.

Both of those beliefs about the lack of usefulness of public choice and social choice theory in talking about core areas of the law and legal process are wrong. The authors make compelling cases, time after time, for the importance of bringing public choice and social choice to bear on almost any area of legal inquiry.

So, I commend this work to you whole-heartedly. You are about to undertake a demanding but highly rewarding intellectual journey.

Preface

The roll-out of a new book is always an exciting moment for academics. As with Ursula in *The Little Mermaid*, *that's what [we] do; it's what [we] live for.*[1] But this particular roll-out is uniquely exciting for several reasons. Most notably, it is the first, and only, law and economics text that takes the capacious perspective on the relevant tools of analysis that we offer. In this single volume, we bring together the perspectives of neoclassical economics (or price theory), interest group theory, social choice theory, and game theory. We also integrate and blend insights from Austrian Economics, Behavioral Economics, and Quantitative Methods.

Part I provides the basic tools of price theory and economic reasoning. Part II covers the core common law subjects, with dedicated chapters (two each) on Tort, Contract, and Property. Part III covers the remaining first year law school curriculum, with one chapter each on Criminal Law and Judicial Process. Part IV broadens the methodological tools of economic analysis, with dedicated chapters (two each) on interest group theory, social choice, and game theory. Finally, Part V provides a comprehensive institutional analysis, presenting two chapters each on the Legislature, the Executive Branch (and Bureaus), the Judiciary, and finally, Constitutions.

This integrative approach allows us to offer comprehensive coverage of neoclassical law and economics in parts I–III, and then to explore in parts IV and V a broader range of topics, sometimes revisiting coverage from those earlier parts with the benefit of new tools, while also introducing new topics that cut across virtually the entire upper level law school curriculum. These coverage areas include *Administrative Law*, *Alternative Dispute Resolution (ADR)*, *Antitrust*, *Bankruptcy Law*, *Choice of Law*, *Constitutional Law I: Structure and Governance*; *Constitutional Law II: Individual Rights*; *Criminal Procedure*, *Election Law*, *Environmental Law*, *Federal Courts*, *First Amendment*, *Legislation*, *International Trade*, and more. Our unique integrative approach, culminating in Part V, explores the implications of the various economic methodologies for the relevant lawmaking institutions, and it incorporates wide-ranging doctrinal and policy-based applications at practically every step. This approach, embracing applications across the law school curriculum, is captured in the book's subtitle: *Private and Public.*

The volume provides the basis for a course that offers a truly unique and comprehensive overview of law school.[2] It is suitable for a seminar or lecture course, and the coauthors have used these materials both ways. As a seminar, these materials allow students, and faculty, to explore countless topics of interest to law and public policy in greater depth, informed by a broad assortment of relevant analytical tools.[3] As a capstone course, it provides a comprehensive positive account of why our legal doctrines and our institutions operate as they do. The book's careful presentation of both the legal and

---

[1] THE LITTLE MERMAID (Walt Disney Pictures 1989).

[2] Although this certainly is no bar prep course, Professor Stearns's students have told him that they think it is a tremendously valuable course to take prior to studying for the bar as it provides a uniquely comprehensive law school overview.

[3] The authors are available to offer a detailed list of suitable seminar paper topics.

economic materials also renders it an excellent fit for instruction in other settings in which students seek an introduction to, or firm foundation in, the implications of the broad tools of economic analysis for law and public policy, including undergraduate and graduate students in business, public policy, economics, and political science.

Although the perspective we offer is largely positive, we do not shy away from pressing normative questions. Some students, and perhaps some faculty, might mistakenly associate *Law and Economics* with a set of predetermined outcomes or with stuffy accounts of stale doctrines. Nothing could be further from the truth. Here is just a partial list of the timely questions that this volume explores:

1. In the heavily criticized decision, *Kelo v. City of New London* (2008), the Supreme Court allowed the City of New London, through its power of eminent domain, to effectuate a private-to-private property transfer, designed, albeit ultimately unsuccessfully, to benefit a large planned development. Does economic analysis, including interest group theory and game theory, support or call into question the *Kelo* ruling?

2. In *Citizens United v. Federal Election Comm'n (FEC)* (2010), the Supreme Court held that private corporations are legal persons for purposes of a First Amendment right to engage in unlimited expenditures that support or oppose a presidential candidate, thereby helping to create a legal basis for Super-PACs. Does economic analysis, including game theory, help to explain whether *Citizens United* was rightly or wrongly decided?

3. In several tragic high-profile incidents, police officers have shot persons of color who, in dominant media accounts, appeared to pose no immediate physical threat, almost invariably without the officers themselves being successfully prosecuted, or in some cases, even indicted. Does the economic analysis of criminal law help to frame the relevant issues that these cases present and to explain the relevant tradeoffs?

4. The doctrine of unconscionability renders voidable certain contracts the terms of which reveal that the person seeking release lacked a meaningful bargaining opportunity; conventional economic analysis has long viewed the doctrine as restricting opportunities for consumer choice in, among other types of contracting, financing schemes. Is there nonetheless a possible economic foundation for the doctrine of unconscionability, or put differently, is it possible that *Williams v. Walker-Thomas Furniture* (D.C. Cir. 1965) was rightly decided after all?

5. In recent decades, an emerging literature has called into question the prevalent practices of civil suit settlement and criminal law plea bargaining. Does the economic analysis of the judicial process help to explain the relevant tradeoffs? And does it help to explain the tradeoffs associated with *Alternative Dispute Resolution* (ADR) mechanisms, such as mediation or arbitration?

6. Despite the broad scientific consensus that human activity has significantly contributed to the emergent problem of global climate change, there is far less consensus as to the most effective means of

addressing the resulting problems. Does economic analysis, including interest group theory, offer helpful insights into the relevant law and public policy tradeoffs?

7. Despite the tremendous benefits that vaccines provide, and the overwhelming consensus in the medical and scientific community that they are safe, vaccines remain controversial, and individuals sometimes seek to extricate themselves and their children from the obligation to be vaccinated. Does economic analysis, and specifically game theory, help to explain mandatory vaccines? Do these tools also help to explain compensation schemes for the small incidence of injuries that occasionally arise?

8. In a notable series of cases, including *Chevron U.S.A. Inc. v. Natural Resources Defense Council, Inc.* (1984); *United States v. Mead Corp.* (2001); and *National Cable and Telecommunications Ass'n v. Brand X Internet Services* (2005), the Supreme Court has vacillated on the extent to which federal courts should defer to agency interpretations of ambiguous provisions within jurisdictional statutes. Does economic analysis help to assess the proper doctrinal framework for agency-deference rules?

9. In the famous (or infamous, depending on your view) decision, *Bush v. Gore* (2000), the Supreme Court, for the first time in history, effectively determined the outcome of a presidential election. Does economic analysis, including social choice theory, help to explain, to justify, or to criticize the case outcome?

10. For many years, culminating in the 2016 election of Donald Trump, one of the major planks of the Republican Party platform was to repeal and replace the Affordable Care Act (ACA), also known as Obamacare. For now, the Act remains in place, but a major component, the "individual mandate," which required consumers to purchase qualified health insurance or pay a tax, was repealed as part of the 2017 tax reform bill. What are the implications of economic analysis for the substantive policies embedded in the Affordable Care Act, and for future repeal or amendment efforts?

11. In *FDA v. Brown & Williamson Tobacco Corp.* (2000), the Supreme Court disallowed the Food and Drug Administration, a federal agency, to regulate tobacco, and in *Massachusetts v. EPA* (2007), the Supreme Court mandated that the Environmental Protection Agency, also a federal agency, regulate, or better justify failing to regulate, greenhouse gas emissions. Does economic analysis, including interest group theory, help to reconcile these seemingly disparate rulings, and if not, does it help to assess which case offers the more compelling approach?

12. In *Planned Parenthood v. Casey* (1992), the Supreme Court rested on stare decisis in declining to overturn *Roe v. Wade* (1973) and in *Lawrence v. Texas* (2003), the Supreme Court overturned the 1986 decision, *Bowers v. Hardwick* (1986), thereby abandoning stare decisis. Does the economic

analysis of stare decisis help to reconcile these seemingly contradictory approaches, and if not, does it help to explain which approach is more sound?

Narrowing the entries for this list was a genuine challenge. We could have generated multiple lists of comparably salient topics. Most of these questions are taken from the Applications at the end of each chapter. There is also a vast array of current, and historical, case and policy illustrations laced throughout the body of each chapter. We do want to emphasize, however, that we did not interweave these or other current topics at the expense of carefully exploring important and longstanding doctrinal materials. Parts II and III especially present in a detailed and user-friendly format, the economic analysis of common law rules and of criminal law and the judicial process. Together with Part I, which presents economic reasoning and price theory, these materials comprise the volume's first ten chapters. Each of the listed questions, and many others, are designed to reinforce core coverage in the body of the chapter that precedes it, and in doing so, to make the academic materials conveyed in the book all the more relevant, and yes, also more fun, for today's law students, especially during classroom discussions.

The analysis further underscores a theme that is central to this volume: economic analysis does not compel any particular results. Economic analysis applies a set of complementary tools that provides the basis for positive, or descriptive accounts. Once that work is done, normative questions invariably arise: are we willing to pay price x to accomplish goal y? Answering that question almost always demands insights from outside economic analysis proper, a point that we repeatedly emphasize.[4] Sometimes the analysis helps to reinforce commonly held intuitions about legal rules drawn from more conventional methodologies; other times, it provides a basis for calling such intuitions into question.

A second major theme of this book involves economic complementarities. Economic analysis is not a monolith, with tools invariably leading to the same result. Quite often legal scholars confronted with an economic analysis, the conclusions of which they find normatively problematic, reject economic analysis altogether, and with that, the richness such analysis often provides. We think that this approach is mistaken. Others gravitate toward the increasingly influential, and fascinating, field of behavioral economics. As this book goes to press, we note Richard Thaler, whose contributions to that field resulted in his having been awarded the 2017 Nobel Prize in Economics. Professor Thaler joins a list of remarkable scholars whose works have been recognized with this prize and whose rich insights we also draw upon in exploring the implications of economics for law and public policy[5]: Kenneth Arrow (1972), Gary Becker (1992), James Buchanan (1986), Ronald Coase (1991), Milton Friedman (1976), F.A. Hayek (1974), John Forbes Nash, Jr. (1993), Douglass North (1993), Elinor Ostrom (2009),

[4] An exception: If a claim is made that a particular policy x, will accomplish result y, and if economic analysis proves that x cannot not succeed in doing so, this does affect the normative merits of x, or, at a minimum, it requires that those pushing policy x support it with a justification other than accomplishing y.

[5] We list in parentheses the year each scholar received the Nobel Memorial Prize in Economic Sciences. *See All Prizes in Economic Science*, NOBELPRIZE.ORG, https://www.nobelprize.org/nobel_prizes/economic-sciences/laureates/ (last visited Oct. 27, 2017).

Thomas Schelling (2005), Amartya Sen (1998), Vernon Smith (2002), George Stigler (1982), William Vickrey (1996), Oliver Williamson (2009), and others.

Those influenced by the growing field of behavioral economics call into question a core assumption of economics, namely individual rationality. We agree that individuals experience any number of heuristic biases, and we do not find this inconsistent with the central premise of economic analysis. By assuming that individuals engage in the cost-effective pursuit of desired objectives, and by recognizing the endless variation in human wants and needs, economic modeling provides the basis for a more robust account of interactive human behavior than alternative methodologies. We also recognize that a complete account of any complex human activity necessarily demands considering more fully all aspects of human capacities, frailties, and predilections.

This volume approaches the critique of economic analysis of law from within, expanding the range of economic methodologies to include interest group theory, social choice, and game theory. We also point out helpful insights from Austrian Economics, Behavioral Economics, and Quantitative Methods. This combination allows for far more robust accounts, including how to frame persistent, yet criticized, features of common law rules, regulatory structures, constitutional structures and doctrines, and even international institutions.

A central tenet of social choice is that no system is "perfect." Every system, like every person, has flaws, but those flaws vary. And the variance often emerges a source of institutional strength. A unique benefit of this blended methodological approach to the economic analysis of law is that it suggests that the whole often exceeds the sum of its parts. Multiple institutions, each with different flaws, and strengths, or multiple rules, each with different limitations, and advantages, can improve the state of the law and the state of the world for those who are affected.

For this reason, we take a different approach to the integration of economic analysis of law than other leading texts. Our trans-methodological approach involves blending neoclassical Law and Economics with interest group theory, social choice, and game theory, plus others, and surveying core common law doctrines, other early applications, such as criminal law and judicial process, along with a comprehensive assessment of the institutions that create law and public policy. Our unique approach lets us interweave materials from the first-year curriculum with others drawn from throughout the upper level curriculum, all with the benefit of new framings and tools.

We anticipate that faculty might approach these materials in various ways. In a one semester course, a professor might wish to focus solely on the conventional L&E core materials (Parts I, II, and III), and perhaps to add on one or two additional methodological overlays (Part IV), such as social choice and game theory. Or the professor might include Part I (methodologies), Part II (the common law), selections from Part IV (advanced methodologies), and selections from Part V (institutions). Alternatively, a professor might choose only to cover the introductory chapter for any of the doctrinal, methodological, or institutional materials. The authors are happy to help in the construction of a syllabus that works best based upon the professor's academic interests and areas of core expertise. The book's breadth is the source of its flexibility and adaptability.

The authors are happy to acknowledge the many outstanding academic contributions to the general fields of law and economics, interest group theory, social choice theory, and game theory. To help those reading this Preface and teaching (or taking) this course, we offer a partial list of leading sources that we have personally benefited from below. We encourage you to avail yourselves of this rich literature. At the same time, we take pride knowing that we have set out a firm foundation, entirely included within this volume, that allows for a comprehensive course (or several alternative courses) without having to assign additional materials. And we should note, we have done so in a manner that, although not devoid of mathematical presentations, is light on math, and for which the core intuitions can also be conveyed, as they are in the text, without math. We also include, where helpful, graphics and tables, thereby appealing to students of differing learning styles.

Finally, leaving the best for last, what most excites each of us about this volume is the unique combination of perspectives and expertise. Max Stearns, Venable, Baetjer & Howard Professor of Law at Maryland Carey Law, became interested in law and economics and public choice at the earliest point in his career, and even as a law student. With this volume, he will have authored (or coauthored) three volumes designed to instruct law students (and others) in the associated tools of price theory, interest group theory, social choice, and elementary game theory. Todd Zywicki, George Mason University Foundation Professor of Law at George Mason's Antonin Scalia Law School, is also a career-long student of economics and public choice, and with Max Stearns, he coauthored *Public Choice Concepts and Applications in Law* (West 2009), which provides much of the basis for parts IV and V of this volume. Max and Todd are particularly pleased that Tom Miceli embraced, and then joined in, this project. Professor Miceli is a Professor of Economics at the University of Connecticut, and he is the author of a leading undergraduate textbook, *The Economic Approach to Law* (Stanford Univ. Press 3d ed. 2017). The book not only combines different economic methodologies, but also the unique perspectives of these authors. The result is a set of materials that asks new questions and applies new tools in confronting long-standing doctrines and lawmaking institutions, along with many of the most pressing problems of law and public policy facing us today. We truly hope that you enjoy what follows!

From Max Stearns

I would like to express enormous gratitude to my generous colleagues and friends, and especially my students. Nearly four years ago, I worked with my terrific editors at West Academic Publishing, and with Todd Zywicki, to develop the idea for this book. A year later, when the first batch of chapters was in draft, I decided to try something unusual. I invited my faculty colleagues who teach in each of the core doctrinal areas now covered in parts II and III of this volume, to read the draft chapters and to come to my class. I began to call those seated to my right "my panel of experts." I was enormously benefited by the insights and dedication of Professors Richard Boldt, Danielle Citron, Martha Ertman, Don Gifford, Mark Graber, Lee Kovarsky, Russell McClain, Paula Monopoli, Mike Pappas, Garrett Power, Bill Reynolds, Michael Van Alstine, and Marley Weiss. The resulting classroom exchanges, often including disagreements over the underlying economic analysis and its implications for relevant institutions and rules, soon emerged a hallmark of the course. (I will continue to invite my colleagues!) Students enjoyed hearing, and participating in, these exchanges, especially as it demonstrated to them something that is often left out of the traditional law school classroom: the professors each come into class with their own perspectives, and try as we might to claim an open mind, inevitably our priors shape how we frame and teach the materials that we cover. Inviting students to pull back the curtain and to see that their faculty often disagree, sometimes profoundly, yet respectfully, is its own educational reward.

As a law student, and throughout my teaching career, I have been fortunate get to know many brilliant scholars who have profoundly influenced my understanding of law, economics, and public policy in ways that undoubtedly find reflection throughout this book. Several of those previously mentioned, and some of those I will mention now, would not associate themselves with law and economics. I have always believed that we learn best when we allow our own intuitions to be challenged, including by those who embrace very different framings. There is an inevitable risk that in listing some, I will inadvertently fail to include others, and I apologize in advance for such inevitable oversight. Even so, it is worth the risk to acknowledge those who have influenced me in ways that have almost certainly improved this project and my scholarship more generally. In addition to those previously listed, I would like to acknowledge and thank John Jeffries, Jr., Glen Robinson, Saul Levmore, Lillian BeVier, Robert Scott, Doug Leslie, Walter Wadlington, Lee Epstein, David Skeel, Nicolaus Tideman, Kenneth Arrow, Henry Manne, Tim Muris, Bill Kovacic, Larry Ribstein, Linda Schwartzstein, Margaret Brinig, Jim Chen, Erin O'Hara, Peter Letsou, Michael Abramowicz, Leslie Henry, Amanda Pustilnik, James Grimmelmann, Josh Wright, Dan Farber, Tom Ulen, Robert Pushaw, Tracey George, Evan Caminker, Omri Ben Shahar, Ariel Porat, Hanoch Dagan, Tsilly Dagan, Roy Partain, Emre Usenmez, Alan Miller, CJ Peters, Eric Rasmusen, David Hyman, and Daniel Sokol. Paul Salamanca provided helpful comments on portions of this manuscript.

I am especially thankful to my students, not just over the past two years, but over the past twenty-six years. I'm an unusual law professor. My two core areas are *Constitutional Law* and *Law and Economics*. To me, these two seemingly disparate areas are inextricably linked; I could not imagine doing either without the other. This explains my early interest in public choice, and especially in social choice theory. These methodologies prove enormously helpful in expanding the conventional law and economics analytical criteria to embrace others in conflict with traditional understandings of efficiency, and also with simple intuitions about majority rule. My students have been extremely patient and generous, as I have always treated the learning process as mutual, gaining far more than I give. Most of my academic work has arisen from my best, if highly imperfect, efforts to figure out complex doctrines well enough to convey them to my students. This has resulted in lengthy published works on standing, stare decisis, Supreme Court voting protocols, the Commerce Clause (dormant and affirmative), the narrowest grounds rule, and tiers of scrutiny, among other topics.

This book has returned me to my earliest interest in law and economics—as a 1L at the University of Virginia Law School, entering as a University of Pennsylvania economics and political science double major—trying to make sense of something entirely new. Relearning these materials now, some thirty years later, has been all the more fascinating to me as a professor. I hope that this volume generates the same enthusiasm for professors and students alike.

I thank Maryland Carey Law for being such a warm and welcoming home to me and my academic work, and for providing the considerable resources necessary for undertaking such a vast and comprehensive project. Sue McCarty has for many years provided such outstanding library support that I have come to refer to her as my secret weapon. Jennifer Smith provided extremely valuable library assistance in preparing several chapters. I benefited from the tremendous support of my talented and dedicated research assistants, each of whom also took my Law and Economics course: Laura Tallerico, Emily Levy, Haneen Daham, and Adam Baig.

Nathan Robertson, Director of Information Policy and Management and Lecturer in Law, and my former student in public choice, provided extremely helpful insights, guidance and support throughout the copyright process. I have been fortunate to work closely with two remarkable members of the law school's support staff. Frank Lancaster, Legal Assistant, personally produced the graphics throughout the book, in his spare time and at home (with a baby no less!), and also helped early on with much additional book-related work. Although I was extremely pleased that Frank received a truly well-deserved promotion here at the law school to Editor, I was also sad to lose him. Elyshia Menkin, Law Faculty Coordinator, has stepped into that role, and she immediately proved herself invaluable to the project, coordinating both permissions and manuscript production, complex processes that each involved many people and lots of moving parts. James Cahoy was my initial Acquisitions Editor at West Academic Publishing, and he was an always helpful soundboard in thinking through this overall project. Although I was sorry to see him move onto another position, Elizabeth Eisenhart, who replaced him in that role, was terrific from the start, helping with many complexities as we saw this book project through to completion.

I thank Dean Donald Tobin and Associate Dean for Academic and Administrative Affairs Barbara Gontrum, with whom I worked closely as Associate Dean for Research and Faculty Development, and who supported me in too many ways to count. This includes allowing me to teach in Aberdeen, Scotland, during the summer of 2016, and supporting a semester of sabbatical leave to (not quite) finish this project.

The Cover Art

During the summer of 2016, while in Scotland, my family and I visited *the National Gallery of Art* in Edinburgh. For the first time, I saw *The Gallery of Cornelis van der Geest*, painted by the Flemish artist, Willem van Haecht, in 1628. Having been raised in a home that was in many respects a museum (see Chapter 14, Part III), I was immediately drawn to the painting, which I later learned depicted the private collection of a spice merchant from Antwerp. Upon reading Erin O'Hara O'Connor's wonderful description of the book as "a veritable treasure trove," I knew that the painting should grace the cover. I hope that like the gallery visitors the artist depicts, our readers will explore the world of ideas within these chapters, in groups or alone, but always with the excitement of seeing something new.

My students are a constant source of inspiration. In *Public Choice Concepts and Applications in Law*, I thanked my parents, Herbert and Audrey Stearns for instilling in me a constant curiosity and a lifelong love of learning. Although they have since passed away, their influence and inspiration continue. My own family, Vered, my ever-patient wife, and

Shira, Keren, and Eric, my wonderful children, have been a never-ending source of love and support. I could not have done this without them.

From Todd Zywicki

Soon after the publication of *Public Choice Concepts and Applications in Law* in 2009, Henry Butler returned to George Mason University Law School, bringing with him a revitalized Law & Economics Center (LEC). Since that time, I have had the opportunity to provide introductory lectures on public choice economics and law & economics to hundreds of state and federal judges from across the United States and even from multiple countries abroad, as well as hundreds of state attorneys general staff from across the country. I have also had the opportunity to teach this material in a more in-depth fashion to hundreds of law professors through various seminars and workshops sponsored by the George Mason Law & Economics Center. Many of those professors have adopted the predecessor to this book, *Public Choice Concepts and Applications in Law*, in their class; many of those judges and AG staff have turned to that book for insight and understanding of public choice economics in doing their jobs. I hope that this larger, more comprehensive book reaches an even broader audience and that those reading it feel that it, too, will help them to be better lawyers, professors, and judges. I thank all of them for their academic and practical perspectives in helping me to better understand how law and economics and public choice are useful in understanding law.

I especially appreciate the support and enthusiasm of Henry Butler, first as Executive Director of the LEC and later as Dean of Antonin Scalia Law School, for the study of law & economics generally and public choice specifically. For many scholars and judges, Scalia Law has become the mothership of law & economics around the United States and the world and Dean Butler is largely responsible for that development. From 2015–2017 I also served as the Executive Director of the LEC and I wish to recognize my colleagues at the LEC for their professionalism and friendship during that period in ensuring that the LEC continued to thrive. Finally, I would be remiss were I not to recognize my debt of gratitude to my graduate school professors at Clemson University who first introduced me to the study of Public Choice—Bill Dougan, David Laband, Roger Meiners, the late Robert Staaf, and Bruce Yandle. I also would like to recognize my many friends and intellectual colleagues in the George Mason Economics Department, and especially Alex Tabarrok, the Executive Director of the George Mason Center for the Study of Public Choice, and Peter Boettke, who has carried the flame of the Virginia School and from whom I have learned so much.

I have taught this material almost every year since *Public Choice Concepts and Applications in Law* was published and I am grateful to my students for their feedback on what worked and what worked not as well. Their insights are hopefully reflected here.

Finally, I want to acknowledge my daughter Claire, whose intellectual curiosity and probing questions amaze me every day; Jeri Curry, whose love, patience, and support every day are a gift that I constantly appreciate and rarely deserve; and Marshall and Colton as we embark on our new life together.

From Tom Miceli

I have been teaching law and economics for over twenty-five years, but exclusively to undergraduate economics majors and graduate students. So when Max and Todd approached me about joining the authorship team for this volume, I viewed it as a unique challenge; namely, how best to communicate the insights that economic theory can bring to law in a rigorous way but without over-burdening students with the technical apparatus that usually accompanies economic analysis. The pre-existing portions of this book—which largely covered public choice topics—served as an admirable model. The resulting product is unique in the field of law and economics, both in its breadth and depth, and has truly been a collaboration of authors with different skill sets, educational backgrounds, and philosophical viewpoints. I think I can speak for all of us, however, in saying that we have learned much from each other in undertaking this project, and hopefully have, in the process, produced a book that conveys the unique perspective that economics brings to the study of law and legal institutions.

My interest in law stems from an undergraduate law-and-economics course that I took during my senior year at Wesleyan University some years ago. Up to that time, I had been an unexcited economics major, but the novelty of that course compared to my prior economics courses, and the skill and passion of my professor, Richard Adelstein, demonstrated to me for the first time the insights that economic analysis can bring to a wide array of social problems, including those outside of traditional market settings. Ironically, that experience inspired me to pursue graduate training in economics, but soon after completing my doctorate, I returned to law and economics as my primary field of research. My hope is that this volume inspires in students the same excitement that I experienced when I first encountered the field. In addition to Richie, I would like to acknowledge the influence that Kathleen Segerson, my long-time co-author and colleague, has had on my career. Early on I recruited Kathy to work on law-and-economics questions concerning tort law, land use issues, and criminal law. Her skills and insights have greatly improved my understanding of the usefulness of economics for understanding law and have made me a better economist. I would also like to thank another co-author and one-time colleague, C.F. Sirmans, for his influence and inspiration. C.F. was already an accomplished scholar in real estate when we began our collaboration, but he foresaw the new insights that the economic approach to law could bring to a wide array of real estate and land use questions. In addition, his econometric skills allowed me to expand my repertoire to include empirical questions. My former graduate student, and now an accomplished scholar, Matthew Baker, and my current colleague, Metin Cosgel, have also been valued co-authors over the years. I am a better scholar for having worked with all of these amazing people. I wish to thank Stanford University Press for its generosity in allowing the adaptation, and in some instances reproduction, of materials from my undergraduate textbook, Thomas J. Miceli, *An Economic Approach to Law* (3rd ed. 2017), especially as these materials related to parts II and III of this volume.

Finally, I would like to again thank Max and Todd for the invitation to join this venture, three decades of students for providing a stimulating intellectual environment, and my family for their enduring support.

A (Partial) Listing of Helpful Works

Richard Adelstein. *The Exchange Order: Property and Liability as an Economic System.* New York: Oxford Univ. Press, 2017.

Peter H. Aranson. *American Government: Strategy and Choice*. Cambridge, MA: Winthrop Publishers, Inc., 1981.

Douglas G. Baird, Robert H. Gertner, and Randall C. Douglas. *Game Theory and the Law*. Cambridge, MA: Harvard University Press, 1998.

James Buchanan and Gordon Tullock. *The Calculus of Consent: Logical Foundations of Constitutional Democracy*. Ann Arbor: University of Michigan Press, 1962.

Guido Calabresi. *The Costs of Accidents: A Legal and Economic Analysis*. New Haven: Yale University Press, 1970.

Robert Cooter and Tom Ulen. *Law and Economics*. 6th ed. 2016. Berkeley, CA. http://scholarship.law.berkeley.edu/books/2/.

Daniel A. Farber and Philip P. Frickey. *Law and Public Choice: A Critical Introduction*. Chicago: University of Chicago Press, 1991.

Daniel A. Farber and Ann O'Connell, *Research Handbook on Public Choice and Public Law*. Northampton, MA: Edward Elgar, 2010.

Michael T. Hayes. *Lobbyists and Legislators: A Theory of Political Markets*. New Brunswick, NJ: Rutgers University Press, 1981.

Richard A. Ippolito. *Economics for Lawyers*. Princeton, NJ: Princeton University Press, 2005.

Nicholas Mercuro and Steven G. Medema. *Economics and the Law: From Posner to Postmodernism and Beyond*. 2nd ed. Princeton, NJ: Princeton University Press, 2006.

Thomas J. Miceli. *The Economic Approach to Law*. 3rd ed. Stanford, CA: Stanford University Press, 2017.

Dennis C. Mueller. *Public Choice III*. New York: Cambridge University Press, 2003.

Dennis C. Mueller, ed. *Perspectives on Public Choice: A Handbook*. New York: Cambridge University Press, 2006.

Mancur Olson. *The Logic of Collective Action: Public Goods and the Theory of Groups*. Cambridge, MA: Harvard University Press, 1971.

A. Mitchell Polinsky. *An Introduction to Law and Economics*. 2nd ed. Boston: Little, Brown, 1989.

Richard Posner. *Economic Analysis of Law*. 9th ed. Austin: Aspen, 2014.

Eric Rasmusen. *Games and Information: An Introduction to Game Theory*. 4th ed. Malden, MA: Blackwell Publishers, 2007.

William H. Riker. *Liberalism Against Populism: A Confrontation Between the Theory of Democracy and the Theory of Social Choice*. San Francisco: W.H. Freeman, 1982.

Steven Shavell. *Foundations of Economic Analysis of Law*. Cambridge, MA: Belknap Press, 2004.

Maxwell L. Stearns and Todd J. Zywicki. *Public Choice Concepts and Applications in Law*. St. Paul, MN: West, 2009.

Maxwell L. Stearns. *Constitutional Process: A Social Choice Analysis of Supreme Court Decision Making.* 1st paperback ed. Ann Arbor: University of Michigan Press, 2002.

Maxwell L. Stearns
Todd J. Zywicki
Thomas J. Miceli

June 1, 2018

Copyright Acknowledgments

The authors thankfully acknowledge permission to reprint materials from the following works:

Altitude Express Inc. DBA Skydive Long Island, Skydiving Contract. Reprinted with permission from Raymond F. Maynard.

WILLIAM J. BAUMOL & ALAN S. BLINDER, ECONOMICS: PRINCIPLES AND POLICY 217 (10th ed. 2006). From Baumol/Blinder. *Economics*, 10E. © 2008 South-Western, a part of Cengage, Inc. Reproduced by permission. www.cengage.com/permissions.

JAMES M. BUCHANAN & GORDON TULLOCK, THE CALCULUS OF CONSENT: LOGICAL FOUNDATIONS OF CONSTITUTIONAL DEMOCRACY (1962). Reproduced with permission from the University of Michigan Press.

Lee Drutman, *Political Divisions in 2016 and Beyond: Tensions Between and Within the Two Parties*, DEMOCRACY FUND VOTER STUDY GROUP Fig. 2 (June 2017), https://www.voterstudygroup.org/publications/2016-elections/political-divisions-in-2016-and-beyond (The 2016 Electorate). Reproduced with permission from Lee Drutman.

Frank H. Easterbrook, *Statutes' Domains*, 50 U. CHI. L. REV. 533 (1983). Reproduced with permission from the University of Chicago Law Review.

Harry T. Edwards, *Collegiality and Decision-Making on the D.C. Circuit*, 84 VA. L. REV. 1335 (1998). Reproduced with permission from the Copyright Clearance Center, Inc.

Einer Elhauge, STATUTORY DEFAULT RULES: HOW TO INTERPRET UNCLEAR LEGISLATION, Cambridge, Mass.: Harvard University Press, Copyright © 2008 by the President and Fellows of Harvard College. Reproduced with permission from Harvard University Press.

David Epstein & Sharyn O'Halloran, *Administrative Procedures, Information, and Agency Discretion*, 38 AM. J. POL. SCI. 697, 698 (1994). Reproduced with permission from Midwest Political Science Association.

William N. Eskridge, Jr., *Politics Without Romance: Implications of Public Choice Theory for Statutory Interpretation*, 74 VA. L. REV. 275, 279 (1988). Reproduced with permission from the Copyright Clearance Center, Inc.

Daniel A. Farber & Philip P. Frickey, *Legislative Intent and Public Choice*, 74 VA. L. REV. 423, 424 (1988). Reproduced with permission from the Copyright Clearance Center, Inc.

MICHAEL S. GREVE, FEDERALISM AND THE CONSTITUTION: COMPETITION VERSUS CARTELS 8–9, 11 (2015). https://www.mercatus.org/system/files/Greve-web-6-3-15.pdf. Reproduced with permission from the Mercatus Center and Michael S. Greve.

HENRY M. HART & ALBERT M. SACKS, THE LEGAL PROCESS: BASIC PROBLEMS IN THE MAKING AND APPLICATION OF LAW 1374–80 (William N. Eskridge & Philip P. Frickey eds., 1994). Reproduced with permission from Foundation Press.

Thomas H. Jackson, THE LOGIC AND LIMITS OF BANKRUPTCY LAW, Cambridge, Mass.: Harvard University Press, Copyright © 1986 by the Presdient and Fellows of Harvard College. Reproduced with permission from Harvard University Press.

Lewis A. Kornhauser, *An Economic Perspective on Stare Decisis*, 65 CHI.-KENT L. REV. 63, 79–80 (1989). Reproduced with permission from Chicago-Kent Law Review.

Darryl J. Levinson & Richard H. Pildes, *Separation of Parties, Not Powers*, 119 HARV. L. REV. 2311 (2006). Reproduced with permission from the Copyright Clearance Center, Inc.

Saul Levmore, *Voting Paradoxes and Interest Groups*, 28 J. LEGAL STUD. 259 (1999). Reproduced with permission from the University of Chicago Press.

Jonathan R. Macey, *Federal Deference to Local Regulators and the Economic Theory of Regulation: Toward a Public-Choice Explanation of Federalism*, 76 VA. L. REV. 265, 268 (1990). Reproduced with permission from the Copyright Clearance Center, Inc.

Jonathan R. Macey, *The Internal and External Costs and Benefits of Stare Decisis*, 65 CHI.-KENT L. REV. 93 (1989). Reproduced with permission from Chicago-Kent Law Review.

McNollgast, *Legislative Intent: The Use of Positive Political Theory in Statutory Interpretation*, LAW & CONTEMP. PROBS., Spring 1994, at 3. Reproduced with permission from McNollgast.

Thomas W. Merrill, *Capture Theory and the Courts: 1967–1983*, 72 CHI.-KENT L. REV. 1039 (1997). Reproduced with permission from Chicago-Kent Law Review.

THOMAS J. MICELI, THE ECONOMIC APPROACH TO LAW, THIRD EDITION (2017). Reproduced with permission from Stanford University Press.

Geoffrey P. Miller, *The True Story of* Carolene Products, 1987 SUP. CT. REV. 397. Reproduced with permission from the University of Chicago Press.

Dennis C. Mueller, **Public Choice II**, A Revised Edition of Public Choice, Edition 2, © Dennis C. Mueller 1989, published by Cambridge University Press. Reproduced with permission from Cambridge University Press.

Dennis C. Mueller, **Public Choice III**, 3rd Edition, © Dennis C. Mueller 2003, published by Cambridge University Press. Reproduced with permission from Cambridge University Press.

Richard A. Posner, *Legal Formalism, Legal Realism, and the Interpretation of Statutes and the Constitution*, 37 CASE W. RES. L. REV. 176 (1986). Reproduced with permission from Case Western Reserve Law Review and Richard Posner.

David G. Post & Steven C. Salop, *Issues and Outcomes, Guidance, and Indeterminacy: A Reply to Professor John Rogers and Others*, 49 VAND. L. REV. 1069, 1078 (1996). Reproduced with permission from Vanderbilt Law Review.

David Post & Steven C. Salop, *Rowing Against the Tidewater: A Theory of Voting by Multijudge Panels*, 80 GEO. L.J. 743, 752 (1992). Reprinted with permission of the publisher, Georgetown Law Journal © 1993.

A.C. Pritchard & Todd J. Zywicki, *Constitutions and Spontaneous Orders: A Response to Professor McGinnis*, 77 N.C. L. REV. 537–50 (1999). Reprinted with permission from the *North Carolina Law Review.*

John M. Rogers, "Issue Voting" by Multimember Appellate Courts: A Response to Some Radical Proposals, 49 VAND L. REV. 997 (1996). Reproduced with permission from Vanderbilt Law Review.

Clinton Rossiter, ed., THE FEDERALIST PAPERS by Alexander Hamilton, James Madison and John Jay. Reproduced with permission from Penguin Random House LLC.

Kenneth A. Shepsle, *Congress Is a "They," Not an "It": Legislative Intent as Oxymoron*, 12 INT'L REV. L. & ECON. 239, 242 n.6 (1992). Reproduced with permission from the Copyright Clearance Center, Inc.

DAVID A. SKEEL, JR., DEBT'S DOMINION: A HISTORY OF BANKRUPTCY LAW IN AMERICA 24–47 (2001). Reproduced with permission from the Copyright Clearance Center, Inc.

Maxwell L. Stearns, *A Beautiful Mend: A Game Theoretical Analysis of the Dormant Commerce Clause Doctrine*, 45 WM. & MARY L. REV. 1, 76–78 (2003). Reproduced with permission from William & Mary Law Review.

MAXWELL L. STEARNS, CONSTITUTIONAL PROCESS: A SOCIAL CHOICE ANALYSIS OF SUPREME COURT DECISION MAKING 41–94 (Chapter 2) (paperback ed. 2002) Reproduced with permission from the University of Michigan Press.

Maxwell L. Stearns, Obergefell, Fisher, *and the Inversion of Tiers*, BALKINIZATION BLOG (Apr. 24, 2016), https://balkin.blogspot.com/2016/04/obergefell-fisher-and-inversion-of-tiers.html. Reproduced with permission from Jack Balkin.

Maxwell L. Stearns, Obergefell, Fisher, *and the Inversion of Tiers*, 19 U. PA. J. CONST. L. 1043 (2017). Reproduced with permission from the Journal of Constitutional Law.

Maxwell L. Stearns, *The Case for Including* Marks v. United States *in the Canon of Constitutional Law*, 17 CONST. COMMENT. 321 (2000). Reproduced with permission from Constitutional Commentary.

Maxwell L. Stearns, *The Misguided Renaissance of Social Choice*, 103 YALE L.J. 1219 (1994). Reproduced with permission from The Yale Journal Co.

Excerpt from https://uspa.org/Find/FAQs/Safety Reproduced with permission from the United States Parachute Association.

Willem van Haecht, *The Gallery of Cornelis van der Geest*, 1628. Reproduced as public domain, via Wikimedia Commons. https://commons.wikimedia.org/wiki/File:The_Gallery_of_Cornelis_van_der_Geest.JPG. This work is on permanent display at *Rubens Huis* (*Rubin Lives On*), Antwerp, Belgium.

Summary of Contents

PART III. EXTENDED APPLICATIONS

PART IV. PUBLIC CHOICE METHODOLOGIES

Table of Contents

PART II. COMMON LAW APPLICATIONS

PART IV. PUBLIC CHOICE METHODOLOGIES

Table of Cases

Table of Authorities

17th Amendment to the U.S. Constitution: Direct Election of Senators, Nat'l Archives Ctr. for Legis. Archives (Aug. 15, 2016), 944

2016 Presidential Primaries Results, Politico (Dec. 13, 2016, 1:57 PM), 744

About the Center, The Center for Study of Public Choice, George Mason University, 435

Abramowicz, Michael & Maxwell L. Stearns, Beyond Counting Votes: The Political Economy of Bush v. Gore, 54 Vand. L. Rev. 1849 (2001), 908

Abramowicz, Michael & Maxwell Stearns, Defining Dicta, 57 Stan. L. Rev. 953 (2005), 582, 839

Abramowicz, Michael, On the Alienability of Legal Claims, 114 Yale L.J. 697 (2005), 378

Abramson, Jeffrey, Death-Is-Different Jurisprudence and the Role of the Capital Jury, 2 Ohio St. J. Crim. L. 117 (2004), 348

Abramson, Paul R. et al., Third-Party and Independent Candidates in American Politics: Wallace, Anderson, and Perot, 110 Pol. Sci. Q. 349 (1995), 963

Abramson, Paul R., et al., "Sophisticated" Voting in the 1988 Presidential Primaries, 86 Am. Pol. Sci. Rev. 55 (1992), 28

Ackerman, Alan T., Incorporation of the Right to Just Compensation: The Fourteenth Amendment vs. the Takings Clause, 1 Brigham-Kanner Prop. Rts. Conf. J. 95 (2012), 288

Ackerman, Bruce A., Beyond Carolene Products, 98 Harv. L. Rev. 713 (1985), 461

Ackerman, Bruce, We the People: Foundations (1991), 12

Adams, James et al., Move to the Center or Mobilize the Base? (Aug. 31, 2006), 734

Adelstein, Richard & Thomas Miceli, Toward a Comparative Economics of Plea Bargaining, 11 Eur. J.L. & Econ. 47 (2001), 404

Adelstein, Richard P., The Moral Costs of Crime: Prices, Information, and Organization, in 12 The Costs of Crime 233 (Charles M. Gray ed., 1979), 315

Adelstein, Richard, Institutional Function and Evolution in the Criminal Process, 76 Nw. U. L. Rev. 1 (1981), 401

Adelstein, Richard, Plea Bargaining: A Comparative Approach, in The New Palgrave Dictionary of Economics and the Law (Peter Newman ed., 1998), 404

Adler, Jonathan H., Conservation Through Collusion: Antitrust as an Obstacle to Marine Resource Conservation, 61 Wash. & Lee L. Rev. 3 (2004), 598

Aivazian, Varouj A. & Jeffrey L. Callen, The Coase Theorem and the Empty Core, 24 J.L. & Econ. 175 (1981), 24, 522

Aivazian, Varouj et al., The Law of Contract Modifications: The Uncertain Quest for a Benchmark of Enforceability, 22 Osgoode Hall L.J. 173 (1984), 154

Akerlof, George A., Writing the "The Market for 'Lemons' ": A Personal and Interpretive Essay, NobelPrize.org (Nov. 14, 2003), 159

Akerlof, George, The Market for "Lemons": Quality Uncertainty and the Market Mechanism, 84 Q.J. Econ. 488 (1970), 159

Alchian, Armen A. & William R. Allen, Exchange and Production: Competition, Coordination, and Control (3d ed. 1983), 35, 941

Alchian, Armen A., Rent, in 4 The New Palgrave: A Dictionary of Economics 141 (John Eatwell et al. eds., 1998), 54, 425

Alchian, Armen A., Uncertainty, Evolution, and Economic Theory, 58 J. Pol. Econ. 211 (1950), 544, 781

Alexander, Larry, Striking Back at the Empire: A Brief Survey of Problems in Dworkin's Theory of Law, 6 Law & Phil. 419 (1987), 855

Alexander, Michelle, The New Jim Crow: Mass Incarceration in an Age of Colorblindness (2012), 325

Allen, Douglas W. & Dean Lueck, Risk Preferences and the Economics of Contracts, 85 Am. Econ. Rev. 447 (1995), 243

Allen, Douglas W., Cropshare Contracts, in 1 The New Palgrave Dictionary of Economics and the Law 569 (Peter Newman ed., 1998), 243

Allen, Douglas W., Homesteading and Property Rights: or, "How the West Was Really Won," 34 J.L. & Econ. 1 (1991), 230

Allison, John A., Chairman, BB&T Corporation, Keynote Address, The Competitive Enterprise Institute's 25th Anniversary Gala (June 11, 2009), 799

Subsidized Weather Insurance, 68 Stan. L. Rev. 571 (2016), 287
Ben-Shahar, Omri, Contracts Without Consent: Exploring a New Basis for Contractual Liability, 152 U. Pa. L. Rev. 1829 (2004), 522
Benston, George, Required Disclosure and the Stock Market: An Evaluation of the Securities Exchange Act of 1934, 63 Am. Econ. Rev. 132 (1972), 627
Bentham, Jeremy, On the Limits of the Penal Branch of Jurisprudence (Philip Schofield ed., 2010) (1789), 308
Bergman, Ben Zion, Torah and Torts: A Reply to Professor Kader, 4 J.L. & Religion 173 (1986), 202
Berman, Harold J. & Charles J. Reid, Jr., The Transformation of English Legal Science: From Hale to Blackstone, 45 Emory L.J. 437 (1996), 595
Bernstein, David E., Lochner v. New York: A Centennial Retrospective, 83 Wash. U. L.Q. 1469 (2005), 456
Bernstein, David E., Rehabilitating Lochner: Defending Individual Rights Against Progressive Reform (2011), 457
Bernstein, Lisa, Custom in Court, 110 Nw. U. L. Rev. 63 (2015), 215
Besen, Stanley M. & Joseph Farrell, Choosing How to Compete: Strategies and Tactics in Standardization, J. Econ. Persp., Spring 1994, at 117, 623
Beshears, John et al., How Are Preferences Revealed?, 92 J. Pub. Econ. 1787 (2008), 559
Besley, Timothy & Stephen Coate, Issue Unbundling via Citizens' Initiatives (Nat'l Bureau of Econ. Research, Working Paper No. 8036, 2000), 1012
Besley, Timothy, Property Rights and Investment Incentives: Theory and Evidence from Ghana, 103 J. Pol. Econ. 903 (1995), 239
Beth, Richard S. & Valerie Heitshusen, Cong. Research Serv. RL30360, Filibusters and Cloture in the Senate (2014), 666
Bhagwati, Jagdish, Directly Unproductive, Profit Seeking Activities, 90 J. Pol. Econ. 988 (1982), 494
Bial, Raymond, The Shaker Village 6 (2008), 224
Bikhchandani, Sushil et al., Learning from the Behavior of Others: Conformity, Fads, and Informational Cascades, J. Econ. Persp., Summer 1998, at 151, 849
Binmore, Ken, Fun and Games: A Text on Game Theory 12 n.8 (1992), 580
Bischoff, Bill, What the New Tax Law Will Do to Your Mortgage Tax Deduction, MarketWatch (Feb. 8, 2018), 438
Black, Duncan, On the Rationale of Group Decision-making, 56 J. Pol. Econ. 23 (1948), 502
Black, Sandra E. & Philip E. Strahan, The Division of Spoils: Rent-Sharing and Discrimination in a Regulated Industry, 91 Am. Econ. Rev. 814 (2001), 424, 789
Black's Law Dictionary 1102 (10th ed. 2014), 854
Blackman, Josh, SCOTUS After Scalia, 11 NYU J.L. & Liberty 48 (2017), 836
Blais, André & Stéphane Dion, Conclusion: Are Bureaucrats Budget Maximizers?, in The Budget-Maximizing Bureaucrat: Appraisals and Evidence 355 (André Blais & Stéphane Dion eds., 1991), 784
Blais, André, Donald E. Blake & Stéphane Dion, The Voting Behavior of Bureaucrats, in Budget-Maximizing Bureaucrat, at 205, 803
Blake, Donald E., Policy Attitudes and Political Ideology in the Public Sector, in Budget-Maximizing Bureaucrat, at 231, 803
Blakeslee, Sandra, Cells that Read Minds, N.Y. Times, Jan. 10, 2006, at F1, 559
Blau, Benjamin M. et al., Key Stakeholders' Stock Returns and the Affordable Care Act, 35 J. Ins. Reg. 1 (2016), 670
Blume, Lawrence & Daniel L. Rubinfeld, Compensation for Takings: An Economic Analysis, 72 Calif. L. Rev. 569 (1984), 284
Blume, Lawrence, Daniel L. Rubinfeld & Perry Shapiro, The Taking of Land: When Should Compensation be Paid?, 99 Q.J. Econ. 71 (1984), 285
Bob, Yonah Jeremy, Court Orders Gov't Pass New Law or Draft All Haredim, Jerusalem Post (Sept. 12, 2017), 959
Boettke, Peter & Todd J. Zywicki, Research Handbook on Austrian Law & Economics (eds. 2017), 7
Bork, Robert H., Coercing Virtue: The Worldwide Rule of Judges 80 (2003), 989
Bork, Robert H., The Antitrust Paradox: A Policy at War with Itself 53 (1978), 690
Boudreaux, Donald J. & A.C. Pritchard, Reassessing the Role of the Independent Judiciary in Enforcing Interest-Group Bargains, 5 Const. Pol. Econ. 1 (1994), 990
Boudreaux, Donald J. & A.C. Pritchard, Rewriting the Constitution: An Economic Analysis of the Constitutional Amendment Process, 62 Fordham L. Rev. 111 (1993), 1014
Bouoiyour, Jamal and Refk Selmi, Bitcoin: A Beginning of a New Phase?, 36 Econ. Bull. 1430 (2016), 625
Box-Steffensmeier, Janet M. et al., The Effects of Political Representation on the Electoral Advantages of House

Feldman, Allan M., Pareto Optimality, in 3 The New Palgrave Dictionary of Economics and the Law, 20
Field, Barry, The Evolution of Property Rights, 42 Kyklos 319 (1989), 245
Fiorina, Morris P., Congress: Keystone of the Washington Establishment 46 (2d ed. 1989), 786
Fiorina, Morris P., Representatives, Roll Calls, and Constituencies 38 (1974), 448, 665
Fiorina, Morris P., Voting Behavior, in Perspectives on Public Choice 391 (Dennis C. Mueller ed., 1997), 432
Fischel, William A., Regulatory Takings: Law, Economics, and Politics 74 (1995), 278
Fischel, William A., The Economics of Zoning Laws: A Property Rights Approach to American Land Use Controls (1985), 261
Fischer, Rebecca B., The History of American Bounty Hunting as a Study in Stunted Legal Growth, 33 N.Y.U. Rev. L. & Soc. Change 199 (2009), 315
Fisher, Ronald, The Genetical Theory of Natural Selection (complete variorum ed. 1999), 575
Fitzgerald, F. Scott, The Great Gatsby 63 (New York: Scribner Paperback Edition, 1995), 95
Flegenheimer, Matt, Senate Republicans Deploy 'Nuclear Option' to Clear Path for Gorsuch, N.Y. Times (Apr. 6, 2017), 666, 961
Fleurbaey, Marc et al., Any Non-welfarist Method of Policy Assessment Violates the Pareto Principle: A Comment, 111 J. Pol. Econ. 1382 (2003), 20
Flynn, Stephanie G., Duty to Mitigate Damages Upon a Tenant's Abandonment, 34 Real Prop., Prob. & Tr. J. 721 (2000), 192
Forced Rider, MIT Dictionary of Modern Economics (D.W. Pearce ed., 4th ed. 1981), 433
Fortin, Jacey & Jonah Engel Bromwich, Cleveland Police Officer Who Shot Tamir Rice Is Fired, N.Y. Times (May 30, 2017), 352
Foucault, Michel, Naissance de la Biopolitique: Cours au Collège de France 1978–1979 (2004), 318
Francis, Peter Jr., The Beads that Did Not Buy Manhattan Island, 67 N.Y. Hist. 4 (1986), 228
Francois, Joseph & Laura M. Baughman, The Unintended Consequences of U.S. Steel Import Tariffs: A Quantification of the Impact During 2002, at 12 (2003), 417
Freeman, Joanne B., Affairs of Honor: National Politics in the New Republic 179 (2002), 640
Freyer, Tony & Andrew P. Morriss, Creating Cayman as an Offshore Financial Center: Structure and Strategy Since 1960, 45 Ariz. St. L.J. 1297 (2013), 997
Fried, Gil, Baseball Spectators' Assumption of Risk: Is It "Fair" or Is It "Foul"?, 13 Marquette Sports L. Rev. 39 (2002), 90
Friedman, Alan E., The Economics of the Common Pool: Property Rights in Exhaustible Resources, 18 UCLA L. Rev. 855 (1971), 614
Friedman, David, Hanged for a Sheep: The Economics of Marginal Deterrence, 22 J. Legal Stud. 345 (1993), 334
Friedman, David, Other Paths, in Law's Order: What Economics Has to Do with the Law and Why it Matters 263 (2000), 314
Friedman, David, Why not Hang Them All? The Virtues of Inefficient Punishment, 107 J. Pol. Econ. S259 (1999), 400
Friedman, Ezra & Abraham L. Wickelgren, A New Angle on Rules Versus Standards, 16 Am. L. & Econ. Rev. 499 (2014), 471
Friedman, James, A Non-cooperative Equilibrium for Supergames, 38 Rev. Econ. Stud. 1 (1971), 590
Friedman, Jeffrey, The Rational Choice Controversy: Economic Models of Politics Reconsidered (ed., 1996), 5
Friedman, Lawrence M., A History of American Law 66 (2d ed. 1985), 266
Friedman, Lawrence M., Law in America: A Short History 109 (2004), 408
Friedman, Milton & Anna Jacobson Schwartz, A Monetary History of the United States, 1867–1960 15 (1965), 624
Friedman, Monroe, Consumer Boycotts in the United States, 1970–1980: Contemporary Events in Historical Perspective, 19 J. Consumer Aff. 96 (1985), 597
Friedmann, Daniel, The Efficient Breach Fallacy, 18 J. Legal Stud. 1 (1989), 200
Friehe, Tim & Thomas Miceli, Marginal Deterrence When Offenders Act Sequentially, 124 Econ. Letters 523 (2014), 334
Frisch, David, Amended U.C.C. Article 2 as Code Commentary, 11 Duq. Bus. L.J. 175 (2009), 215
From Bureaucracy to Business Enterprise: Legal and Policy Issues in the Transformation of Government Services (Michael J. Whincop ed., 2003), 789
Frymer, Paul, Building an American Empire: Territorial Expansion in the Antebellum Era, 1 U.C. Irvine L. Rev. 913 (2011), 230
Fudenberg, Drew & Eric Maskin, The Folk Theorem in Repeated Games with Discounting or with Incomplete

Polinsky, A. Mitchell & Steven Shavell, The Economic Theory of Public Enforcement of Law, 38 J. Econ. Literature 45 (2000), 307
Polinsky, A. Mitchell & Steven Shavell, The Optimal Tradeoff Between the Probability and Magnitude of Fines, 69 Am. Econ. Rev. 880 (1979), 333
Polinsky, A. Mitchell & Steven Shavell, The Optimal Uses of Fines and Imprisonment, 24 J. Pub. Econ. 89 (1984), 324
Polinsky, A. Mitchell & Steven Shavell, The Theory of Public Enforcement of Law, in 1 Handbook of Law & Economics 402 (A. Mitchell Polinsky & Steven Shavell eds., 2007), 308
Polinsky, A. Mitchell & Steven Shavell, The Uneasy Case for Product Liability, 123 Harv. L. Rev. 1437 (2010), 139
Polinsky, A. Mitchell, On the Choice Between Property Rules and Liability Rules, 18 Econ. Inquiry 233 (1980), 254
Polinsky, A. Mitchell, Private Versus Public Enforcement of Fines, 9 J. Legal Stud. 105 (1980), 315
Polinsky, A. Mitchell, Risk Sharing Through Breach of Contract Remedies, 12 J. Legal Stud. 427 (1983), 194
Pond, Shepard, The Maria Theresa Thaler: A Famous Trade Coin, Bull. Bus. Hist. Soc'y, Apr. 1941, at 29, 625
Popatka, John E. & William H. Page, Microsoft, Monopolization, and Network Externalities: Some Uses and Abuses of Economic Theory in Antitrust Decision Making, Antitrust Bull., Summer 1995, at 317, 623
Popper, Andrew F., Luncheon Session, 4 Admin. L.J. 71 (1990), 466
Porter, Robert & Douglas Zona, Detection of Bid Rigging in Procurement Auctions, 101 J. Pol. Econ. 518 (1993), 590
Posner, Eric A. & Adrian Vermeule, Executive Unbound: After the Madisonian Republic (2010), 472
Posner, Eric A. & Cass R. Sunstein, The Law of Other States, 59 Stan. L. Rev. 131 (2006), 849
Posner, Richard A. & Andrew Rosenfield, Impossibility and Related Doctrines in Contract Law: An Economic Analysis, 6 J. Legal Stud. 83 (1977), 194
Posner, Richard A., A Theory of Negligence, 1 J. Legal Stud. 29 (1972), 77
Posner, Richard A., Economic Analysis of Law, 7, 46, 162, 195, 237, 388, 469, 470, 934
Posner, Richard A., Gary Becker's Contributions to Law and Economics, 22 J. Legal Stud. 211 (1993), 391
Posner, Richard A., Gratuitous Promises in the Law, 6 J. Legal Stud. 411 (1977), 154
Posner, Richard A., Legal Formalism, Legal Realism, and the Interpretation of Statutes and the Constitution, 37 Case W. Res. L. Rev. 179 (1986), 391, 657, 695
Posner, Richard A., The Economics of Justice chs. 7 & 8 (1983), 314
Posner, Richard A., The Federal Courts: Challenge and Reform 381 (1996), 838
Posner, Richard A., The Federal Trade Commission, 37 U. Chi. L. Rev. 47 (1969), 794
Posner, Richard A., The Social Costs of Monopoly and Regulation, 83 J. Pol. Econ. 807 (1975), 435
Posner, Richard A., Theories of Economic Regulation, 5 Bell J. Econ. & Mgmt. Sci. 335 (1974), 419
Posner, Richard A., Utilitarianism, Economics, and Legal Theory, 8 J. Legal Stud. 103 (1979), 393
Posner, Richard A., What Do Judges and Justices Maximize? (The Same Thing Everybody Else Does), 3 Sup. Ct. Econ. Rev. 1 (1993), 829
Post, David G. & Steven C. Salop, Issues and Outcomes, Guidance, and Indeterminacy: A Reply to Professor John Rogers and Others, 49 Vand. L. Rev. 1069 (1996), 890
Post, David G. & Steven C. Salop, Rowing Against the Tidewater: A Theory of Voting by Multijudge Panels, 80 Geo. L.J. 743 (1992), 888
Poundstone, William, Prisoner's Dilemma 83 (1992), 582
Powell Papers, Washington & Lee University School of Law, 834
Powell, Stare Decisis and Judicial Restraint, 1991 Journal of Supreme Court History 13, 858
Pramuk, Jacob, Trump Needles Mitch McConnell Over the Senate's 'Horrible' Filibuster Rule, CNBC (Sept. 28, 2017, 10:02 AM), 667
Priest, Dana & William Claiborne, Voters in Several States, D.C. Adopt Limits for Legislators, Wash. Post, Nov. 9, 1994, at A25, 1011
Priest, George L. & Benjamin Klein, The Selection of Disputes for Litigation, 13 J. Legal Stud. 1 (1984), 392, 842
Priest, George L., Procedural Versus Substantive Controls of Mass Tort Class Actions, 26 J. Legal Stud. 521 (1997), 383
Priest, George L., Products Liability Law and the Accident Rate, in Liability: Perspectives and Policies 184 (Robert E. Litan & Clifford Winston eds., 1988), 396
Priest, George L., Products Liability Law and the Accident Rate, in Liability: Perspectives

Richman, William M. & William L. Reynolds, Injustice on Appeal: The United States Courts of Appeals in Crisis (2013), 392
Ridley, Matthew, The Origins of Virtue: Human Instincts and the Evolution of Cooperation 58 (1996), 580
Ridley, Matthew, The Red Queen: Sex and the Evolution of Human Nature (1993), 337
Riker, William H. & Barry R. Weingast, Constitutional Regulation of Legislative Choice: The Political Consequences of Judicial Deference to Legislatures, 74 Va. L. Rev. 373 (1988), 484
Riker, William H. & Steven J. Brams, The Paradox of Vote Trading, 67 Am. Pol. Sci. Rev. 1235 (1973), 439
Riker, William H., Liberalism Against Populism: A Confrontation Between the Theory of Democracy and the Theory of Social Choice (1982), 508, 551
Riker, William H., Political Science and Rational Choice, in Perspectives on Positive Political Economy 163 (James E. Alt & Kenneth A. Shepsle eds., 1990), 736
Riker, William H., The Paradox of Voting and Congressional Rules for Voting on Amendments, 52 Am. Pol. Sci. Rev. 349 (1958), 543, 901
Riker, William H., The Theory of Political Coalitions (1962), 449, 515, 666, 942
Ringleb, Al H. & Steven N. Wiggins, Liability and Large-Scale, Long-Term Hazards, 98 J. Pol. Econ. 574 (1990), 127
Rizzo, Salvador, Trump Administration Botches Basic Civics While Calling for Line-Item Veto, Wash. Post (March 27, 2018), 956
Roberts, Chief Justice John G., Year-End Report on the Federal Judiciary (2008), 829
Roberts, John C., Majority Voting in Congress: Further Notes on the Constitutionality of the Senate Cloture Rule, 20 J.L. & Pol. 505 (2004), 667
Roberts, Sam, Meet Grand Central's Flesh-and-Blood Landlord, N.Y. Times City Room (Jan. 29. 2013), 292
Robinson, Glen O., Public Choice Speculations on the Item Veto, 74 Va. L. Rev. 403 (1988), 446, 672, 955
Robinson, Matthew & Marian Williams, The Myth of a Fair Criminal Justice System, 6 Just. Pol'y J. 1 (2009), 332
Roe, Mark J., Delaware's Politics, 118 Harv. L. Rev. 2491 (2005), 999
Rogers, John M., "I Vote this Way Because I'm Wrong": The Supreme Court Justice as Epimenides, 79 Ky. L.J. 439, 442 (1990), 888
Rogerson, William, Efficient Reliance and Damage Measure for Breach of Contract, 15 RAND J. Econ. 39 (1984), 137, 177
Romano, Roberta, Law as a Product: Some Pieces of the Incorporation Puzzle, 1 J.L. Econ. & Org. 225 (1985), 627, 999
Rosen, Jeffrey, The New Look of Liberalism on the Court, N.Y. Times Mag. (Oct. 5, 1997), 1016
Rosen, Mark D., Was Shelley v. Kraemer Wrongly Decided? Some New Answers, 95 Calif. L. Rev. 451 (2007), 263
Rosenbaum, H. Jon & Peter C. Sederberg, Vigilantism: An Analysis of Establishment Violence, 6 Comp. Pol. 541 (1974), 315
Rosenberg, David & Steven Shavell, A Model in Which Suits Are Brought for Their Nuisance Value, 5 Int'l Rev. L. & Econ. 3 (1985), 375
Rosenkranz, Nicholas Quinn, Condorcet and the Constitution: A Response to the Law of Other States, 59 Stan. L. Rev. 1281 (2007), 849
Ross, Janell & Wesley Lowery, Black Lives Matter Shifts from Protests to Policy Under Trump, Chi. Trib. (May 4, 2017, 7:41 PM), 663
Rossum, Ralph, Popular Election of Senators, Heritage Guide to the Constitution, 944
Rotemberg, Julio J. & Garth Saloner, A Supergame-Theoretic Model of Price Wars During Booms, 76 Am. Econ. Rev. 390 (1986), 593
Roth, Alvin E., Game Theory as a Tool for Market Design, in Game Practice: Contributions from Applied Game Theory 7–18 (Fioravante Patrone et al. eds., 2000), 575
Roth, Alvin E., The National Resident Matching Program as a Labor Market, 275 J. Am. Med. Ass'n 1054 (1996), 575
Rothschild, Michael & Joseph Stiglitz, Equilibrium in Competitive Insurance Markets: An Essay on the Economics of Imperfect Information, 90 Q.J. Econ. 629 (1976), 159
Rottenberg, Simon, The Baseball Players' Labor Market, 64 J. Pol. Econ. 242 (1956), 217
Rouan, Rick, Dimon says Dodd-Frank Puts 'Bigger Moat' Around JPMorgan Chase, Columbus Bus. First (Feb. 5, 2013), 478
Rousseau, Jean Jacques, The Social Contract (Maurice Cranston trans., Penguin Books 1968) (1762), 12
Rowley, Charles K., Introduction, in 1 Public Choice Theory: Homo Economicus in the Market Place xxiv (Charles K. Rowley ed., 1993), 435
Royce, Edward, From Slavery to Sharecropping: The Origins of Southern Sharecropping (1993), 243

Shavell, Steven, The Social Versus Private Incentive to Bring Suit in a Costly Legal System, 11 J. Legal Stud. 333 (1982), 368, 390
Shavell, Steven, Torts in Which Victim and Injurer Act Sequentially, 26 J.L. & Econ. 589 (1983), 92
Shavell, Steven, Uncertainty over Causation and the Determination of Civil Liability, 28 J.L. & Econ. 587 (1985), 119
Shaw, Beth Z., Judging Juries: Evaluating Renewed Proposals for Specialized Juries from a Public Choice Perspective, 2006 UCLA J.L. & Tech. 3, 849
Shepherd, George B. & Morgan Cloud, Time and Money: Discovery Leads to Hourly Billing, 1999 U. Ill. L. Rev. 91, 378
Shepherd, George B., No African-American Lawyers Allowed: The Inefficient Racism of the ABA's Accreditation of Law Schools, 53 J. Legal Educ. 103 (2003), 428
Shepherd, Joanna M., Blakely's Silver Lining: Sentencing Guidelines, Judicial Discretion, and Crime, 58 Hastings L.J. 533 (2007), 388, 408
Shepherd, Joanna M., Fear of the First Strike: The Full Deterrent Effect of California's Two- and Three-Strikes Legislation, 31 J. Legal Stud. 159 (2002), 341
Shepherd, Joanna M., Murders of Passion, Execution Delays, and the Deterrence of Capital Punishment, 33 J. Legal Stud. 283 (2004), 346
Shepsle, Kenneth A. & Barry R. Weingast, Structure-Induced Equilibrium and Legislative Choice, 37 Pub. Choice 503 (1981), 31, 525
Shepsle, Kenneth A. & Barry R. Weingast, The Institutional Foundations of Committee Power, 81 Am. Pol. Sci. Rev. 85 (1987), 525
Shepsle, Kenneth A., Bureaucratic Drift, Coalitional Drift, and Time Consistency: A Comment on Macey, 8 J.L. Econ. & Org. 111 (1992), 752
Shepsle, Kenneth A., Congress Is a "They," Not an "It": Legislative Intent as an Oxymoron, 12 Int'l Rev. L. & Econ. 239 (1992), 17, 526, 687
Sheth, Sonam, Ivanka Trump's New White House Position Could Be an Ethical Minefield, Bus. Insider (Mar. 25, 2017, 9:29 AM), 748
Shick, Blair C. & Irving H. Plotkin, Torrens in the United States: A Legal and Economic History of American Land-Registration Systems 21 (1978), 237
Shleifer, Andrei & Robert W. Vishny, Corruption, 108 Q.J. Econ. 599 (1993), 342
Shontell, Alyson, How to Lose Friends and 'Exfoliate' People—Trump's Son-in-Law, Jared Kushner, is Caught Between 2 Worlds, and His Friends are Cutting Ties, Bus. Insider (Mar. 29, 2017, 8:31 AM), 748
Siegan, Bernard H., Economic Liberties and the Constitution 113 (1980), 456
Silving, Helen, Compensation for Victims of Criminal Violence—A Roundtable, in Considering the Victim 198 (Joe Hudson & Burt Galaway eds., 1975), 311
Skeel, David, Debt's Dominion: A History of Bankruptcy Law in America 24 (2001), 531
Skeel, David, The New Financial Deal: Understanding the Dodd-Frank Act and Its (Unintended) Consequences 19 (2011), 471
Skolnick, Jerome H. et al., The Social Structure of Street Dealing, 9 Am. J. Police 1, 28 (1990), 326
Skowronski, Will, BDC: More Mediation, Less 'Quick Take' to be Used in Property Disputes, Balt. Bus. J. (July 11, 2007, 12:46 PM), 652
Slobogin, Christopher, The Exclusionary Rule: Is It on Its Way Out? Should It Be?, 10 Ohio St. J. Crim. L. 341 (2013), 410
Slonimczyk, Fabián & Peter Skott, Employment and Distribution Effects of the Minimum Wage, 84 J. Econ. Behav. & Org. 245 (2012), 40
Smith, Adam, An Inquiry into the Nature and Causes of the Wealth of Nations 241 (Edwin Cannan ed., Univ. of Chicago Press 1967) (5th ed. 1789), 397
Smith, John Maynard, Evolution and the Theory of Games (1982), 575
Smith, Mitch, Minnesota Officer Acquitted in Killing of Philando Castile, N.Y. Times (June 16, 2017), 352
Snell, Tracy L., Bureau of Just. Stat., Capital Punishment, 2014–2015 (2017), 346
Snodgrass, Mary Ellen, Coins and Currency: An Historical Encyclopedia (2007), 624
Snyder, Edward & James Hughes, The English Rule for Allocating Legal Costs: Evidence Confronts Theory, 6 J.L. Econ. & Org. 345 (1990), 371
Solan, Lawrence M., The Interpretation of Legal Language, 4 Ann. Rev. Linguistics 337 (2018), 657
Somin, Ilya, Democracy and Political Ignorance: Why Smaller Government Is Smarter (2d ed. 2016), 27
Somin, Ilya, Opinion, Gorsuch Is Right About Chevron Deference, Wash. Post: Volokh Conspiracy (Mar. 25, 2017), 779
Somin, Ilya, The Grasping Hand: "Kelo v. City of New London" and the Limits of Eminent Domain (2015), 651
Somin, Ilya, The Limits of Backlash: Assessing the Political Response to Kelo, 93 Minn. L. Rev. 2100 (2009), 1012

Somm, Paul K. & Yannet M. Lathrop, Raise Wages, Kill Jobs?: Seven Decades of Historical Data Find No Correlation Between Minimum Wage Increases and Employment Levels, Nat'l Emp. Law Center Data Brief (May 2016), 40
Sorkin, Andrew Ross, What Timothy Geithner Really Thinks, N.Y. Times Mag. (May 8, 2014), 476
SpearIt, Legal Punishment as Civil Ritual: Making Cultural Sense of Harsh Punishment, 82 Miss. L.J. 1 (2013), 335
Special Issue, Quadratic Voting and the Public Good, 172 Pub. Choice 1 (2017), 500
Spence, David B. & Frank Cross, A Public Choice Case for the Administrative State, 89 Geo. L.J. 97 (2000), 782
Spence, Michael A., Consumer Misperceptions, Product Failure and Producer Liability, 44 Rev. Econ. Stud. 561 (1977), 137, 214
Spier, Kathryn E. & James D. Dana, Jr., Expertise and Contingent Fees: The Role of Asymmetric Information in Attorney Compensation, 9 J.L. Econ. & Org. 349 (1993), 377
Spier, Kathryn E., Litigation, in 1 The Handbook of Law and Economics 259, 301 (A. Mitchell Polansky & Steven Shavell eds., 2007), 370
Spier, Kathryn E., Pretrial Bargaining and the Design of Fee-Shifting Rules, 25 RAND J. Econ. 197 (1994), 373
Spier, Kathryn E., The Dynamics of Pretrial Negotiation, 59 Rev. Econ. Stud. 93 (1992), 383
Spitzer, Matthew L., Multicriterial Choice Processes: An Application of Public Choice Theory to Bakke, The FCC, and the Courts, 88 Yale L.J. 717 (1979), 499, 565
Staff of H.R. Comm. on Oversight & Gov't Reform, 113th Cong., Rep. on the Department of Justice's "Operation Choke Point": Illegally Choking Off Legitimate Business? (2014), 441
Stake, Jeffrey, Inheritance Law, in 2 The New Palgrave Dictionary of Economics and the Law 311, 267
Starr, Ross M., General Equilibrium Theory 31 (2d ed. 2011), 60
State Legislative Term Limits, U.S. Term Limits, 1011
State-Based Exchanges, Ctrs. for Medicare & Medicaid Servs. (Sept. 15, 2017), 773
Stearns, Maxwell L. & Megan J. McGinnis, A Social Choice View of Law and Economics, in Methodologies of Law and Economics 72 (Thomas S. Ulen ed., 2017), 182, 206
Stearns, Maxwell L. & Todd J. Zywicki, Public Choice Concepts and Applications in Law (2009), 6, 394
Stearns, Maxwell L., A Beautiful Mend: A Game Theoretical Analysis of the Dormant Commerce Clause Doctrine, 45 Wm. & Mary L. Rev. 1 (2003), 156, 620, 1002
Stearns, Maxwell L., An Introduction to Social Choice, in Elgar Handbook in Public Choice and Public Law (Daniel Farber & Anne Joseph O'Connell eds., 2009), 499, 541
Stearns, Maxwell L., Book Review, 86 Pub. Choice 379 (1996), 704
Stearns, Maxwell L., Constitutional Process: A Social Choice Analysis of Supreme Court Decision-Making, 499, 541, 877, 909
Stearns, Maxwell L., Direct (Anti-) Democracy, 80 Geo. Wash. L. Rev. 311 (2012), 467, 900, 1011
Stearns, Maxwell L., Election 2016 and the Structural Constitution: A Preliminary Framing, 76 Md. L. Rev. Endnotes 4 (2016), 744
Stearns, Maxwell L., How Outcome Voting Promotes Principled Issue Identification: A Reply to Professor John Rogers and Others, 49 Vand. L. Rev. 1045 (1996), 509, 895
Stearns, Maxwell L., Ideological Blindspots (part IV): The Dimensionality of Trumpism, Blindspot Blog (Apr. 14, 2017), 746
Stearns, Maxwell L., Obergefell, Fisher, and the Dimensionality of Tiers, 19 U. Pa. J. Const. Law 1043 (2017), 499, 544, 872, 903
Stearns, Maxwell L., Obergefell, Fisher, and the Inversion of Tiers, Balkinization (Apr. 24, 2016), 903
Stearns, Maxwell L., Public Choice and Public Law: Readings and Commentary (1997), 24, 394, 425, 482, 558, 621, 693, 839, 937, 998
Stearns, Maxwell L., Reflections on the Aftermath of Election 2016, 77 Md. L. Rev. 271 (2017), 746
Stearns, Maxwell L., Should Justices Ever Switch Votes?: Miller v. Albright in Social Choice Perspective, 7 Sup. Ct. Econ. Rev. 87 (1999), 883
Stearns, Maxwell L., Standing and Social Choice: Historical Evidence, 144 U. Pa. L. Rev. 309 (1995), 621
Stearns, Maxwell L., Standing at the Crossroads: The Roberts Court in Historical Perspective, 83 Notre Dame L. Rev. 875 (2008), 833
Stearns, Maxwell L., Standing Back from the Forest: Justiciability and Social Choice, 83 Calif. L. Rev. 1309 (1995), 621
Stearns, Maxwell L., The Case for Including Marks v. United States in the Canon of

The Federalist No. 59, at 332 (Alexander Hamilton) (Clinton Rossiter ed., 1961), 1008
The Federalist No. 62 (James Madison) (Clinton Rossiter ed., 1961), 945, 1008
The Federalist No. 73, at 411 (Alexander Hamilton) (Clinton Rossiter ed., 1961), 954
The Federalist No. 78 (Alexander Hamilton) (Clinton Rossiter ed., 1961), 701, 988
The Godfather (Paramount 1972), 581
The Informant! (Warner Bros. Pictures 2009), 592
The Nature of the Firm: Origins, Evolution, and Development 18 (Oliver E. Williamson & Sidney G. Winter eds., 1991), 156
The Peevyhouses: The Most Screwed Victims in Case-Law History, PrawfsBlawg (May 9, 2008), 208
The Term-Limited States, Nat'l Conf. St. Legislatures (Mar. 3, 2013), 1011
The White House, Occupational Licensing: A Framework for Policymakers (2015), 485
Thibault, John & Laurens Walker, A Theory of Procedure, 66 Calif. L. Rev. 541 (1978), 358
Thierer, Adam, Who'll Really Benefit from Net Neutrality Regulation?, CBS News (Dec. 21, 2010), 778
Thomas, John R., Formalism at the Federal Circuit, 52 Am. U. L. Rev. 771 (2003), 759
Thompson, Barton H. Jr., The Endangered Species Act: A Case Study in Takings & Incentives, 49 Stan. L. Rev. 305 (1997), 232
Thompson, Neil C. & Jeffrey M. Kuhn, Does Winning a Patent Race Lead to More Follow-On Innovation? (Jan. 2017), 436
Tiebout, Charles M., A Pure Theory of Local Expenditures, 64 J. Pol. Econ. 416 (1956), 245
Tollison, Robert D., Public Choice and Legislation, 74 Va. L. Rev. 339 (1988), 990
Tollison, Robert D., Rent Seeking, in Perspectives on Public Choice, at 506, 436
Tonry, Michael, Malign Neglect: Race, Crime, and Punishment in America (1995), 325
Totty, Evan, The Effect of Minimum Wages on Employment: A Factor Model Approach, 55 Econ. Inquiry 1712 (2017), 40
Treaster, Joseph B. & Abby Goodnough, Powerful Storm Threatens Havoc Along Coast, N.Y. Times (Aug. 29, 2005), 42
Tschoegl, Adrian, Maria Theresa's Thaler: A Case of International Money, 27 E. Econ. J. 443 (2001), 625
Tu, Kevin V. & Michael W. Meredith, Rethinking Virtual Currency Regulation in the Bitcoin Age, 90 Wash. L. Rev. 271 (2015), 625
Tullock, Gordon & Geoffrey Brennan, Why So Much Stability, 37 Pub. Choice 189 (1981), 31
Tullock, Gordon, Public Decisions as Public Goods, 79 J. Pol. Econ. 913 (1971), 795
Tullock, Gordon, The Transitional Gains Trap, 6 Bell J. Econ. 671 (1975), 437
Tullock, Gordon, The Welfare Costs of Tariffs, Monopolies, and Theft, 5 W. Econ. J. 224 (1967), 435
Tullock, Gordon, Trials on Trial: The Pure Theory of Legal Procedure 197 (1980), 394
Tullock, Gordon, Why So Much Stability, 37 Pub. Choice 189 (1981), 525
Tung, Frederick, Before Competition: Origins of the Internal Affairs Doctrine, 32 J. Corp. L. 33 (2006), 627
TV Tropes, Series: Golden Balls, 575
U.S. Gov't Accountability Office, GAO–14–621, Large Bank Holding Companies: Expectations of Government Support (2014), 476
Ulen, Thomas S., The Efficiency of Specific Performance: Toward a Unified Theory of Contract Remedies, 83 Mich. L. Rev. 341 (1984), 200
Ulen, Thomas S., The Public Use of Private Property: A Dual-Constraint Theory of Efficient Governmental Takings, in Taking Property and Just Compensation 163 (Nicholas Mercuro ed., 1992), 277
Umbeck, John, A Theory of Property Rights with Application to the California Gold Rush 90 (1981), 229
Upton Sinclair, The Jungle (1906), 419
Vaccine Injury Compensation Program, U.S. Dep't of Just. (updated Jan. 12, 2017), 603
Valentino, Nicholas A., John Leslie King, & Walter W. Hill, Polling and Prediction in the 2016 Presidential Election, 50 Computer 110 (2017), 744
Varon, Jay N., Promoting Settlements and Limiting Litigation Costs by Means of the Offer of Judgment: Some Suggestions for Using and Revising Rule 68, 33 Am. U. L. Rev. 813 (1984), 372
Vendantam, Shankar, When Crime Pays: Prison Can Teach Some to be Better Criminals, NPR: Morning Edition (Feb. 1, 2013), 339
Vermeule, Adrian, Common Law Constitutionalism and the Limits of Reason, 107 Colum. L. Rev. 1482 (2007), 849
Vernon, J.R., World War II Fiscal Policies and the End of the Great Depression, 54 J. Econ. Hist. 850 (1994), 440
Vickrey, William, Public Economics 29 (Richard Arnott et al. eds., 1994), 512, 551

LAW AND ECONOMICS: PRIVATE AND PUBLIC

PART I

Introductory Methodology

CHAPTER 1

Introduction to the Economic Analysis of Law

Introduction

Legal scholars often apply external methodologies in the study of law. A list of helpful external disciplines includes Anthropology, Critical Studies, Evolutionary Biology, History, Literature, Philosophy, Political Science, Psychology, and Sociology. It also includes Economics. Since the early 1960s, a vast and influential literature has emerged in "Law and Economics." This field boasts numerous books, prestigious peer review journals, and academic conferences that take place within the United States and around the world.

Before describing Law and Economics, it is worth saying a few words about economics itself. Economics is a discipline that embraces several complementary methodologies. These include neoclassical economics, public choice, social choice, game theory, and Austrian economics. It also includes behavioral economics, which bridges economic theory and applied psychology. Although each of these subdisciplines has developed its own analytical tools, with the possible exception of behavioral economics, they generally share a set of common premises and methodologies.

I. COMMON FEATURES OF ECONOMIC ANALYSIS

Positivism: Each of these economics subdisciplines developed with the goal of seeking to explain existing behaviors—of individuals, of groups, or of institutions—that other disciplines, including the alternative complementary methodologies that have been applied to the study of law, found anomalous and thus difficult to understand. Those who work within the tradition of economic analysis thus share a set of tools that grow out of a tradition of "positivism."[1] Positivism means an effort to explain "what is," as opposed to offering a "normative" account that explains what the scholar asserts "should be."[2]

---

1 *See* MILTON FRIEDMAN, *The Methodology of Positive Economics*, *in* ESSAYS IN POSITIVE ECONOMICS 3 (1953).

2 To be sure, economic analysis of law has also generated a literature on how legal rules *should* develop based on specified normative criteria, typically associated with concepts of efficiency. One of the themes of this book is distinguishing positive and normative uses of economic theory, and offering economic accounts

Simplification versus nuance: Each economics subdiscipline employs "models" as a principal means of gaining a positive explanatory insight. Models are tools designed to simplify and capture the essence of something more complex. Effective models create manageable images of a more complex reality, thereby avoiding the clutter and messiness of reality itself. The construction of models inevitably produces the following tradeoff: *Simpler models are more manageable but less nuanced; complex models are more nuanced but less manageable.* In effect, economic modeling constantly seeks to balance the competing criteria of simplification versus nuance as a means of offering insights that are neither so general as to be meaningless nor so specific as to lose the benefits of generalization. The principal benefit of generality is the power to gain important insights in new contexts.

Rationality: The foundational assumption that typically underlies economic models is "rationality." Rationality is a sufficiently important and subtle concept that there are articles and books devoted just to this topic. As a result, we will spend considerable time in this book, including in this chapter, exploring the concept. Rationality is a contested concept both within economic theory and among those who view economics from other disciplinary perspectives. Rationality also forms part of the divide between scholars in the field of behavioral economics on one side, and those who employ the other listed economics subdisciplines on the other.[3] Economists tend to define "rationality" differently from those writing within other disciplines, including law.[4]

Occasionally, those working within a Law and Economics tradition confront the objection: "But you mistakenly assume that people are rational." When you hear this, please compare how the speaker understands rationality with how rationality is used in the relevant economic model. Without agreement on what rationality means, the conversation entails people speaking past one another and thus without advancing common understanding.

Minimalism: Also called "reductionism," minimalism implies an effort to exclude from consideration features that often play a central role in noneconomic accounts of human behavior. Although this relates to the tradeoff in modeling between simplification and nuance, here we emphasize a different aspect. Non-economic accounts of human behavior often consider the nature of individual preferences and how they are formed. Economists generally take preferences as given and claim no particular methodological expertise in devising robust accounts of what particular persons regard as "goods" or "bads." To be sure, economists believe that preference formation is important to a holistic

---

drawn from other subdisciplines when there is a persistent divergence between the state of the law as it exists versus the state of the law as those employing economics tools argue it should be.

[3] One of the central inquiries of behavioral economics is whether observed behaviors are inconsistent with the rationality assumption that pervades much economic analysis, including most notably, neoclassical economics. This implies that rather than accepting the standard definition of rationality as a starting point, behavioral economics sometimes employs a different set of premises about human behavior to create testable hypotheses concerning how individuals manifest rationality. For an overview of behavioral law and economics, see BEHAVIORAL LAW AND ECONOMICS (Cass R. Sunstein ed., 2000). For an article exploring the implications of behavioral law and economics for public choice, see Gary M. Lucas, Jr. & Slavisa Tasic, *Behavioral Public Choice and the Law*, 118 W. VA. L. REV. 199 (2015).

[4] As discussed later in this book, rationality also sometimes takes on different meanings within economic theory itself as seen in the comparison of rationality described later in this chapter and the definition offered in Chapter 3, introducing social choice theory.

understanding of individual behavior and to understanding societal and cultural differences. However, economists prefer to leave such inquiries to those trained in other fields of social science such as anthropology, psychology, sociology, and religion. This is not because the inquiry is unimportant; rather, it is because the economics toolbox has less to say about it.[5]

Testable hypotheses: A benefit of the reductionist economic approach is that it allows for the development of testable hypotheses. By capturing essential features of observable phenomena and by deliberately excluding extraneous details, economists are able to focus on one or a few variables that if changed are most apt to alter incentives, individual behavior, and collective outcomes.[6] An important implication of this approach is that economic models should, in theory, be subject to the possibility of being "falsified," meaning that for any model-driven account of an observed phenomenon there should be a test capable of disproving it.

Although the various subdisciplines within economics generally share these features, notable differences remain. Throughout this book, we will discuss both the commonalities and differences among these various "schools," including where they agree and where they diverge on specific questions of law and public policy. Indeed, one of the features that we believe makes this Law and Economics coursebook unique is that it deliberately brings together schools of economic thought that sometimes lead to differing places on related questions. When we encounter phenomena that a given theory cannot adequately explain, rather than abandoning economic analysis in favor of an account from another discipline, we survey other economic approaches for alternative ways to frame the problem. This approach reveals the power of economic analysis in helping devise competing normative framings, the choice of which ultimately rest on noneconomic grounds.

The specific methodologies associated with each subdiscipline within economics are the product of the kinds of questions they are designed to study. We now consider some of these differing approaches and tools.

A. Subdisciplines of Economic Analysis

Neoclassical economics tends to focus on the study of behaviors of individuals and firms as they operate within private markets; how market mechanisms, including firms, develop and evolve; and how differing markets structures, including competition and monopoly (along with structures in between), affect various equilibrium outcomes. Neoclassical

---

[5] Commentators sometimes simultaneously criticize economic analysis for appearing hegemonic, seeking to explain too much (sometimes called "economic imperialism"), and other times for its self-imposed restrictions, especially with respect to preference formation. *See, e.g., infra* Part V.A (reviewing analysis by Daniel Farber and Philip Frickey, who criticize the extension of economic theory into politics and who further fault those who contend that economics needs no theory as to why some individuals have a preference for voting.)

[6] *See generally* FRIEDMAN, *supra* note 1, at 7–23. For a debate on whether public choice scholarship has lived up to its expectation of developing testable hypotheses capable of falsification, see *infra* Chapter 9 (discussing DONALD P. GREEN & IAN SHAPIRO, PATHOLOGIES OF RATIONAL CHOICE: A CRITIQUE OF APPLICATIONS IN POLITICAL SCIENCE (1994), and THE RATIONAL CHOICE CONTROVERSY: ECONOMIC MODELS OF POLITICS RECONSIDERED (Jeffrey Friedman ed., 1996)).

economics is closely tied to price theory, which studies various market configurations,[7] and which has played a particularly significant role in the development of the influential Chicago School of law and economics.

Public choice applies the tools of economic analysis to nonmarket decision-making, or, perhaps more simply, to politics.[8] These tools have been extended to the study of law and lawmaking institutions.[9] The term "public choice," has generally been understood to have two somewhat different meanings. It is sometimes used to distinguish collective, non-market decision making from "private choice," meaning individual market decision-making. Other times it is used as an umbrella term underneath which we can place specific sub-fields of public choice, including interest group theory, social choice, and game theory. The term public choice has also been used in a more specific sense to be synonymous with interest group theory.[10] We now break these down and describe separately each of the sub-fields of public choice:

Interest group theory studies the incentives and effects of group activity and political institutions. More specifically it focuses on the relationships between private actors and myriad governmental institutions; how firms and groups influence lawmaking bodies, often to gain insulation from competition (called "rent seeking"); and how institutions adapt in response to interest group pressures. Interest group theory plays a particularly significant role in the Chicago public choice school, and also influences other schools.

Social choice theory studies the different implications of a critical aspect of rationality—the assumption of transitive preference orderings (A preferred to B preferred to C implies A preferred to C)—as applied to individuals, on the one hand, and to groups, on the other, and how these differences affect the capacity of institutions to transform individual preferences into collective outputs. Social choice has also been used to study the evolution of institutions and rules, thus influencing the study of constitutional law and lawmaking processes.

Game theory studies interactive individual and institutional behaviors in structured settings as a means of identifying the effects of specified incentives on player strategies

---

7 We provide an introduction to price theory in Chapter 2.

8 In his influential treatise, DENNIS MUELLER, PUBLIC CHOICE III 1 (2003), Dennis Mueller states that public choice applies economics to politics. We agree but we also take a somewhat broader view of the relevant applications. We also include the use of economic tools to study legal doctrines and lawmaking institutions, which might not fall within all readers' understanding of politics. We will occasionally explore related questions concerning how, if at all, to distinguish law from politics.

9 The predecessor to this volume, MAXWELL L. STEARNS & TODD J. ZYWICKI, PUBLIC CHOICE CONCEPTS AND APPLICATIONS IN LAW (2009), was designed to bring together these methods and applications for law students. That book has played a significant role in the development of Chapters 1–2 and 11–24 of this volume.

10 Historically, public choice has also been associated with three "schools," based on prominent academics in Chicago, Virginia, and Rochester. For a more detailed discussion, see STEARNS & ZYWICKI, supra note 9, at xii (associating George Stigler and Gary Becker with the Chicago school; James Buchanan, Gordon Tullock, Robert Tollison, and Nicolaus Tideman with the Virginia school; and William Riker with the Rochester School). In parts IV and V of this volume, we draw upon insights from each of these schools, along with other methodologies.

within single period and iterated (repeated) games.[11] Both social choice and game theory have given rise to vast, often mathematically sophisticated, literatures, and each provides critical insights that cut across economics and other fields.[12]

Austrian Economics studies the limits of information assimilation in conveying relative values and the implications for employing models to predict market responses to changed conditions. This school emphasizes the unique capacity of decentralized market processes to capture and channel disparate information and to move resources to more highly valued uses. Although developed as an intellectual critique of European central planning, associated with socialism, Austrian economics has also been deployed to challenge particular claims associated with the Chicago School of law and economics along with associated normative prescriptions for law and public policy.[13]

Behavioral Economics employs laboratory and natural experiments to study how individuals respond to incentives set out in various formal games, sometimes calling into question the robustness of rationality-driven models. This field, which offers valuable insights into individual and interpersonal human behavior, differs from the other identified subdisciplines of economics in important ways. Economics generally takes individual preferences as given and as revealed through consumer choices. By contrast, behavioral economics, which is closely tied to applied psychology, seeks in part to explain preference formation. This includes identifying certain behaviors that are claimed to defy neoclassical understandings of rationality. Behavioral economics challenges, for example, the assumption that actual choices are the best evidence of true preferences.[14]

Most courses on law and economics select a subset of tools and analytical approaches. Conventional courses have tended to focus on neoclassical economics, often associated with the Chicago School, and to explore common law subject matter, with some extensions into judicial process and criminal law.[15] This approach gained a strong foothold in the legal academy in the early 1980s.[16] The Chicago School offered significant explanatory power with respect to several bodies of common law doctrine, most notably tort, contract, property, and crime. The neoclassical accounts of these and other doctrinal

---

[11] Game theory has been successfully employed to study non-human as well as human actors. Evolutionary biology often employs parallel tools to those employed in game theory. For illustrations involving the Game of Chicken and Hawk-Dove, see *infra* Chapter 16.

[12] Although game theory is not always viewed as a subfield of public choice, we have found that introducing elementary game theory significantly enhances student understanding.

[13] We do not devote a specific chapter to Austrian Economics, but throughout this volume, we introduce concepts drawn from this school as appropriate. *See also* RESEARCH HANDBOOK ON AUSTRIAN LAW & ECONOMICS (Peter Boettke & Todd J. Zywicki eds., 2017).

[14] We also do not devote a specific chapter to behavioral economics. As with Austrian economics, we draw upon relevant insights as is appropriate.

[15] Excellent examples of texts taking this approach include ROBERT COOTER & THOMAS ULEN, LAW AND ECONOMICS (6th ed. 2011), and THOMAS J. MICELI, THE ECONOMIC APPROACH TO LAW (3d ed. 2017). This volume combines the benefits of STEARNS & ZYWICKI, *supra* note 9, with that of MICELI, *supra*, both in terms of selection of methodologies and the range of applications.

[16] Among the reasons was the influence, and controversy, provoked by the first edition of Richard Posner's famous treatise, RICHARD A. POSNER, ECONOMIC ANALYSIS OF LAW (1st ed. 1973), a book now in its ninth edition.

areas were often more robust than explanations offered in the legal literature and even in the judicial opinions themselves.

The Chicago School helped to resolve many longstanding analytical puzzles. By way of example, it offered important insights into the following questions:

> Why does common law condone breach of contract by awarding expectancy damages rather than issuing an injunction when the effect sometimes thwarts contractual performance and allows the breaching party to secure the benefit of a superior market opportunity?
>
> Why doesn't the law systematically impose liability on the party that creates negative externalities, as for example when industrial pollutants are emitted to the detriment of a pre-existing residential community?
>
> Why does the common law sometimes reward the behavior of seemingly bad actors, for example through such doctrines as adverse possession?
>
> Why does the law sometimes impose strict liability on actors who, although they have produced harm, have taken all reasonable, or cost-effective, precautions?

Adherents to the Chicago School contend that these and other seeming doctrinal anomalies can be explained based on models drawn from a fairly simple set of premises. The models that flow from these premises suggest that overall, common law rules tend to improve social welfare, defined here as promoting the "efficient" allocation of resources.[17] In other words, these seemingly counterintuitive legal rules tend to encourage individuals and firms to move resources to more highly valued uses.[18] Assuming this approach provides the basis for a persuasive account, two important related questions remain: (1) How does the common law process accomplish the objective of calibrating those rules so as to promote social welfare? (2) What motivates judges to create rules based on that normative criterion?

Chicago School adherents maintain that law and economics provides the basis for a more robust account of common law rules than competing methodologies. And yet, some doctrines that we identify operate in tension with claims of efficiency as the overriding motivation of common law rules.[19] Several notable treatises offer comprehensive presentations of common law rules assessed against a normative efficiency baseline.[20] This book takes a different approach. To allow for the competing perspectives on Law and

---

[17] We will later revisit the concept of social welfare, and of a social welfare function, to account for other criteria beyond efficient resource allocation. *See infra* Chapters 13 and 14.

[18] For a discussion of the closely related Coase Theorem, see *infra* Part III.

[19] Indeed, you might have noticed that at one point, we claimed that Law and Economics is associated with positivism and at a later point, we observed that those associated with the Austrian school sometimes challenge the Chicago School for its prescriptive accounts. Others, such as Buchanan, criticize Posner's normative claim that judges should seek to promote efficient rules on the ground that such policy decisions should be left to the legislature and that judges should limit themselves to applying that law. See, e.g., James M. Buchanan, *Good Economics—Bad Law*, 60 VA. L. REV. 483 (1974) (arguing in favor of legislative policy making despite its acknowledged imperfections).

[20] *See, e.g.*, POSNER, *supra* note 16; STEVEN SHAVELL, FOUNDATIONS OF ECONOMIC ANALYSIS OF LAW (2004); HANDBOOK OF LAW AND ECONOMICS (A. Mitchell Polinsky & Steven Shavell eds., 2007).

Economics that we provide, we offer a selective presentation of common law rules that are intended to illustrate how to apply relevant economic concepts but without claiming a complete doctrinal overview. This approach allows us to present a positive framework of efficient common law rules that can then be compared with existing common law rules, some of which are reconcilable with the efficiency account and others of which are in tension with it. This comparison allows readers to identify similarities and explore rationales for identified differences.

By way of analogy, students taking the multistate bar exam will study a set of common law rules that don't actually exist in any state jurisdiction. They will also study state-specific common law rules (including what are sometimes referred to as the exceptions to the majority rules) of the jurisdiction in which they seek to practice. Although there is value in understanding the basic structure of rules operating across states, it is also important to recognize the variations.

There is an important difference between the comparison of actual and efficient legal rules on the one hand, and the study of majority common law rules—what the multistate portion of the bar exam tests—and individual state variation on the other. The law and economics analysis of the common law, and of other sets of rules, provides a template that rests on a particular set of policy objectives. These objectives, most notably, include improving social welfare.[21] With the right premises and tools, it becomes possible to construct law and economics models of what "efficient" common law rules should look like, whereas the absence of a clearly defined set of objectives makes it far more difficult to intuit the majority canon of common law rules. Perhaps that explains why law students tend to find the bar exam a somewhat grueling exercise in memorization.[22]

B. Our Methodological Approach

Comparing legal rules that are, and are not, social welfare maximizing helps in assessing possible alternative efficiency accounts that are being missed along with potential norms that compete with efficiency in driving doctrinal development. A central goal of the early materials in this book is to provide students with a framework for making such assessments across the set of materials typically introduced in the first year law school curriculum: tort, contract, property, criminal law, and judicial process (including aspects of civil and criminal procedure).

Obviously even a law and economics course devoted entirely to these subject areas could not fully survey the first-year curriculum. Chapters 3 through 10 will allow students to develop the basis for a coherent understanding of these broader bodies of case law relying on a particular set of simplifying, and we contend, largely non-controversial assumptions.[23] This includes, most notably, individual rationality. These materials convey

[21] Common law rules sometimes rest on such competing concerns as minimizing administration costs or ensuring due process.

[22] For an explanation of how the bar exam ultimately benefits law students by limiting competition and raising fees, see *infra* Chapter 15.

[23] We do not intend to suggest that there is no controversy concerning the foundational assumptions of economic analysis, but rather, we will argue at various points in the book that the controversies often take a different form than what those most critical of law and economics initially claim.

the structure, or architecture, of the common law system and the objectives that a robust positive account—one designed to explain its longstanding features—suggests that this system of law is at least in significant part designed to serve.

This approach to the standard first-year materials provides an apt prelude to the remaining materials in the book. Just as neoclassical economics provides one important simplifying approach to the study of economics, the Chicago School survey of the first-year curriculum offers an important simplifying introduction to the economic analysis of law. As the doctrinal analysis becomes more complex and varied, so too do the tools required to assess it. For other bodies of legal doctrine, including administrative law, aspects of criminal procedure, constitutional law, federal courts, legislation, to name a few, it is not possible to construct a model set of rules that rests exclusively on a single objective such as social welfare maximization, or economic efficiency, without distorting relevant doctrines beyond recognition. For these bodies of law, we need to introduce additional normative criteria and analytical tools. This includes objectives that sometimes operate in tension with social welfare maximization. Most notably, we do not develop these competing objectives by abandoning the economic analysis of law, but rather we do so by broadening it.

As previously noted, public choice traditionally applied the methodology of economics to the subject matter of political science. In recent decades, however, scholars writing in such disciplines as political science, economics, and law have expanded the scope of public choice to study the closely related subject areas of law and the legal process. It is natural to extend public choice to study law and lawmaking institutions. The institutional focus of political science bears striking similarities to the institutional focus of law, especially public law. And yet, as we will see throughout the book, the public choice methodology often provides a point of contrast both to doctrinal approaches to law and to neoclassical law and economics.

In the remainder of this chapter, we consider in more depth several common features that underlie the various economics methodologies applied in this book. For students who have a background in economic theory, much of what follows will be a refresher. For those students for whom this course represents their first entrée into economic reasoning, what follows will be a helpful primer on several foundational economic principles that will be further developed throughout this book. We begin with several foundational assumptions, or principles, which scholars applying the tools of economic analysis generally assume (but do not always state) in their work.

II. FOUNDATIONAL PRINCIPLES OF ECONOMIC ANALYSIS

Economists construct models that are intended to capture or describe important defining characteristics of a broad range of complex real world phenomena. These models allow scholars to construct a manageable image of reality; they are not intended to recreate that underlying complex reality. In this course, we will present numerous models that are intended to help explain common law doctrines, other legal rules, law-making institutions, and a variety of judicial practices and norms. It is important up front to observe that these models are not intended to exclude analyses or insights growing out of other disciplines that study the same phenomena, including those listed in the opening of this chapter. Often the analysis will complement intuitions drawn from other disciplines, and other times it will encourage us to reconsider those intuitions. But any complete analysis will inevitably depend upon a combination of analytical approaches.

The fundamental principles of economics and the accompanying illustrations will draw upon several of the subfields of economic analysis that were previously described. They will also draw upon a range of legal subject matters and institutional settings. Our purpose is not to provide a complete analysis of any of these topics here; we will revisit these in greater depth in later chapters. Rather, it is to set a foundation that will be helpful in further developing an approach to the study of law and lawmaking institutions that is specifically economic in nature.

A. Individual Rationality

Human beings are infinitely diverse and complex creatures who manifest a dizzying array of instincts, passions, and behaviors. Humans are variously impulsive or cautious, analytic or careless, selfish or altruistic, hardworking or lazy, ambitious or content, heroic or cowardly, and compassionate or cruel. Different people hold wide-ranging traits, and individuals often possess peculiar combinations of seemingly inconsistent personal traits. Individuals often exhibit conflicting or erratic behaviors, and even behaviors that seem ill-suited to furthering objectives that they sincerely express a desire to pursue. Individual variation might appear to pose an insurmountable obstacle to scholars seeking to construct models that rest upon common assumptions about individual behavior as the basis for developing testable hypotheses as to how changing an institution or rule might affect such behavior.

Scholars employing an economic methodology tend to avoid setting out strong assumptions concerning individual human desires or motivations. Instead, they rest their models on the seemingly simple assumption of individual rationality. Rationality is distinct from the preferences individuals hold. The assumption of individual rationality means that whatever a person's preferences, she or he is expected to pursue the resulting objectives in a cost-effective manner. Because economists take individual motivations as given, individuals can be as rational in the pursuit of starting or growing a firm for profit as in supporting a charitable cause.

The economic understanding of rationality thus differs from so-called *homo economicus*. Critics of economic analysis sometimes believe that the theory rests upon assuming that individuals are narrowly self-interested. This caricature fails to capture the economist's assumption of individual rationality. Individuals may be motivated by any number of inspirations. While this can, and often will, include the desire to maximize income or profit, it also includes competing concerns, for example, supporting family and friends; gaining intellectual stimulation; increasing leisure; or exhibiting commitments to religion, charity, or a community. Economists assume that *whatever* ends an individual seeks, he or she will do so "rationally." This simple assertion about individual rationality distinguishes an economic approach to the study of human behavior from those associated with other social sciences, including those previously listed.

Economists further assume that while individuals are widely varied in their tastes and preferences, rationality reflects certain constant attributes of human nature. This point is perhaps best illustrated by way of comparison. Consider, for example, the approach to human behavior associated with "republican" philosophy.[24] Such an approach assumes that however selfish individuals may be when operating within the private economic sphere, they are expected to set aside personal motivations in favor of the "public good" when entering the public or political sphere. An influential modern variant, "civic republicanism" contends that ideology or public spiritedness, rather than rational self-interest, is necessary to explain certain political behaviors, including for example why people vote. Scholars embracing this perspective contend that because most voters understand that their votes will almost certainly not control electoral outcomes, economic, or public choice, models are hard pressed to explain voting or to do so other than in a circular manner.[25]

Similarly, some legal scholars contend that ordinary and constitutional politics are distinguished based upon the level of public spiritedness among those participating in the process. Thus, for example, Bruce Ackerman has contended that while self-interested behavior characterizes the rough and tumble of "ordinary politics," those developing constitutions tend to engage in a higher level of public spiritedness that includes focusing on the good of the larger populace.[26]

Now compare the perspective of Nobel Laureate James Buchanan, working in the public choice tradition.[27] Buchanan, like Ackerman, predicts that choices and behavior will differ in the context of constitutional decision making. Unlike Ackerman, however, Buchanan argues that the differing behavior reflects differing incentives within the specific institutional contexts of legislative versus constitutional decision making, as opposed to differing underlying motivations.

Buchanan argues that constitutions tend to be written at a higher level of abstraction and generality than statutes. In general, it is more difficult for individuals to predict where they will be in a post-constitutional regime at the time of constitution drafting than it is to predict how specific pieces of legislation, enacted within an existing constitutional regime, might affect them. As a result, individuals will be more likely to prefer neutral or impartial rules at the constitutional decision-making stage as compared with the stage of enacting legislation. Buchanan's approach is analogous to the "veil of ignorance" thought experiment advanced by philosopher John Rawls.[28] Buchanan predicts that individuals will behave differently in a constitutional choice setting as compared with a legislative

---

[24] To avoid confusion, we are discussing small "r" republicanism, which describes a political philosophy, often associated with JEAN JACQUES ROUSSEAU, THE SOCIAL CONTRACT (Maurice Cranston trans., Penguin Books 1968) (1762), rather than large "R" Republicanism, which instead describes a political party associated with an ideology or bundle of ideologies.

[25] For a more detailed discussion of voting, see *infra* Part V.B.

[26] *See, e.g.*, 1 BRUCE ACKERMAN, WE THE PEOPLE: FOUNDATIONS (1991).

[27] *See* JAMES M. BUCHANAN, THE LIMITS OF LIBERTY (1975); JAMES M. BUCHANAN & GORDON TULLOCK, THE CALCULUS OF CONSENT: LOGICAL FOUNDATIONS OF CONSTITUTIONAL DEMOCRACY (1962).

[28] JOHN RAWLS, A THEORY OF JUSTICE § 24, at 118 (rev. ed. 1999).

setting because of the institutional constraints that confront them, not because their preferences have changed.

Other well-known scholarly traditions, dating to Karl Marx,[29] assume that individual preferences are a product of group or class associations. Marxian economic analysis is premised upon the idea that the ruling class will seek to further its interest at the expense of the working class. In more modern times, legal scholars associated with critical legal studies, critical race theory, and certain strands of feminist scholarship[30] have built on this insight to criticize legal policies that are claimed to benefit elites or, alternatively, to advance policies that help those perceived as marginalized or otherwise disadvantaged.

By contrast, the neoclassical economics tradition questions whether persons, behaving rationally, will seek to pursue interests that benefit a group with which they are associated if doing so simultaneously operates to their individual detriment. For an interesting, and controversial, example that grows out of the neoclassical analysis of labor law, consider the problem of racial discrimination among private companies, or firms. Nobel prize-winning economist Gary Becker has suggested that in competitive labor markets, firms that seek to indulge racial prejudices in the process of hiring or promotions will incur a cost as they are voluntarily restricting their own access to a segment of the labor market. This restriction will place such firms at a competitive disadvantage as compared with those firms that do not discriminate. Over time, the discriminatory, cost-bearing firms will thus be forced either to change their policies, setting aside their personal views on race, or risk falling out of the market as a result of competitive pressures imposed by non-discriminatory firms.[31] One noted criticism of the Becker model is that it responds to the problem of racism by suggesting that as a theoretical matter, it should not exist.[32]

In evaluating the merits of Professor Becker's theory, consider once again the nature of economic analysis. The deliberately reductionist models of interactive human behavior allows economists to construct models capable of empirical testing. Can you think of any tests that one might develop to falsify or reaffirm Professor Becker's theory that, holding all else constant, private market competition should be expected to drive racially discriminatory firms out of the market? Given that racism tragically exists in a host of institutional settings, can Becker's model be extended to explain the circumstances in which it is prone to arise and persist?

More generally, economists are skeptical of claims that individual rationality, and thus behavior, changes as a function of the context in which such behavior takes place. Economists are inclined, for example, to question whether citizens who engage in self-interested private pursuits 364 days a year will shed this predilection on the Tuesday after the first Monday in November (Election Day) thus casting their ballots in a manner that in otherwise uncharacteristic fashion seeks to advance a larger notion of public good.

---

[29] *See, e.g.*, KARL MARX & FRIEDRICH ENGELS, THE COMMUNIST MANIFESTO (Frederic L. Bender ed., W.W. Norton 1988) (1848).

[30] For a helpful introduction to this literature, see MARK KELMAN, A GUIDE TO CRITICAL LEGAL STUDIES (1987); *see also* LESLIE BENDER & DAAN BRAVEMAN, POWER, PRIVILEGE AND LAW: A CIVIL RIGHTS READER (1995).

[31] *See generally* GARY S. BECKER, THE ECONOMICS OF DISCRIMINATION (2d ed. 1971).

[32] *See, e.g.*, Robert E. Suggs, *Poisoning the Well: Law & Economics and Racial Inequality*, 57 HASTINGS L.J. 255 (2005).

Similarly, economists are inclined to question whether a greater degree of public spiritedness better characterizes constitutional politics than ordinary politics. While economists doubt that context or group affiliation alone changes rational motivations, economists believe that institutional incentives can and do shape human behavior.

B. Institutions Matter

Economists are very concerned with how institutions affect individual and group behaviors. In general, such scholars are skeptical about claims that individuals are apt to change their personal *motivations* as they move from one sphere of activity to the next. Economists agree, however, that individual *behavior* often changes with institutional contexts, for example, from acting within a market, to acting within a legislature, to acting within an agency or court.

Merely labeling a setting as different, however, is unlikely to change personal motivations. An individual member of Congress who is motivated to procure special interest legislation for her district or to further partisan concerns associated with her party is unlikely to abandon these goals simply because she is called upon to address a set of questions that are labeled "constitutional" rather than "ordinary" politics. For example, her motivations are likely to remain constant when voting on a prospective judicial nominee, a proposed constitutional amendment, or a decision whether to impeach the President or some other officer. But the constancy of human nature does not imply constancy of individual behavior. Quite the contrary.

A fundamental principle of economics is that individuals respond rationally to changes in incentives. A single user of a fishing pond might be indifferent to concerns of overfishing, whereas a single owner of the pond is more apt to be concerned that stocks remain at a level that allows replenishment. In both contexts, the person is seeking to maximize her return, but the effects of her conduct will vary across these two settings.

Consider also how behavior is affected by a price change over two commodities. If the price of oranges rises relative to the price of grapefruits, then holding all else constant (for example assuming that the same land is hospitable to both crops and that the demand functions for both crops are similar), economists predict that citrus farmers will increase their production of oranges as compared with grapefruits, and conversely, that consumers will purchase fewer oranges and more grapefruits. Changes in the relative price of the two goods affects individual behaviors as reflected in purchasing decisions.

Just as price changes within private markets affect individual purchasing behavior, so too do changes in institutional incentives affect the behavior of affected persons. A fundamental tenet of public choice is that *institutions matter*. By this, economists understand that institutions internalize mechanisms that reward or punish particular behaviors and that individuals, behaving rationally, modify their behavior in response to the resulting institutional incentives.

Nobel prize-winning economist Douglass North has defined "institutions" to be

> the humanly devised constraints that structure human interaction. They are made up of formal constraints (e.g., rules, laws, constitutions), informal constraints (e.g., norms of behavior, conventions, self-imposed codes of

conduct), and their enforcement characteristics. Together, they define the incentive structure of societies and specifically economies.[33]

As an example of the importance of institutions in motivating individual behavior, consider the relative difference in "independence" that judges have in various institutional settings. In the United States, federal judges have a high degree of independence. Article III judges are appointed for life rather than elected for a term of years and serve during "good behavior." This has been interpreted to permit removal only for corruption or malfeasance, rather than for the substantive content, or popularity, of their rulings or written opinions. By contrast, many states have various protocols for electing judges.

Imagine two otherwise identical candidates for judgeships, one of whom is appointed to a federal court and the other of whom is elected to a state court for a term of years. Notwithstanding the nominees' similar ideologies, including their views on the role of the judiciary, it is reasonable to predict that each will behave differently based upon the incentives associated with the two differing institutional settings.[34] Few would deny that federal judges care about how their rulings and opinions are received.[35] We can predict, however, that in contrast with state judges who face reelection pressure, Article III judges are less likely to respond directly to the pressures of popular opinion and are more likely to adhere to their preexisting judicial philosophy, including, perhaps, indulging their ideological views whether or not popular among voters. The specific institutional choices concerning the selection, retention, and removal of judges is thus apt to influence judicial behavior at least some of the time.

As is often the case, policy questions about these and other institutional choices do not admit of a right or wrong answer. A careful economic analysis can, however, help to unmask important—if unstated—assumptions concerning the relevant policy choices. The divergent incentives among judges appointed for life versus judges elected for a term of years likely reflects assumptions concerning who the principals are to whom we wish judges to be most responsive. Elected judiciaries, responsive to the political pressures of current voting constituencies, implicitly view judges as agents of those constituencies. By contrast, independent judiciaries, those relatively isolated from popular political pressures, implicitly view judges as agents of those who enacted the laws that they are now called upon to interpret. Of course if judges or other actors were perfect agents for their respective principals there would be no need to build incentives within institutions that minimize potential divergences between the principal's goals and the agent's actions. Once more, differences in institutional settings, rather than changes in human nature, best explain how relevant actors respond to incentives.

---

[33] Douglass C. North, *Economic Performance Through Time*, 84 AM. ECON. REV. 359, 360 (1994).

[34] For now, we set aside the problem that once the institutional arrangements are put in place, these different judicial institutions attract potential judges who no longer share common approaches to the methodology of judging.

[35] Or as Finley Peter Dunne's Mr. Dooley famously put it: "NO matter whether th' constitution follows th' flag or not, th' supreme coort follows th' iliction returns." FINLEY PETER DUNNE, MR. DOOLEY ON THE CHOICE OF LAW 52 (Edward J. Bander comp., 1963) (1901).

C. Agency Costs

The divergence between the goals of a group of voters or other decision makers and the actions of those they elect or otherwise choose to represent their interests is referred to as "agency costs." Agents, whether they are legislators or judges, are not blank slates. A fundamental tenet of public choice holds that agents are not neutral conduits through which principals further their goals. Instead, the agents themselves possess preferences and motivations that sometimes coincide with, and other times diverge from, those of their principals. James Madison highlighted the problem of agency costs in creating Congress in a famous passage from the *Federalist No. 51*:

> If men were angels, no government would be necessary. If angels were to govern men, neither external nor internal controls on government would be necessary. In framing a government which is to be administered by men over men, the great difficulty lies in this: you must first enable the government to control the governed; and in the next place oblige it to control itself.[36]

Madison was discussing the problem of agency costs in the context of the legislature. But the problem of agency costs also arises in selecting any governmental official, whether the Executive, bureaucrats, or judges. As the preceding discussion shows, in the judicial context, the problem is complicated because before we can identify appropriate measures to reduce agency costs, we must confront the logically antecedent question, who is the principal?

Economic analysis, including public choice, cannot provide an answer as to the optimal degree of judicial independence in a constitutional system. The wide divergences between the federal and state constitutions, and among state constitutions, demonstrate that there is no single correct answer. Public choice can, however, help identify the tradeoffs between accountability, independence, and agency costs, when making these choices, including helping to unmask implicit assumptions concerning whose interests, or which principals, judges are expected to serve.

D. Methodological Individualism

Along with rationality, economic theory rests on the premise of methodological individualism.[37] A careful assessment of any institution demands that one first understand how that institution motivates affected individuals. James Buchanan and Gordon Tullock, two leading public choice theorists, expressed this intuition as follows: "Collective action is viewed as the action of individuals when they choose to accomplish purposes collectively rather than individually, and the government is seen as nothing more than the set of processes, the machine, which allows such collective action to take place."[38] And as

---

[36] THE FEDERALIST No. 51, at 290 (James Madison) (Clinton Rossiter ed., 1961).

[37] Methodological individualism has been an important working assumption within other social sciences since at least the beginning of the twentieth century, including the work of Max Weber, Friedrich von Hayek, and Karl Popper, Joseph Heath, *Methodological Individualism*, *in* THE STANFORD ENCYCLOPEDIA OF PHILOSOPHY (Edward N. Zalta ed., Spring 2015), https://plato.stanford.edu/entries/methodological-individualism/.

[38] *See* BUCHANAN & TULLOCK, *supra* note 27, at 13.

Kenneth Shepsle, another leading public choice scholar, famously put it: "Congress is a 'They,' not an 'It.' "[39]

Methodological individualism thus lies at the foundation of economic analysis, underpinning all models of human interaction and behavior. To illustrate, consider a commodity cartel, such as a cartel for oil production. Considered as a *collective*, the cartel members have a strong incentive to reduce aggregate output, with pro rata allocations among individual producers, in an effort to set the price at the same level as a monopolist who controlled the entire market. And yet, it is well understood that this result is likely to be unstable. The resulting instability arises as a direct consequence of the divergent motivations of the cartel as a whole, on the one hand, and those of its individual members, on the other. Assuming pro rata cuts based, for example, on preexisting market shares or some other formula (such as an average over some set number of years), each *individual* cartel member, behaving rationally, has an incentive to "cheat" by selling just a bit more than the allocated cartel share at a price just below the newly elevated price level. Each individual member of the cartel hopes to get away with modest cheating while also hoping that the remaining cartel members adhere to their quotas, thus sustaining the overall favorable pricing structure. For the cartel as a whole, however, the problem gets much worse. Each cartel member shares the same incentive to benefit from the artificially inflated cartel price, by selling more than the allocated share. Over time, therefore, the cartel output and pricing scheme tends to erode, thereby restoring both the output and price back toward the pre-cartel, competitive level.

Although each of the cartel members would have been better off had all adhered strictly to the allotted quota rather than cheating, the difficulty is that the ultimate production decisions are made individually. Admonishing members to cooperate will not ensure that they do so. The individual firm's goal of maximizing profits does not disappear simply because the firms have collectively identified themselves as a cartel.[40]

E. Free Riding and Forced Riding

Group decision making also gives rise to problems of "free" and "forced" riding, key concepts that are especially significant to public choice theory. Free riding occurs when an individual is able to share in benefit of a collective good without contributing to the cost of its procurement. Free riding occurs most commonly in connection with the provision of public goods.[41] Consider, for example, national defense. Once an army is formed, all Americans benefit from its existence in that the army cannot decide to protect one person's home from invasion, but not her neighbor's. Thus, if an individual pays taxes to support an army, her neighbor also benefits whether or not he contributes. The neighbor has the opportunity, and incentive, to "free ride" on those who pay to provide the public good. Each individual shares this same incentive. If dependent on voluntary contributions, therefore, public goods will tend to be undersupplied. Although the group

---

[39] Kenneth Shepsle, *Congress Is a "They," Not an "It": Legislative Intent as an Oxymoron*, 12 INT'L REV. L. & ECON. 239 (1992).

[40] We will revisit this dynamic in the discussion of the prisoners' dilemma *See infra* Chapter 13.

[41] Geoffrey Brennan & Alan Hamlin, *Fiscal Federalism*, *in* 2 NEW PALGRAVE DICTIONARY OF ECONOMICS AND THE LAW 144, 144 (Peter Newman ed., 1998).

as a whole would be better off if everyone contributed to the provision of such goods, each individual's personal incentive deviates from this collective goal.

Other collective choice situations give rise to "forced riding," the mirror image of free riding. Forced riding occurs when an individual is coerced by other members of the group (such as under majority rule) to contribute to providing a claimed public good despite not receiving a sufficient personal benefit.[42] At the extreme, an individual might even experience disutility from a claimed public good; for instance, a pacifist might claim to be worse off by the provision of national defense. As a less extreme example, consider those who dislike opera but whose taxes subsidize operatic productions or sports detractors whose taxes subsidize the construction of a new stadium. Majority rule does not ensure that those who receive the benefit bear the full cost. Assessed against individual preferences, forced riding risks an *overproduction* of collective goods as compared with a regime in which the beneficiaries fully internalize the marginal cost of procurement.

The problem of forced riding is largely a consequence of the inability to observe subjective individual valuations of public goods and thus the impossibility of assigning contributions based on those valuations. Instead taxes are assessed based on observable characteristics such as incomes or property values, which often fail to align with marginal valuations of the publicly funded goods or services.

F. Structuring Appropriate Micro-Foundations

As the twin concepts of free riding and forced riding demonstrate, in seeking to promote preferred institutional outcomes, it is essential to account for the "micro-foundations" of individual behavior. Effective group performance is impossible unless institutions motivate individuals to act in a manner that furthers the collective body's goals at appropriate levels.

Let us return to the problem of the cartel. Assume once again that contrary to the interests of consumers who prefer competition, the cartel members wish to reduce output in an effort to raise price. An obvious way to align individual and group incentives is to combine the productive capacities into a single firm. The monopolist has an incentive to reduce output and raise price, even though as one of several cartel members, she would prefer to cheat from a quota imposed to achieve the same overall result.

G. Marginal Analysis

Individual incentives come from many disparate sources. Most individuals are influenced by a combination of their family upbringing, cultural identity, religion, socioeconomic circumstances, educational background, and perhaps most obviously, one's internal sense of morality. Thankfully most people do not decide whether or not to commit such horrendous acts as murder, assault, or arson based upon the mere presence or absence of a prohibitive criminal statute. Similarly, most of us take care while driving

[42] This problem arises, for example, in cases of forced subsidization of livestock and agricultural marketing programs, which have been challenged by contributors who do not perceive a proportional benefit to collective advertising. *See, e.g.*, Johanns v. Livestock Mktg. Ass'n, 544 U.S. 550 (2005) (rejecting First Amendment challenge to program that forced subsidization of government advertising and distinguishing cases that struck down similar non-government advertising programs).

because we were raised to think carefully about what we do and to be attentive to how our actions risk affecting others. Unfortunately, the opposite is also true: there is a group of individuals who will engage in harmful activity despite legal prohibitions coupled with considerable sanctions, for example fines or incarceration. Although these observations seem, and indeed are, obvious, they nonetheless raise an important puzzle for the economic analysis of law.

If well-behaved individuals are motivated by personal factors rather than by formal legal rules, and if a subset of individuals will engage in harmful behaviors without regard to such rules, how can law and economics claim to create models describing the likely effect of changes in legal rules on rational individuals or institutional actors? The answer rests on the important economic concept of marginality.

Marginal analysis focuses on the effect of changes in one factor in influencing another, for example how an adjustment in price affects the decision of some consumers to buy or not buy, or how an adjustment to a legal rule motivates some people to engage in, or avoid, a particular activity. There are some goods or services that many consumers will continue to purchase even if the price doubles or even triples, and there are others that consumers will suddenly stop buying even if the price goes up fairly modestly.[43] In each instance, those whose behavior is affected by the price change are "on the margin," whereas those whose conduct is unaffected are "infra-marginal." This also applies to the effect of changes in legal rules on personal and institutional behavior. As with price adjustments, changes in legal rules can only affect the conduct of those who are on the relevant margin affected by the rule change.[44]

Law and economics does not claim that legal rules are responsible for all, or even most, human behaviors. As noted, most observed behaviors are the product of culture, religion, psychology, ethnicity, socioeconomic status, education, and countless other factors that define and enrich personal and group identity. Rather, the analysis assumes that legal rules affect the behaviors of those persons or institutions on the relevant margins of the rules themselves. The number of persons or institutions affected by a change in price or legal rule is an empirical question. Intuitively, however, adjustments in many legal rules are likely to affect the incentives and conduct of considerable numbers of persons or institutions. As a result, modeling the likely impact of adjustments to such rules is an important step in assessing the efficacy of rules and institutions.

H. Politics as an Exchange Model

Disaggregating collective action via the assumption of methodological individualism not only helps to explain the formation and structure of private institutions, but also it transforms the traditional understanding of politics. In contrast with the conventional

[43] For a discussion of price "elasticity," see *infra* Chapter 2.

[44] We will introduce the concept of marginality more formally in Chapter 2. For a discussion of how the concept of marginality helps to explain an anomaly to Adam Smith, namely why such inessentials as diamonds hold considerable value whereas such essentials as water do not. *See infra* Chapter 16 (explaining that Smith lacked the tools to appreciate the effect on price of marginal increases in the availability of goods or services.)

understanding of politics as a search for the "public interest," public choice helps to reframe collective action as an exchange model.[45]

Within this analysis, those who demand government-provided goods and services—voters, interest groups, and lobbyists—offer their support to those elected officials who, in exchange, agree to provide them. Unlike private market exchange, however, the costs and benefits of lawmaking "transactions" affect persons who do not necessarily participate in the bargain. This closely relates to the earlier discussion of free and forced riding.

I. *Pareto Optimality* Versus *Kaldor-Hicks Efficiency* and the Holdout Problem[46]

In theory, even without adhering to a unanimous consent rule as a precondition to collective action, it is possible to ensure outcomes that benefit all persons affected by group decisions. If a proposed change in law is welfare maximizing, those benefiting by the action (the "winners") could compensate those who are harmed (the "losers") and still come out ahead. The winners would thus be made better off, even after compensating the losers, and after receiving compensation, the losers would be no worse off. If such compensation took place, the result would satisfy the most stringent definition of economic efficiency. A change from the status quo to an alternative state is *Pareto superior* if it improves the position of at least one participant without making anyone else worse off. *Pareto optimality* demands that all potential Pareto superior moves have already taken place. When this occurs, any further changes from the status quo would instead effect a wealth transfer between or among participants, with the result that at least one party to the exchange would be made worse off.[47]

In private markets, at least assuming no negative externalities,[48] meaning that persons not party to the transaction are not adversely affected, *Pareto superior* exchanges routinely occur. When an individual purchases a latte for $4, the buyer presumably values the coffee more than the money, and the vendor values the money more than the coffee.

---

[45] We will present the exchange model in more detail in Chapter 11.

[46] For general discussions of these definitions of efficiency, see Allan M. Feldman, *Kaldor-Hicks Compensation*, *in* 2 THE NEW PALGRAVE DICTIONARY OF ECONOMICS AND THE LAW, *supra* note 41, at 417–21; Allan M. Feldman, *Pareto Optimality*, *in* 3 THE NEW PALGRAVE DICTIONARY OF ECONOMICS AND THE LAW, *supra*, at 5–9.

[47] The importance of the Pareto principle in formulating law and public policy has long been the subject of academic debate. *See, e.g.*, Daniel A. Farber, *Autonomy, Welfare, and the Pareto Principle*, *in* LAW AND ECONOMICS: PHILOSOPHICAL ISSUES AND FUNDAMENTAL QUESTIONS 159 (Aristides N. Hatzis & Nicholas Mercuro eds., 2015) (demonstrating theoretical and practical limitations in applying Pareto principle in legal policymaking); Marc Fleurbaey et al., *Any Non-welfarist Method of Policy Assessment Violates the Pareto Principle: A Comment*, 111 J. POL. ECON. 1382, 1383 (2003) (using social welfare function analysis to critique Kaplow and Shavell's assertion that "welfarism and the Pareto indifference condition are equivalent"); Louis Kaplow & Steven Shavell, *Any Non-welfarist Method of Policy Assessment Violates the Pareto Principle*, 109 J. POL. ECON. 281 (2001) (arguing that policy making should be based solely on Pareto criterion, the claimed equivalent to welfarism); Guido Calabresi, *The Pointlessness of Pareto: Carrying Coase Further*, 100 YALE L.J. 1211, 1215–17 (1991) (maintaining that Pareto criterion has limited normative implications because logically, all Pareto improvements should already have taken place).

[48] For a discussion of externalities, see *infra* Part IV.

By contrast, when the government provides goods and services, it uses its coercive power of taxation to fund its programs. When this occurs, not everyone benefits, and without regard to contribution levels, those who do benefit might not do so to the same degree. In theory, those who benefit could pay off those who are disadvantaged, thereby satisfying the condition of *Pareto superiority*. The practical difficulties with such a regime, however, generally make actual compensation implausible.

Under the alternative of *Kaldor-Hicks* efficiency, a change from the status quo is defined as efficient when the *potential* for such compensation exists even though the actual compensation does not occur, meaning when the aggregate gain to winners exceeds the aggregate cost to losers. The intuition is that because the winners' welfare has improved by more than the losers' welfare has suffered (hence the possibility of compensation), the overall result improves social welfare. This more relaxed definition of efficiency, while acknowledging the unavoidable nature of winners and losers in the public procurement of goods or services, provides an important normative foundation for many public programs that, from a practical point of view, cannot satisfy the more stringent Pareto criterion.

In the collective choice setting, the preceding analysis produces an important insight: the best evidence of whether a given collectively chosen policy maximizes social welfare would be the unanimous consent of all members of the affected community. The unanimity benchmark for collective choice, therefore, appears functionally identical to the *Pareto superiority* criterion for market transactions.[49] A unanimity rule for collective choice, however, creates the difficulty that even a single person could prevent the proposed law from passing. An individual might oppose based upon the merits of the proposed change or in a strategic effort to use veto power to demand some other benefit as a precondition to tendering support. In the context of individual market transactions (such as for purchasing a cup of coffee), the problem of the strategic *holdout* does not arise, as an individual lacks the power to impose costs on anyone other than herself. In a collective choice setting, however, the need for consent among all relevant parties can be very expensive, and the costs can include creating opportunities for strategic holdouts.

As a result, although a rule requiring the unanimous assent of those governed as a precondition to coercive governmental action might prevent imposing costs on those who do not benefit from such action, both as a theoretical and as a practical matter, the unanimity norm is impossible to implement. Thus, in judging the merits of a given collective choice institution, it becomes necessary to adopt an alternative to *Pareto* superiority, or its analogue, unanimous consent, such as *Kaldor Hicks* efficiency, and to accept a majority or supermajority decision-making rule.

---

[49] *See* James M. Buchanan, *The Coase Theorem and the Theory of the State*, 13 NAT. RESOURCES J. 579, 588 (1973).

III. THE PROBLEM OF RECIPROCAL COSTS (OR EXTERNALITIES) AND THE COASE THEOREM

In well-functioning markets, with well-defined and freely transferable property rights, the rational actions of individuals not only tend to improve individual welfare, but also to contribute positively to social welfare. Where, however, property rights are poorly defined, or individuals can pass part of their costs of production onto others, one can no longer make this assumption. For instance, a farmer might be able to raise and sell pigs to consumers on mutually beneficial terms. And yet, pig farming also gives rise to odors and pollution that are likely to annoy and harm the farmer's neighbors. If the farmer is not required to compensate his neighbors for the harms created by pig farming, the farmer and his purchasers will not bear the full cost of the activity of raising pigs. At this point, it is no longer possible to infer an increase in social welfare from the transactions that improved the private welfare of the farmer and the purchasers.[50]

This problem, commonly known as *negative externalities*,[51] has long been a major focus of neoclassical economic theory. The influential economist Arthur Cecil Pigou believed that a major challenge facing market economies was ensuring that firms absorb the full costs of their own productive activities, and thus that regulation or taxation was necessary to minimize potential negative externalities.[52]

In his famous essay, *The Problem of Social Cost*,[53] Nobel Prize-winning economist Ronald Coase challenged Pigou's approach to the problem of externalities, claiming it was analytically flawed. Part of the difficulty centered on the indeterminate nature of defining externalities. Any claimed externality can be recast as involving incompatible uses of property, with the result that vindicating the claimed rights of either party imposes genuine costs on the other.[54] Coase claimed that the reciprocal nature of cost undermined the externality framing.

Consider a dental office, with a noisy drill that operates frequently throughout the day, located next door to the home of a nurse who regularly works the night shift. We might say that the dentist's drill imposes an externality on the nurse, who cannot sleep, and issue the nurse an injunction, but we might as easily say that issuing the nurse's injunction imposes an externality on the dentist who can no longer practice in that location. Absent these two competing uses, there is no social conflict. In Coase's analysis,

---

[50] Activities that have externalities are clearly not *Pareto* optimal and may or may not be *Kaldor-Hicks* efficient. Do you see why?

[51] There are also *positive* externalities, as for example, when a developer enters a blighted part of a city and introduces new shopping, employment, and entertainment opportunities with the effect of improving the overall quality of life for those residing there. The existence of these positive externalities, however, does not preclude the simultaneous negative externalities for those residents who are thereby displaced. That is why Kaldor-Hicks efficiency balances the benefits to winners against the burdens on losers.

[52] A.C. PIGOU, THE ECONOMICS OF WELFARE (Palgrave Macmillan 2013) (1920).

[53] R.H. Coase, *The Problem of Social Cost,* 3 J.L. & ECON. 1 (1960).

[54] This can arise in simple binary conflicts or in more complex multiparty conflicts. In the discussion that follows we focus on binary conflicts, but in later discussions, we will consider more complex multilateral bargaining. *See infra* Chapters 7 and 8.

identifying either activity as the source of an externality privileges the competing activity in a conclusory manner. Instead, Coase argued, the legal regime must first identify which of the two parties may properly assert a property right and trigger the necessary legal enforcement mechanisms. The "externality" concept offers little guidance in resolving these issues.

Coase posited that with respect to incompatible uses, the legal system has two overriding functions: first, it must identify which of the competing uses is more socially valuable, and second, it must identify the proper legal mechanism to improve the likelihood that the more highly valued use will be achieved. In Coase's analysis, the legal system's goal is to promote the movement of resources to their more highly valued uses.

Sometimes that results directly from the allocation of property rights, for example, vindicating the claim of the dentist or nurse. On other occasions, however, the legal system accomplishes this by recognizing that the market conditions are conductive to private bargaining, which can reallocate the legal system's initial assignment of rights.

Coase's essay[55] is most well-known for setting out the famous Coase Theorem.[56] The Coase Theorem states that with zero transactions costs and perfect information, resources will flow to their most highly valued uses without regard to the initial allocation of property rights. The Coase Theorem is at once counterintuitive, controversial, and widely misunderstood. One immediate difficulty that Coase confronted was that many critics misunderstood the theorem to imply that transactions costs *are* low, and, as a result, that resource allocation *is* generally efficient and welfare enhancing.[57] Of course there are countless illustrations in the real world of inefficient resource allocations and of costly barriers to welfare-enhancing private market exchange.

What Coase intended, however, was the opposite. Coase posited two preconditions that render liability rules irrelevant to efficient allocation of resources: zero transactions costs and perfect information. Certainly in the real world, there is little reason to assume that transacting is costless. Transactions costs include travel, documentation, and communication. They also include opportunity cost, defined as the time and energy taken from other potentially profitable activities. And perhaps most significantly, although he specified perfect information as a separate condition, the cost of gathering the necessary information with which to enter into transactions is among the greatest cost impediments to contracting.

We now illustrate how Coase's stylized world yields optimal outcomes without regard to the initial assignment of property rights. (This can also be expressed based on which party holds the corresponding liability rule, which controls whether there is a "right" to cause or to be free of a negative externality.) Consider the following hypothetical. Imagine a laundry and a factory that pollutes into a river to the laundry's

---

[55] Coase, *supra* note 53.

[56] *See id.* As demonstrated *infra*, Chapter 13, the term Coase Theorem might be a misnomer because under certain conditions associated with empty core bargaining, even when the theorem's articulated assumptions are satisfied, the predicted efficient resource allocation is not guaranteed.

[57] Coase responded to these criticisms in R.H. COASE, THE FIRM, THE MARKET, AND THE LAW 174–79 (1988).

detriment.[58] The factory is worth $11,000; but by polluting, it reduces the laundry's value from $40,000 to $24,000. Further assume that for the laundry to realize its potential value of $40,000, the factory must cease all pollution, which would require the factory to shut down.

The Coase Theorem posits that in a world with zero transactions costs and perfect information, this efficient result will be achieved—the factory will close and the laundry will operate—regardless of which of the two businesses owns the property right to pollute or to enjoin the pollution. Assume first that the factory owns the right to pollute. The laundry will pay up to $16,000—the difference in its value with and without the factory polluting—to purchase that right from the factory. Because the factory is worth only $11,000 even with the right to pollute, it has a rational incentive to sell its right to pollute, thus allowing the laundry to purchase the right to enjoin the pollution. Conversely, if the laundry owns the right to enjoin the factory's pollution, the factory will not be able to purchase the pollution right from the laundry. The factory values that right at $11,000, $5000 less than the laundry values its contrary right to prevent the pollution. The example illustrates that if the owner of the laundry values the right to be free of pollution more highly than does the owner of the factory to pollute, then regardless of who bears the property right, in a world with zero transactions costs and perfect information, the laundry will ultimately obtain that right.

A critical assumption in the analysis is that the numbers in the example capture all relevant costs. If there are hidden costs, psychological or otherwise, and if such costs are of sufficient magnitude to inhibit the deal, then the result will break down and the efficiency-promoting transaction will not occur, leaving the property right wherever the legal system happened to place it. If that right happened to rest with the laundry, then the efficient result is fortuitously achieved, but if it initially rested instead with the factory, then the transactions costs would suffice to prevent the efficient flow of resources, costing society up to the $5000 premium value that the laundry places on the property right.

Can you identify circumstances in which, even with low transactions costs, the Coasian result is unlikely to arise? If so, could you characterize the implicit impediment to the efficient outcome as a transaction cost? What does the preceding question suggest about the nature of transactions costs as that term is employed in the Coase theorem?[59]

IV. APPLICATIONS: THREE CASE STUDIES[60]

The preceding discussion introduced several important aspects of economic reasoning. We will now introduce three case studies that will help you in developing several insights in the chapters that follow. These case studies are intended to encourage you to think about the power of economic reasoning to tackle foundational questions

---

[58] This is adapted from Varouj A. Aivazian & Jeffrey L. Callen, *The Coase Theorem and the Empty Core*, 24 J.L. & ECON. 175 (1981). *See also* Maxwell L. Stearns, *The Misguided Renaissance of Social Choice*, 103 YALE L.J. 1219, 1234–40 (1994).

[59] We will return to a more detailed discussion of the Coase Theorem in the context of contract law, in Chapter 4, and property law in Chapters 5 and 6.

[60] Portions of the discussion that follow are adapted from MAXWELL L. STEARNS, PUBLIC CHOICE AND PUBLIC LAW: READINGS AND COMMENTARY 64–72 (1997).

about common law doctrine along with our political and legal processes. Although you will gain insights into these examples with new tools introduced throughout the book, for now evaluate them based upon the general intuitions developed in the preceding discussion.

A. The Rational and the Reasonable

In this chapter, we explored the economic concept of rationality. In the next several chapters, which examine the common law doctrines of Tort, Contract, and Property, we consider what the legal system considers "reasonable." We now explore the relationship between these two concepts.[61] Although the concepts are related, we will see that they sometimes diverge. The divergence has notable implications both for common law doctrine and for economic analysis.

Consider first the conventional law and economics understanding of negligence, meaning the failure to take appropriate precautions that could reduce the risk of an accident arising in Tort. The analysis begins with the famous Learned Hand Formula.[62] That formula defines "reasonable," or non-negligent, precautions as those for which the burden (*B*) is lower than the probability (*P*) of causing an accident multiplied by the impact or damage (*L*) should that accident occur. Under this formula, an actor is negligent if she has failed to take a precaution for which $B<PL$. This test has been described as a "threshold rule," meaning that those who fail to meet it are liable for negligence when the other elements in a prima facie negligence suit are met, whereas those who do meet that test are not liable.[63]

An analogous set of threshold rules apply in other common law contexts, for example, in determining whether a non-breaching party provided adequate notice for damages that might not otherwise be anticipated in the event of a breach of contract,[64] or when a property owner seeks to have land fully restored pursuant to a contractual restoration provision following a mining operation even though the cost of doing so would vastly exceed any difference in the fair market value of the affected property.[65]

Whereas the legal system generally seeks to ensure that litigants respond reasonably in circumstances that give rise to litigation, economic analysis also reveals that social welfare is sometimes promoted when individuals pursue their own idiosyncratic objectives. Although such preferences might appear "unreasonable," at least as evaluated against most people's preferences and expectations, the legal system nonetheless often

---

[61] For an analogous discussion, see ROBERT COOTER & THOMAS ULEN, LAW AND ECONOMICS 11–12 (1st ed. 1988) (arguing that as a result of social costs that individual actions sometimes produce, actions viewed as individually rational might be considered unreasonable from a social perspective).

[62] United States v. Carroll Towing Co., 159 F.2d 169, 173 (2d Cir. 1947).

[63] This assumes that the relevant legal standard is negligence as opposed to strict liability or some other standard. When contributory negligence or comparative fault applies, the plaintiff's failure to take appropriate precautions, based on this analysis, can either absolve the defendant of liability (contributory) or require an allocation based on degrees of relative fault (comparative). For a more detailed analysis, see *infra* Chapters 3 and 4.

[64] *See infra* Chapters 5 and 6; *see also* Hadley v. Baxendale (1854), 156 Eng. Rep. 145; 9 Exch. 341.

[65] *See infra* Chapters 5 and 6; *see also* Peevyhouse v. Garland Coal & Mining Co., 382 P.2d 109 (Okla. 1962).

permits individuals to gain the benefit of such pursuits. Recall also that the economist's definition of rationality takes preferences as given and assumes only that individuals will pursue their objectives in a cost-effective manner.

The following are based on more detailed presentations or actual cases discussed in the chapters that follow. For now, preliminarily assess the following:

(1) A skydiving company includes a disclaimer of liability not only for negligent conduct that might lead to a fatal accident, but even for gross negligence, and indeed for any skydiving accident regardless of cause. If someone signs a form contract containing such provisions and a fatal fall resulting from negligence follows, should the contract terms be judicially enforced?[66]

(2) The purchaser of a newly constructed home specifies a particular brand of pipe to be included, but after completion, he learns that the builder used an alternative pipe of equal quality. Should the buyer be able to obtain a judicial order for specific performance to compel removal of the existing pipe in favor of the pipe specified in the contract or damages equivalent to that cost?[67]

(3) At great expense a property owner adds features to her home that are customized to her own tastes, including glass walls with automatic sunblock features, an elaborate play house for her children, and a beautiful swimming pool, in an area in which the demand for such features is uncommon. If the property is taken for a public use through eminent domain, should the owner be able to recover the full cost of her customized home or the substantially lower fair market value?[68]

In these hypotheticals, we might ask if the skydiver (or his estate), the homebuyer, or the property owner, respectively, were behaving rationally by pursuing activities resulting in potential damages greatly in excess of what others might deem reasonable or appropriate. What about the skydiving company, the construction contractor, or the state seeking eminent domain? Were these parties likewise acting rationally in trying to avoid liability altogether or at least the full scope of claimed liability? How should the judicial system reconcile these competing interests to arrive at a reasonable (socially optimal) resolution of the disputes, and why? The chapters on torts, contracts, and property will provide tools that are helpful in addressing these questions.

B. Is Voting Irrational?

Public choice, taken up in part III of the book, applies economic principles, including those developed thus far, to politics and political processes. One foundational aspect of the political process, namely voting, is widely viewed as paradoxical especially when viewed from an economic perspective. The "paradox of voting" is that although virtually no informed voter expects her vote to control the outcome of an election, and although voting is a costly activity, in every election, a considerable percentage of the

---

[66] *See infra* Chapters 3 and 4.

[67] *See infra* Chapters 5 and 6; *see also* Jacob & Youngs, Inc. v. Kent, 129 N.E. 889 (N.Y. 1921).

[68] *See infra* Chapters 5 and 7.

population votes.[69] The obvious costs of voting include not only time and inconvenience, but also becoming sufficiently informed to vote for a desired candidate or group of candidates. As a result, some scholars claim that voting defies "rationality" as that term is understood within economic analysis.

Economists have offered a variety of arguments to "rescue" voting from the claim that it is an irrational activity. The arguments implicate the meaning of rationality. Rationality does not mean narrow self-interest. Instead, individuals may rationally vote because they derive any number of non-pecuniary benefits, or an overall sense of satisfaction, from doing so. Professors Daniel Farber and Philip Frickey have responded as follows:

> Attempts have been made to reconcile voter behavior with the economic model by postulating a "taste" for voting. This explanation is tautological—anything people do can be "justified" by saying they have a taste for doing it.[70]

These scholars ask: "Why is it so difficult to admit that people vote out of political commitment, not personal satisfaction?"[71]

Professors Michael DeBow and Dwight Lee have argued that voting is rational if one views it as a "consumption" activity.[72] Indeed, these scholars claim that knowing that voting is a consumption rather than purely utilitarian activity, might free individuals to vote their conscience, thereby enhancing enjoyment of the act itself.[73] Others have argued that precisely because voters do not internalize the costs and benefits of their electoral decisions, this invites costly and sometimes irresponsible public policy choices.[74] Professors Farber and Frickey have responded in part with a *reductio ad absurdum*: if people derive satisfaction by expecting their votes not to count, they could derive *even more*

---

[69] A rare exception: The November 2017 election between Republican incumbent, David Yancey, and Democrat challenger, Shelly Simonds, for the 94th District in the Virginia House of Delegates, resulted in a tie and was ultimately settled in Yancey's favor by a coin toss. *See* Paul Schwartzman & Laura Vozzella, *Democrat Who Lost Random Drawing for Va. House Seat Concedes to Republican*, WASH. POST (Jan. 10, 2018), https://www.washingtonpost.com/local/virginia-politics/democrat-who-lost-random-drawing-for-va-house-seat-opts-against-recount/2018/01/10/92a4776a-f60c-11e7-beb6-c8d48830c54d_story.html?utm_term=.57bc4553af0f. This produced a 51–49 split in the House of Delegates, favoring Republicans, whereas a Simonds victory would have split the House 50–50. A single additional vote for either candidate would not only have proved decisive in that single race, but also for the composition of the House of Delegates as a whole. *Id.*

[70] Daniel A. Farber & Philip P. Frickey, *The Jurisprudence of Public Choice*, 65 TEX. L. REV. 873, 894 n.129 (1987).

[71] Daniel A. Farber & Philip P. Frickey, *Integrating Public Choice and Public Law: A Reply to DeBow and Lee*, 66 TEX. L. REV. 1013, 1017 (1988).

[72] Michael E. DeBow & Dwight R. Lee, *Understanding (and Misunderstanding) Public Choice: A Response to Farber and Frickey*, 66 TEX. L. REV. 993, 997–99 (1988).

[73] *Id.*

[74] Geoffrey Brennan & James Buchanan, *Voter Choice: Evaluating Political Alternatives*, 28 AM. BEHAV. SCIENTIST 185 (1984). The dispute about whether it is rational to vote at all is separate from the expressed concern among some scholars that the substantive electoral outcomes reflect voter preferences that might be deemed "irrational," see BRYAN CAPLAN, THE MYTH OF THE RATIONAL VOTER: WHY DEMOCRACIES CHOOSE BAD POLICIES (2007), or that that voter incentives might be better aligned with policy preferences that some prefer if government decision making were more localized, see ILYA SOMIN, DEMOCRACY AND POLITICAL IGNORANCE: WHY SMALLER GOVERNMENT IS SMARTER (2d ed. 2016).

satisfaction by locking themselves up in an empty house and shouting support for their favorite candidates.[75]

Consider whether the following theories help to restore the rationality of voting.

1. An Expressive Theory of Voting

Some individuals vote because they value expressing views on important matters of public policy.[76] Such persons might regard doing so as more effective, for example, than shouting in an empty house because even if their votes do not control the outcome, the results are tallied and widely reported. Similar activities that serve an expressive function might include writing letters to the editor of a newspaper or engaging in peaceful demonstration. Because the likely effect of such activities on public policy is minuscule, this theory of voting is often referred to as a *non-instrumental*, meaning the act is an end in itself, rather than a means to the end of affecting a separate outcome, such as who wins an election.

2. A Cost Function of Voting

This theory helps to explain how voters' related behaviors might appear more intuitively rational. If the cost of voting rises, holding all else constant, people are less likely to vote. If people voted purely out of "political commitment" rather than personal satisfaction, the cost of voting would seem to have less influence. This observation is, however, consistent with non-instrumental accounts in that the individual willingness to vote (the demand for voting) tends to decline as the price of voting rises. Available evidence tends to support this claim.[77] Such data include lower turnout in adverse weather and lower voter registration when tied to jury service, a potentially counterintuitive result if voting were motivated by civic virtue. Overall evidence suggests that whatever motivates voting in the first instance, the demand curve for voting appears to slope downward, as is generally consistent with rational behavior respecting the consumption of goods.

3. Possibilities of Strategic Electoral Voting

Some evidence suggests that under specific conditions, individuals vote in a manner that might be described as strategic.[78] For instance, in primary elections, many voters base their votes in significant part on the apparent electoral viability of the available candidates, rather than on which of those candidates is closest to their "ideal point."[79] An ideal point

---

[75] *See* Farber & Frickey, *supra* note 70, at 1017.

[76] *See generally* GEOFFREY BRENNAN & LOREN LOMASKY, DEMOCRACY AND DECISION: THE PURE THEORY OF ELECTORAL PREFERENCE (1993).

[77] Parts of the following discussion are based upon MUELLER, *supra* note 8, at 308–20 (reviewing statistical studies of the "Downsian" model of voting which posits that cost of voting has a negative effect on turnout).

[78] *See generally* Timothy J. Feddersen, *Rational Choice Theory and the Paradox of Not Voting*, J. ECON. PERSP., Winter 2004, at 9 (reviewing literature).

[79] For a discussion of potential strategic voting in the 1988 Presidential primaries, see Paul R. Abramson et al., *"Sophisticated" Voting in the 1988 Presidential Primaries*, 86 AM. POL. SCI. REV. 55 (1992).

is the point along a continuous liberal-to-conservative issue spectrum that most closely corresponds to a voter's ideological preference.[80] Some studies further suggest that voter turnout is higher in elections that are expected to be close.[81]

Are these observed voting behaviors strategic? If so, does that enhance or undermine claims of voter rationality?

4. *Group-Based Model of Vote Mobilization*[82]

Another non-instrumental theory of voting includes the role of certain socioeconomic groups in inculcating voting as a positive value. Examples include especially the well-educated and wealthy, and other identifiable subgroups of voters, such as union members.[83] Citizens are trained through education and social norms to think—perhaps erroneously—that their votes are apt to make a difference in a purely instrumental sense. Indeed, some have suggested that effective democracy depends on such misinformation. Does the incidence of voting among particular groups support or undermine claims that voting is an irrational activity?

5. *Voting as a Game of Cat and Mouse*[84]

Now consider the first of two alternative instrumental accounts of voting. Imagine a world in which everyone understood the voting paradox. Taken to its logical extreme, we might predict that no one would vote. If so, a single individual (whom we will call the "initial voter"), whatever her policy preferences, could completely control the outcome by voting. Some of those who previously declined to vote might now decide to vote to ensure that an idiosyncratic voter does not control the outcome (we will call these the "responsive voters"). Once the responsive voters turn out, this reduces the incentives of the initial voter to cast her ballot. And without the threat that the initial voter poses, the responsive voters lose their incentive to vote. This creates opportunities for a new set of initial voters who, in turn, motivate more responsive voters, and so on.

Some studies suggest that this non-cooperative game can explain why every election produces at least some voters, although these studies also suggest that without including some utility from the act of voting itself, these accounts are necessarily incomplete.[85] Consider how this theory of voting might also relate to the incidence of voting among particular demographic groups. As previously noted, studies have suggested a high correlation between wealth and education, on the one hand, and voting, on the other.[86] This might appear anomalous in that well-educated and wealthy persons are more likely to be aware of the voters' paradox than less educated and poor persons. And yet, educated

---

[80] For a helpful discussion, see Roger D. Congleton, *The Median Voter Model*, *in* 1 THE ENCYCLOPEDIA OF PUBLIC CHOICE 382 (Charles K. Rowley & Friedrich Schneider eds., 2004). For a more detailed analysis of spatial reasoning in public choice modeling, see *infra* Chapters 13 and 14.

[81] *See* MUELLER, *supra* note 8, at 315.

[82] *See id.* at 326–28; Feddersen, *supra* note 77, at 105–12.

[83] Feddersen, *supra* note 77, at 100.

[84] MUELLER, *supra* note 8, at 306–07.

[85] *See id.*

[86] *See id.* at 327. *See also supra* note 83 and accompanying text.

persons who know that that their individual acts of voting are unlikely to control electoral outcomes might also intuit that if they are known to regularly vote, their votes are might be afforded a disproportionate weight relative to their numbers. Even though these voters are unlikely to control the electoral outcome through their individual votes, they might value the signaling effect to those who try to influence outcomes in ways that could harm their interests in the future.

In this analysis, the paradox of voting might result from a somewhat crabbed understanding of each voter's instrumental calculus. The paradox is premised on excluding any potential payoffs *other than* the prospect of influencing the outcome of a given election as the marginal, or decisive, voter. Instead, the instrumental value might also include the signaling value of voting, including conveying that the voter is part of a group that can be relied upon to regularly vote. By voting in non-Presidential elections and regardless of weather conditions, such voters signal that those who would play cat and mouse with them are unlikely to succeed. Does voting to send a signal help to ameliorate the paradox of voting? Or does it merely restore it if, for example, an individual voter typically has a small impact on the overall group signal?

This approach to voting might bring another instrumental benefit. Within the relevant social groups to which such voters belong, the failure to vote might be viewed negatively as it weakens the political signal for the group as a whole.[87] The opposite might also be true. Within the relevant social group, the act of voting might be rewarded, whereas failing to do so might be frowned upon. In this analysis, consistent voters build a form of political capital independent of election-specific outcomes. Does this help to restore the rationality of voting? Why or why not?

6. *The Voter as Minimax-Regret Strategist*[88]

Let us now consider an alternative instrumental voting model. Assume that potential voters register a weak preference as between the two dominant candidates and that they ignore the probabilities of success of those candidates. Assume that a third, fringe candidate, perhaps one affiliated with either the Ku Klux Klan or a neo-Nazi group, enters the race. In this situation, mainstream voters turn out in large numbers to avoid the risk that the fringe candidate might win. The strategy is named minimax regret because the voters are not seeking to optimize their ideal points, but rather they seek to minimize the probability of an outcome that leads to a maximum regret.

Perhaps surprisingly, those who turn out to vote for this reason tend to vote for their first choice candidate even if the second choice candidate stands a better chance of defeating the least favored candidate. Such voters appear to discount the low probability that the fringe candidate will win and the somewhat higher probability that their second choice candidate is more likely to prevent this least favored result from potentially emerging.

---

[87] One recent article suggested, for example, that voting might signal educational status. *See* Nicholas Janetos, *Voting as a Signal of Education* (PIER Working Paper No. 17–010, May 16, 2017), https://papers.ssrn.com/sol3/papers.cfm?abstract_id=2968531.

[88] *See* MUELLER, *supra* note 8, at 307–08.

Perhaps the voter's rationale can be expressed as follows: "Because my vote is almost certainly not going to control the outcome, at the very least I can send a strong signal *against* my least favorite candidate, but if that's the purpose of my vote, I may as well vote for my favorite candidate." Does this further support the intuition that even in the minimax regret context, voters cast ballots because they derive a consumption benefit from doing so?

Questions: Which of these theories do you find most or least persuasive, and why? Do any restore the rationality of voting? Why or why not?

One of the most contentious legal issues in recent years has involved voter identification laws. In 2008, the Supreme Court sustained Indiana's voter ID law against an equal protection challenge.[89] That law allows voters without an ID to cast a provisional ballot provided they show an ID within ten days after doing so. Since then, thirty-three states have enacted some form of voter ID law, several of which have been challenged in lower federal courts, with some challenged provisions struck down.[90] Those who support these laws claim it is a modest requirement that reduces the risk of voter fraud, and those who oppose the laws claim that allegations of voter fraud are overblown, and that the burdens these laws impose disproportionately target poor communities, correlating to communities of color, who are most apt to support Democratic candidates. Which, if any, of the preceding theories best explain the political dynamics behind such laws and why?

C. Is Legislative Logrolling Good or Bad?[91]

Unlike private markets, which generally depend upon the unanimous assent of parties to transactions and which therefore are often presumed to enhance social welfare, legislatures produce law through various majority, and sometimes supermajority, rules. As a result, even if the resulting laws are Kaldor-Hicks efficient, implying that the law is social welfare enhancing overall, winners and losers nonetheless remain.

Legislative processes do not, however, simply involve a series of votes cast on proposed legislation. Instead, they involve a complex framework, one that we will explore in parts IV and V, that includes voting based upon merit, strategic voting or vote trading, and reciprocal commitments made over extended periods of time. Here we consider the peculiar dynamic of vote trading, also known as logrolling.

Logrolling is often thought to be anathema to the "public good" and sound legislative decision-making processes because it permits private interests to attach unrelated, usually narrowly focused private benefits to larger public-regarding legislation. As such, it is often thought that legislative processes should be adapted to prevent or to minimize the power of special interests to attach private legislation (such as "pork barrel" projects) to general-interest bills. Such proposals can take any number of forms, including

---

[89] Crawford v. Marion Cnty. Election Bd., 553 U.S. 181 (2008).

[90] *History of Voter ID*, NATIONAL CONFERENCE OF STATE LEGISLATURES (May 31, 2017), http://www.ncsl.org/research/elections-and-campaigns/voter-id-history.aspx.

[91] For discussions on logrolling's role in legislation, see Gordon Tullock & Geoffrey Brennan, *Why So Much Stability*, 37 PUB. CHOICE 189 (1981); Kenneth Shepsle & Barry R. Weingast, *Structure-Induced Equilibrium and Legislative Choice*, 37 PUB. CHOICE 503 (1981). Further analysis of logrolling will appear *infra* Chapter Nine through Chapter 15.

perhaps most notably the item veto and germaneness rules. On the other hand, if politics actually is an exchange process, then there might be nothing intrinsically wrong with logrolling. Instead, laws that further the public interest will often have unequal distributive effects. Even though welfare is generally enhanced, it is inevitable that certain people will be disadvantaged even by the most benign laws.

Logrolling might sometimes represent a form of side payment from the social surplus created by the adoption of the law to compensate the "losers." Alternatively, logrolling might be viewed as a means through which interest groups extort perks through the political process in exchange for allowing legislation to pass, a process identified with rent seeking.

In politics, as in football, it is generally easier to block than pass. Those empowered for various reasons to prevent the passage of desired legislation might use logrolling simply as a means to get preferred legislative benefits even though the larger legislation does not impose unique costs on them.

Questions: Do you think that logrolling is likely to be a force for good or harm in Congress? If you wished to test this question empirically, how could you falsify either of these competing claims? Can you identify practices in Congress or elsewhere that limit logrolling? Why might some institutions seek to promote logrolling and others seek to inhibit it? Is it possible to allow benign side payments without inviting rent seeking? Why or why not?

Conclusion

The questions presented in this chapter will remain important throughout the course. As you acquire new skills, you might change your thinking about the relationships about the nature of market interactions and about the relationship between markets and lawmaking institutions. In the chapter that follows, we formalize some of the intuitions developed here with a brief introduction to price theory. We then apply several of these concepts to doctrines covered in the first-year curriculum before introducing, in part III, additional methodological tools that will help with more advanced legal materials related to public law.

CHAPTER 2

Elements of Price Theory

Introduction

The material that follows will be a helpful review to some readers and altogether new to others. Students with no formal training in economics or price theory should be able to follow all of the presentations in this book. The materials in this chapter will help by setting out several principles that underlie neoclassical law and economics, interest group theory, social choice, and game theory, each of which are introduced and applied to law and public policy in later chapters. To benefit those who have not previously studied microeconomics, we offer a few introductory comments.

This chapter combines written expositions with graphics. These techniques are mutually reinforcing. Although the relevant concepts can also be expressed algebraically, we believe most students will find our approach more accessible, and we are confident that it does not sacrifice necessary clarity and detail. Most of the graphics are intuitive and easy to follow. Those that are somewhat more challenging will become increasingly manageable as you familiarize yourself with the essential framework.

I. THREE ESSENTIAL INSIGHTS

Many insights from neoclassical law and economics build upon elementary price theory. One such insight is that markets have a special capacity to assimilate certain decentralized information. Without anyone setting out to accomplish this goal, large numbers of individuals, behaving rationally in a private marketplace, contribute meaningful information that allows the market as a whole to signal to both buyers and sellers the relative valuation of countless goods and services. Within this process, the whole is greater than the sum of its parts; markets convey information far beyond the capacity of individuals or groups operating in alternative institutional settings.

A second insight is that subject to specific assumptions, including *initial wealth endowments* and the absence of *externalities*, meaning costs imposed on others from economic activity, individuals behaving rationally within market settings not only benefit themselves, but also will improve social welfare.[1] They do so by contributing to the

[1] Some externalities are positive, with the effect of undervaluing economic activity. Some scholars claim that when using the term rationality, economists imply that individuals behave in a narrowly self-interested manner. *See* Christine Jolls et al., *A Behavioral Approach to Law and Economics*, *in* BEHAVIORAL LAW AND ECONOMICS 13, 20 (Cass Sunstein ed., 2000). More generally, economists use the term to imply that individuals

creation of societal wealth. This important result is referred to as the *First Fundamental Theorem of Welfare Economics* (also sometimes called the *Invisible Hand Theorem*, after Adam Smith's metaphor).[2] When private parties voluntarily transact, they generally anticipate that doing so will produce gains that they can allocate between or among themselves. Typically, the parties share in the resulting gains, although doing so is not necessary to wealth creation.

Economic analysis in general begins with somewhat ambitious assumptions that are helpful in studying specific problems. More sophisticated analyses then relax these assumptions and consider how, if at all, doing so changes the analysis.[3]

The claim that private transactions have the potential to improve social welfare rests on two such assumptions. The first involves externalities and the second involves initial wealth endowments. We assume that parties to privately entered transactions bear all of the relevant social costs of their underlying economic activity. This means that parties do not artificially reduce the cost of those activities by foisting them onto persons who do not share in the resulting gains. When this assumption fails to hold, the parties are said to *externalize* part of the cost of their activities, or to generate *negative externalities*. (*Positive externalities* arise when parties create benefits from their transactions among non-participants to the transaction, and thus to persons who do not bear part of the costs. An example is the provision of public goods, as discussed in Chapter 1.)[4] The second assumption involves initial wealth endowments. Any resource allocation will be affected by the starting point of society's prior wealth allocation. Price theory inevitably begins with an initial set of societal wealth allocations.

These assumptions return us to the *Pareto* condition introduced in Chapter 1.[5] Subject to these two conditions—no negative (or positive) externalities and taking wealth endowments as given—when parties voluntarily enter into market transactions, they produce results that benefit at least one participant without harming anyone else. These are the conditions that define *Pareto* superiority, named after the famous Italian economist, Vilfredo Pareto.[6] Markets possess unique features conducive to activity that satisfies this efficiency benchmark.[7]

---

pursue their objectives, however defined, in a cost-effective manner. Personal objectives can be highly varied, including such altruistic behavior as charitable giving. We employ this broader understanding of rationality throughout the book.

[2] For a more detailed discussion of the First and Second Fundamental Theorems of Welfare Economics, see *infra* Part IV.

[3] Throughout this book, we will repeatedly come back to the assumptions that are expressed here, especially in parts that focus on political influences on regulatory regimes and how those regimes affect market functioning.

[4] *See* Chapter 1, Part II.B.

[5] *See* Chapter 1, Part III.H.

[6] *Vilfredo Pareto*, ENCYCLOPÆDIA BRITANNICA (Aug. 24, 2014), http://www.britannica.com/biography/Vilfredo-Pareto. There is a broad literature on the practical implications of the *Pareto* principle. For a general discussion, see Chapter 1, Part III.H.

[7] We will later see a graphical presentation developed by the philosopher and political economist, Francis Ysidro Edgeworth, which, in effect, demonstrates the mechanism through which transactions produce and allocate wealth through voluntary exchange. *See infra* Figure 2:20. For more background on Edgeworth,

As expressed in a famous economics text by Professors Armen A. Alchian and William R. Allen, exchange is one of the two mechanisms for producing societal wealth; the other is production.[8] By combining various inputs, specifically *factors of production* and *labor*, producers can create outputs the value of which exceeds the opportunity cost of the inputs. As used here, *opportunity cost* means the next best available use of a given activity or factor of production.

To illustrate, assume that a machine enhances the value of outputs of Plant A by $100,000 per year and that the same machine would enhance the value of Plant B's outputs value by $200,000 per year. Using the machine in Plant A creates a forgone opportunity to earn an additional $100,000 per year. The production process combines various factors of production, or inputs, to create goods or services of value in the marketplace. Exchange increases societal wealth by relying on markets to move the resulting goods or services into the hands of those who value them more highly.

A third insight from price theory is a corollary of the second, namely that markets have a special capacity to produce *Pareto*-improving transactions. The corollary is that when legal rules limit the capacity of markets to effectuate voluntary exchange, those rules have the potential to undermine the creation of societal wealth and, in doing so, to reduce social welfare.

Many law courses start with identified illustrations of *market failure.* Claimed market failures are instances in which something appears to prevent market processes from creating social welfare, or conversely, instances in which such processes create social welfare by imposing unique burdens on particular individuals or groups (which is actually a question about the distribution of wealth). These identified market failures are often coupled with proposed regulatory interventions that are designed to remedy the problem. Typically, these take the form of legal rules that restrict some aspect of either production or exchange.

Perhaps for this reason, lawyers and economists often approach common analytical problems from very different starting points. In a course on law and economics, it is important to acknowledge this up front and to articulate clearly those assumptions that underlie these differing perspectives. Economists do not claim that there are no market failures. There are. And we will offer illustrations throughout this volume. On the other hand, economists do not believe that every identified market failure is an actual one or that every recommended regulatory fix will necessarily be improving.

Here we revisit the discussion in Chapter 1 about Ronald Coase and Arthur Cecil Pigou.[9] One of the foundational questions underlying regulatory policy is the extent to which society is, or should be, confident that regulators have properly identified market failures and appropriately tailored their proposed regulatory responses. This will be a central theme throughout this course.

---

see *Francis Ysidro Edgeworth*, ENCYCLOPÆDIA BRITANNICA (June 8, 2001), http://www.britannica.com/biography/Francis-Ysidro-Edgeworth.

[8] ARMEN A. ALCHIAN & WILLIAM R. ALLEN, EXCHANGE AND PRODUCTION: COMPETITION, COORDINATION, AND CONTROL (3d ed. 1983).

[9] *See supra* Chapter 1, Part IV.

A central insight of the economic analysis of law is that conventional legal analysis tends to overlook this step. To the extent this is true, it does so at its peril. Legal scholars sometimes propose regulatory solutions without an independent assessment as to how accurately the claimed market failure has been identified and how effective the proposed regulatory solution is apt to be in improving outcomes. This problem is sometimes referred to as the *nirvana fallacy*. This means the tendency to imagine a perfect alternative to some observed imperfection in the world, for example comparing an actual imperfect market to a theoretically perfect state of competition, and then assuming that a proposed regulatory fix will necessarily be improving.[10]

Law and economics in general, and public choice in particular, encourages those who see perceived market defects to instead consider the following related questions: (1) How confident are we in the ability of political and legal decision makers to identify and respond to claimed market failures?; (2) Is there a risk that failures within the legal system or in political markets might exacerbate, rather than improve upon, the claimed private market failure?; and (3) Are there alternative, non-regulatory methods of structuring institutions so as to improve upon identified problematic outcomes? Answering these questions requires an understanding of how markets function and how regulations can both improve and undermine their functioning.

We now introduce price theory more formally. This returns us to the premise of individual rationality.

II. SUPPLY, DEMAND, AND REGULATORY INTERVENTION

In general, economic theory claims no particular insight into what any specific individual will consider a *good*. Different people like different things. Alice might place a high value on something that Barbara finds wasteful or even a nuisance. The fact that Barbara would not choose to own a pet chinchilla and would pay someone to take it off her hands does not take away from the affection that Alice and like-minded persons hold for these pets.

Rationality implies that for any particular good, those who value it will prefer more of that good to less. As the price of a given good declines, individuals who value it will tend to demand more of it.[11] This so-called *law of demand* holds true whether the good is purely private, for example, a pet or a piece of jewelry, or is collectively provided, for example, public schools or buses. Economists generally depict this intuition graphically, with the amount demanded of a good increasing as an inverse, or negative, function of price. As the price of any given good declines, holding all else constant, individuals, and the market as a whole, will demand more of that good. Figure 2:1 presents the demand function as a downward function of price, simplified as a straight line.

---

[10] *See infra* Chapter 13.

[11] Even if we imagine that most people who favor pet chinchillas would only wish to have one, the assertion still holds. As the price of the pet (and its care) declines, more people who would like to own one, but who could not previously afford it, will be brought into the market, and thus more pet chinchillas will be purchased.

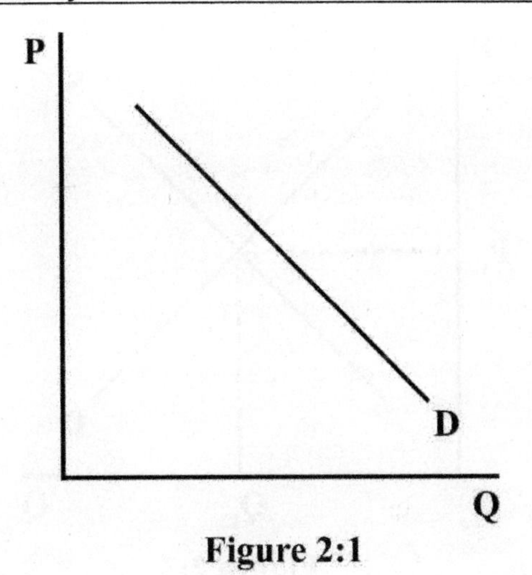

Figure 2:1

The supply function operates on the opposite premise. Holding all else constant, the higher the price that one can command for a good in the marketplace, the more the seller is likely to invest in either producing or procuring that good for sale in the marketplace. Figure 2:2 thus depicts the supply curve as an upward sloping function of price, once more simplified as a straight line.

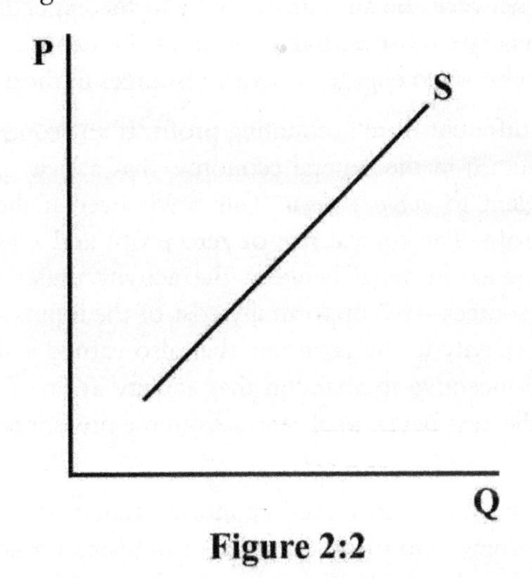

Figure 2:2

Combining the two curves into a single graphic generates an *equilibrium*. This is the point at which supply and demand intersect. The equilibrium corresponds to the point at which the market *clears*. At this unique price and quantity, the amount of the good demanded and supplied precisely match. In Figure 2:3, the market-clearing price and quantity are marked as Pc and Qc respectively, with *c* representing the market-clearing price within a competitive market.

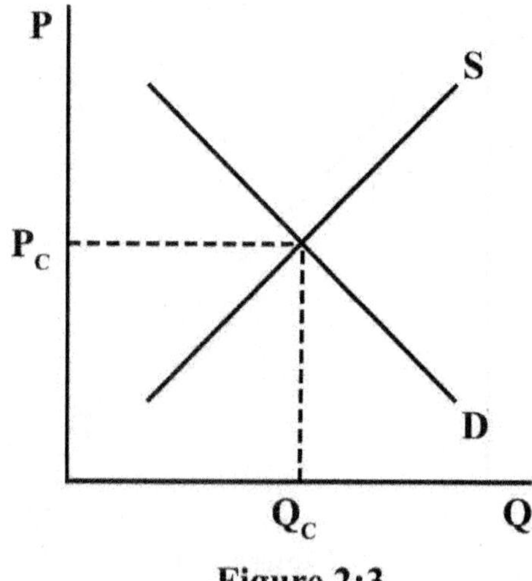

Figure 2:3

Although we will revisit this concept below,[12] it is important here to define the term *profit* as it is used within economic analysis. Economists assume that most of the activities in which people engage or invest resources with the intent of generating income provide a positive financial return. We might think of this *return* as *accounting profit*. This simply means the difference between the amount earned and the expenditures, or the amount actually laid out, to generate those earnings. Without the expectation of such a return, individuals would not choose to engage or invest resources in those activities.

Economic profit is different from accounting profit. If an economic activity produces the standard rate of return in the general economy, that activity produces *zero economic profit,* which is equivalent to *ordinary profit.* This holds even if the activity generates a positive accounting profit. The equivalence of zero profit and a standard rate of return implies that the difference in value between the activity under review and the next available use of the resources—the opportunity cost of the inputs—is zero. If one were engaged in any other activity in the economy that also earned a standard return, there would be no financial incentive to abandon that activity in favor of the activity under review.[13] Subtracting the next best rate of return from the present rate of return produces zero economic profit.

Now imagine that a newly identified economic activity yields positive economic profit. Some people earning zero profit now see a promising economic opportunity. As more individuals abandon their immediate, zero profit, activities to pursue the positive-economic profit activity, the profitability of the latter activity will, over time, be dampened down. If the overall market is operating efficiently, this process will continue until the once positive-profit activity is earning the general rate of return of the economy as a whole, meaning zero economic profit.

---

12 *See infra* Part III.C.

13 To be sure, individuals often leave even higher paying jobs for lower paying ones that they enjoy more, and there is nothing irrational about doing so. The "imputed" income associated with career enjoyment must be included in the analysis to make an appropriate comparison.

We can adapt the very simple model of supply and demand from Figure 2:3, and use it to evaluate how four different sets of regulatory policies can upset a market clearing equilibrium. We proceed with the following illustrations of regulatory policies that prevent market clearance: (1) setting price above market clearance; (2) setting price below market clearance; (3) restricting quantity below market clearance; and (4) forcing quantity above market clearance.

Before proceeding, try to come up with your own illustration of each type of regulatory policy. Some of the policies described below have been enacted based on claims of *market failure*, meaning a perceived defect in market processing with adverse effects concerning price, quantity, or allocation of goods or services. Not all claimed market failures are actual market failures. Sometimes regulations interfere with well-functioning markets, and other times, regulators willingly pay the price of interfering with markets to achieve independent normative objectives. As you read these examples that follow, consider what the consequence of the policy is likely to be for the market-clearing price and quantity, and then compare your results with the examples and analyses that follow.

A. Setting Price Above Market Clearance

Perhaps the most obvious illustration of setting price set above the market-clearing price is a minimum wage law, depicted in Figure 2:4. If we set the minimum wage price *Pmw* above the market-clearing price for unskilled labor *Pc*, where *c* stands for the wage under purely competitive conditions, we observe a dislocation in which the amount of labor that workers are willing to supply exceeds the amount of labor that employers are willing to purchase at the set minimum wage.[14] It is important, however, to recognize that the full extent of this identified gap, identified in the graphic as the *total dislocation*, overstates the dislocation effect of the minimum wage. Although the minimum wage results in a larger supply of labor than demand for that labor at the specified wage, the actual unemployment effect starts from the different baseline of market clearing labor *without* the minimum wage in place. The smaller difference—here representing about half of the total market dislocation—is captured by the quantity at the market-clearing price minus the lower quantity demanded with the minimum wage in place. In the graphic, this is referred to as the *net dislocation*. The remaining part of the dislocation results from newly induced labor spurred by the higher wage, rather than from the forced unemployment of those who would have been working but for the dislocating effect of the minimum wage.

The minimum wage introduces several important policy considerations. Although the minimum wage generally produces the expected effect of increasing unemployment, especially among lower-skilled, young, and minority workers,[15] some studies have found

[14] In conventional textbook presentations, changes in price or quantity are presented through the study of "comparative statics." This is depicted with a shift in either the supply or demand curve (with the other held constant), and then a comparison of the two equilibrium points before and after the change takes place. In the presentation that follows, we are assuming a regulatory intervention that produces a fixed change in price or quantity affected by regulatory fiat. As a result, the change is depicted with a mandated price or quantity depicted as a horizontal line (price) above or below the market-clearing price, or a vertical line (quantity) set higher or lower than the market clearing quantity.

[15] See Jeffrey Clemens & Michael Wither, *The Minimum Wage and the Great Recession: Evidence of Effects on the Employment and Income Trajectories of Low-Skilled Workers* (NBER Working Paper No. 20724, Dec. 2014), http://www.nber.org/papers/w20724.pdf (finding "binding minimum wage increases had significant, negative

either no unemployment effect or a smaller than predicted effect.[16] Although the studies on both sides are contested, empirical findings suggest the possibility that the measured effect on employment is not as large as a simple model might lead us to anticipate.

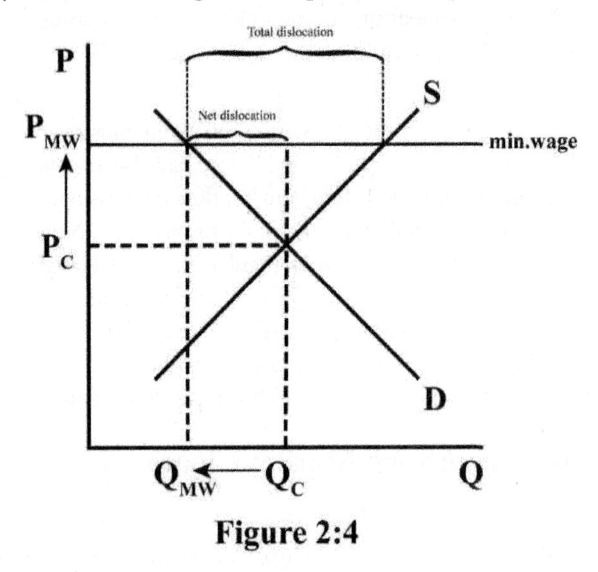

Figure 2:4

It is not possible here to assess that broad literature, but a few observations are appropriate. Consider the possibility that minimum wage laws have a lag effect relative to actual wages paid in most workplace settings for unskilled or relatively low-skilled labor. If so, minimum wage laws that change infrequently over time might not be forcing a higher market wage so much as catching up with preexisting market conditions. Such higher wage laws might offer enacting legislators political benefits. These include claiming to improve the working conditions of those most in need, yet without necessarily generating higher wages for all but a small class of workers, and risking having some workers, including perhaps those identified above, adversely affected.

Do you find this explanation persuasive? Why or why not? To the extent that this is persuasive, does it counsel for a national minimum wage, or for minimum wages to be set at state or local levels? Why? If we have the same minimum wage in two relatively close locations, for example, a major city and a rural area an hour away, does a uniform minimum wage create an opportunity for a positive economic profit? Why or why not?

---

effects on the employment and income growth" of low-skilled workers); Jonathan Meer & Jeremy West, *Effects of the Minimum Wage on Employment Dynamics* (NBER Working Paper No. 19262, Aug. 2013), http://www.nber.org/papers/w19262.pdf (concluding that "the minimum wage impact[s] employment over time, through changes in growth rather than an immediate drop in employment levels").

16 John Schmitt, *Why Does the Minimum Wage Have No Discernible Effect on Employment?*, CENTER FOR ECON. & POL'Y RES. (Feb. 2013), http://cepr.net/documents/publications/min-wage-2013-02.pdf; Fabián Slonimczyk & Peter Skott, *Employment and Distribution Effects of the Minimum Wage*, 84 J. ECON. BEHAV. & ORG. 245 (2012); Paul K. Somm & Yannet M. Lathrop, *Raise Wages, Kill Jobs?: Seven Decades of Historical Data Find No Correlation Between Minimum Wage Increases and Employment Levels*, NAT'L EMP. LAW CENTER DATA BRIEF (May 2016), http://www.nelp.org/content/uploads/NELP-Data-Brief-Raise-Wages-Kill-Jobs-No-Correlation.pdf; Evan Totty, *The Effect of Minimum Wages on Employment: A Factor Model Approach*, 55 ECON. INQUIRY 1712 (2017).

B. Setting Price Below Market Clearance

The second regulatory intervention imposes a lower than market-clearing price. A prominent illustration is rent control. By ordinance, some rental housing, primarily in large cities, is subject to a maximum rent. This is almost invariably set lower than the market-clearing rent. This time, as a result of the regulation, the amount demanded exceeds the amount that those who offer such units are willing to supply at the regulated price. As in the prior example, this total dislocation overstates the net dislocating effect of the regulation. That is because it includes the additional demand for rental property induced by the lower price. The net dislocation, once more taking the pre-regulatory demand as the baseline, is the smaller dislocation to the left of the market-clearing quantity. This reflects the reduced supply caused by the rent ceiling as compared with what the supply would have been absent the rent control law.

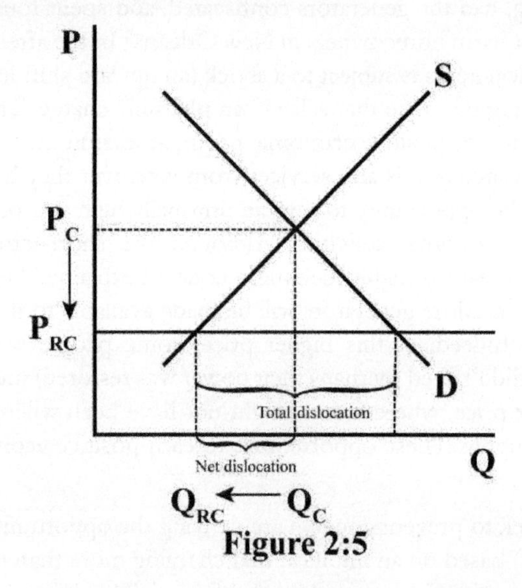

Figure 2:5

Rent control laws have long been criticized as contributing to urban blight.[17] Consider the incentives of property owners who find themselves subject to such ordinances.[18] Rent control lowers the expected return on investment by reducing the present value of the landlord's anticipated income stream. Affected landlords will sometimes have the option to convert such properties into privately owned non-rental units, such as condominiums, that they can then sell, thereby reducing available rental housing stock. Alternatively, some landlords might seek ways to reduce part of the ongoing costs of such properties, including maintenance costs, with the effect of degrading rental housing stock. Finally, some landlords might seek partial additional

---

[17] *See, e.g.*, Paul Krugman, *Reckonings: A Rent Affair*, N.Y. TIMES (June 7, 2000), http://www.nytimes.com/2000/06/07/opinion/reckonings-a-rent-affair.html (explaining that landlords in rent controlled cities will not invest in newer, better quality housing for fear that the municipality will regulate it).

[18] How might this analysis differ for a buyer who acquires a property knowing in advance that it is subject to rent control?

compensation, beyond what is permitted by law, in the form of *under the table payments* (sometimes called *key money*).

There are other examples of price ceilings as well. Consider the following common plea following a natural disaster. The governor gives a speech declaring that those who take advantage of the disaster by *gouging* will be prosecuted to the fullest extent of the law. Let us assume that gouging in this context refers to the efforts of those who supply important goods or services to charge premium prices as a result of scarcity following the disaster. Does the anti-gouging policy benefit those most in need of the affected goods and services?

In one notable example, following Hurricane Katrina, a Kentucky man bought nineteen generators for approximately $1000 each, and drove 600 miles to Mississippi in a rented truck, hoping to sell the generators for double the price, whereupon he was arrested for gouging, had the generators confiscated, and spent four nights in jail.[19] Did this policy benefit or harm homeowners in New Orleans? In the aftermath of the disaster, the demand for critical items is subject to a shock (an upward shift in the demand curve), dramatically increasing the price that sellers can plausibly charge. This new, higher price signals an opportunity for positive economic profit, at least in the short run. Those who can quickly move desired goods and services from wherever they happen to be into the troubled area have the opportunity to earn an unusually high rate of return as compared with their existing economic activities. Although the short-term supply curve for generators in New Orleans is highly inelastic, a concept explained below,[20] it will become more elastic over time. More generators will be made available to the public at a price of $2000 than $1000. Indeed, at this higher price, some people who already owned a generator that they didn't need (perhaps their power was restored) might be willing to part with it at the higher price, whereas they might not have been willing at the lower price, further increasing supply. These opportunities to earn positive economic profit are also referred to as *rents*.

Those who seek to prevent gouging are denying the opportunity to earn such rents (or economic profit) based on an intuition that charging more than the pre-disaster price for those goods or services imposes additional financial burdens on disaster victims and is thus unfair to persons who are already suffering. It certainly seems unfair to profit from the unfortunate circumstances that others are experiencing as a result of a natural disaster.

An economist, however, would approach this analytical puzzle differently. From her perspective, the question becomes how to improve the likelihood that the scarce resources—here generators—flow from places where they have a lower value into New Orleans, where they now have a higher value.[21] This relates to the earlier observation that

---

[19] Joseph B. Treaster & Abby Goodnough, *Powerful Storm Threatens Havoc Along Coast*, N.Y. TIMES (Aug. 29, 2005), http://www.nytimes.com/2005/08/29/us/powerful-storm-threatens-havoc-along-gulf-coast.html; Rafi Mohammad, *The Problem with Price Gouging Laws*, HARV. BUS. REV. (July 23, 2013), https://hbr.org/2013/07/the-problem-with-price-gouging-laws/.

[20] *See infra* at 50.

[21] *See* Michael A. Salinger, Director, Bureau of Economics, Federal Trade Commission, Address to Antitrust Committee of Boston Bar Association: Moneyball and Price Gouging 3–4 (Feb. 26, 2006), https://www.ftc.gov/sites/default/files/documents/public_statements/moneyball-and-price-gouging/060227money

individuals behaving rationally contribute information to markets, which can better signal relative valuations of goods and services than other institutions. Positive economic profit signals that generators are more highly valued in New Orleans than elsewhere. Individuals attuned to such pricing differences realize an opportunity to earn a rent by abandoning their existing economic activity in favor of transporting generators to New Orleans. If the goal is to move generators quickly to New Orleans, the anti-gouging policy might seem ill suited and perhaps counterproductive. In addition, the *gougers* are unlikely to continue earning economic profit through this activity in the longer term. The cost of transporting the resources will eat up some of the rents, and if there are no barriers to others pursuing these rents, market entrants will eventually compete them away until the price just covers the opportunity cost. At that point, the activity will earn zero economic (or ordinary) profit.

Is this a persuasive account of the likely effects of the anti-gouging policies put in place following Hurricane Katrina? Why or why not? Assume that there was no anti-gouging law in the aftermath of Hurricane Katrina. What do you predict would have happened to the price of generators in New Orleans over time, and why?

C. Setting Quantity Below Market Clearance

Now consider a regulation that operates on the quantity of goods sold, rather than on the price. A well-known example involves the wheat quota, imposed during a world-wide glut associated with the Great Depression, and that was sustained in the famous Supreme Court decision, *Wickard v. Filburn*.[22] In *Wickard*, the federal government sustained a congressional scheme by which the Secretary of Agriculture imposed restrictions on the amount of wheat domestic farmers were permitted to grow, relying on regulatory authority under the Commerce Clause in Article I of the United States Constitution. The effect was to reduce the quantity of wheat entering the market, thereby raising the price, rather than to dictate the price at which wheat was sold. The effect is depicted in Figure 2:6.

We will later see that this type of scheme creates strong incentives to cheat and thus to sell above the imposed quota levels.[23] The artificially reduced quantity creates a total market dislocation that induces a greater willingness among wheat farmers to expand their operations, given the restriction on available capacity, even for a substantially lower price, coupled with the desire to benefit from the artificially higher price. By disallowing the forces of supply and demand to adjust, the quota creates a total dislocation that exceeds the smaller net dislocation representing the difference between the original market-clearing price and the artificially raised price resulting from the diminution in available wheat.

---

ballandpricegouging_0.pdf (explaining that preventing price gouging is much like setting a price ceiling and that it prevents needed supplies from being diverted to disaster stricken areas).

[22] 317 U.S. 111 (1942).

[23] This explains why the theory of cartels can be expressed in terms of a multi-lateral prisoners' dilemma. *See infra* Chapter 15.

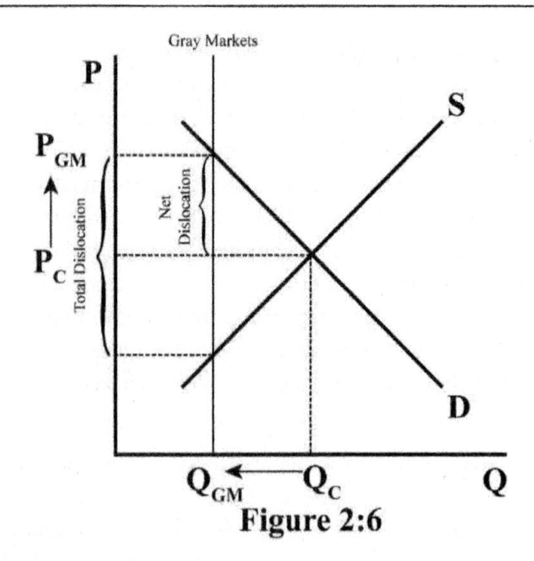

Figure 2:6

A similar dynamic also characterizes goods and services sold in gray markets. These include the unlicensed practice of medicine or law, restrictions on drugs or gambling, and prohibitions against monetized provision of sexual services in most jurisdictions. In each instance, the effect is to raise the price for those who, in spite in the legal ban, continue willingly to procure the goods or services.

Are there sound policy reasons for disallowing the market itself, rather than regulators, to determine whether such goods and services should be permitted to enter the market or in what amounts? In Chapter 15, we will take up the example of the unlicensed practice of law.[24] The data appear to support the claim that requiring attorneys to be licensed increases their earnings. Certainly, licensure provides offsetting benefits to clients, including some assurance that those who hold themselves out as lawyers have the requisite training. An alternative *rent-seeking* argument suggests that a certain professional group with political influence (including lawyers), might seek to limit supply at least in part to raise their earnings, possibly with less regard to the impact on service quality.[25]

Which account best explains the requirement of licensure in law? What about such other professions as medicine or pharmacy? Can you explain why some professions are licensed, whereas others are not? In the absence of legally sanctioned licensure for those professions that require it, the market itself could provide voluntary licensing mechanisms. Which do you think are more likely to be helpful to consumers of legal services? Why?

D. Setting Quantity Above Market Clearance

Finally, we consider what is likely the least intuitive market distortion, mandating an increase in the supply of a good or service that the market would not otherwise provide. Although this might seem implausible, there are illustrations. The most recent example is

---

[24] *See* Chapter 15.

[25] For a fuller discussion of rent seeking behavior, see Chapter 11.

the Patient Protection and Affordable Care Act (ACA),[26] more commonly known as Obamacare. The status of this statute has come into question following the transition from the Obama to the Trump administration. Donald Trump's platform included a commitment to "repeal and replace Obamacare."[27]

The central concern motivating the ACA involved the difficulties associated with health care insurance pooling. Those at low risk (sometimes referred to as "young invincibles") are often disinclined to purchase insurance, and those at high risk, largely due to preexisting medical conditions, often find the resulting exorbitant rates unaffordable. The ACA was designed to increase the number of insureds by forcing low risk individuals to buy insurance and by forcing insurance companies, who would benefit from the increased insurance pooling, to offer affordable coverage to those with preexisting conditions.[28] Overall, the scheme was intended to increase the number of insurance policies entered into the market to reduce the population of uninsured individuals.[29]

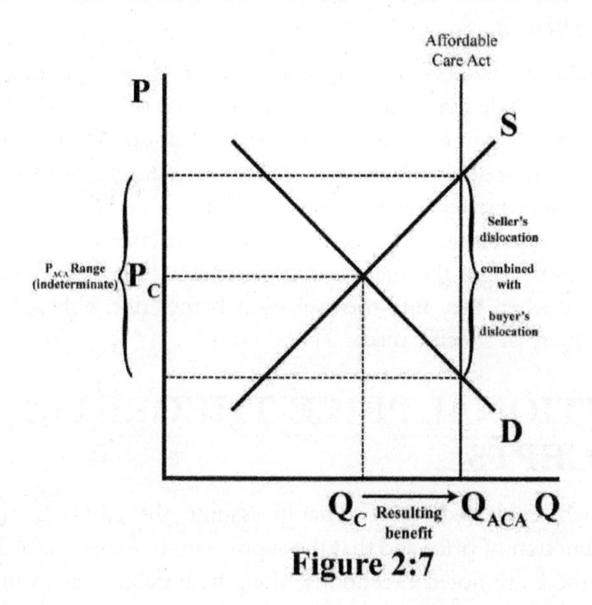

Figure 2:7

The ACA scheme thus forces the purchase of insurance to increase the quantity of premiums paid and forces the provision of policies to decrease the pool of uninsureds. The relationship between the actual and total market distortions take on a somewhat different significance here than in the prior examples. In effect, there are two separate

---

26 Pub. L. No. 111–148, 124 Stat. 119 (2010).

27 For a more general discussion and analysis, see *infra* Chapter 17, which discusses the subsequent repeal of the individual mandate. The analysis that follows explores the implications of the original ACA scheme, which included the mandate.

28 The ACA is an extremely complex statute and includes other features such as state and federal exchanges to satisfy demand that is not met by private insurers. *Id.* We do not offer an analysis of the ACA here, but rather, use it as an illustration of a forced increase in the quantity of a good or service effected by a regulatory scheme.

29 For a more detailed analysis, see Leslie Meltzer Henry & Maxwell L. Stearns, *Commerce Games and the Individual Mandate*, 100 GEO. L.J. 1117 (2012).

dislocations, one for those insureds who would otherwise choose not to enter the market, and one for the insurers who would otherwise choose not to sell to those at high risk, that together comprise the total market dislocation.

In the graphic above, you will see a forced increase in the quantity of policies both purchased and sold. At this higher level of forced purchases and sales, buyers would only be willing to pay a low price, and insurers would correspondingly demand a very high premium. We might be tempted to use the market-clearing price as a baseline, but we do not actually know that this is the meaningful baseline with the newer insureds, including both young invincibles, forced into the pool, and those at high risk now able to purchase insurance. We can say that the premium should lie somewhere between the two extremes of what insurers would charge those at high risk and what young invincibles are willing to pay. That, after all, is the point of forcing broader pooling. These two separate distortions, forcing young invincibles to pay more and forcing insurers to sell for less, add up to the total dislocation. The goal is to have insurers and insureds share these burdens, thus creating a pooling benefit.

Does the goal of reducing the pool of uninsureds justify the resulting market distortion? If you conclude that it does not, can you think of alternative ways to improve insurance pooling other than forcing those who would not otherwise purchase insurance into the pool? How, if at all, is this analysis changed if we assume that when those who are uninsured but who were regarded as low risk become seriously ill, they will nonetheless receive the benefit of medical services, for example, at taxpayer-subsidized emergency rooms? Similarly, how might the analysis change if we assume that those at low risk will seek coverage only when they find themselves at higher risk, either due to age or as a result of the discovery of specific medical conditions?

III. ADDITIONAL PRICE-THEORETIC CONCEPTS

As previously explained, we ordinarily assume that the demand curve slopes downward as a function of price and that the supply curve slopes upward as a function of price. Although there are noted exceptions, along with debates as to their frequency or significance,[30] those are less relevant to the study of law and economics. A more nuanced understanding of the nature of the supply and demand curves is relevant, however, as this affects the efficacy of regulation.

[30] For an interesting counter example of the former, consider claimed illustrations of "Giffen goods," goods for which the income effect of a decline in price overwhelms the substitution effect, thus reducing the quantity demanded as the price declines. For a general discussion, see RICHARD A. POSNER, ECONOMIC ANALYSIS OF LAW 5 (7th ed. 2007); *see also Giffen Paradox*, MCGRAW-HILL DICTIONARY OF MODERN ECONOMICS 254 (2d ed. 1973). For a counter illustration on the supply side, consider the "S" shaped supply curve that has been used to explain why as the price of oil increased in the 1970s, OPEC nations reduced supply, anticipating a greater value of future production as compared with the anticipated value of present investment opportunities. JACQUES CRÉMER & DJAVAD SALEHI-ISFAHANI, MODELS OF THE OIL MARKET (1991).

A. Price Elasticities

The direction of the relationship between price and quantity (positive for supply, negative for demand) captures only part of what is important about these functions. Also significant is how responsive these curves are to price changes. This responsiveness is referred to as the *elasticity* of demand or supply. The concept of elasticity focuses on how an incremental change in price affects the amount demanded (or supplied) of a given good, where both changes are measured in percentage terms.[31]

We begin with demand. When demand for a good is *inelastic*, a significant price increase will not have a correspondingly substantial effect in reducing the quantity demanded of that good. Conversely, when the demand for a good is *elastic*, even a relatively small increase in price will have a relatively large impact on the quantity demanded.

In Figure 2.8, below, we present two demand curves. While both curves are downward sloping (as was the case with the demand curve in Figure 2:1), the first, inelastic, curve, is closer to vertical, and the second, elastic, curve, is closer to horizontal.

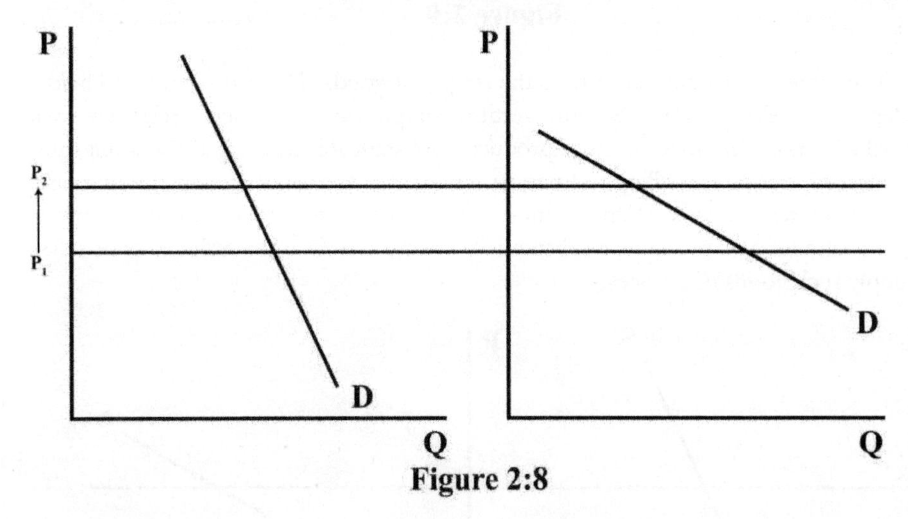

Figure 2:8

We can now illustrate the impact of elasticity by taking these two curves and considering for each how an incremental adjustment in price affects the quantity demanded of the relevant good or service. If we begin with the lower price and raise it to the higher price, we can then compare the effect of the price change, which is the same for each curve, to the change in quantity demanded, which will differ between the two curves. Notice the relatively minor effect in the reduction of quantity demanded for the inelastic demand curve (to the left) as compared with the relatively greater effect in the reduced demand for the elastic demand curve (to the right) as the price increases. The same relationship can be expressed the opposite way; by moving the price down, we

---

[31] Elasticity is not the same thing as slope, although the concepts are related. The problem of using slope to measure the price responsiveness of demand or supply is that slope relies on the units of measure. Thus, for example, if we measured gasoline in gallons versus liters, we would compute different slopes of the demand or supply curves, even though nothing fundamental has changed about costs or consumer preferences. Elasticity avoids this difficulty by computing the percentage changes in quantity relative to the percentage change in price, thus providing a unit-free measure of change.

induce a relatively greater increase in quantity demanded for the elastic, than for the inelastic, demand curve.

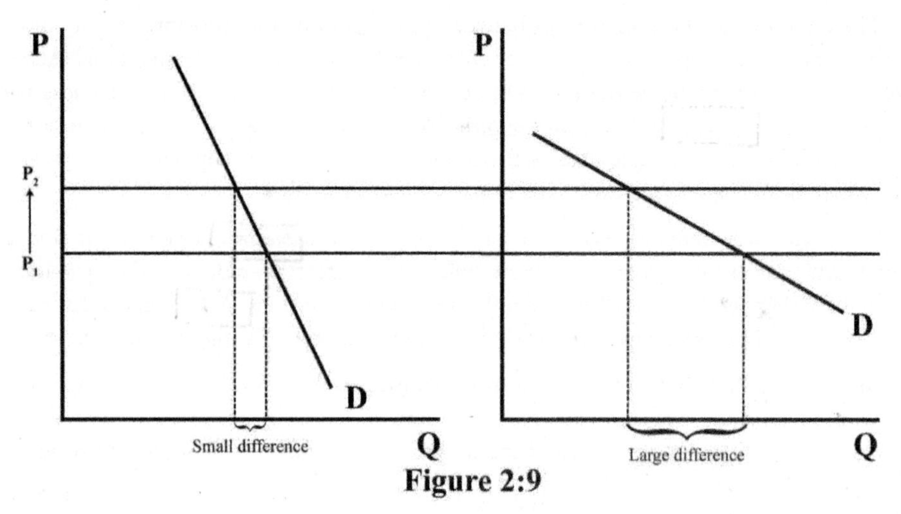

Figure 2:9

The same set of intuitions affects the supply of goods. Thus, in Figure 2:10 below, we depict an inelastic (relatively more vertical) supply curve in which a relatively small upward adjustment in price does not produce a substantial increase in the amount those who sell such goods are willing to bring to the market. We can then compare the same effect on the more elastic (relatively more horizontal) supply curve. The same upward price adjustment now produces a substantially greater effect on the willingness of sellers to supply such goods or services.

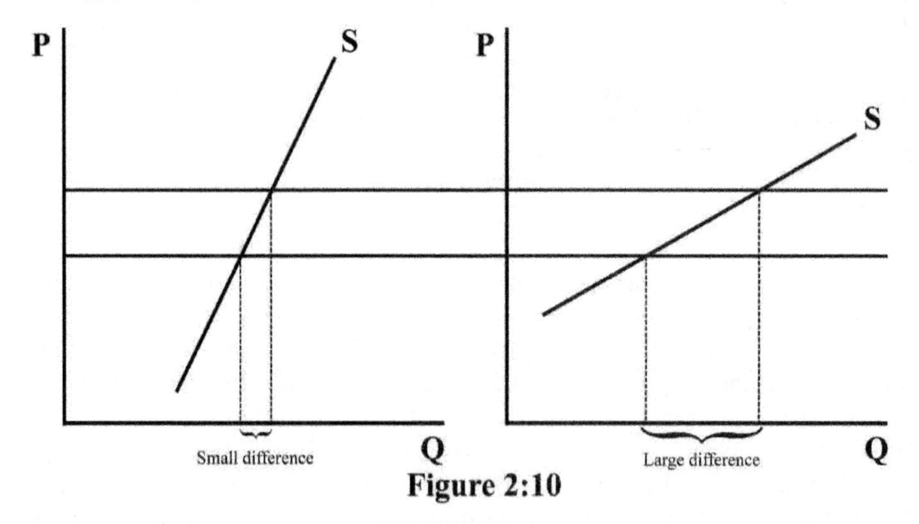

Figure 2:10

Can you identify goods for which the demand curve is likely to be elastic or inelastic? Can you identify goods for which the supply curve is likely to be elastic or inelastic? How does the elasticity of demand for a particular good affect whether a tax on the industry that produces that good is likely to be effective? How does the elasticity of supply affect whether a market is likely to be competitive or non-competitive? We will return to these and related questions below and throughout the book.

The concept of elasticity plays a central role in considering competitive and non-competitive markets. In the discussion that follows, we will see that whether the demand for a given good is elastic or inelastic is greatly affected by the availability of substitutes for those affected goods.

B. Competitive Versus Noncompetitive Markets

Economists distinguish two paradigmatic market situations, competitive and noncompetitive (or monopolistic) markets. Within competitive markets, individual firms are unable to control the market-clearing, or equilibrium, price. The price is determined at the point where supply and demand (Dm) intersect for the market as a whole. Pure competition means that no single firm is sufficiently large within that market to affect the price. For each individual firm, therefore, the price is fixed, meaning that it perceives the demand curve (Di) to be flat (or perfectly elastic). The implication is that if a firm that elected to sell at a price one cent below the prevailing market price could in theory sell an infinite amount. Conversely, if the same firm priced the good one cent above the prevailing market price, it would sell none.

For this reason, within competitive markets, individual firms are *price takers.* As Figure 2:11 suggests, firms operating in competitive markets will sell as much as it is cost effective for them to sell at the prevailing market price over which they have no control.

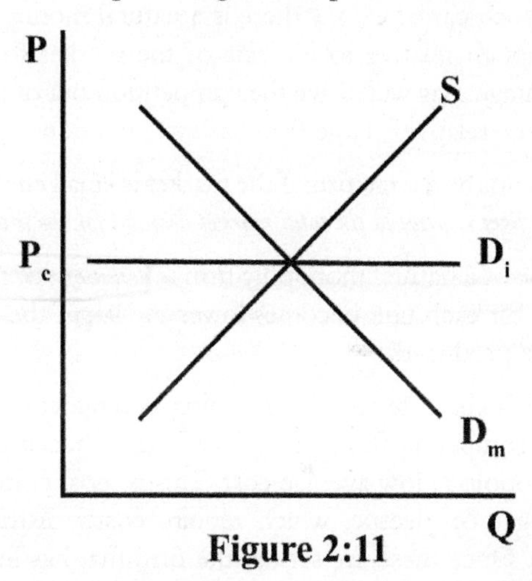

Figure 2:11

We next consider a market in which the seller is a monopolist. (It is important, however, to recognize that most markets operate somewhere between the two analytical poles representing pure competition and pure monopoly. More typically, firms operate within markets in which the sellers possess a limited, not absolute, degree of market power.) Market power implies that the firm is not a price taker. Firms with complete market power are known as monopolists. These firms assume the same position as the aggregate set of firms for a given good or service within a competitive market. Just as the entire set of firms faces a downward sloping, instead of a flat, demand curve, so too does the monopolist. Because the monopolist confronts the demand for the entire market, she is able to affect price by controlling the quantity of goods produced and sold.

Professors William Baumol and Alan Blinder have explained: "There are two basic reasons why a monopoly may exist: barriers to entry, such as legal restrictions and patents, and cost advantages of superior technology or large-scale operations that lead to natural monopoly."[32] The authors add that "It is generally considered undesirable to break up a large firm whose costs are low because of scale economies. But barriers to entry are usually considered to be against the public interest except where they are believed to have offsetting advantages, as in the case of patents."[33]

We have already seen that entrepreneurs pursue opportunities for economic rents in private markets. In Chapter 11, we will introduce the closely related concept of rent seeking, the process through which firms succeed in procuring barriers to entry through the regulatory process. That proves to be one method of obtaining durable economic rents, and much of the literature on public choice focuses on the problematic costs associated with rent-seeking behavior.

Here we consider natural monopoly. Baumol and Blinder explain the conditions that give rise to natural monopoly as follows:

> In some industries, economies of large-scale production or economies of scope (from simultaneous production of a large number of related items, such as car motors and bodies, truck parts, and so on) are so extreme that the industry's output can be produced at far lower cost by a single firm than by a number of smaller firms. In such cases, we say there is a natural monopoly. Once a firm becomes large enough relative to the size of the market for its product, its natural cost advantage may well drive the competition out of business whether or not anyone in the relatively large firm has evil intentions.
>
> A monopoly need not be a large firm if the market is small enough. *What matters is the size of a single firm relative to the total market demand for the product.*[34]

A defining characteristic of a natural monopoly firm is *declining average cost.* This means that the cost of production for each unit becomes lower the larger the scale of the operation in which those units are produced.

When production is characterized by declining average cost, a single monopolistic firm will drive smaller competing firms out of the market because smaller firms cannot match the natural monopolist's low average cost. This is most commonly illustrated with utilities, for example, gas or electric, which require costly distribution networks that operate on a vast scale. Once these are set up, the firm that has invested the large start-up cost is able to offer its services at a lower average cost than potential market entrants.

The major concern with natural monopolies is that once competing firms are driven out, or once potential competitors realize that entry into the market is futile, the dominant

---

[32] WILLIAM J. BAUMOL & ALAN S. BLINDER, ECONOMICS: PRINCIPLES AND POLICY 217 (10th ed. 2006).

[33] *Id.*

[34] *Id.* at 216 (italics in original).

firm, behaving rationally, will reduce its output and raise its price to the monopoly level. This is the traditional justification for regulated or government-run utilities.

More typically, several producers exist in a given market and each has some degree of market power based upon brand name recognition and *product differentiation*.[35] Coca Cola can raise its price relative to Pepsi, and those who are brand-loyal will not immediately switch. If Coca Cola tripled its price relative to Pepsi, however, all but the most loyal fans would develop a taste for Pepsi or another alternative. Because individual firms with market power face downward sloping, rather than flat, demand curves, they are *price setters* rather than *price takers*.

Figure 2:12 illustrates the demand and cost configuration for a firm operating in a noncompetitive market:

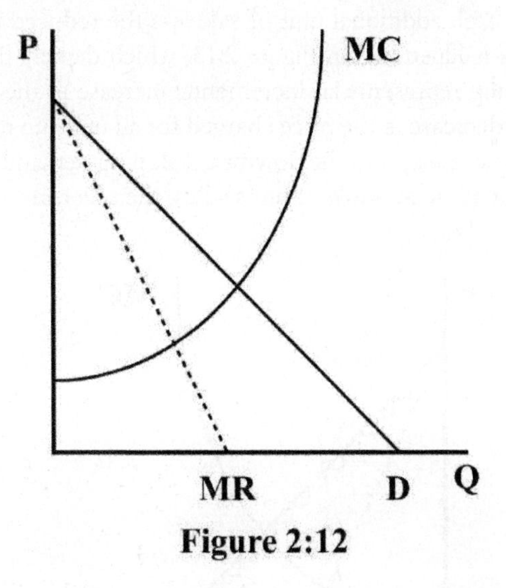

Figure 2:12

The demand curve facing a firm in a noncompetitive market, like that for the market as a whole, slopes downward. Most notably, the monopolist confronts a *marginal revenue curve* (MR). This curve lies beneath the demand curve. To generate this curve, we need to carefully articulate an assumption. The model assumes that that the seller is not able to engage in *price discrimination*. Price discrimination is a process whereby a firm is able to vary the price charged based upon the individual buyer's willingness to pay. If you consider the downward sloping demand curve, you might imagine a series of people each of whom holds different valuations of the relevant good, with those to the left placing the highest value, and those to the right, placing progressively lower values.

From the seller's perspective, it would be ideal to charge each person along the demand curve exactly what she or he would be willing to pay, thus capturing the maximum revenue for the sale of those goods. We assume, however, that the seller is unable to distinguish among buyers in this way, and instead, that she is required to settle on a given

[35] Baumol and Blinder explain that the "rigid requirements make pure monopoly a rarity in the real world," but that "like perfect competition, pure monopoly is a market form that is easier to analyze." *Id.* at 214–15.

price that is charged to all buyers without regard to where they are along the demand curve.

This assumption—that the seller cannot engage in price discrimination—has a substantial consequence for the monopolist as it affects the optimal strategy in decisions respecting price and quantity. That is because for each additional unit that the monopolist would like to sell, it must lower the price not only for *that* unit, but for all units sold to that point. Even though a buyer who places a higher value on that good would be willing to pay more, the seller cannot charge more, and she must take that into account when reducing the price to attract the next buyer. This continues along the entire length of the demand curve.

The marginal revenue curve captures this important intuition. This curve reflects the gains associated with each additional unit of sale less the reduced price for all units sold up to that point. This is illustrated in Figure 2:13, which depicts the declining price as a step function. Each step represents an incremental increase in the quantity sold coupled with a corresponding decrease in the price charged for all units up to that point. Each step reduction in price thus correlates to the downward sloping demand curve because for any additional unit sold (or some multiple of units sold), the seller must lower the price for all buyers at that designated quantity.

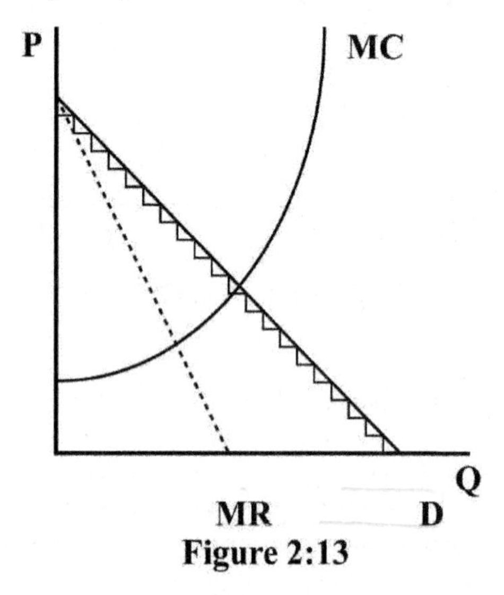

Figure 2:13

Like other businesses, the monopolistic firm is concerned with maximizing profit, not revenue. Consider how the monopolist accomplishes this goal. Behaving rationally, it will sell up to the point where marginal revenue equals marginal cost. That might appear counterintuitive inasmuch as we would not expect a firm to sell at the precise cost to the entrepreneur. Recall that zero economic profit assumes an ordinary rate of return as a result of the concept of opportunity cost. Here too, the marginal cost curve includes opportunity cost, and specifically the forgone opportunity to deploy the same factors of production for the next best market opportunity.

As depicted in Figure 2:14, the rational monopolist will set quantity at the point at which the marginal revenue and marginal cost curves intersect, Qm. At this quantity, the monopolist can then set the price at Pm, the corresponding price along the actual demand curve (as opposed to the marginal revenue curve). Because the marginal cost for any additional unit sold exceeds the marginal revenue associated with the sale of that next unit, it is not cost effective for the monopolistic firm to sell any additional units beyond Qm. Any further output would generate net losses to the firm. That is because in order to sell each additional unit, the firm would have to lower the price not only for that unit, but for all units at that level of output.

Discussion questions and comments: Can you identify any circumstances in which a firm with market power is capable of engaging in price discrimination? If so, what allows that firm, unlike many other firms with market power, to do so? Is all differential pricing for the same good a form of price discrimination? For example, is a designer outfit offered on sale several months after it entered the market the same "product" as when it was first introduced? Is the same meal offered at half price as an "early bird special" an act of price discrimination, or is it two different products, priced accordingly? What about senior citizen discounts offered regardless of the time? Should the legal system be concerned with these examples of differential pricing? If such pricing schemes were banned, who would benefit and who would lose?

Return to the earlier taxation question. If the government imposes a tax on a good for which demand is inelastic, who will ultimately bear the burden of the tax? How does that change for a good for which the demand curve is elastic? Under which set of conditions is a tax more likely to be effective in raising revenue? Why? What if one goal of the tax is to reduce consumption (such as alcohol and cigarette taxes)? In Chapter 3, we will consider whether strict products liability constitutes a form of tax. Assuming it does, is strict liability an appropriate rule as compared with ordinary negligence for defective products? Why or why not?

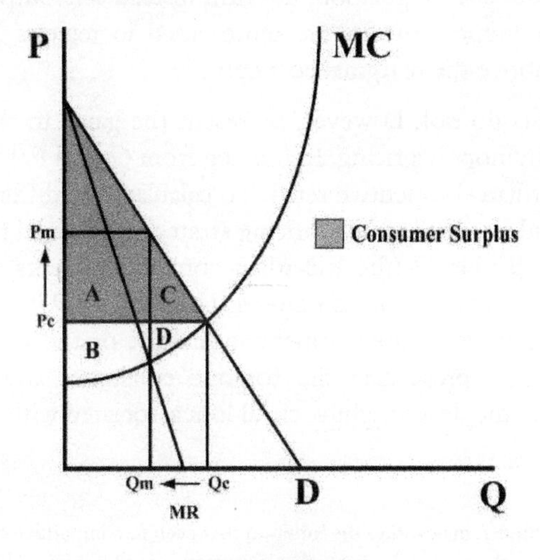

Figure 2:14

Professors Baumol and Blinder state that "barriers to entry are usually considered to be against the public interest except where they are believed to have offsetting advantages" and the authors identify patents as an illustration of when such advantages arise.[36] Why might this be true? Assuming there are such advantages to conferring some degree of monopoly power on those who hold patents, how do we ensure that the legal system does not impose a level of protection for which the costs exceed the benefits? Should copyright and patent be treated similarly for purposes of monopoly protection? Why or why not?

C. Profits and Rents

Monopolistic pricing produces social welfare losses that the preceding analysis helps to identify. To understand the difficulties that monopolistic pricing can produce, it is helpful to focus on three separate but related concepts, some of which were already introduced: *monopoly profit*, sometimes referred to as *economic profit*; *Ricardian competitive rents*; and *monopoly rents*.

As depicted in Figure 2:14, from the perspective of consumers, the ideal result would be for the monopolist to sell a quantity represented as *Qc* and to set price at *Pc*. Assume that through regulation, a firm with market power is forced to set price where marginal cost equals demand. At that point, the price and quantity are the same as those arising under competitive conditions (in which case the marginal cost curve is effectively the supply curve). Under competitive conditions, the rectangle and triangle labeled *A* plus *C*, plus the triangle above represents the consumer surplus, namely the excess of what consumers would be willing to pay for all units from zero up to the equilibrium amount *Qc*. The regions *B* and *D* represent Ricardian competitive rents, namely the ordinary profit that would accrue to a firm selling under competitive conditions. Because the marginal cost curve is upward sloping, and lies below the competitive price up to Q_c, regions *B* and *D* demonstrate the potentially different profit levels of firms operating in a competitive environment.[37] Without such regulation, the firm instead sets output at *Qm* and price at *Pm*. At this point, monopoly profits are represented in regions *A* plus *B*, where the monopoly price lies above the marginal cost curve.[38]

Monopoly profits do not, however, represent the gains to the firm from moving from competitive to monopoly pricing. In moving from *Qc* and *Pc* to *Qm* and *Pm*, the firm has given up its Ricardian competitive rents. To calculate the difference between profits under competitive and noncompetitive pricing strategies, referred to as monopoly rents, we need to subtract *B* plus *D* (the Ricardian competitive rents) from *A* plus *B* (the monopoly profit). Note that $(A+B)-(B+D)=A-D$. Thus, $A-D$ represents the gains from moving from a competitive to noncompetitive market, or the monopoly rents. At the same time, *C* plus *D*, representing the forgone consumer and producer surpluses, respectively, constitute the deadweight societal loss associated with monopoly pricing.

---

[36] *Id.* at 217.

[37] Ricardian competitive rents capture the intuition that even in competitive conditions, some firms will receive greater profits than others, namely those who can produce at lower cost. Thus, for example, even in competitive markets for farmed produce, we would expect, all else being equal, those farms with particularly good soil conditions to receive higher Ricardian competitive rents than farms with poor soil conditions as a result of the differing cost of production. For a helpful discussion of various forms of rent, see Armen A. Alchian, *Rent*, *in* 4 THE NEW PALGRAVE: A DICTIONARY OF ECONOMICS 141–42 (John Eatwell et al. eds., 1998).

[38] This assumes that there are no fixed costs, which would not be reflected in the marginal cost curve.

Discussion questions and comments: Are there any circumstances in which prohibiting monopoly rents might undermine consumer welfare? Consider the following argument. Some markets are characterized by very large start-up costs. Firms willingly incur such costs in anticipation of potential monopoly rents that they will generate, at least in the short to moderate term, which offset that upfront investment. A rule that prohibits monopoly rents potentially inhibits the requisite start-up costs that result in the provision of valuable goods and services to the market. Is this argument persuasive? Does it help to explain the general rule that individual firms with market power are free to earn monopoly profit, but not free to engage in collaborative practices with other firms to earn monopoly profit?[39] What countervailing arguments counsel in favor of limiting the ability of firms to earn monopoly rents? How does this relate to the protection given to those who hold patents or the rights to copyrighted materials?

D. Opportunity Cost, Ordinary Profit, and Economic Profit

The preceding analysis helps explain one of the most important concepts in economics, namely *opportunity cost*.[40] Opportunity cost recognizes that the real cost of activities is not limited to out-of-pocket expenses. It also includes the forgone opportunity associated with the next best use of one's time or resources.

Understanding opportunity cost returns us to the distinction between *economic profit* and *ordinary (or accounting) profit*. Recall that economists often distinguish between competitive environments in which firms earn zero profit and noncompetitive environments in which firms earn economic profit. By zero profit, economists mean ordinary profit, which is equivalent to the generally expected rate of return in the economy. When the return on a particular activity is no better than alternative market opportunities for an entrepreneur's time or resources, then she is earning the generally expected rate of return, meaning zero profit.

By contrast, if another opportunity presents itself that allows a substantially higher rate of return, then the opportunity cost for the present activity has risen, and holding all else constant, rational actors will leave their present (ordinary profit) activity for the alternative (economic profit) activity. As more resources flow toward the activity earning economic profit, the return on that activity will predictably decline toward the normal rate of return.

Questions: How does this relate to the anecdote about the person who invested in purchasing generators to sell in New Orleans in the aftermath of Hurricane Katrina? How do anti-gouging policies affect incentives to pursue economic rents? If you argue that they discourage such opportunities, can you identify countervailing considerations that nonetheless justify such policies?

---

[39] For an article that explores this theme, see David S. Evans & Keith N. Hylton, *The Lawful Acquisition and Exercise of Monopoly Power and Its Implications for the Objectives of Antitrust*, 4 COMPETITION POL'Y INT'L 203 (2008).

[40] For a helpful introduction to opportunity cost, see RICHARD A. IPPOLITO, ECONOMICS FOR LAWYERS 120–24 (2005).

E. Production Schedules, Indifference Curves, and Budget Constraints

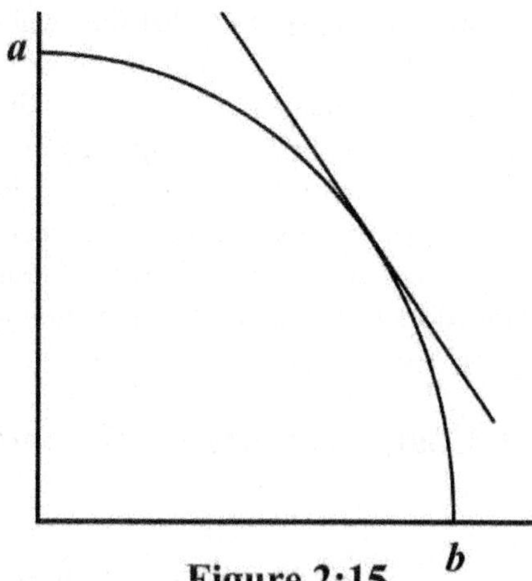

Figure 2:15

The production possibility frontier (PPF), depicted in figure 2:15, represents the potential economic output for an individual, firm, or nation, as between two commodities, labeled *a* and *b*. To determine the maximum value of an individual's *production schedule*, we need to introduce two related concepts: *indifference curves* and *budget constraints*. The PPF is convex. That is because for any individual, the choice of two activities has a specific relationship. If you spent all of your time playing soccer, you could substantially improve your tennis game by giving up a modest amount of time, say an hour, from soccer in favor of tennis. For your second hour sacrificed playing soccer, you would get a slightly reduced benefit in terms of tennis. This relationship continues until you are only playing tennis. Then it plays out in reverse. You earn higher marginal returns playing soccer the first hour you take away from tennis, and for each additional hour you reallocate this way, you get a relatively smaller return. As depicted in Figure 2:16, the convexity of the PPF curve reflects this *diminishing marginal rate of transformation* between the two activities. The more one engages in an activity, the less productive is an additional unit of time in that same activity. Conversely, the less one engages in an activity, the more productive is an additional unit of time in it. This reflects the natural tendency to spend time on the most productive pursuits first.

The convex relationship between two goods can describe the potential production for an individual, and also for society, whether a firm, city, or nation. Like individuals, firms or even nations can choose to specialize in some productive opportunities and to exchange with other nations that make different choices about specialization.

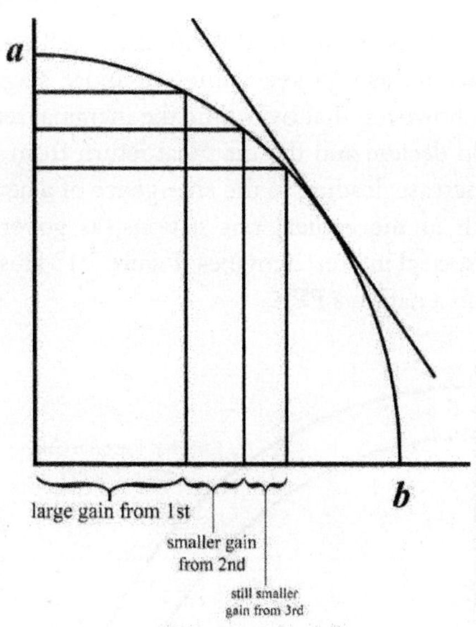

Figure 2:16

In addition, it is worth considering whether there are ways to push out, or pull in, the PPF. Policies that tax productive activities can pull the PPF inward. So can opportunity cost. In a famous study, Mancur Olson demonstrated that, counterintuitively, after World War II, the Axis powers—those who lost the war—exceeded the Allied powers in terms of economic growth.[41] Olson posited that individuals or firms in a given society can seek to earn economic profit in two different ways: (1) by engaging in productive activity, such as staring new businesses, or (2) by seeking protection from competition or a direct wealth transfer through the political process, a process we labeled above as *rent-seeking*. The latter processes include subsidies, preferred tax treatment, and various forms of barriers to market entry by competitors through regulation or tax policy. From the perspective of generating wealth, an individual or firm will rationally be indifferent to the means employed, but from the perspective of social welfare, there is a notable difference between generating wealth through positive-sum production versus seeking rents through zero- or negative-sum protections against competition.

Mancur Olson argued that in the post-War era, the severely damaged industrial sectors in Germany and Japan provided huge potential returns from investment in productive economic activity. At the same time, the nations with decimated political infrastructures presented lower rent seeking opportunities relative to those whose political infrastructures remained intact. Because of the relatively weak governments and the destruction of existing political coalitions that had entrenched rent-seeking activity in the Axis nations, rent seeking required costly new organization and for reliable political coalitions to emerge.

Consistent with the preceding analysis, Olson suggests that the opportunity cost of rent seeking across these groups of nations affected the resulting direction of their production possibility frontiers. Because new productive activity pushes the economy's

[41] MANCUR OLSON, THE RISE AND DECLINE OF NATIONS (1982).

PPF outward, the Axis nations tended to do extremely well economically, whereas the Allied nations with intact infrastructures witnessed more stagnant economic growth. Olson further predicted, however, that over time the marginal return from investment in productive activity would decline and the marginal return from investment in zero-sum political activity would increase, leading to the emergence of a new equilibrium that led to slower economic growth in the earlier Axis nations, as government policies became increasingly affected by special interest activities. Figure 2:17 illustrates the adverse effect of rent-seeking activity on a nation's PPF.

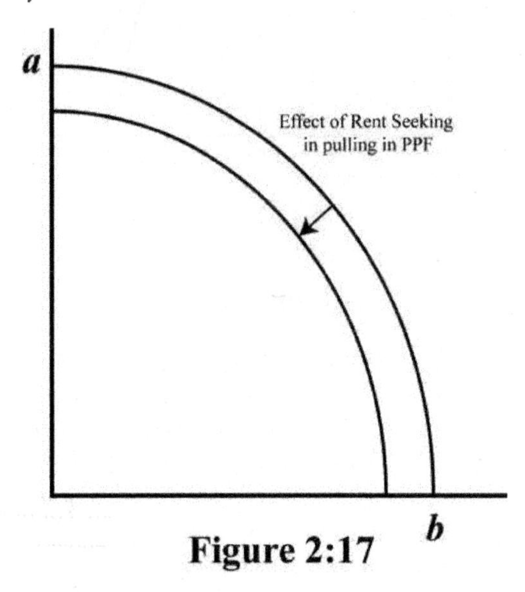

Figure 2:17

Questions: How might taxation policy affect whether the PPF moves outward or is pulled inward? Is it possible to answer this question without first understanding whether the taxation rate is initially optimal, for example, by matching the provision of public goods with the desires of those who are subject to the tax?

Finally, notice that the PPF is affected by choices beyond immediate benefits associated with the goods or services produced. The mechanism of market exchange allows persons, firms, or states to specialize and exchange, thus increasing the value of their outputs. Unlike Robinson Crusoe, whose choice between foraging and building a shelter is strictly limited by how he allocates his individual labor, within markets, individuals routinely produce more of a particular good that they are quite good at producing and then sell those goods on the market.

In contrast with the PPF, which is convex, *indifference curves*, which depict an individual's relative valuation as between two commodities, are concave. This reflects the decreasing marginal utility associated with additional acquired (whether produced or purchased) increments of any one good, *a*, relative to any other good, *b*, or the reverse, decreasing marginal utility for additional acquired increments of *b* relative to *a*. Because the indifference curve plots only *relative* valuation as between two goods, rather than how many of those goods a person can afford, each individual has an infinite number of indifference curves for any potential choice between two commodities or between any given commodity and money, which stands in for a potential basket of all competing commodities.

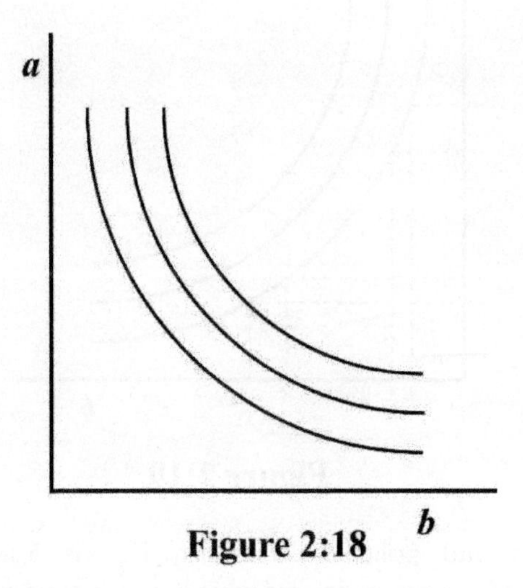

Figure 2:18

As depicted in Figure 2:18, the shape of the curve is easily captured with the following intuition. Imagine that you owned a lot of pens, but no notebooks to write in. You might be willing to give up quite a few pens to get your first notebook, but fewer for the second, and fewer still for a third. Conversely, if you had only notebooks, but nothing to write in them with, you would give up several to get your first pen, but fewer for the second, and still fewer for the third. These relationships are continuous and reflected in the concavity of the curves.[42] In addition, we each have an endless number of indifference curves that fill up the commodity space, reflecting the concept of *non-satiation*—more is always preferred to less.

This analysis is generalizable, and the tradeoffs are reflected numerically in Figure 2:19. In this illustration, when an individual has several of commodity *a* and fewer of commodity *b*, she is willing to give up four of *a* (19–15) to gain just one *b* (from 3 to 4). By contrast, when she has more *b* and fewer of *a*, she will give up only two of *a* (7–5) to gain three more of *b* (from 10 to 13). The analysis works in both directions, and thus can be expressed in terms of how much she is willing to relinquish of *b* to gain additional increments of *a* as a function of how many she has of each good.

---

[42] Indifference curves are sometimes referred to as being convex to the origin, which is the same thing as being concave.

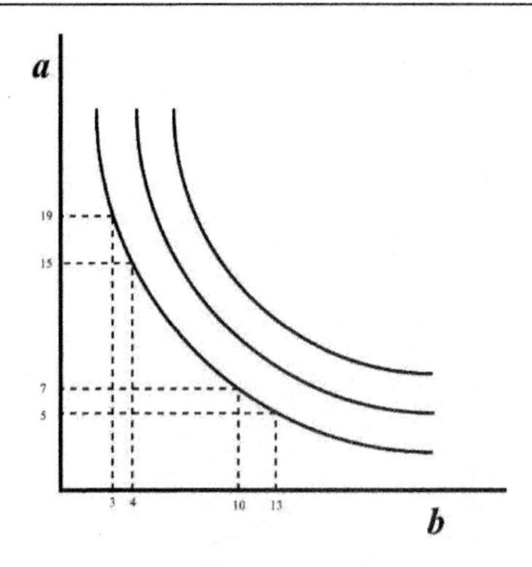

Figure 2:19

The philosopher and political economist, Francis Ysidro Edgeworth, who introduced indifference curves, also devised what is now known as the Edgeworth Box.[43] The presentation involves inverting one set of indifference curves and allowing them to cross another set. Properly analyzed, this device allows us to depict visually how exchange, whether through barter or sales, has the capacity to increase societal wealth. Figure 2:20 juxtaposes two sets of indifference curves, for persons 1 and 2, with respect to two commodities, A and B. To understand the box, note that point one is the origin for person 1, and point 2 is the origin for person two. In other words, the indifference maps for individual two is rotated 180^0 and attached to the map for individual 1. The length of axis A (the vertical axis) is the total quantity of good A available to the two people, and the length of axis B (the horizontal axis) is likewise the total quantity of good B.

Consider any point at which the two curves intersect, representing an initial allocation of the total amounts of A and B between the two people. Now consider how the medium of exchange improves the satisfaction of the two people relative to that initial point. If we take person 1's indifference curve, we can move along it, thereby moving person 2 onto sequentially higher indifference curves, up to the point at which person 1's indifference curve is tangent to (touching, but not overlapping) person 2's highest available indifference curve. At the point at which two curves are tangent, there is no possibility of improving the welfare of one without harming that of the other. In other words, we have reached a *Pareto Optimal* point.

[43] ROSS M. STARR, GENERAL EQUILIBRIUM THEORY 31–40 (2d ed. 2011); IPPOLITO, *supra* note 40, at 6–10.

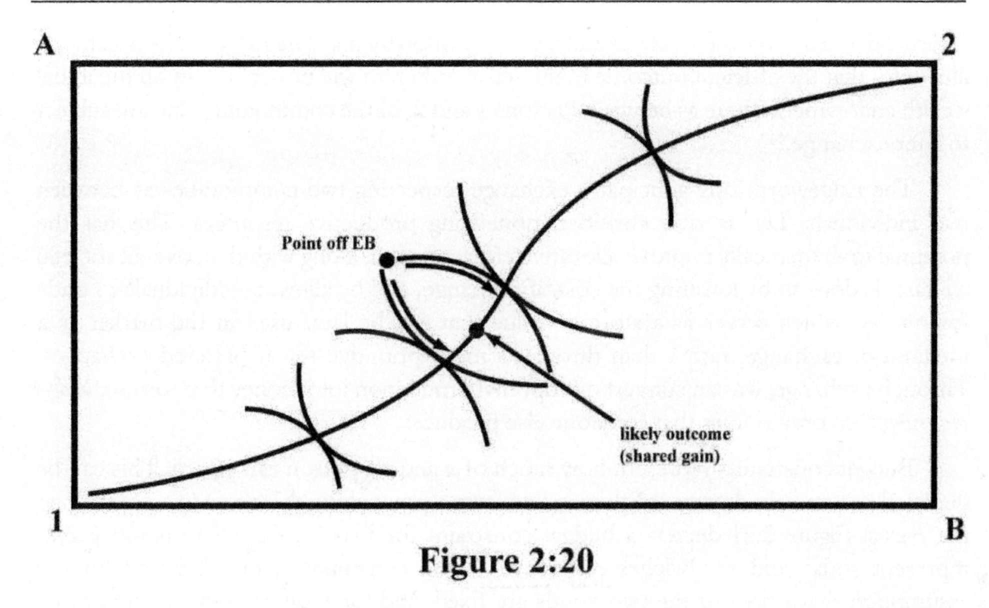

Figure 2:20

In Figure 2:20, we see a line that connects the various tangent points, meaning the aggregated points at which the two participants' indifference curves precisely meet. Connecting these points produces a curved line known as the *contract curve*. For all points along the contract curve, it is not possible to improve one person's welfare without adversely affecting the other person's welfare. To see why, consider moving from one point to another along the contract curve, and notice that although doing so improves the situation for one of the participants by placing him or her on a higher indifference curve, it does so by moving the other participant onto a lower indifference curve.

Let us return to moving from a point off the contract curve to a point on that curve. Consider once more a given point along Person 1's indifference curve through the initial allocation. If we move along Person 1's indifference curve, by definition she is not disadvantaged by this move since she is indifferent to each location along the curve. But person 2 has had his welfare improved. Even so, this might seem unfair. Person 1 might say to Person 2, "The same starting point also sits along one of your indifference curves. So instead of moving along my curve, let's instead move along *your* indifference curve until the tangent point with one of my indifference curves. I will then be at my highest available indifference curve without harming you since you will be indifferent between that point and where we began." Person 2 is just as likely to find this unfair even though, like Person 1 in the earlier example, he is not disadvantaged. In actual transactions, we anticipate that rather than simply benefiting one and leaving the other unaffected, thereby satisfying the stringent *Pareto* criterion, the exchange generates gains that the participating parties can share.

Consider more closely the relationship between the criterion of Pareto optimality and the Edgeworth Box. Each move from a point off the contract curve to a point on the curve is Pareto superior; all points along the contract curve are Pareto optimal. This implies that even in this very stylized universe of two players trading over two commodities, there is not a single point that is "efficient" for the economy as a whole. Recall that we articulated two assumptions underlying price theory. The first involved externalities. The second involved initial wealth endowments. The Edgeworth Box nicely illustrates that the efficient outcome in the sense of Pareto will be dependent on the initial wealth endowments, here as between Persons 1 and 2, of the commodities that are subject to later exchange.[44]

The Edgeworth box anticipates exchange respecting two commodities as between two individuals. Let us now consider monetizing productive resources. This has the potential to dramatically improve allocative efficiency and, along with that, overall societal welfare. It does so by lowering the cost of exchange, and by allowing individuals to trade for money, which serves as a store of value that can be later used in the market as a medium of exchange, rather than through a more primitive set of bartered exchanges. Through exchange, we can convert our optimal production into money that forms a *budget constraint* for commodities that someone else produces.

Budget constraints represent how much of *a* and *b* a person can afford. This can be depicted as a straight downward sloping line from a point along the *a*-axis to a point along the *b*-axis. Figure 2:21 depicts a budget constraint for two goods, where *a* and *b* axes represent sodas and sandwiches respectively. The constraint is drawn based on the assumption that prices of the two goods are fixed, and the individual in question has a fixed income to be spent on the two goods. The budget line thus depicts the combinations of soda and sandwiches that the person can just afford.

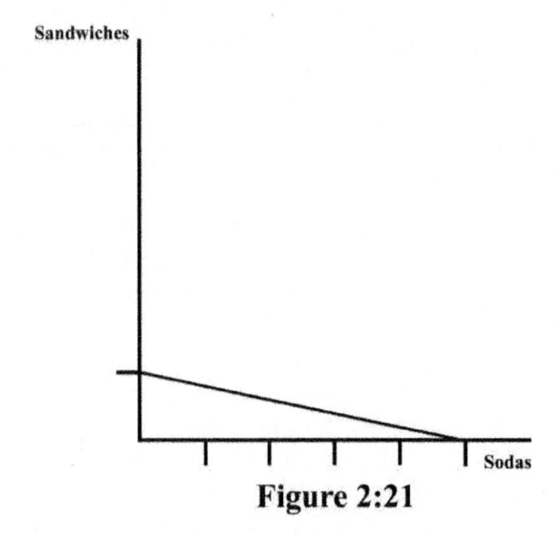

Figure 2:21

To be on the highest indifference curve with respect to two commodities, a person must produce or purchase to the point where an indifference curve is tangent to (meaning it touches but does not overlap), the budget constraint. At this point, the person is achieving the highest level of satisfaction, given the person's income and the prices of the two goods. This is illustrated with a budget constraint respecting two commodities, *a* and *b*, and the potential set of relevant indifference curves in Figure 2:22. If, instead, the indifference curve intersects with the person's budget constraint, she could reallocate

---

[44] Movements along the contract curve, however, might be efficient in the *Kaldor-Hicks* sense.

either purchasing decisions to move onto a higher indifference curve, thus deriving greater utility.

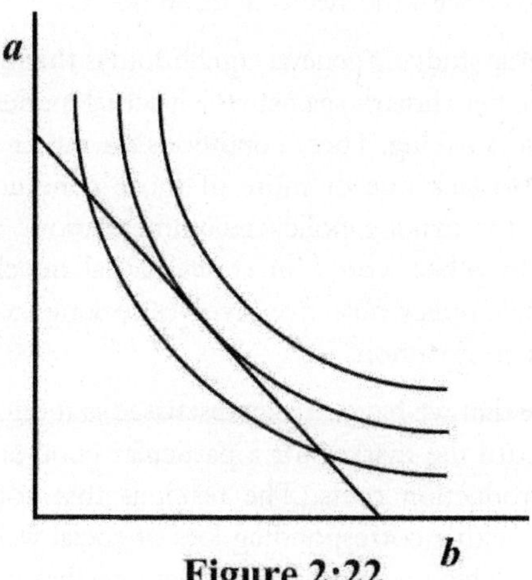

Figure 2:22

IV. GENERAL EQUILIBRIUM AND WELFARE ECONOMICS

General equilibrium concerns the manner in which the independent decisions of all participants in the economy—that is, all consumers and firms—lead, without conscious direction, to the emergence of equilibrium in all markets simultaneously. Moreover, the important theorems of welfare economics demonstrate that, under certain conditions, equilibrium results in the efficient allocation of resources in the sense that no one can be made better off without making others worse off (the criterion of Pareto Optimality). There are at least two reasons for studying general equilibrium.

First, it establishes that the price system can, in principle at least, attain an equilibrium state despite the decentralized and self-interested actions of the various participants. In other words, the market serves as coordination mechanism that results in a socially desirable outcome. This is a very striking conclusion that was first asserted by Adam Smith using his metaphor of the *Invisible Hand*, and it has been proved rigorously by modern economists using the apparatus of mathematics.[45] In fact, the Edgeworth Box diagram shown above is a very simple demonstration of the logic underlying general equilibrium. Recall that it showed, in a simple two-person exchange economy, that starting from any initial allocation of the two goods, consensual trade, or barter, between the two parties will always lead them to a point on the contract curve. Points on that curve represent efficient resource allocations. Further, the Invisible Hand Theorem asserts that there always exists an equilibrium price mechanism (or budget line) that will achieve that outcome in such a way that supply will equal demand for both (all) markets simultaneously. This logic underlies the formal proof of the *existence* of an equilibrium.

[45] The classic reference here is GERARD DEBREU, THEORY OF VALUE: AN AXIOMATIC ANALYSIS OF GENERAL EQUILIBRIUM (1959). For a more recent textbook treatment, see WALTER NICHOLSON & CHRISTOPHER SNYDER, MICROECONOMIC THEORY: BASIC PRINCIPLES AND EXTENSIONS (12th ed. 2017).

The argument extends, with only slight complication, to the case where profit-maximizing firms engage in the production of goods, given the existing endowment of inputs (raw materials and labor) coupled with the available technology.

The second reason for studying general equilibrium is that the conditions needed for its attainment provide the benchmark against which actual markets can be evaluated with respect to economic policy-making. These conditions are rather stringent,[46] and so when actual markets are seen to lack one or more of those conditions, general equilibrium theory provides a basis for making policy recommendations aimed at mitigating the resulting inefficiencies. In other words, in conventional neoclassical economics,[47] an important normative public policy objective involves seeking to correct departures from the conditions of perfect competition.

One such departure that we have already discussed is monopoly, which arises when one or a few sellers control the market for a particular good and therefore can set the price above marginal production costs. The result is that some otherwise beneficial transactions are forgone, with a corresponding loss of social welfare. This analysis helps to explain antitrust laws, which seek to limit structures that conduce to monopolistic pricing strategies. This includes, for example, regulating natural monopolies, such as utilities. These firms are characterized by very large fixed-cost investments, and thus declining average cost, resulting in single firms dominating the relevant market.

A second source of market failure is the existence of externalities, which usually involve the imposition of costs on others who do not receive the benefit of the underlying economic activity. The classic example is pollution, although we will encounter many other examples throughout this book, such as automobile accidents, dangerous products, and boundary encroachments. Externalities risk encouraging producers to overinvest in the underlying activity as a result of failing to account for part of the relevant costs. Some externalities are beneficial, or *positive.* These can include, for example, property improvements, which producers might *underinvest* in to the extent that they fail to realize the full benefits. We will see that many legal doctrines can be characterized based on the objective of encouraging actors to *internalize* externalities, mostly harmful ones but sometimes beneficial ones, which are often regarded as a source of market failure.

A final source of market failure, which relates to positive externalities, concerns the provision of *public goods*. Such goods have two characteristic features: first, those who provide them cannot exclude from the benefits those who fail to contribute to the marginal cost of their procurement; and, second, the value of such goods is not diminished by consumption.[48] More simply, such goods produce benefits that can be widely enjoyed, even if the beneficiaries do not each contribute to the cost. Classic examples include national defense, police protection, and public education. In each instance, once it is provided, no one can be denied the benefits.

---

46 *See* NICHOLSON & SNYDER, *supra* note 45, at Chapter 13.

47 Later in this book, *infra* Chapters 11 *et seq.*, we will consider whether public choice provides a cautionary note with respect to providing government regulators the requisite authority to accomplish these normative objectives.

48 Paul A. Samuelson, *The Pure Theory of Public Expenditure*, 36 REV. ECON. & STATISTICS 387 (1954).

Public goods contribute to market failure because private firms will generally fail to provide, or will underprovide, them given that they cannot capture the full benefits from their provision. This relates to the problem of *free riding* discussed in chapter 1. A common remedy is for the government to provide public goods and to charge all citizens a tax to finance the cost. In effect, a *forced riding* replaces market provision.[49] An important problem for the government, therefore, is to ascertain the desired demand for public goods among the citizenry, and then to properly allocate the cost. Solving this problem is an important function of the political system, as will be detailed in the second half of this book, but it also implicates the judiciary, for example, in the context of *eminent domain.*

The preceding discussion has focused on various departures from efficiency and the role of economic policy in correcting them. Policy makers also care about fairness in the sense of determining how resources are, or should be, distributed. This is a separate issue from efficiency in the sense that it concerns how a pie is divided up, rather than how to enlarge the pie. Even well -functioning markets can lead to a very unequal distribution of wealth; final market distribution depends crucially on how resources are initially allocated. In the Edgeworth Box diagram, for example, free exchange, corresponding to the *Invisible Hand*, implies that markets generally move those good and services within the economy onto the contract curve (the locus of Pareto Optimal allocations) regardless of where they begin. But the final resource allocation as between the players will necessarily depend on the starting points. And if the initial endowment point is skewed in favor of one individual or group, the market alone cannot ensure a more equitable distribution.

General equilibrium theory remains helpful in considering how any given allocation can be achieved most efficiently. This implicates the *Second Fundamental Theorem of Welfare Economics*, another important result from welfare economics.[50] This theorem posits that *any point* on the contract curve can be achieved by a competitive equilibrium provided that suitable lump sum transfers of wealth are possible. Unfortunately, realistic mechanisms for redistributing wealth, such as progressive income taxes or corporate taxes, are not lump sum taxes. As a result, such mechanisms create distortions within markets, potentially exacerbating market inefficiencies. In the end, there is an inevitable trade-off between fairness and efficiency in the formulation of economic policy. As will be detailed later in the book, this trade-off is often at the center of political debates and competition among interest groups.

List of important price theory terms:

externalities, positive and negative (pp. 33–34)

initial wealth endowment (pp. 33–34)

Pareto optimality and superiority (p. 20)

Kaldor-Hicks efficiency (introduced in Chapter 1) (p. 21)

opportunity cost (p. 55)

---

[49] Once again, in the materials on public choice, we will see that animating a demand curve to lobby for such public goods risks an analogous free rider problem. *See infra* Chapter 11.

[50] *See* NICHOLSON & SNYDER, *supra* note 45, at 471–72. This further relates to the analysis by Professors Louis Kaplow and Steven Shavell, discussed *infra* Chapter 8, at 325.

equilibrium and market clearance (pp. 37–39)
total and net market dislocation (p. 39)
price elasticities (demand or supply) (pp. 47–49)
incidence (of a tax or regulation) (implied)
price taker or price setter (pp. 49–54)
competitive and non-competitive markets (pp. 49–54)
marginal revenue (p. 51)
market power (pp. 49–54)
market failure (p. 35)
natural monopoly (p. 50)
declining average cost (p. 50)
barriers to entry (p. 50)
product differentiation (p. 51)
price discrimination (p. 51)
profit: accounting, ordinary, economic (pp. 54–55)
rent: rents, rent seeking, monopoly rents, and Ricardian Competitive Rents (pp. 54–55)
gouging (p. 42)
consumer surplus and producer surplus (pp. 54–55)
deadweight societal loss (pp. 54–55)
indifference curves (pp. 56–60)
budget constraints (p. 62)
First Fundamental Theorem of Welfare Economics (p. 34)
Second Fundamental Theorem of Welfare Economics (p. 65)

PART II

Common Law Applications

CHAPTER 3

Tort Law (Part 1)

Introduction[1]

Tort law is the law of accidents. Although accidents frequently take place among persons who are familiar,[2] tort doctrine is often framed in terms of persons coming together involuntarily. Typically, one person, the tortfeasor, causes a mishap that injures another, the victim. The fortuitous nature of such relationships generally distinguishes tort law from contract law. Contract law involves parties who not only enter into their relationship voluntarily, but who also anticipate that unfortunate contingencies might arise. Contracting parties therefore try, however imperfectly, to contemplate such events in the contract itself. Property law presents cases with either set of characteristics, sometimes involving voluntary, and other times, involuntary, relationships.

Together, these three subjects—Tort, Contract, and Property—form the foundation of the common law. Not surprisingly, a substantial body of early Law and Economics scholarship began in an effort to better explain common law doctrines. Early Law and Economics scholars sought to offer a robust account of doctrinal statements, for example those set out in judicial opinions, that oftentimes failed to stand up to closer analysis or to meaningfully predict future case outcomes. It is appropriate therefore to begin a course on the economic analysis of law with a study of these doctrines.

Classic examples of Tort cases include automobile accidents, medical malpractice, harm caused by defective products, workplace accidents, and environmental harms, such as pollution or exposure to toxic waste. From a doctrinal perspective, the central purpose of tort law is to provide accident victims with a means of redress against tortfeasors, most commonly through damages, meaning financial compensation, and in doing so to create proper incentives for future actors in similar circumstances to avoid causing unnecessary harms. The economic analysis of tort law overlaps with these legal understandings, and, at the same time, it provides the basis for some added nuance and, thus, for a more robust doctrinal account.

In this chapter, we will focus on two essential functions of tort law. First, economic analysis reveals that the doctrines seek to minimize avoidable risk by encouraging

[1] We acknowledge the generosity of the Stanford University Press in allowing the adaptation, and sometimes presentation, of materials drawn from Thomas J. Miceli, *The Economic Approach to Law* (Stanford Univ. Press 3d ed. 2017), for inclusion in Chapters 3 through 10 of this volume.

[2] *See infra* Chapter 4 (discussing warranty cases, medical malpractice, and workplace accidents).

individuals and firms to undertake appropriate risk-reducing precautions and behaviors. This includes providing incentives for all parties who engage in risk-associated activities, including both injurers and victims, to take reasonable steps to minimize the risk and likely impact of accidents. As we shall see, each of us routinely engages in such activities, placing us at constant risk of being either tortfeasors or tort victims. Second, because risk can never be eliminated entirely, at least without incurring unreasonable expenditures, the doctrines further seek to allocate the risk that remains. Specifically, a properly operating tort system allocates "residual risk," meaning the risk that remains after all cost-effective precautions have been taken, to the party who is able to bear it more cost effectively. This party is referred to as either the "cheapest cost avoider" or the "least cost avoider."[3] Sometimes the function of the least-cost avoider is to spread the cost of risk among those who benefit as a group from the risk-creating activities. There is a lot to unpack in this paragraph; we will do so throughout the remainder of this chapter.

Before proceeding, it is worth considering where tort law fits within the larger scheme of doctrines and lawmaking processes that form the early parts of this book.[4] Tort law touches on, and in some instances pierces, the boundaries of several core doctrinal areas. Tort relates to the common law doctrines of Contract and Property inasmuch as together these doctrines help to regulate the marketplace in which a great deal of private conduct takes place. Markets cannot function properly without appropriate background legal rules, and the legal system cannot exist in isolation from the feedback generated by problematic outcomes that result from private behaviors, including private market decisions. In other words, law and markets are intertwined, and the common law doctrines, along with the lawmaking processes that generate them, in a very real sense serve as the connecting tissue.

Tort also touches on, and sometimes overlaps with, criminal law. The boundary between these two sets of doctrines is informed by two principal considerations: first, whether the harmful conduct results from an intent to cause that harm, and second, whether the dangers associated with the particular individual harm are such that the state might choose to take control of the prosecution.[5] These combined bodies of common law and criminal law are also greatly influenced by the formal judicial processes through which they are enforced. This includes processes that govern trials and appeals, the nature and breadth of precedent, and careful consideration of whether and when it is appropriate to allow civil litigation to settle and criminal cases to be plea-bargained. Following the chapters on the common law doctrines, we devote separate chapters to Criminal Law and the Judicial Process. Tort law provides a helpful introduction to the economic analysis of law more generally, and so we begin here.

A logical starting point in the study of tort law is to identify the three contributing factors that comprise the total cost of accidents: (1) victim damages, including bodily harm, property damage, and psychic costs; (2) the cost of precautions aimed at reducing harm, for example, the cost of vehicle safety features and routine vehicle maintenance;

---

[3] *See infra* note 33 and cites therein.

[4] Specifically, we refer to Parts II and III, comprising Chapters 3 and 4, Chapter 5 and 6; Chapter 7 and 8; Chapter 9; and Chapter 10.

[5] There are also instances in which both tort and criminal law cases can proceed in parallel, for example, through prosecutions for murder and civil suits for wrongful death.

and (3) the administrative cost of using the tort system, including attorney's fees and court costs. The analysis in this chapter will focus primarily on the first two of these costs, damages plus precautions, with some commentary on the impact of administrative costs. (We provide a fuller discussion of the costs of using the legal system in Chapter 10 on the judicial process.)

Accidental harm is an unavoidable by-product of many socially valuable activities, including driving, medical procedures, and certain risky occupations. As previously noted, it is not possible to eradicate all risk. Perhaps counterintuitively, it is also not socially desirable as the complete elimination would either entail unacceptably high expenditures on precautions or the abandonment altogether of risk-producing, yet socially productive, activities.[6]

To accommodate the tension between promoting socially desirable activities and avoiding unnecessary accidents that they generate, the legal system has developed various ways of encouraging the reduction of avoidable risk. This includes safety regulations for products, licensing requirements in various professional settings, and criminal penalties for certain risky behaviors. In general, these forms of regulation emerge through legislative processes or the work of regulatory agencies, institutions that we will study after the review of private law.[7] This chapter, and those that immediately follow, are instead concerned with "private" control of risk through common law adjudication. This entails victims of harm—resulting from tortious injury, breach of contract, or the violation of a property right—bringing legal actions as plaintiffs, rather than the government adopting regulations or bringing legal actions of its own.

In addition to promoting victim compensation, tort law is designed to minimize avoidable risks. To prevail in a tort suit, the plaintiff, a tort victim, must establish, first, that he or she was harmed; second, that the defendant caused that harm; and third, that the defendant is responsible for paying compensation.[8] For now, we will assume that the first two requirements, harm and causation, are established.[9] With these issues set aside, we can now focus on whether the tortfeasor should be legally responsible for compensating the plaintiff. Answering this question involves the application of a "liability rule," which specifies exactly how damages from an accident should be divided as between the parties.

We examine three basic liability rules: no liability, strict liability, and negligence. Under a rule of *no liability*, even if it is established that the tortfeasor caused plaintiff's harm, the tortfeasor incurs no legal responsibility to compensate. The doctrine of *caveat emptor*, or "buyer beware," is an illustration of no liability from early products liability law.[10] At the opposite extreme is *strict liability*, under which the tortfeasor is responsible for all of the victim's losses if causation, including cause in fact and legal duty, is established.

---

[6] Indeed, these are really two ways of expressing the concept of cost, the first involving out-of-pocket financial outlays, and the second involving the opportunity cost of forgone economic activity.

[7] *See infra* Chapters 17 and 18; Chapters 19 and 20.

[8] For a formal statement of a prima facie negligence suit, *see infra* note 30, and accompanying text.

[9] We take up problems of causation *infra* Part III.A.

[10] This body of case law arises at the boundary of tort and contract. A product purchaser is in privity with the seller; the victim of the harmful product might not be. In general, products liability, in contrast with warranty law, arises in tort. *See infra* Part IV.

This holds without regard to the level of care that the tortfeasor has taken. Modern products liability law is essentially governed by strict products liability. Finally, under *negligence*, a tortfeasor is liable for the victim's losses only if he is found negligent, or legally "at fault."

Under a negligence regime, potential tortfeasors owe would-be victims a legal duty to undertake all reasonable precautions to avoid accidents. If the plaintiff's injury results from the tortfeasor's failure to meet that duty, she is entitled to compensation; if her injuries resulted despite the tortfeasor's reasonable precautions, however, she is not entitled to compensation. A negligence rule therefore "shields" injurers from liability as long as they undertake reasonable precautions. Aside from products liability and workplace accidents (which are governed by strict liability), negligence is the predominant standard governing the law of accidents.

Negligence is a form of hybrid rule. It combines strict and no liability, with the threshold of "due care" marking the dividing line as to when either attaches. Specifically, if the injurer met (or exceeded) the due care standard, the applicable rule is no liability (i.e., the victim bears the costs of her own harm). However, if the injurer failed the due care standard, he is judged to be negligent and is held strictly liable for resulting injuries caused by his negligence.[11]

Throughout this chapter and others, we will assess legal rules against the concept of efficiency. In later chapters,[12] we will introduce additional criteria beyond efficiency that economic analysis reveals to be relevant in the assessment of legal rules and lawmaking institutions.

As shown in Chapter 1, there are several definitions of efficiency, including *Pareto Optimality (or Pareto Efficiency)* and Kaldor-Hicks efficiency.[13] *Pareto optimality* describes an allocation of resources such that the well-being of no one in society can be improved without harming others. Under this stringent test of efficiency, anyone who would be made worse off by a proposed change can block it. Kaldor-Hicks efficiency identifies those circumstances under which aggregate wealth cannot be increased. Thus, any proposed change that generates a net surplus is permissible as long as those who are benefited gain enough that they could, in theory, fully compensate the losers, thereby making them whole, and still come out ahead. Although Kaldor-Hicks does not demand such compensation, were it to occur these two definitions would merge as the losers would be fully compensated and thus not harmed. Pareto efficiency is thus a special case of Kaldor-Hicks efficiency, meaning that any improvement to the status quo that satisfies Pareto will necessarily satisfy Kaldor-Hicks, whereas the reverse does not hold unless full compensation is provided to those who are harmed, at which point the two understandings of efficiency are the same. Kaldor-Hicks is the predominant efficiency criterion in assessing most legal rules. When a legal rule satisfies Kaldor-Hicks, the law

---

[11] We will later introduce various combined regimes, including comparative negligence, negligence with contributory negligence, and strict liability with dual contributory negligence. *See infra* Chapter 16 (presenting analysis by Louis Kornhauser of relationship in selection of doctrinal regimes over time as a function of technology).

[12] *See infra* Part IV (introducing public choice tools, including interest group theory, social choice, and game theory).

[13] *See supra* Ch. 1 Part III.H.I and notes.

improves overall social welfare as compared with alternative rules that fail this criterion. In the discussion of legal rules that follow, we will generally use Kaldor-Hicks as the baseline for assessing efficiency, and we will specify when our analysis rests on alternative understandings.

In the remainder of this chapter we provide an economic analysis of the foundations of Tort law. Section I begins with a stylized version of accidents in which only the tortfeasor's actions affect accident risk. Although this "unilateral care model" is of limited practical interest since in most accidents both tortfeasor and victim care affect risk, it is nonetheless helpful in developing the initial economic approach to accidents and in preliminarily assessing the incentive properties of the various liability rules. Section II introduces the more realistic "bilateral care model," in which both tortfeasor and victim care affect risk. This model more fully reveals the power of the economic approach to analyze the various forms of negligence. In Chapter 4, we cover several additional topics beyond the basic model.

I. THE UNILATERAL CARE ACCIDENT MODEL

The *model of precaution*,[14] which forms the basis for the economic analysis of tort law, highlights the objective of minimizing the sum of expected damages plus expenditures on precaution, or care. In the simplest version of this model, the "unilateral care model," only the tortfeasor's precaution affects accident risk. Specifically, it is assumed that increases in injurer precaution reduce *expected damages*, defined as the product of the probability of an accident taking place times the accident's severity.[15] In this simple version of the model, other than in choosing the activity in which the injury occurred, the victim is assumed to be passive.[16] Although there are some limited applications of the unilateral care model—for example, when a car veers off the road and crashes into someone's house,[17] or when a surgeon leaves a sponge inside a patient—our primary purpose is to isolate principles that will help in the later study of the more general bilateral care model.[18]

---

[14] This model was originally developed in its current form by John Brown and was in several important respects anticipated by Guido Calabresi, John Brown, *Toward an Economic Theory of Liability*, 2 J. LEGAL STUD. 323 (1973); GUIDO CALABRESI, THE COSTS OF ACCIDENTS: A LEGAL AND ECONOMIC ANALYSIS (1961, 1970); *see also* Robert Cooter, *Unity in Tort, Contract, and Property: The Model of Precaution*, 73 CALIF. L. REV. 1 (1985) (showing the versatility of this model for understanding doctrines in other areas of law beside torts). We will highlight the unifying attributes of this over the next several chapters.

[15] One can specify either the probability of an accident, p, or the resulting damages, D, or both, as decreasing functions of the injurer's care. For purposes of minimizing expected costs, what matters is that the product of the two, pD, is decreasing as a function of injurer care. See STEVEN SHAVELL, ECONOMIC ANALYSIS OF ACCIDENT LAW 5–9 (1987) and WILLIAM LANDES & RICHARD A. POSNER, THE ECONOMIC STRUCTURE OF TORT LAW (1987) for technical treatments.

[16] In the more general "bilateral care" version of the model discussed below, both injurer and victim care affect risk. *See infra* Part II.

[17] This actually happened to the home of Max Stearns!

[18] For simplification, we also assume that the tortfeasor did not suffer an injury.

Before examining how substantive tort law promotes cost-effective precautions, we need to specify the objectives within the model. As noted above, a goal of tort law is to minimize the sum of two sets of costs, the cost of precautions and the expected cost of accidents. Within this model, as the tortfeasor takes additional precautions, he correspondingly lowers the present value of expected damages but at a decreasing rate. At the same time, each additional precaution requires expending more resources. In other words, in terms of expected benefits, these two functions move in opposite directions. The expected benefit of each precaution incrementally declines with additional investments, whereas the cost of precautions rises with each additional investment. Generally, the solution entails a trade-off in the sense that although more care will reduce accident risk, it is not generally desirable (or even possible) to increase care to the point where the risk of an accident is altogether eliminated.

The inability to eliminate the risk of accidents with additional care follows from the principle of diminishing marginal benefits of additional precautions. By way of illustration, a driver can and should (1) engage in routine maintenance, including checking the brakes, tires, airbags, and essential operating systems; (2) ensure that all passengers (including the driver) wear safety belts while the car is in motion; (3) stay reasonably within the posted (or weather-dictated) speed limits; (4) obey traffic and other safety signals; (5) respond carefully to visual cues on and off the road; and (6) avoid alcohol, drugs, or text messaging, each of which interferes with driving performance. Each of these steps incrementally reduces the likelihood of an accident and the severity of an accident should it occur. Even if a driver has undertaken all of these steps, however, there remains the possibility of an unexpected road condition or freak mechanical failure that could cause an accident. There are additional steps that the driver could take to avoid such risk: (7) only drive along familiar neighborhood roads; (8) only drive at times of day when traffic is minimal; (9) don't drive at all except during emergencies; and, the most extreme, (10) leave the car parked in the driveway at all times, or (11) hire a chauffeur. For ordinary drivers, the marginal benefit of most of the latter precautions (7 through 11) are likely overwhelmed by the marginal cost of the restrictions they would impose, although new or timid drivers might follow (7) and (8). This illustrates that the marginal benefit of additional precautions generally declines.

The point is generalizable: As injurers invest in additional increments of precaution for most activities, accident risk will decline but at a decreasing rate.

Figure 3:1 illustrates the preceding discussion graphically. The vertical axis represents expected value in dollars.[19] The downward sloping, convex curve, ED, represents the declining marginal benefit of each additional precaution. The expected return on the first precaution is extremely high in dollar terms (corresponding to the reduced probability of an accident), and for each additional precaution taken, the expected return declines until the curve begins to flatten with a relatively lower return for each further precaution. The cost of care, *X*, is a positively sloped straight line. For ease of exposition, the cost of additional precautions is assumed to increase at a constant rate.

[19] For a related analysis, with accompanying graphics, that demonstrates the role of causation in minimizing the impact of the threshold negligence rule, see Louis Visscher, *Wrongfulness as a Necessary Cause of the Losses—Removing an Alleged Difference between Strict Liability and Negligence*, 2 ECON. ANALYSIS L. REV. 188 (2011). For a further discussion of the impact of causation in affecting this relationship, *see infra* Part III.A.

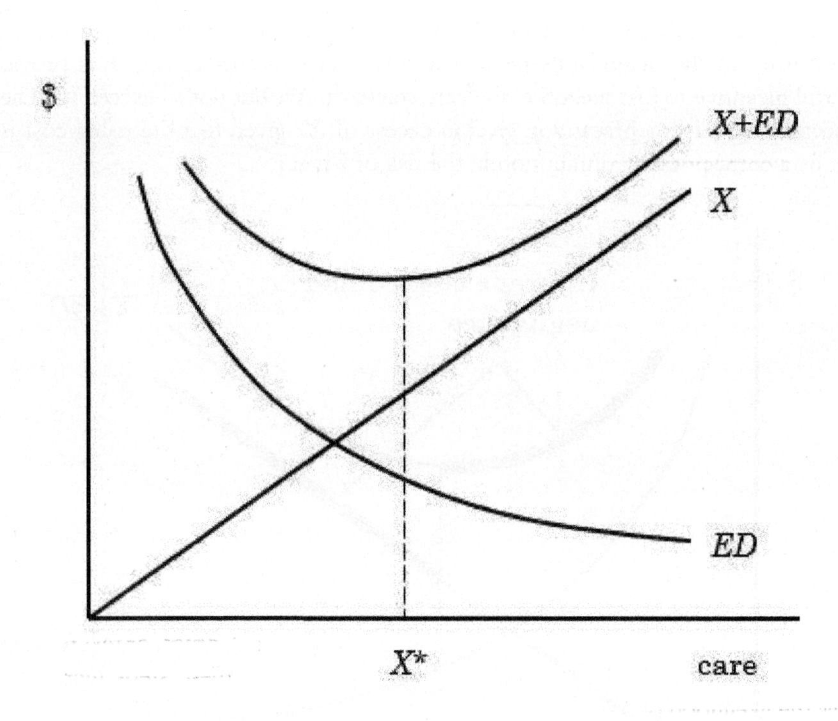

Figure 3:1. Level of injurer care that minimizes overall accident costs.

As previously noted, these curves move in opposite directions. The objective of the tort system within this model is to minimize total costs, represented as *X+ED*, reflected by the U-shaped curve that floats above the two separate cost curves and that represents the sum of costs at each level of care. The point at which the joint costs are minimized is denoted by *X** in the graph. For care levels to the left of *X**, an additional dollar spent on care reduces expected damages by more than a dollar (so *X+ED* declines), whereas for care levels to the right of *X**, an extra dollar of care reduces expected damages by less than a dollar (so *X+ED* rises). Notably the point where the *X* and *ED* curves intersect does *not* generally coincide with the cost minimizing summation, *X**. The critical insight from this basic model is that the choice as to legally required precautions is not set with the goal of minimizing the possibility of accidents; rather it is set at the point at which the marginal cost of additional precautions equals the marginal benefit in reducing expected value in terms of resulting risk. (This point actually occurs where the *slopes* of the two curves are equal in absolute value; although X and ED are total cost curves, summed in X+ED, the slope of each separate curve, ED and X, respectively, capture the marginal benefit and the marginal cost of each additional precaution.)

This analysis helps to emphasize two additional points. First, it explains why the intersection point of the *X* and *ED* curves is inconsequential as these are total cost curves, and why *X** occurs where the slopes of the two curves are equal (in absolute value). Second, it reveals a discontinuity graphically depicted in Figure 3:2. Under a negligence rule, the injurer-defendant's cost curve tracks the *X+ED* curve to the left of *X**. This is the range where $X<X^*$ so the defendant is negligent and hence liable. Then, at *X**, the defendant's cost curve tracks the X curve only. This is the range where he has met or

exceeded the due care standard and so is only responsible for his own cost of care. The discrete drop in the defendant's perceived cost, which occurs at X^*, thus provides a powerful incentive to just meet the due care standard, X^*, but not to exceed it. (There is no incentive to select a precaution level in excess of X^* given that the rising cost is not offset by a corresponding diminution in the risk of harm.)

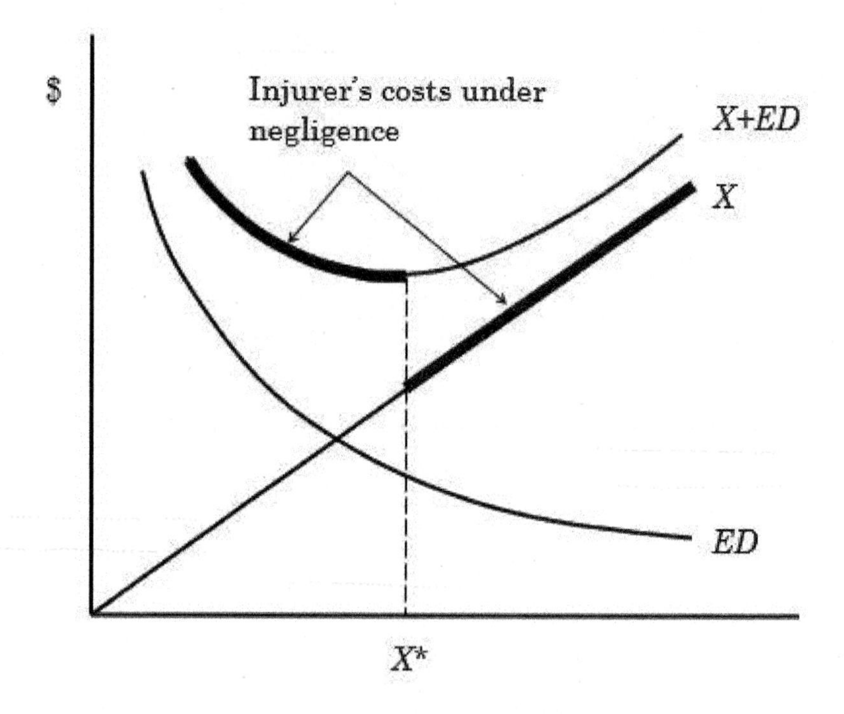

Figure 3:2. Level of injurer care focusing on injurer's cost function

A. Liability Rules

Now consider the actual care choice by the injurer under each of the three liability rules defined above: no liability, strict liability, and negligence. First, under no liability, the injurer will generally avoid costly precautions because she expects to bear none of the damages from an accident. In an extreme case, we might imagine that she undertakes no precautions whatsoever. Within the framework of Figure 3:1, this places the chosen level of care at the vertex, meaning the far left along the horizontal axis, such that X=0. Notice that the overall cost of accidents under this rule is extremely high, as shown by the high assigned dollar value on the *y* axis of *ED*, which also greatly exceeds the cost-minimizing result of setting care at X^*.

Now consider strict liability. One might intuit that with the care rule flipped in this manner, the result is to push the selected standard of care to the opposite end of the X axis, encouraging the tortfeasor to take maximal precaution. In fact, however, Figure 3:1 demonstrates that under strict liability, the tortfeasor is motivated to set the care level at the point that minimizes the sum of these costs, or X^*. That is because although she will have to pay for all of the costs incurred by the victim, she also bears all of the costs of care. For any point to the right of X^*, an additional increment of care will impose costs greater than the expected benefit in terms of reducing the marginal expected cost of a potential accident. The injurer therefore chooses the socially optimal level of care under strict liability because her personal costs coincide with overall social costs. Because this level of care does not eliminate risk altogether, under strict liability the tortfeasor is obligated to bear the remaining residual risk.[20]

Finally, consider the injurer's choice of care under negligence. As described above, an injurer is liable for the victim's accident losses under this rule only if she fails to meet the due care standard as set by the court. However, if she meets or exceeds the standard of care, she is not liable. Clearly, the incentives created by this rule depend on how courts set the due care standard. Tort law sets the relevant legal standard at "reasonableness," meaning the level of care that a reasonable person would choose when faced with the same circumstances as the injurer. The economic theory of negligence law as first described by Posner[21] and Brown[22] equates this standard with the cost-minimizing care level as described above, or X^* in Figure 3:1. The next section argues that consistent with the famous Learned Hand formula,[23] the legal and economic standards coincide. Based on the preceding analysis, we can express this standard as the cost-effective level of precaution, meaning that if the tortfeasor has undertaken too little care, an additional dollar spent on care would provide at least one dollar in return in the expected reduction of the cost of harm from an accident, whereas if she has undertaken such care, an additional dollar spent on care would provide less than a dollar return in the same expected value. This suggests that the analysis provides a positive, or explanatory, account of existing doctrine.[24] The remainder of this section fleshes out this analysis.

It is easy to show that under negligence with due care set at X^*, the injurer will set care at this level. This is true, first, because the injurer has a strong incentive to meet the due care standard in order to avoid paying damages; and second, because there is no expected gain from going beyond this standard, as doing so would involve additional costs that would result in no further reduction in the injurer's liability. Thus, the injurer minimizes his own costs by just meeting the due care standard.

It is important at this point to emphasize the different ways in which strict liability and negligence induce the injurer to take the cost-effective level of care. Strict liability forces the injurer to pay the victim's costs in the event of an accident. If we think of the risk of harm that the tortfeasor creates through her activity as an externality, strict liability taxes that externality, forcing the injurer to internalize the risk of harm that her activity imposes on others.[25] By contrast, negligence establishes a standard of behavior that allows

---

[20] For now, we are not considering the administrative costs on the tort system, or how the tortfeasor might choose to handle the residual risk, for example, through a pricing scheme that allows her to pass it on to consumers of the relevant goods or services, or through insurance.

[21] Richard A. Posner, *A Theory of Negligence*, 1 J. LEGAL STUD. 29 (1972).

[22] Brown, *supra* note 14.

[23] *See infra* note 28 and accompanying text.

[24] Here we distinguish positive analysis, an explanation of why the law takes the form it takes, from normative analysis, an exposition of what one claims the law should be.

[25] Specifically, the rule operates as a Pigouvian tax, with the proceeds going to the tort victim. *See supra* Chapter 1, Part IV (discussing Pigouvian taxation).

the injurer to avoid paying any damages as long as she satisfies the threshold-care standard. This "threshold" feature of negligence, and the way that it creates incentives for efficient behavior, will prove especially important in our discussion of bilateral-care accidents below. It will also prove, not coincidentally, to be a pervasive feature of legal rules across a variety of contexts.

Notice a critical feature about the choice of strict liability or negligence. Provided the tortfeasor fails to take cost-effective precautions, set at X^*, the rules create the same result, with the plaintiff recovering. When the tortfeasor takes the requisite level of care, however, the choice of rule controls whether the plaintiff recovers damages. Under strict liability, the plaintiff recovers, whereas under negligence, he does not. Most important, however, although the choice of rule determines whether the plaintiff recovers, it does not affect the defendant's precaution level. Under either rule, she sets the level of care at X^*. That is because any additional precautions would not be cost effective in the sense that an additional dollar spent on care would result in less than a dollar in expected savings from the reduction of accident risk. The cost of bearing the remaining risk of an accident, or the residual risk, falls on the tortfeasor under strict liability, and it falls on the victim under negligence. We will later see that this allocation of risk, and thus the corresponding choice of tort rule, is sometimes a function of which party is the least cost avoider, meaning which party can bear that risk at lower cost.[26]

B. The Learned Hand Test for Negligence

As shown above, the efficacy of the negligence rule depends on whether the judiciary succeeds in setting the due care standard at the cost-effective level of injurer care in Figure 3:1, defined to be X^*. That raises the question of how the cost-effective care level compares to the articulated legal standard for negligence. In the case *United States v. Carroll Towing Co*,[27] Judge Learned Hand provided what has become a benchmark in applying negligence to assess the proper level of care.

Carroll Towing concerned a barge that slipped away from its moorings and drifted downstream, causing damage to another barge and its cargo. The victim (the owner of the damaged barge) sued the owner of the breakaway barge claiming negligence for the latter's failure to ensure the latter's barge was properly moored. In his decision, Judge Hand wrote the following:

> Since there are occasions when every vessel will break from her moorings, and since, if she does, she becomes a menace to those about her; the owner's duty, as in other situations, to provide against resulting injuries is a function of three variables: (1) The probability that she will break away; (2) the gravity of the resulting injury, if she does; (3) the burden of adequate precautions. Possibly it serves to bring this notion into relief to state it in algebraic terms: if the probability be called P; the injury, L; and the burden, B; liability depends upon whether B is less than L multiplied by P; i.e., whether $B<PL$.[28]

---

[26] *See infra* note 30 and cites therein.

[27] 159 F.2d 169 (2d Cir. 1947).

[28] *Id.* at 173.

This algebraic inequality is now known as the *Hand Test* for negligence. It says that the injurer is negligent if he failed to take a particular precaution, the cost of which is lower than the expected value in reduced damages that it would have provided.

At first glance, the formula seems very similar to the above economic model of accident cost minimization. Indeed, the two can be made to coincide, but for this to occur, some clarification of terminology is required. According to Figure 3:1, the injurer is negligent if $X<X^*$, where the cost-minimizing level of care, X^*, is the point at which the cost of an additional unit of care equaled or exceeded the resulting reduction in expected accident costs. In other words, X^* is the point at which the *marginal costs* of an additional dollar spent on precaution is equal to the expected *marginal benefits* of that additional expenditure. Thus, if we interpret *B* in the Hand test to be the marginal cost of care (represented as the *slope* of the *X* curve in Figure 3:1) and *PL* as the marginal reduction in expected damages from the last incremental dollar spent on care (the *slope* of the *ED* curve in Figure 3:1), then the two tests for negligence precisely coincide. We sometimes refer to this understanding of the Learned Hand Formula as the *Marginal Hand Test.* We can demonstrate this insight with a simple numerical example.

Suppose that the owner of the barge in *Carroll Towing* has three choices concerning the selected level of care: (1) post no attendant, (2) post a daytime attendant, and (3) post a 24-hour attendant. The following table shows the costs and benefits of these options:

Table 3:1. Numerical example of the Hand Test

Care choice	1. Cost of Care (*B*)/**Marginal Cost of Care**	2. Probability of Accident (*P*)	3. Damage (*L*)	4. Expected Harm (Probability times Damage) (*PL*)/**Marginal Benefit**	5. Total Cost (*B*+*PL*)
No attendant	$0	.50	$1000	$500	$500
Daytime attendant	$110/**110**	.10	$1000	100/**400**	210
24-Hour attendant	$250/**140**	.01	$1000	10/**90**	260

In Table 3:1, we list the cost of care, *B*, in column one, the probability of an accident, *P*, in column two, the damage, *L*, in column three, and the Expected Harm (Probability times Damage, or *PL*), in column four. By comparing columns one and four (the non-bolded entries), we observe $B<PL$ for no attendant ($0<\$500$), but $B>PL$ for both a daytime attendant ($\$110>\$100$), and for a 24-hour attendant ($\$250>\$10$). This construction of the Hand Test would suggest that the barge owner should never be found negligent for failing to post an attendant given that the total cost of any available option to have an attendant would exceed the expected damage that would arise for that care level. This interpretation is mistaken, however, in that it fails to compare the *marginal cost* of each successive precaution with the *marginal benefit* of that precaution. The better assessment compares the cost of each marginal increase in care with the benefit of each resulting marginal diminution in the expected cost of the accident, meaning at each care level.

The *Marginal Hand Test* thus asks what the costs and benefits of *incremental units* of care are.[29] Now consider the bold-faced entries in columns one and four. Notice that posting an attendant during the day costs $110 relative to taking no action, and so we set $B=110$ in row two of column one. B is now interpreted to be the *extra* cost of posting the attendant during the day as compared to posting no attendant. Posting the daytime attendant reduces expected accident costs from $500 (=.5×1,000) to $100 (=.1×1,000), so we set $PL=\$400=\$500-\$100$. This is presented in bold in the second row of column 4. Since $100<$400, the marginal Hand Test is satisfied, and we *would* find the barge owner negligent for not posting an attendant during the day.

Suppose next that the owner *did* post a daytime attendant, but the victim claims that he should have posted a 24-hour attendant. Applying the marginal Hand Test to this claim yields $B=\$250-\$110=\$140$ (the bolded entry in row three of column one), and $PL=(.1\times\$1,000)-(.01\times\$1,000)=90$ (the bolded entry in row three of column four). Because posting an attendant for 24 hours instead of just during the day costs an additional $140, but only reduces accident costs by $90, under the marginal Hand Test, the barge owner would *not* be found negligent for remaining with only a daytime attendant. The correspondence between the marginal Hand Test and the economic model can be seen by computing total accident costs for each option in Table 3:1, which equals the sum of column one and the product of columns two and three (i.e., $B+PL$). This summation is provided in column 5, with a progression from 500 (no attendant) to 210 (daytime attendant) to 260 (24-hour attendant). The analysis once more reveals that total expected costs are minimized when the owner posts a daytime attendant. In this reading, the marginal Hand Test fully corresponds with the economic model.

C. Comparing Strict Liability and Negligence

The analysis of the unilateral care accident model has to this point shown that both strict liability and negligence create incentives for injurers to invest in a cost-effective level of care. Table 3:1 helps to explain this intuition. If the owner of the barge that caused the injury were subject to a rule of strict liability, rather than negligence, the cost-benefit analysis as to precaution level would remain the same because the owner's costs would coincide with total costs in column five. That is, it would still be cost effective to hire a daytime guard (incurring a marginal cost of $110 to reduce a marginal risk of harm valued at $400), but it would not be cost effective to go the additional step and hire a 24-hour guard (incurring a marginal cost of $140 to reduce a marginal risk of harm valued at $90). Assuming that there are other ways of managing that risk, perhaps through self-insurance (assuming a large fleet) or insurance with a third party, the barge owner would prefer to set the precaution at the cost-effective level, and manage the residual risk in some other manner.

---

29 *See* Brown, *supra* note 14, at 334–35 (explaining an "incremental" version of the Learned Hand Formula).

Because the choice of strict liability versus negligence does not affect the level of selected care, the question remains whether there is any economic basis for choosing between the two rules. One possibility is administrative costs. Is one rule cheaper for the court to apply? Within a typical negligence suit, the plaintiff must show the following elements: (1) injury caused by defendant's conduct (which can include inaction); (2) a duty of care owed by the defendant; (3) a breach of the duty of care; (4) causation in fact (but for defendant's action or inaction the injury would not have occurred); and (5) scope of liability, more commonly referred to as "proximate cause" (the chain of causation is not too attenuated to assess liability on the defendant).[30] In a negligence action, a negative finding on any of these factors results in a defense verdict. By contrast, for purposes of liability in a strict liability suit, plaintiff need only establish that the defendant's action or inaction was a cause in fact and proximate cause of her injury.[31] As a result, we might expect strict liability to involve lower costs per case because it reduces the need for detailed fact-finding, which often requires resolving contested claims as to the appropriate level of care.

Although this suggests that trials generally will be cheaper under strict liability, the lower requirements of proof also imply that there might be more trials. In assessing whether to file suit, the plaintiff, in consultation with her attorney, will consider the cost of the litigation and the expected recovery, including the possibility of settlement. Holding all else equal, the chance of winning, or of a favorable settlement, will generally be higher under strict liability because the plaintiff only has to prove both aspects of causation, whereas under negligence, she must also prove duty and breach of duty. And as we argued above, behaving rationally, injurers have a strong incentive to undertake precautions that satisfy the legal standard for due care for two reasons: (1) doing so is a cost-effective means of preventing accidents that can result in liability; and (2) doing so avoids liability under a negligence standard. These incentives combine to reduce the basis for negligence-based lawsuits. Overall, the comparison between strict liability and negligence based upon administrative cost grounds is ambiguous. Although lawsuits will be less costly under strict liability, such suits are more likely to be filed. Determining which of these competing factors predominates presents an empirical, rather than a purely theoretical, question.

Another basis for comparison involves the possibility of judicial error. Suppose, for example, that the court systematically errs in measuring victim damages. This will create a source of inefficiency under strict liability, which passes victim costs directly onto injurers. If courts systematically overestimate damages, injurers might take excessive care. Even though the preceding analysis demonstrated that rational actors will take the same level of care under both strict liability and negligence, if courts systematically award excessive damages, this becomes a factor in calculating the optimal level of care by upwardly influencing the value of L in PL (probability times injury) should liability attach, thereby encouraging additional levels of care despite the possible inefficiencies involved.

By contrast, errors in measuring damages will not generally affect incentives under negligence as long as those errors are small, provided that the court accurately sets the due standard of care. Assuming errors are not systematically biased, they should cancel

[30] DAN B. DOBBS, THE LAW OF TORTS § 199 (2016); RICHARD A. EPSTEIN, TORTS § 5.1, at 109–10 (1999); W. PAGE KEETON ET AL., PROSSER AND KEETON ON TORTS § 30, at 164–65 (5th ed. 1984).

[31] Of course under both negligence and strict liability, plaintiff must prove damages.

each other out, thereby encouraging an efficient precaution level under negligence. If instead the court systematically errs in setting the due care standard, that will affect incentives under negligence because of a potential tortfeasor's strong incentive to just meet that standard in order to avoid liability. This problem will not affect incentives under strict liability because the court does not need to calculate a due care standard under that rule. As was the case with administrative costs, the possibility of judicial error has cross-cutting effects on the choice between strict liability and negligence.

A final basis for choosing between the two rules concerns the goal of compensating victims, which strict liability ensures once damages are proven, whereas under negligence, the plaintiff must initially prove that the injurer failed to meet the standard of due care. Thus, only strict liability simultaneously induces cost-effective care by injurers and also ensures victim compensation, meaning without regard to fault. This might appear to strengthen the case for strict liability. The next section, however, highlights a powerful advantage of negligence.

II. THE BILATERAL CARE MODEL OF ACCIDENTS

We now turn to a more realistic setting in which victims as well as injurers affect the risk and severity of accidents. For example, pedestrians decide which side of the street to walk on, patients decide whether or not to follow a doctor's orders prior to surgery, and consumers of dangerous products decide whether or not to properly use those products for their intended purpose.

The basic accident model only needs to be amended slightly to accommodate victim care. With this important modification, the goal of the tort system becomes minimizing the sum of injurer and victim care plus expected accident costs, where the latter are assumed to decrease as a function of the combined levels of care of both parties. In general, the solution to this problem will involve a positive level of care by both injurers and victims. As a first step in analyzing this more general model, the next section examines an important special case.

A. The Least-Cost Avoider Rule

In some accident settings, care by the injurer *or* by the victim is sufficient to prevent an accident from occurring. These are sometimes referred to as *alternative care* accidents.[32] Suppose, for example, that a farmer whose land abuts a railroad track potentially suffers damages when passing trains emit sparks, thereby setting fire to crops planted near the tracks.[33] Let the damage from a fire be $100, but suppose fires can be prevented altogether if either the railroad installs spark arresters on all of its trains at a cost of $75 or if the farmer locates his crops farther back from the tracks at a cost of $50. Although care by either party is risk reducing, and thus cost saving, it is also wasteful for both to invest in

[32] LANDES & POSNER, *supra* note 15, at 61.

[33] *See, e.g.*, LeRoy Fibre v. Chicago, Milwaukee & St. Paul Ry., 232 U.S. 340 (1914); Eric Claeys, *Sparks Cases in Contemporary Law and Economic Scholarship*, *in* RESEARCH HANDBOOK ON AUSTRIAN LAW & ECONOMICS 233 (Peter Boettke & Todd J. Zywicki eds., 2017).

care. The cost-minimizing action in the current example is for the farmer to move his crops and for the railroad to do nothing.

In cases of this sort, Kaldor-Hicks efficiency is accomplished by imposing liability on the party who can avoid harm at the lowest cost, known as the "least-cost avoider."[34] Although both parties could undertake steps to prevent the harm, it is efficient for only one to do so. Because the legal question is not the proper level of care, but rather, which party should undertake it, we can limit our choice of tort rule in this case to either strict liability or no liability. In this example, the efficient rule is no liability. Farmers should bear all fire-induced losses caused by railroad sparks because that rule provides them with proper incentives to avoid planting crops near tracks. By contrast, if the costs were reversed (with the cost of crop relocation at $75 and of spark arresters at $50), the railroad would be the least-cost avoider. In that case, strict liability would be the preferred rule, as it would give the railroad proper incentives to install the arresters.

Actual cases in which either party acting alone can entirely avoid the the risk giving rise to a potential accident, thus resting solely on least cost avoider analysis, are uncommon. More common are cases in which avoiding the risk of injury requires some cost-effective care by both sides. In that setting, neither strict liability nor no liability will induce optimal care by both parties. When only one party is required to take appropriate precautions, the choice between these two rules depends on whether care by the injurer or the victim is more productive in reducing accident risk. However, neither of these binary liability rules can minimize overall costs when both parties must take optimal care to minimize the total cost of accidents.

This conclusion reveals the fundamental challenge in designing an efficient liability rule in bilateral care accident settings, namely, how to create incentives for each party to take cost-effective precautions. A theoretical solution is to impose the full accident costs on the injurer, but then *not award the damages to the victim*, such as with a fine paid to the government.[35] In this regime, both parties could be expected to act as if they were responsible for the full damages and each would then have an incentive to invest in an efficient level of care. Actual liability rules are not structured in this way; instead, the damages award is generally paid to the victim. This reflects both the incentive structure in tort law—absent the anticipated reward of damages, there is generally no incentive to file a lawsuit—and the goal of victim compensation.

The problem of designing an efficient liability rule in bilateral care settings thus reveals a tension between the compensatory and deterrence functions of tort law. In the more common case settings, these functions potentially conflict. This was not the case

[34] The least cost avoider concept finds its origins in the Coase theorem, which, as shown in Chapter 1, treats externalities as reciprocal burdens. R.H. Coase, *The Problem of Social Cost,* 3 J.L. & ECON. 1 (1960); *see also supra* Chapter 1. As applied here, one party can bear the burden at lower cost. Guido Calabresi introduced the term "cheapest cost avoider" in his classic book, GUIDO CALABRESI, THE COSTS OF ACCIDENTS: A LEGAL AND ECONOMIC ANALYSIS (1970). There, he argued that the goal of accident law is to lower the total of the cost of accidents, including the cost of precautions and of the resulting harm. *Id.* He further argued that strict liability imposed on the cheapest cost avoider reduces accident costs as compared with fault-based liability. *Id.*

[35] This is referred to as a "de-coupled" liability rule. In this case, it would not matter for purposes of incentives what is done with the money. The result is similar to what would happen under a tax on damages, where the tax revenue is not given to victims. For a discussion of Pigovian taxes, see *supra* Chapter 1 [Introduction], Part IV.

with the unilateral care model in which strict liability accomplished both goals. The challenge of seeking to properly align the compensatory and deterrence functions within the bilateral care setting underlies the analysis of negligence.

B. Negligence

We begin with "simple negligence." Under this rule the defendant is liable if he failed to satisfy the negligence standard, provided plaintiff proves all the elements in the prima facie negligence case. We will later introduce variations, including "negligence with contributory negligence" and "comparative negligence."[36]

As was true in the unilateral care model, a simple negligence rule sets a due care standard, which we equate to the optimal care of injurers. Injurers continue to have a strong incentive to meet that standard to avoid liability. Anticipating this result, victims will realize that, assuming the defendant behaves rationally, the most likely accidents will result from their own failure to take cost-effective precautions. Since they will bear the burden of those accidents (assuming the defendant was not negligent), the simple negligence rule should encourage plaintiffs, as well as defendants, to undertake due care. The combined incentive for both parties thereby minimizes their overall accident costs.

Professor John Brown first demonstrated this result using game theoretical tools in 1973.[37] Brown showed that under simple negligence, efficient care by both the injurer and victim was a pure-strategy Nash equilibrium. We will explore this concept in more detail in Chapters 15 and 16 on Game Theory. For now, we offer the following definition: A Nash equilibrium is the outcome or set of outcomes that follow from each player's rational strategy in the absence of coordination with the other player or specific information concerning the other player's strategy, and in which no player has an incentive to deviate from their chosen strategy given the other player's rational strategy.[38]

As applied here, each of the two parties anticipates the rational strategy of the other party, which is to employ cost-effective precautions as a means of avoiding liability in the case of the tortfeasor, and of incurring an injury that, as a result of the tortfeasor's proper care level, would go uncompensated, in the case of the victim. Each side thus determines that it is rational to undertake the cost-effective, or efficient, level of care. This means that victims presume that injurers will meet the due care standard and thus avoid liability, and victims also take efficient care to minimize their total costs, which include injuries arising from the residual risk and which thus go uncompensated. The combined effect of this Nash equilibrium is therefore to minimize the joint cost of accidents.

Although the assumptions that give rise to this mutually reinforcing result might seem ambitious, in theory the negligence rule improves the likelihood of this happy outcome. Justice Oliver Wendell Holmes captured this intuition as follows: "as a general proposition people are entitled to assume that their neighbors will conform to the law . . . and therefore . . . are entitled to assume that their neighbors will not be negligent."[39] In

---

[36] In Chapter 21, we will discuss a model that involves "strict liability with dual contributory negligence."

[37] Brown, *supra* note 14.

[38] *See also infra* Chapter 15, at 171 note 21 and cites therein (collecting authorities).

[39] LeRoy Fibre Co. v. Chicago, Milwaukee, & St. Paul Ry. Co., 232 U.S. 340, 352 (1914).

other words, the law encourages individuals in bilateral care settings to form intuitions about how the other party is apt to behave (or in Nash terms, intuitions concerning the other party's rational strategy), and further, it encourages the same individuals, armed with these intuitions, to conform their own conduct to the level of due care (or to employ their own rational strategy).[40] In this "game" the combined strategies generate a single outcome, with both parties undertaking due care, representing the Nash equilibrium.

The following illustration, based on the interaction of a railroad and farmer, further illustrates how a negligence rule promotes mutual care in a bilateral care setting:

Table 3:2. Efficiency of Negligence in Bilateral Care Accidents

Action	Crop damage ($)	Farmer's cost ($)	Railroad's cost ($)	Total cost ($)
No action	100	0	0	100
Farmer moves Crops	75	15	0	90
RR installs arrester	25	0	30	55
Farmer moves crops and RR installs arrester	5	15	30	50

The first column shows the crop damage from railroad sparks for the various combinations of railroad and farmer care. Columns two and three show the cost to the farmer of moving his crops, and to the railroad of installing spark arresters, respectively. Column four shows total costs. Note that total costs are minimized when both parties take care (the bottom row), thereby representing the efficient outcome. Assume that the due care standard for the railroad is to install a spark arrester, and thus, if its failure to do so produces harm to the farmer, it will be found negligent.

Consider first the incentives of the railroad. The railroad assumes that that the farmer, behaving rationally, will move her crops so as to minimize the potential risk of harm that would go uncompensated if the railroad takes appropriate precautions. The railroad then has the choice either to install the arresters, at a cost of $30 (row four), or not to install the arresters, which would leave it liable for the farmer's crop damage of $75 (row two). Clearly, it is cheaper to install the arresters. As for the farmer, she will also presume that the railroad will install the arresters in order to comply with due care, and so her choice is between moving the crops, which involves a total cost of $20 ($15 in care plus $5 in crop damage) (row four), and not moving them, which leaves damage of $25 (row three). Her optimal choice is to move the crops. The resulting outcome is therefore efficient (cost-minimizing).

[40] Below we will examine situations in which individuals confront others who are clearly not behaving in an efficient manner. *See infra* Part II.D.4.

Note the following features of the Nash equilibrium outcome. First, victims are not compensated for losses that follow from residual risk, meaning the risk that remains after both parties in the bilateral care setting take cost-effective precautions. This is a consequence of the conflict, noted above, between the compensatory and deterrence functions of tort law; although the two objectives sometimes converge, in the bilateral care setting in which negligence applies, they diverge with respect to residual risk. Second, the analysis implies that injurers, behaving rationally, will take cost-effective precautions and thus not be found negligent. It is important to remember that accidents can and do arise even when both parties involved undertake appropriate precautions.

In the least-cost avoider example discussed above, we assumed that either party could entirely eliminate the risk of accidents by taking appropriate precautions. Outside that stylized setting, accidents are generally not completely avoidable even when both parties take efficient care, as a consequence of residual risk. Bilateral care predominates in tort because the assumption that either of two parties to a tort could altogether eliminate risk rarely reflects the real world. Even beyond that, the simple model we have examined thus far ignores several aspects of the real world that may cause some parties to behave negligently in equilibrium. The next section examines one reason, specifically heterogeneity across injurers and victims.

C. Varying Costs of Care and the "Reasonable Person" Standard

The discussion thus far has assumed that injurers and victims are largely interchangeable, implying that optimal care strategies will be the same. In reality, of course, this will not be true because people naturally differ in their abilities to assess and respond to risk, whether due to differences in strength, reflexes, ability to make quick judgments, and a host of other personal characteristics. This implies that under negligence law, the due care standard should ideally be calibrated to specific individuals. As a consequence, within the Hand Negligence framework, one might interpret *B*, which we posited represents marginal cost of successive increments of care, as varying with each individual.

The law does not typically apply an individualized standard of care; rather, with limited exceptions, for example, based upon specific skills on which others can reasonably expect to rely,[41] it holds people to a single generalizable standard. That standard is based on the so-called reasonable person test. The hypothetical reasonable person has been defined as "a personification of a community ideal of reasonable behavior, determined by

[41] This includes for example, doctors, lawyers, and other professionals whose care level in the provision of related services is expected to be higher than that of an ordinary person, and within those and other professions, care levels might also vary with degrees of specialization. Professionals tend also to have a lower marginal cost of care due to their considerable professional training and experience. As a result, this raises their X*, which professionals signal to those to whom they offer their services. DOBBS, *supra* note 30, § 284, at 632–33; KEETON ET AL., *supra* note 30, § 32, at 185–86.

the jury's social judgment."[42] Based on this understanding, "Negligence is a failure to do what the reasonable person would do 'under the same or similar circumstances.' "[43]

Reliance on a single standard, as opposed to a set of individualized standards, generates two types of inefficiencies.[44] To simplify, we will place affected persons into three groups.[45] First, for individuals with lower than average costs of care, the reasonable person standard sets care below what their individualized standard of care would otherwise be, because for such individuals, *B* is lower than for the reasonable person. And because such persons can avoid liability by meeting the lower standard, they will tend to take too little care. Second, individuals with slightly higher than average costs of care will have individualized standards that should be lower than the reasonable person standard, as *B* for them is higher than for the reasonable person, but such individuals will nevertheless choose to comply with the higher standard associated with the reasonable person to avoid liability. If we use their own cost of care as the relevant baseline, we might think of the latter group of persons as taking too much care. Finally, for a third group, the costs of care are significantly above the average, and thus their individualized standard is well below the reasonable person standard. These people will actually find it optimal to choose their individually optimal care levels, but as a consequence, they will risk being judged negligent in the event that their reduced care level creates or exacerbates an injury. For this group, the one-size-fits-all negligence rule is equivalent to strict liability given the members' rational decision not to meet the reasonable person standard.

Given that departures from the individually optimal care levels vary in opposite directions from the reasonable person standard, with group one taking too little care, group two taking too much care, and group three taking optimal care, it is not possible to say whether the single standard increases or decreases the accident rate as compared with an individualized negligence standard, or with strict liability, under which all injurers choose their individually optimal care levels. The overall cost of accidents—the sum of damages and injurer care—however, necessarily increases as a consequence of the selection of a single standard. This increase in accident costs, however, must be weighed against the significantly higher litigation costs that would be involved in implementing an individualized standard.

As noted above, the legal regime has partially accommodated these concerns by creating a narrower carve-out for particular categories of individuals falling into the third group. As Landes and Posner observe, only in those "cases where the information costs of departing from the average-man standard are low because the gap between the average individual's due care level and that of the individual defendant is large and palpable, [do] the courts . . . recognize a different standard."[46] Thus persons whom others can observe to be visually impaired, for example by carrying a cane, will not be held to the reasonable

---

[42] KEETON ET AL., *supra* note 30, § 32, at 175; EPSTEIN, *supra* note 24, § 5.1, at 110.

[43] KEETON ET AL., *supra* note 30, § 32, at 175 (quoting Restatement Second of Torts § 283).

[44] LANDES & POSNER, *supra* note 15, at 124–25.

[45] Although for actual individuals there are finer gradations than three, the legal system places individuals within administrable cohorts that approximately correlate to the groupings identified here. In general, the law holds all but a subgroup of category three, those with known or observable limitations, subject to the reasonable person standard despite individual differences in ability to conform to that standard.

[46] LANDES & POSNER, *supra* note 15, at 127.

care standard as applied to contexts in which sighted persons can undertake relevant care with substantially greater ease. Other categories of affected persons include those with intellectual disabilities, children below a certain age, and persons with other visibly observable restrictions.

D. Contributory Negligence

Our discussion of negligence law thus far has focused exclusively on the legal duty of *injurers* to meet the due standard of care. The tort system also imposes duties of care on victims, and state jurisdictions handle this in different ways. Legal regimes include: negligence with contributory negligence, strict liability with contributory negligence, and comparative negligence. After illustrating various forms of contributory negligence, we turn to these other regimes.

Contributory negligence was first introduced in the old English case of *Butterfield v. Forrester*.[47] *Butterfield* involved an injury to a rider who collided with an obstruction that the defendant negligently placed in the road. The court held that, despite the defendant's negligence, the plaintiff could not recover because of his own failure to exercise due care to avoid the obstruction. Specifically, the Chief Judge said:

> A party is not to cast himself upon an obstruction which has been made by the fault of another, and avail himself of it, if he do not himself use common and ordinary caution to be in the right. . . . . One person being in fault will not dispense with another's use of ordinary care for himself.[48]

The contributory negligence standard can be paired with "simple" negligence or with strict liability. We consider each in turn.

1. Negligence with Contributory Negligence (with a Comment on Assumption of Risk)

Under a rule of negligence with contributory negligence, the injurer is liable for the victim's damages only if the injurer failed to take due care and the victim *did* take due care. If the victim did not take due care—that is, if she was found to be contributorily negligent by the court, for example under the Hand Negligence test—the injurer will not be held liable even if he failed to exercise due care. In this regime, the victim's contributory negligence is thus a bar to recovering damages.

Contributory negligence is an *affirmative defense* for the injurer, meaning that the defendant must plead that defense and prove it at trial by a preponderance of the evidence. This means that whereas the victim bears the burden to prove defendant's negligence, the defendant has the burden to prove plaintiff's contributory negligence.[49]

For the same reason that simple negligence satisfies Kaldor-Hicks efficiency, the combined regime of negligence with contributory negligence induces both injurers and

---

[47] (1809) 103 Eng. Rep. 926 (K.B.).

[48] *Id.* at 927 (Chief Judge Lord Ellenborough). The custom in such cases was seriatim opinions, meaning that each judge wrote on his own, rather than for the court.

[49] KEETON ET AL., *supra* note 30, §§ 38, 65.

victims to take cost-effective precautions. With this more nuanced rule, a victim will intuit that the injurer will be motivated to undertake due care to avoid the risk of liability in the event of an accident, and likewise, the injurer will intuit that the victim will be motivated to undertake due care as well, as otherwise, in the event of an accident, the victim will have no chance of recovering at trial, and in equilibrium will bear his own harm. The combined regime—a Nash equilibrium—is mutual care.

It therefore appears that coupling contributory negligence with simple negligence adds nothing to the law in terms of efficiency. Nor does it result in victims being compensated because in the Nash equilibrium, injurers take due care and therefore are not liable. In this sense, the addition of contributory negligence is purely distributional, imposing the cost of accidents for which the plaintiff and defendant are both negligent on the plaintiff, rather than on the defendant, as would be the case under simple negligence. And it is likely that the rule increases administrative costs relative to simple negligence because the court must evaluate whether each party has complied with the relevant standard of care.

Although negligence and negligence with contributory negligence each promote due care on the part of injurers and victims, as a matter of policy should one be preferred to the other? Stated differently, is the selection purely distributional, or does one rule enhance social welfare? Consider the following argument: in some settings, an injurer might be better suited to alert potential victims of appropriate precautions that they should undertake to avoid the risk of injury. In a regime of simple negligence, there is little incentive to provide such notice once the defendant herself has undertaken appropriate care. By contrast, under contributory negligence, by providing notice, the injurer lowers the cost to herself of proving plaintiff's negligence as an affirmative defense by specifying precautions that plaintiff might have failed to undertake.

Can you think of examples in which the addition of contributory negligence creates this potential social-welfare-enhancing incentive? Is it possible that even without the addition of contributory negligence, the injurer's failure to issue the same warnings might itself constitute negligence, thus rendering contributory negligence unnecessary from an efficiency perspective? Why or why not?

a. A Comment on *Assumption of Risk*

One doctrine that bridges these two competing legal regimes and that might therefore offer some insight is *Assumption of Risk*. Although the doctrine today is generally treated as part of comparative negligence, like contributory negligence, assumption of risk was treated historically as an affirmative defense.[50] The most common application arose when a plaintiff voluntarily (and typically unreasonably) encountered a known risk that eventually led to an injury. A classic illustration of assumption of risk involves participating in a sporting activity known to pose considerable danger, such as outdoor rock climbing, with the attendant risk of faulty harnesses or falling debris that could cause

[50] DAN B. DOBBS ET AL., DOBBS LAW OF TORTS § 470 (2016).

a serious accident.[51] Other than by declining to participate, there might be little that an accident victim could do to avoid the risk.

Contributory negligence, by contrast, involves circumstances in which both the injurer and victim can engage in risk-reducing precautions, and in which the optimal outcome (unlike the unilateral care situation) is for both of them to do so. To the extent that the injurer has a comparative advantage in identifying appropriate precautions, including those that both sides might undertake, negligence with contributory negligence might provide incentives to disclose precautions, thereby lowering the cost, with risk reduction by both the injurer and the victim. Assumption of risk encourages the injurer to place the victim on notice of the risk of injuries that are unlikely to be reduced with additional precautions, thus giving the victim the choice to engage in or to avoid the risk-producing activity.

2. *Strict Liability with Contributory Negligence*

Contributory negligence can also be paired with strict liability. Under this rule, a due care standard is set for the victim only, and so injurers are strictly liable unless the victim fails to meet that standard, that is, unless she is found to be contributorily negligent. In this sense, strict liability with a defense of contributory negligence is essentially a *negligence rule for victims*.

The Nash equilibrium, which again encourages cost-effective precautions on both sides, is derived in the same way as under simple negligence, except this time, the roles of the injurer and victim are reversed. Specifically, the victim now has an incentive to meet the due care standard to avoid liability. Because this takes the form of an uncompensated injury, the injurer, who rationally anticipates that she will be held fully liable in equilibrium, also rationally elects efficient care, thereby helping to minimize overall costs.[52]

Our analysis of the three versions of the negligence rule—simple negligence, negligence with contributory negligence, and strict liability with contributory negligence—reveals that each variation yields an efficient outcome in the bilateral care accident model. However, strict liability with contributory negligence differs from the other two in that the injurer bears the residual accident costs in equilibrium (meaning when both sides satisfy the due care standard), thereby compensating the victim. Thus, contrary to the assertion above,[53] there is no necessary conflict between deterrence and compensation in the bilateral care model. Rather, an efficient outcome can be achieved while assigning liability to either the injurer or the victim. This purely distributional choice depends on which of these negligence rules the legal system selects. The fact that strict liability with

---

[51] The once-classic illustration of a spectator at a baseball game hit by a stray ball is more generally handled today as a "no duty" case based on an express disclaimer on an admissions ticket that the ballpark bears no responsibility for such injuries. *See generally* Gil Fried, *Baseball Spectators' Assumption of Risk: Is It 'Fair" or Is It 'Foul"?*, 13 MARQUETTE SPORTS L. REV. 39 (2002) (discussing the history and ongoing validity of foul ball jurisprudence).

[52] This result reveals the mathematical symmetry between injurers and victims in the bilateral care accident model.

[53] *See supra* Part II.D.1.

contributory negligence induces efficient care and compensates victims appears to make it an attractive rule. Despite this, it is not commonly used in tort law.[54]

Are there reasons that are not purely distributional for avoiding strict liability with contributory negligence as the common liability rule in tort? Consider the following argument: outside the context of firms whose economic activities or products pose specific and identifiable risks of injury to others, imposing strict liability imposes too great a cost on persons who, when engaging in ordinary economic activities, might thereby unwittingly become tortfeasors. Although individuals should be expected to undertake appropriate levels of care, including cost-effective precautions that avoid the risk of harm to others, a rule of strict liability would force such unwitting tortfeasors to make difficult choices about engaging in otherwise ordinary activities. Specifically, individuals could choose to avoid many otherwise productive activities, to engage in those activities but to self-insure, or to purchase insurance when possible to do so. And even if individuals take all efficient precautions, strict liability subjects them to potentially high litigation costs. Because all of us are simultaneously potential tortfeasors and potential tort victims with respect to ordinary activities that can cause harm, the general inhibiting effect of strict liability with contributory negligence counsels instead in favor of simple negligence or negligence with contributory negligence.

Do you find this analysis persuasive? Why or why not? If you do find it persuasive, can you think of specific activities that you might avoid or engage in less regularly in a strict liability with contributory negligence regime?

3. Sequential Accidents

Until now, the bilateral care accident model has assumed that injurers and victims make their actual care choices without specific knowledge of that of the other party. In many cases, this is realistic. For example, potential victims of automobile accidents do not know how much other motorists have invested in maintenance of their brakes; surgeons cannot directly verify (beyond self-reporting) whether a patient has complied with all pre-op instructions; and manufacturers of dangerous products cannot know whether consumers will follow proper care instructions in the use of their products. In these situations, parties have to form expectations about what others are doing, and as we have seen, the Nash equilibrium arises when each side's rational expectations are met. Recall that the various negligence rules, each of which coincides with the efficient Nash-strategy equilibrium, compels each party to *presume* that others are complying with the law, including meeting the due care standard. As we have seen, even without specific knowledge of the other party's conduct, the Nash equilibrium result in any of the three negligence regimes we have reviewed is mutual due care.

There is, however, a substantial class of accidents in which the injurer and victim make their decisions sequentially, and thus with the ability of the second mover to observe the behavior of the first before making a decision on the chosen level of care. We will

---

[54] A version of it might be said to have prevailed in products liability prior to the recent trend toward absolute producer liability. *See infra* Part IV.

refer to these as *sequential care accidents.*[55] Under all three of the negligence rules reviewed thus far (simple negligence, negligence with contributory negligence, and strict liability with contributory negligence), if the initial mover chooses to meet the due care standard, the second mover, behaving rationally, will do the same. Thus, the fact that the parties move in sequence doesn't undermine the effect of these rules in promoting mutual due care.

A possible problem arises, however, when the party moving first is *observed* to have been negligent, due to error, inadvertence, or possibly strategic behavior. The question then becomes whether the second mover still has an incentive to exercise due care, or even to take additional, compensating precautions. Once the first mover has been negligent, a Nash equilibrium in which both parties choose due care is no longer possible. The question then arises: which, if any, liability rule motivates the second mover to undertake "second best" efficient precautions (in the Kaldor-Hicks sense) *following* the first mover's problematic behavior?

The answer returns us to *Butterfield v. Forrester*, which introduced contributory negligence. Recall that the case involved a rider who was injured when he ran into an obstruction that the injurer negligently left in the street. *Butterfield* therefore presented a sequential care accident that arose as a result of the victim's actions following the injurer's observed initial negligence. Now consider the incentives that the various negligence rules create for similarly situated victims.

Begin with simple negligence. In this discussion, we will take the victim's anticipated response to its logical extreme, which includes assuming that compensation for injury is complete. This might apply in the context of property damage alone, although even there, potential victims will generally have an incentive to undertake some level of precaution against harm that directly affects them. Based on our earlier analysis, if the victim observes that the injurer has violated the due care standard, the victim has no incentive to take cost-effective precautions. That is because the victim knows that the injurer will be held fully liable for any damages that she suffers. In this analysis, simple negligence therefore does not create appropriate incentives for victim care in a sequential case in which she initially observes injurer negligence.

Now consider how introducing a contributory negligence defense affects incentives in this circumstance. Under this rule, regardless of the injurer's prior behavior, victims cannot collect damages unless they themselves meet the due care standard. This restores the incentive for victims to take appropriate precautions even in the face of observed injurer negligence, as otherwise they will bear their own damages. The conclusion is similar under a rule of strict liability with a defense of contributory negligence under which the victim must meet the due standard of care in order to shift damages back onto the injurer. Regardless of the baseline liability rule (simple negligence or strict liability) to which contributory negligence is attached, the result is to encourage both sides to undertake an appropriate level of care. This argument provides an important economic rationale for

---

[55] *See, e.g.*, Donald Wittman, *Optimal Pricing of Sequential Inputs: Last Clear Chance, Mitigation of Damages, and Related Doctrines in the Law*, 10 J. LEGAL STUD. 65 (1981); Steven Shavell, *Torts in Which Victim and Injurer Act Sequentially*, 26 J.L. & ECON. 589 (1983); Samuel Rea, *The Economics of Comparative Negligence*, 7 INT'L REV. L. & ECON. 149 (1987)); Mark F. Grady, *Common Law Control of Strategic Behavior: Railroad Sparks and the Farmer*, 17 J. LEGAL STUD. 15 (1988).

introducing a contributory negligence defense, and helps to explain the *Butterfield* court's introduction of this defense.

Now let us suppose that the victim is the first mover in a sequential care accident setting. As an illustration, consider another old English case, *Davies v. Mann.*[56] In *Davies*, the owner of a donkey tied it up next to a highway, and the injurer drove by in his wagon, striking and killing the donkey. The court found both parties negligent, the driver for traveling at an excessive rate of speed, and the donkey owner for having left it in harm's way. Under strict liability with contributory negligence and simple negligence with contributory negligence, the owner of the donkey would not be able to recover for his loss, in spite of the injurer's negligence, given his own prior negligence. Thus, even though the driver observed the donkey in the street, and presumably had time to avoid it, under these negligence rules, he lacked an incentive to do so because the contributory negligence standard would have already barred recovery by the donkey's owner. The claimed benefit of contributory negligence where the injurer moved first is therefore absent when the negligent victim moves first. In fact, a simple negligence rule would have better promoted efficient precautions because the injurer would then have had an incentive to meet the due care standard to avoid liability, regardless of the victim's prior negligence. As explained below, the last clear chance doctrine helps restore the burden to the tortfeasor consistent with the operation of a simple negligence rule, and thus despite the victim's prior contributory negligence.

These examples illustrate an important point about the contributory negligence defense. Working with either simple negligence or strict liability as the baseline liability rule, this affirmative defense encourages both parties to a negligence suit to adopt cost-effective precautions when the other party's conduct is unobserved or is simultaneous. That is because in such situations, each party rationally anticipates the behavior of the other party, thereby encouraging an efficient Nash equilibrium. By contrast, when the decisions are sequential, the rational expectation of the other party's conduct is replaced with *actual knowledge* of the other party's conduct. When the first mover is the negligent injurer, contributory negligence helps to restore the incentives of the victim to take appropriate precautions. When the first mover is the negligent victim, however, contributory negligence removes the incentive for care by the injurer, whereas simple negligence without the affirmative defense would restore the incentives of the injurer to take due care. The discussion of last clear chance, which follows, offers a more attractive solution in this sequential situation, and does so without having to eliminate contributory negligence as an affirmative defense (or as part of the comparative fault formulation).[57]

---

[56] (1842) 152 Eng. Rep. 588.

[57] Today, most of the forty-six comparative fault jurisdictions within the United States treat the principle of last clear chance as part of their comparative fault analysis. DAN B. DOBBS ET AL., DOBBS LAW OF TORTS § 226 (2015) ("Although last clear chance and discovered peril doctrines retain none of their original legal force in most states, the facts upon which those doctrines were based are still relevant in determining negligence and comparing fault. In many negligence cases, the defendant creates risks of harm, but harm that might be avoided by any one of several means, including the plaintiff's own efforts to avoid harm.").

4. *Last Clear Chance and Strategic Negligence*

The discussion to this point appears to suggest that in sequential accidents, the optimal rule depends on which party moves first. If the victim moves first, simple negligence is best, whereas if the injurer moves first, contributory negligence, coupled with either strict liability or simple negligence, is best. This is not a particularly satisfying solution because it places a heavy fact-finding burden on the courts, and it does not send a clear signal regarding the applicable liability rule to parties undertaking risk-creating activities.

In *Davies v. Mann*,[58] however, the court introduced a more elegant solution, last clear chance. Under this rule, the party that has the last opportunity to avoid the accident, whether the injurer or the victim, has the legal duty to take appropriate steps to do so without regard to any prior negligence by the initial mover. In cases in which the injurer moves first, such as *Butterfield v. Forrester*[59], last clear chance is essentially equivalent to contributory negligence as it compels the victim to take precaution even in the presence of prior injurer negligence. However, in cases where the injured party moves first, such as *Davies v. Mann*, last clear chance is said to "defeat" contributory negligence because the injurer is compelled to undertake appropriate precautions even in the presence of prior victim negligence. Notice that unlike the regime suggested at the end of the prior subsection, this rule can be expressed in a general and neutral way, favorably affecting victim and injurer incentives based on which party moved second, and thus which has the last clear chance to avoid the accident.

Despite this, Professor Mark Grady has identified a situation in which last clear chance could create problematic incentives.[60] He reasons that first-movers in sequential accidents might have an incentive to take a "strategically" negligent course of action so as to shift some avoidance costs onto second-movers. Consider the following discussion:

> When someone has been negligent in the first place—one hopes, through inadvertence—the best thing left to do is to get the other party to make up for it. But there is a flip side to the coin. If the second party must compensate for errors, the first party may think about the payoff from being deliberately negligent.[61]

Professor Grady illustrates this concept with the following scene from F. Scott Fitzgerald's classic novel, *The Great Gatsby*, which presents a conversation between the narrator, Nick Carraway, and Jordan Baker:

> "You're a rotten driver," I protested. "Either you ought to be more careful or you oughtn't to drive at all."
>
> "I am careful."
>
> "No, you're not."

---

[58] 152 Eng. Rep. at 589.

[59] (1809) 103 Eng. Rep. 926 (K.B.).

[60] Mark F. Grady, *Common Law Control of Strategic Behavior: Railroad Sparks and the Farmer*, 17 J. LEGAL STUD. 15, 19 (1988).

[61] *Id.* at 19.

"Well, other people are," she said lightly.

"What's that got to do with it?"

"They'll keep out of my way," she insisted. "It takes two to make an accident."[62]

This fanciful illustration implies that the last clear chance doctrine might encourage reckless drivers to shift some of the cost of accident avoidance onto those who observe their dangerous driving behavior. Grady argues that courts are sensitive to this possibility and have limited the duty of second-mover (or compensating) precaution to cases in which the likelihood of strategic negligence is small.[63] The problem is distinguishing, after the fact, those cases of prior negligence that involved inadvertence or error from those that involve a deliberate strategy to shift the risk of liability. This might appear to require knowledge of the first-mover's state of mind, or it is possible that the distinction might instead rest on objective factors that correlate with subjective states of mind.

An examination of last clear chance cases suggests a possibly helpful distinction.[64] Historically, last clear chance has been applied in two types of cases: those in which the victim is *helpless* and those in which the victim is *inattentive*. A helpless plaintiff is one who is in a position of danger from which she cannot extricate herself, as when a person walking on a railroad track gets her foot stuck in the rails.[65] By contrast, an inattentive plaintiff is one who merely fails to notice her peril, as when a person standing by the side of the road is hit by a passing vehicle.[66] The risk of strategic behavior is obviously far more likely in cases involving an inattentive plaintiff as it is hard to imagine a victim strategically placing herself in a position of grave peril in the event that the injurer fails to take compensating precautions. Strategic victims are thus more likely to feign inattentiveness in order to "trap" injurers. The greater threat of strategic behavior in these cases suggests at least a possibility that the costs of a duty of compensating precautions might outweigh its benefits.

E. Comparative Negligence

As previously noted,[67] the various combined negligence rules discussed in the last part have largely been superseded by the growing dominance of comparative negligence, which is now the prevailing rule in all but a few states.[68] The principal reason for this

---

62 F. SCOTT FITZGERALD, THE GREAT GATSBY 63 (New York: Scribner Paperback Edition, 1995); Grady, *supra* note 55, at 15.

63 Grady, *supra* note 55, at 18.

64 For purposes of this discussion, we will focus on cases where the victim moves first. This discussion is based on THOMAS MICELI, ECONOMICS OF THE LAW: TORTS, CONTRACTS, PROPERTY, LITIGATION 63–65 (1997).

65 New York Cent. R. Co. v. Thompson, 21 N.E.2d 625 (Ind. 1939).

66 Greear v. Noland Co., 89 S.E.2d 49 (Va. 1955).

67 *See, e.g.*, *supra* notes 50–51 and accompanying text (discussing assumption of risk); *supra* note 58 and accompanying text (discussing last clear chance).

68 This change has occurred primarily by statute rather than by judicial opinion. Memorandum on Uniform Apportionment of Tort Liability Act from Roger Henderson, Reporter, to Gene LeBrun, Chair, Drafting Committee on Apportionment of Tort Liability 6 (July 3, 2000), http://www.uniformlaws.org/shared/docs/apportionment_of_tort_responsibility/atla700m.pdf ("Of the 46 states that have adopted some form of comparative responsibility, ten have been by judicial decision and 36 by legislation.").

conversion seems to have been dissatisfaction with the perceived unfairness of the "all-or-nothing" nature of rules that place full liability on one party when both are in some sense at fault. The unfairness seems especially severe when, for example, contributory negligence bars a slightly negligent victim from recovering against a more obviously negligent injurer. Comparative negligence remedies this problem by apportioning liability according to the relative fault of the two parties.

To illustrate, suppose that a speeding motorist hits a pedestrian who was walking on the wrong side of the road, resulting in medical bills of $100,000 for the pedestrian. If the court determines that 75% of the harm was due to the motorist's negligence, and 25% was due to the pedestrian's negligence, then the pedestrian would be able to recover damages of $75,000 from the injurer. Under negligence with contributory negligence, by contrast, the victim would not have been able to recover at all.

Determining the percentages of relative fault is straightforward in theory. The process involves finding the ratios of the actual care levels to the due care levels on the assumption that the parties' combined due care levels equal 100 percent. To illustrate, imagine a car accident in which x_1 represents person 1's actual care and x_2 represents person 2's actual care. Assume that x^* represents the due care level, here a speed limit of 60, and that each driver falls short of that level of care by speeding, with person 1 driving at 100 and person 2 driving at 80. The parties' relative fault would be calculated as follows: $(x_1-x^*)/(x_2-x^*)$, with the result that person 1 should bear $(100-60)/(80-60)=40/20=2$ times the fault. If total damages are $1,000, then person 1 should bear $667 and person 2 should bear $333. If person 2 is the victim and incurred all of the damages, then person 1 should only have to pay $667 in compensation.

In most cases, however, the calculation would be far more challenging, especially when the types of care are not easily comparable as they are here. This is reflected, for example, in the *Restatement (Third) of Torts: Apportionment of Liability*,[69] and also in the *Uniform Comparative Fault Act*.[70] Both sources invite the jury in such cases to consider two factors: (1) the respective egregiousness of the conduct of each party, and (2) the proximity of each actor's conduct to the resulting harm. This is intended to ameliorate the difficulties of more complex comparisons than the one above, which deliberately forged a set of comparable criteria for each at-fault party.

For a notable example involving more complex comparisons of relative fault, consider the famous McDonald's coffee case.[71] An elderly woman purchased coffee to go in a vehicle that did not contain a cup holder. She was in the passenger seat, with her grandson driving. He parked the car as she held the coffee cup between her knees. As she pulled the lid toward her to remove it, she spilled the contents in her lap, causing third degree burns in her pelvic region and elsewhere, resulting in substantial hospitalization, skin grafting, and ongoing treatments. McDonalds initially declined to settle for more than $800 despite medical expenses and loss of income valued at $18,000. The case was tried

---

[69] RESTATEMENT (THIRD) OF TORTS: APPORTIONMENT OF LIABILITY § 8 (AM. LAW INST. 2016).

[70] UNIF. COMPARATIVE FAULT ACT (1977).

[71] Stella Liebeck v. McDonald's Restaurants, P.T.S., Inc. and McDonald's International, Inc., 994 Extra LEXIS 23, 1995 WL 360309 (Bernalillo Country, N.M. Dist. Ct. 1994); *McDonald's Settles Lawsuit over Burn from Coffee*, WALL ST. J., Dec. 2, 1994, at B6.

to a jury, which found McDonalds grossly negligent, and also found the plaintiff negligent. It assessed McDonalds with 80% fault and plaintiff with the remaining 20%, thus reducing the compensatory damages award from $200,000 to $160,000, and awarding $2.7 million in punitive damages, apparently based on the equivalent of two-days' coffee sales as suggested by plaintiff's counsel. Following the trial, the case was settled for an undisclosed sum reported at lower than $600,000.

The plaintiff's theory was that McDonald's maintained the coffee at a temperature of 180–90° F (82–88° C) and that at this temperature, a brief exposure of 2–3 seconds would cause severe burns, whereas a modestly lower temperature of 160 F (71 C) would allow up to 20 seconds to remove the liquid from skin, thereby abating the severity of the harm. McDonalds contended that maintaining coffee at such high temperatures was customary in the industry and that most traveling purchasers wanted the coffee very hot as they would begin drinking at a later time, although there was also conflicting evidence suggesting that many take-out consumers begin drinking immediately.

The case gained substantial notoriety with many commentators lamenting that it exemplified frivolous litigation.[72] On the other hand, there were several hundred similar incidents against McDonald's for coffee-related burns,[73] and in the aftermath of this suit, the company lowered the temperature of the coffee it served by approximately ten degrees. More notably, it improved the stability of its take-out cups and warnings, thereby reducing the risk of harm.

The seemingly greater fairness of comparative negligence for partly at-fault plaintiffs must be weighed against the rule's efficiency properties, which depend on how the doctrine is formulated. (Just as there are variations on negligence rules, there are also variations on comparative fault.)[74] Economists have shown, however, that as long as the particular form of comparative negligence retains the threshold property for one of the parties—that is, as long as the tortfeasor believes that he or she can avoid liability only by meeting the due standard—then the rule will produce an efficient Nash equilibrium in which both parties, behaving rationally, will undertake due care.[75] In this sense, comparative negligence follows the same basic logical structure as contributory negligence.

The fact that comparative negligence is potentially efficient and seemingly fairer than the other negligence rules provides a strong argument in its favor, and hence explains its popularity. It remains the case, however, that in an efficient Nash equilibrium, meaning when both parties satisfy the due care standard, the victim bears all the residual risk. This is a consequence of the threshold feature of an efficient comparative negligence rule, one

---

72 Hilary Stout, *Not Just a Hot Cup Anymore*, N.Y. TIMES (Oct. 21, 2013), http://www.nytimes.com/2013/10/21/booming/not-just-a-hot-cup-anymore.html.

73 *See* William J. Chriss, *The External Aspect of Legal Ethics, Hot Coffee, and the Noble Lawyer: Attacks on the Profession and Their Massive Ethical and Social Damage*, 19 TRINITY L. REV. 13, 40 (2013) (noting that at trial, Liebeck's attorney "produced evidence that in the ten years before Stella's injuries, McDonald's had received over 700 reports of similar burn incidents . . . .").

74 HARRY SCHULMAN ET AL., LAW OF TORTS: CASES AND MATERIALS 350 (6th ed. 2015) (explaining variations on comparative fault regimes across states based in part on whether the scheme was judicially or legislatively adopted).

75 *See, e.g.*, SHAVELL, *supra* note 15, at 15–17.

that limits the desirability of the rule as a matter of fairness. Of course, the same can be said of negligence and negligence with contributory negligence. The only way to avoid this result is to apply strict liability with or without contributory negligence. Even so, most accidents involve some negligence. Although residual risk is inevitable, cost effective care by both parties typically prevents accidents from occurring. Thus, the actual application of comparative fault will generally involve some sharing of liability, whereas negligence with contributory negligence will foreclose recovery altogether if plaintiff is found negligent.

An important policy question involves whether the administrative cost of simple or comparative negligence is likely to be higher. Imagine that we divide costs into two categories: (1) information costs, meaning the cost of procuring and presenting information to the trier of fact, a judge or jury, and (2) decision costs, meaning the cost of reaching a verdict based on all the evidence presented. If we assume a jury trial, how does the shift from simple negligence to comparative fault affect these two cost functions? One possibility is that comparative fault raises information costs by encouraging additional, and more finely grained, information as to relative fault on both sides, but at the same time, comparative fault might reduce decision costs by facilitating compromise and removing the all-or-nothing implications of contributory negligence. Assuming this is right, is there a way to ascertain which of these two cost functions is apt to dominate? Why or why not?

Notable scholars have also claimed that comparative fault is superior to the other negligence rules because it promotes risk-sharing,[76] and that it better aligns incentives for precautions respecting risk associated with a degree of uncertainty as to the due standard of care.[77] In addition, one scholar has shown that comparative fault is at least as good as various negligence rules, including last clear chance, in motivating second movers in sequential accident settings to take compensating precaution when confronted with observable negligence by the first mover.[78]

III. APPLICATIONS

A. Darnell Michaels v. Tandem Skydiving

Attached as Appendix 1 to this chapter, you will find the contract for *Tandem Skydiving*.[79] It is not necessary to read the entire 7-page document. Pay particular attention to paragraphs 5, 10, and 17. Now assume the following facts. To celebrate her upcoming graduation from the University of Maryland School of Medicine, Mindy Able persuades her fiancée, Darnell Michaels, to take her skydiving. Darnell, a third-year law student at the University of Maryland Carey School of Law, has no interest in diving himself, and he has unsuccessfully tried to dissuade Mindy from diving on several occasions, as have her parents and his parents. Mindy and Darnell are planning to be married during the summer

---

[76] LANDES & POSNER, *supra* note 15, at 82.

[77] Robert Cooter & Thomas Ulen, *An Economic Case for Comparative Negligence*, 61 N.Y.U. L. REV. 1067 (1986).

[78] Samuel Rea, *The Economics of Comparative Negligence*, 7 INT'L REV. L. & ECON. 149 (1987).

[79] *See* Chapter 3 Appendix.

following their May 2019 graduation, and Mindy has agreed to Darnell's request that if and when the couple has children, Mindy will never skydive again.

Upon arriving at *Tandem Skydiving*, on the scheduled date, Mindy and Darnell meet with Mindy's instructor, Teddy Tandem, who informs the couple that Mindy will be videotaped reading and then signing the skydiving contract. At Mindy's request, Darnell reads it initially, and tells Mindy that the terms make him extremely uncomfortable, but that it is ultimately her decision whether she wishes to follow through with the dive. She does, initialing each paragraph, including 5, 10, and 17, and then signing the contract, before heading off for the tandem dive. The record of the events listed below is well documented because the tandem dive was videotaped by another skydiver for an additional fee.

Although the exit from the plane appears to have been uneventful, after the requisite drop, the parachute only partially deployed when initially released. It then fully deployed, causing Teddy not to deploy the backup parachute. But within about 2 to 3 seconds, a seemingly inconsequential tear in the fabric suddenly spread very quickly. Mindy observed the initial partial deployment and began to panic. Ted realized that the full parachute was likely to deploy in time, and he spent the next few seconds trying to provide appropriate verbal assurance to Mindy that the parachute would fully deploy despite the initial mishap. In fact, the expanded tear put Teddy and Mindy into an uncontrolled spin. Although Teddy had deployed the backup chute when he first realized the spin, by then there was not enough time to recover, and the two died in a tragic fall.

Teddy, the owner of the company, was extremely experienced, having been a professional skydiver for over fifteen years, and having owned his own diving company for eight years. Darnell filed suit, claiming a variety of tort-based causes of action, premised on claims of negligence and gross negligence.[80] Darnell seeks compensatory damages and punitive damages. Tandem Skydiving, and its insurer, Parachuting Insurance Inc., moved to dismiss. Assume that the preceding facts are not in dispute.

The following data appears on the *United States Parachute Association* Website:[81]

> The sport of skydiving continues to improve its safety record. In 2016, USPA recorded 21 fatal skydiving accidents in the U.S. out of roughly 3.2 million jumps. That's one fatality per 153,357 jumps—one of the lowest rates in the sport's history! Tandem skydiving has an even better safety record, with one student fatality per 500,000 tandem jumps over the past decade. According to the National Safety Council, a person is much more likely to be killed getting struck by lightning or stung by a bee.
>
> In the 1970s, the sport averaged 42.5 skydiving fatalities per year. Since then, the average has dropped each decade. In the 1980s, the average was 34.1; in the 1990s, the average was 32.3, and in the first decade of the new millennium (2000–2009), the average dropped again to 25.8. Over the past seven years, the annual average continues its decline to 22.1.

---

[80] These include: wrongful death, negligent infliction of emotional distress, reckless infliction of emotional distress, and fraud and misrepresentation.

[81] *Skydiving Safety*, USPA.ORG., https://uspa.org/Find/FAQs/Safety (last visited Mar. 22, 2018).

> With 14 fatalities, 1961—the first year records were kept—stands as the year with the fewest skydiving fatalities. However, USPA was considerably smaller then, with just 3,353 members, and the total number of jumps was far fewer than today.

The website further states:

> In 2016, USPA members in the U.S. reported 2,129 requiring a medical care facility. That's approximately 1 injury per 1,515 skydives.
>
> These safety records stand as a testament to decades of strict safety standards, training policies and programs, including a USPA Safety Day taking place every March, as well as improvements in skydiving equipment over the years.
>
> Skydiving involves inherent risks, but most skydiving accidents result from human error. With proper preparation and good judgment, skydivers can minimize those risks. Thanks to safer equipment, better training and the staffs at more than 240 USPA-affiliated skydiving centers across the country, skydiving continues to become safer.[82]

At trial, uncontested evidence reveals that a new employee of the company, Phil Packer, packed the parachute. The evidence further suggests that Packer failed in either of two respects: (1) he neglected to double check the integrity of the entire chute prior to repacking, a process that might have revealed the initial tear, or (2) following a proper inspection, he accidentally allowed the chute to come into contact with one of the metal components or another sharp object resulting in piercing and a minor tear that compromised the parachute's integrity. The evidence also reveals that given his different level of experience, had Teddy packed the chute himself, he most likely that he would have seen any prior defect and that he would not have allowed any sharp object to come into contact with the chute.

QUESTIONS

1. Based on the economic analysis of Tort law, should the suit be either dismissed or resolved in defendant's favor on motion for summary judgment based on the skydiving contract or, instead, should it proceed to trial?

2. Does your answer depend on whether a jury finds that a cause of the accident was Packer's negligence or gross negligence in either damaging the chute or failing to recognize prior damage?

3. Does your answer depend on whether the jury finds that Teddy Tandem was negligent in failing to maintain focus in the drop, thereby disallowing sufficient time to rely on the back-up chute?

4. Does your answer depend on whether Mindy Able's behavior during the drop contributed to Teddy Tandem's failure to respond more effectively during the dive?

We will revisit this skydiving hypothetic in Chapter 4.

82 *Id.*

B. Tarasoff v. Regents of the University of California[83]

In the landmark case of *Tarasoff v. Regents of the University of California*, a young man had a failed relationship with a woman at the University of California at Berkeley and found himself in a state of deep depression coupled with a record of erratic behaviors. He was successfully persuaded to see a psychotherapist, and in the course of treatment he disclosed his intent to murder the woman with whom he had been involved. As time went on, the treating therapist issued warnings to the police as he was concerned about the stated intent and erratic behavior, but he did not bring the information to the woman herself. After taking a trip, the young man returned to California, whereupon he located and murdered his former girlfriend. The family filed suit against the therapist, his supervisor, and the police.

Following a ruling in the state superior court sustaining defendants' demurrers (roughly equivalent to a motion to dismiss within federal practice), the California Supreme Court issued a partial affirmance and partial reversal and remand. The court ordered the lower court to proceed on the claim against the psychotherapist and his supervisor for failing to notify the victim of the risk of physical harm to her, but not for failing to forcibly commit the patient. The court also affirmed the dismissal against the police. Relevant excerpts from the three main opinions of the Supreme Court of California follow. At the end, you will be asked to evaluate the various opinions based on the economic theory of tort law as set out in Chapter 3.

Tobriner, J., for a majority:

> On October 27, 1969, Prosenjit Poddar killed Tatiana Tarasoff. Plaintiffs, Tatiana's parents, allege that two months earlier Poddar confided his intention to kill Tatiana to Dr. Lawrence Moore, a psychologist employed by the Cowell Memorial Hospital at the University of California at Berkeley. They allege that on Moore's request, the campus police briefly detained Poddar, but released him when he appeared rational. They further claim that Dr. Harvey Powelson, Moore's superior, then directed that no further action be taken to detain Poddar. No one warned plaintiffs of Tatiana's peril.
>
> Concluding that these facts set forth causes of action against neither therapists and policemen involved, nor against the Regents of the University of California as their employer, the superior court sustained defendants' demurrers to plaintiffs' second amended complaints without leave to amend. This appeal ensued.
>
> Plaintiffs' complaints predicate liability on two grounds: defendants' failure to warn plaintiffs of the impending danger and their failure to bring about Poddar's confinement pursuant to the Lanterman-Petris-Short Act (Welf. & Inst.Code, s 5000ff.) Defendants, in turn, assert that they owed no duty of reasonable care to Tatiana and that they are immune from suit under the California Tort Claims Act of 1963 (Gov. Code, s 810ff.).

[83] 551 P.2d 334 (Cal. 1976).

> We shall explain that defendant therapists cannot escape liability merely because Tatiana herself was not their patient. When a therapist determines, or pursuant to the standards of his profession should determine, that his patient presents a serious danger of violence to another, he incurs an obligation to use reasonable care to protect the intended victim against such danger. The discharge of this duty may require the therapist to take one or more of various steps, depending upon the nature of the case. Thus it may call for him to warn the intended victim or others likely to apprise the victim of the danger, to notify the police, or to take whatever other steps are reasonably necessary under the circumstances.
>
> In the case at bar, plaintiffs admit that defendant therapists notified the police, but argue on appeal that the therapists failed to exercise reasonable care to protect Tatiana in that they did not confine Poddar and did not warn Tatiana or others likely to apprise her of the danger. Defendant therapists, however, are public employees. Consequently, to the extent that plaintiffs seek to predicate liability upon the therapists' failure to bring about Poddar's confinement, the therapists can claim immunity under Government Code section 856. No specific statutory provision, however, shields them from liability based upon failure to warn Tatiana or others likely to apprise her of the danger, and Government Code section 820.2 does not protect such failure as an exercise of discretion.
>
> Plaintiffs therefore can amend their complaints to allege that, regardless of the therapists' unsuccessful attempt to confine Poddar, since they knew that Poddar was at large and dangerous, their failure to warn Tatiana or others likely to apprise her of the danger constituted a breach of the therapists' duty to exercise reasonable care to protect Tatiana.

In assessing the critical question of duty of care, the majority continued:

> The most important of these considerations in establishing duty is foreseeability. As a general principle, a 'defendant owes a duty of care to all persons who are foreseeably endangered by his conduct, with respect to all risks which make the conduct unreasonably dangerous.' . . . As we shall explain, however, when the avoidance of foreseeable harm requires a defendant to control the conduct of another person, or to warn of such conduct, the common law has traditionally imposed liability only if the defendant bears some special relationship to the dangerous person or to the potential victim. Since the relationship between a therapist and his patient satisfies this requirement, we need not here decide whether foreseeability alone is sufficient to create a duty to exercise reasonably care to protect a potential victim of another's conduct.
>
> Although, as we have stated above, under the common law, as a general rule, one person owed no duty to control the conduct of another . . . nor to warn those endangered by such conduct (Rest.2d Torts . . . .; Prosser, Law of Torts (4th ed. 1971) s 56, p. 341), the courts have carved out an exception to this rule in cases in which the defendant stands in some special relationship to

either the person whose conduct needs to be controlled or in a relationship to the foreseeable victim of that conduct (see Rest.2d Torts, Supra, ss 315—320). Applying this exception to the present case, we note that a relationship of defendant therapists to either Tatiana or Poddar will suffice to establish a duty of care; as explained in section 315 of the Restatement Second of Torts, a duty of care may arise from either '(a) a special relation . . . between the actor and the third person which imposes a duty upon the actor to control the third person's conduct, or (b) a special relation . . . between the actor and the other which gives to the other a right of protection.'

In discussing the specific roles of a psychiatrist and psychologist, the court concluded:

The role of the psychiatrist, who is indeed a practitioner of medicine, and that of the psychologist who performs an allied function, are like that of the physician who must conform to the standards of the profession and who must often make diagnoses and predictions based upon such evaluations. Thus the judgment of the therapist in diagnosing emotional disorders and in predicting whether a patient presents a serious danger of violence is comparable to the judgment which doctors and professionals must regularly render under accepted rules of responsibility.

We recognize the difficulty that a therapist encounters in attempting to forecast whether a patient presents a serious danger of violence. Obviously we do not require that the therapist, in making that determination, render a perfect performance; the therapist need only exercise 'that reasonable degree of skill, knowledge, and care ordinarily possessed and exercised by members of (that professional specialty) under similar circumstances.' . . . Within the broad range of reasonable practice and treatment in which professional opinion and judgment may differ, the therapist is free to exercise his or her own best judgment without liability; proof, aided by hindsight, that he or she judged wrongly is insufficient to establish negligence.

In the instant case, however, the pleadings do not raise any question as to failure of defendant therapists to predict that Poddar presented a serious danger of violence. On the contrary, the present complaints allege that defendant therapists did in fact predict that Poddar would kill, but were negligent in failing to warn.

The Court added:

We realize that the open and confidential character of psychotherapeutic dialogue encourages patients to express threats of violence, few of which are ever executed. Certainly a therapist should not be encouraged routinely to reveal such threats; such disclosures could seriously disrupt the patient's relationship with his therapist and with the persons threatened. To the contrary, the therapist's obligations to his patient require that he not disclose a confidence unless such disclosure is necessary to avert danger to others, and even then that he do so discreetly, and in a fashion that would preserve the

> privacy of his patient to the fullest extent compatible with the prevention of the threatened danger.

The court concluded:

> For the reasons stated, we conclude that plaintiffs can amend their complaints to state a cause of action against defendant therapists by asserting that the therapists in fact determined that Poddar presented a serious danger of violence to Tatiana, or pursuant to the standards of their profession should have so determined, but nevertheless failed to exercise reasonable care to protect her from that danger. To the extent, however, that plaintiffs base their claim that defendant therapists breached that duty because they failed to procure Poddar's confinement, the therapists find immunity in Government Code section 856. Further, as to the police defendants we conclude that plaintiffs have failed to show that the trial court erred in sustaining their demurrer without leave to amend.

Writing a partial concurrence and partial dissent, Justice Mosk stated:

> I concur in the result in this instance only because the complaints allege that defendant therapists did in fact predict that Poddar would kill and were therefore negligent in failing to warn of that danger. Thus the issue here is very narrow: we are not concerned with whether the therapists, pursuant to the standards of their profession, 'should have' predicted potential violence; they allegedly did so in actuality. Under these limited circumstances I agree that a cause of action can be stated.
>
> Whether plaintiffs can ultimately prevail is problematical at best. As the complaints admit, the therapists did notify the police that Poddar was planning to kill a girl identifiable as Tatiana. While I doubt that more should be required, this issue may be raised in defense and its determination is a question of fact.
>
> I cannot concur, however, in the majority's rule that a therapist may be held liable for failing to predict his patient's tendency to violence if other practitioners, pursuant to the 'standards of the profession,' would have done so. The question is, what standards? Defendants and a responsible amicus curiae, supported by an impressive body of literature discussed at length in our recent opinion in People v. Burnick (1975) 14 Cal.3d 306, 121 Cal. Rptr. 488, 535 P.2d 352, demonstrate that psychiatric predictions of violence are inherently unreliable.
>
> In *Burnick* . . . we observed: 'In the light of recent studies it is no longer heresy to question the reliability of psychiatric predictions. Psychiatrists themselves would be the first to admit that however desirable an infallible crystal ball might be, it is not among the tools of their profession. It must be conceded that psychiatrists still experience considerable difficulty in confidently and accurately *diagnosing* mental illness. Yet those difficulties are multiplied manyfold when psychiatrists venture from diagnosis to prognosis and undertake to predict the consequences of such illness: "A diagnosis of mental illness tells us nothing about whether the person so diagnosed is or is not dangerous. Some mental patients are dangerous, some are not. Perhaps the

psychiatrist is an expert at deciding whether a person is mentally ill, but is he an expert at predicting which of the persons so diagnosed are dangerous? Sane people, too, are dangerous, and it may legitimately be inquired whether there is anything in the education, training or experience of psychiatrists which renders them particularly adept at predicting dangerous behavior. Predictions of dangerous behavior, no matter who makes them, are incredibly inaccurate, and there is a growing consensus that psychiatrists are not uniquely qualified to predict dangerous behavior and are, in fact, less accurate in their predictions than other professionals."

Writing in dissent, Justice Clark stated:

Until today's majority opinion, both legal and medical authorities have agreed that confidentiality is essential to effectively treat the mentally ill, and that imposing a duty on doctors to disclose patient threats to potential victims would greatly impair treatment. Further, recognizing that effective treatment and society's safety are necessarily intertwined, the Legislature has already decided effective and confidential treatment is preferred over imposition of a duty to warn.

The issue whether effective treatment for the mentally ill should be sacrificed to a system of warnings is, in my opinion, properly one for the Legislature, and we are bound by its judgment. Moreover, even in the absence of clear legislative direction, we must reach the same conclusion because imposing the majority's new duty is certain to result in a net increase in violence.

The majority rejects the balance achieved by the Legislature's Lanterman-Petris-Short Act. (Welf. & Inst. Code, s 5000 et seq., hereafter the act.) In addition, the majority fails to recognize that, even absent the act, overwhelming policy considerations mandate against sacrificing fundamental patient interests without gaining a corresponding increase in public benefit.

Justice Clark explained his concern about the ruling's effect on treatment as follows:

First, without substantial assurance of confidentiality, those requiring treatment will be deterred from seeking assistance. . . . It remains an unfortunate fact in our society that people seeking psychiatric guidance tend to become stigmatized. Apprehension of such stigma—apparently increased by the propensity of people considering treatment to see themselves in the worst possible light—creates a well-recognized reluctance to seek aid. . . . This reluctance is alleviated by the psychiatrist's assurance of confidentiality.

Justice Clark concluded:

The tragedy of Tatiana Tarasoff has led the majority to disregard the clear legislative mandate of the Lanterman-Petris-Short Act. Worse, the majority impedes medical treatment, resulting in increased violence from—and deprivation of liberty to—the mentally ill.

QUESTIONS

1. How would you assess the *Tarasoff* ruling based on the economic theory of tort law?

2. Based upon economic analysis of tort law, which of the opinions do you find more persuasive, and why?

3. Is it possible to evaluate *Tarasoff* without studying its empirical effects on patient treatment? Why or why not?

4. Assume that psychotherapists have responded to the ruling, in part, by requiring that patients sign a statement saying that if their therapy reveals what the therapist perceives as a threat of harm to self or others, then patient-client confidentiality will be waived as needed to abate the perceived risk. What if any concern does this raise for the objective of reducing the social cost of *Tarasoff*-like tragedies?

5. If you believe empirical evidence is required, what kind of empirical test could you devise to determine whether the ruling is or is not social welfare enhancing?

IV. CHAPTER 3 APPENDIX

Altitude Express Inc
DBA Skydive Long Island

Date ________

________ Last Name ____ MI ________ First Name

________ Street Address

________ City/ Town ____ State ____ Zip Code

________ Mailing Address

____ Home Phone ____ Mobile Phone ____ E-Mail Address

___/___/___ Birth Date ____ Age ____ Height ____ Weight lbs.

Would you like to be on our mailing list? Yes / No (Please circle one)

Drivers License # ________ Occupation ________

How Did You Hear About Us? ________

Emergency Contact Information:

________ Name ________ Relationship

________ Street Address

________ Home Phone ________ Alternate Phone

Medical Certificate:

USPA recommends that all parachutists either receive an FAA Class III Medical Examination or be examined by a medical physician prior to making parachute jumps. In lieu of these qualifications, members must complete the following medical certificate if they are to participate in parachute jumps.

I hereby certify that I have no physical infirmity, am not under treatment for any physical infirmity or chronic ailment, or injury of any nature, and that I have never been treated for any of the following: cardiac or pulmonary condition or disease, diabetes, fainting spells or convulsions, nervous disorder, kidney or related disease, high or low blood pressure.

I certify that all statements in this application are true and correct to the best of my knowledge, and that the medical facts are correct as stated.

________ **Signature** ________ **Date**

Experienced Skydivers Only:

____ USPA # ____ Exp. Date ________ License Number & Current Ratings

___/___/___ Reserve Pack Date ________ Date of Last Jump & Location ________ Total Number of Jumps

________ Parachute Make & Size

Information we can release: Phone Number / Address / E-mail / None

Last Name

First Name

AGREEMENT, RELEASE OF LIABILITY & ASSUMPTION OF RISK

IN CONSIDERATION of being permitted to utilize the facilities and equipment of ALTITUDE EXPRESS INC., D.B.A. SKYDIVE LONG ISLAND (and its associated entities) to engage in parachute activities, ground instruction, flying and related activities, skydiving, freefall and Tandem jumping, hereinafter collectively referred to as "parachute/ skydiving activities", as defined in paragraph 6 in this contract, I HEREBY AGREE AS FOLLOWS:

1. I understand that this document is a binding contract between myself and the entities described herein as SKYDIVE LONG ISLAND, and I certify that I am of legal age and under no legal disability which would prevent me from entering into a binding contract.

(____)
(Initial)

2. I am aware that "parachuting/ skydiving activities" are **inherently dangerous and may result in injury or death** and agree that the unforeseen may happen and no one can delineate all risks or possibilities of error. Therefore, I specifically include in this Release, any injury resulting from any occurrence, whether foreseen or unforeseen, and whether contemplated or not contemplated which is in any way connected with my "parachuting/ skydiving activities" and/ or on presence of the premises commonly know as CALVERTON ENTERPRISE PARK, the former GRUMMAN FACILITY, The Town of RIVERHEAD, or any other place or entity connected with SKYDIVE LONG ISLAND.

(____)
(Initial)

3. PARTIES INCLUDED: I understand that this Agreement, Release of Liability and Assumption of Risk includes but is not limited to, Ray Maynard, SKYDIVE LONG ISLAND, and any of its officers, board members, and shareholders, its or their agents, customers, associated entities, employees, volunteers, pilots, instructors, jumpmasters, the owners of the aircraft (which shall also include but not be limited to airfoils and balloons), SKYDIVE LONG ISLAND, CALVERTON ENTERPRISE PARK, the former GRUMMAN FACILITY, The Town of RIVERHEAD COMMUNITY DEVELOPMENT AGENCY, and M-GBC, LLC, the owners of any land utilized for "skydiving/ parachuting activities", adjacent property owners, the United States Parachute Association and its members, anyone working with or for SKYDIVE LONG ISLAND, any manufacturer of any piece of equipment or gear which I may use or am using at the time of my **INJURY** or **DEATH** and anyone involved in any way, shape, form, or manner in my "skydiving/ parachuting activities", and specifically including but not limited to tandem or experimental test parachute jumping to include tandem parachute jumping, hereinafter collectively referred to in this Agreement, Release of Liability and Assumption of Risk as SKYDIVE LONG ISLAND.

(____)
(Initial)

4. This entire Contract, Release of Liability and Assumption of Risk is expanded to include all parties mentioned anywhere in the body of the document by name or by category, all vendors or suppliers of materials or equipment for "skydiving/ parachuting activities", including but not limited to the manufacturer of the equipment, its employees, directors, officers and shareholders, and all associated entities, shareholders, partners, employees and all other persons in any way associated with any entity mentioned, either specifically or by implication, in the body of this document.

(____)
(Initial)

5. RISKS CONTEMPLATED: This Agreement is made in contemplation of all "skydiving/ parachuting activities", which for purposes of this agreement shall include but not be limited to all occurrences contemplated or not contemplated, foreseen and unforeseen, instruction, parachute jumping, tandem or experimental test parachute jumping, ground instruction, flying and related activities, the exit from the aircraft, skydiving, freefall, time under the canopy, the landing, any rescue operations or attempts by SKYDIVE LONG ISLAND, whether on or off the designated landing area, or facilities used

by SKYDIVE LONG ISLAND, ground transportation provided to me by any entity in any way associated with SKYDIVE LONG ISLAND, and any activity whatsoever in any way, shape, form, or manner connected with my "skydiving/ parachuting activities" or my presence on or near the facility and grounds of SKYDIVE LONG ISLAND, and/or the airport which is used for my "skydiving/ parachuting activities". These risks shall be referred to for the purposes of this Agreement as "skydiving/ parachuting activities".

(____)
(Initial)

6. PARTIES BOUND BY THIS AGREEMENT: It is my understanding and intention that this Agreement, Release of Liability, and Assumption of Risk be binding not only on myself, but on anyone or any entity, including my estate and my heirs, that may be able to or do sue because of my **INJURY** or **DEATH**. It is further my understanding and agreement that this Release is intended to and does in fact release SKYDIVE LONG ISLAND as defined in paragraph 3 from any and all claims or obligations whatsoever, foreseen and unforeseen, contemplated or not contemplated, arising in any way from my participation in "skydiving/ parachuting activities", even if caused by the negligence or other fault of SKYDIVE LONG ISLAND.

(____)
(Initial)

7. RELEASE OF LIABILITY: I hereby release and discharge SKYDIVE LONG ISLAND from any and all liability, claims, demands or causes of action that I may hereafter have for injuries or damages arising out of my participation in "skydiving/ parachuting activities" **even if caused by negligence or other fault** of SKYDIVE LONG ISLAND.

(____)
(Initial)

8. COVENANT NOT TO SUE: I further agree that I WILL NOT SUE OR MAKE CLAIM AGAINST SKYDIVE LONG ISLAND, CALVERTON ENTERPRISE PARK, or The Town of RIVERHEAD COMMUNITY DEVELOPMENT AGENCY and M-GBC, LLC for damages or other losses sustained as a result of my participation in "skydiving/ parachuting activities" **even if caused by negligence or other fault** of SKYDIVE LONG ISLAND.

(____)
(Initial)

9. INDEMNIFICATION AND HOLD HARMLESS: I also agree to INDEMNIFY and HOLD SKYDIVE LONG ISLAND, CALVERTON ENTERPRISE PARK, The Town of RIVERHEAD COMMUNITY DEVELOPMENT AGENCY, M-GBC, LLC HARMLESS from all claims, judgments and costs, including but not limited to actual attorney's fees, and to reimburse them for any expenses whatsoever incurred in connection with any action brought as a result of my participation in "skydiving/ parachuting activities", including but not limited to actions brought by myself or on behalf of my myself or my estate and further acknowledge that in the event of any lawsuit, this Release can and will be used against me by SKYDIVE LONG ISLAND.

(____)
(Initial)

10. ASSUMPTION OF RISK: I understand and acknowledge that "skydiving/ parachuting activities" are inherently dangerous and I EXPRESSLY AND VOLUNTARILY ASSUME ALL RISK OF DEATH OR PERSONAL INJURY SUSTAINED WHILE PARTICIPATING IN "SKYDIVING/ PARACHUTING ACTIVITIES" WHETHER SUCH RISK IS FORESEEN OR UNFORESEEN, CONTEMPLATED OR NOT CONTEMPLATED, AND WHETHER OR NOT CAUSED BY THE NEGLIGENCE OR OTHER FAULT OF SKYDIVE LONG ISLAND including but not limited to equipment malfunction from whatever cause, inadequate training, any deficiencies in the landing area, rescue attempts, bad landings or any other cause whatsoever, including but not limited to those set forth in paragraph 5, even if those injuries are caused by the negligence or any other fault of SKYDIVE LONG ISLAND.

(____)
(Initial)

11. LIMITATION OF WARRANTY: SKYDIVE LONG ISLAND hereby warrants that the equipment provided by SKYDIVE LONG ISLAND has been previously used for "skydiving/ parachuting activities". This warranty is the only warranty made and is made in lieu of any other warranties, expressed or implied, including but not limited to warranty of merchantability or fitness for a particular purpose.

I have read the above paragraph, acknowledge that I understand it and accept the limitation of warranty.

(____)
(Initial)

12. In the event any agent of SKYDIVE LONG ISLAND is guilty of willful and wanton, or any conduct outside the scope of this contract, I agree that that agent's action shall be beyond the scope of his/her employment and not attributable to anyone on any agency theory, or any other theory.

(____)
(Initial)

13. If I am making a student jump, I understand that I will be wearing a harness which will need to be adjusted by the jumpmaster. If my jump is a tandem jump, I understand that the tandem master will attach my harness to his and that this will put my body in close proximity to that of the tandem master. I specifically agree to this physical contact between the tandem master and myself.

(____)
(Initial)

14. DURATION OF RELEASE: It is my understanding and intention that this Release and Agreement be effective not only for my first jump but for any subsequent jumps or "skydiving/ parachuting activities" and shall be in full force and effect from the signing of this Agreement until such time it is cancelled by SKYDIVE LONG ISLAND.

(____)
(Initial)

15. I hereby agree to waive any and all duty of care, whether by omission or commission, or any other duty which may be owed to me by SKYDIVE LONG ISLAND.

(____)
(Initial)

16. ENFORCEABILITY: I agree that if any portions of this Agreement, Release of Liability and Assumption of Risk are found to be unenforceable or against public policy, that only that portion shall fall, but I specifically waive any unenforceability or any public policy argument that I may make or that may be made on behalf of my estate or by anyone who would sure because of my injury or death.

(____)
(Initial)

17. I am, by reading this paragraph, being made aware that the general rule is that this type of document is to be narrowly construed and ambiguities are to be decided against the person or entity preparing the document. By initialing this paragraph, I expressly waive that rule and specifically agree that this document be broadly construed in favor of SKYDIVE LONG ISLAND and against me and that all ambiguities be resolved in favor of SKYDIVE LONG ISLAND.

(____)
(Initial)

18. It is further agreed between the parties that no matter where venue lies, any lawsuits shall be filed in State Court of Suffolk County, New York. It is further agreed that in the event any lawsuit is filed other than in State Court of Suffolk County, New York or such other locations as SKYDIVE LONG ISLAND shall specify, on motion and at the option of SKYDIVE LONG ISLAND.

(____)
(Initial)

19. I hereby agree to reimburse SKYDIVE LONG ISLAND for loss or damage to any equipment of any kind whatsoever caused by my personal negligence or other wrongdoing.

(____)
(Initial)

20. I hereby authorize SKYDIVE LONG ISLAND or its assignee to take any photographs and videos as they may deem appropriate of myself or my party and to use those photographs and videos in such a manner as they may deem appropriate, including but not limited to uploading them on Facebook, You-Tube, or any other social networking website. I specifically waive any interest, proprietary or otherwise, I may have in such photographs.

(____)
(Initial)

21. I further acknowledge that I have been shown a video featuring an attorney who in general terms has explained the terms and conditions of this Release. I further acknowledge that I have been told that I do not have to go forward at this time and that any monies that I have tendered prior to this date, will be refunded in the event I chose not to continue.

(____)
(Initial)

22. I GIVE UP LEGAL RIGHTS: I understand that by signing this document I am giving up important legal rights and it is my intention to do so.

(____)
(Initial)

23. Even though I may have failed to initial some or all of the paragraphs of this document, I still intend to be bound by all paragraphs. I further understand that this document can only be amended in writing, with the amendment signed by the attorney for the drop zone and myself.

(____)
(Initial)

24. UNDERSTANDING OF AGREEMENT: I HEREBY CERTIFY THAT I HAVE READ AND UNDERSTAND THE CONTENTS OF THIS DOCUMENT AND I WISH TO BE BOUND BY ITS TERMS AND I UNDERSTAND THAT BY SIGNING THIS, I HAVE FOREVER GIVEN UP IMPORTANT LEGAL RIGHTS.

(____)
(Initial)

I UNDERSTAND THAT WHEN I SIGN THIS DOCUMENT, I WILL BE GIVING UP ANY AND ALL RIGHTS WHICH I OR MY HEIRS MAY HAVE TO SUE ANYONE IN ANYWAY, SHAPE OR FORM, ASSOCIATED WITH MY SKYDIVE, EVEN IF THE ENTITY I INTEND TO SUE HAS CAUSED MY INJURY OR DEATH BY THEIR NEGLIGENCE.

I HAVE BEEN GIVEN AN OPPORTUNITY TO READ THIS DOCUMENT. I HAVE DONE SO. I UNDERSTAND ITS CONTENT. I INTEND THAT NOT ONLY I, BUT ALSO MY HEIRS, MY FAMILY AND ANYONE WHO MIGHT ACT ON MY BEHALF IN ANY CAPACITY WHATSOEVER BE BOUND BY ITS TERMS.

READ BEFORE YOU SIGN. YOU ARE GIVING UP IMPORTANT LEGAL RIGHTS.

DATED THE ____________ DAY OF ____________(MONTH), 20________

______________________________________SIGNATURE

______________________________________PRINT YOUR NAME

______________________________________WITNESS SIGNATURE

______________________________________PRINT WITNESS NAME

CHAPTER 4

Tort Law (Part 2)

Introduction

This chapter extends the basic economic model of Tort law from Chapter 3. Section I introduces problems of causation, activity level (as distinguished from level of care), and the role of insurance and litigation costs. Section II discusses products liability law, which implicates parties who sometimes have preexisting relationships. Section III concludes with a brief discussion of medical malpractice, environmental accidents, and workplace accidents.

I. EXTENSIONS OF THE BASIC ACCIDENT MODEL

This section discusses several extensions to the basic accident model, including the meaning and function of causation in tort law, and the impact of activity levels on accident risk. A final section considers liability insurance and litigation costs, the economic function of punitive damages, and the problem of the judgment-proof defendant.

A. Causation

As discussed above, in order to recover damages in a tort suit, the victim must first prove that the injurer "caused" her harm. Until now we have ignored this requirement by assuming that causation was not in dispute. In some accident cases, however, the question of whether or not the injurer caused the victim's injuries is the primary issue to be litigated. In a tort suit, there are two separate but related causation components: *cause in fact* and *scope of liability (or proximate cause)*. To simplify the presentation, we will explore these concepts in the context of the unilateral care model.

1. Cause in Fact

The first notion of causation, *cause in fact*, corresponds to the common sense idea of causation. That is, we say that an injurer's action caused an accident if the accident would not have occurred without the injurer's action or inaction. The test for cause in fact is therefore the "but-for" test. Although our analysis of tort law to this point has ignored this requirement, cause in fact is in one sense implicit in the functional relationship between the level of care and accident risk. That relationship forms the foundation of the economic model of accidents. It is embodied in the downward sloping *ED* (expected damages from failing to take appropriate precautions) curve in Figure 3:1 and in the *PL* (probability of accident times impact) component of the Hand Negligence test.[1]

Mark Grady offered another perspective on cause in fact on which Marcel Kahan then elaborated.[2] According to this view, an injurer is liable for a victim's harm *only if* the injurer was negligent, *and if that negligence caused the victim's harm.* The following example, adapted from Kahan,[3] illustrates the impact of adding the causation requirement to negligence.

Table 4:1. Data for the Cause-in-Fact Example

Action	Cost of care ($)	Accidental cost ($)	Total cost ($)
No net	0	200	200
Net behind goals	50	75	125
Net around rink	100	50	150

Suppose that during a hockey game pucks occasionally fly over the glass and injure fans in the stands. To reduce the risk, the owner of the rink can either install a net behind the goals, which is where most shots go, or she can install nets around the entire rink. The costs and benefits of the various options are shown in Table 4:1. The top row shows the outcome if no action is taken, and the next two show the outcomes with a net behind the goals and around the rink, respectively. Based on the total costs as computed in the final column, the socially optimal (cost minimizing) choice is to install a net behind the goals only. Let us suppose, therefore, that the due standard of care under a negligence rule is set at that level. Thus, the rink owner will be judged negligent if she fails to install a net of any kind and a fan is injured as a result.

Now consider how the negligence rule works in this case, with or without the cause-in-fact requirement. Column 2 in Table 4:2 shows the injurer's costs under a standard negligence rule without a requirement of cause in fact. The first row shows the case where the rink owner negligently fails to install a net behind the goals, which makes him fully liable for the $200 in expected damages. In the other two cases—where he installs a net behind the goals only (row 2) and around the entire rink (row 3)—he is not negligent and therefore only incurs the cost of care. As usual, costs are minimized when parties satisfy the due care standard, making that the optimal strategy.

Now consider column 3, which shows the rink owner's costs under a negligence rule with a cause-in-fact limitation. The only difference is in row 1, where the owner is

---

[1] *See supra* Chapter 3 at 80–82. *See also* Robert D. Cooter, *Punitive Damages for Deterrence: When and How Much?*, 40 ALA. L. REV. 1143 (1989).

[2] Mark Grady, *A New Positive Economic Theory of Negligence*, 92 YALE L.J. 799 (1983); Marcel Kahan, *Causation and Incentives to Take* Care *Under the Negligence Rule*, 18 J. LEGAL STUD. 427 (1989); Louis Visscher, *Wrongfulness as a Necessary Cause of the Losses—Removing an Alleged Difference between Strict Liability and Negligence*, 2 ECON. ANALYSIS L. REV. 188 (2011).

[3] *See generally* Marcel Kahan, *Causation and Incentives to Take* Care *Under the Negligence Rule*, 18 J. LEGAL STUD. 427 (1989) (developing a model of accidents including causation based on fence heights for a cricket field).

negligent. Although she is liable for damages in this case, she is only liable for those damages caused by her negligence, here her failure to install netting behind the goals. However, she is not liable for damages that would have occurred even if she had installed the netting behind the goals. Thus, her liability exposure is the difference between the expected damages with no netting and the expected damages with a netting behind the goals, or $200–$75=$125. In other words, this focuses on marginal cost of liability for no netting, meaning the difference between that cost and the cost of taking the efficient precaution of putting netting behind the goals. In the other two cases, where she installs a net, she is not liable for any damages and therefore only incurs the cost of installing the net, as was true under the standard negligence rule. The important point to notice is that the rink owner's costs are still minimized by just meeting the due standard of care. The only difference is that the reduction in costs from meeting the due standard (i.e., the difference in costs between rows one and two) is less dramatic.[4] This is reflected in Table 4:2.

Table 4:2. Negligence With and Without Cause in Fact

Action	Costs under negligence rule without cause in fact ($)	Cost under a negligence rule with cause in fact ($)
No net	200	125=200–75
Net behind goals only	50	50
Net everywhere	100	100

This discussion—and specifically the reduction in the dramatic discontinuity of liability by the defendant with the added causation requirement—illustrates something fundamental about the tort system.[5] Limiting suits to parties who have experienced an injury for which the injurer's conduct was a cause in fact reduces the potential scope of claimed injuries. Many parties who might be injured some time in the future lose their ability to raise a claim today. This is captured in the famous observation that "negligence in the air . . . will not do."[6] Of course it is possible that such individuals might never be injured as the injurer might alter her conduct prior to causing anyone an injury, or the negligent conduct might continue "in the air" without ever causing harm. In general, negligence suits arise with the coincidence of two unfortunate events, first, the injurer undertakes inadequate precaution, meaning she fails to satisfy the due care standard, and second, the victim happens to be in the wrong place at the wrong time, and is therefore injured as a consequence of the injurer's lack of due care. Do you believe that the inclusion of cause in fact is a sound policy judgment?[7]

---

[4] *See id.* at 440 (demonstrating that analysis is generalizable).

[5] We will later see that this also has implications for other areas of law. *See infra* Chapter 22 (discussing standing doctrine).

[6] Palsgraf v. Long Island R.R. Co., 162 N.E. 99, 99 (N.Y. 1928).

[7] We will later discuss the problem of market-share liability, which also involves a question of case in fact. *See infra* Part III.A.3.

2. *Scope of Liability (or Proximate Cause)*

In addition to cause in fact, a plaintiff must prove that the injurer's action (or failure to act) fell within the scope of liability that resulted in the accident. Although now treated as part of the scope of liability, historically this was commonly expressed in terms of *proximate cause*.[8] That amounts to proving that the connection between the injurer's negligence and the accident is not "too remote." The facts of the well-known case of *Palsgraf v. Long Island* R.R. illustrate this concept:[9]

> Plaintiff was standing on a platform of defendant's railroad after buying a ticket to go to Rockaway Beach. A train stopped at the station, bound for another place. Two men ran forward to catch it. One of the men reached the platform of the car without mishap, though the train was already moving. The other man, carrying a package, jumped aboard the car, but seemed unsteady as if about to fall. A guard on the car, who held the door open, reached forward to help him in, and another guard on the platform pushed him from behind. In this act, the package was dislodged, and fell upon the rails. It was a package of small size, about fifteen inches long, and was covered with newspaper. In fact, it contained fireworks, but there was nothing in its appearance to give notice of its contents. The fireworks when they fell exploded. The shock of the explosion threw down some scales at the other end of the platform many feet away. The scales struck the plaintiff, causing the injuries for which she sues.[10]

It is clear that the actions of the railroad employees satisfied the but-for test for causation in fact. The controlling issue was whether despite this, the railroad should have been absolved of liability for the victim's damages because causation was attenuated, or too remote. The court determined that it should have been and thus ruled in favor of the railroad.

One test for proximate cause is the "reasonable foreseeability test;" could a person placed in the position of the injurer at the time of the events leading to the accident reasonably have foreseen the consequences of his action? From this perspective, proximate cause is a forward-looking test, undertaken from a point in time before the accident occurred. By contrast, cause in fact looks backward, inquiring whether we can construct an account that links the present injury to the claimed negligent conduct as the "but for" cause. As with cause in fact, we are concerned with the consequences of proximate cause in encouraging efficient care.

Although these tests serve overlapping functions, there is an important reason for their combined use. The reasonable foresight test might help to counteract two potential

---

[8] The Restatement (Third) of Torts: Liability for Physical and Emotional Harm replaces the term "proximate cause" with "scope of liability," although even today, most courts and scholars continue to employ the term proximate cause. RESTATEMENT (THIRD) OF TORTS: LIABILITY FOR PHYSICAL AND EMOTIONAL HARM, Spec. Note (AM. LAW INST. 2016). Notably, in *Palsgraf* itself, Judge Cardozo used the term "duty" rather than "proximate cause" even though the case is generally treated, as it is here, as the starting point in introducing the latter concept. *See Palsgraf*, 162 N.E. at 100 ("Even then, the orbit of the danger as disclosed to the eye of reasonable vigilance would be the orbit of *the duty*.") (emphasis added).

[9] 162 N.E. 99.

[10] *Id.* at 99.

biases that could otherwise affect the practical application of the Marginal Hand Test.[11] Recall that for each additional precaution taken, the marginal benefit declines. As a result, and somewhat counter-intuitively, plaintiffs risk being biased in favor of understating the level of precaution that the defendant should have taken. That is because inadequate care is more easily demonstrated for care choices that fall far short of the optimum care level, as the marginal benefit of care is then substantially larger than the marginal cost. This problem is exacerbated by a hindsight bias. After the accident has occurred, it is relatively easy to identify concrete measures that could have been taken to avoid the harm even if from a forward-looking perspective, the failure to undertake that precaution appears far less likely to cause an injury. This is captured in the adage that "hindsight is 20/20."

These combined biases—marginal basis and hindsight bias—create the risk that potential future tortfeasors might place too low a set of expectations on the appropriate level of care than they might had the plaintiff instead focused her claim on more proximate precautions for which the marginal costs and benefits were more evenly balanced. The forward-looking proximate cause test helps counteract these combined biases by putting a lower bound on untaken precautions that plaintiffs can select as the basis for negligence under the Marginal Hand test. If the plaintiff chooses an untaken precaution that appears to be low-cost but that is also attenuated, she risks losing the case on causation grounds.

3. Uncertain Breach of Duty or Causation (and res ipsa loquitur*)*

In some situations, a plaintiff might have difficulty proving which of several defendants breached a duty of care resulting in an accident. This can arise either due to a lack of evidence, or because there are multiple possible causes for his injury. When this is true, injurers may be overly insulated from liability, resulting in insufficient precaution. The law does, however, provide some remedies for this problem. In some cases, for example, the plaintiff may not be able to prove that a specific defendant breached a duty of care, or otherwise caused her harm, even though the circumstances make it more likely than not that one of the defendants did so. When this is true, the doctrine of *res ipsa loquitur* (meaning, "the thing speaks for itself") shifts the burden of proof to the defendant to prove that she did not breach the duty of care or was *not* the cause of the accident.

For example, in *Escola v. Coca Cola*,[12] the plaintiff, a waitress, was injured when a Coca Cola bottle exploded. The plaintiff alleged negligence on the part of the bottler, but she was unable to provide specific evidence of negligence. The court nevertheless held the bottler liable on the ground that the bottle would not have exploded if not for a faulty manufacturing process. There are two possible ways to assess the court's judgment. One is reconcilable with the premise of *res ipsa loquitur*, that the manufacturer was necessarily

[11] This concept was introduced in Chapter 3, *supra* at 80–82.

[12] 150 P.2d 436 (Cal. 1944).

negligent, but that the negligence could not be proven. The other rests on an alternative economic analysis involving risk spreading.[13]

Because *res ipsa loquitur* implies that the bottle would not have exploded but for a negligent manufacturing process, the ruling could be read narrowly to imply that absent specific proof of negligence, manufacturers are liable when there is no other explanation than a lack of due care to explain the injuries attributable to their products. Alternatively, it is possible that even with due care, some minuscule percentage of bottles is apt to come out with a defect that could result in an explosion as a consequence of the problem of residual risk. If so, then even if the defendant undertook all reasonable precautions, the outcome might have been justified on the alternative ground that as between the plaintiff and the defendant, the latter is better suited to carry the burden associated with the residual risk.

This analysis would then transform the case from *res ipsa loquitur* to strict products liability, a subject that we explore more fully below.[14] The two approaches are historically related. Although the doctrine has more longstanding roots,[15] *res ipsa loquitur* gained popularity in part as a response to the increasing complexity of modern consumer products, about which consumers have limited information. Shifting of the burden of proof to defendants reflects their greater knowledge and control of the manufacturing process. In this way, the *res ipsa loquitur* doctrine effectively represents a move in the direction of strict products liability while nominally adhering to the framework of negligence.

Another potential benefit of this approach is in allowing the defendant to spread the cost of insuring against the residual risk to its consumers, a function that plaintiff could not perform if left to carry the residual risk on her own. This is especially likely if the manufacturer is operating along the inelastic portion of its demand function, in which case by imposing liability, it can pass on the risk through a slightly higher price to each consumer. This arguments rests on two related intuitions, one of which is distributional, and the other of which is efficiency-based.

The cost-spreading allows a large number of consumers to subsidize the insurance function, rather than to have the entire burden of the residual risk fall upon the happenstance victim of the accident, for example the waitress injured by the exploding bottle. This aspect is primarily distributional and might accord with various fairness intuitions. In addition, it is also possible that the cost-spreading function enhances social welfare to the extent that it is cheaper for the producer, here Coca Cola, to insure against the residual risk than for each consumer to do so separately.

---

[13] This returns us to the opening discussion of the two goals of tort: (1) minimizing risk through cost effective precautions, and (2) allocating residual risk, including using the allocation for the purpose of risk spreading. *See supra* Chapter 3 Introduction.

[14] *See infra* Part IV.

[15] *See, e.g.*, Byrne v. Bodle (1863), 159 Eng. Rep. 299 (Exch.) (finding liability absent proof of negligence in case involving a barrel that fell out of the factory onto plaintiff's head); Ybarra v. Spangard, 154 P.2d 687 (Cal. 1944) ("[W]here a plaintiff receives unusual injuries while unconscious and in the course of medical treatment, all those defendants who had any control over his body or the instrumentalities which might have caused the injuries may properly be called upon to meet the inference of negligence by giving an explanation of their conduct.").

To be clear, consumers would not buy individual policies for each separate residual risk contingency, such as the risk that a particular manufacturer's glass bottles might explode. Rather, consumers hold policies respecting any number of risks, which might also include a broad set of residual risks associated with the bundle of commodities that they purchase. To the extent that some risks are unknown, however, and thus might not be contemplated by, or fall within the scope of, such policies, the risk-spreading function appears to serve both fairness (or distributional) and efficiency.

The other circumstance in which plaintiffs will have difficulty in proving causation is when there are multiple possible causes of her injuries.[16] Examples include exposure to a toxic substance that increases the risk of incurring a disease for which there is also a natural (background) risk, and when two hunters accidentally fire in the direction of a third but only one bullet hits him.[17] Typically, the tort system limits liability of a given defendant to those situations in which it is more likely than not that his action caused of the harm.[18] If this is interpreted to mean that the likelihood is greater than 50%, then this rule might not satisfy the efficiency threshold inasmuch as actors who have a lower than 50% probability of having caused an accident might still be able to take cost-effective precautions that reduce the risk of harm.

This is most obvious, for example, if we consider a group of injurers. Assume, for example, a *cul-de-sac* in which one neighbor left a sharp tool in the circle that injured a child riding a bicycle. Assume that all residents perform automobile repairs in the circle and that the injury was caused by a common tool or one that the neighbors shared. Further assume that three of the neighbors, A, B and C, each had a 20% chance of leaving the tool, and that the fourth neighbor, D, who owned the shared tool, had a 40% chance. We know that one of the four neighbors caused the injury, but none did so with a probability greater than 50%. Demanding that the plaintiff prove a greater than 50% likelihood that any one neighbor caused the harm would result in a dismissal *even though* leaving the tool in the road was clearly negligent and the risk of injury was foreseeable.

As we observed in discussing the Marginal Hand test and proximate cause, efficiency requires that the threshold liability rule be set such that the marginal cost of the next (foreseeable) precaution be lower than the marginal benefit from taking that precaution. Does setting the probability just over 50% meet this test? Does the "more likely than not" standard cause similarly situated residents to take too little care? If so, how should the preceding hypothetical be resolved?

---

[16] *See, e.g.*, Steven Shavell, *Uncertainty over Causation and the Determination of Civil Liability*, 28 J.L. & ECON. 587 (1985); Thomas Miceli & Kathleen Segerson, *Joint Lability in Torts: Marginal and Infra-Marginal Efficiency*, 11 INT'L REV. L. & ECON. 235 (1991).

[17] *See* Summers v. Tice, 99 P.2d 1 (Cal. 1948).

[18] More formally, we would say that the conditional probability that the injurer's action caused the harm exceeds fifty percent. Bayes' Theorem predicts the likely occurrence of observed phenomenon A based upon its degree of correspondence to observed phenomenon B. Richard Routledge, *Bayes Theorem*, ENCYCLOPÆDIA BRITANNICA, https://www.britannica.com/topic/Bayess-theorem (last visited Sept. 17, 2016). When A is observed along with B, the predictive force of the observed relationship concerning A is referred to as *conditional probability*. When A is observed independently of B, the predictive force of the observed relationship concerning A is referred to as *marginal probability*. For a more detailed analysis, see *infra* Chapter 15. Here the question is whether the observed exposure to a toxic substance or firing of the gun implies a degree of correspondence sufficient to establish causation respecting the observed disease or the observed shooting injury, respectively.

A second approach to dealing with uncertain causation is to hold all possible injurers liable, but only in proportion to their probabilities of causation. For example, in the hunter case, both shooters would bear one half of the harm, or in the *cul-de-sac* case, each neighbor would bear responsibility based on the assessed probability that he left the tool in the circle.

An interesting application of this rule involved multiple manufacturers of a drug that later proved carcinogenic. Because the plaintiff, injured as a result of a medicine her mother used during pregnancy, could not establish which manufacturers had supplied the drug, the court assigned liability in proportion to their market shares at the time.[19] There has been ongoing litigation seeking to assess market share liability in the context of lead-pigment paint poisoning in children, another context in which it is generally not possible to ascertain with certainty which producer provided the offending product.[20] In these cases, the market shares served as a proxy for the probability that a given manufacturer was the actual supplier. This rule appears to fairly allocate liability among producers, at least assuming an accurate assessment by the court of the probable market shares.

The market share liability rule also carries certain drawbacks. For example, as compared with the 51% threshold rule discussed above, the market share rule imposes additional administrative costs by eliminating actual proof of causation in fact. It does so by allowing claims with a lower bar to succeed. In addition, the rule necessarily imposes liability on parties who are not responsible for the particular harm in the sense that only one of the several parties "in the market" actually produced the product causing the specific plaintiff's injury. A counterargument is that if there are numerous plaintiffs, on average market share liability is a reasonable proxy for the percentage of plaintiffs likely injured by each participant's product.

DISCUSSION QUESTIONS

Imagine a case in which one or more victims is able to prove that a particular manufacturer produced the carcinogenic drug or lead-pigment paint that resulted in her injury. Further assume that in the remaining cases, the judicial system has applied market share liability. Should the judicial system revert to the traditional concept of causation when confronted with actual evidence of which manufacturer produced the offending product, thus imposing liability only on that responsible firm, or should it retain market share liability despite proof as to which firm sold the harmful good? Which approach is more efficient, and why?

---

[19] Sindell v. Abbott Labs., 607 P.2d 924 (Cal. 1980).

[20] The case law on market-share liability is limited. In the context of lead-pigment paint, the only precedent is *Thomas v. Mallett*, a case in which the Supreme Court of Wisconsin combined market share liability with comparative fault to devise a theory known as "risk-contribution." 701 N.W.2d 523 (Wis. 2005). This theory assesses market-share liability based on firm market share and advertising during the time frame in which the house that posed the risk to the plaintiff occurred. The ruling was unsuccessfully challenged on substantive due process grounds. Other courts have rejected market share liability in the lead-pigment paint context. *See, e.g.*, Skipworth v. Lead Indus. Ass'n, Inc., 690 A.2d 169 (Pa. 1997). Donald Gifford and Paulo Pasicolan have criticized the extension of market share liability to the lead paint litigation. Donald Gifford, *The Death of Causation*, 41 WAKE FOREST L. REV. 943, 985–88 (2006) (critically evaluating the Thomas decision); Donald Gifford & Paulo Pasicolan, *Market Share Liability Beyond DES Cases: The Solution to the Causation Dilemma in Lead Paint Litigation?*, 58 S.C. L. REV. 115, 118 (2006).

Should the hunting case and the case involving the tool in the *cul-de-sac* be resolved based on probabilities, as with the market share manufacturing context? Why or why not? Should those hypotheticals be resolved in the same way? Is assumption of risk relevant to either case? Is *res ipsa loquitur*? Should the experience levels of the hunters who fired, as compared with the one who was shot, matter to the outcome? Is it fair to allow a verdict against a defendant whose probability of causing harm was 20%? 40%? 50%? Does your answer depend on the gravity of the resulting harm? Should it? Should the cases involving carcinogenic drugs or lead-pigment paint be resolved in the same manner as the cases involving the hunters or the tool in the *cul-de-sac*? Does your analysis turn on the nature of the defendants, and whether they are private individuals or corporations? Should this distinction matter? Do due process or other fairness considerations differ based on the nature of the defendant? To what extent are your answers to these questions informed by economic analysis? To what extent are they informed by other considerations? How should these competing considerations be balanced?

B. Activity Levels

Our analysis of accident law has thus far focused on the efficiency of the care choices of injurers and victims. In many cases, however, an equally important consideration is each party's chosen *activity level*, meaning how frequently or intensively either engages in the risk-creating activity. The risk of automobile accidents, for example, depends not only on how careful the driver is, but also on the number of miles she drives. The risk of accidents caused by dangerous products depends not only on their safety features and consumer care, but also on the number of units sold and the frequency of consumer use. We consider the special problem of products liability below.[21] In this part, we instead focus on non-product accidents between strangers that are affected by activity levels.

From a social perspective, the optimal activity level is a function of the additional benefits derived from that activity and of the additional risks that an incremental increase in that activity poses. Thus, for example, the driver of a car must choose the level of care for each mile driven in addition to how many miles to drive, weighing the appropriate benefits and costs. Our prior analysis assessed various liability rules against incentives to undertake appropriate levels of care. Here we consider the effect of those rules on the choice of activity level. We first derive the basic conclusions in the context of the unilateral accident model in which only injurers choose care and activity level; we then generalize the conclusions to the bilateral accident model.

As we previously saw, under a rule of no liability, injurers will tend to underinvest in care and to over-engage in risks associated with the activity. Because they are not responsible under this rule for harm caused to others, drivers will tend to be less careful during each mile driven and will also tend to drive too many miles. By contrast, under strict liability, drivers are responsible for all harm they cause to others, and they will therefore tend to take appropriate levels of care and to also consider more carefully the frequency and duration of driving.

Now consider the negligence rule. As we have seen, negligence induces injurers to take cost-effective precautions, but because injurers anticipate no liability when they undertake due care, they will tend to over-engage in the activity once they have undertaken

---

21 *See infra* Part II.B.

a given level of care. For some activities the activity level itself is part of due care. For example, following a power outage, a homeowner without an accessible flashlight might walk through the home with a lit candle, placing the home at risk of fire. Further imagine that the homeowner is generally quite responsible and that although she had a working flashlight, and even had extra batteries for it, the bulb died between her last use and the power outage. As soon as she locates a working flashlight or when the power returns, it would be irresponsible of her to continue this activity. The risks associated with walking through the dark house with a lit candle, and the desire to avoid it except when necessary, can be expressed either in terms of due care or in terms of activity level.

More generally, the two inquiries are distinct. This reflects the sense in which negligence combines elements of strict liability with no liability. Specifically, by meeting the due care standard, the injurer generally avoids liability, and by failing to meet that standard, the injurer faces the equivalent of strict liability. In both instances, this holds without regard to activity level. In the efficient Nash equilibrium, tortfeasors are expected to undertake due care, and thus, they expect to be subject to the no liability rule.[22] The overall outcome under negligence is therefore inferior to that under strict liability in terms of incentives with respect to the injurer's activity level. The extent of the resulting inefficiency under negligence depends on the relative impact of the injurer's care and activity level on accident risk, and this will vary across activities.

The comparison between strict liability and negligence becomes ambiguous when we turn to bilateral accidents because now we are concerned with the care and activity choices of victims as well. It turns out that in this case, none of the various liability rules, including the different versions of the negligence rule, can induce the fully efficient outcome. At best, the negligence rules can induce efficient care by both parties and efficient activity by *one* of the parties. The reason for this can be illustrated with the simple negligence rule.

We have seen that the simple negligence rule is generally able to induce efficient care by both parties by setting a due care standard that allows the injurer to avoid liability by undertaking cost-effective precautions, and then imposing liability on the victim. Because the injurer avoids damages, however, he has no incentive to refrain from an excessive activity level, as long as he exercises due care. By contrast, the victim actually bears her damages, and thus she chooses both care and activity level so as to minimize overall costs. The general principle is that the party bearing the residual damages in equilibrium under a given rule will choose efficient care *and* activity level, but the party avoiding liability will choose efficient care but risks choosing an excessive activity level. Thus, among the three liability rules, simple negligence and negligence with contributory negligence will only induce an efficient activity level by the victim, whereas strict liability with contributory negligence will only induce efficient activity by the injurer.[23] The preferred choice depends on which party's activity level is the greater contributor to accident risk.

---

[22] Because this is a unilateral care context, we can treat the rule as assuming that the other party does not take due care, thereby inducing the injurer to take due care to avoid the risk of liability.

[23] A comparative negligence rule with due standards of care will function like simple negligence in this respect.

A possible solution to the deficiency of the various liability rules regarding activity levels would be for the court to define a due care standard for activity level or to incorporate activity level into the due standard of care, as seen, for example, with homeowner with the candle. This might be quite difficult for courts to accomplish. What, for example, is a reasonable number of miles to drive, or even to walk or run? Are the relevant considerations too varied for courts to evaluate activity level? Might "due care" comprise, in more limited fashion, those things for which courts can reasonably set an appropriate standard?

In an article titled "Disgorgement Damages for Accidents,"[24] Professors Robert Cooter and Ariel Porat propose an alternative approach to the calculation of liability for accidents, which has implications for both levels of precaution and activity. The authors maintain that in some tort contexts, calculating damages based on gains to the tortfeasor from an untaken precaution, divided by the probability of harm, is preferred to the more conventional formula, which awards damages based on plaintiff's harm. The practical advantage of what they call the *Disgorgement of Damages for Accidents* ("DDA") measure is that in certain tort contexts the injurer's benefit from the failure to take some precaution will be easier for a court to measure than the victim's harm from the resulting accident. In terms of incentives for care level, DDA imposes on injurers the minimum damage that will induce them to take efficient care, and because damages are lower than under the compensatory measure, DDA strengthens the incentives for victims to take care. With respect to activity levels, the lower damage amount under DDA provides less efficient incentives for the injurer and correspondingly greater incentives for the victim.

In which settings is the Cooter and Porat thesis most apt to apply? Can you think of offsetting concerns that counsel in favor of the traditional damages rule, even in the settings that you identify? How, for example, might the proposal affect plaintiff incentives to litigate? Consider more particularly the possible benefit from the DDA proposal respecting judicial administration costs in assessing damages. In the context of insider trading, where it is likely easier to measure the trader's gain than the harm to the "market," and in some products liability cases, where the plaintiff's harm includes difficult-to-measure pain and suffering or hedonic damages, whereas the gains to the tortfeasor from omitting care might be more easily calculated in terms of profit, do administrative savings justify replacing the traditional rule with DDA? Why or why not? To what extent is the DDA proposal equivalent to replacing actual damages with a Pigouvian tax? If it is equivalent, does that favor the proposal? Why or why not?

Professor Shahar Dillbary explored the relationship between multiple causation and activity levels in an article titled "Causation Actually."[25] Dillbary posits that contrary to conventional understanding, when several actors pursue a course of conduct in which one is the direct cause of injury (such as the one who fires a bullet that hits the plaintiff), all participants can nonetheless be viewed as a *but for* cause of the accident in the sense that absent the dilutive effect that results from imposing liability on multiple actors, none would engage carelessly in the activity. If enough actors are held liable, the expected liability of each could be so diluted that each actor would willingly engage in the activity, however carelessly. Each actor can be defined as a cause of the harm in that but for each

[24] Robert Cooter & Ariel Porat, *Disgorgement Damages for Accidents*, 44 J. LEGAL STUD. 249 (2015).

[25] J. Shahar Dillbary, *Causation Actually*, 51 GA. L. REV. 1 (2016).

participant's careless behavior above a certain participation threshold, the expected liability of each actor would not be adequately diluted to create the incentive to act. Dillbary's model requires that as the number of participants increases, the expected liability remains sufficiently constant, or rises at a slow enough rate, that the expected liability of each actor will be effectively diluted.[26] When the participation effect submerges the individual defendant's risk exposure below a certain level, engaging in activity becomes desirable.

The stylized nature of Dillbary's model can be demonstrated by comparing two related shooting hypotheticals. First, imagine a sporting event in which safe shooting is not cost effective absent some defined precaution, such as constructing a safety wall. If the expected liability that each individual faces is high enough, none would engage in the activity due to the cost of the precaution. If enough actors engage in the activity carelessly, however, and if the additional participant does not adequately increase overall risk, then the dilution effect from increased participation can reach a point such that the activity becomes desirable. If an accident then occurs, each participant, by helping to reduce individual risk exposure through the dilution effect for all members of the group, can be viewed as a but-for cause of the harm. In this model, the activity level is positively correlated to the dilution effect of the shared liability rule. By contrast, if the exposure risk directly and correspondingly increases with group size, for example based on additional required precautions as participation increases, thus counteracting any dilution effect,[27] additional group participation will not motivate an increase in activity level.

Do you agree or disagree with the preceding analysis? If you disagree, how would you propose setting a due care standard for activity level? Do you agree with Professor Dillbary's assessment of the relationship between participation and causation? Can you identify examples in which additional participation does, and does not, have the dilution effect he describes?

C. Further Considerations

This section considers several further extensions to the basic accident model.

1. *Liability Insurance (and Moral Hazard)*

Most people or businesses engaged in risky activities voluntarily purchase liability insurance to protect themselves against damages that they risk incurring or risk imposing on others. In addition, most states require motorists to purchase liability insurance. Among other benefits, this avoids the problem of the judgment-proof defendant, discussed below.

The economic theory of insurance focuses on the social benefits of spreading risk in an optimal way, primarily by shifting it from risk-averse individuals to risk-neutral

---

[26] Although the article uses stylized examples, under Dillbary's model the parties' private benefits, cost of precaution, probability of harm or total damages may increase or decrease with the number of tortfeasors, provided that they do not increase in a manner that prevents this dilution effect. *See id.* at 12–13 (discussing similar examples).

[27] This would occur, for example, if there are no scale economies in the relevant precautions, as there are, for example, in the wall hypothetical.

insurance companies.[28] Our main concern here is how insurance affects incentives for individuals to engage in accident avoidance.

Consider the effect of liability insurance on the care choices of injurers. Holding insurance premiums constant, insurance insulates an injurer from financial risk by transforming an uncertain prospect (i.e., having to make a large damage payment in the event of an accident) into a predictable stream of costs (i.e., premiums). In other words, the injurer makes regular premium payments to the insurance company, and in return, the company pays liability judgments. Setting aside the potential for personal harm to the tortfeasor himself, by substantially reducing the liability risk of accidents, insurance also reduces incentives on the part of drivers to take appropriate precautions. This problem is referred to as *moral hazard*, and it is a source of market failure introduced by insurance. Moral hazard ultimately hurts all insureds. By increasing individual incentives to take risks (or equivalently, by reducing incentives to avoid risks), it generates additional liability costs that are then shared and passed on through higher premiums.

Insurance companies have developed mechanisms to help mitigate moral hazard. One is to condition premiums, to the extent possible, on observable risk-reducing behaviors by insureds. For example, insurers provide premium discounts to those with good driving records and for cars with specified safety features such as antilock brakes, which reduce the risk of collisions, and alarms, which reduce the risk of theft or vandalism. In addition, insurance policies typically include deductibles, amounts charged to the insured for each successfully submitted claim, thus forcing the insured to internalize part of the cost of accidents. The higher the deductible, the greater the insured's incentive to take appropriate precautions. This might include reducing activity levels.

Higher deductibles are also a way to reduce insurance premiums. To that extent, higher deductibles also dilute the risk-sharing benefits of insurance. Unfortunately, this reflects an unavoidable trade-off between risk sharing and incentives for risk-averse individuals.[29] Finally, although we previously assumed constant premiums, premium levels are ultimately tied to driver performance and claims history to the extent possible. The insurance rate structure itself thus helps mitigate moral hazard as higher quality driving records, reflected through claims history and records concerning traffic violations, result in lower insurance premiums.

2. *Litigation Costs*

Although we have occasionally touched on the role of administrative costs in the tort system, until now we have not systematically assessed how litigation costs affect the incentives for parties to invest in accident prevention.[30] Under strict liability, litigation costs tend to lower incentives for injurer care for two reasons.[31] First, the cost of filing suit will deter tort victims from raising relatively small claims for damages, thus allowing

[28] *See, e.g.*, STEVEN SHAVELL, FOUNDATIONS OF ECONOMIC ANALYSIS OF LAW 210–11 (2004).

[29] Steven Shavell, *On Moral Hazard and Insurance*, 93 Q.J. ECON. 541 (1979).

[30] In Chapter 8 we examine in detail how litigation costs affect the resolution of legal disputes more generally. *See infra* Chapter 10.

[31] Keith Hylton, *The Influence of Litigation Costs on Deterrence Under Strict Liability and Under Negligence*, 10 INT'L REV. L. & ECON. 161 (1990).

tortfeasors to externalize such costs. Second, because litigation costs are borne by each side within the United States (under what is known as the "American rule"), unlike in England where the losing party pays both sides' attorney's fees,[32] litigation costs create a further externality that marginally reduces the incentive of tortfeasors to take cost-effective care. (Specifically, injurers ignore the litigation costs of victims.)

Under a negligence rule, the analysis is a bit more subtle. If the negligence standard functions perfectly, all injurers will comply with the due standard of care, and so no victims would file suit because they would not expect to recover any damages. Thus, the efficient zero-litigation cost outcome would, in principle, be achieved. This cannot be an equilibrium, however, because if injurers expect no suits to be filed, they would have no incentive to comply with the due standard. The only equilibrium, therefore, is one in which some injurers to fail to meet the due standard (those with high costs of care), and some victims file suit because there is now a positive probability that they will win (equal to the fraction of injurers who failed to comply with the due care standard).[33] If courts make errors in assessing compliance with the negligence standard, a perfect compliance (or possibly an overcompliance) equilibrium may exist because the possibility of legal error creates an incentive for some victims to file suit.[34]

3. The Problem of the Judgment-Proof Defendant

Injurers sometimes escape liability for damages, besides litigation costs, when they have insufficient assets to pay the victim's losses. This is referred to as the problem of the "judgment-proof" defendant. Injurers who anticipate that they may be unable to pay for any damages that they cause will have inadequate incentives to take care to avoid accidents in the first place, and they will also have an incentive to over-engage in activities that produce risk.

In general, the lower the injurer's assets relative to the potential harm they might cause, the greater the potential externality and resulting inefficiency. A negligence rule might provide greater incentives regarding the injurer's choice of care in the presence of limited assets. Specifically, if the injurer does not anticipate being entirely judgment proof, he will still have an incentive to meet the due care standard to avoid *any* liability. By contrast, under strict liability, he would be liable without regard to the level of care. As a result, he would have a diminished incentive to undertake due care as a means of reducing liability exposure because at some point marginal expenditures yield no corresponding benefit in decreasing exposure.

The problem of the judgment-proof defendant might affect the incentives of both individuals and firms, but the prospect of avoiding liability might also induce firms to alter their organizational structure by, for example, shifting particularly risky activities to

---

[32] James W. Hughes & Edward A. Snyder, *Litigation and Settlement Under the English and American Rules: Theory and Evidence*, 38 J.L. & ECON. 225, 225 (1995).

[33] *See* Janusz Ordover, *Costly Litigation in the Model of Single Activity Accidents*, 7 J. LEGAL STUD. 243 (1978); Hylton, *supra* note 33.

[34] *See* Keith Hylton, *Costly Litigation and Legal Error Under Negligence*, 6 J. LAW, ECON. & ORG. 433 (1990).

subsidiaries protected by limited liability.[35] This is obviously financially beneficial to firms, but harmful to affected victims of the firm's tortious conduct. Not surprisingly, when firms allocate risks for strategic reasons, they are subject to various rules based on fraud that sometimes allow courts to pierce the corporate veil, including treating subsidiaries as part of the parent firm for liability purposes.[36]

The problem of the judgment-proof defendant can also affect firms in other ways. When a firm employee causes an accident with a third party, it is commonplace for the employee to lack the resources to compensate the victim and for the employer to be the "deep pocket." In this context, through the doctrine of *respondeat superior*, the firm will assume the liability on the part of its employee when the tortious conduct arose in the course of employment. The imposition of *vicarious liability*—the employer assuming liability on the part of the employee—thus helps solve the problem of the judgment-proof (or judgment-inadequate) employee.

Because employers generally have the authority to discipline their employees, this doctrine creates an alternative incentive system within the firm to the tort law regime enforced by courts. As William Landes and Richard Posner have observed: "Making the employer liable for his employee's tort serves to enlist the employer as a substitute enforcer of tort law where the primary enforcement mechanism, a tort action against the immediate tortfeasor, is unworkable."[37] This regime is most effective in creating incentives for due care when the firm has the capacity to identify and discipline employees whose conduct places third parties at risk of harm. In many contexts, identifying a specific negligent employee will be fairly easy, as for example, when a delivery person causes a vehicular accident. Other times, this will be more difficult, as when a complex product contains a lurking defect that does not manifest itself in an injury for many years. The ability of the firm to determine when an employee is responsible for an injury and to take appropriate steps will depend on how careful it is in monitoring and recording its own production and other processes.

4. Punitive Damages

As the name implies, punitive damages are awarded to plaintiffs in excess of their actual harm as a means of punishing defendants. Such damages are therefore typically limited to cases in which the defendant's behavior is determined to have been intentional or reckless. In this sense, they resemble criminal fines.[38] Although the functions overlap, the economic theory of punitive damages suggests a somewhat different rationale than that associated with criminal penalties. Criminal penalties are often understood to reflect

---

35 Al H. Ringleb & Steven N. Wiggins, *Liability and Large-Scale, Long-Term Hazards*, 98 J. POL. ECON. 574, 578 n.6 (1990).

36 Another method of accomplishing a similar result is to move assets into a special purpose entity. For a general discussion in the context of Enron, see Steven Schwartz, *Enron and the Use and Abuse of Special Purpose Entities in Corporate Structures*, 70 U. CIN. L. REV. 1310 (2003). For an article exploring the creative structuring of a corporate form to shield assets in the context of the Los Angeles Dodgers, see Douglas G. Baird & Anthony J. Casey, *No Exit? Withdrawal Rights and the Law of Corporate Reorganizations*, 113 COLUM. L. REV. 1 (2013).

37 WILLIAM LANDES & RICHARD A. POSNER, THE ECONOMIC STRUCTURE OF TORT LAW 121 (1987).

38 *See infra* Chapter 9.

the greater difficulty in deterring harmful conduct that is intentional or reckless as compared with conduct that is merely negligent.[39] In the classic law and economics presentation, punitive tort damages seek to impose penalties that compensate for other intentional tortious conduct for which the tortfeasor (or others who are similarly situated) has escaped liability.[40]

As a formal matter, under the Supreme Court decision, *Philip Morris USA v. Williams*,[41] extra-compensatory damages for harms to third parties who might not have pressed their own claims is now treated as a violation of due process, although harm to third parties can be introduced as evidence of egregious conduct, thereby justifying punitive damages for conduct that specifically harmed the plaintiff. In effect, through a circumlocution, a methodology not unlike the traditional economic analysis of punitive damages largely survives provided the presentation of damages is phrased in terms of harm to the specific plaintiff.[42] Punitive damages thus create an incentive on the part of plaintiffs (or their contingency fee attorneys) to bring suit, whereas criminal penalties typically are awarded to the state.[43]

We have already seen two reasons why tortfeasors, especially firms, might escape liability, even though they have the financial ability to pay damages. (Short of garnishment of wages, punitive damages would obviously be useless against judgment-proof defendants.) First, when causation is uncertain, victims have difficulty recovering for their injuries. Second, where contingency fee arrangements are unavailable, the American rule can impose prohibitive litigation costs. Finally, injurers might sometimes seek to conceal culpability for an accident, which might lead to criminal prosecution and civil liability.

Punitive damages on top of compensatory damages can address these problems by increasing the amount of damages injurers expect to pay in those cases where they are held liable. Suppose, for example, that for a particular class of accidents, injurers only face liability for one quarter of the accidents that they actually cause. If average losses per accident are $100,000, then injurers only expect to pay an average of $25,000 per accident (.25 × $100,000), and thus tend to underinvest in care. Multiplying damages in successful cases by a factor of four, yielding a verdict of $400,000 (4 × $100,000), restores *expected* damages per accident to the actual value of $100,000. (This restorative function is referred to as the "punitive multiplier.") Thus, one in four accidents would result in a suit, with damages at $400,000, of which $100,000 is compensatory and $300,000 is punitive. Notice that under this theory, and subject to the necessary phrasing based upon the doctrinal

---

[39] For a more detailed exposition of the tort/criminal law boundary, see *infra* Chapter 9.

[40] On the economic theory of punitive damages, see Cooter, *supra* note 1; A. Mitchell Polinsky & Steven Shavell, *Punitive Damages: An Economic Analysis*, 111 HARV. L. REV. 869 (1998); Catherine M. Sharkey, *Punitive Damages as Societal Damages*, 113 YALE L.J. 347 (2003); *see also* Ciraolo v. City of New York, 216 F.3d 236 (2d Cir. 2000) (Calabresi, J., concurring).

[41] 549 U.S. 346 (2007).

[42] *See generally* Thomas B. Colby, *Clearing the Smoke from* Philip Morris v. Williams*: The Past, Present, and Future of Punitive Damages*, 118 YALE L.J. 392 (2008) (explaining that Williams properly limits damages to the plaintiff's injuries without disallowing "nonpunitive extracompensatory damages" that would force the defendant to internalize the costs of its tortious conduct).

[43] Subject to the preceding caveat, in the analysis that follows, we assume the conventional law and economics multiplier based on claims not pressed.

limits of *Philip Morris*, plaintiffs who actually sue are in effect compensated for the damages suffered by those victims who did not sue, for whatever reason.

How closely does the actual use of punitive damages correspond to this theory? Based on their analysis of cases in which punitive damages have been awarded, Polinsky and Shavell conclude that the correspondence is not close: "Courts . . . do not pay systematic attention to the probability of escaping liability, even though this probability is the central element in determining the appropriate damages multiplier for achieving proper deterrence."[44]

More generally, even in negligence actions, it is customary to set damages at a multiplier of actual proven damages, both for purposes of settlement negotiations and when arguing for damages before the jury. This might reflect the prevalent understanding that contingency fee lawyers recover approximately 35% of the verdict, thereby leaving the plaintiff with the remainder, and, in addition, a similar intuition to that previously discussed for punitive damages: plaintiffs and juries might hold an intuition that even in the absence of intentional conduct, defendants (or their insurers) pay out in only a subset of accidents that result from negligent conduct. In addition, because punitive damages and damages other than for the actual physical injury are generally treated as taxable income by the Internal Revenue Service, this too might encourage jurors to employ a multiplier at trial, and also affecting settlement negotiations.[45] To the extent these explanations are persuasive, the "punitive multiplier" might be different in degree, rather than in kind, as compared with more general recovery in negligence-based tort suits.

In separate works, Professors David Haddock and Keith Hylton have offered an alternative economic perspective on punitive damages, which they contend better accounts case outcomes. The analysis is based on "gain elimination" as opposed to "loss elimination."[46] The objective is to eliminate the gain to defendants from particular tortious acts, rather than to fully compensate victims for the expected value of their losses. The distinction recognizes that some acts lack social value in the sense that the injurer's gain is lower than the victim's loss, rendering the optimal activity level zero. For such activities, any gains that the defendant expects to enjoy above the victims' losses should be eradicated so as to discourage the act altogether.

DISCUSSION QUESTIONS

Is there is a sound economic basis for capping punitive damages, as some states have done? The argument in favor of caps is that they limit incentives to file suit, thereby saving on

---

[44] Polinsky & Shavell, *supra* note 40, at 898.

[45] Commissioner v. Glenshaw Glass Co., 348 U.S. 426 (1955) (treating punitive damages as gross income); 26 U.S.C. § 104(a)(2) Compensation for injuries or sickness (excluding "damages (other than punitive damages) received (whether by suit or agreement and whether as lump sums or as periodic payments) on account of personal physical injuries or physical sickness.") Although settlements provide an opportunity for tax planning, they do not affect the tax treatment of litigation proceeds. Robert W. Wood, Tax Aspects of Settlements and Judgments, BNA Tax Management Portfolio 522—4th, at I.C (last visited Oct. 9, 2017).

[46] *See* David Haddock, Fred McChesney & Menahem Spiegel, *An Ordinary Economic Rationale for Extraordinary Legal Sanctions* 78 CALIF. L. REV. 1 (1990); and Keith Hylton, *Punitive Damages and the Economic Theory of Penalties* 87 GEO. L.J. 421 (1998).

administrative costs. Offsetting this is the concern that capping punitive damages will inhibit their deterrence function as discussed above.[47]

Do you favor caps on punitive damages? Why or why not? Should courts permit punitive multipliers in ordinary negligence actions? Does the multiplier serve to offset the effects of the American rule? Would the system be improved by abandoning the multiplier and shifting to the English rule? Why or why not?

II. PRODUCTS LIABILITY

This section turns to the analysis of products liability, or the law governing product-related accidents. This body of tort law is important in its own right, and also it raises special considerations. The general model of tort law assumes that the parties came together unwittingly, by happenstance, as seen in many of the preceding illustrations. In product-accident settings, the injurer and the victim were typically in a pre-existing contractual relationship before the accident occurred. This general distinction is important in considering the function of the liability system for internalizing accident risk.

Our discussion of products liability begins with a brief overview of the evolution of the relevant doctrine. We then develop an economic model of product-related accidents, the goal of which is to examine the efficiency of the law with respect to the equilibrium output and price of dangerous products, as well as product safety and consumer behavior regarding their use. We conclude by discussing the control of product risk by government (public) regulation versus tort (private) law.

A. Overview of Products Liability Law

The history of manufacturer-based products liability throughout the past century and a half has been characterized by a gradual shift from no liability to strict liability by manufacturers.[48] The change occurred in several phases. The first involved the doctrine of "privity," which barred consumers from suing anyone but the immediate seller of the product, that is, the party with whom the consumer had a direct contractual relationship. This development placed products liability suits within the realm of contract rather than tort. The privity doctrine had the practical effect of insulating manufacturers from liability in most cases, given the increasingly complex process of production and distribution of consumer goods, which placed intermediaries between the manufacturer and the ultimate consumer who suffered the resulting harm.

---

[47] Thomas J. Miceli & Michael P. Stone, *The Determinants of State-Level Caps on Punitive Damages: Theory and Evidence*, 31 CONTEMP. ECON. POL'Y 110 (2013).

[48] LANDES & POSNER, *supra* note 37, ch. 10; RICHARD EPSTEIN, *From Privity to Strict Liability*, *in* MODERN PRODUCTS LIABILITY LAW 23 (1980). Failure to warn and design defect claims tend to operate under a negligence standard, with the latter sometimes operating within the framework of risk utility analysis. RESTATEMENT (THIRD) OF TORTS: PRODUCTS LIABILITY § 2 (AM. LAW INST. 1998). The discussion in the text focuses on manufacturing defects, now also called products liability, which is generally subject to strict liability. *See id.* (explaining that a product is defective when it contains "a manufacturing defect when the product departs from its intended design even though all possible care was exercised in the preparation and marketing of the product").

Despite this difficulty, the privity limitation endured well into the twentieth century, when it was finally abandoned in the famous case of *MacPherson v. Buick*.[49] The *MacPherson* case involved an accident that occurred when one of the wheels on the plaintiff's car broke off, causing injury. Because the plaintiff had bought the car from a dealer rather than the manufacturer, however, the privity doctrine barred him from directly suing the manufacturer. The court nevertheless found that the manufacturer could be held liable because it clearly should have foreseen the possibility of injuries to parties other than the dealership as the immediate purchaser. By abandoning privity, *MacPherson* effectively shifted products liability cases from contract to tort, where they were initially subject to negligence principles. Although this change expanded the scope of manufacturer liability, proving that the manufacturer's negligence caused the victim's harm often continued to pose an insurmountable obstacle.

This problem was eventually overcome by another doctrinal shift, in the middle of the twentieth century, from negligence to strict liability. Although this did not take place with a single case, we have seen one important case in the development: *Escola v. Coca-Cola Bottling Co.*[50] The *Escola* case, you may recall, applied the doctrine of *res ipsa loquitur* ("the thing speaks for itself") in the context of an exploding Coca Cola bottle that injured a waitress. The application of this doctrine effectively relieved plaintiffs of the need to prove negligence on the part of manufacturers of potentially dangerous products. The *res ipsa loquitur* test thus formed part of an eventual shift to strict liability.

A parallel doctrinal development involved warranties for product fitness. Warranties are contractual terms that accompany the sale of products, and that specify, and typically limit, the liability of manufacturers in the event of product failure, including a failure that causes a personal injury. In the mid-twentieth century, these warranty limitations coexisted with the expanding scope of tort liability, creating some confusion regarding the controlling legal principle for product accidents.

The 1960 case of *Henningsen v. Bloomfield Motors, Inc.*[51] brought some needed clarity to this doctrinal area. The *Henningsen* case also involved an automobile accident, this time caused by a failure of the steering mechanism. The sales contract between the purchaser and the manufacturer had included an express warranty that limited liability, and that included an express disclaimer of the implied warranty of merchantability. This was presented in small text on the back of the brief sales contract, and the salesperson did not specifically bring it to the purchaser's attention. This provision thus appeared to bar recovery for the purchaser's wife, who was injured. The court invalidated the disclaimer, finding it a *contract of adhesion*, meaning a contract in which one party sets the terms and the other is given the choice to accept or decline, but with no option to modify.[52] It further ruled that the privity limitation did not apply because the victim, who although not the purchaser, was someone whom the manufacturer could reasonably have foreseen would be a potential user of the vehicle.[53]

---

[49] 111 N.E. 1050 (N.Y. 1916).

[50] 150 P.2d 436 (Cal. 1944).

[51] 161 A.2d 69 (N.J. 1960).

[52] For a discussion of the doctrine of unconscionability, see *infra* Chapter 5.

[53] *Henningsen*, 161 A.2d at 84, 86–87, 97.

With the *Henningsen* decision, the tort and contract approaches to products liability appeared to be converging on a strict liability standard. This was formalized in 1965 with the publication of the *Restatement (Second) of Torts*, which announced that manufacturers were liable for damages caused by any product found to be defective or to have been sold in an unreasonably dangerous condition.[54] The question whether this resulted in a strict liability or negligence rule was unresolved. The determination of whether or not a product was "defective" would presumably have involved a kind of cost-benefit analysis, or Hand Test, implying negligence.[55] For products that are inherently dangerous, however, liability is effectively strict. And indeed, as Professors Tom Ulen and Robert Cooter have observed, some scholars have noted the trend in modern products liability cases toward what they characterize as "absolute liability," sometimes called "enterprise liability," whereby injurers are liable for "almost every injury resulting from the use of their outputs."[56]

B. The Economics of Product-Related Accidents

This section develops an economic approach to product-related accidents, with an emphasis on the elements that make these cases different from accidents between strangers.[57] The first section ignores care choices by manufacturers and consumers and focuses instead on how the assignment of liability affects the determination of equilibrium price and quantity for dangerous products. Later, we extend the discussion to consider the care choices of manufacturers and consumers.

1. Equilibrium Output and Price for Dangerous Products

Our analysis of liability for dangerous products begins with a standard competitive market model with a well-functioning price mechanism. As a benchmark, consider the determination of equilibrium price and quantity for a risk-free ("safe") product. This is depicted by the simple supply and demand diagram in Figure 4:1. The demand curve represents the amount consumers are willing to pay for individual units of the product, and the supply curve represents the manufacturer's cost of producing individual units, also known as the marginal cost curve.[58] The intersection depicts the equilibrium point where supply equals demand, and it determines quantity sold (Q^*) and price (P^*).

---

[54] RESTATEMENT (SECOND) OF TORTS § 402A (AM. LAW INST. 1965).

[55] LANDES & POSNER, *supra* note 37, at 291.

[56] ROBERT COOTER & THOMAS ULEN, LAW AND ECONOMICS 405 (5th ed. 2008); George Priest, *Products Liability Law and the Accident Rate*, *in* LIABILITY: PERSPECTIVES AND POLICY 184 (Robert E. Litan & Clifford Winston eds., 1988); *infra* text accompanying note 68.

[57] These issues were first examined by Steven Shavell, William Landes and Richard Posner. Steven Shavell, *Strict Liability Versus Negligence*, 9 J. LEGAL STUD. 1 (1980); William Landes & Richard A. Posner, *A Positive Economic Theory of Products Liability*, 14 J. LEGAL STUD. 535 (1985).

[58] The negative slope of demand reflects diminishing marginal benefits, and the upward slope of supply reflects increasing marginal costs. *See supra* Chapter 2.

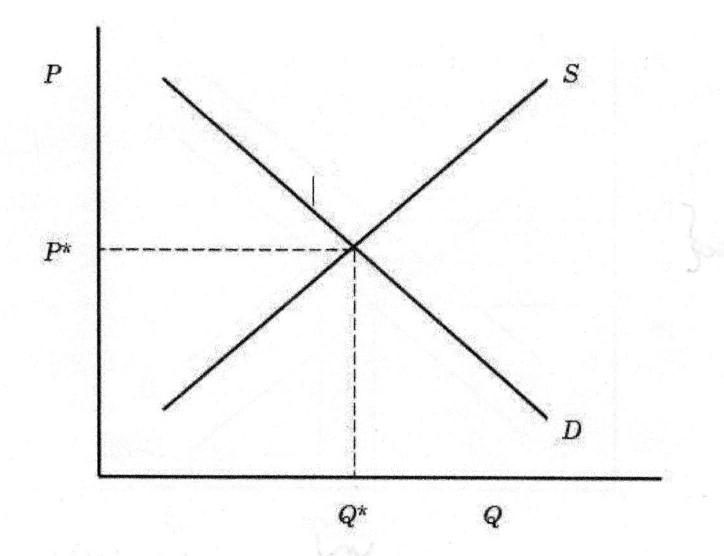

Figure 4:1. Equilibrium price and quantity for a safe product.

Now suppose that there is a risk of an accident from use of the product, and that all parties, at least initially, accurately perceive that risk.[59] Thus, manufacturers and consumers accurately estimate the expected cost of an accident per unit of the product, which we summarize by the expected damage function, *ED*. Recall that this represents the probability of an accident for each unit of the product sold, multiplied by the average loss per accident. In this context, output simultaneously represents the activity level of the manufacturer (the amount they sell) and the activity level of the consumer (the amount they buy). The risk from a dangerous product is therefore proportional to output.

The risk of an accident will affect either demand or supply (or both), depending on the applicable liability rule. For now, consider the extreme cases of strict and no liability. Under strict liability, manufacturers expect to bear all accident costs, so the supply curve shifts up by the full amount of *ED* (i.e., their marginal costs rise by the amount of expected damages per unit of output), whereas the demand curve does not change because consumers expect to be fully compensated in the event of an accident. In other words, consumers behave as if the product is risk-free. Figure 4:2 shows the resulting equilibrium, which occurs at output of Q^{**} and price of P_1. Quantity is lower and price is higher as compared with the risk-free case. By contrast, under a rule of no liability, consumers expect to bear their own losses, and thus, they discount the price they are willing to pay for the product by the full amount of the expected damages per unit. Thus, the demand curve shifts down by the amount *ED*, whereas the supply curve is unchanged. The equilibrium in this case also occurs at output of Q^{**}, but at a lower price, P_0, as shown in Figure 4:2.

59 We consider situations in which consumers misperceive risk below.

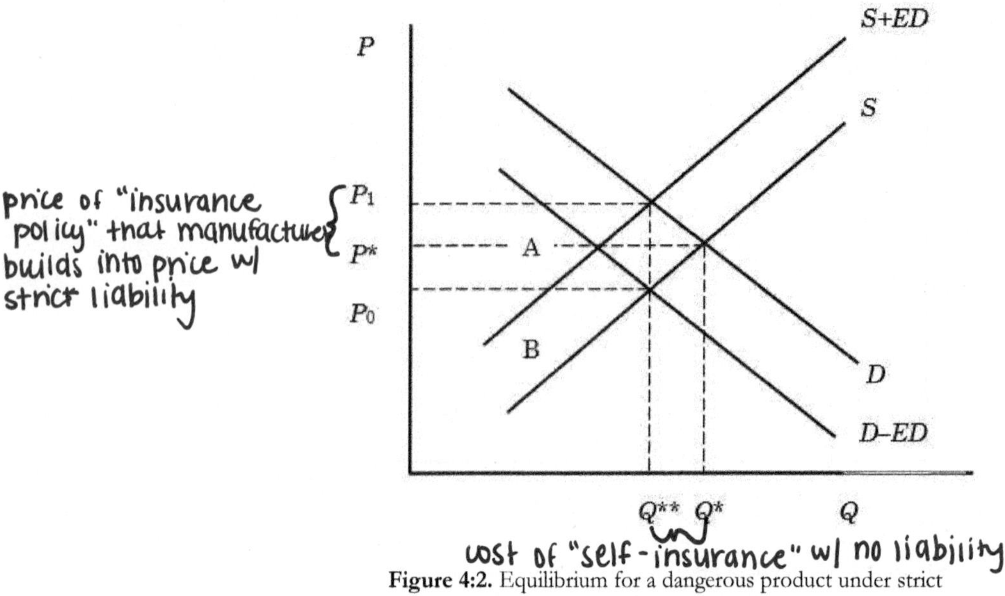

Figure 4:2. Equilibrium for a dangerous product under strict liability (Q^{**}, P_1) and no liability (Q^{**}, P_0).

The fact that the equilibrium output, Q^{**}, is the same under the two liability rules is a general result, and would be true for *any* assignment of liability between the two parties. In other words, equilibrium output is *independent of the assignment of liability*. Further, the equilibrium output coincides with the efficient level of output because it occurs at the point at which the marginal consumption benefit of the last unit, measured by the demand curve, equals the full marginal cost of that unit, including production plus accident costs. The fact that output is both independent of the liability rule and is also efficient is an illustration of the Coase Theorem.[60] This implies that the only consequence of the rule, strict or no liability, is distributional; with either liability rule announced in advance, and with neither party having a comparative advantage in absorbing the risk, the effect is to allocate resources efficiently with the resulting cost difference based on which party covers the risk included in the contract price.

Unlike output, the price is clearly *not* independent of the liability rule. In particular, the price is higher under strict liability as compared to no liability. That is because under strict liability, the manufacturer is in effect selling consumers the product *bundled with an insurance policy for the risk of an accident.* This is analogous to *Henningsen*, in which the ruling disallowed Pontiac to disclaim the implied warranty of merchantability for each car it sold.[61] More generally, as shown in Figure 4:2, in the event of an accident, the victim can sue for damages, which the manufacturer will have to pay.

By contrast, under a rule of no liability, the manufacturer is selling the decoupled product, meaning without the warranty, and thus consumers have to *self-insure* against product risk; that is, they have to pay for their own damages. They can cover these costs in a number of ways: they can pay out of pocket as the need arises; they can set aside some

---

60 *See supra* Chapter 1, Part III (presenting the Coase Theorem).

61 *Henningsen*, 161 A.2d at 97.

money periodically in anticipation of a large future expense; or they can purchase market insurance for risks that manifest themselves in an injury. Which option they choose will depend on the magnitude of the expected damages and their risk tolerance. For example, they are more likely to purchase market insurance, assuming it is available for the relevant category of risk,[62] if they are risk averse and as the expected loss becomes larger.

It is important to note that the price difference between strict and no liability reflects these different modes of covering accident costs. Specifically, under strict liability, the manufacturer acts as the insurer and thus, it must charge a premium to reflect the actuarially fair risk it is assuming. The difference between P_1 and P_0 represents this premium per unit of output, and the area labeled A in Figure 4:2 is the aggregate premium revenue that the firm collects. By construction, it equals the damages per unit (*ED*) multiplied by the equilibrium output (Q^{**}). By contrast, under no liability, the firm only collects revenue equal to area B, the revenue associated with the production costs of a risk-free product, and consumers are responsible for their own accident costs. (The magnitude of those expected costs is the same as that in area A, but it is not paid through the market under a rule of no liability.)

In theory, the two ways of insuring against accident risk are equivalent. Either the firm is the insurer or consumers self-insure, but output and the overall cost to consumers is the same. The situation is similar to the optional service contracts that most manufacturers now offer to cover the costs of repair or maintenance of durable goods such as computers or refrigerators, which consumers are free to purchase or decline.[63]

This raises the question of why the costs of product accidents are not handled in the same way as service contracts, meaning through a voluntary contract solution at point of sale. Indeed, at one time products liability *was* governed primarily by contract, but now, under strict liability, manufacturer insurance for product accidents is compulsory. Below, we offer an economic explanation for this doctrinal shift. We now reconsider the exploding Coca Cola bottle case from the perspective of insurance and least cost avoider analysis.

We previously explained that even when both parties to a tort take cost-effective precautions, there is a residual risk that must be allocated. One approach to its allocation rests on which party can insure at lower cost, either through self-insurance or with a third party insurer.

In the *Escola* case, Coca Cola's ability to absorb the risk is partly a function of its market power, and thus of the *elasticity of demand* for its product. As shown in Figure 4:2 above, to the extent it is operating along the inelastic portion of its demand function, Coca Cola has the power to pass along the additional cost associated with liability for the exploding Coke-bottle risk. If Coca Cola either self insures or purchases a policy to cover

---

[62] ERIC MILLS HOLMES & MARK S. RHODES, HOLMES'S APPLEMAN ON INSURANCE §§ 1.2, 1.3 (1996).

[63] One function of offering an extended product warranty is that the manufacturer can offer a standard warranty to the average consumer at a lower-price while segregating high-intensity or higher-risk users to purchase additional protection. *See* George L. Priest, *A Theory of the Consumer Product Warranty*, 90 YALE L.J. 1297 (1981). Critics of extended warranties argue that they sometimes are purchased by consumers who do not benefit from them, in part because of high-pressure sales pressure. *Just Say "No" to Extended Warranties*, DAVE RAMSEY, https://www.daveramsey.com/blog/just-say-no-to-extended-warranties-dr (last visited Oct. 10, 2017).

the residual risk associated with such unexpected accidents, it can then pass on the cost to its consumers through a slight increase in the price of its bottles, and the consumers will then absorb the insurance premium as part of the purchase price if, instead, however, the victim did not recover damages, that would require each purchaser to be responsible for the residual risk. Each consumer would then be required either to self-insure or to purchase her own insurance from a third party. As previously discussed, this implicates a trade-off in who is better suited to insure against a residual risk, the manufacturer or the consumers, bearing in mind that consumers are apt to insure larger bundles of risk rather than individual risks.

2. *Manufacturer and Consumer Care Choices*

We now turn to manufacturer and consumer care choices. As we have seen, the choice of liability rule did not affect the level of output. The question is whether the same analysis applies to the level of care.

In theory, the answer is yes, and, once more, this follows as a consequence of the Coase Theorem. Consider first the situation under no liability. We saw in the model of accidents between strangers that victims will take efficient care because they bear their own damages, but injurers will not. In the case of products, however, absent producer liability, producers would offer a safe product and demand a higher price to cover the extra cost, which consumers willingly pay because they value safety. As a result, producers supply safe products to the market even though they are not liable for any accident costs. A similar argument can be made under strict liability. In the stranger model, the problem was a lack of victim care; in the case of products, the necessary bargain would involve consumers promising to use the product safely after purchase in return for a lower product price. In both cases, Coasian bargaining at the point of sale theoretically achieves the efficient level of care by injurers and victims regardless of the liability rule.

Attentive readers likely noticed potential problems with the preceding logic. In the case of no liability, the efficient outcome would require consumers to be able to accurately assess the safety features or, more generally, the quality of the product to determine if those features are worth the higher price. There are, however, several alternatives: Government regulators, such as the *Consumer Product Safety Commission*, can set standards for safety and inspect to ensure compliance. Third parties with relevant expertise, such as *Consumer Reports* or *Underwriter's Laboratory*, can also assess quality and safety. And special marketing schemes reinforced by a company's reputation and name-brand can also ensure high quality, as with *Certified Pre-owned Lexus*.[64] The Lexus program allows the manufacture to signal that it is not only willing to warrant its new vehicles at the point of initial sale, but also that it is willing to warrant its used vehicles that satisfy an inspection process several years later. This scheme signals to potential new purchasers that the vehicle is likely to be of particularly high initial quality.

Beyond this, individuals can sometimes inspect goods on their own, although this is of limited value for most complex goods, especially those with potential safety concerns. Especially in circumstances in which it is not possible to personally inspect, for example,

---

[64] Other brands offer similar products, but Lexus was the first to do so. *See* Jim Mateja, *Toyota's Luxury-Car Division Hopes Certified "Pre-Owned" Autos Lure More Customers*, CHI. TRIB., Feb. 18, 1994, at 5C.

the safety of essential vehicle systems and safety features such as airbags, relying on agencies or skilled third parties is essential.

Under strict liability, the problem is reversed. When manufacturers are liable for damage by products that require maintenance, they are dependent on consumer behavior. One solution is to place conditions on warranties. Automobile manufacturers, for example, typically maintain warranties on the condition that the owner complies with a series of preset service visits to ensure that the vehicle is properly maintained. This allows the manufacturer to share costs with the purchaser in a manner that is similar to insurance deductibles in reducing moral hazard.

These approaches are each helpful; none is foolproof. A particular challenge arises when consumers use products in ways not intended by the manufacturer but that create serious risks. An extreme example is using a chainsaw to trim hedges. Adopting the appropriate rule of liability is important in creating proper incentives for care in these cases and in those involving complex products. As previously discussed, there are several available negligence rules: simple negligence, negligence with contributory negligence, comparative fault, and strict liability with contributory negligence. The next section demonstrates that the ability of consumers to accurately perceive risk can narrow these choices.

3. *The Impact of Consumer Perceptions of Risk*

The traditional economic model of accidents, whether involving strangers or parties in privity, assumes that injurers and victims accurately assess the risks that they face. Behavioral economists have argued, however, that this is often an unjustified assumption because people systematically misperceive risk. Some scholars assert that individuals tend to underestimate the likelihood of bad events that occur with relatively high probability, and to overestimate the likelihood of highly visible risks that occur with relatively low probability.[65] If this is true, then such errors in risk assessment could have an important effect on the assessment of the efficiency of the various liability rules.[66] And even if consumers accurately assess risk, the complexity of most modern products makes it difficult to acquire and process the information necessary to compare the costs and benefits of such products.[67]

Fortunately, there is a much more economical way for producers to convey product risks to consumers, specifically through the price mechanism under a rule of strict-products liability. As shown above, when producers are strictly liable, the supply curve shifts up by the amount of the per unit risk (assuming a well-functioning market), resulting in an equilibrium price that reflects the full cost to the consumer, including the expected loss from an accident. Thus, under strict liability, consumers do not need to independently

---

[65] KIP VISCUSI, REFORMING PRODUCTS LIABILITY 62–65 (1991); Christine Jolls, *Behavioral Economic Analysis of Redistributive Legal Rules*, *in* BEHAVIORAL LAW AND ECONOMICS 288, 292–93 (Cass Sunstein ed., 2000).

[66] Michael A. Spence, *Consumer Misperceptions, Product Failure and Producer Liability*, 44 REV. ECON. STUD. 561 (1977); William Rogerson, *Efficient Reliance and Damage Measures for Breach of Contract*, 15 RAND J. ECON. 39 (1984); Thomas J. Miceli et al., *Products Liability When Consumers Vary in Their Susceptibility to Harm and May Misperceive Risk*, 33 CONTEMP. ECON. POL'Y 468 (2015).

[67] LANDES & POSNER, *supra* note 37, at 281.

assess the risk because the quality of the good, including the risk it poses in comparison with others, is signaled by the price. Of course, for this benign story to hold, producers must have accurate knowledge concerning the risks of the products that they market. At a minimum, it is fair to assume that producers hold greater information about such risks for complex consumer products than purchasers. The general historical trend in this area toward strict liability likely reflects this asymmetry in the capacity for risk assessment.[68]

This advantage to strict liability must be balanced against the potential effects on consumer incentives to use products responsibly. (Recall that consumers generally do not have an incentive to take efficient care under strict liability.) The simple solution is to introduce a defense of contributory negligence, which would bar recovery in cases where consumers are found to have used the product improperly, meaning with insufficient care (once again, the perhaps-apocryphal story of a consumer who was injured when he used a chain saw to trim his hedges). Actual products liability law arrived at a rule much like this around the middle to late twentieth century, when producers subject to strict liability were permitted to rest on such affirmative defenses as product misuse and assumption of risk. Toward the end of the twentieth century, however, courts began stripping away such defenses, thereby holding producers liable for some risks that were unforeseen (or unforeseeable).[69]

As a result, some commentators have characterized the current standard for products liability as one of "absolute" or "enterprise" liability, under which producers are liable for any accidents caused by their products.[70] In essence, producers are now insurers against product risk, including for those uses and risks that they could not have anticipated.

C. Regulation Versus Tort Law for Controlling Product Risk

Government regulation and the tort system are alternative methods of controlling product risks and of enforcing product safety. Government regulation of consumer products emerged as a prominent public policy concern during the 1970s, and it has since become an important means for ensuring product safety.[71] This section briefly examines the choice between regulation (public control) and tort law (private control) for mitigating product risk.

Liability provides producers with incentives to invest in cost-effective safety features under the threat of having to pay consumer damages, whereas regulation sets a safety standard with which firms must comply under the threat of legal sanction. In terms of incentives, regulation therefore functions much like a negligence standard. Although compliance with a regulatory standard does not absolutely absolve a tortfeasor of liability,

---

[68] *See* Keith Hylton, *The Law and Economics of Products Liability*, NOTRE DAME L. REV. 2457 (2013), whose risk-utility approach to products liability also cautiously argues that current law probably enhances social welfare.

[69] COOTER & ULEN, *supra* note 56, at 404.

[70] *Id.* at 405; Priest, *supra* note 56; *see also* text accompanying note 56, *supra*.

[71] W. KIP VISCUSI ET AL., *Product Safety*, *in* ECONOMICS OF REGULATION AND ANTITRUST 789 (4th ed. 2005).

it is helpful evidence respecting the chosen standard of care. When the defendant complies with a federal standard, in some instances that can be a complete defense against a state tort claim based upon federal preemption.[72] The different ways that strict liability and negligence work, as previously discussed, shed light on the relative advantages and disadvantages of liability versus regulation.

As we have already seen, strict liability gives manufacturers an incentive to produce safe products by requiring them to pay victim damages. Because it promises full compensation, it simultaneously reduces incentives for consumers to use dangerous products carefully. A regulatory standard, by contrast, improves consumer incentives to use products carefully and to make educated purchase decisions precisely because they are *not* compensated for any damages.[73] In an ideal world, therefore, an appropriately tailored regulatory standard is apt to be more efficient than strict liability because, like a negligence rule, it would give both producers and consumers an incentive to be cautious. The main disadvantages of the regulatory standard are twofold[74]: (1) the difficulty of setting the standard appropriately, and (2) the challenge of ensuring that consumers accurately perceive the risk so that they can make efficient purchase and use decisions. If consumers systematically misperceive risk, as some have argued, they risk making these choices inefficiently. To that extent, strict liability might be preferable as a means of conveying a more accurate risk signal based on the product price.

Both liability and regulation are therefore imperfect alternatives for the control of product risk, with the advantage shifting in the direction of liability as consumer misperceptions become more severe.[75] Other factors that affect the choice between the two approaches include imperfections in the operation of the liability system, such as the problem of the judgment-proof defendant discussed above, and the effect of political influences on the regulatory system, which can distort policies in favor of influential interest groups, which we will explore in part IV.[76]

III. OTHER AREAS OF TORT LAW

This section briefly discusses three other prominent areas of tort law: medical malpractice, environmental accidents, and workplace accidents. Many of the issues discussed above apply to these areas, so the discussion here will focus on the unique features of each.

---

[72] Keith N. Hylton, *Preemption and Products Liability: A Positive Theory*, 16 SUP. CT. ECON. REV. 205 (2008); Richard C. Ausness, *The Case for a "Strong" Regulatory Compliance Defense*, 55 MD. L. REV. 1210 (1996).

[73] This assumes, of course, that ex ante regulation replaces or precludes ex post liability in tort. In fact, however, the two regimes often coexist. A. Mitchell Polinsky & Steven Shavell, *The Uneasy Case for Product Liability*, 123 HARV. L. REV. 1437 (2010).

[74] For now we set aside the discussion, which we return to in part III, and especially Chapters 11 and 12, raising the related concerns of interest group influence in the development of regulatory standards, including potential agency capture by regulated industries. *See infra* Part III.

[75] Miceli et al., *supra* note 66; For an analysis of the choice between liability and regulation in the case of accidents involving strangers, see Steven Shavell, *A Model of the Optimal Use of Liability and Safety Regulation*, 15 RAND J. ECON. 271 (1984).

[76] *See infra* Chapters 11 and 12.

A. Medical Malpractice

Medical malpractice is an increasingly prominent area of tort law. This is partly due to the wider availability of high-risk medical procedures and partly due to a more general overall upward trend in tort claims. Medical malpractice resembles products liability in the sense that the injurer (provider) and victim (patient) have a pre-existing market relationship, and, as a result, contractual principles can theoretically govern the assignment of liability. Despite this, medical patients, like consumers of dangerous products, are not usually well suited to understand the risks, and based on the procedures involved, they are also likely to be infrequent purchasers. As a result, a purely contractual solution will not generally lead to efficient outcomes regarding the assignment of liability. Another factor precluding a contractual solution is the prominence of third-party insurance in the medical marketplace. Because they do not pay the full cost of medical care, moral hazard further distorts patient decisions regarding the consumption of treatment.

Liability for medical malpractice, for example associated with medical procedures, is generally based on negligence, with the due care standard reflecting "customary practice." That is, "the doctor must have and use the knowledge, skill and care ordinarily possessed and employed by members of the profession in good standing."[77] Physicians who are specialized and who hold themselves out as specialists are subject to a standard of care commensurate with others in their field, as opposed to doctors more generally.[78] Customary practice itself therefore varies depending on the level of medical specialization. Failure of a physician to adhere to customary practice is therefore a basis for imposing liability on the physician in the event of an accident.

This raises the question whether adherence to customary practice necessarily shields the physician from liability. In other areas of law, custom does not provide an absolute bar of recovery by plaintiffs if the court determines that an industry custom has lagged behind what would be cost-justified in terms of precautions.[79] In medical practice, however, courts are generally reluctant to find against a physician absent adverse testimony from another physician. This effectively allows the medical profession to set its own standards, a feature largely attributable to the specialized knowledge associated with the field of medicine. Although this can make such claims harder to prove, it is also true that, in general, physicians are subject to a high set of ethical standards concerning patient care.[80]

Partially offsetting the problem of asymmetric information between physicians and patients is the doctrine of *informed consent*. This requires physicians to inform patients beforehand about particular risks involved in their treatment. This duty is limited, however, to disclosure of *material risks*, defined as risks that a reasonable person would find significant or as risks that are customarily disclosed. This reflects a concern about the costs of conveying detailed information when the risk in question is extremely remote.

---

[77] W. PAGE KEETON ET AL., PROSSER AND KEETON ON TORTS 187 (5th ed. 1984).

[78] DAN B. DOBBS ET AL., THE LAW OF TORTS § 298 (2d ed. 2016).

[79] *See, e.g.*, The T.J. Hooper, 60 F.2d 737 (2d Cir. 1932).

[80] Full disclosure: Two of the authors are married to physicians.

(Note the similarity of this logic to that underlying the proximate cause limitation, which, we observed, is also based on a reasonable foreseeability standard.)

A final point regarding malpractice concerns the claim that expanding liability, and the corresponding increase in medical malpractice insurance rates, has caused physicians to practice *defensive medicine*. Professor Patricia Danzon defines the term as follows: "liability-induced changes in medical practice that entail costs in excess of benefits and that would not have occurred in the absence of liability."[81] If courts truly enforce a customary practice standard for determining negligence, however, this should not result in excessive treatment unless the customary practice standard is itself inefficiently stringent. Defensive medicine might therefore signal an evolving legal standard, perhaps reflecting the increasing ability of modern medicine to detect risks. It might also result from greater demand for medical care that is due to the moral hazard problem associated with third-party insurance for health care.

B. Environmental Accidents

Tort liability for environmental harm typically involves unanticipated events, such as oil spills or toxic waste leaks. This is distinguished from continuous and predictable discharge of pollutants as a by-product of a firm's production process, which is the subject of regulatory controls. Two problems impede the use of tort liability for controlling many environmental accidents. The first, referred to as the "dispersed cost" problem, arises because many environmental accidents involve multiple victims. Although the aggregate harm may be large, no single victim is likely to have sustained sufficient harm that would justify incurring the cost of filing a lawsuit.

One solution is a class action suit, which bundles individual claims into a single legal action, thereby achieving significant economies of scale in adjudicating claims. The success of a class action suit typically relies on entrepreneurial attorneys, who exercise substantial control over the disposition of the suit,[82] and who, in addition, stand to gain the most from the settlement or a favorable verdict if the class is large.

The second problem with environmental accidents concerns uncertainty respecting causation. This can happen either because one of many injurers is potentially responsible for the harm, which can arise in various settings, including when several firms dump waste into a landfill, or when there is independent background risk of illness coupled with claimed exposure to a carcinogenic substance. In the case of multiple injurers, the traditional common law rule is "joint and several liability," which allows a plaintiff to collect full damages from any one of the multiple defendants but which allows only a single full recovery. This rule not only overcomes the legal uncertainty over which injurer was the actual cause, but also it allows the plaintiff to go after the defendant with the deepest pockets. The previous discussion of causal uncertainty described two other

---

[81] Patricia Danzon, *Liability for Medical Malpractice*, J. ECON. PERSP., Summer 1991, at 51, 54. There is a literature that investigates whether common practices among physicians are actually motivated by concerns for tort liability or by other considerations, including a belief that juries inaccurately assess liability out of sympathy for injured claimants. *See* David A. Hyman, Myungho Paik, & Bernard Black, *Damage Caps and Defensive Medicine, Revisited*, 51J. HEALTH ECON. 84 (2017).

[82] Jonathan R. Macey & Geoffrey P. Miller, *The Plaintiffs' Attorney's Role in Class Action and Derivative Litigation: Economic Analysis and Recommendations for Reform*, 58 U. CHI. L. REV. 1 (1991).

possible approaches to the assignment of liability in the case of multiple risks: the *probability-threshold rule*, and the *proportional-liability rule*.[83]

Yet another approach to causal uncertainty that some have advocated, especially in the case of risks with a long latency period, is for courts to impose liability at the time of exposure in proportion to the risk incurred. This is contrary to traditional tort principles, which limit recovery to *actual* damages. The advantage of the *tort for risk* rule is that it avoids the problem that injurers might be judgment-proof by the time an illness actually manifests itself. The disadvantage is the possibility of a substantial increase in the volume of lawsuits.[84]

Environmental risks arising from hazardous waste disposal are also governed by statute: specifically, the *Comprehensive Environmental Response, Compensation, and Liability Act (CERCLA)*, enacted in 1980.[85] The primary purpose of this statute was to ensure the cleanup of hazardous waste sites and to impose the cost, when possible, on responsible parties. Under CERCLA, liability is strict and, in the case of multiple polluters, is apportioned based on joint and several liability.

C. Workplace Accidents

We finally consider workplace accidents. This includes those situations in which a worker either causes an injury to a non-worker in the course of employment, or where the worker himself is injured on the job, either due to unsafe working conditions or through the actions of another worker. For accidents where the victim is not another employee, the worker is personally liable if the accident was the result of his negligence, but the employer is also potentially liable under the doctrine of *respondeat superior*, which as we have seen, is a form of vicarious liability.[86] As argued above, the principal economic rationale for this shifting of liability away from the responsible party is that the latter will often lack the resources to compensate the victim, whereas the employer will generally have sufficient resources. The disadvantage is the moral hazard associated with knowing that someone else, the employer, is responsible to pay in the event of your negligence. This problem is mitigated, however, to the extent that the employer can monitor workers and fire, or otherwise discipline, those who behave in a negligent manner.

The second category of workplace accidents involves injuries suffered by workers in the course of their employment. Historically, workers who caused accidents were personally liable if the accident was the result of their negligence, but under the *fellow servant rule*, employers were generally absolved of liability provided that they maintained a reasonably safe workplace. The rationale usually given for this rule was that workers entered an employment situation at their own risk, and in addition, workers were in at least as good a position as the employer to observe and prevent unsafe behavior by their fellow workers. Although such logic may have made sense in the context of the small workplaces that characterized the early days of industrialization, it seems less applicable

---

[83] *See supra* Part III.A.3.

[84] For a formal analysis of a tort for risk, see Thomas Miceli & Kathleen Segerson, *Do Exposure Suits Produce a Race to File? An Economic Analysis of a Tort for Risk*, 36 RAND J. ECON. 613 (2005).

[85] 42 U.S.C. §§ 9601 *et seq.* (2016).

[86] *See supra* Part I.C.3.

in modern work settings that potentially involve large numbers of workers whose behavior cannot be easily observed. For this reason, the fellow servant rule, like the privity limitation for product accidents, was an effective bar of recovery for most industrial accidents prior to the turn of the twentieth century.[87]

That changed with the passage of workers' compensation laws during the early decades of the twentieth century.[88] Under these laws, liability was shifted to employers for any injuries a worker sustained in the course of his or her employment. This included accidents that occurred as a result of another worker's negligence or the victim's own contributory negligence. The rule is thus one of strict employer liability. While this system creates an incentive for employers to maintain a safe workplace, it would seem to significantly reduce incentives for workers to employ due care. This problem is substantially mitigated by the statutory limit on damages schedules for each class of injury when assessed against the suffering from the workplace injury itself. This limitation, like insurance deductibles, enhances worker incentive to take appropriate precautions in order to reduce the expected amount of under-compensation.[89] A further check on workplace safety is provided by the *Occupational Safety and Health Administration (OSHA)*, which was established in 1970 to ensure safe and healthy working conditions.[90] Thus, as was true with potentially dangerous products, there is redundancy in the control of workplace risk.

IV. APPLICATIONS

A. Darnell Michaels v. Tandem Skydiving *Revisited*

Please review question 1 from Chapter 3, which sets out the basic facts. In light of the analysis from this chapter, consider the following variation, which considers incentives both with respect to care levels and activity levels.

Assume that the evidence is indeterminate as to what caused the accident. As the quoted data, introduced with appropriate expert witness testimony, reveal, there is a small category of accidents that are simply anomalies, although there are also some that are caused by human error. There is no way to ascertain on the facts of the case whether this tragic accident was caused by human error or not.

QUESTION

1. Based on the economic analysis of tort law, should the contract operate as a barrier to suit?

2. What theory of liability would create the better incentives on the part of Tandem Skydiving and its customers, including Mary Able, to reduce the social cost of accidents?

---

87 KEETON ET AL., *supra* note 77, at 571–72.

88 DOBBS ET AL., *supra* note 78, § 503.

89 LANDES & POSNER, *supra* note 37, at 311.

90 Occupational Safety & Health Act, Pub. L. No. 91–596, 84 Stat. 1590 (1970).

3. Should the answer to question 2 have any effect on whether the skydiving contract is legally binding?

4. How would you define "appropriate care" in this context?

5. Based on the economic theory of tort law, should the contract be binding only for purposes of Mindy Able's estate or also for any separate cause of action Darnell Michael raises?

6. Assuming that Packer was truly careless and that his carelessness caused the fatal accident, is there a benefit to recognizing his conduct as the basis for negligent and reckless homicide, while disallowing tort recovery based on the contract? How does your answer relate to Pigouvian taxation? To incentives respecting activity levels?

B. Mary Waters v. Calvert's Colors Painting

Assume that from the years 1950 through 1965, three manufacturers of lead pigment paint dominated the Old City, New State market for newly constructed homes: *Albert Paint and Supply*, *Barnett Quality Paints,* and *Calvert's Color Painting.*[91] Each of these companies used lead pigment in its exterior home-painting products, as was then standard-industry practice. The difficulty is that in homes that are not well maintained and in which the paint chips and peels, toddlers often ingest the paint or the chemicals the paint contains, and in doing so subject themselves to considerable and permanent neurological damage.

In the intervening years since these companies dominated the market, the records concerning which houses were painted with paint supplied by each of these manufacturers have been almost entirely lost to history. In a series of cases, including *Ann Amsterdam v. Albert Paint and Supply,* Albert Paint cross-claimed against Barnett Quality Paints and Calvert's Color Painting, and Amsterdam then amended her complaint also to claim against these other defendants. Amsterdam's daughter, Isabel, had ingested lead content from lead pigment paint in her home, causing severe and permanent neurological harm assessed at $5 million in projected damages. Because there was no way to prove which company supplied the paint, the Superior Court of New State allocated liability based on the breakdown of market share in 1958, the year that the home was completed, and thus when it was initially painted. At that time, Albert controlled 40%, Barnett controlled 25%, and Calvert's controlled 35% of the market. The Court apportioned liability on this basis, and affirmed the jury verdict of $20 million based on a multiplier of 400% of actual damages. This ruling was affirmed by the Supreme Court of New State.

Assume the following: Mary Waters purchased her home in Old City, New State, in 2005. Since then, her ten-year old son, Theodore, has experienced severe and permanent neurological damage that doctors have ascribed to lead-pigment paint exposure in their home. The damages are projected at $7 million. Since the landmark *Ann Amsterdam* case, there have been several cases in New State that operate on the principle of market-share liability. As a result, Ms. Waters brought suit against all three manufacturers, whose market shares at the time her house was constructed in 1962 are as follows: Albert 35%, Barnett

[91] In the actual lead paint litigation, the defendants were the lead pigment suppliers to the paint companies. *See, e.g.*, Skipworth v. Lead Indus. Ass'n, Inc., 690 A.2d 169 (Pa. 1997); Thomas v. Mallett, 701 N.W.2d 523 (Wis. 2005). To simplify the presentation without changing the analysis, here we simply refer to multiple paint suppliers based on their market share and assume that each obtains lead pigment from a different source.

20%, and Calvert 45%. Assume that in discovery, the paint manufacturers learned that there is a safe within the Ms. Waters's house that had not been opened since she purchased the house in 2005. Because she did not have the combination, she was ordered to have a locksmith open the safe to ascertain whether the contents included potentially relevant materials. In fact, the safe contained the original architectural drawings, the house specifications, and all of the contract materials for the contractors, subcontractors, suppliers of original appliances, and most notably for the paint. The paint was supplied by Barnett, which, as stated above, held a 20% market share at the time the house was painted.

Assume that the Superior Court of Old State issues the following ruling on the motions to dismiss by Albert and Calvert:

> It is certainly true that in the ordinary course, a defendant cannot be held liable in tort unless he was a cause in fact of the plaintiff's injury. On that basis, it is clear that Albert and Calvert's motion to dismiss are not frivolous, as the documentation reveals with certainty that the paint was supplied by Barnett. This is a highly unusual case, however, and one in which the usual rules that govern the "cause in fact" component of a tort claim cannot be easily applied. Since the landmark case of *Ann Amsterdam v. Albert Paint and Supply*, there have been no fewer than 20 litigated cases, and a larger number of settled cases, in which the courts and the parties have successfully relied upon the principle of market-share liability. In effect, the market-share liability theory has operated as a shield to each manufacturer against the risk of a greater liability exposure than the extant market share based on the best available evidence from when the home was initially painted. It would be illogical to now allow the fact that one or more of the market participants at that time was not the actual supplier to then use that fact as a sword, foisting complete liability on the known supplier, in this case Barnett. I therefore reject the motions to dismiss, but I will stay the trial and allow an interlocutory appeal before the trial proceeds on the specific question whether my denial of the motions to dismiss was proper in this case.[92]

Scenario 1:

1. Assume that you are clerking for Justice Harriet Higgins of the New State Court of Appeals. Applying the economic principles of tort law, how would you advise that she rule in this case, and why? What role, if any, would the *Law of Large Numbers* play in your analysis?

2. How would you rule as a matter of law?

3. Are your answers to questions 1 and 2 consistent, and why or why not?

Scenario 2:

Instead of buying the home in 2005, Mary Waters and her husband, Walter, were the original homeowners and they had the home built to their specifications. Mr. Waters

---

[92] An interlocutory appeal is a special appeal that must be authorized by the trial judge and that takes place before the resolution of all claims, typically before the trial. For the relevant federal rule, see 28 U.S.C. § 1292(b) (2012).

passed away in 1970 of a heart attack, and Ms. Waters lived in the home since then, raising her daughter, Marcia. Marcia since married Greg, and the two then moved in with Mary. In 2005, they had a son, Marcus, who is the victim of the lead-pigment paint poisoning. At trial, there is uncontested evidence that Mary Waters and her daughter did not maintain the paint well, and that if they had done so, ensuring that there was no peeling paint, the likelihood that Marcus would have suffered lead paint poisoning would have dropped by 80%. Assume that the damages are $10 million.

1. Which tort theory provides the best incentives for reducing the social cost of such incidents, and why?

2. Assuming that New State employs comparative fault, how would you assess damages as between the plaintiff and the combined defendants? (For these question, you need not be concerned about market-share liability, and may treat the defendant as a single entity).

CHAPTER 5

Contract Law (Part 1)

Introduction

Contract Law is the body of common law doctrine that governs transactions. Unlike parties to paradigmatic tort cases, parties to contract disputes enter into the initial transaction, and thus their relationship, voluntarily. This fundamental distinction helps to explain important aspects of these two bodies of case law that sometimes align and other times diverge.

Economic analysis helps to identify two primary objectives of a well-functioning system of contract law. First, contract law lowers transaction costs, thereby allowing private parties to more freely move scarce resources to more highly valued uses. Contract doctrine accomplishes this by providing private actors with a set of background, or "off-the-rack," rules that, in general, they can accept implicitly as part of their contract, or they can negotiate in favor of different "tailor made" rules that better suit their needs. This objective facilitates private market transactions.

Second, contract law provides a set of mechanisms for resolving inevitable disputes that arise when contractual relationships break down, most typically (but not always) when one of the parties to a contract has breached or anticipates that the other party will breach.[1] Contract doctrine generally accomplishes this by seeking to replicate the reasonable expectations of the parties at the time of contracting, as opposed to furthering the interests of either party once the contractual relationship has failed, and thus when they are no longer motivated to construe their agreement so as to promote joint gains. This second objective is intended to provide a fair resolution of contract disputes that becomes part of a dynamic feedback loop, informing future contractual negotiations.

Just as economic analysis is helpful in analyzing the law of contract, so too contract law is helpful in explaining something that can get lost in conventional economic analysis. As shown in Chapter 2, as a starting point, economists tend to divide market structures into the extremes of pure competition and pure monopoly, with bilateral monopoly as a special case of the latter. Bilateral monopoly involves a monopolistic supplier and a

---

[1] The latter involves the doctrine of anticipatory repudiation, in which a promisor announces an anticipated breach and places a duty to mitigate the resulting harm on the other side, or which sometimes follows a demand for assurance of performance that may or may not be forthcoming. ROBERT A. HILLMAN, PRINCIPLES OF CONTRACT LAW 335–39 (3d ed. 2014); JOSEPH M. PERILLO, CONTRACTS § 12.3, at 454 (7th ed. 2014).

monopsonistic purchaser, and this combination represents the antithesis of pure competition. In fact, however, whether parties enter into their initial contracts under purely competitive or less-than-competitive conditions, when the contract requires ongoing performance by one or both parties, and when an unanticipated contingency arises that causes the relationship to break down, the parties suddenly find their relationship transformed into a bilateral monopoly.

Nobel Laureate Oliver Williamson captured this intuition as follows:

> Although large-numbers competition is frequently feasible at the initial award stage for recurring contracts of all kinds, idiosyncratic transactions are ones for which the relationship between the buyer and supplier is quickly thereafter *transformed* into one of bilateral monopoly—on account of the transaction-specific costs .... This transformation has profound contracting consequences.[2]

One consequence that follows from this analysis is that contract adjudication typically forces a court to choose whether to further the objectives of the parties as of the time of contract formation (when they faced "large-numbers competition"), or, instead, as of the time of the litigation (when they are in a bilateral monopoly). In this chapter, we will see effective contract doctrine generally takes the former, *ex ante*, perspective.

When contract law operates properly, it reduces the cost of transacting by identifying in advance the circumstances that render promises enforceable. Promises come in many varieties, but only some provide those who experience a broken promise the basis for a legal remedy. That remedy is not always the one that the non-breaching party anticipated or even the one specified in the contract.

These insights raise a number of important doctrinal questions: What are the conditions that determine enforceability? What is the optimal remedy when someone breaks an enforceable promise, thus breaching a contract? Should the court simply order the party who breached to perform (if that is possible), or should it instead order monetary compensation? If it chooses the latter, how should that compensation be assessed? Should it be based on the value of the opportunity that induced the breach, the expected value of performance to the non-breaching party, or some other calculation? Does it matter if the parties specified the damages or mandated specific performance, in the contract itself? The economic theory of contract law, developed throughout this chapter and Chapter 6, seeks to answer these and other related questions. These analyses rest on the general intuition that a central function of contract law is to maximize the gains of contracting parties from their voluntary transactions.

If we set aside the special problems of initial wealth endowments and externalities,[3] contract law facilitates exchanges that satisfy the condition of *Pareto* superiority:[4] Because the exchange is designed to improve the position of at least one of the parties without

---

[2] Oliver E. Williamson, *Transaction-Cost Economics: The Governance of Contractual Relationships*, 22 J.L. ECON. & ORG. 233, 241 (1979) (emphasis in original).

[3] On the endowment effect, see Herbert Hovenkamp, *Legal Policy and the Endowment Effect*, 20 J. LEGAL STUD. 225 (1991). On externalities, see RICHARD A. IPPOLITO, ECONOMICS FOR LAWYERS 228–31 (2005) (generally explaining the effect of external costs on private transactions).

[4] *See supra* Chapter 2 (defining *Pareto* criterion).

harming anyone else, the overall exchange is expected to improve social welfare. More simply: Enforceable voluntary transactions create societal wealth. If Alice values her used car at $5000, and Barbara values it at $7000, by Alice selling the car to Barbara for $6000, each comes out $1000 ahead as compared with the initial state in which Alice has a car that she undervalues and that Barbara would value more highly. The exchange is *mutually beneficial* in that each party shares in the overall *gains from trade*. Mutual benefit arising from voluntary transactions is the defining characteristic of a *free market exchange*. Although other exchanges, such as gift-giving, can also improve social welfare—with the gift benefiting the recipient and the act of giving bringing happiness to the giver—in general, promises to gift do not form the basis for enforceable contracts due to absence of a bargained-for reciprocal promise.[5] In contract law, the reciprocal promise is called *consideration*,[6] although in some cases, the courts allow a promisee (the party to whom the promise is made) to bind a promisor (the party making the promise) based on objectively verifiable *reliance*.[7]

Although contracts are legal devices that facilitate market exchange, not all contractual relationships require written documentation. Formal written contracts are generally not needed when the exchange is instantaneous and information about the nature or quality of the good or service being transferred is easily ascertained. In most states, *The Statute of Frauds* specifies when a written contract is required.[8] In general, when the exchange is executory, meaning that it involves some continuing obligation on both sides to perform; when the price exceeds a set amount; or when there is uncertainty about quality at the time of exchange or some other aspect of performance for which there is a need for verification, a written contract is required. Written contracts help to resolve disputes, especially those that arise in relatively complex transactions. For example, suppose that after Alice sells her car to Barbara, the car turns out to have a hidden defect. A written contract will help to determine the expectations of the parties, and in doing so, will help to resolve such disputes.

Contract disputes generally arise from an unanticipated change in circumstance between the time of contract formation and contract performance and that makes one of the parties dissatisfied with the original terms. Contracting parties sometimes anticipate potential risks that could undermine performance and specify how it should be handled in the contract. For example, Alice's automobile sales contract might include a warranty covering certain defects for a specified period of time. Sometimes, however, the parties leave the resolution of risks to background, or off-the-rack, contracting rules. And when the parties' expectations are unclear, it often falls to courts to interpret the contract against such rules to devise a solution.

As a general matter, the economic analysis of contract law suggests that in resolving such a dispute, courts should inquire how the parties to the contract would have resolved

---

[5] For a possible exception in which the recipient relies to his detriment on the commitment of a gift, thereby rendering the promise enforceable, *see infra* Part I (discussing Hamer v. Sidway, 27 N.E. 256 (N.Y. 1891)).

[6] *See infra* Part I (discussing consideration).

[7] *See infra* Part I (discussing RESTATEMENT (SECOND) OF CONTRACTS § 90). For an extensive discussion on the relationship between § 90 and consideration, see Charles J. Goetz & Robert E. Scott, *Enforcing Promises: An Examination of the Basis of Contract*, 89 YALE L.J. 1261 (1980).

[8] HILLMAN, *supra* note 1, at 132–33; PERILLO, *supra* note 1, § 19.1.

the matter had they anticipated it at the time of contracting and negotiated its resolution in the contract itself. The *ex ante* approach is analogous to the "reasonable person" standard in tort law, except in this context, the court will inquire what reasonable contracting parties would have done had they thought about the problem in advance. This follows from the insight above. At the time of contracting, the parties are structuring their relationship so as to maximize the wealth-producing feature of the contract. They are motivated to do this because by increasing the size of their joint gains, they can each obtain a larger benefit, for example if they split the gains evenly. After a contractual relationship has failed, however, the parties find themselves in a bilateral monopoly, and as a general matter, each party's principal concern is to gain the maximum benefit from the resolution of the dispute without regard to broader social welfare.

Although a simplified vision of contract might suggest that parties generally transact under competitive conditions and that, in doing so, they improve social welfare, the reality is often more complex. Sometimes parties lack the capacity to consent, or they enter into contracts under duress. When this occurs, courts have the power to decline to enforce the contract terms. A contract might also fail to improve social welfare if there are externalities, costs that are borne by a third party and that distort the incentives associated with the transaction. There are a variety of legal methods to address this concern, not all of which involve contract doctrine. For example, permitting requirements prevent the construction of certain buildings or other structures that could adversely affect the property values of those in the community. Similarly, licensing requirements prevent dispensing services for which most individuals cannot themselves assess the qualification of the person holding out claimed expertise. Although the parties might wish to enter into such contracts, the legal system imposes limits and sometimes disallows the contract altogether.

One important limitation on contract law is that contract doctrine does not determine its own domain. The permissibility of excluding certain subjects from permissible contracting, for example, the rendering of legal or medical services without a license, the dispensing of illegal medications, the ban on child labor, and the like, are not controlled by contract law regardless of whether some might view the regulatory restrictions as inhibiting potential social welfare enhancing transactions. The permissible scope of restrictions on contract—or the domain of contract law—is a question of constitutional or statutory law, not contract law.

Another concern involves so-called "take it or leave it" contracts, sometimes referred to as *contracts of adhesion*.[9] Although the paradigmatic illustration of contract involves two parties dickering over terms, this is increasingly uncommon, especially in advanced markets. When an individual enters into a contract with a utility, buys goods or services online, purchases a complex good, or subscribes to a publication, just to name a few, the terms are most commonly set out in advance, and the purchaser must either accept the terms or walk away. An important policy question that we will consider in this chapter is whether consumers are better off in a contracting environment in which they can dicker over terms or in which they face a menu of fixed contracts offered by a variety of vendors from which to choose.

---

[9] *See infra* Part IV.B.

Finally, many contracts for the sale of complex goods, such as cars, computers, and cell phones, involve substantial information asymmetries in which the manufacturer or vendor has an informational advantage as compared with the purchaser. This can also work in the other direction. The purchaser has a substantial informational advantage related to her creditworthiness or to the burdens she might impose for a good under warranty. Despite these difficulties, it is not necessarily advantageous—and indeed it might be disabling—to require full disclosure of any information potentially relevant to contractual performance. Indeed, contract law involves not only markets for commodities or services, but also the often subtle and complex market for information.

The power of contract law to improve social welfare, or to create wealth, depends on transaction costs. This is an implication of the Coase theorem, which you will recall, states that when transaction costs are low and when individuals have full information, resources will flow to their more highly valued uses without regard to the initial allocation of property rights, or the assignment of liability rules.[10] When these conditions hold, parties are more likely to move scarce resources to their preferred uses contractually. In purely competitive markets—markets that rarely characterize the real world—information costs are low because products are interchangeable and because all relevant information is captured in the price. In real-world economies, ones characterized by specialization, by producers with varying degrees of market power, and by complex long-term contractual relationships, it often falls to the legal system, through developing case law, to devise rules that help lower the cost of transacting.

This chapter proceeds as follows. In Part I, we define the elements of an enforceable contract, including consideration and offer and acceptance. In this part, we also review formation defenses that render a contract voidable. These include incapacity or incompetence, renegotiation and duress, mistake and duty to disclose, and unconscionability. In Part II, we introduce breach of contract, including the theory of efficient breach and remedies for breach. Remedies include expectancy damages, reliance damages, and consequential damages. Chapter 6 continues the economic analysis of contract law. In Part I, we review extensions of breach of contract, including mitigation and impracticability. In Part II, we review alternative contract remedies, including specific performance and liquidated damages clauses. And in Part III, we review other self-enforcing contracts: warranties, long term contracts, and non-compete clauses. Each of these chapter concludes with Applications.

I. DEFINING ENFORCEABLE CONTRACTS

We begin with the most fundamental question of contract law: what makes a contract legally enforceable? As previously observed, contracts allow parties to enter into agreements that result in mutual gains. The traditional way that courts have judged such gains is by asking whether at the time of contract formation, three elements were present: *offer*, *acceptance*, and *consideration*. The first two elements, offer and acceptance, indicate that one party, the *promisor*, has made a promise that the other party, the *promisee*, has accepted. Early commentators relied on offer and acceptance to suggest a *meeting of the minds*, although that alone is insufficient to make a promise enforceable. The promisee must

---

[10] *See supra* Chapter 2.

generally also provide *consideration*. Consideration has been defined in various ways, but the critical elements are (a) a bargained-for exchange of legal rights (meaning that it benefits the person to whom it is given or burdens the party who gives it), and (b) a reciprocal benefit.[11]

In general, the amount of consideration is not relevant to the enforceability of a contract; even nominal consideration is adequate. The rule against weighing the value of consideration can be explained on two grounds. First, requiring "adequate" consideration would allow parties to challenge contracts that, in hindsight, resulted in the other party receiving a good deal. Second, the parties themselves are generally better suited than the courts to determine the appropriate price to attach to a contractual obligation.

Typically, consideration is a monetary payment (or a payment in-kind) given in return for the promised delivery of the good or service in question, but it need not take that form. An important counter-example to ordinary consideration that was nonetheless deemed adequate is the famous case of *Hamer v. Sidway*.[12] The case involved a promise by an uncle to his nephew that if the nephew refrained from drinking and smoking until his twenty-first birthday, the uncle would give him $5000. Although the uncle was alive when the nephew turned twenty-one, he awaited payment until the nephew could use the money wisely, and he died before payment was made. After his death, the uncle's estate refused payment on the ground that the uncle's original promise lacked consideration. The court, however, disagreed, stating:

> [The nephew had] used tobacco, occasionally, drank liquor, and he had a legal right to do so. That right he abandoned for a period of years upon the strength of the promise of the [uncle] that for such forbearance he would give him $5,000. We need not speculate on the effort which may have been required to give up the use of those stimulants. It is sufficient that he restricted his lawful freedom of action within certain prescribed limits upon the faith of his uncle's agreement, and now, having fully performed the conditions imposed, it is of no moment whether such performance actually proved a benefit to the promisor, and the court will not inquire into it . . . .[13]

Although the nephew's forbearance in this case appears to constitute substantial consideration, it is worth emphasizing that in general, courts will not *inquire into the adequacy* of consideration. Perhaps the more troubling question is whether the court should have inquired into the form.

---

[11] HILLMAN, *supra* note 1, at 17–18; PERILLO, *supra* note 1, § 4.2. Notably, the RESTATEMENT (SECOND) OF CONTRACTS § 71 abandons the reciprocal benefit: "(3) The [bargained-for] performance may consist of (a) an act other than a promise, or (b) a forbearance, or (c) the creation, modification, or destruction of a legal relation. (4) The performance or return promise may be given to the promisor or to some other person. It may be given by the promisee or by some other person." RESTATEMENT (SECOND) OF CONTRACTS § 71 (AM. LAW INST. 1981). In general courts have continued to adhere to both listed requirements. *See, e.g.*, Estate of Tahilan v. Friendly Care Home Health Serv., Inc., 731 F. Supp. 2d 1000, 1010 (2010); Hyman v. Ford Motor Co., 142 F. Supp. 2d 735, 741–42 (D.S.C. 2001).

[12] 27 N.E. 256 (N.Y. 1891).

[13] *Id.* at 257.

In the RESTATEMENT (SECOND) OF CONTRACTS § 90, the drafters offered an alternative method of enforcing promises that appears to better fit the *Hamer* facts.

> § 90. PROMISE REASONABLY INDUCING ACTION OR FORBEARANCE
>
> (1) A promise which the promisor should reasonably expect to induce action or forbearance on the part of the promisee or a third person and which does induce such action or forbearance is binding if injustice can be avoided only by enforcement of the promise. The remedy granted for breach may be limited as justice requires.[14]

The *Hamer* court intuited that the uncle reasonably should have anticipated that given the extensive nature of the nephew's forbearance in reliance on his promise to pay, it would be unjust to then deny the payment once the forbearance had taken place. The ultimate question is whether at the time the uncle made the promise that the nephew accepted, the two anticipated that regardless of whether the uncle lived until payment would be appropriately rendered on the agreed-upon terms, the uncle's reciprocal promise would still be enforced. One way to justify this reciprocal obligation of payment is to claim that the uncle benefited by anticipating that the nephew's forbearance would result in his leading a more productive life. This would stretch the intuition of consideration, helping to explain the court's disclaiming an inquiry into whether the uncle received an actual benefit. Instead, the court suggested that the nephew's anticipated reliance itself provided the basis for rendering the reciprocal promise to pay binding, thereby anticipating the logic of § 90 of the Restatement.

The following sections discuss cases that approach enforceability from the opposite perspective, in which, despite consideration, courts decline to enforce for other reasons. Specifically, these cases rest on *formation defenses.* The defenses are so named because, if successfully asserted, they provide a basis for asserting that despite features that appear to render the agreement enforceable, a proper contract was never formed. As a legal matter, these defenses render the contract voidable by the party found legally incompetent. This means that the contract is not automatically rendered invalid. Instead, it can be rendered invalid if the defense is exercised; otherwise the promisee may continue to enforce it. In addition, a formation defense will not absolve the party asserting it of all responsibility. The other party may still seek more limited compensation under the doctrine of *unjust enrichment* following from past performance.

A. Mental Incapacity or Incompetence

Courts generally will not enforce contracts entered into by parties judged to be mentally incompetent, either permanently or temporarily, or too young to be able to understand what is in their best interest.[15] Ensuring mental competence is certainly consistent with ensuring a proper meeting of the minds at the time of offer and acceptance. It might also inform whether a party providing consideration understands its value in relation to the reciprocal commitment by the promisee. More simply put, requiring mental competence places the burden on a party who might otherwise seek to

---

[14] RESTATEMENT (SECOND) OF CONTRACTS § 90(1) (AM. LAW INST. 1981).

[15] *Id.* §§ 12, 14, 15.

take advantage of a person who lacks the capacity to understand the commitments associated with contracting. In cases of immaturity or permanent impairment, the decision to invalidate the contract is clear, but there is a competing concern. The possibility of opportunism arises in cases where one party alleges "temporary" incompetence as a way to avoid performance under conditions that, although attractive at the time of the original transaction, have subsequently become unfavorable.[16] In general, courts will hold the contract enforceable unless the circumstances place it into one of the narrow exceptions discussed below.

B. Renegotiation and the Problem of Economic Duress

Courts can also refuse to enforce contracts entered into under circumstances of duress.[17] On its face, this seems like a straightforward effort to ensure that only agreements entered into voluntarily are enforced, but there is some question as to what constitutes legal coercion. Suppose, for example, that someone approaches a business owner and, in return for a payment of $100 a week, provides assurances that the premises will not be burned down or otherwise vandalized. It seems obvious that such a contract would not be enforceable by a court because the business owner accepted the deal under duress.

The problem in this example is that the *offeror* is encouraging the *offeree* to purchase the security of his premises, which already is her right *but for* the implicit threat by the offeror himself. The owner cannot be legally forced to buy something that she already has a legal right to, namely, to be free from harm. Thus, no value is created by the transaction, and indeed, this is a classic illustration of seeking a rent on the threat of otherwise imposing harm to the owner or her property.

The difficulty is not the binary choice: pay or suffer a consequence. This happens in markets all the time. For example, when negotiating the purchase of a car, the buyer might say "give me a discount or I'll go elsewhere." That is perfectly permissible, of course, and is not an example of seeking a rent. Rather, it is an effort to secure a purchase on more favorable terms, perhaps forcing the dealership to choose between allocating more of the contractual surplus to the buyer or relinquishing the sale to a competitor.

These examples do not present difficult legal questions. Greater problems arise in the context of contract modification. This occurs when one party to an existing contract seeks to renegotiate the original terms prior to completion of performance, usually in response to an unforeseen change in circumstances.[18] Although such renegotiations often take place uneventfully, in some cases, one of the parties regrets the changed contract terms and seeks to enforce the original terms instead. The legal question is under what circumstances a party can have the renegotiated terms rendered void, thus restoring the

---

16 One important policy question is whether terms of the contract itself can be offered as evidence of impairment on the ground that "no one in her right mind would have made such an agreement." We will consider this issue, *infra* Part I.D (discussing the Unconscionability Doctrine).

17 States now treat coercion under the doctrine of duress. *See* M.C. Dransfield, Annotation, *Ratification of Contract Voidable for Duress*, 77 A.L.R.2d 426, § 11 (1961).

18 *See, e.g.*, Richard A. Posner, *Gratuitous Promises in the Law*, 6 J. LEGAL STUD. 411, 421 (1977); Varouj Aivazian et al., *The Law of Contract Modifications: The Uncertain Quest for a Benchmark of Enforceability*, 22 OSGOODE HALL L.J. 173 (1984).

original contract terms. Courts traditionally resolved this by applying the *pre-existing duty rule*. This rule held that the modified terms are only enforceable if they were accompanied by new consideration. Absent new consideration, the forced modification resembles the "offer" to not to have a business burned down for a set fee in that, from the offeree's perspective, she was already lawfully entitled to contractual performance on the original terms.

Consider two well-known cases that illustrate the problem of contract modification,[19] and the difficulties associated with the traditional rule. In the first, *Alaska Packers' Ass'n v. Domenico*,[20] the defendant hired a crew of fishermen to go on a salmon-fishing expedition off the coast of Alaska. Once the ship was at sea, however, the crew refused to fish unless the defendant increased their wage. The defendant acquiesced, and the crew completed the job. Once back in port, the defendant refused to pay the renegotiated wage, and the plaintiffs sued. The court found for the defendant, holding that under the pre-existing duty rule the renegotiated wage was invalid on the ground that it was not supported by new and adequate consideration. The fishermen merely completed the job for which they were originally hired.

Now compare *Goebel v. Linn*,[21] a case of claimed economic duress. *Goebel* involved a contract for an ice company to make a delivery to a brewery during the summer at a pre-arranged price. When the delivery date arrived, however, the ice company requested a higher price, claiming that an unusually warm winter had resulted in a reduced supply. Lacking an alternative supply, the brewery, which had a stock of beer that would have spoiled, gave in to the demand, but later refused to pay the higher price, and the ice company sued. At trial, the ice company presented evidence that, as a result of the weather conditions, had it failed to obtain the required price increase, it risked bankruptcy. Although the case appeared analogous to *Alaska Packers,* which refused to honor the revised contract terms, the *Goebel* court upheld the price increase.

Economic analysis provides a basis for distinguishing these two seemingly similar cases. In both cases, the price increase was obtained in response to a change in circumstances, but the nature of those changed circumstances materially differed. In *Alaska Packers'*, the ship's departure from port substantially enhanced the bargaining power of the fishermen as it would have been impractical for the ship-owner to hire a replacement crew.[22] In particular, the crew had two key pieces of leverage that permitted them to extract concessions from the boat owner. First, the salmon fishing season is highly concentrated. Returning the boat to retrieve a new crew would have risked sacrificing the entire fishing season that year. Second, the Alaska Packers' Association had just constructed a new canning factory in Alaska and was counting on the revenues from the fishing season to recoup its capital investment.[23] These factors provided the crew an opportunity to impose costs on the company despite the absence of further bargained for

---

[19] For a related discussion, see Posner, *supra* note 18, at 421–24.

[20] 117 F. 99 (9th Cir. 1902).

[21] 11 N.W. 284 (Mich. 1882).

[22] *See* Todd J. Zywicki, *Libertarianism, Law and Economics, and the Common Law*, 16 CHAP. L. REV. 309, 320 (2013).

[23] *Id.* at 318–20.

consideration. The crew's demand for a higher wage did not reflect any change in the cost of performance and therefore appeared opportunistic.

The crew's demand is characterized by what economists refer to as *appropriable quasi rents*.[24] Opportunities for such rents arise as a consequence of contract-specific investments that, once made, place the other party in a position to extract additional performance obligations from the investing party who stands to lose more if required to walk away and to seek an alternative opportunity, thereby relinquishing the cost of the investment. The classic appropriable quasi-rent context transforms a competitively entered-into relationship instead into a bilateral monopoly. This transformed relationship then creates an opportunity for one party to gain at the expense of the other in a manner that is not consistent with either party's *ex ante* expectations.

A central insight of the transactions cost literature, appropriable quasi-rents become available after parties who have entered into contractual relationships under competitive conditions acquire specialized assets—either human or physical capital—to facilitate performance or receipt of performance of the respective contractual obligations. The resulting bilateral monopoly gives rise to opportunities for strategic, post-contractual behavior. These opportunities can plague long-term contractual relationships or transactions that require substantial investment as a precondition to contractual performance on either side.[25]

One of the foundational insights of law and economics is recognizing the firm as an institution that ameliorates some of the difficulties of long-term contracting.[26] The firm accomplishes this by allowing a single economic entity to coordinate the activities of those who produce positive synergies and then to allocate the gains from their collaborative efforts in a manner that avoids such strategic interactions. Scholars have also recognized that one of the functions that management provides is in allocating the gains that arise from the synergies among contributing factors in a manner that promotes optimal productive incentives within the various components of the firm.[27]

To illustrate the concept of appropriable quasi rents, assume that Alice lives in an old Victorian home painted in a color that is sufficiently uncommon that it must be custom mixed, with unusual architectural features that render access impossible without special equipment, and with wood that is no longer commonly used to build, but that is in need of repair or replacement.[28] To complete the job, Barbara is required to make significant performance-specific investments. Assume for example that the contract is for $15,000, including supplies, and that the nonstandard supplies will cost Barbara $2500.

---

[24] Portions of this discussion in the next few paragraphs are adapted from Maxwell L. Stearns, *A Beautiful Mend: A Game Theoretical Analysis of the Dormant Commerce Clause Doctrine*, 45 WM. & MARY L. REV. 1, 76–78 (2003).

[25] *See* J.A. Brickley & F.H. Dark, *The Choice of Organizational Form: The Case of Franchising*, 18 J. FIN. ECON. 401, 406–07 (1987). *See also* Benjamin Klein et al., *Vertical Integration, Appropriable Rents, and the Competitive Contracting Process*, 21 J.L. & ECON. 297, 301 (1978).

[26] *See generally* R.H. Coase, *The Nature of the Firm*, 4 ECONOMICA 386 (1937), *reprinted in* THE NATURE OF THE FIRM: ORIGINS, EVOLUTION, AND DEVELOPMENT 18, 21 (Oliver E. Williamson & Sidney G. Winter eds., 1991); Brickley & Dark, *supra* note 25.

[27] *See* Williamson, *supra* note 2, at 241.

[28] This example is taken from Stearns, *supra* note 24, at 92–93.

Barbara might be able to return or sell off some specialized supplies in the event that Alice reneges, for example, special ladders. But other supplies—for example, the custom mixed paint and the supplemental wood—are of little or no value other than as used in the performance of the contract with Alice. If Barbara could only recover $500 of the $2500 contract-specific investment, and if the cost and inconvenience of litigating exceed the difference of $2000, Alice could force Barbara to incur up to that amount in additional performance costs as her appropriable quasi-rent. Barbara would be willing to perform unanticipated work up to that amount before it would be economically feasible for her to seek rescission on the ground that the additional demands constitute a material breach.

The *Alaska Packers'* case nicely illustrates the concept of appropriable quasi rents. In that case, the additional costs would include returning to dock, locating a substitute crew, and forgone contractual performance time, possibly costing an entire salmon fishing season. The existing crew was in a position to demand up to the value of these costs as an additional requirement of performance. And they sought to obtain just that in the form of increased wages. In doing so, they were not seeking to enlarge the gains associated with the joint venture that formed the basis of the transaction between them and the ship-owner; rather, they sought to allocate a larger share of the anticipated gains to themselves in a manner that was not reflected in the original contract terms for the reasons previously noted.[29] In effect, the court's holding forced the parties instead to negotiate "on the dock," when operating in competitive markets, rather than in the middle of the ocean, when they are locked into a bilateral monopoly and when the possibility of exiting to pursue another contracting opportunity is unavailable. The *Alaska Packers'* decision thus disallowed this form of opportunistic behavior, thereby preventing the crew from obtaining the sought after appropriable quasi rents, and in doing so, it furthered the *ex ante* expectations of both parties, albeit without satisfying the *ex post* objectives of the crew members.

By contrast, the price increase in *Goebel* appeared to reflect a genuine increase in the cost of ice, one that was unanticipated at the time of contracting. The additional cost was of sufficient magnitude that, without raising the price, and thus if required to perform on the original contract terms, the manufacturer was threatened with bankruptcy. Rather than an instance of appropriable quasi rents, the increased price allowed the ice manufacturer to make the necessary additional investments needed to perform under a costly unanticipated change in conditions. The courts' opposing rulings in these two cases therefore reflected a fundamental difference between the economic circumstances that led to the demand for contract modification. As a result, *Goebel* reflects a sensible departure from an otherwise mechanical application of the pre-existing duty rule.

The RESTATEMENT (SECOND) OF CONTRACTS has essentially adopted the combined approach of these two cases:

> § 89. Modification of Executory Contract
>
> A promise modifying a duty under a contract not fully performed on either side is binding

[29] *See* Zywicki, *supra* note 22, at 319–20. *See also supra* notes 22–23 and accompanying text.

(a) if the modification is fair and equitable in view of circumstances not anticipated by the parties when the contract was made; or

(b) to the extent provided by statute; or

(c) to the extent that justice requires enforcement in view of material change of position in reliance on the promise.[30]

Most notable is subpart (c). In *Goebel*, the ice company experienced a "material change of position in reliance on the promise" for the higher price, in the absence of which its ongoing financial viability was threatened.[31]

DISCUSSION QUESTIONS

One important question that these cases raise is whether courts are well suited to identify circumstances that give rise to appropriable quasi rents as opposed to genuine changes in economic conditions. A related question is whether the parties are better suited to anticipate such changes and to allocate the risk contractually.

Imagine, for example, that in the home improvement hypothetical, Barbara, anticipating the risk that Alice might impose additional performance costs on her, includes in the contract a requirement that Alice, as the homeowner, purchase any job-specific materials and supplies. In doing so, Barbara largely abates the risk that by undertaking the contract-specific investment herself, Alice will then be in a position to impose additional performance obligations.

Can you think of any contractual solution that might have avoided the possibility of post-contractual opportunism in *Alaska Packers' Association*? Can you think of any contractual solution to the risk-allocation problem in *Goebel*? Do your answers to these questions affect whether you believe that the courts in each case ruled correctly? Why or why not?

C. Mistake and the Duty to Disclose

The doctrine of mistake arises when one or both parties hold incorrect beliefs about some material aspect of their contract. Mistaken beliefs are a possible basis for voiding a contract as they sometimes reveal the absence of a meeting of the minds. When the mistake is mutual, there usually is no difficulty in terminating or redrafting the contract, that is, unless one party stands to gain from the mistake. More generally, cases arise from a *unilateral mistake*, where only one party claims to have had a material misunderstanding at the time of contract formation. Professor Anthony Kronman has characterized the underlying issue in mistake cases as follows: "[I]f one party to a contract has reason to know that the other party is mistaken about a particular fact, does the knowledgeable party

---

30 RESTATEMENT (SECOND) CONTRACTS § 89 (AM. LAW INST. 1981).

31 The Uniform Commercial Code addresses modification in Section 2–209. U.C.C. § 2–209 (AM. LAW INST. & UNIF. LAW COMM'N 1977). That section, along with the UCC as a whole, incorporates the requirement of good faith from Section 1–304 into every contract. *Id.* § 1–304. Section 1–201(b)(20) defines "good faith" as "honesty in fact and the observance of reasonable commercial standards of fair dealing." *Id.* § 1–201(b)(20). *See also* 2A LARY LAWRENCE, LAWRENCE'S ANDERSON ON THE UNIFORM COMMERCIAL CODE § 2–209:63 (3d ed. 2016) (citing Roth Steel Prods. v. Sharon Steel Corp., 705 F.2d 134 (1983)) (requiring that modifications are "motivated . . . by an honest desire to compensate for commercial exigencies.").

have a duty to speak up or may he remain silent and capitalize on the other party's error?"[32] Or we might ask: When does a good deal cross the line and become a knowing failure to disclose a material fact?

Unilateral mistake arises in cases of *asymmetric information*. This means that one party to a transaction has superior information about a material aspect of the contemplated transaction. For instance, in the sale of a used car, the owner generally has detailed knowledge about the vehicle's condition—such as its maintenance record or how recently the brakes were replaced—that would be of value to a prospective buyer. In his classic paper, *The Market for Lemons,*[33] Professor George Akerlof showed that the existence of asymmetric information can cause such markets to shrink, and in theory, even to dry up altogether. Because buyers lack specific information about particular used cars put up for sale, they will view all cars as being of "average" quality. Thus, the price will reflect that expectation, which will tend to cause owners of high quality cars to withdraw them from the market where they would otherwise be undervalued. As a result, only those cars at the low end of the quality scale—so-called "lemons"—will remain in the used car market. Economists refer to this problem, which can arise in any market characterized by asymmetric information, as one of *adverse selection*.[34]

The mistake doctrine is concerned with correcting the market failure associated with adverse selection. Of course the rule does not invalidate all contracts in which one party holds a mistaken impression about the transaction. If it did, the doctrine would undermine incentives to invest in acquiring beneficial information before or at the time of contracting, which is often essential to ensuring that contractual exchange is social welfare enhancing. The difficult policy question is how to balance the incentive to invest in pertinent information against the countervailing goal of encouraging agreement over material features of contracts, without which the possibility of a social welfare enhancing exchange is diminished.

Before considering an illustration of the doctrine of mistake, it is worth considering the lemons problem more generally. Although disclosure requirements can improve market functioning by ensuring greater consumer confidence, market mechanisms themselves can also improve the flow of beneficial information. Consider, for example, the Lexus "certified pre-owned vehicles" program, which has since been mimicked by several high-end vehicle manufacturers.[35] Through this program, an authorized dealership

---

[32] Anthony Kronman, *Mistake, Disclosure, Information, and the Law of Contracts*, 7 J. LEGAL STUD. 1, 1–2 (1978).

[33] George Akerlof, *The Market for "Lemons": Quality Uncertainty and the Market Mechanism*, 84 Q.J. ECON. 488 (1970). This paper contributed to Professor Akerlof's receiving the 2001 Nobel Prize in Economics. George A. Akerlof, *Writing the "The Market for 'Lemons'": A Personal and Interpretive Essay*, NOBELPRIZE.ORG (Nov. 14, 2003), http://www.nobelprize.org/nobel_prizes/economic-sciences/laureates/2001/akerlof-article.html.

[34] *See, e.g.*, Michael Rothschild & Joseph Stiglitz, *Equilibrium in Competitive Insurance Markets: An Essay on the Economics of Imperfect Information*, 90 Q.J. ECON. 629 (1976) (examining adverse selection in the market for insurance).

[35] *See* CHESTER DAWSON, LEXUS: THE RELENTLESS PURSUIT 19–20, 127–28 (2011). *See generally* Jen-Ming Chen & Yu-Ting Hsu, *Revenue Management for Durable Goods Using Trade-Ins with Certified Pre-Owned Options*, 186 INT'L J. PRODUCTION ECON. 55 (2017) (discussing certified pre-owned goods, such as Lexus cars, in the context of market segmentation).

warrants its used vehicles—now called "pre-owned"—for a period of several years and tens of thousands of miles. Although most observers are apt to focus on the benefit to the pre-owned car purchaser, consider here the signal that this program sends to potential purchasers of the new vehicles. By signaling that the manufacturer is willing to warrant the vehicle, following a careful inspection process, for several years *after* the initial point of sale, Lexus conveys the vehicle's high quality to prospective new car purchasers, thus enhancing the vehicle's initial value. Similarly, CarMax, which warrants its previously owned vehicles, signals that its cars of various makes and models have been carefully maintained and any remaining defects remedied.[36] In effect, these programs contribute to a *separating equilibrium* in which warranted used cars fetch a considerable premium, whereas those sold privately and "as is" are apt to receive a lower price.

What do these market responses suggest about the Akerlof's theory of lemons? Is the lemons problem a market failure, or is it a useful and informative sorting mechanism? How will you buy your next used car?

1. *Some Examples of Unilateral Mistake*

Consider a person who purchases an item at a garage sale and subsequently discovers, perhaps by watching an episode of *Antiques Roadshow*, that the item is extremely valuable—worth much more than the price she paid. Further, suppose that the seller, after seeing the same TV episode, realizes his mistake and sues to invalidate the sale. What is the appropriate rule? Should the buyer have to return the item, and does it depend on what she knew at the time of purchase?

Consider a boy who goes into a baseball card shop and spots a card with a price tag marked $1200. Both he and the clerk interpret this to mean $12.00, and the boy eagerly buys the card, but when the owner of the shop returns, he informs that clerk that the rare card was actually priced at $1200.00. He therefore sues the boy to have the card returned, citing the doctrine of mistake.[37] Should the boy be required to return the card?

Finally consider the famous case of *Sherwood v. Walker*, which involved a contract for the sale of a cow.[38] The price of the cow was set at $80 based on the (apparently) shared belief that the cow was barren and hence only good for slaughter. Before delivery, however, the cow revealed that she was pregnant, thereby increasing her value to between $750 and $1,000. The seller sought to rescind the contract on grounds of mistake, and the buyer sued to enforce the sale. Citing evidence "tending to show that at the time of the alleged sale it was believed by both [parties] that the cow was barren and would not

[36] *See* Mark Klock, *The Virtue of Home Ownership and the Vice of Poorly Secured Lending: The Great Financial Crisis of 2008 as an Unintended Consequence of Warm-Hearted and Bone-Headed Ideas*, 45 ARIZ. ST. L.J. 135, 142 (using CarMax as an example of using credible signals, such as a good reputation and recognized warranties, to signal "their cars are likely to be superior to Joe's Used Cars."); *CarMax Quality Certified*, CARMAX, https://www.carmax.com/car-buying-process/why-carmax/quality-certified-cars (last visited Aug. 29, 2017) (describing the evaluation and renewal process for pre-owned cars sold by CarMax).

[37] Andrew Kull, *Unilateral Mistake: The Baseball Card Case*, 70 WASH. U. L.Q. 57, 57 (1992). This hypothetical is based on a 1990 Illinois case. Prior to the court's issuance of a decision in the case, the parties settled. The settlement stipulated that the baseball card would be auctioned with the proceeds going to charity. *Id.*; Irmen v. Wrzesinski, No. 90 SC 5362 (Ill. Cir. Ct. DuPage County [Small Claims Div.] filed June 29, 1990).

[38] 33 N.W. 919 (Mich. 1887).

breed,"[39] the court rescinded the contract. In justifying its decision, the court emphasized the difference between mutual and unilateral mistake:

> [I]t must be considered as well settled that a party who has given an apparent consent to a contract of sale may refuse to execute it, or he may avoid it after it has been completed, if the assent was founded, or the contract made, upon the mistake of a material fact,—such as the subject matter of the sale, the price, or some collateral fact materially inducing the agreement; and this can be done when the mistake is mutual.[40]

A dissenting judge, however, doubted that the mistake was in fact mutual:

> There is no question but that the defendants sold the cow representing her of the breed and quality they believed the cow to be, and that the purchaser so understood it. And the buyer purchased her believing her to be of the breed represented by the sellers, and possessing all the qualities stated, and even more. He believed she would breed. There is no pretense that the plaintiff bought the cow for beef, and there is nothing in the record indicating that he would have bought her at all only that he thought she could be made to breed. Under the foregoing facts, . . . it is held that because it turned out that the plaintiff was more correct in his judgment as to the quality of the cow than the defendants, . . . the contract may be annulled by the defendants at their pleasure. I know of no law . . . which will justify any such holding.[41]

The justices writing for the majority and dissent disagreed as to the defendants' beliefs at the time the contract was made, and specifically as to whether the defendants believed that the cow could breed. Their disagreement on whether the contract was enforceable, benefiting plaintiff, or voidable, benefiting defendant, turned on whether the mistake was unilateral or mutual. If the defendant alone believed the cow was barren, then the mistake was unilateral, and because the defendant owned the cow, there was no reason to assume that the plaintiff had greater access to information about the cow's fertility. If the mistake was mutual, then the sale of the fertile cow was a material mistake, and the two parties actually intended any infertile cow of comparable quality that would be appropriate for slaughter.

One difficulty with this approach is that it requires knowledge as to the state of mind of the parties at the time of contracting, which presents difficult matters of proof. Another approach is to inquire whether enforcing the contract encourages investment in socially valuable information or expertise.[42] We will consider additional variations on *Sherwood* in the next subparts after reviewing the 1815 Supreme Court decision, *Laidlaw v. Organ*.[43]

---

[39] *Id.* at 920.

[40] *Id.* at 923 (citations omitted).

[41] *Id.* at 925 (Sherwood, J., dissenting).

[42] The classic discussion of this distinction is Jack Hirshleifer, *The Private and Social Value of Information and the Reward to Inventive Activity*, 61 AM. ECON. REV. 561 (1971). We return to this analysis in the next subpart after considering one additional case that illustrates unilateral mistake.

[43] 15 U.S. (2 Wheat.) 178 (1815). Although this case arose under the "duty of disclose" doctrine, it is subject to the same analysis as the other cases involving unilateral mistake.

Laidlaw involved a contract for the sale of tobacco by Laidlaw to Organ. The contract was set during the British blockade of New Orleans during the War of 1812, as a result of which the domestic price of tobacco was artificially depressed. Earlier on the day of contracting, Organ learned of the signing of the Treaty of Ghent, which concluded the war and would lift the blockade, resulting in a predictably sharp increase in the price of tobacco as a result of reopening foreign markets, thereby ensuring him a large profit. When this information became public, Laidlaw tried to rescind the contract.

Although Chief Justice John Marshall's opinion for the Court can be cited for the proposition of *caveat venditor*, meaning "seller beware,"[44] a fair reading of the case is more nuanced. There was some dispute as to whether the buyer had deliberately withheld information from the seller that the seller expressly inquired about by asking if there was a reason to anticipate a price increase. The Court remanded the case for a jury trial to ascertain such deliberate withholding, but in the absence of such evidence, the opinion suggests that the original contract terms would govern the dispute. The ambiguity arises from two seemingly contradictory statements. On one hand, Chief Justice Marshall stated: "[t]he court is of opinion that he was not bound to communicate it."[45] On the other, he asserted: "[i]t would be difficult to circumscribe the contrary doctrine within proper limits, where the means of intelligence are equally accessible to both parties. But at the same time, each party must take care not to say or do any thing tending to impose upon the other."[46] The remand suggests that the Court was disinclined to allow the buyer to benefit from outright deceit or fraud, but that short of that, the doctrine of *caveat venditor* would control.[47]

2. *Purely Distributive Versus Socially Valuable Information*

Let us now consider the following variation on *Sherwood v. Walker*. A seller offers a supposedly infertile cow. Assume, however, that in one out of fifty such transactions, the cow is actually fertile and that this is common knowledge. Further assume that infertile cows are worth $50, the seller's price, and fertile cows are worth $800. Now assume, as occurred in *Sherwood*, that the cow's fertility is revealed naturally after the contract is signed but before delivery.[48] Can the seller rescind the contract?

---

44 The more common phrase *caveat emptor* means "buyer beware." *Caveat Emptor*, BLACK'S LAW DICTIONARY 267 (10th ed. 2014).

45 *Laidlaw*, 15 U.S. at 195.

46 *Id.*

47 Opinions on this case are varied. For example, Richard Posner appears to endorse the Court's ruling based on the need to create incentives for people to obtain socially valuable information. RICHARD A. POSNER, ECONOMIC ANALYSIS OF LAW 138–39 (8th ed. 2011). Cooter and Ulen, however, suggest that the information in question was purely distributive in the sense that it allowed Organ to profit at Laidlaw's expense, but produced no social value, given that the information was certain to become widely known soon after Organ learned it. ROBERT COOTER & THOMAS ULEN, LAW AND ECONOMICS 26 (1988). Finally, Kronman expresses doubt regarding whether Organ acquired the information casually or as a result of deliberate effort, "for example, by cultivating a network of valuable commercial 'friendships.' " Kronman, *supra* note 32, at 15.

48 As shown below, the fact that revelation occurs before *delivery* is not crucial—what matters is that it occurs before the buyer slaughters the cow.

Assume for now that the answer is "no." If the contract is enforceable, on the rare occasion where it is revealed that the cow is in fact fertile, the buyer gets a substantial windfall, equal to the difference between the value of a fertile cow and a cow for slaughter ($800–$50=$750). But remember that in forty-nine out of fifty cases, the buyer gets exactly what he paid for, a cow for slaughter worth $50. Since it is widely known that one out of fifty cows thought to be infertile actually is fertile, the buyer's *expected* gain equals the average value of a cow of unknown type, or (.02×$800)+(.98×$50)=$65, minus the price of $50, or $15. The seller, on the other hand, receives $50 regardless of whether the cow is or is not fertile. The joint value of a cow with a one in fifty chance of being fertile is $65, and in this example, the $65 value is divided between the seller and buyer such that the buyer receives a premium value of $15.

Now suppose that the seller can have the contract rescinded when the cow turns out to be fertile. In that case, it is the seller who realizes the windfall when the cow turns out to be fertile. That is, the seller retains the $800 value, whereas the buyer receives only those cows worth $50, which is exactly what he paid for. This valuation difference applies not only to the specific sale of the fertile cow; it applies to all sold cows. Thus, the expected value of cows of unknown type is exactly $65, as in the previous example.

This analysis reveals that the choice of rule—to allow or disallow the seller to void the contract—has no effect on the overall value of the cow or of the contract; the choice is merely distributional. That is, it determines which party gets the benefit of the $15 per-cow additional value associated with the one-in-fifty chance that the cow is fertile. And whichever party gets ownership of the fertile cow will put it to its socially optimal use. This follows as an implication of the Coase theorem.[49]

distributional - choosing which party gets the benefit of windfall

One obvious solution to the problem of the fertile cow is for the parties to handle the matter contractually, meaning to have them specify and allocate the risk that the assumption of infertility is mistaken. If the contract specified that in the event the specified cow is later found to be fertile the seller keeps the cow or can recover it after the sale, then the buyer will never agree to pay more than $50. Conversely, if the contract specifies that the buyer can keep the specified cow, whether or not found to be fertile, then the seller and buyer can negotiate the additional $15 value associated with the cow of unknown status between them. Given the possibility of a contractual solution, did the *Sherwood* court reach the correct result by voiding the contract? Does it matter if at the time of the case, 1887, it was not customary to specify what happens in this circumstance following the sale of a cow in the contract itself? Why or why not?

How does this analysis inform the outcome of *Laidlaw*? Did Organ's prior knowledge of the Treaty of Ghent result from productive investment in information or from fortuitous discovery of information that would otherwise be inevitably disclosed? Is it possible to answer this question without knowing, as the remand suggests, whether Organ withheld information from Laidlaw in response to a specific inquiry?

---

[49] *See supra* Chapter 1.

3. *Casual Versus Deliberate Acquisition*

The reason for the irrelevance of the enforcement rule to efficiency in the prior variation on *Sherwood* is that the information about the cow's type was assumed to emerge naturally, that is, without the conscious effort on the part of the buyer or seller. By comparison, one could argue that in *Laidlaw,* allowing Organ to benefit from his fortuitously gained knowledge of the Treaty of Ghent did not result from the investment in socially productive information. Professor Kronman refers to such situations as involving information that is "casually acquired," meaning that no one invested any effort to produce or discover the hidden fact.[50] The facts of *Sherwood* and *Laidlaw* do not reveal evidence of investigative effort, and so it appears that the rulings had only distributional effects.

Let us now alter the *Sherwood* facts slightly and assume that the buyer *can* invest to *deliberately discover* the cow's type before it is otherwise revealed. Assume, for example, that some buyers of supposedly infertile cows are speculators who seek to profit from the discovery of those few that are fertile. Imagine that a test allows these buyers to discover bovine fertility with a high degree of certainty. Finally assume that buyers can administer this test without being observed beyond standing near the cow to check its general quality for slaughter, thereby retaining the resulting information as to each cow's fertility status. (If it were known that the buyer conducted the test, the seller could infer the result by the buyer's decision of whether or not to buy the cow.) Should buyers be allowed to profit from the knowledge that they acquire or should they have a duty to disclose it? Kronman argues in favor of allowing such a buyer to profit from the knowledge he obtains as doing so provides an incentive to invest in discovering socially valuable information.

To evaluate this argument, imagine the following: The buyer spends $10 per cow, without the seller learning of the testing, and is able to identify with near certainty which one of the fifty tested cows is fertile. The consequence is that the buyer can acquire the fertile cow for the purchase price ($50), plus the testing price (up to $500, depending on where in the sequence of testing the fifty cows he discovers the one that is fertile).[51] Assume for simplicity that the buyer had to test all fifty.[52] In effect, the one identified fertile cow now costs the buyer $550, the purchase price of $50, plus the $500 price of testing the entire herd. Because the fertile cow is valued at $800, the buyer is now $250 ahead.

Now compare two sets of facts that flow from this hypothetical. First, without the testing, the fertile cow would reveal herself as such either to the seller or the buyer, but

---

[50] Kronman, *supra* note 32, at 15–16.

[51] Of course, the fact that one in fifty cows is fertile does not mean that upon discovering a fertile cow there can be no other; these are statistically independent events, and it is possible that over two (or many) neighboring herds, each with fifty cows, one rancher has two (or more) fertile cows and the other(s) have none. The assumption that only one of the fifty cows is fertile simplifies the exposition without changing the analysis.

[52] We might imagine, for example, that the test does not produce immediate results, and thus the speculator must test all of the cows initially, or that the speculator is concerned that if stopped midway through the herd upon discovering the fertile cow, the rancher would also become aware of which cow is fertile. This is analogous to a common tactic among collectors who rummage through various flea markets and yard sales seeking valuable rarities. Upon discovering one, savvy collectors will often continue the "search" so as to include non-valuables in the negotiated purchase as a means of avoiding the risk of disclosure.

before slaughter, as happened in the *Sherwood* case. In the second, the cow would have been assumed infertile and slaughtered but for the fertility test. Whether Kronman's thesis that the test is social welfare enhancing might depend on which of these two accounts describes the testing.

In the first hypothetical, whether the test was accomplished or not, the fertile cow would have been revealed as such and would have been used for breeding. In this case, the test allowed the purchaser to secure a rent, associated with the higher value of the fertile cow, equal to $250. But notice that without the test, the buyer or seller would, by assumption, have discovered the fertile cow in advance of slaughter, and would have used her for breeding in any event. And most notably, this would have avoided the $500 investment to test the herd. As a result, when the test results merely in allocating part of the available gain to the buyer, the investment appears socially wasteful. The fertile cow would have been used for its most highly valued use, breeding, without the investment, thereby saving societal resources. In the second hypothetical, when absent the test, the fertile cow would have gone to slaughter, the $500 in testing instead allowed the buyer to capture $250 of the potential $750 loss in value by isolating the fertile cow from the otherwise infertile herd.

The validity of Professor Kronman's thesis that the buyer should keep the cow to encourage socially beneficial investments in information therefore depends on whether the nature of the investment is like the first hypothetical, which involves rent seeking, or like the second, which involves the production of socially valuable information. From the perspective of enhancing social welfare, the deliberate acquisition of information is not, in itself, a basis for protecting the investor's right to that information. In this analysis, when the information generates a purely private benefit, but no corresponding social gain, the court improves social welfare by voiding the contract, thereby discouraging the investment.

The preceding analysis supports the following conclusions: (1) when information is acquired by chance, the choice of enforcement rule has only distributional effects, and therefore allowing or disallowing the contract to be rendered void based on unilateral mistake will have no effect on efficiency; (2) when information that is costly to acquire generates purely distributive effects, imposing a duty to disclose as a means of avoiding unilateral mistake over a material aspect of performance discourages rent seeking behavior; and (3) when information that is costly to acquire generates socially valuable information, meaning information that enhances the net gains from the transaction, failing to require disclosure despite any resulting unilateral mistake promotes benign incentives to invest in the procurement of social-welfare-enhancing information.

Although this approach aligns with economic intuitions, it might not perfectly align with preferred legal policy given problems of uncertainty and enforcement costs. This overall approach leaves us indifferent as to the resolution of cases in category one, above. In addition, it is uncertain whether courts in general have the capacity to sort through these various case categories. More to the point, an important policy question arises as to where the presumption should lie when the case facts are uncertain. For example, if it is unclear whether in a case involving a non-disclosed discovery that was costly to acquire and that places the facts either in categories two or three above, should the court err on the side of assuming rent seeking (category two) or on the side of assuming the acquisition of socially productive information (category three)?

Assuming that it is not possible to ascertain the requisite facts on a per-case basis, which approach do you believe is the preferred default rule, and why? Whichever default rule you select, do you believe it should be rebuttable by contrary evidence? Or should buyers and sellers be able to rely on the selected rule, and make appropriate investments of time and resources, even if it is an imperfect fit in some cases? Why or why not?

As suggested above, the actual facts of *Sherwood v. Walker* seem to conform to category one, suggesting that the court's ruling had no efficiency consequences. Of course, it is possible, and the dissenting judge's comments provide some evidence to support the claim, that the majority was mistaken and that the buyer was a speculator who knew, or at least had a reasonable basis to believe, that the cow was likely to be fertile. If so, how should the court have proceeded? Can you identify additional facts that would help to resolve this question?

Now compare the antique case. The answer there depends on whether the buyer of the item had developed expertise in antiques, or was just lucky. Once more, it depends on whether the case falls into categories two or three, and this is very difficult to ascertain, especially because it is often plausible to claim investment in acquiring expertise. The presumption here matters, especially since failing to encourage such socially beneficial behavior can result in the dissipation of valuable resources.

4. *Unilateral Mistake, Mutual Mistake, and Misunderstanding*

The baseball card case presents yet another difficulty: Whatever might have explained the boy's good fortune, the fact remains that the shop owner had the relevant expertise and had made a simple clerical error in marking the price of a rare card. Such errors are not uncommon. In part for that reason, contract law draws a critical distinction between the *doctrine of unilateral mistake* and the *doctrine of misunderstanding*. As a result of the problems associated with proving subjective intent, as a general rule, contract law bases the resolution of disputes on objective factors. The doctrine of misunderstanding provides an important exception: when there is a misunderstanding that reasonable persons viewing the underlying facts giving rise to the contract dispute would recognize as such, the doctrine allows the disadvantaged party, here the seller, to have the contract rescinded, thereby restoring the parties to their original position.[53]

Economic analysis helps to explain this distinction. Should contract doctrine promote buyer efforts to seek out such clerical errors? This is different from encouraging persons to search out genuine good deals based on acquired expertise, as might have been the case with the antiques example or in *Sherwood*, depending on whether the majority or dissent opinions better characterized the case facts. Those cases implicate the doctrine of unilateral mistake. Since the baseball shop owner already made the requisite investment, allowing the boy to retain the card at the bargain price will not promote investment in socially beneficial information; at best, it gives the boy a windfall at the owner's expense,

---

[53] HILLMAN, *supra* note 1, at 289–90, 350–53; PERILLO, *supra* note 1, § 9.27.

and at worst, it encourages non-socially beneficial investments in finding and exploiting errors. For that reason, the hypothetical instead implicates the doctrine of misunderstanding.

Indeed, the problem in the card case is that the clerk, rather than the owner, was present at the point of sale. Had the owner been present instead, he almost certainly would have caught the error and declined to honor the $12 price. If so, the conflict—one hopes it would not give rise to litigation—would have been guided by the relatively clear rules that govern offer and acceptance.[54] As with an advertisement, the posted price would have not been construed as an "offer," but rather as an invitation to have the buyer make an offer. In this case, the $12 offer is one that the seller could justifiably—and one hopes apologetically—decline.

Now consider the famous 1864 English case, *Raffles v Wichelhaus*,[55] (also known as "the Peerless" case). This landmark case involved mutual misunderstanding rather than unilateral mistake, and demonstrates that without agreement on a material aspect of performance, the contract is voidable on the ground that there has been no meeting of the minds. In *Raffles*, two parties contracted for the delivery of cotton from Bombay to London on the ship "Peerless." Unknown to either party, there were two ships named Peerless on the same route, one making delivery in October, the other doing so in December. The buyer anticipated October delivery, but the actual delivery came with the December ship by the same name, which the buyer refused. The seller claimed that because the ship name was designated in the contract, the buyer was bound to accept. The buyer instead maintained that the ship designation merely signaled that in the event it sank, the contract would thereby be rendered null and void.

The court sided with the buyer, and thus released him from obligation under the contract, thereby announcing the principle that absent a meeting of the minds, there is no contract. In this rare instance, both parties had a reasonable basis for their interpretation of a material contract provision, but because their understandings diverged, the court ultimately determined that no contract had formed.

QUESTIONS AND COMMENTS

In this part, we covered a number of related doctrines: *unilateral mistake*, *mutual mistake*, *misunderstanding*, *mutual misunderstanding*, *caveat emptor*, and *caveat venditor*. Do these combined doctrines create appropriate incentives for parties seeking to contract?

On one reading, these combined doctrines reflect the limits of judicial capacity. Courts are ill equipped to investigate whether parties have invested in socially productive information or simply gotten lucky. Better to err on the side of investing lest we create a disincentive to encourage beneficial economic activity. Except in extreme situations, including a fundamental failure of the meeting of minds (*Peerless*) or a clear indication of a clerical error (the baseball card case), the appropriate rule in situations of mistake is *caveat emptor* or *caveat venditor*, favoring whichever side seeks enforcement.

---

[54] PERILLO, *supra* note 1, § 2.6(d).

[55] [1864] 159 Eng. Rep. 375, 2 H & C 906.

Recall the debate between Coase and Pigou about the possibility of an omniscient regulator imposing taxes that forced actors to internalize the full costs of their economic activities.[56] If it were costless to ascertain whether the party who obtained the benefit of the contract—the sale of a fertile cow for the price of an infertile one, the sale of a valuable antique for a steeply discounted price, the sale of a valuable baseball card for the price of a common one—then it would be appropriate and even beneficial for the legal system to choose a rule that dissuades such non-productive social investments. If, instead, it is costly to accomplish this task, and if, when doing so, courts are prone to error much of the time, then the analysis flips. In that world, the disadvantaged party risks dissipating a rent in seeking to rely on the legal system in an effort to restore herself to a favorable position after realizing that the contract turned out to be disadvantageous. A simpler rule—*caveat emptor* or *caveat venditor*, meaning that the fortunate party gets the benefit of the deal absent the limiting cases of fraud, deceit, or a true absence of the meeting of minds—reduces this potential rent-seeking cost. Do you find this approach persuasive? Why or why not?

Is this a fair reading of these combined legal rules? Is it a sound set of policy outcomes? Is this an area in which doctrine reinforces or thwarts economic intuitions? Why?

D. Unconscionability and Undue Influence

The final reason for invalidating a contract, referred to as the *doctrine of unconscionability*, is based on a claim that the terms or conditions of the contact are grossly unfair to one of the parties. Unconscionability implicates the closely related doctrine of *undue influence*. Professor Richard Epstein has explained that under this doctrine, the court invalidates the contract if its terms make apparent that the party seeking to rescind the contract would not have agreed to it unless incompetent, under duress, mistaken as to a material aspect, or the victim of fraud.[57] The doctrine of unconscionability is different from these other freestanding bases for voiding a contract, however, in that primary evidence of the defect is contained in the terms of the contract itself. When raised successfully, the doctrine of unconscionability shifts the burden to the party seeking enforcement to refute the claim that there existed some sort of market failure, or stated differently, that there was a sound basis for the provision claimed to render the terms of the contract unconscionable.

Two famous cases nicely illustrate the doctrine of unconscionability, and a notable criminal case provides a possible basis for a third. Although there are similarities across these three cases, each also raises unique questions for the economic analysis of the unconscionability doctrine.

We begin with the 1965 case from the United States Court of Appeals for the District of Columbia Circuit, *Williams v. Walker-Thomas Furniture Co.*[58] In *Williams,* two consumers separately entered into a series of purchase contracts over a period of several years in which they bought furniture on credit, paid the balance down, bought additional furniture, paid that down, and so on. This continued until on the final contract, the one that led to the litigation, they defaulted, whereupon the furniture store owner acted upon a

[56] *See supra* Chapter 1.

[57] Richard Epstein, *Unconscionability: A Critical Reappraisal*, 18 J.L. & ECON. 293 (1975).

[58] 350 F.2d 445 (D.C. Cir. 1965).

contractual provision known as a *dragnet security clause*, which allowed the store to reclaim not only the furniture in the most recent transaction, but all of the furniture from the time of the original contracting.

The *Williams* court explained:

> The contract . . . provided that "the amount of each periodical installment payment to be made by [purchaser] to the Company under this present lease shall be inclusive of and not in addition to the amount of each installment payment to be made by [purchaser] under such prior leases, bills or accounts; *and all payments now and hereafter made by [purchaser] shall be credited pro rata on all outstanding leases, bills and accounts* due the Company by [purchaser] at the time each such payment is made." The effect of this rather obscure provision was to keep a balance due on every item purchased until the balance due on all items, whenever purchased, was liquidated. As a result, the debt incurred at the time of purchase of each item was secured by the right to repossess all the items previously purchased by the same purchaser, and each new item purchased automatically became subject to a security interest arising out of the previous dealings.[59]

In reversing the court below, and ruling this provision invalid, the *Williams* court explained the doctrine of unconscionability:

> Unconscionability has generally been recognized to include an absence of meaningful choice on the part of one of the parties together with contract terms which are unreasonably favorable to the other party. . . . In many cases the meaningfulness of the choice is negated by a gross inequality of bargaining power. The manner in which the contract was entered is also relevant to this consideration. Did each party to the contract, considering his obvious education or lack of it, have a reasonable opportunity to understand the terms of the contract, or were the important terms hidden in a maze of fine print and minimized by deceptive sales practices? Ordinarily, one who signs an agreement without full knowledge of its terms might be held to assume the risk that he has entered a one-sided bargain. But when a party of little bargaining power, and hence little real choice, signs a commercially unreasonable contract with little or no knowledge of its terms, it is hardly likely that his consent, or even an objective manifestation of his consent, was ever given to all the terms. In such a case the usual rule that the terms of the agreement are not to be questioned should be abandoned and the court should consider whether the terms of the contract are so unfair that enforcement should be withheld.
>
> In determining reasonableness or fairness, the primary concern must be with the terms of the contract considered in light of the circumstances existing when the contract was made. The test is not simple, nor can it be mechanically applied. The terms are to be considered "in the light of the general commercial background and the commercial needs of the particular trade or case." Corbin suggests the test as being whether the terms are "so extreme as to appear unconscionable according to the mores and business practices of the time and

[59] *Id.* at 447 (emphasis added by court).

> place." . . . We think this formulation correctly states the test to be applied in those cases where no meaningful choice was exercised upon entering the contract.[60]

The *Williams* court ultimately concluded that the terms of Mrs. Williams's contract, including the store's knowledge that she had paid several years of furniture down to about one quarter the purchase price of the final stereo system on which she defaulted, that the store knew she was on welfare and supporting seven children at the time of the final sale, and the obscure nature of the dragnet security clause, were unconscionable, rendering the clause voidable.

Now consider the famous case of *Vokes v. Arthur Murray, Inc.*[61] As in *Williams*, *Vokes* involved a repeated series of transactions between an individual consumer and a business. The *Vokes* case, which can be viewed either as a case of unconscionability or of undue influence, involved a challenge to a set of contracts in which a fifty-one-year-old woman had purchased several thousand hours of dance instruction, influenced by the repeated representation that she had tremendous promise and talent, and that with the right training, she could have a professional dance career. None of this was true.

The *Vokes* court described the case facts as follows:

> [She] embarked upon an almost endless pursuit of the terpsichorean art during which, over a period of less than sixteen months, she was sold fourteen "dance courses" totaling in the aggregate 2302 hours of dancing lessons for a total cash outlay of $31,090.45, all at Davenport's dance emporium. . . . .
>
> These dance lesson contracts and the monetary consideration therefor of over $31,000 were procured from her by means and methods of Davenport and his associates which went beyond the unsavory, yet legally permissible, perimeter of "sales puffing" and intruded well into the forbidden area of undue influence, the suggestion of falsehood, the suppression of truth, and the free exercise of rational judgment, if what plaintiff alleged in her complaint was true. From the time of her first contact with the dancing school in February, 1961, she was influenced unwittingly by a constant and continuous barrage of flattery, false praise, excessive compliments, and panegyric encomiums, to such extent that it would be not only inequitable, but unconscionable, for a Court exercising inherent chancery power to allow such contracts to stand.[62]

In reversing the dismissal of the complaint, the court added:

> [W]here parties are dealing on a contractual basis at arm's length with no inequities or inherently unfair practices employed, the Courts will in general "leave the parties where they find themselves". But in the case sub judice, from the allegations of the unanswered complaint, we cannot say that enough of the accompanying ingredients . . . were not present which otherwise would have

---

[60] *Id.* at 449–50 (citations omitted).

[61] 212 So. 2d 906 (Fla. Dist. Ct. App. 1968).

[62] *Id.* at 907.

barred the equitable arm of the Court to her. In our view, from the showing made in her complaint, plaintiff is entitled to her day in Court.[63]

Finally, consider a criminal prosecution that took place in June of 2015. As reported in the *New York Times*,[64] a psychic procured $713,975 over a period of twenty months from a thirty-two-year-old Brooklyn man after he had been rejected romantically by a woman with whom had been involved after meeting her in a rehabilitation facility in Arizona. The man had traveled to the Arizona clinic for treatment from England, where he had lived, to be treated for acute anxiety. The psychic, who was arrested and charged with Grand Larceny, was the second of two psychics the man had consulted.

The relationship with the psychic developed over a series of separate encounters, with payments beginning at $2500, then $9000, and eventually as high as $90,000. The psychic allegedly told the man that evil spirits were affecting his relationship. In a bizarre twist, at one point the man learned on her Facebook page that his ex-lover had died, and the psychic told him that this proved she was right and that the evil spirits had taken her life. She then assured him that she could have the woman reincarnated through a special gold portal, and even went so far as to tell him that she had seen the woman in a supermarket, after which she set him up to meet her on a date. The man funded these enormous expenditures with earnings from his successful professional career in search engine optimization. At one point, the man slept with the psychic, who told him that she was entirely dependent on him for income because she had to forgo other clients to do his work.

Although the man did not sue the psychic for rescission based on unconscionability, and although it appears the psychic lacked the means for restitution, one might well imagine such a suit had she still had the money that he had paid her.

QUESTIONS AND COMMENTS

Are the two case outcomes, in *Vokes* and *Williams*, sound as a matter of policy? From an economic perspective, do these cases promote social-welfare-enhancing incentives? Why or why not? How do these two cases inform the analysis of the hypothetical contracts suit arising from the psychic case?

Four Alternative Analyses of *Williams*

Consider the following alternative assessments of the *Williams* case:

Version 1: A Neoclassical Law and Economics Analysis: In this analysis, the problem is that, by banning dragnet security clauses, the *Williams* court has raised the cost of credit to individuals like Mrs. Williams who lack access to traditional credit channels such as bank loans or credit cards. The dragnet security clause, although not attractive, opened a possibility of credit to those in need and conditioned the receipt of credit on a remedy that imposed greater burdens on the borrower in the event of a default than benefits to

---

63 *Id.* at 909.

64 Michael Wilson, *Man Who Gave Psychics $718,000 'Just Got Sucked In'*, N.Y. TIMES (Nov. 15, 2015), http://www.nytimes.com/2015/11/16/nyregion/lured-in-by-two-manhattan-psychics-to-the-tune-of-718000.html?_r=0.

the furniture store. That is because the recovered used furniture is rarely going to be of substantial resale value, but it remains of considerable value to the person whose home it occupies. By invalidating the dragnet security clause, the court limited the future borrowing capacity of similarly situated persons, thereby narrowing consumer choice.

In addition, the argument that the clause should be invalidated due to "unequal bargaining power" misconceives the notion of relative consumer power in competitive versus non-competitive markets. In general, consumers are more likely to receive a fair share of the gains from contracting when firms compete for customers, and firms do this by offering consumers increasingly large shares of the available social welfare surplus. Firms lower their costs through form contracts, thereby eschewing opportunities to dicker over terms. When operating in a robust economy, the "bargaining power" that consumers hold manifests itself less in terms of power to negotiate terms within a contract than in terms of selecting among a menu of available fixed-term contracts.

In addition, there is reason to believe that the nature of the cross-collateralization clause was a response to state laws limiting interest rates, or setting "usury" ceilings. A common mechanism for lenders, especially retailers that market goods and credit to their consumers, is to evade such ceilings with onerous collection terms[65] or higher prices.[66] Thus, the elimination of one term might invite other unattractive contract terms. Of course the difficulty for Mrs. Williams is precisely that she did not have an available menu of contracts that would afford her credit to furnish her home. On the other hand, striking the dragnet security clause risked denying her the one avenue to secure credit that had been available.

Version 2: *Positive versus Normative Economic Analysis*: *Williams* helps to illustrate the difference between positive and normative economic analysis. The traditional, neoclassical law and economics analysis suggests the danger that the ruling risks raising borrowing costs to similarly situated purchasers without access to traditional lines of credit, or even worse, risks drying up credit access altogether. One difficulty with this argument, however, is that it implies that economic analysis dictates a policy outcome rather than simply identifying a set of tradeoffs that ultimately must be resolved on independent normative grounds.

The same neoclassical analysis can be extended to any number of "borrowing" methods, some of which most people would intuitively favor prohibiting. Specifically, we can extend the preceding logic to a broad range of lending practices including payday lending, which carries very high prices, and even mob lending. Indeed, we can place these schemes along a spectrum from most to least attractive: (1) commercial credit, (2) family/friend loans, (3) secured credit with dragnet security clauses, (4) payday lending,

---

[65] *See* Todd J. Zywicki, *The Law and Economics of Consumer Debt Collection and Its Regulation*, 28 LOY. CONSUMER L. REV. 167 (2016).

[66] *See* Jones v. Star Credit Corp., 59 Misc. 189 (N.Y. Sup. Ct. 1969) (illustrating with example of inflated pricing to compensate for below-market interest rates). For a general discussion, see THOMAS A. DURKIN ET AL., CONSUMER CREDIT AND THE AMERICAN ECONOMY 483–99 (2014) (describing techniques for circumventing usury ceilings).

(5) mob lending.[67] Cutting off access to any of these sources raises the cost of credit by forcing the borrower into another arrangement with the equivalent of higher interest or more costly enforcement on default, with mob lending almost certainly being the worst, given the risk of physical harm in the event of default.[68]

When the law cuts off a particular method of borrowing, it is certainly true that this raises the borrowing costs and leads some borrowers to seek other, potentially more-expensive, credit alternatives. It is also true, however, that doing so eliminates some problematic features of the prohibited lending arrangement, or at a minimum, it denies those means of lawful sanction. For example, few would argue that we should authorize mob lending because by disallowing the mob to cause escalating bodily injuries on progressive rates of default, the legal system is denying those otherwise in need of it a limited means of credit. We can extend this extreme case to the tradeoffs further up the acceptable levels on the spectrum, with a necessary policy judgment as to whether to allow high interest rates for payday lending, the seizure of personal property for dragnet security clauses, and so on.

The implicit normative claim in the prior analysis (*version 1*) is that we should protect future borrowers from the added costs associated with restricted access to, or the removal of, credit. The positive claim is that the legal system or policy makers must assess the relevant tradeoffs associated with particular lending forms and then make the judgment. This policy tradeoff is informed by economic analysis, but economic analysis alone cannot answer how to balance the tradeoffs between intended and unintended consequences. The result might be that some in Mrs. Williams's situation will have a harder time gaining access to credit, thereby making such transactions more difficult, and it is also possible that in the long term, as with banning mob lending, this will have a benign effect.

Indeed, the *Williams* case facts resemble mob lending in a particular respect. Each time Mrs. Williams borrowed, she paid the debt down, but never to a zero-out balance before the store extended credit again. This process was repeated such that by the time of her default in 1962, the store seized goods she had purchased and paid down (but never completely) as early as 1957. Mob lenders are notorious for also lending, taking payments, and lending more, but without encouraging, or perhaps even allowing, a zero-out balance. The danger of taking "an offer you can't refuse"[69] is that the borrower will find himself in a relationship he cannot exit.

Version 3: *Cross Collateralization and Alternative Lending Structures*: It is possible that *cross-collateralization clauses*—clauses that allow consumers to borrow for one item using as collateral other items they own or possess—in consumer contracts are inefficient. That is because whether or not the contract arose in competitive conditions, once it forms, the parties are left to deal with each other, thereby inviting opportunities for rent dissipation. Certainly that was the case with Mrs. Williams and her relationship with the furniture store. After the contractual relationship began, the store was her only available source of

---

[67] One could array a similar list of remedies upon default, ranging from annoying letters and phone calls, to having to defend a law suit, and even to imprisonment for those failing to pay their debts. *See* Matthew J. Baker et al., *Debtor Prisons in America: An Economic Analysis*, 84 J. ECON. BEHAV. & ORG. 216 (2012).

[68] *See generally The Sopranos* (HBO series 1999–2007); THE GODFATHER (Paramount Pictures 1972).

[69] THE GODFATHER (Paramount Pictures 1972).

credit for home furnishings, and the store's only means of continuing to generate new revenue from Mrs. Williams was to continue extending her credit before the last purchase was fully paid down.

The rent dissipation arises because from the perspective of the store, the collateral is virtually worthless, but there are rents for the consumer because the replacement value to her is high. In other words, the furniture is worth much more to the consumer if she retains it than to the lender if he takes repossession. This can lead to a negotiating process in which the lender extracts too much consumer surplus or forces rent-dissipating negotiations. Because of the anticipated bilateral monopoly problem *ex post*, the arrangement might be well worth banning altogether *ex ante*.

This account relates back to *version 2*: Is the consumer better off by having the dragnet security clause remedy rendered void, and in doing so, being forced to have the furniture store re-price its credit terms? This will most likely mean either a higher up-front down payment or higher interest rates for all purchasers on credit. In effect, by raising the cost of credit this way, the furniture store becomes a *de facto* insurer of those who breach the repayment terms, with all borrowers paying a "premium," the proceeds of which cover those who ultimately default. Notice the analogy to the least-cost-avoider analysis from tort law.[70] Here, the store might be the least-cost avoider because it is able to pass the costs onto all of its customers as a result of the inelastic demand for its products in communities that lack access to conventional means of credit.

Version 4: Some Data: Empirically, the primary tangible effect of *Williams* was to create the rent-to-own industry, thereby forcing low-income consumers who used to be able to make purchases on credit to instead buy through this comparably unattractive arrangement. Some scholars have suggested that the resulting lease terms might result in higher monthly costs and higher total costs if the consumer decides to purchase the goods as compared with the cost of the financing arrangement under the dragnet security clause.[71] The difference is that the lessee is on notice that she does not hold title to the goods until they are fully paid off.

In effect, the result appears to be an example of *regulatory arbitrage*. If you style the transaction as a lease, the law provides very few limits on repossession upon default. Functionally, the two transactions seem to place the purchaser at a similar risk upon default, but subject to a caveat: If the leases are closed out, then the risk of dragging in earlier purchases on prior leases is no longer available to the retailer. The price per lease is undoubtedly higher, but the borrower is in effect paying for the eliminated risk of having her full home of furnishings removed upon default on the final purchase.

Notably, the lease option was legally available to the furniture store prior to the *Williams* case, but retailers instead elected to use secured sales. This might suggest that it is more or less the same transaction, now done in an arguably less-efficient manner (with a greater deadweight loss), yet with the same practical outcome. Alternatively, this datum might mean that when retailers were permitted to do so, they competed solely along the

---

[70] *See supra* Chapter 3.

[71] For a general discussion, see DURKIN ET AL., *supra* note 66, at 517; GREGORY ELLIEHAUSEN, MICHAEL E. STATEN & TODD J. ZYWICKI, CONSUMER CREDIT AND THE AMERICAN ECONOMY 385–88, 584–87 (2014).

dimension of retail price, and the secured-sales approach, with the dragnet security clause, allowed them a lower retail price. Once this option is removed, because all similarly situated retailers are subject to the same rules, all will charge a slightly higher price both for the goods and for the leasing arrangement, with consumers now paying a premium for a reduced risk.

The preceding analysis demonstrates a problem resting the *Williams* result on the retailer's apparent monopoly power or Mrs. Williams's unequal bargaining power. To the extent that Walker-Thomas Furniture has monopoly power, it is still going to extract the available economic rent through one means or another. It can do so through higher down payments, higher interest rates, or some other contract term. But this returns us to the previously discussed relationship between *versions 2* and *3*: Why should the lender use its "bargaining power" against only those who actually default, as opposed to raising the price or interest rate somewhat for all borrowers, with the effect of having the purchasers insure among themselves through this price mechanism against the risk that a subset will default? Whether low-income consumers are better off from being forced into rent-to-own arrangements instead of secured sales raises important empirical and normative concerns, but once again, although economic analysis can sharpen the policy question, it cannot itself resolve the policy tradeoffs.

Vokes and the Psychic Case Revisited

How does the analysis of *Williams* inform the other cases in this subpart? The problem in *Vokes* is not recouping some asset by Ms. Vokes. Rather, it is inducing her into a set of transactions premised on a gross misrepresentation of her talent. Certainly, there is nothing wrong with a proprietor encouraging talented persons to invest in the expertise that they are specially able to impart. The difficulty in *Vokes* is that the dance studio falsely presented to Ms. Vokes that she had talent that she did not. Disallowing this form of egregious misrepresentation will encourage Arthur Murray Dance Studios to locate more promising talent for its elite training and to offer its less ambitious training to a broader group of less talented individuals. In doing so, it will increase the available gains from contracting, whereas its arrangement with Ms. Vokes appears to have taken away from her any possible consumer surplus.

How does the analysis of these cases relate to the psychic? Perhaps you might argue that the contract itself is evidence of delusion, and therefore the contract is voidable on grounds of mental incapacity, thus avoiding the doctrine of unconscionability altogether. The facts might not support that, however, inasmuch as the purchaser of the "services" was successful enough to have generated well over $700,000 worth of spendable assets by the age of thirty-two. Consider also the purchase of lottery tickets. It is a losing bet to be sure. Just as "the house" eventually always wins, so too does the state. Despite this people buy such tickets hoping against hope to become millionaires.

Does a consistent pattern of purchasing lottery tickets mean that those who do so are incompetent? That seems unlikely, and so the question arises whether the sales are unconscionable. They might be, but not legally so. Is this a persuasive analogy to the psychic case? To *Vokes*? Assuming the psychic were not judgment-proof, and that the man sued to void the contracts based on unconscionability, which approach would more effectively lower the risk of future rent dissipation? Does it matter that many individuals "enjoy" spending some money having a psychic tell their fortunes? (Perhaps this is the same sort of satisfaction that lottery ticket buyers enjoy, even though they know it is a losing proposition.) Is disallowing the sort of gouging that occurred in the criminal case going to encourage psychics to pursue the clientele who view their activities as a form of entertainment, and who therefore will place a lower premium on it? If so, does that make the case analogous to *Vokes*? Why or why not?

II. BREACH OF CONTRACT

We have now reviewed several of the conditions that potentially release a party from binding promises pursuant to a contract. The second fundamental question that contract law must answer involves the remedies available to the victim when the other party to an enforceable contract has breached. The economic approach to contract law is often associated with the *theory of efficient breach*. In general, efficient breach sets damages at the level that compensates for the value of anticipated contractual performance, also known as *expectancy damages*. This means placing the non-breaching party in the position she would have been in *but for* the breach. Efficient breach does not require actual performance or injunctive relief. Instead it sets damages at the level that compensates for the breaching party's failure to perform.

The intuition underlying the theory of efficient breach returns us to the distinction between *ex ante* and *ex post* expectations. In a world of uncertainty, conditions arise that sometimes make it unattractive to execute contractual obligations even though the conditions for enforceability are met. Assuming that the goal of contract law is to promote social welfare, defined as moving resources to their more highly valued uses, then when the cost of performance exceeds the benefit, the efficient choice is to breach and pay expectancy damages.

Recall the definition of Kaldor-Hicks efficiency: When a move from the status quo to an alternative state provides gains to the winners that exceed burdens on the losers, the move is regarded as efficient, even though no compensation takes place.[72] The definition of *Pareto superiority* is more stringent: When a move from the status quo to an alternative state improves the welfare of one person without harming others, then the move is regarded as efficient.[73] The theory of efficient breach is rooted in the distinction between these alternative understandings of efficiency.

A party will be induced to breach when the value of the alternative opportunity—known as the *opportunity cost of performance*—exceeds the harm to the other party. When contract doctrine operates effectively, this harm is reflected in the award of damages. This means that a party will prefer to breach when it is Kaldor-Hicks efficient to do so, meaning that the available gains from breach are expected to exceed the losses to the non-breaching party. By setting damages at the non-breaching party's expected value of performance, at least in theory, efficient breach transforms a Kaldor-Hicks efficient breach opportunity into an actual set of *Pareto superior* transactions. It does so by leaving the breaching party better off and no one else harmed, including especially the non-breaching party who is

---

[72] *See supra* Chapter 2.

[73] *See supra* Chapter 2.

compensated at the level that places her in the position she would have occupied but for the breach.

This analysis raises an important, and possibly counterintuitive, jurisprudential insight about contract. If we accept the premises underlying the theory of efficient breach, the goal of contract remedies, and thus of contract law, is not to encourage contractual performance. Rather, the goal is enhance social welfare.[74] This means that contracts themselves are vehicles that pre-commit parties to the allocation of the expected gains from their transaction, rather than vehicles that ensure contractual obligations are executed.

This analysis raises a series of important questions: Is it fair to say that the goal of contract law is to promote social welfare, as opposed to ensuring performance? If so, what happens when one of the parties to the contract *really cares* about performance rather than some objective benchmark equal in market value to expected performance? How, if at all, can such a party signal her desire for actual performance as opposed to its equivalent dollar value, taking the form of expectancy damages? When a party expresses such a signal, should it be enforced? Or will enforcing that signal violate the theory of efficient breach? And finally, why should the breaching party receive all the gains from the superior breach-inducing opportunity, as opposed to being required to negotiate the allocation of those gains with the non-breaching party? Stated differently, does the theory of efficient breach overlook the Coase theorem? Is there an economic rationale for why contract damages rules avoid providing the non-breaching party an opportunity to negotiate for herself part of the social welfare-enhancing gains that induced the efficient breach? If the theory of efficient breach overlooks the Coase theorem, is there something related to breach of contract that the Coase theorem might also overlook? We will explore each of these questions below.

A. The Efficient-Damages Remedy

We begin with the following hypothetical contract. Seller agrees to produce and deliver a good to the buyer for a set price on a specified date. Let V be the gross value of the good to the buyer, let C be the seller's cost of production, and let P be the price, payable on performance. Assume that the actual cost of production, C, is uncertain at the time of contracting, and that it turns out to be higher than anticipated at the time of performance.

This situation arose in *Goebel v. Linn*.[75] Recall that the ice company demanded a higher price for performance than was specified in the contract with the brewer. The cost of the ice depended on how cold the winter was, and neither party could have anticipated that with certainty at the time of contracting.[76] This problem of *cost-uncertainty* applies to

[74] This includes creating incentives for promisors to breach only when doing so promotes social welfare. *See* Steven Shavell, *Damage Measures for Breach of Contract*, 11 BELL J. ECON. 466 (1980); William Rogerson, *Efficient Reliance and Damage Measure for Breach of Contract*, 15 RAND J. ECON. 39 (1984).

[75] 11 N.W. 284 (Mich. 1882).

[76] Recall that in that case, there was evidence that the supplier risked bankruptcy absent the modified price terms, and that the court sustained the modified price terms when the buyer attempted to enforce the contract based on the originally negotiated price. For a discussion, see *supra* Part I.B.

any contract setting in which there is imperfect information about some material aspect of contractual performance conditional on a future event.

Once the cost-uncertainty question is resolved, it is only cost-effective for the promisor to perform if the now-certain cost is lower than the expected value of performance to the buyer, meaning $C<V$. Conversely, where the anticipated performance cost exceeds the expected performance value, or $C>V$, then it is cost-effective for the seller to breach.

1. *Quantifying Expectancy Damages*

We now consider how to derive the efficient damage remedy, D, defined as the expected value of performance to the promisee.[77] As previously noted, the efficient-breach rule induces the promisor to breach when doing so produces a social-welfare gain. The realization of this gain turns on the level at which the anticipated damages are set. The remedy is partly a function of the buyer's *reliance expenditure*, denoted as R. This is the amount of money the buyer, or promisee, invests in anticipation of the seller's expected contractual performance.

In the brewery-ice company example, R is the amount of beer the brewery brews anticipating the delivery of ice. Importantly, the buyer must invest the value of R *before* the seller acquires the necessary information with which to resolve her *cost-uncertainty*. As a result, in the event of breach, the buyer's reliance investment, R, is lost (i.e., the beer spoils), meaning that it is non-salvageable. For now, we will treat the buyer's reliance as a fixed investment; below we will examine the optimal choice of R.

Table 5:1 summarizes the realized returns for the buyer and seller separately, as well as their joint (social) returns, based on the two possible states of performance or breach. In the performance state (top row), the buyer realizes a profit of $V–R–P$, whereas the seller earns a profit of $P–C$. Adding these two amounts, or $(V–R–P)+(P–C)$, yields the joint return of $V–R–C$. The expected value of this expression must have been positive for otherwise the parties would not have entered into the contract. Once C is realized, however, it may or may not turn out to be positive. Notice that the price drops out of the expression for the joint return because it is merely a transfer payment from the buyer to the seller, and hence, it does not affect the overall social value. Put differently, P simply affects the allocation of the social welfare gains between the contracting parties.

---

[77] We define each terms as it is introduced and we also set them out in summary form below Table 5:1, *infra* at p. 184.

Table 5:1. Breach of Contract Illustration

State of the world	Buyer's return	Seller's return	Joint return
Performance	*V–R–P*	*P–C*	*V–R–C*
Breach	*D–R*	*–D*	*–R*

V=Gross Value of Performance

R=Buyer's Reliance Investment

C=Cost of Production

P=Price

D=Damage Remedy

In the breach state, the buyer's return is *D–R*, or the amount of damages he receives from the seller minus his reliance expenditure, a sunk cost at the time of breach. The return for the seller in the breach state consists of the damages payment to the buyer. (Bear in mind that we are only describing the gains from the specific contract in which the breach occurs, and thus we exclude the return to the seller associated with the alternative economic opportunity that induced the breach.) In the breach state, the seller does not incur the cost of performance, and seller is not paid the contract price. The joint return in this case is simply *–R*, the buyer's reliance expenditure, since the damage payment, like the price, is a transfer and drops out of the social return. This return is negative because it is an expenditure that has not been offset by any resulting gain.

We now illustrate the value of identifying these returns in the alternative states within Table 5:1. The final column reveals the condition for efficient breach. This arises when the joint (social) return in the breach state exceeds that for the performance state, expressed in the following algebraic inequality: $-R>V-R-C$. With simple algebra, we now express the condition as $C>V$. This is the condition for breach that we previously identified in which the *cost of performance* exceeds the *expected social value* of the contract, rendering performance no longer efficient.

Notice that the buyer's reliance sunk-cost investment, *R*, is not recoverable in the event of breach, and thus it plays no role in determining when breach is efficient. It might seem unusual that we disallow this expenditure to affect the choice of the seller to breach. In identifying *R* as sunk and not the basis for any separate compensation, however, the model does not imply that the buyer has specifically suffered a loss as a result of incurring that expenditure. Rather, the buyer made that expenditure in anticipation of seller's expected performance. (As we will see below, the optimal choice of *R* accounts for the uncertainty of performance.) The expectancy damages award compensates for the buyer's expected gain from contractual performance and thus offsets buyer's reliance investment. The model simply clarifies that the reliance investment itself, as a sunk cost, does not separately affect seller's decision to breach or perform.

Now consider seller's decision whether to breach after realizing the cost of performance, *C*. From the third column in Table 5:1, we see that the seller will be better off breaching than performing if $-D>P-C$ (damages exceeds the price for performance minus the cost of performance or production cost), or if $C>P+D$ (cost of performance is greater than the price of performance plus damages). The application of the inequality to a particular case turns on the values assigned to the price and damages variables.

We can now assess optimal damages, *D*, meaning the damages level set to induce the seller to breach only when doing so is social-welfare-enhancing. In other words, *D* should only motivate the seller to breach when doing so is Kaldor-Hicks efficient, and when damages are paid, the result should be *Pareto superior*, thereby benefitting seller without harming buyer. To accomplish this, we must make the socially optimal condition for breach, $C>V$, coincide with the seller's actual condition for breach, $C>P+D$. Although the right sides of the two inequalities are not for that reason equal, we equate them here to ensure that the seller compares her realized cost, *C*, to the correct magnitude, which is *V*. This can only happen is $D=V-P$, thereby rendering those values equal. Damages should therefore be set equal to the difference between the *buyer's value of performance* and the *price*. This identified quantity is the same as the buyer's (consumer's) surplus, meaning what the buyer anticipated gaining at the time of contracting.

The final step in the analysis is to compare the measure of damages that we just derived based on the goal of efficient breach to the actual measure that courts employ. As previously stated, the most common measure is *expectancy damages*. This is the amount of money that leaves the victim of breach (here the buyer) as well off as if the contract had been performed. This means that the buyer should be indifferent as between the two states expressed in Table 5:1. As a result, we can now render the buyer's return in each state—with performance or breach—equal: $V-R-P=D-R$ (buyer's return from performance equals buyer's return from seller's breach). We now cancel *R* on both sides, with the result: $D=V-P$. Notice that this is the *same value* computed in the preceding paragraph to ensure efficient breach.

Upon reflection, this conclusion should not be surprising. Because the expectation damage measure fully compensates the victim of the breach based on the expected value of performance, the breaching party internalizes the cost of the breach and therefore should choose to breach only when doing so is social-welfare-enhancing, meaning *after* accounting for the cost of making the non-breaching party whole. In this sense, the economic theory of efficient breach resembles the unilateral care accident model from Chapter 3, where the promisor (the seller) is the "injurer" and the promisee (the buyer) is the "victim."

Expectancy damages operates like strict liability in torts by fully compensating the non-beaching party, thereby properly aligning the promisor's incentives concerning the breach decision. Economic analysis thus reveals this fundamental relationship between these two areas of law.[78] This relationship is intuitive inasmuch as strict liability arises in an analogous bilateral relationship to a contract damages suit. In both instances, there is a single victim of another's conduct. The legal rule determines fault, leaving the question as to what level of damages restores the victim to an equivalent status absent the liability-inducing conduct.

To illustrate, assume that the buyer's valuation of performance (*V*) is $50,000, his reliance expenditure (*R*) is $10,000, and the contract price (*P*) is $30,000. Thus, in the

[78] *See* Robert Cooter, *Unity in Tort, Contract, and Property: The Model of Precaution*, 73 CALIF. L. REV. 1 (1985) (first identifying this relationship).

event of performance, the buyer's profit is $10,000 (=$50,000–$10,000–$30,000). Assume, however, that at the time the contract was made, the cost of performance for the seller (*C*) was uncertain, but was known to lie between $20,000 and $70,000. The condition for efficient performance dictates that once the cost is known, performance should only occur if *C* turns out to be lower than $50,000. Now recall that the seller will actually breach if $C>P+D$, where $D=V-P=\$20,000$ under the expectation damage measure. Thus, the seller will breach if $C>\$30,000+\$20,000=\$50,000$, which matches the condition for efficient breach.

2. *Efficient Breach and the Coase Theorem*

Thus far we have treated cost as falling within an unpredictable range, for example, the performance cost of procuring ice as a function of winter weather conditions. More generally, however, the cost that induces breach arises from a superior economic opportunity. Imagine for example that the manufacturer of custom-made tables has a piece of aged Brazilian rosewood specially commissioned for a table to be sold for $5000. The rosewood costs $1000, and production costs $2000. The buyer, who contracted to purchase the table for $5000, is a wholesaler who will sell it at retail at $7000. Now imagine that a guitar maker wanders in to the table maker's store and learns about the planned construction of the rosewood table. Assume that this particular piece of wood would be uniquely valuable in the construction of a guitar valued at $25,000. Further imagine that the guitar maker offers the table maker $8000 for the piece of Brazilian rosewood.

In this example, if the table maker breaches the contract, under expectancy damages, he would owe the wholesaler the $2000. That is the value of performance (*V*), $7000, minus the contract price (*P*), $5000. By breaching, the seller gains the difference between the opportunity cost of performance, meaning the profit from selling to the guitar maker, minus the damages to the wholesaler. Because the sale to the guitar maker requires no further production by the table maker, the opportunity cost is the price for the wood, $8000, minus the purchase price, $1000, for $7000. If we subtract the $2000 in damages to the wholesaler plus the expected profit from the breached contract of $2000 (the contract price of $5000 minus the cost of the wood, $1000, minus the cost of production, $2000), the table maker comes out ahead by $3000 (which is just the difference between what the new buyer offered and what the original buyer was willing to pay).

Based on the preceding analysis, this is an efficient breach. The table manufacturer was able to make the wholesaler whole, deploy the wood to a more highly valued use (a guitar rather than a table), and gain an additional profit of $3000 over and above the $2000 he would have earned had he performed the original contract. In effect, pursuing the new economic opportunity was Kaldor-Hicks efficient, and by compensating the non-breaching party, the overall transaction was *Pareto superior.*

This neat economic analysis begs an important question. Although it is true that the expectancy damages remedy provides the non-breaching party the value of anticipated performance at the time of contracting, it also provides all the upside gains to the breaching rather than non-breaching party. Why not allow the parties to negotiate the allocation of gains from the superior economic opportunity rather than simply assign them to the party who avoids contractual performance? This is especially puzzling when we consider that the breaching and non-breaching parties are in contractual privity, and thus, in theory, transaction costs should be relatively low. Put more simply: *does the theory of efficient breach overlook the Coase theorem?*

In fact, rejecting expectancy damages in an effort to encourage Coasian bargaining when a contracting party encounters a social welfare maximizing breach opportunity is apt to produce a problematic dissipation of societal resources, thereby obstructing the flow of resources to their more highly valued uses. Although this might seem contrary to the central insight of the Coase theorem, on close reflection, it flows directly from the theorem itself. That is because this is a context in which transactions costs are apt to be predictably high.

Absent the damages rule, social-welfare-enhancing breach transactions might be constrained if the non-breaching party were able to stop the breach by forcing the potential breaching party into a bilateral negotiation to split the gains from the new contractual opportunity. Despite contractual privity, transaction costs are therefore likely to be high in this setting. In this analysis, once the breach is anticipated, each party is apt to view the underlying circumstances from an *ex post* perspective, thus seeking to maximize her share of the available gains, rather than from an *ex ante* perspective, seeking to improve social welfare so as to maximize available gains that can be shared.

This insight can be phrased in various ways, including as a *rent-dissipation game* in which the non-breaching party seeks to gain part of the available rent available to the breaching party.[79] Rent is defined as a return above opportunity cost, and here that is equivalent to performing the original contract. In the course of the bilateral negotiations, the parties can dissipate the value of that rent, thus rendering the otherwise greater performance opportunity less valuable.[80] In addition to avoiding such rent dissipation, the expectancy damages rule promotes the good will capital investment of the breaching party. By contrast, a rule that would deny the opportunity to breach and pay expectancy damages (for example ordering specific performance and requiring the party seeking to breach to negotiate an exit), would threaten to undermine the value of that good will investment.

Although it risks a loss of subjective valuation, the expectancy damages rule is apt to avoid these difficulties by implicitly recognizing the high transactions costs that flipping the rule—giving the non-breaching party contractual enforcement rights and obligating the breaching party to negotiate a release from the duty to perform—would entail. Although the theory of efficient breach might appear to overlook the Coase theorem, on closer analysis, the two are thus reconcilable. The expectancy damages remedy that accompanies efficient breach flows from the Coase theorem in that the regime lowers the cost of moving resources to their more highly valued uses in a predictably high-transaction-cost setting. The rule facilitates breach when the breaching party has been presented with an opportunity that allows her to compensate the non-breaching party and

---

[79] Maxwell L. Stearns & Megan J. McGinnis, *A Social Choice View of Law and Economics*, *in* METHODOLOGIES OF LAW AND ECONOMICS 72 (Thomas S. Ulen ed., 2017).

[80] We can also express this in terms of a cycle created by the parties in privity plus the party offering the superior economic opportunity, and thus seeking to induce the breach, all three of whom would enter an empty core bargaining game, or cycle, in seeking to allocate the gains from superseding the original contract with the social welfare enhancing economic opportunity arising from the breach. *See infra* Part III.B.2. For a general discussion of empty core bargaining and cycling, see also *infra* Chapters 13 and 14.

still come out ahead. Once more this is consistent with the premise that, in general, contract law seeks to improve social welfare, rather than to compel performance.

B. Other Damage Measures

Other possible measures of damages are sometimes appropriate. Under *reliance damages*, for example, the court sets $D=R$, and the buyer is simply restored to his pre-contract level of wealth.[81] In other words, the buyer is made no worse off than if the contract *had not been made*. This contrasts with the expectation measure, which makes the buyer as well off as if the contract *had been performed*. Stated differently, reliance damages restore the non-breaching party to where she was *ex ante*, whereas expectancy damages restore her to where she expected to be *ex post*.

In general, reliance damages tend to induce breach too often given that they are lower than expectancy damages. Stated algebraically, $R<D$ where $D=V-P$. This is intuitive inasmuch as expectancy damages accounts for the anticipated gain of the contract to the buyer as part of the damages remedy. In most contractual settings, the buyer expects positive gains; otherwise she would not have entered into the contract in the first place.

Reliance damages will be lower than expectancy damages whenever the buyer (or non-breaching party) anticipates such gains, and as a result, setting damages at R risks encouraging non-social welfare maximizing breach. To see this more formally, refer to the buyer's return in the performance state in Table 5:1, which equals $V-R-P$ (*expected contract value* minus *reliance costs* minus *price*). This quantity must be positive for the buyer to find the contract profitable, meaning $V-R-P>0$, or adding R on both sides, $V-P>R$. In terms of the numerical brewery-ice company example, $R=\$10,000$, and so reliance damages induces breach whenever $C>P+D=\$30,000+\$10,000=\$40,000$, whereas the efficient threshold for breach is $C=\$50,000$. Thus, the seller breaches too often by failing to internalize the cost of buyer's expected contractual gains. And of course, failing to award any damages for breach would induce even more instances of breach in non-social welfare maximizing circumstances.[82]

C. Efficient Breach and Reliance

To this point, we have treated the reliance investment as fixed, but in reality this is a variable within the non-breaching party's control. With proper incentives, the party will set reliance at the point that maximizes his share of the expected joint value of performance. For example, in the brewery-ice company case, the brewery would have chosen the amount of beer to brew to maximize its expected profit given the anticipated delivery of ice. Assume the buyer's value of performance (its expected revenue) is an

---

[81] More generally, the buyer would be reimbursed for the non-salvageable portion of the reliance investment.

[82] Under a zero-damage measure, the seller will breach whenever $C>P$, or whenever he expects to incur a loss (i.e., $P-C<0$). It follows that it would not generally be efficient for courts to relieve a promisor of the obligation to perform merely because he claims that performance would result in an economic loss. Indeed, in the above example, the seller will incur a loss even though performance is efficient for any realization of C between \$30,000 and \$50,000. We return to this point below in our discussion of various remedies that excuse performance without damages. *See infra* Chapter 6, Part I.B.

increasing function of its reliance expenditure.[83] Simply put, the more beer it brews, the more profit it earns, assuming that is, that the iceman cometh.[84]

The problem is that buyer's reliance expenditure is incurred before the seller's cost of performance is known. In addition, the product of buyer's reliance investment—the beer it brews—is non-salvageable. As a result, the efficient course of action for the buyer is to hedge against the possibility that due to higher production costs, the seller might breach. This possibility should affect how much beer the brewer brews. If the policy goal is to maximize the joint value of contractual performance, then the incentives concerning reliance are endogenous to the contract-damages rule. Stated differently, the measure of damages affects the buyer's optimal decision-making on reliance. To be clear, although the damages rule will affect optimal reliance, the amount of damages awarded does not include those reliance expenditures (at least not directly).[85]

Now consider two extreme scenarios. When performance is certain, the buyer would optimally choose the level of reliance in order to earn the highest possible profit. By contrast, when breach is certain, he would optimally make a zero reliance investment because the entire investment would be lost. Thus, when performance is uncertain, the buyer should optimally invest an intermediate level of reliance, with the amount of the investment proportional to the probability that performance will occur.[86]

The preceding discussion illustrates the buyer's ideal response to uncertainty, but as noted, his actual response will depend on the measure of damages for breach, i.e., the amount he will be compensated in the event of non-performance. We naturally begin with the expectancy damages measure given its desirable property of encouraging only efficient breach. Recall that expectancy damages leaves the buyer indifferent as between breach and performance because the remedy fully compensates the buyer in the event of breach based on the expected value of contract performance. This same feature of expectancy damages risks encouraging the buyer to *overinvest in reliance*; meaning to invest beyond the efficient level. The reason is that the buyer, anticipating being fully compensated for the breach, will behave as if performance is certain, and he therefore will invest in the level of reliance that maximizes profitability based on performance. But we argued above that when there is a risk of breach, it is socially efficient for the buyer to curtail reliance so as to reduce unrecoverable losses should breach occur. In the brewing example, this means that with expectancy damages, the brewer will brew the amount of beer appropriate for certain ice delivery, rather than reducing that amount to hedge against the risk of non-delivery.

We drew an analogy above between expectancy damages and strict liability in torts, and observed that the similarities between the unilateral care accident model and the efficient breach model helps to explain the efficiency of these damages rules. The two contexts are also parallel in risking suboptimal care on the part of the prospective plaintiff.

---

83 Specifically, you would write the buyer's value of performance as $V(R)$, where V is an increasing function of R.

84 *See* EUGENE O'NEILL, THE ICEMAN COMETH (1939).

85 It will affect damages indirectly through its effect on the value of performance, V, given the functional dependence of V on R. *See supra* note 81.

86 Formally, the buyer would choose R to maximize $qV(R)-R$, where q is the probability of performance, $0<q<1$.

The expectancy damages rule fails to induce optimal buyer reliance for the same reason that strict liability fails to induce optimal victim care in the bilateral care accident model. In an extreme case, victims expecting full compensation for their losses under strict liability risk behaving as if they faced no accident risk since the tortfeasor bears the full financial burdens in the event the risk produces an accident. Similar incentives confront buyers who expect full compensation under expectation damages and who therefore invest in reliance without regard to the risk that seller's increased performance cost might induce a breach. Both problems are examples of moral hazard.

In fact, one measure of damages that induces the efficient buyer's choice of reliance is zero damages. Under a no-recovery rule, the buyer would fully account for the loss of his investment in the breach state. Importantly, zero damages does not mean zero reliance; rather it means that the buyer will gauge his level of reliance on the risk of breach. This creates an incentive on the buyer's part to monitor conditions, such as the winter weather where the ice is produced, when making the assessment as to how much to invest in brewing beer. The comparison of the two situations—victim care in torts and buyer reliance in contracts—with regard to economic incentives is precise. The contract model in which buyers decide on reliance and sellers decide on breach *is economically identical to the bilateral care accident model in torts.*[87] Moreover, the inefficiency of strict liability in the tort context is mirrored by the inefficiency of expectation damages in contract with respect to the incentives of the victim to *minimize* resulting harm.

This comparison is not only helpful in demonstrating the conceptual unity between torts and contracts; it also allows us to think about a possible solution to the over-reliance problem based on our analysis of bilateral care torts. In the case of torts, recall, we showed that efficient incentives for both injurer and victim care could be achieved by the use of a negligence rule, which accomplishes this objective because of its threshold feature. In order to recover or to be held non-liable, each actor must first meet a threshold level of care. Although there is no exact analogy to a negligence rule in contract law, it turns out that there is a doctrine that accomplishes the same objective with regard to incentives. It is referred to as the rule of *Hadley v. Baxendale*,[88] based on the famous contract case, or as the *rule of reasonable foreseeability*.[89]

The *Hadley* case concerned a contract between a mill operator and a transport company that called for the latter to transport the mill's broken crankshaft to the manufacturer to have a new one built. When the return of the shaft was delayed due to the transport company's admitted negligence, the mill owner sued for the lost profit. The court, however, held that the mill was only entitled to the losses that could "reasonably be supposed to have been in the contemplation of both parties, at the time they made the contract, as the probable result of the breach of it."[90] In other words, the amount of damages was limited to what could have been reasonably foreseen at the time of breach. The *Hadley* court did allow for the possibility that the mill owner might be unable to avoid especially high reliance costs with no viable means to self-insure, and it noted that when

---

[87] *See* Cooter, *supra* note 78, at 31–32.

[88] [1854] 156 Eng. Rep. 145; 9 Exch. 341. *See* Richard Danzig, Hadley v. Baxendale*: A Study in the Industrialization of the Law*, 4 J. LEGAL STUD. 249 (1975).

[89] 156 Eng. Rep. at 147–48.

[90] *Id.* at 151.

Rule of reasonable forseeability encourages optimal reliance just like negligence in torts

this occurs, the mill owner has the burden to communicate that information to the other party so that the latter can take special precautions to avoid breach.

The significance of the *Hadley* ruling is that it limits damages based on a standard of reasonable expectations, which we have previously equated with *efficient*, or social welfare maximizing, behavior. Specifically, in the context of accident law we argued that a reasonable person would be expected to take cost-effective precautions that are intended to reduce the risk of accidents. (The marginal Hand Test provided the formal basis for this correspondence.) In the current context, reasonable foreseeability equates to efficient, or cost-effective, reliance. For that reason, the *Hadley v. Baxendale* rule limits damages to those that result from reasonable reliance, without regard to the promisee's actual reliance investment.[91]

The *Hadley* rule avoids incentives of the non-breaching party to over-rely because any marginal losses resulting from excessive reliance will not be compensated. Returning to the *Goebel* brewery case, if the buyer had overinvested in the production of beer in anticipation of delivery of the ice (or of receiving full compensation in the event of breach), the court would have limited its damages to the lost profit based on the amount of beer the brewery *should* reasonably have brewed given the possibility of breach. As for the ice company, its incentives for breach remain efficient because it still expects to pay "full" damages, albeit at a level consistent with cost-effective reliance. Thus, the limited expectancy damage measure prescribed by the *Hadley* case, like the negligence rule in tort law, achieves efficient bilateral incentives.

Although this rule raises administrative burdens on courts because it requires knowledge about the promisee's production costs and market conditions in order to calculate the efficient level of reliance, the information burden should be no greater than what is demanded by the marginal Hand Test. That test also requires the court to undertake a cost-benefit calculation for computing due care in accident settings. As we have already seen (and will see again), threshold tests are common in the law, and economic theory reveals why. Such tests provide efficient incentives in bilateral care problems.

D. Consequential Damages and Unavoidably High Reliance

In some contract settings, promisees have unavoidably high reliance investments. For example, the mill in *Hadley* clearly did not have a spare shaft to install while the broken one was being repaired, thus requiring the mill to shut down. The court denied compensation for the lost profits, called *consequential damages*, based on the unforeseeability of the resulting loss. Apparently, it was customary at the time for mills to have spare shafts on hand.

As the *Hadley* court observed, the result might have changed had the factory notified the shipper that the mill's continued operation depended upon having the shaft repaired

[91] This assumes that the non-breaching party has not specially disclosed in advance its planned level of reliance. If it had, the price of the additional risk in the event of breach would be capitalized into the price of the contract.

and returned promptly. If so, consider whether this disclosure would have increased the price of the contract, and if so, what that implies about which party should bear the risk of untimely delivery. A foundational economic insight into contract law involves the ability of parties to contract around legal rules when transactions costs are low. Does the *Hadley* ruling, which puts the burden on the mill operator, or the contrary rule, which would instead place it on the transport company, facilitate the parties' preferred allocation of the risk of delayed delivery? Which of the two possible rules is preferable as an off-the-rack rule against which such bargaining might occur?

Consider another hypothetical involving unavoidably high reliance investments.[92] Suppose, in the era of film photography, a professional photographer purchases a roll of film and then takes pictures of a solar eclipse that she plans to sell to a magazine. When the developer subsequently loses the film, the photographer sues for the lost profit from the expected sale of the pictures. The court, however, merely awards the photographer the cost of a new roll of film based on the argument that a reasonable person could not have foreseen that an ordinary looking roll of film had uniquely valuable pictures. Is this the correct result? If so, is it possible for the photographer in this circumstance to shift the risk onto the developer? As suggested in *Hadley*, the photographer could convey the unique circumstance as to the associated risk prior to contracting, and then choose to contract with the developer only if the latter is willing to take on the risk of loss or damage. Is that the right result? Why or why not?

Consider the following argument: In general, service providers anticipate that those with whom they contract will carry an ordinary level of risk. As a result, the party with the unusual, or extraordinary, level of risk should carry the burden to convey that she wishes to have the other party to the contract take on that risk. If so, the off-the-rack rule should only impose liability for damages that arise from the normal risk situation, with the burden on the party with unusual risk to contract otherwise. This lowers transactions costs by covering most contracting situations. Do you agree? Why or why not?

The next chapter, which continues the economic analysis of contract law, will consider alternative approaches to signaling higher-than-usual levels of reliance within the contract itself. This includes provisions allowing for specific performance and liquidated damages clauses.

III. APPLICATIONS

1. As a general rule, the common law permits contracts with open-price terms. This is also reflected in UCC § 2–305. *Open Price Term*. By contrast, the common law disallows contracts with open-quantity terms except in two limited situations: (1) *requirements contracts* (contracts in which a supplier agrees to provide output consistent with the buyer's demands), and (2) *output contracts* (contracts in which the buyer agrees to purchase the maximum output that the seller chooses to provide). This is reflected in UCC § 2–306. *Output, Requirements and Exclusive Dealings*, which includes a provision of *good faith*. Is the general willingness of contract doctrine to enforce open-term contracts with

[92] This example is adapted from POSNER, *supra* note 47, at 158–59.

respect to price but not with respect to quantity consistent or inconsistent with the economic analysis of contract law set out in Chapter 5, and why?

2. Assume that the following question involves only a potential contract dispute as between Calvin and Cole. Do not address any issues related to potentially unlawful insider trading or other regulatory policies enforced, for example, by the Securities and Exchange Commission (SEC).

Assume the following facts: Acme, a company in New State, produces widgets, but plans to open a new production facility next to its existing location, where it will produce smidgets. A sudden high demand for smidgets, for which copper is a major input, has created this new and valuable business opportunity. As a result of its plans, the price of copper in New State increases by 30%. In addition, the price of real estate in the industrial area in which Acme operates has increased by 20% due to new property that Acme has purchased for its expansion.

Scenario 1: Calvin, a professional dog walker, accidently overhears a conversation between Desmond, the owner of a parcel near Acme's existing plant, and Bart, a low level Acme employee, concerning the sale of Desmond's parcel to Acme. Bart speculates that perhaps Acme is expanding, and given the market, maybe it plans to start making smidgets. Calvin brings the dogs home and goes onto the internet, where he learns that to make smidgets requires a lot of copper. He further learns that the price of copper has gone up 30% in the last two weeks in New State. Calvin has recently inherited $50,000 from a wealthy uncle who passed away, and he immediately uses it to buy 500 shares of Acme stock from Cole at $100 per share. The next day Acme announces its proposed expansion and its plan to start making smidgets. Acme stock suddenly increases in value from $100 to $150, and Calvin immediately sells the Acme stock, which he has now held for twenty-four hours, netting him a quick profit of $25,000. Cole learns how Calvin acquired this information and then sues Calvin for the $25,000 profits. Based on the economic analysis of contract law set out in Chapter 5, how should this case be resolved, and why?

Scenario 2: Assume instead that Calvin is a day trader. He researches information on the internet that leads him to suspect that stock values in particular companies will go up or down, and he looks for coincidences that might elude the ordinary stock purchaser. He notices a rise in the price of copper in New State, and then learns that copper is a major input into the production of smidgets. So he further researches companies in New State that seem to have the technological capability to enter into the smidget market, and he identifies a list of five such companies. Of these five, only Acme is located, or owns property, in an area in which the price of real estate has significantly risen. Calvin buys 500 shares at 100 per share, for $50,000 from Cole, and sells them the next day, following the Acme press release, for $75,000. Cole learns what Calvin has done, and then sues for $25,000 for the profits. Based on the economic analysis of contract law set out in Chapter 5, how should this case be resolved, and why?

Scenario 3: Assume that Calvin is both a computer programmer and a day trader. He has developed a unique program, Info-Monitor, which simultaneously monitors the following: (1) the prices of commodities; (2) real estate values; and (3) markets for new technologies. Using this program, he can identify on an ongoing basis when there is an

"socially useless" – Prof. Miller

apparent market-variability coincidence respecting two or three of these factors that give rise to a likely investment opportunity. This program reports data from which Calvin figures out that Acme is likely to start producing smidgets, and so he buys the 100 shares from Cole at $50,000, and sells them the next day, after the Acme press release, for $75,000. Cole learns what Calvin has done and sues for the $25,000 profit. Based on the economic analysis of contract law set out in Chapter 5, how should this case be resolved, and why?

program is socially beneficial bc of policy reasons → maybe facilitates the movement of capital? Probably not!

when information is costly to acquire increases social welfare, then the duty to disclose would disincentivize investment into acquiring the costly information

Final questions: Would your answer for scenario 1 change if Calvin decided, as a result of his experience, to give up dog walking and become a day trader? Why or why not? Would your answer for scenario 3 change if Calvin decided, as a result of his experience, to give up day trading, and to instead go into the business of directly selling or licensing his newly patented proprietary software, Info-Monitor, to day traders and other professionals? Why or why not?

3. Based on the *doctrine of mutual mistake*, courts faced with a mutual mistake as to a material term in a contract will invalidate the contract entirely. When both parties to a contract seek invalidation, this doctrine is non-problematic. Cases only arise when one party would prefer to have the contract enforced. Based on the economic analysis of contract law can you explain why courts don't take the following alternative approach in these situations: select the contract interpretation that seems more reasonable as between the two parties, and then impose the resulting performance obligation on the side seeking to have the contract voided based on the doctrine of mutual mistake.

4. At page 171, we describe a case reported in the *New York Times* involving a man who expended considerable sums of money on a psychic. Assume that the description of facts reported there, and as summarized in the chapter, are accurate and proven in court. Further assume that the psychic is not judgment proof and, indeed, that she still has all of the money paid for the services she rendered to the then-thirty-two-year-old man. If this suit were litigated as a contract dispute, based on the *doctrine of unconscionability* and the economic analysis of contract law as set out in Chapter 5, how should this case be resolved, and why?

To the degree it is hard to tell, now we have a process cost to avoid making a factfinding distinction. Thus, we should develop a default rule and exception. Default rule should allow people to capitalize on their investment & make exception where plaintiff can prove that unilateral mistake was not socially beneficial.

CHAPTER 6

Contract Law (Part 2)

Introduction

This is the second chapter to explore the economic analysis of contract law. In Part I, we continue the analysis of breach of contract, considering mitigation and impracticability. In Part II, we introduce alternative contract remedies, including specific performance and liquidated damages clauses. And in Part III, we review other self-enforcing contract provisions, including warranties, long-term contracts, and non-compete clauses. Once more, we conclude with Applications.

I. BREACH OF CONTRACT EXTENSIONS

Chapter 5 closed with a discussion of rules that limit incentives to invest in excessive reliance. When the *Hadley v. Baxendale*[1] rule operates properly, it lowers the resulting damages in the event of a breach. In the next subpart, we discuss the obligation to limit damages that arise once the breach has occurred. In both settings, the non-breaching party is obligated to take or avoid actions that create unnecessarily high damage awards against the breaching party. In doing so, these rules avoid unnecessary social welfare losses that might otherwise arise.

A. Mitigation of Damages

In general, courts impose a duty to mitigate on contracting parties.[2] For example, the Restatement (Second) of Contracts § 350 provides that "a party cannot recover damages for loss that could have been avoided by reasonable efforts."[3] The rule is sensible because it creates an incentive for promisees to take reasonable efforts to contain damages after the fact.

As an example, suppose a tenant vacates an apartment prior to the end of the lease. She is then liable for the unpaid rent over the remaining term, but the total amount of damages the landlord can collect is generally limited to the difference between the total

[1] [1854] 156 Eng. Rep. 145; 9 Exch. 341.

[2] Charles Goetz & Robert Scott, *The Mitigation Principle: Toward a General Theory of Contractual Obligation*, 69 VA. L. REV. 967 (1983).

[3] RESTATEMENT (SECOND) OF CONTRACTS § 350 (AM. LAW INST. 1981).

lost rent under the lease and the rent the landlord could have earned if she had made a reasonable effort to find a new tenant.

To illustrate, suppose the monthly rent was $1000, and the tenant vacated six months early. However, a substitute tenant would have been willing to pay $600 a month. Assuming that neither state law nor the lease itself exempts the landlord's duty to mitigate,[4] damages from the original tenant would not be $6000, the forgone rent. Instead, damages would be limited to $2400=($1000–$600)×6, *even if* the landlord chose not to sublet to the substitute tenant. The mitigation rule thus creates an incentive for the landlord to take reasonable steps to reduce the loss from a breach.

The same issue of mitigation of damages arises in the context of tort law. Consider, for example, the Canadian Supreme Court case, *Janiak v. Ippolito*.[5] The *Janiak* Court described the case facts as follows:

> On March 31, 1976 the respondent sustained serious back injuries when his automobile was struck from behind by a vehicle driven by the appellant. Prior to that date the respondent had been employed for eleven years as a crane operator. Since the accident he has been disabled to such an extent that it has been impossible for him to return to work. Liability for negligent driving was admitted by the appellant and the trial was confined to the issue of damages.
>
> The respondent's main injury, according to the medical evidence presented at trial, consisted of a disc protrusion of the cervical spine. Several medical experts testified to the effect that the recommended course of treatment for such an injury would be the surgical excision of the disc together with a spinal fusion. The trial judge accepted the evidence that this type of operation entails an approximately 70 per cent chance of success and that, if successful, could result in an almost 100 per cent recovery for the respondent who could thereafter return to work as a crane operator. The respondent, however, appears to have suffered from a great fear of surgery of any kind and insisted on assurance of a 100 per cent chance of success before consenting to undergo the recommended procedure. As neither his family physician nor his orthopaedic surgeon was able to provide such an absolute guarantee for this or any other type of surgery, the respondent refused to heed the medical advice. Accordingly, his back injuries have not improved and he continues to be disabled and out of work.[6]

As this synopsis states, one of the complicating factors in this case was that Ippolito developed a disabling anxiety about the recommended medical treatment after the injury that prevented him from having the surgery. Although the physicians would not guarantee a successful result, they estimated the probability of success at 70%. As a consequence,

---

[4] *See* Stephanie G. Flynn, *Duty to Mitigate Damages Upon a Tenant's Abandonment*, 34 REAL PROP., PROB. & TR. J. 721 (2000) (discussing splits among the states regarding a landlord's duty to mitigate when a tenant breaches a lease); John Kelly, *A Landlord's Duty to Mitigate in the District of Columbia, Maryland and Virginia*, 24 COM. LEASING & STRATEGY 1 (2011) (discussing the commercial landlord's duty to mitigate in Maryland, Virginia, and the District of Columbia).

[5] Janiak v. Ippolito, [1985] 1 S.C.R. 146 (Can.).

[6] *Id.* at 149.

the Canadian Supreme Court approved a lower court ruling discounting the award of damages by 70% to account for the respondent's failure to mitigate.

The principle difference between the broken lease case and *Ippolito* is that the former arose in a contractual setting, thereby allowing the parties themselves to allocate the assignment of risk in the event that the off-the-rack rule does not suit their needs, whereas the latter arose in tort. Consider a case in which a homeowner leases a bedroom to a college student but is selective in choosing a person who will, in effect, be living in the home. If the homeowner rejects an available sub-tenant because the homeowner is concerned about his cleanliness, should the court offset the award of damages as a result? Or should the homeowner have the power to limit who lives in the home?

Most jurisdictions impose legal restrictions on the permissible bases for excluding a tenant, for example, based on race, gender, religion, or sexual orientation, but there are exceptions for leasing arrangements in such settings as a boarding room within a home.[7] This implies that there is a reduced duty to mitigate when such a lease is broken, potentially leaving the lessee stuck with a greater award of damages in the event of a broken lease in that setting. Does this exception make sense from an economic perspective? Why or why not? Does it make sense from a public policy perspective? Why or why not?

B. Impracticability

The *theory of efficient breach* rests on the premise that it sometimes improves social welfare to break contractually enforceable promises.[8] The theory does not, however, imply that the promisor should thereby escape liability for failing to perform. Indeed, as we have shown, specifying the correct penalty is critical to properly aligning incentives concerning efficient breach.

In this part we consider a related doctrinal difficulty: what should happen if circumstances render contractual performance physically impossible, and thus impracticable? For example, suppose a performer takes ill on the date of a scheduled appearance, or a factory burns down before it can take delivery on a custom-made machine. The related contract *doctrine of impossibility* sometimes excuses the promisor's performance, meaning without imposing a penalty in such cases, thus setting damages at zero.

Recall from the economic analysis of tort law the combined goals of minimizing risk and then allocating residual risk, meaning the inevitable risk that remains even after both parties have taken efficient precautions. The *doctrine of impracticability*, which also captures impossibility, operates on the same premise. Even if the promisee has made an appropriate reliance investment (neither too high nor too low) and the promisor has taken appropriate steps to ensure satisfactory performance, sometimes events arise that render

---

[7] Civil Rights Act of 1964, tit. II, § 201(b)(1) (codified as amended at 42 U.S.C. § 2000a(b)(1)) (exempting from public accommodations law any boarding place with five or fewer rooms and where the owner resides).

[8] *See supra* Chapter 5, Part II (discussing theory of efficient breach).

performance impossible. This is nicely captured in the Scottish idiom: "The best laid plans of mice and men often go astray."[9]

Because impossibility involves residual, and thus unavoidable, risk, the legal response necessarily draws upon the second fundamental tort inquiry mentioned above, namely how to best allocate that risk.[10] The next section reviews the economics of risk sharing and applies it to the related doctrine of impracticability.

1. *Efficient Risk Sharing and Insurance*

Economists generally assume that people are risk averse. This mean that most individuals prefer a certain and predictable income stream to an income stream that fluctuates unpredictably even if the present discounted value of the latter exceeds that of the former. This implies that such individuals will pay a premium roughly equal to the difference in value between the more stable but lower income stream and the less stable but higher income stream. The more such individuals are willing to pay (or the lower the value of the stable income stream they are willing to accept), the more risk averse they are.

To take a simple case, imagine that you have a choice of Option A, a guaranteed income stream of $100 per week, or Option B, a random selection that is 50% likely to yield a guaranteed income stream of $150 per week and an equal likelihood of $70 per week. Since Option B gives you a 50% likelihood of either $150 or $70 per week, the predicted value of that income stream is $110, which is $10 per week higher than Option A, at $100 per week, but with added risk. A risk averse person who elects Option A is, in effect, paying $10 per week to guarantee a certain payment of $100 per week instead of the fluctuating payment, even though the latter has a higher expected value.

People deal with most small risks in their lives by *self-insuring* against them. This usually involves relying on savings to cover costs that arise unexpectedly, such as minor car repairs, appliance repairs, or losing a cheap watch. Very large expenses, however, like a fire or major automobile accident, exceed most people's cash reserves, and so they usually purchase market insurance to cover the associated risks.

Consider, for example, the decision of a homeowner to buy fire insurance. Suppose that the chances of a fire in a given year are one in a thousand (.001), and the resulting loss would be $200,000. The *expected loss* is therefore $200 (=.001×$200,000) per year. A homeowner who is *risk averse* would be willing to pay some amount more than $200 to purchase an insurance policy that would fully cover the loss. The insurance company is willing to offer such a policy because by selling to a large number of households, it can spread the risk, thereby reducing its own financial exposure and making its actuarial risk (fairly) predictable. Assume the insurer sells 1000 home-fire policies for $250 each. The

---

[9] Robert Burns, *To a Mouse, in* POEMS, CHIEFLY IN THE SCOTTISH DIALECT 138 (Kilmarock 1785).

[10] *See generally* A. Mitchell Polinsky, *Risk Sharing Through Breach of Contract Remedies*, 12 J. LEGAL STUD. 427 (1983) (analyzing risk sharing and breach of contract remedies). On the impossibility doctrine, see Richard A. Posner & Andrew Rosenfield, *Impossibility and Related Doctrines in Contract Law: An Economic Analysis*, 6 J. LEGAL STUD. 83 (1977); Victor Goldberg, *Impossibility and Related Excuses*, 144 J. INSTITUTIONAL & THEORETICAL ECON. 100 (1988); Michelle White, *Contract Breach and Contract Discharge Due to Impossibility: A Unified Theory*, 17 J. LEGAL STUD. 353 (1988).

insurer generates $250,000 in annual premiums. Recall that the insurer assessed the actuarial risk of a fire at one claim per thousand households on average per year. Assuming each home is valued at $200,000, that is also the amount of its expected annual payout. The insurer's expected annual profit is therefore $50,000. Of course, in some years the insurer would do worse, and in others it would do better, but based on the statistical property called the *law of large numbers*, a large number of random uncorrelated events will produce a fairly predictable outcome. This will limit the cost of uncertainty, rendering the anticipated $50,000 annual profit on this policy predictable over time.

The preceding example demonstrates the role of insurance in promoting the efficient allocation of risk. In the torts chapter, we saw that liability rules can also serve the same function, for example, by imposing liability on the party that can more effectively spread that risk. For example, in *Escola v. Coca Cola*,[11] the exploding bottle case, imposing the burden of the residual risk on Coca Cola, thereby encouraged the company to spread the risk to its consumers.[12] In effect, by slightly raising the price to cover the contingency that even with careful production processes, a tiny percentage of unexpected injuries might arise, the ruling allows Coca Cola to either purchase insurance or to self-insure, and then to sell the equivalent of "bottle-injury insurance policies" to each of its customers, built into the price of each product.

More generally, when risk is unavoidable, the preceding analysis suggests that it should be assigned to the party who can bear it at the lowest cost. Product manufacturers are expected to have superior knowledge of product risk as compared with consumers, and thus they are usually the lowest cost insurers. In addition, depending on the elasticity of demand for their goods, manufacturers often have the capacity to pass on the increased cost as a means of spreading risk among consumers. By contrast, when the *caveat emptor* rule prevailed in the context of product injuries, the law implicitly assigned the risk of product loss to consumers, who were then forced either to self-insure against injury, or to insure through complex bundled policies, such as homeowners, automobile, or umbrella policies, as opposed to single-category insurance.

Can you identify markets in which the *caveat emptor* rule remains sound for product injuries? For other defects? Does your answer depend on the role of the buyer in ensuring the ongoing quality of the purchased good through regular maintenance and monitoring against defects? Does it depend on the ability of the manufacturer to spread the risk?

The economics of risk sharing and insurance is essential to analyzing the doctrine of impracticability.[13] Although physical impossibility renders performance impracticable and thus precludes performance by the promisor, it does not necessarily rule out liability and damages for non-performance. The policy question thus arises whether assessed damages or discharge of liability better assigns the risk that manifested itself in non-performance. The answer will obviously depend on the specific case facts. Here are some examples that help to set out the general principles.

Suppose that Alice, a factory owner, orders a custom-made machine from Barbara, an equipment manufacturer, to be installed in Alice's factory. Before Alice can take

---

[11] 150 P.2d 436 (Cal. 1944). *See also supra* Chapter 3.

[12] *See supra* Chapter 3.

[13] RICHARD A. POSNER, ECONOMIC ANALYSIS OF LAW 134–38 (8th ed. 2011).

delivery, her factory burns down after it is hit by lightning. Does Alice still owe Barbara the purchase price of the machine? Assume that because the machine was specially made, it has no salvage value other than as scrap.[14] Since the accident could not have been prevented, the allocation of liability depends on which party, Alice or Barbara, is the better insurer against the risk of inability to deliver. Alice, the factory owner, could have purchased market insurance against the risk of fire. Alternatively, Barbara, who built the machine, could have self-insured by charging a premium to all of her customers to cover the possibility that one of them might be unable to take delivery. On these facts, which party seems better suited to absorb the risk? Is the fact that the machine is custom-made relevant to your answer? Why or why not?

As a second example, assume that Abel's, a grocery store chain, enters into a contract [illegible] of produce on a regular weekly schedule. [illegible] ning impossible when weather conditions [illegible] drought or flood. In the event of non- [illegible] from Bart's in the form of any additional [illegible] should Bart's performance obligation be [illegible]

[illegible] n actual cases of impossibility—otherwise [illegible] which party can insure against the risk of [illegible] mpare the following two variations: In the [illegible] rt's is limited to either self-insuring or to [illegible] bel's, the grocery store chain, can more [illegible] hases geographically so that if adverse [illegible] e location, the missing supply can be [illegible] ions that were not affected.

[illegible] food wholesaler who buys from multiple [illegible] re or small local chain. In this case, the supplier, rather than the grocery store, might be able to insure at lower cost precisely because hedging against shortages affecting a subset of suppliers within fluctuating markets is one of the primary functions of a wholesaler. These are two of four combined possibilities reflected in Table 6:1 below:

Table 6:1. Allocating Risk of Impossibility with Wholesaler and Grocer

	Small wholesaler	Large wholesaler
Small grocer	Unclear who bears risk more cheaply	Wholesaler bears risk more cheaply
Large chain grocer	Grocer bears risk more cheaply	Unclear who bears risk more cheaply

The analysis suggests that some cases, those in which only one of the parties can obviously bear the risk at lower cost (the lower left and upper right quadrants), are fairly easily resolved, whereas the others will depend more closely on particular facts. In the

[14] Although the machine manufacturer has a duty to take reasonable steps to find an alternative buyer, by assumption, those efforts are unlikely to be successful on these facts.

lower right corner, where both parties are large and can hedge risk, the allocation of this particular risk might be addressed within the terms of the specific contract, or if not, by their past course of dealing.[15]

The general point of this discussion is that physical impossibility is not a basis *per se* for discharging a contract without penalty. The risk of non-performance, like the risk of an accident when both sides undertake appropriate levels of care, must be borne somewhere, and the preferred rule will allocate that risk to the party who can bear it at lower cost. Of course, the law does not actually require performance when performance is literally impossible. If performance is not conditional, however, it might nevertheless require a party to pay damages resulting from non-performance.

2. *Commercial Impracticability*

A related common law doctrine, now codified in Article 2, § 2–615 of the Uniform Commercial Code,[16] is referred to as *commercial impracticability*. This doctrine typically includes three elements: (1) the occurrence of a circumstance the nonoccurrence of which was assumed as a material element to the contract; (2) the circumstance substantially adds extreme cost or difficulty to contractual performance; and (3) the contract itself did not specify the allocation of the risk that gave rise to the occurrence.[17] Although unavailable at the time, this defense might well characterize the conditions inducing breach in *Goebel v. Linn*[18] a case discussed in Chapter 5 in which the brewery acknowledged that performance would have bankrupted the ice company.

Commercial impracticability differs from the doctrine of impossibility in that it does not involve unexpected circumstances that render performance *physically impossible*; instead it involves unexpected circumstances that render performance *economically burdensome.* This is a difficult burden to satisfy. In the case of *Transatlantic Financing Corp. v. United States*,[19] for example, a ship contracted to make delivery from Texas to Iran, but before performance, the planned route, via the Suez Canal, was blocked, requiring routing around Cape of Good Hope, and thus substantially raising the cost of performance. The court determined that although the first two factors were satisfied, the third was not as it was customary for a shipper to bear the risk of a more costly delivery route when conditions change. In fact, given the knowledge of the parties of unrest in the Middle East, it is possible that the market price itself had already increased, thereby reflecting a risk premium in the shipping price.

---

15 U.C.C. § 1–303(b) (AM. LAW INST. & UNIF. LAW COMM'N 2014) (defining course of dealing as "a sequence of previous conduct between the parties to a particular transaction which is fairly to be regarded as establishing a common basis of understanding for interpreting their expressions and other conduct"). We discuss course of dealing, *infra* at Part III.B.

16 *Id.* § 2–615 ("Excuse by Failure of Presupposed Conditions").

17 *See* Transatlantic Fin. Corp. v. United States, 363 F.2d 312, 315–16 (D.C. Cir. 1966).

18 11 N.W. 284 (Mich. 1882). *See supra* Chapter 5 (discussing *Goebel v. Linn*).

19 363 F.2d at 319 ("While it may be an overstatement to say that increased cost and difficulty of performance never constitute impracticability, to justify relief there must be more of a variation between expected cost and the cost of performing by an available alternative than is present in this case, where the promisor can legitimately be presumed to have accepted some degree of abnormal risk, and where impracticability is urged on the basis of added expense alone.").

As the *Transatlantic Financing Corp.* case reveals, although the analysis of commercial impracticability resembles that of impossibility, there is an important distinction: unforeseen increases in performance costs appear to be the very sort of risk that a promisee intends to shift to the promisor by contract, especially in an *executory contract*, meaning one yet to be fully performed or executed.[20] Otherwise, the promisee would simply hedge against the market herself, and await contracting until the intended time of performance.

Finally, it is ir [illegible] from efficient breach, which arise [illegible] thus raises the opportunity cost of [illegible] y damages rule facilitates the breach [illegible] nal gains from the superior transact [illegible] der commercial impracticability, an [illegible] seek to avoid performance altoget [illegible] l financial loss. Clearly, the promis [illegible] uld prefer the impracticability defe [illegible] imposes a loss on the promisee, wh [illegible]

In general, we [illegible] gh increase in performance costs [illegible] find substitute performance other t [illegible] nisor. For that reason, it might ap [illegible] of commercial impracticability woul [illegible] mance. In fact, however, the legal d [illegible] ght reconcile it with the efficient breach model.[21]

Remember that commercial impracticability does not prescribe a blanket rule of zero damages for breach; rather, it conditions discharge on the realization of exceptionally high performance costs. In this sense, the doctrine operates as a "threshold rule" that leaves the standard measure of expectation damages in place for "normal" performance costs, and only excuses performance without damages for some "high" level of performance costs. The point at which this threshold is reached is not entirely clear from the rule. Economic analysis suggests the following as a possible candidate: The part of performance excused without damages equals performance above the threshold that would produce a social welfare loss, thereby rendering it inefficient.

This threshold rule would transform commercial impracticability into a kind of "negligence rule" for breach of contract. Specifically, if a promisor breaches, and if his realized cost is lower than the legal threshold, he will be assessed full expectancy damages, whereas if part or all of his costs exceed the threshold level, he will incur no damages for that marginal level of performance. And with the threshold set at the efficient level for

---

[20] JOSEPH M. PERILLO, CONTRACTS § 8.3(a) (7th ed. 2014).

[21] *See* Alan Sykes, *The Doctrine of Commercial Impracticability in a Second-Best World*, 19 J. LEGAL STUD. 43 (1990). Professor Sykes questions this doctrinal framing and asks, instead, which party can most efficiently bear the relevant risk, an inquiry that is not embraced within the framework of UCC § 2–615. Consider, for example, the allocation of risks in future contracts, and whether the *Goebel v. Linn* case might be recast as an ancient example of an futures contract for the commodity of ice. Does this alternative framing call the actual case result into question?

breach (which equals the promisee's value of performance, so that impracticability means *C>V*)[22], it is easy to see that the promisor will only breach when it is efficient to do so. The logic is identical to that used to illustrate the efficiency of the negligence rule in torts. Specifically, the threat of full (expectancy) damages deters breach when costs are in the range where performance is efficient (*C<V*), but discharge (zero damages) promotes breach over the range where non-performance is efficient (*C>V*). According to this interpretation of commercial impracticability, therefore, the promisor is induced to breach only when that is the efficient strategy.

In this reading, because damages are in fact zero whenever breach actually occurs, promisees will not be encouraged to over-rely on performance, as they did under the unlimited expectancy damages measure. Thus, in the "bilateral care" version of the contract problem, the threshold interpretation of commercial impracticability, if specified in this manner, achieves an efficient outcome in which promisors breach only when doing so avoids a social welfare loss, and promisees invest only in efficient reliance. Remember that we demonstrated above that the same outcome could be achieved by the "limited" expectancy damages measure (the *Hadley v. Baxendale* rule), which placed an upper limit on damages equal to the promisee's value of performance evaluated at the efficient level of reliance. Although actual damages were not zero in the event of breach under that rule, *marginal* damages were zero because promisees could not be compensated for any losses resulting from reliance expenditures beyond the efficient level.

In terms of incentives, this reading renders the two rules equivalent in terms of motivating promisees to avoid excessive reliance. Both place significant informational burdens on the court, however, as does any threshold rule. The *Hadley v. Baxendale* rule requires the court to calculate the efficient level of promisee reliance in order to determine the preferred compensation level, whereas the commercial impracticability rule requires the court to determine the level of promisor costs at which breach would be efficient. As a general proposition, it is impossible to say which rule would be easier to implement in a given case.

Although this reading might improve the efficiency of contractual performance, it might not characterize the rule's application in *Transatlantic Financing Corp.*[23] In that case, it seems likely that the re-routing that followed the unexpected closing of the Suez Canal resulted in a cost of performance that was not social-welfare-enhancing. To see why, consider whether the parties, had they anticipated this event, would have entered into the same contract. Most likely the transportation company would have demanded a considerably higher delivery price, and it is certainly possible that the United States or its agent, who contracted for these services, would have balked. If so, that implies that overall price required to accommodate the risk would have been too high.

There is, of course, no way to know what would actually have happened in this counterfactual, but the analysis raises the following question: If promisees enter contracts to shift risks onto promisors, is it ever possible to define non-performance that follows from a suddenly excessive performance cost as "inefficient"? Bear in mind that disallowing release from the contract does not necessarily compel performance; rather it

---

[22] For the definition of abbreviated terms used in this chapter, see *supra* Chapter 5, Part II.A.

[23] 363 F.2d 312 (D.C. Cir. 1966).

compels the party seeking release to negotiate non-performance. The exit price might be extremely high, but this too raises a question: Which of the parties is better situated to anticipate the possibility of this sort of risk in advance and to include in the contract a liability-limiting provision? The other contractual solution would have been for Transatlantic Financing to agree to the original contract price *unless* unforeseen events required an alternative routing that raised performance costs. Does this seem a more plausible alternative? Why or why not?

II. ALTERNATIVE CONTRACT REMEDIES: SPECIFIC PERFORMANCE AND LIQUIDATED DAMAGES

In this part, we consider two related alternative contract remedies: (1) specific performance, which is an order by the court for the breaching party to perform the contract as written, and (2) liquidated damages, which is an order to enforce a contractual provision that specifies damages in the event of breach, typically at an amount that exceeds expectancy damages.

A. General Framing

American courts rarely grant specific performance. The remedy is generally limited to cases involving the sale of land or other unique goods, thereby making money damages an inadequate substitute. The absence of an adequate damages measure as a suitable substitute for actual performance strengthens the argument for specific performance, but as the theory of efficient breach suggests, contract law generally avoids compelling performance in favor of breach remedies that enhance social welfare. Despite the risk that specific performance might induce excessive performance, some economists have argued for its wider application.[24]

Liquidated damages clauses allow the parties themselves to specify the level of damages in the event of breach. This might allow an intermediate solution between specific performance and expectancy when the promisee attaches a higher-than-usual value to expected performance, and to that extent, this might seem an attractive alternative to either expectancy damages or specific performance when it is specified. Even so, American courts have been similarly reluctant to enforce liquidated damages clauses. In general, courts allow liquidated damages to be enforced when the parties cannot accurately forecast damages upon breach and when the clause appears to reflect a reasonable estimate of the damages that the promisee is likely to incur.

The UCC has adopted an approach that echoes that at common law. Section 2–718(1) of the UCC states:

> Damages for breach by either party may be liquidated in the agreement but only at an amount which is reasonable in the light of the anticipated or actual

[24] *See, e.g.*, Thomas Ulen, *The Efficiency of Specific Performance: Toward a Unified Theory of Contract Remedies*, 83 MICH. L. REV. 341 (1984); Daniel Friedmann, *The Efficient Breach Fallacy*, 18 J. LEGAL STUD. 1 (1989). For a more formal analysis, see William Rogerson, *Efficient Reliance and Damage Measure for Breach of Contract*, 15 RAND J. ECON. 39 (1984).

> harm caused by the breach, the difficulties of proof of loss, and the inconvenience or nonfeasibility of otherwise obtaining an adequate remedy. A term fixing unreasonably large liquidated damages is void as a penalty.[25]

An interesting feature of both the common law and UCC rules governing liquidated damages is that they appear to disallow the remedy in the circumstance for which it might appear most useful, namely when the promisee attaches a value that *well exceeds* the general expected harm resulting from the failure to perform.

Specific performance does *not* necessarily result in a risk of excessive performance because the promisor can always seek to buy his way out of what he perceives to be an inefficient transaction. As an example, consider a contract for the sale of a parcel of land for which a buyer has agreed to pay $100,000. Suppose that before the transaction is completed, another buyer offers $120,000. Under a money damage remedy, if the seller breaches, the court will award damages equal to the original buyer's expectation interest, which is the difference between his valuation of the land and the price. Suppose it can be determined that he valued the land at $110,000, meaning that damages would be $10,000. The seller will therefore breach, pay the damages, and sell to the new buyer, netting him a gain of $10,000. The outcome is therefore efficient because the higher valuing buyer ends up with the land, and the original buyer has been made whole.

Now consider a specific performance remedy, which orders enforcement of the original contract. One possible outcome is that, after the original transaction is completed, the original buyer resells to the new buyer for a net gain of $10,000. Alternatively, the seller could offer the first buyer some amount of money greater than $10,000 (the first buyer's expected surplus), but less than $20,000 (the premium offered by the second buyer) to cancel the original contract, and then, if mutually agreeable, sell the land to the new buyer. Either way, the land ends up with the higher valuing purchaser. This analysis follows from the Coase theorem, and raises similar transactions costs questions to those explored previously.[26]

How would specific performance work in the brewery-ice company example from Chapter 5, where breach was due to cost uncertainty? Let the value of performance to the brewery, V, be $50,000; the price of performance, P, be $30,000; and the brewery's reliance expenditure, R, be $10,000. In this case, we know that any realized cost for the ice company above $50,000 makes breach efficient. Suppose that the cost is in fact $70,000. Performance will therefore cause the ice company to suffer a net loss of $40,000 (=$30,000–$70,000), so it will offer to pay the brewery some amount up to $40,000 to rescind the contract. The brewery in turn will accept any amount above $20,000 (=$50,000–$30,000), which is its expectation interest. (Remember that the reliance expenditure is sunk, so it does not affect the brewery's minimum buyout price.) Thus, there is room for a potential bargain that would result in performance being cancelled.[27]

---

[25] U.C.C. § 2–718(1) (AM. LAW INST. & UNIF. LAW COMM'N 1977).

[26] *See supra* Chapter 5, Part II.A.2 (illustrating bilateral monopoly and cycling game).

[27] Referring to Table 5:1, *see supra* Chapter 5, at 37, the maximum amount the seller will offer to cancel performance is $C–P$, while the minimum amount the buyer will accept is $V–P$. A buyout is therefore possible if $C–P>V–P$, or if $C>V$, which is the condition for efficient breach.

The critical point of these examples is that under either remedy—money damages or specific performance—the efficient outcome can, in theory, be achieved. The only difference is how that outcome arises. Under money damages, the court dictates the amount of compensation that the original buyer will receive in the event of breach, whereas under specific performance, the buyer is able to participate in the determination of the terms of a breach, either by bargaining directly with the new buyer, or by bargaining with the seller for a buyout. And as previously shown, when we introduce the non-breaching party into the negotiations, there is a risk that bargaining-related transaction costs will result in a dissipation of rents that threatens to avoid the social-welfare-enhancing aspect of having the breaching party pursue the superior economic opportunity. As explored below, this might be more of a problem with specific performance than with the enforcement of liquidated damages clauses.

Specific performance and liquidated damages clauses reallocate a property right to the promisee, whereas the efficient breach affords the promisee only a liability rule.[28] The result is that part of expectancy damages—the right to compensated for the expected value of performance in lieu of actual performance or higher damages—remains with the promisor. The critical inquiry is which of these rules will generally lower the cost of transacting in the sense of encouraging the parties to replicate their true intent from the time of contracting at the point at which their contractual relationship has broken down.

1. Tort Analogy Revisited: Some Ancient Codes

Once more, the relationship between contract and tort remedies is helpful in analyzing this problem. In general, tort law translates all remedies into monetary damages. That might seem especially problematic for severe personal injuries, including, for example, the loss of a limb or injuries to other body parts as a result of a careless accident. There is little doubt that even a large award of monetary damages is rarely adequate for such a loss. Of course the legal system can, in theory, impose increasingly draconian remedies for such harms, and there are precedents for doing so. Such ancient codes as *The Code of Hammurabi* and *The Five Books of Moses* contain prescriptions for "an eye for an eye, a tooth for a tooth."[29] Although even these harsh remedies would not restore the tort victim's lost eye or tooth, they nonetheless recognize the gravity of the harm—perhaps more so than money damages—by forcing the perpetrator to bear it as well.

And yet, some modern commentators have taken the view that this reading of such ancient codes might be mistaken.[30] An alternative reading suggests that the stated remedy provides the basis for an enforceable right—one to be negotiated between the perpetrator and the victim—but with the perpetrator placed in the position of internalizing the full cost of the inflicted harm. The "eye for an eye" affords the victim bargaining rights for a remedy up to the value of the same loss on the perpetrator, and with the hopeful expectation that the actual remedy will never come to that. Stated differently, these ancient

---

[28] For the seminal article on this distinction, see Guido Calabresi & A. Douglas Melamed, *Property Rules, Liability Rules, and Inalienability: One View of the Cathedral*, 85 HARV. L. REV. 1089 (1972). *See infra* Chapter 7.

[29] *Exodus* 21:23–21:27; CODE OF HAMMURABI §§ 196, 200 (L.W. King trans., 2015).

[30] Ben Zion Bergman, *Torah and Torts: A Reply to Professor Kader*, 4 J.L. & RELIGION 173, 175–76 (1986) (citing D. DAUBE, STUDIES IN BIBLICAL LAW (1947)) ("[E]ven in its Biblical origins the law may not have been retaliatory but rather compensatory").

codes facilitate a Coasian bargain *after* the two parties have been forced into a relationship that bears the critical features of a bilateral monopoly. And it accomplishes this without the need for the legal system to impose a specific monetary value on the extreme suffering of the victim, which obviously varies across individuals. Indeed, the ultimate remedies are apt to be highly individualized based on the subjective valuations of both the tort victim and the tortfeasor.

This remedial scheme carries obvious downsides, and one famous literary illustration suffices to make the point. If we set aside the problematic religious stereotyping,[31] *The Merchant of Venice*[32] reveals the risk associated with such *in-kind* remedies: It is possible that some extreme victim (or sociopath) will seek to exact a literal "pound of flesh" (or eye or tooth) rather than treating the stated rule as the tragic starting point for what one hopes will be a constructive Coasian bargain. The problem with *in-kind* remedies is not that the legal system is unable to devise a non-monetary damage remedy when individuals experience unique harms; rather it is that the genuine cost or risk of doing so is potentially far too high.

Indeed, the policy question involved in choosing whether to allow or to prohibit this form of remedy is analogous to the policy decision of whether to allow certain forms of lending that also can result in bodily harm.[33] Thus the same concern affecting tort damages also arises in the setting of contract remedies. Although the parties were already in contractual privity—it is, after all, a contract that broke down—the resulting bilateral monopoly risks creating high bargaining costs. As applied to specific performance, which is the more extreme remedy in the event of a breach, the magnitude of those costs depends on the ability of the promisor to negotiate a buyout from the promisee. And once again, the problem arises as a direct result of the divergence between *ex ante* and *ex post* expectations. In the contract setting, at the time of the initial transaction, the parties seek to maximize their joint gains, and also to allocate those gains between them. At the time of the event that induces breach, neither side is apt to be concerned with improving overall social welfare; indeed enlarging the pie is rarely an option once this occurs. Instead, each side seeks to take the largest share of the available gains, even if at the time of contracting, part of those gains were expected to go to the other party. This is the problem of appropriable quasi rents.[34]

Specific performance provides the non-breaching party an equivalent starting point to "an eye for an eye." Rather than condone the breach and monetize the harm based on reasonable *ex ante* expectations, the remedy forces the breaching party to negotiate based on whatever the expected burdens of performance on the promisor are *ex post.* Liquidated damages provisions place the burden somewhere in between that implied by specific performance and money damages. The specified amount of liquidated damages will almost necessarily lie between the expectancy damages value of breach and the cost of specific performance. We know this because if the cost of expectancy damages exceeded the burden of specific performance, the promisor would simply perform as a means of

---

[31] *See* Nicole M. Coonradt, *Shakespeare's Grand Deception: The Merchant of Venice—Anti-Semitism as "Uncanny Causality" and the Catholic-Protestant Problem*, 11 RELIGION & ARTS 74 (2007).

[32] WILLIAM SHAKESPEARE, THE MERCHANT OF VENICE.

[33] *See supra* Chapter 5, Part I.D.

[34] *See supra* Chapter 5, Intro.

avoiding that greater penalty. And if the liquidated damages were lower than expectancy damages, the promisee would not have bothered to specify damages in the contract.

The question is whether despite the enforcement problems, the inclusion of a specific performance or liquidated damages provision can nonetheless be social-welfare-enhancing. The strongest argument for the enforcement of such a clause is that it signals to the promisor that the promisee places a higher value on a breach than the ordinary promisee in similar circumstances. If enforced, such provisions would, in effect, thereby allocate the higher financial risk associated with non-performance—specifically the subjective, or infra-marginal, value that this specific promisee attaches to performance—onto the promisor. And if the promisor is willing to take on that risk, then the contract price should be expected to compensate the promisor for having done so.

One implication of this analysis is that UCC § 2–718(1), which tracks the common law rule, and which enforces liquidated damages clauses only if the specified amount is "reasonable in the light of the anticipated or actual harm,"[35] might well miss the point of having a liquidated damages clause. The clause is helpful precisely when the promisee holds a subjective valuation to performance that is not otherwise verifiable in the contract terms. We explore this in more detail below.[36]

B. Distribution of the Gains

A second factor affecting the choice between specific performance and liquidated damages versus money damages involves the distribution of the gains from a breach. Assume that Alice, a developer, has several largely indistinguishable lots of land for an intended development, and that based on the high demand in the early sale of lots, including the lot sold to Barb at $100,000, she increases the price to $110,000. After Alice contracts with Barb for the sale of lot 101, a second buyer, Carl, offers Alice $120,000 for that specific lot. Assume that Barb is largely indifferent as between lot 101 and any number of alternative lots, now priced at $110,000, and that she has no reliance-specific investments that could not easily be transferred to another available lot. By contrast, Carl has a special reason to prefer lot 101 to any other within the development, and he is thus willing to pay a premium to acquire it.[37] Based on these assumptions, by breaching her contract with Barb, paying her expectancy damages of $10,000, thereby allowing Barb to acquire an equivalent alternative lot, and then selling lot 101 to Carl for $120,000, Alice is able to improve social welfare and personally gain $10,000.

The question raised by the choice of remedies in this example is not whether the breach should take place. Instead, the two separate inquiries are: (1) who should get the $10,000 surplus? and (2) what is the process through which that question should be resolved? Under expectancy damages, Alice (the promisor) breaches, and after paying Barb her expectancy damages of $10,000, Alice retains the entire surplus.

---

[35] U.C.C. § 2–718(1) (AM. LAW INST. & UNIF. LAW COMM'N 1977).

[36] *See infra* at Part II.A.2.

[37] Once more, the two-markets problem explains the emergence of the opportunity for efficient breach. *See supra* Chapter 5, at 39 (discussing guitar hypothetical).

Now consider specific performance, which gives the promisee (here the original buyer) a property right in contractual performance that the promisor then has to purchase in order to proceed with the social-welfare-enhancing breach. As described above, one possibility is for Barb to enforce the original contract and resell the property at $120,000 to Carl herself, thereby netting herself a gain of $10,000, after purchasing a new lot for $110,000. Alternatively, Barb could negotiate with Alice to allow Alice to avoid performance with her and to sell lot 101 to Carl. Barb and Alice could then negotiate how to split the $10,000 gain. Let's say they split the difference and thus negotiate a buyout price for Barb's purchase contract of $15,000. In this case they share the surplus evenly: Barb receives $15,000, as compared with her expectancy interest of $10,000 from the original contract, a net gain of $5000, and Alice also nets $5000 after selling lot 101 to Carl for $120,000 and paying Barb $15,000.

These examples, along with the earlier discussion of the brewery-ice company case,[38] show that there is a distributional difference between the two remedies for breach. This difference reflects the divergence between the award of gains as between a court-imposed resolution of the dispute with money damages, on one hand, and a negotiated resolution starting with the right to specific performance, on the other. From a fairness perspective, one might argue that because a contract is a promise, the party who breaks the promise should not be allowed to profit from it at the expense of the injured party. This viewpoint argues in favor of specific performance, although as the discussion to follow demonstrates, there are countervailing considerations.

1. *The Coase Theorem Revisited: The Problem of Rent Dissipation*

The preceding analysis overlooks a critical insight of the Coase theorem, namely that resources might not flow to their more highly valued uses *if* transactions costs are high. In that setting, it is possible that the choice as between monetary damages and specific performance is not purely distributional. This returns us once more to the problem of appropriable quasi rents and the distinction between bargaining *ex ante*, when parties seek to maximize social welfare gains so that there is more to divide between them, and bargaining *ex post*, after the contractual relationship breaks down and when each side is principally motivated to take the largest available share of an inevitably smaller pie.

When a contractual relationship has broken down, and each side feels aggrieved, it is less likely that either is motivated to divide the gains evenly. Rather, such breakdowns typically carry with them recriminations, and with that, a sense on both sides of entitlement to whatever shares are part of the spoils. As discussed in Chapter 5, the resulting bilateral bargaining itself threatens to dissipate part, and maybe all, of whatever gains remain. This can also arise in a multiparty setting, which exacerbates the bargaining difficulty even as compared with bilateral monopoly. For example, if Carl, who valued lot 101 at $120,000, approached Alice, the original seller, offering that amount after Barb's purchase, Alice would then need to repurchase the lot from Barb. We might imagine negotiations over the potential $10,000 valuation surplus, assuming that Barb is indifferent as to which lot she takes, with now three parties, Alice, Barb, and Carl,

[38] *See supra* Chapter 5, Part I.B. & Part II.A.1.

depleting that available gain through a rent dissipation game.[39] As explained in Chapter 13, this dynamic can be characterized as a cycle, which like a bilateral monopoly, threatens a dissipation of potential social-welfare-enhancing gains associated with breach. In effect, the expectancy damages rule avoids such high transactions cost challenges that might otherwise arise as a consequence of bilateral or multilateral bargaining.

An additional argument further counsels in favor of expectancy damages. Recall, once more, the illustration with the table manufacturer and guitar maker.[40] It is reasonable to assume that the table manufacture had invested in the goodwill that is associated with becoming known for excellent wood products. Similarly, in the land example, Alice, the developer, invested in the goodwill associated with having many lots available for sale and development. The expectancy damages rule rewards that investment by giving those who are afforded a superior, social welfare enhancing, opportunity the benefit of that opportunity after making whole the promisees with whom they breach. In effect, the expectancy damages rule disallows those in privity of contract to obstruct superior contracts that will often derive from that goodwill capital investment of the promisors, whose contractual commitment is assumed to make them whole *either* by performance or by breach followed by expectancy damages. Finally, notice that the brewery-ice company example did not involve an inducement to breach resulting from such goodwill and a superior market opportunity. As previously noted, the dynamics that give rise to the breach incentive in these two contexts differ, and as applied in the breach context, the expectancy damages rule furthers the objective of avoiding a rent dissipation game in the *ex post* bilateral monopoly setting.

QUESTIONS

Can you identify circumstances suitable for specific performance? If so, do your examples avoid the risk of a rent dissipation game? If not, are they justified on other grounds? Should it be left to contracting parties to determine whether specific performance is a suitable remedy for breach? Why or why not? We have emphasized the transaction costs of negotiating a breach under specific performance, but there are also costs of litigation involved in arriving at a court-imposed money damage remedy. How do these costs affect your answers?

2. *Subjective Value and Breach*

We have shown that under ideal conditions, meaning when transactions costs are low, both specific performance and money damages (under the expectancy damages measure) are able to generate efficient outcomes in cases of breach. There is, however, an important reason why specific performance might be a preferable rule in certain contexts, namely when courts are unlikely to be able to accurately assess buyer's valuation of performance (what we have denoted V). In commercial contracts like the brewery-ice

---

[39] *See* Chapter 5, *supra* at 179–181; *see also* Maxwell L. Stearns & Megan J. McGinnis, *A Social Choice View of Law and Economics*, *in* METHODOLOGIES OF LAW AND ECONOMICS 72 (Thomas S. Ulen ed., 2017). The example in the text is designed to illustrate how bargaining can raise transactions costs, not to illustrate the legal rule governing the conveyance of land. Because land is unique, specific performance is likely to the apply in the event of a breach with respect to property conveyances. PERILLO, *supra* note 20, § 16.2.

[40] *See supra* Chapter 5, Part II.A.2.

company case, measuring this value might be a fairly easy matter because it merely involves determining the profits the brewery would have made from the sale of beer, which can generally be calculated or well estimated with discoverable information. In other cases, however, the buyer's value might be much harder to observe.

To illustrate, consider the well-known case of *Peevyhouse v. Garland Coal & Mining Co.*,[41] which involved a contract between the Peevyhouses, owners of a farm that sat on top of a coal deposit, and the Garland Mining Company. The contract called for the mining company to conduct a strip-mining operation, after which it would restore the land to its pre-mining condition. However, when it came time to perform the remedial work, the mining company reneged, claiming that the estimated cost of the work, $29,000, greatly exceeded the difference in the market value of the farm with or without the remediation. That value was a mere $300. The *Peevyhouse* court sided with the mining company, thereby allowing the breach, and awarding the Peevyhouses damages of $300.[42] By contrast, the dissenting opinion in *Peevyhouse* argued that the plaintiffs were entitled to a specific performance remedy.[43]

On one reading, consistent with the theory of efficient breach, the ruling appears correct. If C=$29,000 and V=$300, breach of the promise to restore the land was clearly efficient, and the court's setting of damages at V (the expectancy value in this case) creates appropriate incentives for the mining company. The problem in this case does not concern these estimated values, which we will assume are correct, but rather, it involves the use of the difference in the *market value* of the land as a true measure of the value of non-performance to the Peevyhouses.

In general, market value is defined to be the maximum amount that someone is *willing to pay* for the land, or for any piece of property, in an arm's length transaction. However, it is not necessarily the minimum amount that the owners of the property are *willing to accept* for it. The price that a buyer is willing to pay and the price that a seller will accept are distinct measures of value. When the buyer's offer price exceeds the landowner's subjective valuation, the transaction proceeds, with a resulting social surplus. By contrast, when the reverse holds and the seller's reservation price (the price she would willingly accept) exceeds the buyer's valuation, no transaction occurs.

Indeed, this is reflected in the widely misunderstood meaning of "for sale" signs, typically in residential neighborhoods. On one reading, the signs signal that the home is available for sale. This is mistaken. All houses are for sale all of the time, but only for the right price. Most of the time, homeowners place a higher, or infra-marginal, value on their homes, and thus their subjective valuation is apt to exceed the offer price of most prospective buyers. The *absence of* a "for sale" sign thus signals that the homeowner holds such an infra-marginal value, and thus, absent unusual conditions, it would be a waste of time to make an offer. By contrast, the "for sale" sign means that whatever subjective valuation the homeowner once had is now past, or at least is small relative to what they perceive is the willingness of buyers to pay. As a result, the homeowner's actual, or subjective, valuation is close enough to the fair market valuation that it is no longer a

---

41 382 P.2d 109 (Okla. 1962).

42 *Id.* at 114.

43 *Id.* at 116 (Irwin, J., dissenting).

waste of time for a prospective buyer to make an offer. And of course, going to the rules of offer and acceptance, the listed price is merely an invitation for the bidder to make an offer, not an offer that the bidder can accept.[44]

In *Peevyhouse*, the owners were not looking to sell their property. They were looking to have it maintained in its present condition following a costly and intrusive strip-mining operation. The ruling disallowed them the benefit of their subjective valuation as part of the remedy despite the inclusion of a restoration clause in the terms of the contract.[45]

Now consider how the owner's subjective valuation is reflected in the simple supply-and-demand diagram in Figure 6:1. The demand curve in the graph represents what buyers are willing to pay for a piece of land, whereas the supply curve is what sellers are willing to accept for it (their *reservation price*, meaning the price below which they will reserve the property for themselves or for a future transaction). When willingness to pay exceeds willingness to accept at the same price, both the buyer and seller are made better off, and so a sale takes place. In the graph, this occurs for all equivalent parcels up to Q^*. The point where the two curves intersect determines the market value of the land—a third measure of value—as indicated by the horizontal line labeled *MV*.[46]

The difficulty is that of the three measures of value—willingness to pay, reservation price (or willingness to accept), and market value—*only market value is observable* and thus verifiable.[47] This is reflected, for example, in the practice among mortgagors to assess value based on the record of sales of comparable properties, as opposed, say, to the statement of subjective valuations of prospective buyers, owners seeking to refinance, or neighbors. And when a tax assessor or a court is faced with the need to put a value on a piece of property, the only practical measure is market value. Notice, however, that for parcels to the right of Q^*—those that are not presently "for sale"—that measure will systematically *undervalue* the land relative to the current owner's subjective valuation as indicated by her reservation price.

---

[44] *See supra* Chapter 5, note 11 and accompanying text.

[45] For this reason, a vote of law professors awarded the Peevyhouses the dubious honor of "most screwed plaintiffs." *The Peevyhouses: The Most Screwed Victims in Case-Law History*, PRAWFSBLAWG (May 9, 2008), http://prawfsblawg.blogs.com/prawfsblawg/2008/05/the-peevyhouses.html. *See also* Adrian Walters, *If You Thought the Peevyhouses Got Screwed, You Are Not Alone . . .*, THE WALTERS WAY (Oct. 17, 2012), https://thewaltersway.wordpress.com/2012/10/17/if-you-thought-the-peevyhouses-got-screwed-you-are-not-alone/ (including images of the Peevyhouse farm).

[46] Not all parcels that sell will necessarily sell for the same price, as individual prices will be determined by bargaining. For the marginal parcel, however, *MV* is the only possible price.

[47] The difference between an owner's willingness to accept and market value is the owner's "subjective value." *See* Timothy Muris, *The Cost of Completion or Diminution of Market Value: The Relevance of Subjective Value*, 12 J. LEGAL STUD. 379 (1983); Herbert Hovenkamp, *Legal Policy and the Endowment Effect*, 20 J. LEGAL STUD. 225 (1991) (discussing related concept of endowment effect, meaning the difference in value persons attached based on possession itself).

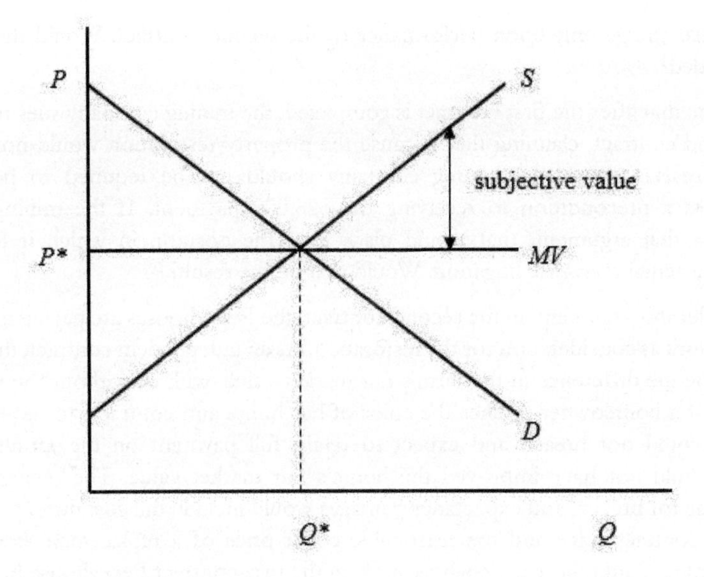

Figure 6:1. Relationship between market value (*MV*) and subjective value.

The Peevyhouses appear to have attached substantial subjective valuation to their land, which implies that they valued performance of the restorative aspect of the contract more highly, indeed much more highly, than was reflected in the $300 market differential of the value of their property. By setting compensation at this market differential, the court therefore likely underestimated *V*, the alternative measure of damages. The result not only seems unfair to the Peevyhouses; it also risks excessive breach.

QUESTIONS AND COMMENTS

It seems intuitive that the Peevyhouse ruling undervalued the restoration for the Peevyhouses. By contrast, the dissenting approach would have restored them to their anticipated position. Even so, specific performance risks a rent-dissipation game, and the difference here, $29,000 as cost of performance and $300 as the differential market value, suggests a broad bargaining range equal to $28,700.

How should the *Peevyhouse* court have weighed these concerns? Is the inclusion of the restorative work in the contract itself relevant to the analysis? Would the Peevyhouses have signed a contract that contained the following provision instead of the restoration provision: "Upon completion of the strip mining, we will ensure that the market value of your property is within $300 of its value prior to the strip mining"? If not, does that suggest the ruling was incorrect? Why or why not?

Might the Peevyhouses have avoided the problem by entering into two separate contracts with the strip mining company? In this variation, the first contract would be a lease to strip mine the land, and the second contract would be to restore the land. Assume that the first contact added to the leasing price the approximate value of the restoration, say $28,000, and that the second contract paid the mining company $28,000 for the restoration work. In effect, the Peevyhouses would be forcing the mining company to pay the value of the restoration to them (equivalent to posting a bond), and would then allow the mining company to recover that additional charge only upon performance of the second contract. Would this approach have succeeded?

Imagine that after the first contract is completed, the mining company sues for the price of the second contract, claiming that because the property restoration would not affect the farm's fair market value, the mining company should not be required to perform the restoration as a precondition to receiving the $28,000 payment. If the mining company succeeded in that argument, that would place it in the position in which it found itself following the actual *Peevyhouse* litigation. Would that be the result?

Consider this argument: in the second contract, the Peevyhouses are paying the expected cost of the work as consideration for the restoration. As an independent contract, the valuation should not be the difference in the farm's fair market value, with or without the restoration. By analogy, if a homeowner dislikes the color of her home and contracts to have it painted, the painter could not breach and expect to retain full payment on the ground that the repainting would not have improved the home's fair market value. The owner would be entitled to sue for breach, and expectancy damages would include the cost difference between the original contract price and the reasonable cover price of a replacement contract with another painter. Would the same analysis apply in the two-contract Peevyhouse hypothetical? Why or why not?

Alternatively, is this a case in which a liquidated damages clause would satisfy the requirements of UCC § 2–718(1)? If the contract specified damages at, say, $28,000 in the event of failing to restore the property, would that "be reasonable in the light of the anticipated or actual harm caused by the breach"? We will return to the problem of subjective value below,[48] and we will consider whether for liquidated damages clauses to be effective, they must hew so closely to the burden of specific performance.

3. *Liquidated Damage Clauses as Self-Enforcing Contracts*

Liquidated damages clauses allow the promisee to assert a valuation for breach between expectancy damages and the burden on the promisor of specific performance. The parties may choose to specify damages for other reasons as well. For example, they may do so to avoid the costs of going to court in the event of breach (especially if the likelihood of breach is high), or because they expect the court to have difficulty in measuring the damages from breach (such as when subjective value is high).

As we have seen, courts do not automatically enforce liquidated damages provisions. They are especially disinclined to do so if the specified amount of damages substantially exceeds what the court perceives to be the actual damages suffered by the victim from a breach. Such excessive amounts are often viewed as being punitive rather than compensatory, and for that reason, courts will generally not enforce these so-called "penalty clauses." The following variation on a famous case nicely illustrates the difficulty with this approach.

Consider *Jacob & Youngs, Inc. v. Kent*.[49] Because the case arose in the context of the provision of services, here the construction of a home, the case implicated the doctrine

[48] *See infra* part II.B.3.

[49] 129 N.E. 889 (N.Y. 1921).

of *express conditions*. For contracts involving the sale of goods the analogous doctrine is *perfect tender*, which allows the buyer to reject when the delivered goods do not conform precisely to the contract description.[50] As the *Jacob & Youngs* case reveals, in the context of service contracts, courts instead favor the doctrine of *substantial performance*, which allows some deviations, subject to an offset for the difference in valuation from promised to actual performance.[51]

In this case, Kent contracted with Jacob & Youngs to have a home constructed, and in the contract, the parties specified use of Reading pipe. Upon completion, Kent discovered that the builder instead used Cohoes pipe, a brand of comparable quality, and refused final payment. The contractor sued. Kent insisted on specific performance, and the *Jacob & Youngs* court, with Judge Cardozo writing, rejected this based on substantial performance. There was no difference in the value of the home post-construction resulting from the use of Cohoes rather than Reading pipe, and the cost of specific performance would have been extremely large, close to a tear down and rebuild.

In our variation, assume that Kent was a marketing director for Reading pipe, and that he planned to entertain prospective clients in his home, including retailers of his product and developers who would use his pipe in their construction projects. Further assume that Kent wishes to make clear to the builder that he holds a special subjective valuation attached to the use of Reading pipe rather than a competing brand, without regard to objective measures of quality. One way to signal this is to specify the pipe in the contract itself. Of course, he tried that, and it failed. Another is to include a specific performance clause, in favor of damages, which, as we have seen, is unlikely to be enforceable. A third approach is to include an "and I really mean it" clause, which expresses that this choice of pipe matters greatly to Kent. Of course, if the valuation difference is minimal or non-existent, as in the actual case, then this too will have no effect.

Finally, assume that Kent includes a liquidated damages provision. Notably, if enforced, this provision need not include damages at or even near the tear down and rebuild cost in the event of deficient performance. Instead, it need only be large enough to make substantial performance, as opposed to perfect tender, unattractive. But for this to work, the specified damages must *exceed* the actual difference between Kent's subjective valuation and the nominal (or nonexistent) difference in market value as between a home built with Cohoes rather than Reading pipe.

---

[50] PERILLO, *supra* note 20, § 11.20. With respect to the sale of goods, the Uniform Commercial Code provides:

> § 2–601. Buyer's Rights on Improper Delivery.
>
> Subject to the provisions of this Article on breach in installment contracts . . . and unless otherwise agreed under the sections on contractual limitations of remedy . . ., if the goods or the tender of delivery fail in any respect to conform to the contract, the buyer may
>
> (a) reject the whole; or
>
> (b) accept the whole; or
>
> (c) accept any commercial unit or units and reject the rest.

U.C.C. § 2–601 (AM. LAW INST. & UNIF. LAW COMM'N 1977).

[51] PERILLO, *supra* note 20, § 11.18(b).

Assume that the construction contract is for $200,000, and the contract states: "In the event that the home is built with pipe other than Reading brand, the builder will offset the amount due by $10,000." Assume that the maximum price difference in the cost of piping is $1000. Whereas a specific performance provision would allow Kent to force upon the builder a cost equal to nearly the full $200,000, the far more modest liquidated damages provision would have signaled clearly that it really matters to Kent that this specific feature satisfy perfect tender rather than substantial performance.

This suggests that a liquidated damages clause is a potentially effective means of signaling subjective valuation, and that the signal can be effective *even if* the specified damages are non-draconian in the sense of equivalence to the full burden of specific performance. At the same time, however, for the clause to be effective, it must exceed actual expected damages based on a measure of differential fair market value (in this case, zero). The damages must simply ensure that the promisor suffer a sufficient financial hit if she fails to perform the material contract term to which it is attached, such as the proposed $10,000 remedy. Nonetheless, if the court viewed the stipulated damages as "excessive," it would decline enforcement.

Economists have advanced additional reasons why courts should enforce liquidated damages clauses.[52] These include the following:

First, damages cannot be known at the time the contract is made but can only be based on the expected loss. Suppose, for example, that in the *Hadley v. Baxendale* case the mill owner and transport company had included a stipulated damages clause requiring the transport company to pay $1000 in the event that it was late in returning the shaft, where the damage amount was based on the average profit earned by the mill over the relevant time period. But suppose that the actual loss turned out to be only $500, as might have been the case if there had been an unusually poor harvest. In this case, the court might interpret the stipulated damage amount to be excessive, even though it was reasonable at the time the contract was made. In terms of incentives for breach, it is, of course, the *expected loss* that matters because that is all that can be known at the time the transport company has to make its decision. Thus, the court's refusal to enforce the clause might be viewed as inefficient because it will result in a systematic underassessment of damages.

Second, promisees might include excessive stipulated damages clauses for reasons other than subjective value. This might include, for example, unavoidably high reliance costs. The *Hadley* case again provides an example: The mill depended upon prompt performance by the transport company because the mill lacked a spare shaft. As we argued above, the efficient course of action in this case is for the promisee to communicate that fact to the promisor so the latter will be particularly careful in carrying out the promised performance. A high stipulated damages amount, which raises the cost of breach, is one way that a promisor can credibly commit to ensuring a high probability of performance. And if breach does occur, the high damage amount will be more likely to adequately compensate the promisee for the resulting losses. Notice, once more, that the damages amount need not equal the full loss value associated with specific performance to be an effective signal.

[52] POSNER, *supra* note 13, at 159–63.

Finally, a promisee might include such a clause when there is a risk that a breach might otherwise go undetected, as when it is due to malfeasance on the part of the promisor or his employees. In this situation, the liquidated damages clause operates like punitive damages in torts, thus providing "excessive" compensation for those breaches that are detected, thereby creating the correct incentives for breach on average.

QUESTIONS AND COMMENTS

Do you believe that the *Kent* case was rightly decided? Why or why not? How would you resolve the variation involving a liquidated damages clause, and why? Does the specific reason that motivated Kent to include the clause matter to your analysis? Why? Notice that one economic justification for enforcing such clauses is the inability to accurately determine damages in advance, with the risk of over stating damages. But another argument depends on subjective valuation, which implies that damages will always exceed the fair market difference between perfect tender and substantial performance. Is it possible to reconcile these two competing intuitions? Why or why not? If not, which should prevail? Why?

III. OTHER FORMS OF SELF-ENFORCING CONTRACTS

In addition to specific performance and liquidated damages, other forms of self-enforcing contracts include warranties, long-term contracts, and non-compete clauses. We consider each in turn.

A. Warranties

Product warranties are guarantees that a product will perform as advertised, backed up by the promise of compensation or replacement in event that the product fails to do so. In this sense, warranties are similar to stipulated damages. The economic theory of warranties is slightly different, however, in that warranties are concerned with performance of the product *after* delivery. Warranty coverage thus depends on production decisions made by the manufacturer, and also on use decisions by the consumer. The situation is therefore economically equivalent to the bilateral care model of products liability in torts, except that here we are concerned with malfunction of the product rather than personal injury to the consumer. Thus, unlike liability coverage, consumer warranties are, in theory, negotiable as between the parties. In practice, however, consumers are usually presented with a menu of take-it-or-leave-it coverage options, sometimes priced based on level or duration of coverage, but generally with no opportunity to dicker over terms.

The Coase theorem would seem to imply that, in a competitive market, manufacturers will achieve a cost-effective level of product quality regardless of the level of warranty coverage. As we argued in the case of products liability, however, this conclusion relies on the assumption that consumers can easily observe or otherwise learn, for example by reputation, of quality and condition, and make their purchase decisions accordingly.[53] In the more realistic case where consumers are unable to observe quality directly, express warranties can serve as a helpful quality signal because producers know that if they sell low quality products, they will be liable for the cost of repairs.[54] Thus, consumers will typically pay a price premium for a product that includes a warranty covering the cost of product failure because they expect the product to be of above-average quality. Warranties convey helpful information in lowering information costs as to the quality of goods.

Warranties do not always cover the *full* cost of repairs; rather coverage is generally limited in scope and/or time. One reason is that full coverage would eliminate any incentive for consumers to use the product carefully and only for its intended purpose. In other words, it would create a moral hazard problem for consumers. Partial warranties therefore represent an efficient response to the bilateral-care nature of the risk of product failure by allocating some risk to consumers.[55]

The analysis to this point has concerned *express* warranties, or warranties that are explicitly included in a sales contract. Developments in products liability in the mid- to late-twentieth century resulted in courts finding an *implied warranty of product fitness* in all sales contracts, which makes producers strictly liable for product-related injuries.[56] From an economic perspective, there is no distinction between product-related costs arising from personal injury versus product failure, and so the preferred legal response should be parallel. The law does not, however, allow producers and consumers to negotiate over the assignment of liability for injury, whereas manufacturers are not obligated to include warranties for repairs or replacements. A possible explanation is that the legal system is more concerned with insuring risk spreading in the context of personal injuries than in the context of failed or defective products. This is especially likely for low cost products for which the risks associated with defects are not terribly burdensome to the consumer.

B. Long-Term Contracts

The final type of self-enforcing contract involves an ongoing relationship between trading partners that consists of a series of repeated transactions. Such relationships are often governed by long-term contracts that economize on the need to renegotiate terms with each transaction. An important advantage of long-term contracts is that they promote transaction-specific investments by the parties (similar to reliance investments) and thereby enhance the value of the relationship. The risk is that such arrangements can create opportunities for opportunistic behavior in particular transactions.

Before proceeding with the analysis of long-term contracts, it is worth mentioning the relationship of such contracts to the formation of a firm. Ronald Coase's theory of the firm suggests that entrepreneurs combine different factors of production into a single

---

[53] One other possibility is to rely on third party intermediaries, such as *Consumer Reports*, to evaluate and compare quality of consumer products.

[54] Michael A. Spence, *Consumer Misperceptions, Product Failure and Producer Liability*, 44 REV. ECON. STUD. 561, 569–71 (1977).

[55] Russell Cooper & Thomas Ross, *Product Warranties and Double Moral Hazard*, 16 RAND J. ECON. 103 (1985).

[56] 5 FOWLER V. HARPER ET AL., HARPER, JAMES & GRAY ON TORTS § 28.16 (3d ed. 2008).

business entity subject to command and control as a means of avoiding problems associated with post-contractual opportunism that might arise if the arrangements were handled entirely by arms-length contracting.[57] Long-term contracting arrangements are designed to overcome similar difficulties, but without permanent structural changes to the entities that enter into the long-term relationships. In effect, long-term contracting falls somewhere in the middle of a spectrum with individual contracts at one end and vertical integration, or the creation of a firm, at the other.

Professors Lisa Bernstein, Robert Scott, and Alan Schwartz have written a series of articles on long-term contracting among large businesses that reveals the limits of the approach codified in § 1–303 of the Uniform Commercial Code. That provision states:

> e) Except as otherwise provided in subsection (f), the express terms of an agreement and any applicable course of performance, course of dealing, or usage of trade must be construed whenever reasonable as consistent with each other. If such a construction is unreasonable:
>
> (1) express terms prevail over course of performance, course of dealing, and usage of trade;
>
> (2) course of performance prevails over course of dealing and usage of trade; and
>
> (3) course of dealing prevails over usage of trade.
>
> (f) Subject to Section 2–209, a course of performance is relevant to show a waiver or modification of any term inconsistent with the course of performance.[58]

This provision states that in long-term contractual relationships, courts are instructed to look at evidence of past dealings when construing the relationship in the event of a breach. Professors Bernstein, Scott, and Schwartz have demonstrated a fundamental problem with this approach, one that goes to the core of the difference between the *ex ante* and *ex post* expectations of contracting parties.[59]

These authors suggest that course-of-dealing evidence arises when the parties to long-term contracts are operating within the productive phase of their relationship, and

---

[57] R.H. Coase, *The Nature of the Firm*, 4 ECONOMICA 386 (1937).

[58] U.C.C. § 1–303 (AM. LAW INST. & UNIF. LAW COMM'N 2001) (Section 1–303 "integrates the 'course of performance' concept from Articles 2 and 2A into the principles of former Section 1–205, which deals with course of dealing and usage of trade."). In the 1990s, the National Conference of Commissioners on Uniform State Laws (NCCUSL) began the process of revising Article 2 of the UCC. Originally intended as a complete revision, the scope was reduced in 2000 to a series of amendments. NCCUSL and the American Law Institute (ALI) approved amended Article 2 and 2A in 2002 and 2003, respectively. In 2011 the Article 2 amendments were withdrawn from the official text of the UCC after no states adopted them. For background information, see *Recommendation of the Permanent Editorial Board for the Uniform Commercial Code to Withdraw the 2003 Amendments to UCC Article 2 and 2A from the Official Test of the Uniform Commercial Code*, 65 CONSUMER FIN. L. Q. REP. 150 (2011). *See also* David Frisch, *Amended U.C.C. Article 2 as Code Commentary*, 11 DUQ. BUS. L.J. 175 (2009); William H. Henning, *Amended Article 2: What Went Wrong?*, 11 DUQ. BUS. L.J. 131 (2009).

[59] Lisa Bernstein, *Custom in Court*, 110 NW. U. L. REV. 63 (2015); Robert E. Scott, *Conflict and Cooperation in Long-Term Contracts*, 75 CALIF. L. REV. 2005 (1987); Alan Schwartz, *Relational Contracts in the Courts: An Analysis of Incomplete Agreements and Judicial Strategies*, 21 J. LEGAL STUD. 271 (1992).

thus when they are anticipating that social welfare is continuing to grow from their ongoing business dealings. Informal accommodations in that setting, for example, allowing expansions of orders, extensions of payment credit, delays on delivery, modifications to order, and the like, work well when the context of the contractual modifications, however informally made, lead to an expanding pie, the benefits of which the contracting parties can then share.

The problem with the UCC rule, these authors claim, is that when the contractual relationship breaks down, the parties are then in an *ex post* relationship.[60] The sorts of informal accommodations that defined the relationship in good times no longer characterize the relationship that has by definition soured. Indeed, the purpose of assigning terms within a written contract, these authors maintain, is in anticipation that the contractual relationships might break down at some point. Remember also that the contracting parties did not choose to combine their factors of production into a single firm. At the point at which the contract does break down, the analysis suggests, the courts should not look to past practices, but to the terms of the contract itself.

C. Non-Compete Clauses

Another context in which long-term contracting arises is employment relationships in which employees need to acquire firm-specific skills in order to undertake certain tasks. It is advantageous to the firm to train its employees, but if the resulting skills are largely transferrable to other firms, there is an opportunity for trained workers to threaten to leave, thereby demanding higher compensation. This risk can blunt firm incentives to train workers in the first place, thus harming both sides.

To illustrate, suppose that an untrained worker is worth $50 to all firms, and that is the wage she would receive. However, if a particular firm invests $25 in training her, the worker would be worth $150 to that firm and $100 to other firms. (Thus, of the $100 in value-added from training, $50 is transferrable.) Training is clearly beneficial in this case because it creates a net increase in value of $75 (=$150–$25–$50), but it is easy to show that the firm will not invest in such training in equilibrium because of the risk of worker exit.

Consider the payoff matrix in Table 6:2, which shows the firm's choices: (Train, Not train), and the worker's choices (Stay, Leave). The social-welfare-maximizing outcome involves the firm investing and the worker remaining with the firm (upper left cell). In that case, the firm pays the worker $75 and earns a profit of $50. Thus, the two parties share the net gain of $125 (=$150–$25). If the firm invests and the worker leaves, however (lower left cell), the worker gets a wage of $100 from another firm, and the original firm incurs the training cost of $25. In the remaining two cases where the firm does not train the worker, the worker gets the unskilled wage of $50 and the firm gets zero. The unique Nash equilibrium of this game is for the firm not to train the worker and for the worker to leave (the bolded lower right cell). Thus, the efficient outcome is forgone.

[60] At the time of Scott and Schwartz's articles, the relevant UCC rule was § 2–208. Section 2–208 was deleted "to conform to the 2001 Revision of Article 1." Section 1–303 currently covers course of dealing, course of performance, and usage of trade. U.C.C. § 2–208 note on status of section (AM. LAW INST. & UNIF. LAW COMM'N 2001).

Table 6:2. Employment Training Example

		Firm	
		Train	Not train
Worker	Stay	$75, $50	$50, 0
	Leave	$100, –$25	**$50, 0**

There are two possible responses to this problem. One is for the parties to enter into an explicit contract that ties the employee to the firm for a certain period of time. An example of this is a *non-compete clause*, which temporarily limits the employment options of workers when they leave a firm. Although, on its face, such a provision seems anti-competitive, the preceding example shows that it can be in the worker's interest to agree to it. Indeed, courts generally honor such clauses provided that they are reasonable in duration and geographic scope.[61] A potential problem of outright bans of such clauses, as is the case in California, is that employers might seek to collude with each other to retain employees in whom they have made large investments.[62] Such collusive agreements have, in fact, been the subject of antitrust litigation.[63] Another response to the firm-specific investment problem is for the firm and employee to split the costs of training, for example, with the employee investing more in the general, or transferrable part, of her education, such as graduate school or law school, and the firm investing more specifically in firm-specific training.

An interesting illustration can be found in professional baseball, where for a long time, teams employed a *reserve clause* to prevent players from leaving for other teams after the owner's team-specific investment. While in operation, the clause informally barred owners from negotiating with players from other teams, even after their contracts had expired; in effect, the team, not the player, owned the rights to the player's labor services.[64] This strategy lasted from the inception of major league baseball in 1876 until the practice was invalidated a century later.[65] Even in the current era of a strong players' union, however, players and owners have collectively bargained for contract terms that tie players to the teams that drafted them until they have completed six years of major league service. The preceding analysis helps to explain why players have agreed to such a clause: The players' union, which represents all players, including minor leaguers who may or may not become major leaguers, agreed to a limited reserve system that allows teams to recoup their investment in training during the first six years of those players who become major

---

61 *See generally* Viva R. Moffat, *Making Non-Competes Unenforceable*, 54 ARIZ. L. REV. 939 (2012) (describing the wide range of enforceability of employee non-compete clauses, from California, where they are generally unenforceable, to most other states, where the clauses are enforceable if they have reasonable limits on duration and geographic range). RESTATEMENT (SECOND) OF CONTRACTS § 188 cmt. D (AM. LAW INST. 1981) (explaining that a non-compete agreement that is too long in duration or too expansive in geographic area violates public policy).

62 *See* RONALD CASS & KEITH HYLTON, LAW OF CREATION: PROPERTY RIGHTS IN THE WORLD OF IDEAS 79–81 (2013).

63 *See id.* at Ch. 5.

64 *See* Simon Rottenberg, *The Baseball Players' Labor Market*, 64 J. POL. ECON. 242 (1956).

65 *See* LEE LOWENFISH & TONY LUPIEN, THE IMPERFECT DIAMOND 18 (1980).

leaguers by not having to pay those new major leaguers their true *market value* (i.e., their *marginal revenue product*). In effect, major leaguers during their first six years are re-paying the team for the training expenses it incurred, both for them and for all players who never made the majors.

Non-compete clauses represent an explicit contractual device for promoting efficient firm investment in workers. It therefore relies on court enforcement. Other contractual provisions are meant to be self-enforcing. Parties engaged in repeat transactions can, for example, establish a reputation for fair dealing and honoring contractual promises.[66] In the above employment training example, self-enforcement of the firm's commitment to train the worker, and the worker's commitment to stay, could take the form of an escalating wage contract. Specifically, the firm could offer the worker an initial wage below the market wage of unskilled workers, with the wage gradually rising during the course of the worker's employment. Under such an arrangement, the worker expects to receive the same lifetime income, but some compensation is deferred. She therefore has a reduced incentive to leave after training because of the "bonus" she expects to receive from staying. In effect, the worker posts a "bond" in her early years that she forfeits by leaving prematurely. Another way to think about this arrangement is that the worker in effect finances his own training costs through a system of deferred compensation. This arrangement might characterize the training of physicians, who during the years of residency and fellowship, earn relatively low wages for their level of training, but who anticipate a larger future income stream.

IV. APPLICATIONS

1. Billy and Molly book their honeymoon trip with "Romantic Resorts" in Waikiki, Hawaii, and reserve the "Honeymoon Suite" with a waterfront view. After arriving at the airport, they are approached by "Own Your Vacation" to spend a few short hours touring a resort facility in Waikiki in exchange for tickets to a full day Hawaiian cruise. They sign up thinking that since they had hoped to go on a cruise, which would be expensive, this was a way to get that with a fairly reasonable commitment but no out-of-pocket cost. When they get to the hotel, they discover that their waterfront view overlooks the pool, which opens daily at 6:00 AM with a program in water aerobics and which includes the "Waikiki Kids Club." The next day, they go on their tour with Own Your Vacation, at which they discover that the "few short hours" is actually a full day in a remote location that they cannot leave. The next day when they go on the cruise, they further discover that it is on an open touring boat that requires bringing your own food; that it is "family friendly," featuring a noisy kid-oriented disc jockey; and that it makes numerous stops all day long. Based on the economic analysis of contract law, how should a suit for breach of contract by Billy and Molly against Romantic Resorts and Own Your Vacation be resolved, and why? Is your economic analysis consistent, or in tension with, contract doctrine, and why?

2. Before Billy and Molly left for their vacation, they hired "Quick Quality Contractors" to install a kitchen in their newly purchased bungalow. The contracting work

[66] For a formal treatment of such an enforcement mechanism, see L.G. Telser, *A Theory of Self-Enforcing Agreements*, 53 J. BUS. 27 (1980).

began one month before the wedding and was supposed to take six weeks, ending the weekend prior to their return from Hawaii. Billy and Molly scheduled their wedding and honeymoon based upon the contractor's representation that the renovation would be completed in six weeks. Because they both had planned to start new jobs the Monday following their Saturday return, it was extremely important that the kitchen be up and running within the specified time frame. When they returned, Billy and Molly discovered that while the old kitchen had been gutted, it would take three-to-four weeks to get their new cabinets and two-to-three weeks at that point to finish the remaining work. This was not due to any mistake on the part of the contractor, but rather was due to the representations by two suppliers about the availability of materials, which proved inaccurate. Based on the economic analysis of contract law as set out in Chapters 5 and 6, what is the proper result if Billy and Molly sue Quick Quality Contractors, and why? How, if at all, does your analysis of the preceding question differ from what it would be under existing contract doctrine, and why? Assume that you had been advising Molly and Billy at the time of contract formation. What steps, if any, might you have encouraged them to take to improve the likelihood of timely contractual performance?

3. Assume the following changes to Application 2: This time the cabinetry is completed on time, but there is a problem with the granite countertops. Billy is taking a new job as a sales representative for Mako Granite, the company that Billy and Molly specifically wrote into the contract to have supply, cut, and install the high-end granite countertops in the kitchen renovation contract, as a subcontractor to Quick Quality Contractors. This provision resulted in adding 10% to the original price of the granite component of the contract ($600 more from the original total of $6000 for the granite, for a sum of $6600). When it came time to deliver the granite, Mako did not have the rare granite specified in the contract, and informed Quick Quality that it would have it within three-to-four weeks. Further assume that Quick Quality knew that Billy and Molly had new jobs and that they needed the kitchen done on time. As a result, Quick Quality located another supplier, Gorgeous Granite, and it ordered the same granite specified in the contract. This included measuring and cutting the granite to fit the countertops. Nowhere on the countertop is the granite supplier identified in any way, and the quality of the final delivery is identical to what Billy and Molly specified in the contract. Finally, assume that Billy had intended to use his kitchen to entertain and to show prospective purchasers the high quality that Mako produces in its granite work. Billy and Molly sue Quick Quality for breach based upon who supplied the granite. Assume that the contract did not specify what would happen in the event that Mako could not supply the materials on time, and if, as a result, Quick Quality located another supplier. What do you believe the preferred outcome to be based on the economic analysis of contract law in Chapter 6, and why?

4. Assume the following changes to Applications 2 and 3: Mako Granite and Quick Quality Contractors regularly contract for high-end kitchen renovations. They have long had an excellent working relationship. It is not unusual for terms of kitchen-supply contracts to be altered, for example, when buyers change their minds at the eleventh hour or when the supplier runs low on a specified stock when a particular granite delivery is due. The contract that Mako and Quick Quality use, which is standard in the industry, specifies that in the event that the supplier does not have the available granite, Quick Quality can find an alternative supplier and Mako will pay the difference in cost, and that if Quick Quality cancels a contract, Mako can sell the granite on the open market, and

Quick Quality will pay the difference between the original contract price and the price realized when the granite is sold. In fact, however, the actual practice in the event of breach has not followed these contract terms. Instead, when Mako is short on supply, Quick Quality typically finds an alternative supplier and the cost is generally close enough that Quick Quality does not bill Mako the difference, and when Quick Quality fails to take delivery of ordered, but unconfirmed, granite,[67] Mako simply restores the precut granite to its general inventory. At the time of the Billy and Molly contract, however, the relationship between Quick Quality and Mako had begun to falter, and when Mako failed to ensure timely delivery on that contract, resulting in a lawsuit, Quick Quality decided to instead make Gorgeous Granite its primary supplier. Quick Quality then chose to enforce the specified contract term, given that the breach forced it to find an alternative supplier at an additional cost of $4000 as a result of the short notice. Based on the economic analysis of contract law, how do you believe this should be resolved, and based on existing doctrine, how do you believe it is likely to be resolved? Are the answers the same, and why or why not?

[67] Assume that delivery does not occur until after the granite supplier sends its own employee to the home to confirm the measurements and to ensure the accuracy of the specifications for cutting.

CHAPTER 7

Property Law (Part 1)

Introduction

Property law governs the establishment, use, and transfer of rights to land and other assets.[1] Economic analysis focuses on the role of property law doctrine in encouraging cost-effective improvements in land and other physical assets and the transfer of assets to those who value them more highly, thereby enhancing social welfare. Secure property rights are a general prerequisite to the efficient operation of markets and are therefore foundational to economic activity more broadly.

As with the materials on tort and contract, the property law unit is subdivided into two chapters. The first part of this chapter focuses on the nature and function of property rights, with an emphasis on how those rights emerge, are defined, and are legally protected, in addition to how property rights more generally influence economic behavior. We also discuss how specific property doctrines facilitate, or in some cases coerce, the transfer of property rights. This part considers how property rules facilitate consensual market exchange of rights both by protecting investments in property and by enforcing contractual transfers of property rights. The analysis reveals that property law doctrine, like contract doctrine, is often *complementary* to markets in providing background, or off-the-rack, rules that facilitate such economic activity as investment and exchange.

Although it is conventional to identify externalities as a source of market failure, as we have seen, a more nuanced analysis recognizes the problem as involving conflicting uses of property, including land, coupled with ill-defined legal rights. For Coasian bargaining to facilitate transfers of rights to those who value them more highly, rights must be clearly defined. Otherwise claimed instances of *market failure* risk becoming a conclusory label leading to a predetermined outcome, rather than a helpful analytical tool in determining how best to accomplish the goal of allocating rights and thereby promoting the creation of social welfare.

As observed above, property law, including common law doctrine and governmental regulation, sometimes serve as a *complement* to markets, thereby allowing a reallocation of rights through private transactions. On other occasions, such rules serve as a *substitute* for market-based mechanisms. Recall that the Coase theorem says that when the cost of

[1] For general discussions of the economics of property law, see Dean Lueck & Thomas J. Miceli, *Property Law, in* 1 HANDBOOK OF LAW AND ECONOMICS 183 (A. Mitchell Polinsky & Steven Shavell eds., 2007) and Robert Ellickson, *Property in Land*, 102 YALE L.J. 1315 (1993).

transacting is low, and thus when markets function well, markets will allocate resources to their more highly valued uses regardless of how legal rights are initially assigned.[2] In this setting, the law is primarily relevant in creating background rules that facilitate private market transactions through which individuals can rearrange prior assignments of rights by means of consensual transfers, and in doing so, achieve mutual gains. When transaction costs are low, therefore, law complements markets in the exercise and transfer of property rights.

By contrast, when transactions costs are high, beneficial reallocations of rights by contractual transfer becomes less likely. When this occurs, the legal assignment of property rights takes on added significance because that assignment will likely be final.[3] In this setting, the role of law is not merely facilitative; rather it becomes determinative. That is because, by definition, the cost of contracting around the initial rights assignment is likely to outweigh the benefit of the transfer.

Chapter 7 is structured as follows: Part I describes the nature and definition of property rights. Part II presents the methods by which property rights may be voluntarily transferred. Part III reviews the conditions under which property owners are sometimes forced to relinquish property rights involuntarily.

Chapter 8 continues the economic analysis of property law as follows: Part I discusses the special case of eminent domain. Part II reviews the doctrine of regulatory takings. Finally, Part III presents a larger perspective on the structure of market transactions in property. Each chapter concludes with applications.

I. THE NATURE OF PROPERTY RIGHTS

Property rights define what people can and cannot legally do with the economic resources under their control, and property law is thus the set of legally enforceable rules that protect an individual's property rights. The analysis that follows will define property rights and discuss how they emerge and are protected.

A. The Definition of Property Rights

The most foundational property right, namely *ownership*, is actually not a single right, but rather is a bundle of rights. Included within that bundle are the following distinct rights: (1) to use the asset, (2) to exclude its use by others, and (3) to sell or transfer the right. In the case of agricultural land, for example, an owner can grow and sell crops, exclude trespassers, and sell or lease to a willing buyer or renter. The law enforces these rights, but not absolutely: As already noted, when one owner's usage rights conflict with another owner's usage rights, the law will sometimes limit the rights of one or both parties. Recall our earlier discussion of Ronald Coase's landmark article, *The Problem of Social Cost*.[4]

---

[2] *See supra* Chapter 1, at 26–29.

[3] The analysis of the efficiency of the various liability rules for assigning accident risk in Chapters 3 and 4 is an example of this role of courts as market substitutes in high transaction cost settings. *See supra* Chapters 3 and 4.

[4] R.H. Coase, *The Problem of Social Cost*, 3 J. L. & ECON. 1 (1960). *See supra* Chapter 1 at 23 (discussing the Coase theorem).

That article, which set out the Coase theorem, described the problem of controlling a rancher's stray cattle so as to minimize the damage to a neighboring farmer's crops. Much of our analysis of property law concerns beneficial limitations on property rights in the presence of such incompatible uses.

In some situations, owners may *choose* to limit their rights by voluntarily transferring one or more "sticks" in their bundle of rights to someone else. The law generally enforces such transactions on the premise that the voluntary division of property rights often enhances the value of the underlying asset. For example, a lease involves the temporary transfer of *use* rights from a property owner (the landlord) to the user (the tenant).[5] Indeed, this follows the insight from contracts that the law generally presumes that voluntary transactions enhance social welfare by creating gains that the parties can share.

At the opposite extreme from private property is *open access property*, which means an absence of individual property rights. In an extreme case in which law enforcement institutions are also lacking, the equilibrium outcome generally entails complete *dissipation* of the asset's value through overuse. This can result in the depletion of mineral deposits or fish stock in a pond as users compete for the scarce resource. Professor Garrett Hardin, an ecologist, famously described this as the *tragedy of the commons*.[6] One theoretical solution is to imagine converting the open access property to private property. If a single person (or firm) owned the scarce resource in its entirety, she would internalize the risk of depletion, and thus have an incentive to use a resource in a manner that captures its full value. In the example of the fishing lake, for example, an individual owner, behaving rationally, would fish to the point at which the stock naturally replenishes.[7]

In some cases, however, open access may be the preferred means of allocating property rights. The prototypical example involves pure *public goods*. Such goods have two defining characteristics: (1) once provided, they are non-excludable, meaning that those who failed to contribute cannot be denied the benefit of their procurement, and (2) their value is not diminished by consumption, meaning that one person's enjoyment does not undermine anyone else's.[8] Economists have shown that, in general, private markets tend to undersupply public goods because those who procure them are unable to capture the full benefits of their investment. For this reason, governments often undertake to provide such public goods as parks, highways, police, and defense. Although the goal is to provide public goods at an optimal level, as we will see in the chapter on interest group theory, some of the same difficulties that limit private market incentives to provide public goods also limit efforts to lobby for governmental procurement of those goods.[9] Because public

---

5 We discuss leases in more detail below. *See infra* part II.B.

6 Garrett Hardin, *The Tragedy of the Commons*, 162 SCIENCE 1243 (1968). *See generally* Steven N.S. Cheung, *The Structure of a Contract and the Theory of a Non-Exclusive Resource*, 13 J.L. & ECON. 49 (1970) (discussing the economic implications of a common resource and a lack of contracting rights and applying these concepts to marine fisheries). The tragedy of the commons is an instance of the more general problem of the Prisoners' Dilemma. *See infra* Chapter 15. For a critical assessment of Hardin's work on the commons, see ELINOR OSTROM, GOVERNING THE COMMONS: THE EVOLUTION OF INSTITUTIONS FOR COLLECTIVE ACTION (2015).

7 In Part I.C below, we consider some examples of how property rights to an open access resource first emerged.

8 *See* Paul A. Samuelson, *The Theory of Public Expenditure*, 36 REV. ECON. & STAT. 387, 387 (1954).

9 *See infra* Chapter 11.

goods, once provided, are freely accessible, the government generally relies on the coercive method of taxation, rather than voluntary contributions, to finance them.

A final form of property ownership, known as *common property*, lies between the extremes of private property and open access. Common property typically describes joint ownership of a resource by a well-defined group. For example, a town might allow its residents' cattle to graze on the "town common," while prohibiting nonresidents from allowing their cattle to do so. Similarly, hunting and fishing grounds, or natural resources like oil or mineral deposits, can be held in common by a limited group of users who mutually agree to the terms of use, thereby reducing, if not altogether avoiding, the tragedy of the commons.[10]

Two notable advantages of common, rather than private, ownership are: (1) exploiting scale economies in usage, and (2) saving on exclusion and monitoring costs, which are necessary to preserve and maintain certain assets, such as fish stock. Common ownership also helps to spread the risk from adverse outcomes, like crop failure, thereby providing a form of social insurance.

Professor Robert Ellickson illustrated this latter concept with the Pilgrims' reliance on cropland as designated common property to prevent starvation in the early Plymouth colony.[11] Historically, religious societies such as the Shakers and various secular utopian communities have adopted communal ownership as a means of promoting egalitarianism among their members.[12] In the absence of market incentives associated with private property, such groups needed to develop alternative mechanisms to motivate appropriate member contributions of labor and resources. Ellickson observed that the Pilgrims eventually allocated each household individual plots for cultivation, thereby creating private property rights over some land as a means of increasing crop yield, while still allowing some sharing. The combined regime served as a means of insurance for those whose individual yields were insufficient. The Shakers encouraged work as a means of worship through the interpretation of religious doctrine, which appears to have helped the community endure from their founding within the United States from 1796 into

---

[10] The Supreme Court has issued conflicting rulings on whether the power to vote can be treated as a kind of commons property. In *Rice v. Cayetano*, the Court relied on the Fourteenth Amendment Equal Protection Clause to strike down a law that limited eligibility to descendants of native Hawaiians for voting for the Board of Trustees of the Office of Hawaiian Affairs, even though the trust fund was created to dispense benefits to such descendants. 528 U.S. 495 (2000). The Supreme Court had previously issued a ruling in tension with this case, upholding a restriction to landowners in the Tulare Water District of the right to vote based on the values of assessed land in the election of the district's board of directors, who were charged with allocating water rights to affected landowners. Salyer Land Co. v. Tulare Water Dist., 410 U.S. 719 (1973).

[11] Ellickson, *supra* note 1, at 1338–39.

[12] *See* RAYMOND BIAL, THE SHAKER VILLAGE 6 (2008). The demise of the Shakers was primarily due to their commitment to celibacy, which meant that conversion of adults and adoption of orphans were the only means of maintaining membership. This declined dramatically in the twentieth century. One active Shaker community continues to survive in Sabbathday Lake, Maine. *Principles and Beliefs*, MAINESHAKERS.COM, http://maineshakers.com/beliefs/ (last visited Aug. 18, 2017). The Shaker website identifies common property as a foundational religious belief: "Community of Goods: The desire to die to self leads the Shaker quite naturally to the pooling of goods. The Christian's task is to live in the present moment and not to store for tomorrow the bread that comes from heaven." *Id.*

modern times, albeit in small numbers.[13] Secular utopian communities have generally failed to thrive over time, perhaps in part due to the tragedy of the commons.

B. Property Rights, Externalities, and Coasian Bargaining

Externalities are prone to arise and persist when property rights are not well defined or enforced. In the canonical example of a polluting factory, suffering neighbors have inadequate protection of their property rights. The legal system generally protects such rights in either of two ways, first through the private law right to sue in tort, and second, through the more recent development of public law regulation, such as restrictions imposed by the Environmental Protection Agency (EPA) on harmful emissions. Both legal regimes seek to force the polluting firm to internalize the harmful burdens of the pollution externality by reassigning the property right to stop the harmful emissions to the victims of the harm.

1. The Rancher and the Farmer

In describing the first of these two legal approaches, Coase illustrated the nature of externalities with a conflict between a rancher and a farmer.[14] In that case, straying cattle from the rancher's herd destroyed the neighboring farmer's crops. The undefined property right involved control of the boundary between the two properties. Coase demonstrated that with clearly defined rights and low transaction costs, placing the property right with either the farmer or the rancher will not affect whether there is a fence to keep the cattle off the farmer's land. Instead, this is controlled by which of the activities—crop cultivation or grazing—is more highly valued, and when the crops are more highly valued, the property right affects only who pays for the fence, a purely distributional question.

Coase posited that if the parties were able to transact at no cost, they would freely bargain around either initial rights allocation, placing the final property right where it is most highly valued. In this analysis, a rule of no liability means that the rancher does not incur damages when his cattle graze on the farmer's adjoining land. The farmer may still block access to the cattle by erecting a fence if that is the least cost option, but the "no liability" rule protects the rancher if the farmer fails to do so.

Assume initially that the farmer's land is more valuable for crops than for grazing, say at $100 per year, rather than $50 per year. Also assume that cattle can be prevented from grazing on the land by construction of a fence around the farmer's land that costs $10. In this example, it is efficient to erect the fence because that yields a net gain of $40. If the rancher holds the right to let the cattle stray, meaning that she would not be liable for any crop damage they cause, then the farmer, seeking to preserve that more highly valued land use, will erect a fence to keep the cattle out. And because the land is more valuable for crops than for grazing, the rancher will not be able to purchase the right to have the fence removed to allow grazing. If, instead, the farmer holds the right, the rancher, who would be liable for resulting damages, will herself pay for the fence at a cost

[13] Metin Cosgel, Thomas Miceli & John Murray, *Organization and Distributional Equality in a Network of Communes: The Shakers*, 56 AM. J. ECON. & SOC. 129, 141–42 (1997).

[14] Coase, *supra* note 4.

of $10 to avoid damages of $100 based on an activity that would provide her a gross benefit of only $50.

Conversely if the land is more valuable for grazing (at $100) than for crops (at $50), then regardless of which party has the initial right, the parties will achieve the efficient outcome in which no fence is built and the cattle stray. If the rancher has the right to let the cattle stray, here meaning that she can, in essence, block the farmer from building a fence, the farmer would only be willing to pay up to $40 to have the fence built, the value of the crops less the cost of the fence. The rancher, however, would demand at least $100. Conversely, if the farmer holds the right to build the fence, the rancher would pay the farmer up to $100 not to build it, which exceeds the $40 net value of the fence to the farmer. Table 7:1 summarizes this discussion.

Table 7:1. Coasian Analysis of Crops Versus Grazing on Adjoining Farmland

	Crops more valued	Grazing more valued
Farmer holds right	Rancher pays for a fence to keep cattle from causing crop damage for which she would be liable.	Rancher pays farmer to take down fence or to not put it up, sharing in the available gains from converting use of farmer's land from crops to grazing.
Rancher holds right	Farmer puts up fence to avoid uncompensated damage from rancher and to preserve higher valued use of cultivation.	Rancher enjoins farmer from building a fence and the cattle stray.

As this discussion reveals, the choice of liability rule does not matter when transactions costs are low. Regardless of who holds the right, when the land is more valuable for cultivating crops, there will be a fence, and when it is more valuable for grazing, there will not be. In the first situation, when the crops are more valuable, the rights allocation merely affects who pays for the fence. In the second, the rancher gains access to the farmer's land regardless of who holds the right initially.

The analysis further demonstrates that in addition to low transactions costs, knowing who holds the right is essential to Coasian bargaining. By contrast, when transaction costs are high, the legal allocation of the property right will control the use of land because the transactions cost will impede Coasian bargaining.

2. Reciprocal Externalities and Coming to the Harm

The preceding discussion demonstrates that careful analysis requires viewing externalities in reciprocal terms. In the prior example, if the cattle graze on the farmer's land, we can say that the rancher has created an externality. Placing the property right with the farmer forces the rancher to internalize her costs. Conversely, if the farmer erects a fence, we could say that the farmer has created an externality by disallowing the rancher's cattle to graze.

Intuitively we might be inclined to define the externality based on the sequence of events. If the farmer arrived first, we might say that the later arriving rancher created an externality by thwarting the farmer's expectation that cattle would not graze on his land. If the rancher arrived first, we might say that by fencing the farmland in, the farmer created an externality by thwarting the rancher's expectation of open adjoining land for grazing. One of Coase's main insights is that the fortuity of sequencing should not necessarily control the property rights allocation. The more significant question is which allocation promotes the more highly valued use, and in the event that the legal regime gets it wrong, which allocation is more conducive to displacing the initial allocation through bargaining.

One further theme that emerges from the analysis returns us to a fundamental insight from the economics of contract law.[15] Notice that because the farmer and rancher own adjoining lands each potentially "externalizes" costs onto each other, placing them in a bilateral monopoly relationship. This dynamic will frequently arise in a property law context. And when this occurs, transaction costs are predictably high, thus emphasizing the importance of allocating initial property rights in a manner that encourages more highly valued uses.

C. The Emergence of Property Rights

We now consider how property rights initially emerge. Harold Demsetz's influential study of the origin of property rights emphasized their role in internalizing externalities.[16] Specifically, Demsetz argued that property rights emerge "when the gains of internalization become larger than the cost of internalization."[17] In the prior example, if we treat the rancher as the source of the externality, the gains of internalizing such costs consist of preventing the resulting harm (e.g., the crop damage), and the costs consist of avoiding the harm in the most cost-effective manner, whether by building a fence, reducing the herd size, or pursuing some other remedy. As the following discussion demonstrates, some historical examples of the emergence of property rights illustrate the ways in which these developments have occurred.

1. *Primitive Property Rights*

The idea of "primitive society" conjures images of people living in a "state of nature" with no rules or governance. In fact, primitive peoples often developed fairly sophisticated property-rights systems.[18] This is not surprising, given the importance of establishing such rights in promoting the production of food, shelter, and protection, all of which are

[15] *See supra* Chapters 5 and 6.

[16] Harold Demsetz, *Toward a Theory of Property Rights*, 57 AM. ECON. REV. 347 (1967).

[17] *Id.* at 350.

[18] Martin Bailey, *Approximate Optimality of Aboriginal Property Rights*, 35 J.L. & ECON. 183 (1992); Paul Rubin, *The State of Nature and the Evolution of Political Preferences*, 3 AM. L. & ECON. REV. 50, 52 (2001).

essential for a society to survive and thrive. The study of primitive societies often reveals social institutions that provide cost-effective methods of ownership and distribution of scarce resources.

In pre-agricultural society, group ownership of resources (common property) was the predominant form of property rights. Early observers tended to mistake common property for lack of property rights, or for open access, thus leading to the mistaken impression that such persons did not appreciate the concept of property rights.[19] But private property in land made little sense in hunting and gathering economies, whereas sharing food among group members was essential for survival. Land-based private property rights began to emerge with the advent of agriculture.

Professor D. Bruce Johnson provides an especially interesting example of a mixed property-rights regime,[20] involving "potlatching" by Native Americans in the Pacific Northwest. Although kinship groups held exclusive rights to different salmon-fishing territories, those groups that were more successful in a given season shared their catch with less successful groups, thereby providing a form of group insurance covering territories with lower than expected yields.

2. *Whaling Norms*

During the mid-eighteenth to mid-nineteenth centuries, whaling was a classic example of an open access resource over which formal property rights did not exist. Professor Robert Ellickson has demonstrated, however, that the high value of whaling products, principally oil and bones, created "a powerful incentive [for whalers] to develop rules for peaceably resolving rival claims to the ownership of a whale."[21] Such disputes arose when, for example, more than one vessel pursued the same whale and each harpooned it, or when a captured whale broke away from a ship and was found by another ship.[22] Although whalers during this time were a diverse group originating from ports in several countries, consistent with Demsetz's property-rights theory, Ellickson observed that whalers nonetheless had developed internationally recognized norms for resolving these inevitable disputes.

As an illustration, Ellickson describes the following norms for deciding on the ownership of a whale.[23] Under the "fast-fish, loose-fish" rule, a whale that was connected

---

[19] *See* Rubin, *supra* note 18, at 184. For one persistent, yet mistaken, illustration, consider the mythic story that Native Americans sold Manhattan to Dutch settlers for $8 and a string of beads. *See, e.g.*, Peter Francis, Jr., *The Beads that Did* Not *Buy Manhattan Island*, 67 N.Y. HIST. 4 (1986). Dennis Zotigh, *America's First Urban Myth?*, NMAI: NAT'L MUSEUM OF THE AM. INDIAN BLOG (Aug. 3, 2011), http://blog.nmai.si.edu/main/2011/08/americas-first-urban-myth.html. The more compelling narrative recognizes that the Native Americans engaged in the transaction likely anticipated at most shared usage rights, rather than the right of exclusion from their home. *See* Paul Otto, *The Dutch, Munsees, and the Purchase of Manhattan Island*, 87 N.Y.S.B.A. J. 10 (2015).

[20] D. Bruce Johnson, *The Formation and Protection of Property Rights Among the Southern Kwakiutl Indians*, 15 J. LEGAL STUD. 41 (1986).

[21] ROBERT ELLICKSON, ORDER WITHOUT LAW: HOW NEIGHBORS SETTLE DISPUTES 191–92 (1991).

[22] A similar problem can arise in the hunting of wildlife. See, for example, the classic case of *Pierson v. Post*, 3 Cai. R. 175 (N.Y. Sup Ct. 1805), which concerned property rights to a fox.

[23] Ellickson notes that one source that captured these norms is Herman Melville's classic whaling novel, *Moby Dick*. ELLICKSON, *supra* note 21, at 191–206.

by a line or other device to a ship, meaning "fastened" or simply "fast," belonged to that ship as against rival claimants.[24] However, if the whale broke away—i.e., became a loose fish—it was up for grabs. A second rule, "the iron holds the whale," assigned exclusive rights in a whale to the whaler who first harpooned it, provided he remained in pursuit.[25] However, once he abandoned pursuit, the whale's status changed to that of a loose fish. A final rule concerned ownership of an appropriately marked and beached finback whale. The difficulty arose when a finder sold the oil to a third party rather than following the custom of notifying the designated intermediary who would then locate the original whaler based on the markings. Once harpooned, finback whales sank to the ocean floor, and thus, unlike other whales, they could not be retrieved until they naturally came ashore at a later time. The marking custom accommodated those who successfully hunted such whales. In a suit against the oil buyer, the United States District Court for the District of Massachusetts granted the value of the oil to the original whaler minus the extraction and preparation costs, and acknowledged that in the ordinary case, the finder is entitled to "reasonable salvage [value] for securing or reporting the property."[26]

Ellickson argues that these rules reflected a rational response to the problem of assigning ownership in a way that maximized value (including the cost of enforcing the governing norms). More important than the specific norms is the general principle: Property rights need not originate from a formal governmental structure, but rather, consistent with Demsetz's hypothesis, they can also arise informally within groups whenever the gains of development and implementation exceed the costs.

3. The Gold Rush

Professor John Umbeck similarly describes the emergence of property rights to mining claims during the California Gold Rush.[27] Initially, given the low estimated value, the law did not formally recognize property rights in lands being mined. That all changed with the discovery of gold at Sutter's Mill in 1848. At first, miners enforced their own claims, principally by carrying guns (referred to as "peacemakers"), but the ironic labeling aside, the resulting violence eventually led to the creation of explicit contractual arrangements providing miners exclusive rights to their claims. In addition, groups of miners formed districts with their own systems of property rights aimed at helping miners enforce their claims. Lacking formal government institutions, the miners thus formed their own.

Finally, in 1872, the U.S. Congress passed mining legislation for the purpose of consolidating and standardizing various territorial laws and customs.[28] *The General Mining Act* established guidelines whereby miners could stake claims and obtain federal patents

---

[24] Louis De Alessi, *Gains from Private Property: The Empirical Evidence*, *in* PROPERTY RIGHTS: COOPERATION, CONFLICT, AND LAW 93 (Terry L. Anderson & Fred S. McChesney eds., 2003) [hereinafter PROPERTY RIGHTS].

[25] This is an example of a "first-possession" rule, as discussed below. *See infra* Chapter 8.

[26] Ghen v. Rich, 8 F. 159, 162 (D. Mass. 1881).

[27] JOHN UMBECK, A THEORY OF PROPERTY RIGHTS WITH APPLICATION TO THE CALIFORNIA GOLD RUSH 90–91 (1981) (describing the "transition from sharing to land allotment contracts.").

[28] The General Mining Act of 1872, 17 Stat. 91–96.

for those claims.[29] Professor David Gerard notes that miners who faced especially high enforcement costs were more likely to seek the greater security of federal patents, which is broadly consistent with Demsetz's property-law origins thesis.[30]

4. *Homestead Laws*

Another early illustration of the development of property rights involves Homestead laws, which awarded property rights to undeveloped and unclaimed western land on a "first-come, first-served" basis. (Of course, this only became possible only after the U.S. government extinguished Native American land rights.[31]) The *Homestead Act*, enacted in 1862, awarded rights in surveyed tracts of land to squatters, conditional on their payment of a $10 fee and a promise to improve the land and reside on it continuously for five years.[32]

At first glance, this might appear to be an inefficient way to allocate land because it fosters a "land rush," which can dissipate commonly shared open access resources, as illustrated by the tragedy of the commons. Professor Douglas Allen has argued otherwise.[33] Allen maintains that land ownership on the western frontier was a risky proposition, owing to competing claims from other settlers and the ever-present threat from Native Americans who were understandably hostile to the expropriation of their land. The federal government was able to provide only limited protection from these threats, and so an alternative form of security was needed. Allen argues that a land rush served this purpose:

> The sudden arrival of tens of thousands of people into a given territory destroyed much of the Indian way of life and forced Indian tribes to accept reservation life or to join the union. The selective and intensive settlement caused by homesteading also reduced the cost of defending any settlement.[34]

In this analysis, homesteading may well have been a cost-effective way to achieve the government's stated goal, namely, of populating the western lands while lowering the cost of securing the newly conferred property rights, albeit at the expense of Native Americans, whose land was thereby appropriated.

---

[29] Land patents imply a combination of process and labor to acquire a property right, which produces an equivalent of fee simple use provided the use of mined land is productive. Dean Lueck, *First Possession as the Basis of Property*, *in* PROPERTY RIGHTS, *supra* note 24, at 215.

[30] David Gerard, *Transaction Costs and the Value of Mining Claims*, 77 LAND ECON. 371, 372 (2001).

[31] *See* Johnson v. M'Intosh, 21 U.S. (8 Wheat.) 543, 570 (1823) ("According to every theory of property, the Indians had no individual rights to land; nor had they any collectively, or in their national capacity . . . ."); Fletcher v. Peck, 10 U.S. (6 Cranch) 87, 142–43 (1810) ("The majority of the court is of opinion that the nature of the Indian title, which is certainly to be respected by all courts, until it be legitimately extinguished, is not such as to be absolutely repugnant to seisin in fee on the part of the state."). *See generally* Paul Frymer, *Building an American Empire: Territorial Expansion in the Antebellum Era*, 1 U.C. IRVINE L. REV. 913 (2011) (exploring the removal of Native Americans from their lands as the first step in the creation of the American empire).

[32] Homestead Act, 12 Stat. 392 (1862).

[33] Douglas W. Allen, *Homesteading and Property Rights: or, "How the West Was Really Won,"* 34 J.L. & ECON. 1 (1991).

[34] *Id.* at 5.

5. *The Rule of First Possession*

The preceding examples illustrate the general principle of establishing property rights by the rule of "first possession."[35] The concept of establishing ownership of an object or resource according to a rule of "first come, first served" strikes most people as intuitively appealing, and for that reason, it also has a long philosophical tradition. "Finders keepers" involves previously owned property, whereas first possession involves property that was not previously owned.[36] Regarding the latter, John Locke argued that when an individual combines his labor with property, as much as 99% of the resulting value might be attributable to labor, the rights to which are owned by the person who engages with the property.[37] Professor Richard Epstein has relied on that intuition to maintain that protecting a person's improvement on property through the establishment of an ownership interest is fundamentally just.[38]

As suggested above, however, some economists have argued that the rule of first possession creates the problematic incentive of racing to acquire possession, resulting in a wasteful dissipation of the asset or rent, analogous to the tragedy of the commons.[39] Professor Dean Lueck argues, however, that the law has developed mechanisms that mitigate this problem. In particular, he notes that the rule of first possession can be effectively applied either to the *stock* or to the *flow* of an asset, based on which poses the lower risk of asset dissipation.[40]

Consider, for example, an underground pool of oil. Ownership of the entire pool—the stock—can be granted to the first person who discovers it. Alternatively, ownership of individual barrels—the flow—can be granted to the driller who first pumps the oil to the surface. Dissipation of the value of the pool can occur under either rule, but in different ways. Granting ownership to the stock establishes exclusive property rights to it, thereby creating incentives for efficient extraction of the oil, but it encourages a race to claim rights to the pool. By contrast, granting ownership to the flow—meaning ownership by the *rule of capture* rather than first possession—avoids a race for first position, but it encourages depletion of the resource as it is equivalent to open access. (Here we assume

↳ both rule of first possession and rule of capture have downsides, specifically racing and depletion

[35] Dean Lueck, *The Rule of First Possession and the Design of the Law*, 38 J.L. & ECON. 393 (1995); Richard Epstein, *Possession as the Root of Title*, 13 GA. L. REV. 1221 (1979). Of course it is ironic to claim superior title to land previously held by earlier possessors, such as Native Americans, based on first possession. The implicit qualifier is "legally recognized" first possession, where the relevant authority for purposes of lawful recognition is the federal government.

[36] *Compare* 1 AM. JUR. 2D *Abandoned, Lost, and Unclaimed Property* § 1 (2016) (explaining that "finders keepers" refers to the rule that the first to discover and take possession of abandon, lost, or mislaid property or a treasure trove receives title), *with* Lueck, *supra* note 35, at 393 ("FIRST possession rules are the dominant method of initially establishing property rights. Such rules grant a legitimate ownership claim to the party that gains control before other potential claimants.").

[37] RICHARD EPSTEIN, TAKINGS: PRIVATE PROPERTY AND THE POWER OF EMINENT DOMAIN 10–11 (1985) (citing JOHN LOCKE, OF CIVIL GOVERNMENT ¶ 27, ¶ 40 (1690)).

[38] *Id.*

[39] *See generally* Lueck, *supra* note 35 (modeling how rent dissipation resulting from first possession can be avoided).

[40] *Id.*

that first possession includes an exclusionary right to prevent all others from capturing access rights to the flow).

The two sources of inefficiency—rent dissipation resulting from (1) the race for first possession, or (2) an open access tragedy of the commons—might not be equally problematic. For example, if there are only a few would-be users and if the resource is abundant, no individual person is likely to seek to extract the entire stock to maintain complete ownership rights. In this case, establishing ownership by the rule of capture will lower the risk of asset or rent dissipation. However, as the resource becomes increasingly scarce, it may become necessary to limit access to the stock itself. Although there are sound reasons for imposing restrictions on the appropriation of groundwater, a scarce resource, this is less likely to hold for the appropriation of ocean water, for example, for purposes of desalination.[41] In the context of a fishing lake or hunting ground, it might be sound policy to place an upper bound on a permissible catch or hunt. In an extreme case, for example endangered species, the optimal policy might be to prohibit hunting altogether, effectively vesting ownership in the government as a means of banning extraction entirely.[42]

II. CONSENSUAL TRANSFERS OF PROPERTY

Having surveyed some of the critical foundations of property rights, we now introduce several specific property law doctrines that promote consensual transfer through market exchange. Our emphasis will be on transfers of land, but the principles apply to other forms of property more generally.

A. Property Transfer

Professors Douglas Baird and Robert Jackson posit that the legal system's role in defining and protecting title of land is essential to promoting efficient property exchange.[43] In an ideal world with complete information, possession of land would perfectly signal legitimate ownership, implying that all previous transfers of land back to the very first possessory claim would have been consensual. In the real world, however, there is no such guarantee, so prospective buyers will sometimes face the risk that a previously defrauded owner—someone who in the past lost title due to error or theft—

---

[41] For a discussion of legal rights associated with desalinization, see Michael Pappas, *Unnatural Resource Law: Situating Desalination in Coastal Resource and Water Law Doctrines*, 86 TUL. L. REV. 81 (2011).

[42] *See* Endangered Species Act, 16 U.S.C. §§ 1531–1544 (2012) (prohibiting the "taking" of endangered species). *See also* Dean Lueck, *The Economic Nature of Wildlife Law*, 18 J. LEGAL STUD. 291, 297–98 (1989); Barton H. Thompson, Jr., *The Endangered Species Act: A Case Study in Takings & Incentives*, 49 STAN. L. REV. 305 (1997) (examining the Endangered Species Act in relation to takings jurisprudence and compensation policies); John D. Echeverria & Michael C. Blumm, Horne v. Department of Agriculture: *Expanding per se Takings While Endorsing State Sovereign Ownership of Wildlife*, 75 MD. L. REV. 657 (2016) (discussing the Court's decision in *Horne v. Department of Agriculture* and the Court's affirmation of the doctrine of sovereign ownership of wildlife). The ESA expired in 1992, and has not been reauthorized. Congress has continued to fund implementation through the annual appropriations bill. *See* M. LYNNE CORN & ALEXANDRA M. WYATT, CONG. RESEARCH SERV. RL31654, THE ENDANGERED SPECIES ACT: A PRIMER (2016).

[43] Douglas Baird & Thomas Jackson, *Information, Uncertainty, and the Transfer of Property*, 13 J. LEGAL STUD. 299 (1984).

will emerge and successfully assert a contrary claim. An optimal system of land title, by which we mean the system that maintains the record of land transfers, will minimize that risk, thereby improving the efficiency of the land market.

The economic analysis of an optimal title system, however, reveals that the goal should not be to *completely* eliminate the risk of error. Elimination of error is costly, requiring maintenance of accurate records and the search of those records by prospective buyers (or their lawyers or other agents). Thus, it is only cost-effective to invest in determining the legitimacy of title up to the point where the marginal benefit of increased security equals the marginal cost of the search.

A formal depiction of this point is shown in Figure 7:1, where the horizontal axis measures "units of security" (denoted by *x*), reflecting greater efforts at searching title, investing in better recording practices, hiring lawyers to interpret ambiguous records, and the like. Greater security of title is valuable because it reduces the likelihood of a legitimate superior claim being asserted in the future. The benefit of greater security is diminishing, however, as reflected by the downward sloping line labeled *MB*. The point at which the line intersects the horizontal axis (i.e., where the *MB* is zero) represents a perfectly secure title and would be the optimal point if security were costless. When the establishment of title security is costly, however, the optimal point occurs at a lower level of security, denoted as x^*, which occurs where the marginal benefit curve intersects the curve representing the marginal cost of increased security (depicted as a horizontal line for simplicity), denoted as *MC*.

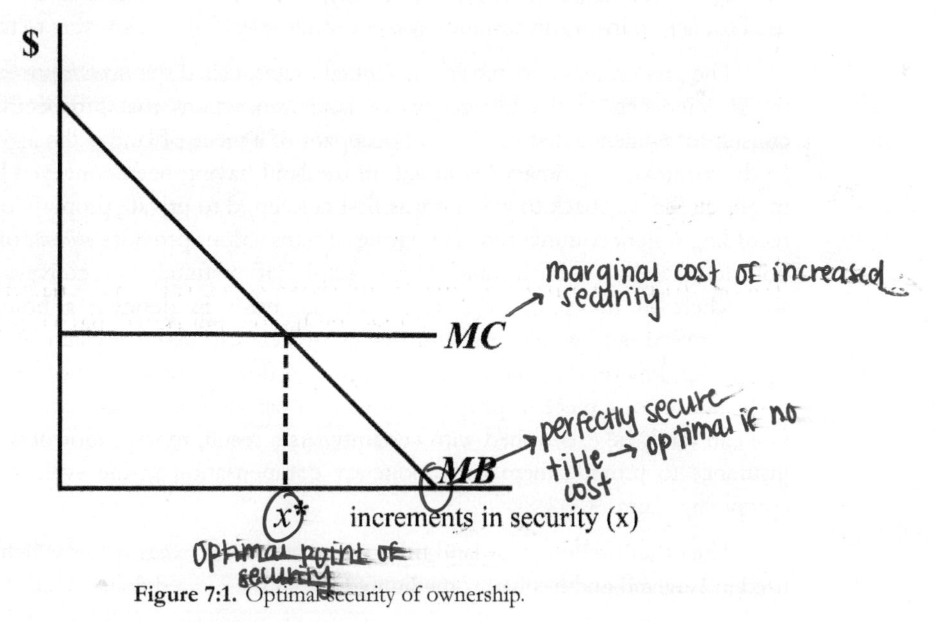

Figure 7:1. Optimal security of ownership.

As discussed more fully in Chapter 9,[44] which examines the economics of criminal law, for example, perfect legal compliance is rarely optimal. Allowing some pollution, some speeding, and yes, some crime, is often the preferred result of a well calibrated enforcement strategy, meaning one that takes both costs and benefits of additional legal

[44] *See infra* Chapter 9.

compliance into consideration. In the specific context of property rights, an externality should only be reduced to the point where the marginal cost of a further reduction exceeds the marginal compliance benefit.

Although most property is susceptible to theft or other forms of coercive expropriation, for low-valued property, mere possession is sufficient to demonstrate ownership. Would-be buyers, therefore, generally invest little or no effort in determining that the possessor is the legitimate owner. As a piece of property becomes more valuable, however, buyers are more likely to want explicit evidence that the possessor is the lawful owner. Thus, for example, a person seeking to buy a used watch will generally be less concerned about its provenance if it is an inexpensive *Timex* than if it is a costly *Rolex*. When property becomes substantially more valuable, such as cars, fine art, or land, evidence of ownership in the form of title (or provenance), is generally an essential component of the transaction.[45]

1. Land Title Systems

An implication of the preceding analysis is that, even with optimal (as opposed to maximum) investment in title security, owners of land (or other valuable property) will occasionally lose ownership involuntarily due to fraud, theft, or error. When that happens, and when the present owner has not engaged in fraud, the law confronts a fundamental question: Should it protect the person wrongfully deprived of title (i.e., the last rightful owner), or the current possessor? The two types of title systems that have historically been used for land transfers in common law countries give different answers to that question.[46]

The predominant system in the United States, called the *recording system*, is based on the maintenance of a public record of land transactions that prospective buyers can consult for evidence that the current occupant of a piece of land is the legitimate owner. In this context, "legitimacy" is based on the land having been conveyed by consensual means all the way back to when it was first converted to private property or to when the recording system commenced. This string of transactions provides *evidence* of title but does not definitively establish title. For example, if a fraudulent conveyance occurred somewhere in the past, or if there was an error in defining a boundary, title is compromised, and a prior rightful owner or heir can assert a claim of full or partial ownership. Lawyers' opinions will sometimes differ on the validity of title, and so with each transfer of a piece of property, interested parties search the record anew. Even so, title can rarely be established with certainty. As a result, most landowners purchase title insurance to provide them with monetary compensation in the event of a successful competing claim.

The other predominant land title system is the *registration system*, which is commonly used in England and has had some limited use in the United States. Under registration, a

---

[45] In Figure 7:1, an increase in the value of a piece of property corresponds to an outward (upward) shift of the *MB* curve, which implies that it is optimal to invest more in security of ownership for more valuable property.

[46] *See* Thomas Miceli & C.F. Sirmans, *The Economics of Land Transfer and Title Insurance*, 10 J. REAL EST. FIN. & ECON. 81 (1995), on which the following is based. *See also* Matthew Baker et al., *Optimal Title Search*, 31 J. LEGAL STUD. 139 (2002) (discussing optimal title search).

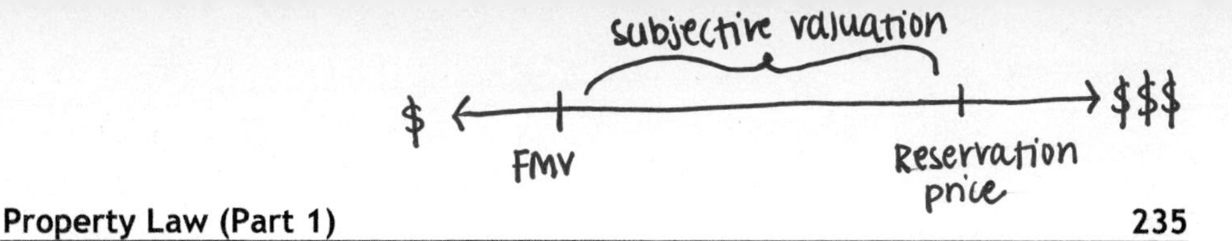

landowner registers title with the government at the time of purchase, at which point there is a judicial search of the record. If no outstanding claims are found, the court certifies that the current owner holds good title against most future claims. And if a successful claimant does come forward, he or she can usually only seek compensation from a public fund financed by land registration fees.

The fundamental difference between these two systems concerns who gets the land in the event of a valid competing claim: Under the recording system it is the claimant; under the registration system it is the possessor. In the analysis that follows, we will consider alternative accounts for these competing rules: (1) an economic (efficiency) basis for claiming one over the other, or (2) a fairness justification going to which party—the innocent possessor or the last rightful owner—is more "deserving" of the land.[47]

To assess the first inquiry, whether there is an efficiency rationale for preferring one of the two systems, we must consider if either approach maximizes the value of land. This depends on whether, in general, the current possessor or the claimant is more likely to place a higher value on contested land. Within a competitive market, we would inquire as to the minimum payment the current possessor would willingly accept to sell the land in a consensual transaction, known as the *reservation price*. As explained in Chapter 6, in general, the possessor's reservation price will exceed *fair market value*, the market-clearing price for the property in competitive conditions. The higher reservation price is a consequence of the possessor's subjective valuation, which equals the difference between these two different valuations, the reservation price and fair market value.

We previously encountered the concept of subjective valuation in the discussion of the *Peevyhouse* case.[48] Subjective valuation also affected the analysis in selecting between expectancy damages, on one hand, or specific performance or liquidated damages, on the other.[49] Justice Oliver Wendell Holmes offered an early insight into the basis for subjective valuation, stating: "[M]an, like a tree in the cleft of a rock, gradually shapes his roots to his surroundings, and when the roots have grown to a certain size, can't be displaced without cutting at his life."[50] This suggests that subjective value is linked to possession and likely grows with the duration of that possession.[51] Stated differently,

---

[47] A third possibility: this is an instance of pure coordination, with neither rule more defensible than the other, but with the need for a clear rule. *See infra* Chapter 16, at 647 (illustrating with alternative rules governing acceptance of offer to form a contract).

[48] *See supra* Chapter 6, at 20–22 (describing "for sale" signs as signaling a diminution in infra-marginal or subjective property valuation).

[49] *See supra* Chapter 6, at 23–26 (discussing Jacob & Youngs, Inc. v. Kent, 230 N.Y. 239 (1921)). Subjective valuation is not unique to land or improvements on land. Experimental economists have shown that subjects attach a higher value to others items that they possess (a *willingness-to-accept valuation*) as compared to what they would pay to acquire those items (a *willingness-to-pay valuation*). The difference between these two measures is *subjective valuation*. *See, e.g.*, Herbert Hovenkamp, *Legal Policy and the Endowment Effect*, 20 J. LEGAL STUD. 225 (1991).

[50] 2 RALPH BARTON PERRY, THE THOUGHT AND CHARACTER OF WILLIAM JAMES 461 (1935) (transcribing the April 1, 1907 letter from Oliver Wendell Holmes to William James in which Holmes describes title by prescription).

[51] Robert Ellickson, *Alternatives to Zoning: Covenants, Nuisance Rules, and Fines as Land Use Controls*, 40 U. CHI. L. REV. 681, 736 (1973).

people enhance the value of their possessions, especially including land, by customizing its use over time to suit their specific needs.

By contrast, a competing claimant is not in possession of the land and may never have been, suggesting that her or his subjective value is apt to be substantially lower. The claimant's valuation is more likely to approximate the property's fair market value. The difference between the valuations of the two parties suggests that in most cases, the current possessor would strictly prefer retaining title to receiving market-value compensation, whereas the claimant would be roughly indifferent between acquiring title or fair market value. The objective of maximizing the value of the land would therefore seem to favor the registration system because in most cases that will leave the land in the hands of the party who assigns it the highest value—namely, the current possessor.

This initial intuition may be premature, however, because if the land is awarded to the claimant, the dispossessed owner can always buy it back, and if the latter does place a higher value on the land, such a transaction will be possible provided that the parties can bargain at relatively low cost. Consider, for example, a parcel of land with a market value of $100,000, but which the current owner values at $150,000, where the extra $50,000 reflects her subjective, or infra-marginal, value. Suppose a claimant arrives and is awarded title, while the owner receives compensation through her title insurance equal to the $100,000 fair market value. Assuming that the parties can bargain, the possessor would be willing to pay up to $150,000 to re-acquire title, whereas the claimant would likely accept an amount above $100,000. Thus, there is room for a mutually beneficial transaction that restores the land to the possessor.

This analysis mirrors the Coasian analysis of specific performance in contract law.[52] Assuming low transactions costs, the result, in both settings, is to move the resource, here real property, to the party who values it more highly even if the legal rule, in this instance the recording-based titling system, initially places it elsewhere. In this low-transaction-cost account, the choice of assignment is purely distributional; with either outcome, the possessor ultimately continues ownership, albeit by having to repurchase it, thus sharing part of the subjective valuation benefit with the rival claimant, rather than by continuing as the rightful owner and retaining that value.

If, however, land transactions are costly, the choice of title system might matter for efficiency, with the preferred system awarding title to the party who will generally value it more highly. In most cases, this might suggest favoring the registration system, which protects the rights of the possessor as against claimants. This rule will also encourage social-welfare-enhancing investments in property within an owner's possession by reducing the risk that a rival claimant might force the owner to relinquish title and thus to forgo any gains in subjective valuation associated with her improvements.[53]

In general, the increase in subjective valuation that results from improvements on land has the potential to raise transactions costs. It does so by forcing the possessor and the successful challenger into a bilateral monopoly negotiation. This creates an opportunity for the rival claimant to seek to expropriate part of the rents associated with

---

[52] *See supra* Chapter 5 (illustrating with efficient breach involving a table maker and guitar manufacturer).

[53] This is analogous to the theory of efficient breach, with expectancy damages encouraging social-welfare-enhancing investments in goodwill by the breaching party. *See supra* Chapter 5.

the possessor's subjective valuation that followed from her specific improvements. The rival claimant has this incentive *even if* he does not specially benefit from the possessor's improvements. All that matters is that the possessor benefits sufficiently that she is willing to pay a premium above the fair market value of the property to remain there. This is another illustration of appropriable quasi rents.[54]

If we vest the right with the claimant, to the extent of her subjective valuation, the possessor will be willing to invest up to that amount to defeat the contrary legal claim. This can take the form of investigating problems with the competing claim, litigation costs, and even seeking to influence decision makers. These expenditures are pure rent seeking in the sense that they are not societally beneficial, but rather are investments in maintaining property that one already enjoys. To be sure, the dispossessed party also has suffered a loss of enjoyment, but the question is which of the two competing rules more generally avoids such rent-dissipating behavior.

Judge Richard Posner has identified a separate trade-off: Although he maintains that registration is more efficient in vesting property title in the party likely to have a higher subjective value, he contends that recordation is more efficient in that it renders the market for title insurance private, whereas registration relies on public funding to reimburse dispossessed property owners confronted with successful competing claims.[55]

Within the United States, the recording system is dominant. Under normal conditions, conflicting land claims are uncommon. This raises the question as to which system works best in the general run of cases. The next section provides some empirical evidence on this question for the United States.

2. *Title Systems in the United States*

A dramatic example of the benefit of land registration was the adoption of the *Torrens Land Registration System* in 1897 by the State of Illinois following the Great Fire of Chicago in 1871, which destroyed all public land records.[56] The need for quick rebuilding placed a high premium on land development, and local officials recognized that the traditional system of land recording would have impeded such investments because of developers' fears that previous owners would come forward and assert title claims. By contrast, the Torrens system provided possessors with stronger property rights and hence sped up redevelopment.[57]

The state began to phase out the land registration system in 1992, and on January 1 of that year, Cook County returned to the recording system.[58] The ongoing reliance on two different recording systems for over a century provided a unique natural experiment that allowed for testing the relative efficiencies of these competing systems of land

---

[54] *See supra* Chapter 5, at 11–13 (discussing appropriable quasi rents).

[55] RICHARD A. POSNER, ECONOMIC ANALYSIS OF LAW 82 (9th ed. 2014).

[56] BLAIR C. SHICK & IRVING H. PLOTKIN, TORRENS IN THE UNITED STATES: A LEGAL AND ECONOMIC HISTORY OF AMERICAN LAND-REGISTRATION SYSTEMS 21 (1978). This system provides an indefeasible title to those properly registered and transfers land via title rather than deed transfer. *Id.*

[57] See *id.* at 17–20, for a history of land registration in the United States.

[58] Thomas J. Miceli et al., *Title Systems and Land Values*, 45 J.L. & ECON. 565, 566 (2002) (noting that the Illinois Torrens statute was repealed in 1996).

conveyance. Two different studies showed a small to moderate savings in the cost of conveyance under registration, primarily attributable to the savings in title-search costs.[59]

The Torrens system was generally more costly on a per-transaction basis as it required each title claim to be litigated in a proceeding similar to a declaratory judgment, albeit without having to search title as far back as under the recording system. Under the *Model Marketable Title Act*,[60] with some exceptions related to land occupation, recording systems need not go back farther than thirty years, thus further reducing the transaction costs associated with the latter system.

Transaction-cost differences, however, do not tell the whole story. As noted, an important advantage of land registration is that it clears title with respect to most future land claims, thereby promoting land development. This advantage will be most important for owners of land subject to a particularly high risk of a future claim. One study found that landowners in Cook County sorted themselves into the competing systems in precisely this way, with higher risk property owners opting for the Torrens system, and with lower risk property owners opting for the recording system.[61] Once this "self-selection" effect was accounted for, the authors showed, land values were slightly higher under the Torrens system, holding all else constant. This suggests that at least when there is a relatively high likelihood of a competing claim, the Torrens system is, in fact, more efficient than the more prevalent recording system.

Despite this, we have seen that Chicago abandoned Torrens in the 1990s following its declining use. One argument for this seemingly counterintuitive result (i.e., abandoning the more efficient system), is that it was never adopted on a sufficiently large scale to fully exploit its benefits. This is attributable to the problem of ***network externalities***, which are savings that arise as the number of users of a product or service (like a land title system) increases.[62] When a network externality is present, the system that eventually becomes dominant is not necessarily the most efficient one. As the impact of the Chicago fire on land markets faded into history, the primary advantage of land registration likewise decreased, thus contributing to its demise.

A possible contributing factor in this story is the lower number of attorneys who specialized in land transactions based on the registration system, as opposed to the recording system, when both were available.[63] Once land claims became increasingly rare, it was easier for those who were engaging in land transactions to go to attorneys with the more familiar expertise, thereby reinforcing the original recording scheme.

---

[59] *See* Joseph Janczyk, *An Economic Analysis of the Land Title Systems for Transferring Real Property*, 6 J. LEGAL STUD. 213 (1977); SHICK & PLOTKIN, *supra* note 56.

[60] MODEL MARKETABLE TITLE ACT (UNIF. LAW COMM'N 1990). Originally referred to as the *Uniform Marketable Title Act*, the name and designation was changed from "Uniform" to "Model" in 1998. *Id.*

[61] Miceli et al., *supra* note 58, at 579.

[62] *See infra* Chapter 13 (describing path dependence and network externalities).

[63] Similar resistance arose in North Carolina and in Minnesota. John Orth, *Torrens Title in North Carolina—Maybe a Hundred Years is Long Enough*, 39 CAMPBELL L. REV. 271, 281 & n.66 (stating "[t]he Torrens system failure in North Carolina may have been partly due to opposition from lawyers, who would lose the fees from frequent title searches."); Note, *Possessory Title Registration: An Improvement of the Torrens System*, 11 WM. MITCHELL L. REV. 825, 833 (1985) (noting resistance from title attorneys as an impediment to broader use of the registration system in Minnesota, since that specialized system employs fewer attorneys).

3. *Title Systems and Economic Development*

Economists have recently begun to recognize the importance of land title systems for economic development. The classic example is the argument by the economist Hernando de Soto that an important impediment to economic growth in South America and other developing countries has been the lack of a well-functioning capital market, which would allow entrepreneurs to transform their primary asset, land, into financial capital.[64] The problem, he claims, is not insufficient wealth, but the absence of strong institutions for protecting land title, which prevents landowners from using their land as collateral for obtaining loans. Although most countries have informal systems for resolving disputes over land claims, more formal and reliable government-backed systems are an efficient means of ensuring that banks are able to use land as security for loans.

Empirical studies showing the positive impact of secure title on land development in underdeveloped countries provide support for this argument,[65] which raises the question of why we do not see more recording systems in such countries. Political corruption is undoubtedly a contributing factor. Another is the network externality problem noted above. For such institutions to become prevalent, they must reach a certain scope and scale, the absence of which can prevent their emergence even when conditions otherwise would appear conducive.[66]

B. Leasing

The discussion of property transfers to this point has focused on land sales, or conveyances of the entire bundle of property rights. This section considers partial transfers, the most common form of which is leasing. A lease is an agreement to divide ownership of an asset, as when a landlord conveys temporary use rights to a tenant. Historically, such agreements were used primarily for farmland; in modern times, however, they are commonly used for housing, commercial real estate, and machinery, including automobiles. This section discusses the law of leases, especially as it pertains to promoting efficient conveyances of land and efficient land use.

1. *Are Leases Contracts?*

In early common law, leases were viewed as conveyances of interests in land and were therefore governed by property law principles. Specifically, the tenant acquired the rights of use and exclusion in return for the promise to pay rent during the lease term. If the tenant failed to pay rent, the landlord could not enter the property and evict the tenant, but instead could only sue for recovery of rent. Correspondingly, the landlord had no duty to maintain the premises during the lease term since the land was, after all, primarily for

---

64 *See generally* HERNANDO DE SOTO, THE MYSTERY OF CAPITAL (2000).

65 *See, e.g.*, Timothy Besley, *Property Rights and Investment Incentives: Theory and Evidence from Ghana*, 103 J. POL. ECON. 903 (1995); Lee Alston, Gary Libecap & Robert Schneider, *The Determinants and Impact of Property Rights: Land Title on the Brazilian Frontier*, 12 J.L. ECON. & ORG. 25 (1996); Thomas Miceli, C.F. Sirmans & Joseph Kieyah, *The Demand for Land Title Registration: Theory with Evidence from Kenya*, 3 AM. L. & ECON. REV. 275 (2001).

66 Thomas Miceli & Joseph Kieyah, *The Economics of Land Title Reform*, 31 J. COMP. ECON. 246, 251 (2003) (citing Janczyk, *supra* note 59).

farming. In most relevant respects, therefore, the tenant became the temporary owner of the property, with all of the associated rights and responsibilities.

This is quite different from modern leases, especially for housing, which are now interpreted by courts as contracts rather than conveyances of property. This reframing had two notable implications. First, courts have found an *implied warranty of habitability*, meaning that the landlord has a duty to maintain the premises in a reasonably suitable condition;[67] and second, the tenant's duty to pay rent is tied to the landlord's fulfillment of her duty. In other words, both parties have ongoing and interdependent obligations that continue beyond the initial transfer of rights. Economic analysis helps to explain this change in legal interpretation of leases.[68]

In a world where leases were primarily for agriculture, tenant farmers supplied the productive inputs, and thus, granting them exclusive rights during the lease term was important to ensuring that they could reap the return from their efforts. A right of entry by landlords, even for failure to pay rent, might invite various forms of opportunistic behavior, such as claiming that nonpayment rendered the lease void after the planting was complete and shortly prior to harvest. The tenant's right of exclusion therefore promoted an efficient crop yield, while still affording the landlord a suit for unpaid rent.

By contrast, as the conveyance of property shifted primarily to the provision of housing, continuous landlord maintenance of essential structures, safety features, heating and plumbing systems, and various appliances became important ongoing inputs. Treating the lease as a mere conveyance of property, and thus as conveying only use rights, did not provide appropriate landlord incentives respecting these features. Redefining residential leases as contracts, by contrast, allowed ongoing mutual obligations. Tenants, therefore, could withhold rent if landlords failed to maintain the unit in a habitable state, and landlords could evict tenants who failed to pay rent on appropriately maintained units. The transformation of leases from conveyance of property rights to contract thus increased the joint value of the lease, meaning both to tenants, who benefited from maintenance, and to landlords, who could charge a premium for the additional services that they provided. As reliance on leases shifted from agricultural to residential, the conversion from relying on principles of property to contract thus improved the efficiency of the conveyances. In doing so, the transition created social welfare gains that both parties can share.

The transformation of leases into contracts was also accompanied by a duty on the part of landlords to mitigate the damages from breach, as previously discussed in Chapter 6.[69] Under property law principles, landlords had no duty to mitigate damages because the tenant was seen as the temporary owner, with exclusive rights of occupancy during the term of the lease. Thus, if the tenant abandoned the land prior to the expiration of the

---

67 *See, e.g.*, Javins v. First Nat'l Realty Corp., 428 F.2d 1071 (D.C. Cir. 1970). *See also* Edward H. Rabin, *The Revolution in Residential Landlord-Tenant Law: Causes and Consequences*, 69 CORNELL L. REV. 517 (1984) (exploring the increased protections tenants received under the law in the 1970s and 1980s from the implied warranty of habitability to rent control).

68 *See generally* Thomas Miceli et al., *The Property-Contract Boundary: An Economic Analysis of Leases*, 3 AM. L. & ECON. REV. 165 (2001) (explaining that an efficiently crafted lease might involve both elements of property and contract law).

69 *See supra* Chapter 6.

lease, the landlord could simply sit tight and sue the tenant for the rent. Under modern leasing law, however, landlords are obligated to take reasonable steps to find a replacement tenant. Otherwise, the landlord is only entitled to the difference between the original rent and the replacement rent she would have obtained had she done so.

As previously discussed, a duty to mitigate reduces losses in the event of breach. Why then do agricultural leases, and some modern commercial leases, fail to include such a duty? At common law, landlords had no duty to mitigate damages in cases of abandoned commercial leases, for example by re-letting, but a number of jurisdictions in recent decades have altered this rule primarily through common law development.[70] Abandonment might be easier to discern in residential settings, and in addition, landlords might have a greater stake in ensuring ongoing habitation of properties that contain equipment in need of regular and proper maintenance.

In some non-residential settings, by contrast, tenants may either be in a better position than the landlord to locate a substitute tenant or might not intend periods of non-use to be a signal of abandonment. For example, farmers may wish to leave some plots fallow during a given season, and commercial users may hold some parts of their leased properties for storage or other contingencies, without regular ongoing usage. The uncertainty in these other contexts implies that the choice of rule might be less important than establishing one with certainty so as to facilitate appropriate bargaining against the background of an available off-the-rack rule.

2. *The Rental Externality and the Law of Waste*

The *rental externality* is an important source of inefficiency in rental agreements, whether for land or durable goods like machinery or cars.[71] This refers to the dilution of incentives for tenants to invest in efficient maintenance of the property during the lease term. The problem is one of moral hazard, and it arises from the fact that tenants do not internalize the cost of their usage beyond the lease period. Lessees have a shorter time horizon than the lifetime of the asset, and as a result, they will tend to over-utilize, or under-maintain, the asset as compared with what the owner would do were she also the tenant or primary user.

The common law doctrine known as *law of waste* helps to address this problem. This doctrine imposes a duty on tenants to invest in reasonable, or cost-effective, maintenance of the asset during the lease period, and to refrain from inflicting damage beyond ordinary wear and tear.[72] The Coase theorem might suggest that a legal duty to invest in cost-effective maintenance is unnecessary because the landlord and tenant could negotiate the proper maintenance level in the lease itself. By providing background rules, however, the common law allows parties to enter into leases at lower cost on the assumption that these

---

70 Carl F. Dixon, *The Landlord's Duty to Mitigate*, 8 PRAC. REAL EST. LAW. 15, 16 (1992).

71 *See* Vernon Henderson & Yannis Ioannides, *A Model of Housing Tenure Choice*, 73 AM. ECON. REV. 98 (1983).

72 *See* JOHN CRIBBET, PRINCIPLES OF THE LAW OF PROPERTY 209–11 (2d ed. 1975). *See also* POSNER, *supra* note 55, at 73 (explaining that tenant farmers lack incentive to improve land in ways that endure after the lease term).

terms capture typical preferences of leasing parties while also allowing them to contract around lease terms that are not suitable to them.

A more serious problem that the law of waste does not entirely resolve is that the landlord lacks the ability to observe, and thus to monitor, the tenant's behavior. As a consequence, there is a risk that some damage the tenant caused might not manifest itself until after the lease term, making it difficult to attribute the resulting cost increase to the specific tenant. Consider a rental car, for example, and its numerous users over a given time frame. Aside from obvious damage, for example following an accident, it is not possible for the rental company to identify who caused damage arising from treatment beyond ordinary wear and tear. Drivers know they can get away with treating rented cars less well than cars they own. Although inspections ameliorate this to some extent with rental housing, even there, treatment of certain equipment, such as kitchen appliances, heating systems, and air conditioning, that exceeds ordinary usage, might be difficult to ascribe to a particular tenant.

Although it is intuitive to think this dynamic places the lessee at odds with the lessor, ultimately the harm from the poor maintenance by some lessees imposes costs on other lessees who take greater care. This follows if we assume that the demand for the leased property or goods is relatively inelastic,[73] thus allowing the lessors to pass on a substantial portion of the increased cost in the leasing price. To the extent that the legal regime helps to promote appropriate levels of care through the doctrine of waste, at least part of the resulting social welfare gain is apt to benefit lessees as well as the property owners.

Rental car companies and landlords are, of course, aware of the moral hazard problem, and therefore charge higher prices or rents up front in order to cover the expected cost of maintenance that they expect to incur over the life of the asset. In a world with low-transactions costs, renters would promise to use an asset with appropriate care in return for a lower rental price. The difficulty, which raises the cost of transactions, is that such promises are not credible. This is similar to consumer promises to use dangerous products with special care.[74] Thus, there is a residual inefficiency. The social welfare gains of rental agreements for housing, cars, and other assets, however, must more than offset this inefficiency; otherwise the rental market would cease to exist.

Although we have discussed moral hazard by tenants or lessees, there is also a reciprocal form of this problem respecting the incentives of the property owners. When landlord inputs affect the preferred maintenance level, as with rental housing, there is likewise an externality inasmuch as landlords do not internalize the use benefits of the asset *during* the lease term. As a result, landlords are apt to maintain the properties less well than they might were they also in possession. As discussed above, however, modern landlord-tenant law imposes a duty on landlords to maintain their units in a habitable state. Although this partially ameliorates the problem, it likely fails to ensure comparable landlord maintenance to owners who are primary occupants.

---

[73] *See supra* Chapter 2, at 15–17 (presenting elasticity of demand).

[74] *See supra* Chapter 3, Part IV.

3. *Sharecropping Contracts*

We conclude this section on leasing by briefly discussing sharecropping contracts, which had once been commonly used in agriculture.[75] Historically in the South, following the Civil War, many plantations were subdivided into smaller lots, and the cultivation was managed through sharecropping contracts, with both newly freed slaves and poor whites working the land. In many accounts, for the new Freedmen, the result was a continuation of slavery under a different name.[76]

One source of difficulty was that the landowners would extend credit on high interest terms and then place liens on the future crops as collateral. This often resulted in landlords taking a substantially larger portion than the original contractual arrangement seemed to anticipate. These arrangements placed the sharecroppers in precarious, and often dire, financial circumstances.[77] Given the overall financial devastation in the South during the post-Civil War period, and the generally insurmountable difficulties that the newly freed slaves confronted, the unfair usages of sharecropping in this period might not be surprising. The analysis here considers whether, despite this tragic history, there is an underlying economic logic to sharecropping arrangements in agriculture or, by analogy, in other work settings.

Under a sharecropping agreement, the landowner supplies the land and sometimes such inputs as seeds and tools, and the farmer supplies the labor. Then at harvest, the two parties share the crop, typically fifty-fifty. One perspective is that sharecropping contracts are designed to ameliorate problematic incentives by inducing both landlords and tenants to contribute to the production of crops as each holds a stake in the final output. Although even a well-functioning sharecropping contract does this imperfectly, the question is whether there is an alternative arrangement that would more effectively accomplish the same goal. The difficulty with sharecropping is that both parties internalize only a fraction of the output and, therefore, farmers are apt to underinvest in effort. Indeed, if we assume that the farmer is the primary contributor of inputs, a leasing arrangement under which the farmer rents the land and owns all of the crops would better align incentives.

Another view is that sharecropping allows the landlord and tenant to share the risks that result from unavoidable uncertainty in crop yields. Under a rental arrangement, the farmer would bear all of the risk, whereas if the landlord hired a farmer at a fixed wage, the landlord would bear all of the risk. Thus, if both the landlord and farmer are risk averse, both might prefer sharecropping as a means of sharing that risk. The difficulty is

---

[75] There is an extensive economic literature on these contracts. *See, e.g.*, STEVEN N.S. CHEUNG, THE THEORY OF SHARE TENANCY (1969); Joseph Stiglitz, *Incentives and Risk Sharing in Sharecropping*, 41 REV. ECON. STUD. 219 (1974); Douglas Allen & Dean Lueck, *Risk Preferences and the Economics of Contracts*, 85 AM. ECON. REV. 447 (1995); Douglas W. Allen, *Cropshare Contracts*, *in* 1 THE NEW PALGRAVE DICTIONARY OF ECONOMICS AND THE LAW 569 (Peter Newman ed., 1998).

[76] Daniel W. Crofts, *From Slavery to Sharecropping*, 23 REVS. AM. HIST. 458 (1995) (reviewing EDWARD ROYCE, FROM SLAVERY TO SHARECROPPING: THE ORIGINS OF SOUTHERN SHARECROPPING (1993), and JULIE SAVILLE, THE WORK OF RECONSTRUCTION: FROM SLAVE TO WAGE LABORER IN SOUTH CAROLINA (1994)).

[77] *See* Donald L. Winters, *Postbellum Reorganization of Southern Agriculture: The Economics of Sharecropping in Tennessee*, 62 AGRIC. HIST. 1, 10 (1988) (describing crop and property liens as a method for securing sharecropper debt).

that crop-yield risk is affected by several considerations, including fluctuations in the quality or quantity of supplies such as seed, variations on labor intensity or skill, and, of course, weather conditions. By contracting with several tenant farmers, the landlord is able to hedge against the risk reflected in differential sharecropper effort. But since the lands subject to sharecropping are in the same general location, even if we assume reasonable inputs by both contracting parties, sharecropping is not an effective means of spreading risk for weather conditions, which is beyond the contracting parties' control.

Given the importance of both production incentives and risk sharing, it is possible that neither a pure wage arrangement nor a pure rental contract, the most likely alternatives to sharecropping, are optimal. As noted above, a pure wage contract shifts all of the risk onto the landowner, and it diminishes the farmer's work incentives as he is no longer the residual beneficiary of his efforts. Conversely, a pure rental contract motivates the farmer, as he is the residual beneficiary, but it forces him to also bear all of the risk, with the result of possible underinvestment, as compared to a regime in which risk is shared. Sharecropping contracts potentially balance these incentives, however imperfectly, by shifting some risk to the landlord while leaving some on the farmer. In addition, poor farmers may lack the up-front cash needed to pay rent. Although there is likely no perfect arrangement, sharecropping might have dominated the alternatives as a result of these risk-reward constraints.

Sharecropping is less common in modern agriculture, but there are modern analogs in other settings. Consider some commonplace employment agreements, including salespeople who earn a base salary plus commission on gross sales, and wait staff who earn lower than minimum wage salaries plus tips, which are sometimes pooled and sometimes retained individually. The commission shifts some of the risk of random sales fluctuations onto the salesperson as an incentive device (given that sales significantly depend on effort), while insuring a base salary. Tipping operates somewhat differently, making the waitperson partly an employee of the restaurant and partly an agent of the patron,[78] with the possible goal of improving service quality by making the waitperson the residual claimant for the variable portion of the patron's bill. Contingency fees for lawyers and commissions for real estate agents can similarly be interpreted as compromises between risk sharing and incentives in the lawyer-client and agent-seller relationships.[79]

QUESTIONS AND COMMENTS

In recent years, tipping customs have come under fire on various grounds, including the accompanying lower-than-minimum wage for affected employees, complaints by patrons as to uncertain tipping norms, and a desire among many to have the pricing of food more clearly reflected on the menu.[80] Alternatively, one might defend the custom on the ground that it

[78] For a study that demonstrates a tenuous relationship between tipping levels and performance quality, see Michael Lynn & Michael C. Sturman, *Tipping and Service Quality: A Within-Subjects Analysis*, 34 J. HOSPITALITY & TOURISM RES. 269, 269 (2010).

[79] *See infra* Chapter 10 Part I.D.1.

[80] *See, e.g.*, Peter Wells, *Leaving a Tip: A Custom in Need of Changing?*, N.Y. TIMES (Sept. 4, 2013), http://www.nytimes.com/2013/09/04/dining/leaving-a-tip-a-custom-in-need-of-changing.html?pagewanted=all&_r=0.

provides a greater upside return for particularly attentive wait staff, and in doing so, that it also provides better service for patrons. Other than context (restaurants rather than farming land), are these trade-offs any different than those in sharecropping? Should the law force a choice among such contractual arrangements or should it let the market sort it out? Which is better for employees? For employers? For customers? Does the efficacy of tipping as an incentive device depend on the quality of the restaurant, and if so, how? Are any of the shared-risk contracting arrangements identified in this discussion specially prone to market failure? Is the answer the same for agriculture, restaurants, legal representation, and home sales? Why or why not?

C. Joint Ownership

Leasing agreements represent a division of ownership rights over time as between two or more specific individuals, for example with one as the landlord and another as tenant. Sometimes a group of property owners will choose to dedicate a portion of shared land as common property. Recall that common property, or joint ownership, exists when more than one individual has rights in the asset. The principal difficulty with joint ownership is the risk of dissipating the value of the property as a result of the tragedy of the commons. For membership above a certain size,[81] effective joint ownership therefore requires governance structures that guard against the risk of group exploitation. This cost will generally grow as membership increases, thus limiting optimal group size. Although individual ownership ameliorates incentives leading to overuse, it also creates exclusion costs, such as defining and enforcing boundaries, which can sometimes result in inefficient underutilization of property.[82]

Consider the example of a health club that allows unlimited access to members but excludes non-members. The advantage of this arrangement over pure private property is that members can share the total cost without having each member duplicate the facilities. This insight provides the basis for the economics of clubs,[83] which can be expressed in various ways. There is an economy of scale in the creation of the health club, with optimal membership and usage above, and below, certain thresholds. There is also a public goods quality to the clubs because use (or consumption) by one member does not generally diminish enjoyment by others. Club theory recognizes, however, that public goods analysis applies only up to a point. Although economies of scale suggest a minimum size, the tragedy of the commons suggests a maximum size. The optimal club size balances the

---

[81] By contrast, joint ownership of marital property likely avoids several of the difficulties associated with tragedy of the commons because of tightly aligned shared interests, for example, enhancing the value of marital assets and ensuring the availability of those assets to children or heirs. For a general analysis of the economics of family law, see THE ECONOMICS OF FAMILY LAW (Margaret F. Brinig ed., 2007).

[82] *See, e.g.*, Barry Field, *The Evolution of Property Rights*, 42 KYKLOS 319, 341 (1989); *but see, e.g.*, Ellickson, *supra* note 1, at 1328–30 (identifying additional costs associated with group rather than individual monitoring because both must monitor against trespassers, but only groups confront problems of cohesion and must employ "intragroup monitoring").

[83] Club theory, which examines the optimal scale for the provision of public goods, RICHARD CORNES & TODD SANDLER, THE THEORY OF EXTERNALITIES, PUBLIC GOODS, AND CLUB GOODS (1986), also underlies theories of fiscal federalism, Wallace E. Oates, *An Essay on Fiscal Federalism*, 37 J. ECON. LITERATURE 1120 (1999). *See also* Charles M. Tiebout, *A Pure Theory of Local Expenditures*, 64 J. POL. ECON. 416 (1956) (distinguishing local expenditures).

cost savings from a larger membership against congestion and overuse as membership expands.

The optimal scale of ownership is also influenced by externalities.[84] In Coase's illustration with cattle straying onto neighboring farmland, one solution is for the rancher and farmer to bargain over access. Another is to have either purchase the other's property and then allocate both lots to their most highly valued uses. Whether by contract or by vertical integration, the final outcome will result in the parties internalizing the costs of their economic activities, thereby promoting the allocation of the land to its highest available use. The merger, however, creates the additional cost of managing and securing the boundary of a larger lot.[85]

The final economic benefit of common ownership, as compared to private property, is risk sharing. Sharing output among a group can insulate members from unavoidable risk. This includes uncertain production when other mechanisms or institutions that limit such risks are unavailable.[86]

1. *Partition Versus Consolidation of Property Rights: Two Sides of the Anti-Commons Coin*

As the preceding examples illustrate, common ownership can serve a useful economic function provided that the governance mechanism avoids over-exploitation resulting from a tragedy of the commons. Some governance structures themselves impede optimal use of jointly owned property, thus inhibiting agreement among divided owners as to a common course of action. This problem can be avoided in two very different ways, first by consolidating the divided rights into a single owner, and second, by dividing the assets into separate lots, with each lot containing the necessary bundle of rights to render it functional or salable. We discuss illustrations of each approach in this subpart.

Professor Michael Heller has referred to the problem of unbundled property rights as the *tragedy of the anticommons*.[87] In a study of divided property rights following Glasnost and the reformation in Russia during the regime of Mikhail Gorbachev, Heller observed that many storefronts in Moscow had empty shelves, whereas kiosks throughout the city were generally well stocked and thriving. Heller theorized that during the period of communist Russia, parties developed intricately divided rights in real property, including stores, and that the disaggregation of property rights blocked any single owner's effective usage rights. By contrast, the more portable kiosks did not interfere with the existing rights of others, and thus kiosks were more adaptable to the transition to a capitalist regime.

The primary structural difficulty involved reassembling the requisite bundle of rights in the stores to allow them to operate or to sell the property. Reassembly of rights proved

---

[84] Ellickson, *supra* note 1, at 1330, 1385.

[85] The question of whether the rancher and farmer should bargain or merge contributed to Coase's analysis of the firm, which has influenced the theory of industrial organization. R.H. Coase, *The Nature of the Firm*, 4 ECONOMICA 386 (1937).

[86] *See supra* Part I.A. (discussing communal ownership of food and other essential goods in the Plymouth Colony).

[87] Michael Heller, *Tragedy of the Anticommons: Property in the Transition from Marx to Markets*, 111 HARV. L. REV. 621 (1988).

prohibitively costly to negotiate. Putting the sticks back into the bundle of rights was akin to squeezing the toothpaste back into a tube. The challenge was not always knowing who held the separate sticks; with divided rights, no prospective buyer would invest in a property whose usage might be blocked by some unknown person holding a partial ownership interest.

A similar difficulty, with a happier outcome, arose in the State of Hawaii, in the context of residential housing. In *Hawaii Housing Auth. v. Midkiff*, the Supreme Court allowed the State of Hawaii to use eminent domain to break up a land oligopoly and to create a process for residents to gain full ownership of the improvements on land and the land itself.[88] Justice O'Connor, writing for the *Midkiff* majority, described the facts as follows:

> Beginning in the early 1800's, Hawaiian leaders and American settlers repeatedly attempted to divide the lands of the kingdom among the crown, the chiefs, and the common people. In the mid-1960's, after extensive hearings, the Hawaii Legislature discovered that, while the State and Federal Governments owned almost 49% of the State's land, another 47% was in the hands of only 72 private landowners. . . . The legislature further found that 18 landholders, with tracts of 21,000 acres or more, owned more than 40% of this land and that on Oahu, the most urbanized of the islands, 22 landowners owned 72.5% of the fee simple titles. The legislature concluded that concentrated land ownership was responsible for skewing the State's residential fee simple market, inflating land prices, and injuring the public tranquility and welfare.[89]

The difficulty in Hawaii was analogous to the Russian storefronts but with one notable difference. In Hawaii, the parties with whom the residents split ownership of the land were known. And yet, as with the storefronts, the disaggregation of rights in the bundle inhibited a robust market, also affecting the transfer in land. The challenge was that the ultimate beneficiaries in the Hawaii case were the residential owners, who after eminent domain, would gain the ability to purchase the land rights, something that the Russian government had not managed to accomplish. Justice O'Connor explained why this was permissible:

> [We] have no trouble concluding that the Hawaii Act is constitutional. The people of Hawaii have attempted, much as the settlers of the original 13 Colonies, did to reduce the perceived social and economic evils of a land oligopoly traceable to their monarchs. The land oligopoly has, according to the Hawaii Legislature, created artificial deterrents to the normal functioning of the State's residential land market and forced thousands of individual homeowners to lease, rather than buy, the land underneath their homes.[90]

In effect, the Court determined that the problem of the anti-commons respecting Hawaiian residential properties was sufficiently compelling to permit eminent domain as

---

[88] Haw. Hous. Auth. v. Midkiff, 467 U.S. 229 (1984).

[89] *Id.* at 232 (citations omitted).

[90] *Id.* at 241–42.

a means of vesting the necessary bundle of rights to restore functionality to the land market.

A similar problem can arise when beneficiaries disagree on the use of joint inherited property. Consider a group of three siblings who inherent equal shares in a single piece of real estate and who cannot agree on how to use it. At common law, there were three ways that one or more of the parties could seek to partition the property: *partition in kind*, *partition by allotment*, and *partition by sale*.[91] Partition in kind means dividing the asset into approximately equal shares among the siblings. Partition by allotment means vesting full title in one sibling with an order to pay the equivalent value of the portions taken to the remaining siblings. And partition by sale means a forced sale with the proceeds split evenly among the siblings.

The availability of these forms of partition vary among jurisdictions, but each offers an alternative way out of the anti-commons problem. These methods vest full title, with all of the sticks in the associated bundle, in smaller physical parcels, to each present owner, or to a single owner, including either a present owner or the successor pursuant to a forced sale. Although physical partition—partition in kind—avoids the inefficiency of the anti-commons problem by creating more functional private property rights, there is a risk of reducing aggregate land value if there are relevant economies of scale such that the undivided asset is more valuable than the sum of the divided parts. This might occasionally characterize land, and it almost invariably characterizes other physical property such as fine art or an automobile.

For this reason, partition includes the alternative means of vesting full title in one of the present owners or by sale to a third party, with proceeds equally divided among the present owners. This solution is also imperfect inasmuch as it forces the owners to accept fair market value, thereby risking a loss in one or more owner's higher subjective valuation.[92] An obvious solution when this occurs is for the sibling with the highest subjective value to buy the others out. Of course, the highest-valuing sibling might be unable to afford it. Another difficulty is that the parties are in a bilateral, or multilateral, monopoly, and if familial relationships have broken down, as sometimes occurs, then the siblings without the high subjective value are in a position to seek part of that gain as an appropriable quasi rent.

QUESTIONS AND COMMENTS

Imagine that three estranged sisters inherit an asset with a fair market value of $100,000 for which one of the sisters, Alice, holds a higher subjective value over the total asset at $150,000, and the other two sisters, Barb and Carly, each value it at fair market value. Which of the preceding rules is most likely to produce the social-welfare-maximizing outcome, and why? Can you identify a solution to the multilateral bargaining problem that is likely to vest full title in the sister who values it most highly? Why or why not? As a matter of fairness,

---

[91] For a general discussion, see Thomas W. Mitchell, *Reforming Property Law to Address Devastating Land Loss*, 66 ALA. L. REV. 1 (2014).

[92] *See* Thomas Miceli & C.F. Sirmans, *Partition of Real Estate: or, Breaking Up Is (Not) Hard to Do*, 29 J. LEGAL STUD. 783 (2000).

should Alice receive the full benefit of her higher subjective valuation, and thus compensate her sisters based on their share of the fair market value? Why or why not?

III. NON-CONSENSUAL TRANSFERS OF PROPERTY

The forced partition of real estate effects a non-consensual transfer of property rights resulting from market failure when bargaining among co-owners breaks down.[93] In this part, we discuss other market failures that can result in non-consensual transfers.

We begin by revisiting the problem of externalities. We then turn to a discussion of involuntary transfers between private individuals, imposed judicially or by regulation. The next chapter considers other contexts that involve market failures in land, including eminent domain and regulatory takings.[94]

A. Control of Externalities

As discussed above, externalities arise when one party's use of property imposes burdens on another's use of property. In this section, we first examine the traditional economic perspective on externalities, commonly associated with the economist Arthur Pigou.[95] In this view, externalities result in harm-creating activity, which must then be controlled with some form of government intervention. The usual prescription is a *Pigouvian tax*, which forces the party identified as causing the externality to internalize the resulting harm. We then compare this perspective with the Coasian approach, which treats externalities as the product of undefined property rights and which then inquires as to which allocation of rights is apt to move resources to their more highly valued uses. The competing analyses provide insight into such doctrinal areas as trespass, nuisance, zoning, and land-use covenants.

1. Pigouvian Taxes

We begin with Coase's example involving a railroad with tracks that border farmland that risks fire from sparks emitted by passing trains. The analysis begins by showing that there are too many trains from a social perspective because the railroad has not accounted for the costs borne by farmers.

This is illustrated in Figure 7:2. The downward sloping Marginal Benefit Curve (*MB*) is the railroad's marginal private benefit from running trains, which equals the marginal social benefit because the railroad internalizes all of the benefits to its customers (i.e., there are no external benefits). The curve labeled MC_P is the railroad's *private* marginal cost, reflecting the cost of its inputs (coal, employees, maintenance of the train and tracks, etc.). The privately optimal number of trains—the level that maximizes the railroad's profit—occurs at the intersection of these curves and is denoted q_P. The curve labeled

---

93 As shown in Chapter 13, this type of market failure can arise as the result of an empty core bargaining game.

94 *See infra* Chapter 8.

95 For a preliminary assessment of this scholarly debate, see *supra* Chapter 1.

MC_S is the marginal *social* cost of running trains, reflecting the railroad's private costs *plus the damage suffered by farmers along the tracks in the form of crop damage*. In other words, it equals MC_P plus the cost of the externality imposed on the farmers. The socially optimal number of trains occurs where the marginal social cost curve intersects the MB curve, at the point labeled q_S. The social optimum therefore involves fewer trains as compared to the railroad's profit-maximizing choice.

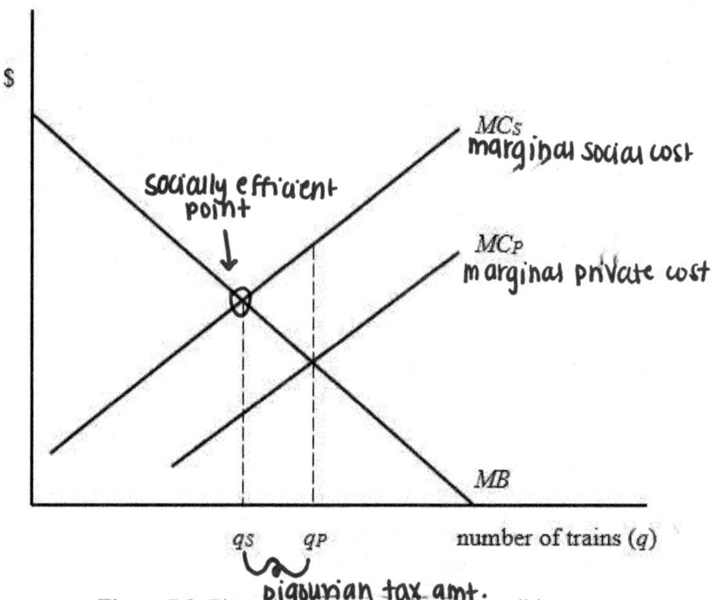

Figure 7:2. Pigouvian tax approach to externalities.

The Pigouvian solution to this inefficiency is to impose a tax on the railroad that forces it to internalize the external harm. If the tax is on a per-train basis, then the amount of the tax should equal the amount of the harm caused per train. That equals the vertical distance between the MC_S and MC_P curves in Figure 7:2.[96] With the tax, the railroad will run the socially optimal number of trains because the profit-maximizing outcome now coincides with the social optimum. Because it forces the railroad to account for its full social costs, the incentive effect of the tax is identical to that of strict liability in torts.[97] In other words, the railroad is fully responsible for all harms that it causes *even if* there are steps that the farmers might have taken to abate the harm.

In the case where the farmer is purely passive, it does not matter whether the revenue from the tax is given to the farmer as compensation for damage or if it is used for some other purpose, such as funding a highway or building a park. The sole purpose of the tax is to align the railroad's financial incentives with the full social cost of its activity. In this sense, the tax differs from strict liability in that the damages need not go to the victim. As

---

[96] The calculation of the tax is more complicated if the externality is not a constant function of the number of trains—that is, if the MC_S and MC_P curves are not parallel. Then the amount of the per-unit tax would be set equal to the vertical distance between the two curves evaluated at the optimal point, q_S. This would shift the MC_P curve up so that it intersects the MB curve at q_S.

[97] *See supra* Chapter 4 (discussing strict products liability).

a result, the Pigouvian tax aligns the injurer's incentives, but it does not necessarily resolve whether the farmer continues to bear the residual risk after the railroad has undertaken all cost-effective precautions to reduce the incidence of spark-induced fires.

An important advantage of the tax over strict liability is that it motivates the farmer not to be passive. Suppose, for example, the farmer can decide how close to the tracks to plant his crops and to store his equipment.[98] This presents the externality as a problem of bilateral care in which the precautions of both the railroad and farmers affect the residual risk and the resulting magnitude of damages. The preferred outcome involves the railroad restricting its number of trains and the farmers planting their crops some distance from the tracks.

As shown in Chapter 3, strict liability properly aligns the incentives of the party that causes harm, but risks undermining incentives to take appropriate precautions on the part of the potential victim. As applied here, the Pigouvian tax, treated as a form of strict liability, will encourage the railroad to reduce the number of trains, but *if* the tax proceeds fully reimburse the farmer for any resulting damage (as would be true under strict liability) it will not encourage farmers to plant their crops farther from the tracks. By contrast, if the Pigouvian tax proceeds are not used to compensate the farmers for resulting damage, then both parties will be motivated to take cost-effective precautions. As we saw in the context of tort, the same bilaterally efficient outcome can be duplicated with a properly structured negligence rule. That is because the railroad would then have an incentive to prove it has undertaken cost-effective precautions in order to avoid liability, and the farmer would then bear the residual damages.

2. *The Coasian Perspective*

As previously shown,[99] in his critique of Pigou's approach to externalities, Coase challenged two assumptions: first, that there is a single "cause" of the harm, and second, that some form of government intervention is necessary to force the injurer to internalize it. We now consider how these two challenges apply to the preceding example.

Pigouvian tax analysis implicitly assumes that the railroad is the cause of the farmer's injury, and, therefore, that it must be made to internalize the cost. Recall that the Coasian analysis treated externalities as arising from undefined property rights.[100] By contrast, the Pigouvian solution awarded the presumptive right to be free from harm to the farmers. The right is presumptive because the tax does not necessarily result in compensation for damages (it can go to the government); rather, it is intended to force an internalization of costs and thus to reduce the offending activity to an efficient level. The Pigouvian tax, or strict tort liability, thus enforces the right by putting a price on it, which the railroad (injurer) then "purchases" up to the point where the benefit of spewing additional sparks just equals its social cost, thereby promoting an efficient activity level.

In this case, where the railroad is identified as the cause of the harm, the Coasian analysis reaffirms the efficiency of the Pigouvian view. Now assume that the disputed

---

[98] *See, e.g.*, LeRoy Fibre Co. v. Chicago, Milwaukee & St. Paul Ry., 232 U.S. 340 (1914).

[99] *See supra* Chapter 1 Part VI.

[100] *See supra* Part I.B.

property right is assigned to the railroad, meaning that the railroads are permitted to spew sparks without incurring a tax or liability. Under the Pigouvian view, the railroad would be expected to expand the number of trains to its profit-maximizing level, q_P in Figure 7:2, and the outcome would be inefficient. A Coasian analysis, however, explains why this might not be the final outcome.

Assuming that one of the parties values the relevant right more highly—either to create a risk of sparks or to have the risk of sparks reduced—there is room for a social-welfare-enhancing bargain between the railroad and farmers. To see why, note that at the railroad's privately optimal outcome, the last train yields zero marginal profit because $MB=MC_P$, but it imposes positive marginal damages on farmers in an amount equal to the vertical distance between MC_S and MC_P at that point. Thus, farmers as a group would be willing to pay up to this amount to the railroad to cut back on the number of trains, and the railroad would accept any amount greater than zero (the private value of the marginal train) to do so. The farmers would thus be willing to "buy" the right to block the marginal train. Such bargaining would in theory continue as long as the value of blocking successive marginal trains to farmers in the form of reduced crop damage (again, the vertical distance between MC_S and MC_P) exceeds the value of running the marginal train to the railroad (the vertical distance between MB and MC_P). Bargaining will therefore occur up to the point where $MC_S–MC_P=MB–MC_P$, or where $MB=MC_S$. In this stylized presentation, this is the efficient point.

In the preceding example, the disputed property right was awarded to the railroad, but farmers, as a group, were able to purchase it up to the point where it was equally valuable to the two parties. This is the opposite of what happened under the Pigouvian approach, where the railroad had to purchase the right. The outcome in both cases was the same, however, with the efficient number of trains being operated. This conclusion—that the outcome will be efficient regardless of the initial assignment of rights, provided that the parties can freely bargain—is a straightforward illustration of the Coase theorem.

Now recall the first assumption implicit in the Pigouvian approach to externalities, that there is a unique "cause" of the harm. The preceding analysis demonstrates the limitation of this approach. In fact, both parties, the railroad and the farmers, are simultaneously "causes" in the sense that if either party were absent, the harm would go away. Coase demonstrated that such harms arise as a "reciprocal" feature of the parties' economic relationship. Borrowing terminology from tort law, both parties are "but-for" causes of the resulting harm.

Coase's critical insight is that it is better to find the rule that maximizes the potential joint gains between the parties to this sort of bilateral relationship, and that the alternative externality analysis obscures that critical inquiry since the harm is inevitably reciprocal in an economic sense. If the parties are able to bargain at low cost, the initial assignment of rights would have distributional consequences, but it would not affect optimal resource allocations, as an inefficient initial allocation can be reassigned by contract. As the following discussion shows, when transactions costs are high, the analysis becomes more complicated.

3. *The Impact of Transaction Costs*

The ability of the parties to bargain to an efficient outcome is, of course, by no means guaranteed. This observation is central to assessing the normative implications of the Coase theorem. For example, if several farmers own the land along the railroad tracks, awarding them the collective right to be free from crop damage might prevent trains from running even if allowing the trains to run is socially optimal. The problem is that the railroad would need permission from each farmer, and a single holdout could undermine that negotiation process. This is especially likely since by doing so, the holdout farmer could seek to extract an inordinately high appropriable quasi rent equivalent to the difference in value between all farmers' land deployed for crops and the added value of restricting some cultivation near the tracks to allow some trains to run.

In effect, multilateral bargaining, coupled with the holdout dynamic, renders transactions costs inordinately high.[101] This structural impediment will likely bar deploying the land to its most highly valued use, that is, unless the legal regime correctly assigns the property-rights allocation initially. That is the second fundamental insight from the Coase theorem. In high transaction-costs setting, the initial assignment of rights becomes critical for achieving the efficient outcome.[102]

This observation helps to connect Pigou's second implicit assumption, namely that some form of governmental intervention is necessary to force the internalization costs as a means of clarifying property rights and of moving resources to their most highly valued uses. The competing accounts—Coase and Pigou—connect in the following sense. In the high transaction cost setting, effective Coasian bargaining is unlikely to occur. As a result, the governmental assignment of rights, whether by a regulation or through the judicial enforcement of a legal claim, is likely to be final.

This analysis is also parallel to those arising under various tort liability rules and rules governing breach and damages under contract law. Because parties to a tort are not able to bargain over the liability rule before an accident occurs, the common law of tort, or superseding legislative rules, must assign the standard of care to ensure efficient use of resources. And because contracting parties often find themselves in a bilateral monopoly setting after the initial contractual relationship has broken down, contract law must likewise establish suitable off-the-rack rules governing breach and damages to ensure the contract is construed so as to maximize social welfare.

The analysis underscores a critical point about the economic analysis of the common law. The factual circumstances that render parties to a lawsuit unable to bargain for a social-welfare-enhancing solution—for example, because they met as strangers in an accident, because the circumstances involve multiple parties and thus invite holdouts, or because of opportunities for appropriable quasi rents distort bargaining incentives—are unimportant. What is important is recognizing that high transaction costs place stress on getting the background legal rule right. Properly calibrated off-the-rack rules are a necessary precondition to moving resources to their more highly valued uses and to ensuring appropriate levels of care, which together insure that when engaging in economic

[101] *See infra* Chapter 8, Part I.A.2 (discussing holdout games in property law).

[102] Harold Demsetz, *When Does the Rule of Liability Matter?*, 1 J. LEGAL STUD. 13, 25–28 (1972).

activity, parties consider both the social benefits and social costs of doing so. This is part of an integrative economic understanding of common law rules, including tort, contract, and property, to which we will return in the next chapter.

4. *Property Rules Versus Liability Rules*

In a classic work, *Property Rules, Liability Rules, and Inalienability: One View of the Cathedral,* Guido Calabresi and A. Douglas Melamed offered an integrative approach to studying the relationship between tort and property.[103] In doing so, they provided an important extension of the Coasian perspective on externalities as it affects the choice of legal rules for the assignment and protection of property rights.[104] Calabresi and Melamed distinguished two types of rules, which they termed *property rules* and *liability rules*.[105] The rules differ as to how they protect a legally defined "entitlement," meaning a right favoring one or the other side in a property dispute.

Consider, once again, Coase's rancher-farmer dispute. The legal entitlement determines whether the farmer has the right to be free from crop damage, or instead whether the rancher has the right to let his cattle stray. Calabresi and Melamed demonstrate that in addition to assigning the initial entitlement, it is equally important to specify the method by which the assignment will be protected.

Assume that the farmer holds the entitlement. If it is protected by a property rule, the rancher must negotiate with the farmer to purchase the right to let her cattle stray. Absent such an agreement, the farmer can enjoin the rancher, thereby forcing him to restrain his cattle or face a fine. Alternatively, if the farmer's entitlement is protected by a liability rule, the rancher can violate it without first obtaining the farmer's consent as long as he is willing to pay compensation for the resulting crop damage after the fact. In other words, the rancher can "take" the farmer's entitlement in a forcible transfer for a price to be set by the court.

The key difference between a property rule and a liability rule therefore concerns the manner in which entitlements are legally exchanged. Under a property rule, exchange can only occur by means of a prior consensual market transaction, whereas under a liability rule it can occur through unilateral action followed by subsequent compensation for resulting damage. The choice of rule tests the limits of the famous assertion: "It's easier to ask forgiveness than it is to get permission."[106] Calabresi and Melamed show that this is true for liability rules but not for property rules. Property rules require *consent* as a

---

[103] Guido Calabresi & A. Douglas Melamed, *Property Rules, Liability Rules, and Inalienability: One View of the Cathedral,* 85 HARV. L. REV. 1089 (1972).

[104] *Id. See also* A. Mitchell Polinsky, *On the Choice Between Property Rules and Liability Rules*, 18 ECON. INQUIRY 233 (1980); Louis Kaplow & Steven Shavell, *Property Rules Versus Liability Rules*, 109 HARV. L. REV. 713 (1996).

[105] They also discuss a third rule, referred to as an *inalienability rule*. *See* Calabresi & Melamed, *supra* note 103.

[106] This quote is frequently, if not definitively, attributed to Rear Admiral Grace Murray Hopper. *See, e.g.*, Elizabeth Dickason, *Looking Back: Grace Hopper's Younger Years*, CHIPS (June 27, 2011), http://www.doncio.navy.mil/Chips/ArticleDetails.aspx?ID=2388 (displaying the cover of the 1986 *Chips Ahoy* magazine with the quote).

precondition to violating them; liability rules allow for asking forgiveness, that is, after court-ordered damages or settlement.

We have already encountered several examples of liability rules. These include all of the tort rules we have studied and the contract rules that award money damages for breach. By contrast, the specific performance remedy for breach is an example of a property rule because it requires performance of the contractual terms, or at least uses that as a starting point for subsequent negotiations. In either situation, a promisor will only breach if she can provide sufficient compensation to the promisee to buy out her performance obligation.

Calabresi and Melamed demonstrate that the policy choice between these two categories of enforcement rules turns on the nature of consent. Although consent ensures mutual gains in a transaction, consent can be obstructed by high transaction costs. The example of the farmer and railroad illustrates the tradeoff between the two categories of rules.

If there is a single farmer along the tracks, it is possible that the two parties would be able to bargain with each other over the assignment of the entitlement so as to maximize the joint value of their activities. In this case, use of a property rule is preferred as it facilitates mutually beneficial (i.e., socially optimal) Coasian bargaining. By contrast, if there are multiple farmers along the tracks, transactions costs are high as a result of the holdout problem. And so there is no assurance that bargaining will succeed in achieving an efficient outcome. In this case, use of a liability rule is preferred because it removes the need for the railroad to negotiate with each farmer before its trains can run. Instead, following the Calabresi and Melamed analysis, the court would set the price of the entitlement and allow the railroad to act unilaterally, thus avoiding the problematic bargaining cost.

Attaining an efficient outcome under a liability rule hinges on properly measuring the farmers' damages. To illustrate, consider the following stylized example, summarized in Table 7:2.

Table 7:2. Illustration of the Choice Between Property Rules and Liability Rules

Number of trains	Crop damage (total/marginal)	Railroad profit (total/marginal)	Net gain ($)
0	0	0	0
1	**500**/500	**600**/600	100
2	**1300**/800	**1200**/600	–100

The first column shows the number of trains, the second column shows the resulting crop damage to farmers along the route (the boldface entry), and the third column shows the railroad's profit (again in boldface). The railroad maximizes its profit by running two trains, but the socially optimal outcome, which maximizes the railroad's profit less the crop damage (column four), is for only one train to run.

Suppose initially that there is a single farmer who sustains all of the damage, and that bargaining between the railroad and the farmer is therefore plausible. Further, suppose that the court assigns the entitlement to the farmer, protected with a property rule. Thus, the farmer can obtain an injunction to prevent the railroad from running any trains. The railroad, however, would be willing to offer the farmer up to $600 to allow the first train to run (the marginal profit), and the farmer would accept any amount above $500 (the marginal injury). Thus, there is room for a bargain, and the first train would run. The parties would not, however, be able to reach a bargain that would allow the *second* train to run. Although the railroad would again offer up to $600 (the marginal profit), its value of the second train, the farmer would demand at least $800 (the marginal injury, meaning the crop damage from adding the second train.) Thus, no transaction would be possible. The final, and efficient, outcome is that only one train would run.

Now consider an example in which the likelihood of successful bargaining is remote. Suppose, for example, that there are several farmers along the tracks whose aggregate damages equal the amounts shown in the table. Even if there is a social gain that would result in allowing the first train to run, a single farmer could block this gain to all the other farmers by refusing to acquiesce unless he receives a disproportionate share of the resulting gains. In the multilateral bargaining setting, this holdout game renders the transaction costs prohibitive, with the socially inefficient result that no trains will run.

Now imagine instead that the court protects the farmers' entitlement with a liability rule and sets the price for the railroad to acquire it at the aggregate damages. The railroad can therefore acquire the entitlement to run its trains without having to negotiate with the farmers, provided that it is willing to pay the damages set by the court. In this case, the railroad will run only one train because its net profit, including the court-imposed damages, now coincides with the net social gain. The railroad therefore internalizes the externality and the outcome is efficient.

The preceding example shows the advantage of liability rules over property rules when transaction costs are high. Specifically, liability rules allow the court to coerce social-welfare-enhancing transfers of entitlements that a property rule could prevent.

It is important to recognize, however, the cost of using liability rules. First, if parties cannot agree to the damages remedy via settlement, they will incur litigation costs, and second, as with any other litigation context, the results might be prone to error. Suppose, for example, that the court erred in measuring the crop damage. If it overestimated the damage from the first train at, say, $700, then the railroad would not have been willing to run the first train. Conversely, if it underestimated the damage from running two trains to be $1100, the railroad would have been willing to run both trains. Based on the assumed values of the respective activities—cultivation versus running the trains—either of these outcomes is problematic. Although liability rules enhance flexibility, the risk of legal error limits their value. In other words, the efficacy of liability rules turns in large part on the ability of courts to properly assess the relevant values.

We previously saw that courts are likely to make systematic errors in estimating damages when victims attach significant subjective value to their entitlements. This is especially true in cases involving land, as exemplified by the *Peevyhouse* case, where market value often understates the owner's true value. This problem will recur in the context of eminent domain, which is an example of a liability rule.

Calabresi and Melamed thus derive the following general principal as a corollary to the Coase theorem: *Courts should use property rules when transaction costs are low, and they should use liability rules when transaction costs are high.* The next two sections provide some illustrations of how the law embodies the logic of this prescription.

5. *Boomer v. Atlantic Cement Co.*

The well-known case of *Boomer v. Atlantic Cement Co.*, nicely illustrates the logic underlying the choice of a property rule or a liability rule.[107] A factory that generated dirt, smoke, and noise harmed a group of nearby landowners. The plaintiffs sought an injunction to have the factory shut down, but the court opted instead to allow it to operate as long as the owner was willing to pay damages to the residents. Thus, the court protected the landowners' entitlement to be free from harm with a liability rule, not a property rule. In defending its ruling, the court reasoned that an outright injunction (property rule protection of the plaintiffs) would have caused the plant to shut down, resulting in the loss of the plant owner's initial investment of $45 million, as well as hundreds of jobs, as compared to the estimated $185,000 in damages suffered by the plaintiffs. The damage remedy instead allowed the plant to continue operating, while compensating the victims.

The court's choice of a liability rule (damages) over a property rule (an injunction) appears to be social-welfare-enhancing given the costly bargaining as a result of anticipated holdouts. The situation, therefore, is similar to the multiple-farmer example above. The liability rule removes this obstacle to moving resources to their more highly valued uses through contract. It is important to remember, however, that in relying on a liability rule, the court must assess the relative aggregate harm from the victims' damages. Although the risk of error in such cases might be high given the related health risks and diminution in property values, the numbers in the *Boomer* case suggest that the value of the plant so far surpassed the harm that even if the court under-compensated victims, the result was likely to have been Kaldor-Hicks efficient.

Although *Boomer* nicely illustrates the problem with multiple parties, we can extend the analysis to demonstrate related negotiating challenges affecting fewer landowners, or even one, creating a simple bilateral monopoly. In the event that the court placed a property right with a single adjoining landowner who was thereby empowered to enjoin the factory, in theory, the plant would have been willing to pay up to $45 million to stay open, even though the assessed harm from the factory running was only $185,000.[108] The wide bargaining range is in fact a reason to expect high bargaining costs, as each side invests considerable effort in obtaining a larger cut of the pie. In a multilateral bargain setting, if all landowners but one acquiesce in a reasonable settlement, the holdout would

---

[107] 257 N.E.2d 870 (N.Y. 1970).

[108] Although this is a likely overestimate, since the plant could be deployed for some alternative use, the valuation difference nonetheless remains dramatic. *See* POSNER, *supra* note 55, at 71. The damages award is only necessary to compensate present owners. Future purchasers will be aware of the factory's entitlement of the property right, and, therefore, any diminution in home values will be capitalized into the sales price.

also force the factory into this bilateral monopoly bargain.[109] Even so, the holdout problem is exacerbated in the multilateral context as each owner has an incentive to be the "last" seller.

6. Trespass and Nuisance Law (with a Comment on Easements by Necessity, Implication, and Prescription)

Trespass and nuisance are the principal common law rules aimed at preventing unwanted infringements on a landowner's property rights.[110] Professor Robert Keeton has stated the difference between the two rules as follows: "trespass is an invasion of the plaintiff's interest in the exclusive possession of his land, while nuisance is an interference with his use and enjoyment of it."[111] Typical examples of trespass involve physical intrusions onto another's land, whether periodic (as when someone occasionally walks across it) or permanent (as when someone builds a structure on it). Common examples of nuisance include pollution and noise.[112]

The usual remedy for trespass is an injunction, a property rule. The would-be trespasser can therefore only continue to invade the property by obtaining the owner's consent, for example, by purchasing an easement or buying the land outright. The remedies under nuisance law are more complicated, and thus they involve a greater degree of discretion on the part of courts. First, the plaintiff must establish that the defendant's intrusion causes "significant harm," where the usual test is whether the burdens of the activity exceed the benefits.[113] Professor Keeton has explained that once this threshold is met, the court may reach one of the following conclusions:

> (1) the social interest is best served by requiring the plaintiff to bear the burden of the type of hardship suffered; (2) the social interest is best served by concluding that the defendant's activity is a socially desirable one under the circumstances and should not be altered or abated, but [the] cost . . . should be borne by the defendant; . . . or (3) the social interest is best served by permitting the plaintiff, . . . to enjoin the activity on the theory that . . . the gravity of the harm outweighs the utility of the conduct.[114]

In other words, the court may issue an injunction halting the activity, invoke a liability rule, or do nothing.

Although remedies for trespass and nuisance do not neatly divide over property rules versus liability rules, the law does treat trespass differently from nuisance. In general, acts

---

[109] Victor Goldberg, *Relational Exchange, Contract Law, and the* Boomer *Problem*, 141 J. INST. & THEORETICAL ECON. 570 (1985).

[110] The discussion in this section is based on Thomas Merrill, *Trespass and Nuisance*, *in* 3 THE NEW PALGRAVE DICTIONARY OF LAW AND ECONOMICS, *supra* note 75, at 617.

[111] W. PAGE KEETON ET AL., PROSSER AND KEETON ON THE LAW OF TORTS 622 (1984).

[112] Attractive nuisance is a related doctrine that holds property owners liable for objects on property that risk attracting children that are not protected. Examples include pools, abandoned vehicles, and swing sets that are not safe from view or properly enclosed. DAN B. DOBBS ET AL., THE LAW OF TORTS § 277 (2d ed. 2016).

[113] KEETON ET AL., *supra* note 111, at 631.

[114] *Id.*

that qualify as trespass tend to arise in low-transaction-cost settings, thus facilitating Coasian bargaining between the trespasser and the landowner. For example, if someone wanted to erect a building near or over a neighbor's boundary, subject to some exceptions described in the following section, it usually would be fairly easy to locate the boundary and negotiate with the owner to purchase the necessary land or usage rights. The same is true if a path across someone else's property is the easiest route to a destination. The protection of an owner's right to exclude others by a property rule in these low-transaction-cost settings is therefore conducive to social-welfare-maximizing transactions that allow the transfer of the right to another party who values it more highly.

a. Easements by Necessity, Implication, and Prescription

The law recognizes limited circumstances in which the risk of high transaction costs that arise with a bilateral monopoly require the judicial vesting of a property right in a party who is seeking to compromise another party's use or exclusion rights in her own land. When this occurs, the court is, in effect, granting one party a limited property right to land owned by another. Three notable illustrations include *easement by necessity*, *easement by implication*, and *easement by prescription*. Each grants a property owner access or usage rights in another's land and does so without requiring the party seeking such access to purchase the right.

Under the doctrine of easement by necessity, the owner of a land-blocked parcel is sometimes permitted to gain an access route over another's land, and when she succeeds, the easement is *appurtenant*, meaning it stays with the land, rather than belonging to a specific individual.[115] "Necessity" is itself necessary but insufficient for such an easement; the court will also inquire as to the expectations of the parties at the time that the lot was conveyed before imposing a burden on the subservient land, meaning the lot through which the dominant land, or the land benefitting from the easement, will gain access. An easement by necessity is not accompanied by compensation, and it does not create a possessory interest; rather, it creates a usage right that can be extinguished with the creation of an alternative means of access, for example, a new road.

Easement by implication arises when a property owner reasonably expects to have access to a main road or waterway, but where the deed document does not establish the right despite expected usage. The required showing for easement by implication is less strict than for easement by necessity. As with easement by necessity, the court will generally focus on the expectations of the parties.

Finally, easement by prescription is a close cousin to *adverse possession*, discussed more fully below.[116] A prescriptive easement arises when a landowner uses neighboring land, for example, as a passage way or to put up a structure, and does so in a manner that satisfies the following conditions: the usage is *open and notorious*; it is *adverse*, meaning it benefits the user to the detriment of the landowner; it is *hostile*, meaning it is an outward use against the landowner's rights; and it is *continuous for the prescriptive period*, meaning that it is not interrupted for the specified period, typically fifteen or twenty years. These are

---

[115] For a more detailed description of each of the easements described here, see JAMES W. ELY JR. & JON W. BRUCE, THE LAW OF EASEMENTS AND LICENSES IN LAND §§ 2:1–:10 (2015).

[116] *See infra* Part III.B.

nearly identical criteria to adverse possession itself, but in the context of easement by prescription, the successful claim involves the right to use land, rather than to gain title.

These easement rules typically arise when parties find themselves in a bilateral monopoly, and when the subservient land owner, if permitted to deny access to dominant landowner, could extract a very high appropriable quasi rent. Easement by prescription looks different from the other two in that it does not involve an access right without which the value of the dominant land is necessarily diminished. But consistent with Holmes's admonition that the true value of land results from improvements, once the continuous and hostile use is established, the affected property is likely to have substantially enhanced value to the party claiming the right.[117] We will expand on this logic in the discussion of adverse possession below.

b. Return to the Cathedral: *Trespass* and *Nuisance* Revisited

In settings where bargaining costs between the infringer and the property owner tend be high, the unqualified protection of the owner's exclusion rights might block efficient transfers of property rights. As seen in *Boomer*, an injunction by the factory's adjoining landowners could have resulted in an inefficient plant closure.[118]

Nuisance cases generally involve harms that are more diffuse. Examples include air and noise pollution. Such cases tend to involve multiple potential plaintiffs and corresponding holdout problems. This dynamic makes bargaining between the polluter and victims difficult, both because larger numbers are often involved and because the harm may be spatially dispersed.

The dividing line between the trespass and nuisance doctrines also helps to mark the boundary between property law and tort law. The right to exclude is an important component of the traditional bundle of property rights, and the law of trespass strictly enforces that right by allowing the owner to exclude infringers. And yet, when the infringement is defined as a nuisance, the legal doctrine sometimes changes course, allowing the owner only a liability rule, and thus a damage remedy. And occasionally it provides no recourse at all. Specifically, those settings where transaction costs between parties to a dispute tend to be low are governed by rules of property law, whereas those settings where the transaction costs between parties tend to be high are governed by the rules of tort law.

Easements by necessity and implication also fit this account by creating conditions in which landowners are able to gain usage rights without subjecting themselves to the difficult bilateral bargaining that could result in subservient landowners extracting a high appropriable quasi rent. And prescriptive easements likewise disallow burdened landowners to exact similar rents after the claimant's considerable and long-term usage investment in land.

---

[117] *See supra* note 50 and accompanying text.

[118] *See supra* Part III.A.5.

7. *Zoning, Land-Use Covenants, and Property-Tax Funded Schooling*

For many types of externalities, common law remedies have been superseded by various regulatory controls.[119] The predominant form of land-use regulation, especially within urban areas in the United States, is zoning.[120] Initially, zoning laws were defended as a means of partitioning different land uses so as to minimize the spillover effects, or externalities, that would otherwise arise from dissimilar uses.[121] In most cities, for example, residential land is separately zoned from commercial and industrial land, often with buffer or transition zones that include more densely populated high-rise and other large-scale residential developments abutting shopping areas and highways.

Scholars have criticized zoning laws as overly blunt and as entailing high administrative costs.[122] Zoning laws, by their nature, impose restrictions on land use and improvements that sometimes conflict with the preferences of residents who live there. Most zoning regimes have procedures that allow for *variances*, which are exceptions that can sometimes be procured pursuant to an administrative proceeding.[123] This might seem counter intuitive inasmuch as residents typically purchase their property subject to existing zoning laws, but very often, those who buy their homes do so based on a complex combination of factors—price, quality of schools, commute, other area amenities—and the zoning restrictions are only one, often minor, consideration.

The history of zoning laws is complicated because although such policies are generally defended on neutral policy grounds, the policies themselves often have other, less benign effects. For example lot-size restrictions, a common zoning practice, can be justified in an effort to better match the provision of public goods and services based on the willingness and ability of communities to pay for them.[124] Homeowners in relatively well-to-do neighborhoods might be said to "have a taste for" matching a high tax base with high quality public schools, beautiful parks, and excellent and responsive police and fire departments. Of course it would seem peculiar to say that residents in lower income neighborhoods, which often disproportionately include persons of color, lack a taste for the same high quality public goods and services. The problem is that the primary funding source for these amenities is property taxes derived from assessed property values. Regardless of preferences, lower income communities lack the capacity to dedicate the same level of resources to such public goods and services. This might be likened to the

---

[119] Merrill, *supra* note 110, at 618–19.

[120] The Supreme Court rejected a due process challenge to a zoning ordinance in *Village of Euclid v. Ambler Realty*, 272 U.S. 365 (1926), and it rejected an equal protection challenge to a zoning ordinance in *Village of Arlington Heights v. Metropolitan Housing Development Corp*, 429 U.S. 252 (1977). For a more detailed economic analysis of zoning laws, see WILLIAM FISCHEL, THE ECONOMICS OF ZONING LAWS: A PROPERTY RIGHTS APPROACH TO AMERICAN LAND USE CONTROLS (1985).

[121] Michelle J. White, *Suburban Zoning in Fragmented Metropolitan Areas*, *in* FISCAL ZONING AND LAND USE CONTROLS 31 (Edwin S. Mills & Wallace E. Oates eds., 1975).

[122] Ellickson, *supra* note 51, at 697–99. *See generally* Michelle J. White & Donald Wittman, *Optimal Spatial Location Under Pollution: Liability Rules and Zoning*, 10 J. LEGAL STUD. 249 (1979).

[123] HERBERT HOVENKAMP ET AL., THE LAW OF PROPERTY: AN INTRODUCTORY SURVEY § 12.1 (16) (5th ed. 2001); WILLIAM B. STOEBUCK & DALE A. WHITMAN, THE LAW OF PROPERTY § 9.29 (3d ed. 2000).

[124] *See generally* Tiebout, *supra* note 83.

inability of low-income consumers to buy luxury goods. When schools and other such merit goods are involved, however, the issue is more complicated as markets will often fail to allocate resources in ways that meet public policy goals.

The Supreme Court confronted this problem in *Village of Arlington Heights v. Metropolitan Housing Development Corp.*[125] In that case a zoning ordinance in the Village of Arlington Heights banned multifamily dwellings in the village center. Metropolitan Housing Development Corporation, which had planned a low-income multi-dwelling project in that location was denied permission, and brought suit, claiming that the restriction violated the Equal Protection Clause of the Fourteenth Amendment. The Supreme Court rejected the constitutional challenge on the ground that the restriction was neutral, despite effects correlated to race and socioeconomic status. It also declined to apply strict scrutiny, a test generally applied against challenged laws that target African Americans and other "suspect classifications." In doing so, the Court constructed a causation analysis that makes it particularly difficult to challenge similar neutral laws that bear a disproportionate adverse impact on persons of color. The Court stated in a famous footnote that even if the challenger is able to demonstrate that some chose the zoning policy in part based on racial exclusion, the Village could succeed in having the policy sustained if it could prove that absent that illicit intent, it would have enacted the policy on race-neutral grounds.[126]

In *San Antonio Independent School District v. Rodriguez*,[127] the Supreme Court separately upheld a complex scheme in Texas that allowed public school funding based on property-tax revenues derived from assessed property values. The policy included a state-implemented scheme to distribute proceeds from wealthier to less-well-off communities. Despite the offset, the overall scheme generated substantially greater per-pupil educational resources within well-off communities as compared with communities of lower socioeconomic status, again disproportionately affecting persons of color.

These cases are not atypical. More generally, assessed property values as the basis for tax-funded public largesse afford relatively wealthy neighborhoods the means to fund substantially higher quality public goods and services than is the case of lower income communities. This difference is apt to persist even when combined with some methods of redistribution, as shown in *Rodriguez*.

An alternative account of zoning laws and property-tax based provision of public goods is that such schemes allow wealthier communities to retain more of the benefit of their higher level property tax contributions. Two-acre lot zoning communities, for example, preserve a certain look and feel, one that the residents find highly attractive. At the same time, minimum lot size zoning allows those who reside in the high-value properties to retain more of the tax benefits within their own community, thereby inhibiting those who live nearby from receiving spillover benefits from the resources that the higher tax revenues provide.[128] This type of zoning is therefore sometimes referred to

---

[125] 429 U.S. 252 (1977).

[126] *Id.* at 270 n.21.

[127] 411 U.S. 1 (1973).

[128] *See* Tiebout, *supra* note 83; Bruce W. Hamilton, *Zoning and Property Taxation in a System of Local Government*, 12 URB. STUD. 205 (1975).

as *fiscal zoning*, as distinguished from *externality zoning*. Fiscal zoning makes it cost-prohibitive for low-income families to move in, once more with a disproportionate effect on communities of color, whereas externality zoning is designed to ensure that particular conflicting land uses do not undermine one another.

An alternative to zoning is land-use covenants. These are explicit limitations on what a landowner can do with her land. Historically, these practices have also been fraught with difficulty. Covenants have included racial and religious exclusions.[129] In *Shelley v. Kraemer*,[130] the Supreme Court struck down such covenants as violating the Fourteenth Amendment Equal Protection Clause in the context of the sale of a house to an African American family.

Today, we continue to see reliance on alternative covenants, not based on race or other prohibited categories, but rather in condominiums, housing co-ops, and homeowners' associations, typically as a means of supplementing background regulatory rules.[131] Some residential communities also rely on covenants, for example, to limit permissible paint colors; to require specific roofing materials, such as slate; and to impose specific requirements for lawn and yard maintenance. These sorts of land-use covenants are designed to avoid *neighborhood externalities* in settings where multiple households live in close proximity to one another, and where departing from certain home maintenance norms risks lowering the values of surrounding homes.[132] In this sense, such covenants resemble externality zoning, but they tend to be more fine-grained.

In general, these sorts of restrictions are appurtenant, meaning attached to the land, rather than belonging to the specific property owner. This lowers the transaction cost of ensuring that newcomers abide by the relevant terms, as they do not have to be renegotiated with each transfer of ownership. If they are efficiently designed, these restrictions increase the value of the property to which they are attached by minimizing the effects of externalities. The efficacy of covenants, however, is generally limited to small-scale externalities within a limited group of properties or over a small geographic area. Control of larger scale externalities more typically falls within the realm of nuisance law and public regulation.[133]

---

[129] Yi-Seng Kiang, *Judicial Enforcement of Restrictive Covenants in the United States*, 24 WASH. L. REV. & ST. B.J. 1, 4–5 (1949) (listing the wide variety of restrictive covenants that existed at the time, including those based on race, on religion, and on national origin).

[130] 334 U.S. 1 (1948). This case got around the problem that the Fourteenth Amendment bans "state action," rather than private conduct, by claiming that judicial enforcement of such covenants creates state action. One noted difficulty is that this is generally true of the judicial enforcement of any lawful private agreement. The Court has thus generally cabined this feature, limiting its force to the specific context of race. *See* Mark D. Rosen, *Was* Shelley v. Kraemer *Wrongly Decided? Some New Answers*, 95 CALIF. L. REV. 451, 458 (2007).

[131] Henry Hansmann, *Condominium and Cooperative Housing: Transactional Efficiency, Tax Subsidies, and Tenure Choice*, 20 J. LEGAL STUD. 25 (1991); Armand Arabian, *Condos, Cats, and CC&Rs: Invasion of the Castle Common*, 23 PEPP. L. REV. 1 (1996) (discussing covenants, conditions, and restrictions imposed by condominium developments); Robert Ellickson, *Cities and Homeowners Associations*, 130 U. PA. L. REV. 1519 (1982) (comparing the legal statuses of cities and homeowners associations).

[132] Roger E. Cannaday, *Condominium Covenants: Cats, Yes; Dogs, No*, 35 J. URB. ECON. 71 (1994).

[133] Ellickson, *supra* note 51. *See also infra* Chapter 8.

QUESTIONS AND COMMENTS

Zoning laws and restrictive covenants raise an important efficiency question. Assume a set of restrictions that does not implicate racial or socioeconomic considerations, but rather that imposes requirements on residents, some of whom find them outdated. For example, imagine a neighborhood once characterized by houses of a particular color or set of colors and slate roofs, and that also bans particular vehicles such as flatbed trucks or recreational trailers that are within the view of the street, as opposed to those that are housed in enclosed garages. Now imagine that a subset of families within the community finds these restrictions both dated and costly in the sense that it is substantially more expensive to maintain and replace aging slate than conventional shingles, and, in addition, many families enjoy trucks, many of which are high end and visually attractive, and these homeowners do not wish to store them separately as doing so adds cost and undermines their accessibility.

In a lawsuit to strike down these restrictions, who should prevail, the party seeking to avoid the restrictions, or the neighborhood association charged with enforcing them? Alternatively, should the association have the authority to grant variances at the request of specific homeowners? Why or why not?

Consider the following alternative analyses:

Version 1: By imposing a restriction on land use, the zoning laws reduce the subjective value, in the sense of enjoyment, of the homeowner's land. She might prefer a novel color, the more convenient use of her truck, and to save money by avoiding the maintenance of a costly roof that in her view is no more attractive than newer conventional materials. If the homeowner's association can grant exceptions that are generally attractive and that save homeowners cost and convenience, it can thereby improve social welfare. Failing to grant such variances undermines homeowner choice, reducing efficiency.

Version 2: Prospective homeowners face a menu of options when choosing communities in which to reside. Some have stringent zoning laws or other restrictions; others do not. The analysis is analogous to that of "take it or leave it" contracts in Chapters 5 and 6. The better understanding of efficiency in this context applies at the level of the community subject to applicable covenants, not at the level of the homeowner seeking to avoid them through individual variances. Homeowners associations should be required to enforce the literal terms of the restrictions, that is unless doing so violates the law, as for example in the case of once-discriminatory restrictive covenants.

Which of these two accounts better promotes social welfare? Why? Can you think of a way to test your intuition with empirical evidence?

B. Adverse Possession

Adverse possession is sometimes oxymoronically described as "legal theft" of land as it allows a person to claim full title to another person's land, without the need to pay for it, provided that the claimant occupies the land for a statutorily set period of time, generally fifteen-to-twenty years, and fulfills other specified requirements. These typically include the following: the *disseisor*, or the party seeking to dispossess the title holder, must be in *actual possession*; that possession must be *hostile* to that of the owner; it must be *open and notorious*; it must be *continuous* (without significant periods of disruption); and it must be *exclusive*, meaning not coextensive with the title holder.[134] Adverse possession operates, in effect, as a statute of limitations on the right of the titleholder to exclude a trespasser. This time-limited property rule allows the *disseisor* to force the titleholder to relinquish title in the event that she does not exercise her legal right to enforce the law of trespass in a timely manner.

We previously observed that the right to exclude is an important component in the bundle of property rights. As a result, the doctrine of adverse possession appears in tension with a basic tenet of property law. Some have defended the rule as preventing landowners from "sleeping on their rights," that is, from allowing their land to remain idle for a very lengthy period of time.[135] But notice that adverse possession does not require an owner to develop land. Indeed, it is often appropriate to avoid improvements, which can be irreversible, for extended periods. And sometimes, the option value in future development exceeds a property's present use value. Others defend the doctrine along with statutes of limitations more generally.[136] As time passes, evidence of title deteriorates, thereby making title costlier to establish. In the modern era of record keeping, this too seems a weak argument for expropriation without compensation.

A better economic argument for adverse possession returns to the prior discussion of the complexities of titling schemes and the related problem of uncertain ownership.[137] The underlying risk for current owners involves potential claims from previous owners who were wrongfully displaced. This risk inhibits the incentives for investing in optimal land improvements. One way to strengthen the current owner's rights, and thus to promote social-welfare-enhancing improvements, is to extinguish claims filed after a specified period of time. Notice that a shorter duration strengthens the current owner's rights. A statutory length of zero might therefore appear to provide the current owner with complete protection from the time of purchase going forward, which is effectively what land registration (the Torrens system) does.

The difficulty is that the preceding analysis views ownership only by looking backward. It asks what statutory length provides the *current possessor* with the maximum protection against past claims. We get a different answer, however, if we recognize that the current owner is himself subject to the risk of losing title in the future—whether to a squatter, boundary encroacher, or as a result of fraud or error—especially if he is an absentee landowner waiting for the optimal time to develop. From this forward-looking

---

[134] Some states also require the claimant to pay taxes on the land, or to show "color of title." For a discussion, see Richard A. Epstein, *Past and Future: The Temporal Dimension in the Law of Property*, 64 WASH. U. L.Q. 667 (1986); Robert C. Ellickson, *Adverse Possession and Perpetuities Law: Two Dents in the Libertarian Model of Property Rights*, 64 WASH. U. L.Q. 723 (1986); Thomas W. Merrill, *Property Rules, Liability Rules, and Adverse Possession*, 79 NW. U. L. REV. 1122 (1984–1985).

[135] *See* Merrill, *supra* note 134, at 1130–31; *but see* Henry W. Ballantine, *Title by Adverse Possession*, 32 HARV. L. REV. 135, 135 (1918).

[136] *See, e.g.*, Epstein, *supra* note 134, 677–80.

[137] *See* Jeffry Netter et al., *An Economic Analysis of Adverse Possession Statutes*, 6 INT'L REV. L. & ECON. 217 (1986); Thomas Miceli & C.F. Sirmans, *An Economic Theory of Adverse Possession*, 15 INT'L REV. L. & ECON. 161 (1995); Matthew Baker et al., *Property Rights by Squatting: Land Ownership Risk and Adverse Possession*, 77 LAND ECON. 360 (2001).

perspective, the current owner would like an unlimited length of time to be able to recognize an encroachment on his rights and have it corrected.

These combined, backward- and forward-looking perspectives, reveal an inevitable trade-off: the current owner as the potential *victim of a past claim* would like a zero duration statute, whereas the current owner as a potential *future claimant* himself would like an infinitely long duration statute. The optimal length balances these two considerations. Of course, there is no way to come up with a specific number, and actual lengths vary by state, although a period of fifteen-to-twenty years is fairly typical. The point is that the law has settled on such intermediate length to balance these competing intuitions.

C. Transfer of Property Through Inheritance

Inheritance law governs the transfer of wealth, including land, from one generation to the next. For the most part, the law enforces the expressed wishes of testators regarding how they desire to dispose of their wealth, but historically there have been some limitations. Here, we discuss two historical restrictions specifically pertaining to the inheritance of land, the first of which has been abandoned: *primogeniture* and the *rule against perpetuities*.

The rule of primogeniture prescribed that all lands must descend, most often, to the oldest son or male heir upon the owner's death. The traditional justification for this rule is that it prevented land from becoming excessively fragmented, a concern that was particularly acute in the context of an agricultural economy.[138] Prior to the American Revolution, southern colonies, which were predominantly agricultural, preserved the tradition, whereas the New England colonies largely rejected it.[139]

Although the preservation of scale economies might have been a good reason to interfere with the desires of testators, especially as land became scarce and given the high costs of reassembling fragmented parcels,[140] the question remains as to why the law did not allow the testator to bequeath all of his land to the "most deserving" heir, rather than to the eldest, and without regard to sex? There is no easy answer to these questions, but one possibility is that if we assume the need to preserve the entirety of the asset due to economies of scale, giving landowners discretion over the disposal of their land might create a wasteful rent-dissipation contest as siblings actively compete for the inheritance.[141] By contrast, a legal rule that pre-determines a single beneficiary, such as primogeniture, discourages such competition among potential heirs and also provides an

---

[138] Matthew Baker & Thomas Miceli, *Land Inheritance Rules: Theory and Cross-Cultural Analysis*, 56 J. ECON. BEHAV. & ORG. 77, 78, 97 (2005).

[139] LAWRENCE FRIEDMAN, A HISTORY OF AMERICAN LAW 66 (2d ed. 1985).

[140] For a discussion of the problem of fragmentation, see Heller, *supra* note 87 (describing the Tragedy of the Anti-Commons). *See also infra* Chapter 8 (discussing problem of land assembly in context of eminent domain).

[141] James Buchanan, *Rent Seeking, Noncompensated Transfers, and Laws of Succession*, 26 J.L. & ECON. 71 (1983); Baker & Miceli, *supra* note 138, at 78. For a stylized illustration of this problem motivated by King Lear, see *infra* Chapter 13, at 556–560.

incentive for all but the oldest male child to seek an alternative means of financial support.[142]

A second limitation on inheritance is the *Rule Against Perpetuities*, which asserts that no interest in land is valid unless it must vest within twenty-one years after the death of anyone alive at the time of creation of the interest.[143] Professor Jeffrey Stake notes that the purpose of the rule "is to prevent people from attempting to control ownership beyond the generation they know well, their children."[144] The rule is thus said to be a limitation on "dead hand" control of land. Parents can seek to impose limits on the actions of their children, but the rule limits their ability to exert control further into the future.

This partial limitation embodies a trade-off between the benefits of being able to impose constraints on heirs known to be spendthrifts, and the costs of limiting future (unknown) generations from being able to control their assets, often in response to unforeseen contingencies.[145] Once again, the law strikes a trade-off between competing economic intuitions.

Synopsis

In this chapter, we reviewed several essential features of property law. In the next chapter, we consider a variety of extended doctrines affecting property rights and transfers, some voluntary, others involuntary, and we offer a broader economic theory of the common law that integrates the three doctrinal areas covered thus far: tort, contract, and property.

IV. APPLICATIONS

1. Billy and Molly have gotten over that whole honeymoon fiasco, and they have finally settled into their bungalow, at #2208 Lovely Lane, Old City, New State. After a challenging first year of new jobs and in their new home, they decided to take a vacation. This time, they were a bit more savvy, relying on friends' recommendations and published reviews, and they settled on a two-week trip at a beach resort in Cancun, Mexico. Billy

---

[142] One need go no further than the *Book of Genesis* for confirmation that such schemes do not eliminate rent-dissipation games. *Genesis* 27:5–30 (describing successful scheme by Rebekah and Jacob to avoid having Esau receive his birthright based on primogeniture).

[143] Professor John Chipman Gray expressed the rule as follows: "No interest is good unless it must vest, if at all, not later than twenty-one years after some life in being at the creation of the interest." JOHN CHIPMAN GRAY, THE RULE AGAINST PERPETUITIES § 201 (4th ed. 1942). In the fourth edition, Gray states the above expression of the rule as well as the expression of the rule from the first edition of his treatise: "No interest subject to a condition precedent is good, unless the condition must be fulfilled, if at all, within twenty-one years after some life in being at the creation of the interest." Gray explains the first edition expression "to be correct if we assume that 'condition' includes not only all uncertain future acts and events but also all certain future events with the exception of the termination of preceding estates." Not making this assumption results in the fourth edition iteration of the rule. *Id.*

[144] Jeffrey Stake, *Inheritance Law*, *in* 2 THE NEW PALGRAVE DICTIONARY OF ECONOMICS AND THE LAW, *supra* note 75, at 311, 319.

[145] In Thomas J. Miceli & C. F. Sirmans, *Time-Limited Property Rights and Investment Incentives*, 31 J. REAL EST. FINANCE & ECON. 405 (2005), the authors formalize this trade-off based on a theoretical framework that unifies several legal doctrines involving time limits, including the Rule Against Perpetuities, patents, and adverse possession laws.

and Molly took their vacation during the first two weeks of July, 2017, and it turned out that the neighbors on each side of their home did as well.

Lovely Lane is a tree-lined residential street with similar bungalows on both sides of the street. If you are facing Billy and Molly's house, #2204 is on the left and #2212 is on the right. The houses numbered 2208 and 2212 are yellow, whereas #2204 is blue. The remaining houses on their side of the street, including #2200 and #2216, are all white. Well before Billy and Molly moved in, the street numbers, which are painted onto the curbs, had been fading on both sides of the street. The mail-delivery persons know the neighborhood well, as do most of the delivery workers, for example, from *FedEx* and *UPS*. Although there are occasional mishaps, these are uncommon and only a minor inconvenience.

Version 1: When Billy and Molly returned from their very enjoyable trip, they were stunned to see that their roof, which was in great need of replacement, was brand new! Their neighbors, Holly and Walter, who live in #2212, also returned from their two-week vacation from the Galapagos Islands, only to discover that somehow their neighbors seemed to have gotten their new roof. In the contract, Walter and Holly specified the proper street number, 2212 and stated that the house was yellow. Before contracting, Holly met with Shelly Shingle, owner of Shingle's Shingles, of the famous logo: *Our Shingles Don't Hurt!* Holly did not meet with Roger Roofer, the head of the installment team, but she did speak with him by telephone and mentioned that there are two neighboring yellow houses, that the numbers were not well marked, and that hers was easy to locate as it was next door to the white house numbered 2216. She didn't mention that the number for that house was also fading, and that although her roof needed replacement, the roof on #2208 looked even worse. The roof contract price was $6000. Assume that the new roof improves the value of Billy and Molly's home by $3000. Shingle's Shingles sues Billy and Molly for damages when they decline to pay for their new roof. Based on the economic theory of property law set out in Chapter 7, what should the rule governing this case be? Should Shingle's Shingles be allowed to recover damages and, if so, in what amount?

Version 2: Billy and Molly have a perfectly fine roof, and no one touches it during their vacation. When they return, however, they are stunned to see that the Great Oak in their back yard now has a beautiful tree house, the kind that they had only seen in magazines. They could not be more thrilled. Although they have no children yet, they do plan to start a family, and they had even talked about the possibility of constructing a tree house on that very tree, but they never imagined they would have one quite as fancy, with separate rooms, a built-in ladder, and even a pulley system to send up food and drinks. Holly and Walter also have a Great Oak, and they had contracted with Tommy's Tree Homes before they left, for $8000, intending this as a special present for their seven-year-old twin daughters, Betsy and Matilda, upon their return. Assume that the tree house improves the value of Billy and Molly's home by only $500 as it is classified as an "over-improvement on land," meaning an enjoyable improvement for those who did it, but one that will not be reflected by a corresponding change in the fair market value of the home given the overall nature of the community and land values. Further assume that Billy and Molly would not have built the tree house, but that they are delighted to have it. If Tommy's Tree Homes sues Billy and Molly demanding payment, applying the economic analysis of law, what should the outcome be and why?

Version 3: Assume that while Billy and Molly take their vacation, Holly and Walter stay home where they construct a set of chicken coops on the side of their property closest to Billy and Molly. Holly plans to set up a new business named *One Cluck Away*. A large sign, posted in front of the home, has a picture of a hen next to several eggs, and it reads: "Farm Fresh Eggs are Never More than One Click (or Make that One Cluck!) Away, at *hollyseggfarm.com*." Billy and Molly are distraught when they realize that they are constantly bombarded with the sounds and smells of hens on their adjoining property. Assume the following additional facts: Nothing prohibits raising hens or having a small business in this neighborhood, but general property law principles do apply. Several neighbors own small businesses that they run out of their homes. (As one example, Calvin, who lives in #2209, directly across the street, runs a highly successful business as a day trader and as the proprietor of a software program, Info Monitor.) Further assume that the clucking could be abated by relocating the coops to another available part of the property of Holly and Walter, and by putting up a sound barrier, at a total cost of $5000. Holly believes that she will be able to earn $10,000 per year as supplemental income with this business after an initial startup period of one year. If Molly and Billy sue Holly and Walter to stop the clucking, based on the economic theory of property law, what should the outcome be and why? Nuisance problem → not intruding on land of neighbor

Final questions: Based on your knowledge of property law, how, if at all, do your answers to these questions differ from property law doctrine, and if you answers are different, can you explain why the economic theory of property departs from the relevant doctrine?

2. Old City, New State has two different types of resident-owned high-rise units: condominiums and cooperatives. The basic difference is that in a condominium, the resident owns the actual unit in the form of a deeded property, whereas in the case of cooperatives, all of the residents own shares equal to the assessed value of their units in relation to that of the larger building. One of the benefits of the cooperative arrangement is that because the residents are effectively partners in a building complex, they can exert substantially greater control over sales of individual units (or technically transfers of shares with access and use rights in the units) than is the case with condominiums for which similar restrictions would risk violating laws prohibiting restrictive covenants based on protected classifications, including race, sexual orientation, and gender, among other categories.

Version 1: Awful Paul of the punk rock band *Crooked Dealers* wants to move into the prestigious cooperative, Old Town Views, where Marissa Marcus, a highly successful painter and the owner of the penthouse suite, has agreed to sell that suite to him at a stunning $15 million dollars, the highest price ever paid for a unit in the entire state. The other residents are less entertained by this idea, especially since the band has a raucous reputation and as Awful Paul, by all media accounts, is aptly named. The cooperative owners would prefer to avoid the paparazzi, the parties, the noise, and more generally, the attention. Pursuant to the cooperative rules, they vote to disallow the transfer based on a provision that allows a collective veto when the intended transfer would threaten to compromise the "lifestyle and enjoyable experience of other residents." Ms. Marcus is considering suing the Old Town Views Governance Board for infringing on her property rights. Based on the economic theory of property law, how should this dispute be resolved, and why? How would it be resolved based on your understanding of actual doctrine?

Version 2: An Old City ordinance prohibits restrictive covenants or other similar devices that could be used to avoid the more direct vehicles for discrimination based on race, sexual orientation, nationality, or gender, and that are loosely or vaguely worded so as to justify the exclusion of persons based on these criteria for other nominal reasons. Assume that Awful Paul is Hispanic, as are the other members of *Crooked Dealers*. How, if at all, does that change your answers to any of the questions in Version 1, and why?

3. Assume that a homeowner's association in Quiet Gardens, a residential community of one-story ranchers, includes the following provision:

At all times, residences must maintain lawns at a height no greater than 1 1/4–1 1/2 inches, and must remove snow along walkways and driveways within 24 hours of the end of the snowfall. All houses must be maintained with slate roofs with no more than 5 visibly chipped pieces of slate, and no house may be painted with colors that are not on the approved list (provided in a separate document). No additional structures beside the house, garage, and a single shed with dimensions satisfying the conditions of approval (also listed in a separate document) are permitted. No vehicles may be kept in the street parking or in the garages other than sedan vehicles or sports utility vehicles. No trucks of any kind are permitted.

Version 1: In 2005, Fred and Melinda purchased a home in Quiet Gardens. Fred is the owner and manager of a Ford Dealership, Fred's Ford, and he drives a 2015 Ford F150, a truck, which is perfectly maintained, and which allows him to bring supplies such as car parts, maintenance equipment, and the like, from various businesses to his dealership. The dealership is a thirty-minute drive from his new home, and many of his suppliers are in the opposite direction, making it especially burdensome to go to the dealership initially and then to leave from there to go to his suppliers. Assume that in 1950 when the community was built, many trucks were unattractive, unlike Fred's well-kept F150. Even so, the homeowner's association has sent Fred a letter informing him that he can no longer park his truck at his home, even in his garage. Under the economic analysis of property law, what is the preferred result and why? Based on your knowledge of property doctrine, how would this be resolved? If your answers differ, can you explain why?

Version 2: Fred drives a specially equipped vehicle that is also off the permissible vehicle list, one that allows his wife, who uses a wheelchair, to gain access with a platform.[146] In addition, he has installed a ramp to the home, which further violates the terms of residency. The homeowner's association informs Fred that he has thirty days to remove the ramp and that he cannot park his special vehicle on the property. Under the economic analysis of property law, what is the preferred result and why? Based on your knowledge of property doctrine, how would this be resolved? If your answers differ, can you explain why?

4. There is an extreme shortage of kidneys for transplant in the United States. You cannot sell a kidney in the United States or enter into a binding contract to exchange one, but you can donate one. In addition, when individuals elect to be organ donors, their donations often do not occur because most hospitals give the surviving family members

---

[146] For this question assume that the *Americans with Disabilities Act*, 42 U.S.C. § 12101 *et seq.* (2012), does not apply.

rights of refusal (which are frequently exercised). One way to view this is that the law disallows individuals one of the rights in the bundle with respect to their own body parts, namely the right to transfer ownership. Does the economic analysis of property rights help to inform whether organ sales should be allowed, and why or why not?

5. Along with most legal systems, ours allows, and even encourages, intergenerational wealth transfers. This can inhibit productive incentives by those who inherit considerable wealth, thus facilitating the accumulation of wealth within families, also known as "dynastic wealth." This produces much-criticized anomalies, some of which have gained political attention, including the very high percentage of wealth owned by a tiny percentage of the population. Does the economic analysis of property rights, or economic analysis more generally, help to inform the analysis of this policy, and if so how?

CHAPTER 8

Property Law (Part 2)

Introduction

In this chapter, we continue our survey of the essential doctrines of property law by covering eminent domain and regulatory takings, two important forms of involuntary transfer of property rights. We then offer a synopsis of the various themes that have emerged over the previous chapters based on a broader theory of law and markets. The analysis helps to integrate the economic analysis of the doctrines of tort, contract, and property, thus completing this part of the course book on the economic analysis of the common law.

I. EMINENT DOMAIN

The government's power of eminent domain is authorized by the Takings Clause of the Fifth Amendment, which says, "nor shall private property be taken for public use, without just compensation."[1] The terms of the clause express two limitations on government takings: first, the acquired land must be put to *public use*, and second, the owner must be paid *just compensation*.

Although private citizens cannot generally coerce transactions in land, even if they claim a higher value, eminent domain vests such power in the government. Expressed in terms of the Cathedral,[2] we can draw the following distinction: Private owners of land generally have a property interest protected by a property right as against other *individuals* who claim a higher value in their land.[3] By contrast, the same owners have a property interest protected by only by a liability rule as against the government, provided the conditions for a taking are met. So individuals must negotiate the purchase of others' private lands, but the government can coerce the transaction. The question is why?[4] We

---

1 U.S. CONST. amend. V.

2 Guido Calabresi & A. Douglas Melamed, *Property Rules, Liability Rules, and Inalienability: One View of the Cathedral*, 85 HARV. L. REV. 1089 (1972).

3 As we have seen, some forms of easement and the doctrine of adverse possession are exceptions to this general rule. *See supra* Chapter 7.

4 Some readers might object that *Kelo v. City of New London*, 545 U.S. 469 (2005), effectively allowed a private developer to "take" private property. We discuss *Kelo*, *infra* Part I.A.3. For now, suffice to say that the formal mechanism through which the Supreme Court permitted the acquisition of Mrs. Kelo's property to occur was nonetheless through a governmental taking.

explore this question in the course of discussing the two principal restrictions on takings: (1) public use, and (2) just compensation.

A. Public Use

Typically, eminent domain is used for such public purposes as highways, airports, schools, or parks. Although there are exceptional cases, as a general matter, the requirement that the acquired land be put to a public use is typically met. The controversial cases relating to public use in modern times usually involve economic development plans that are largely private, but that proponents anticipate will enhance the value, and thus the tax basis, of the affected property.[5] Not surprisingly, such cases sometimes result in litigation. A recent high profile example is the case of *Kelo v. City of New London*,[6] which we discuss below. In this subpart, we develop an economic analysis of the public use requirement, which will lay a foundation for that later analysis.

In an important economic analysis of eminent domain, Professor Thomas Merrill distinguished the *means* and the *ends* with respect to a government-sponsored project.[7] The *means* concern the manner of acquisition, whereas the *ends* concern the intended use of the acquired land. A literal interpretation of *public use* implies that the ends analysis predominates and that takings are permissible only if the eventual goal is to convert the acquired land to some form of public good, including those previously identified.[8] In fact, however, because of its coercive qualities, eminent domain litigation has often focused on the means through which land is taken.

An economic perspective on the means-ends distinction turns on the nature of two potential sources of market failure: the free-rider problem associated with the provision of public goods, and the holdout problem associated with assembling lands needed to provide the public goods.[9]

1. *The Free-Rider Problem*

As previously explained, public goods have two defining characteristics: first, once they are provided, it is impractical to exclude others from their benefits; and second, the consumption by some does not diminish the ongoing value of those goods to others.[10] As a result, the benefits of public goods cannot be denied to those who have failed to contribute to the cost of their procurement. This is the classic *free-rider problem*. Examples of public goods include national defense, criminal law enforcement, and public roads, coupled with rules, markers, and equipment designed to promote traffic safety.[11] The free-

---

[5] Historical instances in which eminent domain was used to further largely private enterprises concerned the construction of railroads in the nineteenth century, as we will note below, see, e.g., *infra* Part I.A.3.

[6] 545 U.S. 469 (2005).

[7] Thomas W. Merrill, *Economics of Public Use*, 72 CORNELL L. REV. 61 (1986).

[8] *See supra* Chapter 1; *supra* at 18–19 (identifying public goods associated with takings).

[9] For a more detailed introduction to free riding and holdouts, see *infra* Chapter 11.

[10] *See supra* Chapter 2 at p. 67, note 48 (citing Paul Samuelson presentation).

[11] Economists historically included lighthouses as an illustration, that is, until Ronald Coase's trenchant analysis, R.H. Coase, *The Lighthouse in Economics*, 17 J.L. & ECON. 357 (1974), which demonstrated that lighthouses were funded through licensing contracts. More generally, Coase's historical analysis of lighthouse

rider problem makes it difficult, perhaps impossible, for profit-maximizing firms to recover the cost of public goods, and as a result, private markets tend to undersupply them. For this reason, some economists have argued that the government should take over the provision of public goods, or at least subsidize them to ensure that the efficient quantity is supplied.[12] To overcome the free-rider problem, the government can use its coercive power of taxation to compel consumers to contribute to the cost of provision.[13] In this way, a *forced purchase* of public goods has the potential to compensate for the undersupply of such goods within private markets.[14]

It is important to recognize, however, that this solution to the public-goods problem is necessarily imperfect, or second best. The government can never exactly replicate a hypothetical efficient market outcome, due to the absence of a pricing mechanism. Only pricing provides a means of fully assessing the relative marginal valuations of costs and benefits to each individual. Moreover, value is inherently subjective in that each person differently internalizes that costs and benefits of goods and services, including those that the government provides.[15] With respect to private market exchanges the problem of determining whether an individual values a good or service is ameliorated by the principle of *revealed preferences*, meaning by signaling value through voluntary market exchange. Because the government lacks information on subjective values, it cannot precisely match tax payments to individual benefits, which would allow for tax-based price discrimination, thereby better matching payments with beneficiaries.[16] How much a given person pays in practice depends on the nature of the tax, whether based on income, property value, or sales. These revenue-generating measures typically bear little, if any, relationship to the benefits that the person receives from the public good. Inevitably some individuals will overpay and others will underpay if we assume as a benchmark their subjective valuations.

2. The Holdout Problem

Most large-scale development projects, whether public or private, require the assembly of separate tracts of land. This is especially true in urban areas where land ownership tends to be fragmented and few, if any, large undeveloped swaths of land

provisions suggests that simply because a particular service appears to have some properties of a public good does not necessarily mean that the good or service will be undersupplied by private action.

[12] For an argument that the logic of public goods does not compel public provision, but only that the government facilitates their provision through some means, including enhancing private market mechanisms, see John Hasnas, *Reflections on the Minimal State*, 2 POL., PHIL. & ECON. 115 (2003). Of course, as a result of the collective action problem in motivating governmental action, see *infra* Chapter 11, facilitating private procurement of public goods can itself be understood as the government provision of a public good.

[13] For an analysis demonstrating the fundamental public choice dilemma that lobbying for the provision of public goods possesses public goods qualities, see *infra* Chapter 11.

[14] For a discussion of the obverse problem of forced riding, here meaning the forced contribution to public goods or services for which some do not perceive a benefit, see *supra* Chapter 1.

[15] It is important to distinguish subjective valuation, which is individual, from willingness to pay, which is influenced by external market functions, and thus implicates opportunity cost. By way of example, an individual who holds a higher subjective valuation of a commodity than is reflected in the market price will still be willing to pay only the market price.

[16] In theory, sophisticated demand-revealing tax schemes can be designed to better match tax payments and benefits, but they are generally impractical. *See* ANTHONY B. ATKINSON & JOSEPH E. STIGLITZ, LECTURES ON PUBLIC ECONOMICS 482–518 (1980).

remain. The problem that land assemblers face is that once the planned assembly becomes public knowledge, individual owners realize that they can impose substantial costs on the buyer by refusing to sell.[17] The reason is that the project usually cannot go forward until all or most of the land is acquired, and so each seller holds a kind of monopoly power that she can exercise by holding out for prices well in excess of prior fair market value or even her prior subjective valuation.[18] The source of the problem is technological in the sense that, in general, each parcel is essential to the completion of the overall project.[19]

The underlying dynamic returns us to the problem of appropriable quasi rents. The problem in land assembly is conceptually analogous to that which the railroad would have faced had it been required to separately obtain the permission of all farmers abutting its tracks before running any trains, or that the factory owner in *Boomer* would have faced had the court issued an injunction requiring him to negotiate with each individual neighbor to avoid being shut down. Each of those situations requires the "assembly" of separate property rights as a precondition to facilitating a more highly valued economic activity.

The prior analysis, however, revealed that these problems can generally be avoided with the use of a liability rule, which results in a *forced sale* that transfers the rights to the more highly valued user. This also applies here. Substituting protection in the form of a liability rule via eminent domain, rather than a property right, avoids the holdout game and thus facilitates the necessary transfer of rights consistent with the property's more highly valued use. With the power of eminent domain, owners have no choice but to sell at a price set by the court, typically fair market value, thereby allowing the assembly of parcels, and the project, to proceed.

3. An Economic Theory of Public Use

Free riders and the holdout problem are distinct sources of market failure with different solutions. Free riding is an impediment to the provision of public goods, and can be avoided with forced funding through taxation. Holdouts arise in the context of land assembly and are avoided by forced sales through eminent domain. However, neither free riders nor holdouts are necessarily interdependent. Together these phenomena produce four theoretical combinations, depicted in Table 8:1.[20]

---

[17] For a discussion of how the Walt Disney Company assembled contiguous parcels with straw purchasers, see *infra* Chapter 11.

[18] There is a large literature on this problem. *See, e.g.*, Lloyd Cohen, *Holdouts and Free Riders*, 20 J. LEGAL STUD. 351 (1991); Michael A. Heller, *The Tragedy of the Anticommons: Property in Transition from Marx to Markets*, 111 HARV. L. REV. 621 (1998); Thomas Miceli & Kathleen Segerson, *Land Assembly and the Holdout Problem Under Sequential Bargaining*, 14 AM. L. & ECON. REV. 372 (2012).

[19] For a discussion that assesses the implications of this problem and how it has the potential to transform a holdout game into a chicken game, see *infra* Chapter 16.

[20] *See* THOMAS J. MICELI, THE ECONOMIC THEORY OF EMINENT DOMAIN 33 (2011).

Table 8:1. Sources of Market Failure and Corresponding Remedies Implied by Means-Ends Analysis

	No Free Riding	Free Riding
No Holdout	**Case 1:** **No Tax; No Eminent Domain** General private transactions with limited need for government intervention **Solution:** Leave to market in the absence of market failure	**Case 2:** **Tax; No Eminent Domain** **Problem:** Insufficient public goods, but not land-based **Solution:** Taxation and public provision, but without eminent domain
Holdout	**Case 3:** **No Tax; Eminent Domain** **Problem:** Land assembly to facilitate the creation of a land-based project with public purpose **Solution:** Reliance on eminent domain to avoid holdout game	**Case 4:** **Tax; Eminent Domain** **Problem:** Insufficient public goods and land assembly required to provide them **Solution:** Governmental intervention through combined taxation and eminent domain

In *Case 1*, depicted in the upper left quadrant, neither a free-rider nor a holdout problem is present, so there is no need to use coercive taxation to compel purchases or to use eminent domain to force sales. This characterizes most transactions in which market exchange is conducive to a social-welfare-enhancing outcome.

The opposite extreme is *Case 4*, depicted in the lower right quadrant, where there is both a free-rider and a holdout problem. This often characterizes large-scale public goods like highways and airports where eminent domain is needed to assemble the necessary land, and taxation is needed as the source of funding. In this situation, public purpose is not controversial because both the means and ends push toward justifiable reliance on eminent domain.[21]

In *Case 2*, depicted in the upper right quadrant, there is a free-rider problem but no holdout problem. Here, it is appropriate for the government to provide the good in question and to fund it with taxation. However, there is no need for it to rely on eminent

[21] Thomas S. Ulen, *The Public Use of Private Property: A Dual-Constraint Theory of Efficient Governmental Takings*, *in* TAKING PROPERTY AND JUST COMPENSATION 163, 165 (Nicholas Mercuro ed., 1992) (arguing that the "dual constraint" in the takings doctrine of (1) just compensation, and (2) public use, improves the efficiency of eminent domain).

domain as the provision does not require the assembly of separate parcels of land. If some land is required to facilitate the provision of the public good, the government should then be required to purchase it, along with any other required inputs, in a market transaction. An example is a local government's provision of police and supporting requirements for public safety, a public good within the jurisdiction. The government can use taxation to compel residents to contribute to the cost of maintaining a police force, but it would not be justifiable for it to use its eminent domain powers to conscript police officers, obtain a fleet of cars, or to gather other necessary inputs.[22] Although the government might be tempted to bypass the market based on the logic of the ends approach to public use, Professor Thomas Merrill and Professor William Fischel have argued that the risk of such misuse of eminent domain is limited.[23] Litigation and other transaction costs will generally more than offset the savings of bypassing the market in cases that fit the dynamic of *Case 2*.

That leaves *Case 3*, in the lower left quadrant, in which there is no free-rider problem, but there is a holdout problem. This is the situation in most so-called *private takings* cases where a land developer, possibly acting under the auspices of a governmental agency, has to assemble land for a large-scale development project. Eminent domain is justified in this case by the means approach to overcome holdouts. Historically, courts have tended to act in accordance with this logic, for example by allowing railroad, canal, and water-powered mill builders the right to use eminent domain. Professor Merrill has observed that in authorizing the use of eminent domain, however, courts have generally tried to justify their actions in terms of the ends approach.[24] Specifically, courts have sought to find the public benefits that would flow from the project rather than justifying the takings on holdout grounds.

This judicial approach to public use is epitomized by *Kelo v. City of New London*,[25] which concerned a proposed use of eminent domain by the City of New London, Connecticut for a large-scale urban redevelopment project.[26] The plaintiffs in the case claimed that the public use requirement was not satisfied because the bulk of the land was to be used for private development, including a significant portion turned over to a large pharmaceutical company for the construction of a research facility. In a controversial five-to-four decision, the U.S. Supreme Court nevertheless upheld the use of eminent domain. Using language reflective of the ends approach, the Court noted that:

> The City has carefully formulated an economic development plan that it believes will provide appreciable benefits to the community, including—but by no means limited to—new jobs and increased tax revenue. . . . Because that

---

[22] ROBERT COOTER, THE STRATEGIC CONSTITUTION 289 (2000).

[23] Merrill, *supra* note 7; WILLIAM A. FISCHEL, REGULATORY TAKINGS: LAW, ECONOMICS, AND POLITICS 74 (1995).

[24] Merrill, *supra* note 7, at 67.

[25] 545 U.S. 469 (2005).

[26] In Chapter 16, we revisit this case based upon two sets of competing intuitions, a holdout game and a game of chicken.

> plan unquestionably serves a public purpose, the takings challenged here satisfy the public use requirement of the Fifth Amendment.[27]

The dissenting Justices objected to the forcible transfer of land from one private party to another, claiming that the majority analysis permits what is essentially private benefit "so long as the new use is predicted to generate some secondary benefit to the public—such as increased tax revenue, more jobs, maybe even esthetic pleasure."[28]

Prior to *Kelo,* precedents on the use of eminent domain for private development had been mixed. In *Berman v. Parker*,[29] the Supreme Court allowed the taking of a department store that was not blighted as part of a comprehensive development scheme in the District of Columbia, pursuant to a congressional act, to eliminate urban blight and to promote urban development. Justice Douglas, writing for a majority, reasoned that the planning commission charged with the urban development had determined the need for a more comprehensive approach, stating:

> If owner after owner were permitted to resist these redevelopment programs on the ground that his particular property was not being used against the public interest, integrated plans for redevelopment would suffer greatly. The argument pressed on us is, indeed, a plea to substitute the landowner's standard of the public need for the standard prescribed by Congress. But as we have already stated, community redevelopment programs need not, by force of the Constitution, be on a piecemeal basis—lot by lot, building by building.[30]

Until *Kelo*, the most well-known development takings case was issued by the Michigan Supreme Court. In the 1981 decision, *Poletown Neighborhood Council v. City of Detroit*,[31] the Michigan Supreme Court sustained a development taking that condemned an entire neighborhood to allow the creation of a General Motors plant, with the hope that it would bring new jobs and economic growth. In *County of Wayne v. Hathcock*,[32] decided in 2004, however, the Michigan Supreme Court disallowed eminent domain in Wayne County Michigan to create a 1300-acre business and technology park, and in so doing, overturned *Poletown*. Although the Michigan cases were decided based on the state constitution, the principles are the same, and both state and federal courts routinely cite each other's cases in this area.

The analytical problem that these cases highlight is that virtually any successful large-scale development project will produce some spillover benefits to the public in the form of jobs and enhanced tax revenues. As Professor Matthew Parlow has observed, relying on these secondary benefits to satisfy the Fifth Amendment (or state-counterpart) public-purpose requirement encourages budget-constrained local governments to join with

---

[27] *Kelo*, 545 U.S. at 483–84.

[28] *Id.* at 501 (O'Connor, J., dissenting).

[29] 348 U.S. 26 (1954).

[30] *Id.* at 35.

[31] 304 N.W.2d 455 (Mich. 1981).

[32] 684 N.W.2d 765 (Mich. 2004).

developers who seek to acquire and redevelop "underperforming" properties as a means of improving tax revenues.[33]

One response to this doctrinal analysis, which focuses on the meaning of public purpose, is that the underlying economic justification for eminent domain is the problem of holdouts. Although this might be true descriptively, judges appear disinclined to rest takings cases on this basis as a result of the text of the Takings Clause itself. The Fifth Amendment does not express itself in terms of structural impediments to transacting. Despite this, given the enormous financial stakes associated with large-scale economic development, some jurists have implicitly taken this approach.

Consider the following justification for allowing the use of eminent domain in a state takings case concerning the right of mine operators to build access roads:

> Now while it may be admitted that hotels, theaters, stage coaches, and city hacks, are a benefit to the public, it does not, by any means, necessarily follow that the right of eminent domain can be exercised in their favor. The truth is, that there is a wide distinction between railroads and hotels, and, also, between the business of mining and that of conducting theaters. A railroad, to be successfully operated, must be constructed upon the most feasible route; it cannot run around the land of every individual who refuses to dispose of his property upon reasonable terms. In such cases the law interferes, and takes the private property of the citizen upon payment of just compensation.[34]

This analysis fairly clearly rests on a holdout rationale. Similarly, Justice Douglas, writing in *Berman*, expressed the concern that if "owner after owner . . . resist[s] these redevelopment programs on the ground that his particular property was not being used against the public interest, integrated plans for redevelopment would suffer greatly."[35] At least implicitly, this too rests on the concern for holdouts.

Private-development takings cases are also analogous to the occasional forced sales in non-takings settings. As we have seen, property doctrine sometimes permits what amounts to private takings when it imposes a liability rule, rather than a property rule, as the remedy for an external harm. By awarding damages, rather than injunctive relief, the *Boomer* court, for example, effectively conveyed the equivalent of eminent domain power to the factory against the competing claim of the neighboring plaintiffs.[36] As with eminent domain, the ruling was most easily justified in terms of the holdout problem inevitably confronting the factory had it been required to negotiate with all affected parties following an injunction.

Also recall the contract case *Peevyhouse v. Garland Coal & Mining Co.*[37] The *Peevyhouse* court permitted the functional equivalent of a private taking by awarding damages rather than an injunction that would have compelled the mining company to restore the land to

---

33 Matthew J. Parlow, *Unintended Consequences: Eminent Domain and Affordable Housing*, 46 SANTA CLARA L. REV. 841 (2006).

34 Dayton Gold & Silver Mining Co. v. Seawell, 11 Nev. 394, 411 (1876).

35 348 U.S. 26, 35 (1954).

36 FISCHEL, *supra* note 23, at 76; Victor P. Goldberg, *Relational Exchange, Contract Law and the* Boomer *Problem*, 141 J. INSTITUTIONAL & THEORETICAL ECON. 570 (1985).

37 382 P.2d 109 (Okla. 1962).

its pre-mining condition. We suggested that the damages ruling was problematic inasmuch as it disallowed the homeowner the benefit of his subjective valuation associated with having the property restored. Injunctive relief, in the form of specific performance (a property rule) would have forced the mining company to bargain with the promisee for an acceptable buy-out price. On the other hand, this form of relief might have allowed the landowner to compel a far greater payment than even the subjective valuation of the restored property, albeit with the payment capped at the full restoration cost. One difficulty is that it is simply impossible to know how sincere a homeowner is in expressing subjective valuation in such circumstances, which is why courts rely on market value compensation, as discussed below.

QUESTIONS AND COMMENTS

The explanation for the court's reliance on the ends approach to justify private takings no doubt reflects the Fifth Amendment's wording. Of course that constraint does not apply in the context of common law nuisance or the selection of damages rules in various contract law settings; and certainly the language matters. Holdouts can arise in any number of settings, including those that do, and that do not, obviously justify a taking.

Assume, for example, a residential neighborhood with quarter-acre residential lots and homes selling for a quarter of a million dollars, all with convenient access to a highway or an alternative route producing, in general, a twenty-five-minute commute to a major city. Now imagine a developer identifies this as an attractive neighborhood for an alternative development that mixes higher end homes on half-acre lots with townhouses and condominiums. Assume further that the lot value for the development exceeds the fair market value of the homes, but that due to a holdout, the developer anticipates that the separate bargains will not work. Some owners might insist on several million dollars for their lots, without which the project is thwarted. This presents a classic holdout game, and it has been played out in several real-world settings.

In the chapter on game theory, we will see illustrations that include the successful effort by the Walt Disney Company to acquire land for the development of its Florida theme park. Certainly that too was subject to holdouts, but Disney did not benefit from eminent domain. Instead it relied on straw purchasers who negotiated separately with homeowners for undisclosed principals. This thwarted attempts to hold out, but undoubtedly misled the sellers.

Does the public purpose doctrine help to explain when holdouts do or do not justify exercising takings power? Must the holdout be coupled with something else, making the holdout itself a necessary, but insufficient, condition? If so, what is that something else? Is economic analysis helpful in answering this question? Why or why not? We will revisit these questions, along with *Kelo*, in Chapter 16.

B. Just Compensation

1. *Just Compensation Equals Fair Market Value*

The second requirement for the use of eminent domain is that the landowner must receive *just compensation*. No specific guidance is offered as to what exactly that means. One could argue that a taking should replicate, to the extent possible, a market exchange, and compensation should therefore reflect an estimate of what the price for the land would have been in a consensual transaction. This returns us to the discussion of the "for sale" sign in Chapter 7. Recall the intuition that a "for sale" sign does not actually signal what it literally says: All houses are always for sale, but only at the right price. The absence of the sign signals that the owner presently values it more highly than fair market value, making a consensual transaction on mutually agreeable terms unlikely.

In his classic work on takings, Professor Richard Epstein suggested an alternative possibility, arguing the amount of compensation should "leave the individual owner in a position of indifference between the taking by the government and retention of the property."[38] We have already seen one difficulty with this approach: although it would ensure the owner her subjective valuation, it would also create opportunities for appropriable quasi rents and for holdouts in cases where the buyer has to acquire contiguous properties to effectuate the development scheme. In effect, Epstein's proposal would be like placing a "for sale" sign in front of everyone's house, but to make all prospective buyers aware that price always corresponds to seller's subjective valuation. As applied to eminent domain, this would give each seller protection of her land as against the government unless the price paid is equivalent to a fully voluntary arms-length transaction. Of course, the government can negotiate such transactions without the power of eminent domain, but this approach would not provide a tool to overcome holdouts.

In practice, these two definitions of just compensation—fair market value and full valuation—are compatible if the owner has no subjective value. Professor Merrill has described this as follows:

> [Market value compensation] awards the condemnee what he would obtain in an arm's length transaction with a third party, but [it] does not compensate him for the subjective "premium" he might attach to his property above its opportunity cost. In some cases, such as those involving undeveloped land, there may be no subjective premium. But in other cases, the premium may be quite large. . . .[39]

Professor Ellickson observes that subjective value is likely to be especially high for family homes, and its magnitude will be positively related to the duration of residence.[40]

The problem of subjective value in eminent domain situations is not merely one of undercompensating landowners. Because market-value compensation under eminent domain systematically undercompensates landowners as compared with what they would willingly accept in a consensual transaction, it potentially leads to excessive transfer of

---

[38] RICHARD A. EPSTEIN, TAKINGS: PRIVATE PROPERTY AND THE POWER OF EMINENT DOMAIN 182 (1985).

[39] Merrill, *supra* note 7, at 83.

[40] Robert C. Ellickson, *Alternatives to Zoning: Covenants, Nuisance Rules, and Fines as Land Use Controls*, 40 U. CHI. L. REV. 681, 736 (1973). Several explanations associated with behavioral economics have been offered for the source of subjective value. These include the "endowment effect" and the "offer-ask" disparity. Economists universally accept subjective value as a legitimate method of assessing economic value, at least in some circumstances. *See* FISCHEL, *supra* note 23; Herbert Hovenkamp, *Legal Policy and the Endowment Effect*, 20 J. LEGAL STUD. 225 (1991); Jack L. Knetsch & Thomas E. Borcherding, *Expropriation of Private Property and the Basis for Compensation*, 29 U. TORONTO L.J. 237 (1979).

land to the government.[41] The point is illustrated in Figure 8:1, where the downward sloping *MB* curve represents the marginal benefit of land in public use, while the horizontal *MC* curve represents the actual value of the land to the current owners, including any subjective value.[42]

The efficient transfer of land to the government is determined by the intersection of these curves, and is labeled q^* in the graph. The market value of the land, labeled *MV*, is drawn below the *MC* curve for all landowners, reflecting a positive subjective value. If the government makes its taking decision by comparing the value of the land in public use to the compensation it has to pay, then it will acquire q' parcels, which exceeds the efficient level. Thus, based upon subjective valuation, too much land will be taken.

There is, however, a possible offsetting effect that helps justify setting compensation below the true subjective value of the land. That has to do with the spillover benefits that accompany any large-scale economic development. If a highway or railroad is built, properties along the route (but not too close) will increase in value, and existing businesses will likewise benefit from a government-sponsored urban redevelopment project.

Although these external benefits should be captured by the *MB* curve in Figure 8:1, in practice they might not be, in which case q^* is artificially low.[43] Suppose, for example, that the true social marginal benefit is represented by the dashed curve labeled MB_S. In this case, the efficient amount of land to be acquired occurs at the intersection of MB_S and *MC*, which in the example shown is closely approximated by the actual amount of land actually taken under market-value compensation. The reason is that the undercompensation serves as an implicit subsidy that offsets the spillover benefits from the project.

There are two important caveats to this analysis: First, there is no guarantee that the amount of the undercompensation will correspond to the spillover benefits from a given project. The graph suggests that they are roughly equal, but nothing ensures that as a general result.[44] Second, the cost of the implicit subsidy falls entirely on owners whose land is taken, rather than on the beneficiaries of the spillover benefits who ideally would bear a fair share of the financial burden. In effect, this normative justification rests on Kaldor-Hicks, rather than Pareto, efficiency, meaning that the winners win more than the losers, whose property is taken, lose.

---

41 D. Bruce Johnson, *Planning Without Prices: A Discussion of Land Use Regulation Without Compensation*, *in* PLANNING WITHOUT PRICES 63, 65 (Bernard H. Siegan ed., 1977).

42 For ease of presentation, we assume all owners hold the same subjective value.

43 For example, Professor Daryl Levinson asks why we should assume that the government internalizes the social benefits of public projects. Daryl J. Levinson, *Making Government Pay: Markets, Politics, and the Allocation of Constitutional Costs*, 67 U. CHI. L. REV. 345 (2000). Even if governments do internalize the benefits within their jurisdictions, some benefits may spill across jurisdictional boundaries, especially for municipal takings.

44 In an interesting historical effort at a more targeted subsidy, state courts in the early nineteenth century sought to promote railroad construction by use of the *benefit-offset principle*. Under this doctrine, if only a portion of a person's land was taken by eminent domain, the amount of compensation paid for that portion could be reduced by any increase in the value of the untaken portion resulting from its proximity to the railroad. William Fischel notes that despite the sound economic logic, the result nonetheless operated to the detriment of those subject to a partial taking given that others whose land was not taken received the same positive externality without the forced subsidy. FISCHEL, *supra* note 23, at 80–84 (citing Harry N. Scheiber, *The Road to* Munn*: Eminent Domain and the Concept of Public Purpose in the State Courts*, 5 PERSPS. AM. HIST. 327 (1971)).

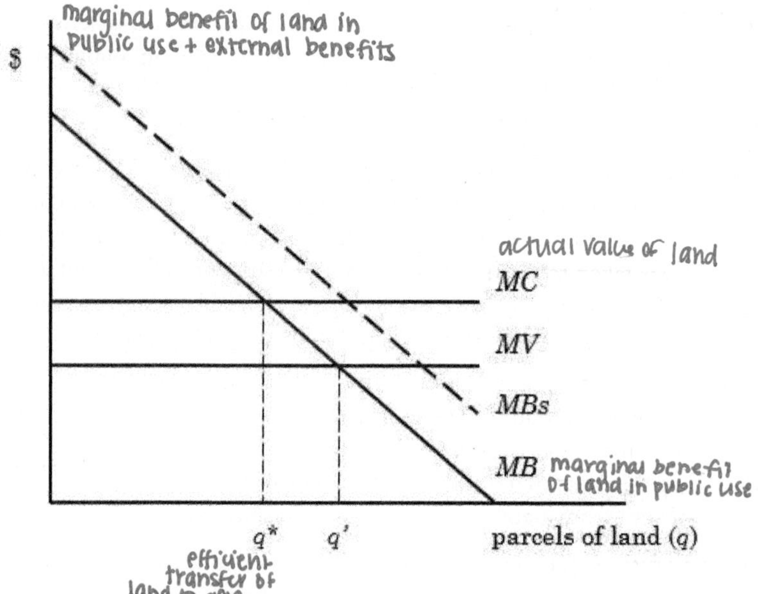

Figure 8:1. Impact of market-value compensation on the taking of land.

2. Compensation as Insurance

Thus far we have considered two questions: (1) does just compensation leave owners indifferent as between a taking and no taking? and (2) does just compensation provide the government with incentives for the efficient acquisition of land? The answer is no to both, under market-value compensation. In this section, we consider an alternative rationale for just compensation, namely insuring landowners against the risk of a taking. Lawrence Blume and Daniel Rubinfeld argue that because most people are risk averse, they suffer disutility from the prospect of not being compensated for a random decline in their wealth, for example, due to an accident, a fire, or an unanticipated government taking.[45] Risk aversion is the reason that people buy insurance against accidents and fires, and therefore, according to this argument, why the government should pay them just compensation for takings.

This rationale, however, raises the question of why the government needs to be the insurer. Blume and Rubinfeld claim that private insurance against takings risk is not generally available because it is sufficiently rare that insurance companies would have difficulty properly calculating an actuarially fair premium. Of course it is also possible that the absence of government compensation might spur such a market. Professor Louis Kaplow argues that insurance against takings could potentially create a moral hazard problem regarding land-use decisions.[46] An offsetting factor is that if the government is the primary insurer, it might strategically alter its taking decisions to favor uninsured parcels, or it might refuse to insure parcels that it plans to take. Blume and Rubinfeld argue that to avoid these problems, government insurance against takings must be

---

[45] Lawrence Blume & Daniel L. Rubinfeld, *Compensation for Takings: An Economic Analysis*, 72 CALIF. L. REV. 569 (1984).

[46] Louis Kaplow, *An Economic Analysis of Legal Transitions*, 99 HARV. L. REV. 509 (1986).

mandatory, a result accomplished by the Fifth Amendment requirement of just compensation.

In a highly influential article on takings law, Professor Frank Michelman argued for just compensation based on what he called the "demoralization costs" of non-payment.[47] These costs are similar to the disutility of risk aversion, but in the case of takings they arise not from random events, like fires. Instead, these costs involve the "risk of majoritarian exploitation," which is a purposeful effort to redistribute wealth from those whose property is taken to those with political and constitutional power.[48]

3. Compensation and Land-Use Incentives

In a classic article, Lawrence Blume, Daniel Rubinfeld, and Perry Shapiro addressed the effect of compensation on land-use decisions.[49] These authors conclude that in order to induce landowners faced with a taking risk to make cost-effective investments in their land, *no compensation* should be paid. This *no-compensation result* was initially surprising for two reasons, first, because of its perceived unfairness, and second, because of its departure from the constitutional requirement of just compensation. Despite this, the result is an intuitive solution to the moral hazard problem. The following example illustrates the point.

Table 8:2. Data for Deriving the No-Compensation Result

Project	Investment	Gross Return	Net Private Return	Expected Social Return
1	$500	$10,000	$9,500	$27,500
2	$5000	$15,000	$10,000	$27,000

Consider a landowner who is deciding between two investment projects, the data for which are shown in Table 8:2. Project 1 requires an up-front, non-salvageable investment of $500 and yields a gross return of $10,000, while Project 2 requires an investment of $5000 and yields a gross return of $15,000. Because Project 2 offers a higher net return, as shown by column four, it would be both the privately and socially optimal choice of the landowner.

But now suppose there is a twenty-percent chance that the land in question will be taken for a public project that will be worth $100,000.[50] We assume that the landowner is aware of the risk before he makes his initial investment. Even so, the investor will consider the expenditure a sunk cost at the time of the taking; that is, if the land is taken, the initial

---

[47] Frank I. Michelman, *Property, Utility, and Fairness: Comments on the Ethical Foundations of "Just Compensation" Law*, 80 HARV. L. REV. 1165 (1967).

[48] FISCHEL, *supra* note 23, at 148–50.

[49] Lawrence Blume, Daniel L. Rubinfeld & Perry Shapiro, *The Taking of Land: When Should Compensation be Paid?*, 99 Q.J. ECON. 71 (1984).

[50] If the project involves assembly, then $100,000 is the proportional share of the overall value attributed to this particular parcel.

investment is lost.[51] Based on these assumptions, we now show that the *socially* optimal choice is Project 1.

To see this, compute the expected social returns from the two projects as follows:

Project 1: –$500+(.8)($10,000)+(.2)($100,000)=$27,500

Project 2: –$5000+(.8)($15,000)+(.2)($100,000)=$27,000

Project 1 therefore yields the higher return once the possible public use of the land is accounted for. The reason project one is now optimal is that the risk of a taking results in a significantly larger loss of the initial investment under Project 2. Now consider the actual decision of the landowner, and suppose initially that compensation is full as required by the Fifth Amendment. Thus, whichever project the owner chooses he will be fully compensated for his loss in the event of a taking. (We will ignore subjective value here and assume that the landowner's valuation coincides with the market value.) In this case, the landowner chooses Project 2, which maximizes his net private return. This "overinvestment" represents the moral hazard problem associated with full compensation.

Consider next the outcome under zero compensation. In this case, the landowner will compute the expected private returns from the two projects as follows:

Project 1: –$500+(.8)($10,000)+(.2)(0)=$7,500

Project 2: –$5,000+(.8)($15,000)+(.2)(0)=$7,000

In this case, he opts for Project 1, the efficient choice. Notice that the *difference* between the two returns in the above calculation, $500, is exactly the same as the difference between the social returns computed above. This is a general result, thus explaining why zero compensation is efficient.[52]

The no-compensation result is contrary to taking doctrine at least as applied to direct condemnations.[53] Although there may be additional problems with this rule, the intuition developed here seems compatible with results observed in certain areas of tort and contract law. In these settings, a robust account of the doctrines we have reviewed emphasizes the incentive function of the selected compensation rule.

Regardless of the context, the principle is the same: if a party expects to be fully compensated for a loss, her incentives to take appropriate steps to avoid the harm is substantially diminished and perhaps even eliminated. Thus, accident victims have substantially diminished incentives to take care under strict liability; promisees tend to rely excessively under an expectation damages regime; and landowners tend to over-invest under a regime that compensates them fully, including their subjective valuation,

---

[51] This timing of events is not as restrictive as it might initially appear. New public projects are continually being proposed, and therefore private land is perpetually at risk of being taken.

[52] The reason the differences are the same is that the expressions for the social returns differ from the corresponding private returns by a constant that is equal to the expected social value of the land.

[53] For a discussion of other reasons why a zero compensation rule might seem problematic, see *infra* Chapter 12; Chapter 16.

following a taking. The economic analysis of these doctrines thus reveals important connections across these seemingly disparate doctrines.[54]

The no-compensation result understandably attracted enormous attention among economists and legal scholars, mostly in the form of various counter-arguments to justify paying some compensation. We have already discussed the most common of these arguments: namely, to prevent excessive taking of land by the government, and to provide insurance against taking risk.[55] These, and other, goals must therefore be traded-off against the inefficiency from over-investment in land subject to a taking.

QUESTIONS AND COMMENTS

Although the Fifth Amendment requires just compensation for eminent domain, the preceding analysis also applies to other policies influencing property development. Consider, for example, the program administered by FEMA for relief following natural disasters; some instances of relief are non-controversial.[56] Sometimes funding is used to support rebuilding on beachfront communities in the aftermath of a hurricane.[57] Beneficiaries are often persons with sufficient wealth to purchase and build vacation properties. What implications does the preceding analysis have for granting relief in these situations?

The just compensation requirement in the Eminent Domain Clause has been construed to mean fair market value rather than investment cost or subjective value. Although this does not eliminate moral hazard, as would a rule of zero compensation, it certainly mitigates moral hazard when compared with these alternative valuation measures. As we have seen, however, fair market value undercompensates property owners whose subjective valuation is not the product of moral hazard, and instead is the product of what society encourages individuals and families to do: invest in their homes, schools, and communities more generally. Doing these things also enhances a homeowner's subjective valuation.

Is it possible that just compensation assessed at fair market value is simply the best the law can do? Or is there a way to calibrate compensation to address the moral hazard problem when it genuinely arises, but without undermining subjective value that is not the product of strategic behavior by the property owner?

II. REGULATORY TAKINGS

To this point, our discussion of eminent domain has focused on direct physical acquisitions, or condemnations, of property. Government regulations that limit the uses

---

[54] *See* Robert Cooter, *Unity in Tort, Contract, and Property: The Model of Precaution*, 73 CALIF. L. REV. 1 (1985).

[55] MICELI, *supra* note 20, at 85–112, provides an overview of the large literature that has arisen in response to Blume, Rubinfeld, and Shapiro, *supra* note 49.

[56] *See The Disaster Declaration Process*, FEMA (last updated Apr. 6, 2017, 10:24 AM), https://www.fema.gov/disaster-declaration-process (describing the formal disaster declaration process, including information on damage assessment, types of declarations, appeals, and post declaration actions).

[57] For a general analysis, see Saul Levmore, *Coalitions and Quakes: Disaster Relief and Its Prevention*, 3 U. CHI. L. SCH. ROUNDTABLE 1 (1996); *see also* J. Peter Byrne, *The Cathedral Engulfed: Sea-Level Rise, Property Rights, and Time*, 73 LA. L. REV. 69 (2012); Omri Ben-Shahar & Kyle Logue, *The Perverse Effects of Government-Subsidized Weather Insurance*, 68 STAN. L. REV. 571 (2016); Christopher Serkin, *Passive Takings: The State's Affirmative Duty to Protect Property*, 113 MICH. L. REV. 345 (2014).

to which a piece of property may be put without actually taking the physical property, for example, through a transfer of title, are much more common. Examples include zoning, environmental and safety regulations, and historical landmark designations. Historically, courts have granted governments broad powers to impose these types of regulations in the public interest without triggering a need to compensate the affected landowners for the resulting loss in property value. Courts have therefore treated regulations differently from outright takings, which require compensation.

This dichotomy between regulation with no compensation versus takings with just compensation has long presented a puzzle. Economists often view these two legal interventions as different in degree rather than in kind, and more specifically, they tend to focus on valuation effects on the property, not the form that the regulation takes. From this perspective, an outright taking of property represents one end of a continuum that includes numerous methods through which the state can remove sticks from the bundle of associated property rights.

This raises the question: Is a regulation ever so burdensome that it must be treated as a taking requiring just compensation? We begin with a brief overview of the doctrinal tests that courts have relied upon to answer the "just compensation" question. We then develop two alternative economic theories that each provide valuable insight into regulatory takings.

A. Legal Tests for Compensation

We begin with the 1887 decision, *Mugler v. Kansas*.[58] In *Mugler*, a state statute outlawed the operation of breweries in Kansas following passage of a state constitutional amendment banning intoxicating liquors. Mugler, the owner of a newly constructed brewery, was convicted of violating the statute. Before the Supreme Court, Mugler claimed that his conviction violated the Due Process Clause of the Fourteenth Amendment and the Eminent Domain Clause of the Fifth Amendment.[59]

The Court denied the claim on the grounds that the state had the power to pass laws prohibiting activities deemed "injurious to the health, morals, or safety of the community,"[60] and that in using these powers a state may regulate the noxious use of property without triggering the need for just compensation when there is no physical taking. The *noxious use* doctrine has been construed broadly to permit state regulatory

[58] 123 U.S. 623 (1887).

[59] Although earlier cases had rested on the Fourteenth Amendment Due Process Clause to accomplish the same result, the Takings Clause, which is contained in the Fifth Amendment, was formally incorporated to apply to the States in *Penn Central Transportation Co. v. City of New York*, 438 U.S. 104 (1978). Alan T. Ackerman, *Incorporation of the Right to Just Compensation: The Fourteenth Amendment vs. the Takings Clause*, 1 BRIGHAM-KANNER PROP. RTS. CONF. J. 95, 97 (2012). For a discussion of the early history of state takings, including reliance on state constitutions in the pre-Reconstruction Amendment period, see MARK A. GRABER & HOWARD GILLMAN, COMPLETE AMERICAN CONSTITUTIONALISM, VOL. 1: INTRODUCTION AND THE COLONIAL ERA 311–12 (2015) (the colonial background); HOWARD GILLMAN, MARK A. GRABER & KEITH WHITTINGTON, AMERICAN CONSTITUTIONALISM: VOL. II, RIGHTS AND RESPONSIBILITIES 222–26 (2013) (cases); *id.* at 163 (general law).

[60] *Mugler*, 123 U.S. at 668.

powers without triggering compensation given that nearly all regulations can be justified as furthering public health, safety and morals.

The Supreme Court took a more restrictive view of state police powers affecting private property in the 1922 decision, *Pennsylvania Coal Co. v. Mahon*.[61] The *Pennsylvania Coal* case concerned the Kohler Act, a Pennsylvania law that required mining companies to leave enough coal in the ground to prevent subsidence, or surface cave-ins. The Pennsylvania Coal Company had deeded surface rights to a plot of land to Mahon, while retaining the rights to mine beneath. When the company notified Mahon of its intent to mine, Mahon sued to enjoin the operation, claiming a right to have his surface rights protected against the risk of subsidence. Under earlier Pennsylvania law, a surface rights owner had no such protection unless he also purchased a *support estate*, which would ensure the requisite pillars of coal beneath the surface property.

Rather than rely on *Mugler* and hold the diminution of value in the mining rights was a valid regulation pursuant to state police powers, the Court, with Justice Holmes writing, reasoned that "while property may be regulated to a certain extent, if regulation goes too far it will be recognized as a taking."[62] The Court further reasoned that the public safety concern could have been adequately addressed with the posting of appropriate signs, adding "We are in danger of forgetting that a strong public desire to improve the public condition is not enough to warrant achieving the desire by a shorter cut than the constitutional way of paying for the change."[63]

This argument forms the basis for the *diminution of value test* for compensation, which suggests that compensation might be due if a regulation goes "too far" in reducing the landowner's value. The Court did not specify when exactly that threshold is met, although it did reason that on the case facts, the required support altogether eliminated the possibility of undertaking the mining operation.

Justice Louis Brandeis wrote a strong dissent, arguing that the majority had effectively abandoned the *Mugler* noxious-use doctrine. Specifically, Brandeis rejected the claim that private benefit to Mahon from the Kohler Act negates the more general public purpose of the mining restriction. Brandeis stated:

> [T]he purpose of a restriction does not cease to be public, because incidentally some private persons may thereby receive gratuitously valuable special benefits. . . . Furthermore, a restriction, though imposed for a public purpose, will not be lawful, unless the restriction is an appropriate means to the public end. But to keep coal in place is surely an appropriate means of preventing subsidence of the surface; and ordinarily it is the only available means.[64]

In his book on regulatory takings, Professor William A. Fischel questioned the *Mahon* Court's factual assumptions, most notably that the mining operation would have inevitably forced subsidence on Mahon's property.[65] Based on his review of historical

---

[61] 260 U.S. 393 (1922).

[62] *Id.* at 415.

[63] *Id.* at 416.

[64] *Id.* at 417–18.

[65] FISCHEL, *supra* note 23.

records, he determined that such mining was routinely undertaken and that the mining companies ensured adequate support to protect the interests of those with surface rights. In the *Mahon* case, however, the mining company expressly reserved mining rights, and Pennsylvania law at the time recognized a support estate, which was not included as part of the estate that Mahon purchased.

In a 1987 decision, *Keystone Bituminous Coal Ass'n v. DeBenedictus*[66] a case with some striking similarities to *Mahon*, the Supreme Court reversed course and sustained the Bituminous Mine Subsidence and Land Conservation Act (Subsidence Act), enacted in 1966, and several related regulations, against a challenge by four mining companies who argued that the regulatory regime created a taking. The mining companies challenged two provisions. Section 4 "prohibit[ed] mining that causes subsidence damage to three categories of structures . . .: [1.] public buildings and noncommercial buildings generally used by the public; [2.] dwellings used for human habitation; and [3.] cemeteries."[67] And Section 6 "authorize[d] the [Department of Environmental Resources] to revoke a mining permit if the removal of coal causes damage to a structure or area protected by § 4,"[68] and if the mining company has not undertaken several specified steps to abate the harm or protect the financial interests of those who are harmed.

Writing for the majority, Justice Stevens emphasized the following distinctions with *Mahon*. First, whereas the earlier statute benefited a narrow group of homeowners, this statute protected a far broader group of identified beneficiaries. Second, in the intervening decades, impressions as to the public interest at stake had changed, as indicated by the Subsidence Act, which was longstanding before the planned mining operations. Third, unlike in *Mahon*, the courts had determined that the mining operations constituted a public nuisance warranting the listed protections in Section 6. And finally, the value of the property with the restriction in place was greater in *DeBenedictus* than in *Mahon*.

Chief Justice Rehnquist, writing in dissent, emphasized the similarities across the two cases, rejecting the majority's claimed distinctions. He also found the diminution in value to the mining companies sufficiently severe to treat the case as a taking.

QUESTIONS AND COMMENTS

In *Mahon*, which party's reliance interests were undermined by the injunction issued to Mahon pursuant to the Kohler Act? To the extent that the planned mining operation posed a special risk to Mahon, was this a context in which the parties were not well suited to structure the conveyance of the relevant property rights by contract, rather than having them judicially enforced after the deed was conveyed? Was a contractual solution plausible in *DeBenedictus*? Might the difference in terms of plausible contracting have explained Justice Stevens' focus on the broader class of beneficiaries in the latter case? Why or why not?

---

[66] 480 U.S. 470 (1987).

[67] *Id.* at 476.

[68] *Id.* at 477.

Return to the Law of Regulatory Takings

In the 1978 decision, *Penn Central Transportation Co. v. City of New York*,[69] the Supreme Court rejected a takings challenge to the application of a historical landmark designation in New York City to deny permission to construct a fifty-five-story high-rise above Grand Central Terminal. Penn Central claimed that the restriction thwarted the air rights above the terminal, undermined its investment-backed expectations, and rendered continued use of the property non-profitable.

In denying the challenge, the Supreme Court, with Justice Brennan writing, articulated what has become known as the three-part *Penn Central* test:

> [T]he Court's decisions have identified several factors that have particular significance. The economic impact of the regulation on the claimant and, particularly, the extent to which the regulation has interfered with distinct investment-backed expectations are, of course, relevant considerations. So, too, is the character of the governmental action. A "taking" may more readily be found when the interference with property can be characterized as a physical invasion by government, than when interference arises from some public program adjusting the benefits and burdens of economic life to promote the common good.[70]

In other words, the Court is more likely to characterize a regulation as a taking when: (1) the economic impact on the claimant is particularly significant, creating an unacceptable diminution in value; (2) the regulation thwarts an investor's "distinct investment-backed expectations"; and (3) the character of the regulation is tantamount to a "physical invasion by the government" as opposed to a regulatory program with an associated balancing of benefits and burdens.

The Court distinguished *Mahon* based on the effect of the regulation on investment-backed expectations, stating:

> Because the statute [in *Mahon*] made it commercially impracticable to mine the coal, and thus had nearly the same effect as the complete destruction of rights claimant had reserved from the owners of the surface land, the Court held that the statute was invalid as effecting a "taking" without just compensation.[71]

As applied to *Penn Central*, the Court determined that unlike in *Mahon*, balancing these considerations did not require finding a taking. Specifically, the Court observed that the restriction did not undermine the use of all air space above the terminal, but did note that the historical landmark designation was at odds with tearing down major parts of the structure that motivated the initial designation. The Court further reasoned that the investors were able to develop other related parts of their property near the terminal, thus raising the question as to when a regulatory restriction on part of a property means a taking of the whole. This has become known the *denominator problem*, meaning that if the restriction is evaluated against the larger property the investors owned, then the regulated fraction is much smaller than if assessed against only the terminal. Finally, the Court

---

69 438 U.S. 104 (1978).

70 *Id.* at 124.

71 *Id.* at 127–28.

rejected the argument that the ongoing use as a terminal undermined investment-backed expectations simply because with the restriction in place, the property would generate a lower income stream than if the requested construction had been approved. In fact, the company that owned the terminal had been in bankruptcy, and after the ruling, although ownership did not change hands, it was eventually publicly run.[72]

Perhaps the most notable factor in the *Penn Central* test is the third: The Court implicitly took the position that regulations provided general benefits, here the chance to see an early twentieth-century Beaux-Arts masterpiece, with costs imposed on the terminal owners. The Court declined to treat those burdens as it would a physical taking. This left open the question as to how far a regulation had to go before it shifted character and was tantamount to a taking that triggered just compensation.

The Supreme Court addressed this question in the final case we will consider: *Lucas v. South Carolina Coastal Council*.[73] *Lucas* involved a land developer who had purchased two beachfront lots in 1986 for $975,000, in South Carolina, that he planned to develop for residential use. Although the construction required a permit, based on existing South Carolina law, he anticipated approval. In 1988, however, the South Carolina legislature enacted the Beachfront Management Act, which prohibited beachfront development in an effort to prevent beach erosion. The permit was therefore denied, and the developer brought suit claiming that the near total diminution in value constituted a taking for which just compensation was required.

The Supreme Court, with Justice Scalia writing for a majority, agreed. The Court held that a regulation that effects a complete diminution in the value of property, thereby entirely undermining a purchaser's investment-backed expectations, is a taking requiring just compensation. Scalia stated:

> We think, in short, that there are good reasons for our frequently expressed belief that, when the owner of real property has been called upon to sacrifice *all* economically beneficial uses in the name of the common good, that is, to leave his property economically idle, he has suffered a taking.[74]

Scalia added that the state could nevertheless avoid paying compensation if it demonstrated that the land use contemplated by the developer would have constituted a nuisance under the state's common law, thereby implicating the noxious-use doctrine, but the applicability of the exception on the case facts seemed implausible.

B. An Economic Theory of Regulatory Takings

The preceding survey is sufficient to demonstrate the seemingly tangled law of regulatory takings. In this section we develop two sets of alternative economic theories that are designed to bring coherence to this doctrinal area.[75] We begin with an analysis

---

[72] Sam Roberts, *Meet Grand Central's Flesh-and-Blood Landlord*, N.Y. TIMES CITY ROOM (Jan. 29. 2013), https://cityroom.blogs.nytimes.com/2013/01/29/grand-centrals-flesh-and-blood-landlord/.

[73] 505 U.S. 1003 (1992).

[74] *Id.* at 1019 (emphasis in original).

[75] The first of the two theories was initially developed in Thomas J. Miceli & Kathleen Segerson, *Regulatory Takings: When Should Compensation be Paid?*, 23 J. LEGAL STUD. 749 (1994).

that focuses on the incentive function of compensation, which has been a common theme linking the various doctrines reviewed here and in the preceding chapters. We will specifically focus on the role of the compensation rule in simultaneously providing incentives for landowners to make appropriate land-use decisions in the face of a regulatory risk, and for the government to make suitable regulatory decisions. This twofold objective poses a challenge because, based on our preceding analysis of physical takings, full compensation risks encouraging landowners to overinvest as a result of the moral hazard problem, and anything less than full compensation risks excessive governmental regulation when regulators fail to fully internalize the costs of the restrictions they impose.

The first theory combines insights from the work of Professor Michelman with that of Professors Thomas Miceli and Kathleen Segerson. We begin with an influential test for compensation proposed by Professor Frank Michelman.[76] Michelman emphasized the *demoralization costs* that landowners and their sympathizers bear in the absence of compensation. He realized, however, that these costs must be balanced against the *settlement costs* that the government incurs if required to pay compensation. Michelman's solution is a balancing test in which compensation is paid if demoralization costs exceed settlement costs, and in which no compensation should be paid when the opposite condition holds.

Now consider an alternative *threshold rule* proposed by Professors Miceli and Segerson, which is aimed at addressing the land-investment and over-regulation choices. Recall that we previously observed similar bilateral-care-type problems in specific tort and contract law settings. The authors' study of those areas suggested the following threshold rule as a possible solution to regulatory takings: If the government imposes an *in*efficient regulation (i.e., if it over-regulates), it will be required to pay the landowner full compensation for the lost value of the land. However, if the government imposes an efficient regulation, it will not be required to pay compensation. The threshold for compensation is therefore taken to be the efficiency of the government's action.

This rule would provide a parallel solution in property to the Learned Hand negligence test in tort. Miceli and Segerson prove the efficiency of this rule in the same way that that negligence proves efficient in the bilateral care model of accident law. The analysis begins by considering the behavior of a budget-constrained governmental agency. The threshold rule would deter the agency from enacting excessive regulations because of the "threat" of having to pay compensation. Compensation thus serves as a penalty for excessive regulation in the same manner that the threat of liability under negligence deters injurers from exercising too little care. The authors further claim that in the Nash equilibrium, the threshold rule would motivate landowners to invest efficiently in their land prior to the enactment of a regulation because owners would rationally anticipate that governments will only impose efficient regulations, and therefore that compensation will be zero in the event of a regulation. And as shown above, zero compensation eliminates the moral hazard problem for landowners, resulting in efficient investment.

Miceli and Segerson reconcile their model with Michelman's less formal analysis. The authors suggest that if the proposed threshold rule equates the demoralization costs

---

[76] Michelman, *supra* note 47.

of not paying compensation with the risk of excessive governmental regulation, and if it further equates the settlement costs of paying compensation with landowner moral hazard, then the framings achieve the same result.[77]

We now introduce an alternative analysis, and then compare the analyses in assessing the preceding cases. This analysis focuses on two underlying analytical difficulties with regulatory takings, one of which is epistemological, here meaning that it raises questions that are conceptually impossible to resolve, and the other of which is practical, meaning that even if we could resolve them as a theoretical matter, it would be impossible to devise a system of rules that could practically account for the identified difficulties.

We begin with the epistemological problem. One difficulty with regulatory takings, and with takings more generally, is that assessing relative claims of efficiency requires knowledge as to the subjective valuations that individuals whose property is either taken, or subject to a costly regulation, attach to their property or its planned usage. In some situations, this is a tractable question, at least in theory. For example, in *Penn Central*, it is possible to construct models that will project the cost and future income streams from the existing use of the terminal, on one hand, versus the potential use as a fifty-five-story high-rise, on the other. Because this is a business investment, it is unlikely that from the perspective of the financiers there is a subjective valuation associated with either approach. The greater difficulty is assessing the subjective value, or pleasure, that countless individuals enjoy when viewing the existing Beaux-Arts architecture.

For some, this is a feature of design that they miss altogether as they rush from train to taxi, whereas for others it is a major destination to be relished during a trip to Manhattan. In addition to individual observers, the planned construction would also have affected surrounding buildings, including obstructed views that they previously enjoyed. In theory we might ask everyone who enjoys the historical building what they would willingly accept to forgo that benefit, and then figure out a rough annual benefit calculated prospectively on a discounted-present-value basis. We could then compare that to the difference in value to the developers. This would, in effect, allow us to test the Miceli and Segerson thesis concerning whether the *Penn Central* decision creates or thwarts efficiency, defined here as social welfare maximization.

The epistemological challenge is the same one that motivates the Kaldor-Hicks standard for efficiency more generally. Even if it were possible to identify all affected persons to ask these questions, there is no reason to assume that the answers would be sincere. Individuals strongly opposed to the construction would have an incentive to overstate their opposition. Similarly, developers have an incentive to overstate the downside of not proceeding and the upside of doing so.

Part of the difficulty is that unlike in private markets, where revealed preferences signal personal valuations of goods and services, and where the aggregation of disparate decisions helps identify a market-clearing price, and thus an objective measure of fair market value, there is no mechanism with which to let markets clear on the enjoyment of a landmark site. Certainly there are sites that people pay to see, but in a city like New York, there are many sites that people enjoy simply by passing by or even walking through. Stated differently, because the landmark holds the characteristics of a public good, there

[77] FISCHEL, *supra* note 23, at 158.

is no method of effective price discrimination that would allow us to capture that beneficial information.

The same epistemological problem respecting valuation arises more broadly in zoning. If we were to extend an efficiency analysis to regulatory takings, then in theory, this should apply to zoning as well since zoning laws likewise benefit some persons and impose direct costs on others. This is captured in the concept of *mutual reciprocity of advantage*. Despite this, the Supreme Court has upheld zoning laws as non-compensable regulations, and this is likely because of the intractable judicial difficulties that would arise were the courts to venture into the territory of assessing relative efficiencies of such laws.

In general, the Court has allowed laws that impose restrictions on land use, whether through zoning laws or more targeted regulations that impose specific costs on a narrower group of property owners. By contrast, the Court treats any physical invasion of property rights by the government as a taking. And in a very narrow category of case, epitomized by *Lucas,* it treats a regulation that entirely depletes the purchaser of valuation in the land as it would a physical taking. An alternative way to read this body of case law is that the Court seeks to avoid the intractable challenges of valuation in land-use regulation, including zoning law, in general, but that it recognizes that in extreme cases, such as in *Lucas*, the regulation goes so far that the property owner is left ultimately with a title document but nothing more in terms of valuable sticks in the bundle of rights.

QUESTIONS

Which account better characterizes the case law, that offered by Michelman, Miceli and Segerson, or the alternative account provided above? Why? If you are persuaded by the Miceli and Segerson account, how would you propose handling the epistemological challenges? If you are persuaded by the alternative account, how do you reconcile the intuition that many land-use regulations impose greater financial burdens on property owners than the physical taking of part of their property? Is economic analysis helpful in answering these questions? Why or why not?

III. A SUMMING UP: THE GENERAL TRANSACTION STRUCTURE

The preceding chapters have demonstrated the power of economic analysis to offer a unifying theory of the common law. This theory emphasizes the relationship between legal doctrines and market decision making in improving the movement of land and other scarce resources to their more highly valued uses. We have seen that the costs of judicial administration and practical difficulties in ascertaining valuations can inhibit the neat equilibrium results observed in simplifying efficiency-based models. Even so, there is great value in having a coherent framework against which to assess actual legal doctrine. One major benefit of this approach is in finding commonalities across different fields of law.

In this part we will offer an integrative approach that draws upon the lessons from the preceding chapters. The analysis relies on the Coase theorem, which holds that, with low transaction costs, resources will flow to their more highly valued uses without regard to liability rules, and its corollary that, depending on the presence or absence of high transaction cost, the choice between property rules and liability rules can control the ultimate allocation of resources.[78] We now develop a theory that we refer to as the *General Transaction Structure* of the common law.[79] The analysis begins with a hypothetical that sets up four possible combinations of legal rules and that explores their effects on resource allocation.

Before proceeding, some clarification as to the terminology will be helpful. Within this model, a party protected with a property right has the power to enjoin the other party, thus preventing her from creating or continuing an externality. The concept of externality will sometimes coincide with Pigouvian intuitions. A neighboring homeowner with the property right to enjoin a polluting factory might be said to avoid suffering an ongoing harm that the factory has caused, thereby forcing the factory to internalize the full cost of its economic activity. On the other hand, if the property right vests with the factory, the legal rule prevents the homeowner from externalizing the full cost of enjoying her home onto the factory, instead requiring that she internalize those costs by undertaking the necessary abatement costs herself. From an economic perspective, the external costs arise from ill-defined property rights—does the factory have the right to emit pollutants or does the homeowner have the right to full enjoyment absent the pollutants?—rather than from non-economic intuitions of cause and effect.

A similar dynamic arises with rights protected by a liability rule. A party protected with a liability rule does not have the right to an injunction but does have a right to have the other party compensate with money damages for the burden associated with minimizing the externality. Once more, the concept of externality is reciprocal and thus treats external costs as a function of ill-defined property rights. A party burdened by a conventional externality—the factory polluting to the homeowner's detriment—has the right to damages as a means of minimizing the burden of the external harm in lieu of injunctive relief or the purchase of the right to continue unabated. Conversely, if the factory is protected with a liability rule, it can require the homeowner to cover its abatement costs if that is the lower cost method of reducing the resulting burden. We now illustrate these general concepts with the following hypothetical.

Imagine that Albert and Bonnie Chelsea (ABC) purchase a lot on which they construct an expensive home. Shortly after moving in, ABC discover that they are backyard neighbors with a business named *Doggy Overnight and Grooming* (DOG), a kennel and grooming facility. Although ABC enjoy their own fairly tame Chow Chow, they are distressed by the incessant barking, day and night, and the not-infrequent stray dogs that enter their yard to do their business, leaving a mess to clean up. They are especially worried as Bonnie is expecting their first child, and they fear that the noise will disrupt her sleep and that with DOG located as it is, their yard will not be suitable for their child to enjoy as a toddler.

---

[78] *See supra* Chapter 1.

[79] In addition to R.H. Coase, *The Problem of Social Cost*, 3 J.L. & ECON. 1 (1960) and Calabresi & Melamed, *supra* note 2, this approach is based on the work of Alvin K. Klevorick, *On the Economic Theory of Crime*, *in* NOMOS XXVII: CRIMINAL JUSTICE 289 (J. Roland Pennock & John Chapman eds., 1985), and JULES L. COLEMAN, MARKETS, MORALS, AND THE LAW ch. 2 (1988).

Table 8:3 depicts four possible outcomes of the dispute, depending on which party is assigned the entitlement (in this case, the right to control the noise and straying dogs), and whether that assignment is protected by a property rule or a liability rule. We might imagine that the resulting property right should vest with ABC because this is a residential neighborhood and DOG is operating a business that disrupts the enjoyment of a neighboring home. Alternatively, we might imagine the property right vesting with DOG, who was there first, even though ABC apparently were unaware of the business until after the home was built on the adjacent lot. As previously explained, these juxtaposed framings highlight the necessarily reciprocal nature of the externality consistent with the Coase theorem.

Table 8:3. The General Transaction Structure

		Assignment	
		Homeowner	Doggie Overnight & Grooming
	Property Rule	ABC can enjoin DOG, forcing DOG to relocate or to purchase the right to continue operating from ABC.	DOG can continue to operate unabated.
Enforcement rule	Liability Rule	ABC can recover damages from noise and harms from stray dogs as needed to take remedial steps to abate the externality, which DOG will pay if lower cost than undertaking its own abatement.	ABC can compel DOG to abate the externality if doing so is lower cost, but ABC must cover those expenses, for example, soundproofing, fencing, or possibly DOG's relocation.

Assume first that the court assigns the entitlement to ABC and protects them with a property rule (upper left cell). ABC can then enjoin the operation of DOG. For DOG to continue to operate, it would have to purchase that right from ABC or relocate at its own expense. By contrast, if the court protects ABC's entitlement with a liability rule (lower left cell), ABC can only recover damages from DOG for the noise and occasional nuisance associated with the dogs going into their yard. The damages will cover the cost of ABC's abatement, including fencing, soundproofing, and the residual damages for those externalities that cannot be eliminated entirely. If the court correctly calibrates the damages, DOG will either pay them or the parties will negotiate for DOG to abate the damages on its own if it is less costly than the damages award, for example, by putting up its own soundproof walls and better fencing its facility, and then pay a smaller sum for the residual harm that remains.[80] In these two examples, the notion of harm and the direction of causation is consistent with Pigou's understanding of the externality (i.e., DOG causes the harm to ABC), and the goal of the damages award is to force DOG to internalize its costs.

The next two alternatives introduce a more reciprocal, or Coasian, understanding of the externalities. Assume that the court assigns the entitlement to DOG and protects it with a property rule (upper right cell). In that case, ABC has no right to force DOG to abate the noise or stray dogs, although the family could construct soundproof walls and a fence at its own expense, and can also offer to pay DOG to do so if that is less costly. Finally, imagine that the court instead protects DOG's entitlement with a liability rule (lower right cell). In this case, we still assume the need to abate the nuisance, and this can be done by having DOG take the same steps as before—construct soundproof walls and a better fence—but the cost of doing so falls on ABC as the reciprocal source of the externality. If ABC had not moved in, DOG would not suffer the need to take these remedial measures. If these more modest measures prove inadequate, then ABC can compel DOG to move, but ABC must cover the expenses as the party who is *creating* the externality that DOG's property right protects.

As emphasized in our discussion of the Coasian approach to externalities above, the choice among these various options depends on the ability of the two parties to bargain. Assume that DOG and ABC can bargain costlessly. A property rule is then preferable to a liability rule because it promotes a consensual resolution rather than requiring judicially assessed damages, for example, the disutility to ABC of the barking and stray dogs, if ABC has the right, or any costs of remedial measures or relocation, if DOG has the right.

The initial assignment of the right is primarily a distributional issue because it determines who must pay to acquire that right if it is not vested with the party who values it more highly in the first instance. Thus, if ABC wins and is protected with a property right, DOG must purchase the right to lift the injunction or move. Conversely, if DOG wins and is protected with a property right, it can let its dogs bark and stray, and ABC must pay DOG to limit the noise and stray dogs or to relocate. Either way, however, the efficient outcome is achieved through bargaining, with minimal judicial involvement. We have seen this play out now in several settings within contract and property. Provided transactions costs are low, a property right will facilitate the movement of resources to their more highly valued uses through contract, and the ruling itself effects a purely distributional, rather than an efficiency-based, consequence.

We have also seen, however, that bilateral monopoly itself, which characterizes the relationship between ABC and DOG, threatens to raise transaction costs. If, for example, either party, ABC or DOG, initially owned both lots and sold one to the other, the parties would have negotiated mutually beneficial restrictions on use that maximize the value of both lots. Instead, the parties unwittingly found themselves as neighbors, stuck in a relationship in which each seeks to maximize its *ex post* position. If ABC wins the property right, for example, and if the noise is not particularly problematic but would cost DOG a

[80] DOG may alternatively choose to relocate if the cost of abatement exceeds its cost of relocating.

lot to abate, then they are in a position to extract an *appropriable quasi rent* through a more costly settlement than would be required to reduce the burden of the externality to ABC. Conversely, if DOG holds the property right and if it would cost ABC quite a lot to abate the noise, DOG has a reduced incentive to engage in reasonable low cost measures that could improve ABC's enjoyment.

With high transaction costs, a liability rule could be more efficient as it avoids the risk of such bilateral negotiations. As we have seen, this heightens judicial involvement because the court must assign both the entitlement (i.e., deciding the winner) and the price of the resulting harm (i.e., the measure of damages). If the winner is ABC, the homeowner cannot enjoin DOG's operation and can only obtain damages from the resulting diminution in the enjoyment of the property. DOG will either abate on its own, pay the damages, or relocate, whichever is cheaper. Either way, DOG will continue to operate, here or elsewhere. Conversely, within this model, if DOG wins, and if its interest is protected with a liability rule, ABC can compel DOG to abate the harm but ABC must cover the costs, including either steps to reduce the noise and stray dogs, or even DOG's possible relocation.

As previously shown, an appropriate damages regime will encourage the party that loses to take cost-effective measures to reduce or eliminate the externality if doing so is cheaper than the expected damages award. We have seen this dynamic in various settings within tort, contract, and property in which the expected costs of transacting are high, and thus where the best the court could do is assess damages incurred by the winning party and hope that it has accurately measured the damages.

The preceding argument helps to explain the relationships between the legal rules and market decision making. When consensual transactions are feasible, they are the preferred method for allocating resources, limiting the role of the court in enforcing the resulting contracts. In this way, the legal system provides the necessary backdrop for private exchange to take place that will promote the efficient allocation of resources. However, when transaction costs inhibit bargaining, then it may be efficient for a court to take on a greater role in allocating resources by imposing a liability remedy and setting the price of exchange.

We now illustrate the versatility of this simple framework with several applications from the areas of torts, contracts, and property law. The canonical Pigouvian approach to externalities corresponds to the lower left cell, where DOG (injurer) is compelled to pay damages equal to the harm suffered by ABC (victim). The damages remedy can either take the form of a Pigouvian tax, or it can take the form of strict tort liability. As argued in Chapters 3 and 4, the two are equivalent in terms of incentives for injurer abatement, although they differ in terms of how they are administered and who receives the revenue. The tax is imposed by a public agency and liability results from a private damages suit. The victim receives the revenue under judicially enforced strict liability, but not necessarily so under the tax regime.

The *Boomer* case similarly corresponds to the outcome in the lower left cell, given that the factory was ordered to pay damages to the victims as a condition for remaining in operation.[81] A damages remedy for breach of contract also falls into this category if we

[81] Boomer v. Atlantic Cement Co., 257 N.E.2d 870 (N.Y. 1970). *See supra* Chapter 7, Part III.A.5.

analogize the party committing the breach (the promisor) to the "injurer" and the promisee to the "victim."

In the farmer/rancher case, from Chapter 7, the upper left cell again reflects the assignment of the entitlement to the farmer (victim), but protects it instead with a property rule. This represents the outcome under the law of trespass, where victims can enjoin unwanted intrusions onto their property. In the context of contract law, it represents a specific performance remedy whereby the victim of a breach can ask the court to enforce the original promise. Thus, breach can only occur as a result of a buy-out.

Recall that in discussing the *Peevyhouse* case[82] in Chapters 6 and 7, we considered whether specific performance would have promoted a better outcome through bargaining, or whether, instead, the bilateral monopoly rendered bargaining implausible. If we assume high transactions costs, then this would place the case in the lower left cell in Table 8:3, consistent with the case outcome, whereas if we assume low transaction costs, it would go into the upper left cell, contrary to the ruling.

In the two cells on the right side of Table 8:3, DOG wins the entitlement. By analogy to the farmer/rancher illustration, this assignment effectively reverses the roles of injurer and victim by requiring the farmer to pay for any "damages" that the rancher incurs in abating the damages inflicted by his cattle. Once more, this is consistent with Coase's intuition about the reciprocal nature of externalities as a function of ill-defined property rights. In the upper right cell, this assignment is protected by a property rule, meaning that the farmer has to bribe the rancher to reduce his herd or otherwise restrain the cattle. This is analogous to the common law doctrine of "coming to the nuisance," which sometimes protects pre-existing land uses against damage claims filed by newcomers.[83]

By contrast, the lower right cell represents an assignment of the entitlement to DOG, or the rancher, protected by a liability rule. A famous illustration of this outcome is the case of *Spur Industries, Inc. v. Del E. Webb Development Co.*[84] In *Spur*, a land developer encroached upon a pre-existing cattle feedlot and sued to have it shut down as a public nuisance. The lower court enjoined the feedlot on that basis, and, although sustaining that ruling, the appeals court treated it as a special injunction on the ground that the developer came to the nuisance, and thus found the developer responsible for the feedlot's relocation costs. Although formally the feedlot was enjoined, within this model, the feedlot continued to hold a right that was protected by a liability rule, one that required the developer to cover its abatement cost, in this case relocation.

The *Spur* ruling thus challenges the conventional notion of causation that is implicit in the Pigouvian view of externalities. Although the feedlot was the seeming source of harm, having been found a public nuisance and given that its operation created the offensive odors, the externality was reciprocal in the Coasian sense because the harm only materialized when the developer arrived on the scene. The court exploited the reciprocal nature of the externality by awarding the entitlement to the feedlot by virtue of its priority in time. *Spur* thus stood *Boomer* on its head.

---

[82] Peevyhouse v. Garland Coal & Mining Co., 382 P.2d 109 (Okla. 1962).

[83] Donald Wittman, *First Come, First Served: An Economic Analysis of Coming to the Nuisance*, 9 J. LEGAL STUD. 557 (1980).

[84] 494 P.2d 700 (Ariz. 1972).

The General Transaction Structure helps to classify the various settings in which parties are able to bargain effectively once clear property rights are defined. It also identifies the conditions in which parties are apt to find themselves in a bilateral monopoly, or other high transaction costs settings, thus requiring greater judicial involvement. The analysis highlights the reciprocal nature of external costs, and the various forms of remedy that can potentially come into play. In so doing, the framework helps underscore the critical relationship between legal rules and private market negotiations in affecting the efficient allocation of resources, as we have seen in various settings within tort, contract, and property.

IV. APPLICATIONS

1. Town Hills is located in an old section of Old City, New State. The neighborhood is close to downtown Old City, within about three miles of restaurants, shops, theaters, and other businesses. Even so, Town Hills has suffered over the past fifteen years as a result of an increasing amount of street crime and break-ins, abandoned homes, and overall neighborhood blight. Town Hills is also a community that has been marked as a *food desert*, meaning that there are very few healthy eating options within a reasonable walking distance for residents, and bus service is spotty at best.

Many of the residents, who are poor and persons of color, do not own their own vehicles. The Town Hills community was primarily characterized by row homes with an average fair market value of $100,000 each, and small free-standing homes on 1/8 acre lots, with an average fair market value of $150,000. Only two-thirds of the row homes were occupied, with many abandoned and boarded up, and these were interspersed between occupied units. Many of the row home and free-standing homes were in ill states of repair.

During her successful campaign for Old City Mayor, Mildred Jenkins promised not only to clean up Town Hills, but to do more; she promised to make Town Hills a model community, a place that all residents of Old City will be proud of whether they lived there or elsewhere, and a place that other cities throughout the United States will seek to emulate.

Under Jenkins' plan for "New Town Hills," the city would use eminent domain coupled with a complex *Valuation-and-Incentive Credit Scheme* (VICS), to acquire all of the properties. Jenkins' overall development plan was as follows: After the properties were acquired, she would have a group of major developers come in, each taking a part of the New Town Hills project. One would build new high-rise condominiums, another would build townhomes, and a third would build quarter- and half-acre zoned housing. The condominiums would have one-to-three bedrooms, with prices estimated at $225,000 to $340,000, the townhomes would have three-to-five bedrooms and would be priced at $350,000 to 600,000, and the free-standing homes would be priced from $500,000 to $650,000 for the quarter acre lots and from $650,000 to $1.25 million for the half-acre lots. The developers would also construct a recreation area, with indoor and outdoor pools, tennis courts, and basketball courts. There would also be a new shopping area, including a theater and several restaurants, and also a high-end grocery store featuring organic and locally sourced foods. As one example, it would feature eggs and produce from a thriving local business known as *hollyseggfarm*.

Mayor Jenkins, a lawyer, is well versed in economic analysis, having majored in Economics at the University of Maryland at College Park, and having taken a course in Law and Economics at the University of Maryland Carey School of Law. She was well aware of the potential for holdouts, namely property owners who might undermine her campaign pledge, and so she included the following as part of her ingenious VICS scheme: Town Hills property owners who contracted to sell their properties by May 1, 2017 would receive a 20% bonus above assessed fair market value (FMV); owners who contract to sell by June 15, 2017, would receive a 10% bonus above FMV, and those who sell on or after June 16, 2017, would receive FMV. Finally, in response to input during many town hall informational sessions, Mayor Jenkins included the following additional features as part of her plan:

> Town Hills property owners who sell their property and who purchase a home in the newly developed Town Hills community, would receive an additional inducement of 20% of the final eminent domain FMV, separate from the preceding timing-based inducements, along with a special mortgage-assistance program. To ameliorate the traffic congestion problem raised by many residents, any purchaser who sells a property in Old City and purchases a home in the New Town Hills development and who commits to owning only a single car per home unit for these cars (whether a condo, townhome, or free standing house), will receive an additional inducement of $25,000 toward the purchase price of the new home. And any seller of a home in Old City who purchases a home in the New Town Hills development and who purchases an electric car will receive an additional $15,000 inducement toward the purchase price of a new home. Each inducement requires three years in the home and adherence to the stated condition(s); otherwise, there is a substantial tax penalty that is enforceable anywhere within New State. (This is now reflected in the New State Property Tax Code.)

Version 1: Several residents of Town Hills find the overall scheme unfair. They cannot afford the new homes even with the inducements being offered. The only way that they could come close is to sell early, and then to commit to having one car, which would have to be electric. For the seller of a $100,000 home this creates a potential benefit of $80,000. Even if such an owner sells her home for the full fair market value, this leaves a considerable shortfall against the newly constructed housing, for example, $45,000 to get a newly constructed one-bedroom condominium. They contest the plan as an illegal taking.

Based on the economic analysis of property law, how should their dispute be resolved? How would it be resolved under general principles of property law? If there is a difference, can you explain why?

Version 2: Assume the Jenkins plan is approved and goes into effect. Assume that Molly and Billy, who live across town, rented, rather than owned, their bungalow. Although they liked their neighborhood well enough, they could never quite get over the feeling that, for some reason, their neighbors were not as fond of them. Molly is now pregnant with their first child, and despite an amazing tree house on their property, she and Billy are intrigued by the proposed New Town Hills development. They already own an electric car, and they want to buy the lower end single family home, presently priced at

homeowners maybe best target for these regulations bc they want to incentivize those who are invested in the community long term
→ Billy and Molly are renting, so they might not fit within the public goals

Billy and Molly wouldn't contribute to the public benefit goals? But also, they want to purchase a home, which would probably be considered a benefit

Who are incentives for? people who own property in Old Town, the comm. being redeveloped
→ Billy & Molly don't own a home & don't live in targeted neighborhood

But, the vehicle incentive goals should apply to them bc the goals are not geographically limited, per their terms

$500,000, although that is rat … nts to which those selling within th … driving one car and for buying an el … y, that would result in a total credit … operty for the early sale, plus $20,0 … 00 for driving one car, plus $15,000 … rchase price to $420,000, which mo … (Molly is considering going to law school at night, and thinks that this might help her decide), seeking a declaratory judgment that they are entitled to the full extent of these credits.

Based on the economic analysis of property law set out in Chapters 7 and 8, how should this suit be resolved? How should it be resolved based on general principles of property law? If the results differ, can you explain why?

General questions: Evaluate the overall scheme in light of the economic analysis of property law, and under general principles of property law. How, if at all, do your answers vary, and if they do, can you explain why?

2. The following are extensions of the Chapter 7 applications that also involve Molly and Billy:

Banning whole category of transactions that are socially valuable requires a strong justification
→ Homeowners may have a regulatory takings claim
• Public nuisance commission seriously undermines the regulatory taking

Denominator problem - figuring out the value is being taken
→ problem here, the treehouse value is $8000

Scenario 1: Assume that after Walter and Ho … daughters the new tree house (although without … one mistakenly built at Billy and Molly's house) … in the local magazine, *Old City Home & Garden.* … adorning Old City homes with fancy tree house … year-old boy suffers a tragic fatal accident by falling from his family's less-well-constructed tree house. Mayor Jenkins encounters serious resistance in the City Council when she proposes passing an ordinance that would make … To avoid that difficulty, she instead uses her authority under eminent domain to acquire land that a separate commission deems a public … requisite finding that the high risk of injury re… then announces that the city will use its power of … within Old City, and will provide all affected homeowners "just compensation" equal to the full difference in fair market value betwee… without the tree house. For Holly and Walter … removes a treehouse that cost them $8000, in a… Under the economic theory of property law set out in Chapters 7 and 8, how should this be resolved? Based on your understanding of property law, how would it likely be resolved? If there is a difference in your answers, can you explain why?

Scenario 2: For this question only, assume that Mayor Jenkins grandparents in the tree house in Holly and Walter's yard and, more generally, makes her plan prospective from the announced date of implementation. Assume that the neighbors on the other side of the house of Holly and Walter, at 2216 Lovely Lane, Carl and Crystal Careless, also have a large oak tree in their back yard. But unlike the tree on which Holly and Walter built their treehouse, at 2212, the Careless tree is ailing, and without serious maintenance taking the form of pruning, it has a 30% chance of falling onto the property of Holly and Walter within the next six-to-nine months. This is especially dangerous since Holly and Walter's twins, Betsy and Matilda, spend so much time in their tree house. Holly and Walter have begged their neighbors to take appropriate steps to take care of this risk, but to no avail. (Walter thinks that [illegible] to Holly's having moved their hen houses that support her business to C[illegible] Holly hires an arborist, Trudy's Trees, and has Trudy, the pr[illegible] Trudy informs Holly that her intuitions ar[illegible]s risk that the tree could fall on the [illegible]tructed tree house. Trudy estimate[illegible] removal of the tree would cost $1[illegible] economic theory of property law s[illegible]lved? Based on your understandin[illegible]f your answers differ, can you expl[illegible]

Scenari[illegible]om Chapter 7. How, if at all, does [illegible]apter? If your view has changed, w[illegible]

3. [illegible] some students will enjoy giving it a [illegible]*cient than the Income Tax in Redistribu*[illegible] Shavell, posit that social welfare is enhanced w[illegible] common law rules of tort, contract, and property are efficient, an[illegible]on of wealth instead takes place through the system of tax and transfer.[85] For this [illegible]ion, we focus solely on the common law subjects studied in the preceding Chapters, 3 through 8. On one reading, the authors state a tautology: If the state of the common law is inefficient, this implies that there is a potential to improve social welfare, meaning to create more wealth, by rendering the system efficient. Once that additional wealth has been generated, using the tax system to redistribute it is necessarily the more efficient means of doing so than is relying on the common law. That is because the tax-and-transfer approach does not entail the social welfare diminution associated with having inefficient common law rules. On the other hand, throughout the chapters on the common law doctrines, we have seen a number of conceptual difficulties with rendering some common law rules maximally efficient. Some of the difficulties result from transactions costs problems, and others arise from epistemological difficulties in ascertaining subjective valuations. We have also seen that such seemingly inefficient rules tend to persist despite claims of some scholars as to their inefficiency.

How, if at all, does the Kaplow and Shavell thesis relate to the discussion of General Equilibrium and Welfare Economics in Chapter 2? To what extent, if any, do the conceptual difficulties analyzed in that discussion, or in the preceding chapters, concerning the efficiency or inefficiency of specific common law rules, help in assessing the Kaplow and Shavell thesis? Do you agree with the thesis? Why or why not? To what extent is your answer informed by economic analysis? If the answer is "not entirely" then what other considerations inform your views? How do you think Professors Kaplow and Shavell might respond?

---

[85] Louis Kaplow & Steven Shavell, *Why the Legal System Is Less Efficient than the Income Tax in Redistributing Income*, 23 J. LEGAL STUD. 667 (1994).

PART III

Extended Applications

CHAPTER 9

Criminal Law

Introduction

In this chapter, we offer an economic analysis of criminal law. We begin with a fundamental question: why do we have a system of criminal justice at all? Many offending behaviors recognized as crimes are also torts. The economic analysis of these two fields requires careful consideration of how they relate. A possible distinction between tort and criminal law rests on the intuition that some persons who commit criminal acts are "irrational" in the sense that tort-based incentives do not discourage their harmful behaviors toward others. For this to work, must we assume a *rational offender*, meaning one immune to tort sanctions yet responsive to criminal sanctions? This chapter looks closely at the rational offender assumption more generally as it relates to both criminal law and tort.

Applying economic modeling to criminal law invites a second analytical challenge related to the complex objectives of the criminal justice system. Scholars have identified up to six functions of the system of criminal justice: (1) *general deterrence*, (2) *specific deterrence* (which includes *restraint*)[1]; (3) *retribution*; (4) *rehabilitation*; (5) *education* (which can also be included within *rehabilitation*); and (6) *restoration*. Although economic modeling has implications for each of these goals, the leading model, developed by the Nobel Prize winning economist Gary Becker, focuses on one: how criminal law improves general deterrence.[2] This narrower focus might cause some to question the model's value. We believe that in addition to the importance of the specific analysis of general deterrence, by situating this model within this larger set of objectives, the economic analysis of criminal law provides the basis for additional inquiries into the efficacy and fairness of the criminal justice system.

---

[1] Restraint limits opportunities for criminality through actual detention; specific deterrence also includes the disincentive for further criminality as a consequence of detention. *See* 1 WAYNE R. LAFAVE, SUBSTANTIVE CRIM. L. § 1.5(a)(2) (2d ed. 2015) (explaining restraint as a purpose of punishment); Richard S. Gebelein, *Delaware Leads the Nation: Rehabilitation in a Law and Order Society; A System Responds to Punitive Rhetoric*, 7 DEL. L. REV. 1, 2 (2004) ("Incapacitation: This is the ultimate form of specific deterrence."); *see also* Meghan J. Ryan, *Judging Cruelty*, 44 U.C. DAVIS L. REV. 81, 108 (2010) ("Specific deterrence is the notion that punishing an offender will deter that specific offender from committing crimes in the future.").

[2] Gary S. Becker, *Crime and Punishment: An Economic Approach*, 76 J. POL. ECON. 169 (1968). The model has been the subject of much research since its original publication. For a survey, see A. Mitchell Polinsky & Steven Shavell, *The Economic Theory of Public Enforcement of Law*, 38 J. ECON. LITERATURE 45 (2000).

Although, like the Becker model, this chapter will focus primarily on general deterrence, it is important to articulate up front the full range of objectives.[3] General deterrence involves the incentive effect of the threat of punishment in inhibiting criminal conduct. Specific deterrence, by contrast, involves incapacitating the offender, for example, through incarceration, house arrest, or other forms of punishment, for at least some period of time. It also includes the resulting disincentive for that specific offender to engage in future criminal activity. Retribution views punishment as expressing societal condemnation of the offending activity and of the person who engaged in it. Rehabilitation means using at least part of the sanctions following a criminal conviction to improve the prospect that the offender might re-enter as a productive member of society, for example, through job training, civic education, and counseling, both during and after incarceration. This explains the overlap with education. Restoration means seeking to redress the specific harms, to the extent feasible, to the specific victims of the criminal act and to society though fines, other means of compensation, or meaningfully related acts of public service.

In addition to this broader set of functional objectives, we recognize that the criminal justice system implicates a range of societal concerns associated with due process, racial inequality and justice, and socioeconomic disparities. Although we cannot offer a comprehensive treatment of these important issues, we will touch on them in this chapter and elsewhere in this book. Of course most individuals who avoid criminal behaviors do so for a broad range of reasons. These include commitment to community, moral precepts, education, family, religion, and myriad other factors that generally fall outside the realm of legal incentives. As previously discussed,[4] economic analysis of law rests on the narrow claim that properly calibrated rules provide the basis for benign incentives *on the margin*. After considering why we have a specific body of criminal law, and a corresponding system of criminal justice—or stated somewhat differently, after exploring how tort law differs from criminal law—this chapter will develop an economic model of general deterrence. This model focuses on the *marginal impact of legal rules* in affecting benign incentives related to criminal law.

The central premise of the economic approach to crime control is that the threat of criminal penalties, whether in the form of fines or imprisonment, will have a deterrent effect on individuals who are contemplating criminal acts, and that the appropriate choice of penalties will lower the crime rate.[5] Although many criminals are undeterred by applicable tort remedies, the economic analysis of criminal law nonetheless assumes that many potential offenders are rational in a meaningful sense. The model assumes that most potential offenders weigh the benefits of criminal acts against the burden associated with

---

[3] ARTHUR W. CAMPBELL, LAW OF SENTENCING § 2:1 (3d ed. 2004) (listing deterrence, incapacitation, rehabilitation, and retribution); WAYNE R. LAFAVE, CRIMINAL LAW § 1.5 (5th ed. 2010).

[4] *See supra* Chapter 1.

[5] As previously noted, the modern version of the economic theory of crime began with the seminal work of Becker, *supra* note 2, but precursors to Becker's ideas can be found as far back as CESARE BECCARIA, ON CRIMES AND PUNISHMENTS (Henry Paolucci trans., 1963) (1767) and JEREMY BENTHAM, ON THE LIMITS OF THE PENAL BRANCH OF JURISPRUDENCE (Philip Schofield ed., 2010) (1789). For a comprehensive survey, see A. Mitchell Polinsky & Steven Shavell, *The Theory of Public Enforcement of Law*, *in* 1 HANDBOOK OF LAW & ECONOMICS 402 (A. Mitchell Polinsky & Steven Shavell eds., 2007) and Steven D. Levitt & Thomas J. Miles, *Empirical Study of Criminal Punishment*, *in* 1 HANDBOOK OF LAW & ECONOMICS *supra*, at 455.

expected punishments.[6] Although some criminals are entirely undeterred by such incentive effects, the system of criminal law can still function reasonably well by focusing on the effect of sanctions on those who are responsive to them. The distinction between those who can and cannot be rationally deterred broadly relates to the distinction between general and specific deterrence. By applying criminal sanctions to, among others, those who do not respond to incentives with properly calibrated sanctions, we can more effectively deter those who do, in fact, rationally weigh the costs and benefits of committing criminal acts.

We refer to this conception as the *rational offender assumption*. The analysis is analogous to the study of residual risk in tort. Recall that the economic model of tort demonstrates that tort doctrine seeks to minimize avoidable risk—that which can be reduced with cost-effective precautions—and then to allocate residual risk to the party who can bear it at lowest cost. The system of criminal law likewise seeks generally to deter rational offenders, knowing that it will not deter all offenders. At that point, criminal law seeks to punish those who are not deterred. This includes two groups: (1) those who rationally commit crime because they value doing so more than the threatened criminal sanction, and (2) those who are otherwise unresponsive to the threat of a criminal sanction. Although incapacitating both groups can further the objectives of deterrence, criminal law does not always treat the two groups in the same manner. Some crimes are committed by individuals who are mentally impaired, either permanently or temporarily. Criminal law has employed various standards to assess mental competence under the guise of *insanity*. Insanity is a legal rather than psychological term.[7] Other crimes are committed by individuals acting out of passion, which by impairing rational judgment, is sometimes a mitigating factor.

Deterrence presumes the ability of persons to be deterred, and thus relies on the assumption that those considering criminal activity have some ability to rationally assess the benefits of planned criminal activity against the risk of punishment times the anticipated sanction if they are apprehended. Building on this assumption, the economic theory of criminal law posits that society should structure punishments, including the form they should take and the investment in apprehending offenders, so as to minimize the net costs of crime to society. Once more, there is an analogy to the economic model of tort, which posits that a well-functioning tort system seeks to minimize the social cost of accidents, including the costs of precautions and the cost of accidents themselves.

This chapter lays out the standard economic model of law enforcement and examines the extent to which the model's prescriptions match actual criminal justice policies. In those cases where theory and practice diverge, we offer some possible explanations as to why. We also survey the large and growing empirical literature on crime, which seeks both to evaluate the validity of the economic model (i.e., to test its predictions), and to better understand the impact of various criminal law enforcement policies. Finally, we pursue several extensions of the basic theory, including the likely

[6] As we will see, this means incorporating the probability of apprehension times the resulting punishment if caught into the decision calculus to commit a crime. *See infra* Part II.

[7] For a discussion of insanity, see *infra* notes 91–99 and accompanying text.

impact of corruption among law enforcers, the economics of the death penalty, and the debate over gun laws.[8]

I. WHY DO WE HAVE A SYSTEM OF CRIMINAL LAW?

Although crimes and torts are both harmful acts that society seeks to deter, the legal system controls them in very different ways. Tort law is privately enforced by means of lawsuits filed by victims, and criminal law is publicly enforced by police and prosecutors acting as agents of the state. Penalties and procedural rules are also very different in the two areas.[9] In this part, we offer some reflections on the tort-criminal law boundary and relate the analysis to defining features of the criminal justice system.

A. The Role of Intent

The offending behaviors observed in tort and in criminal law intersect in curious ways. An obvious, yet superficial, division is that tort law involves accidental conduct, whereas criminal law involves intentional harms. This is obviously oversimplified. Just as there are *intentional torts*,[10] which are subject to damages once defined as punitive,[11] so too there are crimes of negligence (e.g., negligent homicide) and even of strict liability (e.g., statutory rape).

Before assessing the relationship between intent and the tort-criminal law boundary, it will be helpful to review the relevant states of mind defined within criminal law. For conduct to be classified as criminal, a statute must specify each of two contributing factors. The first, *mens rea* ("guilty mind") or *scienter*, means a requisite state of mind. The second, *actus reus* ("guilty act") means the legally prohibited conduct that, combined with the requisite mens rea, creates the basis for criminality. Here we are focused on mens rea.[12]

Although, as noted above, there are crimes of strict liability and negligence, most criminal law presumes one of the following mental states: *recklessness*, meaning knowingly taking a risk of harm; *knowledge*, meaning awareness that the harm will result; and *intent*, meaning the desire to bring the harm about.[13] The mens rea states thus progress along a

---

[8] We defer several procedural aspects of the criminal justice system to Chapter 10, which studies the judicial process. These features include, for example, plea bargaining, the bail system, judicial sentencing discretion, and the privilege against self-incrimination.

[9] See the discussion of civil and criminal procedure in Chapter 10.

[10] Consider, for example, wrongful death, which is a tort, but that does not require proof of intent or even reckless conduct.

[11] As we have seen, *supra* Chapter 4, this is complicated by the Supreme Court ruling in *Philip Morris USA v. Williams*, 549 U.S. 346 (2007), *cert. dismissed as improvidently granted*, 556 U.S. 178 (2009).

[12] *Mens Rea*, BLACK'S LAW DICTIONARY (10th ed. 2014).

[13] *See* 1 LAFAVE, *supra* note 1, § 5.4(b) (explaining that "criminal" negligence requires more fault than civil negligence, meaning greater knowledge or a higher degree of risk); *see also id.* § 5.1(c) (explaining the basic mental states—intent, knowledge, recklessness, and negligence).

spectrum from least to most severe: strict liability, negligence, recklessness, knowledge, intent.

As we have seen, some torts also involve intentional conduct.[14] When they do, the tort system provides a basis for punitive damages. Such damages are generally designed to compensate for actions coupled with a state of mind that quite literally "adds insult to injury."[15] More generally, however, the tort system calibrates incentives respecting conduct that is careless, or negligent. In cases involving unilateral care, it does so by encouraging cost-effective precautions by the potential tortfeasor, and in the more common cases involving bilateral care, it does so by encouraging cost-effective precautions by both the potential tortfeasor and victim. Indeed, even when the tort standard is strict liability, the economic model of tort demonstrates that the incentive effect is the same as for negligence, namely promoting cost-effective precautions. The ultimate consequence in the choice of rule is to allocate residual risk as between the tortfeasor and victim.

Within tort, some conduct that would not rise to the level of intent might satisfy the standard for recklessness. For example, when a factory owner allows conditions that cause pollution, a rancher permits her cattle to stray, or a railroad fails to take precautions that result in the engines spewing sparks, we can often infer that the tortfeasor knowingly assumed a risk of harm. Formal inquiries into the tortfeasor's mental state, however, are not part of a prima facie negligence case outside the intentional tort context. In negligence actions, for example, the tortfeasor's mental state instead enters indirectly through an assessment that compares the marginal cost to the marginal benefit times the likely impact of a potentially effective forgone precaution.[16]

On one reading, this analysis suggests that intent is irrelevant in distinguishing tort and criminal law. Both systems employ a range of overlapping mental states and assign liability, or criminal responsibility, based on increasing culpability. The tort system has little difficulty assigning liability for conduct that overlaps with criminal law, and so viewed, the principal difference might be whether the victim or the state receives any compensatory component of the applicable sanction.[17]

---

[14] *See supra* Chapter 3, Part III.C.4.

[15] The idiom "to add insult to injury" is commonly attributed to the early Roman fabulist, Phaedrus, but is likely older. Christine Ammer, *Add Insult to Injury*, *in* THE AMERICAN HERITAGE DICTIONARY OF IDIOMS 3 (2d ed. 2013) (tracing phrase to fable involving bald man hitting himself on the head without killing the fly who had bitten him there).

[16] FOWLER V. HARPER ET AL., HARPER, JAMES AND GRAY ON TORTS § 16.9 (2007) (describing the factors in assessing unreasonable risk: likelihood of harm, seriousness of injury, and value of the interest to be sacrificed)

[17] *See* Susan R. Klein, *Redrawing the Criminal-Civil Boundary*, 2 BUFF. CRIM. L. REV. 679 (1999). By contrast, in civil law systems the injured party may bring a civil action seeking damages "at the same time as the public action and before the same court." CODE DE PROCÉDURE PÉNALE [C. PR. PÉN.] [CRIMINAL PROCEDURE CODE] art. 2, 3 (Fr.). Specifically, in France a victim "may initiate criminal proceedings . . . or join existing proceedings" as a *partie civile*. Helen Silving, *Compensation for Victims of Criminal Violence—A Roundtable*, *in* CONSIDERING THE VICTIM 198, 200–01 nn.251 & 253 (Joe Hudson & Burt Galaway eds., 1975). *See generally* Anne-Marie de Brouwer & Marc Groenhujsen, *The Role of Victims in International Criminal Proceedings*, *in* INTERNATIONAL CRIMINAL PROCEDURE 149 (Göran Sluitert & Sergey Vasiliev eds., 2009) (examining the

If tort law were entirely successful in dealing with external harms caused by others, we might conclude that there is no need for a separate body of criminal law. This analysis also implicates *Philip Morris USA v. Williams*.[18] Until *Philip Morris*, the damages multiplier for computing punitive damages was designed to account for the likelihood that although there were several victims of the tortfeasor's offending conduct, only a subset successfully prosecuted their claims. The damages remedy thus compensated for those who failed to do so, providing, in effect, a bounty for the subset who did. Under *Philip Morris*, however, such damages must be based solely on reprehensibility, although knowingly affecting large numbers of persons can inform that judgment. In addition, criminal enforcement is public, thereby supplanting the private damages remedy, except to the extent that a parallel tort action is permitted. More generally, channeling a case into the tort or criminal justice system might have distributional, rather than incentive-based, consequences, primarily affecting whether any award directly benefits the state or the victim.

An alternative account of the tort-criminal law boundary focuses precisely on incentives. This analysis emphasizes the role of intent in allocating incentives to target particular forms of harmful activity. We begin by considering the limits of the tort system's method of deterrence, most commonly monetary damages. Consider the two central goals of the tort system: (1) creating incentives for efficient precautions, and (2) allocating the residual risk that inevitably remains to the lowest cost bearer. As noted above, most criminal offenses require states of mind beyond negligence.

When the offending conduct meets the threshold of recklessness (knowingly taking a risk of harm), knowledge (awareness of the consequence of harm), or intent (desiring to impose harm), encouraging cost-effective precautions misses the point. The would-be criminal is seeking to offend or, at a minimum, is indifferent to offending. This means she is willing to cause harm, whether or not the victim has undertaken reasonable, or cost-effective, precautions. Indeed, she is sometimes *hoping* to do just that. And so, even if the potential victim has undertaken appropriate precautions, the offender is often sufficiently committed to the offending activity that she will pursue an alternative pathway toward accomplishing it.

The tort system, which encourages appropriate, or cost-effective, precautions is unlikely to provide a sufficient response in these circumstances precisely because the offender is looking to get around such precautions. In addition, it will often be *inefficient* for potential victims to undertake the requisite precautions themselves—those that go above and beyond due care—to thwart someone who is looking to commit a crime against them. Inefficient precautions are socially wasteful in that they are undertaken purely to protect oneself from another who is seeking to impose harm.[19] This is equivalent to rent dissipation. And if large numbers of people who feared being victimized by criminal acts took such above-and-beyond precautions, then the resulting social welfare loss would be potentially enormous. On the other hand, it is efficient for society as a whole to invest in stopping those who are unwilling to be deterred by cost-effective precautions, and in apprehending and punishing such individuals. And indeed, in this analysis, criminalization

evolving role of the victim in criminal proceedings in various international jurisdictions and the International Criminal Court).

[18] 549 U.S. 346 (2007).

[19] They are, however, *privately* productive to the would-be victim.

might be understood as imposing special sanctions against offenders who risk encouraging potential victims to incur the wasteful costs of above-and-beyond precautions, as opposed to cost-effective precautions. Societal investment in countering criminal activity sends appropriate signals to other would-be offenders who might be rationally deterred from committing future harmful acts, coupled with the requisite mens rea, typically recklessness or higher.

This analysis suggests that because tort damages will not prove effective for persons who are beyond the reach of cost-effective deterrence, the criminal justice system vests enforcement power with the government, rather than with the victims of crime. At the same time, many crimes target individual persons, and it would be inappropriate to prevent some personal means of redress. Tort thus offers parallel remedies for victims of many crimes, as in the case with civil suits for wrongful death, which is subject to the lesser *preponderance of the evidence* standard, as opposed to the *beyond a reasonable doubt* standard applicable in criminal law.

Recall that tort doctrine is premised on the intuition that when individuals engage in socially beneficial activities, they sometimes unintentionally cause harm to others. Tort law thus provides a method of compensating victims and of encouraging cost-effective precautions by both tortfeasors and victims. In general, the legal system has determined that the failure to take appropriate precautions when undertaking socially productive activity is not a crime. This returns us to the mens rea continuum of relevant mental states: strict liability, negligence, recklessness, knowledge, and intent. The criminal justice system imposes increasing levels of criminal culpability for the same actus reus, or criminal act, when that act corresponds with increasing levels of mens rea or scienter.[20] In general, crimes with reduced levels of *scienter* are limited to offenses that have historically been defined as severe, including sexual activity with minors (statutory rape) or the taking of a life (wrongful death). Most criminal activity instead requires the higher level mental states of recklessness, knowledge, or intent.

Tort and nuisance law are generally adequate to address such problems as a polluting factory, a rancher whose cattle stray, or a railroad whose engines spew sparks, and this can be accomplished through privately prosecuted lawsuits. Indeed, the feedback loop that arises from common law litigation itself encourages parties to internalize the relevant costs, thereby discouraging the offending activity. Such rules either directly inhibit the offending behavior or they provide a backdrop for renegotiating relevant rights when the legal rule initially favors the lower valued activity and when transaction costs are low.

In contrast with common law rules, which are announced in cases based on events that have already occurred, criminal laws must be specified in advance. Defining offending conduct as criminal after it has taken place is known as an *ex post facto* law, and is constitutionally prohibited.[21] The common law of tort, contract, and property, by contrast,

---

[20] *See* H.L.A. HART, *Negligence, Mens Rea and Criminal Responsibility*, *in* PUNISHMENT AND RESPONSIBILITY: ESSAYS IN THE PHILOSOPHY OF LAW 136–57 (1968).

[21] Two separate, but related, rules have this effect: the Ex Post Facto Clause, which prohibits retroactively criminalizing conduct, U.S. CONST. art. 1, § 9, cl. 3; and *Bouie v. City of Columbia*, 378 U.S. 347 (1964), which prevents the retroactive diminution of the prosecutorial standard, and which operates under the Due Process Clause of the Fifth Amendment, as applied to federal prosecutions, and the Fourteenth Amendment as applied to state prosecutions.

defines which party has the legal right following the offending conduct (and it also sets a standard to be followed by those engaged in the same, or substantially similar, conduct in the future). Although the rancher might intentionally let her cattle stray, and in doing so recklessly damage the farmer's crops, she did not intentionally violate *the law*. The legal dispute between the rancher and farmer involved which of the two parties had the relevant property right to begin with. Had this been known, the parties could have rested on the existing legal rule or bargained for a preferred one. By contrast, intending, or knowing of, a problematic consequence is insufficient for a criminal prosecution *unless* the problematic conduct was defined as criminal beforehand.

As you read the remainder of this chapter, consider which of these accounts better explains the relationship between tort and criminal law. Does the overlap of mental states render the choice primarily distributional with respect to the compensatory aspects of the sanction imposed? Or does the relative cost-effectiveness of undertaking precautionary measures targeting those who hold the most commonly prosecuted criminal states of mind provide an efficiency rationale for the coexistence of the two bodies of law? We will consider each of these questions throughout this chapter.

B. Imperfect Detection

Another justification for public enforcement concerns the cost to victims of identifying, and bringing suit against, the party responsible for their injuries. When the cost is high, some injurers will escape punishment under a purely private tort-based enforcement system. Public enforcement helps to overcome this problem by transferring investigatory and prosecutorial responsibility to the state. As we have also seen, there are private solutions to the under-detection problem.[22] One is suggested by the once dominant understanding of punitive damages discussed above and detailed in Chapter 4.[23] Linking punitive damages to the prevalent non-enforcement of private rights relates to the difficulty of inadequate detection. By inflating damages in inverse proportion to the probability of detection, such damages force internalization based on *expected damages*. From the perspective of cost internalization, it does not matter whether this is accomplished in a private tort system or through the system of criminal law. The choice is purely distributional as between the victim and the state.

A second response to under detection is for private firms to seek out offenders. This approach risks possible inefficiencies. First, there are significant scale economies associated with the detection and apprehension of offenders. These arise from the high fixed costs of establishing a police force, and the avoidance of duplicative activities concerning the collection and maintenance of a registry of information about current and past offenders. A single agency performing these functions might carry with it the benefits of a natural monopoly. Organizing that agency as a public entity might also ameliorate some risks of monopoly exploitation of victims by a private firm. To be sure there are

---

[22] Throughout much of history, law enforcement was entirely private. *See, e.g.*, DAVID FRIEDMAN, *Other Paths*, *in* LAW'S ORDER: WHAT ECONOMICS HAS TO DO WITH THE LAW AND WHY IT MATTERS 263–80 (2000) (providing some examples from modern history); RICHARD A. POSNER, THE ECONOMICS OF JUSTICE chs. 7 & 8 (1983) (discussing law enforcement in primitive society, where rudimentary bureaucracy renders state enforcement of criminal law implausible).

[23] *See also* case cited *supra* note 11 and accompanying text.

offsetting concerns. Information technology substantially lowers the cost of gathering investigative data, and the state monopoly itself can create its own exploitation risk.

In addition, private prosecution of offenders might fail adequately to account for two associated public harms arising from criminal activity:[24] first, the fear among other members of the public of becoming a future crime victim to the extent that tort-based deterrence proves inadequate;[25] and second, the risk of excessive private retribution, known as *vigilantism*. Private enforcers working exclusively for victims will not necessarily account for the full extent of these social harms, and the resulting underinvestment in apprehension might fail to minimize potential social welfare losses.

A possible alternative solution involves a system of public rewards, such as bounties, that reflect the true social cost of a given act. Under such a system, the government would, in effect, subsidize private enforcers to account for the social benefit of apprehension. By analogy, on the civil side, *qui tam* actions afford private parties a bounty for prosecuting certain statutorily specified civil law violations.[26]

Such systems create their own difficulties, as seen, for example, in the early period in the American West. Consider, for example, an arrangement whereby state-funded bounty hunters undertake the task of law enforcement.[27] If the first firm to apprehend an offender collects the fine, then firms will have an incentive to overinvest in enforcement in a race to be first.[28] The situation mirrors the problem of rent dissipation under a rule of first possession, which is also reflected in the context of patent races. Government control of both the reward and the apprehension effort, through a scheme of public enforcement, helps to avoid these difficulties.

Although the history is complicated,[29] public enforcement is also helpful in abating vigilantism. Public law enforcement renders private enforcement *and punishment* for actual or alleged criminal activity illegal. The United States has had a tragic history of such

---

[24] Richard P. Adelstein, *The Moral Costs of Crime: Prices, Information, and Organization*, *in* 12 THE COSTS OF CRIME 233 (Charles M. Gray ed., 1979).

[25] The idea is similar to Michelman's demoralization costs, which recall, arose from uncompensated government takings of land. *See also supra* Chapter 8.

[26] David Freeman Engstrom, *Private Enforcement's Pathways: Lessons from Qui Tam Litigation*, 114 COLUM. L. REV. 1913 (2014); William E. Kovacic, *Whistleblower Bounty Lawsuits as Monitoring Devices in Government Contracting*, 29 LOY. L.A. L. REV. 1799 (1996).

[27] Eric Helland & Alexander Tabarrok, *The Fugitive: Evidence on Public Versus Private Law Enforcement from Bail Jumping*, 47 J.L. & ECON. 93 (2004); Jonathan Drimmer, *When Man Hunts Man: The Rights and Duties of Bounty Hunters in the American Criminal Justice System*, 33 HOUS. L. REV. 731 (1996) (studying the historical evolution and modern significance of bounty hunters); Rebecca B. Fischer, *The History of American Bounty Hunting as a Study in Stunted Legal Growth* 33 N.Y.U. REV. L. & SOC. CHANGE 199 (2009) (studying the history and impact of bounty hunting as allowable under the common law in the United States.)

[28] *See* Gary S. Becker & George J. Stigler, *Law Enforcement, Malfeasance, and Compensation of Enforcers*, 3 J. LEGAL STUD. 1 (1974); William Landes & Richard A. Posner, *The Private Enforcement of Law*, 4 J. LEGAL STUD. 1 (1975); A. Mitchell Polinsky, *Private Versus Public Enforcement of Fines*, 9 J. LEGAL STUD. 105 (1980).

[29] *See* DAVID MARK CHALMERS, HOODED AMERICANISM: THE HISTORY OF THE KU KLUX KLAN 56–57 (1981) (describing the Ku Klux Klan's involvement in law enforcement, in particular assisting Arkansas authorities during Prohibition); WYN CRAIG WADE, THE FIERY CROSS: THE KU KLUX KLAN IN AMERICA 36, 46 (1998) (describing the Ku Klux Klan as a "vigilante army" that was often allowed to inflict terror, pain, and death by complacent local authorities). For a general overview of vigilantism, see H. Jon Rosenbaum & Peter C. Sederberg, *Vigilantism: An Analysis of Establishment Violence* 6 COMP. POL. 541 (1974).

behavior, not limited to the treatment of newly freed slaves by the Ku Klux Klan, including lynching and treacherous behavior toward blacks and members of other minority groups.[30] The state monopoly on criminal law enforcement makes such behavior illegal, and indeed, renders it criminal in its own right.

C. Criminal Sanctions and the General Transaction Structure

A final explanation for this separate body of law relates to the function of criminal law in enforcing the *General Transaction Structure*, as laid out in Chapter 8. Recall that this structure accomplished two things: (1) defining the institutional arrangement by which legal entitlements, or rights, should be assigned, and (2) establishing the manner in which such entitlements can be transferred. In doing so, the common law furthers the goal of maximizing social welfare by moving resources to their more highly valued uses. A key element of this structure concerns the choice between property rules and liability rules.

Recall that property rules facilitate consensual, or market, transfers, whereas liability rules result in court-ordered, and thus coercive, transfers. In general, the choice between property and liability rules depends on the magnitude of transaction costs. When transaction costs are low, property rules are preferred, and when transaction costs are high, liability rules are preferred. Within this analytical framework, the role of criminal law is to provide a mechanism for enforcing the General Transaction Structure.[31]

Suppose, for example, that an individual possesses a legal entitlement protected by a property rule. Assume that in Coase's farmer/rancher dispute, the farmer has the right to be free from crop damage caused by the rancher's cattle, and that he can enforce that right by obtaining an injunction against stray cattle. If the rancher still allows the cattle to stray, and if the court simply requires him to pay for the crop damage, then we would say that the rancher had succeeded in "transforming" the farmer's property rule into a liability rule.

In theory, the same interpretation could be applied to the theft of a watch, or any other property: If the court merely required the thief to compensate the victim for the value of the stolen good, the thief would violate the efficient transaction structure. Although the result would be an efficient exchange in the sense that the watch moves to the higher valuing user, its illegality reflects the preference for consensual exchange when transaction costs are low. This is the counterargument to the *efficient theft* paradox, which is often used as a critique of the property rule-liability rule framework. Critics of takings, a form of liability rule, argue that the result is to legitimize governmental theft.[32] Of course

---

[30] SHERRILYN A. IFILL, ON THE COURTHOUSE LAWN: CONFRONTING THE LEGACY OF LYNCHING IN THE TWENTY-FIRST CENTURY (2007).

[31] Guido Calabresi & A. Douglas Melamed, *Property Rules, Liability Rules, and Inalienability: One View of the Cathedral*, 85 HARV. L. REV. 1089 (1972); Alvin Klevorick, *On the Economic Theory of Crime*, *in* NOMOS XXVII: CRIMINAL JUSTICE 289 (J. Roland Pennock & John Chapman eds., 1985); JULES COLEMAN, MARKETS, MORALS, AND THE LAW 28–66 (1988).

[32] Roy Whitehead, Jr. & Lu Hardin, *Government Theft: The Taking of Private Property to Benefit the Favored Few*, 15 GEO. MASON U. C.R. L.J. 81 (2004); James Audley McLaughlin, *Majoritarian Theft in the Regulatory State: What's a Takings Clause for?*, 19 WM. & MARY ENVTL. L. & POL'Y REV. 161 (1995).

lawful takings in high-transaction-cost settings are by definition not thefts, whereas violations of property rules by private persons in low-transaction cost settings are.

Once we accept the idea that any transfer can be judged economically efficient if the recipient values the item being transferred more than the party surrendering it, then one can argue that consent, in itself, is no longer relevant to judging efficiency. This characterizes transfers under liability rules, but applying the same logic, it can be extended to actual theft. When a piece of property is protected by a property rule, society has deemed that it should only be transferred consensually, and within the General Transaction Structure framework, we can say that this is because the transaction costs of using the "market" are low. Thus, there needs to be a sanction aimed at deterring involuntary transfers, or thefts, when this occurs even though the property transfer itself might in some sense be deemed "efficient." In other words, society wants to direct transactions to the marketplace in those settings where markets function well.[33]

Although differential wealth undoubtedly contributes to the motive of many who engage in theft, it is important to separate the problem of price, which applies to any commodity beyond the means of a person who wishes to have it, from the problem of transaction costs, which instead involves a structural impediment to a market transaction, taking wealth allocations as given. When we further consider that the victim acquired the good through a consensual transaction sometime in the past, it is also likely that she holds a subjective valuation not reflected in the market price, whereas the thief is apt to seek the good for its fair market value, for example to resell in a grey market, which typically discounts value as compared with lawfully acquired goods.

This argument for criminalizing theft has an attractive quality. Specifically, it situates an important aspect of criminal law within the broader framework of the law's role in promoting the efficient allocation of resources. The criminal law accomplishes this by channeling transactions into markets when they function well, and into an alternative dispute mechanism when they do not.

QUESTIONS AND COMMENTS

The law sometimes allows bargaining over the outcome as between two landowners, for example when the rancher's cattle stray onto the farmer's land. Although the rancher has taken the use rights from the farmer, this is not treated as theft. And yet, when one person takes another's watch, the law treats that as theft. Both involve one person taking property, or a property right, from another.

Although the watch hypothetical assumed that the victim values the object more highly than the thief, is that generally likely to be true? And if it is not true, does that change the analysis as to whether compensatory damages, as opposed to criminal sanctions, are appropriate? If you believe that the victim is generally likely to value the watch more highly, then criminalization appears efficient. Why, then, does the law not make the same assumption respecting the land use rights of the farmer, who, we presume, also purchased her land in a lawful market transaction?

[33] This point is made in Calabresi and Melamed's seminal paper, *supra* note 31, and then extended by Klevorick, *supra* note 31.

Is the watch case more likely than the farmer/rancher dispute to produce a wasteful rent dissipation in order for the original rights holder to retain what is hers? How, if at all, is the rent-dissipation story different from claiming that the victim holds a higher subjective valuation than the party encroaching on her rights, either by stealing the watch or letting the cattle stray? If these economic accounts meaningfully differ, why doesn't the law treat the diminution in subjective value as a crime more generally, as seen, for example, in *Peevyhouse v. Garland Coal & Mining Co.*,[34] where the mining company refused to restore a property owner's land following a mining operation despite a contractual obligation to do so? Which analysis better accounts for these outcomes, preserving subjective valuation or avoiding wasteful rent dissipation? Why?

II. THE ECONOMIC THEORY OF CRIMINAL LAW

Gary Becker's economic theory of crime progresses in two stages.[35] The first stage concerns the decision of individual offenders regarding whether or not to commit a crime. In making this decision, offenders are assumed to compare the benefits from committing the act to the expected punishment, including the probability of apprehension, which the offender takes as given. As previously noted, the rational offender assumption is an essential component of the Beckerian theory. Aggregating this decision across all potential offenders produces what we can label a *supply curve of crime*.[36] The probability of apprehension, which affects this curve, depends on the variables that influence the law enforcement policy.

The second stage of Becker's theory involves an effort to improve society by optimizing the social welfare function as it relates to crime. A *social welfare function* means a ranking over different societal states from less to more desirable.[37] These rankings are based upon specified assumptions about the relative costs and benefits of the various states of the world, in this instance states of the world that vary based on different approaches to criminal law enforcement.

A. The Supply of Crime

Potential offenders expect to receive some monetary, or equivalent, *gain* from committing an illegal act, denoted as g,[38] which they then compare to the value of the expected punishment. If the gain exceeds the expected punishment, they commit the act, but if it does not, they refrain. The expected punishment is computed as the *probability of*

[34] 382 P.2d 109 (Okla. 1962).

[35] Becker, *supra* note 2.

[36] Although Becker does not use this terminology, Michel Foucault used the term in lectures on criminality and punishment at the Collège de France in 1979 and 1978. *See* MICHEL FOUCAULT, NAISSANCE DE LA BIOPOLITIQUE: COURS AU COLLÈGE DE FRANCE 1978–1979 (2004) (transcribing Foucault's 1978 and 1979 lectures).

[37] Becker, *supra* note 2, at 204. In Chapters 13 and 14, we will revisit this concept (discussing Arrow's theorem, which demonstrates the impossibility of constructing a social welfare function that meets a set of specified conditions designed to capture the fairness and rationality of group decision making).

[38] The gain need not be explicitly monetary, but for expositional purposes we assume the ability to translate the gain into a monetary equivalent.

apprehension, p, times the sanction, which might consist of a *fine*, f, a *prison term*, t, or a combination of both. In the case of a prison term, we assume that the offender can attach a *dollar cost* based on the opportunity cost per unit of time in prison, c, multiplied by the length of the *prison term*, t, resulting in ct. For example, this could represent the income the offender could have earned, but it also includes the obvious disutility of incarceration, which is the flip side of the value of freedom. The overall expected punishment is therefore equal to $p(f+ct)$. The following inequality captures the incentive of a potential offender to commit a criminal act:

$$g > p(f+ct),$$

Otherwise, he will be deterred.

As an example, let $p=.1$, $f=\$10,000$, $t=6$ (measured in months), and $c=\$1000$ per month. Then the expected punishment equals

$$(.1)[\$10{,}000+(6)(\$1{,}000)]=\$1{,}600$$

Thus, only those offenders who expect a gain greater than $1600 will commit the act.

Now suppose that potential offenders vary in their gains from committing the act in question, ranging from $0 to $2000, and that expected offender returns are uniformly dispersed over this range. Thus, one fifth of offenders have a gain exceeding the expected punishment of $1600.[39] This is shown graphically in Figure 9:1, where the 45^0 line shows the gain, and the horizontal line at $1600 shows the expected punishment. The supply of crime therefore consists of the 20% of potential offenders to the right of the intersection.

It follows from the graph that an increase in any combination of the policy variables—the probability of apprehension, the fine, or the length of the prison term—will reduce the supply of crime by increasing the expected punishment. This reflects the deterrent effect of punishment. For example, an increase in the prison term to eight months, all else equal, will raise the expected punishment to $1800, thereby reducing the crime rate from 20% to 10%. This is shown by the upward shift of the horizontal line in Figure 9:1, which also moves the intersection point upward and to the right. Similar effects would arise from increasing the fine or increasing the probability of apprehension.

[39] Specifically, the fraction of the overall range of offenders that lies between $1600 and the upper bound of $2000 is equal to $400/$2000=.2, or one fifth of the total.

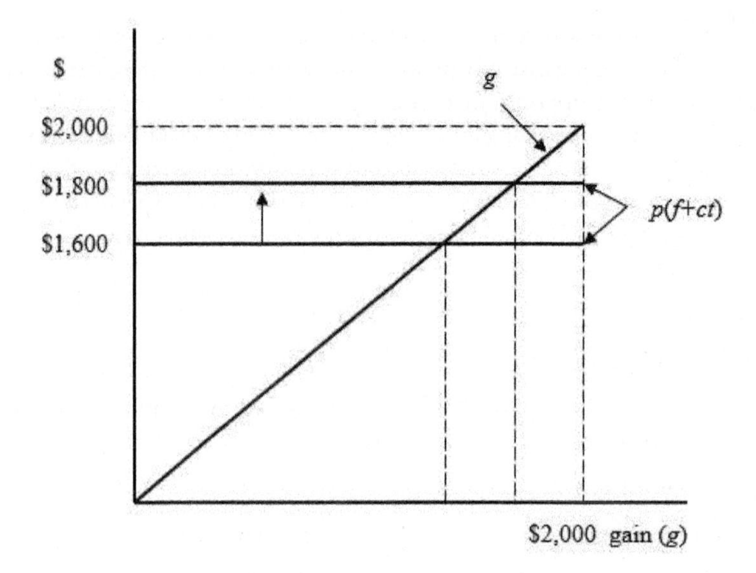

Figure 9:1. The supply of crime.

B. Optimal Punishment

As previously noted, within Becker's model, the enforcement authority selects the policy variables that define the penalty structure in an effort to improve the state of society, meaning its relevant social welfare function. In this case, that function depends on the net social harm from crime. The specific components of the welfare function are: (1) the harm to victims (measured in dollars), (2) the cost of apprehending and punishing offenders, and, in most versions of the model, (3) the gain to offenders from committing the criminal act. Although including the gain to offenders does not typically change the nature of the outcome, this aspect has, not surprisingly, generated considerable debate.

In his commentary on Becker's original model, which included the offender's welfare gains, George Stigler asked: "What evidence is there that society sets a positive value upon the utility derived from murder, rape, or arson? In fact, the society had branded the utility from such activities as illicit."[40] While Stigler's position is compelling for these identified crimes, other acts deemed criminal might benefit the offender in ways that are also socially valuable. Consider, for example, a man who speeds to the hospital with his pregnant wife; a lost hiker who breaks into a cabin for food; or a student who parks illegally, yet safely, to get to an exam on time. In each of these admittedly unusual cases, the "crime" in question would seem to be a worthwhile act. Of course there are difficult cases in between, including euthanasia for terminally ill patients, procuring marijuana in states where its use remains illegal as a prescribed means to reduce the suffering from diseases the symptoms of which conventional medicines fail to reach, and certain forms of civil disobedience, for example, being arrested while protesting for a just cause.

---

[40] George J. Stigler, *The Optimum Enforcement of Laws*, 78 J. POL. ECON. 526, 527 (1970). *See also* Jeff L. Lewin & William N. Trumbull, *The Social Value of Crime?*, 10 INT'L REV. L. & ECON. 271 (1990).

Given the broad range of offenses classified as criminal, the decision whether to include the benefit to the perpetrator within the social welfare function raises important ethical questions. One consideration is the gravity of the relevant criminal act. The literature on criminal law draws a distinction, albeit a discredited one, between offenses that are *malum in se*, meaning harmful of their own force, or *malum prohibitum*, meaning harmful because they are legally prohibited.[41] To be sure, a violent sociopath might derive great pleasure from obviously horrific criminal acts. If our goal is simply to tally gains and losses, the criminal's gains are still gains. On the other hand, if including the pleasure the perpetrator derives from activity worthy of profound societal condemnation risks changing the calculus against criminalization, weighing those gains exacerbates the societal loss, thereby strengthening the argument for exclusion.

One way to reconcile these competing positions is to claim that the criminal's utility is included, but is offset by the value attached to society's moral condemnation, both of the activity and of the criminal's enjoyment of that activity. This requires a rather esoteric set of calculations, in addition to seemingly intractable measurement difficulties. Economic analysis is not terribly helpful in resolving the philosophical question. Given that Becker included the gain and that doing so does not generally affect the general nature of the outcome, we will proceed consistently with that aspect of the model. In doing so, we also observe that excluding this factor would have the predictable consequence of encouraging increasingly severe punishments for more egregious crimes by removing this offsetting gain.

We are now ready to derive the elements of a theoretically optimal punishment policy. To simplify the analysis, we will first derive the optimal structure of penalties—that is, the choice between fines and prison—based on the assumption that the *probability of apprehension*, p, is fixed. Later, we will relax the assumption of a fixed probability and consider assessing an optimal enforcement strategy, in addition to an optimal structure of penalties.

1. Fixed Probability of Apprehension

We first consider the case of fines alone by fixing the *prison term*, t, at zero. Then we allow a choice between the two modes of punishment, fines and prison.

a. Fines Alone

Under a fine-only policy, the expected punishment is simply the fixed probability of apprehension times the fine, or pf. The condition for an offender to commit a crime therefore reduces to $g>pf$. The noteworthy feature of a fine is that the cost of increasing it is in theory zero.[42] By contrast, increased prison terms positively affect the cost function.

We assume that the crime in question imposes *harm on society*, denoted as h, which represents the dollar cost or equivalent value of any resulting harm, whether to property or person. To claim that a given criminal act is "efficient," the gain to the offender must

---

[41] LAFAVE, *supra* note 3, § 1.6(b).

[42] In fact, increasing the fine results in more revenue for the government. This is not counted as a social welfare gain, however, because it is merely a transfer from the offender to the government.

exceed the harm to society, or $g>h$. Comparing this with the offender's decision rule above, we see that the two will coincide when $pf=h$; that is, when the expected fine is set equal to the harm. Solving this for the optimal fine, yields:

$$f^*=h/p$$

Thus, the optimal fine for a given criminal act equals the harm from that act divided by the probability of apprehension. And since $p<1$ (the criminal justice system cannot eliminate *all* criminal activity), it follows that the fine should *exceed* the harm. The analysis is the same as that used to explain the now-discredited understanding of punitive damages for intentional torts.[43] As an example, if the harm from the act is $1500, and the probability of apprehension is .1, then the optimal multiplier is ten, resulting in a fine of $15,000.

Consider the following implications, which flow from the preceding analysis. First, the optimal fine is equivalent to a Pigouvian tax, or strict tort liability, adjusted to account for imperfect detection. This reflects the intuition that as with tort law, a central purpose of criminal law involves internalizing those externalities that produce social welfare losses. Second, for the purposes of setting the optimal fine, the enforcement authority does not need to account for the perpetrator's benefit from committing the crime; it only needs to assess the resulting societal harm. This avoids the intractable difficulties associated with calculating offender benefits. Third, crimes that are definitely inefficient are easily accounted for by simply assuming that the societal harm from the act, h, exceeds the maximum benefit to the offenders, thereby producing a social welfare loss. Thus, in our earlier example depicted in Figure 9:1, if $h>\$2000$, there could never be an "efficient" crime, and thus, within the framework of this model, setting the optimal fine as prescribed above produces a successful general deterrent.

In the case of crimes that are definitely inefficient, the harm-based fine derived above is "excessive," meaning it is higher than necessary to achieve complete deterrence. For rational offenders,[44] it is sufficient to set a fine, f, as follows:

$$f^*=g/p$$

That is, an offender should be required to disgorge his or her gains from committing the act, with the penalty suitably adjusted to reflect imperfect detection. Rational offenders will then anticipate no expected gain from committing the act and so will be deterred from doing so.[45]

There are three important caveats to this analysis:

The first caveat is that the analysis assumes offenders are risk neutral. For criminals who are risk preferring, not Becker's normal case, a low probability of a high penalty, one that fully offsets the potential gains, might not be an adequate deterrent. Assume, for example, that the probability of detection for a given offense, valued at $6000, is one-

---

[43] *See* Chapter 3 Section III.C.4; *see also supra* note 11.

[44] As previously noted, this will not deter those who are defined as "irrational" in the sense of beyond the reach of incentives, and for whom only specific, rather than general, deterrence, can ensure they will not commit criminal acts. *See supra* note 7; *infra* notes 91–99 and accompanying text.

[45] Keith Hylton, *The Theory of Criminal Penalties and the Economics of Criminal Law*, 1 REV. L. & ECON. 175 (2005).

third, and thus the enforcement authority calculates the optimal penalty, f^*, at 300% of expected gains, or $18,000. For risk-neutral (and risk-averse) criminals, this will be a deterrent since a penalty of $18,000 applied in one-out-of-three crimes equals (or exceeds) the expected gain from each criminal act, $6000. However, this penalty structure will *not* deter a risk-loving criminal because the risk itself—the uncertainty about being caught—confers utility.

This returns us to the distinction between general and specific deterrence. Within the framework of Becker's model, risk-neutral or risk-averse offenders may be deterred with a penalty structure that is not apt to deter risk-preferring offenders. For risk-preferring criminals, such penalties will not operate as a general deterrent, leaving specific deterrence as a primary means of preventing certain criminal acts.

The second caveat is that it is important to recognize that a "benefit-based" fine operates efficiently only if two conditions are met: first, if we assume that the relevant crime should be completely deterred; and, second, if we can more readily assess the offender's gain than the societal harm from the criminal act. An example where the latter condition might be met is insider trading since it is almost certainly easier for the enforcer to observe the offender's monetary gains than to estimate the full extent of societal losses, for example to other market participants.[46]

More generally, it is rarely optimal entirely to eliminate criminal activity. As with any other activity, the marginal cost of criminal enforcement is a rising function, whereas the marginal benefit of enforcement is a declining function. This is the criminal law analogue to the marginal Learned Hand formula in tort, which seeks to equate marginal costs and benefits to determine the appropriate recovery. For most non-violent criminal acts, meaning those for which the harm either is financial or can readily be translated into monetary equivalents, there is a cost spectrum that captures detection and prosecution. At some point, the relative costs of enforcement will exceed the relative benefits of detection and prosecution *even if* the overall category of crime is one worth prosecuting. With appropriate penalties in place, we can reduce crime in a cost-effective manner, but this does not mean altogether eliminating criminal activity. A subset of criminal activity—akin to residual risk in tort—will remain even when the enforcement authority undertakes cost-effective enforcement.

The preceding discussion involved non-violent crime. For violent criminal activity, the enforcement authority generally devotes a very high percentage of its resources to pursuing leads to protect potential victims. Of course there is always some resource constraint, and so there is an aspect of triage involved in the pursuit of all criminal activity, but in this context, the decisions are more apt to be framed based on the likelihood of successfully preventing physical harm than based on the simpler cost-benefit analysis outlined above.

---

[46] For a discussion of disgorgement as an alternative to harm as the basis for awarding tort damages, see *supra* Chapter 4 note 23 and accompanying text (discussing the Cooter and Porat disgorgement thesis). Whether or not insider trading is a crime that should definitely be deterred, however, has long been debated. HENRY G. MANNE, INSIDER TRADING AND THE STOCK MARKET (1966); Hayne E. Leland, *Insider Trading: Should It Be Prohibited?*, 100 J. POL. ECON. 859 (1992).

The third caveat involves applying a *reductio ad absurdum*, meaning the danger of taking the preceding analysis to its logical and absurd extreme conclusion. A classic illustration involves speeding, a misdemeanor. We typically observe police stops with escalating penalties based on the egregiousness of the driving behavior. In theory, we could dramatically reduce enforcement costs by imposing a super high penalty and apprehending only a tiny fraction of offenders. The forfeiture of a house, or, taking this to the complete extreme, imposing the death penalty, would undoubtedly provide general deterrence even with a very low chance of being apprehended. One might construe the Eighth Amendment prohibition against cruel and unusual punishment to prevent implementing such a scheme, although, in general, the clause has not been successfully employed in cases involving penalties claimed to be excessive.[47] More generally, due process, or simple principles of fairness, demands proportionality in attaching penalties to criminal offenses. We return to this concern below in assessing the relationship between optimal punishment under the Becker model and actual criminal sanctions.

b. Fines and Imprisonment

We now extend the model to allow the use of imprisonment instead of, or in combination with, fines. For now, we continue to assume that the probability of apprehension is fixed. As noted above, one of the main differences between fines and imprisonment is that imprisonment is costly.[48] In terms of its general deterrent effect, the preceding specification of the rational offender model implies that an appropriately tailored prison term has the same deterrent effect as a monetarily equivalent fine. Among the most important, if controversial, implications of the economic model of law enforcement therefore follows: *it is socially optimal for fines to be used to the maximum extent possible before a prison term is imposed.*[49]

The analysis raises important implications that are affected by socioeconomic status, and thus that map onto concerns of race and other demographic considerations. We begin by sketching the formal model as Becker presented it, and then consider these complicating dynamics and their normative implications.

The model generally assumes that the offender's wealth sets the upper limit on potential fines. Given that offenders have varying levels of wealth, the optimal fine can be specified as the lower of either the expression derived above, h/p,[50] or the offender's wealth. Returning to the above example where h=\$1500 and p=.1, the optimal fine is therefore \$15,000 or the full extent of offender's wealth if the latter is lower. If the wealth

---

[47] LAFAVE, *supra* note 3, § 3.5(f), at 148–49. Justice Powell, in his separate concurrence in *Bowers v. Hardwick* suggested that imposing a criminal sanction for consensual same-sex sodomy might violate the Eighth Amendment. 478 U.S. 186, 197 (1986), *overruled by* Lawrence v. Texas, 539 U.S. 558 (2003).

[48] There has also been a movement to have criminals pay for the cost of their incarceration after release. Tina Rosenberg, Opinion, *Paying for Their Crimes, Again*, N.Y. TIMES (June 6, 2011), http://opinionator.blogs.nytimes.com/2011/06/06/paying-for-their-crimes-again/. *See also* Leah A. Plunkett, *Captive Markets*, 65 HASTINGS L.J. 57 (2013).

[49] A. Mitchell Polinsky & Steven Shavell, *The Optimal Uses of Fines and Imprisonment*, 24 J. PUB. ECON. 89 (1984).

[50] Recall that h is harm, and p is the probability that the fine will be imposed.

constraint does not set upper limits, meaning that the imposed penalty can apply to future income or other sources of acquired wealth, the optimal prison term is zero.

In the case where the offender's wealth is lower than the optimal fine, however, the model suggests that a fine alone will result in under-deterrence. Assume, for example, that an offender's total wealth equals $10,000, which is the maximum fine he can be assessed if caught. This makes his expected fine (.1)($10,000)=$1000. Thus, if a fine is the only available sanction, the potential criminal might choose to commit the crime if $g>\$1000$ even though the penalty was set to deter the crime if $g>\$1500$. The model therefore implies that a poor offender on these facts risks committing too many crimes. This is the same dynamic as a judgment-proof actor risking too many negligent acts because he is immune from the usual tort sanction of monetary damages.

One way to read this model is to suggest that the risk of under-deterrence justifies supplementing fines with prison. Because prison is costly to impose, however, it will only be optimal to use it as a supplement to the fine if the benefit of greater deterrence equals or exceeds the social cost of imprisonment. This implies that reliance on prison will be most beneficial for those offenders whose wealth falls far below the harm from a given act because in that case the benefit of additional deterrence will be the greatest. It follows that the poor will be more likely to receive prison time under this theory, all else equal.

As previously noted, this analysis leads to potentially difficult normative implications. We touch on a few here. First, notice once more that the model assumes risk neutrality. We previously noted that risk-preferring individuals are willing to take greater risks given the relatively low probability of apprehension even if the present value of the crime is *lower than* the present value of the penalty times the risk of being caught. Now consider the possible opposite dynamic with very poor criminals. For those with wealth below the properly assessed penalty, f^*, if we assume that the result of successful prosecution is total wealth disgorgement (and possibly a lien on future-acquired assets), then we might also imagine that such persons are especially prone to being risk-averse given the financial impact to him or her of the criminal activity. The impact of the same fine for a poor person is apt to greatly exceed the impact of the same penalty for a person of financial means. This, of course, raises empirical questions that are difficult to test given the stylized nature of the assumptions built into the model. For example, we do not generally see wealth-based penalty schemes that we can compare with uniform penalty schemes for the same offense.

Second, the analysis implies that if we are limited to fixed penalty schemes, and if present wealth proves insufficient for poor persons to pay a levied fine, then this might justify incarceration to make up the differential value in the penalty. If a monetization scheme were implemented such that those with means could simply pay fines, and those who could not do so were sent to prison, this would exacerbate the already disproportionate representation of persons of color in prison. There is an influential literature on the burdens that this dynamic has created not only for the inmates themselves, but also for their families and the communities in which they live.[51]

---

[51] *See, e.g.*, MICHELLE ALEXANDER, THE NEW JIM CROW: MASS INCARCERATION IN AN AGE OF COLORBLINDNESS (2012); MICHAEL TONRY, MALIGN NEGLECT: RACE, CRIME, AND PUNISHMENT IN AMERICA (1995).

Finally, recall that calibrating appropriate criminal penalty schemes involves a marginal Learned Hand-type assessment of penalties times probabilities of apprehension. This means that the enforcement authority will assess the marginal costs of identification and prosecution, and thereby favor going after those who they can apprehend at lower cost. Another dynamic that operates to the detriment of relatively poor criminals, who also tend to reside in urban areas, is that it is relatively easier to identify and prosecute their criminal activity as compared with similar crimes committed in suburban or rural communities.[52] This, for example, has been particularly acute with respect to low-level drug crimes, including trafficking in, and possession and use of, marijuana, further exacerbating the race and socioeconomic dimensions of criminal law enforcement.

QUESTIONS AND COMMENTS

A possible alternative way to assess the impact of penalties focuses on the opportunity cost of fines versus imprisonment. Notice that the Becker model uses market valuation to assess the impact of fines or the alternative of imprisonment. Consider the following alternative approach. Assume a criminal act with a penalty of $10,000 or one year in prison. A convicted criminal who earns, say, $80,000 or more per year will likely find a way to pay the fine and to avoid imprisonment. By contrast, a convicted criminal with an income below, say, $25,000 likely has no way to avoid prison. The fine or penalty scheme would thus result in those with limited financial resources going to prison and those with greater resources avoiding prison in favor of the fine. Of course for the relatively wealthier criminal, the impact of the fine is minuscule as compared with its impact on the poor criminal.

Within the Becker model, the two sets of convicted criminals are treated equivalently based on the market valuation of the penalty. From an opportunity-cost perspective, however, elevating the fine based on means might provide a comparable level of deterrence as compared with a lower penalty assessed against poorer criminals. And for truly wealthy criminals, virtually no fine will suffice. Consider, for example, the incarceration of Bernie Madoff.[53] Was imprisonment the only means of imposing a meaningful penalty on him? Of course poor criminals typically lack the opportunity to implement high-level Ponzi schemes, making the comparison imperfect.

This analysis suggests three possible approaches: (1) apply the Becker model, which would use incarceration to substitute for the inability to assess fines against poor criminals; (2) apply the Becker model, but limit the judicial choice of prison or fines consistently without regard to the ability of the individual convicted of the crime to pay the entire fine; or (3) recast the Becker model to use opportunity cost as compared with market valuation in assessing the impact of the penalty on specific criminals or on criminals that possess a specific set of characteristics associated with socioeconomic status. Which of these seems the most fair? Fair to whom? Is it problematic to elevate sanctions simply because a person has greater financial means? Is that any better than using imprisonment to levy a punishment only on those who lack the means to pay an equivalent (based on market value) fine? Which approach do you prefer? Why?

---

[52] Jerome H. Skolnick et al., *The Social Structure of Street Dealing*, 9 AM. J. POLICE 1, 28 (1990).

[53] Judgment, ECF Doc No. 100, 4, United States v. Madoff, No. 09 Cr. 213 (S.D.N.Y. June 29, 2009).

c. Probation and Parole

Imprisonment is not the only form of non-monetary sanction that can be used in conjunction with fines. There are also three forms of supervised release: *probation* (supervised release in lieu of imprisonment), *parole* (early supervised release from prison), and *house arrest* (a closely monitored substitute for imprisonment). All three represent efforts to mitigate the cost of imprisonment while still allowing some supervision or monitoring of convicted offenders. Although these alternatives to prison impose lower societal costs, they are also less burdensome to offenders, thereby diluting their deterrent effect. On the other hand, prison itself can create great public burdens as those who are incarcerated for extended periods of time are more prone to recidivism, develop fewer marketable skills, and risk suffering considerable psychological harms.[54] The targeted use of these alternative forms of punishment offers important benefits as part of a comprehensive law enforcement policy, including improving prospects for meaningful societal reintegration after the punishment is complete.

Probation is often an effective sanction for individuals with no prior criminal history and convicted of minor offenses, who suffer a high cost from the stigma associated with criminal conviction, and for whom the risk of recidivism is low. Imposing actual prison time on these individuals is therefore largely unnecessary in terms of specific deterrence, although the reduced penalty might compromise general deterrence. As for parole, its main benefit is to give offenders an incentive to behave well while in prison, thereby lowering the cost of detention and perhaps contributing to productive use of prison time that might benefit the inmate on release. The Department of Corrections in most jurisdictions has few vehicles for motivating positive behavior in general, and the prospect of parole is among the most powerful.[55] Parole also has both specific and general deterrent effects among inmates, potentially reducing the incidence of in-prison crime both for the person who receives it, and for others hoping to do so.

The absence of the prospect of release for good behavior diminishes incentives to behave cooperatively while incarcerated. For this reason, such punishments as *life without eligibility for parole* or *three-strikes laws*, which incarcerate for life for a third offense without regard to its gravity, have potentially counterintuitive effects in terms of prison discipline.

The combined use of probation and parole allow the re-incarceration of convicted criminals who break the parole terms. Similarly those on house arrest risk incarceration if they break the restrictive terms, such as wearing monitoring anklets or leaving the permitted confines of the home other than during permitted times, such as during work release.[56] These combined prison alternatives lower the cost to the criminal justice system

---

[54] Shelley Johnson Listwan et al., *The Pains of Imprisonment Revisited: The Impact of Strain on Inmate Recidivism*, 30 JUST. Q. 144 (2011).

[55] Joan Petersilia, *Beyond the Prison Bubble*, 75 FED. PROBATION 1 (2011); Michael R. Geerken & Hennessey D. Hayes, *Probation and Parole: Public Risk and the Future of Incarceration Alternatives*, 31 CRIMINOLOGY 549 (1993).

[56] Jamie S. Martin et al., *Offenders' Perceptions of House Arrest and Electronic Monitoring*, 48 J. OFFENDER REHABILITATION 547 (2009); Brian K. Payne & Randy R. Gainey, *The Influence of Demographic Factors on the Experience of House Arrest*, 66 FED. PROBATION 64 (2002).

of administering penalties, and also create environments that are more suitable to successful reintegration into society.

2. *Optimally Chosen Probability of Apprehension*

We now turn to a more general characterization of the optimal enforcement policy in which the criminal justice regime can affect both the probability of apprehension and the magnitude and nature of the selected punishment. The choice of p (probability of apprehension) involves discretion over expenditures on police in addition to the costs associated with operating the judicial system. We first consider a fine-only regime in which p and f (fine) are chosen optimally, and later allow a choice of prison in conjunction with fines.

a. Fines Only

Professor Gary Becker first derived the conclusion that the optimal enforcement strategy in a fine-only regime should involve a maximal fine coupled with a low probability of detection.[57] Recall that in the fine-only case with a fixed p, if we assume that rational criminals are risk neutral, the optimal fine was equal to h/p. In the case where p can also be adjusted, the outcome is very different. Risk neutrality implies that rational offenders care only about the *expected* fine, pf.[58] Thus, the enforcer can achieve any desired level of deterrence by setting the appropriate *product* of p and f. This is equivalent to selecting the desired intersection point in Figure 9:1. However, raising p is costly as more police have to be hired, whereas raising f is not. This implies that that within this simple model, an optimal enforcement policy should always involve raising f as much as possible, and correspondingly lowering p, to achieve the target value of pf, although as previously noted, this can lead to seemingly absurd results.[59] Based on these assumptions, the fine should first be set at the offender's wealth, and the probability of apprehension should then be correspondingly lowered to achieve the target level of deterrence.

This conclusion is illustrated in Figure 9:2, where the negatively sloped, convex curve represents those combinations of p and f that yield a constant product pf. Since this achieves a fixed level of deterrence, it represents a "constant crime" line.[60] This follows the same logic as indifference curves, which trade off the marginal utility derived from alternative goods for individuals.[61] Here, we consider the marginal utility of the two "goods" in affecting general deterrence: fines and imprisonment. The criminal justice system is indifferent to the choice among the combined elements of p and f that each point along the curve represents in terms of the resulting deterrence effect.

---

[57] Becker, *supra* note 2.

[58] The conclusion would be different if they were risk-averse or risk-loving. See the *discussion infra* Part II.B.2.b.

[59] *See supra* Part II.B.1.b.

[60] Mathematically, the curve is a rectangular hyperbola.

[61] *See supra* Chapter 2.

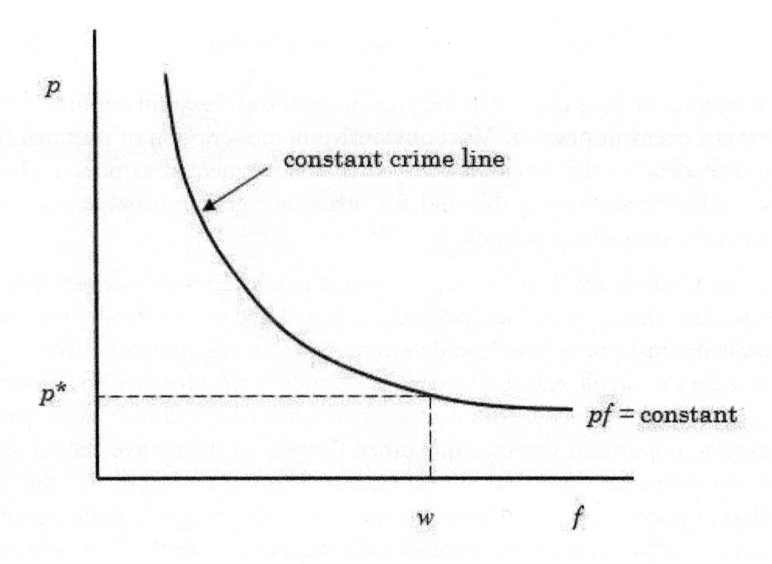

Figure 9:2. Cost-minimizing combination of *p* and *f* when offenders are wealth-constrained.

Although the system is indifferent to points along the curve from a deterrence perspective, explaining why it is a constant crime line, it is not indifferent from a cost perspective. Given that it is costly to raise *p* but costless to raise *f*, movement downward and to the right along this line lowers the enforcement costs of achieving the given level of deterrence. The cost-minimizing strategy, therefore, is to continue to raise *f* until it reaches the offender's wealth, indicated by the point labeled *w* in the graph, and then to set the probability of apprehension at the corresponding point on the curve, labeled *p**.

b. Fines and Imprisonment

Finally, consider the case where all policy variables, *p*, *f*, and *t*, can be freely chosen by the enforcement authority. In this case, because adjusting the probability of apprehension and the prison term are both costly, it remains optimal to raise the fine as high as possible before increasing either of the other two variables. Thus, the fine should, once more, be set at offender's wealth, and the other two variables should be increased to the point where their marginal deterrence benefit of each equals its marginal costs. Unfortunately, there is no simple formula like $f=h/p$ for describing the optimal value of those variables—it depends on their relative costs and benefits. That is because the enforcer is combining two costly inputs to produce the desired level of deterrence: (1) enforcement costs raise *p*, and (2) incarceration costs to raise *t*. This is therefore analogous to a firm choosing an optimal combination of capital and labor. Generally, the optimal solution is described by an equality between the *marginal rate of substitution* of capital and labor based upon the relative prices of the inputs. Because the analysis depends on the relative prices and productivity of each inputs, we cannot write a general formula for how much of each input to use. The same intuition applies here respecting fines or imprisonment.

c. Why Are Actual Fines Not Maximal?

The optimal policies derived in the previous sections depart in important ways from actual law enforcement practice. Most obviously, the prescription of maximal fines (i.e., equal to offenders' wealth levels) is rarely if ever implemented as policy. This section offers several explanations for this and for other divergences between the model and actual criminal enforcement policies.

Varying offender wealth. The first explanation as to why fines are not generally maximal is impracticality. The apprehension rate cannot be tailored to an offender's wealth, as the theoretically optimal policy based on deterrence alone would prescribe (see Figure 9:2). This is true for the simple reason that a given offender's wealth cannot be observed until *after* he or she is apprehended. Although apprehension rates will vary based on resource commitments, population density, and other factors, an alternative model assumes a constant apprehension rate for all offenders. This is analogous to the common assumption in price theory that firms cannot effectively engage in price discrimination within private markets, except in specified circumstances. If we think of penalties as the "price" of committing a crime, then the model suggests that likewise, the enforcement authority cannot price discriminate based on the ability of the criminal to pay at a given fine level. The analogy is imperfect, however, inasmuch as sentencing guidelines do allow some flexibility based on the past criminal record of individuals convicted of crime.

Given the general constraint on customizing penalties, it turns out that the optimal enforcement policy involves setting $f=h/p$ for individuals with wealth greater than h/p, and $f=w$ for individuals with wealth lower than h/p. Following this analysis, only offenders at the low end of the income distribution pay their full wealth as a fine. Individuals who face a fine of h/p are optimally deterred, whereas those who face a fine equal to their wealth risk being under-deterred. This analysis, once again, mirrors that applied to judgment-proof tortfeasors.

Given this structure of criminal fines, Professors A. Mitchell Polinsky and Steven Shavell have posited that it is optimal to increase the apprehension rate to the point where the reduction in under-deterrence at the low end of the income distribution just equals the marginal cost of raising p in the form of more resources being devoted to apprehension.[62] The reduction in under-deterrence occurs because a higher p lowers the value of h/p, thereby allowing more individuals to pay the optimal fine.

Criminal Offenses and Proportionality of Punishment. Perhaps the most important limit on the imposition of high fines or prison terms is the widely shared intuition that punishments should be proportional to crimes. It is important to recognize that proportionality operates at two levels, first, ensuring that the punishment is adequate to the offense, and second, ensuring that it is not excessive in light of the offense. These two proportionality objectives are in tension.

We begin with the consideration of adequacy. If the "proportionality norm" means that punishments should literally be proportional to harms in this sense, then the rule $f=h/p$ satisfies the requirement for a fixed p. However, if proportionality means that

---

[62] A. Mitchell Polinsky & Steven Shavell, *A Note on Optimal Fines When Wealth Varies Among Individuals*, 81 AM. ECON. REV. 618 (1991).

punishments should *not exceed* harms, then the rule fails whenever $p<1$.[63] That is because when the probability of apprehension is lower than 100%, optimal deterrence requires an increased fine, rendering punishment disproportionate to the offense. For example, if the probability of a $1000 theft is 50%, optimal deterrence requires a fine of $2000, which is twice the harm. Basing the fine on a criminal's wealth at the low end also risks violating proportionality given that pre-existing wealth bears no necessary correlation to the seriousness of an offense, and thus might require supplementation. And basing the fine on wealth at the high end only satisfies proportionality if the resulting fine is lower than or equal to the ratio h/p.

All told, the analysis implies that concerns for proportionality find their origins in intuitions separate from Becker's pure deterrence model. Such external considerations include due process, fairness, enforcements costs, and the relative incidence of penalties on differing demographic groups that are affected by, among other factors, socioeconomic circumstances.

Within the United States, judicial discretion also affects how the proportionality norm is handled. The goal of deterrence, which, as we have noted, is the main objective of the Becker model, is forward-looking, meaning that it seeks to prevent future crime. In its simplest form, the model predicts that this goal is best achieved by stiff sentences rarely applied. Ideally, within this framework, extreme punishments, because they successfully deter crimes, never have to be imposed, although as previously noted, this can lead to potentially absurd results.[64]

By contrast, proportionality is backward-looking in the sense that it focuses on the characteristics of the offense and the criminal after the crime has occurred. At this stage of the criminal process, there is evidence that the criminal justice system is in part concerned with the risk that judges and juries might sometimes impose overly harsh punishments.[65] Sometimes judges and juries themselves might be concerned that criminal sanctions are excessive as applied to particular offenses. An extreme example of this practice is *jury nullification*, whereby a jury declines to convict a defendant despite evidence that satisfies the legal standard of "beyond a reasonable doubt" to avoid imposition of what jurors perceive as an unjust punishment or because they believe that there is something problematic with classifying the underlying behavior as criminal.[66] Ultimately, the criminal justice system seeks to balance the competing values of deterrence and fairness.[67]

---

63 H.L.A. HART, *Punishment and the Elimination of Responsibility*, *in* PUNISHMENT AND RESPONSIBILITY 161–62 (1968).

64 *See supra* Part II.B.1.b.

65 *See* ROBERT DAWSON, SENTENCING: THE DECISION AS TO TYPE, LENGTH, AND CONDITIONS OF SENTENCE 201 (1969); Donald Wittman, *Punishment as Retribution*, 4 THEORY & DECISION 209, 233–34 (1974) (giving anecdotal evidence); *see also* Joel Waldfogel, *Criminal Sentences as Endogenous Taxes: Are they "Just" or "Efficient"?*, 36 J.L. & ECON. 139 (1993) (giving empirical evidence); Andrew Wistrich & Jeffrey Rachlinski, *Judging the Judiciary by the Numbers: Empirical Research on Judges*, 13 ANN. REV. L. & SOC. SCI. 203 (2017) (using experimental and field studies to demonstrate judges may deviate from impartiality).

66 WAYNE R. LAFAVE ET AL., CRIMINAL PROCEDURE § 22.1(g) (5th ed. 2009).

67 *See, e.g.*, Thomas Miceli, *Criminal Sentencing Guidelines and Judicial Discretion*, 26 CONTEMP. ECON. POL'Y 207 (2008).

Equal treatment of rich and poor. Another fairness consideration concerns the comparable treatment of defendants without regard to their relative wealth. The prescription that the fine should be equated to the offender's wealth implies that the rich and the poor will be treated differently; as previously noted, Becker's formal model carries the implication that the wealthy will pay higher fines and the poor will be more likely to face prison time. This problem is exacerbated by obvious racial implications as persons of color are disproportionately represented in lower socioeconomic groups, and also within prison populations. Actual criminal law policy instead rejects tailoring of punishments based on an offender's wealth, although myriad factors nonetheless contribute to these disparities.[68]

One commentator has criticized the criminal justice system as imposing excessive imprisonment on wealthy criminals as an antidote to the perception that persons of wealth otherwise "buy their way out of prison."[69] Other commentators take the juxtaposed position that the criminal justice system is rigged against the poor, including disproportionately persons of color.[70] This returns us to the opening discussion of the competing goals of the criminal justice system.

The Becker model views penalties strictly in terms of their deterrent effect and the costs of imposing them, revealing no qualitative difference between a monetary penalty and deprivation of liberty other than in terms of the marginal impact on general deterrence. Many observers, however, regard as unfair the reality that offenders who are poor are more apt to find themselves incarcerated. Although the Supreme Court has not treated wealth as the basis for heightened scrutiny under equal protection, and it has generally rejected equal protection challenges based on racial correlations in this context,[71] there is a wide perception that the criminal justice system is administered unfairly,[72] and this claim is in tension with the implications of the pure deterrence model.

Requiring all persons to face the same punishment without regard to wealth, and thus the ability to pay a fine, will bias punishments toward broader use of imprisonment.

---

[68] Most notably, this includes the responsiveness and quality of legal representation. The racial disparities are also affected by bail and the ability to pay. Cynthia E. Jones, *"Give Us Free": Addressing Racial Disparities in Bail Determination*, N.Y.U. J. LEGIS. & PUB. POL'Y 919 (2013) (arguing that broad decision-making power in bail determination proceedings leads to officials considering improper factors, such as wealth of the accused and race, in the bail determination process); Matthew Clair & Alix S. Winter, *How Judges Think About Racial Disparities: Situational Decision-Making in the Criminal Justice System*, 54 CRIMINOLOGY 332 (2016) (examining "judges subjective understandings of the cause of racial disparities in the criminal justice system" through interviews with judges on their decision-making processes and strategies).

[69] John Lott, *Should the Wealthy Be Able to "Buy Justice"?*, 95 J. POL. ECON. 1307 (1987).

[70] ALEXANDER, *supra* note 51; Michael Pinard, *Collateral Consequences of Criminal Convictions: Confronting Issues of Race and Dignity*, 85 N.Y.U. L. REV. 457 (2010).

[71] *See, e.g.*, San Antonio Indep. Sch. Dist. v. Rodriguez, 411 U.S. 1 (1973) (rejecting claim that wealth effect of school funding scheme justifies heightened scrutiny); Washington v. Davis, 426 U.S. 229 (1976) (rejecting high racial correlation of adverse testing result as a basis for applying heightened scrutiny); McCleskey v. Kemp, 481 U.S. 279 (1987) (rejecting the Baldus study as proof of purposeful discrimination in death penalty case).

[72] Matthew Robinson & Marian Williams, *The Myth of a Fair Criminal Justice System*, 6 JUST. POL'Y J. 1 (2009); Monica Anderson, *Vast Majority of Blacks View the Criminal Justice System as Unfair*, PEW RES. CTR.: FACT TANK (Aug. 12, 2014), http://www.pewresearch.org/fact-tank/2014/08/12/vast-majority-of-blacks-view-the-criminal-justice-system-as-unfair/.

The additional cost will likely require a lower apprehension rate, and with it, a diminution in deterrence. Efforts to equalize the treatment of rich and poor are apt to be only partially successful because those with means are able to hire private lawyers who handle fewer cases. The result is to lower the conviction rates of wealthy persons charged with crime or to secure more favorable plea bargains.[73]

Cost of false convictions. Two types of errors can occur in criminal prosecution: wrongful acquittals and wrongful convictions. As we explore more fully in Chapter 10, the high standard of proof for criminal conviction, as well as other procedural safeguards for defendants, reflect a particular social aversion to wrongful convictions. Despite this higher standard of proof, some errors will inevitably occur. If we assume that society suffers a greater loss from punishing an innocent person than from freeing a guilty one, this implies a potential social welfare loss inevitably associated with increases in the severity of the punishment, including fines. When this cost is accounted for, optimal fines will not generally be maximal.[74] This provides an additional reason, separate from proportionality, for disfavoring maximal fines.

Other costs of imposing fines. In addition to the cost of wrongful punishment, there might be other costs associated with imposing and collecting fines. First, offenders might seek to shelter their wealth, thereby imposing collection costs on the government. Second, as fines increase, offenders might increasingly seek to evade detection, thereby increasing apprehension costs.[75] For example, as speeding fines increased, wealthy drivers were more likely to rely on technologies that reliably signaled speed traps, although today, individuals with cell phones can download programs with this feature at almost no cost.

Risk-averse versus risk-preferring offenders. Except as noted, we have assumed that offenders are risk-neutral, meaning that they only care about the *expected fine*, or pf. If offenders are risk-averse, however, then greater uncertainty of punishment—i.e., lowering p and correspondingly raising f—itself imposes a cost on offenders. In that case, a maximal fine is no longer necessarily optimal.[76] This works by introducing variance in the possible punishment; along with a lower probability of apprehension comes a higher penalty should it occur. For risk-averse offenders, even though the overall cost of engaging in criminal activity is the same when these two variables are properly adjusted, the value of the reduced-probability-higher-penalty regime imposes greater cost than the certain-apprehension-fixed-penalty regime. As a result, for risk-averse criminals, we can avoid imposing the maximal fine and still achieve the same level of deterrence by offsetting with the added risk of a higher fine for those who are actually apprehended.

This conclusion holds without the need to include the utility of the offense to those who commit them within the social welfare function. Instead, the desirability of lowering p and raising f is simply a means of calibrating optimal deterrence while also accounting

---

73 For a discussion of plea bargaining, *see infra* Chapter 10.

74 *See* John Harris, *On the Economics of Law and Order*, 78 J. POL. ECON. 165 (1970); Thomas Miceli, *Optimal Criminal Procedure: Fairness and Deterrence*, 11 INT'L REV. L. & ECON. 3 (1991).

75 Arun Malik, *Avoidance, Screening and Optimum Enforcement*, 21 RAND J. ECON. 341 (1990).

76 A. Mitchell Polinsky & Steven Shavell, *The Optimal Tradeoff Between the Probability and Magnitude of Fines*, 69 AM. ECON. REV. 880 (1979).

for the cost of judicial administration. The difficulty remains, however, in ascertaining the risk preference of potential criminals.

Although his earlier model began with the premise of risk neutrality, Gary Becker also posited that offenders might tend to be risk-preferring.[77] If so, then the greater *certainty* of punishment is itself a deterrent, and the preceding conclusions are reversed. Consider an earlier illustration: Recall that we assumed a 33% chance of apprehension for a given offense, and that to compensate, we set the penalty at 300% of the value of the offense, with these values known in advance. A would-be criminal who is risk-preferring would assume a two-thirds chance of succeeding, and a one-third chance of a really big loss if she did not succeed. As a result, for a risk-preferring criminal, we would have to raise the penalty level to compensate for the *reduced* deterrent effect of uncertain apprehension.

Marginal deterrence. The final argument against maximal fines is marginal deterrence. This means that to deter offenders from committing more harmful acts, punishments need to increase along with the increased marginal harm. Thus, for example, if breaking and entering, and armed robbery, were punishable with the same sanction, offenders would not be marginally deterred by the sanction from committing the latter act. This argument suggests that punishments should generally rise with degrees of harm, and that sanctions should be less than maximal for all but the most harmful acts.[78]

The implications for optimal punishment can be difficult to assess. The reason, as we have seen, is that deterrence can be achieved by raising the probability of apprehension as well as the magnitude of the sanction. Thus, marginal deterrence can be achieved with maximal sanctions if more effort is devoted to apprehending offenders who commit more harmful acts. Only if the probability of apprehension cannot be tailored to specific crimes will it be optimal to lower actual sanctions for less harmful acts.

One complication is that with marginal analysis, there is an outer limit for the maximal crime. Thus, the punishment for lesser crimes has to be reduced incrementally down to the initial offense. As a practical matter, therefore, it would only be possible to fully deter the most egregious offenses.

QUESTIONS AND COMMENTS

Consider three-strikes laws in California and other jurisdictions.[79] These schemes are designed to deter repeat offenders by providing no relief for a third offense regardless of its gravity, with the result of life without eligibility for parole. If you were setting optimal punishment policy, how would you advise the California legislature with respect to this

---

[77] Becker, *supra* note 2, at 178.

[78] Both Cesare Beccaria and Jeremy Bentham anticipated marginal analysis of criminal penalties. *See supra* note 5 and accompanying text; Steven Shavell, *A Note on Marginal Deterrence*, 12 INT'L REV. L. & ECON. 345, 345 (1992). In addition, George Stigler relied on marginal analysis in his critique of Becker's model. Stigler, *supra* note 40. For recent formal analyses, see Shavell, *supra*; David Friedman, *Hanged for a Sheep: The Economics of Marginal Deterrence*, 22 J. LEGAL STUD. 345 (1993); Tim Friehe & Thomas Miceli, *Marginal Deterrence When Offenders Act Sequentially*, 124 ECON. LETTERS 523 (2014).

[79] David Schultz, *No Joy in Mudville Tonight: The Impact of Three Strike Laws on State and Federal Corrections Policy, Resources, and Crime Control*, 9 CORNELL J.L. & PUB. POL'Y 557 (2000).

scheme, and why? What about life without eligibility for parole more generally? What about other lengthy sentences that exceed an inmate's life expectancy?

C. Repeat Offenders

As noted above, increasingly harsh punishments for repeat offenders are a pervasive feature in a variety of contexts. In addition to three-strikes laws, this also includes criminal and regulatory enforcement, punishment of sports infractions, and even school discipline. Although such schemes appear to be politically popular,[80] they are difficult to justify on the basis of economic theory. For the limited category of crimes for which the benefits to the perpetrator exceed the societal costs (including forgone enforcement costs of apprehension and punishment) there is no obvious basis for punishing repeat offenders more harshly per offense. By way of analogy, if we assume no special costs associated with the repeated nature of the offense, this would be akin to charging repeat customers higher prices for any number of commodities or services.

In the more common case in which the social harm from an act exceeds the benefit for all offenders, meaning that the offense is not efficient, a policy of setting the expected value of the punishment equal to the harm should be sufficient to deter rational offenders from committing the crime. If some offenders choose to commit it anyway, there is no reason on deterrence grounds to threaten punishing them more harshly for future violations as a matter of general deterrence, although, as discussed in the next section, additional sanctions might be justified on grounds of specific deterrence (e.g., incapacitation).

If we assume the probability of apprehension is not fixed, but rather is a variable that is calibrated to reduce enforcement costs, it is especially difficult to then further impose a regime of increasing fines. Given that the model is premised on a maximal penalty to compensate for the reduced risk of apprehension even for the initial offense, increasing penalties beyond those needed to ensure that the present value of risk times punishment deters offenses is in tension with the larger criminal justice model.

As the arguments in the previous section demonstrate, however, several observed features of actual punishment practices require that we modify features of the standard Becker model. This includes relaxing some of its core assumptions or introducing social values beside efficiency that bear on the determination of criminal punishments. In the discussion that follows, we relax some of the model's core assumptions and we also introduce some non-efficiency values in an effort to better explain observed features of the criminal justice system that are inconsistent with the model's predictions.

One possibility, first suggested by Professor George Stigler, is that individuals might sometimes commit first offenses "by accident," such as when they are unsure of the law in question, or perhaps because they acted inadvertently.[81] In this setting, several authors

---

[80] *See, e.g.*, SpearIt, *Legal Punishment as Civil Ritual: Making Cultural Sense of Harsh Punishment*, 82 MISS. L.J. 1 (2013); Walter L. Gordon III, *California's Three Strikes Law: Tyranny of the Majority*, 20 WHITTIER L. REV. 577 (1999).

[81] Stigler, *supra* note 40, at 528–29.

have shown that increasing the penalty for repeat offenders may be optimal because repeat offenders are more likely to have acted intentionally.[82]

An alternative interpretation is that repeat offenses are an objective means of inferring heightened mens rea. Recall that mens rea, or scienter, is the mental state that accompanies the criminal act, or actus reus. This is captured in Stigler's intuition that a first offense might be "by accident." By contrast, second or third offenses are more likely to be with specific knowledge, and perhaps intent. In general, a higher scienter increases the gravity of the charged offense, and thus warrants a higher level of punishment.

Another approach, first suggested by Professors A. Mitchell Polinsky and Daniel L. Rubinfeld, is that because various offenders might differ in their gains from crime, they might also represent different threats to society.[83] An escalating penalty scheme can help sort those who value the crime more, and who thus pose a greater societal harm by eliminating from the pool of repeat offenders those who are deterred with the initial sanctions. This implies that that some offenders are beyond rational deterrence. Such offenders either hold infra-marginal valuation from repeat offenses (meaning that the marginal gain from successive offenses exceeds the marginal increase in expected penalty from those offenses), or they suffer a cognitive impairment that renders them somehow immune to the relevant incentive effects that generally motivate others. This relates to the legal standards for insanity, which we take up below.

With respect to rational offenders, the analysis of repeated offenders further implies that escalating punishments assume that those who contemplate repeated crimes consider the *lifetime* punishment from first embarking on a criminal career. Thus, *backloading* penalties deters such rational offenders while saving on the (wasteful) cost of punishing them as habitual offenders since they will forecast the relevant costs and benefits in advance.[84] In this way, escalating penalties balance the gains from deterrence against the costs of punishment.

An alternative argument for escalating penalties is that the scheme offsets the *learning-by-doing* effect of repeat crime, which raises the cost of apprehending experienced criminals.[85] Offsetting this effect, however, is the likelihood that enforcers will pursue

[82] C.Y. Cyrus Chu, Sheng-Cheng Hu & Ting-Yuan Wang, *Punishing Repeat Offenders More Severely*, 20 INT'L REV. L. & ECON. 127 (2000); Winand Emons, *Subgame-Perfect Punishment for Repeat Offenders*, 42 ECON. INQUIRY 496 (2004).

[83] A. Mitchell Polinsky & Daniel Rubinfeld, *A Model of Optimal Fines for Repeat Offenders*, 46 J. PUB. ECON. 291 (1991).

[84] Thomas Miceli, *Escalating Penalties for Repeat Offenders: Why Are They so Hard to Explain?*, 169 J. INSTITUTIONAL & THEORETICAL ECON. 587 (2013).

[85] Kyung Hwan Baik & In-Gyu Kim, *Optimal Punishment When Individuals May Learn Deviant Values*, 21 INT'L REV. L. & ECON. 271 (2001). For an article demonstrating that individuals "with an incarceration history earn significantly higher annual illegal income from criminal activity compared with [individuals] without an incarceration history," see Donald T. Hutcherson, *Crime Pays: The Connection Between Time in Prison and Future Criminal Earnings*, 92 PRISON J. 329 (2012).

repeat offenders more aggressively,[86] and that enforcers might also learn from experience, thereby becoming more effective in their pursuit of repeat offenders.[87]

Another argument for escalating penalties arises from the stigma associated with criminal punishment.[88] One source of this stigma is the reduced labor market opportunities for individuals with a criminal record. This feature of the criminal sanction is problematic, and it also has complex implications for the economic model. The threat of stigma associated with a criminal conviction enhances the potential specific deterrence for first-time offenders. It does so by raising the opportunity cost of committing a crime. For example, the presence of stigma would shift the cost line upward in Figure 9:1, thereby lowering the crime rate for any punishment scheme. However, once an individual *has* a criminal record, the impaired opportunities for legitimate employment then lower the opportunity cost of committing *additional* crimes.[89] The marginal stigmatic effect of additional convictions might be lower than the marginal cost of the first conviction in terms of the potential harm to employment prospects. Thus, optimal criminal penalties can be lowered for first-timers and raised for repeaters. An escalating scheme might achieve a desired level of deterrence.[90]

D. The Insanity Defense

Insanity is a legal, rather than psychological or psychiatric, term. Its meaning has evolved throughout history within England and the United States. Under the *M'Naghten* test, a person was deemed insane, and thus not legally culpable for a criminal act, if he met two alternative criteria: first, he did not understand the nature and quality of his actions, and second, if he did, he did not understand the implications of those actions, meaning that they are wrong.[91] This test governed within English law for many years, and was also applied within the United States.

A difficulty with the *M'Naghten* test is that it disallowed an insanity plea for individuals who, although understanding the nature of the harm they caused, cognitively could not control their actions as a consequence of an "irresistible impulse."[92] The

[86] David A. Dana, *Rethinking the Puzzle of Escalating Penalties for Repeat Offenders*, 110 YALE L.J. 733, 739–57 (2001).

[87] Nuno Garoupa & Mohamed Jellal, *Dynamic Law Enforcement with Learning*, 20 J.L. ECON. & ORG. 192 (2004). This analysis can also be expressed in terms of a Red Queen game. LEWIS CARROLL, THROUGH THE LOOKING-GLASS, AND WHAT ALICE FOUND THERE 50 (Henry Altemus 1897). For a discussion of Red Queen games in evolutionary biology, see generally MATT RIDLEY, THE RED QUEEN: SEX AND THE EVOLUTION OF HUMAN NATURE (1993).

[88] *See* Eric Rasmusen, *Stigma and Self-fulfilling Expectations of Criminality*, 39 J.L. & ECON. 519 (1996); Dana, *supra* note 86, at 772–76; Patricia Funk, *On the Effective Use of Stigma as a Crime-Deterrent*, 48 EUR. ECON. REV. 715 (2004); Thomas J. Miceli & Catherine Bucci, *A Simple Theory on Increasing Penalties for Repeat Offenders*, 1 REV. L. & ECON 71 (2005).

[89] This appears consistent with Hutcherson, *supra* note 85.

[90] A final possible explanation for escalating penalties is that they serve to educate the public about the social acceptability of particular activities or behaviors. Dana, *supra* note 86, at 776–83. Low initial penalties send a message that a particular act is not acceptable, and increasing penalties for repeat offenses strengthens that signaling effect as the behavior becomes more entrenched.

[91] M'Naghten's Case, [1843] 8 Eng. Rep. 718.

[92] *R v. Byrne* [1960] 2 Q.B. 396.

irresistible impulse test was applied within England in the case of *R. v. Byrne*,[93] and within the United States most notably in the case of Lorena Bobbitt, who was acquitted of criminal charges after cutting off her husband's penis following claims of sexual and other physical abuse.[94]

The *Durham* test works a compromise between the *M'Naghten* and *Irresistible Impulse* tests, inquiring whether the crime was the product of the defendant's mental disease, such that without the disease, she would not have committed the crime.[95] Within federal practice, the application of the more liberal *Durham* test has largely been abandoned.[96]

The *Model Penal Code* provides that "[a] person is not responsible for criminal conduct if at the time of such conduct as a result of mental disease or defect he lacks substantial capacity either to appreciate the criminality [wrongfulness] of his conduct or to conform his conduct to the requirements of law."[97] This rule provides for a complete defense. Within federal practice, the Comprehensive Crime Control Act, enacted in 1984, requires that "at the time of the commission of the acts constituting the offense, the defendant, as a result of a severe mental disease or defect, was unable to appreciate the nature and quality or the wrongfulness of his acts;" this must be established by "clear and convincing evidence."[98] The Insanity Defense Reform Act of 1984[99] sets out related provisions applied to sentencing. The federal standard has been described as a partial return to the *M'Naghten* standard, which assesses the ability of the criminal defendant to distinguish right from wrong.

Although the Becker model does not specifically address the various insanity tests, consider whether individually or separately they meaningfully capture individuals who are beyond the reach of sanctions contained within criminal law that are designed to motivate rational actors. One way to construe these tests is that they are attempts to avoid imposing criminal sanctions on those who cannot respond rationally to such sanctions, but who are, nonetheless, an ongoing danger to themselves or others.

E. Specific Deterrence (Including Incapacitation)

Our discussion of crime control thus far has focused primarily on how criminal law enforcement reduces social harm through its effect on general deterrence. For offenders who are not susceptible to general deterrence, the principal means through which society can prevent further offenses is specific deterrence, including incapacitation and its later effect in discouraging future crime.[100] Undoubtedly, this was the primary motivation for

---

93 *Id.*

94 Russell D. Covey, *Temporary Insanity: The Strange Life and Times of the Perfect Defense*, 91 B.U. L. REV. 1597, 1623 (2011).

95 Durham v. United States, 214 F.2d 862 (D.C. Cir. 1954). The test originated in the New Hampshire case, State v. Pike, 49 N.H. 399 (1870).

96 United States v. Brawner, 471 F.2d 969, 975–78, 1039 (D.C. Cir. 1972) (overturning reliance on *Durham* test).

97 MODEL PENAL CODE § 4.01 (AM. LAW INST. 1985).

98 18 U.S.C. § 17.

99 18 U.S.C. § 4241.

100 *See* source cited *supra* note 2 and accompanying text.

the once-popular three-strikes laws, which prescribed life imprisonment for persons repeatedly convicted of criminal acts.[101] The goal of incapacitation might also provide an explanation for the apparent and dramatic "over-use" of prison within the United States as compared to the prescriptions of the Becker model, which, you may recall, reserves prison for use only when fines alone cannot practically accomplish the deterrence objective.

Professor Steven Shavell has argued that the economic theory of incapacitation implies that potentially dangerous individuals should be kept in prison only for as long as the harm they would impose on society if released exceeds the cost of further detention.[102] Whether or when release becomes desirable, however, depends on offsetting effects. On one hand, offenders may become less dangerous the longer they are in prison, either because harmfulness declines with age, or because imprisonment has been accompanied with successful efforts at rehabilitation. On the other hand, prison itself is an often-brutal environment, one fundamentally at odds with rehabilitation. Many prisoners become more dangerous with time served and thus "hardened" criminals without regard to the nature of the original offense. In this context, hardening might mean having the opportunity to study and network with older, more seasoned, offenders, creating greater criminal opportunities on release.[103] Sometimes the stigma of having "served time" prevents meaningful reintegration by inhibiting beneficial employment prospects on release, thus encouraging, or at least inviting, recidivism. Whether *softening with age* or the *hardening with imprisonment* dominates raises difficult empirical questions. It is possible that both intuitions are correct, but each intuition has greater effect over different age ranges for convicted criminals. In other words, incarcerated criminals might harden to some set point, after which they begin to soften with age.

F. Some Empirical Evidence

We conclude our survey of the economic model of crime with a brief review of empirical evidence that relates to the preceding analysis. We first summarize tests of the deterrent effect of criminal punishments, which is crucial in assessing the model's usefulness for formulating policy. We then discuss the relationship between crime rates and the business cycle. Later, in Section III, we also offer some empirical evidence on the death penalty and gun laws.

1. *Testing the Deterrent Effect of Punishment*

In 2007, Professors Steven D. Levitt and Thomas J. Myles surveyed the large empirical literature designed to test the implications of the economic theory of crime.[104]

---

[101] There are, of course, less drastic, but perhaps less effective, forms of incapacitation, such as house-arrest or revocation of a driver's license.

[102] Steven Shavell, *A Model of Optimal Incapacitation*, 77 AM. ECON. REV. 107 (1987).

[103] *See* Shankar Vendantam, *When Crime Pays: Prison Can Teach Some to be Better Criminals*, NPR: MORNING EDITION (Feb. 1, 2013), http://www.npr.org/2013/02/01/169732840/when-crime-pays-prison-can-teach-some-to-be-better-criminals (quoting Donald Hutcherson: "Spending time in prison leads to increased criminal earnings . . . On average, a person can make roughly $11,000 more [illegally] from spending time in prison versus a person who does not spend time in prison." (citing Hutcherson, *supra* note 85)).

[104] Levitt & Myles, *supra* note 5, at 455.

With respect to the deterrent effect of law enforcement, they cite several studies that found a negative relationship between the crime rate, on one hand, and both greater hiring of police and longer prison sentences, on the other. With respect to police, they conclude: "the marginal benefit in reduced crime associated with hiring an additional police officer in large urban environments . . . [is] roughly in line with the marginal cost."[105] This implies that the scale of police forces is close to efficient levels.

Although Levitt and Myles find that crime rates decline in response to longer prison terms, in contrast with policing, they conclude from empirical evidence that "it appears that the current scale of incarceration is above the socially optimal level."[106] This conclusion is in line with recent claims by many politicians that incarceration rates in the United States are excessively high, especially for minorities. Although the prison population has leveled off in recent years, America still has about 25% of the world's prisoners despite having 5% of the world population.[107]

One difficulty with such correlative studies is sorting out cause and effect. Does hiring more police or increasing prison terms reduce crime due to deterrence or due to incapacitation? Distinguishing the two is important both for policy reasons and for assessing the rational offender assumption, which depends only on deterrence. Several studies have therefore explicitly tried to sort out the separate effects. For example, Professors Daniel Kessler and Steven Levitt looked for changes in the crime rate following the 1982 sentence-enhancement laws in California.[108] An immediate drop in crime would support finding a general deterrence effect because the longer prison terms had not yet taken effect. This would imply that the threat of longer incarceration, rather than incapacitation or specific deterrence, caused the drop in crime. The authors did indeed find evidence of a reduction in crime, thus strengthening the case for general deterrence.

Professors Jonathan Klick and Alexander Tabarrok identified an ingenious natural experiment to test the effect of increased police presence on the level of crime based on terror alerts in Washington, D.C.[109] The authors recognized that following terror alerts in the George W. Bush Administration, there was a corresponding increase in police presence, and they used public data to test the effect of the presence on criminal activity. They found a reduction in crime as a negative function of increased police presence, especially in the area of Washington's National Mall. Because the terror alerts themselves were random from the perspective of general expected criminal activity, this allowed the

---

[105] *Id.* at 469.

[106] *Id.* at 471.

[107] Minorities, particularly African-Americans and Hispanics, are disproportionately represented in the prison population despite committing crimes at the same rates as whites. *See* ASHLEY NELLIS, SENT'G PROJECT, THE COLOR OF JUSTICE: RACIAL AND ETHNIC DISPARITY IN STATE PRISONS (2016); E. ANN CARSON & ELIZABETH ANDERSON, BUREAU OF JUST. STAT., PRISONERS IN 2015 (2016). *See also American Prisons: The Right Choices*, THE ECONOMIST (June 20, 2015), http://www.economist.com/news/briefing/21654578-americas-bloated-prison-system-has-stopped-growing-now-it-must-shrink-right-choices.

[108] Daniel Kessler & Steven D. Levitt, *Using Sentence Enhancements to Distinguish Between Deterrence and Incapacitation*, 42 J.L. & ECON. 343 (1999).

[109] Jonathan Klick & Alexander Tabarrok, *Using Terror Alert Levels to Estimate the Effect of Police on Crime*, 48 J.L. & ECON. 267 (2005).

authors to isolate the effect of increased police presence as a general deterrent, and the authors found a statistically significant effect.

Passage of three-strikes laws by several states also provided an opportunity to disentangle deterrence and incapacitation. In a cross-state study, Professors Carlisle E. Moody and Thomas B. Marvell found that such laws actually increased the homicide rate by as much as 30% over the long run.[110] This appears counterintuitive, and yet, one reading, based on marginal deterrence, helps to reconcile the result: given that offenders facing the maximal penalty (life imprisonment) for a crime have no incentive to refrain from committing further, more harmful, acts in an effort to avoid apprehension, it might be less surprising that the third, triggering event is the more serious offense of homicide.

Professor Joanna M. Shepherd criticized the results of the Moody and Marvell study, arguing that the authors failed to account for the possibility that passage of three-strikes laws may have been a *response to*, rather than a *cause of*, higher murder rates.[111] This problem is referred to as a *simultaneity bias*. After correcting for this, Shepherd found that three-strikes laws in California reduced the rate of covered crimes, not only by repeat offenders—those who would have been subject to the maximal sanction—but also by first-time offenders, thus providing further evidence in favor of a general deterrence effect of prison.

In a separate study, Steven Levitt used a different strategy to distinguish deterrence and incapacitation.[112] He recognized that adults face harsher penalties than juveniles for most crimes, and he posited that if the deterrence hypothesis is sound, criminals transitioning into the adult system should be deterred to a greater extent than they had been as juveniles by the threat of harsher punishments. Levitt's study confirmed this hypothesis of a greater deterrence effect.

2. The Effect of the Business Cycle on Crime Rates

One implication of the rational offender hypothesis is that certain offenses, those that target financial gain, should increase when general economic conditions decline. As the economy worsens and opportunities for legal employment decline, crime should become more attractive to those individuals who would consider it as a possible substitute for lawful income. The idea is similar to the above discussion of the stigma effect of criminal conviction, which we argued caused an erosion of labor-market options and thereby reduced the deterrent effect of criminal penalties by lowering the opportunity cost of crime.

Two studies have employed this logic to test the deterrence hypothesis, and both supported the theory.[113] Using data from 1949 to 1997, the studies showed that the unemployment rate is a significant positive determinant of the rate of property crimes.

---

[110] Thomas B. Marvell & Carlisle E. Moody, *The Lethal Effects of Three-Strikes Laws*, 30 J. LEGAL STUD. 89 (2001).

[111] Joanna M. Shepherd, *Fear of the First Strike: The Full Deterrent Effect of California's Two- and Three-Strikes Legislation*, 31 J. LEGAL STUD. 159, 169–70 (2002).

[112] Steven D. Levitt, *Juvenile Crime and Punishment*, 106 J. POL. ECON. 1156 (1998).

[113] *See* Philip Cook & Gary Zarkin, *Crime and the Business Cycle*, 14 J. LEGAL STUD. 115 (1985); Steven Raphael & Rudolf Winter-Ebmer, *Identifying the Effect of Unemployment on Crime*, 44 J.L. & ECON. 259 (2001).

Specifically, a drop of 1% in the unemployment rate resulted in a decline of between 1.6% and 5% in the property crime rate. By contrast, the studies did not find a significant effect of unemployment on the rate of violent crimes. This supports the rational offender model inasmuch as property crimes are much more likely to be motivated by the desire for economic gain, which increases with adverse economic conditions, whereas violent crimes are more likely to be motivated by non-financial considerations, and thus, such crimes are less apt to be affected by general changes in economic conditions.

III. EXTENSIONS OF THE BASIC THEORY

This part examines several extensions of the basic economic theory of law enforcement. Specifically, we discuss the problem of corruption of law enforcement agents, the impact on crime of the death penalty and gun control laws.

A. Corruption of Law Enforcement Officers

All legal systems are potentially subject to corruption, and economic analysis has been applied to study the nature of corruption, its causes, and how to structure institutions so as to limit corruption and its effects.[114] The focus here will be on corruption of the police, those on the front line of enforcing criminal law. We specifically consider the possibility that police might accept bribes in return for not reporting a criminal violation, or might frame an innocent person and then demand payment for not turning him in.[115]

There are many reasons to be disturbed by such egregious behavior when it occurs, including, most notably, abuse of the public trust. Without suggesting that diluting the deterrence function of the criminal law is the most important concern, we now focus on this effect. Bribery reduces deterrence by lowering the payment an offender expects to make when apprehended for a crime.[116] Assume a fine of $1000 for a theft of property valued at $100. If the police officer avoids charging the perpetrator in exchange for a $200 bribe, then the efficacy of the set penalty, valued at ten times the valuation of the offense, has been reduced to two times that valuation. The problem becomes more complex if we account for the implications of a criminal record, which might well exceed the cost of the fine itself and which therefore further contributes to the deterrent effect of the criminal law. If the fine is $1000 and the criminal record for the misdemeanor imposes an expected cost of $5000, then in theory the perpetrator might be willing to pay an unscrupulous police officer up to $5999 to avoid the higher cost combined criminal sanction.

The incentive problem is exacerbated by the potential for a repeat play relationship between the officer and the perpetrator. This might, for example, be the case with members of organized-crime families or gangs who pay regular bribes to evade criminal prosecution, and who, in doing so, significantly supplement the pay of officers who are

---

[114] *See, e.g.*, Andrei Shleifer & Robert W. Vishny, *Corruption*, 108 Q.J. ECON. 599 (1993) (studying corruption related to bribes for governmental largesse).

[115] The analysis is based in part on A. Mitchell Polinsky & Steven Shavell, *Corruption and Optimal Law Enforcement*, 81 J. PUB. ECON. 1 (2001).

[116] Offenders worried about the stigma from conviction, however, might be willing to pay more than the nominal fine.

"on the take." Of course the officers themselves are subject to criminal prosecution, and there are complex structures within police departments for internal investigations.[117]

Another form of police corruption involves framing persons who have not committed a crime. *Framing* lowers the deterrent effect of criminal law by diverting the focus of prosecution onto non-perpetrators, and in doing so, it also lowers the opportunity cost of crime. Specifically, it lowers the cost of engaging in criminal acts by discounting the possibility that the actual culprit will be apprehended and by reducing the differential returns between legal and illegal activity.

B. Entrapment, Solicitation, and Inducement to Commit Criminal Acts

Another form of police malfeasance, similar to framing, is *entrapment.* This occurs when a criminal defendant claims that *solicitation* by an undercover police officer unlawfully encouraged him to commit a crime that he otherwise would not have committed. As a general proposition, solicitation itself is not against the law if it merely provides the perpetrator an opportunity to commit a criminal act that he was otherwise inclined to commit. When solicitation crosses the line to *inducement*, thereby encouraging the perpetrator to commit a crime that he was not otherwise inclined to commit, the perpetrator can raise entrapment as an affirmative defense. This typically entails having the criminal defendant prove by a preponderance of the evidence that the police crossed the prohibited line, transforming lawful solicitation into prohibited entrapment, although some jurisdictions require the state to disprove entrapment beyond a reasonable doubt.

Entrapment differs from framing in that the defendant is not claiming factual innocence; rather he is claiming that the actions of the police unduly contributed to his guilt. From a deterrence perspective, the entrapment defense is meant to discourage excessive police enforcement of criminal laws, meaning enforcement efforts aimed at individuals who did not intend to engage in criminal behavior, and thus who are less in need of being deterred.

The application of the entrapment defense, however, is problematic because the defendant actually *did* commit a crime. And it is possible that in many such cases, the police believe that the perpetrator will engage in the criminal activity with or without police involvement, but involve themselves to gain needed evidence for a successful prosecution. One complicating factor arises when the resulting charges against the entrapped perpetrator are used as leverage to gain testimony against others whom the police would otherwise have difficulty prosecuting.[118]

The economic theory of crime provides two possible justifications for the use of an entrapment defense. First, a defendant could argue that although he was in fact seeking a criminal opportunity—for example, to buy drugs or hire a prostitute—he would not have found one *but for* the solicitation by the undercover police officer. Since the law does not

---

[117] *See* OFFICE OF COMMUNITY ORIENTED POLICING SERVS., U.S. DEP'T OF JUSTICE, STANDARDS AND GUIDELINES FOR INTERNAL AFFAIRS: RECOMMENDATIONS FROM A COMMUNITY OF PRACTICE (Aug. 21, 2009) (explaining the recommended procedure for investigating citizen complaints against police).

[118] This gives rise to a potential prisoners' dilemma. For an exploration of the prisoners' dilemma in various contexts, including criminal law, see *infra* Chapter 15.

punish merely for holding criminal intent (mens rea) that is not coupled with a criminal act (actus reus), absent the contrived criminal opportunity, there would have been no basis for the offense.[119] The alternative argument is that the criminal act induced by the entrapment itself forms *actus reus*, which combined with the state of mind, provides the basis for a criminal conviction. The fact that such individuals imposed no *actual* harms is fortuitous, and when *solicitation* does not rise to *inducement,* the criminal law treats the underlying acts accordingly.

A second justification for an entrapment defense is that although the defendant was caught in a sting, he might not have committed the alleged criminal act had the police not sufficiently sweetened the deal as compared with ordinary opportunities, to make it worthwhile. This argument posits that the defendant was not sufficiently predisposed to commit the alleged crime but for the slightly more attractive circumstances associated with the entrapment itself. And so, *but for* the inducement by the officers, the opportunity cost of the criminal act for the defendant was too high.

One difficulty is that this opportunity-cost argument rests on intuitions about the offender's state of mind at the time of the offense, something that is not directly observable. Professor Dru D. Stevenson has argued that in response to this difficulty, courts have tended to judge entrapment based on observable behavior of the police—for example, whether they appeared to be overly zealous—rather than based upon evidence of the defendant's state of mind.[120]

C. The Death Penalty

Capital punishment is undoubtedly among the most controversial criminal justice policies. Globally, its use has been on the decline.[121] Within the United States, this has long been a contentious issue. Today, relatively few counties lead in executions nationwide.[122] After steady declines in executions during the early to mid-twentieth century, in its 1972 decision, *Furman v. Georgia*, the Supreme Court held five-to-four that capital punishment was unconstitutional.[123] The majority agreed only on a one paragraph per curiam opinion that was split over two groups: Justices Stewart, White, and Douglas, focused on the apparent arbitrariness associated with race, albeit without specifically finding a violation of the Fourteenth Amendment Equal Protection Clause.[124] Justices Brennan and Marshall claimed more broadly that the death penalty itself was cruel and

---

[119] *See* STEVEN SHAVELL, FOUNDATIONS OF ECONOMIC ANALYSIS OF LAW 564–65 (2004).

[120] Dru D. Stevenson, *Entrapment and the Problem of Deterring Police Misconduct*, 37 CONN. L. REV. 67 (2004).

[121] *See, e.g., On the Way Out—with Grisly Exceptions*, THE ECONOMIST, July 4, 2015, at 50–51.

[122] *See* Lee Kovarsky, *Muscle Memory and the Local Concentration of Capital Punishment*, 66 DUKE L.J. 259 (2016); *The Clustering of the Death Penalty*, DEATH PENALTY INFO. CTR., http://www.deathpenaltyinfo.org/clustering-death-penalty (last visited Aug. 28, 2017) (showing that, as of January 1, 2013, "15 counties accounted for 30% of the executions in the U.S. since 1976").

[123] 408 U.S. 238 (1972).

[124] *Id.* at 239–40.

unusual punishment in violation of the Eighth and Fourteenth Amendments.[125] Chief Justice Burger, and Justices Blackmun, Powell, and Rehnquist, dissented.[126]

State legislatures responded to the challenge by enacting procedures intended to satisfy the discredited regime struck down in the 1972 *Furman* decision. In the 1976 decision, *Gregg v. Georgia*,[127] the Supreme Court, with Justice Potter Stewart writing, rejected constitutional challenges to the newly enacted death penalty laws and set forth the requirements for a constitutionally permissible scheme.[128] These include that the guilt/innocence and sentencing phases be bifurcated, that the first phase provide objective and reviewable criteria for death eligibility, and that the second phase provide an opportunity for the jury to carefully assess and weigh those factors that might mitigate the offense, thereby warranting a lesser penalty, against the aggravating factors presented by the state.

More recently the mechanisms of execution have themselves come under constitutional attack. In 2015, the Supreme Court sustained Oklahoma's lethal injection protocol against a constitutional challenge alleging that its lack of proven efficacy constituted cruel and unusual punishment.[129] Although nineteen states have abolished capital punishment as of 2015, Table 9:1 shows that the rate of executions in the United States had for a number of years been on the rise since its constitutionality was re-established in *Gregg*. Beginning in the year 2007, those numbers began to decline, and this is reflected most notably in the lower yearly average from the years 2010 through 2016. The data appear below.

Although the death penalty raises a host of normative questions, here we inquire as to whether it is a deterrent for the limited category of capital murder offenses to which it applies within relevant jurisdictions. In one sense, capital punishment offers a nearly ideal test of the general deterrence hypothesis. The alternative to the death penalty is almost invariably life imprisonment without the possibility of parole. Setting aside the limited category of in-prison crime, both penalties involve permanent incapacitation.[130] Any negative effect on the crime rate, therefore, can only be due to deterrence. Actual testing of the death penalty's general deterrent effect, however, presents significant empirical challenges.

---

[125] *Id.* at 257 (Brennan, J., concurring); *id.* at 314 (Marshall, J., concurring).

[126] *Id.* at 375 (Burger, C.J., dissenting).

[127] 428 U.S. 153 (1976) (introducing the use of "aggravating" and "mitigating" factors in the penalty phase of capital punishment cases).

[128] For an excellent history, see CAROL S. STEIKER & JORDAN M. STEIKER, COURTING DEATH: THE SUPREME COURT AND CAPITAL PUNISHMENT (2016).

[129] *See* Glossip v. Gross, 135 S. Ct. 2726 (2015).

[130] Levitt & Myles, *supra* note 5, at 474.

Table 9:1. Executions in the United States, 1930–2016

Period	Number Executed	Yearly Average
1930–1939	1,667	166.7
1940–1949	1,284	128.4
1950–1959	717	71.7
1960–1967	191	23.9
1968–1976	0	0
1977–1989	120	9.2
1990–1999	478	47.8
2000–2009	590	59.0
2010–2016	254	36.3 (for seven-year span)

Source: *Statistical Abstract of the U.S.*, various years, and *Bureau Of Justice Statistics: Prisoners Executed.*[131]

Professor Isaac Ehrlich, the first economist to systematically address this issue, relied on data from the 1930s to the 1970s (i.e., prior to the 1972 to 1976 hiatus), and found a significant deterrent effect for the death penalty as compared with life without eligibility for parole.[132] By contrast, Professor Lawrence Katz relied on data from 1950 to 1990 (i.e., spanning the pre- and post-hiatus period) and found no such additional deterrent effect.[133] A third set of studies that focused solely on the post-hiatus data (i.e., from 1977 on) found a significant deterrent effect.[134]

---

[131] *Statistical Abstracts of the United States: Prisoners Executed under Civil Authority by Sex and Race*, U.S. CENSUS BUREAU, https://www2.census.gov/library/publications/2011/compendia/statab/131ed/tables/12s0352.xls (last visited Apr. 3, 2018); *Prisoners Executed*, BUREAU OF JUST. STAT., https://www.bjs.gov/index.cfm?ty=pbdetail&iid=2079 (last visited Apr. 3, 2018). Since 2010, the number of executions have gone down each year, with twenty executions in 2016. *Id.* There are several possible causes, including fewer death penalty sentences, death row inmates dying of age/natural causes due to aging, death sentence reversals, and state administrative challenges in obtaining lethal injection drugs. *See* TRACY L. SNELL, BUREAU OF JUST. STAT., CAPITAL PUNISHMENT, 2014–2015 (2017); Rebecca Hersher, *Death Sentences and Executions Are Down, But Voters Still Support Death Penalty Laws*, NPR (Dec. 21, 2016, 12:06 AM), http://www.npr.org/sections/thetwo-way/2016/12/21/506183108/death-sentences-and-executions-are-down-but-voters-still-support-death-penalty-l; Jennifer Horne, *Lethal Injection Drug Shortage*, COUNCIL OF ST. GOV'TS: E-NEWSLETTER (2017), http://www.csg.org/pubs/capitolideas/enews/issue65_4.aspx.

[132] Isaac Ehrlich, *Capital Punishment and Deterrence: Some Further Thoughts and Additional Evidence*, 85 J. POL. ECON. 741 (1977); Isaac Ehrlich, *The Deterrent Effect of Capital Punishment: A Question of Life and Death*, 65 AM. ECON. REV. 397 (1975).

[133] Lawrence Katz et al., *Prison Conditions, Capital Punishment, and Deterrence*, 5 AM. L. & ECON. REV. 318 (2003).

[134] *See* H. Naci Mocan & R. Kaj Gittings, *Getting Off Death Row: Commuted Sentences and the Deterrent Effect of Capital Punishment*, 46 J.L. & ECON. 453 (2003); Hashem Dezhbakhsh et al., *Does Capital Punishment Have a Deterrent Effect?: New Evidence from Postmoratorium Panel Data*, 5 AM. L. & ECON. REV. 344 (2003); Joanna M. Shepherd, *Murders of Passion, Execution Delays, and the Deterrence of Capital Punishment*, 33 J. LEGAL STUD. 283 (2004).

In a review of these post-hiatus studies, Professors John J. Donohue and Justin Wolfers concluded that the incidence of the death penalty is sufficiently rare that changing the design variables even slightly rendered the claimed findings non-robust. The authors stated:

> Our key insight is that the death penalty—at least as it has been implemented in the United States since *Gregg* ended the moratorium on executions—is applied so rarely that the number of homicides it can plausibly have caused or deterred cannot be reliably disentangled from the large year-to-year changes in the homicide rate caused by other factors.[135]

The death penalty obviously raises a host of questions beyond any claimed marginal deterrence effect. These include: the impact of quality counsel on the death penalty, the socioeconomic divergence of its application, the overwhelmingly disparate application correlated with race, and also with the differential race of the victim and perpetrator.[136] A separate consideration involves the relative cost of life incarceration versus the death penalty with the various appeals that commonly precede either execution or relief in favor of an alternative sentence.

To be sure, death penalty supporters find it ironic that opponents rely on, among other bases, the cost of protracted delays that the appeals they pursue impose on the judicial system as a basis for repealing the death penalty.[137] And yet, our system does include legal processes that death row inmates are lawfully entitled to pursue, and the cost of ensuring that a person convicted of a capital offense and sentenced to death has had her or his constitutional rights protected prior to execution is a legitimate cost consideration in assessing the penalty's efficacy. Excluding the cost of ensuring the lawful administration of the death penalty would bias the results and render the analysis incomplete.

Undoubtedly the most critical cost associated with the death penalty is the risk of wrongful punishment. As recent cases in which condemned prisoners have been released based on DNA evidence reveal, even the substantial safeguards put in place for capital cases cannot entirely eliminate error.[138] An interesting aspect of this cost is whether the distinction between a possibly erroneous execution is different in kind from other

---

[135] John J. Donohue & Justin Wolfers, *Uses and Abuses of Empirical Evidence in the Death Penalty Debate*, 58 STAN. L. REV. 791, 794 (2006).

[136] David C. Baldus et al., *Comparative Review of Death Sentences: An Empirical Study of the Georgia Experience*, 74 J. CRIM. L. & CRIMINOLOGY 661 (1983); *but see* McCleskey v. Kemp, 481 U.S. 279 (1987) (rejecting the Baldus study as a basis for striking down the death penalty). *See also* John Wooldredge et al., *Victim-Based Effects on Racially Disparate Sentencing in Ohio*, 8 J. EMPIRICAL LEGAL STUD. 85 (2011); Jefferson E. Holcomb et al., *White Female Victims and Death Penalty Disparity Research*, 21 JUST. Q. 877 (2004); Theodore Eisenberg et al., *Forecasting Life and Death: Juror Race, Religion, and Attitude Toward the Death Penalty*, 30 J. LEGAL STUD. 277 (2001).

[137] Knight v. Florida, 528 U.S. 990, 992 (1999) (Thomas, J., concurring) ("It is incongruous to arm capital defendants with an arsenal of 'constitutional' claims with which they may delay their executions, and simultaneously to complain when executions are inevitably delayed."); Alex Kozinski & Sean Gallagher, *Death: The Ultimate Run-on Sentence*, 46 CASE W. RES. L. REV. 1, 24–25 (1995); *see also* Jeremy J. Schirra, *Killing Them with Procedure: A New Cruel and Unusual Punishment*, CRIM. L. BRIEF, Spring 2011, at 5.

[138] For a website that collects this information, see *The Innocence List*, DEATH PENALTY INFO. CENT., http://www.deathpenaltyinfo.org/innocence-list-those-freed-death-row (last visited Aug. 28, 2017).

erroneous punishments, including extended incarceration. There is ample literature taking the position that "death is different,"[139] and in some obvious respects it is.

A central claim of the death-is-different literature involves the finality associated with wrongful execution. Of course wrongful incarceration is also final in the sense that its adverse psychological and other consequences can never be undone. Reparations cannot compensate for the lost freedom and other resulting harms. The marginal deterrence effect as between life without eligibility for parole versus the death penalty remains but one aspect of the debate over the death penalty, a topic that will continue to be debated based on a wide range of normative considerations.

D. Gun Laws and Crime

Another controversial issue in the area of criminal justice policy is the question of gun control. Few would argue against keeping guns out of the hands of criminals and others who are a danger to themselves or to society. Supporters of the right to bear arms, as expressed in the Second Amendment, maintain that the problem is how to accomplish that goal without simultaneously depriving law-abiding citizens of the right to own guns.

The history of the right "to keep and bear Arms" is complicated. The Second Amendment to the United States Constitution states: "A well regulated Militia, being necessary to the security of a free State, the right of the people to keep and bear Arms, shall not be infringed."[140] One of the fundamental interpretive questions involves the relationship between the prefatory clause, which grounds the operative clause in the context of well-regulated militia, and the operative clause, which includes no express limitation on "the right of the people to keep and bear Arms."

The scholarly literature on the meaning of the Second Amendment is more extensive than the Supreme Court case law.[141] In the 1939 decision, *United States v. Miller*, the Supreme Court held that the Second Amendment did not create an enforceable individual right.[142] That ruling lasted for nearly seventy years. The Court reversed course in the 2008 decision, *District of Columbia v. Heller*, declaring an individual right to keep and bear arms in the context of a challenge to a gun control law in the District of Columbia.[143] And then

---

[139] *See, e.g.*, Raoul G. Cantero & Robert M. Kline, *Death Is Different: The Need for Jury Unanimity in Death Penalty Cases*, 22 ST. THOMAS L. REV. 4 (2009); Jeffrey Abramson, *Death-Is-Different Jurisprudence and the Role of the Capital Jury*, 2 OHIO ST. J. CRIM. L. 117 (2004).

[140] U.S. CONST. amend. II.

[141] *See, e.g.*, Akhil Reed Amar, *The Second Amendment: A Case Study in Constitutional Interpretation*, 2001 UTAH L. REV. 889; Robert H. Churchill, *Gun Regulation, the Police Power, and the Right to Keep Arms in Early America: The Legal Context of the Second Amendment*, 25 LAW & HIST. REV. 139 (2007); Saul Cornell, *Commonplace or Anachronism: The Standard Model, the Second Amendment, and the Problem of History in Contemporary Constitutional Theory*, 16 CONST. COMMENT. 221 (1999); Glenn Harlan Reynolds, *A Critical Guide to the Second Amendment*, 62 TENN. L. REV. 461 (1995); Don B. Kates, *A Modern Historiography of the Second Amendment*, 56 UCLA L. REV. 1211 (2009); Nelson Lund, *The Second Amendment, Political Liberty, and the Right to Self-Preservation*, 39 ALA. L. REV. 103 (1987); Sanford Levinson, *The Embarrassing Second Amendment*, 99 YALE L.J. 637 (1989). Nelson Lund, *The Second Amendment, Political Liberty, and the Right to Self-Preservation*, 39 ALA. L. REV. 103 (1987).

[142] 307 U.S. 174 (1939).

[143] 554 U.S. 570 (2008).

in the 2010 case, *McDonald v. City of Chicago*,[144] the Court extended that right to apply against municipalities and states through the constitutional doctrine of incorporation, in that case as applied to a restriction by the City of Chicago.[145]

Among the most contentious academic and political questions related to crime, as shown below, is the effect of gun control laws on the crime rate. In theory, one can examine the effect of gun laws either by looking across states and asking whether those with stricter gun laws exhibit higher or lower levels of crime, or one could look at a given jurisdiction that enacts a gun law and ask how the new law affected the crime rate within that state. Both approaches are subject to biases. In the cross-sectional approach, for example, states with higher crime rates may be more likely to enact strict gun laws, which might falsely lead one to conclude that stricter laws caused crime to increase. And in conducting intra-state time-series studies, one would have to control for all factors besides the new gun law that could affect crime rates in order to avoid a spurious correlation.

The economist most closely associated with gun law research is John Lott, who used data from all 3054 counties[146] in the United States for the period 1977 to 1992 to examine the effect of concealed-carry laws—laws that allow citizens to carry concealed handguns—on the crime rate. Lott claimed that these laws lowered the crime rate, reflecting a deterrent effect.[147] Lott's conclusions, however, have been subject to substantial criticism, as summarized by Ian Ayres and John Donahue, who generated an opposite result and who concluded that "it is probably wise to push for more study than for more laws."[148] The Ayers and Donahue study has also been criticized for the selective application to a five-year period, based on the observation that the same methodology will generate opposite result if the period for analysis is extended.[149]

The debate over guns laws, like that over capital punishment, will no doubt continue, as will studies of their effect on crime rates. It is also worth considering whether time-limited studies adequately address the long-term implications of the wide availability of guns. Guns are long-term durable goods, and even when they are acquired by responsible

---

144 561 U.S. 742 (2010).

145 Through the incorporation doctrine, the Supreme Court has now applied all but three of the substantive protections in the Bill of Rights against the states. LAFAVE ET AL., *supra* note 66, § 2.4–2.6. The Court has accomplished this by construing the Fourteenth Amendment Due Process Clause to include in its substantive protections those rights, specified within the Bill of Rights, with the exception of the right to a jury trial for cases in excess of $20, the right to indictment by a grand jury (indictment by information is adequate), and the right not to have troops quartered in peacetime. Until the *McDonald* case, the list of unincorporated rights also included the Second Amendment.

146 At the time of Lott's research the number of counties in the United States was 3054; today the number of counties is 3142. *Annual Estimates of the Resident Population for Counties: April 1, 2010 to July 1, 2016*, U.S. CENSUS BUREAU, https://www.census.gov/data/tables/2016/demo/popest/counties-total.html (for total number of United States Counties click on "United States" under the heading "Annual Estimates of the Resident Population for Counties: April 1, 2010 to July 1, 2016) (last visited Aug. 31, 2017).

147 JOHN R. LOTT, MORE GUNS, LESS CRIME (1998).

148 Ian Ayres & John J. Donohue III, *Nondiscretionary Concealed Weapons Laws: A Case Study of Statistics, Standards of Proof, and Public Policy*, 1 AM. L. & ECON. REV. 436, 466 (1999) (reviewing JOHN R. LOTT, MORE GUNS, LESS CRIME (1998)).

149 The authors studied the initial five-year period after the passage of "shall issue laws," the timing of which varied from state to state. Carlisle E. Moody & Thomas B. Marvell, *The Debate on Shall-Issue Laws*, 5 ECON. J. WATCH 269, 272–73 (2008).

owners, persons who maintain them appropriately and who obtain proper training on use and storage, there is no guarantee that the guns will be passed on to others who are also responsible and who will exercise comparable precautions and care. The growing stash of guns, estimated in the US at 300 million (bear in mind the population is 319 million), is the product of generations of previously accumulated guns.[150]

One of the most common arguments against gun control laws is that they will only affect those who seek to acquire guns legally. This is partly true inasmuch as there is a large stock of guns available for illegal acquisition. But is it possible that the empirical studies might be focusing on the wrong question? If the goal is not to immediately reduce the incidence of crime, but to reduce the growing stock of available guns over time, then gun control laws, combined with other incentive programs to remove guns that are already available, will work toward reducing the availability of guns for illegal acquisition. The relevant time line to assess the effect of such a policy might be long, but it is also true that decisions spanning back decades have affected present gun-related crime rates.

Second Amendment advocates claim that if law-abiding citizens have guns, they can defeat those who use guns for violent crime. Consider whether this too rests on problematic, or at least ambitious, assumptions. These include ensuring that those who are law abiding will choose to acquire guns, will have a loaded weapon ready at the precise time when a gun crime is going to take place, and, most importantly, will have the knowledge and temperament to use the gun effectively under intensely stressful and life-threatening conditions. If any of these conditions are not met, then the wide availability of lawful guns is less likely to be a meaningful antidote to pervasive gun crime. Of course it is also true that awareness of the availability of lawful guns might, in some circumstances, discourage gun crime. In general, the empirical studies on gun control consider the effect of gun laws on overall crime or overall violent crime. An additional question involves the frequency with which lawfully acquired guns are used to successfully overtake illegally obtained guns employed in the course of criminal activity.

QUESTIONS AND COMMENTS

Does economic analysis affect your intuitions about the death penalty? Gun control laws? Do you believe that these are issues for which appropriate empirical evidence will eventually "resolve" the underlying policy questions? Why or why not? If not, are there other questions that economic analysis can help to answer that relate to these policy questions? What are they?

One of the principal arguments by Second Amendment rights advocates does not involve the beneficial use of guns against perpetrators. Rather, it involves the claim that such rights are necessary to avoid government tyranny. Can you devise an empirical test for the guns-prevent-tyranny hypothesis? Why or why not? If you conclude guns do prevent tyranny, are there countervailing considerations that would nonetheless justify restricted access to guns? If you conclude that guns do not prevent tyranny, are there countervailing benefits to gun ownership that nonetheless favor an individual right to bear arms?

[150] WILLIAM J. KROUSE, CONG. RESEARCH SERV., RL32842, GUN CONTROL LEGISLATION 8 (2012).

IV. APPLICATIONS

1. In 2015, the FBI demanded that Apple provide a back door into a cell phone in its possession. This cell phone was used by one of the now-deceased perpetrators in a shooting in San Bernardino, California that resulted in the deaths of fourteen persons and in serious injuries to twenty-two additional victims.[151] The FBI was concerned that the attackers might have had connections to terrorist cells within the United States and abroad, and, if so, that there were possible further plans for domestic attacks. The technical details surrounding this matter are highly complex, and the purpose here is not to explore them in depth. Rather, it is to simplify (with the admitted risk of oversimplification) the details as needed to consider what, if any, implications the economic analysis of criminal law might have held for the order by a federal district court judge in California compelling Apple to comply with the FBI's demand for cooperation.[152]

The FBI had relied on the *All Writs Act*[153] (rather than issuing a *subpoena*) to make two related requests: (1) that Apple construct a new version of its *iOS* operating system that can be installed on the *IPhone 5C* and that will allow the FBI to gain access to the phone data without the problems associated with delay and an eventual wall resulting from the limited permissible attempts to unlock the phone with entered key data; and (2) that Apple prospectively create a back door to its phone-operating systems so that upon future events of this sort, the FBI can more quickly access the relevant information, potentially abating further attacks. Apple declined these requests, claiming, among other arguments: (1) that it lacked the present technology to unlock the phone and that it had no obligation to create it, although it did not deny the capacity to do so; (2) that by doing so for the then-current iPhone and by creating a prospective back door to its locking technology on future iPhones, Apple would threaten the privacy of its users; (3) that doing so would invite unscrupulous public officials in nations abroad, where Apple sells its products, to compel such access for dissidents and other persons who, although running afoul of domestic law in those countries, are engaging in conduct that many in the United States would find defensible, even commendable.

As demonstrated in this chapter, the economic analysis of criminal law reveals certain insights that operate in parallel to those operating in the economic analysis of tort law. In one framing, the goal is to minimize the sum of criminal activity plus enforcement costs, similar to the goal in tort of minimizing the sum of precautions and accident costs, as reflected in Figure 3:1.[154] This provides the basis for much of Professor Gary Becker's general deterrence model for crime.

---

[151] Adam Nagourney et al., *San Bernardino Shooting Kills at Least 14; Two Suspects Are Dead*, N.Y. TIMES (Dec. 2, 2015), https://www.nytimes.com/2015/12/03/us/san-bernardino-shooting.html.

[152] Matt Zapotosky, *FBI Has Accessed San Bernardino Shooter's Phone Without Apple's Help*, WASH. POST (Mar. 28, 2016), https://www.washingtonpost.com/world/national-security/fbi-has-accessed-san-bernardino-shooters-phone-without-apples-help/2016/03/28/e593a0e2-f52b-11e5-9804-537defcc3cf6_story.html?utm_term=.8889ec1e1679n (noting the alternative method the FBI used allowed it to "withdraw the case").

[153] 28 U.S.C. § 1651 (2012).

[154] *See supra* at 77.

How, if at all, does Becker's model help to assess the competing positions of the FBI and Apple in this case? How do you think that the case should have been resolved? Are your answers to these two questions the same? Why or why not?

2. In a series of recent high profile events, police officers have taken the lives of persons of color under circumstances that, although contested, have been presented in dominant media accounts to suggest the absence of a credible and immediate physical threat to the officer's physical well being.[155] The factual events in Baltimore, Maryland involving Freddie Gray have been resolved by a series of acquittals for those cases brought to trial, and with the others dismissed. No federal charges were brought against the officers.[156] Although the cases have been legally resolved, the factual circumstances in Ferguson, Missouri involving Michael Brown; and New York City, involving Eric Garner, and many others, remain disputed.

On many occasions, prosecutors have failed to bring charges, grand juries have failed to indict, and of juries have failed to convict police officers in these sorts of tragic circumstances, with the result of setting off substantial urban unrest, sometimes leading to violence, injuries, and related criminal activity. As stated in Question 1, one premise of the Becker model is that the criminal justice system seeks to minimize the social costs of crime and the administrative costs of criminal law enforcement. In this context, the economic analysis poses a puzzle: The failure to successfully prosecute police officers charged with serious criminal activity—taking the lives of individuals, who are persons of color and who, although suspected of criminal activity, did not appear to present an adequate justification based on an immediate physical threat to the officer—substantially raises the risk, and thus the cost, of future criminal activity.

There are different methods of framing this problem. Just as the underlying factual predicates to these shootings are contested, so too are the circumstances that have led to the failures to indict some officers and to convict others in similar cases. Some prominent scholarly and media accounts claim that police officers receive a degree of solicitousness within our system of criminal justice that is not afforded to criminal defendants more generally, and even less so for persons of color. Assume for purposes of this question that the failure to indict or to convict in such cases is at least in substantial part a by-product, or peculiar feature, of our somewhat arcane system of criminal justice. This includes the conferral of various protections associated with due process, broadly understood. These protections apply to all suspects and criminal defendants, including police officers, and although they have different consequences from case to case, they tend to benefit police officers who are often viewed as particularly credible by jurors serving on grand or petit juries.

---

[155] *See, e.g.*, Mitch Smith, *Minnesota Officer Acquitted in Killing of Philando Castile*, N.Y. TIMES (June 16, 2017), https://www.nytimes.com/2017/06/16/us/police-shooting-trial-philando-castile.html; Jacey Fortin & Jonah Engel Bromwich, *Cleveland Police Officer Who Shot Tamir Rice Is Fired*, N.Y. TIMES (May 30, 2017), https://www.nytimes.com/2017/05/30/us/cleveland-police-tamir-rice.html; Rebecca Ruiz, *Officers Won't Be Charged in Black Man's Shooting Death in Louisiana*, N.Y. TIMES (May 2, 2017); Lucia Walinchus & Richard Pérez-Peña, *White Tulsa Officer is Acquitted in Fatal Shooting of Black Driver*, N.Y. TIMES (May 17, 2017), https://www.nytimes.com/2017/05/17/us/white-tulsa-officer-is-acquitted-in-fatal-shooting-of-black-driver.html.

[156] Rebecca R. Ruiz, *Baltimore Officers Will Face No Federal Charges in Death of Freddie Gray*, N.Y. TIMES (Sept. 12, 2017), https://www.nytimes.com/2017/09/12/us/freddie-gray-baltimore-police-federal-charges.html.

To the extent that this explains the failure to indict or to convict officers in these circumstances, society could reduce the social cost of crime by more willingly charging and prosecuting such officers as this would help to abate the pent up demand for justice when such tragic circumstances arise.

This suggests a fundamental tension in our system of criminal justice as it applies to such incidents, and with that, three possible approaches: First, if we conceive the due process rights as belonging solely to the criminal defendant, we risk exacerbating the risk of criminal activity following such high profile and racially charged events. Second, if we conceive the rights associated with the criminal process, including charging and trial, as vested more broadly in the public interest, we can possibly lower the risk of unrest, but at the cost of relaxing protections for the police officers who find themselves as criminal suspects, as subject to grand jury proceedings, or as criminal defendants in these circumstances. Third (a variation on the first), given these pressures, we might cast due process as a figurative firewall between the rights of those charged with criminal offenses and the interests of society. In this framing, we would limit the economic analysis of crime to prospective general deterrence rather than to deterrence of other criminal activity, including any unrest associated with any unsuccessful effort to indict or convict police officers in these cases.

Question 1: Does the economic analysis of criminal law inform the choice of framing? If so, how? If not, why not? Which framing do you find most persuasive, and why? How, if it all, is your answer affected by the economic analysis of criminal law set out in this chapter?

Question 2: Consider the related question of *victim impact statements*. In *Payne v. Tennessee*, 501 U.S. 808 (1991), the Supreme Court rejected a constitutional challenge to introducing such statements in the sentencing phase of a capital murder trial. Since then, forty-four states have adopted laws permitting their use. Does the economic analysis of criminal law help to assess whether the Supreme Court reached the right result in *Payne*? Why or why not? How does this question relate to the three alternative framings described above?

3. In recent years, university policies designed to curb campus sexual assaults have come under intense scrutiny.[157] These policies are, in large part, motivated by requirements of Title IX of the Civil Rights Act of 1964, a portion of the United States Education Amendments of 1972,[158] and related litigation. These policies do not follow a criminal law model, and they do not afford those charged with offenses, such as rape and sexual assault, with due process protections, including the requirement of proof beyond

---

[157] For criticism of such policies see Jacob Gersen & Jeannie Suk, *The Sex Bureaucracy*, 104 CALIF. L. REV. 881 (2016); Janet Halley, *Trading the Megaphone for the Gavel in Title IX Enforcement*, 128 HARV. L. REV. F. 103 (2015); Emily Yoffe, *The Uncomfortable Truth About Campus Rape Policy*, THE ATLANTIC (Sept. 6, 2017), https://www.theatlantic.com/education/archive/2017/09/the-uncomfortable-truth-about-campus-rape-policy/538974/. For defenses of these policies see Michelle J. Anderson, *Campus Sexual Assault Adjudication and Resistance to Reform*, 125 YALE L.J. 1940 (2016); *Sexual Assault on Campus: Working to Ensure Student Safety: Hearing Before the S. Comm. on Health, Education, Labor, and Pensions*, 113th Cong. (June 26, 2014), https://www.gpo.gov/fdsys/pkg/CHRG-113shrg22618/pdf/CHRG-113shrg22618.pdf (testimony of Catherine E. Lhamon, Assistant Sec'y Off. for C.R., U.S. Dep't of Educ.); Kirsten Gillibrand, Opinion, *Betsy DeVos is Betraying Our Students*, COSMOPOLITAN (Sept. 13, 2017), http://www.cosmopolitan.com/politics/a12229492/betsy-devos-kirsten-gillibrand-title-ix-sexual-violence/ (Gillibrand is the junior Senator from New York State).

[158] 20 U.S.C. §§ 1681–88 (2012).

a reasonable doubt, before a penalty can be imposed. At the same time, the imposed penalties are not criminal, but rather, are administrative, including forcing students found to violate such university policies to leave the institution for a period of time, or permanently, typically with the results marked on the student's transcript or other administrative records. Such a record can block a successful transfer to another institution.

In addition to these administrative policies, many campuses have adopted written policies demanding affirmative consent for progressive stages of sexual activity.[159] Although these policies have been the subject of debate, one argument in their favor is that the policies reduce the administrative burden of resolving contested factual circumstances that can arise in such settings, including the possibility of a claimed misunderstanding as to the level of consent that had been given prior to sexual activity. In effect, these policies shift the burden to the person seeking to advance sexual activity to obtain verbal or other affirmative consent.

This combined regime has allowed faster administrative responses and resolutions to alleged incidents of campus sexual assault. Some commentators have argued that these policies produce consequences for the alleged perpetrator that are as damaging as criminal convictions but without the benefit of protections associated with a criminal process. Does the economic analysis of criminal law help to inform the wisdom and efficacy, or lack thereof, of these policies? Why or why not? If economic analysis is not helpful, what is the preferred methodology for such assessments?

4. Another public policy that has come under increasing scrutiny involves sex offender registries.[160] Although most are unsympathetic to persons convicted of violent sex crimes, there are two notable considerations. First, those placed on the registries are often listed for life. Second, the list of covered offenses typically also includes such non-violent offenses as consensual intercourse between two minors, classified as statutory rape, and even some instances of public urination. The consequences for those placed on the registry can be devastating, including limiting access to housing, education, and jobs. Does the economic analysis of law help to evaluate sex registry laws? Why or why not?

---

[159] Jessica Bennett, *Campus Sex . . . With a Syllabus*, N.Y. TIMES (Jan. 9, 2016), https://www.nytimes.com/2016/01/10/fashion/sexual-consent-assault-college-campuses.html?_r=1. *See* Univ. of Calif., Sexual Violence and Sexual Harassment Policy (2016), https://policy.ucop.edu/doc/4000385/SVSH (stating "[c]onsent is *affirmative, conscious, voluntary, and revocable*.") (emphasis in original); SUNY Policies on Sexual Violence Prevention and Response (Dec. 1, 2014) (updated June 2015) (defining affirmative consent as "a knowing, voluntary, and mutual decision among all participants to engage in sexual activity. Consent can be given by words or actions, as long as those words or actions create clear permission regarding willingness to engage in the sexual activity. Silence or lack of resistance, in and of itself, does not demonstrate consent.").

[160] Individuals arrested for public urination may be charged with indecent exposure or public lewdness, which, in some states, requires registering as a sex offender. According to a 2007 report by Human Rights Watch, "[a]t least 13 states require registration for public urination, two limit registration to those who committed the act in view of a minor." HUMAN RIGHTS WATCH, NO EASY ANSWERS: SEX OFFENDER LAWS IN THE US (Sept. 11, 2007), https://www.hrw.org/report/2007/09/11/no-easy-answers/sex-offender-laws-us#page. *See also Unjust and Ineffective*, THE ECONOMIST (Aug. 6, 2009), http://www.economist.com/node/14164614. The 2007 Human Rights Watch report further states "[a]t least 29 states require registration for consensual sex between teenagers." HUMAN RIGHTS WATCH, *supra*.

Consider the special case of chemical castration as an alternative to incarceration for those convicted of sex crimes and with a predisposition toward recidivism. Does the economic analysis of law help to evaluate this alternative sanction? Why or why not?

5. In several nations (mostly European), including Finland, Sweden, Denmark, Croatia, Germany, and Switzerland, the system of criminal fines is not fixed per offense, but rather is graded based on the income of the offender.[161] For relatively light offenses, such as minor traffic violations, fines are fixed, but for more serious violations, those accompanied by a possible prison sentence, the regime includes "day fines." These fines are typically assessed at a modest lower bound, and up to one-half-day's wages times the number of days for which the scheme applies the fine. In Finland, for example, the rate is calculated at one-sixtieth of the monthly earnings per day. In effect, this is a form of fine-based price discrimination. Not all nations are enamored of this idea, and a brief experiment in England and Wales was abandoned after one year, from 1992 to 1993.

How, if at all, does the economic analysis of criminal law inform this alternative approach to imposing fine-based criminal sanctions? Would you support its implementation in the United States? Why or why not? How, if at all, is your answer informed by economic analysis? By other concerns? Which predominate, and why?

[161] For a discussion of day fines in Europe, see Elena Kantorowic-Reznichenko, *Day Fines: Reviving the Idea and Reversing the (Costly) Punitive Trend*, AM. CRIM. L. REV. (forthcoming 2018); Elena Kantorowicz-Reznichenko, *Day-Fines: Should the Rich Pay More?*, 11 REV. L. ECON. 481 (2015). *See also* Joe Pinsker, *Finland, Home of the $103,000 Speeding Ticket*, THE ATLANTIC (Mar. 12, 2015), https://www.theatlantic.com/business/archive/2015/03/finland-home-of-the-103000-speeding-ticket/387484/.

CHAPTER 10

Legal Process

Introduction

The preceding chapters presented substantive doctrine through the lens of economic analysis. In general, they did not focus on the procedures through which those doctrines emerged. The relationship between lawmaking processes and substantive legal rules is also an important consideration in the economic analysis of law and lawmaking institutions. As a result, not only do we explore this theme here as it relates to the prior substantive bodies of law set out in Chapters 3 through 8, but also we will revisit it as we develop additional analytical methodologies in later chapters.[1]

Legal process is highly relevant to the materials that we have introduced thus far, and with the benefit of tools drawn from neoclassical economic analysis, we can develop important insights into the relationship between the common law rules of tort, contract, and property, and the statutory body of criminal law, on one side, and the decision-making processes that brought them about, on the other. In this chapter we undertake a systematic analysis of legal process as it relates to these bodies of legal doctrine.

Since the rules and procedures for civil versus criminal cases differ in important ways, we will treat them separately. As we will see, however, the general approach to each has considerable similarities. This should not be surprising given that the objectives of the two systems, as seen for example in the discussion of the *General Transaction Structure*, substantially overlap.[2] In this chapter, we will see that from the perspective of judicial process, these bodies of law further overlap in seeking to arrive at accurate judgments while also using judicial resources in a cost-effective manner. In this framework, trials are viewed as complex processes designed to reach a decision under conditions of uncertainty.

Achieving more accurate outcomes necessarily entails greater cost. This includes, most obviously, a greater expenditure of resources. As we will also see, these can include important non-pecuniary costs, for example relaxing certain protections against those charged with criminal offenses. This concern finds reflection in rules governing standards of proof, admissible evidence, and the processes governing appeals. It is also evident in practices that affect—and that are often designed to promote—out-of-court settlements (or, in the case of criminal prosecutions, plea bargains). One of the important implications

1 *See, e.g.*, Chapter 13 and 14, Chapters 15 and 16, and Chapter 23 and 24.

2 *See supra* Chapter 6 and Chapter 9.

of the criminal justice system, in particular, is that it is not designed as a universal quest for truth. Indeed, the combination of rules and practices will often have the effect of inhibiting the quest for truth in response to other considerations. For now, we can simply acknowledge that processes designed to uncover truth, meaning factual accuracy, on one hand, and justice, meaning fairness of the overall process, especially to vulnerable litigants such as criminal defendants, on the other, do not uniformly push in the same direction.[3]

Despite this tension, there is no doubt that the legal system is concerned with the accuracy of judicial proceedings, with the creation of precedent, and with overall administrative costs. The common law comprises the accumulation of countless published appellate judicial decisions that form the body of precedent governing future cases. As our study of the various areas of the law has shown, those rules are also crucial in motivating incentives for *current* behavior outside the formal process of adjudication. Judicial decisions have two distinct features: first, they resolve immediate disputes, and second, they create precedent that influences the development of substantive doctrine. Because the second feature has an important public goods aspect to it, it is critical to consider what motivates the creation of precedent.

Scholars who perceive an underlying economic logic within the common law are necessarily interested not only in substantive doctrine, but also in the lawmaking function of the judicial process. As the preceding chapters have shown, several generations of scholars have discerned a set of efficiency properties from the various bodies of common law doctrine.

> Tort law creates incentives that reduce avoidable risk and then allocates the inevitable residual risk to those who can generally bear it at the lowest cost.
>
> Contract law offers a set of default off-the-rack rules that contracting parties will ordinarily accept, thereby reducing the cost of contracts when transactions costs are high, and allowing customization when transactions costs are low.
>
> Property law structures rights and liabilities in land and other valuable assets in a manner that helps to move scarce resources to their more highly valued uses.

Of course there are many counterexamples that thwart this simplified presentation of such rules, several of which we explored in Chapters 3 through 8. But to the extent that the common law and criminal law exhibit patterns conforming to this general structure, or that this structure offers a more robust analysis than competing accounts, this raises an important puzzle for the positive economic analysis of law: What forces move judicial lawmaking toward efficiency?

Before proceeding, we begin with a point of terminology. This chapter will touch on materials that include the *Federal Rules of Civil Procedure* ("FRCP"); substantive rules of *Criminal Procedure*, which is a body of constitutional common law doctrine; and various institutional rules that are common across common law-based judicial decision-making processes. In earlier generations of legal education, these and other materials formed the

---

[3] John Thibault & Laurens Walker, *A Theory of Procedure*, 66 CALIF. L. REV. 541 (1978) ("The initial step in stating a theory of procedure is to recognize the fundamental dichotomy between the potential dispute resolution objectives of 'truth' and 'justice.' ").

basis for a course in *Judicial Process* or *Legal Method*.[4] In most law schools, for better or worse, those courses have generally fallen out of favor. Although this chapter and others in this volume are not a substitute for such a course, we do acknowledge substantial overlapping content and methodology.

The chapter is organized as follows. We first describe the basic structure of a legal dispute, beginning with the filing decision by the plaintiff and culminating with some sort of resolution of the dispute, for example, dropping the complaint, settling out of court, or taking the case through trial and a possible appeal.[5] Our analysis will begin with the decision to settle or go to trial, an important choice that has been subject to economic modeling. It turns out to be fairly easy to explain why most cases settle given the high costs of trial. The greater challenge is explaining why any cases ever go to trial. The same paradox confronts criminal trials versus plea bargaining.

We then extend the model to explain several additional features of the judicial process. These include the selected burden of proof; the rules governing pretrial discovery; the English versus the American rule for allocating legal costs; and FRCP Rule 68, a limited rule that affects the process through which some cases filed in federal court are settled prior to trial.[6] We also consider several related aspects of the adjudicatory process: the problems of frivolous lawsuits, class action litigation, contingent legal fees, court delay, legal error, and the lawmaking function of trials. Additional rules discussed in this chapter include FRCP, 11, 23, 50, and 56.

We then turn to specific aspects of the criminal judicial process. Our primary focus involves plea-bargaining, the criminal law counterpart to out-of-court settlements in civil litigation. Although many of the same considerations apply, plea-bargaining raises special concerns, most notably the question of whether its prevalence increases the risk that innocent defendants will plead guilty to avoid the risk of greater sanctions following a criminal trial. We also consider the bail system, sentencing guidelines, and judicial sentencing more generally, and we conclude with a discussion of constitutional issues related to the rule against self-incrimination, unreasonable searches and seizures, and forfeiture of assets used in criminal enterprises.

I. THE CIVIL ADJUDICATORY PROCESS

A civil lawsuit is a complex multi-stage process. It begins with the plaintiff filing a complaint against a defendant seeking legal redress, most commonly in the form of monetary damages for harm that the defendant allegedly caused. Because suits are costly, however, most disputes do not result in litigation. In fact, a RAND study found that with the exception of motor vehicle accidents, the majority of personal injury victims never file

[4] Bradley Scott Shannon, *Where Have You Gone, Judicial Process?*, 84 FORDHAM L. REV. RES GESTAE 24 (2016); Richard B. Cappalli, *The Disappearance of Legal Method*, 70 TEMP. L. REV. 393 (1997).

[5] Other options include, but are not limited to, the following: cross claims; counter claims; motions for failure to state a claim upon which relief can be granted, to dismiss, or to set aside the verdict; and post-verdict settlements.

[6] FED. R. CIV. P. 68.

suit at all.[7] Once a suit is filed, the plaintiff and defendant, in consultation with their lawyers, typically engage in pretrial bargaining. In the vast majority of cases, the result is an out-of-court settlement. For example, in 2014, only 1.1% of all civil cases filed in U.S. District Courts reached trial.[8]

This high settlement rate turns out to be quite consistent with what economic theory would predict. Consider, for example, a victim who incurred damages of $100,000 as a result of an accident allegedly caused by the defendant. Assume strict liability, and that if plaintiff proves causation, both parties anticipate she will prevail at trial. Further assume that expected judgment is $100,000, equaling the plaintiff's damages, and that it would cost each party $10,000 in legal costs (time and lawyer fees) to try the case.

It is easy to see how the parties can gain from bargaining. The total anticipated cost to defendant of going to trial is $110,000 (the verdict plus expected costs), and the total anticipated benefit to the plaintiff is $90,000 (the verdict minus expected costs). The $20,000 difference, which equals the joint trial costs, constitutes the "settlement range," or the joint gain from avoiding trial. Any payment between $110,000 and $90,000 will improve the position of the two parties as compared with going to court and dissipating a potential $20,000 surplus. If the parties split the surplus evenly, the payment would be $100,000, which equals plaintiff's claimed damages. Settlement, therefore, replicates the outcome of a trial by fully compensating the victim while saving the wasteful trial costs.

The analysis helps explain why settlements are dominant. The more challenging question is why any cases go to trial. The next section reviews the principal models economists have developed to answer that question.

A. The Settlement-Trial Decision

The most significant factor affecting the decision to go to trial is uncertainty as to the expected outcome. In the preceding example, we assumed that the parties held symmetric information, including accurate beliefs as to which side would prevail at trial, the expected value of the judgment, and the trial costs. Such perfect information is rare, but in this simple example, it allows identifying a precise settlement range, or bargaining surplus, of $20,000, if the parties avoided trial. For cases to go to trial, the outcome must instead be uncertain, *and* the parties must hold different beliefs about that outcome, meaning that uncertainty alone is not sufficient to result in a trial. Economic models attribute this dynamic to two possible sources of imperfect information: *mutual optimism* and *asymmetric information*.

---

[7] DEBORAH HENSLER ET AL., RAND INST. FOR CIVIL JUSTICE, R-3000-HHS/ICJ, COMPENSATION FOR ACCIDENTAL INJURIES IN THE UNITED STATES 110 (1991), https://www.rand.org/content/dam/rand/pubs/reports/2006/R3999.pdf].

[8] *See* ADMINISTRATIVE OFFICE OF THE U.S. COURTS, U.S. DISTRICT COURTS—CIVIL CASES TERMINATED, BY NATURE OF SUIT AND ACTION TAKEN, DURING THE 12-MONTH PERIOD ENDING MARCH 31, 2014, at tbl.C-4 (2015), http://www.uscourts.gov/file/10248/download.

1. *The Mutual Optimism Model*

The earliest models of the settlement-trial decision simply assumed that the two parties might hold different beliefs about the outcome of trial.[9] The potential divergence reflected either uncertainty concerning the applicable law, as interpreted by the judge or as applied by the trier of fact (judge or jury), or differing intuitions concerning the facts that would be proved at trial.

We begin with a simple model. P_p and P_d represent the respective probabilities, as assessed by plaintiff and defendant, that plaintiff will prevail at trial. J represents plaintiff's expected judgment against the defendant if plaintiff wins (which we assume the parties agree upon),[10] and C represents the trial costs for each party (which we assume are known and equal).[11] Plaintiff's expected value of trial is therefore P_pJ-C (plaintiff's expected probability of winning times the judgment minus costs), and thus the minimum amount she would accept in a settlement. Likewise, the defendant's expected cost of a trial is P_dJ+C (defendant's expected probability of losing times the judgment plus costs), and thus the maximum amount he would offer to settle rather than go to trial. A settlement is therefore possible if $P_dJ+C> P_pJ-C$ (meaning if the expected losses to the defendant exceed the expected gains to the plaintiff). Simplifying the inequality produces the following:

$2C > (P_p-P_d)J$ (settlement condition).

The left side of the inequality represents the total litigation costs. The right side represents the difference in the expected values of going to trial as assessed by the plaintiff and defendant. And so settlement is possible if the sum of the litigation costs *exceeds* the difference in assessed probability as between the parties of the plaintiff prevailing times the expected judgment. Otherwise, the parties can be expected to go to trial.

Let us now consider the following implications of this settlement condition. First, if $P_p=P_d$, the parties agree on the probability that plaintiff will prevail, and thus a settlement will always be possible given that $2C>0$. This holds regardless of the value of J. By contrast, as shown below, when P_p and P_d diverge, the likelihood of going to trial is affected by the value of J. However, so long as there is agreement on the probability of the outcome, there is no difference in the *expected value* of the suit, and thus, the cost of litigating will exceed the potential benefits of going to trial. The condition of equal expectations of plaintiff prevailing was met in the numerical example above, where we assumed that $P_pJ=P_dJ=\$100,000$. As demonstrated there, the benefit of a settlement is exactly equal to the savings in total trial costs, or $2C$.

Second, the model predicts that a trial will take place if the inequality in the settlement condition is reversed, $2C<(P_p-P_d)J$ (anti-settlement condition). In that case, the

---

9 *See* William Landes, *An Economic Analysis of the Courts*, 14 J.L. & ECON. 61 (1971); John Gould, *The Economics of Legal Conflicts*, 2 J. LEGAL STUD. 279 (1973); Robert Cooter & Daniel Rubinfeld, *An Economic Analysis of Legal Disputes and Their Resolution*, 27 J. ECON. LITERATURE 1067 (1989).

10 This is a simplifying assumption that if relaxed, such that the parties hold differing expected values for J, will not affect the model's basic conclusions. *See* Cooter & Rubinfeld, *supra* note 9.

11 The assumption of costless settlement is stronger than necessary; the analysis holds provided that settlement is less costly than trial. *Id.*

parties' difference in the expected value of trial will necessarily exceed the combined litigation costs, thus eliminating the possibility of settlement. Note that a necessary, albeit insufficient, condition for this to be true is that $P_p > P_d$. That is, under this model, a trial can only be justified if the plaintiff holds a more favorable view of the strength of her case than the defendant does of his.[12] (Remember that P_d, the defendant's assessed probability of *plaintiff winning*, equals his assessed probability of the *defendant losing*.) When $P_p > P_d$, the parties's respective assessments are characterized by *mutual optimism*; each holds a positive view of the chances of prevailing at trial.

Finally, assuming that $P_p > P_d$, under the preceding *settlement condition*, a trial is more likely under either of two conditions: first, as the costs of trial ($2C$) fall, and second, as the expected judgment at trial (J) increases. The first condition is obvious: higher trial costs encourage the parties to settle. The second condition provides that as the "stakes," meaning the expected money judgment, rise, so too does the probability of taking the case to trial.

Before considering the implications of asymmetric information on the trial-settlement decision, consider two limitations to the mutual optimism model. First, even in a case in which the preceding settlement condition is met, the parties might proceed to trial. Because legal disputes produce a bilateral monopoly (the two sides are stuck with each other until the dispute is resolved one way or another), the potential gains by the settlement condition might be depleted in the course of negotiations.[13]

Second, as noted, the parties' disagreement regarding the outcome of a trial could be attributable to different assessments of legal precedent, especially when relevant legal doctrines are changing, or to divergent expectations about how facts will develop at trial. The process of discovery, which helps narrow the gap concerning factual disputes and which thus limits information asymmetries, enhances the likelihood of settlement, but the process is costly and imperfect, allowing divergencies to remain.[14]

2. *The Asymmetric Information Model*

Like the mutual optimism model, the asymmetric information model attributes trials to the parties' differing beliefs about the outcome of a trial. In contrast with the mutual optimism model, however, the asymmetric information model attributes those different beliefs to the implications of private information concerning pertinent facts held by one

---

[12] To keep the analysis simple, we are excluding the possibility of counterclaims by the defendant.

[13] As we will see in Chapters 13 and 14, the possibility of a breakdown in bargaining also increases with additional parties as a result of cycling, or empty-core bargaining, dynamics.

[14] We noted this point *supra* notes 9–10, and accompanying text (citing study by Cooter and Rubinfeld). In cases where the plaintiff seeks an injunction in addition to (or instead of) damages, the model becomes more complicated, leading to the prediction that differing assessments of the stakes at trial will not necessarily result in a trial. Such a model is applicable, for example, in nuisance and patent infringement cases, where plaintiffs seek both to collect damages for past harms, and to enjoin future harm. Such cases have the potential to result in "reverse settlements," where the plaintiff actually pays the defendant to settle. This can happen if the cost of an injunction to the defendant is very high relative to the cost of going to trial. *See* Keith Hylton & Sungjoon Cho, *The Economics of Injunctive and Reverse Settlements*, 12 AM. L. & ECON. REV. 181 (2010).

party.[15] For example, in a tort case the defendant might have private information about facts that would demonstrate whether or not he was negligent. Or the plaintiff might have private information about whether she sustained an actual injury, or whether she was contributorily negligent.[16] In either case, the asymmetry will lead to divergent beliefs as to the expected value of going to trial.

The formal asymmetric information model is more complicated than the mutual optimism model, but the central idea can be conveyed with an illustration. Suppose there are two types of plaintiffs, those with *strong* cases and those with *weak* cases. The plaintiffs with strong cases will win at trial with probability P_s=.9, whereas those with weak cases will win with probability P_w=.3. As above, J=$100,000 (the damages sought by the plaintiff), and C, the cost of trial, equals $10,000 for all parties. Assume initially that the defendant can distinguish the two types of plaintiffs.

Table 10:1 shows the expected values of a trial for the strong and weak plaintiffs, and the corresponding expected costs for the defendant. Since we are assuming that beliefs are symmetrical, a settlement is possible in both cases, with the settlement amount falling between the defendant's cost and the respective plaintiff's valuation. Thus, if the parties split the surplus, the settlement amount for a strong plaintiff will be $90,000, whereas the settlement amount with a weak plaintiff will be $30,000.

Table 10:1. Data for Asymmetric Information Model Example

		Plaintiff's expected value	Defendant's expected cost
Plaintiff type	Strong	P_sJ-C=$80,000	P_sJ+C=$100,000
	Weak	P_wJ-C=$20,000	P_wJ+C=$40,000

Now imagine, instead, that the defendant cannot distinguish the two types of plaintiffs, although he knows the fraction of each within the plaintiff population. In this case, a defendant facing a plaintiff of unknown type has two possible strategies. The first is to offer a settlement amount of $80,000, which is the lowest amount that plaintiffs with a strong case will accept. This is referred to as a "pooling strategy" because both types of plaintiffs will accept the offer, and each case settles with certainty. The expected cost of this strategy to the defendant is $80,000 regardless of which type of plaintiff he is facing.

The second strategy is to offer $20,000, which is the lowest amount that weak plaintiffs will accept. This second strategy is referred to as a "separating strategy" because the two types of plaintiffs are expected to respond differently to it. Specifically, weak plaintiffs will accept the offer and settle, whereas strong plaintiffs will reject the offer and opt for trial. The cost of the strategy to the defendant therefore depends on the fraction of the two types within the plaintiff population. Assume the population is evenly divided between weak and strong plaintiffs. Thus, there is an equal probability that a given plaintiff

---

[15] For early versions of this model, see Lucian Bebchuk, *Litigation and Settlement Under Imperfect Information*, 15 RAND J. ECON. 404 (1984); Barry Nalebuff, *Credible Pretrial Negotiation*, 18 RAND J. ECON. 198 (1987).

[16] Although both parties will generally have private information, for expositional purposes, the model assumes that only one party is privately informed.

is weak and will settle, or is strong and will go to trial. If we assume that all of the weak plaintiffs accept the $20,000 settlement offer and that all strong plaintiffs reject it, then the defendant's expected cost of the separating strategy is (.5)($20,000)+(.5)($100,000)=$60,000 per case. Notice that this is lower than the per-case cost of the pooling strategy, which is $80,000. Thus, in this example, the separating strategy is cheaper, even though half the cases end up at trial.

If instead we assume that the fraction of strong cases is .8 and the fraction of weak cases .2, the separating strategy now has an expected cost of (.2)($20,000)+(.8)($100,000)=$84,000, which is greater than the cost of the pooling strategy. In this case, the defendant would rather settle all cases despite the fact that a subset of those cases are weak.

The trade-off between the two strategies is that the pooling strategy saves the cost of a trial, but involves overcompensating weak plaintiffs. Based on these assumptions, a smaller fraction of weak cases increases the likelihood that the defendant would prefer the pooling strategy.[17] Trials are therefore more likely to occur as the fraction of weak cases in the population of cases increases. Notice, however, that the cases that *end up at trial* under the separating strategy will be the strong ones (a point that we will return to below). The model also implies, consistent with optimism model, that trials are less likely as the cost of trials increase, and more likely as the stakes of the case increase.

B. Procedural Rules and Legal Costs

Below we discuss several specific aspects of civil procedure through the lens of the settlement-trial decision framework. Our focus will be on how these rules affect the cost of litigation and thus incentives to settle. Where appropriate, we will also consider the influence of these rules on the accuracy of trial outcomes.

Before doing so, we consider when a case, or particular claims within it, may be dismissed as a matter of law versus when a claimant is lawfully entitled to present the case or particular claims to a trier of fact, either a judge or jury. The distinction between these two methods of disposing of legal claims is important because the economic analysis of settlement versus trial relates to both, but with different implications. In general, the models assume that the claimant is lawfully entitled to pursue presented claims in court, but this depends on whether there is a legal basis for allowing the claim to proceed. Even if there is no legal basis, however, it is costly for a defendant to ascertain and prove the lack of merit to the satisfaction of the judge, who has the authority to dismiss the claim as a matter of law prior to trial.

Nuisance suits typically involve non-meritorious claims that impose costs on defendants as a precondition to having a claim dismissed, and thus, that invite opportunities for settlement. Such suits create a benefit to the plaintiff analogous to appropriable quasi rents.[18] In the subpart that follows, we briefly review the rules that

---

[17] The general formula for the threshold fraction of strong types, denoted by a, is $a=[(P_{h}-P_{l})J]/[2C+(P_{h}-P_{l})J]$, so, in the example, any fraction of weak types smaller than .75 favors pooling.

[18] *See supra* Chapters 5 and 6.

allow the court to determine the legal bases upon which to dismiss legal claims without allowing them to go to trial.[19]

1. Judgment as a Matter of Law and Summary Judgment

There are two principal federal rules that govern this area of law, *Federal Rule of Civil Procedure (FRCP) Rule 50. Judgment as a Matter of Law in a Jury Trial; Related Motion for a New Trial; Conditional Ruling*, and *FRCP Rule 56—Summary Judgment*. The rules are similar in many respects; the principal distinction involves the stage at which the defending party seeks to have the suit or claims within it dismissed as a matter of law. In general, Rule 56 applies until thirty days following completion of discovery, and Rule 50 applies either after all evidence on particular claims, or on the case as a whole, is taken, and before verdict, or up to twenty-eight days following the verdict. Under earlier practice, a motion after evidence but prior to verdict was referred to as a *Directed Verdict*, and a motion to set aside an adverse jury verdict was referred to as either *Judgment Notwithstanding Verdict*, or *JNOV* for the Latin, *Judgment Non Obstante Verdicto*.

Each of these motions, *Summary Judgment*, *Directed Verdict*, or *JNOV* implies that at the stage at which it is moved, the court should be able to determine as a matter of law whether the claimant should be permitted to proceed to have the fact finder resolve the legal claims. Under Rule 56(a), "The court shall grant summary judgment if the movant shows that there is no genuine dispute as to any material fact and the movant is entitled to judgment as a matter of law."[20] To avoid summary judgment, the nonmovant cannot rest solely on allegations in the pleadings; instead, Rule 56(c) provides:

> (c) **Procedures**.
>
> (1) *Supporting Factual Positions*. A party asserting that a fact cannot be or is genuinely disputed must support the assertion by:
>
> (A) citing to particular parts of materials in the record, including depositions, documents, electronically stored information, affidavits or declarations, stipulations (including those made for purposes of the motion only), admissions, interrogatory answers, or other materials; or
>
> (B) showing that the materials cited do not establish the absence or presence of a genuine dispute, or that an adverse party cannot produce admissible evidence to support the fact.[21]

Rule 50(a) provides:

> (a) Judgment as a Matter of Law.
>
> (1) *In General*. If a party has been fully heard on an issue during a jury trial and the court finds that a reasonable jury would not have a legally sufficient evidentiary basis to find for the party on that issue, the court may:

---

[19] For a related analysis, see Keith Hylton, *When Should a Case be Dismissed? The Economics of Pleading and Summary Judgment Standards*, 16 SUP. CT. ECON. REV. 39 (2008); Daniel Klerman, *The Economics of Civil Procedure*, 11 ANN. REV. L. & SOC. SCI. 353 (2015).

[20] FED. R. CIV. P. 56(c).

[21] FED. R. CIV. P. 56(a).

(A) resolve the issue against the party; and

(B) grant a motion for judgment as a matter of law against the party on a claim or defense that, under the controlling law, can be maintained or defeated only with a favorable finding on that issue.

(2) *Motion.* A motion for judgment as a matter of law may be made at any time before the case is submitted to the jury. The motion must specify the judgment sought and the law and facts that entitle the movant to the judgment.[22]

The procedures for defeating a motion under for Rule 50(a) are simpler because at the time the motion is advanced, formal evidence has been taken, and thus, the parties need not rest in allegations in the pleadings, supported by discovery.

Rule 50(b) states:

(b) Renewing the Motion After Trial; Alternative Motion for a New Trial. If the court does not grant a motion for judgment as a matter of law made under Rule 50(a), the court is considered to have submitted the action to the jury subject to the court's later deciding the legal questions raised by the motion. No later than 28 days after the entry of judgment—or if the motion addresses a jury issue not decided by a verdict, no later than 28 days after the jury was discharged—the movant may file a renewed motion for judgment as a matter of law and may include an alternative or joint request for a new trial under Rule 59.[23]

The primary distinction between moving for judgment as a matter of law under Rule 50(a) versus (b) is that the jury has not yet reached a verdict in the former, whereas it has, presumably in plaintiff's favor for all or part of the claims, in the latter. For the trial judge, there is often a benefit to awaiting the jury verdict because if the jury rejects the claim for which the motion for directed verdict was initially advanced, the court need not rule that the claim was deficient as a matter of law. On the other hand, setting aside a verdict after it is rendered places the court in opposition to the jury, possibly further thwarting the expectations of the claimant.

In addition to these procedural rules, the possibility of settlement is affected by the specific burden the claimant must satisfy both to get a case to trial and to persuade the trier of fact at the trial itself. The next subpart discusses these issues.

2. *The Burden of Proof*

The burden of proof determines which party, the plaintiff or the defendant, has the responsibility to convince the court that she or he ought to prevail in a case. This involves two related concepts: first, plaintiff must produce evidence that would allow a reasonable fact finder to determine that she has met her obligation with respect to each element in a legal claim (the "burden of production"), and second, plaintiff must persuade the trier of fact that her evidence meets the requisite standard of proof (the "burden of persuasion").

---

22 FED. R. CIV. P. 50(a).

23 FED. R. CIV. P. 50(b).

Generally speaking, the burden of proof operates as a default rule. When the plaintiff fails to meet the requisite burden, which changes with each stage of litigation, the court will dismiss the suit or rule against her on the merits. In other words, plaintiff must persuade the court that it has met the burden of production to get the case to the trier of fact. Although plaintiff generally would not have an incentive to file a frivolous suit if she anticipated losing at trial,[24] assigning this burden to plaintiffs in civil cases nonetheless reduces litigation costs by discouraging the filing of non-meritorious claims that might be intended to encourage settlement for its nuisance value. If, for example, the defendant carried the burden of production, this would encourage excessive claims. Plaintiffs could file suit, and knowing defendant carried the burden of production, anticipate that defendant will prefer to settle, rather than to incur the related costs. If the defendant had the burden of production, in theory, plaintiffs could file and then extract a settlement up to the defendant's cost of initially meeting that burden, even if the suit is totally frivolous. In civil litigation the burden of persuasion is by a preponderance of the evidence, or just over fifty percent. In theory, how that is allocated should have less of an impact in encouraging excessive litigation than the burden of production. We discuss this below in the context of the "standard of proof."

3. Discovery

Once a case has been filed, the parties begin the process of pretrial negotiation. During this period, the rules of discovery compel parties, upon request, to share particular information about their cases with their opponents. Usually, this takes the form of *interrogatories*, questions that one side can submit to the other, and *depositions*, interviews under oath with the other side's witnesses. The legal requirement that parties show their cards in this manner is easily explained as a means of promoting settlement.[25]

To see why, let us return to the settlement condition above, and recall that the principal source of trials in the mutual optimism model is the *disagreement term* depicted as $P_p - P_d > 0$. Within the formal model, a trial will take place only when this term is positive. To the extent that the parties' differing expectations about the outcome at trial is based on private information, misapprehensions about the other party's case, or simple bias, discovery will tend to reduce that disparity, thereby enhancing the likelihood of revealing a settlement range. Discovery likewise helps ameliorate information asymmetries by revealing likely evidence supporting or opposing each side's case.[26]

In addition to encouraging settlement, discovery affects the value of settlements. To illustrate, suppose that the required sharing of information results in the parties' agreeing

---

[24] *See* Bruce L. Hay, *Allocating the Burden of Proof*, 72 IND. L.J. 651, 658 (1997). Professor Hay offers the following analysis: respecting the burden of persuasion:

> Now consider the plaintiff's decision to file suit. From the foregoing it is evident that the plaintiff will not file a meritless claim. This is true no matter who bears the burden of proof: under either allocation, she would lose the case, and thus have no reason to waste her time and money taking it to court. Accordingly, the plaintiff will file suit only if her claim is meritorious, regardless of the burden allocation.

See id.

[25] Robert Cooter & Daniel Rubinfeld, *An Economic Model of Discovery*, 23 J. LEGAL STUD. 435 (1994).

[26] Steven Shavell, *Sharing Information Prior to Settlement or Litigation*, 20 RAND J. ECON. 183 (1989).

on the probability that plaintiff will prevail at trial, which we call the "true" probability, P. In this case, we know that a settlement is always possible. If we make the reasonable assumption that the parties split the surplus from the settlement (the combined trial costs, $2C$), then as previously shown,[27] the settlement amount exactly equals the expected judgment at trial, PJ. That is because under the stated conditions, settlement replicates the expected trial outcome, but without trial costs. In the above example, if after discovery the parties agree that the expected judgment at trial is $100,000, and trial costs are $10,000 each, plaintiff's expected value of a trial is $90,000, and the defendant's expected cost of trial is $110,000. An equal split of the $20,000 surplus puts the settlement exactly in the middle, at $100,000.

Although discovery promotes settlement, there are potential offsetting costs. Because compliance is generally mandatory, and subject to fairly stringent limits on abuse,[28] a party can make requests simply to gain a strategic advantage. Suppose, for example, that a plaintiff has an expected value of trial equal to $20,000, which represents the minimum amount she would accept in a settlement. If the defendant makes a discovery request that would cost $5,000 in combined legal fees and personal time, the plaintiff would be willing to settle for $15,000 rather than complying. This strategy is especially effective in cases where the parties have asymmetrical resources, such as when a single individual with an hourly fee attorney sues a large corporation with salaried attorneys.[29]

4. *The English Rule Versus the American Rule*

Calls for tort reform in the United States have included proposals to switch from the *American rule*, under which plaintiffs and defendants each pay their own litigation costs, to the *English rule*, under which the loser pays the winner's litigation costs. (The English rule is therefore sometimes referred to as the "loser pays" rule.) Advocates claim that the English rule carries the following benefits: (1) increasing the settlement rate by raising the expected litigation cost for the side with the weaker case, and (2) reducing frivolous lawsuits as a consequence of the implicit threat of having to cover both sides' costs. The remainder of this section evaluates these claims based on the preceding mutual optimism model,[30] although the conclusions are the same under the asymmetric information model. We conclude with some related empirical and experimental evidence.

a. Settlement Under the English Rule

The first step in comparing the settlement rates under the two rules is to derive the plaintiff's expected value of trial and the defendant's expected cost of trial under the English rule. Following the prior notation, the plaintiff's expected value of trial is P_pJ–(1–

---

27 *See supra* at p. 382.

28 *See* Charles Yablon, *Stupid Lawyer Tricks: Discovery Abuse*, 96 COLUM. L. REV. 1618 (1996); Frank H. Easterbrook, *Discovery Abuse*, 69 B.U. L. REV. 635 (1989).

29 Of course this might be offset by representation on a contingency fee basis. For a discussion of contingent fees, see *infra* at p. 375.

30 The analysis follows Steven Shavell, *The Social Versus Private Incentive to Bring Suit in a Costly Legal System*, 11 J. LEGAL STUD. 333 (1982) and Cooter & Rubinfeld, *supra* note 9. For a comparable analysis using the asymmetric information model, see Bebchuk, *supra* note 15.

$P_p)2C$. The first term is the plaintiff's judgment if she wins, J, multiplied by the probability of winning, P_p. The second term is the cost if she loses, which equals the combined trial costs ($2C$), multiplied by the probability of losing, $1-P_p$. The corresponding expression for the defendant's expected cost of trial is $P_d(J+2C)$. This represents the defendant's expected cost of losing, equal to the sum of the judgment plus total trial costs multiplied by the probability of losing. (When the defendant wins, he incurs no cost because his trial costs are reimbursed.)

Under the English rule, a settlement is possible if the defendant's cost of trial (the maximum he would be willing to pay to settle) exceeds the plaintiff's value of trial (the minimum amount she would accept). Settlement is therefore possible if $P_d(J+2C) > P_pJ-(1-P_p)2C$, or if

$2C > (P_p-P_d)(J+2C)$ (settlement condition—English rule).

If the total litigation costs (2C) exceed the difference in plaintiff's and defendant's expected probabilities of prevailing multiplied by the sum of the expected judgment plus the total litigation costs, then it is possible to settle. Now compare this to the preceding settlement condition under the American rule. Although the left-hand sides of the two conditions are the same, the right-hand side is larger under the English rule. This implies that settlement is *less likely* under the English rule because a smaller disagreement will prevent settlement for given values of J and C. For our example with J=\$100,000 and C=\$10,000 a value of $P_p-P_d>.20$ will result in a trial under the American rule, but a value of $P_p-P_d>.17$ will result in trial under the English rule.

The intuitive explanation for the lower predicted settlement rate is that the stakes of a trial are larger under the English rule because the allocation of legal costs is now determined by who wins, whereas under the American rule, both sides pay their own costs regardless of who wins, thus reducing the stakes of going to trial. A switch to the English rule therefore has the same effect on the settlement rate as an increase in J, holding all other factors constant. As the stakes of trial rise, the probability of settlement declines. By including the litigation costs as part of the stakes, the stakes rise, thereby exacerbating the impact of the parties' differential risk assessment of going to trial.

The analysis is actually more complicated because, until now, we have held all other factors constant, but the change in rule affects other considerations as well. For example, litigants are apt to invest more effort in trying to prevail at trial under the English rule precisely because more is at stake.[31] This will tend to make $2C$ larger under the English rule, which, as we have seen, increases the likelihood of settlement. Likewise, if litigants are risk-averse, the English rule will tend to promote settlement because trials are now riskier.[32] Once these factors are accounted for, the theoretical prediction about the effect of a switch to the English rule on the settlement rate is ambiguous.

---

31 John Hause, *Indemnity, Settlement, and Litigation, or I'll be Suing You*, 18 J. LEGAL STUD. 157 (1989).

32 This is because the difference between the returns from winning and losing is larger under the English rule, which increases the risk. For example, the difference between winning and losing for the plaintiff under the American rule is J, but it is $J+2C$ under the English rule. A similar difference exists for the defendant under the two rules.

b. Filing Suit Under the English Rule

The other claimed advantage of the English rule is discouraging meritless suits. To assess this claim, compare the expected value of a suit to plaintiffs under the two rules. Whichever rule promises a higher expected return, all else equal, will result in more suits being filed. Using the expressions derived above, a suit is more valuable to plaintiffs under the English rule if $P_pJ-(1-P_p)2C>P_pJ-C$, or if $P_p>1/2$. The first inequality provides conditions under which the expected value under the English rule exceeds that under the American rule. This is set out as follows: the expected gains to plaintiff from prevailing minus the expected costs from losing (the value under the English rule) are greater than expected gains of winning minus individual court costs (the value under the American Rule). Solving this demonstrates that suits are more valuable under the English rule if the probability of plaintiff winning (as judged by the plaintiff and her lawyer) exceeds 1/2.[33] In other words, plaintiffs with *stronger cases* will be more likely to file under the English rule.[34] This conclusion supports the intuition that weaker claimants are discouraged under the English rule by the risk of having to pay the winner's trial costs.[35]

c. Compliance with Legal Standards

The analysis to this point has focused on the impact of the cost-shifting rule, taking as given the occurrence of a legal wrong (accident). In this respect, we have only considered how the rule affects post-accident costs (filing and litigation). However, the manner in which litigation is expected to unfold will have an impact on the decisions of potential litigants regarding compliance with legal standards before an accident occurs. Thus, a complete analysis of the effects of the cost-shifting rule must also include the rule's impact on compliance costs and damages. Using a model that incorporates injury, avoidance, and litigation costs, Keith Hylton has shown that the English rule generally performs best in minimizing the sum of these costs. This result obtains because the English rule creates the largest differential between the expected liability of defendants found liable or not liable, thereby maximizing the deterrence effect of litigation.[36]

d. Evidence on the Impact of the English Rule

In theory, given the general similarities in the U.S. and English common law systems, the different court reimbursement rules in the United States and England provide the basis for a natural experiment on the impact on settlements. In practice, however, substantial differences remain making it difficult to isolate this one variable. To date no scholar has undertaken such a test.

---

[33] The threshold of ½ is a consequence of our assumption that the two sides have equal trial costs. More generally, it would be $Cd/(Cp+Cd)$, where Cp is the trial cost for plaintiffs and Cd is the trial cost for defendants.

[34] John J. Donohue III, *Opting for the British Rule, or If Posner and Shavell Can't Remember the Coase Theorem, Who Will?*, 104 HARV. L. REV. 1093 (1991).

[35] Professor Kathryn Spier has demonstrated that the same conclusion emerges from the asymmetric information model. Kathryn E. Spier, *Litigation*, *in* 1 THE HANDBOOK OF LAW AND ECONOMICS 259, 301 (A. Mitchell Polansky & Steven Shavell eds., 2007).

[36] Keith Hylton, *An Asymmetric-Information Model of Litigation*, 22 INT'L REV. LAW & ECON. 153 (2002).

There are, however, two other sources of evidence on the likely impact of the English rule, one from a localized natural experiment in the State of Florida, and the other from laboratory studies. The natural experiment involved a Florida statute that mandated the use of the loser-pays rule for medical malpractice cases from 1980 to 1985. Because this is a jurisdiction within the United States, many more factors were held constant as compared with other state jurisdictions, thus allowing a rare opportunity to test the impact of this one rule change.

In two studies, James Hughes and Edward Snyder used data from over 10,000 cases,[37] and they reached the following conclusions: First, the English rule increased the trial rate. This is consistent with the predictions drawn from the mutual optimism model and the asymmetric information models in cases involving risk-neutral litigants with fixed trial costs. Second, the English rule resulted in more claims being dropped, supporting the intuition that it discourages weaker claims, which might include, for example, claims shown to be non-meritorious in the course of discovery. Third, the English rule resulted in a higher plaintiff-success rate, higher average judgment at trial, and higher settlement amount. Although the case sampling is limited, these results are consistent with the intuition that overall the English rule encourages higher quality litigated cases.

One experimental study found that the English rule resulted in a higher settlement rate than the American rule.[38] This is consistent with the theoretical predictions respecting the special case in which litigants are either risk-averse or anticipate spending more resources on trials under the English rule. It is difficult to know how much weight to place on these results, however, because they were derived from controlled experiments rather than actual cases in which parties had the benefit of legal counsel and in which real claims were at stake.

5. Federal Rules of Civil Procedure Rule 68: Offer of Judgment

Federal Rules of Civil Procedure Rule 68 provides:

Rule 68: Offer of Judgment.

(a) Making an Offer; Judgment on an Accepted Offer. At least 14 days before the date set for trial, a party defending against a claim may serve on an opposing party an offer to allow judgment on specified terms, with the costs then accrued. If, within 14 days after being served, the opposing party serves written notice accepting the offer, either party may then file the offer and notice of acceptance, plus proof of service. The clerk must then enter judgment.

(b) Unaccepted Offer. An unaccepted offer is considered withdrawn, but it does not preclude a later offer. Evidence of an unaccepted offer is not admissible except in a proceeding to determine costs.

---

37 *See* Edward Snyder & James Hughes, *The English Rule for Allocating Legal Costs: Evidence Confronts Theory*, 6 J.L. ECON. & ORG. 345 (1990); James Hughes & Edward Snyder, *Litigation and Settlement Under the English and American Rules: Theory and Evidence*, 38 J.L. & ECON. 225 (1995).

38 Don L. Coursey & Linda R. Stanley, *Pretrial Bargaining Behavior Within the Shadow of the Law: Theory and Experimental Evidence*, 8 INT'L REV. L. & ECON. 161 (1988).

(c) Offer After Liability is Determined. When one party's liability to another has been determined but the extent of liability remains to be determined by further proceedings, the party held liable may make an offer of judgment. It must be served within a reasonable time—but at least 14 days—before the date set for a hearing to determine the extent of liability.

(d) Paying Costs After an Unaccepted Offer. If the judgment that the offeree finally obtains is not more favorable than the unaccepted offer, the offeree must pay the costs incurred after the offer was made.[39]

Rule 68 has some peculiar features that have affected its efficacy. Intuitively, if the defendant offers a settlement that is declined and then prevails, obtaining a favorable verdict, it would seem the rule should apply to the fees from the time the offer was made. The specific wording of subpart (d) however limits the application to when the plaintiff obtains a judgment lower than the settlement offer, as opposed to when the defendant prevails at trial, thus precluding relief in that circumstance.[40] In addition, the rule has generally been construed not to apply to lawyers' fees, subject to narrow exceptions when there is a statutory right to recover such fees.[41] As a result, the rule applies to the more limited administrative costs such as filing fees and copying.[42]

In the analysis that follows, we evaluate the implications of this rule, as applied in the context of the mutual optimism model and in the narrow class of cases in which lawyer's fees are recoverable. In such settings, the rule encourages settlement by "penalizing" plaintiffs who reject "reasonable" offers. We now consider if this is the likely result.[43]

Within this narrow class of cases, Rule 68 has the potential to modify the American rule by stating that if the plaintiff rejects a properly timed settlement offer, and if following trial, the ultimate judgment and verdict for plaintiff are lower than the offer, the plaintiff must pay the defendant's costs incurred from the time the offer was made. To examine the impact of this provision, we define a to be the probability that the trial judgment is lower than the rejected offer, conditional on the plaintiff's winning. The resulting expected value of a trial for the plaintiff is $P_pJ–C–P_paC$, where the final term is the expected penalty under Rule 68. That term, P_paC, equals the probability of plaintiff victory, times the probability that the judgment is less than the rejected offer, which is then multiplied by defendant's trial costs. The combined value therefore is plaintiff's expected

---

[39] FED. R. CIV. P. 68. *See also* Geoffrey Miller, *An Economic Analysis of Rule 68*, 15 J. LEGAL STUD. 93 (1986) (discussing rule).

[40] A possible rationale: If the rule covered a defense verdict and if defendant anticipates prevailing at trial, she could always offer to settle at $1, and upon prevailing ensure that plaintiff covers her costs, in some instances also including attorney's fees.

[41] *See* Delta Airlines v. August, 450 U.S. 346 (1981).

[42] *See* Jay N. Varon, *Promoting Settlements and Limiting Litigation Costs by Means of the Offer of Judgment: Some Suggestions for Using and Revising Rule 68*, 33 AM. U. L. REV. 813 (1984). In diversity jurisdiction cases, the court will refer to state law to determine if the rule covers attorney's fees. Laura T. Kidwell, Annotation, *Application and Construction of State Offer of Judgment Rule—Determining Whether Offeror Is Entitled to Award*, 2 A.L.R. 6th 279 (2005). For a more recent decision on the use of Rule 68 offers in class-action litigation, see Campbell-Ewald Co. v. Gomez, 136 S. Ct. 663 (2016) (resolving a long-standing circuit split on whether unaccepted offers of judgment could moot the named plaintiff's complaint in a class action, and holding that they do not).

[43] Miller, *supra* note 39.

value of judgment at trial *minus* the costs *minus* the expected value of covering the other side's costs having rejected the settlement offer. The corresponding expected cost of trial for the defendant is $P_dJ+C-P_{d}aC$, where the final term is the expected reimbursement of trial costs based on the defendant's assessment of the plaintiff's probability of winning with a judgment lower than the settlement offer. Here the combined value is defendant's expected value of judgment at trial *plus* costs, *minus* the expected value of the plaintiff covering defendant's post-offer court costs.

The resulting settlement condition, computed in the same manner as above, is

$2C > (P_p-P_d)J-(P_p-P_d)aC$ (settlement condition—Rule 68 with lawyers' fees included).

This means that settlement is expected when the combined trial costs for both parties exceed the difference in plaintiff's and defendant's probabilities times judgment minus the same difference times aC, the probability of a lower-than-settlement offer times relevant costs. Compared to the corresponding settlement condition under the American rule, and assuming mutual optimism, the addition of Rule 68 can improve the likelihood of settlement. In the asymmetric information model, results are indeterminate and might vary depending on which party is privately informed and on whether such private information concerns the probability of plaintiff winning or the amount of the expected judgment.[44] In their experimental analysis, Professors Don Coursey and Linda Stanley found that Rule 68 increased the settlement rate as compared to the standard American rule.[45]

The mutual optimism model predicts that the settlement amount will be lower under Rule 68 as compared with the standard American rule given that the rule worsens the plaintiff's bargaining position. While this might reduce the number of filed suits, that result will also reduce the deterrent effect of the threat of lawsuits.

C. Frivolous Suits

A common criticism of the civil justice system is that it is beset by *frivolous lawsuits*. Although this term does not have a precisely defined meaning, in general lawyers attach this label to suits with little or no merit that are filed primarily to obtain a settlement. For example, imagine a suit that has no merit, such that $PJ=0$, meaning that plaintiff has no chance of prevailing based on the law, a lack of damages, or both. Alternatively, imagine a suit with some merit, $PJ>0$, but with an expected judgment that is lower than expected trial costs, so that $PJ-C<0$. Together, these represent *negative expected value* (NEV) suits, with $PJ=0$ as a special case. Taking such cases to trial is inefficient despite their possible

---

44 Spier, *supra* note 35, at 303–04; Kathryn E. Spier, *Pretrial Bargaining and the Design of Fee-Shifting Rules*, 25 RAND J. ECON. 197 (1994). *See also* Tai-Yeong Chung, *Settlement of Litigation Under Rule 68: An Economic Analysis*, 25 J. LEGAL STUD. 261 (1996); Lucian Arye Bebchuk & Howard F. Chang, *An Analysis of Fee Shifting Based on the Margin of Victory: On Frivolous Suits, Meritorious Suits, and the Role of Rule 11*, 25 J. LEGAL STUD. 371 (1996); Amy Farmer & Paul Pecorino, *Conditional Cost Shifting and the Incidence of Trial: Pretrial Bargaining in the Face of a Rule 68 Offer*, 2 AM. L. & ECON. REV. 318 (2000).

45 Coursey & Stanley, *supra* note 38.

merits. Because the value of the suit is expected to be consumed by the litigation costs, filing such suits is, to that extent, socially wasteful.[46]

Under the American rule, it might appear irrational for a defendant to make settlement offers for NEV suits. Because taking NEV suits to trial would not be profitable, the trial threat is not credible, at least assuming that the plaintiff is unwilling to invest more in litigation costs than she anticipates recovering. This implies that suits for which the sole purpose is to obtain settlement should never be filed in the first place. Despite this, under certain conditions, NEV suits can yield positive settlement value.

1. *How NEV Suits Can Succeed*

NEVs might sometimes succeed based on information asymmetries.[47] To illustrate, assume once more that two types of plaintiffs differ in their probability estimates for success at trial. Assume that plaintiffs with strong cases have a probability of victory at trial equal to .9, whereas plaintiffs with "weak" cases have a zero probability of victory. Let J=$100,000 and C=$10,000 for all parties. Recall that a defendant who cannot distinguish between different types of plaintiffs has two possible strategies. The first is to make a pooling offer of $80,000, which is the lowest amount that plaintiffs with strong cases will accept rather than go to trial; and the second is to make a separating offer, which in this case will be zero, the lowest amount that plaintiffs with weak cases will "accept."

Recall that the anticipated per-case cost of the pooling strategy is $80,000 because both types of plaintiffs will accept the offer and settle. The expected per case cost of the separating strategy (offering zero) depends on the percentage of the two types of plaintiffs in the population. For now assume that there are equal numbers of each, so the percentage is .5. In contrast with the pooling strategy, the per-case expected cost of making a settlement offer of zero is (.5)($100,000)=$50,000. This equals the cost of going to trial with the strong plaintiffs, $100,000, multiplied by the fraction of strong plaintiffs in the population, .5. Because the weak plaintiffs drop their suits, the per-case cost under the separating strategy is cheaper than under the pooling strategy. In this example, NEV suits fail to obtain positive settlement amounts, and all strong cases go to trial.[48]

Now imagine that we increase the fraction of strong cases to .9. In this case, the per-case expected cost of the separating strategy becomes (.9)($100,000)=$90,000, which exceeds the $80,000 per-case cost of the pooling strategy. Here it is optimal for defendants to settle all cases, even though they know that ten percent of the filed cases are frivolous. Intuitively, if strong cases represent a large enough fraction of all suits, it pays the defendant to pay off some frivolous plaintiffs in order to avoid the cost of trial with plaintiffs holding strong claims.

---

[46] For a discussion of class action litigation, see *infra* at p. 404.

[47] *See* Lucian Arye Bebchuk, *Suing Solely to Extract a Settlement Offer*, 17 J. LEGAL STUD. 437 (1988); Avery Katz, *The Effect of Frivolous Litigation on the Settlement of Legal Disputes*, 10 INT'L REV. L. & ECON. 3 (1990).

[48] It follows that it would be unprofitable for plaintiffs with NEVs to file suit in the first place, given a positive filing cost. Incorporating the filing decision complicates the model but does not alter the basic result. *See* Katz, *supra* note 47.

Professors David Rosenberg and Steven Shavell offer a different argument for the success of NEV suits.[49] In this model, after a plaintiff files suit, the defendant has to incur some defense costs to file a motion for summary judgment.[50] Once the defendant make the initial investment, a plaintiff with a NEV suit will drop the case rather than proceed to trial. However, the defendant may prefer to settle at the earlier stage rather than incurring those early costs. Assume, for example, that the cost of an initial defense (for example, hiring a lawyer) is $1,000. The defendant would then be willing to pay up to $1,000 to settle even a known frivolous suit, one that would be dismissed as a matter of law with the requisite showing, which requires proving "no genuine issue of material fact," backed up by credible proffers in the pleadings. Thus, as long as the plaintiff's filing cost is less than $1,000, NEV suits will be profitable. Notice that assigning the burden of production to the plaintiff in civil cases tends to make this strategy less attractive as it imposes some up-front costs on the plaintiff.

Professor Lucien Bebchuk has also argued that the sequencing in which the parties incur various litigation costs affects the profitability of filing NEV suits.[51] Bebchuk focuses on how legal costs are divided over the course of the litigation process. He posits that even if the case has a negative expected value at the time of filing, it can still garner a settlement if at the time that the case reaches the courthouse steps the *remaining costs* to the plaintiff are lower than the expected judgment (i.e., the threat to go to trial is credible at that point going forward). This follows from the intuition that legal costs incurred up to the point of settlement negotiations are sunk, and thus the plaintiff's threat to proceed to trial at that point remains credible based solely on the anticipated costs to the defendant going forward.

Applying a process known as *backwards induction*, under specified circumstances, Bebchuk shows that it is rational for the defendant to settle as soon as the case is filed.[52] The model implicitly assumes complete information over litigant costs at each stage, and it allows for uniform or rising costs over time in supporting its conclusion. In Bebchuk's analysis, anticipating the continuing cost of litigation in each discrete future stage of litigation, to avoid the rising incremental costs, it becomes rational for the defendant to offer a settlement in the earliest possible period, namely at the filing of the suit.

2. *Ways of Discouraging NEVs*

Conventional wisdom holds that frivolous suits should be discouraged as a waste of societal resources. As previously shown, some therefore argue for a switch to the English

[49] David Rosenberg & Steven Shavell, *A Model in Which Suits Are Brought for Their Nuisance Value*, 5 INT'L REV. L. & ECON. 3 (1985).

[50] For a discussion of summary judgment, see *supra* at p. 385.

[51] Lucian Arye Bebchuk, *A New Theory Concerning the Credibility and Success of Threats to Sue*, 25 J. LEGAL STUD. 1 (1996).

[52] Backward induction is a process whereby the two parties elect strategies in the present period based on their rational response to other party's expected strategy in the period that immediately follows, reasoning back from the final period of play in a sequential game. Based on this process, for a predicted series of *n* rounds of play, the parties treat each period, *n*, *n-1*, *n-2*, and so on, down to the present period, as creating the same incentives as they would confront in a single period game. For a more detailed explanation of this process, see *infra* Chapter 15.

rule, which discourages the filing of suits with a low probability of success. But consider a NEV case with a high probability of victory but low expected damages. The English rule enhances the case's value because the losing party pays the winning party's fees regardless of the size of the judgment. This renders the effect of the English rule on NEV suits ambiguous.[53]

Federal Rules of Civil Procedure Rule 11 potentially discourages frivolous claims in U.S. federal courts. Rule 11(b) provides:

> (b) Representations to the Court. By presenting to the court a pleading, written motion, or other paper—whether by signing, filing, submitting, or later advocating it—an attorney or unrepresented party certifies that to the best of the person's knowledge, information, and belief, formed after an inquiry reasonable under the circumstances:
>
> (1) it is not being presented for any improper purpose, such as to harass, cause unnecessary delay, or needlessly increase the cost of litigation;
>
> (2) the claims, defenses, and other legal contentions are warranted by existing law or by a nonfrivolous argument for extending, modifying, or reversing existing law or for establishing new law;
>
> (3) the factual contentions have evidentiary support or, if specifically so identified, will likely have evidentiary support after a reasonable opportunity for further investigation or discovery; and
>
> (4) the denials of factual contentions are warranted on the evidence or, if specifically so identified, are reasonably based on belief or a lack of information.[54]

Rule 11(c) Provides:

> (c) Sanctions.
>
> (1) *In General.* If, after notice and a reasonable opportunity to respond, the court determines that Rule 11(b) has been violated, the court may impose an appropriate sanction on any attorney, law firm, or party that violated the rule or is responsible for the violation. Absent exceptional circumstances, a law firm must be held jointly responsible for a violation committed by its partner, associate, or employee.[55]

Rule 11(d) exempts discovery from the scope of Rule 11. In effect, Rule 11 authorizes federal judges to impose monetary sanctions—usually in the form of an order to pay the defendant's legal costs—against plaintiffs whose cases are determined to be frivolous.[56] Although Rule 11 has the potential to inhibit frivolous suits, as with Rule 68, it has been

---

[53] Spier, *supra* note 35, at 307.

[54] FED. R. CIV. P. 11(b).

[55] FED. R. CIV. P. 11(c).

[56] The scope of Rule 11 was substantially narrowed in the 1993 amendments. *See* FED. R. CIV. P. 11, Advisory Committee Notes.

applied rarely. As a result, despite this potential social welfare benefit, Rule 11 has generally not been forceful in deterring frivolous litigation.[57]

Some repeat-player defendants discourage NEV suits by developing a reputation for refusing to settle. This tactic is sometimes associated with insurance companies and manufacturers of dangerous products.[58] The success of this strategy depends on the credibility of the *defendant's* threat to go to trial in situations where that would not be the rational strategy for dealing with a single case in isolation. The approach is most apt to succeed as part of a larger caseload management strategy.

Finally, consider the extent to which any claimed social impact of NEV suits should account for the potential deterrent function of lawsuits.[59] Once this deterrence function is accounted for, the social undesirability of frivolous suits becomes less clear. The reason is that when litigation is costly, some plaintiffs with meritorious claims (i.e., with $PJ>0$) are discouraged from filing suit. Although this saves judicial resources, it also dilutes deterrence because injurers expect to escape responsibility for some damages that they caused. Professors Thomas Miceli and Michael Stone have argued that when this dilution effect is accounted for, the social desirability of discouraging frivolous (NEV) suits becomes less obvious.[60]

D. Contingency Fees for Lawyers

In the United States, plaintiffs' personal injury lawyers routinely represent their clients in a contingency fee arrangement whereby compensation is based on a percentage of the recovery, whether by settlement or at trial. The typical share is one-third.[61] Some nations disallow such arrangements.[62] A large literature has arisen to explain both the existence of contingent fees for lawyers and to assess their impact on legal representation and the judicial process.[63]

---

[57] *See* Charles S. Fax, *Does the Proposed Amendment to Rule 11 Solve a Problem or Create One?*, LITIG. NEWS, Summer 2011, at 11.

[58] Thomas J. Miceli, *Optimal Deterrence of Nuisance Suits by Repeat Defendants*, 13 INT'L REV. L. & ECON. 135 (1993).

[59] This effect has two components, the deterrence effect of damages awards and the separate lawmaking function of lawsuits, which takes the form of a public good, see *infra* Section I.G.

[60] Thomas J. Miceli & Michael P. Stone, *"Piggyback" Lawsuits and Deterrence: Can Frivolous Litigation Improve Welfare?*, 39 INT'L REV. L. & ECON. 49 (2014) (maintaining that frivolous suits serve a beneficial deterrence function by not shielding injurers from some cases that would not be filed due to litigation costs.)

[61] Some contingency fee contracts vary the recovery depending on whether the case is settled or tried. Herbert M. Kritzer, *Seven Dogged Myths Concerning Contingency Fees*, 80 WASH. U. L.Q. 739 (2002).

[62] *Id.*

[63] *See, e.g.*, Thomas J. Miceli & Kathleen Segerson, *Contingent Fees for Lawyers: The Impact on Litigation and Accident Prevention*, 20 J. LEGAL STUD. 381 (1991); Kathryn E. Spier & James D. Dana, Jr., *Expertise and Contingent Fees: The Role of Asymmetric Information in Attorney Compensation*, 9 J.L. ECON. & ORG. 349 (1993); Daniel L. Rubinfeld & Suzanne Scotchmer, *Contingent Fees for Attorneys: An Economic Analysis*, 24 RAND J. ECON. 343 (1993); Bruce L. Hay, *Contingency Fees and Agency Costs*, 25 J. LEGAL STUD. 503 (1996); Rudy Santore & Alan D. Viard, *Legal Fee Restrictions, Moral Hazard, and Attorney Rents*, 44 J.L. & ECON. 549 (2001).

1. *Rationale for Contingency Fees*

The contingency fee arrangement has been justified on three principal bases. First, the arrangement allows those who could not otherwise afford representation based on hourly fees to obtain representation through an alternative means of compensation that involves sharing in any recovery. In effect, the lawyer "loans" his or her services to the client, and requires "repayment" only if the representation is successful. Second, the arrangement creates a sharing of the risk of an uncertain trial outcome between the lawyer and client. Third, the contingent fee arrangement has been presented as a partial antidote to the agency problem that pervades many long-term contracting arrangements, including those for legal representation. According to principal-agent theory, the structure of the compensation scheme is important in inducing appropriate effort by agents in circumstances prone to the problem of moral hazard.[64] This problem is apt to arise when the principal either cannot observe, or cannot properly evaluate, the agent's work effort. In this analysis, the contingency fee structure encourages the lawyer to work diligently on behalf of the client.

There is an important caveat to the latter analysis. The claimed antidote to the principal-agent problem is offset by a critical insight from portfolio theory.[65] Although the client typically holds claims associated with a single suit, the contingency fee lawyer holds a portfolio of claims.[66] Some of the claims will prove meritorious, and thus profitable to pursue with considerable zeal, and others will prove less likely to be profitable after initial investigation, including discovery. Experienced lawyers will have strong intuitions concerning the relative strength of potential individual claims when taking on clients, although those will often change as the lawyer acquires additional information. The revised intuitions as to the likelihood of success and the potential value of each suit are certain to influence the lawyer's advice concerning such strategic considerations as whether to settle and, if so, in what amount.

Some commentators have suggested that the lawyer agency-cost problem might be ameliorated if the lawyer (agent) purchased the plaintiff's (principal's) legal claims for an agreed-upon fee, which would then form the basis for plaintiff's compensation. The lawyer would then pursue the claim entirely on her own.[67] This would potentially avoid the portfolio difficulty inasmuch as it would transform the contingency to 100% of the

---

[64] *See* RICHARD A. IPPOLITO, ECONOMICS FOR LAWYERS 375–79 (2005); George B. Shepherd & Morgan Cloud, *Time and Money: Discovery Leads to Hourly Billing*, 1999 U. ILL. L. REV. 91, 124–25.

[65] Shepherd & Cloud, *supra* note 64, at 104. The analysis here is similar to the analysis in Chapter 7 of sharecropping, or other shared-risk labor, incentives. Recall that in the sharecropping context specifically, the landlord can often diversify risk by managing multiple tenants, with differing work capacities, whereas the tenant is generally stuck with a single tract of land, and the attendant risks associated with weather and soil conditions.

[66] Other businesses that operate on this model include book publishing, with the publisher holding a portfolio of manuscripts only a subset of which, such as *Law and Economics: Private and Public*, are apt to become commercial best sellers, and, of course, venture capital, now popularized though *Shark Tank*. SHARK TANK (ABC), http://abc.go.com/shows/shark-tank.

[67] *See, e.g.*, Michael Abramowicz, *On the Alienability of Legal Claims*, 114 YALE L.J. 697 (2005); Robert Cooter, *Towards a Market in Unmatured Tort Claims*, 75 VA. L. REV. 383 (1989).

recovery. We might imagine a market for legal claims, with lawyers bidding to purchase rights to pursue particular claims of those who hold them.

This theoretical arrangement creates obvious complications. For example, the agency-cost problem is now flipped, with the "client" and his potential witnesses now less motivated to cooperate as needed to pursue the claim in a manner that achieves its maximum value. The resulting complexity could undermine traditional understandings of the attorney-client relationship. Conversely, we might imagine the lawyer pursuing some claims with greater zeal than an individual client whose enthusiasm for a potentially profitable but prolonged legal battle is inversely affected by immediate financial need. If we treat the client's valuation as a baseline, this could result in the excessive pursuit of claims.

Perhaps for these reasons, the law generally disallows the sale of legal claims,[68] although it does allow contingency fees. As suggested above, the distinction likely rests on promoting shared risk between the lawyer and client. Indeed, under standard contingency fee contracts, the plaintiff continues to hold the larger share.[69] The arrangement further ensures that the client, who has intimate knowledge of the factual predicates to the legal claims, remains actively involved at each decision-making juncture, including those that relate to valuation and the choice of settlement or trial. A contingency ensures that plaintiffs retain a stake in the outcome of the case all the way to its conclusion.[70]

2. *The Impact of Contingency Fees*

Contingency fees potentially affect the incentives of plaintiffs and their lawyers regarding the choice between settlement and trial.[71] So far, we have derived the formal settlement conditions of various cost rules under the assumption that the plaintiff and her lawyer were acting jointly based on the overall benefits and costs of going to trial. Under a contingent fee arrangement, however, plaintiff and her lawyer will potentially have conflicting interests.

---

68 Charles R. Korsmo & Minor Myers, *Aggregation by Acquisition: Replacing Class Actions with a Market for Legal Claims*, 101 IOWA L. REV. 1323, 1343 (2016) (discussing the historical prohibitions on the sale of legal claims); Keith N. Hylton, *The Economics of Third-Party Financed Litigation*, 8 J.L. ECON. & POL'Y 701 (2012) (discussing related issues, including recent state laws that have narrowed past prohibitions and of the legal status of funds used to finance litigation).

69 An important exception: Class action litigation, in which, although the lawyer holds a smaller percentage as compared with the aggregated claims, she holds a much larger share than any individual claimant, whose overall share is typically minuscule. *See infra* at p. 404.

70 The logic here is similar to that used in Chapter 4 to explain partial product warranties, given that an accident could be due to a combination of defective production and consumer misuse. Russell Cooper & Thomas Ross, *Product Warranties and Double Moral Hazard*, 16 RAND J. ECON. 103 (1985). Partial coverage is a response to this dual moral-hazard problem. In Chapter 14, we will also consider the role of case orderings in affecting substantive doctrine, and the resulting incentives of lawyers to time cases for maximal doctrinal effect. This problem, known as *path manipulation*, is potentially exacerbated in a regime in which lawyers own the right to press what were traditionally their clients' legal claims.

71 *See* Geoffrey Miller, *Some Agency Problems in Settlement*, 16 J. LEGAL STUD. 189 (1987); John J. Donohue III, *The Effects of Fee Shifting on the Settlement Rate: Theoretical Observations on Costs, Conflict, and Contingency Fees*, LAW & CONTEMP. PROBS., Summer 1991, at 195.

Consider first the plaintiff's preferences under a contract that pays the lawyer one-third of any recovery following settlement or trial.[72] The lowest settlement amount S that the plaintiff would accept must now satisfy the condition: $(2/3)S>=(2/3)P_pJ$, or $S>=P_pJ$.[73] Assuming that the defendant's offer to settle is the same as computed above under the American rule (i.e., P_dJ+C), then the settlement condition from the *plaintiff's* perspective with a contingency fee is as follows:

$C > (P_p–P_d)J$ (plaintiff's settlement condition—contingent fee)

In other words, plaintiff will prefer to settle when the difference between the assessments of plaintiff prevailing as assessed by the two parties, times the judgment, has a lower value than one party's lawyer's fees, here equal to what defendant saves by settling rather than trying the case. This implies that the plaintiff will be *more* willing to go to trial than when the plaintiff and her lawyer acted jointly in the decision-making process, reflecting the fact that under contingency-fee representation, the plaintiff incurs no out-of-pocket lawyer's fees by opting for a trial.

Now compare what would happen if the plaintiff's lawyer controlled the settlement decision. The minimum settlement the lawyer will accept must satisfy $(1/3)S>=(1/3)P_pJ–C$ (one third of the settlement value must equal or exceed the lawyer's share of the expected recovery minus lawyering costs, which are fully borne by the lawyer). Using simple algebra to rearrange this yields the lawyer's condition for a settlement:

$4C > (P_p–P_d)J$ (lawyer's settlement condition—contingent fee)

Notice that the right side of the two settlement conditions are the same $(P_p–P_d)J$, which we can call the *disagreement term*, namely the parties' differing assessments of the likelihood of plaintiff prevailing times the expected value of judgment. Clearly, the left sides of the two settlement conditions differ. Plaintiff will prefer to settle as long as the disagreement term is of lower value than one side's lawyering fees, whereas the contingency fee lawyer would prefer to settle even if the disagreement term is of lower value than four times lawyer's fees. The critical difference is that unlike her client, the lawyer internalizes not only the available settlement range reflecting the other side's lawyering fees, but also the full cost of her client's lawyering fees, subject to a triple multiplier as a result of the one-third contingency. This increases the expected trial cost for the lawyer, and thus also increases the settlement range as compared with the client.

This demonstrates that the lawyer's incentives under a contingency fee arrangement are more strongly biased toward settlement. Combining these settlement conditions reveals that contingency fees bias plaintiffs toward trial and bias lawyers toward settlement. The actual outcome will therefore depend on which party ultimately controls the settlement decision. Although contingency fees help to align the interests of clients and lawyers, they do so imperfectly.

Because plaintiffs pay only on recovery, thus incurring no financial risk in filing suit, contingency fees have been blamed for encouraging frivolous litigation. To some extent

[72] For expositional purposes, we ignore that possibility of differing contingency rates based upon whether the suit settles or goes to trial.

[73] For expositional purposes, we assume that plaintiff's lawyer incurs all of the trial costs, C. It therefore ignores non-monetary costs of trial.

this is ameliorated by the lawyer's gatekeeping function since, in theory, lawyers are only interested in cases for which they anticipate a positive net return.[74] Indeed, with a contingency rate of one-third, lawyers will decline representation in some suits even holding a positive expected value. Specifically, some suits for which $(1/3)P_pJ-C<0$ (representing a negative return for the contingency fee lawyer) will have $P_pJ-C>0$ (representing a positive return for the suit as a whole). Using the plaintiff's incentives as a baseline, contingent fees may actually result in too few suits being filed.

This conclusion fails to account for the impact of asymmetric information on NEV suits. When a contingency fee arrangement is incorporated into this model, the effect on total litigation costs turns out to be less certain.[75] Fewer cases are filed under a contingent fee as compared with an hourly fee, reflecting contingency fee lawyer incentives, but more cases go to trial due to information asymmetries.[76] The combined impact on overall litigation costs is therefore ambiguous.

E. Class Action Litigation

Under *Federal Rule of Civil Procedure 23*, a nominal plaintiff can have a class certified, thereby combining the claims for the class as a whole into a single suit. Rule 23(a) provides as follows:

> Rule 23—Class Actions
>
> (a) **Prerequisites**. One or more members of a class may sue or be sued as representative parties on behalf of all members only if:
>
> (1) the class is so numerous that joinder of all members is impracticable;
>
> (2) there are questions of law or fact common to the class;
>
> (3) the claims or defenses of the representative parties are typical of the claims or defenses of the class; and
>
> (4) the representative parties will fairly and adequately protect the interests of the class.

Rule 23(b) provides that a class may be certified provided:

> the court finds that the questions of law or fact common to class members predominate over any questions affecting only individual members, and that a class action is superior to other available methods for fairly and efficiently adjudicating the controversy.

Rules 23(c) sets out the requirements for certification, notice, and judgment respecting issues, classes, and subclasses.

The case law respecting class action litigation is complex and beyond the scope of this chapter. Class action litigation is important to the economic analysis of law, however,

---

[74] We hold aside for now the implications of portfolio analysis. *See supra* notes 65 and 66, and accompanying text.

[75] Thomas J. Miceli, *Do Contingent Fees Promote Excessive Litigation?*, 23 J. LEGAL STUD. 211 (1994).

[76] In the asymmetric information model the conflict over settlement between the plaintiff and her lawyer does not arise because settlement is dictated by the defendant's strategy.

and it is also controversial both because of its effects on lawyer incentives and because of the claimed burdens it imposes on defendants to settle once a class is certified, and thus without regard to the merits of the underlying suit. Class action litigation has given rise to two economic models, which push in opposite directions viewed from a social welfare perspective.

The first model picks up on the preceding principal-agent analysis.[77] In general, the true stakeholder in class action litigation from a financial perspective is the contingency fee lawyer. Consider, for example, a case involving a large class of 100,000 claimants, each holding a claim valued at $20, for a total initial valuation of $2 million. With a one-third lawyer's contingency fee and a damages multiplier of 3, the value to each claimant is a mere $40, whereas for the lawyer, the value is $2 million, or one-third of the total expected $6 million recovery.

No individual claimant would rationally press a legal claim valued at $40 given the time investments and other associated costs. By contrast, the lawyer has a strong incentive on these facts to seek class certification and to pursue the claim. Scholars have observed that for this very reason, the most vital juncture in class action litigation is the question of class certification.[78] Once the class is certified, the settlement range strongly favors plaintiff, and more specifically, his contingency-fee attorney. Consider whether this helps to explain Rule 23(e), which states: "The claims, issues, or defenses of a certified class may be settled, voluntarily dismissed, or compromised only with the court's approval."[79] In addition, the divergent incentives between the class action lawyer and her client skews in favor of early settlement. Professor John C. Coffee has observed that the class action attorney is apt to prefer investing only up to the point that maximizes her fees, as opposed to maximizing the judgment.[80] In this analysis, the attorney seeks to settle based on the relationship between expenses incurred relative to expected return, often favoring early settlement.[81]

The second model views class action litigation in Pigouvian terms. In this model, regardless of whether the recovery principally benefits the client or the attorney, the effect is benign if it forces the internalization of costs in a manner that reduces the risk of harmful personal injuries or if it inhibits sharp business practices that individuals bear on a small scale but that produce large windfalls for the offending firm.[82] In effect, this model presents class action litigation as a privately imposed regulatory regimen through the

[77] John C. Coffee Jr., *Understanding The Plaintiff's Attorney: The Implications of Economic Theory for Private Enforcement of Law Through Class and Derivative Actions*, 86 COLUM. L. REV. 669 (1986).

[78] *See* Richard A. Nagareda, *Class Certification in the Age of Aggregate Proof*, 84 N.Y.U. L. REV. 97 (2009). Professor Nagareda states:

> With vanishingly rare exception, class certification sets the litigation on a path toward resolution by way of settlement, not full-fledged testing of the plaintiffs' case by trial. In terms of their real-world impact, class settlements can be quite significant, potentially involving dollar sums in the hundreds of millions or requiring substantial restructuring of the defendant's operations.

Id. at 99.

[79] FED. R. CIV. P. 23(e).

[80] Coffee, *supra* note 77.

[81] *Id.* at 690. For a similar dynamic affecting real estate agents versus clients, see STEVEN D. LEVITT & STEPHEN J. DUBNER, FREAKONOMICS 71–75 (2005).

[82] Gerald A. Wright, *The Cost Internalization Case for Class Actions*, 21 STAN. L. REV. 383 (1969).

mechanism of Pigouvian taxation, with the tax proceeds going to the lawyer and her clients. Myriam Gilles and Gary Friedman, for example, rely on a Pigouvian analysis to criticize the agency model, although they acknowledge that the high stakes of class certification risks collusive behavior between the defendant and class action lawyers.[83]

As a general matter, courts are not supposed to assess the legal merits of proposed class action claims at the time of class certification, but instead must focus on such questions as commonality. In *In Re Rhone-Poulenc,* Judge Richard Posner, writing for the United States Court of Appeals for the Seventh Circuit, assessed the probability that a proposed class of thirteen hemophiliacs would prevail based on the prior rejection of the claims of twelve of the class members, as opposed to assessing the merits of the underlying legal claims. Professor George Priest commended Posner's analysis on the ground that once a class is certified, without regard to the merits, defendants are often financially coerced into settlement given the enormously high stakes.[84]

Which of these two models do you believe best describes class action litigation? Do you believe that class action litigation is harmful or benign? Why? Consider how NEV suits are affected by class action litigation. Assume that for each individual member of the plaintiff class the expected suit value is negative, but that for the certified class, the value is positive. How does the litigation model for NEV suits relate to the incentive structure of tort law, which economic analysis demonstrates is designed in large part to minimize the sum of accident costs, as shown in Figure 3.1? Does the combination of the relevant economic models favor or disfavor class action tort litigation? Why?

F. Court Delay

Court delay has been blamed for impeding accurate and fair trial outcomes and timely victim compensation. Because well over ninety percent of cases settle, delays might appear to affect only a small fraction of cases. In fact, however, Professor Daniel Kessler found that trial delay is also a significant source of delay in settlement.[85] We offer two explanations for why that is the case.

First, Professor Kathryn Spier has demonstrated that in a dynamic model where the pretrial period is broken into discrete time periods, settlements will cluster into the initial and final periods, as is reflected in the following U-shaped settlement pattern:[86]

---

[83] Myriam Gilles & Gary B. Friedman, *Exploding the Class Action Agency Costs Myth: The Social Utility of Entrepreneurial Lawyers,* 155 U. PA. L. REV. 103 (2006).

[84] George L. Priest, *Procedural Versus Substantive Controls of Mass Tort Class Actions,* 26 J. LEGAL STUD. 521, 521 (1997) ("[U]niform settlement and zero litigation is an extraordinary empirical fact, neither predicted by nor consistent with *any* current economic model of litigation and settlement. It is reflective of the huge uncertainty and, therefore, the risk that attends judgment of a mass tort claim by a lay jury." (footnote omitted)).

[85] Daniel Kessler, *Institutional Causes of Delay in the Settlement of Legal Disputes,* 12 J.L. ECON. & ORG. 432 (1996).

[86] Kathryn Spier, *The Dynamics of Pretrial Negotiation,* 59 REV. ECON. STUD. 93 (1992).

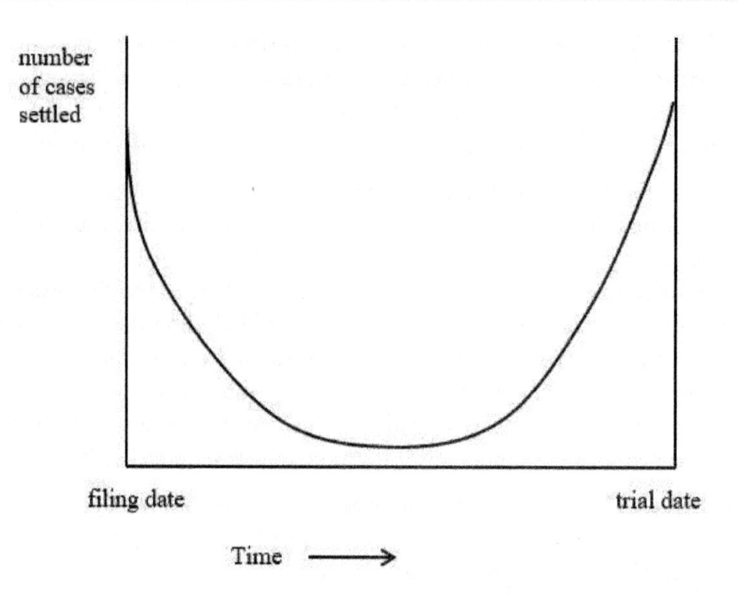

Figure 10:1. Pattern of settlements during the pretrial period.

In this model, the bulk of cases will either settle immediately, or on the courthouse steps.

As an alternative explanation, Professor Thomas Miceli shows that defendants can use trial delay strategically to lower their costs.[87] Suppose, for example, that plaintiffs differ in their discount rates, meaning that some are less patient than others in seeking to obtain a settlement or judgment, but that defendants cannot distinguish among them. Defendants can then use delay as a sorting device.

Consider a case with an estimated $100,000 trial value, but for which trial is scheduled one year from now. Assume there are two types of plaintiffs, those with a discount rate of 10% and those with a discount rate of 5%. The first type is therefore more impatient than the second. The "impatient" plaintiff will settle for $100,000/1.1=$90,909 today rather than waiting for trial, whereas the "patient" plaintiff will settle for $100,000/1.05=$95,238 today. The analysis is identical to that involving a defendant confronting asymmetric information concerning weak and strong plaintiffs. Thus, the defendant can either offer $95,238 now, which both types of plaintiffs will accept (the pooling strategy), or it can offer $90,909, which the impatient plaintiff will accept but the patient plaintiff will reject, preferring to wait for trial (the separating strategy). As before, the per-case cost of the pooling strategy is $95,238, whereas the per-case cost of the separating strategy depends on the fraction of each type of plaintiff in the population, in addition to the defendant's own discount rate, given that absent settlement, payment takes place in one year.

To illustrate, suppose there are equal numbers of each plaintiff type, and the defendant's discount rate is 8%. The present value of the cost of the separating strategy is as follows:

(.5)($90.909)+(.5)($100,000)/(1.08)=$91,751

[87] Thomas J. Miceli, *Settlement Delay as a Sorting Device*, 19 INT'L REV. L. & ECON. 265 (1999).

This is lower than the per-case price of the pooling strategy.[88] On these facts, the defendant can lower its financial exposure by relying on delay as a sorting device across plaintiffs.

As with frivolous suits, the conventional wisdom is that trial delay is a pressing policy concern that is in need of a remedy.[89] This analysis explains how defendants might strategically use delay to reduce costs through a separating equilibrium strategy producing settlement versus trial cohorts based on differential plaintiff discount rates.[90] Increasing the settlement rate through delay as a result of differential plaintiff discount rates reduces litigation costs, and, at the same time, reduces the deterrent effect of lawsuits. Counterintuitively, the latter effect might lead firms to take greater risks, resulting in an increased number of disputes. Because these factors push in opposite directions, as a purely theoretical matter, the overall effect is ambiguous. In addition, two factors not accounted for in this argument are the precedent-setting effect of lawsuits, discussed below, and the separate normative goal of ensuring that legal disputes achieve a just resolution, which is a common rationale for efforts to reduce delay.

G. Judicial Error

Another source of inefficiency in the legal process is the risk of judicial error, which is an unavoidable consequence of decision making under uncertainty. Although the rules of civil and criminal procedure are in large part designed to reduce error risk (as discussed below), as in other contexts, reducing risk does not entirely eliminate error. On the civil side, this means mistakenly finding or declining to find liability. In the criminal law context, it translates to the two paradigmatic types of legal error: false convictions and false acquittals. Borrowing language from statistics, wrongful convictions or findings of liability are referred to at *Type 1 errors* (false positives), whereas wrongful acquittals or findings of no liability are referred to as *Type 2 errors* (false negatives).[91] Increasing either type of errors reduces the deterrent effect of the law.[92]

To see why, consider a person who sometimes engages in a dangerous activity that yields him benefits, B, but that also causes expected damages to others, D. If the person expects to face strict liability for the damages, he will only engage in the activity if $B>D$, which satisfies the condition of Kaldor-Hicks efficiency (the injurer's gain exceeds the victims' losses). Now assume that when the injurer engages in the activity, he is wrongly absolved of liability with probability a (a type 2 error), and when he does not engage in the activity he is wrongly found liable with probability b (a type 1 error). In this case, his expected gain from engaging in the activity is $B-(1-a)D$ (the benefit of the activity, less the discounted probability of being found liable for a resulting injury times expected damages), whereas his cost of not engaging is $-bD$ (the probability of being found wrongly

[88] The separating strategy is preferred in this example for any $r>.043$.

[89] One often-proposed remedy is alternative dispute resolution (ADR). *See* Steven Shavell, *Alternative Dispute Resolution: An Economic Analysis*, 24 J. LEGAL STUD. 1 (1995).

[90] H.S.E. Gravelle, *Rationing Trials by Waiting: Welfare Implications*, 10 INT'L REV. L. & ECON. 255 (1990).

[91] *See infra* Chapter 20.

[92] *See, e.g.*, I.P.L. Png, *Optimal Subsidies and Damages in the Presence of Legal Error*, 6 INT'L REV. L. & ECON. 101 (1986); Thomas J. Miceli, *Optimal Criminal Procedure: Fairness and Deterrence*, 11 INT'L REV. L. & ECON. 3 (1991).

culpable despite not having taken the risk of injury times the expected damages). Given the payoffs, this person will rationally engage in the activity if $B-(1-a)D>-bD$ (meaning if the gains from doing so, as defined above, exceed the costs of not doing so, also as defined above). This can be simplified as follows: $B>(1-a-b)D$.

Notice that the value attached to D in this equation, which includes the impact of type 1 *and* type 2 error, is lower than it was absent the risk of error. Thus, the injurer engages in the activity too often, given a positive probability of either type of error (i.e., $1-a-b<1$, which implies $a+b>0$). Increases in the probability of either error reduce deterrence.[93] Legal error of either type has this dampening effect on deterrence because it reduces the accuracy of courts in assigning legal responsibility.

The law embodies various mechanisms for minimizing legal error. We discuss two: the standard of proof for conviction, and the appeals process.

1. *Standard of Proof*

The primary procedural protection intended to reduce the risk of legal error in a trial is the standard of proof for conviction (also known as the *burden of persuasion*, as noted above). Essentially, this represents the minimum degree of certainty that the trier of fact, the judge or the jury, must reach before finding liability in a civil case, or finding guilt in a criminal case. Assuming it operates properly, the standard should be set to minimize the sum of the costs of type 1 and type 2 error.[94]

To illustrate, consider a criminal trial. After hearing evidence from both sides, the trier of fact assesses the probability that the defendant is guilty, given by θ, which is some number between zero and one. Given evidentiary uncertainty and other random factors, θ is an imperfect assessment of the defendant's actual guilt or innocence, and it measures the strength of the case against the defendant. Assuming that, in general, there is more available evidence against factually guilty defendants, θ should on average be larger for those who have committed the offenses for which they are charged. This will not be universally true, of course, as some defendants who committed the underlying acts will have successfully covered their tracks, and others who did not commit the offenses will be framed or implicated by circumstantial evidence.

These ideas are captured in the concept of a *probability density function*. This means there is a distribution, approximated in a bell-shaped curve. If we select a random variable from that function, it is more likely to fall within those values with more entries, meaning the middle, than with fewer, meaning the end points. Imagine that the value of θ represents the realization of a random variable in any particular case drawn from a probability density function in which $f_G(\theta)$ applies if the defendant is actually guilty, and $f_I(\theta)$ applies if the defendant is actually not guilty. The probability density function of a random variable shows the chance of picking any particular value of θ in a random draw. For a bell shape, picking intermediate values is most likely. These two functions,

---

[93] It seems reasonable to assume that $1-a>b$, which implies that "guilty" defendants are more likely to be convicted than innocent defendants; otherwise the legal system would be entirely ineffective in deterring harmful behavior.

[94] *See* Thomas Miceli, *Optimal Prosecution of Defendants Whose Guilt Is Uncertain*, 6 J.L. ECON. & ORG. 189 (1990); Edward K. Cheng, *Reconceptualizing the Burden of Proof*, 122 YALE L.J. 1254 (2013).

associated with findings of guilty or not guilty, drawn as bell-shaped curves in Figure 10:2, overlap, with f_G shifted to the right (i.e., toward higher realizations of θ) as compared with f_I. This implies that drawing a high value of θ is more likely if the defendant is actually guilty, but is still possible even if the defendant is actually innocent.

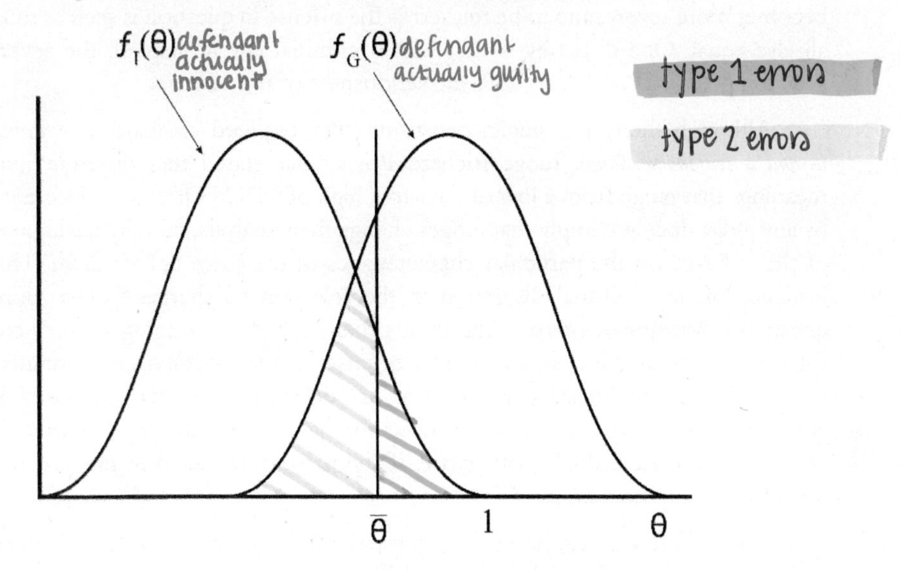

Figure 10:2. The standard of proof for conviction and the probabilities of legal error.

In this setting, the standard of proof specifies a threshold, $\bar{\theta}$, such that the defendant is found guilty if $\theta \geq \bar{\theta}$ and acquitted if $\theta < \bar{\theta}$. In civil cases, the standard of proof is *preponderance of the evidence*, which means that $\bar{\theta}$ just exceeds 50%, whereas in criminal law the standard is *beyond a reasonable doubt*, which although not precisely defined as a percentage term, might be construed to mean that $\bar{\theta}$ exceeds 90%. (For current purposes, the specific value of $\bar{\theta}$ is not important; in the discussion that follows, we explain why these standards differ.)

For the standard of proof shown in Figure 10:2, it should be evident that there will be both false convictions and false acquittals. The false convictions (type 1 errors) are those realizations of θ that are drawn from the density function f_I but that fall to the right of $\bar{\theta}$. The total number of these errors is the area under f_I and to the right of $\bar{\theta}$. Likewise, the false acquittals (type 2 errors) are those realizations of θ that are drawn from f_G but that fall to the left of $\bar{\theta}$. The number of these errors is the area under f_G and to the left of $\bar{\theta}$. Note that there is an inevitable trade-off in the relationship between the incidence of these two errors because a change in the standard of proof in either direction will increase the number of one type of error while reducing the number of the other. A stricter standard of proof (i.e., a higher $\bar{\theta}$) will reduce the number of false convictions but will increase the number of false acquittals. Conversely, a more lenient standard of proof (i.e., a lower $\bar{\theta}$) will have the opposite effect.

We are now in a position to derive the optimal standard of proof based on the assumed goal of minimizing the overall cost of the two types of legal error. The trade-off between the two types of error suggests that an intermediate standard of proof will be optimal, but exactly how stringent it should be will depend on the relative costs of wrongful convictions versus wrongful acquittals. We can assume that the cost of wrongful convictions increases with the severity of the sanction for conviction, whereas the cost of wrongful acquittals increases with the harm caused by the defendant's action. Thus, we would expect the standard of proof to be strengthened as the threatened sanction becomes more severe, and to be relaxed as the offense in question is seen as more serious, all else equal. One difficulty is that within criminal law in general, the severity of the sanction positively correlates with the seriousness of the offense.

Although there is a single, constitutionally required standard in criminal trials,[95] *beyond a reasonable doubt,* Judge Richard Posner has stated that different judges apply meanings that range from a low of 75% to a high of 95%.[96] Of course different meanings by any judge does not imply that judges change their analysis, thereby raising the standard of proof based on the particular characteristics of the cases before them. There is also evidence of prosecutorial discretion in the selection of charges.[97] The more difficult question is how juries interpret the standard and whether, in doing so, they compensate for the severity of the charge or of the offense. In the most extreme circumstance, the practice of jury nullification involves a jury declining to apply the stated legal rules governing conviction despite the prosecutor having met the legal standard of proof beyond a reasonable doubt; otherwise, if the prosecutor failed in her proffer, the jury would acquit on the merits.

Given these caveats, let us now compare the differing standards of proof for civil and criminal cases. The higher standard in criminal cases suggests a strong aversion to wrongful convictions as compared with wrongful acquittals. This seems intuitive given the threat of imprisonment and the stigma associated with having a criminal record that results from a conviction. The standard of proof reflects the intuition that in the criminal law context, society is more concerned with type 1 errors (false convictions) than type 2 errors (false acquittals). By contrast, there is less reason to believe that either of the two types of errors is more costly in a civil context as is reflected by the *preponderance of the evidence* standard applied in civil litigation, which equals just over fifty percent.

As a final point, note that there are two ways in which the incidence of both types of errors can be simultaneously reduced. The first is through increased spending on evidence gathering, and the second is by improvements in technology that increase the ability to distinguish between the innocent and the guilty. Examples of the latter include fingerprint and DNA evidence, although neither has eliminated problems of proof.[98] In theory, such improved technology would cause the two density functions in Figure 10:2 to diverge, thus allowing a more accurate distinction between those who are and who are not guilty. Although this is socially desirable, the resulting benefits must be weighed against the cost of the additional resources needed to gather more evidence or to develop and use such technologies.

---

[95] *In re* Winship, 397 U.S. 358 (1970).

[96] RICHARD A. POSNER, ECONOMIC ANALYSIS OF LAW § 22.4, at 829 (2011).

[97] For a general discussion, see Joanna Shepherd, Blakely's *Silver Lining: Sentencing Guidelines, Judicial Discretion, and Crime*, 58 HASTINGS L.J. 533, 558 (2007).

[98] *See* Rick Visser & Greg Hampikian, *When DNA Won't Work*, 49 IDAHO L. REV. 39 (2012); Jacqueline McMurtrie, *Swirls and Whorls: Litigating Post-Conviction Claims of Fingerprint Misidentification After the NAS Report*, 2010 UTAH L. REV. 267.

2. *Appeals*

The losing side in a legal proceeding generally has the ability to appeal that ruling to a higher court. The appeals process is designed to correct errors made by lower courts. In a criminal proceeding, the prosecution cannot appeal an acquittal,[99] but it is permitted to appeal certain rulings of law that interfere with prosecution, such as the dismissal of an indictment or a judicial decision setting aside a jury verdict of guilty. In the event that an intermediate appellate court reverses a conviction (appeals from convictions are available in all states[100]), the state may also further appeal that reversal to the state's highest court.

In civil litigation, the plaintiff can appeal questions of law or fact, but the standards of review differ significantly. For questions of law the standard is *de novo* review, implying no deference, whereas for questions of fact, the standard is typically *clearly erroneous*, implying broad deference. Defendants can also appeal counterclaims under the same legal standard.

The appeals process demonstrates the comparative advantage of the two judicial functions split between trial and appellate courts. Trial courts take evidence, often based on testimony of witnesses, and they apply legal rules to the facts brought before them or refer such determinations to a jury. Appellate courts do not see the witnesses, and they typically include panels of three judges who have expertise on substantive rules of law. The different standards of review described above reflect the differing institutional comparative advantages as between trial and appellate courts respecting their judicial functions.

Modeling the appellate process is complicated because the social welfare function has to weigh the following factors: the benefits of error correction to the appellant, the additional costs to the parties and the legal system, and the potential precedent that the appeal might produce. In addition, in federal practice and in most state jurisdictions, the first appeal following a criminal conviction is "of right" but the second is discretionary. The United States Supreme Court, and most state courts of highest jurisdiction, have discretionary docket control respecting most or all appeals. This further complicates modeling inasmuch as the parties have greater control over what gets docketed in the first appellate process and substantially less control in the second.[101] This distinction implies that the first appellate process might be more closely tied to concerns of error correction at the level of the individual case, and that the second might be driven instead by the broader concept of error correction affecting the governing body of precedent.

H. The Lawmaking Function of the Judicial Process

We now consider the role of the judicial process in creating precedent. As our analysis of the various substantive areas of law in prior chapters has demonstrated, legal

---

[99] This is prohibited by the Double Jeopardy Clause of the Fifth Amendment as applied to federal prosecutions, and the Fifth and Fourteenth Amendments as applied to state prosecutions. WAYNE R. LAFAVE ET AL., CRIMINAL PROCEDURE § 25.3 (2015).

[100] *Id.* § 27.3.

[101] In Chapter 24, we describe models respecting particular features of the appellate process as it affects Supreme Court decision making.

rules establish incentives for people to behave in certain socially desirable ways, whether they are engaging in risky activities, entering into contracts, or investing in property or improvements. As seen in this chapter, these common law rules develop through complex judicial processes. Our study of these processes can shed light on how such rules develop and how, if at all, they promote the various objectives of the common law revealed by economic analysis.

1. *The Social Versus Private Value of Lawsuits*

The first step in understanding the lawmaking function of the judicial process is to examine the difference between the social and private value of lawsuits.[102] The private value of a lawsuit represents the net gain to the plaintiff, as examined in the above analysis of the settlement-trial decision, whereas the social value involves the effect of the suit, through its signaling or precedential impact, in affecting compliance with the law.[103] We illustrate the difference between the two values in the context of a simple accident model where the controlling legal rule is strict liability.[104]

Consider an accident that imposes a loss of $1,000 on a victim, and in which the cost of bringing suit is $500. Under a rule of strict liability the plaintiff will win at trial with certainty, and so the *private value* of the suit to the plaintiff is the difference of $500. Thus, the plaintiff will bring suit. The social value of the suit, however, concerns the incentive it creates for injurers in general to invest in accident avoidance. Suppose, for example, that injurers can spend $50 in precaution to reduce the probability of an accident from .5 to .4, and that it also costs an injurer $500 to defend himself at trial if an accident occurs and the plaintiff sues. The threat of a lawsuit, which in this case is credible, will induce the injurer to invest in precaution because if he does not invest, his expected costs will be (.5)($1,000+$500)=$750 (.5 times the sum of expected liability plus the cost of the suit), whereas if he does invest his expected costs will be $50+(.4)($1,000+$500)=$650 (the cost of precaution plus .4 times the same sum). Investing in precaution thus saves him $100 on average.

It does not necessarily follow, however, that suits improve social welfare. To determine if they do, we need to compare the *total social costs* if suits are filed with total social costs if suits are not allowed. In this example, total social costs with suits are given by $50+(.4)($1,000+$500+$500)=$850 (the precaution cost plus .4 times the sum of the expected liability plus *both sides'* court costs), whereas total social costs without suits are (.5)($1,000)=$500 (.5 times expected liability with no legal costs). This is therefore an example in which *suits are not socially valuable.* Although the threat of suits induces injurers to take care, thereby reducing the number of accidents and expected accident costs, suits also require both parties to incur litigation costs of $500, which in this case exceeds the marginal savings from injurer care.

---

[102] *See* Steven Shavell, *The Social Versus Private Incentive to Bring Suit in a Costly Legal System*, 11 J. LEGAL STUD. 333 (1982) (addressing this question).

[103] By signaling we mean the publicity that attends trials and appeals independent of the formal precedent the cases establish.

[104] The analysis is more complicated under a negligence rule, but the basic conclusion that the social and private value of lawsuits diverges remains the same.

In this example, therefore, suits are *privately valuable but not socially valuable.* It is important to emphasize, however, that by altering the numerical assumptions, it is possible to generate a different result. For example, if injurer precaution reduced the probability of accidents from .5 to .1 but everything else was the same, suits would be both privately and socially valuable because now, total costs with a suit would be $250. Similarly, holding to the initial assumptions, but reducing victim damages to $400 would make the suit socially valuable but not privately valuable (because victim damages are less than the cost of bringing suit).

The analysis reveals that there is no necessary relationship between the social and private value of lawsuits. The divergence between these values arises from two sources: first, under the American rule, plaintiffs disregard defendant's trial costs in deciding whether or not to file, a negative externality; and second, as a general matter, individual plaintiffs do not account for the deterrent effect of a suit in inducing injurers to invest in precautions against accidents, a positive externality. These two effects tend to work in opposite directions. Defendant's costs reduce the social benefit of litigation, whereas the deterrent effect increases the social benefit of litigation.

The preceding conclusion, that there is a divergence between the social and private incentives to bring suit, implies that the parties to a lawsuit are not necessarily maximizing their joint wealth. In other words, there are gains to be had if they could enter into agreements to somehow avoid litigation. Two such mechanisms are available: *waiver agreements*, in which potential plaintiffs waive their claims for compensation from defendants; and agreements to enter into *arbitration* rather than litigation. Professor Keith Hylton has demonstrated that if potential litigants are able to negotiate such agreements costlessly, and if they expect those agreements to be enforced, then litigation will be brought only when it is socially desirable.[105]

The analysis in this section has assumed that a given rule (strict liability) is in place, and that the sole function of the lawsuit is to enforce that rule. Another possible benefit of litigation is the prospect of supplanting an inefficient rule with an efficient one. Once more, other than the effect of the ruling on this specific case outcome, as a general matter, the plaintiff does not internalize that larger social benefit. Because of this, there is a risk that the "lawmaking" function of litigation will be undersupplied from a social perspective. The next section explores this function of the legal process.

2. *Evolution of the Law*

Although earlier scholars had also explored related issues,[106] then-Professor Richard Posner and Professor William Landes were the first to systematically assess the common law from the perspective of economic efficiency.[107] Landes and Posner advanced the

---

[105] This conclusion is a consequence of the Coase Theorem. *See* Keith Hylton, *Agreements to Waive or to Arbitrate Legal Claims: An Economic Analysis*, 8 SUP. CT. ECON. REV. 209 (2000).

[106] Early writers include Aaron Director and Ronald Coase. For a discussion of the early history of law and economics, see HENRY G. MANNE, AN INTELLECTUAL HISTORY OF THE GEORGE MASON UNIVERSITY SCHOOL OF LAW (1993), https://www.law.gmu.edu/about/history.

[107] *See* Richard A. Posner, *Gary Becker's Contributions to Law and Economics*, 22 J. LEGAL STUD. 211 (1993) (crediting Becker with getting Landes and Posner to collaborate); Richard A. Posner, *Legal Formalism, Legal Realism, and the Interpretation of Statutes and the Constitution*, 37 CASE W. RES. L. REV. 179, 185 (1986).

broad claim that the common law embraced an underlying economic logic, much of which finds reflection in the preceding chapters. Their early work did not, however, focus on the mechanism that might help to produce this seemingly benign result.

In later work, Richard Posner considered this question as well. In the discussion that follows, we consider the work of Richard Posner, and of several other scholars, who have considered not only whether economic analysis helps to explain legal doctrine, but also whether it helps to identify the motivations of decision makers or the features of the judicial process that might move the common law toward or away from efficiency.

a. The Selection of Cases for Trial

The vast majority of civil cases (more than ninety-five percent) end up settling before they ever reach trial. The evolution of the common law, however, depends entirely on those few cases that not only reach trial, but that are also appealed and that result in a published opinion that can be cited as precedent.[108] The method by which cases are chosen for trial is therefore a critical first step in thinking through how the common law evolves. Unfortunately, since we know very little about cases that settle, the nature of the resulting *selection bias*, meaning the process for choosing which cases end up settling and which cases end up being litigated, must largely be inferred from a theoretical construction of the settlement-trial process. The two models developed above, the mutual optimism and asymmetric information models, offer the bases for different predictions about the nature of this bias.[109]

Recall that under the mutual optimism model, a critical feature that explains why cases go to trial is the divergent expectations of the plaintiff and defendant respecting the likely trial outcome. Professors George Priest and Benjamin Klein argue that parties are likely to experience an increasingly large divergence in expectations the closer the case facts are to supporting victory for either party under the prevailing legal standard, meaning when each side has an approximately equal chance of winning.[110] This theory has given rise to the so-called "50% rule," meaning the prediction that cases reaching trial should result in a roughly 50% win rate for plaintiffs.

The asymmetric information model generates different predictions about which cases end up going to trial. In one of the preceding illustrations,[111] we assumed that the plaintiff possessed private information about the relative strength of her case, and that in the separating equilibrium, those plaintiffs with weak cases accepted the defendant's settlement offer, whereas those plaintiffs with strong cases opted for trial. That model thus predicts that cases reaching trial should have a high probability of plaintiff victory. Suppose, however, that the asymmetry is reversed and that the defendant has private information about the strength of its case, for example, knowledge as to whether

---

[108] Within the federal system, not all, or even most, appellate court decisions are published. WILLIAM M. RICHMAN & WILLIAM L. REYNOLDS, INJUSTICE ON APPEAL: THE UNITED STATES COURTS OF APPEALS IN CRISIS (2013).

[109] DOUGLAS G. BAIRD, ROBERT H. GERTNER & RANDAL C. PICKER, GAME THEORY AND THE LAW 260–61 (1994).

[110] George Priest & Benjamin Klein, *The Selection of Disputes for Litigation*, 13 J. LEGAL STUD. 1 (1984).

[111] *See supra* at 383.

disclosures at trial might reveal its employees to have been negligent. In that situation, defendants with weak cases will settle and those defendants with strong cases will go to trial, which implies that cases reaching trial should have a low probability of plaintiff victory. This shows that the kind of cases that reach trial might vary depending on the information structure. In combination, this reveals that *any* probability of plaintiff victory at trial is possible.[112]

Although there is no clear prediction regarding the plaintiff win rate for cases that reach trial, both the mutual optimism and asymmetric information models predict that cases with higher stakes (i.e., larger plaintiff damages) are more likely to be tried rather than settled. This turns out to be crucial for answering the question posed in the next section.

b. Does the Common Law Evolve Toward Efficiency?

The first "wave" of law and economics scholarship was motivated to explain common law rules in terms that transcended the doctrinal accounts expressed in published judicial opinions. As the preceding chapters demonstrate, law and economics scholars employed neoclassical microeconomic theory to identify linkages between bodies of case law and incentives to move resources to their most highly valued uses, whether the relevant body of doctrine involved contract, tort, or property.

We now turn to the institutional mechanisms, or decision-making processes, that affect the development of efficient—and sometimes inefficient—common law rules. Using the principles of economic reasoning, we evaluate whether it is possible to identify conditions that are likely to render common law courts more or less prone to producing efficient case results, even if not captured in formally articulated doctrines, and that prove consistent with an efficient understanding of governing rules. We also identify what such conditions are likely to be and how they might have changed over time. Our analysis begins with the perspective of judges as "suppliers" of efficient law, then shifts to the demand by litigants, and then returns, once more, to the supply side.

i. Why Do Judges Supply Efficient Common Law?

Professor Richard Posner has posited that judges are likely to prefer supplying efficient rules because such rules are social welfare enhancing.[113] Posner states: "[T]he economic norm I call 'wealth maximization' provides a firmer basis for a normative theory of [judge-made] law than does utilitarianism."[114] Professor Todd Zywicki has suggested four problems with this assumption:[115] first, judicial preferences are not susceptible to empirical verification; second, many judges appear as concerned with redistributive as with efficiency objectives; third, normative goals respecting efficiency might change in different historical periods; and finally, it is not obvious that even judges holding a strong

[112] *See* Keith Hylton, *Asymmetric Information and the Selection of Disputes for Litigation*, 22 J. LEGAL STUD. 187 (1993); Steven Shavell, *Any Frequency of Plaintiff Victory is Possible*, 25 J. LEGAL STUD. 495 (1996).

[113] Richard A. Posner, *Utilitarianism, Economics, and Legal Theory*, 8 J. LEGAL STUD. 103 (1979).

[114] *Id.* at 103.

[115] Portions of this discussion are adapted from Todd J. Zywicki, *Rise and Fall of Efficiency in the Common Law: A Supply-Side Analysis*, 97 NW. U. L. REV. 1551, 1563 (2003).

preference for efficiency as a legal norm have the expertise or empirical evidence needed to meaningfully effectuate that goal.[116]

Whatever the merits of these respective positions, the question remains whether the efficiency of the common law depends on individual judicial predilections. In a series of influential articles, two scholars claimed that common law efficiency does not depend upon judicial preferences, but rather that it depends upon the dynamics of litigant behavior.

ii. A Demand Side Analysis of Common Law Efficiency[117]

Paul Rubin, a Professor of Economics, sought to untangle the common law efficiency question in a manner that avoided the assertion that the common law is efficient because judges have a taste for efficiency.[118] Rubin proposed a demand-side explanation of common law efficiency where the tendency toward the efficient common law doctrine arises from an "invisible hand" process of private litigation, and thus does not rely on the preferences of individual jurists.

Rubin claimed that common law efficiency is a function of the balance of interests on both sides of the case. One way to conceptualize the value of a precedent to a litigant takes the form of a stream of rents that result from future favorable settlements or more predictably favorable judicial rulings. Favorable precedents are of the greatest value to those who anticipate being repeat players. For instance, in tort cases, firms are disproportionately likely to be defendants and thus to favor pro-defendant rules, whereas plaintiffs' lawyers are likely to prefer liability-expanding rules.[119] In other cases, for example, one involving a car accident between two private parties, neither of the parties ordinarily expects to be a repeat player, and thus each litigant is principally concerned with the immediate case outcome. In still other cases, anticipated repeat players appear on one side of the case but not the other.

Rubin argues that at least to some extent the outcome in a case will reflect the resources that parties invest in the case. Repeat players will generally be more willing to invest more in creating a beneficial precedent than non-repeat players. Rubin envisions three paradigmatic cases. In the first, both parties are interested in the precedent and are

---

116 *Id.* (footnote omitted).

117 Portions of this discussion are based upon MAXWELL L. STEARNS, PUBLIC CHOICE AND PUBLIC LAW: READINGS AND COMMENTARY 779–84 (Anderson 1997), and MAXWELL L. STEARNS & TODD J. ZYWICKI, PUBLIC CHOICE CONCEPTS AND APPLICATIONS IN LAW 466–71 (2009).

118 Paul H. Rubin, *Why Is the Common Law Efficient?*, 6 J. LEGAL STUD. 51, 53 (1977) [hereinafter *Why is the Common Law Efficient?*]. For other works on this issue, see Martin J. Bailey & Paul H. Rubin, *A Positive Theory of Legal Change*, 14 INT'L REV. L. & ECON. 467, 476 (1994); Paul H. Rubin, *Common Law and Statute Law*, 11 J. LEGAL STUD. 205 (1982); Paul H. Rubin et al., *Litigation Versus Legislation: Forum Shopping by Rent Seekers*, 107 PUB. CHOICE 295 (2001); Paul H. Rubin & Martin J. Bailey, *The Role of Lawyers in Changing the Law*, 23 J. LEGAL STUD. 807 (1994). *See also* GORDON TULLOCK, TRIALS ON TRIAL: THE PURE THEORY OF LEGAL PROCEDURE 197–206 (1980).

119 *See* Todd J. Zywicki & Jeremy Kidd, Meaningful Tort Reform (2010), http://papers.ssrn.com/sol3/papers.cfm?abstract_id=2273943; Todd J. Zywicki, *Public Choice and Tort Reform* (Geo. Mason Law & Econ. Research Paper No. 00–36, 2000), https://www.law.gmu.edu/assets/files/publications/working_papers/00-36.pdf (exploring whether defense lawyers are likely to have symmetrical or asymmetrical incentives as compared with plaintiffs' lawyers in seeking liability-reducing rules).

thus willing to invest accordingly, with a resulting tendency toward efficiency. Rubin explains:

> If rules are inefficient, there will be an incentive for the party held liable to force litigation; if rules are efficient, there will be no such incentive. Thus, efficient rules will be maintained, and inefficient rules litigated until overturned.[120]

In the second, only one party has an interest in the precedent (as distinguished from the judgment). Rubin argues:

> [T]here will be pressure for precedents to evolve in favor of that party which does have a stake in future cases, whether or not this is the efficient solution. This is because a party with a stake in future decision[s] will find it worthwhile to litigate as long as liability rests with him; conversely, a party with no stake in future decisions will not find litigation worthwhile.[121]

Finally, in the third, neither party has an interest in the precedent. Rubin suggests that the result is a tendency toward random drift in the law, meaning that the current rule generally will persist, regardless of its efficiency or inefficiency.

Rubin maintains that in the formative period of the common law, the conditions for the evolution of efficient precedent prevailed. During the nineteenth century (and presumably before) both common law and statutory rulemaking were dominated by individual interests acting independently, rather than by organized interests acting collectively. As a result, the parties to the dispute generally had equal stakes in case outcomes. Moreover, legal relations were likely to have been more reciprocal in nature because prior to large-scale industrialization, legal interactions were largely between private individuals who were unlikely to systematically be either plaintiffs or defendants. Under conditions of reciprocity, there was a tendency to support efficient (and fair) rules rather than those that systematically favored one side. Rubin argues that over time this symmetry broke down and that several identifiable areas of law came to be dominated by repeat players who invested in securing law that favored their interests. He claims that this characterized law for manufacturers in the nineteenth century and, in recent decades, certain bodies of tort law that are driven by plaintiffs' tort lawyers who have been able to litigate strategically to promote preferred tort doctrine.[122] As a result, Rubin claims, the common law has tended to deviate from its traditional orientation toward efficiency in those doctrinal areas.[123]

Professor George Priest responded to Rubin's analysis with a model that rests neither on judicial predilection nor on precedent capture as the dominant force moving the common law toward efficiency.[124] Priest suggests an ingenious mechanism that rests instead entirely on the incentives respecting the individual case ultimately presented for review in a common law court. Priest posits that inefficient common law rules provide

---

[120] *See* Rubin, *Why is the Common Law Efficient?, supra* note 118, at 53.

[121] *Id.* at 55.

[122] Rubin & Bailey, *supra* note 118, at 814–17.

[123] Paul H. Rubin, *Public Choice and Tort Reform*, 124 PUB. CHOICE 223 (2005).

[124] *See* George L. Priest, *The Common Law Process and the Selection of Efficient Rules*, 6 J. LEGAL STUD. 65 (1977).

the potential for greater gains from displacement than do efficient common law rules. This difference in potential gains arises because efficient rules are already social welfare maximizing, whereas inefficient rules are social welfare reducing. (At best, displacing an efficient rule with an inefficient rule produces distributional consequences, and at worst it also produces a social welfare loss.) As a result, potential litigants themselves will generally perceive greater opportunities for gain from the litigation process when they are disadvantaged by an inefficient, rather than by an efficient, common law rule. Further, Priest argues that inefficient rules will tend to be characterized by higher stakes:

> For the set of all legal disputes, the stakes will be greater for disputes arising under inefficient rules than under efficient rules. Inefficient assignments of liability by definition impose greater costs on the parties subject to them than efficient assignments. . . . It follows, therefore, that other factors held equal, litigation will be more likely for disputes arising under inefficient rules than for those arising under efficient rules.[125]

This argument connects the Priest mechanism to the litigation models above, which, recall, predicted that higher stakes will result in a greater likelihood of trial.

In this analysis, even if the judges themselves were indifferent to the efficiency of the common law, the aggregation of potential litigants would have a stronger incentive to litigate more cases challenging inefficient than efficient common law rules. Thus in a regime in which each judge simply flipped a coin to resolve each case, the law of large numbers would gradually, but inexorably, move the common law in the overall direction of efficiency.

Priest explains that even if an individual judge or small group of judges holds a preference for announcing inefficient common law rules, the ability to move common law doctrine in their preferred direction will succeed only if relatively few jurists hold such a view.[126] If a high percentage of jurists issue decisions in contravention of efficiency considerations, under Priest's model, this creates many opportunities for gains through the litigation process to bring cases that seek to supplant inefficient with efficient common law rules. The process then moves the common law back in the direction of efficiency. Only if relatively few jurists move the common law away from efficiency such that the aberrational results are not quickly identified as such, does the then-smaller subset of inefficient common law rules have a substantial likelihood of persisting.

In later works, Priest has offered arguments suggesting a movement away from common law efficiency, for example, in such areas as tort doctrine.[127] Priest attributes this transformation to an intellectual revolution among judges who have come to adopt

---

[125] *Id.* at 67.

[126] We can express Priest's seeming counterintuition as an illustration of the fallacy of composition. *See infra* Chapter 13 (explaining that for some individual phenomena the occurrence of which generates a predicted result, multiplying the incidence of the phenomenon can inhibit rather than enhance the result.)

[127] *See* George L. Priest, *Products Liability Law and the Accident Rate*, *in* LIABILITY: PERSPECTIVES AND POLICIES 184 (Robert E. Litan & Clifford Winston eds., 1988); George L. Priest, *The Modern Expansion of Tort Liability: Its Sources, Its Effects, and Its Reform*, J. ECON. PERSP., Summer 1991, at 31.

modern redistributive goals for tort law and who have imposed those ideological views on the law.[128]

iii. Supply Side Redux: Judicial Competition and Common Law Efficiency

Professor Todd Zywicki has supplemented the models developed by Rubin and Priest with a supply-side analysis that explains what he characterizes as the rise and fall of efficiency in the common law.[129] Zywicki observes that during the formative centuries of the English common law system, England had a competitive or "polycentric" legal order. Unlike current legal systems, during the Middle Ages, multiple courts with overlapping jurisdictions existed side-by-side throughout England. These courts included ecclesiastical (church) courts, law merchant courts, local courts, the Chancery court, three different common law courts, the King's Bench, the Court of Common Pleas, and the Exchequer Courts. For most legal matters a litigant could bring a case in several different courts. For instance, church courts had jurisdiction over all matters related to testamentary succession, but if the deceased owed a debt at the time of death this suggested the possibility of jurisdiction in other courts as well.

Judges were paid in part from the litigant filing fees, thus providing competitive incentives respecting the scope of jurisdiction and the expansion of judicial dockets.[130] As Adam Smith, writing in the eighteenth century, observed:

> The present admirable constitution of the courts of justice in England was, perhaps, originally in a great measure, formed by this emulation, which anciently took place between their respective judges; each judge endeavouring to give, in his own court, the speediest and most effectual remedy, which the law would admit, for every sort of injustice.[131]

Smith also noted that requiring judges to compete for fees motivated them to work harder and more efficiently, thereby removing incentives to shirk or to indulge in personal preferences.[132] Zywicki claims that judicial competition motivated litigants to engage in beneficial forum-shopping, thereby helping to drive the early common law toward efficiency. He further claims that in the United States, a similar, albeit somewhat attenuated system, arose under the regime of *Swift v. Tyson*,[133] which permitted the

---

[128] *See* George L. Priest, *Puzzles of the Tort Crisis*, 48 OHIO ST. L.J. 497 (1987); George L. Priest, *The Current Insurance Crisis and Modern Tort Law*, 96 YALE L.J. 1521 (1987); George L. Priest, *The Invention of Enterprise Liability: A Critical History of the Intellectual Foundations of Modern Tort Law*, 14 J. LEGAL STUD. 461 (1985).

[129] *See* Zywicki, *supra* note 115, at 1581–1621.

[130] 1 WILLIAM HOLDSWORTH, A HISTORY OF ENGLISH LAW 252–55 (A.L. Goodhart & H.G. Hanbury eds., 7th ed. rev. 1956); 2 ADAM SMITH, AN INQUIRY INTO THE NATURE AND CAUSES OF THE WEALTH OF NATIONS 241 (Edwin Cannan ed., Univ. of Chicago Press 1967) (5th ed. 1789).

[131] SMITH, *supra* note 130, at 241–42.

[132] *Id.* at 241 ("Public services are never better performed than when their reward comes only in consequence of their being performed, and is proportioned to the diligence employed in performing them.").

[133] 41 U.S. 1 (1842).

development of competing systems of law as between state and federal courts, a regime that was superseded by the *Erie* doctrine.[134]

Professor Daniel Klerman has challenged some of Professor Zywicki's conclusions. Klerman argues that because early common law courts allowed plaintiffs to select the forum, interjurisdictional competition spurred the development of pro-plaintiff rules. Klerman rests this conclusion on the fact that in early common law courts, judicial compensation was based upon fees, thus furthering a pro-plaintiff bias. Klerman acknowledges that to some extent this bias was constrained by Chancery courts, to which disputes could be removed.[135] Klerman further observes that this pro-plaintiff bias began to change as a result of statutes enacted in 1799 and 1825 that shifted judges to a salary-based compensation system, stripping them of their right to collect fees from litigants. Klerman claims that this reform led to the adoption of a variety pro-defendant rules instead.

Consider the implications of Zywicki's analysis of law merchant courts for Klerman's assessment of common law courts. Zywicki claims that competing jurisdiction among courts produced a more efficient set of common law rules. Is it possible to identify mechanisms that would push courts of overlapping jurisdiction in the direction of a distributional, or pro-plaintiff bias, on the one hand, or toward efficiency, on the other?

Consider the following argument. If plaintiffs have complete control over where to file suits, the resulting competition might motivate pro-plaintiff rules as this would increase the size of dockets along with corresponding fees. Alternatively, if more efficient common law rules create social welfare gains that can be shared as between plaintiffs and those with whom they contract or otherwise engage during the course of repeat business, then plaintiffs might instead be motivated to bargain for the selection of more efficient courts *ex ante* and to share in any resulting gains. Which of these accounts seems more plausible and why?

Consider also the following observation by legal historian Thomas Scrutton:

> If you read the [common] law reports of the seventeenth century you will be struck with one very remarkable fact; either Englishmen of that day did not engage in commerce, or they appear not to have been litigious people in commercial matters, each of which alternatives appears improbable.[136]

Scrutton claims that most commercial disputes were heard outside the common law courts, and instead in law merchant courts. Does this help to answer the preceding question? Why or why not?

Zywicki has shown that Lord Mansfield's incorporation of law merchant principles and practices into the common law during the mid-nineteenth century established many

---

[134] Erie R.R. v. Tompkins, 304 U.S. 64 (1938).

[135] Daniel Klerman, *Jurisdictional Competition and the Evolution of the Common Law*, 74 U. CHI. L. REV. 1179 (2007).

[136] Thomas Edward Scrutton, *General Survey of the History of the Law Merchant*, 3 SELECT ESSAYS IN ANGLO-AMERICAN LEGAL HISTORY 7, 7 (Ass'n of American Law Schools ed., 1909). In some situations these were the "Staple Courts" which decided disputes that arose among traders on markets for various staple goods, such as wool and cotton. *See* Bernard Edward Spencer Brodhurst, *The Merchants of the Staple*, *in* 3 SELECT ESSAYS, *supra*, at 16–17; *see also* A.T. CARTER, A HISTORY OF ENGLISH LEGAL INSTITUTIONS 241–71 (1902).

of the efficiency-enhancing rules for which he claims the common law became known. Zywicki further explains that the polycentric legal order in which the common law emerged as a result of judicial competition, spurred in part by the judges' own financial incentives, produced an additional beneficial effect. Specifically, it allowed dissatisfied parties to opt out of disadvantageous legal regimes and into preferable ones. For instance, merchants rarely resorted to common law courts, opting instead for law merchant courts, thus limiting the reach of sometimes archaic common law rules in commercial transactions.[137] Zywicki explains that the possibility of judicial exit through forum shopping removed a critical element in the power of courts to promote rent seeking litigation.[138] He further maintains that this regime reduced incentives to invest in procuring inefficient precedents. Zywicki argues that this historical analysis bolsters Rubin's intuition that during its early formative period, the common law tended toward efficiency.

Zywicki attributes the subsequent tendency toward inefficient common law rules to the demise of competing courts in the United States and England. He further claims that the reduced ability of litigants to choose their court or to exit inefficient courts raised the agency costs associated with judicial decision making. Zywicki contends that his thesis is also consistent with Priest's claim that there has arisen a fundamental philosophical transformation of the judiciary. Under a system without competing courts, Zywicki claims, judges have a much greater ability to infuse ideology into their opinions.

Do you find Zywicki's alternative supply-side account of common law efficiency persuasive? Is it consistent with the insights of Rubin and Priest? While Zywicki focuses on the *Erie* doctrine's effect on limiting federal-state judicial competition, what about the role of state-state competition? How does this affect the efficiency of common law in the United States? Is the elimination of federal-state competition more or less important than state-state competition in facilitating efficient common law? Why? Legal commentators have long observed that early federal diversity jurisdiction was at least in part a social welfare program benefiting business going to more distant locations that reduced the risks associated with being subject to unpredictable or even hostile state laws.[139] Does this insight support arguments for preferring to avoid state-state or federal-state competition? Why? How might Klerman respond to the preceding analysis? Which model do you find more persuasive? Why?

---

[137] *See* CARTER, *supra* note 136, at 261.

[138] The analysis here anticipates some of the arguments that will be made in Chapter 23 or 24 regarding of federalism and jurisdictional competition.

[139] For relevant discussions, see William Howard Taft, *Possible and Needed Reforms in the Administration of Justice in the Federal Courts*, 45 ANN. REP. A.B.A. 250, 259 (1922) (observing that "[n]o single element in our governmental system has done so much to secure capital for the legitimate development of enterprises throughout the West and South as the existence of federal courts there, with a jurisdiction to hear diverse citizenship cases."); William L. Marbury, *Why Should We Limit Federal Diversity Jurisdiction?*, 46 A.B.A. J. 379, 380 (1960) (noting the "value to our present-day economy in a system which guarantees to the citizen who moves beyond the borders of his own community the protecting mantle of the federal judiciary. . . . [E]nterprise is definitely encouraged by the fact that the federal courts are available under such circumstances."); Robert J. Pushaw, Jr., *Article III's Case/Controversy and the Dual Functions of Federal Courts*, 69 NOTRE DAME L. REV. 447, 507 (1994) (citing numerous Framers and Ratifiers, as well as secondary sources, in support of this historical account).

II. CRIMINAL PROCEDURE

We now turn our attention to the criminal judicial process. Criminal procedure encompasses the set of rules applied to criminal defendants from the time of arrest, through trial, and following a conviction, through sentencing. The economic analysis of criminal procedure bears substantial similarities to that civil procedure, and so we focus here on a subset of features that are unique to the criminal process. Part of the discussion will necessarily implicate substantive criminal law in addition to the procedural rules. This includes the next subpart, which considers whether to evaluate criminal law as a regulatory system or as a market for the price of crime.

We begin by noting that, despite its similarities to civil procedure, criminal procedure includes numerous pro-defendant procedural protections that are not available for civil defendants. The most commonly advanced reason for this difference, as noted in our discussion of the divergent standards of proof for conviction in the two arenas, is the presumed high cost of false convictions for criminal defendants, owing to the risk of imprisonment and the social stigma associated with criminal conviction. A complementary argument is that the pro-defendant bias is needed to restrain the discretion of various agents in the criminal justice system. One concern is that the maximand of prosecutors and of judges, especially those who are elected, and thus who are politically accountable, might include conviction records, which could be in tension with a more neutral dispensation of justice.[140] There is an accompanying risk: beyond the potential unfairness to those charged with criminal offenses, the resulting incentives might undermine the accuracy of signaling the social cost of unlawful acts.

A. Is Criminal Law a Regulatory System or a Market?

In an influential article, then-Professor Frank Easterbrook argued that the structure of criminal law can be usefully interpreted as a market system aimed at placing an efficient "price" of crime.[141] The analysis flows from the economic analysis of crime developed in Chapter 9. In that framing, criminal penalties establishing prices for certain socially harmful activities help deter would-be offenders. Easterbrook focuses on prosecutorial charging discretion and judicial sentencing discretion, features that permit actors to make decentralized decisions based on case-specific information. The resulting pricing system tailors sentences to crimes, which he claims improves efficient deterrence. Easterbrook further maintains that curtailing discretion, for example through mandatory sentences, will impede the efficiency of this market function.

Professor Stephen Schulhofer has criticized this analysis, claiming that unfair sentences often emerge as a by-product of unlimited prosecutorial and judicial discretion.[142] He specifically points to the "unwanted disparities in the treatment of similarly situated offenders" that characterizes such a system.[143] He further argues that

---

[140] *See* Keith Hylton & Vikramaditya Khanna, *A Public Choice Theory of Criminal Procedure*, 15 SUP. CT. ECON. REV. 61 (2007). *See also* David Friedman, *Why not Hang Them All? The Virtues of Inefficient Punishment*, 107 J. POL. ECON. S259 (1999).

[141] Frank Easterbrook, *Criminal Procedure as a Market System*, 12 J. LEGAL STUD. 289 (1983).

[142] Stephen J. Schulhofer, *Criminal Justice Discretion as a Regulatory System*, 17 J. LEGAL STUD. 43 (1988).

[143] *Id.* at 80.

discretion undermines deterrence because it clouds the signal to would-be offenders regarding the consequences of their actions. In effect, Schulhofer argues that if this is a market, excessive discretion leads to its own "market failure" in pricing crime. More fundamentally, Schulhofer argues that using the market analogy to describe the system of criminal justice is flawed. Instead, Schulhofer views criminal justice as a regulatory system subject to top-down control by policy makers.

Professor Richard Adelstein offers a compromise view that emphasizes the price-setting function of criminal law, but that also posits that this body of law is subject to a fundamental "market failure" because of informational problems.[144] In Adelstein's view, the criminal justice system is best characterized as an evolutionary process involving an interplay between legislatures, which send broad signals about criminal penalties with the goal of optimizing deterrence, and courts, which seek to individualize punishments to crimes based on case-specific facts. Imperfect detection and concerns about justice in individual cases create an inherent tension between these institutions' *ex ante* and *ex post* perspectives, with the overall system seeking to balance those conflicts. We revisit this tension in our discussion of sentencing guidelines below.

B. Plea Bargaining

Plea bargaining, the criminal analog to pretrial settlement, is likely among the most important aspects of criminal procedure. As in civil cases, the vast majority of criminal cases (often over ninety percent) are resolved by plea bargains rather than by trial. Unlike civil settlements, however, the practice of plea bargaining is often viewed with skepticism. Among the concerns is the risk that innocent defendants will be induced by the promise of a lesser charge to plead guilty. At the same time, the problem of caseloads has placed considerable stress on plea bargaining as a way conserve on scarce judicial resources. Supreme Court case law on plea bargaining has emphasized this trade-off.

In *Santobello v. New York*,[145] the Court recognized the necessity of plea bargaining as a way of conserving on resources:

> Properly administered, [plea bargaining] is to be encouraged. If every criminal charge were subjected to a full-scale trial, the States and Federal government would need to multiply many times the number of judges and court facilities.[146]

The Court admonished, however, that this concession to reality must not overshadow the primary function of the criminal justice system, namely, to punish the guilty and to avoid punishing the innocent. In the landmark case of *Brady v. United States,* the Court expressed the concern that "offers of leniency [might] substantially increase the likelihood that defendants, advised by competent counsel, would falsely condemn themselves."[147] These concerns are exacerbated by plea bargaining, which results in a waiver of otherwise available constitutional protections.

---

[144] Richard Adelstein, *Institutional Function and Evolution in the Criminal Process*, 76 NW. U. L. REV. 1 (1981).

[145] 404 U.S. 257 (1971).

[146] *Id.* at 260.

[147] 397 U.S. 742, 758 (1970).

1. *Economic Models of Plea Bargaining*

The standard economic approach to plea bargaining emphasizes the same factor that tended to promote the settlement of civil cases—namely, the mutual benefit to plaintiffs and defendants of avoiding the costs of trial. An important difference, however, is that the state, in the person of the prosecutor, takes on the role of the "plaintiff," and even from an ex ante perspective, the criminal defendant does not have the option of another party with whom to deal. In effect, the state is the monopolistic seller of "deals" to the criminal defendant, and except in those cases in which the defendant holds information of substantial value to the state, the state is likely to extract most or all of the negotiated surplus because of its advantage in resources. Notably, the victim of the crime is not a party to the case. In theory, the prosecutor represents the interests of the entire community rather than the individual victim, and therefore should pursue whatever societal concerns are embedded in the delegated range of prosecutorial discretion, for example, which claims to pursue and how aggressively to pursue them. In reality, of course, these goals are apt to be heavily influenced and perhaps dominated by budgetary considerations, the personal ambitions of the prosecutor, such as the desire for re-election or other political office, or any number of other political considerations.

Professor William Landes initially modeled plea bargaining based on the assumption that the prosecutor seeks to maximize the expected punishment of offenders, subject to a budget constraint.[148] Although this objective reflects the social goal of achieving maximal deterrence, recall that the economic model of crime assumes the separate goal of cost-effective deterrence, which accounts for enforcement costs. The defendant seeks to minimize the combined cost of expected punishment plus legal representation. Given this formulation, the process of negotiating over a pretrial settlement is analytically parallel to that employed when discussing civil cases. Specifically, the negotiation consists of the prosecutor offering a reduced sentence in exchange for the defendant's guilty plea, thereby saving the state and the defendant the cost of a trial. Trials can nevertheless arise if the parties are either mutually optimistic about the outcome of a trial, or if one party holds private information about the strength of the case.

The model assumes away an important complication that distinguishes plea bargaining from civil settlement negotiations. The prosecutor has a constitutional obligation under *Brady v. Maryland* to disclose exculpatory evidence,[149] whereas the criminal defendant does not have a reciprocal duty to disclose testimonial evidence to the prosecutor.[150] As a result, at least in theory, the process of discovery in criminal law favors the defendant.

Professor Gene Grossman and Michael Katz have developed an alternative model that emphasizes the role of plea bargaining in sorting innocent and guilty defendants.[151] Assume that innocent defendants have a probability of conviction at trial equal to P_i, and that guilty defendants have a probability of conviction equal to P_g. Further assume that

[148] William M. Landes, *An Economic Analysis of the Courts*, 14 J.L. & ECON. 61 (1971).

[149] Brady v. Maryland, 373 U.S. 83 (1963).

[150] For a discussion of testimonial versus nontestimonial evidence in criminal discovery, see *infra* note 149, and cites therein.

[151] Gene Grossman & Michael Katz, *Plea Bargaining and Social Welfare*, 73 AM. ECON. REV. 749 (1983).

$P_g > P_i$, reflecting greater evidence against guilty defendants. The dollar value of the sanction on conviction is S, and defendant's trial costs are C. The overall expected cost of going to trial is therefore higher for the guilty defendant than for the innocent defendant as reflected in this inequality:

$$P_gS+C > P_iS+C.$$

Now consider the possible strategies of a prosecutor who cannot distinguish between the two types of defendants. She has three possible strategies: (1) refuse to offer a plea bargain, and go to trial with both types; (2) make a plea offer of S_p that will be accepted by guilty defendants and rejected by innocent defendants, meaning that the cost of S_p to guilty defendants is lower than that a trial, whereas the cost of S_p to innocents is higher than that of a trial, or expressed algebraically, $P_gS+C > S_p > P_iS+C$; and (3) make a plea offer that both types will accept, meaning $P_gS+C > P_iS+C > S_p$.

The prosecutor's optimal choice will depend on her objective. If we suppose that she primarily cares about saving trial costs, but that she also wants to balance that against the cost of inducing guilty pleas by innocent defendants, her choice will be between options (2) and (3). Option (2), the "separating strategy," involves some trial costs but reduces (or in this simple example, eliminates) the likelihood of guilty pleas by innocent defendants, whereas option (3), the pooling strategy, aims to avoid all trial costs but with the problematic feature of inducing innocent defendants to also plead guilty.

Notice a disturbing implication of the separating strategy. It avoids wrongful guilty pleas by encouraging all innocent defendants go to trial, but because all guilty defendants plead guilty, the end result is that any convictions following trial are wrongful! This result follows from the assumption that $P_g > P_i$, meaning that all guilty defendants have a higher probability of conviction at trial than do all innocent defendants. More realistically, of course, the situation will resemble that in Figure 10:2, where the defendant's probability of conviction is a random variable that can take any value for either type of defendant within individual cases, but higher values will be more likely for guilty defendants because, on average, there will be more evidence against them. In that scenario, there can be no perfect separating equilibrium outcome. As a result, plea bargaining will not necessarily prove better than trials in sorting innocent and guilty defendants.

Finally, Professor Jennifer Reinganum has developed a model based on asymmetric information in which defendants hold private information about the strengths of their cases.[152] Recall that this is legally plausible because although the prosecution is constitutionally obligated to disclose exculpatory evidence to the defense, the defense is not obligated to disclose evidence of guilt to the prosecutor, at least through testimony.[153] The results are analogous to the asymmetric information model in the context of civil cases. Specifically, we would expect defendants with weak cases (i.e., high probabilities of conviction at trial) to accept plea bargains and defendants with strong cases (i.e., low probabilities of conviction) to opt for trial. This outcome involves an imperfect sorting of innocent and guilty defendants, with most guilty pleas being made by truly guilty

---

[152] Jennifer Reinganum, *Plea Bargaining and Prosecutorial Discretion*, 78 AM. ECON. REV. 713 (1988).

[153] This follows from the combination of the *Brady* rule and the Fifth Amendment privilege against self-incrimination. LAFAVE ET AL., *supra* note 99, §§ 20.3, 20.5. The state can, however, compel non-testimonial evidence, for example, finger prints, saliva, or blood samples. Schmerber v. California, 384 U.S. 757 (1966).

defendants (because they have higher probabilities of conviction on average), and most trials involving truly innocent defendants (because they have lower probabilities of conviction on average).

2. *The Impact of Plea Bargaining on Deterrence*

Because of the prominence of plea bargaining in the criminal justice system, it is important to consider the potential impact of the practice on deterrence. The economic theory of crime discussed in Chapter 9 envisioned a single enforcement authority with the power to pursue the goal of optimal deterrence. Specifically, the enforcer could specify a penalty structure (i.e., a probability of apprehension and a sanction level) and could credibly commit to carrying it out. Plea bargaining potentially interferes with that objective by creating an additional stage of sentencing discretion during which objectives other than deterrence, for example reducing the risk of error avoidance, ensuring sentencing proportionality, or furthering the prosecutor's personal political ends, potentially predominate.

As we argued in Chapter 9, some commentators claim that prosecutors resist imposing what they perceive to be overly harsh sentences by exercising discretion either to drop cases or to reduce the charge in cases that they elect to pursue.[154] If so, plea bargaining acts as a potential impediment to the imposition of high-penalty, low-probability enforcement schemes that a simplistic reading of the economic model of crime might suggest. Plea bargaining also potentially reduces the ability of future offenders to predict the punishments that they will face. These factors help to explain why plea bargaining reduces the deterrent function of criminal law.

3. *A Comparative View*

Unlike in the United States, within the inquisitorial systems of continental Europe, plea bargaining is at least theoretically prohibited.[155] Professor John Langbein has suggested that to accommodate the caseload problem, civil law systems instead simplify the trial process and weaken the procedural protections of defendants compared to trials in the United States.[156] This raises an interesting comparative law question regarding the desirability of prosecutorial discretion: under what conditions will a regime of compulsory prosecution better promote the goals of the criminal justice system than a regime with broad plea bargaining?[157]

The answer depends on the criminal justice system's underlying values. Consider, for example, aversion to wrongful punishments, which we have argued is a particular concern of the criminal justice system in the United States. Some convictions of innocent defendants are inevitable (as depicted in Figure 10:2), but plea bargaining actually *lowers* the cost of false convictions by encouraging some innocent defendants against whom

---

[154] *See supra* Chapter 9, note 65.

[155] Richard Adelstein, *Plea Bargaining: A Comparative Approach*, *in* THE NEW PALGRAVE DICTIONARY OF ECONOMICS AND THE LAW (Peter Newman ed., 1998).

[156] John Langbein, *Land Without Plea Bargaining: How the Germans Do It*, 78 MICH. L. REV. 204 (1979).

[157] The discussion is based on Richard Adelstein & Thomas Miceli, *Toward a Comparative Economics of Plea Bargaining*, 11 EUR. J.L. & ECON. 47 (2001).

there is nonetheless probative evidence to plead guilty to a lesser charge rather than having to face the prospect of a harsher punishment on conviction for a more serious charge at trial. Although the Supreme Court has expressed concern that plea bargaining can result in wrongful guilty pleas, Judge Frank Easterbrook has expressed a somewhat different view:[158] Easterbrook posits that there is

> no reason to prevent [an innocent] defendant from striking a deal that seems advantageous. If there is injustice here, the source is not the plea bargain. It is, rather, that innocent people may be found guilty at trial.[159]

This follows from the simple observation that the alternative to a guilty plea is the trial itself. Although plea bargains result in certain punishment, for some defendants the option to plead guilty and avoid a risky trial may reduce the potentially higher cost of wrongful conviction.

Alternatively, if society places a higher value on avoiding wrongful acquittals, compulsory prosecution may be a better system because it gives truly guilty defendants less ability to escape conviction for more serious criminal charges and punishment through a plea. Consistent with this perspective, continental legal systems typically do not afford criminal defendants the privilege against self-incrimination. Although it is not permissible to draw adverse inferences from the defendant's failure to testify in the U.S. system, as we will show below, the existence of the privilege nonetheless helps make innocent defendants' denial of guilt more credible. Based on these observations, Professors Richard Adelstein and Thomas Miceli maintain "that plea bargaining is more likely to evolve in systems that emphasize the protection of innocent defendants, and systems that stress punishing the guilty are more likely to be able to sustain a regime of compulsory prosecution."[160]

C. The Bail System

An important difference between the civil and criminal justice systems is that criminal defendants often face the possibility of detention during the pretrial period based on the concern that they may flee the jurisdiction and evade prosecution. Offsetting this is the presumption of innocence and the fact that imprisonment substantially impedes a defendant's ability to assist in preparing his defense. The bail system provides a partial solution designed to accommodate these competing factors. Bail allows defendants who are deemed to be a flight risk to post a monetary bond that they would forfeit if they fail to show up for trial.[161]

Setting the optimal bail is similar to setting the optimal criminal fine in the sense that both are intended to deter a prohibited act. The main difference is that the bail amount must be posted by the defendant up-front (i.e., before fleeing), so there is no need for probability scaling—if a defendant jumps bail, he forfeits the bail with certainty. Like the optimal fine, the optimal bail amount will vary by individual because defendants pose

---

[158] Easterbrook, *supra* note 141, at 320.

[159] *Id.*

[160] Adelstein & Miceli, *supra* note 157, at 60.

[161] William M. Landes, *The Bail System: An Economic Approach*, 2 J. LEGAL STUD. 79 (1973).

different risks of flight and of committing further crimes. The ability of defendants to afford bail is also an issue, but this problem is partially offset by the existence of bail bondsmen, who post the bail in return for a fee. And although a defendant is more likely to flee when someone else posts the money (a type of moral hazard problem), bail bondsmen will have an incentive to protect their investment by monitoring defendants, as well as by charging a premium to reflect the flight risk.

A common criticism of the bail system is that minority defendants are charged higher bail, holding constant the risk of flight. Professors Ian Ayres and Joel Waldfogel used bail bond fees to test this proposition based on the intuition that market-determined fees should reflect a defendant's true flight risk.[162] Their findings did, in fact, show that "judges in setting bail demanded lower probabilities of flight from minority defendants," holding all other factors constant.[163]

D. Sentencing Guidelines and Judicial Discretion

Judges historically enjoyed considerable discretion in setting criminal sentences under so-called indeterminate sentencing. Although, in theory, this allowed judges to tailor sentences to the individual convicted criminal's circumstances, it also raised concerns about sentencing disparities that were difficult to justify based on observable case facts. Beyond these fairness concerns, indeterminate sentencing also interfered with the price-signaling function of criminal penalties, which promotes the general deterrence objective of criminal law.

Based on these and other considerations, Congress enacted the Federal Sentencing Guidelines in 1987, which greatly curtailed judicial sentencing discretion.[164] The guidelines specified sentencing ranges based on the criminal history of the offender and the seriousness of the crime. Judges were generally bound to select a sentence from within more narrow specified bands. The process for setting up the guidelines involved delegation to an agency housed within Judicial Branch that included, among other appointees, a number of federal judges appointed by the President, with the recommended guidelines going into effect unless overturned by Congress within the statutorily specified period of 180 days.[165] The guidelines have since been held advisory only, on the ground that mandatory sentencing guidelines violated the Seventh Amendment right to a jury trial.[166] To the extent that the guidelines cabin judicial discretion, they raise an important question concerning the optimal relationship between congressional policy and judicial sentencing discretion in setting criminal penalties.

---

[162] Ian Ayres & Joel Waldfogel, *A Market Test for Race Discrimination in Bail Setting*, 46 STAN. L. REV. 987 (1994).

[163] *Id.* at 993.

[164] The guidelines were part of the Comprehensive Crime Control Act, Pub. L. No. 98–473, 98 Stat. 2027 enacted on October 12, 1984. See The U.S. Sentencing Guidelines: Implications for Criminal Justice (Dean J. Champion ed., 1989) for an overview of the law and its implications.

[165] The Supreme Court rejected a constitutional challenge to the statutory scheme in *Mistretta v. United States*, 488 U.S. 361 (1989). *See also* Blakely v. Washington, 542 U.S. 296 (2004) (applying the same rule to state sentencing guidelines).

[166] United States v. Booker, 543 U.S. 220 (2005); *Blakely*, 542 U.S. 269.

The basic trade-off concerns the conflicting goals of fairness in sentencing (i.e., fitting punishments to crimes after the fact) and deterrence. Broadly speaking, judges will be in a better position to pursue fairness in sentencing because they will be more familiar with the specific facts of criminal cases that appear before them. By contrast, the legislature, or an agency pursuant to a delegation, will be better able to create broad policy that is designed to further general deterrence as the penalty ranges are set more firmly in advance.

The sentencing guidelines, which set out *ranges* that were intended as binding, but are now advisory, can be interpreted as a compromise between these competing objectives.[167] At one extreme, as the range shrinks to a single point, sentences are fixed and inflexible, which might be preferred from the perspective of deterrence, but which can result in sentences that appear unfair in specific cases. This is especially likely if the legislature pursues a low-probability-of-apprehension, high-penalty scheme, as a strict reading of the economic analysis of criminal might be seen to imply. Illustrations of this rigid approach include the much-criticized three-strikes law operating in California, which sometimes results in severe penalties for a minor third offense. Conversely, indeterminate sentencing allows judges extremely broad discretion, but reduces deterrence by clouding the signaling function. A fixed range with flexibility within the range might suitably balance these goals.

Several empirical studies have sought to examine the effect of sentencing guidelines on both fairness and deterrence. Two studies specifically looked at whether the guidelines reduced sentencing variance. One study looked at 77,201 criminal cases decided between 1981 and 1993 and found that sentence differences based solely on random judicial assignment *declined* after the enactment of guidelines,[168] whereas another study using cases from 1981 to 1995 found that sentence variance attributed to judges actually *increased*.[169] The problem, however, is not variance *per se*, but rather, it is "unwarranted disparities among defendants with similar records who have been found guilty of similar criminal conduct."[170] Professor Joel Waldfogel therefore specifically asked whether the guidelines removed only "unwarranted" discretion.[171] His results suggested that the original guidelines would not be effective in removing undesirable discretion while allowing judges the discretion to tailor sentences to cases based on relevant differences.

It seems likely, however, that the actual enactment of the guidelines was not motivated primarily by fairness concerns, but rather by a desire for increased deterrence. Crime rates were rising throughout the 1970s and into the early 1980s when the guidelines were being debated. Legal historian Lawrence Friedman has observed that "the demand for tougher and tougher laws fueled the movement to get rid of [indeterminate

---

167 The following discussion is based on Thomas Miceli, *Criminal Sentencing Guidelines and Judicial Discretion*, 26 CONTEMP. ECON. POL'Y 207 (2008).

168 *See* James M. Anderson et al., *Measuring Interjudge Sentencing Disparity: Before and After the Federal Sentencing Guidelines*, 42 J.L. & ECON. 271 (1999).

169 *See* Chantale LaCasse & A. Abigail Payne, *Federal Sentencing Guidelines and Mandatory Minimum Sentences: Do Defendants Bargain in the Shadow of the Judge?*, 42 J.L. & ECON. 245 (1999).

170 Sentencing Reform Act of 1984, 28 U.S.C. § 991 (b).

171 Joel Waldfogel, *Selection of Cases for Trial*, *in* THE NEW PALGRAVE DICTIONARY, *supra* note 155.

sentencing]."[172] If so, it appears, that the guidelines did not have this intended effect. Using data from 1960 to 2000, Professor Joanna Shepherd found that "in states with guidelines, the guidelines are associated with approximately an 8% increase in the violent crime and a 7% increase in property crime, after controlling for other variables."[173] It remains to be seen whether the subsequent relaxation of sentencing guidelines will result in the exercise of greater discretion by judges, and if so, how this will affect the crime rate.

E. Three Issues of Criminal Procedure

We conclude this section by discussing three important doctrinal issues that pertain to criminal procedure: the privilege against self-incrimination, the prohibition against unreasonable searches and seizures, and asset forfeiture laws.

1. The Privilege Against Self-Incrimination

The Fifth Amendment privilege against self-incrimination gives criminal defendants the right to remain silent from the time of custody and interrogation and the right to refuse to testify at trial.[174] This includes the right to have the jury instructed not to draw adverse inferences from the failure to testify.[175]

Although there are reasons other than guilt for declining to speak with investigative officers or for refusing to testify, for example, being cross-examined with respect to past criminal conduct,[176] in most instances it is fair to assume that those who have not committed the offenses with which they are charged will wish to protest their innocence so as to avoid trial, or to testify at trial to persuade the jury in their favor. For this reason, the privilege is sometimes viewed as protecting those most likely to be guilty. In the absence of the rule, those who committed the underlying offense and who wished to avoid self-incriminating statements would be forced to lie to the police and to perjure themselves at trial, acts which are themselves serious criminal offenses.[177] Of course, some who are guilty cooperate with police or prosecutors, for example to give information respecting other guilty parties in exchange for a better deal, and some even testify on their own behalf, for example, at sentencing as a means of explaining their conduct in the hope of a reduced sentence.

One curious feature of the privilege is that by disallowing juries to draw an adverse inference from the failure to testify, the rule appears to make it more difficult to distinguish those who are or are not guilty.[178] In fact, one might argue that the privilege actually benefits the innocent by making their protestations of innocence more credible.[179]

---

[172] LAWRENCE M. FRIEDMAN, LAW IN AMERICA: A SHORT HISTORY 109 (2004).

[173] Joanna Shepherd, Blakely's *Silver Lining: Sentencing Guidelines, Judicial Discretion, and Crime*, 58 HASTINGS L.J. 533, 535 (2007).

[174] LAFAVE ET AL., *supra* note 99, § 6.5.

[175] *Id.* § 24.5.

[176] *Id.*

[177] *Id.*

[178] For a general discussion, see POSNER, *supra* note 96, § 29.3, at 958.

[179] Daniel Seidmann & Alex Stein, *The Right to Silence Helps the Innocent: A Game-Theoretic Analysis of the Fifth Amendment Privilege*, 114 HARV. L. REV. 430 (2000).

To show this, imagine that the privilege is not available. In this case, guilty defendants would also be forced to take the stand, and they would risk having to perjure themselves to avoid incrimination. The result is a pooling equilibrium in which claims of innocence under oath lose their persuasive force. Allowing criminal defendants to remain silent without permitting an adverse inference, however, is more likely to result in many guilty defendants taking that option, thereby promoting a partial separating equilibrium that improves the value of claims among those who choose to testify as to their innocence.

To illustrate, assume that out of 100 defendants, 25 are innocent. If all defendants protested their innocence on the stand, then the claim of any one defendant would be believable only 25% of the time. However, if under a rule against self-incrimination, two-thirds, or 50 of the 75 guilty defendants, chose *not* to testify, then the claim of innocence by a given defendant would be believable 50% of the time (i.e., 25 guilty and 25 innocent defendants would claim innocence). One interesting question is whether this would motivate a larger number of guilty defendants to testify so as to protest their innocence as a result of the added aura of credibility. Of course if prosecutors can prove that such defendants are lying, that makes this a highly risky strategy in addition to exposing the defendants who take it to the additional charge of perjury.

2. The Prohibition Against Unreasonable Searches and Seizures

The Fourth Amendment of the Constitution protects citizens from unreasonable searches and seizures. Judge Richard Posner has suggested that the use of a reasonableness standard represents a balancing of costs and benefits, a kind of Hand test, for determining when searches should be allowed.[180] To illustrate, assume the search cost, C, represents the invasion of a suspect's privacy, including the reputational loss from the inference of guilt people draw from mere suspicion; the benefit of a search is the product of the likelihood that probative evidence of a crime will be found, P, and the benefit from a conviction, B, representing the social welfare that results from apprehension and conviction. In this framing, a search is reasonable if the cost is less than the expected benefit, or if $C<PB$.

Under the Fourth Amendment, the principal means of enforcing this requirement is that, when feasible, police have to obtain a warrant from a judge before conducting a search.[181] When applicable, the warrant requirement ensures that an impartial magistrate has to make a determination that there is probable cause to believe that the target of the search was involved in a crime. This provides an important safeguard against random searches or searches of individuals who might be targeted for illicit purposes. In the preceding framework, it ensures that P is sufficiently large that the product, PB, outweighs the cost of the invasion of privacy.

The remedy for unlawful searches is the "exclusionary rule," which holds that any evidence gathered in an unlawful search (a search without a warrant that does not satisfy

---

[180] POSNER, *supra* note 96, § 29.2, at 955.

[181] Courts have recognized exceptions, including exigent circumstances, and they have permitted general searches without probable cause, for example, traffic stops, airport metal detectors, and more recently, more invasive airport searches. LAFAVE ET AL., *supra* note 99, §§ 3.6, 3.9.

one of the exceptions to that requirement) cannot be used in a trial against the target of the search, sometimes referred to as the "fruit of the poisonous tree."[182] The rule is controversial in that it results in discarding probative evidence of defendant's guilt, and it might over-deter the police from conducting searches. Assume, for example, that the court interprets "probable cause" to mean $P \geq .5$ and therefore refuses to issue a warrant in cases where $P < .5$. This will result in some otherwise efficient searches—those for which $C < PB$—being forbidden. As a result, there will actually be a bias against searches where B, the benefit of a conviction, is large.

Some scholars have proposed replacing the exclusionary rule with an alternative remedy for illegal searches, for example, a tort suit against the offending officer.[183] One empirical question is whether the threat of tort liability will have the same effect in deterring inefficient searches (applying the Hand test), or otherwise unconstitutional searches, as does the exclusionary rule.

There are at least two drawbacks of the tort remedy, however. First, juries might be reluctant to assess liability against a police officer who turned up evidence, even if illegally, against a truly guilty defendant. Second, tort liability might not deter the planting of evidence by police if courts are unable to distinguish illegally obtained evidence from legitimate evidence after the fact. By contrast, the exclusionary rule with a warrant requirement requires police to convince an impartial magistrate that probable cause exists in advance, which makes planting of evidence much more difficult. Thus, when there is a risk of police corruption, the exclusionary rule enhances the ability of courts to distinguish the innocent from the guilty while also protecting the privacy rights of citizens.[184]

One complication for the preceding model involves its assumptions as to the prerequisites for a warrant. Applying that framework, assume that there are six possible suspects, for example gang members, A through F, in a case involving the murder of a member of a different gang. Further assume that the probability of finding evidence, P, for the homes of A through E is 15%, but that for F it is 25%. The precise percentages are unimportant, but the essential inquiry involves how to calculate probable cause when one member of a larger group holds a statistically significantly higher P as compared with the rest of the relevant cohort but still below 50%.

Assume that a P of 25% would not suffice in the individual-suspect case, as was assumed above where P was set at greater than 50%. Does this change in a context in which the percentage for the aggregate group of suspects, A through F, well exceeds 50%, but the percentage for F, which although higher than that for other individuals, A through E, is only 25%? In addition, what if there is a high likelihood that searching the home of F is apt to provide strong evidence as to whether there is incriminating evidence in one or more of the homes of A through E? Assume for example that the police believe that there is an 80% chance that one of the gang members, A through F, had the gun used in

[182] Weeks v. United States, 232 U.S. 383 (1914); Mapp v. Ohio, 367 U.S. 643 (1961).

[183] Kit Kinports, *Culpability, Deterrence and the Exclusionary Rule*, 21 WM. & MARY BILL RTS. J. 821 (2013); Christopher Slobogin, *The Exclusionary Rule: Is It on Its Way Out? Should It Be?*, 10 OHIO ST. J. CRIM. L. 341 (2013).

[184] Dhammika Dharmapala & Thomas Miceli, *Search, Seizure, and False (?) Arrest: An Analysis of Fourth Amendment Remedies When Police Can Plant Evidence*, *in* RESEARCH HANDBOOK ON ECONOMIC MODELS OF LAW (Thomas J. Miceli & Matthew Baker eds., 2013).

the crime, and that the head of the gang, F, is most likely to have relevant information in his home that might lead the police to know where to find the gun as among the homes of A through E. Should this satisfy the requirement for a warrant? How would this fit within the preceding economic analysis of probable cause?

3. *Asset Forfeiture Laws*

A final issue concerns laws allowing government seizure of assets used in the commission of a crime. Seizure of assets originally arose out of admiralty law, where it was used to enforce customs duties and to combat piracy, and the Supreme Court upheld these early laws.[185] The practice was revived for use during the Prohibition era and again in the 1970s and 80s in the war on drugs.[186] Today it remains a standard, though controversial, weapon in the arsenal of law enforcement agencies.[187]

Property can be seized under both criminal and civil law. Under criminal law, the owner of the asset must be convicted of a crime before the owner's property can be seized, whereas under civil law no conviction is needed because the proceeding is technically against the property itself rather than its owner.[188] Thus, under civil forfeiture, assets can be seized from parties who are not themselves guilty of a crime, and the burden of proof shifts to the owner of the assets to prove no knowledge that the property was being used for criminal activity, or that the owner took all reasonable steps to prevent said use.[189] For example, if individuals are selling drugs from a rented apartment or from their parents' home, the property can be seized.

From an economic perspective, the question is whether the threat of seizure is an effective deterrent of crime, even when the alleged criminal does not own the asset in question. (In this sense, seizure is not the same as disgorgement of an offender's criminal gains, or a benefit-based sanction.) If the asset is an essential input in the commission of certain crimes, then the answer in general is yes because the threat of seizure will be reflected in the rental price of the asset, which raises the cost of crime to the offender. The policy is not costless, however, because owners of assets that may be used for criminal activity will not in general be able to distinguish legal and illegal users up front, and so the rental premium will create a market distortion. Thus, optimal seizure should balance its deterrence benefits against the deadweight loss in the rental market for such assets.[190] The fact that law enforcement agencies can profit from the sale of seized assets, however, creates a real risk of overuse, or of outright abuse, given the difficulty asset owners often have in proving their innocence after the fact. Critics therefore argue that judicial oversight of the practice is an important check on its use.[191]

---

185 Roger Pilon, *Can American Asset Forfeiture Law Be Justified?*, 39 N.Y.L. SCH. L. REV. 311 (1994).

186 *Id.*

187 *Id.*

188 *Id.*

189 *Id.*

190 *See, e.g.*, Thomas J. Miceli & Derek Johnson, *Asset Forfeiture and Criminal Deterrence*, 34 CONTEMP. ECON. POL'Y 119 (2015).

191 Eric L. Jensen & Jurg Gerber, *The Civil Forfeiture of Assets and the War on Drugs: Expanding Criminal Sanctions While Reducing Due Process Protections*, 42 CRIME & DELINQUENCY 421 (1996).

III. APPLICATIONS

1. *The American versus the English Rule and FRCP 68: What would Coase say?*

As we have seen, the American rule requires each side to pay her own lawyer's fees, whereas the English rule requires the loser to pay the winner's lawyer's fees. Federal Rule of Civil Procedure ("FRCP") 68 offers a modest modification to the American rule, requiring the plaintiff to cover defendant's costs, usually excluding lawyer's fees, if the plaintiff's verdict is lower than a pre-judgment offer of settlement. The efficacy of this rule is further undermined by the quirk that it does not apply if the defendant actually wins a favorable trial verdict. We have also seen models that demonstrate some ambiguity in the implications of the rule choice as between the American and English rules for settlement, but overall the literature appears to suggest a stronger disincentive to file frivolous, or Negative Economic Value ("NEV"), suits under the English rule.

Assuming that most litigation is funded by insurers rather than the direct parties, for example, in cases involving auto insurance claims, products liability claims, and the like, does the rule choice matter? Is it possible that the additional expectation of frivolous claims is reflected in insurance premiums, thus rendering the choice of rule largely irrelevant viewed from a Coasian perspective? Why or why not?

2. In recent years, there has been substantial attention paid to unpublished appellate court opinions, espe [illegible] peals. What implications, if any, does [illegible] ency of common law development [illegible] ls all decided appellate court opinio [illegible] published be better or worse from a social welfare perspective? Why or why not?

Under *Erie Railroad Co. v.* [illegible][192] In theory, all common law in div [illegible] sion, including rulings from the rele [illegible] mon law courts.

Is it be possible that in at [illegible] might be a feature rather than a bug in the federa [illegible] ions improve the efficacy of *Eri* [illegible] ersity jurisdiction cases, no federal d [illegible] blish the resulting opinion. (Bear [illegible] rrow exceptions not relevant here, [illegible] this proposed rule would improve [illegible] sses? Why or why not? Would you support the rule? To what extent is your answer informed by economic analysis? To what extent is it informed by other considerations?

In recent years, courts have struggled with how to treat so-called unpublished opinions. Even calling them "unpublished" is a misnomer as these are now readily available in online databases and are even collected and printed in the *Federal Appendix*. How, if at all, does the free availability of such opinions affect your analysis? In 2006 the

---

[192] 304 U.S. 64, 78 (1938).

Federal Judicial Conference added *Federal Rule of Civil Procedure* 32.1,[193] which provides that federal courts may not prohibit the citation of so-called unpublished opinions, athough the rule leaves unresolved the question of the precedential authority of those opinions.

3. In addition to the phenomenon of unpublished opinions, there has been an increased push toward *Alternative Dispute Resolution*. This sometimes includes *mediation* and other times *arbitration*. Here we consider arbitration. Many arbitrated disputes arise from form contracts, for example involving cruises and the purchase of some complex goods or services, thereby limiting access to a judicial forum if a dispute arises.

Do the models set out in this chapter or in the remaining materials we have studied help to assess whether such clauses, typically presented on a take-it-or-leave-it basis, should be judicially enforced? Do the models help to assess whether these clauses are likely to be efficient? Are those the same questions? Why or why not?

4. In the criminal justice system, plea bargaining has generated substantial concern. This chapter discussed the risk that the threat of a harsher punishment following a conviction might motivate an innocent defendant to plead guilty to a lesser charge. In Chapter 15 we will study the prisoners' dilemma ("PD"). This question assumes basic familiarity with that concept, which we will later introduce more formally.[194]

One problem with plea bargaining is the incentive of prisoners to strike deals in exchange for testifying against another defendant. Indeed, that is the classic presentation of the PD. In light of this problem, would you support or oppose a rule that allows those who have engaged in plea bargains in these circumstances to have their pleas reconsidered in the event that they are subsequently found to be factually innocent? What are the competing considerations? Do any outweigh the concern for actual innocence? Why or why not?

5. The rule of *Brady v. Maryland*[195] requires the state to disclose exculpatory evidence to the defense. There is no rule requiring the defense to disclose testimonial incriminating evidence to the prosecution, but the state may compel the production of some non-testimonial incriminating evidence. By contrast, in civil litigation, the discovery rules are symmetrical. One explanation for the asymmetry within our criminal justice system is that the defense is in a disadvantageous position at the hands of the state. On the other hand, the state has the higher burden of proof, beyond a reasonable doubt,

---

[193] Rule 32.1 states in full:

Rule 32.1 Citing Judicial Dispositions

(a) Citation Permitted. A court may not prohibit or restrict the citation of federal judicial opinions, orders, judgments, or other written dispositions that have been:

(i) designated as "unpublished," "not for publication," "non-precedential," "not precedent," or the like; and

(ii) issued on or after January 1, 2007.

(b) Copies Required. If a party cites a federal judicial opinion, order, judgment, or other written disposition that is not available in a publicly accessible electronic database, the party must file and serve a copy of that opinion, order, judgment, or disposition with the brief or other paper in which it is cited.

FED. R. CIV. P. 32.1.

[194] For an explanation of the prisoners' dilemma, see *infra* Chapters 15 or 16.

[195] 373 U.S. 83 (1983).

meaning that the criminal defendant need only raise reasonable doubt to prevail. Compare this with the preponderance of the evidence standard in civil litigation, which imposes a more uniform burden on both sides.

Would the system of criminal justice be improved if the rules of discovery in that context were also reciprocal? Would you support a proposal to render them reciprocal? Why or why not? To what extent if any is your opinion informed by economic analysis? By other considerations? Which considerations are most important and why?

PART IV

Public Choice Methodologies

CHAPTER 11

Interest Group Theory (Part 1)

Introduction

In order to aid the American steel industry in March 2002, President George W. Bush imposed tariffs on imported steel that ranged from 8% to 30%,[1] depending on the type of steel.[2] The tariffs aided the steel industry by dramatically increasing the market price of steel in the United States. At the same time, however, this price increase was passed on to producers who relied upon steel inputs, including, for example, automobile manufacturers, producers of machinery, and the construction industry. The resulting price increases were substantial. One study estimates that over 200,000 jobs were lost in the United States in industries employing steel in the first year of the tariff alone, a number that exceeds the total employment in the entire United States steel industry.[3] By contrast, the same study estimates that the tariffs saved fewer than 10,000 jobs within the steel industry at a cost of between $450,000 to $584,000 per job. Some manufacturers were able to pass along part of the raised cost of steel inputs to end users in the form of higher prices. This strategy was most effective in those industries for which demand for goods was relatively inelastic,[4] including, for example, in the markets for certain automobiles,

[1] *See* Proclamation No. 7529, 3 C.F.R. 15 (2003) ("To Facilitate Positive Adjustment to Competition from Imports of Certain Steel Products"). The action was taken by President Bush pursuant to Article 2.1 of the World Trade Organization (WTO) Agreement on Safeguards, Agreement on Safeguards, Apr. 15, 1994, Marrakesh Agreement Establishing the Trade Organization, Annex 1A, Legal Instruments—Results of the Uruguay Round, 33 I.L.M. 1125 (1994) (setting forth the rules for application of safeguard measures pursuant to Article XIX of the General Agreement on Tariffs and Trade, GATT 1994: General Agreement on Tariffs and Trade 1994, Apr. 15, 1994, Marrakesh Agreement Establishing the World Trade Organization, Annex 1A, 1867 U.N.T.S. 187, 33 I.L.M. 1153 (1994) [hereinafter GATT 1994]), which permits a country to impose "safeguard measures" if "serious injury" could result to domestic producers as a result of unfair trade practices such as the improper dumping of goods. *See* WORLD TRADE ORGANIZATION, TRADING INTO THE FUTURE 29–32 (2d ed. 2001). The procedures for implementing safeguards are codified in U.S. law at 19 U.S.C. § 2253 (2012).

[2] For an informative discussion of the steel tariffs, see Robert Read, *The Political Economy of Trade Protection: The Determinants and Welfare Impact of the 2002 US Emergency Steel Safeguard Measures*, 28 WORLD ECON. 1119 (2005). The steel tariffs were lifted twenty-one months later in December 2003 following an adverse ruling by the WTO that the tariff violated the GATT 1994. *Id.* at 1132–33.

[3] JOSEPH FRANCOIS & LAURA M. BAUGHMAN, THE UNINTENDED CONSEQUENCES OF U.S. STEEL IMPORT TARIFFS: A QUANTIFICATION OF THE IMPACT DURING 2002, at 12 (2003) (study was prepared by Trade Partnership Worldwide for the Consuming Industries Trade Action Coalition (CITAC)).

[4] For a discussion of price elasticities, see Chapter 2.

motor vehicle parts, machine goods, and construction inputs. Nonetheless, some analysts determined that the net effect of the tariffs, including the increased cost of consumer goods and jobs lost within manufacturing industries relying upon steel inputs, was substantially greater than the benefits in terms of jobs retained or gained within the steel industry itself.

The 2002 steel tariffs are far from unique in American history. In 2009, then-newly-elected President Barack Obama imposed a stiff tariff on imports of Chinese tires. A 2012 analysis estimated that the increased total cost to American consumers resulting from the tariff in 2011 was $1.1 billion.[5] Moreover, although the tariff saved up to 1200 jobs in the American tire manufacturing industry, the loss of income for consumers led them to reduce their consumption of other retail products. The study estimated that the tire tariffs resulted in a net *reduction* of overall employment of 2531 jobs. Each job saved in the American tire manufacturing industry was estimated to cost $900,000 per job. And these estimates do not include the American jobs lost in other industries when China imposed a retaliatory tariff on chicken parts.

In *Federalist No. 10*, James Madison famously expressed fear that transient majorities, or "factions," would form with the power to deploy the machinery of government to their advantage. Madison posited that one of the principal missions of constitutionalism is to divide and control the government to make more difficult the possibility that factional violence would form and operate the machinery of government to the detriment of the electorate. Madison's thesis represents a major contribution to American political theory. And yet, the examples of the steel tariff and Chinese tire tariff raise the possibility that as a description of how the United States system of governance actually operates, the theory might be incomplete.[6]

How did the steel industry succeed in acquiring a protective tariff when weighed in terms of the number of people, the number of firms, or the value of economic activity, the aggregate economic losses exceeded that industry's resulting gains?[7] For those who might assume that governmental processes generally conduce to the "public interest," the steel and the Chinese tire tariffs appear to provide an important pair of cautionary tales. The analysis becomes even more significant if it reveals a fundamental limitation of the public interest view of legislative procurement of goods and services.

tariffs on imported steel confer a rent on domestic steel producers

This chapter will begin the process of constructing simple models designed to explain important features of the political process. Although we will emphasize familiar processes within the United States, several of the insights that we develop can be generalized to alternative political systems. The analysis will explore the conditions under

---

[5] Gary Clyde Hufbauer & Sean Lawry, *US Tire Tariffs: Saving Few Jobs at High Cost*, POL'Y BRIEF: PETERSON INST. INT'L ECON. (2012), https://piie.com/publications/pb/pb12-9.pdf.

[6] It is also often believed that the President will be less responsive to special interests than a typical member of Congress because the President has the incentive to consider the interests of the entire country and thus to internalize the costs of inefficient policies. *See* Peter H. Aranson, Ernest Gellhorn & Glen O. Robinson, *A Theory of Legislative Delegation*, 68 CORNELL L. REV. 1, 41 (1982). Yet the steel tariff was imposed by the President interpreting GATT and was only repealed after an adverse ruling by the WTO. What might explain the President's behavior in this case? For a discussion, see Read, *supra* note 2, at 1126–27, 1133–34.

[7] For an analysis establishing that these various measures reveal losses exceeded gains, see Read, *supra* note 2, at 1129–31.

which majoritarian or minoritarian factions, meaning interest group coalitions that produce majority alliances or influential minority interest groups, are likely to thrive within U.S., or other, political processes; how those processes are structured to limit or to harness such interests; and what the implications of such processes are for the procurement of various forms of public and quasi-private legislative goods.

The chapter proceeds as follows: Part I juxtaposes public and private interest models of government. Part II presents the economic theory of regulation beginning with the Chicago School. Part III sets out a more general theory of regulation, drawing upon other public choice traditions, culminating in the Wilson-Hayes matrix. Part IV sets out several applications drawn from prominent Supreme Court cases.

I. PUBLIC AND PRIVATE INTEREST MODELS OF GOVERNMENT

This part compares public and private interest models of government. We begin with the *public interest model* of government regulation, which dominated throughout much of the twentieth century. This view came into prominence with the rise of the industrialized era. Both within the media and popular culture, there was a strong perceived need for the government to provide benign intervention to combat the increasingly horrific working conditions associated with early industrialization. For one prominent example, consider Upton Sinclair's famous 1906 novel, *The Jungle*, which, in widely exposing the unsafe and unsanitary conditions associated with the meat packing industry at the turn of the twentieth century, provided a strong impetus for the creation of the Food and Drug Administration.[8]

The development of economic science provided a strong theoretical foundation for relying upon the government to correct widely perceived imperfections within market processes identified as *market failures*. Regulatory advocates recognized that self-interest did not invariably align with the public good and believed that proper government intervention was necessary to ensure that markets produced socially optimal, or at least preferred, results.

Then-Professor Richard Posner described the commonly held public interest theory of government as follows: "This theory holds that regulation is supplied in response to the demand of the public for the correction of inefficient or inequitable market practices."[9] Posner further ascribed two assumptions to the resulting public interest theory of regulation: (1) "that economic markets are extremely fragile and apt to operate very inefficiently (or inequitably) if left alone," and (2) "that government regulation is

---

[8] UPTON SINCLAIR, THE JUNGLE (1906) (Sinclair first published the novel in 1905 as a serial in the journal, *Appeal to Reason*, with the intent of highlighting issues of immigrant labor and poor working conditions). For alternative accounts, see Marc T. Law & Gary D. Libecap, *The Determinants of Progressive Era Reform: The Pure Food and Drugs Act of 1906, in* CORRUPTION AND REFORM: LESSONS FROM AMERICA'S ECONOMIC HISTORY 319 (Edward L. Glaeser & Claudia Goldin eds., 2006) (noting influence of producer groups); Gary D. Libecap, *The Rise of the Chicago Packers and the Origins of Meat Inspection and Antitrust*, 30 ECON. INQUIRY 242 (1992).

[9] Richard A. Posner, *Theories of Economic Regulation*, 5 BELL J. ECON. & MGMT. SCI. 335, 335 (1974).

virtually costless."[10] These premises are often assumed to hold without the benefit of careful analysis.[11]

Assessing these premises returns us to the theoretical disagreement between the economists Arthur Cecil Pigou and Ronald Coase.[12] Pigou claimed that where property rights were imperfectly defined, property owners, acting in their self-interest, were motivated to engage in profitable economic activities even when those activities generated substantial *negative externalities* such as pollution. Because owners of polluting firms did not internalize the full social cost of production, Pigou claimed, the quest for profit thrust a wedge between the level of output chosen by a self-interested private actor and the socially optimal level of the activity. The resulting market failure implied that left to its own devices, the market, or market actors, tended to produce too many goods for which all costs were not internalized, with the effect of passing real costs onto others who did not benefit from the economic activities. Pigou proposed resolving this difficulty by, among other means, imposing a tax that resulted in the full internalization of the costs of economic activity.

The public interest model assumes that the government can identify various deficiencies in private market orderings, such as the negative externality of pollution, and then appropriately calibrate legal rules to ensure that private actors fully internalize such costs. By better aligning private and social costs of economic activities, Pigouvian regulation would promote socially beneficial outcomes.

Pigou's argument has been subject to two critiques, each reflecting the insight that along with private market failures, so too government regulatory responses are prone to imperfection. The first critique rests on information costs. Even well-intentioned regulators face daunting challenges in collecting and processing the information necessary to identify market failures and to devising solutions that will ameliorate and improve upon the market imperfections such that the benefits of regulation exceed the costs. The second critique focuses on the concern that those empowered to regulate are often subject to political pressures that run counter to the goal of dispassionately furthering Pigouvian objectives.

Coase's critique of regulation focused on the first problem, that of the efficient collection and use of information by government regulators. Coase challenged the assumption that government is capable of collecting and using all of the information needed to identify and correct market failures. The government, even if theoretically capable of operating as a Pigouvian central planner, is unlikely to actually do so in practice. Thus, whereas the public interest model of government rests upon identified market failures as compared with a theoretically perfectly functioning market capable of aligning private and social costs, public choice identifies the failings of an idealized view of regulation in which the government can costlessly correct market failures.

---

10 *Id.* at 336.

11 For a summary list of various asserted bases for regulation and a summary of competing theoretical models of government regulation, see SUSAN E. DUDLEY & JERRY BRITO, REGULATION: A PRIMER (2d ed. 2012), especially Chapter 2, *Theories of Regulation: Why Do We Regulate?*.

12 *See supra* Chapter 1, at Part III (discussing Pigou and Coase).

Public choice provides the foundation for the second critique. Public choice is not concerned with theoretically ideal institutions, whether markets, legislatures, or other institutions.[13] Rather, it is concerned with identifying the relative strengths and weaknesses of real world institutions and assessing when particular decision-making responsibilities are better channeled toward one institution or another. Public choice models treat regulatory processes as a type of political market such that outcomes are apt to reflect the push and pull of various economic interests jockeying for available gains. Just as private markets can fail when profit-seeking individuals disregard social costs, self-interested private actors engaged with political bodies can thwart optimal regulatory outcomes as measured against public interest theory benchmarks. Whereas Coase focuses on the problem of assuming regulatory omniscience, public choice scholars focus on the problem of failing to recognize regulatory self-interest.

Not long after the rise of industrialization, political scientists began to critically assess the public interest understanding of benign government processes. One famous illustration, E.E. Schattschneider's study of the 1930 Smoot-Hawley Tariff,[14] demonstrates some of the conceptual difficulties that reemerged in the 2002 steel tariffs.[15] The Smoot-Hawley Tariff differs from the more recent steel tariffs in that it resulted from a federal statute rather than from an executive proclamation. Through a series of logrolls, Congress managed to endorse a combination of prohibitive tariffs that benefited various industries, but did so at tremendous cost to the national economy. Schattschneider's analysis, which rests on a pluralist understanding of politics,[16] views Congress as a neutral conduit that rubber-stamped an industry-negotiated pact, one primarily reached outside formal political processes. Modern public choice analysis builds upon pluralism but recognizes the importance of modeling the interest of legislators themselves in interacting with various other forces, including constituencies, lobbyists, and actors within other branches of government. The public interest view of government stands in stark contrast with this pluralist understanding, and also public choice theory.

As the examples of the steel and tire tariffs, and the discussion of the Smoot-Hawley Act, demonstrate, the public interest model imperfectly describes the workings of actual political processes. At a minimum, these examples might illustrate the possibility that political actors, and Congress as an institution, sometimes depart from the public interest

---

[13] *See* Harold Demsetz, *Information and Efficiency: Another Viewpoint*, 12 J.L. & ECON. 1 (1969) (describing the nirvana fallacy that "pervades much public policy economics"); *see also infra* Chapter 13, at Part I.F.2.

[14] Tariff Act of 1930, Pub. L. No. 71–361, 46 Stat. 590 (codified as amended at 19 U.S.C. §§ 1202–1681b).

[15] E.E. SCHATTSCHNEIDER, POLITICS, PRESSURES AND THE TARIFF (photo. reprint 1963) (1935).

[16] Pluralist theory, a precursor to the modern theory of public choice, viewed the legislature as a conduit through which special interest groups accomplished their own legislative outcomes. *See* EARL LATHAM, THE GROUP BASIS OF POLITICS: A STUDY IN BASING-POINT LEGISLATION 35 (1952) (positing that "[the] legislature referees the group struggle, ratifies the victories of the successful coalitions and records the terms of surrenders, compromises, and conquests in the form of statutes."); THEODORE J. LOWI, THE POLITICS OF DISORDER, at xviii–xix (1971) (positing that "[the] basis of pluralism and quiescence is the organized group and group interactions, with political man holding the whole together through delegation and negotiation."); Maxwell L. Stearns, *The Public Choice Case Against the Item Veto*, 49 WASH. & LEE L. REV. 385, 400 n.94 (1992) (collecting authorities on pluralism). A major difference between pluralism and the modern theory of public choice is that the latter accounts for the independent role of political actors, based upon their personal motivations, in affecting institutional outcomes. Stearns, *supra*.

in favor of producing outcomes that benefit special interest groups. Public choice theorists often contend that interest group influence on legislative outcomes is commonplace, with the effect of producing narrow tax exemptions, protective tariffs, industry subsidies, and competitive restrictions or barriers to entry. They further recognize that special interest provisions are often contained within a larger piece of legislation or regulation that might otherwise be conducive to advancing the public interest. Whereas Madison expressed the concern that governmental processes would allow majoritarian factions to benefit at the expense of the public, assessing what we will call the *microfoundations of collective decision making* allows us to appreciate how well organized narrow interest groups frequently prevail within Madison's complex constitutional scheme even though it was designed to improve legislative accountability and to limit factional violence.

What became known as *capture theory* further influenced the development of public choice. This theory reflects the often-observed phenomenon that regulatory agencies, ostensibly established to rein in wayward industries, often appear to be controlled by those very industries, with the consequence of thwarting the public interest objectives the agencies were originally called upon to serve. Richard Posner describes the central insight as follows:

> This formulation is more specific than the general interest group theory. It singles out a particular interest group—the regulated firms—as prevailing in the struggle to influence legislation, and it predicts a regular sequence, in which the original purposes of a regulatory program are later thwarted through the efforts of the interest group.[17]

Capture theory further contributed to developing a positive theory of the regulatory process by helping to describe some of its frequently observed, yet problematic, features.

Capture theory nonetheless remained an incomplete account of regulatory dynamics. For example, it failed to offer a compelling theoretical explanation as to why bureaucracies are more apt to be prone to interest group influence than legislatures, which were assumed less likely to succumb to such pressures. In addition, the theory did not account for the reality that in some instances, the initial impetus for the regulatory regime, and even the creation of the relevant agency itself, was motivated by the regulated industry, rather than by the public, and then followed by industry capture. For example, Richard Posner has observed that there is ample evidence that the Interstate Commerce Commission (ICC) was founded at the behest of the railroad industry in order to cartelize the industry.[18] Capture theory also tended to focus on the role of industry in redeploying regulatory processes to their advantage, without considering that other interests, such as consumer groups or public interest groups, engage in similar strategies, and that sometimes competing industries, or other interests, vie for regulatory influence. For example, although the ICC regulated competition among different firms within the railroad

---

17 Posner, *supra* note 9, at 341–42.

18 *See id.* at 352. The ICC was established as an independent agency in 1887 by the Interstate Commerce Act, "designed to prevent railroads from practicing price discrimination, because discrimination was undermining the railroads' cartels." *Id.* at 337. During the twentieth century, the ICC's jurisdiction grew to include other common carriers, as did the ICC's enforcement and investigatory powers. In 1995, the ICC was terminated and the commission's functions were shifted to other agencies and departments. *See* Paul Stephen Dempsey, *The Rise and Fall of the Interstate Commerce Commission*, 95 MARQ. L. REV. 1151, 1185 (2012).

industry, it also regulated interstate trucking and barges, which were often competing industries. As shown below, public choice, which builds on these theories, helps to provide a more comprehensive account of the regulatory process and of various interest groups in seeking to influence that process.

A. Rents, Quasi-Rents, and Rent Seeking

We can now more fully appreciate the concept of economic rents, introduced in Chapter 2. Recall that an economic rent arises when an economic activity, for example labor, earns a return that exceeds the opportunity cost of the income-producing asset. Monopolists earn economic rents through innovation, product differentiation, or restrictions on outputs with the effect of commanding a price paid for the resulting goods or services that is higher than that dictated in a competitive market. Our concern here is the latter method, also known as rent seeking.

Restrictions on the ability of potential competitors to supply the same or similar goods results in *economic rents* for those who capture the market. Those exempt from competition are thus able to supply their goods at a price that exceeds the opportunity cost, or next best use, of the various factors of production. A firm with market power can extract economic rents by restricting supply, thereby raising prices.[19] The monopolist receives rents equal to the difference between the level of profit available under conditions of monopoly and that available under competitive conditions. The following graphic illustrates the monopolistic pricing strategy and the resulting economic rents:

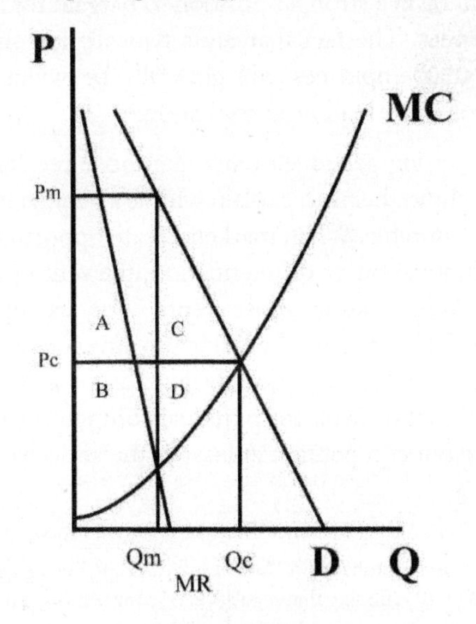

Figure 11:1

Figure 11:1 illustrates the social welfare loss of monopoly. The triangular areas *C* and *D* represent the resulting social *deadweight loss*. These triangles represent forgone beneficial exchanges that would have been conducted absent the monopolistic pricing strategy. Area *C* represents the forgone consumer surplus and area *D* represents the

[19] For a more detailed discussion, see Chapter 2.

forgone producer surplus. These *deadweight loss triangles* are often referred to as *Harberger triangles*, named after the economist Arnold Harberger, who was the first to formalize the analysis and to measure the social loss resulting from monopolistic practices, including those resulting from price regulations and taxes.[20] A principal normative justification for antitrust law, for instance, is to "recoup" these deadweight losses for the economy by preventing a monopolist from restricting supply and thereby raising prices.

As previously shown, the area *A–D* is equivalent to the monopolistic rent minus the forgone producer surplus in Figure 11:1. This represents the economic rent, which is largely a wealth transfer from consumers to producers resulting from monopolistic pricing, and the corresponding reduction in output and increase in price. Another way of generating economic rents is through the enactment of regulations that restrict competition and allow producers to raise prices above competitive levels. Consider the steel tariff. Steel tariffs raise the price of imported steel relative to domestic steel. But they also allow domestic steel producers to increase prices to just below that of imported steel even though they do not pay the tax. The steel tariff proceeds are paid directly to the federal government, and yet, the resulting price increases are a direct wealth transfer from consumers to domestic steel producers.

The distribution of economic rents among the various stakeholders in the benefiting firms, primarily shareholders and employees, depends on how these groups negotiate. In general, however, we can predict some "sharing" of rents between employees and owners of the firm,[21] largely depending on each group's relative bargaining power. For instance, unionized employees might be in a stronger position to bargain for a greater share of rents than nonunionized employees. The fact that rents typically are shared between owners and employees suggests that employees will generally be willing to provide political support for protectionist or other beneficial regulation.[22]

monopoly rent - excess cost that a firm can charge above the market price present if there was competition

While monopolistic pricing generates rents like those resulting from protectionist regulatory policies, public choice helps to explain why as a general matter the latter source of rents is likely to be more durable. When markets create opportunities for monopolistic pricing through product innovation or differentiation, the rent opportunity attracts new entrants that tend to compete away those rents. For example, markets produce opportunities for monopolistic pricing when start-up investments are sufficiently high that the average cost of the goods in question declines as a result of economies of scale. Declining average cost makes it difficult for potential competitors to enter the market, as a single firm tends to drive out competition at least in the short to moderate term.

---

20 *See* James R. Hines, Jr., *Three Sides of Harberger Triangles*, J. ECON. PERSP., Spring 1999, at 167.

21 *See* Sandra E. Black & Philip E. Strahan, *The Division of Spoils: Rent-Sharing and Discrimination in a Regulated Industry*, 91 AM. ECON. REV. 814 (2001) (finding that regulation of competition in the banking industry resulted in rent-sharing with banking employees); *see also* Marcello Estevão & Stacey Tevlin, *Do Firms Share their Success with Workers? The Response of Wages to Product Market Conditions*, 70 ECONOMICA 597 (2003); Pedro S. Martins, *Rent Sharing Before and After the Wage Bill*, 41 APPLIED ECON. 2133 (2009).

22 For instance, the United Steelworkers of America were vigorous political supporters of the decision to impose steel tariffs. *See* Read, *supra* note 2, at 1125–26. The United Auto Workers (UAW) also provided strong support for federal bailout proposals of the automobile industry in 2008. Matthew Doland & John D. Stoll, *UAW Faces Prospect of More Concessions*, WALL ST. J., Nov. 17, 2008, at A4 (noting that "the UAW is standing shoulder-to-shoulder with the [auto] companies in an intense public campaign to plead for a federal bailout").

Familiar paradigms include electrical utilities, mail systems, and airplane and automobile manufacturers, each of which is characterized by extraordinarily high start-up costs. In most circumstances, however, even these industries eventually invite new entrants and thus competition. Federal Express competes with the United States Postal Service, oil distributors compete with natural gas, and although the market remains concentrated, several manufacturers compete in the production of automobiles and airplanes. But one need not resort to this sort of large-scale industry to illustrate the proposition of market power. While large-scale natural monopoly is uncommon,[23] conditions that characterize natural monopoly, such as declining average cost for the relevant range of outputs, arise within many start-up industries. In nearly every industry, for at least some period of time, high start-up costs give rise to economies of scale and declining average costs. Over time, however, the perceived opportunities for the resulting *quasi-rents*—rents that result from temporary market conditions that allow prices above the opportunity cost for the relevant factors of production[24]—encourage others to incur the necessary initial investments to offer competing market products.

By contrast, government-conferred rents are usually created by erecting barriers to entry. These include restrictive licensing and permit regimes, which limit the erosion of rents through market competition. Governmentally created rents are also more permanent because whereas some coordinated monopolistic activity is subject to regulatory enforcement under antitrust laws, regulatory schemes with anticompetitive effects are generally exempt from such laws.[25]

II. THE ECONOMIC THEORY OF REGULATION[26]

In two articles written in the 1970s, George Stigler and Sam Peltzman consider the circumstances under which legislators, behaving rationally, are likely to confer rents, along with the nature of the rents that private interests, behaving rationally, are likely to seek. In *The Theory of Economic Regulation*,[27] George Stigler challenged the intuition that most regulation is imposed upon industries to benefit the public, instead positing that much

---

[23] For a discussion of natural monopoly, see *supra* Chapter 2.

[24] Fred McChesney defines *rent* as, "returns to the owner of an asset in excess of the level of returns necessary for him to continue using the asset in its current employment. Thus, a rent is any return above what the owner would earn in the asset's next-best alternative use." FRED S. MCCHESNEY, MONEY FOR NOTHING: POLITICIANS, RENT EXTRACTION, AND POLITICAL EXTORTION 10 (1997). As McChesney notes, economists have never agreed on a precise definition of rent, especially in contrast to the term *quasi-rent*, which refers to *temporary* returns on assets above opportunity cost. *Id.*; *see* Armen A. Alchian, *Rent*, *in* 4 THE NEW PALGRAVE: A DICTIONARY OF ECONOMICS 141–42 (John Eatwell et al. eds., 1998). We follow the general convention of public choice economics and use *rent* to refer to returns above the asset's opportunity cost, regardless of whether temporary or permanent.

[25] *See* Parker v. Brown, 317 U.S. 341 (1943) (finding state government actions exempt from the Sherman Act); *see also* TODD ZYWICKI ET AL., FED. TRADE COMM'N, REPORT OF THE STATE ACTION TASK FORCE (2003), https://www.ftc.gov/sites/default/files/documents/reports/report-state-action-task-force-recommendations-clarify-and-reaffirm-original-purposes-state-action/stateactionreport_0.pdf.

[26] Portions of the discussions that follow are adapted from MAXWELL L. STEARNS, PUBLIC CHOICE AND PUBLIC LAW: READINGS AND COMMENTARY 120–21 (1997).

[27] George J. Stigler, *The Theory of Economic Regulation*, 2 BELL J. ECON. & MGMT. SCI. 3 (1971).

regulation is affirmatively acquired by industries to secure monopolistic rents. Stigler questioned why, for example, the oil industry, in which the supply is relatively elastic (output is sensitive to changes in price), lobbied for import quotas rather than for import tariffs or direct cash grants. If the regulation had been aimed at protecting domestic production capabilities for national defense purposes, as industry interests then claimed, tariffs could have achieved that with all costs paid into the national treasury rather than to industry participants. Direct cash grants or subsidies also would have produced the stated objective of ensuring a domestic oil supply at a substantially lower cost to consumers than import quotas.

Quotas, unlike tariffs, limit market supply and thereby prevent competitive market entry from dissipating rents. Stigler posited that the industry preference for quotas reflected the desire of producers, operating in a market typified by elastic supply, to prevent potential market entrants from sharing the benefits of regulation. He further demonstrated that state licensure requirements often serve the same purpose of inhibiting market entry and of securing monopolistic rents for the industry acquiring the regulation.

Stigler considered when legislators, behaving rationally, are likely to provide regulatory benefits sought by industries. His analysis suggests that well organized and small groups (especially those without significant opposition), that are best able to confer regulatory benefits upon their members, are most likely to engage in effective rent seeking, meaning affirmative lobbying efforts to secure beneficial legal protections against competition; whereas large and diffuse groups are not.[28] Behaving rationally, legislators are apt to be responsive to these sorts of constituent pressures, as responsiveness furthers reelection prospects.

Sam Peltzman explained the significance of Stigler's insight as follows:

> In one sense, Stigler's work provides a theoretical foundation for [a] "producer protection" view [of regulation]. . . . Stigler . . . realized that the earlier "consumer protection" model comes perilously close to treating regulation as a free good. In that model the existence of market failure is sufficient to generate a demand for regulation, though there is no mention of the mechanism that makes that demand effective. . . . Since the good, regulation, is not in fact free and demand for it is not automatically synthesized, Stigler sees the task of a positive economics of regulation as specifying the arguments underlying the supply and demand for regulation.[29]

Peltzman refined Stigler's model to link regulatory output not only to the size and organization of the lobbying group, but also to the votes gained or lost in response to the implemented regulation. Peltzman explained:

> Stigler is asserting a law of diminishing returns to group size in politics: beyond some point it becomes counterproductive to dilute the per capita transfer. Since the total transfer is endogenous, there is a corollary that diminishing

---

[28] These themes are also explored in MANCUR OLSON, THE LOGIC OF COLLECTIVE ACTION: PUBLIC GOODS AND THE THEORY OF GROUPS (1965).

[29] Sam Peltzman, *Toward a More General Theory of Regulation*, 19 J.L. & ECON. 211, 212 (1976).

> returns apply to the transfer as well, due both to the opposition provoked by the transfer and to the demand this opposition exerts on resources to quiet it.[30]

By focusing on votes rather than group size, Peltzman was able to incorporate a factor into his model that was only a detail in Stigler's original formulation: "[T]he costs of using the political process limit not only the size of the dominant group but also their gains."[31] In the resulting model, regulation occurs not merely from a bidding process in which optimally formed industry groups win, but also it arises as a result of a more subtle and complex process through which the suppliers of regulation, namely the legislators, weigh the gains derived from the prospective transfer against the costs borne in terms of lost votes.

In a comment on the Stigler and Peltzman articles, Gary Becker posited that competitive political forces might serve to reduce the relative size of those deadweight societal losses that result from industry regulation. Thus, whether quotas, tariffs, or subsidies predominate in a particular industry is likely a function of which is the most cost-effective, and thus efficient, form of wealth transfer, meaning a transfer that creates the smallest deadweight loss. For Becker, this insight explains the choice of regulatory form in terms other than the common belief that "voters are systematically fooled about the effects of policies like quotas and tariffs that have persisted for a long time."[32]

Consider whether the economic theory of regulation supports heightened judicial scrutiny as a means to minimize legislatively procured rents. Some scholars, whose works we will later discuss, have proposed imposing judicial barriers to enforcing the products of legislative rent seeking. At least since the New Deal, however, the Supreme Court has not gone along. One potential silver lining, suggested by Becker, is that if we are willing to accept that at least some regulation is a form of wealth transfer, rather than a vehicle for promoting the public good, we need not worry terribly much about the form that the regulation takes. The regulatory equivalent of Adam Smith's invisible hand will move wealth transfers to their most cost-effective form.

A. Attorney Licensing

Based on the above analysis, consider the age-old regime of attorney licensure. By requiring membership in a state bar, the licensure regime limits the supply of lawyers in each jurisdiction. From a public interest perspective, licensing of professional services can be justified on the ground that consumers might find it difficult to determine the quality of these services. But by restricting supply, the bar also allows lawyers to raise their prices above what the prevalent market price for legal services would be in the absence of the licensure regime, with the effect of facilitating rents for those admitted to practice law.

In setting admissions standards to the bar, lawyers might be tempted to take into account (perhaps subconsciously) their financial self-interest in restricting the supply of lawyers, thus increasing their own salaries in addition to pursuing the more benign goal

---

[30] *Id.* at 213.

[31] *Id.*

[32] Gary Becker, *Comment*, 19 J.L. & ECON. 245, 246 (1976). To be clear, Becker is not addressing the normative merit of the redistributive policy, but only the extent to which the choice among available policies generating a wealth transfer affects the size of the resulting deadweight loss.

of protecting consumers against incompetent lawyers. This temptation is especially strong given that the bar is a self-regulatory regime, meaning that members of the bar, working through their state supreme courts, set the standards for the entry of new lawyers into the profession.[33]

This unusual, non-legislative process adds to the difficulties of consumers organizing to oppose consumer welfare-reducing rules adopted by the bar.[34] A 2011 study of the impact of lawyer licensing in the U.S. estimated that the licensing of lawyers raised the salaries of entry-level lawyers by an estimated $10,000–$23,000, and that higher prices for lawyers' services, and the resulting reduction in access to lawyers' services, had the overall effect of reducing consumer welfare by approximately $800 million.[35] Moreover, it appears that the difficulty of passing the bar exam is set not to guarantee a certain minimum level of competency to practice law, as would be consistent with the public interest theory of the bar. Instead, the bar failure rate generally correlates with the number of test takers, suggesting that the exam is more difficult to pass as the number of applicants to the bar rises, regardless of the applicants' merits.[36] A cynical view might suggest that while law students lament the need to study for and pass the bar exam, it is lawyers themselves, rather than prospective clients, who most benefit from the licensure regime.

The supply restriction might also have distributional consequences. For instance, to the extent that the bar requirement is set higher than necessary to protect the public, this might disproportionately burden minority lawyers seeking admission to the bar.[37] Although the licensure regime certainly benefits consumers of legal services by ensuring a higher degree of professionalism, greater accountability, and more uniform standards, it also undoubtedly provides financial benefits to lawyers through reduced competition and correspondingly higher fees.

The net result might also be to price legal services above what some persons in need might be able to afford.[38] One indication of the resulting social welfare loss is the growing market for services that lawyers traditionally provided through alternative and lower cost means. Some such services do not even require the assistance of any professional, for example computer software that makes it easier for consumers to write a will or to file for bankruptcy.

---

[33] James C. Cooper, Paul A. Pautler & Todd J. Zywicki, *Theory and Practice of Competition Advocacy at the FTC*, 72 ANTITRUST L.J. 1091, 1101–02 (2005); *see also* Einer R. Elhauge, *The Scope of Antitrust Process*, 104 HARV. L. REV. 667 (1991).

[34] *See* Cooper, Pautler & Zywicki, *supra* note 33, at 1101–02.

[35] *See* Mario Pagliero, *What Is the Objective of Professional Licensing? Evidence from the US Market for Lawyers*, 29 INT'L J. INDUS. ORG. 473 (2011).

[36] Mario Pagliero, *The Impact of Potential Labor Supply on Licensing Exam Difficulty in the US Market for Lawyers*, 48 BRIT. J. INDUS. REL. 726 (2010).

[37] George B. Shepherd, *No African-American Lawyers Allowed: The Inefficient Racism of the ABA's Accreditation of Law Schools*, 53 J. LEGAL EDUC. 103 (2003).

[38] Even within the regulated legal profession there is substantial variety in the quality of lawyers and of fee arrangements and rates. Lawyers who charge high rates for high-expertise services today likely would be unaffected by open entry, as the primary source of their pricing power is their unique expertise. Lower-rate lawyers providing less-sophisticated services, however, likely would see greater competition and lower wages.

As a result of the licensure regime, lawyers need not fear entry of unlicensed lawyers undercutting their prices. Not surprisingly, however, lawyers might well be motivated to lobby against the provision of services by unlicensed individuals that at one time required, but are now exempt from, provision by licensed practitioners of law.[39] In addition, through various regulations prohibiting the *Unauthorized Practice of Law*, governments promise to prosecute and punish those who provide legal services without being properly licensed.

The practice of law can be analogized to a *regulated monopoly* in which lawyers earn economic rents for their services. As shown in the discussion that follows, economic theory predicts that at least some of these rents should be dissipated. What are some of the ways in which the economic rents of the practice of law are dissipated? Why does law school in the United States take three years to complete and cost so much?

B. Steel Tariffs and Rent Seeking Revisited: The Elusive Welfare Loss Triangle

In light of the preceding analysis, reconsider the steel tariffs. Assume that a protectionist tariff will benefit the steel industry by a total of $10 million. Further assume that there is only one manufacturer of steel or a sufficiently low number that the producers are able to coordinate outputs to affect price. In theory, the steel industry would be willing to pay up to $10 million in campaign contributions and other forms of lobbying expenditures to have the steel tariff enacted. If no other costs were involved, including most notably the opportunity cost of alternative uses of firm assets, the steel industry would be willing to pay as much as $9,999,999 to secure the resulting $1 quasi-rent, or profit above normal returns.

With some simplifying assumptions, we can now illustrate not only the potential burdens that the tariffs impose on intermediate producers and ultimate consumers of steel products, but also explain why the pressure in favor of the tariff is likely stronger and more persistent than pressure in opposition.[40] Consider the tariff from the perspective of the myriad purchasers of steel. These include intermediate purchasers who use steel as inputs in production of direct consumer products or as indirect inputs into other production processes and who under certain conditions can pass at least some of the costs on to consumers who purchase their products. While it is not necessary to set out numbers, we can explain the essential intuition that the tariff imposes considerable costs

---

[39] *See* Cooper, Pautler & Zywicki, *supra* note 33, at 1101–02. For instance, the bars in some states have attempted to expand the definition of the *practice of law* to apply to many services that can be competently performed by non-lawyers, such as title companies, at much lower cost. Requiring lawyers to perform these ministerial services is estimated to add several hundred dollars to the price of a home closing with no discernible benefit to consumers. *See* Letter from R. Hewitt Pate, Acting Ass't Att'y Gen. et al., to the Standing Comm. on the Unauthorized Prac. of Law, St. Bar of Ga. (Mar. 20, 2003), https://www.ftc.gov/sites/default/files/documents/advocacy_documents/ftc-and-department-justice-comment-georgia-state-bar-standing-committee-unlicensed-practice-law/v030007.pdf (opinion letter from the FTC and the Department of Justice addressing the "performance of certain real estate closing-related activities by nonlawyers.").

[40] In a later discussion of the Wilson-Hayes matrix, we will place this analysis in the larger context of legislation that variously benefits or burdens broad to narrow constituencies. *See infra* note 100 and accompanying text.

overall, perhaps greater costs than gains, without generating sufficient opposition to prevent its enactment.

Numerous industries use steel as one of the factors of production, including construction, and manufacturers of automobiles and industrial machines.[41] Each producer has varying degrees of market power based, for example, upon product differentiation, brand recognition, and goodwill. In general, market power does not arise as a consequence of some form of industry monopoly, but rather as a result of some combination of these other factors. For example, purchasers are not indifferent between which brands of cars or appliances they buy, or even which they buy within a specific price range. Some consumers strongly prefer Toyota, whereas others strongly prefer Honda. And within any given brand, some strongly prefer sedans, sports cars, minivans, SUVs, or hybrids in any of these categories. Although consumers hold strong preferences and will pay more for their favored products, few, if any, consumers are entirely unconcerned about price. Despite brand loyalty, a consumer who generally prefers a Toyota Camry might consider a Honda Accord, or vice versa, if the price or features resulting from a particular promotion are substantially more attractive.

Consumer products typically are not fungible. Depending upon a producer's degree of market power, it will be more or less able to pass on increased costs to end consumers through higher prices. If we assume that steel is not a good that admits of ready substitutes as a factor of production (at least in the short run), then the demand for steel is relatively inelastic. This means that intermediate purchasers will absorb, at least as an initial matter, most of the burdens of the tariffs through costs that the producers of steel pass on to them: in this example, approximately $10 million. In turn, they will tack part of that additional cost onto their own products in the form of higher prices. How much they will successfully pass on, versus how much they will absorb in the form of lost profits, is a function of their relative market power over the goods they produce and sell. While *incidence analysis*, which studies the ability of various industries to pass on costs, would be required to determine where the ultimate burdens of the tariffs fall, our immediate purpose is instead to evaluate the likely impact of interest groups on the creation of the steel tariff. To simplify, assume that the intermediate producers each year are able to pass on most, or all, of the additional costs to the hundreds of thousands of purchasers of products in which steel is a major factor of production.

If there are 100,000 such purchases in a given year, which is likely a very low estimate, then the average added cost per consumer is approximately $100. If the costs are passed on over several years, the figure will be substantially lower. And, of course, to the extent that the producers themselves bear part of the cost through lost profits, the cost to consumers is further reduced. Prices fluctuate based upon numerous factors, and few

---

[41] In a 2000 study, it was estimated that there were approximately 193,000 steel-using firms in the United States, of which about 98% were small businesses with fewer than 500 employees. Read, *supra* note 2, at 1131. Recent surveys estimate the number of persons employed by U.S. manufacturers that use steel as an input at 6.5 million, in addition to an estimated 6.8 million workers in the U.S. construction industry, which accounts for 42% of domestic steel consumption. Daniel R. Pearson, *If Trump Wins on Steel, US Manufacturers Lose*, CNN (Aug. 2, 2017, 8:20 AM), http://www.cnn.com/2017/08/02/opinions/steel-trump-higher-prices-opinion-pearson/index.html (citing BUREAU LAB. STAT., ECONOMIC NEWS RELEASE: EMPLOYEES ON NONFARM PAYROLLS BY INDUSTRY SECTOR AND SELECTED INDUSTRY DETAIL (2017), https://www.bls.gov/news.release/empsit.t17.htm).

consumers will focus on the precise cost of each factor when making a major purchasing decision. But for simplicity, let us assume that consumers do focus on the precise cost or that lost information is freely available, perhaps on the invoice.

Consider whether from the perspective of 100,000 purchasers of steel products *each year*, it is rational to invest in opposing the steel tariff. One might imagine that as, with the producers, it is rational for each consumer to invest up to the full value of the passed-on cost, here $100, in opposing the tariff. And yet, consumers face additional obstacles to effective lobbying. A core insight from interest group theory is that when the size of the affected group is large and diffuse, it is unlikely that such opposition will effectively mobilize, thereby making it a challenge to recoup the value of the forgone welfare loss triangle that results from such tariffs.[42]

C. Free Riding and the Logic of Collective Action

In *The Logic of Collective Action*, public choice theorist Mancur Olson argued that when groups are small and well organized, as appears to be the case with domestic steel producers, they are well positioned to lobby in favor of beneficial legislative procurements.[43] By contrast, when groups are large and diffuse, as is the case with the consumers of products for which steel is a major factor of production, they are poorly positioned to lobby for or against such procurements.

While numerous problems can inhibit effective lobbying, the most important for our immediate purposes returns us to the phenomenon of *free riding*.[44] Each individual consumer will rationally decline to invest in opposition to the extent that successful lobbying efforts benefit consumers of such products generally. Each person or firm hopes that other similarly situated consumers will lobby in his or her place. Of course, the incentive to free ride is general, and so it is rational for the group as a whole to decline to make the necessary investment in opposition to the procurement of the tariff. This is so even though the aggregate benefit of the lobbying might well exceed even the financial benefits the tariff affords the steel industry.

1. *Information Costs, Rational Ignorance, and the Timing of Payoffs*

The preceding analysis assumes that consumers freely obtain information about particular factors of production for the goods they purchase. That assumption is certainly ambitious. Information is costly. Complex consumer goods have a sufficiently large number of inputs that it would be impractical for most consumers to educate themselves

---

[42] As this book goes to press, the Trump administration is also considering imposing steel import tariffs. *See* Joe Deaux, *Trump Still Determined to Impose Steel Tariffs, Says Nucor CEO*, Bloomberg (Sept. 29, 2017), https://www.bloomberg.com/news/articles/2017-09-29/trump-still-determined-to-impose-steel-tariffs-says-nucor-ceo; Mark O'Hara, *Steel Tariffs Might Be on President Trump's Radar*, Mkt. Realist (Oct. 5, 2017, 9:53 AM), http://marketrealist.com/2017/10/steel-tariffs-might-president-trumps-radar/. Peter Baker & Ana Swanson, *Trump Authorizes Tariffs, Defying Allies at Home and Abroad*, N.Y. TIMES (Mar. 8, 2018), https://www.nytimes.com/2018/03/08/us/politics/trump-tariff-announcement.html.

[43] *See* OLSON, *supra* note 28, at 53–65.

[44] *See supra* Chapter 1.

concerning the precise costs of any individual factor, such as the price of steel, and how that cost affects the overall price. Economists have dubbed this problem *rational ignorance*.[45] Given the cost of acquiring information, the low likelihood that the information could be used productively, and the obvious difficulties of free riding, relatively few consumers will rationally invest in researching regulatory processes that benefit specific industries at their expense. Consider the extent to which the combination of rational ignorance and free riding helps to explain the steel tariffs.

The prior discussion assumed that both the benefits to the steel producers and the cost to affected consumers was borne at a single time, or within a single year. That is almost certainly not the case. The steel producers did not immediately realize the full $10 million estimated value of the tariffs, and consumers did not bear the entire burden at one time, or even within a single year. Instead, the benefits to the producers and the costs to consumers were spread over several years, and most likely even decades, in the form of more highly priced goods and services.[46]

The same is true for virtually all legislatively conferred rents, including those associated with professional attorney licensure. In each case, the value of the barrier to competition (from foreign producers in the case of steel and from unlicensed practitioners in the case of attorneys) is spread over a sufficiently long period that the burden such a regime poses for any individual consumer is substantially further reduced. For end consumers, the effect, predictably, is to exacerbate both the free rider and rational ignorance problems.

More recently, theorists have debated whether rational ignorance produces random or systemic effects in inhibiting such potentially welfare-enhancing policies as free trade. In *The Myth of Democratic Failure*, Donald Wittman argues that although voters are likely to be rationally ignorant respecting such policies, this alone should not skew political outcomes if voter errors are not systematically biased and thus are randomly distributed over policy options.[47] Economist Bryan Caplan instead claims that because voter preferences on such issues are subsidized through political processes as a result of the

---

[45] Rational ignorance means that individuals will decline to invest in obtaining information where the marginal costs of gathering that information exceed the expected marginal benefits. For a general discussion, see Morris P. Fiorina, *Voting Behavior*, *in* PERSPECTIVES ON PUBLIC CHOICE 391, 396 (Dennis C. Mueller ed., 1997) (citing ANTHONY DOWNS, AN ECONOMIC THEORY OF DEMOCRACY 238–59 (1957)). *See also* JAMES M. BUCHANAN, PUBLIC FINANCE IN DEMOCRATIC PROCESSES: FISCAL INSTITUTIONS AND INDIVIDUAL CHOICE 7–9 (1967).

[46] This analysis, however, would not hold for a firm seeking to acquire a company that benefits from a tariff. *See* PAUL A. SAMUELSON & WILLIAM D. NORDHAUS, ECONOMICS 700–02 (16th ed. 1998) (explaining effect of a tariff). For the firm seeking to be acquired, the present value is a function of the additional predicted income stream, discounted to present value, associated with the tariff. *Id.* at 252–54 (explaining general formula for present value). As a result, the steel tariffs represent a one-time capital gain to the acquired firm, but no gain to the acquiring firm. *See* RICHARD A. BREALEY & STEWART C. MYERS, PRINCIPLES OF CORPORATE FINANCE 41–43 (6th ed. 2000) (defining an asset that pays a fixed sum for a specified time as an annuity and describing its valuation).

[47] DONALD A. WITTMAN, THE MYTH OF DEMOCRATIC FAILURE: WHY POLITICAL INSTITUTIONS ARE EFFICIENT (1995).

forced-rider problem, their ability to indulge welfare-reducing policy preferences might systematically and adversely skew public policy over a range of issues.[48]

2. *Group Size Revisited*

The effects described above might well be different for small and organized groups. An affected interest group will have considerable motivation to factor in the potential financial benefit of a conferred quasi-rent. While this requires such groups to calculate the *discounted present value* of the expected stream of economic benefits to be generated over the life of the regulation in question, this is essential to assessing the potential value of the proposed regulation and to evaluating how much it is worth investing in lobbying. The interest group will have to discount the stream of benefits in light of the following: (1) the time-value of money ($1 million ten years from now is worth far less today than $1 million next year), and (2) the probability that the law might be repealed in any given year, as actually occurred within less than two years in the case of the steel tariffs following a World Trade Organization (WTO) ruling.[49] Whatever the discount times probability yields, it remains rational for the benefiting group to invest up to that amount as a means of securing the present value of the stream of rents. This calculation informs cost-effective, or rational, rent-seeking activity.

3. *Implications for Government Policy*

Olson's insight, that small and well-organized groups are well positioned to lobby for beneficial legislation, also helps to explain how rent-seeking activity generally occurs. Olson's theory predicts that interest group activity typically disproportionately affects the details of the legislative and regulatory processes, rather than the structure of general rules.

For example, consider the structure of the United States income tax code. Olson's focus on the effectiveness of narrow groups seeking concentrated benefits and imposing dispersed costs suggests that instead of lobbying for system-wide changes to rules, such as lower marginal personal tax rates or corporate tax rates, particular firms or industries will tend to lobby for targeted tax benefits or loopholes that confer firm- or industry-specific benefits. Targeted loopholes typically will be less transparent to the general public and less expensive to provide, thereby reducing pressure to offset the lost tax revenues with higher taxes elsewhere, or by cutting expenses or funding through deficit spending. Lobbying for narrow tax preferences also tends to make policing free riding easier, thereby overcoming collective action problems by concentrating the benefits of the program while dispersing the costs. Although each targeted tax benefit is less expensive than a broader tax overhaul benefit, Olson's argument suggests that this dynamic will be replicated across the tax code, resulting in myriad preferential tax loopholes, increased complexity, and increased efforts by private actors to direct their activity toward tax-preferred economic activity instead of those activities most likely to increase social welfare.

---

[48] BRYAN CAPLAN, THE MYTH OF THE RATIONAL VOTER: WHY DEMOCRACIES CHOOSE BAD POLICIES (2007). A *forced rider problem* arises when a person "value[s] the pecuniary and non-pecuniary benefits of belonging to an organization which enforces membership at less than the pecuniary and non-pecuniary costs." *Forced Rider*, MIT DICTIONARY OF MODERN ECONOMICS (D.W. Pearce ed., 4th ed. 1981).

[49] *See supra* note 2, and cites therein.

Does the major tax overhaul during the first year of the Donald Trump administration[50] reinforce or undermine the preceding analysis? Consider two possibilities. First, the ambitious nature of the overhaul affecting personal and corporate rates, including reliance on the latter to attract new business, undermines Olson's theory by demonstrating the capacity for major tax reform. Or second, the rarity of such massive reform, with the last major tax overhaul taking place during the Ronald Reagan administration,[51] reinforces the Olson model by demonstrating that this overhaul, with Republicans controlling both Houses of Congress and the Presidency, arose as the product of a very specific combination of political factors, including taking place in advance of an interim election that might alter the composition of the House, thereby thwarting a future opportunity for similarly broad reform. Which account do you find more persuasive, and why?

D. The Geometry of Rent Seeking[52]

To understand the economic significance of rent-seeking legislation, it will be helpful to reconsider the market power paradigm[53]:

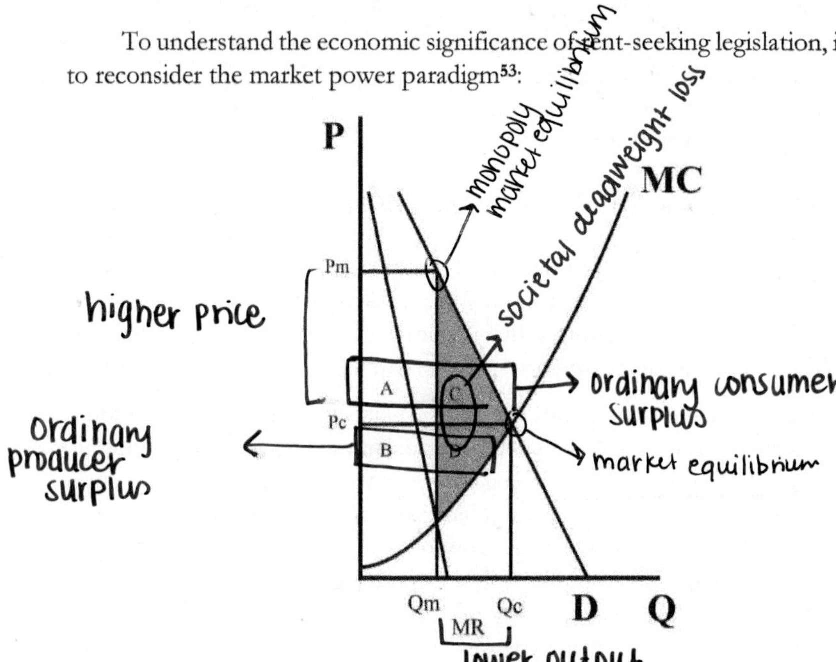

Figure 11:2

The shaded area in Figure 11:2, depicting the forgone consumer and producer surpluses resulting from the monopolistic pricing strategy, represents a societal deadweight loss. If the firm produced to the point where the marginal cost curve intersects the demand curve, societal welfare would improve as more of the relevant goods are produced and sold at a lower price. The monopoly rents, A–D, that arise in noncompetitive markets provide industries with incentives to attempt to secure market power through the political process.

[50] Tax Cut and Jobs Act of 2017, Pub. L. No. 115–97, 131 Stat. 2054.

[51] Tax Reform Act of 1986, Pub. L. No. 99–514, 100 Stat. 2085.

[52] Portions of the discussion to follow are based upon STEARNS, *supra* note 26, at 120–25.

[53] *See supra* Chapter 2.

As Professor Charles K. Rowley has observed: "[D]uring the 1960s . . . economists [tended to] dismiss the welfare cost of tariffs and monopolies as unimportant in view of the minute values associated with the Marshallian deadweight loss triangles of lost consumers' surplus associated with their existence."[54]

In a famous paper, *The Welfare Costs of Tariffs, Monopolies, and Theft*,[55] Gordon Tullock challenged the intuition that deadweight loss triangles imposed a relatively small cost on society by demonstrating additional costs to monopoly power, and in particular monopoly power created and protected through the process of regulation.[56] In what Rowley describes as "arguably [The Virginia School's] single most important contribution to public choice,"[57] Tullock posited that the deadweight loss represented by forgone consumer and producer surpluses does not represent the full costs of rent seeking. Instead, he argued that the full value of monopoly rents might be dissipated in the very process of rent seeking.[58] Given the value of monopoly power, we would expect interest groups, behaving rationally, to expend significant resources in attempting to secure legislatively conferred rents. The resulting costs constitute a further deadweight societal loss that might well offset the value to the acquiring firm of the resulting monopoly rents.

Figure 11:2 helps to illustrate Tullock's essential insight.[59] As previously noted, the areas $C+D$ (forgone consumer and producer surplus respectively) are the deadweight cost of monopoly, or *Harberger Triangles*. The area A was recognized as a simple wealth transfer from consumers to producers that takes the form of a monopoly rent. Tullock observes, however, that producers would be willing to expend the full value of the monopoly rent, here depicted as the rectangular area A minus the forgone producer surplus D, to secure its value. The process of expending up to the value of the economic rents in pursuit of

---

[54] Charles K. Rowley, *Introduction*, *in* 1 PUBLIC CHOICE THEORY: HOMO ECONOMICUS IN THE MARKET PLACE, at xxiv (Charles K. Rowley ed., 1993).

[55] Gordon Tullock, *The Welfare Costs of Tariffs, Monopolies, and Theft*, 5 W. ECON. J. 224 (1967).

[56] *Id.* at 226, 232; *see also* Richard A. Posner, *The Social Costs of Monopoly and Regulation*, 83 J. POL. ECON. 807 (1975).

[57] Rowley, *supra* note 54, at xxiv. The Virginia School of Political Economy emerged in the mid-twentieth century at the University of Virginia and developed at other Virginia universities, such as Virginia Polytechnic Institute and George Mason University. The Virginia School focused on public choice theory and included the work of scholars such as, James M. Buchanan, Gordon Tullock, and Dennis C. Mueller. *See* Roger D. Congleton, *Buchanan and the Virginia School*, *in* METHOD AND MORALS IN CONSTITUTIONAL ECONOMICS 23 (Geoffrey Brennan et al. eds., 2013); *About the Center*, THE CENTER FOR STUDY OF PUBLIC CHOICE, GEORGE MASON UNIVERSITY, https://publicchoice.gmu.edu/about (last visited Apr. 3, 2018).

[58] Tullock, *supra* note 55, at 226, 232.

[59] In Tullock's original formulation, he presented a flat marginal cost curve, which did not account for area B plus D, representing forgone Ricardian competitive rents. The presentation in the text presents the analysis based upon an upward sloping marginal cost curve to render the analysis consistent with the presentation in Chapter 2. For an individual monopolist, competitive rents are dissipated in the acquisition of factors earning such rents, rendering the marginal cost curve flat. By contrast, with an industry seeking to cartelize, some member firms will have previously earned competitive rents due to special personal skills or other superior inputs, such as land. Controlling output to raise price potentially produces winners and losers, and the costs of cartelizing might exceed the benefits for some firms sacrificing competitive rents. Although the marginal firm earns no such rents, the aggregate firms gain the benefit of monopolistic profit less competitive rents, which, as previously shown, equals A minus D. =

acquiring that rent is known as *rent dissipation*.[60] The full social cost of rent seeking can be estimated as the sum of the Harberger deadweight loss triangles (areas *C+D*) *plus* the so-called Tullock amount (area *A–D*), or areas *A+C*. In equilibrium the analysis suggests that all rents will be fully dissipated. Generating accurate estimates of the social welfare losses that result from rent-seeking activity has proven elusive, but, as Tullock maintains, these losses will be substantial when the costs of rent dissipation are included.[61]

Rent-seeking expenditures reduce social wealth in a number of ways, including diverting resources from productive activity toward lobbying for purely redistributive transfers.[62] These costs include the efforts and expenditures of those seeking monopoly rents, such as hired lobbyists and managerial time, all of which could instead be deployed to productive economic activities. Public choice theorists posit that as rent seeking becomes more lucrative, politicians and regulators will increase their efforts to secure positions that provide them with the power to confer rents. Just as firms will rationally invest in rent seeking, so too legislators will invest time and other resources in securing positions that empower them to respond to rent-seeking efforts. Ambitious legislators will tend to concentrate on those regulatory areas more likely to be the subject of rent-seeking activity, such as appropriations committees, as compared with committees that, although equally important from a public interest perspective, lack such opportunities. The incentive to rent seek distorts activities of other economic actors by diverting attention away from socially productive activities. Consider whether top legal talent is more fruitfully deployed, for example, in drafting commercial contracts or other activities that increase social wealth or in facilitating or directly lobbying on behalf of industry. Alternatively, might lobbyists be analogized to sales persons, who, by explaining beneficial features of proposed legislation, thereby add value?

Tullock's observation that parties engaged in rent seeking will dissipate much of the potential gains in the process of pursuing those rents generates a corollary: rent-seeking expenditures are simply lost to the economy. Eliminating a tariff or removing a barrier to entry can increase social welfare, but it cannot restore the loss associated with the dissipated rent. At the same time, the value to the rent-seeking party will be embedded in the value of the underlying asset itself. Thus, eliminating the preferential policy will also generate major losses to the parties that have previously invested in rent seeking, meaning that eliminating policies that generate rents holds substantial redistributional consequences. The efficiency gains from reducing deadweight loss typically will be broadly

---

[60] Note that the phenomenon is not limited to political rent seeking. For instance, the acquisition of a patent right provides the patent holder with a monopoly rent during the enforcement period. The opportunity to collect these monopoly rents will tend to encourage overinvestment in research designed to produce a patented product relative to one that is not patentable. As an example, it is often observed that there might be a "patent race" to invent a new drug before a competitor does so, leading to heightened investment in attempting to be the first to patent the drug and thereby win the prize of a legal monopoly for the period of the patent. *See* Neil C. Thompson & Jeffrey M. Kuhn, Does Winning a Patent Race Lead to More Follow-On Innovation? (Jan. 2017), http://www.law.northwestern.edu/research-faculty/searlecenter/events/innovation/documents/Thompson_Kuhn_Patent_Race.pdf.

[61] *See* Robert D. Tollison, *Rent Seeking*, *in* PERSPECTIVES ON PUBLIC CHOICE, *supra* note 45, at 506, 512–14 (summarizing studies).

[62] *See* James M. Buchanan, *Rent Seeking and Profit Seeking*, *in* TOWARD A THEORY OF THE RENT-SEEKING SOCIETY 3 (James M. Buchanan, Robert D. Tollison & Gordon Tullock eds., 1980).

dispersed, whereas those who suffer large wealth losses will tend to be highly concentrated, making it very difficult politically to lobby for deregulation.

As a result of this asymmetry, Tullock identified what he called the *transitional gains trap*.[63] Consider taxi medallions. To operate a taxi in New York City, the driver or taxi owner must own a taxi medallion. In 1937, New York City initially provided for 16,000 taxi medallions for taxi operators, a figure that dwindled to under 12,000 a few years later, where it remained constant for many years. By 2013 the number of medallions had only risen to 13,437.[64] The result was that in 2013 the price for a single taxi medallion—and thus the oligopoly right to operate a taxi—had surged as high as $1.3 million.[65] In 2017, there were only 13,587 medallions, even though the population of New York City (and demand for taxi rides) had grown multifold during that period.[66]

Within a few years of medallions being sold for $1.3 million, however, ride-sharing services Uber and Lyft entered the New York City market. As of 2017, it was estimated that there were over 50,000 Uber and Lyft drivers in the city.[67] The result was that within a few years the price of a taxi medallion plummeted to as low as $170,000 for a medallion put up for sale on October 6, 2017.[68] Although the introduction of ride-sharing services meant substantially greater convenience and lower prices for consumers, it resulted in a huge capital loss to the owners of taxi medallions, who paid as much as $1.3 million for a taxi medallion that was worth merely one-eighth of that a few years later.

As discussed above, licensed lawyers in the United States earn economic rents as a result of rules that protect them from competition, increasing their lifetime earnings. How might this be reflected in the cost and duration of legal education? Would you expect prospective lawyers to capture all of those gains?

A more general example within the United States involves the mortgage interest tax deduction within the Internal Revenue Code. Homeowners can deduct from their federal income taxes interest payments made on primary residential mortgages.[69] The policy is designed to promote home ownership, yet the home ownership rate in the United States is similar to that in many other countries, most of which do not have the mortgage interest

---

[63] Gordon Tullock, *The Transitional Gains Trap*, 6 BELL J. ECON. 671 (1975).

[64] NEW YORK CITY TAXI & LIMOUSINE COMMISSION 2013 ANNUAL REPORT 8 (2013), http://www.nyc.gov/html/tlc/downloads/pdf/annual_report_2013.pdf.

[65] *See* Danielle Fufaro, *Taxi Medallions Reach Lowest Value of 21st Century*, N.Y. POST (Apr. 5, 2017), http://nypost.com/2017/04/05/taxi-medallions-reach-lowest-value-of-21st-century/.

[66] *Id.* By July 2017 several owners were offering to sell for as little as $220,000. *See* NYCITYCAB.COM, https://nycitycab.com/Business/TaxiMedallionList.aspx (last visited Oct. 23, 2017) (listing medallions for sale). Moreover, during that month the overwhelming number of transfers of taxi medallions were via foreclosure, as owners who had financed their acquisition of a high-priced taxi medallion defaulted on their loans when the underlying medallions plummeted in value. *See* NYC TAXI AND LIMOUSINE COMMISSION, MEDALLION TRANSFERS, http://www.nyc.gov/html/tlc/html/about/medallion_transfers.shtml (last visited Oct. 23, 2017) (listing medallion transfers by month and year).

[67] Fufaro, *supra* note 65.

[68] *See* NYCITYCAB.COM, *supra* note 66 (listing medallions for sale).

[69] I.R.C. § 163 (Westlaw through Pub. L. No. 115–140). *See also* Jonathan Gruber, Amalie Jensen & Henrik Kleven, *Do People Respond to the Mortgage Interest Deduction? Evidence from Denmark* (NBER Working Paper No. 23600, 2017), http://www.nber.org/papers/w23600 (finding that the mortgage interest deduction has no effect on rates of homeownership).

tax deduction. That is because the mortgage interest deduction subsidizes home purchases relative to renting, thereby shifting the demand curve for home purchases. This increase in demand increases the purchase price of homes. Thus, the benefit of the mortgage interest deduction is capitalized into the price of home sales. The overall equilibrium result of the combined effects of the subsidy provided by the mortgage interest deduction, and the higher home prices that result, is an empirical question. As noted above, studies find that the equilibrium result raises home prices on average but without changing the level of home ownership as compared with countries lacking the mortgage interest deduction. Does interest group theory help to explain this result? What would happen to the average price of a home in the United States if this deduction were eliminated or reduced, as recently occurred?[70] What other effects might the presence of the mortgage interest deduction have for the economy?[71] Would you advise eliminating this deduction altogether? Why or why not?

1. *The Rise and Decline of Nations*[72]

In his influential book, *The Rise and Decline of Nations*,[73] Mancur Olson took the preceding analysis a significant step further. Olson linked the tendency of interest group influence—or rent seeking—over time to the decline in the rate of economic growth in Western democracies after World War II.[74] Olson demonstrated that those countries whose economic and political infrastructures were harmed most severely during World War II—Germany, Italy, and Japan—sustained the strongest economic development over the next twenty-five years, while those whose economic and political infrastructures remained intact—Australia, New Zealand, the United Kingdom, and the United States—performed most poorly during the same period.

Although it might appear counterintuitive that the military victors in World War II would become the subsequent economic losers and vice versa, the result makes more sense when we reconsider it from the combined perspectives of rent seeking and opportunity costs. At any given time, there are two different ways for a producer to earn money in an economy. They can either produce new goods in the competitive market, or they can engage in rent seeking. When a nation's political infrastructure is gutted, rational

[70] The Tax Cut and Jobs Act of 2017 reduced the limits on deductibility of mortgage interest for married couples from $1,000,000 to $750,000, and it generally eliminated the deductibility of home equity loans. *See* Tax Cut and Jobs Act of 2017, Pub. L. No. 115–97, § 11043, 131 Stat. 2054, 2086–87 (codified at I.R.C. § 163); Bill Bischoff, *What the New Tax Law Will Do to Your Mortgage Tax Deduction*, MARKETWATCH (Feb. 8, 2018), https://www.marketwatch.com/story/what-the-new-tax-law-will-do-to-your-mortgage-interest-deduction-2018-02-09. *See also* Benjamin H. Harris, *What Changes in the Mortgage Interest Deduction Would Mean for Home Prices*, TAXVOX BLOG: URB. INST. & BROOKINGS INST. TAX POL'Y CTR. (June 5, 2013), http://www.taxpolicycenter.org/taxvox/what-changes-mortgage-deduction-would-mean-home-prices (estimating that elimination of the deductions for mortgage interest payments and property taxes would reduce home prices by 11.8% on average for the twenty-three cities studied).

[71] *See* Gruber et al., *supra* note 69 (finding that the mortgage interest deduction induces consumers to buy larger and more expensive homes and incur higher levels of debt than they otherwise would).

[72] Portions of the discussion that follows are based upon STEARNS, *supra* note 26, at 121–23.

[73] MANCUR OLSON, THE RISE AND DECLINE OF NATIONS: ECONOMIC GROWTH, STAGFLATION, AND SOCIAL RIGIDITIES (1982).

[74] *Id.* at 74–117.

firms will make a different calculation concerning the extent to which they deploy resources across these two activities. Not only are rent-seeking opportunities likely to be scarcer in a regime with a compromised political infrastructure, but also the ability of the government to issue the necessary commitments (or bonds) that confer regulatory protections that will remain in place is diminished. Conversely, politically conferred rents are likely to be more durable in more stable regimes. And because the present discounted value of those rents will be higher as a result of more durable bonds, rational firms will be increasingly willing to make the necessary investments to secure those rents in stable regimes, which have well-established political infrastructures.

Olson's analysis suggests that substantially reducing rent-seeking behavior requires radical, rather than narrow or incremental, institutional reform. Olson demonstrated that rent seeking not only imposes significant economic costs that can pull the production possibility frontier inward,[75] but also, it can inhibit ordinary economic growth that otherwise would push the frontier outward over time.[76] In light of the significant societal loss that rent seeking represents, public choice theorist Dennis Mueller has posited: "The task of reform is to design institutions that allow and encourage those forms of competition that create rents by creating additional consumer and citizen surpluses, and discourage competition designed to gain and retain existing rents."[77] Still others have posited that even if we can devise such institutional reforms, their adoption will simply relocate—but not eliminate—rent seeking. Thus, William H. Riker and Steven J. Brams explain:

> Of course, when vote trading is banished from the legislature, political compromise goes on someplace else politically antecedent to the legislature. Thus in state legislatures and city councils with disciplined parties, it is in the majority caucus or in the mind of the boss that the compromise takes place. In England, the Cabinet serves as one place of compromise and very probably something like vote trading goes on there. Since the Cabinet situation is unstructured in comparison with the Parliamentary situation, however, it is probably hard to identify the trades and compromises that do occur.[78]

Recall that the production possibility frontier, Figure 11.3, reproduced from Chapter 2,[79] represents the potential economic output for an individual, firm, or nation, as between two commodities.

An individual is capable of producing two forms of output, *a* and *b*, such that for each commodity the person experiences decreasing marginal productivity. Producing the first unit of *b* would require this person to forgo relatively little in her production of *a*, and producing each additional unit of *b* would require this person to forgo producing a somewhat larger quantity of *a*. Conversely, producing additional increments of *a* requires relinquishing larger and larger increments of *b*.

---

75 *See* Chapter 2.

76 *See* DENNIS C. MUELLER, PUBLIC CHOICE III 555 (2003).

77 DENNIS C. MUELLER, PUBLIC CHOICE II 245 (1989).

78 William H. Riker & Steven J. Brams, *The Paradox of Vote Trading*, 67 AM. POL. SCI. REV. 1235, 1238 (1973).

79 *See supra* Chapter 2.

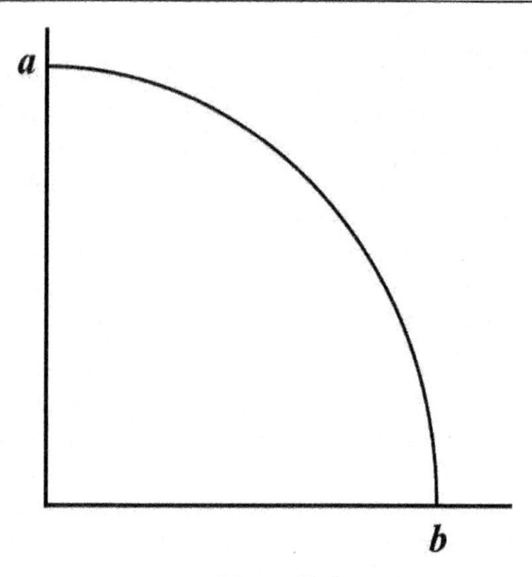

Figure 11:3

The production possibility frontier can be used not only to depict the production potential for an individual or firm, but also, on a larger scale, it can depict the maximal output of an industry, state, or nation. Industries maximize their economic output when they produce at the most highly valued point along their production possibility frontier. Olson's analysis of the post-World War II economies of the former Allied and Axis powers not only reflects diminished opportunities for rent seeking, but also, it potentially reflects more profitable private market opportunities in nations whose economic and political infrastructures had been destroyed. There was great pent-up postwar demand for new goods in those economies destroyed by the war and thus great economic opportunities for private sector development. By contrast, consider those nations that suffered less infrastructure damage. In the aftermath of a booming wartime economy, which succeeded in pulling the affected nations out of the Great Depression,[80] industries within those nations were likely already producing at or near their production possibility frontiers. If so, the potential profits that such industries were capable of generating from rent seeking were high, sometimes higher than, the potential profits such industries were capable of generating from the next best available investment activity. Mueller captures this insight as follows:

> To temper the resistance of [interest] groups to the losses they would experience by eliminating those programs that facilitate rent seeking, even greater gains must be offered. Perhaps this observation explains why it is sometimes politically easier to eliminate or reduce a large group of restrictions on trade than just a few. The deregulation movement in the United States [in the 1980s during the Reagan Administration appeared to have been successful] because it attacked regulations in many industries. To come fully to grips with

[80] J.R. Vernon, *World War II Fiscal Policies and the End of the Great Depression*, 54 J. ECON. HIST. 850, 850 (1994) ("What ended the Great Depression? In the traditional view, the answer is World War II, a conclusion that appears in the works of numerous economist and historians.").

the rent-seeking problem, one must think in terms of radical reforms; fundamental redefinitions of property rights.[81]

If Olson is correct, then his analysis would require weighing the benefit of societal and institutional stability against the cost of rent seeking. The calculus is especially daunting given that to the extent institutional reform is successful, meaning that it is a stable solution to prior rent-seeking activity, we might once again expect to see rent seeking rearing its ugly head.

Todd Zywicki has argued that Olson's thesis, which focuses historically on the "radical reforms" associated with the devastation following World War II, might not account for other opportunities for broad deregulatory agendas that also can spur sustained economic growth.[82] Zywicki notes that Olson's book was published in 1982, which corresponded with the beginning of the Reagan era. In this period, although the United States infrastructure was not under threat of decimation, Zywicki maintains that the broad deregulatory agenda had the effect of creating policies that helped set in motion almost two decades of nearly uninterrupted economic growth. Zywicki further maintains that for entrenched rent-seeking arrangements to remain sufficiently stable to resist such broad regulatory reforms, the rent-seeking beneficiaries must include not only affected interest groups, but also the political actors.[83]

More recently, for example, Zywicki observes that since the federal government bailed out American banks during the 2008 financial crisis, politicians and regulators have more frequently imposed pressure on banks to accomplish various political objectives, such as the Operation Choke Point initiative during the Obama Administration. Zywicki observes that some allege that in implementing this policy, the Department of Justice and federal banking regulators improperly pressured banks away from providing services to companies in certain legal but controversial industries, such as payday lenders and firearms dealers.[84] Similarly, Zywicki claims, the bailouts of General Motors and Chrysler resulted in mutual benefits to private companies and interest groups, including the United Auto Workers, and to politicians, who conveyed to their constituents the benefits of regulations that increased manufacturing of small, high-mileage cars.

Zywicki suggests that Olson's analysis might have been more robust historically than prospectively at the time he was writing. Zywicki further claims that these contemporary political bargains might prove durable and thus detrimental to long term economic growth

---

[81] MUELLER, *supra* note 77, at 245 (citing James M. Buchanan, *Reform in the Rent-Seeking Society*, *in* TOWARD A THEORY OF THE RENT-SEEKING SOCIETY, *supra* note 62, at 359).

[82] Todd Zywicki, *Rent-Seeking, Crony Capitalism, and the Crony Constitution*, 23 SUP. CT. ECON. REV. 77 (2015).

[83] *Id.* at 90.

[84] *See* Letter from Bob Goodlatte, Chairman House Judiciary Comm. et al., to Hon. Jeff Sessions, U.S. Att'y Gen. et al. (Aug. 10, 2017), https://judiciary.house.gov/wp-content/uploads/2017/08/081017-Choke-Point-Letter.pdf (requesting repudiation of Operation Choke Point, citing pressure placed on financial institutions to not provide service to industries, such as payday lenders and firearms dealers); Victoria Guida, *Justice Department to End Obama-era 'Operation Choke Point'*, POLITICO (Aug. 17, 2017, 10:41 PM), http://www.politico.com/story/2017/08/17/trump-reverses-obama-operation-chokepoint-241767; For details on the program, see STAFF OF H. COMM. ON OVERSIGHT & GOV'T REFORM, 113TH CONG., REP. ON THE DEPARTMENT OF JUSTICE'S "OPERATION CHOKE POINT": ILLEGALLY CHOKING OFF LEGITIMATE BUSINESS? (2014).

as a result of the emerging symbiotic relationship between politicians and the affected interest groups. Zywicki concludes that a more complete model must account for the role of politicians and regulators as active participants not only in the process of generating and distributing rents but also in obtaining reciprocal benefits that forge such ongoing relationships.

E. Rent Seeking in Equilibrium: The Case of Campaign Finance Reform

A corollary of Mancur Olson's analysis of rent seeking and economic growth following World War II suggests that, behaving rationally, economic actors will allocate resources until the marginal value of private market production and of rent-seeking expenditures are approximately equal. Thus, if the economic returns to rent seeking increase over time, public choice predicts that interest groups will invest increasingly greater resources pursuing rent-seeking activities.

Consider the important and controversial question of why campaign expenditures on political activity have historically risen over time. In a provocative article, John R. Lott, Jr.[85] posits "a simple explanation" that campaign expenditures are increasing because the government is getting bigger. The explanation is straightforward: "[T]he more transfers the government has to offer, the more resources people will spend to obtain them."[86] And "[a]s government has more favors to grant, the effort spent to obtain those favors should increase."[87] As the size of government grows, the government, by definition, will have greater ability to transfer wealth. Even public goods such as national defense and highway construction will have important private good elements susceptible to rent-seeking activity. In other words, if the government has the power to enact laws or regulations that can substantially benefit certain firms or industries (such as a narrowly tailored tax break or a congressional earmark), then there will be potential beneficiaries who will rationally invest in rent seeking in an effort to capture those benefits. Similarly, if the government has the power to enact laws or regulations that can impose substantial costs on particular firms (such as a tax increase or strict regulation), those firms will rationally invest in rent seeking to prevent the imposition of the cost. Controlling for other possible factors that might have increased the costs of campaigns during that time (such as increases in the costs of television advertising), Lott concludes that the near-180% increase in federal campaign spending and 136% per capita real expense increases for House and Senate races from 1976 through 1994 resulted primarily from the increased opportunities that the growing federal and state governments presented for rent seeking.

Lott concludes that the conventional approach of addressing increasing campaign expenditures by imposing spending or contribution caps is misguided. Although spending caps might reduce the direct monetary expenses of campaigns, they are not likely to alter the total social cost of political campaigns, and, ironically, such limits might even increase social costs by forcing them into less cost-effective forms, including in-kind contributions,

---

[85] John R. Lott, Jr., *A Simple Explanation for Why Campaign Expenditures Are Increasing: The Government Is Getting Bigger*, 43 J.L. & ECON. 359 (2000).

[86] *Id.* at 363.

[87] *Id.*

rather than direct payments to a candidate. The changed form of contribution, however, does not mean that the overall portion of societal wealth devoted to supporting campaigns has diminished.

Lott further observes that the forms that these contributions can take is nearly infinite and that the corresponding range of governmental transfers is quite broad. Lott states: "If the hypothesis presented here is correct, increased abilities to transfer wealth in any form (for example, regulations or expropriation of property) should lead to increased campaign expenditures."[88] Lott claims that his empirical results, which use government expenditures as a proxy for an increased ability to transfer wealth, support his hypothesis. Lott asserts, therefore, that the policy debate potentially misses the critical insight that the difficulties associated with excessive campaign spending cannot be solved by limiting campaign donations.[89] This would simply change the form of payments. Attempts to reduce campaign contributions focus primarily on the symptoms rather than the causes of growing campaign finance. For example the Bipartisan Campaign Reform Act of 2002, commonly referred to as the McCain-Feingold Campaign Finance Act, attempts to regulate the form, timing, and substance of political activity.[90]

Alternatively, consider the vast increase in campaign expenditures by corporate entities following the Supreme Court's controversial decision, *Citizens United v. Federal Election Comm'n*.[91] (We present an excerpt of *Citizens United* with analytical questions in Chapter 15.[92]) For now, suffice to say that the decision lifted a regulatory ban on direct spending by corporations, holding that such entities are First Amendment persons for purposes of such expression. The decision is widely credited with authorizing the creation of super PACs, and thus a dramatic corporate spending increase in political campaigns.[93] Does this suggest that the prior regime, which disallowed unlimited corporate campaign expenditures, had the opposite effect of holding back such spending? If Lott's thesis holds, because the decision in *Citizens United* did not spur an increase in the size of government or the availability of government largesse, should the outcome have mattered to the level of corporate campaign expenditures? Why or why not? Given the effect of *Citizens United* on corporate campaign spending, does this suggest that Lott's model is incomplete?

Consider also how this relates to the McCain-Feingold Campaign Finance Act,[94] after which several regulatory loopholes were identified. Among other problems, the

---

[88] *Id.* at 364.

[89] *Id.* at 362.

[90] Bipartisan Campaign Reform Act of 2002, Pub. L. No. 107–155, 116 Stat. 81 (codified as amended in scattered sections of 2 U.S.C.). The doctrinal history is complex, and others attribute the creation of super-PACs to the subsequent United States Court of Appeals decision, *SpeechNow.org v. Fed. Election Comm'n*, 599 F.3d 686 (D.C. Cir. 2010).

[91] 558 U.S. 310 (2010).

[92] *See infra* Chapter 15 (Applications).

[93] *See* R. SAM GARRETT, CONG. RESEARCH SERV., R42042, SUPER PACS IN FEDERAL ELECTIONS: OVERVIEW AND ISSUES FOR CONGRESS (2016). James A. Kahl, Citizens United, *Super PACs, and Corporate Spending on Political Campaigns: How Did We Get Here and Where Are We Going?*, 59 FED. LAW. 40 (2012).

[94] Bipartisan Campaign Reform Act of 2002, Pub L. No. 107–155, 116 Stat. 81.

loopholes facilitated the formation of private 527 groups.[95] These groups have been able to engage in political activity beyond the act's reach. If the loophole for 527 groups were closed, would that be likely to eliminate the amount of social resources expended on political campaigns? Why or why not? Is the history of the McCain-Feingold Act in tension with that of *Citizens United*? Why or why not?

F. Rent Extraction

Professor Fred McChesney has demonstrated that through the phenomenon of *rent extraction*, legislators can generate the equivalent of the social welfare loss associated with rent seeking even absent a specific effort by an interest group to direct resources toward securing legislatively produced rents. Assume that a protectionist licensing scheme is enacted that promises a stream of benefits over the next ten years at an expected value of $1 million per year. Further assume that six years after the law was passed, a member of Congress on the relevant committee that oversees this program announces that she is considering initiating proceedings to have the law repealed.

At this point, if the law remains effective, the interest group will receive four more years of economic rents at $1 million per year. How do you predict an interest group would respond to the proposed legislative action? Interest group theory suggests that behaving rationally, the interest group would be willing to invest up to the present discounted value of the $4 million income stream with the program in place to avoid its repeal. McChesney refers to this scheme as *rent extraction* or *rent extortion*, which he likens to a sort of political blackmail. The politician essentially coerces various forms of contributions or support in exchange for not affirmatively harming the interest group either by taking away an existing benefit or imposing a new cost.[96]

Alternatively, even if there is no quasi-private benefit to protect, the same legislator could approach industry leaders with the threat to impose a costly new regulation. For example, a member of Congress on the committee that oversees the Medicare Program could approach leading pharmaceutical makers proposing reimbursement caps that are substantially lower than those currently allowed under Medicare. The pharmaceutical industry might respond by offering various forms of political support in exchange for leaving the present higher reimbursement caps in place. In this analysis, it is even possible that the legislator could succeed in rent extraction even if she had no intention of imposing the lower reimbursement caps, provided that her threat appears credible to the pharmaceutical industry leaders.[97]

---

[95] The Congressional Research Service defines 527 groups as "groups registered with the Internal Revenue Service (IRS) as Section 527 political organizations that seemingly intend to influence federal elections in ways that may place them outside the [Federal Election Campaign Act] definition of a political committee. GARRETT, *supra* note 93, at 2 n.6. *See* 26 U.S.C. § 527 (2012).

[96] MCCHESNEY, *supra* note 24, at 124.

[97] *See id.* at 45–68 (presenting McChesney's empirical support). A politician's credibility will turn on her or his willingness to occasionally act upon such threats. It does not matter if the interest group already "paid" for the law at the outset, as those investments are sunk costs.

G. Bootleggers and Baptists

One insight that emerges from the foregoing analysis is that for interest groups and lobbyists to successfully work political processes, they cannot be entirely selective in choosing with whom to negotiate. The frequent observation that politics makes strange bedfellows has a theoretical analog in public choice. Consider Bruce Yandle's *Bootleggers and Baptists model* of regulation.[98] In Yandle's analysis, regulations can emerge out of the confluence of the narrow economic self-interest of groups working together with more public-spirited parties. Yandle offers the example of so-called Sunday Blue Laws which have long existed in many states (especially in the southern United States, but also in Massachusetts), forbidding the sale of alcoholic beverages on Sundays.

Yandle observes that two very different groups, indeed groups that one would not expect to associate with each other, might agree to offer strong support for such regulation. First, there were those who he refers to as the Baptists, morally motivated teetotalers who support these laws out of a sense of moral and religious conviction concerning the social benefits of temperance. Yandle observes, however, that there is a second group who might support these laws for less charitable or altruistic motives, the so-called Bootleggers, producers of illegal "moon-shine whiskey," who essentially had a monopoly on the sale of liquor one day a week. While one might have assumed that Baptists and Bootleggers are ideological opponents—as indeed they generally are—on this one issue the two groups share a strong common interest, albeit for opposing reasons.

Similarly, prior to its demise, the notorious Enron Corporation was a staunch supporter of the Kyoto Protocol, an international treaty aimed at reducing harmful emissions. Enron was heavily invested in alternative energy sources. Although one would expect Enron and various environmentalist groups typically to oppose one another on issues of environmental regulation and policy, the Kyoto Protocol benefited Enron because it raised the costs of using traditional fuels and thus increased the cost-effectiveness—and thus the demand for—the novel alternatives in which Enron was invested.[99]

III. TOWARD A GENERAL MODEL OF REGULATION

This chapter has laid the foundation for analogizing legislative and regulatory processes to a market in which interest groups demand legislation and politicians provide it. As a first approximation, that model is helpful even if it fails to capture the full variety of types of legislation that legislatures provide. That requires a more complex model that can identify the conditions under which the legislature is likely to provide various forms of legislation, including quasi-private goods or public goods, and also under which the legislature is unlikely to legislate in any degree of specificity and instead might elect to

---

[98] BRUCE YANDLE, THE POLITICAL LIMITS OF ENVIRONMENTAL REGULATION: TRACKING THE UNICORN 23–28 (1989).

[99] *See* Bruce Yandle & Stuart Buck, *Bootleggers, Baptists, and the Global Warming Battle*, 26 HARV. ENVTL. L. REV. 177 (2002) (applying Yandle's theory of Baptists and Bootleggers to explain the political support for the Kyoto Protocol).

delegate to administrative agencies. While the analysis is necessarily simplified—most legislation will not fit neatly into a single category—it is nonetheless a starting point in assessing the dynamics of legislative processes, procurement, and compromise.

A. The Wilson-Hayes Matrix[100]

Two public choice theorists, James Q. Wilson and Michael T. Hayes, have used these insights to create a model of four legislative categories designed to predict which supply and demand configurations will tend to produce too much public action as well as which ones produce too little.[101] For simplicity, Wilson and Hayes divide the benefits associated with legislation into general benefits to the public at large, for example, defense, and narrow or special interest benefits, for example, an industrial subsidy or tariff. Similarly, Wilson and Hayes divide the costs associated with legislation into those that are distributed widely, for example, the former federal fifty-five miles per hour speed limit, and those that are distributed narrowly, for example, rent control. While the costs and benefits of most legislation fall between these extremes, these categories, depicted in Table 11.1, remain useful in constructing the analytical paradigm.

The difficulty with categorizing legislation between the extremes of conferring narrowly distributed and widely distributed benefits or between imposing narrowly distributed and widely distributed costs is exacerbated by the tendency of interest groups to characterize government policy in favorable terms. Thus, it is strategically beneficial for special interest groups to characterize special interest goods, for example, a particular defense contract, as benefiting the general public, for example, by claiming that it will help the national defense. Professor Glen O. Robinson has offered a useful definition that helps to respond to this problem:

> We can roughly define "public goods" as those in which there is some symmetry in the distribution of benefits and costs (within some near-term time period), whereas "private goods" are those where distribution of benefits and costs is asymmetrical; benefits are concentrated in a particular geographic region or special group, whereas costs are distributed more broadly over the general population.[102]

The traditional, or public interest, view of Congress is that members follow their interest to collectively supply goods benefiting the general public and bargain only as to detail. The irony highlighted by public choice theory is that individual members of society are least likely to lobby for such goods. Because no one can be excluded from the benefits of such classic public goods as a police force or national defense, individuals will free ride in their efforts to lobby for such legislative procurements, waiting for others to do so on their behalf. Because everyone engages in this behavior, the model predicts that goods

---

[100] Portions of the following discussion are based upon STEARNS, *supra* note 26, at 402–11.

[101] *See generally* JAMES Q. WILSON, POLITICAL ORGANIZATIONS 332–37 (1973); MICHAEL T. HAYES, LOBBYISTS AND LEGISLATORS: A THEORY OF POLITICAL MARKETS (1981). While Wilson first posited these four categories, Hayes, relying upon the works of several public choice theorists, substantially developed the original model.

[102] Glen O. Robinson, *Public Choice Speculations on the Item Veto*, 74 VA. L. REV. 403, 408–09 (1988).

providing benefits to the general public tend to be undersupplied. Although everyone benefits from them, no one is willing to incur the necessary costs to procure them.

Table 11.1. The Four Box Static Model[103]

	Widely Distributed Benefits	**Narrowly Conferred Benefits**
Widely Distributed Costs	***Legislative Characteristics:*** This desired category of legislation tends to be undersupplied as constituents express too little pressure in support; alternatively when pressure is brought on both sides, legislatures sometimes delegate to avoid the resulting conflict. ***Illustrations:*** • Desired legislative responses to various environmental crises, e.g., waste management or global warming • National fiscal management, e.g., social security reform.	***Legislative Characteristics:*** Because small organized groups exert pressure disproportionately to numbers in political processes, legislatures tend to oversupply special interest legislation. ***Illustrations:*** • Tariffs • Industry subsidies
Narrowly Conferred Costs	***Legislative Characteristics:*** Given the fear that factional violence (as asserted by Madison in *The Federalist No. 10*), or interest group politicking (the modern equivalent), will disadvantage unpopular minorities, congressional processes include numerous features that tend to enlarge successful coalitions above minimum winning size. ***Illustration:*** • Rent Control	***Legislative Characteristics:*** Because intense interests directly conflict, legislators prefer to delegate to agencies, hoping to shift blame for resulting failures while claiming credit for resulting successes; legislators can also benefit from simply threatening regulatory delegation and can benefit from monitoring agencies. ***Illustration:*** • National Labor Relations Board

103 STEARNS, *supra* note 26, at 407.

Alternatively, there is a stronger incentive to lobby for goods that provide narrow and direct benefits to identifiable groups. The free rider phenomenon is not eliminated altogether, but it is reduced to the extent that individuals can be excluded from the group benefiting from the legislation. The problem here is analogous to that of cheaters in a cartel.[104] To avoid having potential beneficiaries of narrow benefit legislation cheat by not contributing to lobbying efforts, special interest lobbyists will try, where possible, to make the legislative benefits divisible and excludable.

The problem with lobbying incentives is the same with respect to the costs of collectively supplied goods as it is with respect to the benefits. For public goods with widely distributed costs, one would expect minimal lobbying in opposition, just as one would expect minimal lobbying in support of goods conferring widely distributed benefits. Similarly, for goods imposing costs on a narrow group, one would expect greater lobbying in opposition, subject to the same free rider or cheating problem that occurs with goods that confer narrow benefits. In sum, lobbying efforts in favor of or in opposition to legislation will increase in proportion to the degree to which benefits are narrowly conferred or costs are narrowly imposed.

The same factors driving the demand for legislation are at work in driving the supply. Just as constituents will press more vigorously for legislation conferring narrow and excludable benefits, legislators will supply legislation more readily when they can credibly claim credit with their constituents for having procured the legislative benefit.[105] An individual Member of Congress is aware that constituents will be dubious of claims that he or she was single-handedly responsible for a major legislative success. Legislators also know that constituents will be more willing to give credit for narrow and discrete legislative procurements aiding their district. In addition, one theorist claims that Members of Congress expect their constituents to remember votes against their interests longer than votes in their favor.[106] If so, this creates an obvious dilemma for legislators faced with some constituents who would benefit by proposed legislation at a price borne by other constituents. Legislators can avoid this problem by exercising a third option beyond supplying or not supplying legislation. Specifically, they can delegate decision-making responsibility to agencies or courts.

Members of Congress can be expected to exercise this third option in instances in which one constituent group benefits directly at the expense of another, whether the costs and benefits of the legislation are widely or narrowly distributed. Legislators can use delegation as a means to let both sides claim victory in the legislative process, while blaming the agency at some future date for imposing the legislative cost. Frequently, regulation results in the interest groups *capturing* the agency such that the ensuing regulation is closer to the model of legislation under the old pluralist theory typified in

[104] *See supra* Chapter 1, at Part II.D.

[105] *See generally* DAVID R. MAYHEW, CONGRESS: THE ELECTORAL CONNECTION 52–54 (2d ed. 1974). Mayhew explains that because individual Congressmen cannot convincingly take credit for grandiose legislation, and because constituents are aware of immediate legislative procurements, Congressmen seek legislation that provides "particularized benefits" to their constituents. Particularized benefits must be given to an identifiable group and on an *ad hoc* basis so that a Congressman can have an identifiable role in their procurement. *Id.*

[106] *See* MORRIS P. FIORINA, REPRESENTATIVES, ROLL CALLS, AND CONSTITUENCIES 38–39 (1974) (explaining influence on Congressmen of "the ungrateful electorate").

E.E. Schattschneider's study of the Smoot-Hawley Act.[107] In essence, the interest groups win at the expense of the general public.

As shown in Table 11.1, Wilson and Hayes combine these demand and supply configurations to create four legislative categories. Although Congress was traditionally expected to provide legislation fitting with the widely distributed benefits/widely distributed costs category, public choice theorists posit instead that such legislation is most likely to be undersupplied. Because of the conflicting demand pattern in which all constituents receive a slight benefit and incur a slight cost, and because lobbying efforts are not likely to be intense on either side, legislators will respond with inaction, or with symbolic action in the form of delegation. One method Congressmen can use to increase the likelihood that a proposed bill in this category will secure enough votes for passage is to agree to attach to the bill legislation falling within another category in which the incentive for lobbying is stronger. This explains not only how non-germane riders come into being, but also why the Wilson-Hayes matrix is arguably most important for its dynamic legislative-bargaining implications.

The widely distributed benefits/narrowly conferred costs category is characterized by weak lobbying in support of legislation and strong lobbying in opposition, and is thus conflictual. Examples might include: broad environmental regulations, for example to combat climate change or other threats, which impose costs on industry; efforts to curtail spending on a large scale to curb the deficit, which impose costs on costly program beneficiaries; or programs to overhaul infrastructure, which impose costs on a variety affected businesses or residents. Legislators faced with these conflicting demand configurations are likely either to do nothing or to delegate.

The United States system of lawmaking contains numerous protections against the formation of majoritarian factions, including such constitutional protections as bicameralism, presentment, and constitutional judicial review.[108] In addition, numerous internal practices, including complex committee structures and calendaring rules, make the passage of legislation more difficult, and thus make majoritarian interest group politics more costly and thus less likely. These and other institutional protections or impediments to the passage of legislation are especially important in this context. In fact, one could argue that these protections, referred to as ***negative legislative checkpoints***, or ***veto gates***[109] are in place to slow down or to stop legislation that benefits the public at large at a cost borne largely or entirely by a narrow interest group.

B. Minimum Winning Coalitions and Negative Legislative Checkpoints

Negative legislative checkpoints, or veto gates, serve to increase the size of coalitions necessary to succeed in passing legislation.[110] William Riker, who developed the theory of

[107] For a discussion of pluralism, see *supra* Part I.

[108] *See* U.S. CONST. art. I, § 1; *id.* art. I, § 7, cl. 1 & 2; *id.* art. III.

[109] *See* STEARNS, *supra* note 26, at 410 (defining *negative legislative checkpoints*); McNollgast, *Legislative Intent: The Use of Positive Political Theory in Statutory Interpretation,* LAW & CONTEMP. PROBS., Winter & Spring 1994, at 3, 7 (defining *veto gates*). The following discussion uses these terms interchangeably.

[110] *See generally* WILLIAM H. RIKER, THE THEORY OF POLITICAL COALITIONS 32–46 (1962).

minimum winning coalitions, reasoned that, in theory, the most stable coalition in a legislative body will comprise one more than 50%. A larger coalition can benefit its membership by excluding others from the generalized benefits until a simple majority is achieved.[111] Riker's theory is most easily understood as the public choice analog to Madison's theory of factions. In essence, these congressional processes and the constitutional impediments to the rapid formation of successful majority factions reduce the possibility that a simple majority will be a successful coalition.[112]

Protection against minimum winning coalitions is especially important in the widely distributed benefit/narrowly conferred cost category. It is in this category that the interests of distinct minority groups are in the greatest danger of being thwarted by the legislative process. Professor Peter Aranson has observed that legislative coalitions are more stable as they approach minimum winning size within state legislatures, as compared with Congress, which tends toward larger coalitions.[113] If so, this is likely attributable to the relatively larger number of veto gates at the federal level.

The narrowly conferred benefits/widely distributed costs paradigm is characterized by strong demand for legislation and weak lobbying in opposition. When this occurs, public choice theory predicts enactment of legislation favorable to the active lobbying group. The most important legislative byproduct of this category is the rider, often one that is not germane to the overall substance of the underlying legislation to which it is attached. The skewed lobbying incentives in this category result in the legislative process of *logrolling*, with the effect of broadly conferring quasi-private goods as a means of achieving legislative compromise. Logrolling is the process by which legislators trade votes for each other's narrowly conferred benefit/widely distributed cost items in exchange for their own. The predicted result is a proliferation of pork barrel appropriations, the sum total of which may leave everyone worse off than had no legislation been passed at all. Not surprisingly, perhaps, the logrolling problem is exacerbated in large part by the very veto gates designed to protect special interests from general benefit legislation enacted at their expense. The same legislators empowered to slow down or stop bills encroaching on the rights of particular interest groups also can use their power to coerce items conferring narrow benefits on other special interest groups.

The final category, narrowly conferred costs/widely distributed benefits, like the first configuration, is conflictual. But unlike in the first configuration, lobbying efforts here are intense on both sides. This is a classic situation in which legislators will opt out by delegating their authority to either an agency or to courts. Examples include the National

---

[111] Riker's theory includes specific limitations. *See id.* at 32 ("In person, zero-sum games, where side-payments are permitted, where players are rational, and where they have perfect information, only minimum winning coalitions occur.").

[112] *See* Harold H. Bruff, *Legislative Formality, Administrative Rationality*, 63 TEX. L. REV. 207, 219–20 (1984) (explaining that devices such as House Rules Committee agenda controls and the threat of presidential veto serve to increase size of winning coalitions); RIKER, *supra* note 110, at 89–101 (observing that historically, successful coalitions are larger than minimum winning size); PETER H. ARANSON, AMERICAN GOVERNMENT: STRATEGY AND CHOICE 367 (1981) ("To pass, bills usually require more than simple majorities, because unconvinced lawmakers can use any number of lethal and dilatory strategies for defeating, or delaying, or substantially modifying them.").

[113] *See* ARANSON, *supra* note 112, at 65.

Labor Relations Act,[114] establishing the National Labor Relations Board, and the Labor Management Relations Act,[115] vesting federal district courts with authority to resolve disputes over labor-management contracts. Delegation allows legislators to claim credit for creating legislative benefits while blaming the agency or courts for imposing the costs.

Although rent seeking is often associated with the procurement of quasi-private goods through the legislative process, it is important to recognize that public goods often generate rent-seeking behavior and thus result in rent dissipation. Part of the problem is definitional. While "national defense" is generally characterized as a public good, the government does not provide national defense generically. Instead, it selects particular tanks, planes, or ships to buy, companies to contract with, and localities in which to place various bases. Embedded in the provision of national defense, therefore, are many decisions that have the potential to substantially enrich particular industries, firms, or communities, especially those in districts of influential politicians. Large defense contractors actively lobby and contribute to political campaigns in the hopes that their firms will be selected for lucrative defense contracts. For the same reasons that the Wilson-Hayes matrix predicts a tendency to oversupply quasi-private goods, it also implies that once the decision to supply a public good is made (such as national defense) there will be a strong tendency toward privatizing substantial aspects of the public goods provision.

The Wilson-Hayes matrix has implications for several public policy proposals. While we will reconsider these issues throughout the book, for now consider whether the tendency to favor special interest over general interest legislation provides support for such proposals as the item veto, single subject amendments, or the balanced budget amendment. Does the same tendency favor greater judicial scrutiny of legislation, especially special interest legislation? To what extent do these questions require one first to assess the proper baseline for evaluating the proper extent of interest group influence on the political process?[116]

IV. APPLICATIONS: INTEREST GROUP THEORY AND LAW

Interest group theory raises profound questions for the study of law. These include foundational questions that concern many of the Supreme Court's most famous and familiar constitutional decisions. In this section, we reexamine a few such cases from the perspective of public choice. We invite you to consider the extent to which insights from interest group theory affect the manner in which you now view the underlying issues that these cases present. In addition, consider more generally whether the analysis informs your understanding of the proper role that judges play, or should play, within our constitutional system of governance when construing constitutional challenges of the sort presented in the cases described below.

---

[114] 29 U.S.C. §§ 151–169 (2012). Section 153 of the Act establishes the National Labor Relations Board. *Id.* § 153.

[115] 29 U.S.C. §§ 141–197 (2012).

[116] *Cf.* Einer R. Elhauge, *Does Interest Group Theory Justify More Intrusive Judicial Review?*, 101 YALE L.J. 31 (1991).

A. Lochner v. New York

In *Lochner v. New York*,[117] the Supreme Court, with Justice Peckham writing, confronted a constitutional challenge under the Fourteenth Amendment Due Process Clause to the Labor Law of New York. That statute prohibited bakers from working more than sixty hours per week and more than ten hours per day. The case arose at the intersection of the relatively broad understanding concerning the scope of state police powers and a substantive reading of the Due Process Clause to protect certain economic liberties, including the right to contract. The case raised the question whether in the exercise of its police powers, New York could effectively prohibit private contracting in this employment setting. Justice Peckham framed the inquiry as follows:

> If the contract be one which the State, in the legitimate exercise of its police power, has the right to prohibit, it is not prevented from prohibiting it by the Fourteenth Amendment. Contracts in violation of a statute, either of the Federal or state government, or a contract to let one's property for immoral purposes, or to do any other unlawful act, could obtain no protection from the Federal Constitution, as coming under the liberty of person or of free contract. Therefore, when the State, by its legislature, in the assumed exercise of its police powers, has passed an act which seriously limits the right to labor or the right of contract in regard to their means of livelihood between persons who are *sui juris* (both employer and employee), it becomes of great importance to determine which shall prevail—the right of the individual to labor for such time as he may choose, or the right of the State to prevent the individual from laboring, or from entering into any contract to labor, beyond a certain time prescribed by the State.[118]

While the State claimed that regulating the hours of bakers was necessary to promote the general health and safety, as well as that of the bakers themselves, Justice Peckham found the argument attenuated:

> The mere assertion that the subject relates though but in a remote degree to the public health, does not necessarily render the enactment valid. . . .
>
> . . . .
>
> . . . There must be more than the mere fact of the possible existence of some small amount of unhealthiness to warrant legislative interference with liberty. It is unfortunately true that labor, even in any department, may possibly carry with it the seeds of unhealthiness. But are we all, on that account, at the mercy of legislative majorities? A printer, a tinsmith, a locksmith, a carpenter, a cabinetmaker, a dry goods clerk, a bank's, a lawyer's or a physician's clerk, or a clerk in almost any kind of business, would all come under the power of the legislature, on this assumption. No trade, no occupation, no mode of earning one's living, could escape this all-pervading power, and the acts of the legislature in limiting the hours of labor in all employments would be valid,

---

[117] 198 U.S. 45 (1905).

[118] *Id.* at 53–54.

> although such limitation might seriously cripple the ability of the laborer to support himself and his family.[119]

Justice Peckham then specifically addressed whether bakers were in need of unique legislative protection, as urged by the state:

> [W]e think that such a law as this, although passed in the assumed exercise of the police power, and as relating to the public health, or the health of the employees named, is not within that power, and is invalid. The act is not, within any fair meaning of the term, a health law, but is an illegal interference with the rights of individuals, both employers and employees, to make contracts regarding labor upon such terms as they may think best, or which they may agree upon with the other parties to such contracts. Statutes of the nature of that under review, limiting the hours in which grown and intelligent men may labor to earn their living, are mere meddlesome interferences with the rights of the individual, and they are not saved from condemnation by the claim that they are passed in the exercise of the police power and upon the subject of the health of the individual whose rights are interfered with, unless there be some fair ground, reasonable in and of itself, to say that there is material danger to the public health or to the health of the employees, if the hours of labor are not curtailed.
>
> . . . .
>
> . . . Adding to [a legitimate series of bakery inspection requirements] a prohibition to enter into any contract of labor in a bakery for more than a certain number of hours a week, is, in our judgment, so wholly beside the matter of a proper, reasonable and fair provision, as to run counter to that liberty of person and of free contract provided for in the Federal Constitution.[120]

Justice Peckham concluded that "[u]nder such circumstances the freedom of master and employee to contract with each other in relation to their employment, and in defining the same, cannot be prohibited or interfered with, without violating the Federal Constitution."[121]

In his dissenting opinion, Justice Harlan challenged both the premises of Peckham's analysis and the Court's application on its own terms. Justice Harlan began by discussing the Supreme Court's role in assessing the proper scope of the State's exercise of police powers:

> It is plain that this statute was enacted in order to protect the physical well-being of those who work in bakery and confectionery establishments. It may be that the statute had its origin, in part, in the belief that employers and employees in such establishments were not upon an equal footing, and that the necessities of the latter often compelled them to submit to such exactions as unduly taxed their strength. Be this as it may, the statute must be taken as

119 *Id.* at 57, 59.

120 *Id.* at 61–62.

121 *Id.* at 64.

> expressing the belief of the people of New York that, as a general rule, and in the case of the average man, labor in excess of sixty hours during a week in such establishments may endanger the health of those who thus labor. Whether or not this be wise legislation it is not the province of the court to inquire. Under our systems of government the courts are not concerned with the wisdom or policy of legislation.[122]
>
> . . . What the precise facts are it may be difficult to say. It is enough for the determination of this case, and it is enough for this court to know, that the question is one about which there is room for debate and for an honest difference of opinion. There are many reasons of a weighty, substantial character, based upon the experience of mankind, in support of the theory that, all things considered, more than ten hours' steady work each day, from week to week, in a bakery or confectionery establishment, may endanger the health, and shorten the lives of the workmen, thereby diminishing their physical and mental capacity to serve the State, and to provide for those dependent upon them.
>
> If such reasons exist that ought to be the end of this case, for the State is not amenable to the judiciary, in respect of its legislative enactments, unless such enactments are plainly, palpably, beyond all question, inconsistent with the Constitution of the United States. We are not to presume that the State of New York has acted in bad faith. Nor can we assume that its legislature acted without due deliberation, or that it did not determine this question upon the fullest attainable information, and for the common good.[123]

In arguing that the law should be upheld as a proper exercise of the State's police powers, Justice Harlan relied upon several studies discussing the safety conditions for bakers:

> Professor Hirt in his treatise on the "Diseases of the Workers" has said: "The labor of the bakers is among the hardest and most laborious imaginable, because it has to be performed under conditions injurious to the health of those engaged in it. It is hard, very hard work, not only because it requires a great deal of physical exertion in an overheated workshop and during unreasonably long hours, but more so because of the erratic demands of the public, compelling the baker to perform the greater part of his work at night, thus depriving him of an opportunity to enjoy the necessary rest and sleep, a fact which is highly injurious to his health." Another writer says: "The constant inhaling of flour dust causes inflammation of the lungs and of the bronchial tubes. The eyes also suffer through this dust, which is responsible for the many cases of running eyes among the bakers. The long hours of toil to which all bakers are subjected produce rheumatism, cramps and swollen legs. The intense heat in the workshops induces the workers to resort to cooling drinks, which together with their habit of exposing the greater part of their bodies to the change in the atmosphere, is another source of a number of diseases of various organs." . . . The average age of a baker is below that of other workmen;

---

[122] *Id.* at 69 (Harlan, J., dissenting).

[123] *Id.* at 72–73.

> they seldom live over their fiftieth year, most of them dying between the ages of forty and fifty.[124]

Finally, consider the following passage from Justice Oliver Wendell Holmes's dissenting opinion:

> This case is decided upon an economic theory which a large part of the country does not entertain. If it were a question whether I agreed with that theory, I should desire to study it further and long before making up my mind. But I do not conceive that to be my duty, because I strongly believe that my agreement or disagreement has nothing to do with the right of a majority to embody their opinions in law. . . . The Fourteenth Amendment does not enact Mr. Herbert Spencer's Social Statics. . . . [A] constitution is not intended to embody a particular economic theory, whether of paternalism and the organic relation of the citizen to the State or of *laissez faire*.[125]

DISCUSSION QUESTIONS

1. Does public choice provide a means of assessing the various opinions in *Lochner*? One possible answer is that the case turns strictly on a matter of the substantive interpretation of the Fourteenth Amendment Due Process Clause. While that view might help to explain Chief Justice Holmes's dissent, it does not explain the extent to which Justices Peckham, for the majority, and Harlan, in dissent, relied heavily on their own understandings of both the factual nature of the baking profession and their understandings of the wisdom, or lack thereof, of the legislative processes that resulted in the challenged law.

2. Do the analyses that Justices Peckham and Harlan offer turn on assumptions concerning the effectiveness of the political process in New York in reflecting the popular will or wisdom of legislative policy? Does the majority's analysis rest upon a notion of political market failure? If so, what is that intuition based upon? Does Harlan's discussion of the studies concerning the safety of the baking industry overcome such claims? Why or why not?

3. In another passage, the majority asserts: "It is impossible for us to shut our eyes to the fact that many of the laws of this character, while passed under what is claimed to be the police power for the purpose of protecting the public health or welfare, are, in reality, passed from other motives."[126] What does this mean? What does Justice Harlan mean when he asserts: "It is plain that this statute was enacted in order to protect the physical well-being of those who work in bakery and confectionery establishments," and that "[w]e are not to presume that the State of New York has acted in bad faith."[127] Does Harlan believe that legislators are invariably sincere in their motives? That the legislative motives were sincere in this case? Should it matter if public choice theory, or available empirical evidence, demonstrates that sometimes legislative motives might be insincere, or that they might have been insincere respecting the legislation at issue before the Court?

---

124 *Id.* at 70–71.

125 *Id.* at 75 (Holmes, J., dissenting).

126 *Id.* at 64 (majority opinion).

127 *Id.* at 69, 73 (Harlan, J., dissenting).

Two Interest Group Perspectives

Professor Bernard Siegan provides an interest group analysis of the statute under review in *Lochner*.[128] Siegan questions the dissent's assumption that the motivation for the law, as was claimed, was to protect the physical and economic well-being of the bakers. For example, he observes that the bakers' pay might be reduced along with the reduction in hours, making it more difficult for the bakers to support themselves and their families. In addition, he suggests that the law might not be the product of a benign motivation to protect bakers from the potential health risks associated with long hours, but rather to protect bakers working at larger industrial bakeries that already complied with the various safety and hours regulations reflected in the New York law, at the expense of smaller, often immigrant-owned bakeries, that did not. Siegan explains:

> In New York, as elsewhere, the baking industry was split between sizable bakeries whose plants had been specifically built or fully converted for such purposes, and small bakeries, operating out of limited, often subterranean quarters not originally intended for such use. . . . The New York trend was also toward bigger operations. . . .
>
> Contemporary articles in the *New York Times* reported that sanitary, health, and working conditions in the small bakeries were far below those in the large ones. . . .
>
> Working hours were [also] much longer in the small bakeries than in the large ones, and the maximum hours provision hit employers and employees of the former much more. . . . [W]orkers in some small bakeries . . . remained on the business premises (if not actually on the job) from twelve to as many as twenty-two hours a working day. The workday in the larger firms . . . met or was close to the statutory maximum of ten hours.
>
> . . . [The] restrictions on working hours meant higher labor costs for the small bakers, who, due to competition from the corporate bakers, were limited in the amount they could pass on in the form of higher prices. A number of the small bakers would have to terminate their businesses.
>
> The effect on the larger bakeries would be far less adverse. They were much closer to the hour standard, and unlike the small bakeries, they might sustain a modest increase in costs if they had to hire more workers. However, extra production costs would be offset by the lessened competition from the small bakeries, which would lead to higher prices.[129]

Also consider Professor David Bernstein's complementary analysis,[130] which posits that larger corporate bakeries also had unionized work forces, whereas smaller, immigrant-owned bakeries did not:

> The larger New York bakeries tended to be unionized, and were staffed by bakers of Anglo-Irish and (primarily) German descent; the latter group came to dominate the Bakery and Confectionery Workers' International Union. . . .

---

[128] BERNARD H. SIEGAN, ECONOMIC LIBERTIES AND THE CONSTITUTION 113–20 (1980).

[129] *Id.* at 116–18.

[130] *See* David E. Bernstein, Lochner v. New York: *A Centennial Retrospective*, 83 WASH. U. L.Q. 1469 (2005).

The smaller bakeries employed a hodgepodge of ethnic groups, primarily French, Germans, Italians, and Jews, usually segregated by bakery and generally working for employers of the same ethnic group. Employees of smaller bakeries were generally not unionized, especially among the non-Germans.

By the mid-1890s, bakers in large bakeries rarely worked more than ten hours per day, sixty hours per week. However, these bakers were concerned that their improved situation was endangered by competition from small, old-fashioned bakeries, especially those that employed Italian, French, and Jewish immigrants. These old-fashioned bakeries were often located in the basement of tenement buildings to take advantage of cheap rents and floors sturdy enough to withstand the weight of heavy baking ovens. Unlike the more modern "factory" bakeries, which operated in shifts, the basement bakeries often demanded that workers be on call twenty-four hours a day, with the bakers sleeping in or near the bakery during down times. Workers in such bakeries often worked far more than ten hours per day.

Union bakers believed that competition from basement bakery workers drove down their wages.[131]

Bernstein sees the eventual New York State law as the outcome of a coalition that included reformers concerned about public health and the bakers' union, which wanted to put small basement bakeries that generally failed to meet the new sanitary standards out of business. Bernstein claims that the bakers' union, which was well organized at the time, as opposed to the baking industry, which was less well organized, provided the impetus behind the law. Eventually, the bakery owners became better organized and decided to fund Mr. Lochner's challenge to the maximum hours provisions of the Labor Law of New York in part because they believed that those provisions were only being enforced against nonunion bakeries. While Bernstein claims that large corporate bakeries were supporters of the provisions of the law that gave them a comparative advantage in the market over smaller rivals, he also observes that a coalition of organized labor and public health reformers procured the challenged labor law.[132]

DISCUSSION QUESTIONS

1. How, if at all, do the analyses by Professors Siegan and Bernstein affect your thinking about the relative merits of the various *Lochner* opinions? Assuming that these commentators are correct that the New York law was largely motivated by the desire of larger, unionized bakeries to limit competition by smaller bakeries, does this provide a normative justification for striking the law down? How, if at all, might this analysis change if, as Bernstein suggests, the challenged law arose from a Bootleggers and Baptists coalition that was at least partly motivated by concerns for public health and safety?

2. Does the federal judiciary have the institutional competence to make appropriate assessments concerning the political forces that support or oppose a given piece of legislation?

---

[131] *Id.* at 1476–77 (footnotes omitted).

[132] *See* DAVID E. BERNSTEIN, REHABILITATING *LOCHNER*: DEFENDING INDIVIDUAL RIGHTS AGAINST PROGRESSIVE REFORM (2011).

Should the answer to this question affect how the Supreme Court analyzes cases like *Lochner*? Why or why not?

3. Does the analysis suggest that conventional presentations that pit the interests of management against the interests of labor fail to recognize that often the relevant competition giving rise to protectionist laws is labor against labor, or management against management? If so, should this affect the judicial approach to cases like *Lochner*? Why, or why not?

B. West Coast Hotel v. Parrish

In the landmark case *West Coast Hotel Co. v. Parrish*,[133] which overturned *Adkins v. Children's Hospital*,[134] the Supreme Court sustained a minimum wage law for women.[135] This case is widely understood to represent the end of the *Lochner* era. The Court not only signaled the end of the era of economic substantive due process in its holding, but also in its broad assertion: "What is this freedom? The Constitution does not speak of freedom of contract. It speaks of liberty and prohibits the deprivation of liberty without due process of law."[136]

Ultimately, the choice between the *Lochner* regime, which allows the federal judiciary to check market regulations that interfere with private contracting, and the *Parrish* regime, which permits legislatures, both state and federal, to regulate markets in a manner that thwarts at least some mutually agreeable transactions, comes down to institutional competence. The *Lochner* regime presumes market transactions to be beneficial because they are mutually entered into, whereas the *Parrish* regime presumes legislative limits on the market to be permissible because legislative processes are assumed to represent majoritarian preferences. Building upon an insight from Chapter 2, the Pareto superiority criterion, we can construct a simple analysis that reveals the inevitability of this ultimate choice, either to prefer market transactions or democratic decisions, in at least some sets of circumstances.

Market transactions are presumed to be welfare enhancing because they are entered into with the mutual consent of the contracting parties. The participants would not engage in the exchange if at least one participant (and probably both participants) did not expect to be made better off as a result. But logrolling also involves the mutual consent of those who agree to the relevant vote trades. Ironically, however, a regime that steadfastly honors mutually agreeable legislative trades, for example *Parrish*, creates the possibility, and perhaps the actuality, of legislation that inhibits certain forms of private market contracting, for example, contracts to work below the minimum wage or above the maximum number of hours. Conversely, a regime that steadfastly honors mutually agreeable private market exchange, for example *Lochner*, creates the possibility, and perhaps the actuality, of preventing legislation that is the product of mutually agreeable

---

[133] 300 U.S. 379 (1937).

[134] 261 U.S. 525 (1923) *Adkins* was a 1923 Supreme Court case challenging a 1918 law enacted by Congress guaranteeing a minimum wage to women and children working in the District of Columbia. The Court, citing *Lochner*, held the law violated due process and was unconstitutional. *Id.* at 545, 548–50.

[135] 300 U.S. at 398–99. *Parrish* concerned the Washington State Minimum Wages for Women Act which required a minimum wage be fixed for women and children. *Id.* at 386–88.

[136] *Id.* at 391.

exchanges in the form of logrolls among legislators, producing such laws as minimum wages or maximum hours. In a constitutional system, it is inevitable that at some point, the judiciary will be forced to confront this choice because there is no set of mechanisms that can invariably protect both sets of mutually agreeable exchanges.

One could avoid this seeming dilemma by claiming private transactions that do not produce externalities are Pareto superior, while legislative logrolling invariably affects parties other than the members of the legislature, and thus they invariably produce externalities and cannot be assumed Pareto superior. The difficulty, however, is that ultimately this is an argument of definition. Economists making this argument are focusing solely on externalities among other private market actors, for example in the case of pollution. But, by insistently honoring private market exchanges, such as contracts below specified minimum wages, economists disregard potential harm to actors in an altogether different institution, namely legislators who, responding to constituent pressures, or based on their own normative assessments, wish to enact minimum wage laws. Only by defining such actors as outside the scope of the model can one claim that private market transactions should be vindicated against contrary laws on the grounds that they uniquely satisfy the Pareto principle.

Of course, the same is true with respect to those who seek to protect legislative compromise. It would also be a mistake to claim that such laws are invariably desirable because legislators have agreed to enact them. This calculus fails to consider the potential negative effects within the private market. Those who hold strong laissez faire views will be inclined to dismiss the significance of the concern about thwarting laws they deem socially detrimental, and those who are more skeptical of private markets and who are favorably inclined toward market regulation will hold a contrary view. The point here is not to demonstrate that either set of views is right or wrong. Rather it is to demonstrate that one cannot guarantee both sets of concerns simultaneously; there is a necessary choice, or at least the potential for a choice, that tests the outer limits of concerns for protecting the market and concerns for protecting democratic decision making. The history of the doctrine of economic substantive due process suggests that the Supreme Court has changed its mind over time with respect to this fundamental question, as demonstrated in the *Lochner* and *Parrish* decisions.

C. United States v. Carolene Products

Consider next the famous case *United States v. Carolene Products Co.*,[137] a case that was decided one year after *West Coast Hotel Co. v. Parrish*.[138] *Carolene Products* is notable not only because it provides a theoretical justification for low-level scrutiny of economic regulation, in this case a challenge to a prohibition against lower cost filled milk, but also because in its famous *footnote four*, it offers an express and influential theory concerning those defects in political processes that might provide a normative justification for applying strict scrutiny to certain forms of legislation.

In *Carolene Products*, Justice Stone, writing for a majority, sustained the Filled Milk Act, a federal statute that "prohibit[ed] the shipment in interstate commerce of skimmed

[137] 304 U.S. 144 (1938).

[138] 300 U.S. 379 (1937).

milk compounded with any fat or oil other than milk fat, so as to resemble milk or cream,"[139] as an adulterated product deemed injurious to the public health, against a challenge based upon the Fifth Amendment Due Process Clause and the Commerce Clause. The Court relied upon an earlier case, *Hebe Co. v. Shaw*,[140] for the proposition that "a state law which forbids the manufacture and sale of a product assumed to be wholesome and nutritive, made of condensed skimmed milk, compounded with coconut oil, is not forbidden by the Fourteenth Amendment."[141] The Court did not rest solely on precedent, however, asserting:

> [A]ffirmative evidence also sustains the statute. In twenty years evidence has steadily accumulated of the danger to the public health from the general consumption of foods which have been stripped of elements essential to the maintenance of health. The Filled Milk Act was adopted by Congress after committee hearings, in the course of which eminent scientists and health experts testified. An extensive investigation was made of the commerce in milk compounds in which vegetable oils have been substituted for natural milk fat, and of the effect upon the public health of the use of such compounds as a food substitute for milk. . . . [T]he House Committee on Agriculture . . . and the Senate Committee on Agriculture and Forestry . . . concluded . . . that the use of filled milk as a substitute for pure milk is generally injurious to health and facilitates fraud on the public.[142]

While the Court relied upon such legislative findings and the underlying testimony, it further noted that such findings were not necessary to sustain the Act. The Court continued:

> Even in the absence of such aids the existence of facts supporting the legislative judgment is to be presumed, for regulatory legislation affecting ordinary commercial transactions is not to be pronounced unconstitutional unless in the light of the facts made known or generally assumed it is of such a character as to preclude the assumption that it rests upon some rational basis within the knowledge and experience of the legislators.[143]

In the famous footnote four that followed this passage, Justice Stone, joined by a plurality of four, stated:

> There may be narrower scope for operation of the presumption of constitutionality when legislation appears on its face to be within a specific prohibition of the Constitution, such as those of the first ten amendments, which are deemed equally specific when held to be embraced within the Fourteenth.
>
> It is unnecessary to consider now whether legislation which restricts those political processes which can ordinarily be expected to bring about repeal of

[139] *Carolene Prods.*, 304 U.S. at 145–46.

[140] 248 U.S. 297 (1919).

[141] *Carolene Prods.*, 304 U.S. at 148.

[142] *Id.* at 148–49 (citations omitted).

[143] *Id.* at 152.

> undesirable legislation, is to be subjected to more exacting judicial scrutiny under the general prohibitions of the Fourteenth Amendment than are most other types of legislation. . . .
>
> . . . .
>
> Nor need we enquire whether similar considerations enter into the review of statutes directed at particular religious, or national, or racial minorities. [P]rejudice against discrete and insular minorities may be a special condition, which tends seriously to curtail the operation of those political processes ordinarily to be relied upon to protect minorities, and which may call for a correspondingly more searching judicial inquiry.[144]

The Court's argument in footnote four that the majoritarian political process generally protects individuals, but that "discrete and insular minorities," such as racial or religious minorities, may be entitled to special protection by the judiciary, underlies John Hart Ely's well known book, *Democracy and Distrust*.[145] In Ely's analysis, the true vice of factions is in failing to protect groups that systematically are disadvantaged, in part due to numbers and in part due to organizational abilities, within traditional political processes. As a result, Ely maintains, heightened scrutiny of laws that adversely affect specified racial minorities and women are normatively justified by perceived failures in political markets.

Consider Professor Bruce Ackerman's response to this analysis.[146] Following Mancur Olson, Ackerman contends that although the size of minority groups might be a weakness, their insularity might be a strength, at least when compared with other non-insular groups. Thus, Ackerman states:

> Other things being equal, "discreteness and insularity" will normally be a source of enormous bargaining advantage, not disadvantage, for a group engaged in pluralist American politics. Except for special cases, the concerns that underlie *Carolene* should lead judges to protect groups that possess the opposite characteristics from the ones *Carolene* emphasizes—groups that are "anonymous and diffuse" rather than "discrete and insular." It is these groups that both political science and American history indicate are systematically disadvantaged in a pluralist democracy.[147]

Are there reasons to suspect that those groups that have traditionally benefited from the Court's treatment of *Carolene Products* footnote four, namely African Americans and other demographic minorities, might lack some of the benefits that Ackerman ascribes to groups characterized by such attributes as discreteness and insularity? If so, why? As you also read Professor Geoffrey Miller's complementary analysis below, consider whether it is possible that Ackerman's analysis commits a category mistake, meaning that it equates as discrete and insular minorities two separate groups in the Wilson-Hayes matrix:[148] those minorities who seek protections from laws benefiting majority groups at their expense

---

144 *Id.* at 152–53 n.4 (citations omitted).

145 JOHN HART ELY, DEMOCRACY AND DISTRUST: A THEORY OF JUDICIAL REVIEW (1980).

146 Bruce A. Ackerman, *Beyond* Carolene Products, 98 HARV. L. REV. 713 (1985).

147 *Id.* at 723–24.

148 *See supra* Table 11.1 (The Four Box Static Model).

(the lower left), on one side, and special interest groups seeking quasi-private legislation at the expense of a diffuse electorate (the upper right), on the other? If so, which box is the target of Ackerman's analysis, and which box is the target of footnote four?

Professor Geoffrey P. Miller has offered a critical account of the *Carolene Products* opinion, in which he claims that the result was to prevent access to a low cost product for those consumers most in need.[149]

> Filled milk was a technological innovation in the canned milk industry, an industry that was itself a response to the technological difficulties of bringing fluid milk to markets. The problem of dairy marketing has always been the perishability of fluid milk. . . . The early decades of the twentieth century saw rapid development of transportation, refrigeration, and pasteurization, facilitating the creation of home delivery systems of bottled milk. Even so, there remained a demand for fluid milk that resisted spoilage. Many homes, especially in poorer areas, did not have refrigerators; and it was useful for all [illegible] have some extra fluid milk on hand for emergencies. Canned [illegible]se needs.[150]

[illegible]clusion that filled milk was a wholesome and economical milk product, [illegible]urt's public interest justifications for the law as being "patently bogus," [illegible]the law to the influence of the dairy industry.[151] Filled milk, which was [illegible]im milk . . . to which has been added, or which has been blended or [illegible]any fat or oil other than milk fat,"[152] sold for a much lower price than [illegible]has had no fat removed or added. Much of the profit for dairy farmers [illegible]butors (such as Borden) came from sales of fluid and condensed whole [illegible]creased consumption of filled milk threatened to divert millions of [illegible]to the market, thereby "driving down the price of that commodity."[153] Finally, in 1923 the federal Filled Milk Act was enacted, which prohibited the shipment in interstate commerce of filled milk, and by 1937, thirty-one states had also banned the manufacture or sale of filled milk, three states had enacted effectively similar legislation, and three states had imposed conditions and regulations on the manufacture and sale of filled milk.[154] "The effect of the federal statute, coupled with prohibitory state legislation," Miller observes, "was to drive most producers out of business."[155] Miller concludes:

> The battle over filled milk seems well-described by interest group theory. The most plausible inference is that the statute was enacted at the behest of a coalition of groups intent on advancing their own economic welfare at the expense of less powerful groups. An impressionistic view of the events

---

149 Geoffrey P. Miller, *The True Story of* Carolene Products, 1987 SUP. CT. REV. 397.

150 *Id.* at 400.

151 *Id.* at 399.

152 Filled Milk Act, 21 U.S.C. § 61 (2012).

153 Miller, *supra* note 149, at 404.

154 *Id.* at 410.

155 *Id.*

> surrounding the statute's enactment supports this inference: the sponsors were from big dairy states, while the chief opponents were from cotton states.[156]

Miller also conducted an empirical analysis that generally supported his conclusions. He observes:

> In the *Carolene Products* footnote, Justice Stone suggested that special protections were needed for "discrete and insular minorities" because such groups would not be adequately served by the political process. The statement, if meant as a general observation about American politics, is obviously misplaced. Public choice theory demonstrates that, in general, "discrete and insular minorities" are exactly the groups that are likely to obtain disproportionately large benefits from the political process.
>
> The insights of public choice theory are amply demonstrated by the battle over filled milk, where one discrete minority—the nation's dairy farmers and their allies—obtained legislation harmful to consumers and the public at large. To be sure, the legislation discriminated against another discrete minority—the filled milk industry—but this fact simply reflects the complexity of the dairy industry. Filled milk producers, if they had not been trumped by a politically more powerful group, might themselves have been able to obtain special legislative favors to the detriment of the public interest.[157]

Does this analysis affect your thinking about the deferential approach that the *Carolene Products* Court took to the statute under review? About its less deferential approach in cases involving discrete and insular minorities? Miller posits:

> The political theory underlying the *Carolene Products* footnote, now a half-century old, needs to be updated. The results of that process may call in question the Supreme Court's policy of blind deference to legislation favoring special industrial interests. Is it time to re-examine the wisdom of "see-no-evil, hear-no-evil" as the prevailing philosophy in economic regulation cases?[158]

DISCUSSION QUESTIONS

1. To what extent is the Supreme Court's deferential standard of review in *Carolene Products* based on its embedded assumptions about how the legislative process operates? Does the Court provide any justification for its assumptions?

2. Is the filled milk industry the sort of discrete and insular minority that the Supreme Court had in mind in *Carolene Products* footnote four? Is it possible that Professor Miller has also committed a category mistake that the Wilson-Hayes matrix helps to identify?[159]

---

156 *Id.* at 423.

157 *Id.* at 428 (footnote omitted).

158 *Id.*

159 *See supra* note 100, and accompanying text.

3. Should the Court carefully scrutinize both economic regulation and legislation affecting discrete and insular minorities? What might the costs of such a regime be? To what extent are your answers informed by public choice?

CHAPTER 12

Interest Group Theory (Part 2)

Introduction

In Chapter 11, we introduced the related concepts of interest group theory and rent seeking. As that chapter demonstrated, public choice helps to identify certain process-based biases that emerge from political structures that potentially thwart expectations as compared with majoritarian preferences. Government regulation, for example, does not always result from a perceived need to correct a market failure, and at least in some instances, it might be better understood as acquired by, rather than imposed upon, the affected industry as a means of helping to protect members from competition.

This chapter further considers how interest group theory sometimes reinforces and other times questions intuitions derived from neoclassical law and economics. The analysis reveals that as with law and economics itself, the implications of public choice do not uniformly point in one direction. Part I compares and contrasts traditional law and economics with public choice, using case studies involving the power of eminent domain and the requirement of just compensation; regulating economic crises based on rules or standards, and regulation of greenhouse gases. Part II considers some challenges to the methodology of public choice. And part III provides applications.

I. LAW & ECONOMICS AND PUBLIC CHOICE COMPARED AND CONTRASTED

Public choice economics begins with the premises that there is a market for political activity and that institutional outputs, taking the form of government action or inaction, can be meaningfully assessed using economic assumptions concerning how various actors operate within the framework of relevant institutions. Institutions, the rules that constrain or shape human activity,[1] such as voting rules and the allocation of decision-making authority within and across different units of government, provide incentive structures within which individuals act. Sometimes individuals interact within institutional structures in ways that align aggregate preferences with preferred outcomes, thereby producing laws and regulations that further the public interest. In some situations, however, the products of such interactions appear less desirable even when viewed strictly from the perspective of participant preferences.

---

[1] Douglass C. North, *Institutions*, J. ECON. PERSP., Winter 1991, at 97.

Some scholars ascribe the potential divergence between constituent preferences and legislative outputs to the seeming ubiquity of rent-seeking efforts, both at the legislative and agency levels. Provided the government has the capacity to confer valuable benefits, or to impose costly punishments, on private interests, such actors, behaving rationally, will invest resources to try to secure the upside gains and to forestall anticipated burdens. The economic concept known as *marginal rates of substitution* helps to explain this intuition.[2] If along the relevant margin, a firm can achieve an expected higher rate of return from pursuing a regulation that inhibits competition or that provides a subsidy, as compared with investing the same capital in research and development or in the production of its goods or services, public choice theory predicts that the firm is apt to adjust its capital in favor of lobbying or *corridoring* activity.[3] This holds even if the aggregate effect of many firms engaging in a like strategy is to reduce the production of societal wealth overall.

Some scholars further posit that public choice suggests that it is ill-advised to ignore the inevitability of such interest group pressures when designing lawmaking processes. James Buchanan has described the need to account realistically for activities that affect political processes as "politics without romance," emphasizing political activity as it actually takes place, with real people interacting in real-world institutions.[4] At the same time, public choice theory is neither nihilistic nor a source of despair; it recognizes in many instances that government regulation is appropriate and welfare improving notwithstanding ubiquitous rent-seeking pressures. In effect, public choice counsels that it is neither sound to ignore the costs of government imperfections due to rent-seeking pressures that can result in welfare-reducing outcomes, nor to ignore the potential benefits of government regulation that can arise in spite of those imperfections.

Scholars generally agree that it is crucial when evaluating government conduct to account for all costs. This includes costs associated with rent seeking and any associated regulatory distortions that might thwart constituent expectations. Professor Todd Zywicki, along with other scholars, maintains that government environmental regulation is often distorted by rent-seeking pressures and the self-interested behavior by firms seeking to use environmental regulation to gain a competitive advantage over rival firms and industries.[5] Eliminating the power to regulate such matters would obviously also eliminate incentives to engage in related rent-seeking behavior. Despite this, there are many contexts, including an array of environmental regulations, that even after netting out the distortion costs, remain social-welfare enhancing. The mere fact that government regulation might be distorted by rent-seeking pressures should not be understood to counsel against the regulation; rather, public choice counsels assessing the full set of costs and benefits, as Buchanan would say, "without romance."[6] Recognizing the potential for ubiquitous interest group involvement might offer some insights into how to regulate

---

[2] *See supra* Chapter 9, at 27.

[3] Corridoring is used to describe interest group efforts to influence regulatory processes (walking the corridors of the agencies), and is analogous to lobbying in the hallways of Congress. Andrew F. Popper, *Luncheon Session*, 4 ADMIN. L.J. 71, 76 (1990) (defining the term and attributing its coinage to Theodore Lowi).

[4] James M. Buchanan, *Politics Without Romance: A Sketch of Positive Public Choice Theory and Its Normative Implications*, *in* THE THEORY OF PUBLIC CHOICE—II 11 (James M. Buchanan & Robert D. Tollison eds., 1984).

[5] *See* Todd J. Zywicki, *Environmental Externalities and Political Externalities: The Political Economy of Environmental Regulation and Reform*, 73 TUL. L. REV. 845 (1999).

[6] Buchanan, *supra* note 4.

most effectively, including, most notably, how to design institutions, in order to harness interest group influence in a productive manner so as to minimize the divergence between constituent desires and enacted policy.[7]

Public choice also offers an important extension of the economic insight known as the *theory of the second best*.[8] The theory of the second best has been used to explain the functioning of private markets, and the benefits they are able to provide in deploying resources to their more highly valued uses, even though market institutions invariably depart from the ideas of perfect competition. Problems can include imperfect information, information asymmetries, varying degrees of market power, and problems of cost internalization. Efforts to correct a perceived market failure in one area might decrease overall efficiency if it creates a more problematic distortion in another area. In some circumstances, allowing an identified market failure to persist can be more efficient than incurring the costs, some known, and others not, of seeking to eradicate it. This also implicates public choice inasmuch as problematic political institutions, including inevitable interest group influence, can serve as one potential source of resulting inefficiencies arising from attempts to correct market failure.

Thus, in situations in which government intervention is generally thought to be appropriate or social welfare increasing, public choice can provide insights on how to best structure regulations or rules to increase the likelihood that government regulation will accomplish its intended purpose and how best to minimize the adverse consequences of rent seeking or rent dissipation in the pursuit of that goal. For example, in some instances, ambitious regulatory solutions might also be more apt to fall victim to such interest group pressures than modest approaches. A regulatory strategy that would appear to be the most direct and efficient approach in an ideal world might prove to be especially vulnerable to interest group distortions. In some circumstances, therefore, a more modest regulatory approach with smaller overall benefits might be preferable. This is consistent with the understanding that public choice does not counsel any particular ideological agenda; whichever agenda they pursue, however, regulatory proponents should be as, or more, concerned that the policies they seek to accomplish are meaningfully effectuated.

The remaining discussion in this part offers specific public choice insights into policies informed by the theory of second best. In situations in which government intervention or regulation is thought to be warranted, what can public choice tell us about how to effectively structure those regulatory interventions?

[7] For analyses along these lines, see Maxwell L. Stearns, *The Public Choice Case Against the Item Veto*, 49 WASH. & LEE L. REV. 385 (1992) (relying on interest group theory to argue against the item veto, which by unbundling the packaging of legislation would eliminate the power of interests to help in the process of procuring desired public interest legislation); Maxwell L. Stearns, *Direct (Anti-)Democracy*, 80 GEO. WASH. L. REV. 311 (2012) (demonstrating the capacity of legislatures, in comparisons with judicial review or plebiscites, to harness combined interest group pressures and those advocating for public goods in producing legislative packaging).

[8] *See* R.G. Lipsey & Kelvin Lancaster, *The General Theory of Second Best*, 24 REV. ECON. STUD. 11 (1956).

- What does public choice add?

A. Law & Economics and Public Choice Contrasted: The Case of Eminent Domain and "Just Compensation"

The concepts of rent seeking and rent dissipation have significant implications for the economic analysis of law and for legal doctrine. In this section, we will analyze the Fifth Amendment's requirement of "just compensation" in the government's exercise of power under the Eminent Domain Clause.[9] Specifically, we will contrast Richard Posner's law and economics analysis of just compensation and eminent domain with an alternative public choice analysis.

Assume the government needs to acquire a particular parcel of property for some public purpose for which there are no realistic market alternatives, such as to build a school or to preserve a historic landmark. Forcing the government to purchase the property through a consensual market transaction with the owner provides the landowner with the incentive to hold out and to act opportunistically by trying to extract a price that exceeds her true subjective valuation of the property. As a result, to avoid bilateral monopoly bargaining, which could defeat the project, the government is vested with the authority of eminent domain. This power effectively converts the owner's property right into a liability rule, subject to just compensation, rather than affording the owner the power to enjoin the transfer.[10] Enabling the government to compel the transfer, however, risks the flip side of the holdout problem: whereas the absence of eminent domain power risks disallowing the government to acquire properties for which it holds a true higher value, the power of eminent domain, by not compelling voluntary market transactions, risks having the government take property that the original owner values more highly than the government.

1. *A Law and Economics Analysis of Eminent Domain and Just Compensation*

To address these second-order concerns respecting potentially inefficient takings, standard law and economics analysis maintains that the requirement of just compensation works to minimize this risk: if the government is going to take property, it should be required to pay fair market value to prevent the potential resulting inefficiency in which the property is better left in private hands. Just compensation requires that the government pay the prevailing market price. If that price exceeds the value that the government places upon the property, the government will forgo the taking because it will not be willing to pay more than the value it attaches to the land. Conversely, if the government values the land more highly than fair market value, it can compel the taking, compensate the owner, and still potentially improve societal welfare. We say potentially because as a result of strategic holdouts, there is no objective way to ascertain whether claimed higher subjective valuation is sincere or strategic. In this analysis, the just

---

[9] U.S. CONST. amend. V ("[N]or shall private property be taken for public use, without just compensation"). The Eminent Domain Clause, also known as the Takings Clause, applies to state and local governments through the Fourteenth Amendment Due Process Clause. We consider other aspects of eminent domain, *supra* Chapter 8, and *infra* Chapter 16.

[10] *See supra* Chapters 7 and 8 (discussing property rules and liability rules in property law).

compensation requirement ensures that the government is more likely to take property when it actually places a higher value on its proposed use than the landowner.[11]

Richard Posner claims that this traditional law and economics account of the just compensation requirement is incomplete and that it is not necessary to pay fair market value to prevent inefficient takings.[12] To illustrate, assume a taking that involves the acquisition of a single parcel, and that, as compared with the government, the landowner places a higher value on her property. Posner maintains that under the standard economic assumption of no transaction costs, a welfare-reducing taking will not occur even absent the just compensation requirement. Posner posits that a property owner who is about to have her land seized will not sit idly by and acquiesce in the taking. Instead, she will rationally invest up to the value of the resource to be taken, including hiring lawyers or lobbyists, to fight it. To simplify, assume that the property owner could simply pay off the government to let her retain land she values more highly, rather than to have the government acquire it and to deploy it to a lower-valued use. If the government is indifferent as between this particular parcel and one for which the owner does not hold the same higher subjective value, the government can take the payoff, purchase the other property, and still come out ahead.

This result follows from the Coase theorem: In a world without transactions costs, the resources will flow to, or remain in, the hands of the person who values it most highly without regard to liability rules.[13] To be sure, the removal of the just compensation requirement has distributional consequences, but per Coase, it does not have efficiency consequences. By contrast, if, as compared with the homeowner, the government places a higher value on the property, the government would be willing to invest more in lawyers and other resources to take the land than the owner would be willing to invest to block the taking. In that case the land will be reallocated to its highest-valued use. Thus, Posner concludes, the outcome, as a matter of efficiency, is independent of the requirement of just compensation.[14]

2. *An Alternative Public Choice Analysis of Eminent Domain and Just Compensation*

Although Posner's analysis reveals the limits of the standard economic account of the just compensation requirement, public choice demonstrates that Posner's alternative economic analysis might be incomplete.[15] Posner's analysis focuses solely on the deadweight loss resulting from a potentially inefficient government taking. Todd Zywicki offers an alternative positive justification for requiring just compensation that rests on public choice. Zywicki maintains that Posner fails to account for the social cost of this

---

[11] This assumes that the government fully internalizes the costs in engaging in these sorts of projects. Given the problem of agency costs, as described in Chapter 1, however, it may be that the incentives of those individuals who make the actual decisions are not fully aligned with that of the government or the constituents as a whole.

[12] RICHARD A. POSNER, ECONOMIC ANALYSIS OF LAW § 3.7, at 56 (7th ed. 2007).

[13] *See* Chapter 1, *supra* part IV.

[14] In effect, Posner's argument is an application of the Coase theorem. Do you see why?

[15] *See* Todd J. Zywicki, *The Political Economy of Takings Law: Reflections on Public Use and Just Compensation* (working paper, 2011) (on file with author).

regime, which includes the additional expenses Gordon Tullock associates with rent seeking or rent dissipation.[16] These losses include the very expenses that Posner properly identifies as ameliorating the risk of the inefficient taking, namely the expenditures on lawyers and lobbyists necessary to block it. The resulting rent dissipation depletes resources expended for the sole purpose of blocking a transfer that risks moving land from a more to less highly valued use. Although lobbying reduces the risk of realizing the deadweight loss (the lost triangle) associated with the ultimate property transfer, the expenditures themselves comprise an independent social-welfare loss (the dissipated rectangle).[17]

In Zywicki's analysis, rather than encouraging socially wasteful expenditures on lawyers and political activity, the just compensation requirement reserves the value of the land to the property owner. Such expenditures might appear to be a simple wealth transfer, but they are not. In the absence of the inefficient taking, these expenditures would not arise, freeing the lawyers and lobbyists to engage in more highly valued activity. There may still be some remaining litigation over the proper value to assign to the property to ensure that a taking is efficient with the just compensation requirement in place, but the requirement substantially narrows the range of conflict and thus the range of expenditures for rent seeking or rent avoidance. By contrast, eliminating the just compensation requirement risks facilitating a wasteful rent-seeking game and thus inviting a substantial social-welfare loss.

Assume, for example, the owner subjectively values her land at $120, the fair market value is $100, and the government values it at $100. If the government is required to pay just compensation, the $100 will be simply a wealth transfer from the government to the private owner. This transfer will have distributional consequences (a transfer of $100 to the landowner), but it will not result in a loss of social wealth through rent dissipation, as the government will, in this simplified example, have no incentive to hire lawyers and others to fight for the taking. The government will have to pay $100 regardless, either to lawyers or to the landowner, and, all else equal, it is apt to prefer the more expeditious, and predictable, strategy. This means one with less conflict that also reduces the rent-dissipation risk. On the other side, the landowner will have an incentive to spend up to $20 (rather than $120) on lawyers and lobbyists, because the $100 payment substantially reduces her risk of suffering a capital loss, thereby reducing wasteful rent dissipation. Thus, under Posner's stated assumptions, the result will be the same as far as which party owns the land. The result in terms of wasteful rent dissipation, however, varies depending on whether or not the government is required to pay just compensation.

B. The Economics of Rules Versus Standards in Financial Regulation

Public choice theory can also provide important insights into the longstanding debate over the use of rules versus standards in governmental activity and the design of

[16] Richard Posner has acknowledged this caveat to his argument. *See* RICHARD A. POSNER, ECONOMIC ANALYSIS OF LAW § 3.7, at 59 n.6 (6th ed. 2003) (citing Zywicki, *supra* note 15) (acknowledgement omitted in later editions).

[17] *See supra* Chapter 11, Figure 11:1.

institutions that address particular social problems.[18] An important illustration involves financial services regulation in the United States and the issue of banks deemed too-big-to-fail.[19]

1. Financial Crises and Too-Big-to-Fail Banks

Consider the problem of very large banks that pose a systemic risk to the economy if they become insolvent, sometimes called *too-big-to-fail.* These large and complex entities present complicated regulatory challenges. The unique structure of the financial services industry, the highly concentrated nature of the leading banks, and the deep and ongoing regulatory entanglement between banks and their regulators pose an illuminating case study for public choice and the law.

Beginning in 2007 and accelerating in 2008, the global financial system spiraled into chaos, largely as a result of mortgage-related investments. In the United States, as in other parts of the world, government officials responded with extraordinary interventions into the economy that were intended to stabilize the financial system. In the United States, the Bush administration pursued a series of ad hoc interventions, beginning with the bailout of the investment bank, Bear Stearns, in the spring of 2008, that was followed by a series of summary mergers between failed savings and loans and mortgage companies with existing banks. Following the unexpected collapse of the investment bank Lehman Brothers—largely as a result of a surprise government decision *not* to provide an expected bailout of that firm[20]—the government finally abandoned its strategy of ad hoc, piecemeal responses. Instead, it proposed a comprehensive legislative strategy through the enactment of the Emergency Economic Stabilization Act of 2008.[21] Among other provisions, the Act created the Troubled Asset Relief Program (TARP).[22]

TARP made available up to $700 billion in federal funding to stabilize the financial system. TARP was a centerpiece of myriad programs and initiatives by various governmental and related entities to ameliorate the crisis caused by widespread mortgage delinquencies and resulting foreclosures.[23] As initially proposed, the funds targeted the purchase of so-called toxic assets (mainly subprime mortgage loans and related securities) to remove those assets from bank balance sheets. Eventually, the program was repurposed, and the funds were used to make direct investments in an effort to recapitalize banks.[24] Although causation remains unclear, despite a deep recession the financial system eventually recovered, and the economy improved. In 2009, under the guidance of the Obama administration, TARP funds were used to help bail out General

---

[18] *See* Pierre J. Schlag, *Rules and Standards*, 33 UCLA L. REV. 379 (1985); Louis Kaplow, *Rules Versus Standards: An Economic Analysis*, 42 DUKE L.J. 557 (1992); Ezra Friedman & Abraham L. Wickelgren, *A New Angle on Rules Versus Standards*, 16 AM. L. & ECON. REV. 499 (2014).

[19] GARY H. STERN & RON J. FELDMAN, TOO BIG TO FAIL: THE HAZARDS OF BANK BAILOUTS (2004).

[20] *See* DAVID SKEEL, THE NEW FINANCIAL DEAL: UNDERSTANDING THE DODD-FRANK ACT AND ITS (UNINTENDED) CONSEQUENCES 19–40 (2011).

[21] Emergency Economic Stabilization Act of 2008, 12 U.S.C. §§ 5201–5241 (2012).

[22] *See* SIMON JOHNSON & JAMES KWAK, 13 BANKERS 164–68 (2010).

[23] For an overview and summary of the various programs established during this period, see Jonathan G. Katz, *Who Benefited from the Bailout?*, 95 MINN. L. REV. 1568 (2011).

[24] *See id.*

Motors and Chrysler, funding uses that arguably were outside of the intended scope of TARP.[25]

Some scholars applying tools from law and economics have praised these extraordinary government interventions by the Bush administration, and later by the Obama administration, as a necessary and appropriate use of government discretion to address the financial crisis. This position has been most forcefully articulated by law Professors Eric Posner and Adrian Vermeule.[26] They endorse the ad hoc flexible approach of the Bush administration's response, arguing that the President needs broad discretion to respond in times of economic crisis. They maintain that tying the President's hands with rigid legal rules will limit the President's ability to take actions necessary to restore stability to the financial system. Posner and Vermeule state: "The Fed and Treasury did not simply apply general norms established by a policymaking Congress. The nature of the crisis, including the overwhelming uncertainty, *forced* these two agencies to take an ad hoc approach."[27] Posner and Vermeule conclude that emergency actions taken in response to the crisis were effective at stabilizing the economy.

Assume that Posner and Vermeule are correct that some government action was appropriate in theory and useful in practice.[28] Does it necessarily follow that the most effective method of accomplishing financial system stability involves vesting the President with broad and largely unconstrained discretion? Consider whether an alternative approach might have achieved similar ends more effectively.[29]

Posner and Vermeule blame the government for stoking the crisis by choosing not to bail out Lehman Brothers in September 2008.[30] Professor David Skeel has argued that their analysis is incomplete. Skeel contends that Posner and Vermeule fail to consider a major reason that the Lehman Brothers failure was so disruptive, which grows out of moral hazard problems created by the Bear Stearns bailout. In response to that bailout, Lehman Brothers rejected efforts by the government to merge the company with other

---

[25] *See* Gary Lawson, *Burying the Constitution Under a TARP*, 33 HARV. J. L. & PUB. POL'Y 55 (2010); *see also* Robert K. Rasmussen & David A. Skeel, Jr., *Governmental Intervention in an Economic Crisis*, 19 U. PA. J. BUS. L. 7, 27 (2016) (noting that then-Treasury Secretary Henry Paulson publicly stated that he did not intend to use TARP funds to bail out General Motors and Chrysler).

[26] ERIC A. POSNER & ADRIAN VERMEULE, EXECUTIVE UNBOUND: AFTER THE MADISONIAN REPUBLIC (2010).

[27] *Id.* at 38 (emphasis added).

[28] Richard Kovacevich, who served as CEO of Wells Fargo during the financial crisis, has challenged this premise. *See* Richard Kovacevich, *The Financial Crisis: Why the Conventional Wisdom Has It All Wrong*, 34 CATO J. 541 (2014). Kovacevich argues that the government's interventions and the manner in which they were executed actually exacerbated the crisis, rather than dampening it. Kovacevich criticizes the government's decision (described in more detail below) to force all of the largest banks to take TARP funds, in some cases against their wishes, as happened with Wells Fargo. Although the government maintained that this funding would improve market stability if all of the solvent banks also accepted money, Kovacevich instead argues that this exacerbated instability by leading investors to infer that all banks were in trouble even though some who received such funding were not. For purposes of the current discussion, we simply assume that the government's interventions were effective and focus on the manner in which those programs were executed.

[29] *See* Todd Zywicki, *The Rule of Law During Times of Economic Crisis*, *in* ECONOMIC AND POLITICAL CHANGE AFTER CRISIS: PROSPECTS FOR GOVERNMENT, LIBERTY, AND THE RULE OF LAW 36 (Stephen H. Balch & Benjamin Powell eds., 2016).

[30] POSNER & VERMEULE, *supra* note 26, at 38.

financial institutions, which might have saved it, assuming instead that like Bear Stearns, should it fail, the government would also provide the necessary financial support. This seemed especially likely given that Lehman Brothers was a larger and more systemically important financial institution.[31]

Skeel further claims that rather than taking steps to prepare for an orderly bankruptcy, Lehman Brothers engaged in a game of chicken with the government by threatening an expensive, and potentially catastrophic, failure in the event that it was not bailed out, and that it continued to expect a government bailout virtually up until the moment of its bankruptcy filing.[32] Skeel observes that Lehman Brothers' bonds continued to trade with no apparent risk premium up until the time of its bankruptcy filing, which suggest that market participants expected that it would be bailed out.[33] As a result, the decision of the government not to bail out Lehman Brothers, after having previously bailed out Bear Stearns, caught market actors by surprise and made the Lehman Brothers' failure much more disruptive than it otherwise might have been.

Posner and Vermeule focus on the potential benefits to the economy of providing the President with discretionary authority to undertake ad hoc responses to the financial crisis. Skeel's response suggests that this argument might overlook the risk that the government's discretionary activity had the potential to exacerbate the disruption caused by Lehman Brothers' failure, thereby worsening the overall impact on the economy.[34] In a perfect world, unaffected by interest group politicking, rent-seeking, rent-extraction, and strategic behavior by market participants, providing the President with unconstrained authority to take such discretionary actions might be sound policy. On the other hand, with those pervasive elements, the question becomes more complicated. Skeel thus suggests that the Posner and Vermeule analysis implicitly assumes that the government's response to a financial crisis is most accurately described by the public interest model of government. In that model, the President, as the principal governmental actor, is motivated to promote the public interest, and his efforts are expected to be largely undistorted by interest group influences (such as lobbying by large banks for government bail outs) or strategic behavior by private market actors that try to force the government into particular actions.

Todd Zywicki has argued that although elevating standard-based discretionary decision making over rule-based decision making potentially enables the government to engage in more targeted and fine-tuned interventions, enlarging the scope of government discretion potentially creates heightened opportunities for interest groups to manipulate

---

31 *See* SKEEL, *supra* note 20, at 19–29 (discussing "The Lehman Myth").

32 The *chicken game* is discussed in Chapter 16.

33 *See* SKEEL, *supra* note 20, at 29 fig. 2.3.

34 *See* Kovacevich, *supra* note 28; *see also* ROGER KOPPL, FROM CRISIS TO CONFIDENCE: MACROECONOMICS AFTER THE CRASH (2015); JOHN A. ALLISON, THE FINANCIAL CRISIS AND THE FREE MARKET CURE 164 (2013) (arguing that it was "the inconstancy and arbitrariness of government policy makers" that rattled the capital markets, not Lehman's failure). Some commentators claim that the government's announcement of TARP might have precipitated the crisis by causing a panic, rather than settling markets. *See* ALLISON, *supra*, at 165; *see also* John B. Taylor, *Causes of the Financial Crisis and the Slow Recovery*, *in* ACROSS THE GREAT DIVIDE: NEW PERSPECTIVES ON THE FINANCIAL CRISIS 51 (Martin Neil Baily & John B. Taylor eds., 2014).

outcomes to further private interests.[35] In Zywicki's analysis, one benefit of rule-based decision making is encouraging predictably consistent treatment of similarly situated persons or entities. In this instance, Zywicki claims, it would have potentially averted the risk that the government, by singling out particular banks, such as Bear Stearns, for favorable treatment, and others, such as Lehman Brothers, for unfavorable treatment, would send an unanticipated shock to the economy.[36] He further contends that in the world of the second best, a rule-based policy (such as "no bail outs" or "always bail out") might be more effective than an ad hoc policy, even if a more discretionary policy might, in theory, generate more optimal results.

Consider the example of the actual practice by which TARP funds were allocated during the financial crisis. By its terms, the TARP legislation set specific criteria for funding eligibility, including ascertaining the degree of institutional solvency. A study of those who supported the enactment of the TARP program and those who received benefits suggests that these criteria might not have been applied consistently in practice. An analysis of political support for TARP found that the likelihood of a politician voting in favor of TARP legislation correlated positively with the amount of financial support she or he received from the financial services sector.[37] In the dispersal of TARP funding, banks with senior executives or members of their board of directors who were former employees of the United States Treasury Department or bank regulators were more likely to receive TARP funds than those that did not.[38] Other studies found that the likelihood of receiving TARP funds, the amount of TARP funds received, and the value to a particular bank of the enactment of TARP correlated with the degree of political connectedness and clout of the bank. Further, the likelihood of particular politicians voting in favor of the bailout correlated with the degree of political support offered by the financial services industry that politicians or regulators overseeing the industry received.[39]

Zywicki explains that the Treasury Department also forced some banks to take bailout money that they did not want and that those banks claimed not to need.[40] Those banks were then required to pay back those funds at substantial cost to shareholders.[41] Zywicki recounts that both John Allison,[42] CEO of BB&T at the time, and Richard

---

[35] *See* Todd J. Zywicki, *Rent-Seeking, Crony Capitalism, and the Crony Constitution*, 23 SUP. CT. ECON. REV. 77 (2016).

[36] *Id.*

[37] Jim F. Couch et al., *An Analysis of the Financial Services Bailout Vote*, 31 CATO J. 119 (2011); Michael Dorsch, *Bailout for Sale? The Vote to Save Wall Street*, 155 PUB. CHOICE 211, 221 (2011).

[38] *See* Ran Duchin & Dennis Sosyura, *The Politics of Government Investment*, 106 J. FIN. ECON. 24 (2012).

[39] These studies are summarized in Zywicki, *Crony Capitalism*, *supra* note 35.

[40] *See id.*

[41] *See* Kovacevich, *supra* note 28 (noting that Wells Fargo was forced to take bailout money over its objections); Andrew Martin, *Give BB&T Liberty, But Not a Bailout*, N.Y. TIMES (Aug. 1, 2009), http://www.nytimes.com/2009/08/02/business/02bbt.html (reporting comments of former BB&T CEO John Allison that BB&T was forced by the federal government to accept bailout money over its objections).

[42] *See* ALLISON, *supra* note 34, at 170–71. Allison argues that one benefit to the government of forcing healthy banks, such as BB&T, to accept TARP funds was that the government knew loans to those institutions would be paid back. This would make the program look more successful in the eyes of the public, increasing

Kovacevich, CEO of Wells Fargo, have reported that their banks were forced to take TARP funds even though they claimed that they did not need those funds.[43]

Although interest group theory helps to explain some of these dynamics, it might be less helpful in devising specific solutions. Zywicki posits that whereas standard law and economics analysis, such as that offered by Posner and Vermeule, focuses on the benefits of discretionary action during a crisis, public choice theory provides the basis for a more comprehensive analysis of the resulting costs.

How might one go about weighing the benefits of government discretion (as identified by Posner and Vermeule) against the accompanying costs? What are the criteria for measuring the success of a government program once all costs are taken into account? Should other values be included that might evade a conventional cost-benefit analysis? If so, what are these values? Do you think that TARP was sound in its adoption and implementation? Why or why not? Whose analysis, Posner and Vermeule, Skeel, or Zywicki, do you find more persuasive, and why?

2. *Interest Groups and the Post-Financial Crisis Regulatory Regime*

Consider the related question concerning the problem of banks deemed too-big-to-fail, which arose in the post-2008 recession-crisis era. In response to the financial crisis, Congress passed the Dodd-Frank Financial Reform Act, a massive piece of legislation, the primary purpose of which was to stabilize the financial system and to eliminate the need for future bailouts. The legislation creates multiple new rules and institutions to ensure that in the event of insolvency, a large bank will be liquidated and not bailed out.[44] The primary vehicle established by Dodd-Frank is the Orderly Liquidation Authority (OLA), which, as the name suggests, is designed to force the orderly liquidation of insolvent financial firms.[45] Executing Dodd-Frank has required extensive compliance costs, including hundreds of rulemakings, comprising thousands of pages, with the consequence of substantial burdens on regulated firms.[46]

---

public approval for the initiative. Keep this example in mind when you consider the discussion of bureaucratic behavior and bureaucratic incentives in Chapter 20.

[43] *See* Mark Calvey, *Former Wells Fargo CEO Dick Kovacevich Blasts TARP: An 'Unmitigated Disaster'*, S.F. BUS. J. (Jun. 13, 2012), https://www.bizjournals.com/sanfrancisco/blog/2012/06/wells-fargo-dick-kovacevich-occupy-tarp.html (quoting Richard Kovacevich). Documents subsequently released by the U.S. government confirmed that the position of Treasury Secretary Henry Paulson was that the country's nine largest banks "would be required" to take TARP money whether they wanted to or not. *See* Sara Lepro, *First Nine Banks Were Forced to Take Bailouts*, BOSTON.COM (May 15, 2009), http://archive.boston.com/business/articles/2009/05/15/first_nine_banks_were_forced_to_take_bailouts/.

[44] For an overview of the Dodd-Frank legislation and its key provisions, see SKEEL, *supra* note 20.

[45] *See* SKEEL, *supra* note 20, at 117–54 (discussing Dodd-Frank's rules for resolving financial distress among insolvent firms).

[46] According to one estimate by the American Action Forum, as of 2016 Dodd-Frank had imposed more than $36 billion in final rules costs and 73 million paperwork hours. *See* Sam Batkins & Dan Goldbeck, *Six Years After Dodd-Frank: Higher Costs, Uncertain Benefits*, AM. ACTION F.: INSIGHT (July 20, 2016), https://www.americanactionforum.org/insight/six-years-dodd-frank-higher-costs-uncertain-benefits/.

Despite the law that is designed to address the TBTF problem, several empirical studies have found that there remains a continuing TBTF subsidy for large banks. The subsidy is reflected in a smaller risk premium that TBTF banks must pay to finance their ongoing operations.[47] This finding is consistent with the assumption that large banks retain an implicit government guarantee that they will not be forced to liquidate in the event of insolvency. Leading Republican and Democratic politicians have argued that Dodd-Frank does not actually eliminate the TBTF problem.[48] Many experts claim that the regime designed by Dodd-Frank probably would work effectively if it was invoked in a crisis.[49]

If the Dodd-Frank structure could be used to address the problem of bailouts of TBTF institutions, why do many in the affected industry, and several scholars, contend that it has not worked successfully? Todd Zywicki argues that although the Dodd-Frank regime may be viable in theory, it fails to address the *political* challenges associated with restricting bank bailouts. Zywicki claims that the Dodd-Frank insolvency regime does not provide a credible commitment that political officials actually will follow Dodd-Frank, rather than employ bailouts during a crisis, *even if* the regulatory structure might have worked had it been property implemented. Zywicki contends that in a crisis, politicians tend to favor short-term strategies that seem likely to stabilize immediate situation, such as bailouts, and thus tend to discount the long-term consequences, such as the moral hazard problems associated with bailouts, along with the corresponding incentive of large banks to take on excessive risks and thus to become highly leveraged.[50] Given the trade-

---

[47] *See* U.S. GOV'T ACCOUNTABILITY OFFICE, GAO–14–621, LARGE BANK HOLDING COMPANIES: EXPECTATIONS OF GOVERNMENT SUPPORT (2014); INT'L MONETARY FUND, IMF SURVEY: BIG BANKS BENEFIT FROM GOVERNMENT SUBSIDIES (Mar. 31, 2014), http://www.imf.org/external/pubs/ft/survey/so/2014/POL033114A.htm. Other studies have found that the TBTF subsidy persists but on a smaller scale. *See* JOHN LESTER & ADITI KUMAR, DO BOND SPREADS SHOW EVIDENCE OF TOO BIG TO FAIL EFFECTS? EVIDENCE FROM 2009–2013 AMONG US BANK HOLDING COMPANIES (2014). One study concludes that the TBTF subsidy has been eliminated. *See* Bhanu Balasubramnian & Ken Cyree, The End of Too-Big-to-Fail? Evidence from Senior Bank Bond Yield Spreads Around the Dodd-Frank Act (June, 2012), https://papers.ssrn.com/sol3/papers.cfm?abstract_id=2089750.

[48] *See, e.g.*, Remarks by Senator Elizabeth Warren on Citibank and Its Bailout Provision (Dec. 12, 2014), https://www.warren.senate.gov/?p=press_release&id=686 ("If this Congress is going to open up Dodd-Frank in the months ahead, let's open it up to get *tougher*—to create more bailout opportunities. If we are going to open up Dodd-Frank, let's open it up so that, once and for all, we *end Too Big to Fail.* I mean let's really end it—not just say we did. . . . Let's pass something—anything—that would help break up these giant banks.") (remarks of Democratic Senator); Andrew Ross Sorkin, *What Timothy Geithner Really Thinks*, N.Y. TIMES MAG. (May 8, 2014), https://www.nytimes.com/2014/05/11/magazine/what-timothy-geithner-really-thinks.html (" 'Does TBTF still exist? Yeah, of course it does." (quoting former Democratic Treasury Secretary Timothy Geithner); REPORT PREPARED BY THE REPUBLICAN STAFF OF THE COMMITTEE ON FINANCIAL SERVICES, U.S. HOUSE OF REPRESENTATIVES, FAILING TO END "TOO BIG TO FAIL": AN ASSESSMENT OF THE DODD-FRANK ACT FOUR YEARS LATER 97 (113th Congress, Second Session, July 2014), https://financialservices.house.gov/uploadedfiles/071814_tbtf_report_final.pdf (concluding that "the Dodd-Frank Act further entrenched the problem of 'too big to fail' by giving regulators even greater control over our financial system and a virtually unlimited pot of taxpayer money to bail out financial institutions when regulation inevitably fails.").

[49] Randall D. Guynn, *Are Bailouts Inevitable?*, 29 YALE. J. ON REG. 121 (2012).

[50] Empirical studies have found that banks that received TARP funds were more likely to take greater risks than banks that did not before the crisis. *See* Deniz Igan, Prachi Mishra, & Thierry Tressel, *A Fistful of Dollars: Lobbying and the Financial Crisis*, 26 NBER MACROECON. ANN. 195 (2011).

off between the short-term political benefits of averting financial instability, on one side, and the long-run costs of market instability, and even a possible recession, on the other, rational politicians will tend to support bailouts. Zywicki argues that this tendency will be even stronger in a situation such as that created by Dodd-Frank, in which the procedures themselves are novel and untested and thus associated with political risks given the uncertainty as to whether they will actually succeed. Moreover, Zywicki notes that Dodd-Frank itself was passed along a party-line vote in Congress over substantial Republican opposition. This raises the additional question of whether any Republican President would be willing to rely on its procedures in the event of a crisis. Bankers in TBTF institutions might therefore come to expect bailouts regardless of other regulatory interventions that appear to commit the government to a contrary policy.

Michael Munger and Richard Salsman characterize the problem follows: "[T]he premise of [TBTF] is that a government promise not to act violates time consistency; states may commit to allowing large firms to fail, but by now 'everyone knows' that no government will stand by, passively, amid systemic failure, even if, by intervening, it further boosts the degree of moral hazard."[51] Vern McKinley observes that experience during the last financial crisis suggests that in times of crisis, such expectations tend to be self-reinforcing; when markets expect bailouts, not providing them, as occurred with Lehman Brothers, can trigger market uncertainty.[52]

In Zywicki's larger analysis, although the OLA insolvency regime might appear efficient it risks failing to consider the short-term incentives that politicians face to bail out failing firms to stave off a deeper crisis. Zywicki maintains that experience during the financial crisis suggests that courts will be reluctant to insist upon rigid adherence to legal rules when faced with the claimed need for extraordinary government action.[53] He further observes that public choice is helpful in assessing these additional dynamics in a second-best world. He believes that this implies two options: either accept the reality that very large banks will be bailed out in the event of insolvency (and regulate them accordingly so as to reduce the risk of moral hazard and systemic risk) or break up large banks so as to avoid having a category of banks deemed TBTF.[54] These alternatives have different costs and benefits that must be measured against those of Dodd-Frank. Zywicki claims that this analysis avoids the potential mistake of comparing Dodd-Frank as intended, but not necessarily as implemented, against the risk of a financial crisis. Zywicki concludes that when the de jure legal regime (no bailouts) differs from the de facto legal regime

---

[51] Michael C. Munger & Richard M. Salsman, *Is "Too Big to Fail" Too Big?* 11 GEO. J.L. & PUB POL'Y 433, 438 (2013).

[52] *See* VERN MCKINLEY, FINANCING FAILURE: A CENTURY OF BAILOUTS 270–75 (2012) (collecting quotes from Treasury Secretary Henry Paulson regarding the need to bail out large banks because that response was expected by the markets).

[53] *See* POSNER & VERMEULE, *supra* note 26 (noting that courts and the rule of law impose minimal constraints on U.S. presidents during periods of financial crisis); Todd J. Zywicki, *Economic Uncertainty, the Courts, and the Rule of Law*, 35 HARV. J.L. & PUB. POL'Y 195 (2012). Zywicki contends that these problems are exacerbated by judicial reliance on such doctrines as standing and mootness, which, in the Chrysler bankruptcy case, resulted in failing to resolve several contentious case issues. *See* Todd J. Zywicki, *The Chrysler and General Motors Bankruptcies*, *in* RESEARCH HANDBOOK ON CORPORATE BANKRUPTCY LAW (Barry Adler ed., forthcoming 2019).

[54] For an argument along these lines, see Munger & Salsman, *supra* note 51.

(bailouts), the result might be to raise the cost and risk of financial regulation as a consequence of the resulting uncertainty as to the government's potential response in an economic crisis.[55]

Moreover, although Dodd-Frank was intended to regulate large banks and to reduce systemic risk, empirical evidence indicates that the compliance costs have fallen disproportionately on small banks. Marshall Lux and Robert Greene maintain that although certain regulatory compliance costs have fallen specifically on larger firms (such as the costs of complying with Dodd-Frank's special rules for banks considered to pose systemic risk to the economy), the overall costs of regulation have fallen disproportionately on smaller banks that lack comparable economies of scale in regulatory compliance.[56] Professor Peter B. Pashigian has argued that the costs of regulation are often relatively more expensive for small firms than for large firms to bear.[57] In particular, the costs of many regulations that have a substantial fixed-cost component (such as the apparatus to satisfy certain paperwork obligations), do not scale proportionally to the size of the firm's operations. As JPMorgan Chase & Co. CEO Jamie Dimon observed, Dodd-Frank has "widened the moat" in the competitive position between TBTF institutions and others.[58] Similarly, Goldman Sachs CEO Lloyd Blankfein announced in 2010 that the bank would be "among the biggest beneficiaries" of Dodd-Frank as its regulatory costs and regulatory-created profit opportunities would be particularly advantageous to large banks that could bear those costs more easily than smaller competitors.[59] In fact, some commentators claim that efforts to reform or repeal some elements of Dodd-Frank have met with opposition from larger banks that recognize the competitive advantages provided by some elements of the Dodd-Frank regime.[60]

---

[55] Some scholars claim that many of the important effects of Dodd-Frank have been consistent with public choice predictions. Some provisions, such as the Durbin Amendment, which imposed price controls on the interchange fees that large banks could assess on debit card transactions, reflect strong interest group pressures. *See* TODD J. ZYWICKI, GEOFFREY A. MANNE & JULIAN MORRIS, UNREASONABLE AND DISPROPORTIONATE: HOW THE DURBIN AMENDMENT HARMS POORER AMERICANS AND SMALL BUSINESSES (2017).

[56] Marshall Lux & Robert Greene, *The State and Fate of Community Banking* (M-RCBG Assoc. Working Paper No. 37, 2015), https://www.hks.harvard.edu/centers/mrcbg/publications/awp/awp37 (noting that the assets of small banks have shrunk twice as fast after Dodd-Frank's enactment as compared to before); Hester Pierce, Ian Robinson & Thomas Stratmann, *How Are Small Banks Fairing Under Dodd-Frank?* (George Mason University Mercatus Ctr., Working Paper No. 14–05, 2014), https://www.mercatus.org/publication/how-are-small-banks-faring-under-dodd-frank.

[57] *See* Peter B. Pashigian, *The Effect of Environmental Regulation on Optimal Plant Size and Factor Shares*, 27 J.L. & ECON. 1 (1984).

[58] Rick Rouan, *Dimon says Dodd-Frank Puts 'Bigger Moat' Around JPMorgan Chase*, COLUMBUS BUS. FIRST (Feb. 5, 2013), http://www.bizjournals.com/columbus/blog/2013/02/dimon-says-dodd-frank-puts-bigger.html.

[59] Timothy P. Carney, *Goldman and JPMorgan Sit Safely Behind the Walls of Dodd-Frank*, WASH. EXAMINER (Feb. 12, 2015), http://www.washingtonexaminer.com/goldman-and-jpmorgan-sit-safely-behind-the-walls-of-dodd-frank/article/2560179.

[60] *See* Olivia Oran, *Big Banks' Relationship with Dodd-Frank: It's Complicated*, REUTERS (Nov. 23, 2016), https://www.reuters.com/article/us-usa-trump-banks/big-banks-relationship-with-dodd-frank-its-complicated-idUSKBN13I1YA; Norbert J. Michel, *Why Big-Wig Financial Execs Love Dodd-Frank*, THE HERITAGE FOUNDATION (Jul. 14, 2016), www.heritage.org/government-regulation/commentary/why-big-wig-financial-execs-love-dodd-frank.

Are you persuaded by this public choice assessment of Dodd-Frank? Why or why not? Do you believe that the resulting regulatory regime provides the basis for a credible commitment that the government will not bail out failed banks? If not, what do you see as the alternatives? If you accept Todd Zywicki's presentation of the trade-offs, what else would you want to know before deciding whether to keep the current OLA regulatory regime or, instead, to simply break up large banks? How might the various financial regulatory agencies respond to proposals that would eliminate the risk of bailouts, thereby also eliminating many of the costs and the regulatory complexity of the current regime? Consider the following observation: Some commentators believe that one contributor to the financial crisis was the lack of regulatory competence coupled with interest group capture of government regulatory agencies. To the extent that Dodd-Frank increases regulatory complexity and further empowers agencies, does this inform the preferred regulatory model? Why or why not?

C. International and Private Rulemaking Bodies

We now consider international and private rulemaking institutions. Consider, for example, the challenge of regulating global climate change. Because of the manner in which greenhouse gasses are emitted, effective regulation of carbon dioxide emissions should be accomplished on a global scale. From a regulatory perspective, however, reduction of greenhouse gas emissions presents a classic prisoners' dilemma,[61] and corresponding free rider problem: while all countries benefit over the long run from reducing emissions, reducing emissions is costly, both financially and politically. As a result, each country has an incentive to free ride on the efforts of other countries to reduce emissions without incurring the corresponding costs. And yet, international regulation raises the question as to which institutions would best promote necessary transnational agreements to adopt and implement such policies. Possible candidates include multilateral treaties and the United Nations, although it is also possible that new intergovernmental organizations might be formed specifically to address this environmental issue.

Each possible forum for collective action presents different decision-making rules and different opportunities for influence over the process. Designing effective domestic environmental regulation is complex, and those complexities deepen as we approach these subjects on a global scale. As Bruce Yandle and Stuart Buck observed, for example, much of the contentiousness over the 1997 Kyoto Protocol on Climate Change dealt less with the objectives of the treaty than with the cost allocations to various industries and nations.[62] Global environmental regulation provides a major opportunity for interest groups and nations to use regulation as a means of imposing costs on economic rivals. Yandle and Buck claim that this regime invited substantial interest group influence respecting the regulatory details. They present the resulting agreement as the product of a *Bootleggers and Baptists* negotiation, combining interests that sought to ameliorate climate change (a Baptist goal) with interest groups, and nations advancing protectionism (a

---

[61] For a more detailed discussion of the prisoners' dilemma, see *infra* Chapter 15.

[62] *See* Bruce Yandle & Stuart Buck, *Bootleggers, Baptists, and the Global Warming Battle*, 26 HARV. ENVTL. L. REV. 177 (2002). *See also supra* Chapter 11, Part II.G.

Bootlegger goal). Their analysis suggests that substantive policies are inextricably linked to questions as to the most effective means of implementation.

Other "legislative" bodies potentially implicate similar issues. Today, much of the development of private contract and commercial law is delegated to two private organizations, the American Law Institute (ALI),[63] which publishes the various *Restatements of Law*, and the Uniform Law Commission (ULC), which publishes among other things the *Uniform Commercial Code* (UCC). Each body comprises collections of experts, whose goal is to clarify and improve the law, and both bodies are extremely influential. Judges around the country frequently refer to, and rely upon, the ALI Restatements, and virtually every state has adopted the UCC (often with qualifications).

The authoritative and influential nature of these bodies provide them with considerable influence on the development of the law. In some respects, these organizations constitute quasi-private legislatures, although their works are not binding sources of law for any jurisdiction. The membership of these organizations are not elected by the public at large, yet the organizations wield substantial power to influence the content of the law across many jurisdictions.[64] Professors William Barker and Jonathan Macey have argued in separate works that as awareness of the influence that these organizations have on the law has grown, interest groups have sought to influence their proceedings and deliberations.[65] Mark Chenoweth has noted that these bodies tend to be heavily influenced by the perspectives of the professoriate, which is not necessarily representative of the public at large. For example, the Restatement process has been criticized as being "aspirational" rather than as merely restating the law.[66]

Do you agree with this analysis? Is there anything necessarily wrong with experts, here law professors and experienced practitioners, having a disproportionate influence over a process that relates to and benefits from their expertise? Do you believe that interest groups are apt to have an oversized influence on a process that is dominated by such experts, including law professors, whose incomes and careers do not depend upon catering to those interests? To the extent that the influence of professors on ALI deliberations is known, along with any perception that the Restatements sometimes take an aspirational approach, courts and legislatures are able to take this into account. The membership of the ALI is publicly available.[67] Are you concerned about the role these private quasi-legislative bodies play or the role that particular groups have in influencing them? Consider also that to become law, the ULC must have its proposals adopted through formal legislative processes. The ULC ultimately adds a step, and not an easy one,

---

[63] Disclosure: Maxwell Stearns is a member of ALI.

[64] *See* Larry E. Ribstein & Bruce H. Kobayashi, *An Economic Analysis of Uniform State Laws*, 25 J. LEGAL STUD. 131 (1996); Alan Schwartz & Robert E. Scott, *The Political Economy of Private Legislatures*, 143 U. PA. L. REV. 595 (1995).

[65] *See* William T. Barker, *Lobbying and the American Law Institute: The Example of Insurance Defense*, 26 HOFSTRA L. REV. 573 (1998); Jonathan R. Macey, *The Transformation of the American Law Institute*, 61 GEO. WASH. L. REV. 1212 (1992).

[66] *See, e.g.*, Mark Chenoweth, *Does the American Law Institute Have an Ethics Problem on Its Hands?*, FORBES (June 30, 2017), https://www.forbes.com/sites/wlf/2017/06/30/does-the-american-law-institute-have-an-ethics-problem-on-its-hands/#7097492a2c9d.

[67] MEMBER DIRECTORY, AM. L. INST., https://www.ali.org/members/directory/ (last visited Oct. 23, 2017) (listing names and affiliations of ALI members alphabetically).

thereby making legislative change more, rather than less, costly for affected groups. How does that affect your analysis?

Consider also Justice Scalia's critique of the Restatement process, as set out in a 2015 Supreme Court case. Justice Scalia stated that "modern Restatements . . . are of questionable value, and must be used with caution."[68] In particular, he claimed that "[o]ver time the Restatements' authors have abandoned the mission of describing the law, and have chosen instead to set forth their aspirations for what the law ought to be."[69] Scalia further stated that the Restatement "should be given no weight whatever as to the current state of the law, and no more weight regarding what the law ought to be than the recommendations of any respected lawyer or scholar."[70] Do you agree? Why or why not? Does the fact that ALI Restatements are vetted by vast numbers of experts belie the claim that they should bear no more influence than the views of a respected professor or scholar? Do you think that the significant role played by the ALI and ULC in shaping the law is appropriate? Why or why not?

Consider again the global climate change regulation. If you conclude that international bodies are prone to interest group influence respecting such regulation, what alternative would you propose? Given the overwhelming consensus of the scientific community that human activity has substantially contributed to global climate change, coupled with varying models, many of which are frightening in terms of the predicted impact on large populations,[71] should efforts to address this global problem account for concerns that interest group influence might risk distorting resulting policies? What role should public choice economics play in choosing the processes through which such policies are set? If international agreements, especially affecting developing nations, fail, should industrialized nations, such as the United States, enact laws unilaterally? Is this an area in which there is a risk that excessive reliance by some on public choice intuitions risks blocking vitally needed regulatory reform? Why or why not?

II. NORMATIVE DEBATES OVER INTEREST GROUP THEORY AND INTEREST-GROUP-THEORY-BASED LEGAL SCHOLARSHIP

In this section, we consider two normative critiques of public choice, with a particular emphasis on interest group theory, and on the legal scholarship relying upon it. We begin with Professor Einer Elhauge's article, *Does Interest Group Theory Justify More Intrusive Judicial Review?*[72] Elhauge answers the title question in the negative. The article presents two central arguments, the first of which is of particular importance to this

---

68 Kansas v. Nebraska, 135 S. Ct. 1042, 1064 (2015) (Scalia, J., concurring in part and dissenting in part).

69 *Id.*

70 *Id.*

71 *See generally* IPCC, CLIMATE CHANGE 2014: SYNTHESIS REPORT 7–16 (2015), https://www.ipcc.ch/pdf/assessment-report/ar5/syr/SYR_AR5_FINAL_full_wcover.pdf.

72 Einer R. Elhauge, *Does Interest Group Theory Justify More Intrusive Judicial Review?*, 101 YALE L.J. 31 (1991).

chapter. We then consider the critique by Professors Donald Green and Ian Shapiro, set out in their book, *Pathologies of Rational Choice Theory*.[73]

A. The Problem of Baselines[74]

Elhauge's analysis responds to claims by an impressive cadre of legal scholars who rely upon public choice to identify claimed defects in political processes and who, based on identified defects, advocate less judicial deference to legislative outcomes.[75] Elhauge advances two arguments that together represent a broadside attack on the literature relying on interest group theory to advocate changes in judicial interpretation of statutes:

> First, any defects in the political process identified by interest group theory depend on implicit normative baselines and thus do not stand independent of substantive conclusions about the merits of particular political outcomes. Accordingly, expansions of judicial review cannot meaningfully be limited by requiring threshold findings of excessive interest group influence. Further, the use of interest group theory to condemn the political process reflects normative views that are contestable and may not reflect the views of the polity.
>
> Second, even if interest group theory succeeds in demonstrating defects in the political process, that would not justify the leap to the conclusion that more intrusive judicial review would improve lawmaking. The litigation process cannot be treated as exogenous to interest group theory because that process is also subject to forms of interest group influence that would be exacerbated if judicial review became more intrusive. More generally, when one makes the necessary comparative assessment, interest group theory does not establish (as it must to justify more intrusive judicial review) that the litigation process is, overall, less defective than the political process.[76]

In essence, Elhauge's major critique of normative legal scholarship that relies upon interest group theory is that it invariably presumes, usually without acknowledgement, that having identified tendencies toward some degree of interest group influence in the political processes, that input is *excessive*. The problem is that it is never clear what the proper level of interest group input actually is, and thus the critical question—*excessive as compared with what?*—is not asked.

Elhauge further adds that the difficulty with such scholarship is that by identifying a given level of interest group influence, and claiming it disproportionate, the reader risks assuming a different baseline concerning interest group influence than would be the case absent the interference of interest group theory. Elhauge explains:

---

[73] DONALD P. GREEN & IAN SHAPIRO, PATHOLOGIES OF RATIONAL CHOICE THEORY: A CRITIQUE OF APPLICATIONS IN POLITICAL SCIENCE (1994).

[74] Portions of the discussions that follow are adapted from MAXWELL L. STEARNS, PUBLIC CHOICE AND PUBLIC LAW: READINGS AND COMMENTARY 246–53 (1997).

[75] Elhauge includes the following scholars and reviews many of their articles in his analysis: Erwin Chemerinsky, Frank Easterbrook, Richard Epstein, William Eskridge, Jonathan Macey, Jerry Mashaw, Gary Minda, William Page, Martin Shapiro, Bernard Siegan, Cass Sunstein, and John Wiley. Elhauge, *supra* note 69, at 33.

[76] Elhauge, *supra* note 72, at 34.

> More generally, . . . interest group theory can be seriously misleading unless one recognizes and identifies the nature of the implicit normative baseline. Unawareness that an implicit baseline exists can mislead one into believing that value-neutral defects in the political process justify expanding judicial review. Unawareness of the content of that implicit baseline can mislead one into applying normative standards different from the standards one would otherwise apply.[77]

Elhauge evaluates a large number of potential normative baselines that one could use interest group theory to advance. Although Elhauge views all of the potential baselines as contestable, his larger point is that once a baseline is selected, one can apply it directly to a proposed policy change without the intermediate step of considering the policy in question through the lens of public choice.

At one level, Elhauge's analysis appears irrefutable. As with economic analysis generally, interest group theory is a set of positive tools.[78] Proper economic analysis uses models to suggest the likely implications of a proposed policy change—and also to suggest means of testing a given thesis—but it cannot of its own force evaluate the merits of the resulting trade-offs. Such conclusions lie outside the scope of the economic models and necessarily rest, as Elhauge phrases it, on "implicit normative baselines."[79] This suggests that those reading normative scholarship resting upon public choice (we might say based upon any theory) must not only assess the care with which the public choice analysis (or whatever relevant analysis) is undertaken, but also must identify any unexpressed normative baselines capable of biasing the resulting analysis.

The second part of Elhauge's analysis suggests that virtually any baseline is contestable. This raises an important set of concerns as well. How does one select a baseline or set of baselines with which to evaluate proposals that are made in the name of public choice? If public choice demonstrates tendencies of political processes to favor one set of inputs over another, or one interest group over another, how does one select a baseline to inform the judiciary as to how best to proceed in assessing the resulting laws? As explored more fully in the applications in Chapter 11, for example, should the possibility that large bakeries or labor unions motivated the challenged law in *Lochner v. New York*,[80] or that large dairy producers influenced the filled milk ban in *United States v. Carolene Products*,[81] change the analysis or outcomes in those cases? Would such findings counsel different results than would be the case if we instead accepted the premise that in both cases, the legislatures' goals were simply to protect bakers' health and consumers of baked goods, in *Lochner*, and consumers of dairy products, in *Carolene Products*, respectively? Also, how are we to assess whether, as Elhauge also suggests, courts are also susceptible to interest group influence, thus calling into question their ability to check against interest-group driven laws, assuming that the operative baseline suggests such

---

[77] *Id.* at 49.

[78] It is also worth noting that Professor Elhauge carefully distinguishes the positive use of public choice from the normative legal scholarship that relies upon public choice insights to advocate changes in the proper scope or level of judicial review. *See* Elhauge, *supra* note 72, at 48.

[79] Elhauge, *supra* note 72, at 34.

[80] 198 U.S. 45 (1905).

[81] 304 U.S. 144 (1938).

influence to be excessive? Is there a coherent methodology, perhaps but not necessarily including one drawn from economics, for selecting among baselines? Should we assume that one baseline or set of baselines invariably applies? Might different baselines apply to different institutions? If so, how would one make such an assessment?

B. The Problem of Testability

In 1994, Professors Donald Green and Ian Shapiro wrote *Pathologies of Rational Choice Theory*.[82] This book presented a major attack on public choice that, unlike the Elhauge analysis, rested primarily on methodological grounds. The authors' analysis, which generated a strong response from public choice scholars,[83] rests on two principal bases. The primary difficulty, the authors claim, is that there has been a lack of empirical support for some of the strongest rational choice claims, an observation that later scholars have challenged.[84] For example, Green and Shapiro posit that: "Focusing centrally on [the works by such leading theorists as Kenneth Arrow, Anthony Downs, and William Riker], we claim that to date few theoretical insights derived from rational choice theory have been subjected to serious empirical scrutiny and survived."[85] In addition, the authors claim, public choice theorists have been willing to rest upon relatively thin evidence, but well-developed theoretical models, to advance ambitious normative proposals. The authors observe:

> Too often prescriptive conclusions . . . are floated on empirically dubious rational choice hypotheses, as when Riker and Weingast argue that the susceptibility of majority rule to manipulation justifies robust court-enforced constitutional constraints on what legislatures may legitimately do, as was undertaken by the U.S. Supreme Court during the *Lochner* era.[86]

There is no denying the importance of resting proposed policy changes on sound empirical testing and falsifiable theses. As you continue through this book, consider the extent to which, if any, those advancing proposals to change existing practices offer sufficient empirical support or rest instead on purely theoretical justifications. Further consider the nature of empirical verification. Is this limited to inferences drawn from large number data sets, or does it also include reliance upon public-choice-based models to offer robust accounts of otherwise anomalous phenomena, such as bodies of case law that are in tension with more conventional legal analysis? Is there a danger that insisting

---

[82] GREEN & SHAPIRO, *supra* note 73.

[83] *See* Symposium, *Pathologies of Rational Choice*, 9 CRITICAL REV. 25 (1995) (including as symposium contributors: Jeffrey Friedman, Robert P. Abelson, Dennis Chong, Daniel Diermeier, John Ferejohn, Debra Satz, Morris P. Fiorina, Stanley Kelley, Jr., Robert E. Lane, Susanne Lohmann, James Bernard Murphy, Peter C. Ordeshook, Norman Schofield, Kenneth A. Shepsle, and Michael Taylor).

[84] For a presentation claiming that since the Green and Shapiro book was published, a large literature has developed within public choice offering testable hypotheses, see Tonja Jacobi, *The Judiciary*, *in* RESEARCH HANDBOOK ON PUBLIC CHOICE AND PUBLIC LAW 234, 253–54 (Daniel A. Farber & Anne Joseph O'Connell eds., 2010) (claiming that "Green and Shapiro's criticism has lost much of its bite; nevertheless some issues with empirical testing of public choice hypotheses remain.").

[85] GREEN & SHAPIRO, *supra* note 73, at 9.

[86] *Id.* at 11 (citing William H. Riker & Barry R. Weingast, *Constitutional Regulation of Legislative Choice: The Political Consequences of Judicial Deference to Legislatures*, 74 VA. L. REV. 373, 378 (1988)).

upon the former method demands proffers from presently unavailable evidence and that those making contrary proffers might rely on available data that are problematic proxies for the underlying inquiry? More generally, consider the extent to which public choice, broadly defined to include social choice and game theory, is helpful in providing positive explanations for existing, and sometimes counterintuitive, practices that conventional legal analysis has proved ill-equipped to explain. Consider also how this relates to the neoclassical law and economics analysis of common law rules. To what extent does providing a more robust positive theory serve as a form of empirical testing of rational choice models designed to explain underlying phenomena? Consider also whether this benefit of public choice responds to Elhauge's analysis claiming no need to engage in the intermediate step of developing economic models to assess questions of law and public policy? When evaluating proposals to maintain the status quo or to accept a proposed change, how does one select a proper normative baseline? These are questions that we will revisit in the next chapters, which introduce the tools of social choice theory.

III. APPLICATIONS: INTEREST GROUP THEORY AND LAW

This section presents two cases in which interest group theory provides insights to regulatory questions that judges have been forced to squarely confront in recent years. The first case, *North Carolina State Board of Dental Examiners v. Federal Trade Commission*,[87] raises the question of how judges should apply the federal antitrust laws to regulations promulgated by a professional licensing board comprising members of the regulated industry. The second case, *Sensational Smiles v. Mullen*,[88] addresses how courts should approach a state law the purpose of which is to protect an industry and its members from competition, an issue we will return to in more detail in Chapter 17.

A. North Carolina State Board of Dental Examiners v. Federal Trade Commission

According to frequently cited estimates by labor economists Morris Kleiner and Alan Krueger, the percentage of American workers who work in jobs that require professional licensure grew from less than 5% of workers in the 1950s to 29% in 2008.[89] Not surprisingly, this growth in licensing and its effects on the economy and workforce have drawn the attention of policy makers, including the Obama administration, which issued a related report on the regulatory implications of this trend.[90]

To the extent that it addresses potential market failures that arise from information asymmetries as between consumers and service providers, especially in highly specialized and technical service areas, occupational licensing is social-welfare enhancing. In these

---

[87] 135 S. Ct. 1101 (2015).

[88] 793 F.3d 281 (2d Cir. 2015), *cert. denied*, 136 S. Ct. 1160 (2016).

[89] *See* Morris M. Kleiner & Alan B. Krueger, *Analyzing the Extent and Influence of Occupational Licensing on the Labor Market*, 31 J. LAB. ECON. S173 (2013).

[90] *See* THE WHITE HOUSE, OCCUPATIONAL LICENSING: A FRAMEWORK FOR POLICYMAKERS (2015), https://obamawhitehouse.archives.gov/sites/default/files/docs/licensing_report_final_nonembargo.pdf.

contexts, it can be difficult for consumers to determine either qualification or quality without some third-party imprimatur, which professional licensure helps to provide. In an occupation that requires highly technical skill, leading industry members seem well suited both to set qualifications and to ascertain if those qualifications are met. At the same time, allowing members of a licensed profession to set their own qualification standards invites opportunities to erect barriers to entry, thereby providing those members a financial benefit. This also implicates issues related to antitrust law.

North Carolina State Board of Dental Examiners v. Federal Trade Commission[91] involved a Federal Trade Commission (FTC) order challenging a rule of the North Carolina Dental Board. The rule prohibited nondentists from offering specified teeth whitening services or products. The Supreme Court upheld the FTC challenge, concluding that because the actions of the state regulatory board were not adequately supervised by the state government, the rule was prohibited under the Sherman Act and did not fall within the Act's state-action exception, announced in *Parker v. Brown*.[92] Justice Kennedy wrote the majority opinion in *North Carolina State Board of Dental Examiners v. Federal Trade Commission*, joined by Chief Justice Roberts, and Justices Ginsburg, Breyer, Sotomayor, and Kagan. Justice Alito wrote a dissent, joined by Justices Scalia and Thomas.

In his majority opinion, Justice Kennedy noted that under North Carolina law, the practice of dentistry was considered "a matter of public concern requiring regulation."[93] The State Board of Dental Examiners was created to regulate the practice of dentistry,[94] and is responsible to "create, administer, and enforce licensing system for dentists."[95] As part of its scope of responsibilities, the Board has the authority to file suit to enjoin any person from engaging in the unlicensed practice of dentistry.

The Board has eight members, including six practicing dentists elected by other dentists, a licensed hygienist, and a consumer, appointed by the Governor.[96] Board members may serve no more than two consecutive three-year terms.[97] The Act does not provide a mechanism for a public official to remove a member of the Board.[98] The Board has the authority to promulgate rules and regulations governing the practice of dentistry in the state.[99]

Beginning in the 1990s, North Carolina dentists started offering teeth-whitening services. By 2003, nondentists, including cosmetologists who operated mall kiosks, began to offer comparable services. The Court explained:

> [Nondentist providers] charged lower prices for their services than the dentists did. Dentists soon began to complain to the Board about their new

---

[91] 135 S. Ct. 1101 (2015).

[92] 317 U.S. 341 (1943).

[93] *North Carolina Dental Board*, 135 S. Ct. at 1107 (citing N.C. GEN. STAT. ANN. § 90–22(a) (West 2013)).

[94] *Id.*

[95] *Id.*

[96] *Id.* at 1108.

[97] *Id.*

[98] *Id.*

[99] *Id.*

competitors. Few complaints warned of possible harm to consumers. Most expressed a principal concern with the low prices charged by nondentists.

Responding to these filings, the Board opened an investigation . . . . A dentist member was placed in charge of the inquiry. Neither the Board's hygienist member nor its consumer member participated in this undertaking. The Board's chief operations officer remarked that the Board was "going forth to do battle" with nondentists. The Board's concern did not result in a formal rule or regulation reviewable by the independent Rules Review Commission, even though the Act does not, by its terms, specify that teeth whitening is "the practice of dentistry."

Starting in 2006, the Board issued at least 47 cease-and-desist letters on its official letterhead to nondentist teeth whitening service providers and product manufacturers. Many of those letters directed the recipient to cease "all activity constituting the practice of dentistry"; warned that the unlicensed practice of dentistry is a crime; and strongly implied (or expressly stated) that teeth whitening constitutes "the practice of dentistry." In early 2007, the Board persuaded the North Carolina Board of Cosmetic Art Examiners to warn cosmetologists against providing teeth whitening services. Later that year, the Board sent letters to mall operators, stating that kiosk teeth whiteners were violating the Dental Practice Act and advising that the malls consider expelling violators from their premises.

These actions had the intended result. Nondentists ceased offering teeth whitening services in North Carolina.[100]

In 2010 the FTC filed an administrative complaint charging the Board with having violated section five of the Federal Trade Commission Act. The complaint alleged that "the Board's concerted action to exclude nondentists from the North Carolina teeth whitening market constituted an anticompetitive and unfair method of competition."[101] The Board defended, claiming its activities fell within the state action immunity exception to the antitrust laws. The Administrative Law Judge ruled in favor of the FTC, and the United States Court of Appeals for the Fourth Circuit affirmed.

Affirming that ruling, the Supreme Court noted that resolving the issue required balancing two potentially incompatible goals: the federal government's interest in promoting competition through the antitrust laws, and the traditional power of the states under principles of federalism to accomplish other social goals:

Federal antitrust law is a central safeguard for the Nation's free market structures. In this regard it is "as important to the preservation of economic freedom and our free-enterprise system as the Bill of Rights is to the protection of our fundamental personal freedoms." The antitrust laws declare a considered and decisive prohibition by the Federal Government of cartels, price fixing, and other combinations or practices that undermine the free market.

---

[100] *Id.* (internal citations omitted).

[101] *Id.* at 1109 (internal citations omitted).

> The Sherman Act serves to promote robust competition, which in turn empowers the States and provides their citizens with opportunities to pursue their own and the public's welfare. The States, however, when acting in their respective realm, need not adhere in all contexts to a model of unfettered competition. While "the States regulate their economies in many ways not inconsistent with the antitrust laws," in some spheres they impose restrictions on occupations, confer exclusive or shared rights to dominate a market, or otherwise limit competition to achieve public objectives. If every duly enacted state law or policy were required to conform to the mandates of the Sherman Act, thus promoting competition at the expense of other values a State may deem fundamental, federal antitrust law would impose an impermissible burden on the States' power to regulate.
>
> For these reasons, the Court in *Parker v. Brown* interpreted the antitrust laws to confer immunity on anticompetitive conduct by the States when acting in their sovereign capacity. That ruling recognized Congress' purpose to respect the federal balance and to "embody in the Sherman Act the federalism principle that the States possess a significant measure of sovereignty under our Constitution." Since 1943, the Court has reaffirmed the importance of *Parker*'s central holding.[102]

As Justice Kennedy explained, in the earlier case, *California Retail Liquor Dealers Ass'n v. Midcal Aluminum*, the Court had articulated a two-pronged test under *Parker*.[103] That test was designed to balance the competing goals of preserving free market competition and respecting state regulatory authority. Justice Kennedy stated:

> A nonsovereign actor controlled by active market participants—such as the Board—enjoys *Parker* immunity only if it satisfies two requirements: "first that 'the challenged restraint . . . be one clearly articulated and affirmatively expressed as state policy,' and second that 'the policy . . . be actively supervised by the State.' " The parties have assumed that the clear articulation requirement is satisfied, and we do the same. While North Carolina prohibits the unauthorized practice of dentistry, however, its Act is silent on whether that broad prohibition covers teeth whitening. Here, the Board did not receive active supervision by the State when it interpreted the Act as addressing teeth whitening and when it enforced that policy by issuing cease-and-desist letters to nondentist teeth whiteners.[104]

The Court noted that where states exercise their sovereign power, they are permitted to enact anticompetitive laws. But the Sherman Act "does not always confer immunity where, as in this case, a State delegates control over a market to a non-sovereign actor."[105] The Court further noted that the danger of anticompetitive action is greatest when the state government delegates its authority to active market participants:

---

[102] *Id.* at 1109–10 (internal citations omitted).

[103] *Id.* at 1110 (citing Cal. Retail Liquor Dealers Ass'n v. Midcal Aluminum, 445 U.S. 97, 105 (1980)).

[104] *Id.*

[105] *Id.*

> Limits on state-action immunity are most essential when the State seeks to delegate its regulatory power to active market participants, for established ethical standards may blend with private anticompetitive motives in a way difficult even for market participants to discern. Dual allegiances are not always apparent to an actor. In consequence, active market participants cannot be allowed to regulate their own markets free from antitrust accountability. Indeed, prohibitions against anticompetitive self-regulation by active market participants are an axiom of federal antitrust policy. So it follows that, under *Parker* and the Supremacy Clause, the States' greater power to attain an end does not include the lesser power to negate the congressional judgment embodied in the Sherman Act through unsupervised delegations to active market participants.
>
> *Parker* immunity requires that the anticompetitive conduct of nonsovereign actors, especially those authorized by the State to regulate their own profession, result from procedures that suffice to make it the State's own. The question is not whether the challenged conduct is efficient, well-functioning, or wise. Rather, it is "whether anticompetitive conduct engaged in by [nonsovereign actors] should be deemed state action and thus shielded from the antitrust laws."[106]

The Court held:

> *Parker* immunity does not derive from nomenclature alone. When a State empowers a group of active market participants to decide who can participate in its market, and on what terms, the need for supervision is manifest. The Court holds today that a state board on which a controlling number of decision-makers are active market participants in the occupation the board regulates must satisfy *Midcal*'s active supervision requirement in order to invoke state-action antitrust immunity.[107]

To lawfully displace competition, the Court noted, a state must either adopt clear policies or it must delegate that authority to nonsovereign agencies in a manner that ensures active supervision.[108] The Board did not claim its anticompetitive conduct was pursuant to such state regulatory supervision, and thus the Court concluded that those activities were not entitled to immunity under *Parker*.[109]

In his dissent, Justice Alito did not express disagreement with the concerns raised by the majority regarding the potential dangers of a licensing board controlled by active market participants. Rather, he disagreed with applying antitrust laws to enforce this policy against the Board. He wrote:

> Today, however, the Court takes the unprecedented step of holding that *Parker* does not apply to the North Carolina Board because the Board is not structured in a way that merits a good-government seal of approval; that is, it is made up

---

[106] *Id.* at 1111 (internal citations omitted).

[107] *Id.* at 1114 (internal citations omitted).

[108] *Id.* at 1115.

[109] *Id.* at 1116.

> of practicing dentists who have a financial incentive to use the licensing laws to further the financial interests of the State's dentists. There is nothing new about the structure of the North Carolina Board. When the States first created medical and dental boards, well before the Sherman Act was enacted, they began to staff them in this way. Nor is there anything new about the suspicion that the North Carolina Board—in attempting to prevent persons other than dentists from performing teeth-whitening procedures—was serving the interests of dentists and not the public. Professional and occupational licensing requirements have often been used in such a way. But that is not what *Parker* immunity is about. Indeed, the very state program involved in that case was unquestionably designed to benefit the regulated entities, California raisin growers.
>
> The question before us is not whether such programs serve the public interest. The question, instead, is whether this case is controlled by *Parker*, and the answer to that question is clear. Under *Parker*, the Sherman Act (and the Federal Trade Commission Act) do not apply to state agencies; the North Carolina Board of Dental Examiners is a state agency; and that is the end of the matter. By straying from this simple path, the Court has not only distorted *Parker*; it has headed into a morass. Determining whether a state agency is structured in a way that militates against regulatory capture is no easy task, and there is reason to fear that today's decision will spawn confusion. The Court has veered off course, and therefore I cannot go along.[110]

Justice Alito contends that the only relevant question in the case is whether the North Carolina Board of Dental Examiners is a state agency, which it is.[111] After articulating a number of reasons that he thought demonstrated that the Board so qualified, Alito stated:

> As this regulatory regime demonstrates, North Carolina's Board of Dental Examiners is unmistakably a state agency created by the state legislature to serve a prescribed regulatory purpose and to do so using the State's power in cooperation with other arms of state government.
>
> The Board is not a private or "nonsovereign" entity that the State of North Carolina has attempted to immunize from federal antitrust scrutiny. . . . North Carolina did not authorize a private entity to enter into an anticompetitive arrangement; rather, North Carolina *created a state agency* and gave that agency the power to regulate a particular subject affecting public health and safety.[112]
>
> Justice Alito further reasoned:
>
> The Court's analysis seems to be predicated on an assessment of the varying degrees to which a municipality and a state agency like the North Carolina Board are likely to be captured by private interests. But until today, *Parker* immunity was never conditioned on the proper use of state regulatory

---

[110] *Id.* at 1117–18 (Alito, J., dissenting).

[111] *Id.* at 1119–20.

[112] *Id.* at 1121 (emphasis in original).

> authority. On the contrary, in *Columbia v. Omni Outdoor Advertising, Inc.*, we refused to recognize an exception to *Parker* for cases in which it was shown that the defendants had engaged in a conspiracy or corruption or had acted in a way that was not in the public interest. The Sherman Act, we said, is not an anticorruption or good-government statute. We were unwilling in *Omni* to rewrite *Parker* in order to reach the allegedly abusive behavior of city officials. But that is essentially what the Court has done here.[113]

Finally, Justice Alito criticized the majority on the basis that it would create uncertainty for states seeking to regulate market practices:

> Not only is the Court's decision inconsistent with the underlying theory of *Parker*, it will create practical problems and is likely to have far-reaching effects on the States' regulation of professions. As previously noted, state medical and dental boards have been staffed by practitioners since they were first created, and there are obvious advantages to this approach. It is reasonable for States to decide that the individuals best able to regulate technical professions are practitioners with expertise in those very professions. Staffing the State Board of Dental Examiners with certified public accountants would certainly lessen the risk of actions that place the well-being of dentists over those of the public, but this would also compromise the State's interest in sensibly regulating a technical profession in which lay people have little expertise.
>
> As a result of today's decision, States may find it necessary to change the composition of medical, dental, and other boards, but it is not clear what sort of changes are needed to satisfy the test that the Court now adopts. The Court faults the structure of the North Carolina Board because "active market participants" constitute "a controlling number of [the] decisionmakers," but this test raises many questions.[114]

Justice Alito concluded:

> When the Court asks whether market participants control the North Carolina Board, the Court in essence is asking whether this regulatory body has been captured by the entities that it is supposed to regulate. Regulatory capture can occur in many ways. So why ask only whether the members of a board are active market participants? The answer may be that determining when regulatory capture has occurred is no simple task. That answer provides a reason for relieving courts from the obligation to make such determinations at all. It does not explain why it is appropriate for the Court to adopt the rather crude test for capture that constitutes the holding of today's decision.[115]

---

113 *Id.* at 1122 (internal citations omitted).

114 *Id.* at 1122–23 (internal citations omitted).

115 *Id.* at 1123.

DISCUSSION QUESTIONS

1. The majority opinion places great weight on the composition of the Board, which is controlled primarily by actively practicing dentists. The Court is thus concerned that the Board will be self-serving (either consciously or unconsciously) rather than promoting the public interest. Justice Alito's dissent acknowledges that reality but argues that it is irrelevant given the scope of the state action exception to the antitrust laws and given the limits of judicial competence to discern when agencies pursue policies as a result of capture, rather than for more public serving purposes. Which argument do you find more persuasive, and why?

2. Justice Alito argues that the majority opinion implicitly rests on the idea that the legality of a state's regulatory action depends upon whether the regulation itself is a "proper use of state regulatory authority." He further argues that the *Parker* test does not include this qualifier on the scope of the state action exception to the antitrust laws, and thus, that the motives for the anticompetitive conduct are irrelevant. Should motive analysis matter in this context? Why or why not?

3. Assume that Justice Alito's analysis had been controlling for the Court, thereby insulating even self-interested licensing board activity from antitrust scrutiny. How do you think private actors might respond? Consider the comments of then-Director of the FTC's Office of Policy Planning, Todd Zywicki, before the Japanese Fair Trade Commission in 2003:

> A successful competition policy must target threats to competition from two fronts. One front involves purely private efforts to undermine competition, such as price-fixing and bid rigging. The other, often more subtle, front involves private efforts to convince governments to suppress competition—in other words, rent-seeking. As long as governments have existed, interested businesses have asked government officials to give them an advantage over their competitors. These efforts have often succeeded. Typically promulgated under the banner of consumer protection, or the "public or national interest," many regulations artificially reduce the number of competitors and limit the ability of existing companies to compete. Public restraints often can harm consumers for far longer than private restraints. Cartels inevitably fall apart over time, but anticompetitive laws can last indefinitely. Public restraints can be open and notorious and are far easier to enforce. While private cartelists may cheat on their agreements, public cartels may be enforced through the government.
>
> Attempting to protect competition by focusing solely on private restraints is like trying to stop the flow of water at a fork in a stream by blocking only one of the channels. Unless you block both channels, you are not likely to even slow, much less stop, the flow. Eventually, all the water will flow toward the unblocked channel. The same is true of antitrust enforcement. If you create a system in which private price fixing results in a jail sentence, but accomplishing the same objective through government regulation is always legal, you have not completely addressed the competitive problem. You have simply dictated the form that it will take. It is a hollow victory to break a price-fixing cartel if its members successfully lobby for a government granted authority to set prices collectively.[116]

---

[116] Todd J. Zywicki, Director, Off. Pol'y Planning, Fed. Trade Comm'n, Address at the Competition Policy Research Center, Fair Trade Commission of Japan, Inaugural Symposium: Competition Policy and Regulatory Reform: Means and Ends, How Should Competition Policy Transform Itself? Designing the New

Do you agree or disagree with Zywicki's thesis? Is it possible that rather than diverting the flow, blocking access to one means of anticompetitive conduct makes finding an alternative pathway more costly? Is Zywicki's theory consistent with the theory of second best? Why or why not? Based on the discussion in this chapter and Chapter 11, to what extent do you think that the political process will correct efforts by self-interested actors seeking to use government regulation to accomplish anticompetitive ends that would otherwise be illegal under the antitrust laws? Is imperfectly countering anticompetitive conduct better than not countering it at all?

4. In *The FTC and State Action: Evolving Views on the Proper Role of Government*, former FTC officials John Delacourt and Todd Zywicki argue that the Court's adoption of the *Parker* doctrine in 1943 during the New Deal implicitly rested on the Court's assumptions that government activity was animated by the public interest model of regulation.[117] *Parker* arose from the challenge by a California raisin farmer to a mandatory state program that controlled the marketing and sale of agriculture products, including raisins, with the intent to control the price of those products.

Delacourt and Zywicki contend that the Court's opinion was premised on accepting core principles of New Deal economics, especially the belief that markets for agricultural products were prone to instability and to boom and bust cycles, thus requiring active government involvement to stabilize prices. Delacourt and Zywicki contend that although the underlying theory on which the case rests is less widely accepted, the legal doctrine persists. They further argue that *Parker* rests implicitly on the Court's assumption that regulatory activity is animated by the public interest model of government. The authors inquire whether, in light of what they regard as changed economic wisdom, the doctrine should be reformulated. To what extent is the majority's opinion in *North Carolina Dental Board* consistent with Delacourt and Zywicki's hypothesis that theories of regulation play an implicit role in the evolution of legal doctrine in this area?

An alternative approach would counsel that the judiciary is ill suited to ascertain which schools of economic reasoning are dominant or whether a presently dominant school, however defined, should be treated as controlling. In this analysis, the judiciary should exhibit a certain degree of modesty, especially since it is prone to making profoundly costly errors when resting its rulings on social science analysis over which the members of the judiciary lack the requisite training and expertise. The *Parker* ruling, in this analysis, can be justified based on intuitions concerning core institutional competence, rather than resting simply on economic intuitions that some scholars now question.

Which approach, that articulated here, or the one embraced by Delacourt and Zywicki, is more persuasive? Why?

5. In striking down the Board's rule against nondentist teeth whiteners, Justice Kennedy, writing for the *North Carolina Dental Board* majority, was joined by Chief Justice Roberts and all four members of the Court's liberal wing. Justice Alito's dissent was joined by Justices Scalia and Thomas, and these three jurists are often identified with the Court's conservative wing. Is this judicial lineup surprising? Why or why not? Do you think the

---

Competition Policy 3–4 (Nov. 20, 2003), https://www.ftc.gov/public-statements/2003/11/competition-policy-and-regulatory-reform-means-and-ends-how-should (citing generally MANCUR OLSON, THE RISE AND DECLINE OF NATIONS 75–117 (1982).

[117] John T. Delacourt & Todd J. Zywicki, *The FTC and State Action: Evolving Views on the Proper Role of Government*, 72 ANTITRUST L.J. 1075 (2005).

dissenting Justices believe the challenged regulations were meritorious or that they voted to allow them to remain in place for other reasons? If the latter, what were those reasons? Assuming that both liberal and conservative Justices disapproved of the merits of the Board policy, and further assuming that this also captures the general sentiment of the citizens of North Carolina, why might elected officials in North Carolina have not repealed the law? In your opinion, should a judge's understanding of the political process that generated a particular law or regulation be relevant to its rulings? Why or why not?

B. Sensational Smiles v. Mullen

Consider the opinion of Judge Guido Calabresi of the United States Court of Appeals for the Second Circuit, and a leading law and economics scholar, in the case of *Sensational Smiles v. Mullen*.[118] *Sensational Smiles* dealt with a ruling issued by the Connecticut State Dentistry Board that declared certain teeth-whitening procedures must be performed by licensed dentists. The rule specified that only a licensed dentist could shine a light emitting diode (LED) lamp at the mouth of a patient during a teeth-whitening procedure. Sensational Smiles challenged the state regulation, claiming it violated Equal Protection and Due Process Clauses because no rational relationship exists between the rule and the government's legitimate interest in the public's oral health.

The Second Circuit upheld the regulation against the constitutional challenge. Specifically, Judge Calabresi reasoned that even if the purpose and effect of the regulation was to transfer wealth to licensed dentists by protecting them from competition against lower-cost providers of teeth whitening services, that constitutes a legitimate public purpose. Calabresi wrote:

> In sum, given that at least *some* evidence exists that LED lights may cause some harm to consumers, and given that there is some relationship (however imperfect) between the Commission's rule and the harm it seeks to prevent, we conclude that the rule does not violate either due process or equal protection.
>
> This would normally end our inquiry, but appellant, supported by amicus Professor Todd J. Zywicki, forcefully argues that the true purpose of the Commission's LED restriction is to protect the monopoly on dental services enjoyed by licensed dentists in the state of Connecticut. In other words, the regulation is nothing but naked economic protectionism: "rent seeking . . . designed to transfer wealth from consumers to a particular interest group."[119] Zywicki Br. at 3. This raises a question of growing importance and also permits us to emphasize what we do not decide, namely, whether the regulation is valid under the antitrust laws. See *N. Carolina State Bd. of Dental Examiners v. F.T.C.*

[118] 793 F.3d 281 (2d Cir. 2015), *cert. denied*, 136 S. Ct. 1160 (2016).

[119] In the field of public choice economics, "rent-seeking" means the attempt to increase one's share of existing wealth through political activity. *See* Anne O. Krueger, *The Political Economy of the Rent-Seeking Society*, 64 AM. ECON. REV. 291 (1974); Jagdish Bhagwati, *Directly Unproductive, Profit Seeking Activities*, 90 J. POL. ECON. 988 (1982); *see also* Dist. Intown Properties Ltd. P'ship v. D.C., 198 F.3d 874, 885 (D.C. Cir. 1999) ("While the resulting proposals are naturally advanced in the name of the public good, many are surely driven by interest-group purposes, commonly known as "rent-seeking.' "). [Footnote in original].

(holding that dental board was not sufficiently controlled by the state to claim state antitrust immunity).

> In recent years, some courts of appeals have held that laws and regulations whose sole purpose is to shield a particular group from intrastate economic competition cannot survive rational basis review. See *St. Joseph Abbey v. Castille* ("[N]either precedent nor broader principles suggest that mere economic protection of a particular industry is a legitimate governmental purpose[.]"); *Merrifield v. Lockyer* ("[M]ere economic protectionism for the sake of economic protectionism is irrational with respect to determining if a classification survives rational basis review."); *Craigmiles v. Giles* ("[P]rotecting a discrete interest group from economic competition is not a legitimate governmental purpose."). The Tenth Circuit, on the other hand, has squarely held that such a protectionist purpose is legitimate. See *Powers v. Harris* ("[A]bsent a violation of a specific constitutional provision or other federal law, intrastate economic protectionism constitutes a legitimate state interest."). We join the Tenth Circuit and conclude that economic favoritism is rational for purposes of our review of state action under the Fourteenth Amendment.[120]

The Second Circuit then reviewed a line of Supreme Court cases requiring judicial deference to state economic regulations and concluded,

> These decisions are a product of experience and common sense. Much of what states do is to favor certain groups over others on economic grounds. We call this politics. Whether the results are wise or terrible is not for us to say, as favoritism of this sort is certainly rational in the constitutional sense.[121]

Sensational Smiles rejected the contrary conclusion of the United States Court of Appeals for the Fifth Circuit in *St. Joseph Abbey v. Castille*, a case challenging a rule restricting who may sell caskets.[122] In *St. Joseph Abbey*, the Fifth Circuit stated:

> As a threshold argument, the State Board urges that pure economic protection of a discrete industry is an exercise of a valid state interest. . . . As we see it, neither precedent nor broader principles suggest that mere economic protection of a particular industry is a legitimate governmental purpose, but economic protection, that is favoritism, may be well supported by a post hoc perceived rationale as in *Williamson* [*v. Lee Optical Co.*,]—without which it is aptly described as a naked transfer of wealth.[123]

The *St. Joseph Abbey* court then discussed and rejected both of the State's claimed rationales for the rule, that it was justified by consumer protection and health and safety concerns. After finding that the only rational justification for the law was economic protectionism, the court concluded:

---

[120] *Sensational Smiles*, 793 F.3d at 285–86.

[121] *Id.* at 287.

[122] 712 F.3d 215 (5th Cir. 2013). In *St. Joseph Abbey v. Castille* a Benedictine abbey challenged rules issued by the Louisiana Board of Embalmers and Funeral Directors as unconstitutional. Specifically, the abbey challenged the rule giving funeral homes the exclusive right to sell caskets. *Id.*

[123] *Id.* at 221–23.

> The great deference due to state economic regulation does not demand judicial blindness to the history of a challenged rule or the context of its adoption nor does it require courts to accept nonsensical explanations for regulation. The deference we owe expresses mighty principles of federalism and judicial roles. The principle we protect from the hand of the State today protects an equally vital core principle—the taking of wealth and handing it to others when it comes not as economic protectionism in service of the public good but as "economic" protectionism of the rulemakers' pockets. Nor is the ghost of *Lochner* lurking about. We deploy no economic theory of social statics or draw upon a judicial vision of free enterprise. Nor do we doom state regulation of casket sales. We insist only that Louisiana's regulation not be irrational—the outer-most limit of due process and equal protection—as Justice Harlan put it, the inquiry is whether "[the] measure bears a rational relation to a constitutionally permissible objective." Answering that question is well within Article III's confines of judicial review.
>
> The funeral directors have offered no rational basis for their challenged rule and, try as we are required to do, we can suppose none.[124]

In *Sensational Smiles*, Judge Droney filed an opinion concurring in the judgment in which he rejected the majority opinion's position that mere economic protectionism is inadequate to sustain a law without some legitimate public purpose being advanced as well. Judge Droney wrote: "In my view, there must be at least some perceived public benefit for legislation or administrative rules to survive rational basis review under the Equal Protection and Due Process Clauses."[125] Judge Droney went on to hold that the State Dental Board's ruling was rationally related to the "state's legitimate interest in protecting the public health" and thus was valid under that standard of review.[126]

DISCUSSION QUESTIONS

1. In later chapters, we will revisit the question of how judges should approach special interest legislation. In the meantime, consider the various costs and benefits of the approach taken by the Second and Fifth Circuits in these cases, and consider which approach you find more persuasive. Might the widespread acceptance of interest group theory increase judicial tolerance of rent-seeking behavior and of regulation animated by the desire to transfer wealth to interest groups?

2. Judge Calabresi suggests that interest group control over some regulatory outcomes is simply another word for "politics." Do you agree? If not, how would you define politics? Assuming this is politics, is conveyance of wealth from one group to another the sole basis for sustaining the law *even if* there is no apparent public interest rationale?

Consider Professor Maxwell Stearns's alternative analysis: Legislative processes are invariably complex and dynamic. Securing public interest legislation requires accommodations that include payoffs to interest groups. Sometimes these payoffs are reflected in the public

---

[124] *Id.* at 226–27.

[125] *Sensational Smiles*, 712 F.3d at 288 (Droney, J., concurring in part and concurring in the judgment).

[126] *Id.*

interest statutes themselves; other times they find reflection in separate bills, some of which are then enacted as statutes. The judiciary lacks the capacity to unpack such complex arrangements and to ascertain what might have happened without the interest group payoff. If the interest group involvement was essential to gaining the larger beneficial legislation, this provides the basis for upholding the payoff despite the wealth transfer. In this analysis, the court sustains interest group payoffs not *because of the wealth transfer* but *in spite of* it as a means of facilitating other important aspects of the legislative bargaining process. Which approach to judicial deference, this one, which finds reflection in Maxwell L. Stearns,[127] or that of Todd Zywicki, as shown in his brief in *Sensational Smiles*? Why?

3. How does Elhauge's discussion of baselines relate to the question of whether "economic protectionism" standing alone is a legitimate governmental interest or whether interest group influence is a synonym for "politics," as Judge Calabresi states?

4. In *St. Joseph Abbey*, the district court found that the state regulatory rules advanced no public purpose, and it rejected the consumer protection and public health and safety rationales advanced by the State of Louisiana. The Fifth Circuit noted that the extensive training the law requires of aspiring funeral directors does not include instruction on caskets or how to counsel grieving consumers; nor did the rule regulate any element of casket design or pricing. The law also failed to advance any apparent public health or safety rationale. Indeed, Louisiana law did not require a casket for burial or regulate the requirements for casket design or construction. The court concluded that the only remaining justification for the law was to protect the economic interests of funeral home directors, which the Fifth Circuit held to be insufficient to sustain the law. Do you agree with that finding? Whether you agree or disagree with it, do you agree with the court's resolution of the case? Why or why not? Is this analysis responsive to Green and Shapiro's contention that public choice theory lacks empirical validation? Is this a context in which the type of evidence likely to satisfy social scientists differs from the type of evidence likely to satisfy a court? Why or why not?

5. What impact, if any, should the acceptance of different regulatory theories (public interest, capture theory, and public choice theory) have for judicial review of economic regulation? Consider this question later in the book when you revisit these issues in Chapter 17.

[127] *See* sources cited *supra* note 7.

CHAPTER 13

Social Choice (Part 1)[1]

Introduction

The study of social choice emerges from a deceptively simple insight. Economic theory assumes as a condition of rationality that individuals hold transitive preference orderings, meaning *A* preferred to *B* preferred to *C* implies *A* preferred to *C*. Social choice reveals that the assumption of transitivity cannot be extended to groups of three or more individuals selecting among three or more options through a method of unlimited majority rule. Instead, the preferences of group members sometimes cycle over options such that *ApBpCpA*, where *p* means preferred to by simple majority rule.[2]

This simple insight enjoys an impressive historical pedigree that dates back to two French philosophers writing contemporaneously with the founding and constitutional framing periods in the United States.[3] Since the 1950s, social choice has generated a rich literature that boasts a prominent Nobel Prize in Economics for Arrow's Impossibility Theorem, or simply Arrow's Theorem, awarded to economist Kenneth Arrow in 1972.[4] Social choice also informs a considerable legal literature that studies the nature and competence of institutions, including elections, legislatures, courts, and agencies or bureaus.

Both interest group theory and social choice study institutions. Whereas interest group theory disaggregates institutions and studies at a granular level the incentives of institutional constituencies or members, social choice begins by taking member

---

1 Portions of this chapter are adapted from MAXWELL L. STEARNS, CONSTITUTIONAL PROCESS: A SOCIAL CHOICE ANALYSIS OF SUPREME COURT DECISION MAKING 41–94 (Chapter 2) (paperback ed. 2002), Maxwell L. Stearns, *The Misguided Renaissance of Social Choice*, 103 YALE L.J. 1219 (1994) [hereinafter *Misguided Renaissance*], and Maxwell L. Stearns, *An Introduction to Social Choice*, *in* ELGAR HANDBOOK IN PUBLIC CHOICE AND PUBLIC LAW (Daniel Farber & Anne Joseph O'Connell eds., 2009) [hereinafter *Introduction*].

2 Following convention, our analysis begins by assuming individual rationality, defined here to require holding transitive preference orderings. We then compare individual rationality to possible cyclical preferences within groups of three or more individuals, each of whom satisfies the rationality criterion. In a later analysis, we revisit the assumption of individual transitivity and identify the conditions under which rules or norms can motivate cycle-like preferences for an individual or pair. *See infra* Chapter 14. For a discussion of multicriterial decision making, see Matthew L. Spitzer, *Multicriterial Choice Processes: An Application of Public Choice Theory to* Bakke, *The FCC, and the Courts*, 88 YALE L.J. 717, 719–20 (1979). *See also* Maxwell L. Stearns, Obergefell, Fisher, *and the Inversion of Tiers*, 19 U. PA. J. CONST. LAW 1043 (2017).

3 For a brief discussion of this history, see Stearns, *Misguided Renaissance*, *supra* note 1, at 1221–28.

4 *See id.* at 1224.

preferences as given. Social choice then studies the mechanisms by which institutions transform member preferences (or inputs) into collective decisions (or outputs). The study of these processes often proves essential to understanding institutional policy formation and implementation. A central insight of social choice is that how well institutions perform in their policy or lawmaking role is not simply a function of the preferences that constituents hold; it also depends on the quality of the processes through which institutions transform preferences into outputs. Social choice studies how group decision making affects these important processes.

This chapter proceeds as follows. Part I introduces several foundational social choice concepts. These include majority rule, the median voter theorem, cycling, the Condorcet criterion, path dependence, agenda setting, minimum winning coalitions, and Arrow's Theorem. This part also provides a summary of notable proposals advanced by legal scholars relying on social choice theory. Part II adds another layer to social choice analysis that helps to place these and other normative proposals for institutional reform within a broader context. The analysis explains the important role of institutional complementarity in improving the quality and rationality of institutional outputs. The analysis also helps to recast social choice—and in particular Arrow's Theorem—as a set of positive tools that can be used in comparative institutional assessment. In this part, we introduce several related concepts including the fallacy of composition, the isolation fallacy, the nirvana fallacy, empty core bargaining games, and structure-induced equilibria.

Chapter 14 relies upon social choice to expand the set of normative criteria, or baselines, that arise from economic analysis, but extend beyond efficiency, for evaluating institutions and rules. Part I begins with a study of parliamentary rules that shows how social choice helps to explain institutional adaptation as a means of improving the quality of institutional decision-making processes and outputs. Combining these baselines proves essential in comparative institutional analysis. Part II reintroduces the Arrow's Theorem criteria and provides a preliminary comparative assessment of the most important institutions in the formation of public law and policy.[5] This part also explores the important concept of dimensionality and discusses the implications of Arrow's insight for the construction of decision-making rules.[6] Part III introduces the concept of multicriterial decision making and considers its implications for common law and constitutional rules. Each chapter concludes with applications.

---

[5] Part V of this book, and in particular Chapters 17 through 24, provides a more detailed comparative institutional account based upon the full range of tools introduced in part IV.

[6] For a discussion of alternative voting protocols, including Borda Counts, Coombs Voting, Hare Voting (or Single Transferable Voting), Copeland Voting, Plurality Voting, and Approval Voting, see Stearns, *Introduction, supra* note 1. The discussion reveals each rule's respective strengths and weaknesses, and assesses its relative Condorcet efficiency—meaning its probability of securing a Condorcet winner when one is available—as compared with the remaining voting alternatives, under specific conditions. For an analysis of the quadratic voting, see Special Issue, *Quadratic Voting and the Public Good*, 172 PUB. CHOICE 1 (2017). This methodology is designed to elicit the marginal cost for each successive vote in the procurement of public goods as a means of calibrating the demand and supply for such goods.

I. THE PROBLEM OF SOCIAL CHOICE

A. Foundations: Majority Versus Plurality Rule

An obvious starting point in the study of group decision making is *majority rule*. At first blush, majority rule appears simple. In making a cake for five children, if three prefer chocolate to vanilla, and two prefer vanilla to chocolate, assuming the cake will have one flavor, chocolate it is![7] In practice, majority rule is anything but simple. Depending upon the context, majority rule is often difficult, and sometimes impossible, to justify. One obvious problem is identifying strength of preference. Suppose that one of the two children who prefer vanilla is severely allergic to cocoa, the main ingredient in chocolate. Most would concede, we hope, that majority rule is no longer appropriate.

Several problems are immediately apparent: What if, instead, the child just intensely dislikes chocolate? Is majority rule still inappropriate? If so, what should replace it? Perhaps we might ask the children how strongly they feel about their choice of flavors. How might you expect them to respond? Can you think of a mechanism that would discourage the children from exaggerating? Is the risk of exaggeration limited to children? Why or why not?

For now, we will set aside the problem of intensity of preferences and focus on another limitation of majority rule. What happens when no option has first choice majority support? When this occurs, decision makers need to consider alternative voting protocols. One obvious alternative is *plurality rule*. Plurality rule selects as the winner that option that receives the most votes, which can be less than a majority. With only two options, an odd number of voters, and no abstentions, majority and plurality rule coincide. With three or more options, plurality rule can identify a winner even when majority rule does not.

In the absence of a first choice majority winner, is the plurality choice always defensible? Why or why not? Can you identify circumstances in which the socially superior choice receives *fewer* votes than the plurality winner? Is it possible that selecting the plurality option might in some circumstances violate foundational principles of majority rule?[8]

To answer these questions, we need to consider another voting alternative, one that returns to the concept of rationality. Here we focus on a different aspect of rationality than the cost-effective pursuit of desired objectives. In social choice, individual rationality connotes *transitive preference orderings*. If A is preferred to B and if B is preferred to C, then

---

[7] For a formalization of the special properties of majority rule, consider May's Theorem, which holds that "D is determined only by the values of D_i, and is independent of how they are assigned. Any permutation of these ballots leaves D unchanged." DENNIS C. MUELLER, PUBLIC CHOICE III, at 134 (2003) (describing May's Theorem, which holds that only simple majority rule satisfies the conditions of decisiveness, anonymity, neutrality, and positive responsiveness).

[8] Writing in 1770, Jean-Charles de Borda provided an early analysis demonstrating that plurality rule sometimes fails to capture the will of the voters. *See* Robert J. Weber, *Approval Voting*, J. ECON. PERSP., Winter 1995, at 39 (discussing Jean-Charles de Borda, *Mémoires sur les Élections au Scrutin*, *in* HISTOIRE DE L'ACADEMIE ROYAL DES SCIENCES (1781)).

we assume A is preferred to C. The median voter theorem, described below, helps to illustrate the implications of this proposition.

B. The Median Voter Theorem

The *median voter theorem* is the analytical starting point for a great deal of interest group theory and social choice analysis.[9] We begin with the basic model. We later relax some of the simplifying assumptions to bring the model closer to actual institutions.[10]

Assume a one-stage election in which the policy positions of the candidates and the preferences of the voters can be expressed along a single dimensional scale. This scale represents extreme liberal to extreme conservative views of public policy over the relevant set of issues. Each voter has a preferred position along this ideological continuum, known as an *ideal point*. Assume each voter prefers whichever candidate expresses a set of policy positions closest to that voter's ideal point. Further assume that the electorate has ninety voters with preferences evenly clustered in nine groups of ten. Each group occupies a specific ideological increment that represents a degree of liberalism or conservatism spread along the single dimensional scale.

Imagine an election between two candidates. Candidate *R*, a Republican, occupies position 9, the most conservative position along the spectrum. Candidate *D*, a Democrat, occupies position 1, the most liberal position along the spectrum. The median voter theorem posits that if these two candidates are primarily motivated to be elected or reelected, behaving rationally, they will eventually modify, or water down, their extreme policy positions until they converge at or near the ideal point of the median voter or voters, represented at position 5.[11] Figure 13:1 depicts this result.

The median voter theorem posits that as each candidate seeks to maximize support, she or he will gravitate toward the median electoral position in an effort to capture a larger segment of the electorate. The model assumes full electoral participation and that each voter's primary objective is to secure electoral victory for the candidate who is closest to her or his ideal point.[12] Based upon these assumptions, provided that there is some policy distance between *R* and *D* (with *R* to the right of *D*) after the candidates' general convergence toward the median voter, the voters will not punish the candidate who remains closest to their respective ideal points by declining to vote or by voting for the

---

[9] Duncan Black initially introduced the model, *see* Duncan Black, *On the Rationale of Group Decision-making*, 56 J. POL. ECON. 23 (1948), that Anthony Downs popularized in AN ECONOMIC THEORY OF DEMOCRACY (1957). For an informative review of the literature, see Roger D. Congleton, *The Median Voter Model*, *in* THE ENCYCLOPEDIA OF PUBLIC CHOICE 382 (Charles K. Rowley & Friedrich Schneider eds., 2004).

[10] In the next subsection, for example, we relax the assumption of a single dimensional scale to introduce the concept of cycling.

[11] In the context of spatial competition in markets, Harold Hotelling achieved a similar result, predicting that two shops competing along a single street would rationally converge at the midpoint of the street, thwarting the socially superior outcome of placement at distances 25% and 75% along the street. The preferred result would allow all consumers to travel no more than a 25% along the street to get to one of the shops, whereas the Nash equilibrium result requires some to travel as much as 50% along the street. Harold Hotelling, *Stability in Competition*, 39 ECON. J. 41 (1929).

[12] The full electoral participation assumption is a necessary consequence of the assumption that voters seek to move policy toward their ideal point. Can you explain this result?

other side's preferred candidate. Otherwise, a voter would be voting for a candidate farther from her or his ideal point, pushing policy opposite to the preferred direction.

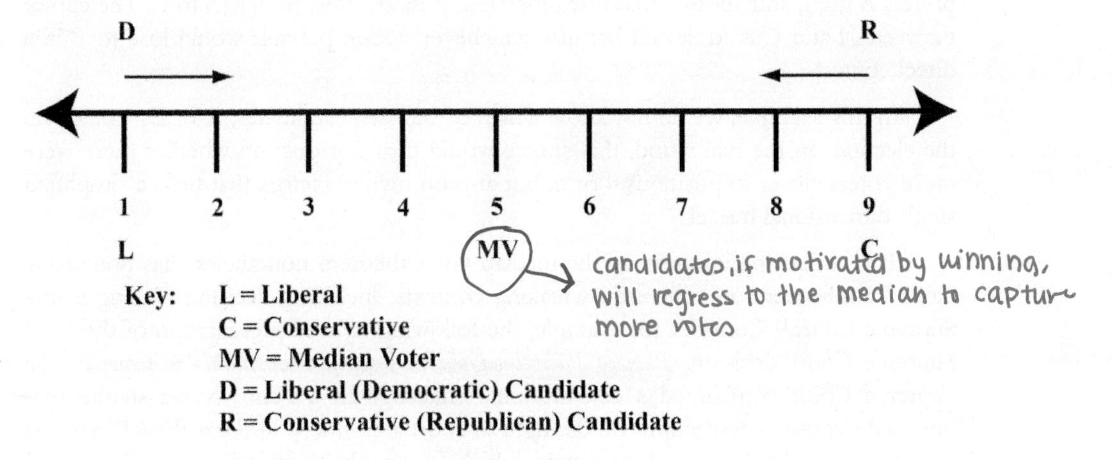

Figure 13:1

The median voter theorem predicts that the pure Nash equilibrium outcome for the two candidates converges at or near the median voter,[13] position 5 on this nine-point scale. While this model rests upon admittedly strong simplifying assumptions, exploring its internal logic is helpful before relaxing the assumptions to better reflect actual voting contexts. In the model's most basic application, the two candidates converge upon indistinguishable platforms, leaving the voters with no meaningful choice. Of course, in any large number electorate, a single identifiable median voter is unlikely.[14] Imagine for example that in their convergence toward the median voter, candidates *R* and *D* retain a slight difference in platforms, such that *D* occupies position 4, whereas *R* occupies position 6. Each candidate is one increment to the left or right of the median (position 5) in the direction of her or his electoral base.

Now imagine that the voters divide into three broad constituencies, liberals (*A*), moderates (*B*), and conservatives (*C*), each occupying a three-point range along the nine-point ideological spectrum. Thus, *A* occupies positions 1 through 3; *B* occupies positions 4 through 6; and *C* occupies positions 7 through 9. Given that none of these constituencies capture a majority, how will the election affect the ultimate set of adopted policies? Consider how the voting camps rank the available policy packages, *ABC*.

The median voter theorem assumes that all voters behave rationally and vote consistently with their internally transitive preferences. Voters whose ideal points occupy the ends of the political spectrum (*A* or *C*), thus rank second the policy position closest to their ideal point (*B*), and rank last the position farthest from their ideal point (*C* or *A*). The liberal voters rank their preferences *ABC*, and the conservative voters rank their preferences *CBA*. The second and third choices of the moderate voters do not matter.

---

[13] We introduced this concept in Chapter 3 or 4, and will reintroduce it in greater detail in Chapter 15.

[14] As we will see, however, this does not mean that there are no median voters in other contexts. For a discussion of actual median voters in the Supreme Court, see *infra* Chapter 22. *See also* STEARNS, *supra* note 1, at 97–156.

Whether they rank their preferences *BAC* or *BCA*, assuming all vote sincerely in a regime of direct comparisons over the three options, a majority (conservatives and moderates) prefers *B* to *A*, and another majority (liberals and moderates) prefers *B* to *C*. The choice between *A* and *C* is irrelevant because whichever option prevails would lose to *B* in a direct contest.

In this example, we do not know which of our two candidates, *R* or *D*, would win the election. In the real world, this choice would turn not only on whether there were more voters closer to positions 4 or 6, but also on myriad factors that belie a simplified single dimensional model.

The underlying intuition of the median voter theorem nonetheless has potentially helpful applications in concrete lawmaking contexts, including decision making in the Supreme Court.[15] Consider for example, the following stylized presentation of the 1992 Supreme Court decision, *Planned Parenthood of Southeastern Pennsylvania v. Casey*.[16] The Supreme Court confronted a constitutional challenge to a Pennsylvania statute that imposed a series of restrictions on the right to abort announced in *Roe v. Wade*.[17] Assume that the Court divides into three camps, which for simplicity we will refer to as Liberal (*L*), Moderate (*M*), and Conservative (*C*). Further assume that the Liberals prefer to maintain the original *Roe* holding, which would result in striking down all of the restrictive provisions of the challenged abortion laws. Assume that the Conservatives prefer to overrule *Roe* outright, thus rejecting any constitutional right to abort and sustaining all challenged provisions. Finally, assume that although the Moderates would not necessarily endorse *Roe* on first principles, based on stare decisis, they retain some version of a right to abort, albeit in a weaker form than the Liberals prefer. The Moderates proceed to redefine *Roe* in a manner that preserves the essential right to abort, but that gives states somewhat broader regulatory power over abortion. Applying the new standard, the Moderates sustain all but one challenged abortion regulation, which demands that women seeking an abortion first notify their spouses.

---

[15] For a more detailed analysis that links the following analysis to the narrowest grounds rule, see *infra* Chapter 22, Part I.C.1.B. *See also* STEARNS, *supra* note 1, at 129–38.

[16] 505 U.S. 833 (1992).

[17] 410 U.S. 113 (1973).

Table 13:1. *Casey* Through the Lens of *Marks*

(L) Blackmun and Stevens (concurring)	(M) O'Connor, Kennedy, and Souter (plurality)	(C) Rehnquist, Scalia, White, and Thomas (dissenting)
Strike down all restrictive provisions based upon either *stare decisis* or analysis of merits of original *Roe* decision.	Strike down only spousal notification provision, based upon *stare decisis* revision of *Roe*.	Uphold all provisions based upon critical analysis of merits of original *Roe* decision.

Broad abortion right ←→ Narrow abortion right

Table 13:1[18] captures these three *Casey* positions, cast along a single dimensional scale, with the liberal position (*L*) providing a broad abortion right, the moderate position (*M*) seeking to modify but retain *Roe*, and the conservative position (*C*) declining to provide any abortion right and seeking to overrule *Roe*. In this example, there are two Supreme Court justices voting for *L*, three voting for *M*, and four voting for *C*, although the specific numbers do not matter provided that any two-group combination forms a majority. Since the three positions can be cast along a single dimensional scale, we can assume that if asked to rank the three options, the Liberals will choose *LMC*, and the Conservatives will choose *CML*. The second and third ordinal rankings of the Moderate camp (*MCL* or *MLC*) are, once more, irrelevant. Either way, *M* emerges the dominant outcome, where dominant means that no other option contains the requisite majority support to displace it in a direct binary comparison.

The median voter theorem reveals a decisional rule in the absence of a first-choice majority candidate that is sometimes in tension with plurality rule. The theorem implies that when preferences align along a single dimensional scale, and when there is no first-choice majority candidate, voters will prefer candidates somewhat distant from their ideal point, including one occupying a median position, as compared with a more distant candidate.

In a three-candidate race, the median-voter outcome will sometimes defy plurality rule. To see why, imagine an electoral distribution in which fewer voters occupy the median position *B* than either of the extreme positions *A* or *C*.[19] Assume that the liberals (*A*) hold 40% of the electorate, the moderates (*B*) hold 25% of the electorate, and the conservatives (*C*) hold 35% of the electorate. Figure 13:2 depicts this distribution of voters above the incremental policy positions one through nine:

---

[18] STEARNS, *supra* note 1, at 129 tbl.3.6 (*Casey* through the lens of *Marks*).

[19] The same analysis would apply if the median position received the second largest number of votes.

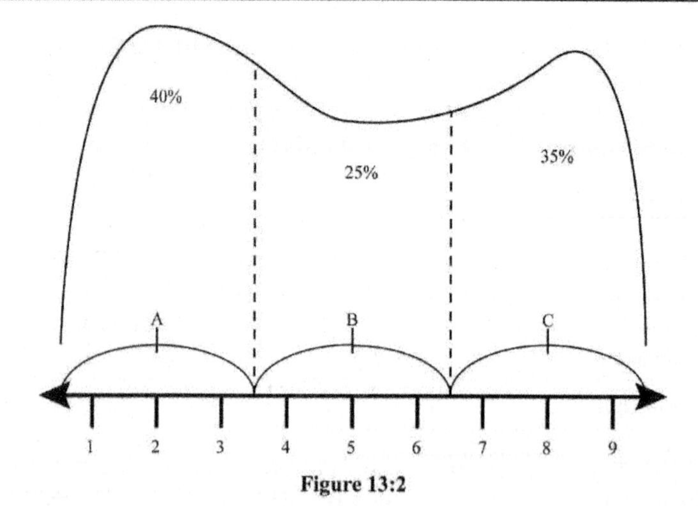

Figure 13:2

As before, assume the policy positions divide into ideological clusters *A*, *B*, and *C*, and that the voters occupying each position rank order their choices among these positions. Although *B* emerges as the median outcome, with 25% support among voters, *A* obtains plurality support, with 40%, and *C* comes in second, with 35%. Under plurality rule, option *A* would prevail. Applying the early analysis, however, which assumes that those occupying the extreme positions, *A* and *C*, rank position *B* as a second choice over the opposite extreme position (*C* and *A* respectively), *B*, the median outcome, emerges as the preferred choice.[20]

Given the preferences, which platform, *A* or *B*, is the preferred result? As previously noted, in the actual *Casey* opinion, option *L* received two votes, option *M* received three, and option *C* received four. Which rule, plurality voting or the median voter theorem, is more suitable in that setting?[21] Which voting rule, plurality or median voter, is generally preferred? Is it possible that each is preferred in some contexts, yet is disfavored in others? If so, what might those contexts be?

To answer these questions, we must once again revisit rationality as understood in social choice. The analysis that follows demonstrates that the median voter theorem is a special case of preferences in the absence of a first-choice majority candidate. Identifying the circumstances that are, or are not, conducive to generating a dominant median outcome is important in developing a social choice analysis of institutions and rules.

C. Rationality Revisited: Cyclical and Non-Cyclical Preferences

We begin, once more, with a deceptively simple insight that underlies the social choice understanding of rationality. Imagine that three persons are choosing among three options *A*, *B*, and *C*. The options can represent virtually anything, including political

[20] As explained below, *see infra* pp. 507–508, option *B* is the Condorcet winner, named for the French philosopher who described this result in 1785. *See also* Stearns, *Misguided Renaissance*, *supra* note 1, at 1221.

[21] Keep this question in mind as you read the discussion of the narrowest grounds doctrine, *infra* Chapter 22, Part I.C.1.B, *see also infra* Chapter 14, note 61, and accompanying text.

candidates, particular public policy proposals, or even the flavor of a cake. Once again, we generally assume that *A* preferred to *B* preferred to *C* implies *A* preferred to *C*. In selecting ice cream flavors, for example, if Alice likes coffee more than chocolate, and chocolate more than vanilla, we infer that she likes coffee more than vanilla. This does not, of course, mean that Alice is forever barred from selecting vanilla over coffee, as she might if she had coffee several nights in a row.[22] But if asked whether she likes coffee more than vanilla, most would think it odd if Alice chose vanilla, given her remaining preferences.

Social choice reveals that this simple assumption respecting individual rationality, namely that persons generally hold transitive preference orderings, cannot be ascribed to groups seeking to transform individually rational (or transitive) preferences into collective outputs. The median voter theorem illustrates how, in the absence of a majority candidate, group preferences along a single dimensional continuum tend to converge on the median position. The theorem rests on specific assumptions about aggregating member preferences into group preferences. By relaxing those assumptions, we can see why the median voter model fails to capture all of the important dynamics of social choice.

To keep the analysis simple, assume that three persons (P1, P2, and P3) are choosing among three options, or alternatively that each person represents a constituency such that any two-group combination forms a majority. Assume that after the members disclose their first choices over options *ABC*, they discover that none holds the same preference, and thus there is no first-choice majority candidate. After making this discovery, each member discloses her or his ordinal preference rankings from most-to-least preferred, as follows:

P1: *ABC*

P2: *BCA*

P3: *CAB*

Since there is no first-choice majority candidate, the members take a series of pairwise votes, meaning votes between two available options, hoping to select a winner. Assume that each member votes sincerely, meaning consistently with the above rankings in each direct comparison.

As between options *A* and *B*, *A* wins, with P1 and P3 defeating P2. As between options *A* against *C*, *C* wins, with P2 and P3 defeating P1. Thus far, the voting has revealed that *C* is preferred to *A* and *A* is preferred to *B*. If an individual, such as P3, held these preferences, we would infer that she also prefers *C* to *B*. Social choice reveals that unlike P3, when the group aggregates the preferences of all participants through unlimited binary comparisons, it achieves a different result. With these preference orderings, the group prefers *B* to *C*, with P1 and P2 defeating P3. The final pairwise contest thus reveals an intransitivity, or cycle, over options *ABC*, such that *CpApBpC*.

---

[22] It also does not mean that at some future time, Alice might not change her mind and acquire a taste for a flavor that she once disliked, thereby transforming her preferences. But once this occurs, we would once again presume that she holds her now updated preferences in a similar transitive fashion.

This example illustrates the voting paradox, also called the Condorcet paradox after a French philosopher who described it in an essay in 1785.[23] Simply put, the paradox is that transitivity, assumed to be a basic tenet of individual rationality, cannot be assumed for groups of three or more individuals selecting among three or more options. Assume that each individual holds transitive preference orderings, such that P1 prefers *A* to *C*, P2 prefers *B* to *A*, and P3 prefers *C* to *B*. When taking pairwise majority votes, the result for the group is intransitive, or a cycle.

In addition to writing about the paradox, Condorcet proposed an important, if partial, solution to the problem concerning how to transform individual preferences that lack a first-choice majority outcome into a normatively defensible group outcome. Condorcet's proposed voting rule substantially aligns with the intuition underlying the median voter theorem. Condorcet proposed that when an available option would defeat the remaining options in direct pairwise comparisons, now referred to as the Condorcet winner, that option should prevail.

To illustrate, consider three persons selecting among options *ABC*, this time with the following slightly modified preferences: P1: *ABC*; P2: *BCA*; and P3: *CBA*. We have only altered P3's second and third ordinal ranking (from *AB to BA*); the remaining preferences are unchanged. Once again, there is no first-choice majority candidate. Now apply Condorcet's proposed method. As between *A* and *B*, *B* wins, with P2 and P3 defeating P1; and as between *B* and *C*, *B* wins, with P1 and P2 defeating P3. The choice between *A* and *C* is irrelevant (*C* wins, with P1 losing) because option *B*, the Condorcet winner, defeats each alternative in a direct comparison. Institutions or rules that ensure that available Condorcet winners prevail are said to satisfy the Condorcet criterion.

The Condorcet criterion is an important benchmark for evaluating the decision-making competence of institutions. As the median voter theorem demonstrates, the criterion is closely linked to the concept of majority rule and one person, one vote. Professor William Riker observed, "when an alternative opposed by a majority wins, quite clearly the votes of some people are not being counted the same as other people's votes."[24] Consider, once again, an electorate in which a plurality of 40% prefer the liberal platform, *A*; 25% prefer the moderate platform, *B*; and 35% prefer the conservative platform, *C*. Although the liberal platform holds plurality support, that outcome would suppress a majority (moderates and conservatives) who prefer the moderate to the liberal platform. Similarly, the conservative platform would suppress a majority (liberals and moderates) who prefer the moderate platform to the conservative platform. Because the liberals and conservatives each rank the moderate platform *B*, with only 25% of the vote, as their second choice (with preferences *ABC* and *CBA* respectively), that option defeats *A* and *C*, with 40% and 35% of the vote respectively, in direct comparisons. Thus, selecting option *B*, the median position, with only 25% first-choice support, vindicates majority rule, whereas selecting option *A*, the plurality candidate, with 40% first choice support, does not.

---

[23] *See* Stearns, *Misguided Renaissance*, *supra* note 1, at 1221.

[24] WILLIAM H. RIKER, LIBERALISM AGAINST POPULISM: A CONFRONTATION BETWEEN THE THEORY OF DEMOCRACY AND THE THEORY OF SOCIAL CHOICE 100 (1982).

This intuition is reflected in the *Casey* decision as shown in Table 13:1.[25] By specifying the membership in each of the three camps in *Casey*—liberal, moderate, and conservative—we can see once more a potential divergence between outcomes dictated by the competing logic of the Condorcet criterion and plurality rule. As previously noted, two Justices, Blackmun and Stevens, embraced the liberal position, voting to strike down all the restrictive Pennsylvania abortion provisions. Three Justices, O'Connor, Kennedy, and Souter, embraced the moderate position, voting to sustain all but the spousal notification provision. And four Justices, Rehnquist, Scalia, White, and Thomas, embraced the conservative position, voting to sustain all challenged provisions. While a majority of five Justices (the liberals and the moderates) voted to strike down the spousal notification provision, in a regime of plurality rule, the four conservative dissenters, the largest unified coalition, would instead control, sustaining the spousal notification provision along with the remaining challenged provisions.[26] By contrast, applying the Condorcet criterion, the coalition embodying the median position along the spectrum of how far abortion rights extend expresses the holding. The result is to strike down the spousal notification provision (with the liberal and moderate justices controlling) and to sustain the remaining provisions (with the moderate and conservative justices controlling).

Despite the Condorcet criterion's normative appeal, two important limitations prevent some important institutions from adopting rules that satisfy it. First, as we have already seen, depending upon the preferences of the group members, there might not always be a Condorcet winner. When there is no Condorcet winner, rules that meet the Condorcet criterion and thus allow separate majority votes over all available pairwise comparisons produce an intransitivity or cycle.[27] Second, as we saw in the simple example involving the choice of vanilla or chocolate cake where one child was allergic to cocoa, majority rule fails to account for the differing levels of interest that participants have in the outcome due to the disparate intensities with which they hold their preferences. The Condorcet criterion is grounded in majority rule, meaning one person, one vote, regardless of individual stakes in the outcome, and like majority rule, it fails to account for intensity of preference.

To illustrate, imagine a decision concerning how much money to allocate for a park renovation, with three proposals: low, moderate, and high. Each proposal is of comparable quality and the differences are due to the scope of the proposed renovation. Assume that there are three city council members, each holding a different first choice and each agreeing that the only issue is the scope of the project. We might imagine convergence toward the moderate expenditure, with those preferring the low and high

---

25 *See supra* p. 545 (presenting stylized discussion of *Casey*).

26 Although the discussion simplifies the opinions by avoiding partial concurrences and partial dissents, this does not change the analysis. The discussion further assumes sincere voting, implying that a change in the voting regime will not change the position each justice takes on the merits of each challenged provision. For a discussion of how a change in voting protocols threatens to compromise this assumption, see STEARNS, *supra* note 1, at 117–22. *See also* Maxwell L. Stearns, *How Outcome Voting Promotes Principled Issue Identification: A Reply to Professor John Rogers and Others*, 49 VAND. L. REV. 1045 (1996).

27 Whereas the *Casey* opinions are conducive to finding a Condorcet winner, we will see other Supreme Court cases in which there is no Condorcet winner, implicating alternative decision-making rules that thwart the Condorcet criterion in favor of alternative normative considerations. *See infra* Chapter 22, parts I and II (discussing outcome voting and stare decisis).

expenditures ranking the moderate position as a second choice and the opposite extreme expenditure as a third choice. If so, the moderate outcome emerges a Condorcet winner. Imagine, instead, that only the high expenditure will include access ramps to the various activities for children suffering certain physical limitations, including reliance upon wheelchairs. Assume that although the members whose first choices are the low and moderate expenditures would prefer to conserve resources for some other public works project, the intensity of their opposition to the larger expenditure is lower than the intensity of support by the one member for the more expensive plan whose constituency includes parents of children with disabilities hoping to enjoy the newly renovated park. In this case, although the moderate proposal, the Condorcet result, operates consistently with majority rule, taking into account intensities of preference, the socially preferred outcome might instead be the more costly renovation. Although the Condorcet criterion is important, it remains only one of several competing benchmarks in evaluating collective decision-making processes.

As this example (along with the earlier ice cream cake example) illustrates, the Condorcet criterion generalizes the principle of majority rule beyond the limited context in which group preferences include a first-choice majority candidate. As such, the Condorcet criterion carries with it the same strengths (including operating consistently with democratic norms) and weaknesses (including failing to account for preference intensities) as simple majority rule.

D. Cycling, Path Dependence, and Agenda Setting

As previously explained, one limitation of voting rules that satisfy the Condorcet criterion is the risk of cycling. A cycle implies that for any possible outcome, another is preferred in a regime of direct pairwise comparisons by simple majority rule. Because this result holds for all possible outcomes, when members hold such preferences, rules that satisfy the Condorcet criterion fail to guarantee a stable outcome.

We can think of rules that satisfy the Condorcet criterion as having the characteristic feature of unlimited majority veto. Pairwise comparisons remain available until there no longer exists a majority whose preferences would be thwarted by the proposed outcome. As we have seen, however, when group preferences cycle, such a stable outcome is not possible because for any proposed outcome, some majority prefers an alternative. To illustrate, reconsider the first set of preferences above: P1: *ABC*; P2: *BCA*; and P3: *CAB*. Even assuming each participant holds transitive (rational) preferences, a regime of unlimited pairwise voting yields an intransitivity for the group as a whole. Thus, the group prefers *A* to *B* (with P2 losing) and *B* to *C* (with P3 losing), but *C* to *A* (with P1 losing), or *ApBpCpA*.

Although groups possessing such preferences cannot select a winner without thwarting the preferences of a majority in a potential pairwise comparison, groups characterized by such preferences do not forever remain in the throes of cycling. Rather, assuming the group does not opt for inaction, thereby defaulting to the status quo, the cycle is inevitably embedded in whichever outcome the group selects. To explain why, we must identify a characteristic feature of rules that satisfy the Condorcet criterion. Such rules allow the same number of pairwise contests as available alternatives (in this instance, three pairwise votes over three alternatives). By contrast, when decision rules limit the number of pairwise contests relative to available options and when member preferences cycle, provided the members vote sincerely, the substantive outcome will turn on the order, or path, in which options are voted. To be sure, path-dependent outcomes can be stable. They might even be predictable if we understand the preferences of the person who controls the agenda, referred to as the *agenda setter*, and if participants are somehow prevented from voting strategically. At the same time, however, path-dependent outcomes thwart the preferences of at least one majority that would have preferred an alternative outcome in a suppressed binary, or pairwise, comparison.

To illustrate we return once more to the example with cycling preferences (*ABC*, *BCA*, *CAB*). With only two votes over the three options, and assuming that members vote sincerely, we will induce a path toward a determinate result. If we begin with *A* versus *B* (*A* wins) followed by *C* versus *A* (*C* wins), the path leads to *C*. Only by bringing back option *B*, which was defeated in the first round, and pitting it against option *C*, do we formally reveal the cycle. If we knew all ordinal rankings in advance, we could intuit that option *C* thwarts the majority preferences of P1 and P2, who form a majority preferring option *B* to option *C*. Once again, although path dependence leads to a stable outcome, with full disclosure or with the later disclosure of suppressed preferences, we can discover an embedded cycle. Of course, participants will not always possess, or have the means of acquiring, such information. As a result, non-Condorcet rules have the potential to produce path-dependent results that appear to have majority support. After all, the outcome ultimately selected follows a series of separate majority votes. The voting process might therefore lend normative legitimacy to the eventual outcome even if that outcome thwarts the preferences of a majority that would have favored an alternative in a direct pairwise comparison.

Path dependence is the flip side of agenda setting. Assuming that members vote sincerely based on their ordinal preferences, then when group preferences are intransitive, a rule allowing two votes over the three options empowers the agenda setter to control the outcome. By positioning the votes such that the option that would defeat her first choice is itself defeated in the first round of voting, the agenda setter can produce a voting path that leads directly to her first choice.[28] In devising rule-making procedures, therefore, an important consideration is controlling the power of the person who sets the voting path.

To what extent are judicial or legislative outcomes likely to be path dependent? Can you identify an institution that grants agenda-setting power to one or more participants? If so, can you identify mechanisms that limit such agenda-setting power? Do you recall having been disadvantaged or benefited by agenda setting? If you were disadvantaged, can you identify strategies that might have facilitated a better result?

---

[28] We have already seen the path leading to *C*. If, instead, the agenda setter most prefers option *A*, she would first present *B* versus *C* (*B* wins), then *B* versus *A* (*A* wins). Option *C*, the sole option that would defeat *A* in a direct pairwise contest, was defeated in the first round. And if the agenda setter most preferred option *B*, she would first present *C* versus *A* (*C* wins), and then present *C* versus *B* (*B* wins). Option *A*, the sole option that would defeat option *B* in a pairwise contest, was defeated in the first round.

E. A Brief Comment on Arrow's Theorem

While we provide a more detailed introduction to Arrow's Impossibility Theorem (or simply "Arrow's Theorem") in Chapter 14,[29] we now offer a brief summary. Arrow's Theorem generalizes the voting paradox.[30] In effect, the theorem proves that any decision-making rule designed to "solve" the potential impasse resulting from cyclical preferences necessarily violates some other important norm associated with fair, or democratic, decision making. Kenneth Arrow posited a group of conditions, which William Vickrey later simplified to four.[31] Arrow proved that no institution can simultaneously satisfy those conditions while also guaranteeing the ability to translate the individually rational, or transitive, preferences of members into rational group orderings.[32] At its most basic level, Arrow's Theorem exposes an inevitable tension confronting collective decision-making bodies. The tension is between ensuring rational (transitive) outcomes, on one side, and adhering to a set of fair or democratic norms, on the other.

Before briefly describing the fairness conditions, it is worth noting their somewhat technical quality. In his proof, Arrow set out these conditions with mathematical precision. What follows is a non-mathematical description based on William Vickrey's simplified proof. Even these descriptions are easier to understand in the context of specific applications, which we will provide, along with a more detailed overview, in the next chapter. Our immediate purpose is more limited. By introducing Arrow's fairness conditions, we hope to convey that the problem of cycling (the inverse of rationality) is but one consideration in the inevitably complex tradeoffs that Arrow's Theorem reveals for the study of institutions and rules.

Arrow's fairness conditions are as follows:

(1) *range*: the collective decision-making rule must select its outcome in a manner that is consistent with the members' selection from among all conceivable ordinal rankings over three available alternatives;

(2) *independence of irrelevant alternatives*: in choosing between paired alternatives, participants are assumed to decide solely based upon the merits of those options and without regard to how they would rank options that might be introduced later;

(3) *unanimity*: if a change from the status quo to an alternate state will improve the position of at least a single participant without harming anyone else, the decision-making body must so move; and

---

[29] *See infra* Chapter 14, Part II.

[30] *See* RIKER, *supra* note 24, at 116.

[31] STEARNS, *supra* note 1, at 81, 344–45 n.91. *See also* William Vickrey, *Utility, Strategy, and Social Decision Rules*, 74 Q.J. ECON. 507 (1960), *reprinted in* WILLIAM VICKREY, PUBLIC ECONOMICS 29 (Richard Arnott et al. eds., 1994).

[32] For a discussion of the relationships between the criteria as described in Kenneth Arrow's original analysis, in William Vickrey's simplified proof, and here, see STEARNS, *supra* note 1, at 344–45 n.91, 346–47 n.104, 337 n.22, 347–48 n.112.

(4) *nondictatorship*: the group cannot consistently vindicate the preferences of a group member against the contrary will of the group as a whole.[33]

This preliminary description helps to reveal the tradeoffs institutions inevitably confront in developing decision-making rules. We have seen, for example, the potential conflict between an institutional commitment to cycle avoidance, on the one hand, and to unlimited majority rule or veto power, on the other. The Arrovian fairness conditions reveal this as one of several normative values in potential conflict. Other conflicting normative commitments include ensuring that decision makers express sincere preferences, that members are able to register cardinal (meaning strength of) preferences, that mutually beneficial exchanges are honored, and that various disproportionate allocations of power among members are avoided. Arrow's Theorem helps to situate these normative commitments within a framework that allows for greater precision in evaluating the tradeoffs necessary to ensuring proper institutional functioning.

The inability of any single institution to satisfy all of these conditions while ensuring rational, or transitive, group outputs raises an important question: Which normative concerns should take priority? Ralph Waldo Emerson famously deemed "a foolish consistency . . . the hobgoblin of little minds."[34] We might imagine that rationality, meaning the demand to reconcile each member's binary preferences with transitive group preferences, thereby avoiding the inconsistency of a cycle, is less important than it first appears. Should institutions sacrifice rationality to satisfy the other Arrovian fairness conditions?

We must first consider these questions: Why is rationality at least potentially important? And how should rationality be traded off against other fairness considerations grounded in democratic norms? Here is a possible answer: institutions that sacrifice rationality cannot ensure socially significant outputs, at least if we define that to mean avoiding an outcome that a present majority disfavors as compared with an available alternative. Conversely, institutions that do ensure rationality cannot guarantee a stable outcome when preferences cycle.

Ensuring socially significant outcomes, or ensuring stable outputs, might not be vital to all institutions, but certainly these concerns will be important to some. Although path-dependent outcomes are potentially stable, they inevitably embed thwarted majority preferences. When members with cyclical preferences demand collective decision, endless majority veto power might threaten that obligation. The continuing veto process might threaten the legitimacy, or the collective willingness to accept, the eventual outcome.[35] Institutions that generate path-dependent outcomes elevate the concern for outputs with the appearance of legitimacy, even when they embed cyclical preferences, over at least one of Arrow's fairness conditions. Do you see why this result is inevitable?

---

[33] STEARNS, *supra* note 1, at 84–94.

[34] RALPH WALDO EMERSON, *Self-Reliance*, *in* ESSAYS: FIRST SERIES 37 (Everyman's Library ed. 1906) (1841) ("A foolish consistency is the hobgoblin of little minds, adored by little statesmen and philosophers and divines.").

[35] Legitimacy implies a willingness to accept an outcome based on respect for the process that generates that outcome, as opposed to based on agreement with the merits of the outcome. STEARNS, *supra* note 1, at 35–36 (discussing the social value derived from institutions that can produce outcomes rather deriving value based upon merit of the outcome).

By proving that no institution can simultaneously ensure transitive outputs and satisfy the specified fairness conditions, Arrow's Theorem exposes inevitable tradeoffs between the need for stable outcomes, on one side, and ensuring fair collective processes, on the other. One critical implication is an inevitable tradeoff between rules that ensure transitive outputs and rules that prevent minorities from exerting power disproportionate to their numbers.[36] Unlimited majority veto has the potential to block any possible outcomes when preferences cycle. At some point, the only viable method of ensuring stable outputs might be vesting ultimate decision-making power in a minority or an individual. Rules designed to avoid indecision resulting from cycling thus risk allowing an individual or minority group to control, or manipulate, the agenda for the group as a whole. Social choice thus implicates not only the paradox of voting, meaning the possibility that individually transitive preferences might combine into cyclical group preferences, but also the tension between rationality and Arrow's fairness conditions.

F. Implications for Institutional Reform: Veto Gates (Negative Legislative Checkpoints) and Minimum Winning Coalitions

Given the abstract nature of Arrow's Theorem, it is helpful to introduce some specific proposals for institutional reform that rely upon it. Several of the proposals that follow are guided by assumptions about the relative competence of appellate courts and legislatures. These assumptions implicate not only Arrow's Theorem and the problem of cycling, but also specific institutional features that developed at least in part in response to the difficulty of aggregating collective preferences. Exploring these normative proposals helps lay the foundation for later social choice analyses of courts and legislatures.

1. *Congressional Practices that Affect Transformation of Preferences into Outputs*

A group of legal scholars has questioned whether the risk of institutional cycling undermines the general presumption of judicial deference to legislative policymaking.[37] Whether or not cycling is understood to mean a perpetual state of indecision—with each proffered alternative defeated by another, a process repeated *ad infinitum*—Congressional roadblocks to passing legislation, known as "negative legislative checkpoints" or "veto gates,"[38] certainly raise the cost of securing proposed legislation. James Madison's theory of factions, grounded in the earlier work of David Hume, gives these legislative practices an historical pedigree and seeming constitutional legitimacy. Given Madison's premise set out most clearly in *The Federalist No. 10*, that rapidly forming majoritarian factions should

---

36 We do not mean that substantive outcomes cannot favor discrete or historical minorities, racial or otherwise, without violating Arrow's fairness criteria. An institution meeting some combination of Arrow's combined conditions could choose to further any normative policy concerning antidiscrimination, affirmative action, or something else entirely.

37 For an introduction to this literature, see Stearns, *Misguided Renaissance, supra* note 1, at 1225–27.

38 For a discussion of these terms, *see supra* Chapter 11, notes 110–116, and cites therein.

be feared,[39] such devices as bicameralism, presentment, various elaborate committee structures, calendaring rules, and even the contested Senate filibuster might have the benefit of broadening coalitions needed to pass legislation.

These practices therefore have an important theoretical foundation in the theory of minimum winning coalitions.[40] Recall that, based on specified conditions, Professor William H. Riker posited that legislative coalitions become increasingly stable as they approach minimum winning size, meaning a simple majority.[41] This theory is the public choice analogue to the Madison-Hume theory of factions. Riker posited that supermajorities tend to break down in favor of simple majority coalitions because the smaller the successful coalition, the larger each member's *pro rata* share of the resulting gains.

Consider a legislature with nine members in which the successful coalition shares a benefit equal to one hundred. An over-weighted coalition of seven would provide each member a *pro rata* benefit of just over fourteen (one hundred divided by seven), whereas a simple majority coalition of five would provide each member a larger pro rata benefit of twenty (one hundred divided by five). Absent any structural impediments, coalitions larger than a bare majority tend to decompose into simple majority coalitions. A principal concern raised by both Riker and Madison is that absent barriers to simple majority coalitions, legislative processes might routinely redistribute wealth or other benefits from broad constituencies to successful narrow-majority coalitions, or factions.

Although veto gates (negative legislative checkpoints) afford defenses to factional legislation by enlarging coalitions, they also produce a paradox. By vesting minority groups with blocking or veto power, these roadblocks provide opportunities for strategic behavior, including demanding rents as a precondition to supporting (or declining to thwart) the often critical path that shapes the substance of enacted legislation. These institutional practices thus contribute to normative criticisms concerning Congress's ability to rationally aggregate collective preferences and to proposals to expand the judicial lawmaking authority through statutory interpretation and implementation.

2. *Social Choice Implications for Institutional Competence as Between Congress and the Judiciary*

Based on the defects that they ascribe to legislatures grounded in insights from social choice, prominent legal scholars challenge legal doctrines that confer broad deference to legislative policy making. One group of scholars, including Professors William Eskridge, Lynn Stout, and Jonathan Macey, has challenged a premise underlying rational basis scrutiny. These scholars question the presumption that absent an identified constitutional violation, federal courts should assume that legislatures have rationally processed the

---

[39] *See* THE FEDERALIST No. 10 (James Madison).

[40] *See supra* Chapter 2, Part III.A.

[41] Riker's theory provides that "[i]n *n*-person, zero sum games, where side-payments are permitted, where players are rational, and where they have perfect information, only minimum winning coalitions occur." WILLIAM H. RIKER, THE THEORY OF POLITICAL COALITIONS 32 (1962). *See also supra* Chapter 2, Part III.B.

preferences of their members and constituents in light of relevant policy considerations.[42] Instead, based upon social choice insights demonstrating the difficulties with collective preference aggregation, these scholars advocate a more liberal construction of statutes and broader constitutional judicial review as needed to further their respective visions of the public good.

Other scholars, most notably Professors Daniel Farber and Philip Frickey, have cautioned against relying on social choice to enhance judicial power, claiming instead that to the extent that social choice calls legislative decision making into question, the methodology supports institutional reform within Congress itself rather than a transfer of decision-making authority to the courts.[43] Farber and Frickey argue that social choice analysis belies purely pluralist conceptions of legislation. As a result of legislative features that have developed in part in response to potential cycling, they posit that unbridled pluralism is conducive to zero-sum pluralist politicking, the modern-day equivalent to Madison's theory of factions. These scholars contend that social choice theory proves consistent with their preferred small "r" republican vision of politics, which tends to favor broad electoral participation. Whether focusing upon judicial or legislative reform, these scholars are part of a neo-republican scholarly tradition that is concerned with ensuring that institutions properly represent broad constituencies and protect their preferences against the often challenging realities of American politics.

Evaluating these and other such proposals for institutional reform, whether targeted to courts or legislatures, requires a comparative institutional analysis. Arrow's Theorem proves helpful in undertaking this analysis in a manner that avoids the pervasive *nirvana fallacy*.[44] Scholars commit this fallacy when they identify a perceived institutional defect and then propose fixing the problem by shifting decisional responsibility somewhere else without first assessing whether the alternative institution would be better or worse at performing the assigned task.

Other commentators have focused on the implications of social choice for decision making in collegial courts. Because appellate courts, including the Supreme Court, are collective decision-making bodies, social choice also reveals potential defects in the judicial process.[45] Responding to such arguments, Professors Farber and Frickey have suggested that if the problem of cycling applies to both legislatures and the judiciary, then as a tool of analysis, social choice leaves us at an impasse. The authors explain:

---

[42] *See, e.g.*, William N. Eskridge, Jr., *Politics Without Romance: Implications of Public Choice Theory for Statutory Interpretation*, 74 VA. L. REV. 275, 279 (1988); Jonathan R. Macey, *Promoting Public-Regarding Legislation Through Statutory Interpretation: An Interest Group Model*, 86 COLUM. L. REV. 223, 261–66 (1986); Lynn A. Stout, *Strict Scrutiny and Social Choice: An Economic Inquiry into Fundamental Rights and Suspect Classifications*, 80 GEO. L.J. 1787, 1799, 1823 (1992).

[43] *See generally* DANIEL A. FARBER & PHILIP P. FRICKEY, LAW AND PUBLIC CHOICE: A CRITICAL INTRODUCTION (1991); Daniel A. Farber & Philip P. Frickey, *Legislative Intent and Public Choice*, 74 VA. L. REV. 423 (1988).

[44] For a famous discussion of the nirvana fallacy, see Harold Demsetz, *Information and Efficiency: Another Viewpoint*, 12 J.L. & ECON. 1 (1969).

[45] *See, e.g.*, Frank H. Easterbrook, *Ways of Criticizing the Court*, 95 HARV. L. REV. 802, 818–31 (1982); *see also* Einer R. Elhauge, *Does Interest Group Theory Justify More Intrusive Judicial Review?*, 101 YALE L.J. 31, 101–08 (1991).

> In a sense, the . . . thesis [that cycling plagues both courts and legislatures] proves too much. If chaos and incoherence are the inevitable outcomes of majority voting, then appellate courts (which invariably have multiple members and majority voting rules) and even the 1787 Constitutional Convention are equally bankrupt. As a result, the . . . thesis is bereft of any implications for public law, since it tells us to be equally suspicious of *all* sources of law. If we accept the thesis as to legislatures, we are left with nowhere to turn.[46]

We do not evaluate each of these proposals in this chapter.[47] Instead, we offer a framework that helps to evaluate these and other claims. The analysis explores not only the nirvana fallacy, but also the fallacy of composition and the isolation fallacy. Together, these tools provide a basis for using social choice to better appreciate several existing institutional norms and functions. The analysis reveals that social choice offers the basis for developing the normative foundations of several enigmatic features of constitutional lawmaking.

II. INSTITUTIONS RECONSIDERED: THE FALLACY OF COMPOSITION, THE ISOLATION FALLACY AND THE PROBLEM OF TIMING

To illustrate the fallacy of composition, we introduce two hypotheticals. The first is inspired by Shakespeare's *The Tragedy of King Lear*,[48] and the second is based upon a 1992 Supreme Court case, *New York v. United States*.[49] The analysis demonstrates that *even if* each institution is separately prone to cycling, collective decision-making bodies operating together can reduce cycling, thereby improving their quality of outputs.

A. The Fallacy of Composition

The fallacy of composition is the assumption that if phenomenon X produces result Y, more of phenomenon X will produce more of result Y. For a simple illustration, imagine a proposed housing development in which the basic model house is brick. An individual purchaser could make her house distinctive by instead selecting a stone façade. But now imagine that every purchaser shares this intuition and thus seeks to render her or his home distinctive with this strategy. After several home buyers follow the strategy, a stone façade no longer renders a home distinctive. Indeed, a home buyer could make her home distinctive by instead opting for brick. Of course, the same problem would arise if everyone mimicked that strategy.

Similarly, an individual homeowner could make her house safer against burglary by installing an alarm. While sophisticated burglars can get past most alarms, holding all else

---

[46] FARBER & FRICKEY, *supra* note 43, at 55.

[47] For a more detailed critique, see Stearns, *Misguided Renaissance, supra* note 1.

[48] WILLIAM SHAKESPEARE, THE TRAGEDY OF KING LEAR. For an earlier presentation of this example, see STEARNS, *supra* note 1, at 54–58.

[49] 505 U.S. 144 (1992).

constant,[50] alarms divert would-be burglars in favor of homes that lack alarms and can thus be broken into with less effort and at lower risk. Of course, if most or all homeowners in the housing complex install an alarm, the diversionary benefit is dramatically reduced. While each alarmed home is somewhat more difficult to burgle, the larger benefit of encouraging would-be burglars to thieve elsewhere is substantially diminished. In both examples, phenomenon *X* (a stone façade or a house alarm) produced result *Y* (distinction or a reduced risk of burglary relative to neighboring homes) *only if* a relatively small number of actors followed the distinguishing strategy. If most or all homeowners followed the same strategy, the benefits of distinction are substantially reduced and perhaps eliminated.

B. Implications for Collective Decision Making

We now return to the context that motivated our discussion, namely the problem of cycling in collective decision-making institutions. Professors Farber and Frickey aptly expressed the concern: If the problems revealed in Arrow's theorem are a universal feature of collective decision-making bodies, then the insights of social choice might leave us "nowhere to turn."[51] If each institution is susceptible of cycling, does social choice imply that no institution can avoid the difficulty?

In fact, however, when we apply the fallacy of composition in this context, we see that two collective decision-making bodies that independently cycle can reduce cycling by operating together. The critical insight is that even when two institutions cycle, they do not necessarily cycle in response to the same underlying phenomena. The different triggers to institutional cycling imply that although phenomenon *X* (an institution processing member preferences) produces result *Y* (generating occasional cycling), more of phenomena *X* (multiple institutions processing member preferences) can avoid or reduce result *Y* (thus inhibiting cycling).

In some respects, this is old news. The United States Constitution, after all, establishes two lawmaking bodies, Congress and the Supreme Court. These bodies were never intended to operate entirely in isolation from each other. And as we will see, several Supreme Court doctrines allocate decisional responsibility between these two branches in a manner that promotes their collective rationality.[52]

The important question, then, becomes which factual predicates cause cycling in one lawmaking institution while inhibiting it in the other. The most important difference in these factual predicates is timing. Institutions are more likely to cycle *after* being confronted with the need to allocate the benefits of an unanticipated gain or the burdens of an unanticipated loss.[53] Conversely, institutions are less likely to cycle when constructing rules that apply generally and prospectively, and thus *before* the circumstances arise that generate such a gain or loss.

---

[50] This includes the assumption that an alarm does not signal higher value of contents in the home to steal.

[51] *See* FARBER & FRICKEY, *supra* note 43, at 55.

[52] *See infra* Chapter 16.

[53] *See* Stearns, *Misguided Renaissance*, *supra* note 1, at 1242 (positing that negotiations concerning how to allocate capital gains or losses are prone to generating cycling).

To demonstrate the generality of this proposition, we offer two illustrations. In the first, private actors are prone to cycling and the legislature breaks the impasse. In the second, the legislature is prone to cycling, inviting the judiciary to break the impasse. The critical point is that there is nothing inherent about the legislature that causes, or that breaks, cycling. Rather, any multimember institution can itself cycle or can limit cycling elsewhere. The result in each instance depends upon the nature of each institution's interaction with the factual predicate, or the timing, that motivates (or inhibits) cycling.

C. The Problem of the Empty Core Among Private Actors

The next two examples rely upon a game theoretical concept known as the empty core.

The first hypothetical will take as its inspiration William Shakespeare's *The Tragedy of King Lear*.[54] In the original story, an aging Lear vainly disinherits his youngest and most beloved daughter, Cordelia, because unlike her sisters, Goneril and Regan, Cordelia was unwilling to express her love for him in unconditional terms as a precondition to taking her share of the kingdom. Cordelia claimed that while she loved him dearly as a father, her foremost love would be for her yet unchosen husband. As the story unfolds, we learn the devastating consequences of both Cordelia's disinheritance and the premature conveyance to Lear's other daughters.

Our adaptation involves a more modern dysfunctional family. Professor Lear, an eccentric mathematics professor who has recently won $30 million in the lottery, has long been estranged from his three daughters who are also estranged from each other. Because the daughters have not had any contact with Lear since their mother died ten years before, they are unaware that he won the lottery five years ago. Assume that the full lottery proceeds were distributed as a single lump sum with no discounting. Upon winning the lottery, Lear did not change his reclusive lifestyle. Instead, he placed the proceeds into a trust fund, planning to pass the money to his daughters under specified conditions. Five years after winning, Lear was diagnosed with a fatal disease with six months to live. After receiving the diagnosis, Lear saw an opportunity to construct a controlled high stakes social choice experiment with real players.

Lear immediately contacted the administrator of the trust and had the trust's terms modified as follows. If the terms governing the distribution of the corpus of Lear's trust for the lottery winnings were satisfied by the time of his death, the full proceeds of the trust would then be distributed in accordance with the terms of his daughters' agreed upon division of the trust assets. Failing that, the corpus of the trust would pass into the residuum of Lear's will, from which it would be used to endow the new Lear Institute, a research center devoted to studying applied social choice and game theory.

The relevant provisions of the trust require that the full proceeds be distributed based upon the consent of any two of Lear's three daughters, subject to two conditions. First, the allocations must be agreed to by two of the three daughters by no later than 5:00 p.m. for ten days prior to Lear's death and must remain unchallenged for ten days. The first submitted plan that meets this ten-day rule without being superseded by another plan

54 WILLIAM SHAKESPEARE, THE TRAGEDY OF KING LEAR.

will be final. Second, after any distribution plan is submitted, any daughter (or daughters) will forfeit her (or their) shares by seeking to alter the distribution by any means other than through a superseding coalition that independently satisfies the ten-day filing rule. Filing an action to enforce prior agreements in a court of law or equity is prohibited. The daughters can allocate shares however they wish, provided they do so privately and legally. Upon receiving a plan for final distribution that satisfies the ten-day rule, the trust administrator shall immediately notify Lear of its terms. Otherwise, the full corpus of the trust shall pass to the residuum of Lear's will.

Before considering how the daughters might respond, a few general comments about the hypothetical will be helpful. Under the terms of the trust, the daughters are expected to agree to an outcome governing the distribution of what will be an extremely valuable windfall. Any daughter can try to supersede any proposed solution with an alternative provided that she forms a new coalition and files in time to meet the ten-day rule before Lear's death. Although the daughters may employ any background decision-making rules they wish, they completely forfeit the money if they pursue legal enforcement. A minimum of two out of the three daughters must agree upon, and submit in writing, a planned distribution, with the goal of satisfying the ten-day rule. No single daughter can disrupt a pending plan other than by forming a superior coalition and filing a superseding plan subject to that rule. Finally, although the daughters know that Lear is terminally ill, no one knows when he will die, and thus each later-filed plan increases the risk that his death will cut short the necessary ten-day filing period.

Now consider the options confronting the daughters. One obvious solution exists: Each daughter could take $10 million and the three now wealthier sisters could go on with their lives. Based upon this intuition, Professors Farber and Frickey have posited that in such cycling games, simple and obvious *fairness solutions* (also called *value solutions*), like equal division, prove practical and potentially stable.[55] Indeed, this solution might also be a *Schelling Point*.[56]

This hypothetical is a classic illustration of an *empty core* game, a game that reveals the features of the Condorcet paradox. The empty core implies that for any existing coalition, there exists an alternative "superior" coalition that can improve the payoffs for both the excluded party and a defector. Because this holds true for any potential coalition, no coalition is stable. By contrast, a game has a core, producing a stable solution, when, for a coalition or set of coalitions, there is no alternative superior coalition that will improve the plight of an excluded party and a defector. Because the Lear game has an empty core,

---

[55] The authors state:

> [T]his solution is a sort of equilibrium. It is true that any player could offer an amendment that would beat th[e] [equal division] outcome—but what would be the point of doing so and thereby setting off a round of endless cycling? In a sense, the existence of massive cycling provides the basis for a new form of equilibrium adopted precisely to avoid the cycles.

Farber & Frickey, *supra* note 43, at 434. As the following discussion demonstrates, despite the normative appeal of equal division, this is not a pure Nash equilibrium in a cycling game; instead, that result requires changing the payoffs to eliminate the cycle.

[56] *See* THOMAS C. SCHELLING, THE STRATEGY OF CONFLICT 57 (1960) (introducing the concept of "focal point[s] for each person's expectation of what the other expects him to expect to be expected to do," which was later named after Schelling).

for any proposed solution. an alternative will be favored by a newly formed coalition, generating a cycle.

To simplify, assume a pool of $30, where each dollar represents $1 million. Further assume that Goneril and Regan begin by submitting a plan for each to take $15 each. We can now see how each of the following sequential coalitions can displace the original plan, but without any remaining stable:

Regan/Goneril: 15/15

Cordelia/Regan: 10/20

Goneril/Cordelia: 10/20

Regan/Goneril: 10/20

For each proposed coalition, the displaced sister approaches the less advantaged sister in the prior round, improving that sister's payoff along with her own, at the expense of the previously advantaged, and now newly displaced, sister. First, Cordelia breaks up the Regan/Goneril (15/15) coalition in favor of a Cordelia/Regan (10/20) Coalition. Second, Goneril breaks up that coalition in favor of a Goneril/Cordelia (10/20) Coalition. And finally, Regan breaks up that coalition in favor of a Regan/Goneril (10/20) coalition. Assume that each superseding coalition is accomplished prior to completion of the 10-day rule. The coalitions have come full circle, restoring the Goneril, Regan coalition, albeit with altered payoffs. The final listed coalition is no more stable than it was in the initial round.

It might appear that the whole problem would be solved if, as previously suggested, the three sisters simply agreed to submit a written plan calling for the fairness solution of equal division. But this too is unstable. After the $10/$10/$10 plan is submitted, Goneril can approach Regan, offering to cut Cordelia from the coalition and proposing an alternative (Goneril, Regan) coalition with a $15/$15 split. That, of course, is the starting point in the empty core game shown above.

We can only speculate, of course, what the final outcome would be and whether the daughters would reach a satisfactory resolution lasting ten days without a later filing before their father's death, or whether, as a result of efforts by the excluded sister to improve her payoff by forming a new coalition, the daughters would ultimately force the trust corpus into the residuum of their father's will, with each sister taking nothing. It is also important to observe that even if they succeeded in forming a successful coalition that meets the requirements under Lear's will, say the fairness solution, that result necessarily embeds a thwarted majority that would prefer a superior coalition. Again, this is true for any coalition in the game. The point is not to predict the outcome. It is sufficient to note that the cycle will either prevent a final timely disposition of assets or will produce an outcome disfavored by an alternative majority.

Lawmaking institutions sometimes have a comparative advantage over private individuals, like the Lear sisters, in avoiding cycling games. And yet, under alternative conditions, lawmaking bodies themselves are prone to cycling, thereby benefiting by working with other institutions. As the next variation on the Lear hypothetical demonstrates, institutional comparative advantage in avoiding cycling is a function of timing. Empty core bargaining problems arise when parties negotiate after the facts emerge that produce an unanticipated gain or loss.

Let us now modify the hypothetical to allow the sisters to legally enforce any interim agreements that they reach without sacrificing any of the resulting gains. Assume that Lear's trust does not prevent the sisters from suing for breach, and that the standard remedy is expectancy damages.[57] Recall that expectancy damages restore the non-breaching party to the position that she would have been in had the breaching party fully performed. While it is not possible to predict which coalition might initially form that would give rise to a contract action following a breach, for any coalition that does form, this contract remedy will restore stability in favor of the earlier, pre-breach result.

To illustrate, assume that Goneril and Regan submit the original plan for each to receive $15. Cordelia offers Regan to form a superior coalition, in which Regan receives $20 and Cordelia receives $10. In contrast with the prior hypothetical that led to a cycle, in this example, if she behaves rationally, Regan will decline. If Regan enters into the superior coalition with Cordelia, she will gain $5 (receiving $20 rather than $15), but will risk forfeiting $15 to Goneril in compensatory damages, placing her in an inferior position relative to honoring the original bargain. The principle is generalizable. Once any coalition has formed, an expectancy damages rule ensures that any gains to the defector from forming a superior coalition with the initially excluded daughter will be depleted by the damages award.[58]

The contract damages rule will not necessarily avoid any possible cycling. It might, instead, shift the cycle back to pre-contractual negotiations. While any coalition that formed would be stable with such a rule in place, at the negotiating stage, the same empty core problem has the potential to rear its ugly head. Preliminary coalitions can, in theory, form and reform, prior to any formal agreements that, once breached, give rise to a contract damages action.

Does this help to explain why contract law demands the formation of an actual contract rather than an interim agreement during negotiations as a precondition to an action for breach of contract?[59] While expectancy damages avoid a cycle once an actual agreement is formed, as the next variation on the Lear hypothetical will demonstrate, this is not the only solution to the problem of cycling in the context of intestacy.

A legislature not only can induce stability among private actors facing an unanticipated gain or loss by enacting a liability rule, for example through expectancy

---

[57] For ease of exposition, we assume immediate judicial enforcement. For a discussion of the expectancy damages rule, see *supra* Chapter 6. *See also* JOSEPH M. PERILLO, CALAMARI & PERILLO ON CONTRACTS § 14–C, at 490–91 (6th ed. 2009). The same analysis would apply if the contract regime permitted injunctive relief.

[58] For a somewhat more complex presentation that explores the empty core bargaining game and its relationship to the Coase theorem, see Varouj A. Aivazian & Jeffrey L. Callen, *The Coase Theorem and the Empty Core*, 24 J.L. & ECON. 175 (1981). *See also* R.H. Coase, *The Coase Theorem and the Empty Core: A Comment*, 24 J.L. & ECON. 183 (1981). For a general discussion of this illustration and Coase's response, see Stearns, *Misguided Renaissance, supra* note 1, at 1234–40.

[59] For a provocative alternative proposal, see Omri Ben-Shahar, *Contracts Without Consent: Exploring a New Basis for Contractual Liability*, 152 U. PA. L. REV. 1829 (2004) (suggesting a basis for contractual liability in the absence of mutual assent taking the form of formal acceptance).

damages; it can also do so by creating a property right.[60] Assume that Lear dies intestate. Although left to their own devices the sisters have the potential to cycle over the various allocation schemes, the problem is avoided in the laws of virtually every state, providing that siblings take in equal shares.[61]

To see why the legislature can devise this simple and compelling solution when the sisters seem unable to do so, consider the different incentives that confront the sisters, as private actors, versus the legislature. While the sisters are motivated by the desire to maximize their individual payouts once the potential windfall is announced, the legislature is instead motivated to announce rules that apply generally and prospectively. If successful, the legislative rule will mirror what the parties would have agreed to prior to the announcement of the windfall. After a windfall is announced, the sisters are no longer negotiating from *ex ante* frame of reference, as is critical to avoid strategic behavior. In this game, the legislature is well suited to replicate the more beneficial *ex ante* perspective on their behalf and, for that reason, it can devise a solution that limits cycling when combined with the sisters acting privately.

This analysis returns us to the claim that because all institutions are theoretically prone to cycling, social choice leaves us "nowhere to turn."[62] The response involves the fallacy of composition. If the separate institutions prone to cycling, here the private actors seeking to allocate a large windfall and the legislature seeking to devise an off-the-rack rule, cycle in response to different factual phenomena, by operating together they are able to reduce, and perhaps even avoid, cycling.

The same analysis applies with respect to the expectancy damages rule. Once again, assume that the legislators have no stake in the outcome of any particular set of coalitions that form among siblings negotiating in the absence of a will. The obvious facilitating rule then places the improperly excluded party who was victim of a breach in a position to sue, and thus to be restored to where she would have been but for the breach. This rule will generate a stable outcome, albeit one that thwarts an available superior coalition, regardless of which coalition initially forms. To be clear, while each of these rules—equal division among siblings absent a will or expectancy damages following a breach—ensures a stable outcome, neither avoids an embedded set of preferences that can be characterized in terms of a cycle. The outcome remains stable because the legal rule ensures that there is no basis for supplanting the off-the-rack outcome (following the property rule), or it ensures that the cost of displacing an agreed-upon outcome exceeds any resulting gain (following the contract rule).

Lawmaking bodies are not always prone to devising benign *ex ante* solutions. As the next hypothetical will demonstrate, legislatures can also fall prey to the adverse

---

[60] For a general discussion distinguishing liability and property rules, see *supra* Chapters 5 or 6.

[61] *See supra* Chapters 7 or 8 (discussing replacement of primogeniture with equal division). *See also* WILLIAM M. MCGOVERN JR. & SHELDON F. KURTZ, WILLS, TRUSTS AND ESTATES: INCLUDING TAXATION AND FUTURE INTERESTS § 2.2, at 54–56 (5th ed. 2017). In the event that this off-the-rack, or one-size-fits-all, rule turns out not to fit for particular parents, those parents, again in virtually all states, are free to supersede it by the express terms of their will.

[62] *See* FARBER & FRICKEY, *supra* note 43, at 55.

consequences of relative timing, and thus to cycling, sometimes inviting a judicial response to break the impasse.

D. Legislative Cycling: Location of Toxic-Waste Disposal Facility

The next hypothetical is based upon the 1992 Supreme Court decision, *New York v. United States*.[63] The *New York* Court struck down the take-title provisions of the Low-Level Radioactive Waste Policy Amendments of 1985. These amendments were enacted after a series of unsuccessful regulatory initiatives designed to ensure adequate facilities for storing low-level radioactive waste. The amendments solved this problem by imposing sufficient sanctions such that individual states would be motivated either to become self-sufficient or to join in a pact with other states that collectively would be self-sufficient.

Under the terms of the amendments, states that failed within a specified time frame to join a successful regional waste-disposal pact with other states or to become self-sufficient by creating their own in-state waste disposal facilities were required to take title to low-level radioactive waste or to compensate producers for any resulting liability. Although the amendments produced a series of three compliance incentives that were intended to ensure self-sufficiency on the part of states by the end of 1992, Justice O'Connor, writing for the *New York* Court, determined that only the take-title provisions exceeded Congress's powers under the Commerce Clause, or alternatively, under the Tenth Amendment.

The case facts revealed that by December 31, 1992, the compliance deadline under the 1985 amendments, only New York had failed to either join a regional pact or to create an in-state disposal facility for low-level radioactive waste. New York then filed suit to challenge the take-title provisions as exceeding the permissible scope of Congress's regulatory powers under the Commerce Clause. The facts further revealed that while New York had initially decided to join a regional pact, it later opted instead to create an in-state disposal facility. The New York State Assembly eventually rejected each of five proposed sites, with the result that New York was the only noncompliant state and thus the only state subject to the onerous take-title provisions.

Consistent with the preceding analysis, the following simplified rendition of the *New York* facts demonstrates how the state legislature is prone to cycling under the federal regulatory requirements. Imagine that instead of five proposed sites there are three, *ABC*. Consider the incentives among the legislators representing those districts or for any three groups of legislators such that any two groups comprise a majority. The general problem of course is that no legislator wants the facility in her own district, a phenomenon that environmentalists refer to as Not In My Back Yard, or simply NIMBY. Assume that *AB* form a majority, voting to place the facility in *C*. *C* can offer *A* a sufficient legislative perk to form a superior *CA* coalition, with the result of instead voting to place the facility in *B*. *B* can now propose a similar deal to *C* if *C* defects in favor of a superior *BC* coalition, voting to place the facility in *A*. Now *A* can make a similar promise to *B*, reforming the now superior *AB* coalition, and once again voting to place the facility in *C*. At this point

[63] 505 U.S. 144 (1992).

the coalitions have come full circle, *AB*, *BC*, *CA*, *AB*, with the facility voted to be placed in *C*, *B*, *A*, *C*. Of course, no outcome is stable because, like the Lear game, this game has an empty core.

Why is the state legislature itself prone to cycling in this example when in the prior example involving the allocation of assets in the absence of a will, the state legislature succeeded in eliminating the cycling problem among the sisters? When faced with allocating the proceeds of a large unanticipated windfall, the sisters were not concerned with devising the best or most equitable public policy respecting the division of assets among siblings in the absence of a will. Instead, each sister rationally engaged in whatever strategy maximized her personal gain. In this empty core game, these combined strategies produced a cycle. By contrast, the legislators, when developing a prospective regime governing rules of heredity in the absence of a will, sought to devise a fair and general solution.

That is a characteristic feature of off-the-rack rules, whether taking the form of contractual rules (the expectancy damages rule) or property rights (the equal division rule). Unlike the sisters who were motivated by *ex post* gain, the legislators approached the problem as if the relevant facts giving rise to a potential cycle had not yet occurred. Even though the legislators are prone to cycling when they are confronted with a legislative capital loss (allocating the burdens of a newly imposed regulation that requires locating a waste facility), they are able to inhibit cycling among private actors when constructing a general and prospective off-the-rack rule. This beneficial result occurs *even though* both private actors and legislators are sometimes prone to cycling.

E. Why So Much Stability? Connecting Interest Group Theory and the Problem of Cycling

In a famous essay posing this question, Professor Gordon Tullock questioned the practical significance of cycling in the face of generally stable institutional outcomes.[64] Tullock noted that, while the literature on legislative cycling is extensive, observed legislative cycling is practically nonexistent. Tullock proposed that the solution to the apparent gulf between the theoretical prediction of frequent legislative cycles and the empirical observation of stable legislative outcomes results from logrolling, or vote trading. Tullock maintained that logrolling promotes stable legislative outcomes by allowing legislators to register cardinal values, rather than mere ordinal rankings, when selecting among alternatives.

In an important series of articles, Professors Kenneth Shepsle and Barry Weingast questioned logrolling as a general explanation of the absence of observed cycling, demonstrating that when participants lack different intensities of preference, logrolling itself conduces to cycling.[65] With equal intensities, vote-trading mechanisms manifest the underlying cycle in a different form. Shepsle and Weingast argue instead that a variety of

---

[64] Gordon Tullock, *Why So Much Stability*, 37 PUB. CHOICE 189 (1981).

[65] Kenneth A. Shepsle & Barry R. Weingast, *Structure-Induced Equilibrium and Legislative Choice*, 37 PUB. CHOICE 503 (1981) [hereinafter *Structure-Induced Equilibrium*]; Kenneth A. Shepsle & Barry R. Weingast, *The Institutional Foundations of Committee Power*, 81 AM. POL. SCI. REV. 85 (1987); *see also* DENNIS MUELLER, PUBLIC CHOICE III, at 104–08 (1989).

institutional structures in Congress, including committees, calendaring rules, the filibuster, and bicameralism—devices that include previously identified negative legislative checkpoints or veto gates—induce stability by raising the cost of identifying and commodifying potential cyclical preferences. In effect, these combined mechanisms raise the costs of working bills through the legislature, and, in doing so, they reduce the likelihood of revealing thwarted majority preferences, thereby inhibiting potential cycles.

This account provides an important conceptual link between interest group theory and social choice theory by offering a positive account for lawmaking structures that reduce the incidence of observed cyclical preferences. At the same time, because of the tendency of interest groups to exploit these very devices, they are also an important subject matter for interest group theory. Even accepting that these features diminish legislative cycling, the normative implications of such structures for legislative outcomes remains uncertain.

In a separate article, Professor Shepsle responded to an argument by Professors Farber and Frickey that questioned the practical importance to legislatures of the theoretical literature on cycling.[66] Farber and Frickey stated: "Arrow's Paradox is both fascinating and illuminating, but it may have little direct relevance to legislative practice."[67] Professor Shepsle addressed this assertion by considering the normative significance of cycle-breaking rules for legislative outcomes in light of the theoretical possibility of suppressed cycles. Professor Shepsle responded:

> The authors are confused by the fact that even in voting processes victimized by the Arrow result, we are sometimes able to identify equilibria. These equilibria, however, are strongly affected by the underlying incoherence of majority preferences and, because of this, lack a compelling normative justification. Arrow's theorem does not necessarily entail constant flux and indeterminacy; rather, it implies that the manner in which majority cycling is resolved is arbitrary or otherwise morally indefensible.[68]

In effect, Shepsle suggests that Farber and Frickey have focused on the wrong question. Farber and Frickey observe the absence of cycling and infer that cycling must

---

[66] Professors Farber and Frickey have separately relied upon such concepts as the *Yolk*, *Uncovered Set*, and *Strong Point* to explain why we do not observe cycling in legislatures. Although modeled differently, each concept rests on the intuition that legislative cycling is avoided in favor of a stable center of gravity that represents a set of outcomes capable of defeating *most* alternatives in direct comparisons. FARBER & FRICKEY, *supra* note 43, at 54 ("The 'sense of the legislature' or the legislative center of gravity corresponds to the solution sets (yolk, strong point, uncovered set or whatever) of recent formal models."). By definition, the set of options that satisfies one or more of these criteria does not defeat *all* alternatives in direct comparisons. As a result, depending upon the stakes involved and the intensity with which a potentially thwarted majority prefers an alternative to an option falling, for example, within the yolk, the concept cannot offer a complete account for the failure of observed legislative cycling. The authors have also suggested that the desire to avoid cycling itself can prevent cycling. FARBER & FRICKEY, *supra* note 43, at 434 (positing that "the existence of massive cycling provides the basis for a new form of equilibrium adopted precisely to avoid the cycles"). For this thesis to succeed, the participants must value avoiding cycling sufficiently to change the nominal payoffs in a manner no longer characterized by a cycle. If not, then the cycle persists; but if so, the cycling problem is alleviated by assuming that the payoffs are no longer conducive to cycling.

[67] Daniel A. Farber & Philip P. Frickey, *The Jurisprudence of Public Choice*, 65 TEX. L. REV. 873, 904 (1987).

[68] Kenneth A. Shepsle, *Congress Is a "They," Not an "It": Legislative Intent as Oxymoron*, 12 INT'L REV. L. & ECON. 239, 242 n.6 (1992).

therefore not be a significant real world concern. But Shepsle notes that the absence of observed cycling outcomes does not imply an absence of cycling preferences. Instead, Shepsle maintains, the failure to observe cycling suggests the presence of legislative structures that promote stable outcomes by raising the cost of disclosing, and thus acting on, preferences that reflect voting cycles. Even if cyclical preferences are common, Congress can produce stable outcomes—outcomes that Shepsle and Weingast refer to as "structure-induced equilibria"[69]—by effectively suppressing (or embedding) cycling preferences.

Shepsle claims that the real problem is not legislative instability resulting from cycling, but rather the potential arbitrariness of the results that cycle-suppressing rules generate. While these rules can produce stable outcomes, the outcomes nonetheless embed a set of underlying cyclical preferences. For Shepsle, this implies that the ultimate set of chosen outcomes, regardless of their stability, lack an adequate normative justification as compared with forgone legislative outcomes.[70] Stated differently, because cycle-breaking rules might thwart majority preferences for an alternative outcome, Shepsle contends that there is no compelling normative justification for crediting the actual outcome more than other theoretical outcomes that the legislature might have selected.

To evaluate the moral significance of structure-induced equilibrium outcomes, we must distinguish what Shepsle labels the normative *justification* for such outcomes from what we will instead label the normative *legitimacy* of such outcomes.[71] Legitimacy refers to societal acceptance of outcomes based upon the quality of the processes that generated them.[72] By contrast, justification, as Professor Shepsle uses the term, refers to a merits-based comparison, relying upon legislative preferences, as between the selected outcome and forgone alternatives.[73] A similar analysis can be applied to courts. For instance, a group might unanimously agree with a rule that courts should follow precedent in subsequent cases even if the practice leads to occasionally unsatisfactory results. The general rule—follow precedent in materially indistinguishable cases—would legitimate even some disfavored outcomes because the precedent regime is grounded in a more general legal principle.[74]

Because structure-induced equilibrating rules make it difficult to distinguish socially significant outcomes (in the sense of being Condorcet winners) from those that are the arbitrary product of voting rules (and thus no more meritorious than rejected outcomes),

---

69 *See* Shepsle & Weingast, *Structure-Induced Equilibrium*, *supra* note 65.

70 *See* Shepsle, *supra* note 68, at 241–42.

71 Professor Stearns initially developed this argument in STEARNS, *supra* note 1, at 41–94.

72 Thus, the 8 OXFORD ENGLISH DICTIONARY 811 (2d ed. 1989), defines *legitimate* as "Comfortable to law or rule; sanctioned or authorized by law or right; lawful; proper," and further describes its etymology as follows: "[T]he word expresses a status which has been conferred or ratified by some authority. . . ."

73 Professor Riker suggests the same comparison when he discusses potential outcomes based upon the presence, or absence, of agenda manipulation. Professor Riker observes that:

> The[] consequences [of social choice] are either that power is concentrated in society or that any system of voting can be manipulated to produce outcomes advantageous to the manipulators or at least different from outcomes in the absence of manipulation.

RIKER, *supra* note 24, at 137.

74 For a discussion demonstrating that the regime of precedent breaks cycles that manifest over groups of cases, see *infra* Chapter 22, I.D.2.

Shepsle suggests that actual outcomes should be regarded as normatively suspect.[75] But the distinction between legitimacy and justification challenges Shepsle's conclusion that cycle-breaking practices, which produce structure-induced equilibria, render selected legislative outcomes normatively problematic. Even if a legislative outcome lacks independent merit in comparison with a forgone alternative, the overall set of outcomes might be legitimated by acceptance of the process that generated them. In other words, the social significance of a selected outcome can be assessed based on comparative merit, inquiring how it compares to a forgone alternative under majority rule, or based on the legitimacy, inquiring whether it is accepted as a result of the fairness, including notice, of the decision-making rule.

To summarize, the pervasiveness of theoretical cycling among all collective decision-making bodies does not imply that social choice undermines institutional competence across the board. Rather, it suggests the need to consider the differences between or among institutions and how institutions combine to ameliorate each other's deficiencies. In addition, within institutions, procedures that raise the cost of identifying preferred alternatives to a proposed outcome can also inhibit cycling. While structure-induced equilibrating rules might render outcomes path dependent (with the result that other potential outcomes are preferred by thwarted majorities), those outcomes might nonetheless be accepted as legitimate if the participants regard the generative processes as fair.

F. A Preliminary Comparison Between Legislatures and Appellate Courts

Legislative rules and customs raise the cost of discovering formal intransitivities through voting. Even so, when legislative stakes are high—either because of contentious policy disputes or based on fiscal concerns—skilled legislators will seek to discover such preference structures informally. Legislators are unlikely to observe cycles as such. Instead, legislators can discover information with which to infer that a majority prefers an alternative to any proposed outcome. Legislators who realize the absence of a normative justification for moving ahead when no proposed bill or amendment has adequate support might pursue a strategy that defaults to the status quo. Thus, a combination of formal and informal mechanisms allow legislative bodies to discover and to decline to act when faced with intransitive preferences.

By contrast, as a general matter, appellate courts are institutionally obligated to issue a collective decision, i.e., to decide the case or cases properly before them, regardless of whether a Condorcet-winning option exists. Later in this book, we will consider Supreme Court decision-making rules that encourage the formal resolution of cases even when member preferences embed a cycle.[76] When this occurs, the case result inevitably thwarts the preferences of some majority on the Court.

---

[75] For similar analyses to that offered by Shepsle in the legislative context, see RIKER, *supra* note 24, at 192–95, and in the judicial context, see Frank H. Easterbrook, *Statutes' Domains*, 50 U. CHI. L. REV. 533, 547–48 (1983).

[76] For a more detailed analysis, see STEARNS, *supra* note 1. *See also infra* Chapter 15, Part I.C and I.D.2.

In addition to having the option of inaction, legislatures possess one other important means of avoiding the difficulties of cyclical preferences that appellate courts lack. Whereas appellate judges are widely expected not to trade votes across issues within cases or across cases,[77] legislators have the capacity to vote trade, or logroll, within and across bills. As Professors Shepsle and Weingast have observed, when intensities of preference are uniform, vote trading can reintroduce cycling.[78] Most often, however, given the varying stakes of proposed legislation for legislators and their constituents, intensities of preference are unlikely to be uniform.

To see how vote trading can improve results when preferences are not uniform, consider Professor William Eskridge's hypothetical, designed to illustrate the limits of legislative competence:

> Assume that Legislator *A* controls the agenda, so that Decision 1 is the last to pair up, winning against Decision 3. In addition, assume that the social benefit of Decision 1 is 100 (55% of which accrues to District *A* and 45% to District *B*) and that the social benefit of Decision 3 is 120 (shared equally by the three Districts). Obviously, from the collective point of view, the best decision is Decision 3 . . ., yet a coalition of *A* and *B* will vote for Decision 1. This is not only unfair to *C* (which gets no benefit even though it pays taxes), but is collectively wasteful as well (to the tune of 20).[79]

Eskridge maintains that this suboptimal result, creating a social welfare loss to *C*'s detriment, arises because the legislators vote solely in accordance with their immediate ordinal assessments over options. Now consider whether vote trading might avoid this undesirable outcome. If the same legislators anticipate future interactions, legislators *A* and *B* are apt to anticipate potential for gains from trade.

In this instance, excluding *C* from the coalition produces a welfare loss of 20 to the entire group. If *A* is willing to forgo a payoff of 15 (55 from Decision 1 minus 40 from Decision 3) and if *B* is willing to forgo a payoff of 5 (45 minus 40), thus incurring a combined loss of 20, the entire group, *ABC*, offsets this loss with a gain of 40, for a marginal net gain to the group of 20, a substantial welfare enhancement.

Although *C* receives all of the immediate benefit (an increased payoff from 0 to 40), provided that *C* promises a future payoff to *A* and *B* between the 20 they gave up from forgoing Decision 1 and the total of 40 that *C* has now gained from Decision 3, Decision 3 becomes the more likely result. On these assumptions, as compared with Decision 1, Decision 3 is not merely Kaldor-Hacks efficient; it becomes Pareto superior, making *C* better off without harming *A* or *B*.

---

[77] This is not to suggest that judges never engage in strategic behavior in seeking to promote desired policy objectives in a given case. *See generally* LEE EPSTEIN & JACK KNIGHT, THE CHOICES JUSTICES MAKE (1998). As explained *infra* Chapter 21, such behavior is generally limited to compromise along a unidimensional issue continuum within a case, almost invariably toward the median, rather than across issues within a case or across cases. For a competing normative account, see ROBERT D. COOTER, THE STRATEGIC CONSTITUTION 205–09 (2000) (proposing that broader judicial commodification of preferences through vote trading might be welfare enhancing).

[78] Shepsle & Weingast, *Structure-Induced Equilibrium*, *supra* note 65, at 506–07.

[79] Eskridge, *supra* note 42, at 284.

The same intuition helps to explain how, by allowing individuals to register cardinal utilities over options, vote trading can avoid a cycle. While ordinally ranked preferences can generate cycles in a regime of unlimited majority rule over binary comparisons, with cardinal values, many or most theoretical cycles prove inconsequential in the real world. Assume that three legislators possess paradigmatic cyclical preferences (1: *ABC*; 2: *BCA*; and 3: *CAB*) and that following a regime of path-induced voting, the likely result, benefiting legislators 2 and 3, is to produce result *C*. Despite the participants' ordinal rankings, it is quite possible that legislators 2 and 3 care less about the choice among options than does legislator 1, who winds up with her last choice. If so, legislator 2 or 3 might be willing to support an alternative outcome favoring legislator 1 in exchange for that legislator's future reciprocal accommodation. As Gordon Tullock posited, with different intensities of preference, vote trading can eliminate cycles.[80]

Sometimes social welfare is improved by declining to select an available Condorcet winner, and logrolling also helps to accomplish this. This follows from the limitation that the Condorcet criterion does not account for intensity of preferences. Imagine that the legislators hold the following preferences yielding *B* as the Condorcet winner: 1: *ABC*; 2: *BCA*; 3: *CBA*. While legislator 1 ranks option *B* second, it is possible that she significantly prefers option *A* and that legislators 2 and 3 do not care very much about the legislative issue. If so, legislators 2 and 3 might be willing to subordinate their ordinal ranking over these options to produce a more beneficial result for legislator 1 in exchange for a reciprocal future commitment.

Now compare the mechanism of private market exchange. As shown in the Lear hypothetical, private actors can cycle over options. This is most apt to occur when markets are *thin*. This implies a lack of competition, which results in limiting options as to who market actors must deal with (the sisters are stuck with each other in trying to sort out how to respond to their father's will) or in failing to attach meaningful prices, reflecting cardinal values. In *thick* markets, characterized by robust competition, the price mechanism allows commodification of preferences, which restores cardinal values, with the effect of rendering many theoretical cycles inconsequential.[81]

While the practices discussed above potentially frustrate majoritarian preferences, consider whether they are nonetheless meritorious. The nirvana fallacy implies that when evaluating a given institutional practice, we must not only assess the immediate outcome or set of outcomes that provoked a given instance of dissatisfaction; we must also ask whether the institution would function better overall if the practice were changed. In addition, to rely upon social choice to justify a shift in decision-making responsibility from one organ of government to another—say from a legislature to a court—we must undertake the following comparative analysis. We must first identify each institution's Arrovian deficiency based upon its combined internal rules and structures. We must then determine which institution, warts and all, is better suited to the task in question. After some applications, which follow, Chapter 14 begins this comparative institutional analysis.

---

[80] *See* Tullock, *supra* note 64, at 190.

[81] For an interesting hypothetical that illustrates this proposition with a three-way empty core bargaining game and that illustrates the difficulty that such games pose for the Coase theorem, see *supra* note 58, and cites therein.

III. CASE AND STATUTORY ILLUSTRATIONS

The applications in this chapter examine the phenomenon of cycling as it relates to American bankruptcy law. Cycling over bankruptcy law potentially arises in two different contexts. First, Professor David Skeel has argued that the history of federal bankruptcy law in the United States illustrates the phenomenon of cycling. During the nineteenth century, Skeel argues, Congress cycled over whether the country should have a permanent national bankruptcy law. For much of the nineteenth century, Skeel maintains, there was no stable majority coalition in support of a permanent bankruptcy law. Instead, temporary coalitions formed during periods of national financial crisis, but once the crisis passed, the coalition in support of bankruptcy legislation would also lapse. Every state, however, had its own system of debtor-creditor laws, so in the absence of a national bankruptcy law, debtor-creditor relations were governed by state laws. In 1898 Congress enacted a new bankruptcy law for the first time, and that law turned out to be permanent. The Bankruptcy Code that exists today is a direct descendent of the 1898 Bankruptcy Act. We will refer to the history that surrounds this legislation as a *macro* analysis of bankruptcy law.

Second, we look at the phenomenon of potential cycling *within* bankruptcy cases. The process of a successful Chapter 11 reorganization eventually culminates in the proposal of a plan of reorganization by the debtor, a process that is governed by a variety of complex substantive rules and which creditors and other claimants in the case must vote to approve. The Chapter 11 process itself is potentially susceptible to cycling among creditors. We examine several rules that govern the bankruptcy process to explore the question whether they reflect a concern about the potential for cycling in the contexts that give rise to bankruptcy cases and, if so, whether the bankruptcy rules satisfactorily address those concerns. We can conceive of this aspect of cycling as a *micro* analysis of bankruptcy law.

A. "Macro" Cycling: Cycling over Proposed Bankruptcy Legislation in the Nineteenth Century

The Bust-and-Boom Pattern of Nineteenth-Century Bankruptcy Legislation[82]

The nineteenth-century bankruptcy debates have long been seen as fitting a loose, bust-and-boom pattern. In times of economic crisis, Congress rushed to pass bankruptcy legislation to alleviate widespread financial turmoil. Once the crisis passed, so too did the need for a federal bankruptcy law. . . . The traditional account is inaccurate in some respects and, as we will see, it does not explain why bankruptcy suddenly became permanent in 1898. But it provides a convenient framework for describing the first century of bankruptcy debate.

Agitation for bankruptcy legislation rose to a fever pitch at roughly twenty-year intervals throughout the nineteenth century. A depression starting in 1793 led to the first federal bankruptcy law in 1800—an act that Congress

[82] DAVID A. SKEEL, JR., DEBT'S DOMINION: A HISTORY OF BANKRUPTCY LAW IN AMERICA 24–47 (2001) (footnotes omitted).

> repealed three years later. Congress went back to the drawing board in the 1820s, when financial crisis and controversy over the Bank of the United States prompted calls for another bankruptcy law. The debates never came to fruition, however, and it was not until 1841, following the Panic of 1837, that Congress passed its second bankruptcy law. The 1841 act lasted only two years, when defections from the party that had won its passage, the Whigs, led to repeal. The cycle came around once more on the eve of the Civil War, with the Panic of 1857 putting bankruptcy back on the agenda, and setting the stage for the 1867 act. The 1867 act lasted longer than its predecessors, with a movement for repeal leading to an amendment instead in 1874. But by 1878, the nation was once again without a federal bankruptcy law. . . .
>
> Congress passed three federal bankruptcy laws prior to 1898: the Bankruptcy Acts of 1800, 1841, and 1867. Together, the acts lasted a total of sixteen years. The absence of a federal bankruptcy law did not leave a complete vacuum in debtor-creditor relations, of course. Most states had insolvency laws on the books. . . . In times of financial panic, states also responded by passing stay laws imposing moratoria on creditor collection. Proponents of federal bankruptcy legislation emphasized both the wide variation in these laws and their serious constitutional limitations, such as the inability of state law to bind out-of-state debtors.[83]

Skeel explains that today bankruptcy is seen primarily as a device for allowing debtors to discharge debt. Originally, however, one major purpose of federal bankruptcy law in America was to promote a more effective collection of debts, especially interstate collection. The inclusion of the Bankruptcy Clause as an enumerated power of the U.S. Constitution, for instance, was in large part designed to permit Congress to override debtor-friendly laws similar to those enacted by the states under the Articles of Confederation, most notably to protect farmers.[84] Not surprisingly, therefore, substantive views on the propriety of various proposed bankruptcy policies tended to divide based upon geographical region. Skeel writes:

> Because southerners feared that northern creditors would use bankruptcy law as a collection device to displace southern farmers from their homesteads, the strongest opposition to federal bankruptcy came from the South. Many western lawmakers opposed bankruptcy legislation for similar reasons. Lawmakers from the commercial northeastern states, by contrast, were much more likely to view federal bankruptcy legislation as essential to the promotion of commercial enterprise.
>
> In addition to geography, lawmakers' views on bankruptcy also tended to divide along party lines. The Federalists (later Whigs, and then Republicans) promoted bankruptcy as essential to the nation's commercial development. Jeffersonian Republicans (later Democratic Republicans, and then Democrats), on the other hand, sought a more agrarian destiny and insisted that bankruptcy

---

[83] *Id.* at 24–25 (footnotes omitted).

[84] *See* Todd J. Zywicki, *Bankruptcy*, *in* THE CONCISE ENCYCLOPEDIA OF ECONOMICS 31 (David R. Henderson ed., 2d ed. 2008), http://www.econlib.org/library/Enc/Bankruptcy.html.

legislation would encourage destructive speculation by traders. Northeastern Federalists were the leading cheerleaders for federal bankruptcy legislation, and southern and western Jeffersonians were the staunchest opponents.[85]

Skeel argues that the bankruptcy debates of nineteenth-century America illustrate a phenomenon of legislative cycling:

> Rather than two positions, lawmakers divided into at least three camps, and sometimes more—and these camps crossed party lines. By considering the competing views in slightly more detail, and by analogizing these views to a voting irregularity that political scientists call *cycling*, we can begin to see how deeply unstable bankruptcy was for over a hundred years.
>
> . . . Daniel Webster, like the famous Supreme Court justice Joseph Story, argued for an expansive and permanent federal bankruptcy framework. John Calhoun embodied the opposing view that federal bankruptcy legislation would be a serious mistake. Not coincidentally, Webster was a Whig from a commercial state, Massachusetts, whereas Calhoun was a states' rights advocate from the agrarian South.
>
> Senator Henry Clay of Kentucky, a Whig and member along with Webster and Calhoun of the "Great Triumvirate" of famous senators, represented a third, and similarly influential, view of bankruptcy. Clay was willing to support bankruptcy legislation, but only if the law was limited to voluntary bankruptcy. Clay shared the fear of many bankruptcy opponents that northern creditors would use bankruptcy to displace southern farmers from their homesteads, but he believed voluntary bankruptcy would minimize this risk while enabling financially strapped debtors to obtain relief.[86]

Skeel likens the story in terms to a legislative cycle:

> A vexing problem when lawmakers (or decision makers of any kind, for that matter) hold a multiplicity of views on a single subject is that their voting may lead to irrational or unstable outcomes. At its extreme, the competing views can lead to the phenomenon of cycling. . . .
>
> Although the views will be described in stylized form, the overall pattern is not simply hypothetical. The senators I will use for purposes of illustration held views very close to the positions I will attribute to them, and Congress's ever-shifting stances on bankruptcy law in the nineteenth century may well have reflected the kinds of uncertainties we are about to explore.
>
> Assume that three senators, Benton, Webster and Clay, must choose among three options: not passing any bankruptcy law (No Bankruptcy); passing a complete bankruptcy law [that permitted both voluntary and involuntary bankruptcy] (Complete Bankruptcy); or passing a law that permits only voluntary bankruptcy (Voluntary Only). . . .

---

[85] SKEEL, *supra* note 82, at 26.

[86] *Id.* at 28.

Of the three options we are considering, Benton would prefer not to pass any bankruptcy law (No Bankruptcy). If a bankruptcy law must pass, his next choice would be a complete bankruptcy law that included involuntary bankruptcy and brought corporations within its sweep (Complete Bankruptcy). His least favorite alternative is Voluntary Only.

As a fervent nationalist, Daniel Webster strongly favors an expansive bankruptcy law that provides for both voluntary and involuntary bankruptcy (Complete Bankruptcy). So strongly does he believe in the importance of bankruptcy to the health of the national economy that he would accept Voluntary Only bankruptcy as a second choice. His least favorite option is No Bankruptcy.

Henry Clay sees voluntary bankruptcy as an opportunity to alleviate the dire financial straits of many of his constituents. But he strongly opposes involuntary bankruptcy, fearing that many debtors who might otherwise recover from their financial distress would be hauled into bankruptcy court by their creditors. Clay's first choice is thus Voluntary Only, his second choice No Bankruptcy, and his last choice Complete Bankruptcy.

Table 13.2. Cycling Among Bankruptcy Options in the Nineteenth Century

Senator	*First Choice*	*Second Choice*	*Third Choice*
Benton	No Bankruptcy	Complete Bankruptcy	Voluntary Only
Webster	Complete Bankruptcy	Voluntary Only	No Bankruptcy
Clay	Voluntary Only	No Bankruptcy	Complete Bankruptcy

Professor Skeel explains that the positions in the table fail to yield a Condorcet winner, and thus are prone to cycling when voted upon over binary pairs. Skeel states that "If the senators continued to vote and voted in accordance with their preferences, the votes would [disclose a] cycle." Skeel adds:

> This kind of voting irregularity can arise in either of two ways. If a group of existing voters hold inconsistent views, cycling can occur at the time of a particular vote, as in the illustration we have just considered. But cycling can also take place intertemporally. Even if a clear majority of legislators held Benton's views today, next year's majority might hold the views I have attributed to Webster; and two years down the road might be a Clay year.

I should emphasize—as several readers of this book emphasized to me—that true cycling only occurs under the restrictive conditions defined in Arrow's Theorem. If lawmakers agreed that one option belongs on the left, one in the center, and one on the right, for instance, their preferences would not be cyclical even if they sharply disagreed about the best choice. In view of this, let me emphasize that the principal point of this section is simply that the multiplicity of views contributed to Congress's inability to reach a stable outcome on federal bankruptcy legislation throughout the nineteenth century. Whether lawmakers' inconstancy reflected true cycling, or merely a garden-variety case of shifting legislative outcomes, the point remains the same.

Moreover, it is quite possible that the bankruptcy debates did indeed reflect true legislative cycling. If legislators hold consistent preferences, they will ordinarily gravitate toward a stable outcome even if there are sharply divergent views on what the outcome should be. Yet no such outcome emerged in the bankruptcy debates until late in the century. One is hard-pressed to think of another legislative issue on which Congress flip-flopped so continuously and for so long.

* * *

From the 1830s on, lawmakers' views were repeatedly splintered among the options we have considered—Complete Bankruptcy, Voluntary Only, and No Bankruptcy—along with variations on these themes. In the twentieth century, Congress has developed institutional structures that can assure stability even in the face of inconsistent preferences. One of these, delegation of gatekeeping authority to a committee, dates back to the early nineteenth century. Because the relevant oversight committee determines whether existing legislation is reconsidered, committees have the power to prevent a new Congress from promptly reversing the enactments of its predecessor. In theory the Judiciary Committee, which has overseen bankruptcy issues since 1821, could have served this purpose. But committees played a less prominent role in the nineteenth century, in part because both Congress and congressional committees operated on a part-time basis. Neither the Judiciary Committee nor any stable block of lawmakers in Congress was in a position to act as agenda setter and provide the kind of stable outcome we see in other contexts where lawmakers hold inconsistent preferences.

Even a brief overview of the debates that led to the 1841 and 1867 acts gives a flavor of the instability that came from the multiplicity of views. The 1841 act was the brainchild of the Whig party, which had made bankruptcy law a crucial plank in the platform that brought them the presidency and control of the Senate the year before. In the face of strong opposition, the Whigs secured the necessary votes for enactment through a controversial log-rolling campaign that obtained votes for bankruptcy in return for votes on a land distribution bill. . . .

Even before the bill took effect, a vote to repeal passed the House when a small group of southern Whigs reversed their earlier support for the

> legislation, and a similar proposal fell only one vote short in the Senate. The defection of several more Whigs . . . brought the coalition tumbling down. Less than two years after it went into effect, President Tyler (who had assumed the presidency after President Harrison died) signed the repeal legislation and the 1841 act was gone. . . .
>
> The debates on the 1867 bankruptcy act, which dated back to the early 1860s, were complicated by the onset of the Civil War. When the war finally ended, the Republicans held large majorities in the House and Senate, which strengthened the support for a bankruptcy bill that included involuntary as well as voluntary bankruptcy. . . . Although it lasted longer than either of its predecessors, the 1867 act was deeply unstable from the moment it was enacted. In both 1868 and 1872, lawmakers amended the law to soften its effects on debtors, and a move to repeal it led to further concessions to debtors in 1874. By 1878, the act had few defenders, and it was repealed by large majorities of both parties in both houses.
>
> The 1898 act would bring these instabilities to an end, but each of the competing views remained very much in evidence throughout the deliberations that preceded it. . . . [I]n debates that began in 1881 and spanned almost two decades, the Senate voted for . . . Complete Bankruptcy in 1884, as did the House in 1890 and 1896, and Complete Bankruptcy finally prevailed in 1898 in the form of the 1898 act. Proponents of Voluntary Only bankruptcy . . . also had their moments, as the House passed a Voluntary Only bill in 1894, and the Senate passed a somewhat similar bill before agreeing to Complete Bankruptcy in 1898. Throughout this time, opponents of bankruptcy managed (sometimes on the merits, sometimes because Congress ran out of time to act) to preserve the No Bankruptcy status quo.[87]

In 1898 Congress finally enacted a bankruptcy law that, with several major overhauls, has remained a permanent piece of legislation. Thus, the 1898 legislation brought an end to the century of legislative turmoil that had frustrated the enactment of a permanent bankruptcy law in the nineteenth century.

Skeel asks, "Why, after a century of legislative turmoil, did Congress finally enact a permanent bankruptcy law in 1898?"[88] He identifies several factors, but ultimately posits that the most important factor bringing about the permanence of the 1898 act was the growth of a specialized bankruptcy bar to administer the new system, a development that was triggered by the massive railroad reorganizations of the late-nineteenth and early-twentieth centuries. In short, bankruptcy lawyers had the incentive, organization, and political influence to retain a permanent bankruptcy law that earlier coalitions of interest groups had difficulty procuring in the first place. The bankruptcy bar exerted continuing influence by promoting a lawyer-centered litigation system that stands in stark contrast with the more typical administrative bankruptcy systems that characterize most western legal systems. This influence, Skeel notes, is reinforced by the historical accident that jurisdiction over bankruptcy law is in the Judiciary Committee of Congress, rather than

[87] *Id.* at 28–33.

[88] *Id.*

such other committees as Banking or Financial Services. Lawyers are repeat players before the Judiciary Committee, thus possessing potentially greater influence there than would likely be the case on other subject-driven committees. On the Financial Services Committee, for example, banking interests are likely to exert comparatively greater influence than the organized bar. Finally, during the course of the twentieth century, bankruptcy law came to be seen as a highly technical, largely non-ideological area of law. This understanding of bankruptcy reinforced the influence of bankruptcy lawyers on the legislative process by allowing them to couch their recommendations in terms of nonpartisan technical advice. In reality, as Skeel notes, bankruptcy lawyers have an incentive to increase the scope of bankruptcy law along with the expense and complexity of bankruptcy procedures, as has been consistent with historical developments throughout the twentieth century.

Consider as an alternative whether the primary actors in the legislative process, creditors, debtors (such as farmers), and corporate management, might have been willing to offer *conditional* support for a permanent bankruptcy system. This might arise if their support was conditioned on the superiority of the proposed regime to a continuation of the No Bankruptcy regime, meaning the continued reliance on state law over related matters of debt collection and debtor relief. During the nineteenth century, various groups preferred no bankruptcy system to the particular state systems imposed during various economic crises.

This reading might be plausible to the extent that bankruptcy lawyers saw the creation and maintenance of a bankruptcy system *as an end in itself*. Because bankruptcy lawyers earn their living from bankruptcy filings, they have a direct stake in the continued existence of a bankruptcy system. The details of the particular system might, in some respects, prove less important than the existence of stable regulatory infrastructure for bankruptcy law that depends in large part for its administration on a developed bankruptcy bar. In this analysis, the bankruptcy bar would serve as a residual claimant for the continued existence of the bankruptcy system itself, ensuring that even if legislative cycling or shifting preferences occurred, it would do so *within* the accepted framework of the continued existence of some bankruptcy regime rather than through ongoing proposals to create, or displace, the bankruptcy system in wholesale fashion. Bankruptcy lawyers might prefer a system that produces a greater number of bankruptcy filings and perhaps even more expensive and complex bankruptcy procedures, goals that appear to have become more prominent during subsequent rounds of bankruptcy reforms during the twentieth century.

In 2005, Congress passed a comprehensive bankruptcy reform law that tempered some of the highly pro-debtor elements of the 1978 Code. Professor Todd Zywicki has argued that the balance struck in this legislation can be further explained using the insights from Skeel's model of the interaction between creditors, bankruptcy lawyers, and ideology.[89] In 2005, Zywicki argues, these same forces were present but the balance was struck differently. Most importantly, the Republican takeover of Congress in 1994 shifted the ideological center of gravity in Congress away from the debtor-friendly orientation of the past to a new focus on personal financial responsibility. Zywicki observes that the

---

[89] Todd J. Zywicki, *The Past, Present, and Future of Bankruptcy Law in America*, 101 MICH. L. REV. 2016 (2003) (reviewing SKEEL, *supra* note 82).

Republican Party is also generally tied less closely to lawyers than Democrats, and its electoral victory therefore weakened the interest group influence of lawyers over Congress. Finally, a dramatic growth in bankruptcy filings during the 1980s and 1990s, from about 250,000 annual consumer filings at the beginning of that period to about 1.5 million per year at the end, despite a period of steady prosperity and low unemployment, strengthened creditors' claims that the bankruptcy system was overly vulnerable to fraud and abuse. The interaction of these various factors produced a different winning coalition than in the past, pushing the bankruptcy laws in a more conservative direction.

DISCUSSION QUESTIONS

1. Skeel notes that during the nineteenth century, the Supreme Court consistently adopted broader readings of the Bankruptcy Clause of Article I, Section 8 of the Constitution ("To establish . . . uniform Laws on the subject of Bankruptcies throughout the United States"), thereby providing Congress broad latitude in crafting federal bankruptcy law. Skeel suggests that by increasing the *range* of options open to Congress, the expansive interpretation the Supreme Court gave to the Constitution's Bankruptcy Clause during the nineteenth century exacerbated the problem of instability and promoted cycling. Assuming that the Supreme Court could anticipate at the time of making a decision that one interpretation would be more likely to result in cycling than another, should it take this into account in its decision? Does social choice justify a normative conclusion that a judge should prefer a narrow interpretation that reduces the likelihood of cycling over a broader one that encourages cycling? In answering this question, note that a narrower interpretation of the Bankruptcy Clause promotes stability but does so by restricting the range of options available to Congress. Does social choice theory provide a normative basis for choosing between ensuring stability versus adhering to range?

2. Although Congress has exclusive power under Article I, Section 8, of the Constitution to enact laws on the subject of bankruptcies, this power is layered over a preexisting foundation of state debtor-creditor law. This preexisting legal framework means that Congress's failure to enact a federal bankruptcy law creates a default rule of deferring to such state laws. Doing so may not result in an optimal bankruptcy regime, but it does create a functional status quo outcome, meaning that the result need not be catastrophic. "No Bankruptcy" is therefore both a theoretical and practical option, although perhaps subject to certain substantive biases that render this system suboptimal (such as a tendency to prefer in-state interests over out-of-state interests). In this sense, the presence of a workable default rule made it less essential for Congress to act except in times of crisis. This combination of factors might have the unintended consequence of promoting cycling. Absent this workable *status quo*, would Congress have felt a greater urgency to reach agreement on bankruptcy law and to prevent cycling? Why or why not?

3. Skeel notes that given the presence of legislative cycling, one option available to legislators to break the cycle would be the adoption of some institutional rule or actor with the authority to limit range through agenda-setting power. If so, what practical alternatives can you identify for where to vest such power? Consider the following possibilities. First, some congressional committee (such as the Judiciary Committee) could use its agenda-setting power to prevent status quo-altering legislation from reaching the floor of Congress. Second, a well-organized interest group (such as the bankruptcy bar) could use its external influence to restrict the range of practical outcomes available to Congress by effectively excluding the preferences

of less organized groups from practical consideration. Third, the Supreme Court could through constitutional interpretation limit the range of options available for Congress to consider. Fourth, the Constitution could preempt any state authority with respect to debtor-creditor law, thereby eliminating "No Bankruptcy" as a theoretical or practical alternative. Finally, the legislature could permit logrolling and thereby relax the requirement of sincere voting or *independence of irrelevant alternatives*. Are these the only options? If not, what other options might have been available to nineteenth century lawmakers to create a stable bankruptcy law? What criteria might you use to select among these or other alternatives?

B. "Micro" Cycling: Cycling Inside Bankruptcy

Consider whether the problem of cycling that might have characterized nineteenth century federal legislation is endemic to the problem of bankruptcy. To illustrate, consider a stylized debtor-creditor arrangement in which the debtor owes $1.5 million but holds assets valued at $500,000, resulting from a combination of questionable business decisions and a failing economy. To simplify, assume three creditors, each owed $500,000. Each creditor wants to gain a maximum payoff even if this requires depleting all assets of the debtor's firm, while the debtor seeks to remain an ongoing concern. Assume that the three entities seek to resolve their financial relationships with a regime of majority decision-making over the debtor's assets. For any solution with majority support that is selected, a superior coalition can displace that proposed solution in favor of another majority preferred solution.

It is easy to translate this into a simple empty-core bargaining game. If the two creditors, *A* and *B*, form a coalition to split all of the debtor's assets (250, 250), where each increment represents one-thousand dollars, then creditor *C*, can approach *B* and propose a superior coalition in which *B* receives 300, but leaves *C* with assets worth 200. Creditor *A* can now approach Creditor *C* and propose a new coalition in which *C* now receives a higher payoff of 300, while *A* receives a payoff of 200. Creditor *B* can now approach *A* and propose a superior payoff to *A* of 300, with *B* receiving 200. At this point the game has come full circle with coalitions *AB*, *BC*, *CA*, *AB*, but of course that result is no more stable than it was in the first round.

Within the Bankruptcy Code, there are numerous provisions that establish debt priorities and voting rules so that not all creditors sit in equal positions concerning a debtor. For instance, bankruptcy law generally requires that substantive entitlements that are created outside bankruptcy law are preserved in bankruptcy unless there is some compelling reason to alter the substantive rules in bankruptcy.[90] This rule is generally justified as a means of preventing the problem of "forum-shopping" between non-bankruptcy courts and bankruptcy courts with the goal of using bankruptcy proceedings to further non-bankruptcy objectives including redefining state law entitlements rather than to further bankruptcy policies. The so-called absolute-priority rule requires that all claimants with a higher level of priority against the debtor are supposed to be paid first before subsequent claimants are paid. For instance, under a strict application of the absolute priority rule, creditors are entitled to be paid in full before any assets of the estate

[90] This rule is typically associated with the Supreme Court's decision in *Butner v. United States*, 440 U.S. 48 (1979).

are distributed to shareholders or the debtor. Courts have recognized some modest exceptions to the absolute priority rule.[91]

The rules for confirmation of a debtor's plan of reorganization are also complicated and contain numerous voting rules and substantive limitations. For instance, a debtor's plan can be confirmed by a bankruptcy judge only if at least one "impaired" class of creditors (i.e., a class of claimants that is paid less than full value for its claim) votes in favor of the plan.[92] An entire class of claims is deemed to accept a plan if the plan is accepted by creditors that hold at least two-thirds in amount and more than one-half in number of the allowed claims in the class.[93] To prevent "gerrymandering" of claims in order to engineer plan approval, one provision allows only "substantially similar" claims to be classed together.[94]

DISCUSSION QUESTIONS

Do you think that these provisions help to ameliorate the theoretical cycles described above? Why or why not? Why do the rules for approval of the plan by a class require a positive vote by both a majority of the claimants by number and a supermajority of the dollar amount of the claims? Bankruptcy practice also permits the selling of claims, thereby allowing original creditors of the bankrupt debtor to sell their claims in the case to others and thus permitting certain creditors to amass larger numbers of claims and claim amounts than would otherwise be the case. This also potentially gives the creditor greater authority over the plan's terms. Does social choice theory provide any insight on whether this "claims trading" activity is likely to be welfare-enhancing?

Is there any connection between the macro-and micro-analyses of bankruptcy law? Is it possible that the bankruptcy regime ultimately adopted as a result of the history Professor Skeel describes places stress on specific bankruptcy applications in a manner that potentially generates cyclical preferences? Stated differently, is it possible that the regime produces rules that embed cycles in the selected outcomes? Why or why not?

---

[91] For a discussion, see SKEEL, *supra* note 82, at 233–34.

[92] 11 U.S.C. § 1129(a)(10) (2012). Under § 1126(f), holders of unimpaired claims are deemed to have accepted the plan.

[93] 11 U.S.C. § 1126(c) (2012).

[94] 11 U.S.C. § 1122(a) (2012).

CHAPTER 14

Social Choice (Part 2)[1]

Introduction

Chapter 13 introduced the problem of social choice. The chapter described several voting protocols, the median voter theorem, cycling, the Condorcet criterion, path dependence, agenda setting, minimum winning coalitions, and Arrow's Theorem. It also discussed the role of institutional complementarity in improving the quality and rationality of outputs, and identified several analytical fallacies used in assessing normative proposals to change institutional responsibilities based upon perceived processing deficiencies.

This chapter continues the introduction to social choice. Part I introduces a helpful study of parliamentary rules. The study provides a basis for expanding the set of normative criteria used in comparative institutional analysis. It further reveals how institutions adapt to improve the quality of their outputs in response to specific challenges. Part II demonstrates that the Arrow's Theorem criteria provide the basis for a positive comparative assessment of institutions. The analysis focuses on appellate courts and legislatures, the principal lawmaking institutions, in addition to agencies and markets. Part III explores the conditions that give rise to intransitive preferences, and introduces the concept of multi-criterial decision making. This concept reveals that even fewer than three persons, indeed an individual, can, under specified conditions, experience a phenomenon akin to cycling. The chapter concludes with applications.

---

1 Portions of this chapter are adapted from MAXWELL L. STEARNS, CONSTITUTIONAL PROCESS: A SOCIAL CHOICE ANALYSIS OF SUPREME COURT DECISION MAKING 41–94 (Chapter 2) (paperback ed. 2002), Maxwell L. Stearns, *The Misguided Renaissance of Social Choice*, 103 YALE L.J. 1219 (1994) [hereinafter *Misguided Renaissance*], and Maxwell L. Stearns, *An Introduction to Social Choice*, *in* ELGAR HANDBOOK IN PUBLIC CHOICE AND PUBLIC LAW 88 (Daniel Farber & Anne Joseph O'Connell eds., 2009) [hereinafter *Introduction*].

I. INSTITUTIONAL ADAPTATION AND ARROW'S THEOREM

A. A Social Choice Analysis of Parliamentary Rules

In a study of parliamentary rules, Professor Saul Levmore posits that the staging of these rules improves the overall rationality and fairness of legislative outputs.[2] In addition to explaining how legislative bodies make decisions, Levmore's study expands the breadth of normative criteria used in evaluating institutions. This contributes to a broader comparison of legislatures, courts, and agencies, and markets.

Levmore studied many sets of parliamentary rules written in the mid-nineteenth century, including Robert's Rules of Order. He determined that when Condorcet-winning options are likely to be available, the selected decision-making rules generally satisfy the Condorcet criterion. By contrast, when it is more likely that the various options before the legislature or assembly lack a Condorcet winner, parliamentary rules tend to vary significantly.

Levmore assumes the drafters were almost certainly unaware of the Condorcet paradox, meaning that group preferences sometimes cycle when aggregated in a regime of endless majority rule. Even so, Levmore posits that the participants in various legislative assemblies pushed the rules in a manner consistent with an observable pattern resulting from having confronted *avoidable dissatisfaction*. This arises when the rules produce a non-Condorcet winner despite the availability of a Condorcet winner. When this occurred, Levmore posits, the thwarted majority coalition likely pressured those controlling the proceedings to replace the existing rule with one better suited to generating satisfactory outcomes. Levmore illustrates his hypothesis with the following hypothetical five-member assembly. Assume each member holds the following ordinal rankings over five alternatives, ABCDE.[3]

P1: *ABCDE*

P2: *ABCED*

P3: *CBDEA*

P4: *CBEAD*

P5: *EDBCA*

Although option *B* is no one's first choice, it is a Condorcet winner. Imagine that the voting rule is plurality with a runoff, such that each member votes her first choice and, absent a majority winner, the two top candidates run off against each other. In this regime, option *B* will be suppressed in the first round of voting. There is no first choice majority candidate and, as between the two top first choice candidates, *A* and *C* (each with two votes), *C* prevails, with P1 and P2 losing.

---

[2] *See generally* Saul Levmore, *Parliamentary Law, Majority Decision Making, and the Voting Paradox*, 75 VA. L. REV. 971 (1989).

[3] This discussion is adapted from Stearns, *Misguided Renaissance*, *supra* note 1, at 1254.

Now assume that this result emerged with respect to a high stakes legislative matter. After the meeting, P1, P2, and P5 discuss the outcome and with little effort, they realize they form a majority preferring *B* to *C*. With somewhat greater effort, involving the remaining members of the assembly, they might learn that *B* defeats each remaining alternative in a direct pairwise contest. Even without that step, they might reason that consistent with majority rule, *C* should not have defeated *B*. At the next meeting, these members might express their dissatisfaction with the earlier proceedings and propose replacing the problematic *plurality and runoff* regime with an alternative voting protocol that better respects majority preferences.

If the new voting regime also thwarts the Condorcet criterion, this process is likely to repeat itself. Through continuous tinkering, frustrated majorities will eventually seize upon a rule that satisfies the Condorcet criterion, for example *motion-and-amendment voting*.[4] At that point, by resolving the problem of avoidable dissatisfaction, the assembly will have settled on a stable rule, although, as shown below, other difficulties might emerge. Assuming no change in preferences, under the newly adopted voting regime, if P3 moves to adopt option *C*, P1 can then move instead to substitute option *B*. The motion to amend will get majority support (P1, P2, and P5), and because option *B* is a Condorcet winner, any other motion to amend (seeking to supersede *B* with *A*, *D*, or *E*) would fail. The resulting motion to approve option *B* would pass, and motion-and-amendment voting would emerge as the stable voting rule.

This simple story is noteworthy in two critical respects. First, it demonstrates the importance of an economic benchmark potentially in tension with efficiency against which to evaluate the competence of parliamentary decision-making rules. While the Condorcet criterion and efficiency do not invariably conflict, there are circumstances where they might. While option *B* in the prior example is a Condorcet winner, it might nonetheless be an inefficient public policy choice. For example, that option might set a minimum wage so high that an industrious class of minimally skilled workers is rendered unemployable, or place a ceiling on rents so low that landlords are thereby discouraged from maintaining properties in sound repair or are encouraged to convert them for sale as condominiums, thereby thwarting an otherwise profitable rental market. Second, the example explains an evolutionary process toward rules satisfying the Condorcet criterion that does not, in any way, depend upon familiarity with the Condorcet paradox or social choice. Rather, through a simple process of adaptation, rules that continue to serve their intended purposes remain, whereas those that do not are supplanted.

The analysis does not imply that the adaptive process is random. Legislators think carefully about how to respond effectively to the difficulties that confront them.

---

4 An important clarification: For this regime to succeed, the motion-and-amendment voting procedure must permit at least as many binary comparisons as options. Unlimited motion-and-amendment voting necessarily satisfies this criterion. If, instead, the regime prevents reconsideration of an option defeated in an earlier round of voting, and if that option would defeat the ultimately successful option, then the restrictive regime prevents participants from revealing, at least through the formal voting process, whether the selected outcome is a Condorcet winner or is instead the arbitrary product of a voting path. For an informative discussion in the context of Congressional voting procedures, see William H. Riker, *The Paradox of Voting and Congressional Rules for Voting on Amendments*, 52 AM. POL. SCI. REV. 349, 355–56 (1958) (identifying restrictions on permissible amendments relative to options that prevent members of Congress from determining if outcomes are Condorcet winners).

Sometimes they seize upon the best result quickly; other times they stumble along the way. To the extent that individuals consciously adopt beneficial strategies that affect the evolution of institutions and rules, they simply quicken the pace of beneficial adaptation. The pace of adaptation, however, is separate from the evolutionary process itself.[5]

1. *Dimensionality and Symmetry: The Foundations of Cycling*

In some instances, there will be no Condorcet winner, and thus not all dissatisfaction is avoidable. One foundational insight of social choice is that as options increase, the likelihood of a Condorcet winner decreases.[6] As more options are introduced, so too are arguments for preferring among them. Introducing more options therefore increases the number of dimensions along which to assess those options normatively. Professor Max Stearns explains that "Dimensions are normative scales of measurement used to evaluate virtually anything that is being compared."[7] Identifying a Condorcet winner presupposes a shared dimension, or frame of reference, thereby allowing choices to be ranked along a common scale. Increasing the dimensions along which participants assess options reduces the likelihood that participants will grade their choices along a common normative scale as required to identify a Condorcet winner. Absent a common scale of measurement, the probability that a Condorcet-winning option exists declines. Increasing the number of options thus increases the probability of cycling.[8]

The relationship between choices, or options, on one side, and dimensions or analytical framings, on the other, is both subtle and important. Professor Donald Saari has ascribed the problem of cycling to "the curse of dimensionality."[9] As we will see,

---

[5] *See* Armen A. Alchian, *Uncertainty, Evolution, and Economic Theory*, 58 J. POL. ECON. 211 (1950). Thus, for example, whether or not the first person to try vertical integration had in mind solving a potential long-term bilateral negotiating problem, or, instead, was simply a power monger, to the extent that the strategy worked to avoid difficult bilateral negotiating problems among the affected actors, it was destined to survive. Future economic actors facing such problems, again whether or not they held a rudimentary intuition consistent with the economic theory of the firm, might opt to mimic the initial entrepreneur's strategy for no other reason than that he is doing better than they are under similar conditions. For a seminal discussion of the theory of the firm, see R.H. Coase, *The Nature of the Firm: Origin*, 4 J.L. ECON. & ORG. 3 (1988).

[6] William V. Gehrlein, *Condorcet's Paradox*, 15 THEORY & DECISION 161, 192 (1983) ("The results suggest that the probability of the no-winner form of Condorcet's paradox increases as the number of dimensions in the attribute space increases. The probability also tends to increase as the number of candidates increases."); Bradford Jones et al., *Condorcet Winners and the Paradox of Voting: Probability Calculations for Weak Preference Orders*, 89 AM. POL. SCI. REV. 137, 138 (1995) ("As is apparent, Condorcet winners become less likely as (1) the number of alternatives increases and (2) the number of individuals increases.").

[7] Maxwell L. Stearns, Obergefell, Fisher, *and the Dimensionality of Tiers*, 19 U. PA. J. CONST. LAW 1043, 1048 (2017), Stearns explains:

> People routinely evaluate information along analytical dimensions. Some dimensions involve simple binaries—black versus white, male versus female—although as used to sort individuals, such simple schemes sometimes fail. Other scales are more nuanced, for example, continuous gradations of height or weight.

See id. (footnote omitted).

[8] For a graphical presentation that illustrates this concept, see *infra Appendix A*.

[9] DONALD G. SAARI, DISPOSING DICTATORS, DEMYSTIFYING VOTING PARADOXES 13–15 (2008).

whether dimensionality is a curse or a blessing depends on the nature of the substantive choices under review and whether a cycle might help avoid a problematic result.

A single dimension can accommodate an infinite number of options, and yet in some instances, two dimensions are required to accommodate as few as three options. Professor Stearns explains:

> People often combine multiple criteria along a single dimension. Larger objects tend to be heavier, allowing us to rank modes of transportation—a scooter, a bicycle, a car—in a sequence that captures both size and weight. Sometimes combined alignments break down. Adding [an aloft] hot air balloon—larger than a car yet lighter than a scooter—forces the need to split the dimensions of size (scooter, bicycle, car, *then* hot air balloon) and weight (hot air balloon *then* scooter, bicycle, car).[10]

The Supreme Court decision, *Planned Parenthood of Southeastern Pennsylvania v. Casey*,[11] demonstrates that a single case can sometimes collapse multiple doctrinal issues along a single dimension. Some Justices assessed *Casey* based on their preferred substantive analysis of the claimed constitutional right to abortion, whereas others assessed the case based solely on the separate issue of the stare decisis effect of *Roe v. Wade*,[12] thereby avoiding a formal assessment of the merits of the claimed constitutional right. Despite the two separate doctrinal inquiries, we can easily cast the *Casey* opinions along a single dimension, from a relatively broad to a relatively narrow abortion right. The *Casey* opinions can be ranked along this unidimensional scale because those who preferred a strong form of abortion right also preferred a strict application of stare decisis respecting *Roe*, whereas those who preferred a weak abortion right also preferred a weak application, or outright rejection, of *Roe* as precedent.

The preferences of the Justices on opposing ends of the *Casey* Court—the liberals and the conservatives respectively—were *symmetrical.* This means that opposite resolutions of the dispositive, meaning controlling, case issues—(1) is there a fundamental right to abortion?, and (2) does *Roe v. Wade* control *Casey* as a matter of stare decisis?—also led the liberal and conservative Justices to opposite resolutions respecting the judgment for the case as a whole. Although *Casey* presented two substantive issues, the issues flattened along a single dimension such that the opinions could be cast according to the strength or weakness of the abortion right, however determined.

In other cases, however, judicial preferences are *asymmetrical,* thus revealing a problem of dimensionality.[13] In those cases, the Justices who resolve the dispositive issues in opposite fashion reach the same judgment for the case as a whole, whereas the Justices resolving one issue in favor of each opposing camp dissent, thus voting for an opposite

---

[10] *See* Stearns, *supra* note 7, at 1043. Stearns explains that one can sort infinite integers along either of the following binary dimensions: *odd/even* or *prime/non-prime.* And yet, sorting the three-integer sequence *234* based upon the criteria of odd, even, prime, and non-prime requires splitting over two dimensions. That is because number 2, the sole even prime, thwarts the assumption that primes are odd. *Id* at 1067–68.

[11] 505 U.S. 833 (1992). *See supra* Chapter 13 Table 13:1.

[12] 410 U.S. 113 (1973).

[13] *See infra* Chapter 22, Part I.1.A (demonstrating multidimensionality and asymmetry in Kassel v. Consol. Freightways Corp., 450 U.S. 662 (1981), and Arizona v. Fulminante, 499 U.S. 279 (1991)).

judgment. These less common cases reveal an impasse concerning whether the various judicial camps care more about the resolution of one or more of the controlling case issues or instead about the outcome for the case as a whole.

The same analysis applies in both the legislative or judicial contexts. As institutions introduce more options, they increase the risk that members called upon to assess the options will discover a problem of dimensionality, meaning an inability to assess options on a common normative scale. When this occurs, there is a heightened probability of asymmetry and thus that group preferences will cycle.

2. *Return to Parliamentary Rules*

As applied to parliamentary rules, a legislative body is sometimes likely to have a large number of options, for example, when selecting an annual budget or when choosing among dates for an election or other event. Even seemingly similar options can add dimensionality and thus increase the likelihood of cycling. If there are only a few dates, then decision makers are more likely to register their perspectives along a common normative dimension, for example, the desire for an early or late adjournment. Similarly, if there are few proposed budgetary allocations, voters are more likely to assess choices along the common dimension of how much to allocate to the project in question. With such preferences, and assuming sincere voting, there is a natural pull toward a median position. But as options increase, some voters will base preferences on criteria that are out of keeping with such a single dimensional scale, and will instead factor in such concerns as avoiding meeting on particular holidays or on certain days of the week, or how the choice will affect other parts of the calendar. In the budgetary context, some will evaluate choices not only based on the expenditure, but also based on other available projects, quality at each expenditure level, or even the symbolism associated with allocating larger or smaller funds to particular projects.

Because increasing options reduces the likelihood of a Condorcet winner, it also increases the likelihood of thwarted majority preferences. When preferences cycle, any given option thwarts some majority that would prefer another outcome. For this reason, Levmore posits that dissatisfied majorities are once again likely to force tinkering with the rules.[14] This time, however, the resulting dissatisfaction is unavoidable, and further tinkering will not push the rules toward a stable alternative. Instead, as Levmore explains, there is likely to be substantial variation across different sets of parliamentary rules, a result supported by his survey.

Within an important subset of these varied parliamentary rules, Levmore discovered an apparent common thread. As previously discussed, voting rules that do not satisfy the Condorcet criterion generally ground outcomes in the order in which votes are taken. As a consequence, whoever is afforded the authority to set the voting agenda will possess disproportionate power. By contrast, when a decision-making body employs a rule that satisfies the Condorcet criterion and when a Condorcet winner is available, once more assuming sincere voting, a dominant outcome emerges without regard to the order in

---

[14] Levmore, *supra* note 2, at 1024 ("[W]ell-informed and clever chairpersons can manipulate motion-and-amendment voting by recognizing favored members first so that their motions need not survive a great many votes.").

which votes are taken. All rules that satisfy the Condorcet criterion produce a Condorcet winner when one is available. By contrast, rules that defy the Condorcet criterion vary in the results that they produce whether or not there is an available Condorcet winner. Rules that do not meet the Condorcet criterion also vary in their susceptibility to *agenda manipulation*, for example, by a committee chair.[15]

When options are unlikely to include a Condorcet winner, the legislature might elect to modify the motion-and-amendment procedure to prevent reconsideration of previously defeated options. In contrast with the unlimited motion-and-amendment procedure, which ensures a Condorcet winner when one is available, but which cycles absent a Condorcet winner, this regime produces an outcome with or without a Condorcet winner. Recall that without at least the same number of pairwise contests as options, it is not possible to determine whether the outcome is a Condorcet winner or is instead the arbitrary product of a voting path. By prohibiting reconsideration of defeated alternatives, this voting regime ensures an outcome, but risks preventing the requisite number of binary comparisons to determine that outcome's social significance, or merit, in comparison with forgone alternatives.

Based upon this intuition, Professor Riker criticized a rule employed in both houses of Congress permitting only "four amending motions to a bill or resolution."[16] Riker contended that the rule had the potential to mask voting cycles and thus to produce outcomes he deemed arbitrary. Although Riker is certainly correct that, with more than five options, this voting rule has the potential to mask a cycle by preventing the requisite number of binary comparisons relative to options, his observation invites two qualifications. First, as Riker recognized, if the legislative preferences cycle, expanding the number of permissible amendments will reveal the cycle, but will not provide a means of ensuring a stable outcome over alternatives.[17] Second, even a formal limit on the number of permissible votes relative to options might not prevent legislators from discovering cycling preferences through various informal mechanisms, especially with high stakes.

As in other professional settings, important legislative matters are often resolved well in advance of formal meetings, which sometimes ratify results that, by the time of the meeting, are a *fait accompli*. Consider, once more, *structure-induced equilibrating rules*.[18] Perhaps ironically, these very practices can also function as venues for the informal discovery of cycling preferences, thereby helping to avoid problematic voting paths. If so, the practical effect is to create focal points at which to expand the number of iterations,

---

[15] For a classic illustration of agenda manipulation, see Michael E. Levine & Charles R. Plott, *Agenda Influence and Its Implications*, 63 VA. L. REV. 561, 572 (1977) (describing manipulated voting scheme in context of flying club to acquire authors' preferred aircraft fleet and confirming results in lab experiments).

[16] Riker, *supra* note 4, at 354.

[17] Recognizing this problem, Riker observed:

> Even if both houses were to provide this method of discover[ing potentially cyclical preferences], they would still need a procedure for resolving the intransitivities discovered. . . .
>
> . . . But, as Arrow has shown, an intransitivity, once in existence, cannot be eliminated simply by juggling the techniques of counting.

Id. at 364.

[18] *See supra* Chapter 13, Part 11.AE.

beyond what is allowed by formal rules, to discover voting cycles and to blunt adverse agenda strategies.

While these arguments provide a partial response to Riker's concerns about path dependence when opportunities to amend are limited, there is little doubt that prohibiting reconsideration of defeated alternatives affords committee chairs tremendous power over the critical voting path. Chairs determine, for example, who gets the floor and, very often, the order in which issues are raised. As Levmore explains, motion-and-amendment voting favors early motions because after an original motion is proposed, members can propose amendments to that motion, and amendments to that amendment (termed *an amendment in the second degree*) and to that amendment (amendments in the third degree) and so on. Voting begins at the outer edge, pitting the highest ordinal amendments against each other, the victor against the next highest ordinal amendment, until the successful amendment is directly voted against the original motion. In contrast with later amendments that must survive a series of successive rounds to be voted against the original motion, the original motion itself need only survive a single round, against the final surviving amendment, before it (or the amendment that replaces it) is voted up or down.

Because motion-and-amendment voting favors early motions, Levmore posits that the regime affords committee chairs substantial agenda-setting power. It does so by allowing chairs to favor early proponents and then to order amendments so that problematic options raised in the form of later amendments can be eliminated in early rounds of voting.[19] Levmore concludes, therefore, that while motion-and-amendment voting works well when there are few options to consider (because it locates Condorcet winners thus eliminating avoidable dissatisfaction), it is likely to produce dissatisfaction as larger numbers of options become available. At that point, the regime invites the threat of strategic agenda setting.

This insight provides the basis for Levmore's next step in analyzing the development of parliamentary rules. Levmore suggests that when there are likely to be several potential options, a good defensive strategy against agenda setting is a switch to *succession voting.* While motion-and-amendment favors early motions, succession voting favors relatively late motions.[20] In this regime, motions are voted upon in the order in which they are raised until a motion secures the requisite majority to pass. In addition, under this regime defeated options cannot be reconsidered. Thus, the regime ensures a result even when preferences cycle. Because it is more difficult for the chair to control the order in which motions will be advanced than to sequence options already presented, it is generally more difficult to manipulate succession voting than motion-and-amendment voting.

Once again, however, succession voting, which violates the Condorcet criterion, threatens occasional avoidable dissatisfaction, for example, when there are relatively few

19 *See* Levmore, *supra* note 2, at 1028.

20 *See id.* at 1024–25. Levmore explains that "In contrast [with motion and amendment voting], succession voting often favors later—but not too late—entries into the fray, but since it is difficult for the chair to judge the quantity of alternatives yet to be proposed, it is difficult to position one's favorite correctly." *Id.* at 1025. The danger of being too late is that under this voting rule, the first motion to secure a majority wins. As a result, a relatively late successful option will foreclose potentially preferred options not yet introduced.

options available. Levmore thus observes one more evolutionary step involving, for example, the selection among either dates or budgetary allocations. Structuring votes over such options raises important social choice implications. As we have already seen, increasing options on such issues can produce more than a single dimension and thus introduce the risk of cycling. And yet, options pertaining to such matters as dates or budgetary allocations are often conducive to a natural sequencing, including most obviously early-to-late or low-to-high (or the reverse). Although there are obviously exceptions, such issues are often likely to include a Condorcet-winning option representing the median choice among participants on a single dimensional scale. One way to increase the likelihood of choosing an available Condorcet winner is to base the order of consideration on an underlying logical sequence. This can take the form of an *incremental voting rule*, for example, working from the top down or the bottom up. Importantly, when the logical sequencing structure rests along a single dimensional scale, the voting protocol will yield the same outcome—the Condorcet winner—regardless of the end of the spectrum (high or low, early or late) at which voting begins.

Professor Levmore summarized the evolutionary process affecting parliamentary rules as follows:

> The codes can be regarded as evolving along the lines of, or as having adopted, the following reasoning: (1) employ the motion-and-amendment process when there are few alternatives because it promises to find any Condorcet choice without encouraging unavoidable dissatisfaction; (2) when there are numerous alternatives likely to be proposed, facilitate a switch to succession voting because a Condorcet winner is quite unlikely and the switch will make it difficult for the chair to manipulate the order of recognition to unfairly influence the outcome; and (3) when succession voting exposes unavoidable dissatisfaction, tinker with the order in which proposals are considered.[21]

Levmore found paradoxical the departure from motion-and-amendment voting in favor of a *plurality voting rule* for the selection of committee chairs given the relatively low cost of repeated votes within legislative assemblies.[22]

A possible explanation lies in risk that rules that satisfy the Condorcet criterion might lead to an impasse absent a Condorcet winner. When choosing whether and how to resolve *issues*, legislatures often avoid formal decisions, whether as a result of cycling or following a decision to leave the *status quo*. By contrast, when choosing among *people* to fill positions, inertia is generally not an option even when preferences cycle, because committee chairs and other official positions are essential to conducting business. As

---

21 *Id.* at 1026–27.

22 Levmore offers two tentative explanations for this seeming anomaly, first a comparison to *round robin voting*, which, although meeting the Condorcet criterion, allows one candidate to wait out all other votes and run only in the final election, potentially undermining perceptions of fairness, *id.* at 1018–21, and second, noting that single round plurality voting, or a *plurality with a runoff*, reduces transactions costs relative to round-robin voting. *Id.* at 1017. Levmore observes that "[i]t is interesting, but not terribly helpful, to note that plurality voting often concerns a choice among *individuals* while motion-and-amendment voting often involves decision-making with regard to *issues*." *Id.* at 1013 n.122.

Levmore's study reveals, when legislatures choose among people, rules thus gravitate away from the Condorcet criterion.[23]

Can you think of other voting contexts that favor a non-Condorcet rule? If so, what is it about the institutional context that demands an outcome even when preferences cycle? Might such rules differ in a legislative versus judicial context? Why or why not?[24]

B. A Comment on Baselines

As the preceding analysis demonstrates, social choice reveals several normative dimensions for assessing the quality of institutional outputs and the processes that institutions employ to generate them. While these baselines grow out of economic analysis, they extend beyond both the traditional concerns for improving social welfare, defined in terms of efficiency, and the Condorcet criterion. This chapter and Chapter 13 exposed no fewer than five baselines:

(1) Respecting the democratic norm of majority rule (the Condorcet criterion),

(2) Ensuring that a collective decision is made whether or not preferences cycle (rationality),

(3) Controlling or limiting agenda manipulation (promoting fairness),

(4) Encouraging principled rather than strategic decision making (ensuring merit-based decisions), and

(5) Allowing commodification of preferences when individuals hold different intensities of preference for particular outcomes (improving social welfare).

Broadening economic analysis to include these, and perhaps other, baselines promotes a substantially richer analysis than applying any single baseline. What is missing is a framework for assessing the tradeoffs that these, or other, criteria produce in the design of collective decision-making institutions.

The analysis thus far has been directed at understanding potential institutional *objectives*: what are the goals that society ascribes to particular institutions? The next section, which revisits Arrow's Theorem, is directed at the question of institutional *capacity*: what does social choice reveal about the ability of institutions to satisfy those objectives?

II. ARROW'S THEOREM

Arrow's Theorem proves that all institutions contain some inherent weakness or set of weaknesses, at least as compared with what Arrow defined as a minimally acceptable set of benchmarks for assessing institutional competence. Whether the identified weaknesses of any given institution are a reason for serious concern, or simply the price

---

[23] *See id.* at 1013 n.122. Consider also Levmore's comparison of two non-Condorcet rules in this context, plurality voting and round-robin voting. Levmore suggests that as between the two, plurality voting appears fairer in this context because round-robin voting allows some to wait out multiple rounds, while forcing others to undertake numerous direct comparisons in the interim. *Id.* at 1020–22 & nn.137–38.

[24] We will revisit these questions in Chapters 17 or 18 and Chapters 21 or 22. *See also* STEARNS, *supra* note 1 (using social choice to distinguish legislative and judicial voting processes).

of doing business, turns in large part on the specific functions we expect our institutions to perform. As you read the discussion that follows, consider how Arrow's various normative criteria help to inform our understanding of the quality of institutions as well as the choice among institutions for various functions in a constitutional democracy.

A. A Closer Look at Arrow's Theorem

Professor and Nobel Laureate Kenneth Arrow set out to create a set of governing rules to be used by a planning authority that would simultaneously satisfy a fundamental tenet of rationality, namely the ability to ensure that the authority's collective decisions satisfy the minimal criterion of transitivity, and several seemingly noncontroversial assumptions about fair collective decision-making processes.[25] Although then unaware of the work of the Marquis de Condorcet, Arrow ultimately demonstrated that any effort to fix the problem of collective indeterminacy or irrationality that results from the problem of cycling will necessarily violate at least one important condition that people would commonly, or at least intuitively, associate with fair collective decision making. Arrow's Theorem has therefore aptly been characterized as a generalization of the Condorcet paradox.[26] Arrow proved that no collective decision-making body can simultaneously satisfy four seemingly noncontroversial assumptions about fair collective decision making and guarantee the ability to produce collective results that satisfy the basic condition of transitivity. Thus, whereas Condorcet demonstrated that the general assumption of individual rationality cannot be extended to groups, Arrow demonstrated that devices designed to cure collective irrationality will undermine collective fairness in some fundamental way.

Before explaining the four conditions that Arrow presumed essential to fair collective decision making, a few comments on methodology will be helpful. While the term "fairness" is admittedly general, Arrow defined each fairness condition with mathematical precision in his axiomatic proof, and defended each condition on credible normative grounds. That is not to suggest that every fairness condition is equally important or that all fairness conditions have been universally accepted on normative grounds, at least in all contexts. For now, it is sufficient to note that individually and collectively, the various fairness conditions are sometimes at odds with both traditional economic understandings of efficiency and rationality. Rationality is defined here to mean ensuring the power to translate internally transitive member preferences into transitive orderings for the group as a whole.

---

[25] For a discussion of Arrow's initial results and how Arrow corrected an error in his first proof, see STEARNS, *supra* note 1, at 344–45 n.91. With one modification, see STEARNS, *supra* note 1, at 336–37 n.104 (explaining history of range criterion in works by Arrow and Vickrey, and as presented by Mueller, and how the more stringent definition presented in the text conforms to the alternative presentations), following DENNIS C. MUELLER, PUBLIC CHOICE III, at 582–91 (2003), we are employing the definitions from William Vickrey's more accessible proof, *see* William Vickrey, *Utility, Strategy, and Social Decision Rules*, 74 Q.J. ECON. 507, 508–09 (1960), *reprinted in* WILLIAM VICKREY, PUBLIC ECONOMICS 29 (Richard Arnott et al. eds., 1994), in lieu of those set out in Arrow's revised proof. For an explanation, including a comparison to Arrow's original and revised proofs, see STEARNS, *supra* note 1, at 344–45 n.91, 346–47 n.104, 347–48 n.112.

[26] *See* WILLIAM H. RIKER, LIBERALISM AGAINST POPULISM: A CONFRONTATION BETWEEN THE THEORY OF DEMOCRACY AND THE THEORY OF SOCIAL CHOICE 116 (1982).

In an important respect, the whole of Arrow's Theorem is greater than the sum of its parts. Even if one rejected the normative validity of Arrow's understanding of collective rationality or one or more of his claimed fairness conditions,[27] this would not undermine the power of the theorem as a positive tool in establishing benchmarks for a meaningful comparison of institutions and rules. That seeming counterintuition is closely linked to the *nirvana fallacy*. Recall that scholars commit the nirvana fallacy when they identify a defect in an institution or rule and then propose either shifting decisional authority elsewhere, or devising a different governing rule, without having first assessed whether the proposed alternative would improve or exacerbate the problem.[28]

Voltaire notably captured this intuition, stating: "the perfect is the enemy of the good."[29] Surprisingly, perhaps, in undertaking comparative institutional analysis, it is more difficult to ascertain what is good than it is to define what is perfect. Arrow did not set out to define a perfect institution, but rather, an adequate one that honored what he regarded as basic conditions of rationality and fairness. Even so, Arrow proved the impossibility of achieving his seemingly modest objectives. In doing so, Arrow provided a credible combined set of normative benchmarks for meaningful comparative institutional analysis. Whether or not Arrow's Theorem defines the "perfect," what we will now frame as *Arrow's Corollary* defines the "good enough," or more to the point, the "good enough for our purposes."

Arrow's Theorem proves that no single collective decision-making body can simultaneously satisfy four specified conditions: *range* (the outcome must be consistent with the members' selection among any conceivable ordering over three options), *unanimity* (the *Pareto* criterion, but with a twist), *independence of irrelevant alternatives* (in choosing among options presented, the decision makers are to decide based solely upon the merits and without regard to how they would rank options that might later be introduced), and *non-dictatorship* (the decision-making rule cannot systematically honor the preferences of an individual against the contrary preferences of the group as a whole), while ensuring the ability to produce collective results that are rational (transitive).[30] We will provide more detailed definitions of each of these terms below and connect the definitions with several of the previously described examples.

We now present a corollary to Arrow's Theorem:[31] Because *no* collective decision-making body can ensure compliance with all five stated criteria (the four fairness conditions plus collective rationality), any collective decision-making body that functions, meaning simply that it issues collective decisions, has necessarily sacrificed at least one

---

[27] Professor William Riker, for example, strongly questioned the validity of *independence of irrelevant alternatives*. *See id.* at 130. Professors Richard Pildes and Elizabeth Anderson have questioned the validity of collective rationality (or transitivity). *See* Richard H. Pildes & Elizabeth S. Anderson, *Slinging Arrows at Democracy: Social Choice Theory, Value Pluralism, and Democratic Politics*, 90 COLUM. L. REV. 2121, 2146–58, 2192 (1990). For a response to these arguments, see Stearns, *Misguided Renaissance, supra* note 1, at 1249–50 (discussing independence) and 1251–52 nn.114 & 115 (discussing rationality), and STEARNS, *supra* note 1, at 41–94.

[28] *See* Chapter 13 note 44 and accompanying text.

[29] Voltaire, *La Bégueule: Conte Moral* (1772), http://www.archive.org/details/labgueulecontem00voltgoog ("Le mieux est l'ennemi du bien.").

[30] *See supra* note 25, and cites therein (describing Arrow's Theorem criteria).

[31] *See* STEARNS, *supra* note 1, at 82–83 (describing Arrow's Corollary and its implications for constitutional process).

(and possibly more than one) of those five criteria. This corollary implies that adherence to all of the five criteria is not essential to the functioning of institutions. Moreover, conditions that are essential to the functioning of some institutions are more easily sacrificed in, and might even prove detrimental to the functioning of, others.

This argument rests on the following normative assertion: As a society, we do not reject all of our collective decision-making bodies—including markets, state legislatures and Congress, state and federal appellate courts, and agencies—as inherently irrational or unfair even though we are sometimes dissatisfied with the particular results that these institutions produce.[32] This implies that there is a standard for evaluating our collective decision-making institutions, which, although falling short of the combined Arrow's Theorem criteria, nonetheless renders them generally acceptable, or good enough.

Because they are simultaneously unattainable, the combined Arrow's Theorem criteria serve as objective standards by which to assess institutions, knowing that each separate institution will necessarily fail to meet at least one. As previously noted, Arrow's proof says nothing about which of the criteria are most (or least) important in any given institutional setting. For that reason, Arrow's Theorem informs institutional *capacity*, but not institutional *objectives*. If we use Arrow's Theorem as the benchmark for comparative institutional assessments, we can determine the nature of each institution's *different* capacities and, notably, each institution's deficiencies. Based upon identified deficiencies, we can then assess whether the existing allocation of decisional authority is less bad than the alternative allocations that would result from the various proposals for institutional reform. In addition, by applying the same analysis to rules within institutions, we can, once again, evaluate proposed changes to those rules to see if they are likely to improve or worsen whatever problems in institutional functioning the proponents seek to cure.

Comparative institutional analysis implicates the fallacy of composition and the related *isolation fallacy*. One important method of improving institutional fairness and rationality, including, for example, in Congress and the Supreme Court, is through the combined operation of more than one institution in a manner that allows each to compensate for the other's deficiencies. Evaluating institutions as if they were operating in isolation undervalues their overall quality by ignoring how complementary institutions compensate for each other's differing strengths and weaknesses. One important example involves the evolution of initial Supreme Court rules away from the Condorcet criterion (for example, outcome voting and stare decisis) and the evolution of Congressional rules and practices toward the Condorcet criterion (for example, motion-and-amendment voting combined with informal practices at veto gates that help identify thwarted majority preferences or voting cycles).

This is not to suggest that the Supreme Court generally misses available Condorcet winners,[33] or that Congress invariably finds them. Instead, the analysis shows that the starting point for the rules in each institution reflect their general obligations to either resolve matters properly before them or their power to remain inert when confronted

---

[32] *See id.* at 83.

[33] For a discussion of how the narrowest grounds rule operates to locate available Condorcet winners even when there is no majority first choice opinion, see *id.* at 124–39 (discussing narrowest grounds doctrine) and *infra* Chapter 22, Part I.C.1.B.

with proposals lacking sufficient support to justify a collective decision to supplant the status quo.

These starting rules often combine with companion rules that further improve each institution's outputs. In the Supreme Court, the narrowest grounds rule reduces the risk of missing available Condorcet winners notwithstanding the non-Condorcet outcome-voting rule, which ensures that the institution satisfies its obligation to resolve cases properly before it even when preferences cycle.[34] And in Congress, as we have already seen, structure-induced equilibrating rules raise the cost of locating intransitive preferences notwithstanding the power to pass on proposed legislation without formal action.[35] Simply put, the starting point in the development of these rules is substantially informed by the different institutional responsibilities that arise in the event that member preferences are prone to cycling.

B. A More Detailed Application

We will now set out a more detailed analysis of Arrow's Theorem that ties together several of the concepts developed in this chapter and that provides a basis for future applications of social choice to specific institutions and rules. Applying Vickrey's simpler proof,[36] Arrow's Theorem establishes that no single institution can simultaneously satisfy four conditions of fairness and ensure collective rationality. We now provide a detailed definition of each of the fairness criteria and link these definitions to the earlier discussion.

Range (and the *Condorcet criterion*): Range requires that when a group is selecting among three options, the outcome be the universal product of a rule that permits all members to rank all three options in any order.[37] This admittedly cryptic-sounding condition—one that ensures adherence to the Condorcet criterion—becomes intuitive when we consider an application. For three options *ABC*, there are six potential sets of ordinal rankings. While we can easily list all six (*ABC*, *ACB*, *BAC*, *BCA*, *CAB*, *CBA*), mathematically, this is intuitively expressed as three factorial. This means that for the first-choice ranking, the decision maker can select among all three options, *ABC*; for the second-choice ranking, having already selected one option, the decision maker can select between the remaining two, *AB*, *AC*, or *BC*. And for the final choice ranking, the decision maker has no choice. Having already selected two of the three options only one remains. Three factorial, or the product of these three choice sets (3x2x1), equals six.

Range has two components, one governing each member's free choice in ranking options, and the other governing the nature of the rule used to process the combined rank orderings into a group output. Adhering to range requires that each decision maker be permitted to select from any of the potential six combinations of ordinal rankings so that none is off-limits. Range also requires that the decision-making rule select an outcome

---

[34] *See infra* at Chapters 22, Part II.2.

[35] *See infra* at Chapters 22, Part II.2.

[36] *See* Vickrey, *supra* note 25, at 509–11.

[37] For a more detailed discussion of the history of this criterion, see STEARNS, *supra* note 1, at 336–37 n.104.

that honors, and thus that operates consistently with, each member's selection from the various sets of ordinal rankings.

When broken down into its constituent parts, the range criterion appears intuitive. If participants are not permitted to rank all options in the order of their choosing (thus barring selection from all combined ordinal rankings over options), then whoever decides which combined rankings are off-limits can exert disproportionate power relative to the other participants over the ultimate decision. It is for that reason that adhering to range furthers democratic norms. We have already seen some examples. Recall that in a group with non-Condorcet-winning preferences (P1: *ABC*, P2: *BCA*, P3: *CAB*), a regime that permits unlimited pairwise voting will disclose a cycle, such that *ApBpCpA*. If, instead, range is restricted so that the ranking *CAB* is off-limits, then out of the six potential ordinal rankings (*ABC*, *ACB*, *BAC*, *BCA*, *CAB*, *CBA*), P3 might select *CBA*, the only remaining option that ranks *C* first. If the remaining preferences are unaffected, then *B* would emerge the winner as against *A* and *C*, even though with the true ordinal rankings disclosed, *A* defeats *B*. If given the power, P2 might exclude ranking *CAB* because doing so is likely to produce a voting path leading to his preferred outcome, *B*, although it does so at the expense of P3 who ranks *C* first and *B* last. Notice that in this example, excluding *CAB* effectively prevents option *A* from winning even though that is the only option capable of defeating *B*.

In two important institutional contexts, the range criterion is relaxed as a means of ensuring collective outcomes even when members hold preferences that cycle. As we have already seen, in selecting committee chairs, parliamentary rules avoid motion-and-amendment procedures in favor of plurality voting. This non-Condorcet rule effectively violates range by disallowing the necessary final pairwise comparison to disclose that when all relevant binary comparisons are considered, the members' preferences cycle. In effect, some members are prevented by the order of voting from expressing preferences for all candidates based on a full assessment of each person's ordinal rankings, thus relaxing range. To paraphrase George Orwell, when range is relaxed some person's votes are more equal than others.[38]

Appellate courts also relax range to meet their collective obligation to resolve properly docketed cases even when judicial preferences cycle. The Supreme Court's collective obligation to produce a judgment in a case that is properly before it, for example, prevents the Court from employing a case decision rule that satisfies the Condorcet criterion. A regime of unlimited pairwise comparisons by majority rule, for example, has the potential to produce a collective impasse. This does not mean, of course, that the Supreme Court must *always* produce a judgment, as, for example, when it determines that *certiorari* has been granted improvidently or when a case is remanded following a recently issued governing case. But even then, the Court must affirmatively select a method of disposition through collective action. In addition, the Court is not obligated to resolve issues in the manner the litigants prefer. More broadly, appellate courts generally lack the degree of agenda control that the Supreme Court exercises through its power of certiorari. Even in the Supreme Court, however, each decision-making juncture—from deciding whether to decide a case, to deciding whether a case is

---

[38] GEORGE ORWELL, ANIMAL FARM 88 (Alfred A. Knopf 1993) (1946) ("All animals are equal, but some animals are more equal than others.").

justiciable, to deciding the merits of a case—requires some formal, if *de minimis*, collective institutional decision. When judicial preferences cycle, a regime that adhered to range would instead threaten an impasse. As we will demonstrate in more detail in the chapter on the judiciary,[39] the practice of an odd number of Supreme Court justices voting on a judgment almost always ensures an outcome in the case even though the justices might hold combined preferences that embed a cycle.

By contrast, as we have seen, various legislative practices allow Congress to remain inert when members discover preferences that cycle. While range thus marks an important distinction between rules employed in appellate courts and legislatures, including the Supreme Court and Congress, this does not mean that legislative preferences endlessly cycle. In Congress, the combination of structure-induced equilibrating rules and logrolling, which allows members to register intensities of preference, generate equilibrium results.[40] Even with these combined institutional arrangements, Congressional rules are generally better suited to satisfying the Condorcet criterion than those in the Supreme Court. Through informal means, members of Congress have the capacity to locate Condorcet winners even when formal rules appear to limit all necessary binary comparisons over options. When stakes are sufficiently high, members of Congress can negotiate outside formal voting and thus reveal preferences that encourage inaction or discourage adverse voting paths. In contrast with the Supreme Court, which is generally obligated to issue judgments in cases properly before it, Congress has no parallel obligation even to vote on each proposed bill. Instead, Congress allows countless legislative proposals never to become bills, and the vast majority of bills that are proposed simply to die.

In addition, Congressional practices sometimes improve the quality of outputs by avoiding the Condorcet criterion in favor of other norms. Remember that the Condorcet criterion does not account for intensities of preference. In a group with the following ordinal preferences, P1: *ABC*; P2: *BCA*; and P3: *CBA*, although *B* is the Condorcet winner, it might also be an inferior social alternative to another option, for example *C*. If, for example, P1 is nearly indifferent among all options, she might happily forgo voting for *B* in a contest with *C*, thereby allowing *C* to prevail, in exchange for the support of P2, who least prefers option *A*, in some other matter. Thus, through the commodification of preferences, legislators sometimes produce results that, while thwarting the Condorcet criterion, are nonetheless beneficial for all participants to the exchange.[41]

Unanimity and *Independence of Irrelevant Alternatives*: Unanimity is defined as follows: "If an individual preference is unopposed by any contrary preference of any other individual, this preference is preserved in the social ordering."[42] Although unanimity is equivalent to the efficiency criterion of *Pareto superiority*, introduced in Chapter 2, the different contexts

---

[39] *See infra* Chapter 22.

[40] *See* Maxwell L. Stearns, *The Public Choice Case Against the Item Veto,* 49 WASH. & LEE L. REV. 385, 397–98 (1992). Such devices include elaborate committee structures, bicameralism, filibusters, and formal limits on the number of permissible amendments for pending legislation. *See supra* at Chapters 11, Part III.A.

[41] Of course, this does not mean it is helpful to society. *See infra* p. 557 (discussing tension between unanimity in legislatures and markets).

[42] MUELLER, *supra* note 25, at 583. For a discussion of the origin of this condition, see STEARNS, *Misguided Renaissance, supra* note 1, at 88–92, 347–49 nn.112–130.

in which these terms apply have the potential to invite some confusion. Within the study of private markets, a move from the status quo to an alternative state is defined as *Pareto superior* if it benefits at least one participant without harming others. An outcome is *Pareto optimal* if no further *Pareto superior* moves are available, meaning that all potential welfare-improving moves have already taken place. At this point, any further changes from the existing allocation of resources will necessarily have distributional consequences, benefiting some at the expense of others.

Economists generally regard private markets as uniquely suited to producing wealth by facilitating *Pareto superior* transactions. When an individual purchases food from a supermarket, the buyer values the food more than the money and the supermarket values the money more than the food; if not, the transaction would not take place. If we set aside such problems as initial wealth endowments and externalities, and assume away illegal or coercive tactics such as fraud or duress, then it is a fair supposition that market transactions are the product of unanimous consent. Because people voluntarily engage in market exchange, it is also fair to assume that they do so with the intent to improve their position. Private market exchanges are thus likely to improve the utility of at least one, and probably both, of the affected parties to the resulting transaction.[43] Otherwise they would not have bothered.[44]

The difficulty with applying the *Pareto* criterion in the context of lawmaking is that mutually assented-to trades in legislatures, or *logrolling*, have the potential to inhibit wealth-producing private market exchange. As Oliver Wendell Holmes famously observed, "[r]egulation means the prohibition of something."[45] Regardless of the wisdom of the underlying regulatory policy, legislation that restricts private market transactions elevates legislative unanimity over private market unanimity. For most regulatory policies to succeed, they must inhibit at least some potential *Pareto superior* private market transactions. Conversely, constitutional doctrines that invalidate such regulation elevate private market unanimity (or *Pareto superiority)* over legislative unanimity.[46]

Does this analysis help to explain the tradeoffs discussed in Chapter 11 in the doctrinal transformation from *Lochner v. New York*,[47] decided in 1905, to *West Coast Hotel*

---

[43] Exchange is one of two mechanisms for wealth creation; the other, of course, is production.

[44] Thus, price theory is conceptually an adjunct to the theory of social choice, rather than the other way around. *See* James M. Buchanan, *Social Choice, Democracy and Free Markets,* 62 J. POL. ECON. 114 (1954).

[45] Hammer v. Dagenhart, 247 U.S. 251, 277 (1918) (Holmes, J., dissenting).

[46] To be clear, legislative decision making usually requires approval by majority rule, and not unanimous legislative consent. The unanimity criterion, however, does not apply at the level of final legislative approval, but rather at the level of individual exchanges that occur during the process of logrolling. For this reason, private market transactions actually proceed with a lower level of social consensus than legislative transactions. When two private market actors unanimously transact business, barring any legal prohibitions to the deal, the exchange proceeds. There is no need for additional consent by other market participants. By contrast, when two legislators engage in a logroll through their unanimous consent, that exchange acquires no force unless and until it is ratified by several majority voting procedures that incorporate it into a successful bill that the President then signs or vetoes. The level at which the unanimity criterion is applied in the two settings, however, is not the ratification of the exchange (or of the vote trade) but rather the exchange or vote trade itself.

[47] 198 U.S. 45 (1905).

Co. v. Parrish,[48] decided in 1937? Is the social choice analysis of these doctrines consistent or in tension with the implications of interest group theory? Why?

An extensive public choice literature posits that legislative processes at both the federal and state levels are systematically biased in favor of regulatory policies that tend to undermine private market efficiency.[49] Recall that in his article, *Does Interest Group Theory Justify More Intrusive Judicial Review?*, Professor Einer Elhauge posited that interest group theory itself cannot answer whether interest group involvement in legislative processes is excessive because one must first apply a normative baseline concerning the proper extent of interest group influence.[50] Does social choice theory help the analysis by offering a basis for comparing alternative normative baselines? Why or why not?

Independence of Irrelevant Alternatives: To fully appreciate unanimity, we must now introduce another Arrovian fairness condition, namely *Independence of Irrelevant Alternatives*. The criterion is defined as follows: "The social choice between any two alternatives must depend only on the orderings of individuals over these two alternatives, and not on their ordering over other alternatives."[51] Independence thus requires that each decision maker base her pairwise choice solely upon the relative merits of the presented alternatives, without strategic considerations. Prohibited strategies can include trying to anticipate, and thus derail, a disfavored voting path by voting other than for one's first choice as needed to prevent an adverse outcome, or trying to improve one's utility through vote trading.

The independence criterion might well be the most counterintuitive and, indeed, controversial, of Arrow's fairness assumptions. The objection to independence can be expressed quite simply: If you or some other decision maker are influenced in selecting between options *A* and *B* by the presence (or absence) of option *C*, who is to say that *C* is irrelevant to your decision such that you should make the choice as if lacking this additional information? Despite this objection, both Condorcet and Arrow embraced independence, albeit for different reasons. Condorcet's intuition proves significant to evaluating Congress, while Arrow's intuition proves significant in evaluating the Supreme Court.

Whereas range is generally relaxed in the Supreme Court in order to promote the Court's ability to ensure collective judgments in each case, it is generally honored in Congress, which has the power to remain inert when preferences cycle or to commodify preferences when cyclical preferences fail to capture the real stakes due to different preference intensities. The intuition underlying Arrovian independence is largely opposite. Subject to a caveat described below, Supreme Court Justices are generally presumed to adhere to independence, whereas members of Congress are understood regularly to violate independence.

---

[48] 300 U.S. 379 (1937).

[49] For one of the leading articles, see Peter H. Aranson, Ernest Gellhorn & Glen O. Robinson, *A Theory of Legislative Delegation*, 68 CORNELL L. REV. 1 (1982).

[50] Einer R. Elhauge, *Does Interest Group Theory Justify More Intrusive Judicial Review?*, 101 YALE L.J. 31, 101–08 (1991). For a more detailed analysis of Elhauge's argument, see MAXWELL L. STEARNS, PUBLIC CHOICE AND PUBLIC LAW: READINGS AND COMMENTARY 246–53 (1997).

[51] MUELLER, *supra* note 25, at 584; *see also* STEARNS, *supra* note 1, at 89 & n.119. For a discussion of the origins of this condition, see STEARNS, *supra* note 1, at 89–92, 349 n.130.

Influenced by the republican philosopher Jean-Jacques Rousseau, Condorcet proposed that in choosing among options, legislators should focus solely upon the merits of presented alternatives so that in each successive contest, better options are selected, until the best option emerges.[52] In Condorcet's understanding, upon entering the public sphere either as legislators or voters, individuals are expected to subordinate their personal objectives in favor of the best interest of society.[53] By contrast, Arrow's intuition is influenced less by republican philosophy than by foundational assumptions of welfare economics. For Arrow, independence was necessary to avoid the difficulty that economists associate with interpersonal utility comparisons.[54] Within markets, individuals routinely signal their own relative utility through their willingness to pay, or what economists label *revealed preferences*.[55] Indeed, to that extent, social choice theory provides a basis for understanding the comparative advantage of markets, at least under standard assumptions including no externalities and no coercion or duress, relative to other institutions in the creation of wealth. The problem that Arrow confronted was in seeking

---

[52] *See* Stearns, *Misguided Renaissance*, *supra* note 1, at 1250 n.108 (discussing Rousseau's influence on Condorcet and collecting authorities).

[53] KEITH MICHAEL BAKER, CONDORCET: FROM NATURAL PHILOSOPHY TO SOCIAL MATHEMATICS 230 (1975) ("All men, Rousseau and Condorcet agreed, have the right to follow their own opinion. But reason dictates that on entering political society, they consent to submit to the general will—or, in Condorcet's phrase, 'the common reason'—those of their actions that must be governed for all according to the same principles.").

[54] *See* MUELLER, *supra* note 25, at 591 ("It was the desire to establish a welfare function that was not based upon interpersonal utility comparisons that first motivated Arrow."); Gary Lawson, *Efficiency and Individualism*, 42 DUKE L.J. 53, 61 & n.26 (1992) (citing economists and legal scholars for the proposition that "it is impossible to make interpersonal comparisons of utility" (internal citations omitted)). Consider also Professor Robin West's discussion of interpersonal utility comparisons:

> As many modern moral philosophers have argued, and as (nonlegal) economists generally concede: we can make these comparisons, and we do make these comparisons, every day. We can sympathize with one person's subjective grief and another's subjective annoyance, compare the two subjective experiences, and decide the former is of greater weight, magnitude, intensity, and importance than the latter, even when neither subjective experience is reflected in a contract, a vote, or a price. We can even make comparisons of the intensity of that most arbitrary of subjective experiences, namely culinary taste: we might compare Johnny's revulsion to the taste of candy with Susan's indifference and decide that Johnny hates the candy more than Susan likes the bubble gum. We can do this even if neither party has committed to the trade. . . . We look at Johnny's scrunched-up face, and we share with him a pale version of his nauseous reaction to what is causing his physical response.

Robin L. West, *Taking Preferences Seriously*, 64 TUL. L. REV. 659, 683–84 (1990).

Of course, Professor West is correct that individuals routinely make such comparisons. She is also correct that in assessing observed preferences, we actually do share a "pale version of" the other person's emotional reaction. For an accessible discussion, see Sandra Blakeslee, *Cells that Read Minds*, N.Y. TIMES, Jan. 10, 2006, at F1 (reviewing literature on *mirror neurons*). The concern Arrow and other economists have expressed, however, is that virtually any regulatory regime that includes preference intensities will invite strategic behavior among participants. Notice that West's familiar illustration (at least for those with children), involves the revelation of preferences after the fact that caused the sincere reaction. When asking children to select among several choices for dinner, each of which is one child's favorite, would we expect comparable expressions of candor to Johnny's unplanned "scrunched-up face." Why or why not? Notice also that the larger the regulatory stakes, the greater the incentives for strategic behavior. Is this an adequate response to West? Why or why not? Is her argument an adequate response to Arrow's inclusion of independence? Why or why not?

[55] For discussions of revealed preferences, see John Beshears et al., *How Are Preferences Revealed?*, 92 J. PUB. ECON. 1787 (2008); P.A. Samuelson, *A Note on the Pure Theory of Consumer's Behaviour*, ECONOMICA, Feb. 1938, at 61.

to develop a rule-making system that lacked a pricing mechanism through which to express cardinal utility. The difficulty is that absent such a mechanism, systems that seek to quantify and compare interpersonal utilities are likely to invite posturing or other forms of strategic behavior. Does this help to explain the difficulties with the chocolate or vanilla cake hypothetical that opened Chapter 13? If so, how?

The unanimity and independence criteria operate in tension. Unanimity encourages methods that discover cardinal values and individual strategies that enhance individual utility. Independence demands nonstrategic or principled decision making without regard to the effect on eventual outcomes. Within legislatures, individual legislators can vote sincerely or can enter into unanimous exchanges, or logrolls, thus voting strategically rather than sincerely on the merits of each proposal. The logrolling process demands careful attention to voting agendas and considerable foresight about the relationships between immediate decisions and future options. Effective legislating involves strategizing and vote trading. Thus, while logrolling promotes unanimity, it thwarts independence. Conversely, norms against strategic judicial voting promote independence (an element of principled voting) at the price of sacrificing potentially unanimous vote trades that would improve the likelihood of ruling closer to the ideal point of the participating jurists.[56]

Legal academics commonly presuppose that judges engage in principled, rather than strategic, decision making.[57] And yet this raises a puzzle. Are appellate judges somehow less well equipped than legislators to trade votes? Appellate courts have far fewer members than most legislative bodies, and the judges acquire substantial information regarding each others' preferences and anticipate repeated rounds of play. Given that the circumstances are ripe for enforcing agreements, it is not difficult to imagine incorporating a judicial custom or norm that would facilitate some form of judicial logrolling. And yet, even in as high-stakes a context as the Supreme Court, documented instances of vote trading across cases, or even across issues within cases, appear to be rare or nonexistent.[58]

To be sure, recent studies of the papers of retired Supreme Court Justices demonstrate that individual justices sometimes change their minds between their initial case assessments, as indicated in their preliminary post-argument conference votes, and the final case dispositions.[59] This tends to happen when justices need to compromise to secure a majority, without which the case would produce a holding but not establish a precedent. The result is often to produce a narrower holding, quite possibly a Condorcet winner, than the preferred broader holding for the justice making the compromise.[60]

---

[56] *But cf.* ROBERT D. COOTER, THE STRATEGIC CONSTITUTION 205–09 (2000) (presenting games in which jurists could improve the likelihood of achieving preferred policies within and across cases through vote trading).

[57] *See, e.g.*, Lewis A. Kornhauser & Lawrence G. Sager, *The One and the Many: Adjudication in Collegial Courts*, 81 CALIF. L. REV. 1 (1993).

[58] For an informative discussion of Justice Powell's rejection of an overture for a vote trade by Justice Brennan, see JOHN C. JEFFRIES, JR., JUSTICE LEWIS F. POWELL, JR. 303–04 (1994).

[59] *See generally* LEE EPSTEIN & JACK KNIGHT, THE CHOICES JUSTICES MAKE (1998).

[60] *See generally* Maxwell L. Stearns, *The Case for Including* Marks v. United States *in the Canon of Constitutional Law*, 17 CONST. COMMENT. 321 (2000). A challenge to this rule is pending as this book goes to press. *See* Hughes v. United States, No. 17–155 (argued Mar. 27, 2018). Professor Stearns, with other law professors,

How do these judicial strategies compare to Congressional logrolling? Can you identify relevant similarities and differences? How do these judicial practices relate to Arrovian independence and unanimity? Are there judicial norms that temper actual judicial vote-trading behavior? Why is there so little, if any, evidence of Supreme Court justices trading votes over issues within cases or across cases? What role, if any, do published opinions play in your analysis? Among the federal circuit courts of appeals, it is commonplace to issue written opinions that are unpublished, and that are generally non-precedential.[61] To the extent that the preceding analysis characterizes appellate courts versus legislatures more generally, how does this affect the analysis? Why don't members of Congress defend their votes in writing? Should proposals to shift decision-making responsibility between these two institutions take account of these very different institutional norms?[62]

To the extent that there is a tension between unanimity and independence, which criterion is more important? Is it possible to answer that question outside a specific institutional context? Why or why not? If not, what does that suggest about the Arrow's Theorem conditions?

Non-dictatorship: Non-dictatorship is defined as follows: "No individual enjoys a position such that whenever he expresses a preference between two alternatives and all other individuals express an opposite preference, his preference is always preserved in the social ordering."[63] Non-dictatorship appears the most obvious fairness condition in any collective decision-making institution. In fact, however, Arrow's Theorem proves that to preserve transitive orderings in a system that meets the other fairness conditions set out above, it is inevitable that someone be vested not merely with substantially disproportionate decisional authority, but also with authority that violates non-dictatorship. Although there are certainly different power levels among members of Congress, for example based on seniority and which party is in control, as a formal matter, at least with respect to recorded voting, each institution satisfies the non-dictatorship criterion.[64] These customs or rules do not give decisive significance to one participant at the expense of the contrary preferences of all members, at least not all of the time, and thus for matters brought to a vote, as a formal matter, each member has an equal vote on bills presented for decision. No member's contrary preference is consistently preserved in the social ordering.

---

filed an amicus curiae brief in that case. Brief of Law Professors in Support of Neither Party, *Hughes* (filed Jan. 26, 2018).

[61] There are important departures from the norm of published opinions. *See, e.g.*, WILLIAM M. RICHMAN & WILLIAM L. REYNOLDS, INJUSTICE ON APPEAL: THE UNITED STATES COURTS OF APPEALS IN CRISIS (2012) (criticizing the accelerating trend away from written opinions in all cases as unjust); Erica S. Weisgerber, Note, *Unpublished Opinions: A Convenient Means to an Unconstitutional End*, 97 GEO. L.J. 621, 626 (2009) (arguing that unpublished opinions written in the interests of efficiency are "of lesser quality"). Even unpublished slip opinions are accompanied by a judgment and thus a collective action on the part of the deciding court. And, in addition, they remain written and subject to scrutiny by other judges of the court, and also by the public, even if, in general they cannot be cited as authority. *See generally* Patrick J. Schiltz, *Much Ado About Little: Explaining the Sturm und Drang over the Citation of Unpublished Opinions*, 62 WASH. & LEE L. REV. 1429 (2005).

[62] For a related discussion, see STEARNS, *supra* note 1, at 92. *See also* Chapter 13.

[63] For a discussion of the origins of this condition, see *id.* at 92–94, 339 n.130.

[64] Of course, Arrow's Corollary implies that another condition is necessarily violated in each institution.

It is still worth discussing the occasional unequal power distributions within these institutions. In the Supreme Court, as in most appellate courts, the Chief Justice (or in the case of the federal circuits, the chief judge) truly is the first among equals in terms of the weight attached to her or his vote.[65] Even so, the Chief Justice does possess a significant source of disproportionate power, which occasionally vests in other senior members of majority coalitions. When the Chief Justice votes with the majority, he assigns the opinion; when the Chief Justice votes in dissent, the senior Justice voting with the majority assigns the opinion.[66] Although this practice does not formally violate non-dictatorship, the power differential raises important concerns.[67] In addition, through the *Rule of Four*, a minority is given power to control the Court's docket through the writ of *certiorari*. Here again, the rule does not vest the same justices with power over all certiorari petitions against the contrary will of the Court.[68] Those in a successful minority of four in one round might well find themselves in the unsuccessful majority of five in the next.

Within Congress, the various structures that allow individual members to block legislation, or even appointments, afford such members disproportionate power relative to their colleagues.[69] While each member has an equal vote as a formal matter, Congress effectively allows some members to exert more power than their nominal votes might otherwise suggest. But here too, the power is not unlimited. In the event that a committee chair abuses her or his power, other members can engage in a variety of retaliatory measures intended to limit such abuses in the future.

C. Summary

As stated above, the whole of Arrow's Theorem is greater than the sum of its parts. Even if one or more individual criteria are normatively suspect, the Theorem provides a framework for analyzing and comparing institutions in a manner that avoids the nirvana fallacy. It does so by demonstrating the ability of a given institution to relax criteria that

---

[65] Compare, for example, the power of the Vice President in his capacity as President Pro Tem of the Senate, to cast a deciding vote in the event of a tie. This occurred early in the Trump Administration, making Mike Pence the first Vice President ever to cast the deciding vote for a Cabinet nominee, confirming Betsy DeVos as Secretary of Education. Emmarie Huetteman & Yamiche Alcindor, *DeVos Confirmed for Education by Pence's Vote*, N.Y. TIMES, Feb. 8, 2017, at A1.

[66] Saul Brenner & Harold J. Spaeth, *Majority Opinion Assignments and the Maintenance of the Original Coalition on the Warren Court*, 32 AM. J. POL. SCI. 72 (1988).

[67] For example, the practice might violate the Anonymity criterion of May's Theorem, *see supra* Chapter 13, note 7, and cite therein. In addition, Warren Burger as Chief Justice sometimes voted against his preferred position to control the opinion and narrow its scope as compared to how the opinion would have been written had he dissented. *See* BOB WOODWARD & SCOTT ARMSTRONG, THE BRETHREN: INSIDE THE SUPREME COURT 64–65 (1979).

[68] For a general discussion, see Maxwell L. Stearns, *The Rule of Four*, *in* 4 ENCYCLOPEDIA OF THE SUPREME COURT OF THE UNITED STATES 298 (David S. Tanenhaus ed., 2008).

[69] For example, Senator Marco Rubio blocked a vote on the appointment of Roberta Jacobson as Ambassador to Mexico due to her involvement in the opening to Cuba during the Obama Administration. *See* Carol Morello & Ed O'Keefe, *How a New U.S. Ambassador Got Confirmed and Government Gets 40 New Reports*, WASH. POST (Apr. 29, 2016), https://www.washingtonpost.com/world/national-security/how-a-new-us-ambassador-got-confirmed-and-government-gets-40-new-reports/2016/04/29/1ebb59e0-0e41-11e6-8ab8-9ad050f76d7d_story.html; *see also* Helen Dewar, *Sen. Helms's Gavel Leaves Weld Nomination in Limbo: Chairman Thwarts Majority Call for Hearing*, WASH. POST, Sept. 13, 1997, at A1.

are inessential to—or that might actually harm—its functioning. Table 14:1 summarizes the preceding discussion and analysis.[70] As you read the applications that follow in the remainder of this book, consider the implications of Arrow's Theorem and of Arrow's Corollary as a means of gaining insight into the relevant institutions and rules.

Table 14:1. The Supreme Court and Congress Through an Arrovian Lens

Arrovian Criterion	Supreme Court	Congress
Range	Collective obligation to produce results prevents the Supreme Court from employing Condorcet-producing rules.	Collective ability to remain inert has allowed Congressional rules coupled with informal practices to evolve toward Condorcet criterion. In addition, cardinalization of preferences enables members of Congress to achieve collectively rational results while occasionally thwarting the Condorcet criterion.
Unanimity	Vote trading is inhibited in the Supreme Court by publication of written opinions and judgment-based decision making.	Vote trading is encouraged, thus producing *Pareto superior* legislative exchanges, which potentially undermine private market efficiency.

[70] STEARNS, *supra* note 1, at 93 tbl.2.4.

Independence of Irrelevant Alternatives	Judgment-based decision making and publication of written opinions raise the costs of strategic voting among justices; strategic interactions that remain are generally toward median position on the Court and operate along single-dimensional scale within individual cases.	Congressmen regularly vote strategically, thus cardinalizing their preferences over issues and bills.
Nondictatorship	Generally adhered to, opinion assignment power and power of certiorari provide occasional disproportionate power to minorities on the Court.	Compromised by practices that afford disproportionate power to committee chairs and to individual congressmen, limited by informal quasi-market checks when the stakes are high.
Condorcet Criterion	Evolution of important rules, including outcome voting and stare decisis are attributable to the Court's ability to employ Condorcet-producing rules. These rules should be evaluated in conjunction with companion rules, e.g., the narrowest grounds rule and standing, which help to improve the Court's overall rationality and fairness.	Important congressional voting rules have evolved toward Condorcet criterion, except when Congress lacks the power to remain inert, including in selecting legislative leaders. Some limited rules appear to defy Condorcet criterion, but common voting practices provide quasi-market solution, thus restoring Condorcet criterion when stakes are high.

III. CYCLING WITH FEWER PARTICIPANTS: MULTI-CRITERIAL DECISION MAKING

Until now, we assumed collective intransitivity, or cycling, is a function of the number of persons involved in the decision-making process. The standard presentation of social choice, as seen in the introduction to Chapter 13, assumes that each member holds transitive preferences over options, and demonstrates that under conditions lacking a Condorcet winner, when the preferences are combined, the result is a cycle. Specifically, with member preferences P1: ABC; P2: BCA; and P3: CAB, we discover that in a regime of unlimited binary comparisons, the group cycles such that ApBpCpA, where p means "preferred to by simple majority rule."

In a book titled *Why the Law is so Perverse*,[71] Professor Leo Katz focuses on another strand of social choice involving *multicriterial decision making*.[72] Despite the daunting terminology, the intuition is fairly easily explained. If we assume that the decision makers are required to accommodate norms that rest along competing analytical dimensions when choosing among alternatives, it is possible to specify conditions replicating a cycle with fewer than three persons or camps. Indeed, it is possible with an individual.

In what he presents as a parable, Professor Katz provides an intuitive illustration.[73] Katz imagines an accident involving a married couple, Al and Chloe, in one car, and Bea, driving another. Al suffers a sufficiently severe injury that he risks losing a leg, whereas Chloe suffers a minor injury risking permanent damage to a finger. Bea has an intermediate injury. Al and Chloe arrive first at the Emergency Room, and the doctor explains they are short staffed and he has time to treat only one of them safely. Al explains that although his injury is more severe, and although she is not a professional musician, Chloe's life work is playing the piano. Her sense of personal fulfillment matters deeply to them both, and so he wishes to forgo his treatment in favor of hers. The doctor agrees. Bea then arrives at the Emergency Room, and she insists upon being prioritized over Chloe given her relatively more severe injury. The doctor agrees. Al then insists upon being treated ahead of Bea, since his injury is more severe, and the doctor agrees. Al then instructs the doctor to prioritize Chloe for the reasons previously explained. The doctor agrees. At this point Bea speaks up, starting the cycle anew.

Professor Max Stearns summarizes the resulting anomaly as follows:

> In [this] fanciful illustration, Katz demonstrates how competing rules of triage and free exchange (the Pareto principle) can create a confounding cycle for a physician with time to treat only one of three patients involved in an automobile crash: one member of a married couple, Al and Chloe, with Al suffering a relatively severe, and Chloe, a relatively minor, injury, and another woman, Bea, with a moderate injury. If Al and Chloe prioritize Chloe's treatment over Al's, then under the Pareto principle, Chloe is treated first. Under triage, Bea takes priority over Chloe. And under triage again, Al takes

[71] LEO KATZ, WHY THE LAW IS SO PERVERSE (2011).

[72] For a classic article exploring this concept, see Matthew L. Spitzer, *Multicriterial Choice Processes: An Application of Public Choice Theory to* Bakke, *The FCC, and the Courts*, 88 YALE L.J. 717 (1979).

[73] KATZ, *supra* note 71, at 25–28.

> priority over Bea. Then under Pareto, Chloe regains priority. This combination generates a treatment cycle: Chloe p Al p Bea p Chloe, where p means preferred to under the conflicting multicriterial decision making of triage and Pareto. This holds even if only a subset of patients participates in the formal decision making at a given time.[74]

What generates this cycle are the competing demands along the dimensions of triage and Pareto, or efficiency narrowly defined.

Professor Maxwell Stearns has separately offered an account of a personal cycling dynamic involving his inheritance of a vast historical collection that neither he nor his sister had the capacity to absorb. The collection was significant historically, but with considerable content that was of insufficient value or quality to gift to a museum and whose provenance made most of the items a challenge to sell. The collection also had a strong sense of cohesion, meaning that the whole was in many respects greater than the sum of the parts.

Stearns explains the resulting cycle as follows:

> Step 1: I realize that I cannot absorb the entire collection into my home, and so I plan to convey it, either by gift, if possible, or sale.
>
> Step 2: I then realize that I want to have a remembrance, and so I plan to keep selected special items, those that have the most meaning, within or across collections.
>
> Step 3: I further realize that the collection (and the various sub-collections) has its own integrity, and represent a cohesive whole that is compromised if divided up, and so if I take a part, I must take the whole.
>
> Step 4: I realize that I cannot take the entire collection, and so I plan to convey it . . . . .
>
> The cycle is complete.[75]

This example illustrates two points about multicriterial decision making. First, although this involves one decision maker, the challenge arises because the choices implicate two dimensions: (1) a practical dimension, with "retain the entire collection" (impractical) at one extreme and "convey the entire collection by gift or sale" (somewhat more practical) at the other; and (2) a coherence dimension, prioritizing holding the entirety of the collection together, as much as possible, whether retained or conveyed. We might imagine ranking graded options along the first dimension from most to least (or least to most) preferred: (1) take it all, (2) take part, (3) take none. And yet, although position (2) seems a middle ground, it is plausible to rank it last since it alone violates the coherence dimension. The example further illustrates that *multipeaked along a single dimension* implies that the preferences ultimately rest along more than one dimension. That is because the initial dimension fails to capture the ultimate stakes.

---

[74] Stearns, *supra* note 7, 1083 n.180 (addressing an example adapted from LEO KATZ, WHY THE LAW IS SO PERVERSE 25–29 (2011)).

[75] Maxwell Stearns, *Collecting's Existential Crisis*, BLINDSPOT BLOG (Apr. 26, 2017), https://www.blindspotblog.us/single-post/2017/04/26/Collectings-Existential-Crisis.

Professor Stearns explains that multicriterial decision making holds potentially broad implications. In a legislative or judicial context in which there are only two dominant camps, or framings of an issue, it is possible to generate multicriterial decision making, and thus a cycle, based on how those two camps assess a discredited framing from the past. Stearns relates this to the implications of Jim Crow for the debates over whether equal protection demands color blindness or allows race-based affirmative action. Stearns explains:

> Dimensionality, and cycling, arises not only from positions people hold over choices, but also from background rules or conceptual framings that affect those choices. In multicriterial decision making, background rules combine with present options to forge dimensionality. . . . During the Jim Crow era, the two dominant positions were Jim Crow and color blindness. Today, with Jim Crow thankfully discredited, only color blindness and the modern liberal position are creditworthy.
>
> Recall that with preferences P1: ABC, P2: BCA, P3: CAB, the group will discover a cycle such that BpCpApB, where p means preferred to by simple majority rule. But even if a decision maker is removed, the cycle can persist due to a combination of remaining preferences and governing rules. Rules extend the preferences of past participants to the decision-making process. Indeed, rules *are* the formal extension of past decision makers' preferences.
>
> If P3 plans to retire, she might encourage P1 and P2 to embrace a rule that captures all or part of her preferences. Imagine the proposed rule provides that when choosing either between B and C or between B and A, P3's preferences, which least favor B, must be credited. The rule would discourage either P1 or P2, working with P3's replacement, P4, from enacting either of their last choices. When combined with the ordinal preferences of P1 and P2, the P3 rule replicates the earlier forward cycle. Although cycling is often viewed unfavorably, a cycle might be preferable to the risk that P4 will team up with either P1 or P2 to produce P3's least preferred result.
>
> This dynamic can arise when present jurists frame equal protection options based upon conflicting understandings of discredited positions from the past. Modern liberals infer from Jim Crow the need to avoid racial subordination even if doing so means condoning occasional reliance on race to benefit a once subordinated group. Color-blinds infer from Jim Crow that regardless of how it is characterized, any reliance on race is harmful and must be prohibited. Despite its general condemnation, Jim Crow has forged ongoing multicriterial decision making.[76]

Professor Katz posits that the problem of multicriteriality embeds many anomalies within the law. He inquires why we so often eschew seemingly intermediate, or simply alternative, options. For example, Katz asks why we disallow voluntary torture as an alternative to prolonged incarceration; why we disallow the sale of organs, but allow giving them away voluntarily; and why we generally disallow specific performance in favor of

---

[76] Stearns, *supra* note 7, at 1083–84.

monetary damages.[77] In each example, and many others, the result is to prevent an option that might make the choice between those that remain less stark and that the affected parties might prefer.

One interesting implication of Katz's analysis is whether the law sometimes removes a particular issue dimension from the decision path to force a choice along the dimension that remains. Can you think of examples from the common law that have this effect? Can you think of regulatory examples? In either instance, would the law be improved by allowing consideration of choices arising along the now-prohibited dimension? Why or why not? Does Stearns's illustration of cycling by one person hold any doctrinal significance? Can you identify circumstances in which the legal system, by removing a personal option, implicating an alternative choice dimension, might help facilitate more benign, or responsible, conduct?

IV. APPLICATIONS

1. Interest Groups and Legislative Cycling

Professor Saul Levmore has argued that the presence of legislative cycles might increase the influence of interest groups on the legislative process, and in fact, might help promote the formation of interest groups.[78] Levmore explains:

> Interest groups act where there are cycling majorities or other aggregation anomalies and, therefore, where there are excellent opportunities to influence agenda setters or to bargain for the formation of winning coalitions. Instability attracts political activity.[79]

The presence of underlying preferences that are susceptible of cycling, Levmore explains, suggests that legislative outcomes are often determined by "procedures and institutions," such as the presence of those with agenda-setting power or the structure of voting rules, "rather than coherent or stable majority preferences." Where this is the case, he argues, "Political activity is a relatively attractive investment."[80] Levmore explains:

> First, participation and subsequent investment may be most profitable when victory does not require overcoming a clear or stable majority winner. . . . As contributors and political entrepreneurs evaluate investments, it is likely to turn out that many of the best available projects are those in which costs are low because procedures, rather than underlying preferences, need to be influenced. This approach stresses a rational, or expected-value, calculation by contributors and groups.
>
> A second approach makes room for quasi-rational actors who choose strategies that might plausibly advance their ends efficiently, but in settings where there is insufficient pressure to root out imperfect strategies. . . . [I]mperfectly informed interest groups might invest where the probability of victory (rather than its expected value) is high—and . . . where there is no stable

[77] KATZ, *supra* note 71, at 15–25.

[78] Saul Levmore, *Voting Paradoxes and Interest Groups*, 28 J. LEGAL STUD. 259 (1999).

[79] *Id.* at 259.

[80] *Id.* at 261.

winner the chance of bargaining for victory or influencing the agenda setter is greatest.

Levmore further explains that:

> It seems likely that an interest group would have more trouble gaining for its members something that a majority of the citizenry (or legislature) unambiguously opposes than it would have extracting a law or subsidy that did not appeal to any absolute majority of the relevant voters but that was not opposed by a clear majority.

Thus, Levmore concludes that:

> [A]n interest group will invest more where procedure determines outcome, but it may invest either less or yet more depending on whether it also expects to be opposed by a competing organized group. Where there is no Condorcet winner and there is a competing organization, the probability of victory drops (compared to the case where there is no organized competition) but the likelihood of a loss increases if one does nothing. My secondary conjecture is that one should find increased investment where there is no Condorcet winner, regardless of expected opposition.[81]

In this analysis, special interest legislation might arise not only due to the greater and more persistent pressures from interest groups, as compared with the diffuse public, as explained by Mancur Olson and as reflected in the Wilson/Hays analysis presented in Chapter 11, but also on the specific dynamics of legislative cycling, and the ability of interest groups to exploit those cycles.

Does this analysis bolster arguments for applying greater than conventional rational basis scrutiny to economic regulation? Why or why not? How does this relate to Einer Elhauge's inquiry, *Does Interest Group Theory Justify More Intrusive Judicial Review?* Elhauge's argument against greater judicial review as a function of increased interest group involvement in the political process relates to the problem of unarticulated baselines concerning the appropriate level of such involvement. Does Levmore's analysis avoid this problem? If so, how? If not, why not?

2. Licensure, Contract Formation, and Multicriterial Decision Making

Leo Katz has demonstrated that cycling can arise with fewer than three persons choosing among three or more options. Indeed, when faced with multicriterial decision making, one or two actors can experience conditions resembling a cycle. In Katz's example involving the three injured persons seeking medical care, the cycle arises as a result of infusing concerns for a Pareto-improving trade, favoring the care of Chloe (with a minor injury), over Al (with a severe injury), at the expense of Bea (with a moderate injury). In actual medical practice, a physician would not have the option even to consider trading off the triage dimension for the desire of a patient to prioritize someone's less severe injury. Removing that option avoids the cycle in actual practice by eliminating one choice dimension, namely Pareto, but in doing so, it raises the very question at the core of Katz's inquiry: Why?

---

[81] *Id.* at 272–73 (footnote omitted).

Why are physicians required to limit their care to triage in this setting, rather than allowing the patients to ask for, or even bid for, reprioritization? Can you think of exceptions that allow physicians to favor some patients, with less significant injuries, over others, whose injuries are more severe? Consider, for example, boutique medical practices.[82] The basic model is that members of the practice pay an annual fee, say $2500, to have access to the physician, who in turn, takes on fewer patients and thus has the capacity to offer those she cares for greater attention. The physician has a guaranteed base income comprising the total fees less costs. Assuming the membership is 100 families and no additional costs, that ensures an annual income of $250,000 before treating any patients. This also suggests that for those with the means and inclination to join as members, the physician will attend to their needs *even if* the needs of non-members of the practice are greater. How does this relate to the Katz parable? Is allowing such practice structures sound public policy? Why or why not? How does your answer relate to the problem of multicriterial decision making? To dimensionality?

This dimensionality problem is not unique to medicine, and even within medicine it arises in other ways. Physicians are also not permitted, under prevailing professional norms, to treat patients in a manner that is not consistent with standard medical care.[83] Consider, for example, the requirement that a hospitalized patient seeking to leave a doctor's care prematurely sign a statement attesting that he is doing so "against medical advice." If the contractual arrangement between doctor and patient were unrestricted, would this be necessary? Similarly, a physician can, and in some instances must, decline to treat patients seeking procedures that are not consistent with the expected standard of medical care *even if* the patient and physician would otherwise agree to that procedure.

The same holds for legal services. Lawyers are not allowed to contract with their clients to avoid the lawyer's professional obligations in the course of legal representation. Neither medical nor legal services may be dispensed without license, and both professions impose obligations that can prevent arrangements that the professional and the patient or client might prefer. Can you identify examples? Are those you identify justified? Why or why not?

Katz gives, as an example of the anomaly of multicriterial decision making, the inability to trade off time in prison for a period of voluntary torture. He notes that the latter would be far less costly, both to the state and to the prisoner. Why is this disallowed?

---

[82] *See* Frank Pasquale, *The Three Faces of Retainer Care: Crafting a Tailored Regulatory Response*, 7 YALE J. HEALTH POL'Y & ETHICS 39, 63–64 (2007) ("Given most retainer care physicians' commitment to a unitary standard of care, such patients are not 'skipping in front of' other patients within retainer practices. However, they only attained this level of care by effectively outbidding those unable or unwilling to pay the required retainer. Moreover, considering the baseline of primary care availability, they are far 'ahead' of those in non-retainer practices. The average American waits several days for an office visit, is subjected to more delays once at the doctor's office, and more than half of such visits last less than twenty minutes. By contrast, retainer patients get near-immediate access through traditional visits, house-calls, and even e-consultations and phone calls."); John Kirkpatrick, *Concierge Medicine Gaining Ground*, PHYSICIAN EXECUTIVE, Sept. 1, 2002, at 24.

[83] Tim Cramm et al., *Ascertaining Customary Care in Malpractice Cases: Asking Those Who Know*, 37 WAKE FOREST L. REV. 699, 702–03 (2002) ("[T]he physician is held to a standard of customary care—the physician's performance must be of such a nature that the patient could have expected to receive the same or virtually similar treatment no matter who treated the patient.").

Should it be? Does your answer relate to social choice? If so, how? If not, what are the alternative bases for disallowing such arrangements?

3. Agenda Setting and the Rule of Four

The Supreme Court's Rule of Four is among the more anomalous rules governing the judicial process. Rather than having a majority vote on which cases to take onto the Court's docket, which is almost entirely discretionary, the docket is, with rare exception, governed by the Rule of Four. Because the Supreme Court has nine members, assuming full participation, this obviously violates the Condorcet criterion.

Can you think of a justification for this minority voting rule? Unlike dispositions on the merits, certiorari votes are generally not defended with written opinions. Can you think of a rationale for this feature of the Rule of Four? Does your explanation relate to social choice? If so, how?

V. APPENDIX A: SINGLE PEAKEDNESS VERSUS MULTIPEAKEDNESS, AND UNIDIMENSIONALITY VERSUS MULTIDIMENSIONALITY

This Appendix will illustrate the conceptual relationships between (1) single-peakedness and multipeakedness, and (2) unidimensionality and multidimensionality with helpful graphics. We begin with a group with well-tamed, or Condorcet-producing, preferences.

Imagine an assembly with three members or three coalitions, such that any two form a simple majority. The assembly seeks to allocate funds for a bridge repair. The proposed amounts, in increments of $10,000, are 1, 2, and 3, each of which is the first choice of one of the three members. As demonstrated in Figure 14:1 below, we can chart the collective preferences, such that the vertical axis represents the legislators, A, B, and C, and the horizontal axis represents the allocations, 1, 2, and 3.

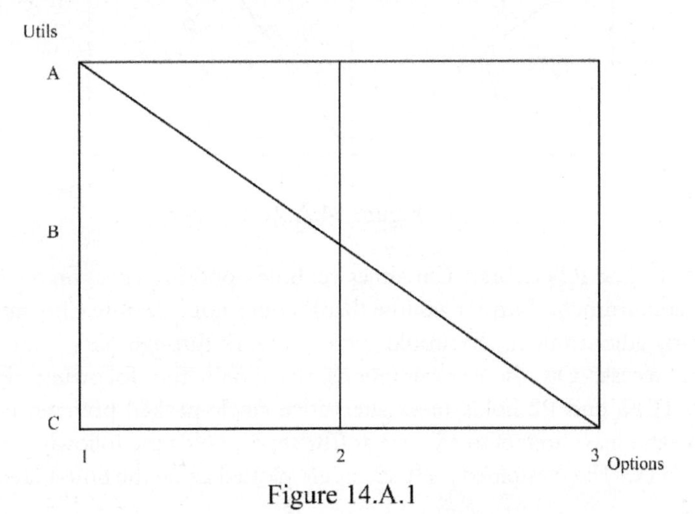

Figure 14.A.1

The legislators' first choice preferences can be cast along a single-peaked curve, sloping downward, from most to least preferred. Whether it employs top-down or bottom-up voting, the assembly will settle on the same result, 2, as the dominant median position, or Condorcet winner. Even with such well-tamed preferences, however, an alternative voting regime might produce a more extreme, non-Condorcet outcome. A committee chair who most prefers to allocate 3 might first present the middle position, 2, hoping for its defeat by those who prefer the opposing extremes, then present 1, hoping those who prefer at least level 2 funding will defeat it as well. If only option 3 remains for an up or down vote, it might pass if the sole remaining alternative is to forgo the bridge repair entirely. This anomaly helps to illustrate Professor Saul Levmore's insight that when there is likely to be a Condorcet winner, parliamentary rules tend to structure vote orderings to improve the likelihood that such options prevail.

Now consider combined preferences that lack a Condorcet winner. We can express this in two ways. We begin with multipeakedness along a single dimension. Imagine that for one of the assembly members, the low position is the first choice, the high position is the second choice, and the middle position is the last choice. This is less counterintuitive than it first appears. Assume, for example, that the assembly is selecting a date for terminate the session, and the options are Thanksgiving (T), Christmas (C), or December 31 (N). While these dates can be cast along a unidimensional continuum, representing the order of the dates, for the voter who least prefers the middle position, ranking preferences results in two peaks at the extremes over a valley in the middle. For this voter, the time-based dimension fails to capture the relevant stakes.

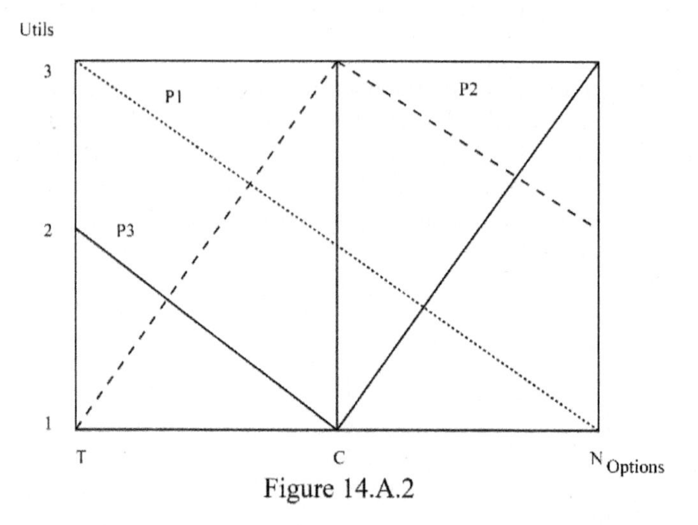

Figure 14.A.2

Assume P1 and P2 celebrate Christmas yet hold opposing views on the merits of an early or late adjournment. Further assume that P3 does not celebrate Christmas, and that absent an early adjournment, she would prefer to work through New Year to lengthen the summer recess. On these assumptions, P1 holds the following single-peaked preferences: TCN, and P2 holds these alternative single-peaked preferences: CNT. By contrast, P3, who least prefers to adjourn at Christmas, holds the following multi-peaked preferences: NTC. The combined preferences are plotted along the time-based dimension in Figure 14.A.2. In a regime of direct pairwise comparisons, we discover that separate majorities prefer N to T and T to C, but C to N, producing the cycle: CpNpTpC.

We can now express the same cycle as resulting from single-peaked preferences resting along two issue dimensions.[84] For the three decision makers, the selection of adjournment date implicates two issues rather than one, first, whether to break early or late, and second, whether to break specifically to celebrate Christmas. By expanding the issue space to accommodate these two choice dimensions, we can transform P3's previously multi-peaked preferences on a single dimension into uni-peaked preferences along a multidimensional spectrum.

Table 14.A.3 casts each adjournment date based upon how it aligns along each of the two dimensions:

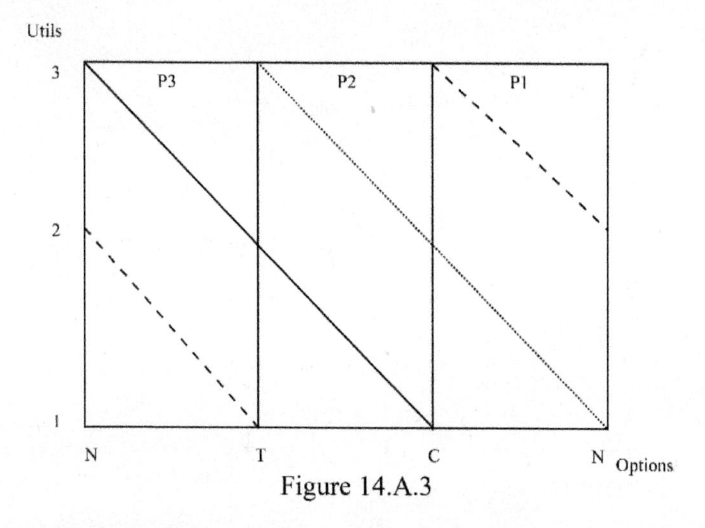

Figure 14.A.3

In this analysis, option C implies lengthening summer recess and breaking to celebrate Christmas, option N implies breaking to lengthen summer recess, but not to celebrate Christmas, and option T implies not lengthening summer recess and breaking to celebrate Christmas. P1, who does not care about lengthening summer recess and who celebrates Christmas, ranks his preferences TCN. P2 who wishes to lengthen summer recess, but who, failing that wishes to break for Christmas, ranks his options NCT. Finally, P3, who wishes to lengthen summer recess but who does not celebrate Christmas, ranks her preferences NTC.

Figure 14.A.3, which uses utilities as a proxy for the value that the members place on each choice of adjournment date,[85] casts the preferences over the three options over the relevant two dimensions. The result is that each member's preferences are uni-peaked across two dimensions. To visualize this, imagine cutting the figure from the page and

---

[84] *See* P. ORDESHOOK, GAME THEORY AND POLITICAL THEORY: AN INTRODUCTION 56–65 (1986) (observing that "the existence of multipeaked preferences implies that the issue space is not unidimensional, but multidimensional.").

[85] To simply demonstrate the visual presentations of relationships among options, the graphics use continuous lines to connect discrete utilities assigned to each alternative. This should not be interpreted to imply that the utilities are continuous between selections among discrete options.

rolling it into a tube, bringing the left and right sides, representing N, together. The result is three continuous sets of single peaked preferences descending over two dimensions, reflecting the ranked policy choices depicted in Table 14.A.1.

The important point for our purposes is that the two graphic depictions represented in Figure 14.A2 (multipeakedness across a unidimensional issue spectrum) and Figure 14.A.3 (single peakedness across a multidimensional issue spectrum), express precisely the same underlying phenomenon. That is because the problem of dimensionality is what causes multipeakedness along a single dimension. And as noted throughout, dimensionality, however captured, is the phenomenon that gives rise to cycling.

CHAPTER 15

Game Theory (Part 1)

Introduction

This chapter, and Chapter 16, introduce several basic tools from elementary game theory. We have already introduced some game theoretical concepts,[1] which we will explore in greater depth here and apply in the remaining chapters. Game theory complements the other analytical tools we have introduced: price theory, interest group theory, and social choice theory. It also offers the basis for deeper insights into the functioning of markets, and into questions of law and public policy.

Game theoretical literature is extensive, covering surprisingly diverse subject areas. These include behavioral economics, psychology, evolutionary biology, international relations, markets, and the interpretation of biblical texts.[2] Game theory has even influenced TV game shows.[3] The legal literature applying game theory is sufficient to justify its own course treatment.[4] These two chapters are not a substitute for such a course or for a course in game theory more generally. Instead, our goal is to introduce a select

---

[1] *See supra* Chapters 3 and 4 (discussing John Brown torts model).

[2] *See, e.g.*, COLIN F. CAMERER, BEHAVIORAL GAME THEORY: EXPERIMENTS IN STRATEGIC INTERACTION (2003) (applying game theory to behavioral economics); THOMAS C. SCHELLING, THE STRATEGY OF CONFLICT (1981) (applying game theory to psychology); Andrew M. Colman, *Thomas C. Schelling's Psychological Decision Theory: Introduction to a Special Issue*, 27 J. ECON. PSYCHOL. 603, 603–08 (2006) (same); JOHN MAYNARD SMITH, EVOLUTION AND THE THEORY OF GAMES (1982); RONALD FISHER, THE GENETICAL THEORY OF NATURAL SELECTION (complete variorum ed. 1999) (applying game theory to evolutionary biology); James D. Fearon, *Rationalist Explanations for War*, 49 INT'L ORG. 379, 379–414 (1995) (applying game theory to international relations); Alvin E. Roth, *Game Theory as a Tool for Market Design*, *in* GAME PRACTICE: CONTRIBUTIONS FROM APPLIED GAME THEORY 7–18 (Fioravante Patrone et al. eds., 2000) (applying game theory to markets); Alvin E. Roth, *The National Resident Matching Program as a Labor Market*, 275 J. AM. MED. ASS'N 1054, 1054–56 (1996) (applying game theory to labor markets); STEVEN J. BRAMS, BIBLICAL GAMES: GAME THEORY AND THE HEBREW BIBLE (rev. ed. 2002) (applying game theory to biblical texts). Jacob Glazer & Ariel Rubinstein, *A Study in the Pragmatics of Persuasion: A Game Theoretical Approach*, *in* NEW PERSPECTIVES ON GAMES AND INTERACTION 121 (Krzysztof R. Apt & Robert Van Rooij eds., 2008) (applying game theory to pragmatic linguistics).

[3] *See Series: Golden Balls*, TV TROPES, http://tvtropes.org/pmwiki/pmwiki.php/Series/GoldenBalls (last visited Oct. 1, 2017).

[4] For a book dedicated to that topic, see DOUGLAS BAIRD ET AL., GAME THEORY AND THE LAW (1994).

subset of games that allow for greater insight into the materials reviewed thus far and for those that follow.

While game theory has fascinating historical antecedents,[5] the formal discipline is generally traced to two mathematics professors, the Hungarian-born John Von Neumann and the German-born Oskar Morgenstern.[6] After circulating a series of research papers that described specific games,[7] Von Neumann and Morgenstern published a seminal book in 1944 that pulled together various strands of the emerging discipline of game theory.[8]

A great deal of game theoretical literature presents itself in the form of stylized, and sometimes complex, mathematical models. Such models allow scholars to eliminate unnecessary detail and to focus instead on particular features of interest. One important difference between game theory and neoclassical economic analysis involves assumptions concerning knowledge versus uncertainty. While law and economics scholars have tended to employ models premised upon complete knowledge (or costless information),[9] game theorists often design models specifically intended to explore the implications of incomplete knowledge, asymmetric information, or ignorance.[10]

This chapter focuses on a game likely to be familiar to some readers, the prisoners' dilemma. This game models the behavior of two prisoners each of whom lacks specific knowledge concerning the other's strategy.[11] More complex variations of the prisoners' dilemma (or of other single period games) consider the implications of introducing degrees of certainty or uncertainty at separate decision-making junctures, referred to as *nodes*.[12] This more nuanced analysis improves the realism of the models, but at the trade-off of reduced generality. One reason is that, in such games, which are sometimes

---

[5] For an interesting overview, see Paul Walker, *A Chronology of Game Theory* (Oct. 2005), http://www.econ.canterbury.ac.nz/personal_pages/paul_walker/gt/hist.htm. For one fascinating illustration, Walker notes that Professors Robert J. Aumann and Michael Maschler have offered a compelling game theoretic account, grounding the outcome in the *nucleoli* of coalition games, of an otherwise anomalous Talmudic passage concerning the division of an estate among multiple creditors that appears to defy both equal and proportional division. *See* Robert J. Aumann & Michael Maschler, *Game Theoretic Analysis of a Bankruptcy Problem from the Talmud*, 36 J. ECON. THEORY 195 (1985).

[6] Robert J. Leonard, *From Parlor Games to Social Science: von Neumann, Morgenstern, and the Creation of Game Theory 1928–1944*, 33 J. ECON. LITERATURE 730 (1995).

[7] John von Neumann, *On the Theory of Parlor Games*, 100 MATHEMATICAL ANNALS 295 (1928).

[8] OSKAR MORGENSTERN & JOHN VON NEUMANN, THEORY OF GAMES AND ECONOMIC BEHAVIOR (Princeton University Press 2004) (1944).

[9] Can you see why these are two ways of saying the same thing? The distinction in the text is more a matter of emphasis than definition. Economist Frank Knight, for example, modeled behavior based upon incomplete information or ignorance. *See, e.g.*, FRANK H. KNIGHT, RISK, UNCERTAINTY AND PROFIT (1921). Early law and economics scholarship has tended toward adopting complete information models. By contrast, those writing in the tradition of behavioral economics, or applied psychology, emphasize the role of law and norms in encouraging benign choices in a world of costly information, especially given the natural human tendency to favor default options. *See, e.g.*, CASS R. SUNSTEIN & RICHARD H. THALER, NUDGE: IMPROVING DECISIONS ABOUT HEALTH, WEALTH, AND HAPPINESS (2008).

[10] ERIC RASMUSEN, GAMES AND INFORMATION: AN INTRODUCTION TO GAME THEORY (4th ed. 2007).

[11] For a more detailed analysis of the prisoners' dilemma, see *infra* pp. 578–603.

[12] For a general discussion, see RASMUSEN, *supra* note 10, at 43–46.

formatted as a decision tree,[13] the ultimate resolution depends on the outcomes within each *subgame* that comprises the larger game. In addition, in more complex games, player strategies and combined outcomes—or equilibria—can turn on slight alterations in assigned values.[14] This includes the discount rate assigned for future benefits associated with cooperation or costs of defection in each round of play.[15]

In earlier chapters, we presented analyses that can now be formalized in terms of the prisoners' dilemma or various multiple pure Nash equilibrium games introduced in Chapter 16. Selecting the correct game is essential to analyzing a legal doctrine or decision-making rule. As Professors Douglas Baird, Robert Gertner, and Randal Picker have observed,[16] failing to appreciate the broader spectrum of available games when assessing questions of legal policy can result in wrongly assuming that coordination difficulties invariably reflect an underlying prisoners' dilemma.[17] Applying the incorrect game can thus lead to important prescriptive errors.

This chapter will focus on the prisoners' dilemma, in single period and in iterated form. This represents the simplest game because it conduces to a single dominant "Nash equilibrium" result. We will consider several variations on the prisoners' dilemma, including a game with endless iterations (or rounds of play) and a game with a known end period, and show how those alternative sets of conditions affect the predictions of the model. The chapter concludes with applications.

Chapter 16 will present three games that are more complex in that each admits of more than a single pure Nash equilibrium. Instead, these games conduce to a combination of outcomes, any of which is possible depending on the selected player strategies in a given round of play. Two of the available outcomes correspond to what game theorists refer to as pure Nash equilibria and two others correspond to non-pure Nash equilibria.[18] The chapter presents the driving game (or multiple Nash equilibrium bargaining game); the battle of the sexes; and the game of chicken (or Hawk-Dove).

In each of these two chapters, we introduce the terminology used to describe the games and their implications. Such concepts include *normal form games*, *extended form games*, *single period games*, *iterated games*, *pure Nash equilibrium*, *non-pure Nash equilibrium*, *backward induction*, and *unraveling*. We also introduce several related concepts including *Bayes' theorem*, *trigger strategy equilibria*, and *tit for tat strategies* (and several variations on simple tit for tat).

---

[13] In these chapters, we present only simple form illustrations with single matrices. Decision-tree presentations are referred to as *extended form* games. As Ian Ayres has explained, "Extensive form representation is especially appropriate for games with *asymmetric* or *incomplete* information." Ian Ayres, *Playing Games with the Law*, 42 STAN. L. REV. 1291, 1301 (1990) (reviewing RASMUSEN, *supra* note 10).

[14] These values can, for example, represent degrees of knowledge or predictability. In the parlance of game theory, altering these values can affect which equilibria predominate both within sub-games and within the larger games that the sub-games comprise. *See* RASMUSEN, *supra* note 10.

[15] For a discussion of discount rates, see *infra* pp. 631–632.

[16] BAIRD ET AL., *supra* note 4.

[17] *See also* Richard McAdams, *Beyond the Prisoners' Dilemma: Coordination, Game Theory, and the Law*, 82 S. CAL. L. REV. 209 (2009). A related insight from game theory shows that the payoffs attached to those options that the players in the game rationally avoid nonetheless can have profound effects on the ultimate outcome of a game. BAIRD ET AL., *supra* note 4, at 14–17 (providing illustration).

[18] BAIRD ET AL., *supra* note 4, at 37.

While our choice of selected games and concepts is not comprehensive, we refer to other works throughout our discussion that provide detailed presentations of other games.

I. THE SINGLE-PERIOD PRISONERS' DILEMMA

A. The Basic Game

Imagine that Alex and Brad are arrested and held in separate cells. They cannot communicate and as a result they can neither make any agreements nor enforce any agreements that they might have made in the past. The police present each prisoner with the same offer: If both prisoners remain silent, each will be charged with a misdemeanor and face six months in prison. If Alex testifies against Brad and Brad remains silent, Alex will be released without charge (thus serving no time) and Brad will be charged with a class one felony and receive an expected sentence of five years. If Brad testifies against Alex and Alex remains silent, the payoffs are reversed with Brad receiving no time and Alex serving five years. If both prisoners testify then they will each be charged instead with a class two felony and face an equally certain sentence of three years. We present this simple form game in the following matrix.

Table 15:1. The Classic Prisoners' Dilemma

Payoffs for (Alex, Brad)	**Brad cooperates**	**Brad defects**
Alex cooperates	6 months, 6 months	5 years, no time
Alex defects	no time, 5 years	**3 years, 3 years**

Table 15:1 sets out the *payoffs*, or expected results for each player based upon the combined strategies, in this game. Unless otherwise indicated, in this and all future matrices, the Nash outcome (or set of outcomes) is presented in bold. The payoffs, listed in the order of (column, row), are *reciprocal*, meaning that the incentives are the same for both Alex and Brad. In this game, the payoffs to cooperation and defection are viewed narrowly from the perspective of the opposing parties in the game, here the prisoners, rather than from that of other affected persons, for example the prosecutor or society. A prisoner *cooperates* by remaining silent, thus failing to incriminate the other prisoner, and conversely, a prisoner *defects* by testifying against the other prisoner so as to obtain a lighter sentence.

If both Alex and Brad cooperate, each receives a relatively lenient six-month sentence. Alternatively, if Alex cooperates and Brad defects, Alex is given the harshest available sentence, five years, while Brad is released without charge. Conversely, if Alex defects and Brad cooperates, Alex is released, while Brad is sentenced to five years. If both Alex and Brad defect, then each is sentenced to three years.

The prisoners' dilemma game is an example of a *non-cooperative game* with a single pure Nash equilibrium. This unique solution arises because as a result of the payoffs, each player pursues a predictable strategy that is independent of the other player's actual strategy. Whether a given player cooperates or defects, it is rational for the other player to defect to obtain the benefit of a higher payoff. Because these payoffs are reciprocal, the incentives are identical for Alex and Brad. If Alex cooperates, Brad improves his payoff from six months to no time by defecting, and if Alex defects, Brad improves his payoffs from five years to three years by defecting. The same incentives hold true for Alex in the event that Brad cooperates or defects. Thus, the optimal strategy for Alex is to defect regardless of what Brad does, and the optimal strategy for Brad is to defect regardless of what Alex does.

It is important to consider the assumptions that underlie this game. First, the game assumes that each player seeks to maximize his *individual* payoffs without regard to the payoffs to the other player.[19] From the perspective of both players combined, the best outcome is mutual cooperation, with a total joint sentence of one year (six months each). If one cooperates and the other does not, the joint sentence is five years. And if both defect, the joint sentence is six years. Thus, mutual defection yields the lowest joint payoff of all combined strategies. And yet, mutual defection emerges as the dominant strategy.

Second, note that in this game what is optimal for the players may not be optimal from a larger societal perspective. While the joint value to Alex and Brad is maximized when both cooperate, the joint value to society might well be maximized if both defect. This is certainly true if Alex and Brad are actually guilty of having committed a serious offense. Outside the criminal context, prisoners' dilemmas also have the potential to produce benign outcomes. Business cartels, for example, can be viewed as creating multilateral prisoners' dilemmas, subject to the same dynamics as the simpler prisoners' dilemma with two players. While the cartel as a whole benefits when members "cooperate," thus moving output and pricing from a competitive to a monopolistic level,[20] consumers benefit when the cartel members defect, thereby restoring competitive production levels and pricing. Defection will increase the cheater's share of the market, but by incrementally raising output levels and lowering price, it risks the eventual demise of the cartel. Because prisoners' dilemmas sometimes produce benign societal outcomes, an important public policy inquiry involves identifying those circumstances in which placing individuals or institutions within, or removing them from, a prisoners' dilemma benefits society.

Third, the prisoners' dilemma game involves mutual ignorance in that neither player has specific knowledge concerning the other player's strategy. Even without such knowledge, however, this game produces a determinate outcome, or pure Nash equilibrium. A Nash equilibrium is the outcome or set of outcomes that result from each player's rational strategy absent coordination or specific information about the other player's strategy, and in which no player has an incentive to deviate given the other player's strategy.[21] Thus, a pure Nash outcome arises when no player, acting alone, could improve

---

[19] One might couch this in terms of rationality, subject to the caveat that it is not necessarily irrational to hold preferences that include concern for the welfare of others. In this simple form game, however, the numbers are assumed to capture the full payoffs for each player.

[20] For a general discussion, see *supra* Chapter 1, Part II.D.

[21] BAIRD ET AL., *supra* note 4, at 21 (describing Nash equilibrium as the solution concept to the principle that "The combination of strategies that players are likely to choose is one in which no player could do better

her or his payoff through a unilateral move to an alternative strategy.[22] Mutual defection, with each player being sentenced to three years, is a pure Nash equilibrium in this game because neither player acting alone can improve upon it by altering her conduct. And yet, the outcome is inferior to the alternative strategy of mutual cooperation for both Alex and Brad. This undesirable outcome emerges from each player's rational strategy as a response to the payoffs and the other player's possible strategies.

This familiar game provides a foundation for many basic features of game theoretical analysis. The prisoners' dilemma is shown above in its *normal form*.[23] This form of game identifies the players, the available player strategies, and the payoffs that result from each combination of player strategies.[24] Although the prisoners' dilemma matrix specifies payoffs for each combined set of strategies, it is the relationship between and among payoffs, as opposed to the nominal payoffs themselves, that motivates each prisoner's strategy. In this game, the combination of individual strategies drives the outcome toward mutual defection. We can change the nominal payoffs without changing the prisoners' dilemma provided that the numbers render defection the rational strategy for each prisoner without regard to the other prisoner's strategy.

As with any game, it is possible that the assumptions used to generate the payoffs fail to actually capture the stakes. Other factors not captured in these numbers might motivate one or both prisoners to respond differently, thus avoiding this seemingly problematic result. For example, it is possible that loyalty, morality, or guilt might motivate Alex or Brad to decline to testify against the other despite the resulting personal consequences. In police dramas, for example, it is commonplace for a parent who feels guilty about the plight of her or his child to "take the fall" by declining to testify.[25] And yet, if we focused only on the threatened sanctions that the police presented to each party, and set aside emotional factors, the incentives would form the basis for a classic prisoners' dilemma.

By way of contrast, consider the doctrine of spousal privilege.[26] This rule prevents the state from forcing a husband and wife into a prisoners' dilemma, at least when prosecuting either spouse is impossible without the other spouse's incriminating

---

by choosing a different strategy given the strategy the other chooses. The strategy of each player must be a best response to the strategies of the other"). KEN BINMORE, FUN AND GAMES: A TEXT ON GAME THEORY 12 n.8 (1992) (stating that Nash equilibrium "arises when each player's strategy choice is a best reply to the strategy choice of the other players."); MATTHEW RIDLEY, THE ORIGINS OF VIRTUE: HUMAN INSTINCTS AND THE EVOLUTION OF COOPERATION 58 (1996) ("The definition of a Nash equilibrium is when each player's strategy is an optimal response to the strategies adopted by other players, and nobody has an incentive to deviate from their chosen strategy.").

[22] Some texts define the Nash concept to require that "each player adopts a particular strategy with certainty." BAIRD ET AL., *supra* note 4, at 313.

[23] ROBERT GIBBONS, GAME THEORY FOR APPLIED ECONOMISTS 3 (1992); BAIRD ET AL., *supra* note 4, at 7–8, 312.

[24] BAIRD ET AL., *supra* note 4, at 7–8.

[25] *Spoiler Alert*: Or for a spouse following an affair! *See The Affair, Season 2* (Showtime television broadcast 2015).

[26] FED. R. EVID. 501 incorporates common law privileges and has been construed to incorporate the longstanding spousal privilege. For a general discussion, see Bruce I. McDaniel, Annotation, *Marital Privilege Under Rule 501 of Federal Rules of Evidence*, 46 A.L.R. FED. 735 (1980).

testimony. Why might the legal system seek to avoid allowing prosecutors to construct a prisoners' dilemma as between spouses, but not as between a parent and child? Should there be a more general familial testimonial privilege? Why or why not?

While it is possible to incorporate psychological or other factors into the matrix payoffs, doing so has the potential to change the anticipated rational behavior. Depending upon the specific changes, the altered payoffs might transform the prisoners' dilemma into a different game with a different equilibrium solution. As with economic rationality, game theory does not imply that personal motivations are invariably self-interested. In constructing a game, however, it is critically important that the specified payoffs capture the incentives. Given the payoffs in prisoners' dilemma set out in Table 15:1, the pure Nash equilibrium operates to the detriment of each prisoner as compared with the alternative of mutual cooperation.

B. The Prisoners' Dilemma in a World of Organized Crime

Consider the role of organized crime operations such as the Mafia or urban gangs in affecting prisoners' dilemma payoffs. Assume two mobsters are arrested and that the police provide each with the necessary incentives to testify against the other, or to remain silent, so as to form a prisoners' dilemma. Further assume, however, that each mobster knows that if he defects, he will be subject to severe punishment from within the organized crime syndicate that far exceeds the maximum punishment that the prosecutor threatens to impose. The nature of organized crime thus changes the payouts in what otherwise might have looked like a prisoners' dilemma game, thereby limiting the prosecutor's ability to induce a mutual defection strategy. In assessing the nature of this game, therefore, it is important to consider not only the payoffs that the prosecutor produces, but also the *total* individual payoffs, which include the private punishment imposed by the mob for defection.

The mob can also lower the cost of imprisonment, for example, by supporting an incarcerated mobster's dependents and promising work and income upon discharge.[27] In addition, because many organized crime organizations are family-based, psychological interdependency among the members has the potential to alter payoffs that otherwise resemble a prisoners' dilemma by increasing the value of cooperative strategies.[28]

---

[27] Such accommodations reduce, without eliminating, the cost of doing time, and take the form of "an offer he can't refuse." *Cf.* THE GODFATHER (Paramount 1972) (depicting Don Corleone extending such an offer to a non-mobster). Inmates associated with organized crime, or with urban street gangs, might also experience other benefits within prison systems, including prestige and protections against violence, given the risk of retaliation inside the prison, or upon release, by affiliated mob members.

[28] Consider for example the famous blood oaths that members of mob families take. The members of such organizations must swear absolute obedience to their superiors, putting the crime family ahead of their own family, and being prepared to sacrifice their lives should the mafia boss order it, a result instilled in part through such rituals. LETIZIA PAOLI, MAFIA BROTHERHOODS: ORGANIZED CRIME, ITALIAN STYLE 5, 67–70 (2003).

Finally, consider the famous "witness protection program," established by federal government.[29] To what extent does this program change the payoffs to cooperation as a countermeasure to mob-driven sanctions that inhibit the prosecutorial goal of encouraging mobsters to break ranks and defect? Does this program help to restore a benign prisoners' dilemma among coordinated criminals that organized crime has undermined? Why or why not?

II. THE ITERATED PRISONERS' DILEMMA: THE CASE OF PRECEDENT

We will now present a variation on the normal form prisoners' dilemma. This involves the possibility of endless iterations rather than a single round of play. To do so, we consider a highly stylized model of appellate court judging and the incentives of jurists to cooperate or defect from a regime of adherence to precedent. We do not suggest that this game accurately captures the dynamics of precedent in a multimember court. As we will see later in this book, there is a large literature on precedent and the motivations of judges to follow or avoid it.[30] Instead, we rely on this familiar context to explore the implications of three different prisoners' dilemma games: (1) a single period game, (2) a game with *endless iterations*, and (3) an iterated game with a *known end period*.[31] As we will see, even this more nuanced presentation fails to capture what might be better described as a spectrum, rather than discrete games.[32] When we revisit the discussion of precedent, we will consider a range of explanations, some relying on benefits to the judges themselves and others relying on societal benefits, for this common law judicial practice.[33] We now begin by translating the single-period prisoners' dilemma into a judicial context.

A. The Single-Period Judicial Prisoners' Dilemma

Imagine a judicial system in which each trial decision is subject to appeal before an appellate court consisting of a single judge. Each appellate court judge has the power to determine the legal principle used to decide the case before her, and also to determine

---

[29] This program was created as the product of a series of cases beginning in the 1960s through the work of, among others, Attorney General Robert Kennedy, as part of the war on organized crime. 18 U.S.C. § 3521 (2012). The Witness Security Program was authorized by the Organized Crime Control Act of 1970 and amended by the Comprehensive Crime Control Act of 1984. For a general discussion, see Douglas A. Kash, *Hiding in Plain Sight: A Peek into the Witness Security Program*, FBI LAW ENFORCEMENT BULL. May 2004, at 25, 27–28.

[30] *See infra* Chapter 21, Part I.B and Chapter 22, Part II.

[31] For a discussion of the historical origins of repeated games in the prisoners' dilemma context, see RIDLEY, *supra* note 21, at 58–60; *see also* WILLIAM POUNDSTONE, PRISONER'S DILEMMA 83–89; 101–31 (1992) (discussing history of prisoners' dilemma research including studies at RAND).

[32] *See infra* note 63, and accompanying text (discussing probabilistic end periods).

[33] In Chapters 21 and 22, we adapt the model set out below to study the scope of opinions, materiality, and vertical stare decisis on pyramidal common law courts. *See infra* Chapter 21, Part I.B.2. For general presentations of a similar game to that set out in the text, see Michael Abramowicz & Maxwell Stearns, *Defining Dicta*, 57 STAN. L. REV. 953, 1004–11 (2005); Erin O'Hara, *Social Constraint or Implicit Collusion?: Toward a Game Theoretical Analysis of Stare Decisis*, 24 SETON HALL L. REV. 736 (1993); Eric Rasmusen, *Judicial Legitimacy as a Repeated Game*, 10 J.L. ECON. & ORG. 63 (1994).

whether and to what extent she should respect prior decisions on similar points of law issued by other appellate judges on the same court.

Although the model can be generalized to include additional judges without affecting the results, to further simplify exposition, assume an appellate court with only two judges, Alice and Barb, each of whom adjudicates randomly assigned appeals. While some appeals present issues of first impression, meaning questions of law not previously resolved, more often the appeals present legal questions that either Alice or Barb have previously resolved. Assume that Alice and Barb hold different views on the underlying questions of legal policy with respect to an important subset of such cases.

Now consider how the judges view their obligation with respect to precedent if they anticipate only a single round of play and how their incentives might change if they instead anticipate multiple rounds of play. The single period game reflects a classic prisoners' dilemma. Each judge prefers to decide cases consistently with her own view as to how to resolve the legal merits, unimpeded by her colleague's prior, and sometimes contrary, rulings.[34] At the same time, each judge prefers that the other respect as precedent her rulings in cases implicating the same governing principles of law as this enhances her imprint on legal policy.

Before formalizing the prisoners' dilemma, we can capture its intuition. Each judge prefers to constrain her colleague to her own prior construction of legal materials without being reciprocally constrained. Assuming that there is a benefit to a regime of precedent, these incentives likely thwart that regime in favor of each judge deciding cases as she prefers even when a given case presents a question of law that her colleague has previously resolved.[35]

To formalize the game, we now translate the concepts of defection and cooperation into the context of judicial decision making. Cooperation means adhering to the other's decisions as precedent and defection means disregarding such decisions—failing to afford them precedential status. In addition, we will specify the payoffs, meaning the anticipated benefits of cooperation, and the anticipated costs of unilateral or mutual defection. There are two essential benefits associated with a precedent-based legal system.[36] First, a system of precedent affords each judge a more lasting imprint on the law, even though, at the same time, it prevents each judge from imposing that imprint in cases subject to a contrary precedent.[37] Second, a precedent-based regime generally enhances the stability of law. Those outside the legal system will benefit from knowledge that particular rules of law are

34 While there is a large literature that seeks to explore judicial motivations, it is unnecessary here to engage this debate. *See infra* Chapters 21 and 22 (reviewing literature). Whether we view the judges as policy makers or as legal formalists who differ in good faith on the substantive construction of governing legal sources, the stare decisis game remains the same.

35 To be clear, the judges might adhere to each other's decisions when they agree on the merits, but that is different than adhering to precedent as precedent. The obligation of precedent assumes that judges will apply even decisions with which they disagree simply because they resolve materially indistinguishable points of law. O'Hara, *supra* note 33, at 736.

36 For a discussion of other benefits to stare decisis, see *infra* Chapters 21 and 22, Parts I.B and I.C. (reviewing literature).

37 Professor O'Hara aptly labels this benefit eliminating "non-productive competition," meaning a constant state of flux in which each judge announces her preferred view of legal policy only to have it contradicted by a colleague's contrary ruling in a later round of play. O'Hara, *supra* note 33, at 738.

not a random consequence of which judge happens to decide the case, but rather are the product of a growing and stable body of precedent developed over the course of large numbers of cases with random assignments.

Assume that each judge benefits from a regime of respect for precedent both in individual terms by having a more lasting imprint on the law (the first benefit) and in institutional terms by being part of a judiciary with the added prestige associated with more reliable case law upon which society can rely (the second benefit). Further assume that despite these benefits, at the level of the individual appeal, each judge continues to place a greater value on her independent resolution of underlying legal policy. Each judge thus prefers that while the other judge respects her prior decisions as precedent, she retains the flexibility to ignore precedents with which she disagrees.

Assume that adhering to precedent provides payoffs to each judge of ten, and that unilateral defection produces payoffs of twelve for the defector and five for the cooperator. Even with unilateral defection, the cooperator receives the benefit of a stable body of case law (the second benefit), but faces the prospect of losing her preferred imprint on substantial bodies of developing doctrine (the first benefit). In the event that neither judge adheres to precedent, each receives a payoff of seven,[38] which reflects some influence on the law, albeit in a random and temporary manner (unless and until the other judge decides a similar case to the contrary), but without the personal or institutional benefits of a precedent-based system.

Table 15:2 depicts the underlying judicial prisoners' dilemma.

Table 15:2. Prisoners' Dilemma Confronting Appellate Judges

Payoffs for (Alice, Barb)	Barb cooperates	Barb defects
Alice cooperates	10, 10	5, 12
Alice defects	12, 5	**7, 7**

Although this game, unlike Table 15:1, depicts the payoffs with positive integers, the game remains the same. Without regard to what the other judge does, it is rational for each judge to defect and thus to avoid the obligation of precedent. If Alice adheres to precedent, then Barb can improve her payout from ten to twelve by defecting, and if Alice defects, Barb can improve her payout from five to seven by defecting. The payoffs are reciprocal, and thus the pure Nash equilibrium is mutual defection, with payoffs of (7, 7). This result obtains even though each judges would receive higher individual payoffs (10, 10) in a regime of mutual cooperation, respecting each other's opinions as precedent.

[38] We assume that the benefit of this random influence on the law exceeds the cost of sacrificing the general benefit of precedent (the second benefit) in a regime that is dominated by the other judge.

B. The Iterated Judicial Prisoners' Dilemma

Now assume that Alice and Barb anticipate future interactions over multiple periods.[39] Each judge anticipates that her strategy in any given period, including the first, potentially affects the other judge's incentives in a later period. Evaluating how future iterations affect judicial incentives and behavior now involves a two-step process. First, we need to identify the changed incentives in future periods of play (or in the final period if we know when the game ends), and then, through a process of *backward induction*, assess the consequences of the outcome in each subsequent period concerning how the game is played in the immediately preceding round. We continue this process of backward induction until we return to the initial period of play.

We begin by assuming that the judges do not know when the game will end and that they therefore act in each round as if there will be a future round of play. Although obviously no game can go on forever, for expositional purposes, we refer to this game as involving endless iterations. We then relax this assumption and consider how introducing a known end period affects incentives in each round of play. To identify the payoffs in a late period (when the final period is unknown) or the final period (when it is known), we need to consider how the possibility of future iterations can alter the judges' incentives to cooperate by adhering to precedent, or to defect, thus producing a regime without the benefit of precedent. As we will see, the anticipated future interaction has the potential to alter the calculations in each period of play from those in a standard prisoners' dilemma to an alternative set of payoffs that yields mutual cooperation as the pure-Nash equilibrium.

Assume first that there is no known end period, and, therefore, that within any given round, the judges anticipate a subsequent round of play.[40] This version of the game produces a benefit from cooperation that the single period game, depicted in Table 15:2, does not capture. While we provide a matrix that expresses these payoffs numerically below, for now consider the intuition. The most notable factor influencing the change in payoffs is that mutual cooperation now produces an anticipated stream of future benefits over many periods, rather than just a one-shot benefit. Conversely, defection produces an anticipated set of forgone benefits if the result is an endless stream of mutual defections.[41]

Robert Axelrod has aptly described this phenomenon as the "shadow of the future."[42] The idea is that the anticipated benefits of repeated mutual cooperation versus repeated mutual defection in some cases will be sufficiently large to outweigh even the cost of enduring an isolated instance of the other player's defection in a given round of

---

[39] For simplicity, assume that each iteration, or subgame, represents a discrete number of cases or a specific judicial term and that each judge issues all decisions on the same day, for example, at the end of the term.

[40] These stylized assumptions allow us to introduce an important benefit of cooperation that is not captured in the single period game and that, as shown below, is potentially eliminated through the process of backward induction or unraveling. *See infra* pp. 640–641 (describing unraveling).

[41] As in the prior discussions, it is also important to emphasize here that in the payoff matrix, table 15:3, the numbers are relevant only for the relationships they create for the individual and combined strategies as opposed to specific values associated with a discounted income stream from future cooperation or defection.

[42] ROBERT AXELROD, THE EVOLUTION OF COOPERATION 12 (1984).

play. If so, then each player is rationally motivated to cooperate in each single round of play (or within each *subgame*). Notably, in this game, the result obtains whether or not the other player cooperates or defects.

This result rests on an important assumption about the *discount rate*, meaning the present discounted value of the benefits of future cooperation or the present discounted cost of future defection.[43] To achieve the benefits of future cooperation, the discount rate must be low enough that players do not treat the repeated game as if only immediate payoffs are controlling. Depending upon how heavily one discounts the value of future rounds of play, game theorists can model the iterated prisoners' dilemma to produce mutual cooperation, mutual defection, or anywhere in between.[44] In the discussion that follows we assume a sufficiently low discount rate to generate the possibility of mutual cooperation. Based upon this assumption, the pure Nash equilibrium strategy shifts from mutual defection (the outcome of the single period game) to mutual cooperation (the outcome of a game with endless iterations).

Alice rationally anticipates that Barb will obtain two benefits if Alice cooperates by adhering to Barb's opinions as precedent: first, the specific benefit of enhancing the value (or durability) of Barb's decisions, and second, the general benefit of improving reliance on the rule of law and thus the prestige of the court on which Alice and Barb sit. As a result, Alice anticipates that Barb will seek to reward her cooperative behavior in the next round by adopting a similar cooperative strategy. Once again, these payoffs are reciprocal, and so Barb anticipates that Alice has the same incentives to reward Barb's adherence to her cases as precedent. Based upon these assumptions, each judge is motivated to cooperate in each subgame, whether or not the other judge cooperates (adheres to precedent) or defects (disregards precedent). Mutual cooperation thus emerges as the dominant strategy as each judge seeks to avoid the danger of incurring the lower individual payoffs resulting from an ongoing stream of defections.

Table 15:3. Iterated Prisoners' Dilemma Respecting Precedent

Payoffs for (Alice, Barb)	**Barb cooperates**	**Barb defects**
Alice cooperates	**15, 15**	10, 12
Alice defects	12, 10	8, 8

We can translate this game into a matrix with altered payoffs and incentives. The changed payoffs reflect the altered incentives in any single period within the iterated game resulting from anticipated future rounds of play. As shown in Table 15:3, if Alice cooperates, it is also in Barb's interest to cooperate as doing so raises her payoffs from ten to fifteen. This reflects the value of having her decisions honored as precedent and of anticipating a continued regime of adherence to precedent. Conversely, if Alice defects,

[43] For a discussion of discount rates, see RASMUSEN, *supra* note 10, at 486; RICHARD A. IPPOLITO, ECONOMICS FOR LAWYERS 338–40 (2005).

[44] This result is known as the folk theorem of the iterated prisoners' dilemma, because even before it was formalized, it formed part of the general understanding among those who employed game theoretical tools. BAIRD ET AL., *supra* note 4, at 307–08; *see also* Eric Rasmusen, *Folk Theorems for the Observable Implication of Repeated Games*, 32 THEORY & DECISION 147 (1992).

thereby reducing Barb's immediate influence on the law, it nonetheless remains in Barb's interest to cooperate. Despite the immediate short-term loss, reflected in the reduced payoff from fifteen to ten, cooperation still produces the benefit of an anticipated stream of mutual cooperation in later rounds. By contrast, while punishment allows Barb an immediate imprint on the law, that benefit is smaller than the cost of inciting an endless stream of mutual defection, with the resulting lower payoff of eight.

Once again, these payoffs are reciprocal, and so Alice and Barb have the same incentives. In this game, each judge is motivated to cooperate in each future round of play without regard to whether the other judge abides or avoids precedent in a given round of play. The mutual cooperation regime dominates as a result of the anticipated losses that punishment will invite in each future round.

While the preceding analysis suggests that under some circumstances each judge will suffer isolated instances of defection without imposing punishment, this does not mean that Alice or Barb will reward a constant stream of defection with cooperation. If Alice repeatedly defects, then beyond some point, Barb might punish that defection even at the risk of producing a perpetual stream of mutual defection, with correspondingly low payoffs. The number of defections required to generate punishment depends upon the specific strategy each player employs regarding how to respond to defection by the other player. In the subpart that follows, we will consider several of the potential strategies that the players might employ.

1. Tit for Tat Strategies: From Committed Pacifist to Grim Trigger

In Robert Axelrod's analysis of *tit for tat* strategies, he demonstrates a variety of circumstances in which the most effective strategy is to mimic the behavior of the other party to the game.[45] Cooperation yields cooperation and defection yields defection. In games yielding this strategy, imposing the *tit* as punishment for the *tat* is not an end in itself. Rather, the punishment is intended as a credible signal designed to motivate future cooperative behavior.

The Axelrod strategy can be understood as a form of contingent cooperation, meaning that each player signals a desire to behave cooperatively (or nicely) as a function of the other player's demonstrated willingness to reciprocate. Axelrod has demonstrated that in a variety of contexts, tit for tat is an optimal strategy, yielding the highest payoffs, even though it requires nothing more elaborate than simple period-by-period mimicking behavior.

It is important to note, however, that although tit for tat is an effective strategy over the long run, it is not necessarily optimal in all short-run instances or in all contexts. For instance, tit for tat is not likely to prove an effective strategy if the other player has committed (or bonded) to a defection strategy; if there is a high probability that the game will soon end; or if, contrary to the game with Alice and Barb, the discount rate is sufficiently high. Thus, in some settings, it is better to follow a more aggressive

[45] Robert Axelrod & William Hamilton, *The Evolution of Cooperation*, 211 SCIENCE 1390–96 (1981); AXELROD, *supra* note 42; Jonathan Bendor, *Uncertainty and the Evolution of Cooperation*, 37 J. CONFLICT RESOL. 709 (1993); Robert Axelrod & Douglas Dion, *The Further Evolution of Cooperation*, 242 SCIENCE 1385 (1988).

punishment strategy, namely *two tits for a tat* or the more extreme *grim trigger*, while in others it is better to follow a more lenient strategy, for example a *tit for two tats* or the more extreme *committed pacifism*. Two tits for a tat punishes twice for one defection and a tit for two tats punishes once after two defections. The most severe punishment strategy is grim trigger, which disallows the other player to induce cooperation after a single instance of defection. Conversely, the most lenient strategy is committed pacifism, meaning that regardless of what the other player does, no punishment will follow. We present a range of strategies, from strict to lenient, along a single dimension in Figure 15:1.

Figure 15:1 Spectrum of Potential Punishment Strategies

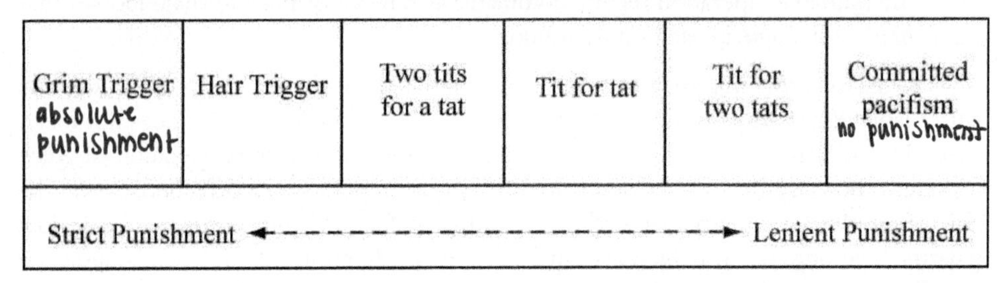

Grim Trigger
Hair Trigger
Two tits for a tat
Tit for tat
Tit for two tats
Committed pacifism
Strict Punishment
Lenient Punishment

The optimal strategy in any circumstance depends on a combination of factors. These include the anticipated value of mutual cooperation, the plausibility that the other player will construe leniency as a signal to restore the benefits of mutual cooperation, or the risk that she will instead view it as a sign of weakness to be exploited. Most importantly, except in the extreme cases of grim trigger and committed pacifism, the players have the potential to alter their strategies over time as they update their information about the other player's likely response to their selected strategy.

Axelrod has demonstrated that, in general, some form of *contingent nice* strategy, including tit for tat, tends to prevail over extreme strategies.[46] Can you identify circumstances favoring more extreme strategies? What about unilateral disarmament? Is this a beneficial strategy to avoiding war? Does the answer depend on whether the other side has armed solely as a defensive measure (a result dispelled by the disarmament) or instead has done so with aggression in mind? Conversely, grim or even *hair trigger*—meaning a rapid punishment for even slight provocations just short of grim trigger—risks devastation when signals are potentially ambiguous and the other side's good faith disagreement is misread as an act of aggression.

Does the generations-long family feud between the Hatfields and McCoys illustrate the dangers of hair-trigger strategies?[47] What about the *three-strikes rule*, which results in permanent incarceration upon the third conviction, regardless of the severity of that offense? Is this game better characterized as a *tit for three tats* or as grim trigger on the third offense? If the latter, is there a sound justification for imposing a grim trigger strategy at that stage? Why or why not? Is the contract law doctrine of anticipatory repudiation an

---

[46] AXELROD, *supra* note 42, at 176.

[47] Although the Hatfield/McCoy feud is the most famous, such family feuds were not uncommon in the nineteenth century in the Appalachian region. For an analysis linking such feuding strategies to a Scottish highland culture in which fending off threats to goat herds demanded a reputation for the herder's immediate willingness to exact revenge, see MALCOLM GLADWELL, OUTLIERS: THE STORY OF SUCCESS 164–70 (2008).

illustration of grim trigger? Why or why not? How is the choice of strategy in each instance affected by the discount rate?

Let us now return to the judicial context. Depending on the payoffs from mutual cooperation, Alice and Barb might fear an end to precedent as the judicial equivalent to feuding. As a result, each might elect to engage in a softer strategy, between committed pacifism and grim trigger, hoping to restore the preferred regime of precedent. Notice also that if the iterated prisoners' dilemma game is played among a larger number of players, for example an appellate court with several judges rather than two, the risk of defection might be more severe. Without some degree of tolerance, even a good faith dispute among a subset of judges might threaten to destroy a cooperative norm that is beneficial to the larger group. This is especially true if there is no practical means to mete out punishment to only defectors, as might be the case for example if jurists meet in panels of three, rather than in isolation. And even with our two-judge illustration, some legitimate disagreements over the scope of governing precedent is inevitable. It might therefore be preferable to follow a *benefit of the doubt* strategy (a tit for several tats) rather than to assume that each contested application of precedent is necessarily a defection and thus to follow a simple tit for tat strategy.[48]

Axelrod further suggests that cycles of retribution have the effect of leaving money on the table, meaning that the players forgo valuable benefits of cooperative equilibria that can be obtained through more accommodating strategies. Depending upon the strategies that players follow, they might also invite other, competitor institutions to come in and employ more beneficial cooperative strategies at the expense of those who follow excessively myopic or grim forms of punishment. Alternatively, depending on the magnitude of the resulting losses from short-sighted punishment strategies, existing institutions might modify their structures to produce incentives facilitating more benign results.

Is it possible that common law judicial systems impose a strong cooperation (respect precedent) norm so that individual trigger-happy jurists (those who would punish perceived defection with actual defection) get reined-in, thereby promoting a benefit of the doubt strategy that is conducive to mutual cooperation? If so, does that make the payoffs from Figure 15:3 more plausible in this context of precedent than those in Figure 15:2? Why or why not? Do cooperative norms respecting precedent more likely arise as a consequence of the hierarchical judicial structure of common law systems, and thus through vertical precedent, or through mutual cooperation in a repeat game on the same level court? (We will reconsider these questions in Chapter 21). Can you identify circumstances in which groups trapped in a cycle of retaliation might simply be displaced by another group with more cooperative internal norms?[49]

---

[48] The converse is also true; it is not even necessary that the defecting party actually intend to defect. Indeed, it is not necessary that she defect at all so long as any action is *perceived* as a defection by the other party, with the result of prompting retaliation.

[49] For a general discussion, see Todd J. Zywicki, *Was Hayek Right About Group Selection After All?*, 13 REV. AUSTRIAN ECON. 81 (2000).

2. *Trigger Strategy Equilibrium*

When players adopt an optimal set of strategies as needed to generate beneficial cooperation, the combined result is sometimes referred to as a *trigger strategy equilibrium*. This means that the ultimate outcome of the iterated prisoners' dilemma game turns on the values associated with cooperation or defection and the optimal strategies needed to reward cooperation or to punish defection. As noted above, the maintenance of a cartel is an example of a prisoners' dilemma game. In this context, game theorists have relied upon the concept of trigger strategy equilibrium to identify optimal strategies for members to monitor and punish defection from agreed-upon production quotas, thereby maintaining a cooperative equilibrium.[50] Each individual cartelist has an incentive to cheat on the agreement by secretly increasing production and lowering price. If the cartel members reciprocate defection with further defection, the cartel breaks down. If, on the other hand, cartel members never punish defection, the result is an unsustainable unilateral defection benefiting the defectors and harming the remaining producers as the defectors benefit from the artificially raised price, while also having a negative effect on that price through the higher production levels. In general, private cartels are very difficult to sustain, especially as the number of participants increases. As in the judging context, some good faith disputes inevitably emerge in which producers disagree as to whether particular production levels are or are not compliant with the cartel terms. Although some degree of tolerance might be necessary to sustain multilateral cartel relationships (thus avoiding the grim trigger), endless tolerance makes the cartel impossible to sustain (thus avoiding committed pacifism). Trigger strategy equilibria represent possible equilibrium solutions to the problem of punishment in response to an instance (or several instances) of defection as required to bring the defector back into the fold of cooperation.

As applied to the context of judging, the analysis suggests that Alice will sometimes cooperate even faced with Barb's defection. It does not imply, however, that Alice's patience is unlimited. Beyond a certain defection level, Alice will punish Barb's by also defecting. As in the cartel, the goal is to calibrate the optimal level of tolerance for defection with the proper frequency (and level) of punishment. There is a spectrum of strategies that the players can employ.[51] As Axelrod demonstrates, however, neither extreme strategy is likely to produce the highest payoffs over time. Instead, the players are more likely to settle on an intermediate strategy that condones some defection but that, beyond a certain point, imposes punishment. Moreover, the optimal strategy might change over time as the other party alters her or his conduct, thus explaining why the extreme strategies of committed pacifism or grim trigger, which disallow such calibration over time, are rarely optimal. To evaluate how strategies might change over time, it is helpful to consider the probabilistic framework known as *Bayes' theorem*.

---

[50] For a general discussion, see, e.g., Robert Porter & Douglas Zona, *Detection of Bid Rigging in Procurement Auctions*, 101 J. POL. ECON. 518 (1993); Joseph E. Harrington, Jr., *Detecting Cartels*, *in* HANDBOOK OF ANTITRUST ECONOMICS 213 (Paolo Buccirossi ed., 2008).

[51] For a general discussion, see James Friedman, *A Non-cooperative Equilibrium for Supergames*, 38 REV. ECON. STUD. 1 (1971).

3. *Bayes' Theorem: The Importance of Updating Information*

Bayes' theorem relies upon observation of the relationship between two random phenomena in the past to make predictions about the relationship between those phenomena in the future.[52] Whether we are discussing business cartels seeking to optimize output and price, or appellate judges seeking to optimize the value of a precedent-driven system, each decision maker will rationally base her or his behavior on expectations concerning the behavior of other players in the game. Bayes' Theorem predicts the likely occurrence of observed phenomenon *A* based upon its degree of correspondence to observed phenomenon *B*. When *A* is observed along with *B*, the predictive force of the observed relationship concerning *A* is referred to as *conditional probability*. When *A* is observed independently of *B*, the predictive force of the observed relationship concerning *A* is referred to as *marginal probability*. Bayes' theorem posits that prior observed occurrences of *A* as a function of *B* and independent of *B* provide meaningful probabilistic data concerning the likelihood that *A* will occur in future periods. Most notably, the probabilities concerning *A* occurring in the future adjust along with changed observations regarding the incidence of *A* as a function of, or independent of, *B* in the past.[53]

Formally, Bayes' Theorem applies to efforts to determine the other player's *type*, meaning if she is a cooperator or a defector. Sometimes this can be discerned within a single period, but not always. In more complex games, the theorem can be extended to assess a more refined reading of type, such as *defector*, unless subject to a particular level of meted out punishment; otherwise *cooperator*. Newly acquired information in each round helps to locate the point that will tip a potential defector to behave cooperatively instead. As applied to trigger strategy equilibria, Bayes' theorem implies that decision makers seeking to motivate others to cooperate will try to gauge the other party's cooperative behavior as a function of decisions to punish or not to punish defection.

In this analysis, the purpose of punishment is not retribution, but to provide credible information that will make predictions of future behavior more reliable. For instance, the failure to respond to defection with punishment might provide a signal that one is a pushover who can be taken advantage of on a consistent basis, and responding with full

---

[52] Steven C. Salop, *Evaluating Uncertain Evidence with Sir Thomas Bayes: A Note for Teachers*, J. ECON. PERSP., Summer 1987, at 178.

[53] Bayes' theorem does not imply a causal connection between *A* and *B* even when probabilistic data supporting conditional probabilities as between the two phenomena are highly significant. For example, the conditional probability that (*A*) people carry umbrellas when (*B*) drivers use windshield wipers is high. The fact that drivers use windshield wipers, however, obviously does not cause people to carry umbrellas. Conversely people carrying umbrellas does not cause drivers to use windshield wipers. Instead, rain, an independent factor, causes both observed phenomena, and for that reason, the correlation, or conditional probability, between the two events is significant. Despite the lack of a causal relationship, it is reasonable to predict that when we next observe drivers using windshield wipers (or people carrying umbrellas), we are likely also to observe people carrying umbrellas (or drivers using windshield wipers), based upon a high conditional probability. For an illustration involving a claimed link between night time lighting for children and myopia, see Karla Zadnik et al., *Myopia and Ambient Night-time Lighting*, 404 NATURE 143 (2000) (providing alternative account linked to hereditary nature of myopia and an increased probability that myopic parents will use nighttime lighting for their children than non-myopic parents).

force for even a slight provocation might signal recklessness and thus a person to be avoided. It is not necessary that one meet every defection with punishment, so long as the failure to do so does not cause the other party to believe that one will never respond with punishment.

In the context of appellate judging, if Alice observes Barb defecting and immediately punishes her, she might then witness Barb continuing to defect, leading to an endless stream of defection. Alternatively, if Alice does not punish Barb's defection, she might observe Barb cooperating in the next round. This might mean that she misread the earlier signal, and that the perceived defection was a good faith disagreement on the scope of a precedent. Alternatively, it might mean that Barb is only inclined to defect on rare occasions, and that Alice is better off condoning such rare defections than risking an end to the general regime of mutual cooperation. If Alice continues to watch Barb and witnesses another defection, she might impose a punishment (a tit for two tats). If at this point, Barb declines to defect for an even longer period of time, Alice might infer that she has hit upon an effective strategy and thus continue to adhere to it. We do not, of course, suggest that a single change in strategy will produce a stable and benign result. This merely illustrates the kind of adjustments required to facilitate improved strategies over time.

This simple story suggests that in selecting among strategies, Alice benefits from observing Barb's behavior in each given round of play and from updating her response accordingly. It is possible that Alice's tit for two tats strategy yields a sufficiently low level of defection by Barb that Alice sticks with it and views the occasional additional defection by Barb as the price of securing the larger benefits of mutual cooperation over time. Or it is possible that further refinements prove necessary over time.[54]

4. *Quality-Adjusted Pricing as Affecting Success or Failure of Cartels*

The ability of a party to defect from a cartel or other agreement is also affected by the likelihood that other members to the cartel can detect and punish cheating. As detection costs rise, it becomes easier to cheat and to avoid punishment. This is especially notable when cartel members cheat by adjusting the quality of the goods they sell, rather than simply by reducing price for goods of the same quality as sold by other cartel members. Commodity cartels are more likely to be sustainable than those for complex, or bundled, goods and services in which improved quality is a substitute for reduced price.[55]

If, for example, airlines tried to fix the prices of fares, some airlines would be tempted to cheat on the agreement by providing tastier meals, better customer service, friendlier flight attendants, free movies, or more comfortable seating. Indeed, this is just

---

[54] In this game, the conditional probability was how much defection follows from a given punishment, and the marginal probability is how much defection arises independently of punishment. This distinction is important because in a world with imperfect information, it is possible that judges appear to defect based upon good-faith disagreement over whether a claimed precedent is controlling in the case they are deciding. If so, some defection arises with or without punishment, simply due to disagreement, while other defection arises as a rational consequence of the selected punishment strategy.

[55] For an example of a worldwide cartel in the production of the commodity lysine, see KURT EICHENWALD, THE INFORMANT (2000). This was made into an enjoyable Steven Soderbergh movie starring Matt Damon in 2009. *See* THE INFORMANT! (Warner Bros. Pictures 2009).

what occurred in the 1970s, when prior to deregulation of the airline industry, the Civil Aeronautics Board (CAB) set the fares for all airline transportation at above-market rates.[56] Airlines competed for passengers by providing amenities such as in-flight lounges and other luxuries, all of which disappeared following deregulation and the accompanying reduction in airline fares back toward a market-clearing price. Because it is more costly to monitor all aspects of quality with complex services like air transit, quality-adjusted pricing makes cartel enforcement more difficult than for commodities.[57] Similarly, if it is difficult to punish a particular defector (say because that party is substantially larger than other members of the cartel or because it is a governmental entity), then the cartel will be unstable. Absent the ability to effectively monitor and punish cheating, cartels generally cannot be maintained over time.

In the context of judging, this analysis implies that Alice might not always be able to determine whether Barb has defected from a regime of mutual respect for precedent. The complexities of distinguishing holding and dicta, and of determining whether case distinctions are legitimate or an effort to avoid precedent, raise the cost of enforcing a regime of precedent and increase the risks associated with imposing punishment. Do these nuances make the task of developing a regime of precedent on the same level court implausible? Why or why not? If you conclude that they do, can you think of other mechanisms that create the benefits of precedent without imposing such costs?[58]

5. Extensive Form Games and Subgame Perfection

As previously stated, one danger of an excessively strict punishment strategy is that premature punishment (following a good faith disagreement that was not intended as a defection) might wrongly signal a willingness to forgo the benefits of mutual cooperation.[59] The critical point is that for mutual cooperation to emerge as the dominant strategy, each juncture, or subgame, in the iterated game must produce mutual cooperation. Professor Eric Rasmusen has explained that to generate this seemingly happy outcome, the game must satisfy the condition of "subgame perfectness."[60] Rasmusen explains:

---

[56] Paul L. Joskow & Roger G. Noll, *Economic Regulation*, *in* AMERICAN ECONOMIC POLICY IN THE 1980S, at 367, 380–82 (Martin Feldstein ed., 1995).

[57] For a related discussion involving the difficulty of cartelizing to end payola, the practice of paying to get favored radio or other media play in the music industry, as a result of the difficulty in detecting cheating, see Ronald H. Coase, *Payola in Radio and Television Broadcasting*, 22 J.L. & ECON. 269 (1979).

[58] We will revisit this question in Chapters 21 and 22 (discussing pyramidal courts and vertical precedent).

[59] Julio J. Rotemberg & Garth Saloner, *A Supergame-Theoretic Model of Price Wars During Booms*, 76 AM. ECON. REV. 390 (1986) (demonstrating that in cartel context, an observed production increase leads to an inference problem regarding cheating, or reflecting, instead, a shock in demand, and thus makes difficult assessing whether to pull the trigger strategy).

[60] RASMUSEN, *supra* note 10, at 108. Although each subgame pure equilibrium is a Nash equilibrium, not all Nash equilibria are subgame pure equilibria. Instead, depending on such factors as discount rates and punishment strategies, some Nash solutions for the overall game might include rounds of play without subgame perfection. Robert Gibbons, *An Introduction to Applicable Game Theory*, J. ECON. PERSP., Winter 1997, at 127, 135 (noting that "to be subgame-perfect, the players' strategies must first be a Nash equilibrium and must then fulfill an additional requirement" and that "[t]he point of this additional requirement is, as with backward induction, to rule out Nash equilibria that rely on non-credible threats.")

A strategy profile is a **subgame perfect Nash equilibrium** if (a) it is a Nash equilibrium for the entire game; and (b) its relevant action rules are a Nash equilibrium for every subgame.[61]

This means that in each round of play, Alice and Barb need to give each other, if perceived to defect, the benefit of the doubt to avoid a cycle of defection. It is not impossible to recover from punishment following defection, but as previously stated, the likelihood of this result depends upon the value each side attaches to cooperation and defection and on how each side updates its strategies based upon information from the other player. Occasional defection followed by punishment might not render a cycle of defection inevitable, but it does lower the likelihood of mutual cooperation, holding all else constant. Depending on the valuations attached to the cooperation regime, there is a risk that the players might, in fact, wind up leaving the money on the table. In the next and final variation of the prisoners' dilemma, we consider another difficulty that can shift the potentially benign mutual cooperation outcome back to mutual defection.

6. Backward Induction and Unraveling

The final difficulty that can affect the outcome in an iterated prisoners' dilemma game is unraveling. Assume for now that in an endless iterated prisoners' dilemma, the result is mutual cooperation. This result follows from the assumption of endless rounds of play and the possibility of punishment in each future period. Of course, there are never actual endless rounds of play in any game, although it is possible that neither player knows when the game will end, and thus whether she or the other player will make the final move. We will now assume, instead, that the players anticipate a specific period at which their interactions will end. In this variation on the game represented in Table 15:3, we can introduce the concepts of *backward induction* and *unraveling* to demonstrate how this changed assumption affects incentives at each decision node.

To simplify, assume that the judges anticipate six periods of play, after which the game stops. We begin by considering the players' incentives in period six, the final known period.[62] In period 6, there is no longer any promise of reward or threat of punishment in the very next period, because there will be no period 7 in which such rewards or threats can be carried out. As a result, in period 6, the judges have the same incentives to cooperate or defect as they had in the single period prisoners' dilemma, depicted in Table 15:2. Now consider the incentives in the second-to-final period. In period 5, each judge knows that in the final period 6, the result will be mutual defection without regard to whether she cooperates or defects in period 5. As a result, there is no effective possibility of reward for cooperation or punishment for defection. Regardless of what each player does, period 6 will produce a regime of mutual defection. Since the judges in period 6 will behave as if they had defected in period 5, regardless of what the other judge does, the dominant strategy is defection. Through backwards induction, we see that this game unravels, meaning that the benefits of an iterated prisoners' dilemma game, as reflected in Table 15:3, revert from the last period through the first to those of a standard prisoners'

---

[61] RASMUSEN, *supra* note 10, at 109. *See also* Ayres, *supra* note 13, at 1305 ("A combination of strategies is a perfect Nash equilibrium if the strategies satisfy the Nash requirements for every subgame.").

[62] Because the prior game did not have a known end period, we instead modeled incentives based upon a future period in which the players continued to anticipate a subsequent sound of play.

dilemma, as reflected in Table 15:2. As a result, with a known end period, the incentives among the players are the same as if the game had only a single period. The anticipated benign outcome, mutual cooperation, in a game with endless iterations, unravels in favor of mutual defection, beginning with the last known period of play and all the way down to the initial period of play when there is a certain end period.

As the preceding discussion demonstrates, the game theoretical analysis does not suggest a simple binary choice between a game with endless iterations (yielding cooperation) or a game with a known end period (yielding mutual defection). Until now we have assumed that while the judges do not know each other's strategies, they do have information concerning whether there is an opportunity to reward cooperation or punish defection in a subsequent round of play.

An alternative is to introduce uncertainty or a *probabilistic end period* in the game itself. Game theorists have demonstrated that depending upon assumptions concerning degrees of certainty and the discount rate, it is possible to construct games in which, absent complete information about when the game will end, parties nonetheless retain mutual incentives to engage in cooperative strategies.[63] As previously noted, within such games, a great deal turns on the values assigned to the discounted future benefits of anticipated cooperation within each round of play. By changing those values, even slightly, modelers can affect outcomes within particular subgames and within the overall game, thus inviting, once again, concerns about subgame perfectness and perfectness for the overall game.

7. *Questions and Comments*

Article III judges, who hold life tenure (and thus for whom there might be no known end period), embrace a regime of precedent. So too do state judges who are often appointed for previously identified terms of years.[64] Does this help to resolve the origins of precedent, or does it make the analysis more difficult? Does the preceding game theoretical analysis help to identify the conceptual origins of the common law regime of precedent?[65] Why or why not? Scholars also debate whether a system of law founded on precedent generally provides better, more predictable, or more stable doctrine than civilian regimes, which nominally eschew precedent in favor of code law interpreted in

---

[63] Drew Fudenberg & Eric Maskin, *The Folk Theorem in Repeated Games with Discounting or with Incomplete Information*, 54 ECONOMETRICA 533 (1986).

[64] Gary M. Anderson, William F. Shughart II & Robert D. Tollison, *On the Incentives of Judges to Enforce Legislative Wealth Transfers*, 32 J.L. & ECON. 215, 220 (1989) (discussing variations in tenure of state court judges in contrast to the life tenure of federal judges).

[65] We are not drawing a historical distinction between precedent and stare decisis. In early jurisprudential history, precedent was linked to large bodies of case law relied upon to establish a proposition of law. *See* Harold J. Berman & Charles J. Reid, Jr., *The Transformation of English Legal Science: From Hale to Blackstone*, 45 EMORY L.J. 437, 444–51 (1996). Stare decisis, meaning the obligation to abide by a particular decision on a point of law as precedent, is a more recent development. *See id.* at 513–16 (discussing use of case method in influencing conventional understanding of stare decisis); *see also* Hart v. Massanari, 266 F.3d 1155, 1175 (9th Cir. 2001) (Kozinski, J.) ("Case precedent at common law thus resembled much more what we call persuasive authority than the binding authority that is the backbone of much of the federal judicial system."). In modern jurisprudence, the terms are used interchangeably and we use them in that fashion in this discussion.

decisions that, at least in theory, only govern the immediate case.[66] What are the trade-offs between a precedent and non-precedent regime? Does the preceding analysis help to explain whether judges would rationally create a regime of precedent if the obligation to respect precedent did not otherwise exist? Why or why not? We will revisit these questions in Chapter 21.

In a hierarchical judicial system, inferior judges adhere to precedent when they fear reversal by a higher court. But do judges adhere to horizontal precedent of a co-equal court? What about when precedent threatens to constrain the result in a particularly important case? What happens if a particular judge does not follow precedent? Do other judges on the same level court impose punishment, or does punishment, if imposed at all, arise from elsewhere? Is it possible to punish an isolated defector without harming the regime of precedent for the court as a whole? Why or why not? If not, does this mean that the regime of precedent operates independently of the actions of individual judges on the court? And if that is true, does that imply that precedent is more likely to take vertical or horizontal form? Why?

Which, if any, of the games described thus far is most relevant in answering these questions? Do judges only adhere to precedent when they anticipate endless future periods? Do judges ever anticipate that there will be no end point? Based on probabilistic end periods, does that matter to the regime of precedent? What about state systems that appoint judges for periods of years, and thus with certain end periods? Why do they adhere to precedent? Does the unraveling problem prevent reliance upon game theory in developing a coherent account of precedent? If so, what alternative explanations can you devise? Is it possible that some structural features of the judiciary impose precedent without relying upon a trigger strategy equilibrium?[67]

C. Is the Prisoners' Dilemma Good or Bad?

We have now seen an illustration of a benign prisoners' dilemma (from a social perspective), namely the classic case involving persons who have committed serious offenses. And we have seen a potentially problematical prisoners' dilemma involving the breakdown in the stability of precedent in the law. Can you identify other examples of prisoners' dilemmas that produce net positive and net negative societal results? Can you identify mechanisms that help to resolve the problems that prisoners' dilemmas create in the negative case, or mechanisms that help to facilitate a prisoners' dilemma in the positive case? Is it fair to say that one objective of a well-functioning legal system is to facilitate beneficial prisoners' dilemmas and to devise solutions to problematical ones? If so, are judges well suited to the task of identifying good versus bad prisoners' dilemmas? Why or why not? How, if at all, does your answer relate to the debate described in Chapter 1 between Coase and Pigou?

---

[66] Abramowicz & Stearns, *supra* note 33, at 953; Todd J. Zywicki, *A Unanimity-Reinforcing Model of Efficiency in the Common Law: An Institutional Comparison of Common Law and Legislative Solutions to Large-Number Externality Problems*, 46 CASE W. RES. L. REV. 961, 996–1004 (1996); JOHN HENRY MERRYMAN & ROGELIO PÉREZ-PERDOMO, THE CIVIL LAW TRADITION: AN INTRODUCTION TO THE LEGAL SYSTEMS OF WESTERN EUROPE AND LATIN AMERICA (3d ed. 2007).

[67] *See infra* Chapter 21, Part I.B.5; *see also* Abramowicz & Stearns, *supra* note 33, at 953.

Consider the following additional examples of good and bad prisoners' dilemmas. Competitive markets place sellers in a prisoners' dilemma relationship with other sellers and buyers in a prisoners' dilemma relationship with other buyers. All firms would benefit if they could combine their strategies to restrict production and raise prices; all consumers would benefit if they could also combine their strategies to coordinate demand and reduce prices. Antitrust law generally seeks to break up cartels, or to prevent firms from adopting schemes that result in monopolistic pricing strategies, in favor of a larger number of competitive firms or practices more likely to promote competitive pricing.[68] Competitive markets, by definition, involve a large number of producers and consumers.

While the standard prisoners' dilemma is generally presented with two players, competitive markets nonetheless have the characteristic features of a benign multilateral prisoners' dilemma. Given the large numbers of players involved in competitive markets, producers and consumers are generally unable to create effective agreements to coordinate their behaviors. This holds true of both production levels, in the case of sellers, and consumption levels, in the case of buyers. It also applies to enforcing any agreements that producers or consumers previously made.[69] Assuming that these characterizations are fair, are restraints on monopoly or anticompetitive policies equivalent to a legal effort to create or perpetuate a benign prisoners' dilemma?

In some contexts, promoting competition might contradict other goals, complicating the claim that competition invariably corresponds to a good prisoners' dilemma. Consider an open-access resource, such as a fishery in a lake.[70] The fish in the lake should be harvested at a rate that maintains the long-term viability of the fish population, thereby maximizing the revenue stream over time. A single owner of the lake would harvest the fish accordingly. Where the lake is open to anyone, however, the fishermen are in a mutual prisoners' dilemma. If one fisherman forgoes a catch or throws back a fish that is too small so that it can be caught at a more optimal time, he runs the risk that a subsequent fisherman will not be as restrained. Indeed, the incentive of each fisherman, acting rationally, would be to catch as many fish as possible before others do, leading to a rapid depletion of the number of fish in the lake. If fishermen can overcome their collective-action problems and control access to the fishery, they can prevent the

---

[68] As David Evans and Keith Hylton have observed, antitrust law does not prohibit every method of exploiting monopoly power, including most notably decisions to charge a monopoly price. While antitrust law regulates specific problematic conduct that results in monopolistic strategies, according to the authors, it simultaneously balances the pricing concern against the dynamic incentives to undertake entrepreneurial efforts targeted toward innovation. Because the potential for monopoly profit is often an inducement to investing in an area characterized by high start-up costs, large scale economies, and declining average cost, the authors maintain that antitrust law sometimes applies a lighter hand when pursuing individual firms with monopoly power than firms engaged in combined pricing strategies with other firms. *See* David S. Evans & Keith N. Hylton, *The Lawful Acquisition and Exercise of Monopoly Power and its Implications for the Objectives of Antitrust*, 4 COMPETITION POL'Y INT'L 203 (2008).

[69] *See generally* Monroe Friedman, *Consumer Boycotts in the United States, 1970–1980: Contemporary Events in Historical Perspective*, 19 J. CONSUMER AFF. 96, 108 (1985) (acknowledging difficulty of measurement but positing that consumer boycotts are generally unsuccessful). For an interesting analysis of the various pressures that affect the success of boycotts, see Sankar Sen et al., *Withholding Consumption: A Social Dilemma Perspective on Consumer Boycotts*, 28 J. CONSUMER RES. 399 (2001).

[70] H. Scott Gordon, *The Economic Theory of a Common-Property Resource: The Fishery*, 62 J. POL. ECON. 124 (1954).

depletion of the resource. On the other hand, their efforts might run afoul of the antitrust laws, which forbid agreements to reduce competition. Some scholars have urged that the antitrust laws be modified or applied in such a manner as to permit private agreements among competitors when necessary to prevent the depletion of a common pool resource.[71]

Consider also the case of labor unions. Unions seek to cartelize labor. Why might the legal system willingly facilitate a solution to a supply side prisoners' dilemma affecting the sale of labor when it exhibits a contrary inclination respecting coordination in the production and sales of goods and services?[72] To the extent that collective bargaining succeeds in raising wages above what would otherwise prevail in the free market, it has the potential to produce unemployment, especially among unskilled, young, and minority workers. Is permitting collective bargaining, and thereby restricting competition among employees for jobs and wages, a beneficial solution to a problematic prisoners' dilemma game, or is it instead a means of allowing a cartel that thwarts what would otherwise be a socially beneficial prisoners' dilemma game akin to market competition more generally? How can you tell? To what extent, if any, are your answers to these questions informed by game theory? To what extent, if any, is it informed by interest group theory? Is this a context in which intuitions drawn from game theory and interest group theory run in different directions? If so, how should the resulting policy questions be resolved? And by whom?

Now consider various environmental enforcement regimes, for example, the Clean Air Act,[73] the Clean Water Act,[74] or the Endangered Species Act.[75] Are these statutes motivated by concerns that, left to their own devices, firms would engage in practices that thwart expressed societal interests in preserving the quality of water, air, and endangered species and their habitats? Are they further motivated by the concern that, again, left to their own devices, firms and states in which they operate are in a prisoners' dilemma in which each would prefer that others comply with restrictive regulatory practices, while reserving the power to cheat in an effort to facilitate profitable economic activity in conflict with these policy concerns? Or are they devices to cartelize industries, raise prices, and create barriers to entry? Or both? Can you tell whether these regulations are solving a prisoners' dilemma game or creating a cartel in response to what otherwise would be a socially beneficial prisoners' dilemma game?

We do not suggest that such large bodies of case law as antitrust, environmental law, and labor law can be captured in a simple prisoners' dilemma analysis. Instead, we hope to demonstrate that the prisoners' dilemma, along with the games in Chapter 16, provide a helpful starting point or perspective in considering the normative foundations of these and other regulatory regimes. Can you identify other bodies of case law or regulatory law

---

[71] *See* Jonathan H. Adler, *Conservation Through Collusion: Antitrust as an Obstacle to Marine Resource Conservation*, 61 WASH. & LEE L. REV. 3 (2004). We will revisit this model of the common pool resource in the context of bankruptcy in the applications.

[72] *See* Coronado Coal Co. v. United Mine Workers of Am., 268 U.S. 295 (1935) (applying the Sherman [Anti-Trust] Act against a union's strike).

[73] 42 U.S.C. §§ 7401–7671 (2012).

[74] 33 U.S.C. §§ 1251–1387 (2012).

[75] 16 U.S.C. §§ 1531–1544 (2012).

that can be explained in terms of creating a benign, or thwarting a harmful, prisoners' dilemma? Can you identify contrary examples in which the legal system has facilitated a harmful prisoners' dilemma or undermined a beneficial one? If you do identify such cases, do the other tools introduced in this book help to explain the resulting anomaly?

III. APPLICATIONS

1. In this chapter's final section, we observed that prisoners' dilemmas are neither inherently good nor bad. It all depends on the particular context in which the game is played. This includes Supreme Court cases. In this application, we present two cases, and ask you to consider whether, in each case, the Court has placed the relevant players in, or removed them from, a prisoners' dilemma, and whether the relevant game is good or bad from a social perspective. Put differently, has the Supreme Court, in each case, improved social welfare by accurately capturing the underlying game-theoretical stakes, or has it undermined social welfare by thwarting them?

We begin with the 1905 Supreme Court decision, *Jacobson v. Massachusetts*. *Jacobson* involves a Massachusetts compulsory vaccine law for small pox, which the Court sustained. The second is the 2010 Supreme Court decision, *Citizens United v. Federal Election Commission*. That case involves a successful First Amendment challenge to a federal statute that banned certain corporate election-related activity, including expenditures. Our presentation of the second case focuses on those aspects relevant to the underlying game.

JACOBSON V. MASSACHUSETTS[76]

MR. JUSTICE HARLAN delivered the opinion of the court:

This case involves the validity, under the Constitution of the United States, of certain provisions in the statutes of Massachusetts relating to vaccination.

The Revised Laws of that commonwealth, chap. 75, § 137, provide that 'the board of health of a city or town, if, in its opinion, it is necessary for the public health or safety, shall require and enforce the vaccination and revaccination of all the inhabitants thereof, and shall provide them with the means of free vaccination. Whoever, being over twenty-one years of age and not under guardianship, refuses or neglects to comply with such requirement shall forfeit $5.'

An exception is made in favor of 'children who present a certificate, signed by a registered physician, that they are unfit subjects for vaccination.' § 139.

[Pursuant to this state authority in 1902 the city of Cambridge passed a regulation requiring smallpox vaccinations. Jacobson, the plaintiff, refused to be vaccinated and challenged the law.]

. . . .

What, according to the judgment of the state court, are the scope and effect of the statute? What results were intended to be accomplished by it? These questions must be answered.

[76] 197 U.S. 11 (1905) (internal citations and quotation marks omitted).

. . . .

[For] nearly a century most of the members of the medical profession have regarded vaccination, repeated after intervals, as a preventive of smallpox; that, while they have recognized the possibility of injury to an individual from carelessness in the performance of it, or even in a conceivable case without carelessness, they generally have considered the risk of such an injury too small to be seriously weighed as against the benefits coming from the discreet and proper use of the preventive; and that not only the medical profession and the people generally have for a long time entertained these opinions, but legislatures and courts have acted upon them with general unanimity.

. . . .

[We] assume, for the purposes of the present inquiry, . . . at least as a general rule, that adults not under the guardianship and remaining within the limits of the city of Cambridge must submit to the regulation adopted by the board of health. Is the statute, so construed, therefore, inconsistent with the liberty which the Constitution of the United States secures to every person against deprivation by the state?

The authority of the state to enact this statute is to be referred to what is commonly called the police power . . . . Although this court has refrained from any attempt to define the limits of that power, yet it has distinctly recognized the authority of a state to enact quarantine laws and 'health laws of every description;' . . . . [T]he police power of a state must be held to embrace, at least, such reasonable regulations established directly by legislative enactment as will protect the public health and the public safety. . . .

We come, then, to inquire whether any right given or secured by the Constitution is invaded by the statute as interpreted by the state court. The defendant insists that his liberty is invaded when the state subjects him to fine or imprisonment for neglecting or refusing to submit to vaccination; that a compulsory vaccination law is unreasonable, arbitrary, and oppressive, and, therefore, hostile to the inherent right of every freeman to care for his own body and health in such way as to him seems best; and that the execution of such a law against one who objects to vaccination, no matter for what reason, is nothing short of an assault upon his person. But the liberty secured by the Constitution of the United States to every person within its jurisdiction does not import an absolute right in each person to be, at all times and in all circumstances, wholly freed from restraint. There are manifold restraints to which every person is necessarily subject for the common good. On any other basis organized society could not exist with safety to its members. Society based on the rule that each one is a law unto himself would soon be confronted with disorder and anarchy. Real liberty for all could not exist under the operation of a principle which recognizes the right of each individual person to use his own, whether in respect of his person or his property, regardless of the injury that may be done to others. This court has more than once recognized it as a fundamental principle that 'persons and property are subjected to all kinds of restraints and burdens in order to secure the general comfort, health, and prosperity of the state; of the perfect right of the legislature to do which no question ever was, or upon acknowledged general principles ever can be, made, so far as natural persons are concerned . . . 'The possession and enjoyment of all rights are subject to such reasonable conditions as may be deemed by the governing authority of the country essential to the safety, health, peace, good order, and morals of the community. Even liberty itself, the greatest of all rights, is not unrestricted license to act according to one's own will. . . . The good and welfare of the commonwealth, of which the legislature is primarily the judge, is the basis on which the police power rests in Massachusetts.

Applying these principles to the present case, it is to be observed that the legislature of Massachusetts required the inhabitants of a city or town to be vaccinated only when, in the opinion of the board of health, that was necessary for the public health or the public safety. The authority to determine for all what ought to be done in such an emergency must have been lodged somewhere or in some body; and surely it was appropriate for the legislature to refer that question, in the first instance, to a board of health composed of persons residing in the locality affected and appointed, presumably, because of their fitness to determine such questions. . . . Upon the principle of self-defense, of paramount necessity, a community has the right to protect itself against an epidemic of disease which threatens the safety of its members. It is to be observed that when the regulation in question was adopted smallpox, according to the recitals in the regulation adopted by the board of health, was prevalent to some extent in the city of Cambridge, and the disease was increasing. If such was the situation,—and nothing is asserted or appears in the record to the contrary,—if we are to attach any value whatever to the knowledge which, it is safe to affirm, in common to all civilized peoples touching smallpox and the methods most usually employed to eradicate that disease, it cannot be adjudged that the present regulation of the board of health was not necessary in order to protect the public health and secure the public safety. Smallpox being prevalent and increasing at Cambridge, the court would usurp the functions of another branch of government if it adjudged, as matter of law, that the mode adopted under the sanction of the state, to protect the people at large was arbitrary, and not justified by the necessities of the case. . . . There is, of course, a sphere within which the individual may assert the supremacy of his own will, and rightfully dispute the authority of any human government,-especially of any free government existing under a written constitution, to interfere with the exercise of that will. But it is equally true that in every well-ordered society charged with the duty of conserving the safety of its members the rights of the individual in respect of his liberty may at times, under the pressure of great dangers, be subjected to such restraint, to be enforced by reasonable regulations, as the safety of the general public may demand. . . . The liberty secured by the 14th Amendment, this court has said, consists, in part, in the right of a person 'to live and work where he will'; and yet he may be compelled, by force if need be, against his will and without regard to his personal wishes or his pecuniary interests, or even his religious or political convictions, to take his place in the ranks of the army of his country, and risk the chance of being shot down in its defense. It is not, therefore, true that the power of the public to guard itself against imminent danger depends in every case involving the control of one's body upon his willingness to submit to reasonable regulations established by the constituted authorities, under the sanction of the state, for the purpose of protecting the public collectively against such danger.

. . . .

Whatever may be thought of the expediency of this statute, it cannot be affirmed to be, beyond question, in palpable conflict with the Constitution. . . .

. . . .

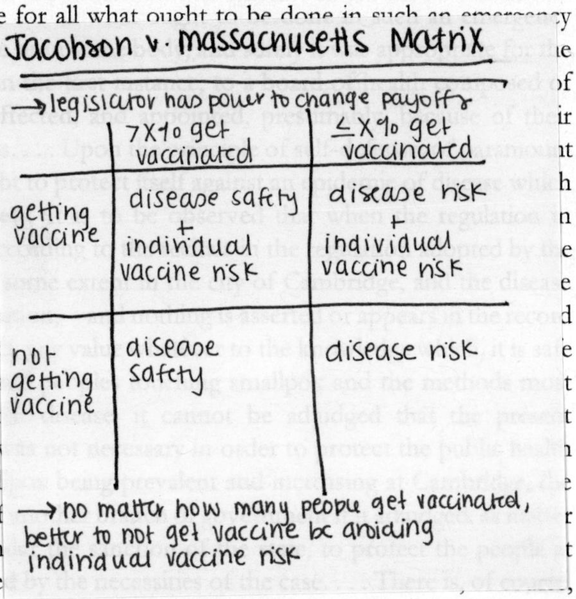

Risks involved
(1) small percentage of harm from vaccine itself
(2) risk of harm to society if no herd immunity

forcing cooperation benefits society
→ allowing defection would be bad for the public as a whole
→ removing individual from prisoners dilemma benefits society

Benefits
(1) vaccination reduces risk of harm from disease
(2) not being vaccinated and avoiding harm plus preserving individual liberty

The fact that the belief is not universal is not controlling, for there is scarcely any belief that is accepted by everyone.

. . . .

The defendant offered to prove that vaccination 'quite often' caused serious and permanent injury to the health of the person vaccinated; that the operation 'occasionally' resulted in death; that it was 'impossible' to tell 'in any particular case' what the results of vaccination would be, or whether it would injure the health or result in death; that 'quite often' one's blood is in a certain condition of impurity when it is not prudent or safe to vaccinate him; that there is no practical test by which to determine 'with any degree of certainty' whether one's blood is in such condition of impurity as to render vaccination necessarily unsafe or dangerous; that vaccine matter is 'quite often' impure and dangerous to be used, but whether impure or not cannot be ascertained by any known practical test; that the defendant refused to submit to vaccination for the reason that he had, 'when a child,' been caused great and extreme suffering for a long period by a disease produced by vaccination; and that he had witnessed a similar result of vaccination, not only in the case of his son, but in the cases of others.

These offers, in effect, invited the court and jury to go over the whole ground gone over by the legislature when it enacted the statute in question. The legislature assumed that some children, by reason of their condition at the time, might not be fit subjects of vaccination; and it is suggested-and we will not say without reason-that such is the case with some adults. But the defendant did not offer to prove that, by reason of his then condition, he was in fact not a fit subject of vaccination at the time he was informed of the requirement of the regulation adopted by the board of health. It is entirely consistent with his offer of proof that, after reaching full age, he had become . . . a fit subject . . . .

It seems to the court that an affirmative answer to these questions would practically strip the legislative department of its function to care for the public health and the public safety when endangered by epidemics of disease. . . .

. . . .

We now decide only that the statute covers the present case, and that nothing clearly appears that would justify this court in holding it to be unconstitutional and inoperative in its application to the plaintiff in error.

The judgment of the court below must be affirmed.

It is so ordered.

MR. JUSTICE BREWER and MR. JUSTICE PECKHAM dissent.

DISCUSSION QUESTIONS

1. Does the mandatory vaccine law solve a game theoretical problem? If the case involves a prisoners' dilemma, who are the players? Does the Court place the players in a prisoners' dilemma or remove them from it? Is the game "good" or "bad"? Do your answers affect whether the Court properly resolved the case? Why or why not?

2. The Court notes that the state's police power permits it to effect quarantine laws. How does the analysis of a quarantine laws relate to that of compulsory vaccination law? Do they involve the same game? Why or why not?

Under the National Childhood Vaccine Injury Act of 1986, Congress created a mechanism for persons injured through the mandatory vaccine process to obtain financial recovery without going through the tort system. On the webpage for the Vaccine Injury Compensation Fund, the program is described as follows:

About the National Vaccine Injury Compensation Program[77]

> The VICP is a program designed to encourage childhood vaccination by providing a streamlined system for compensation in rare instances where an injury results from vaccination.
>
> Over the past 12 years, the VICP has succeeded in providing a less adversarial, less expensive and less time-consuming system of recovery than the traditional tort system that governs medical malpractice, personal injury and product liability cases. More than 1,500 people have been paid in excess of $1.18 billion since the inception of the program in 1988.
>
> Individuals who believe they have been injured by a covered vaccine can file a claim against the Department of Health and Human Services (HHS) in the U.S. Court of Federal Claims seeking compensation from the Vaccine Trust Fund. The Department of Justice (DOJ), which represents HHS, consistently works to ensure that fair compensation is awarded in every case that meets the eligibility criteria. If found eligible, claimants can recover compensation for related medical and rehabilitative expenses, and in certain cases, may be awarded funds for pain and suffering and future lost earnings. Often, an award is more than $1 million. By protecting the Trust Fund against claims by those who have not suffered a vaccine-related injury, DOJ helps to preserve the Fund for future deserving claimants. Regardless of a claimant's success under the Program, reasonable attorneys' fees and costs are paid.
>
> Vaccines covered under the program include those that protect against diphtheria, tetanus, pertussis (whooping cough), measles, mumps, rubella (German measles), and polio. The program continues to evolve consistent with medical science, and recently, HHS expanded coverage to four new vaccines: hepatitis B, varicella (chicken pox), Hemophilus influenzae type b, and rotavirus; pneumococcal vaccine will soon be covered, too.
>
> Another positive result of the program is that costly litigation against drug manufacturers and health care professionals who administer vaccines has virtually ceased. Although an individual who is dissatisfied with the Court's final judgment can reject it and file a lawsuit in state or federal court, very few lawsuits have been filed since the program began. The supply of vaccines in

---

[77] *Vaccine Injury Compensation Program*, U.S. DEP'T OF JUST. (updated Jan. 12, 2017), https://www.justice.gov/civil/vicp.

the U.S. has been stabilized, and the development of new vaccines has markedly increased.

QUESTIONS

compensates those who comply, but are harmed

1. How, if at all, does the National Vaccine Injury Compensation Program affect the nature of the game in *Jacobson*, and the soundness of the policy endorsed by the ruling?

2. The fund operates on a concept of *residual risk*, introduced in Chapters 3 and 4. Although the *Jacobson* Court did not use this term, it was fairly explicit that even when a vaccine is properly administered, some persons might suffer adverse consequences from the vaccine, and that there is no way to determine in advance who might be so affected. How does the problem of residual risk relate to the game theoretical problem of vaccines?

allocating residual risk removes some of the incentive to defect, meaning that it increases the likelihood of mutual cooperation → compensates for the discount rate that one may receive if they defect and others comply, therefore making the decision between defection and cooperation a closer call for those who would otherwise be inclined to defect

Consider the following analysis: As a result of herd immunity, overall risk is reduced when the vaccine is administered widely. The consequence of such a program, however, is that some will bear the burden of the residual risk, realizing an illness that they might not have gotten but for the vaccine. With the fund in place, those individuals continue to bear that risk, but in the event that the risk manifests itself in injury or death, the fund partially offsets the resulting financial burdens for the victim or her family, albeit subject to a preset amount (akin to a regime of workers' compensation), rather than in tort. Although VICP allows for the filing of a state or federal suit for those dissatisfied with relief under the program, apparently few such claims are filed. The program also allows recovery of reasonable attorney's fees regardless of success, which would generally not be true of lawsuit within the United States. In the vaccine context, is it appropriate to allocate residual risk, as between the government on the one hand and the individual on the other, in the manner achieved by VICP? Why or why not?

CITIZENS UNITED V. FEDERAL COMMUNICATIONS COMMISSION

Citizens United, a nonprofit corporation, released a critical documentary, titled "Hillary" in January 2008, which targeted then-senator Hillary Clinton, who was running in the Democratic Primary for President. Citizens United sought to broadcast the documentary on cable television's on-demand programming. Relying on the Bipartisan Campaign Reform Act (BCRA), which prohibited corporations from broadcasting advertisements advocating the election or defeat of a candidate within thirty days of a primary, the Federal Election Commission banned the broadcast. The decision was upheld by a three-judge panel of the United States District Court, and the case was appealed to the U.S. Supreme Court, which by a 5–4 decision reversed, ruling for Citizens United.[78]

Central to the case was whether corporations hold the same First Amendment rights as individuals to make independent expenditures during political campaigns, as distinguished from making direct contributions to campaigns. In ruling that they do, the Court overturned *Austin v. Michigan Chamber of Commerce* (1990), and partially overturned *McConnell v. Federal Election Commission* (2003).

---

[78] Citizens United v. Fed. Election Comm'n, 558 U.S. 310 (2010).

JUSTICE KENNEDY delivered the opinion of the Court.

The law before us is an outright ban, backed by criminal sanctions. Section 441b makes it a felony for all corporations—including nonprofit advocacy corporations—either to expressly advocate the election or defeat of candidates or to broadcast electioneering communications within 30 days of a primary election and 60 days of a general election. . . .

. . .

Section 441b's prohibition on corporate independent expenditures is . . . a ban on speech. As a "restriction on the amount of money a person or group can spend on political communication during a campaign," that statute "necessarily reduces the quantity of expression by restricting the number of issues discussed, the depth of their exploration, and the size of the audience reached." *Buckley v. Valeo* (1976). Were the Court to uphold these restrictions, the Government could repress speech by silencing certain voices at any of the various points in the speech process. . . .

. . .

[T]he First Amendment stands against attempts to disfavor certain subjects or viewpoints. . . . [I]t is inherent in the nature of the political process that voters must be free to obtain information from diverse sources in order to determine how to cast their votes. . . .

We find no basis for the proposition that, in the context of political speech, the Government may impose restrictions on certain disfavored speakers. . . .

. . .

Austin v. Michigan Chamber of Commerce (1990) "uph[eld] a direct restriction on the independent expenditure of funds for political speech for the first time in [this Court's] history." . . . . [T]he *Austin* Court identified a new governmental interest in limiting political speech: an antidistortion interest. *Austin* found a compelling governmental interest in preventing "the corrosive and distorting effects of immense aggregations of wealth that are accumulated with the help of the corporate form and that have little or no correlation to the public's support for the corporation's political ideas."

. . .

If the First Amendment has any force, it prohibits Congress from fining or jailing citizens, or associations of citizens, for simply engaging in political speech. If the antidistortion rationale were to be accepted, however, it would permit Government to ban political speech simply because the speaker is an association that has taken on the corporate form. . . . If *Austin* were correct, the Government could prohibit a corporation from expressing political views in media beyond those presented here, such as by printing books. . . .

* * *

Austin's antidistortion rationale would produce the dangerous, and unacceptable, consequence that Congress could ban political speech of media corporations. Media corporations are now exempt from § 441b's ban on corporate expenditures. Yet media corporations accumulate wealth with the help of the corporate form, the largest media corporations have "immense aggregations of wealth," and the views expressed by media corporations often "have little or no correlation to the public's support" for those views. Thus, under the Government's reasoning, wealthy media corporations could have their voices diminished to put them on par with other media entities. There is no precedent for permitting this under the First Amendment.

. . .

The Government contends further that corporate independent expenditures can be limited because of its interest in protecting dissenting shareholders from being compelled to fund corporate political speech. This asserted interest . . . would allow the Government to ban the political speech even of media corporations. Assume, for example, that a shareholder of a corporation that owns a newspaper disagrees with the political views the newspaper expresses. Under the Government's view, that potential disagreement could give the Government the authority to restrict the media corporation's political speech.

. . .

. . . *Austin* should be and now is overruled. We return to the principle established in *Buckley* and *First National Bank of Boston v. Bellotti* (1978) that the Government may not suppress political speech on the basis of the speaker's corporate identity. No sufficient governmental interest justifies limits on the political speech of nonprofit or for-profit corporations.

CHIEF JUSTICE ROBERTS, with whom JUSTICE ALITO joins, concurring.

The Government urges us in this case to uphold a direct prohibition on political speech. It asks us to embrace a theory of the First Amendment that would allow censorship not only of television and radio broadcasts, but of pamphlets, posters, the Internet, and virtually any other medium that corporations and unions might find useful in expressing their views on matters of public concern. Its theory, if accepted, would empower the Government to prohibit newspapers from running editorials or opinion pieces supporting or opposing candidates for office, so long as the newspapers were owned by corporations—as the major ones are. First Amendment rights could be confined to individuals, subverting the vibrant public discourse that is at the foundation of our democracy.

The Court properly rejects that theory, and I join its opinion in full. . . .

JUSTICE SCALIA, with whom JUSTICE ALITO joins, and with whom JUSTICE THOMAS joins in part, concurring.

. . .

. . . All the provisions of the Bill of Rights set forth the rights of individual men and women—not, for example, of trees or polar bears. But the individual person's right to speak includes the right to speak *in association with other individual persons*. Surely the dissent does not believe that speech by the Republican Party or the Democratic Party can be censored because it is not the speech of "an individual American." It is the speech of many individual Americans, who have associated in a common cause, giving the leadership of the party the right to speak on their behalf. The association of individuals in a business corporation is no different . . . .

. . . The Amendment is written in terms of "speech," not speakers. Its text offers no foothold for excluding any category of speaker, from single individuals to partnerships of individuals, to unincorporated associations of individuals, to incorporated associations of individuals—and the dissent offers no evidence about the original meaning of the text to support any such exclusion. We are therefore simply left with the question whether the speech at issue in this case is "speech" covered by the First Amendment. No one says otherwise. . . . We should celebrate rather than condemn the addition of this speech to the public debate.

JUSTICE STEVENS, with whom JUSTICE GINSBURG, JUSTICE BREYER, and JUSTICE SOTOMAYOR join, concurring in part and dissenting in part.

* * *

In the context of election to public office, the distinction between corporate and human speakers is significant. Although they make enormous contributions to our society, corporations are not actually members of it. They cannot vote or run for office. Because they may be managed and controlled by nonresidents, their interests may conflict in fundamental respects with the interests of eligible voters. The financial resources, legal structure, and instrumental orientation of corporations raise legitimate concerns about their role in the electoral process. Our lawmakers have a compelling constitutional basis, if not also a democratic duty, to take measures designed to guard against the potentially deleterious effects of corporate spending in local and national races.

* * *

. . . . Campaign finance distinctions based on corporate identity tend to be less worrisome . . . because the "speakers" are not natural persons, much less members of our political community, and the governmental interests are of the highest order. Furthermore, when corporations, as a class, are distinguished from noncorporations, as a class, there is a lesser risk that regulatory distinctions will reflect invidious discrimination or political favoritism.

. . .

The Framers took it as a given that corporations could be comprehensively regulated in the service of the public welfare. Unlike our colleagues, they had little trouble distinguishing corporations from human beings, and when they constitutionalized the right to free speech in the First Amendment, it was the free speech of individual Americans that they had in mind. While individuals might join together to exercise their speech rights, business corporations, at least, were plainly not seen as facilitating such associational or expressive ends. Even "the notion that business corporations could invoke the First Amendment would probably have been quite a novelty," given that "at the time, the legitimacy of every corporate activity was thought to rest entirely in a concession of the sovereign." . . . In light of these background practices and understandings, it seems to me implausible that the Framers believed "the freedom of speech" would extend equally to all corporate speakers, much less that it would preclude legislatures from taking limited measures to guard against corporate capture of elections.

. . .

. . . [I]n *Austin*, we considered whether corporations . . . could be barred from using general treasury funds to make independent expenditures in support of, or in opposition to, candidates. We held they could be. Once again recognizing the importance of "the integrity of the marketplace of political ideas" in candidate elections, we noted that corporations have "special advantages—such as limited liability, perpetual life, and favorable treatment of the accumulation and distribution of assets"—that allow them to spend prodigious general treasury sums on campaign messages that have "little or no correlation" with the beliefs held by actual persons. In light of the corrupting effects such spending might have on the political process, we permitted the State of Michigan to limit corporate expenditures on candidate elections to corporations' PACs, which rely on voluntary contributions and thus "reflect actual public support for the political ideals espoused by corporations." . . .

. . .

On numerous occasions we have recognized Congress' legitimate interest in preventing the money that is spent on elections from exerting an " 'undue influence on an officeholder's judgment' " and from creating " 'the appearance of such influence,' " beyond the sphere of *quid pro quo* relationships. . . . Corruption operates along a spectrum, and the majority's apparent belief that *quid pro quo* arrangements can be neatly demarcated from other improper influences does not accord with the theory or reality of politics. It certainly does not accord with the record Congress developed in passing BCRA, a record that stands as a remarkable testament to the energy and ingenuity with which corporations, unions, lobbyists, and politicians may go about scratching each other's backs—and which amply supported Congress' determination to target a limited set of especially destructive practices.

. . .

. . . The legislative and judicial proceedings relating to BCRA generated a substantial body of evidence suggesting that, as corporations grew more and more adept at crafting "issue ads" to help or harm a particular candidate, these nominally independent expenditures began to corrupt the political process in a very direct sense. The sponsors of these ads were routinely granted special access after the campaign was over. . . . Many corporate independent expenditures, it seemed, had become essentially interchangeable with direct contributions in their capacity to generate *quid pro quo* arrangements. In an age in which money and television ads are the coin of the campaign realm, it is hardly surprising that corporations deployed these ads to curry favor with, and to gain influence over, public officials.

. . .

. . . Unlike natural persons, corporations have "limited liability" for their owners and managers, "perpetual life," separation of ownership and control, "and favorable treatment of the accumulation and distribution of assets . . . that enhance their ability to attract capital and to deploy their resources in ways that maximize the return on their shareholders' investments." Unlike voters in U. S. elections, corporations may be foreign controlled. Unlike other interest groups, business corporations have been "effectively delegated responsibility for ensuring society's economic welfare"; they inescapably structure the life of every citizen. " '[T]he resources in the treasury of a business corporation,' " furthermore, " 'are not an indication of popular support for the corporation's political ideas.' " . . .

It might also be added that corporations have no consciences, no beliefs, no feelings, no thoughts, no desires. Corporations help structure and facilitate the activities of human beings, to be sure, and their "personhood" often serves as a useful legal fiction. But they are not themselves members of "We the People" by whom and for whom our Constitution was established.

. . .

. . . At bottom, the Court's opinion is thus a rejection of the common sense of the American people, who have recognized a need to prevent corporations from undermining self-government since the founding, and who have fought against the distinctive corrupting potential of corporate electioneering since the days of Theodore Roosevelt. It is a strange time to repudiate that common sense. While American democracy is imperfect, few outside the majority of this Court would have thought its flaws included a dearth of corporate money in politics.

[S]ome corporations have affirmatively urged Congress to place limits on their electioneering communications. These corporations fear that officials will shake them down for supportive ads, that they will have to spend increasing sums on elections in an ever-escalating arms race with their competitors, and that public trust in business will be eroded. . . . A system that effectively forces corporations to use their shareholders' money both to maintain access to, and to avoid retribution from, elected officials may ultimately prove more harmful than beneficial to many corporations. It can impose a kind of implicit tax.

Citizns United Matrix

	B silent	B spends
A silent	A no gain, but retains valu; B no gains, but retains valu	A is disadvantaged compared to B; B benefits from rent seeking & undiluted message
A spends	B disadvantaged compared to A; A benefits from rent seeking & undiluted behavior	A no gain & loses valu; B no gain & loses valu

JUSTICE THOMAS, concurring in part and dissenting in part. . . .

QUESTIONS

1. Can *Citizens United* be characterized in terms of a prisoners' dilemma? If so, who are the players? Is it a game in which the Court has extricated corporations from a problematic prisoners' dilemma or instead, a game in which the Court has placed corporations within such a prisoners' dilemma? Do the majority, concurrences, and dissent, disagree on the structural aspects of the game? If not, should that matter to the outcome? If so, which analysis is most persuasive, and why? Which position does the majority take? Which position does Justice Stevens take in dissent?

2. What are the differing views on quid pro quo corruption? Which is more persuasive, and why? How does this analysis relate to the larger prisoners' dilemma analysis?

3. What is the basis for the differing views of how to treat corporations for First Amendment purposes? How does this relate to the game theoretical analysis? Consider, in particular, the final paragraph of Justice Stevens's dissenting opinion, and compare that with the defense of corporate speech in the other opinions. Which of these views is more persuasive, and why?

4. This case generated tremendous backlash. In an unusual incident during his second State of the Union address, President Barack Obama stated: "*Last week, the Supreme Court reversed a century of law to open the floodgates for special interests—including foreign corporations—to spend without limit in our elections. Well, I don't think American elections should be bankrolled by America's most powerful interests, or worse, by foreign entities.*"[79] Justice Samuel Alito was criticized, having been observed in the front row, mouthing "*Not true.*" Does the game theory analysis, or subsequent developments, help to determine which side had the better position?

Bankruptcy Revisited

In Chapter 13 we viewed bankruptcy through the lens of social choice and cycling, and we saw how bankruptcy procedures might address cycling problems that arise in the multiparty bankruptcy negotiations. Professor Thomas Jackson has analyzed bankruptcy as the solution to a prisoners' dilemma, or a common pool problem. As you read the following excerpts, consider the relationship between these two accounts.

The Role of Bankruptcy Law and Collective Action in Debt Collection[80]

> Bankruptcy law can be thought of as growing out of a distinct aspect of debtor-creditor relations: the effect of the debtor's obligation to repay [particular creditors] when the debtor does not have enough to repay everyone in full. Even then, however, a developed system exists for paying creditors without bankruptcy. The relevant question is whether that existing system of creditor remedies has any shortcomings that might be ameliorated by an ancillary system known as bankruptcy law.
>
> To explore that question, it is useful to start with the familiar. Creditor remedies outside of bankruptcy (as well as outside other formal, non-bankruptcy collective systems) can be accurately described as a species of "grab law," represented by the key characteristic of first-come, first-served. The creditor first staking a claim to particular assets of the debtor generally is entitled to be paid first out of those assets. It is like buying tickets for a popular rock event or opera: the people first in line get the best seats; those at the end of the line may get nothing at all.[81]

Professor Jackson proceeds to discuss the varieties of non-bankruptcy "grab" law, including security interests, judicial liens, garnishment, or statutory liens. In general, those rules provide that the first creditor to "perfect" its interest gets paid in full before any other "junior" claimants. Jackson explains:

> A solvent debtor is like a show for which sufficient tickets are available to accommodate all prospective patrons and all seats are considered equally good. In that event one's place in line is largely a matter of indifference. But when there is not enough to go around to satisfy all claimants in full, this method of

[79] Address Before a Joint Session of the Congress on the State of the Union, 2010 DAILY COMP. PRES. DOC. 1, 8 (Jan. 27, 2010).

[80] The following discussion is taken from THOMAS H. JACKSON, THE LOGIC AND LIMITS OF BANKRUPTCY LAW 7–19 (1986).

[81] *Id.* at 8–9.

ordering will define winners and losers based principally on the time when one gets in line.

The question at the core of bankruptcy law is whether a *better* ordering system can be devised that would be worth the inevitable costs associated with implementing a new system. In the case of tickets to a popular rock event or opera, where there must be winners and losers, and putting aside price adjustments, there may be no better way to allocate available seats than on a first-come, first-served basis. In the world of credit, however, there are powerful reasons to think that there is a superior way to allocate the assets of an insolvent debtor than first-come, first-served.

. . . Because creditors have conflicting rights, there is a tendency in their debt-collection efforts to make a bad situation worse. Bankruptcy law responds to this problem. Debt-collection by means of individual creditor remedies produces a variant of a widespread problem. One way to characterize the problem is as a multiparty game—a type of "prisoners' dilemma." As such, it has elements of what game theorists would describe as an *end period* game, where basic problems of cooperation are generally expected to lead to undesirable outcomes for the group of players as a whole.[82] Another way of considering it is as a species of what is called a *common pool* problem, which is well known to lawyers in other fields, such as oil and gas.

. . . Imagine that you own a lake. There are fish in the lake. You are the only one who has the right to fish in that lake, and no one constrains your decision as to how much fishing to do. You have it in your power to catch all the fish this year and sell them for, say, $100,000. If you did that, however, there would be no fish in the lake next year. It might be better for you—you might maximize your total return from fishing—if you caught and sold some fish this year but left other fish in the lake so that they could multiply and you would have fish in subsequent years. Assume that, by taking this approach, you could earn (adjusting for inflation) $50,000 each year. Having this outcome is like having a perpetual annuity paying $50,000 a year. It has a present value of perhaps $500,000. Since (obviously, I hope) when all other things are equal, $500,000 is better than $100,000, you, as sole owner, would limit your fishing this year unless some other factor influenced you.

But what if you are not the only one who can fish in this lake? What if a hundred people can do so? The optimal solution has not changed: it would be preferable to leave some fish in the lake to multiply because doing so has a present value of $500,000. But in this case, unlike that where you have to control only yourself, an obstacle exists in achieving that result. If there are a hundred fishermen, you cannot be sure, by limiting your fishing, that there will be any more fish next year, unless you can also control the others. You may,

[82] *Id.* at 9–11. [After explaining the difference between a single period game, a game that is expected to be infinitely repeated, and a game with a known end period, Jackson explains:] "Although insolvency may signal an end to relationships with one debtor, many creditors will still favor cooperation because of repeat dealings with each other. But not all will expect such repeat dealings, and destructive races to assets can be caused by a few 'bad apples.' " *Id.* at 10–11, n.10.

then, have an incentive to catch as many fish as you can today because maximizing your take this year (catching, on average, $1,000 worth of fish) is better for you than holding off (catching, say, only $500 worth of fish this year) while others scramble and deplete the stock entirely. If you hold off, your aggregate return is only $500, since nothing will be left for next year or the year after. But that sort of reasoning by each of the hundred fishermen will mean that the stock of fish will be gone by the end of the first season. The fishermen will split $100,000 this year, but there will be no fish—and no money—in future years. Self-interest results in their splitting $100,000, not $500,000.

What is required is some rule that will make all hundred fishermen act as a sole owner would. That is where bankruptcy law enters the picture in a world not of fish but of credit. The grab rules of nonbankruptcy law and their allocation of assets on the basis of first-come, first-served create an incentive on the part of the individual creditors, when they sense that a debtor may have more liabilities than assets, to get in line today (by, for example, getting a sheriff to execute on the debtor's equipment), because if they do not, they run the risk of getting nothing. This decision by numerous individual creditors, however, may be the wrong decision for the creditors as a group. Even though the debtor is insolvent, they might be better off if they held the assets together. Bankruptcy provides a way to make these diverse individuals act as one, by imposing a *collective* and *compulsory* proceeding on them. Unlike a typical common pool solution, however, the compulsory solution of bankruptcy law does not apply in all places at all times. Instead, it runs parallel with a system of individual debt-collection rules and is available to supplant them when and if needed.

. . . [A] less allegorical and more precise analysis is necessary. . . . Debtor has a small printing business. Potential creditors estimate that there is a 20 percent chance that Debtor (who is virtuous and will not misbehave) will become insolvent through bad luck, general economic downturn, or whatever. (By insolvency, I mean a condition whereby Debtor will not have enough assets to satisfy his creditors.) At the point of insolvency . . . the business is expected to be worth $50,000 if sold piecemeal. Creditors also know that each of them will have to spend $1,000 in pursuit of their individual collection efforts should Debtor become insolvent and fail to repay them. Under these circumstances Debtor borrows $25,000 from each of four creditors, Creditors 1 through 4. Because these creditors know that there is this 20 percent chance, they can account for it—and the associated collection costs—in the interest rate they charge Debtor. Assume that each party can watch out for its own interest, and let us see whether, as in the example of fishing, there are reasons to think that these people would favor a set of restrictions on their own behavior (apart from paternalism or other similar considerations).

Given that these creditors can watch out for their own interests, the question to be addressed is *how* these creditors should go about protecting themselves. If the creditors have to protect themselves by means of a costly and inefficient system, Debtor is going to have to pay more to obtain credit. Thus, when we consider them all together—Creditors 1 through 4 *and*

Debtor—the relevant question is: would the availability of a bankruptcy system reduce the costs of credit?

. . . .

. . . Does that advantage exist in the case of credit? When dealing with businesses, the answer, at least some of the time, would seem to be "yes." The use of individual creditor remedies may lead to a piecemeal dismantling of a debtor's business by the untimely removal of necessary operating assets. To the extent that a non-piecemeal collective process (whether in the form of a liquidation or reorganization) is likely to increase the aggregate value of the pool of assets, its substitution for individual remedies would be advantageous to the creditors as a group. This is derived from a commonplace notion: that a collection of assets is sometimes more valuable together than the same assets would be if spread to the winds. It is often referred to as the surplus of a going-concern value over a liquidation value.

Thus, the most obvious reason for a collective system of creditor collection is to make sure that creditors, in pursuing their individual remedies, do not actually decrease the aggregate value of the assets that will be used to repay them. In our example this situation would occur when a printing press, for example, could be sold to a third party for $20,000, leaving $30,000 of other assets, but the business as a unit could generate sufficient cash so as to have a value of more than $50,000. As such it is directly analogous to the case of the fish in the lake. . . .

. . . Consider what the creditors would get if there were no bankruptcy system (putting aside the ultimate collection costs). Without a collective system all of the creditors in our example know that in the case of Debtor's insolvency the first two creditors to get to (and through) the courthouse (or to Debtor, to persuade Debtor to pay voluntarily), will get $25,000, leaving nothing for the third and fourth. And unless the creditors think that one of them is systematically faster (or friendlier with Debtor), this leaves them with a 50 percent chance of gaining $25,000, and a 50 percent chance of getting nothing. A collective system, however, would ensure that they would each get $12,500.

Would the creditors agree in advance to a system that, in the event of Debtor's insolvency, guaranteed them $12,500, in lieu of a system that gave them a 50 percent chance of $25,000—payment in full—and a 50 percent chance of nothing? Resolution of this question really turns on whether the creditors are better off with the one than the other. There are two reasons to think that they are . . . . First of all, if these creditors are risk averse, assurance of receiving $12,500 is better than a 50 percent chance of $25,000 and a 50 percent chance of nothing. . . .

One other possible advantage of a collective proceeding should also be noted: there may be costs to the individualized approach to collecting (in addition to the $1,000 collection costs). . . .

> These various costs to using an individual system of creditor remedies suggest that there are, indeed, occasions when a collective system of debt-collection law might be preferable. Bankruptcy provides that system. . . .[83]

Viewing bankruptcy as solving a collective action problem, Jackson argues, helps to explains many of the important provisions of bankruptcy law:

> This approach immediately suggests several features of bankruptcy law. First, such a law must usurp individual creditor remedies in order to make the claimants act in an altruistic and cooperative way. Thus, the proceeding is inherently *collective.* Moreover, this system works only if all the creditors are bound to it. To allow a debtor to contract with a creditor to avoid participating in the bankruptcy proceeding would destroy the advantages of a collective system. So the proceeding must be compulsory as well. But unlike common pool solutions in oil and gas or fishing, it is not the exclusive system for dividing up assets. It, instead, supplants an existing system of individual creditor remedies . . . .
>
> Note that the presence of a bankruptcy system does not mandate its use whenever there is a common pool problem. Bankruptcy law stipulates a minimum set of entitlements for claimants. That, in turn, permits them to "bargain in the shadow of the law" and to implement a consensual collective proceeding outside of the bankruptcy process. . . .[84]

DISCUSSION QUESTIONS

1. Jackson argues that one justification for the normative force of a bankruptcy system is that creditors acting behind a "veil of ignorance" would implicitly consent to bankruptcy rules in the event of the debtor's insolvency because they all would be better off by being forced to participate in this collective system. Is that a satisfactory normative justification? Does that rationale apply for so-called involuntary creditors as well? If so, why do creditors demand security interests to improve their priority in bankruptcy?

2. Does Jackson's argument support making bankruptcy mandatory in all debtor-creditor relationships or should parties be allowed to contract around bankruptcy? Imagine a corporation's charter that provides: "In the event of insolvency, this corporation will not seek bankruptcy relief"? Would such notice to prospective creditors justify avoiding bankruptcy in the event of illiquidity, even if the result is to risk the first-come-first-served problem that Jackson identifies? Why or why not?

3. Jackson states: "The formal bankruptcy process would presumably be used only when individual advantage-taking in the setting of multiparty negotiations made a consensual deal too costly to strike—which may, however, occur frequently as the number of creditors

---

[83] JACKSON, *supra* note 80, at 9–16 (footnotes omitted) (citing Thomas H. Jackson, *Bankruptcy, Non-Bankruptcy Entitlements, and the Creditors' Bargain*, 91 YALE L.J. 857 (1982)). *See also* Garrett Hardin, *The Tragedy of the Commons*, 162 SCIENCE 1243 (1968); Gary D. Libecap & Steven N. Wiggins, *Contractual Responses to the Common Pool: Prorationing Crude Oil Production*, 74 AM. ECON. REV. 87 (1984); Alan E. Friedman, *The Economics of the Common Pool: Property Rights in Exhaustible Resources*, 18 UCLA L. REV. 855 (1971).

[84] JACKSON, *supra* note 80, at 17.

increases."[85] How does this analysis relate to the social choice account of bankruptcy rules as a function of cycling? More generally, what is the relationship between Jackson's account of bankruptcy as seeking to avoid a prisoners' dilemma or common pool game, on the one hand, and the social choice account of bankruptcy as seeking to avoid a problem of legislative cycling or cycling over debtor/creditor financial interests, on the other?

→ in bankruptcy setting, there is an obvious end of interactions. such ends will not encourage mutual cooperation because each creditor knows that eventually, they will not be punished for defecting or rent seeking activity

[85] *Id.* at 17.

CHAPTER 16

Game Theory (Part 2)

Introduction

This chapter builds upon the analysis from Chapter 15, which focused on the prisoners' dilemma in its various forms. In this chapter, we present three games, each of which displays additional layers of complexity. Unlike the prisoners' dilemma, the games in this chapter have more than one outcome corresponding to a pure Nash equilibrium. In these games, the player strategies, when combined, can yield any of four outcomes. Two such outcomes are *pure Nash equilibria*, and the other two are not pure Nash equilibria. Because each player can elect either of two strategies, we cannot predict which of the four outcomes will obtain in any given game when they play simultaneously.[1] By contrast, when the players select their strategies sequentially, the likelihood of settling on a pure Nash equilibrium outcome rises considerably.

In two of the games, the *driving game* and *battle of the sexes*, the players settle upon a pure Nash equilibrium outcome when their selected strategies turn out to be coordinated. In the driving game, this happens when both drivers remain right or left, and in the battle of the sexes, it happens when the two spouses settle on the same activity. By contrast, in the *game of chicken*, the players settle on the pure-Nash equilibrium when they each assume a different role, thereby failing to coordinate, with one choosing to drive straight and the other choosing to swerve. Along with the details of the games, we provide illustrations. We conclude the chapter with Applications that help to test the implications of these games.

I. GAMES WITH MORE THAN ONE PURE NASH STRATEGY EQUILIBRIUM

The following games yield two outcomes that correspond to a pure Nash equilibrium and two outcomes that correspond to non-pure-Nash equilibrium. This result can arise when the players follow mixed strategies that randomize over options (for example selecting either of two available strategies fifty percent of the time), in an effort to anticipate the likely strategy of the other player. While such strategies produce an expected

[1] DOUGLAS BAIRD ET AL., GAME THEORY AND THE LAW 37 (1994) ("The alternative to a pure strategy equilibrium is a mixed strategy equilibrium, in which, in equilibrium, each player adopts a strategy that randomizes among a number of pure strategies.").

(or ex ante) payoff, referred to as a *mixed strategy equilibrium*, the actual (or ex post) value will depend on the strategy selected by the other player. Sometimes the mixed strategy will produce the desired payoff, but if so, it is only because of the fortuity of a correct guess. Alternatively, when the mixed strategy results in an incorrect guess, meaning a failure to match the strategy of the other player, the result is a lower set of payoffs for both players than would have been available had the players instead adopted strategies that resulted in the benefits, and higher payoffs, produced from mutual cooperation. Once again, we will provide illustrations using normal form games, and then consider how the Nash concept conduces to a solution or set of preferred solutions in each game.

We begin with the simplest version of games with multiple Nash equilibria and then add increasing complexity. First, consider the driving game. This game involves an intuitive problem of pure coordination, one in which no one strategy is inherently superior to any other and the only basis for preference is assumed to be ensuring that the two players cooperate, meaning that they act consistently. As we will see, however, even a mutual desire for beneficial coordination does not ensure that the players necessarily succeed. One obvious function for government operating in its regulatory capacity is in facilitating incentives to encourage benign pure Nash equilibrium results in coordination games. We then introduce the battle of the sexes. The outdated label should not detract from the game's important central insight. In contrast with the driving game, two players might agree on the benefit of combined outcomes in which their choices align, yet disagree as to the relative benefits and burdens of the two possible aligned strategies. And finally we introduce the game of chicken. This unfortunate normal form game depicts conditions under which two players seek to best each other in a context in which one or both players can adopt strategies that in combination prove capable of producing severe, even deadly, consequences. We then introduce an alternative equilibrium concept, *non-myopic equilibrium*,[2] to demonstrate why the apparent Nash outcome might not invariably obtain.

Together these games help to generalize the public policy inquiry with which we ended our discussion of the prisoners' dilemma in Chapter 15. What role does the state have in seeking to transform problematical games into benign games, thereby promoting beneficial results for the parties involved and for society? Within games that admit of more than a single pure Nash equilibrium strategy, what role does the state have in encouraging courses of play that lead players to preferred (pure) over disfavored non-pure-Nash equilibrium outcomes?

A. The Driving Game

Assume that we are in the early part of the twentieth century, with the advent of automobiles. While some relatively wealthy individuals drive, cars remain scarce and, as a result, rules governing their operation are rudimentary.[3] Assume that in a given

---

2 STEVEN J. BRAMS, THEORY OF MOVES (1994).

3 In fact, in the earliest period there were no testing requirements for a driver's license, and, of course, traffic rules were extremely limited. *See* M.G. LAY, WAYS OF THE WORLD: A HISTORY OF THE WORLD'S ROADS AND OF THE VEHICLES THAT USED THEM 173–97 (1992) (describing "recording . . . individual drivers and vehicles in a register," drivers' licenses as a "revenue-raising measure," and the gradual development of rules of the road).

jurisdiction there are no rules governing whether automobiles should be driven on the left or right side of the road. To simplify, assume that there are only two drivers, Anne (*A*) and Bob (*B*), and that neither much cares which side of the road she or he drives on. Both do care, however, that whichever convention one follows the other follows as well. Thus, while each driver least prefers that one drive on the left at the same time that the other drives on the right, each is indifferent as between a rule requiring both to drive on the left or both to drive on the right. Table 16:1 captures the payoffs in this game.

Table 16:1. The Driving Game

Payoffs for (A, B)	B drives left	B drives right
A drives left	**10, 10**	0, 0
A drives right	0, 0	**10, 10**

The payoffs reflect the intuition that the driving game involves a problem of pure coordination. If driver *A* drives left, and if driver *B* initially drives right, driver *B* can improve his payoffs from 0 to 10 by shifting and also driving left. Conversely, if driver *A* drives right, and driver *B* initially drives left, driver *B* can again improve his payoffs from 0 to 10, this time by shifting and also driving right. Neither left nor right driving is inherently superior, but it is vital that both players follow the same strategy. The payoffs are reciprocal, and so, if driver *B* is the initial mover, *A's* incentives to conform to *B's* behavior are the same as for *B* when *A* was is initial mover. The effect is to motivate the second driver to follow the selected strategy of the first driver.

In contrast with the prisoners' dilemma, which yields a single pure Nash equilibrium outcome in either single period or iterated form, the driving game produces two pure Nash equilibrium outcomes (right/right or left/left) in a single round of play. And yet, the game will not necessarily produce either of the available pure Nash equilibria as the actual outcome in a given round of play.

In the hypothetical, we assumed that either driver *A* or driver *B* was the initial mover. Imagine instead that the two drivers make their selection at the same time, and thus without the benefit of either driver observing the other driver's selected strategy. Each driver will rationally try to anticipate the other driver's strategy without knowing that strategy and with a fifty percent chance of being correct. If driver *A* anticipates that driver *B* will drive right, driver *A* will drive right. Because driver *A* makes his choice without actual knowledge of driver *B*'s strategy, however, despite their best efforts to coordinate, the two drivers might inadvertently select opposing strategies to their mutual detriment. If the players employ mixed strategies, each randomizes over options (selecting right or left fifty percent of the time),[4] with the possibility of an outcome that is not a pure-Nash equilibrium. Sometimes the mixed strategies will produce the desired effect (right/right or left/left), but when that happens, the benign result follows from the fortuity of a correct guess. Alternatively, when the mixed strategies result in an incorrect guess, failing to match the strategy of the other player, the result is a lower set of payoffs for both players than would have been available had the players stumbled upon a coordinated outcome.

---

[4] This is, in fact, the unique mixed strategy equilibrium.

The two disfavored results (left/right or right/left) are not pure-Nash, and neither would likely obtain had either player known in advance of the strategy selected by other player, as, for example, when the players make their choices sequentially. When the players choose their strategies simultaneously, however, there is nothing in the game itself that dictates what the actual outcome will be.

The game's most obvious application, for which it is named, is driving. State law regulates most aspects of highway safety, including selecting the side of the road on which to travel. While in the United States, we drive on the right side of the road (with left-side steering wheels), this solution is not unique.[5] England and Australia, for example, employ the opposite, but still pure-Nash equilibrium, regime of driving on the left side of the road (with steering wheels on the right). Neither of these two regimes is superior to the other, which is why each represents a pure Nash equilibrium strategy. But of course either is superior to the non-pure Nash outcomes of right/left or left/right driving.

A more complex illustration of the driving game arises in the context of the dormant Commerce Clause.[6] Numerous states have highway safety laws that specify particular means of transporting goods through the state. On occasion, the safety laws of one state run up against those of a neighboring state. When this occurs, the conflicting legal regimes threaten to impose considerable costs on those transporting goods in interstate commerce. On several notable occasions, conflicting laws of this sort have given rise to

---

[5] The history of right side driving in the United States appears to be path dependent. Historians trace right-side driving to the technology of the Conestoga wagon, in the mid-eighteenth century. For a discussion, see LAY, *supra* note 3, at 199–200. Lay explains:

> A major impetus for right-hand driving in the United States came from the design of the Conestoga wagon, which had led to the winning of the West. The wagon was operated either by the postilion driver riding the left-hand near horse—called the wheel horse—or by the driver walking or sitting on a "lazy board" on the left-hand side of the vehicle. He kept to the left in both cases in order to use his right hand to manage the horses and operate the brake lever mounted on the left-hand side. Passing therefore required moving to the right to give the driver forward vision.

Id. at 199. *See also* Richard F. Weingroff, *On the Right Side of the Road,* U.S. DEP'T OF TRANSP.: FED. HIGHWAY ADMIN., https://www.fhwa.dot.gov/infrastructure/right.cfm (last updated June 27, 2017). For the first time in over forty years, a sovereign nation executed a road-side driving switch. Prime Minister Tuilaepa Sailele Malielegaoi ordered the tiny Pacific island nation of Samoa to switch from right to left driving (and a prospective switch from left to right steering wheels) effective September 9, 2009, to allow Samoan workers to import cheaper used cars from in Australia and New Zealand, which follow British driving convention. *See* David Whitley, *Samoa Provokes Fury by Switching Sides of the Road,* THE TELEGRAPH: MOTORING NEWS (July 3, 2009, 11:00 PM), http://www.telegraph.co.uk/motoring/news/5732906/Samoa-provokes-fury-by-switching-sides-of-the-road.html. While this met considerable internal resistance, in part due to the capital loss to left side steering wheel vehicle owners resulting from the altered secondary market, *see* Patrick Barta, *Shifting the Right of Way to the Left Leaves Some Samoans Feeling Wronged,* WALL ST. J., Aug. 24, 2009, at A1, the switch suggests that the path-dependent account of coordinated driving regimes is not necessarily limited to contiguous states. *See infra* pp. 679–680. Ultimately the switch is reported to have gone smoothly. *See* Associated Press, *Samoa Switches Smoothly to Driving on the Left,* THE GUARDIAN (Sept. 8, 2009) https://www.theguardian.com/world/2009/sep/08/samoa-drivers-switch-left (explaining that steering wheels can be either left or right). *Samoa to Allow Left-Hand Drive Vehicles Again,* RNZ PACIFIC (Mar. 6, 2017), https://www.radionz.co.nz/international/pacific-news/325925/samoa-to-allow-left-hand-drive-vehicles-again (reporting that Samoa would allow 100 imports per month of private vehicles, thus allowing imports from the United States again).

[6] The discussion that follows is based upon Maxwell L. Stearns, *A Beautiful Mend: A Game Theoretical Analysis of the Dormant Commerce Clause,* 45 WM. & MARY L. REV. 1 (2003).

constitutional challenges under the dormant Commerce Clause.[7] Two prominent illustrations are *Bibb v. Navajo Freight Lines*,[8] and *Kassel v. Consolidated Freightways*.[9]

In *Bibb*, Illinois law required that trucks use curved mudflaps. This conflicted with the contrary laws of forty-five other states that instead required straight mudflaps. Compliance with both regimes was impractical as it would require changing mudflaps at the border of Illinois and neighboring states. In *Kassel*, Iowa prohibited, with notable exceptions,[10] the use of sixty-five-foot twin trailers, rigs that the surrounding states permitted.[11] Once again, the law was problematic in that it ran up against those of the surrounding states favoring the banned rig.

How might game theory help characterize the challenged Illinois and Iowa laws? Are these non-coordinated laws the product of a driving game or of some other game? If they are the product of a driving game, why then did Illinois and Iowa enact laws out of keeping with those of surrounding states, rather than replicating the laws of such states to facilitate the flow of interstate commerce? Are there situations in which an individual state might actually prefer to produce a mixed strategy equilibrium? What would the benefits be? Consider the following.[12]

Among the most elementary intuitions of economic analysis is the law of diminishing returns. As a general matter, as one acquires more units of a given good, the marginal value or utility derived from acquiring each successive unit declines.[13] There are, however, notable exceptions to this important principle. Marginal values have the potential to rise, rather than decline, in cases involving *positive network externalities* or *path dependence*.[14] These

---

7 The Commerce Clause provides Congress the power "To regulate Commerce with foreign Nations, and among the several States, and with the Indian Tribes." U.S. CONST. art. I, § 6, cl. 3. While the clause is an express delegation of authority to Congress to regulate commerce, almost from its inception, the Supreme Court construed the clause to limit the power of states to interfere with interstate commerce. For a detailed history and analysis, see Stearns, *supra* note 6.

8 Bibb v. Navajo Freight Lines, Inc., 359 U.S. 520 (1959).

9 Kassel v. Consol. Freightways Corp., 450 U.S. 662 (1981).

10 These exceptions included: the use of oversize vehicles for shipments from border cities to adjoining states, where the cities passed ordinances to permit their use; Iowa truck manufacturers shipping trucks up to seventy feet; and shipping oversized mobile homes from points in Iowa to Iowa residents. *Id.* at 666.

11 Other regions, including New England and most Southeastern states, employed the Iowa regime. *Kassel*, 450 U.S. at 687–88 (Rehnquist, J., dissenting).

12 This analysis is developed more fully *infra* pp. 621–637.

13 This is reflected in the convex to vertex slope of indifference curves. *See supra* Chapter 2. Diminishing marginal utility resolves what Adam Smith considered an economic anomaly, namely why water, an essential good, is relatively valueless as compared with diamonds, an inessential luxury good. KARL E. CASE & RAY C. FAIR, PRINCIPLES OF MACROECONOMICS 341 (7th ed. 2004); MAXWELL L. STEARNS, PUBLIC CHOICE AND PUBLIC LAW: READINGS AND COMMENTARY, at xxi (1997); ALFRED MARSHALL, PRINCIPLES OF ECONOMICS 13 (8th ed. 1920).

14 For general discussions of path dependence, see Maxwell L. Stearns, *Standing Back from the Forest: Justiciability and Social Choice*, 83 CALIF. L. REV. 1309 (1995) (linking the modern standing doctrine to stare decisis-induced path dependence and the corresponding incentive of ideological interest groups to manipulate case orderings to effect favorable doctrine); Maxwell L. Stearns, *Standing and Social Choice: Historical Evidence*, 144 U. PA. L. REV. 309 (1995) (providing historical and case support for social choice theory of standing doctrine); Oona Hathaway, *Path Dependence in the Law: The Course and Pattern of Legal Change in a Common Law System*, 86 IOWA L. REV. 601 (2001) (relating theories of path dependence to judicial behavior).

related concepts are particularly helpful in assessing the nature of the driving game as played among states.

Assume a nation with two states and in which State A enacts a policy of right driving (left steering wheels). This law provides a clear benefit to in-state drivers by inhibiting avoidable collisions caused simply by the absence of an announced coordinated driving strategy. But if neighboring State B possesses a contrary driving regime (left driving, right steering wheels), then the value of State A's law is limited to those driving in that jurisdiction. In this instance, the marginal value of the law rises if State B enacts a coordinated driving regime, thereby facilitating the flow of vehicular traffic between the two bordering states. Now expand the scope to include a nation, like the United States, with a large number of contiguous states. The phenomenon of increasing marginal utility continues as other adjoining states, States C, D, and E, embrace the same driving regime. As each state coordinates with the policy initially selected by State A, the marginal utility for drivers, along with that of the affected states, rises.

The driving regime's value is not a function of its merit in comparison with alternative driving regimes. Rather, it is a function of the regime's coordination with those of adjoining states. Had the initial moving state elected a left driving regime (with right steering wheels), the increasing marginal utility would have attached to the continued selection of that alternative regime. The value of the regime is independent of its normative merit and is instead a function of the emerging path of coordinated interstate policy.

The phenomenon of path dependence also helps to assess strategies respecting the implementation of developing technologies. Scholars have long noted, for example, that the modern keyboard, labeled *QWERTY* after the top left row of lettered keys, is a function of early key punch technology that was designed to spread out the most commonly hit keys on a typewriter to avoid jamming malfunctions.[15] The concern was diminished with the advent of electronic typewriters, and eliminated entirely in the age of digital word processing and computers.

In the 1930s, August Dvorak devised a new typing system that reassigned the most commonly used letters to the strongest fingers. His alternative never gained popularity despite the claim of several commentators that it is technically superior to QWERTY. One account of the seeming anomaly is that Dvorak failed due to path dependence.[16] The issue is not merely the somewhat significant personal learning curve for individuals to master a new typing system. In addition, virtually all text-based data entry systems throughout the world based on using the English alphabet, and also many that are not,

---

[15] Paul A. David, *Clio and the Economics of QWERTY*, 75 AM. ECON. REV. 332 (1985); S.J. Liebowitz & Stephen E. Margolis, *The Fable of the Keys*, 33 J.L. & ECON. 1 (1990); *see generally* Michael L. Katz & Carl Shapiro, *Network Externalities, Competition, and Compatibility*, 75 AM. ECON. REV. 424–40 (1985).

[16] Paul A. David, *Path Dependence, Its Critics and the Quest for 'Historical Economics,' in* EVOLUTION AND PATH DEPENDENCE IN ECONOMIC IDEAS: PAST AND PRESENT 15–40 (Pierre Garrouste & Stavros Ioannides eds., 2001). For detractors from this conventional account, see STAN J. LIEBOWITZ & STEPHEN E. MARGOLIS, WINNERS, LOSERS, AND MICROSOFT: COMPETITION AND ANTITRUST IN HIGH TECHNOLOGY 140 (1999); Liebowitz & Margolis, *supra* note 15, at 21 ("[T]he evidence in the standard history of QWERTY versus Dvorak is flawed and incomplete. . . . [T]he claims for the superiority of the Dvorak keyboard are suspect."). Detractors do not claim QWERTY is superior. Rather, they claim that Dvorak's alternative has not been proven superior.

have developed technologies around the QWERTY keyboard.[17] Path dependence implies that even a superior technology developed at a later time might fail if the industry path strongly favored an earlier, even inferior, technology. This is known as a *lock-in effect*, due to existing technology that becomes locked-in.

The intuition underlying increasing marginal utilities due to path dependence can also be expressed in terms of *positive network externalities*. As more and more people began to use QWERTY, the cost of operating consistently with that technology was reduced, and the marginal benefit of being part of a common system increased. Similar accounts relying upon path dependence and positive network externalities have been suggested to explain the dominance of VHS technology over Betamax in recording video[18] and the use of Windows operating systems over alternatives offered, most notably, by IBM and Apple.[19]

1. Regulation Versus Standards

The preceding analysis raises two important questions. First, when does achieving the benefits of positive network externalities demand no more than common standards for conducting business or legal affairs? And second, when is it helpful, or even necessary, for the government to, instead, issue binding regulations requiring reliance on common standards?[20]

In the discussion that follows we provide three illustrations of standard setting: mediums of exchange, states of incorporation and choice of law, and securities regulation. The examples explore the role of standard setting in solving potential coordination difficulties, and of government in providing, and sometimes mandating, such standards.

a. Three Stories of Mediums of Exchange: The Dollar and Euro, the Maria Theresa Thaler, and Bitcoin

We begin with the evolution of money as a means of facilitating trade and the role of government in standardizing money. We then discuss the role of the U.S. Dollar and

---

[17] Not only do other nations with romance languages use QWERTY, but systems with altogether different alphabets, e.g., Mandarin or Hebrew, routinely code those alphabets onto QWERTY keyboards. *See* Neville Holmes, *The Profession as a Culture Killer*, COMPUTER, Sept. 2007, at 111–12 (discussing China's reliance on QWERTY).

[18] Stanley M. Besen & Joseph Farrell, *Choosing How to Compete: Strategies and Tactics in Standardization*, J. ECON. PERSP., Spring 1994, at 117–18.

[19] For related discussions, see John E. Popatka & William H. Page, *Microsoft, Monopolization, and Network Externalities: Some Uses and Abuses of Economic Theory in Antitrust Decision Making*, ANTITRUST BULL., Summer 1995, at 317, 321–23. Network externalities in the operating system market are tied not only to human investment, but also to the availability of other applications. *Id.* at 335–40. For an interesting first-person discussion of the economic effects that led to Windows dominance over OS/2, see Posting of Gordon Letwin to comp.os.ms-windows.misc (Aug. 17, 1995), http://gunkies.org/wiki/Gordon_Letwin_OS/2_usenet_post. For a critical account of these path dependence claims, see Liebowitz & Margolis, *supra* note 15, at 5.

[20] For example, the United States and Europe have taken markedly different approaches to standard-setting in cellular phone networks. For a discussion, see Neil Gandal et al., *Standards in Wireless Telephone Networks*, 27 TELECOMM. POL'Y 325 (2003); Luís Cabral & David Salant, *Evolving Technologies and Standards Regulation*, 36 INT'L J. INDUS. ORG. 48 (2014). *See also* Dan Saugstrup & Anders Henten, *3G Standards: The Battle Between WCDMA and CDMA 2000*, INFO, 2006 No. 4, at 10, 14–15.

the Euro, the Maria Theresa Thaler in the Austrian empire and major parts of the Arab world even after de-monetization, and the emergence of Bitcoin as an anonymous electronic currency.

Early historians claimed that money as a medium of exchange emerged through spontaneous ordering to allow individuals to coordinate their behavior into a larger network.[21] Because money serves both as a store of value and as a measure of relative valuation, it creates the possibility of robust market exchange by avoiding the need for barter. Historically, units of currency have included scarce goods such as salt, clam shells, and beads.[22] Over time, monetary systems have tended to standardize around reliance upon scarce metals, such as gold and silver.[23] The value of the standardization of money in promoting a system of exchange, and in providing a means of storing value, is demonstrated by the spontaneous "invention" of money throughout human history.

In the United States throughout most of the nineteenth century, private banks issued paper currency backed by precious metals. Today, many banks issue credit cards and debit cards that are almost universally accepted and redeemed against the assets of the issuing bank. Over time, the central government has assumed the role of issuing various forms of currency. Inflationary government monetary policies during the eras of the Revolutionary War and Articles of Confederation led to a ban on issuance of paper currency in the Constitution.[24]

Early governmental issuances of paper money during the first half of the nineteenth century were intended to fund government operations during emergencies, such as during the War of 1812, but such issuances were not declared legal tender. The federal government first issued "greenbacks," which "postponed" redemption into gold, during the Civil War, declaring them "legal tender."[25] In 1870, the Supreme Court struck down the *Legal Tender Act* as violating the Constitution, only to reverse itself in 1871 following a change in the membership of the Court.[26] Within the United States today, the Federal Reserve issues currency that is declared legal tender for all debts public and private.[27]

---

[21] Carl Menger, *On the Origins of Money*, 2 ECON. J. 239 (1892).

[22] *See generally* MARY ELLEN SNODGRASS, COINS AND CURRENCY: AN HISTORICAL ENCYCLOPEDIA (2007) (providing encyclopedic overview of types of currency used throughout world history, including shell money, bead currency, and salt money).

[23] *See* JEAN-FRANÇOIS SERVAL & JEAN-PASCAL TRANIÉ, THE MONETARY SYSTEM: ANALYSIS AND NEW APPROACHES TO REGULATION 38–40 (2014); Irena Asmundson & Ceyda Oner, *What Is Money?*, 49 INT'L MONETARY FUND: FINANCE & DEVELOPMENT (2012), http://www.imf.org/external/pubs/ft/fandd/2012/09/basics.htm.

[24] *See* Todd J. Zywicki, *The Coinage Clause*, *in* THE HERITAGE GUIDE TO THE CONSTITUTION 114 (2005).

[25] *See* Kristin L. Willard, Timothy W. Guinnane & Harvey S. Rosen, *Turning Points in the Civil War: Views from the Greenback Market*, 86 AM. ECON. REV. 1001 (1996); *see generally* MILTON FRIEDMAN & ANNA JACOBSON SCHWARTZ, A MONETARY HISTORY OF THE UNITED STATES, 1867–1960 15–85 (1965) (describing what the authors call "The Greenback Period" in United States monetary history).

[26] Hepburn v. Griswold, 75 U.S. (8 Wall.) 603 (1870) (invalidating the Legal Tender Act); Legal Tender Cases, 79 U.S. 457 (1871) (overruling *Hepburn*). A change in Court personnel involving the appointments of Justices William Strong and Joseph Bradley is credited as effecting this change in outcome. For an historical analysis, see Charles M. Fairman, *Reconstruction and Reunion: 1864–88*, 6 THE OLIVER WENDELL HOLMES DEVISE HISTORY OF THE SUPREME COURT OF THE UNITED STATES 713–63 (1971).

[27] 31 U.S.C. § 5103 (2012).

Compare this account with a famous numismatic example. For many years, a large part of the world relied upon the *1780 Maria Teresa Thaler* even though it was a non-mandated foreign national currency. While the coin was first minted in 1741, the Austrian government continued to strike the coin with the same date, 1780, following Maria Teresa's death.[28] The Maria Teresa Thaler rapidly emerged as the leading coin throughout the Austrian empire and later through major parts of the Arab world. The coin set such a remarkable standard that the Austrian government continued issuing the 1780 imprint even after it was demonetized in the 1850s, allowing its continued use as a trade coin.[29] In effect, the coin's prestige allowed it to emerge as the dominant medium of exchange throughout a large part of the world. Indeed, it was so popular that other nations tacitly approved its use by declining to impose an alternative medium of exchange.

Today, throughout many parts of the world, the Dollar or Euro has become a *de facto* "coin of the realm" at least in major urban centers where such currencies are regarded as relatively stable gauges of value and can be converted at low cost into local currency. In effect, at various times, systems around the world have customized their business financing around the standards set by forms of currency issued by Austria, the United States, or the European Union, rather than based upon a superimposed regulatory system focused on a single mandated medium of exchange.

Finally, consider the more recent history of emerging virtual currencies, most notably *Bitcoin*.[30] Bitcoin is entirely virtual, and was created anonymously with a complex computer algorithm. This had the unique benefit of allowing a slow and somewhat predictable rate of growth to meet increasing demand without risking rapid deflation through monetization. Bitcoin's primary benefit to users, aside from investment speculation, is anonymous electronic transacting. Bitcoin operates as virtual electronic cash. The sole means of access to a personal Bitcoin *wallet* is an individual *electronic key*, which, if lost, is equivalent to losing cash in a physical wallet or purse. Bitcoin facilitates non-traceable transactions, which, not surprisingly, has led to concerns as to its use on websites trafficking in illicit goods or services.[31] An important tradeoff between government-established currencies, on one hand, and Bitcoin, on the other, involves relative instability of value, characterized by Bitcoin's somewhat rapid fluctuations,[32] on

---

[28] *See* Adrian Tschoegl, *Maria Theresa's Thaler: A Case of International Money*, 27 E. ECON. J. 443, 444–45, 452 (2001) (providing history and noting that at the time of publication, the coin was still being struck in limited quantities for collectors). Re-strikes of the Maria Theresa Thaler are available from the Austrian Mint. MODERN RE-STRIKES MARIA THERESA TALER—PROOF, MÜNZE OSTERREICH, https://www.muenze oesterreich.at/eng/Produkte/Maria-Theresa-Taler-proof (last visited Sept. 27, 2017).

[29] Shepard Pond, *The Maria Theresa Thaler: A Famous Trade Coin*, BULL. BUS. HIST. SOC'Y, Apr. 1941, at 29. Numismatists are able to distinguish early coinage from later issuances bearing the same date. *Id.* at 26.

[30] For a general discussion of Bitcoin, see Kevin V. Tu & Michael W. Meredith, *Rethinking Virtual Currency Regulation in the Bitcoin Age*, 90 WASH. L. REV. 271–348 (2015). For the initial paper introducing Bitcoin, see Satoshi Nakamoto, *Bitcoin: A Peer-to-Peer Electronic Cash System*, BITCOIN.ORG (2008), https://bitcoin.org/ bitcoin.pdf.

[31] Not surprisingly, an emerging literature questions whether and how to regulate Bitcoin. *See* Tu & Meredith, *supra* note 30. Such regulation might risk the benefit of Bitcoin as an anonymous medium of exchange.

[32] Historically Bitcoin has experienced rapid price fluctuations following its initial meteoric rise in value, although in recent years, its value has stabilized somewhat. *See* Jamal Bouoiyour & Refk Selmi, *Bitcoin: A Beginning of a New Phase?*, 36 ECON. BULL. 1430, 1431 (2016) (stating that the volatility of Bitcoin has

one side, versus nontraceability, on the other. Although cash transactions can be anonymous, unlike Bitcoin transactions, they are cumbersome, and they are impractical in e-commerce.

QUESTIONS AND COMMENTS

What implications does the history of the emergence of money hold for governmental standardization of currency? Would the United States be better served without a central unit of currency declared as legal tender by the federal government? If so, what would most likely replace it? Does the history of the Maria Theresa Thaler or of Bitcoin help to answer these questions? Why or why not? Is there an overriding benefit to some form of national currency standardization? If not, can you explain its prevalence in the modern world? What role do such currencies play in reducing transactions costs domestically or internationally?

In the absence of a central currency, would a dominant substitute emerge, or would a large number of competing currencies emerge? Are creditors, or debtors, systematically better off with a national currency? Why? Is the benefit of a central currency outweighed by the risk that the government will inflate the currency to reduce the national debt? Does this risk help answer whether national currencies tend to favor creditors or debtors? Why? Are there mechanisms that can abate the inflationary risk? Has this risk been realized in recent years? Decades? How, if at all, does this relate to the valuation fluctuations in Bitcoin? Are governments or private entities better suited to issuing effective bonds against the devaluation resulting from inflation? Why?

Does Bitcoin offer the basis for a natural experiment respecting whether the national provision of a currency as a medium of exchange is wealth generating as compared with reliance upon privately produced mediums of exchange? Or is the principal function of Bitcoin—anonymous electronic transacting—too specific for meaningful comparative analysis? Does it matter that Bitcoin's creator was, and remains, anonymous? Why or why not? As the use of Bitcoin has become more common, and as debates have arisen as to whether it should be regulated, other virtual currencies have also emerged.[33] How, if at all, does this affect your analysis of Bitcoin? Of the likely value of other emerging virtual currencies? Why? Does Bitcoin have an advantage over other virtual currencies as a consequence of path dependence and positive network externalities? Why or why not?

---

consistently declined since 2015); Luke Graham, *Bitcoin Price Bounces Back by Nearly $1,000 as Market Moves on from Recent Drama*, CNBC (Sept. 18, 2017, 7:21 AM), https://www.cnbc.com/2017/09/18/bitcoin-rebounds-digital-currency-recovers-32-percent.html; Alexandria Arnold, *Bitcoin's Valuation Is Confusing Currency Analysts*, BLOOMBERG TECH. (June 7, 2017, 2:25 PM), https://www.bloomberg.com/news/articles/2017-06-07/bitcoin-perplexes-currency-analysts-as-valuation-debate-grows; Jonathan Todd Barker, *Why is Bitcoin's Value So Volatile?*, INVESTOPEDIA (May 16, 2017, 9:55 AM), http://www.investopedia.com/articles/investing/052014/why-bitcoins-value-so-volatile.asp.

[33] *See* Ryan Farell, *An Analysis of the Cryptocurrency Industry*, WHARTON RES. SCHOLARS 130 (2015) (stating that since the release of Bitcoin over 550 new cryptocurrencies have emerged); Tu & Meredith, *supra* note 30; Prableen Bajpai, *The 6 Most Important Cryptocurrencies Other Than Bitcoin*, INVESTOPEDIA (Apr. 21, 2017, 10:00 AM), http://www.investopedia.com/tech/6-most-important-cryptocurrencies-other-bitcoin/.

b. States of Incorporation and Contractual Choice of Law

We now consider the flexibility among firms in choosing their state of incorporation and the ability of contracting parties, in at least some circumstances, to choose the governing legal regime through contractual choice of law. Delaware, a tiny state, has become the dominant standard for corporate chartering in the United States. Professor Roberta Romano ascribes Delaware's dominance to the relatively high percentage of its state revenues derived from corporate chartering activity.[34] Because corporate chartering accounted for 16.9% of those revenues, Romano posited that Delaware was able to issue a credible bond against radical changes in its corporate law.[35] Other states could mimic Delaware Corporate Law (as Nevada has done),[36] but they could not issue a comparable bond not to change their corporate law.

Although incorporating in Delaware is notably more costly than in other states, for relatively large corporations, the expense nonetheless remains minor.[37] Many companies with a more significant presence in other states are legally based in Delaware, thereby rendering their governance subject to Delaware law as a result of the *Internal Affairs Doctrine*.[38] In the context of transacting, many parties include choice of law clauses that specifically rely upon the law of other jurisdictions to govern potential legal disputes that might arise. And in some instances, firms designate arbitration in lieu of a state-based legal system.[39]

---

34 Roberta Romano, *Law as a Product: Some Pieces of the Incorporation Puzzle*, 1 J.L. ECON. & ORG. 225, 240 (1985).

35 Romano was writing in 1985 and based her analysis on then-current and historical data. For recent data on revenues from corporate charters, see DELAWARE DIVISION OF CORPORATIONS, 2015 ANNUAL REPORT, https://corp.delaware.gov/Corporations_2015%20Annual%20Report.pdf (last visited Apr. 4, 2018) (stating "[g]eneral fund revenue collections by the Division of Corporations" accounted for 26% of the state's general fund revenues).

36 Jonathan R. Macey & Geoffrey P. Miller, *Toward an Interest-Group Theory of Delaware Corporate Law*, 65 TEX. L. REV. 469, 488 (1987).

37 Lucian Arye Bebchuk & Assaf Hamdani, *Vigorous Race or Leisurely Walk: Reconsidering the Competition over Corporate Charters,* 112 YALE L.J. 553, 573 (2002) (noting that "[i]ncorporation in Delaware involves a franchise tax that is nonnegligible, though not substantial for most publicly traded firms"). The cost differential is not that of *establishing* a corporation, but results from "franchise fees" for Delaware firms. *See* ANTHONY MANCUSO, INCORPORATE YOUR BUSINESS app. A (2d ed. 2004). These fees can range from $175 to $200,000 based upon the number of shares in the incorporated Delaware firm and the method of calculation. *See How to Calculate Franchise Taxes*, DELAWARE DEPARTMENT OF STATE, https://corp.delaware.gov/taxcalc.shtml (last visited Oct. 1, 2017). For a discussion of the incidence of such fees on various companies based upon size, see Marcel Kahan & Ehud Kamar, *The Myth of State Competition in Corporate Law*, 55 STAN. L. REV. 679, 690–99 (2002) (presenting tables showing marginal revenues from annual taxes and franchise fees by state).

38 For a general discussion of the Internal Affairs Doctrine, see Frederick Tung, *Before Competition: Origins of the Internal Affairs Doctrine*, 32 J. CORP. L. 33 (2006). *See also* LARRY E. RIBSTEIN & PETER V. LETSOU, BUSINESS ASSOCIATIONS (4th ed. 2003); Larry E. Ribstein & Erin A. O'Hara, *Corporations and the Market for Law*, 2008 U. ILL. L. REV. 661. George Stigler, *Public Regulation of the Securities Markets*, 37 J. BUS. 117 (1964) (same); George Benston, *Required Disclosure and the Stock Market: An Evaluation of the Securities Exchange Act of 1934*, 63 AM. ECON. REV. 132 (1972) (providing interest group account of Securities Act of 1934).

39 For informative discussions of contractual choice of law, see ERIN A. O'HARA & LARRY E. RIBSTEIN, THE LAW MARKET (2009); Andrew T. Guzman, *Choice of Law: New Foundations*, 90 GEO. L.J. 883 (2002); Erin A. O'Hara & Larry E. Ribstein, *From Politics to Efficiency in Choice of Law*, 67 U. CHI. L. REV. 1151 (2000).

Do these two illustrations—corporate chartering and contractual choice of law—support the intuition that at least in some circumstances, parties can benefit from a uniform standard, and thus from positive network externalities, without the burdens of mandatory regulation? Can you identify circumstances in which this is less likely to be true and when it is better to have the legal system mandate the governing standard? Is game theory helpful in answering these questions?

c. Securities Exchanges

Consider also the Securities and Exchange Commission (SEC). The SEC sets standards for publicly held corporations in a variety of contexts, including the sale and acquisition of stock. In addition, the SEC sets standards for domestic stock exchanges, including most notably the New York Stock Exchange (NYSE). As a result of these regulations, firms and individuals buying registered stocks do so knowing that the companies in question have satisfied detailed reporting requirements and will be held accountable should they contravene various legal prohibitions, for example, the prohibition against insider trading.

While this regime has the benefit of ensuring a common set of standards governing private market exchange for publicly held corporations, consider whether this could be accomplished absent uniform regulation. Some legal historians have argued that the SEC was established in large part to impose barriers to entry, protecting large securities dealers that were recognized by regulated exchanges.[40]

To what extent are the potential benefits of competition, such as lowering barriers to entry, offset by the path-dependent or lock-in effects of a dominant exchange, such as the NYSE? Would competition increase the risk among traders of forgoing assurances respecting insider trading or disclosures in corporate filings? If an unregulated, or privately regulated, system of securities exchange is welfare enhancing, why do nearly all large industrialized nations have nationally regulated securities exchanges?[41] Which regime is more likely to provide better protections to investors in this area: a national regulatory standard, state-by-state standards, or private standards?

In other settings, private organizations create their own set of standards for the assessment of quality, for example, organizations that set standards for vegetarian, vegan, and kosher foods; vehicle fuel efficiency; and quality assessments for numerous goods and services. In recent years, commentators have taken to task food producers who rely

---

[40] *See, e.g.*, Paul G. Mahoney, *The Political Economy of the Securities Act of 1933*, 30 J. LEGAL STUD. 1 (2001) (setting out interest group account of the founding of the SEC).

[41] Franco Barbiero, *Federalizing Canada's Securities Regulatory Regime: Insights from the Australian Experience*, 24 NAT'L J. CONST. L. 89, 90 (2008) ("Since Australia centralized the regulation of its capital markets under a federal banner in 1991, Canada has remained the only developed country in the world with a provincially regulated regulatory regime."). Barbiero further notes that out of the 183 members of the International Organization of Securities Commissions in 2008, Canada and Bosnia-Herzegovina are the only two lacking a national securities regulator (Bosnia has 2). *See id.* at 90–91. Canadian securities are regulated by Canada's thirteen provincial and territorial governments. *Id.* at 90. Bosnia-Herzegovina's securities are regulated by the country's two autonomous entities, the Federation of Bosnia and Herezegovina and the Republika Srpska. EUR. BANK FOR RECONSTRUCTION & DEV., COMMERCIAL LAWS OF BOSNIA AND HERZEGOVINA 22 (2014).

on "organic" labels, claiming that absent governmental regulations, the claim is meaningless.[42] Similar problems have arisen in the context of health-related products that do not fall within the jurisdiction of the Food and Drug Administration (FDA).[43] In other settings, firms are more likely to advertise that their products comply with private rather than with governmental standards. For example, we are more apt to see firms advertise "approved by Underwriters Laboratory," than "compliant with all applicable governmental regulations." Can you explain this seeming discrepancy?

2. Overcoming Positive Network Externalities

In several of the preceding examples of coordinated activity, early movers hold an advantage over newer entrants. Depending upon the strength of the positive network effect, this advantage might remain *even if* the later-introduced product is regarded as technically superior. Consumers will weigh the benefits of sacrificing the positive network externalities against the marginal technological improvements associated with the later-introduced goods or services. Of course, if the value of the new technology is substantial enough, this will eventually overwhelm the burden of departing from a path-induced technology regime.

For a simple and familiar illustration, consider some well-known children's toys. Various toy systems have their own standards for interlocking with other toys by the same manufacturer and in some instances with similar products offered by competitors. While *Lego* building blocks will not interlock with *Playmobil*, Lego offers a large assortment of products that interlock with their basic system. By contrast, while *Thomas the Tank Engine and Friends* and *BRIO* toy train systems are competitors, they interlock with each other, thus allowing the toys to be used interchangeably.

While systems involving interactive toys might appear trivial, they illustrate an important economic principle. Parents who purchase a basic Lego set will have some incentive to have the child acquire other Lego toys that operate consistently with that system. But if Playmobil offers a building set with features that Lego lacks (or the reverse) that the child very much wishes to have, few parents would consider themselves permanently "locked in" to the exclusion of the other toy system. Of course, for many parents, although children's toys can be costly, they are not prohibitively so, and thus children often have different toys operating on incompatible systems.

For more expensive systems, however, purchasers might be less willing to acquire a new technology simply because it offers some marginal improvements over a costly

---

[42] For a discussion of the problems surrounding "organic" food labeling see Chenglin Liu, *Is "USDA ORGANIC" A Seal of Deceit?: The Pitfalls of USDA Certified Organics Produced in the United States, China, and Beyond*, 47 STAN. J. INT'L L. 333 (2011). *See also* Valerie J. Watnick, *The Organic Foods Production Act, the Process/Product Distinction, and a Case for More End Product Regulation in the Organic Foods Market*, 32 UCLA J. ENVT. L. & POL'Y 40 (2014); *see also* PETER LAUFER, ORGANIC: A JOURNALIST'S QUEST TO DISCOVER THE TRUTH BEHIND FOOD LABELING (2014).

[43] For a general discussion of the problems with regulating dietary supplements and other products outside the scope of FDA regulation, see Michael A. McCann, *Dietary Supplement Labeling: Cognitive Biases, Market Manipulation, and Consumer Choice*, 31 AM. J.L. & MED. 215 (2005). *See also* Diane E. Hoffman et al., *Probiotics: Achieving a Better Regulatory Fit*, 69 FOOD & DRUG L.J. 237 (2014).

system already in place. Prior to technology that allowed low-cost customization,[44] few businesses were willing to offer employees a menu of keyboard options, including QWERTY and Dvorak. Similarly, even now many employers elect one among several competing word processing or operating systems, for example Word or WordPerfect, or Windows or Mac OS, rather than allowing employees to make this election individually. In each of these illustrations, market forces have primarily determined whether the continued benefit of positive network externalities outweighs the cost of declining to adapt to a newly developing technology.

How, if at all, might this differ when lawmaking institutions select among two or more competing technologies? As we have already seen, state laws affecting various aspects of transportation have the potential for positive (or negative) network effects. In assessing claims under the dormant Commerce Clause doctrine that a contrary state law thwarts beneficial coordination among states, the federal judiciary is called upon to assess whether the challenged law provides sufficient benefits to justify allowing a single state to thwart the common practices of other states. Does this help to explain the Supreme Court's occasional reliance on a balancing test in such cases?[45] If so, what normative principles should the Court consider in striking an appropriate balance? Should the Court be skeptical of claims that state laws that are out of sync with those of neighboring states are genuinely motivated by highway safety concerns, rather than by potential strategic considerations?

Does the creation of positive network externalities help further explain the cases of *Bibb* and *Kassel*? While highway safety laws that facilitate the flow of interstate commerce produce positive network effects for affected states, they also have the potential to impose burdens on pass-through states and corresponding opportunities for strategic behavior. Consider the perspective of a state that is primarily a throughway for interstate commerce benefiting surrounding states. For the pass-through state, the common regime might add to costs of highway maintenance and increase risks of vehicular accidents, all with relatively minor corresponding benefits to in-state residents or industry. While the surrounding states benefit from a common network of coordinated laws, a burdened state might benefit from deliberately departing from that framework, thereby forging a mixed strategy equilibrium.[46]

Under existing dormant Commerce Clause doctrine, a state's desire to reduce the financial burdens of highway maintenance by shifting such burdens onto neighboring states, for example by discouraging in-state commercial traffic, is not a permissible justification for interfering with the coordinated regime of surrounding states. States that depart from otherwise common regulatory regimes must defend their laws on alternative

---

[44] With modern computer operating systems, keyboard customization is a standard, cost-free feature. *See* APPLE SUPPORT, *macOS Sierra: Use Dvorak Keyboard Layouts*, APPLE (Mar. 28, 2017), https://support.apple.com/kb/PH25652?locale=en_US; *see also* MICROSOFT SUPPORT, *Change Your Keyboard Layout*, MICROSOFT, https://support.microsoft.com/en-us/help/17424/windows-change-keyboard-layout (last updated Aug. 31, 2016).

[45] For an article claiming that the Supreme Court does not actually apply a balancing test in these cases, see Donald H. Regan, *The Supreme Court and State Protectionism: Making Sense of the Dormant Commerce Clause*, 84 MICH. L. REV. 1091 (1986).

[46] For a more elaborate account that develops this theory and evaluates it against the relevant case law, see Stearns, *supra* note 6.

grounds, and they typically do so based upon concerns for highway safety. When the Court confronts such a case, it is forced to consider whether the claimed benefits of the nonconforming law outweigh the costs of burdening an otherwise common regulatory regime that facilitates the flow of commerce among states.

Does this analysis help to explain the Supreme Court's decisions to strike the challenged laws in *Bibb* and *Kassel*? Does it help to explain why the Court achieved these results using a balancing test even though the Court has routinely stated that highway safety laws are an area of deference to states? Whether or not this explains these rulings, does the analysis provide a sound normative justification? Why or why not? Do these cases suggest the need for central regulatory enforcement in the context of challenged state highway safety regulations, as opposed to a standard around which states can conform their conduct? Why or why not? Does your answer to the preceding questions help to explain why, in contrast with general constitutional cases, which are binding on Congress, Congress has the power to overturn dormant Commerce Clause rulings with ordinary legislation?

B. The Battle of the Sexes

We will now consider another simple form game that, like the driving game, has four possible outcomes and in which two outcomes correspond to pure-Nash strategy equilibria and the other two correspond to non-pure-Nash equilibria. Unlike the driving game, however, the selection between these two pure Nash outcomes is not a simple matter of coordination. While the players care very much about having a coordinated strategy, they differ substantially on which available coordinated strategy to prefer.

Let us begin with a married couple. The wife is a football fan while the husband significantly prefers attending the theater. While each is willing, on occasion, to indulge the other's preference, the husband and the wife each derive significantly greater enjoyment from her or his preferred activity than from engaging in the spouse's preferred activity. At the same time, however, the level of satisfaction that each spouse derives from either activity depends in large measure on whether she or he is joined in that activity by the spouse. Thus, while the husband and the wife each prefer their own first-choice activity, each would prefer to instead join the spouse in the second-choice activity to engaging in the first choice activity alone. The payoffs in this game are reflected in Table 16:2 below.

Table 16:2. The Battle of the Sexes

Payoffs for (H, W)	**W attends theater**	**W attends football**
H attends theater	**10, 7**	5, 5
H attends football	3, 3	**7, 10**

In this game, the husband (*H*) and wife (*W*) each prefer different outcomes. If husband and wife each attend theater, husband's first choice activity, then husband receives the highest available payoff of ten, while wife receives the second highest available payoff of seven. Conversely, if both attend the football game, wife's first choice activity, these payoffs are reversed, with wife obtaining a payoff of ten and husband obtaining a payoff of seven. If each attends her or his first choice activity alone, each receives a payoff of five. Conversely, if each attends her or his lesser preferred activity alone (husband going to the game; wife going to theater), each receives a payoff of three.

With knowledge of the other's strategy, either spouse could improve her or his payoff unilaterally by conforming to the other spouse's strategy. The final combination of strategies—each going to the less preferred activity—is not a null set. Imagine, for example, that each spouse is trying to anticipate the other's behavior but, unable to communicate and hoping to surprise the other, each pursues the other's first choice strategy. Alternatively, each spouse might mistakenly assume that the other has committed to her or his first-choice strategy and thus try to mimic that strategy. Either approach generates the lower left-hand solution.[47]

Given the payoffs in this game, each player hopes that both will engage in her or his first-choice activity, but, failing that, hopes to engage together in the spouse's first-choice (and her or his second-choice) activity, rather than attending a first-choice activity alone. And of course, the least preferred option is for each spouse to engage in the other's first-choice activity alone. As indicated in the table, this game, like the driving game, generates two possible outcomes that each correspond to a pure-Nash equilibrium: (theater, theater) and (football, football). It also generates two possible outcomes that do not: (theater, football) and (football, theater). As before, if the players randomize their strategies, then any of the outcomes might obtain, although the formal assigned values affect the relative probabilities over some outcomes.[48]

One consequence of this game is the incentive to issue some kind of bond through which either spouse commits to the first-choice activity. Consider, for example, the husband's incentives when theater tickets become available. Assume that he purchases tickets and immediately notifies his wife. The wife then confronts a choice of going to the game alone or joining her husband. Given the incentives, she gains more (with a payoff of seven) attending the theater than attending the football game alone (with a payoff of five). And because the payoffs are reciprocal, the same is true if instead the wife had purchased two football tickets first on the same terms. To what extent is repeat play a solution to the problem that this game presents? If it is not, would you be best off seeking guidance from a game theorist or a marriage counselor?

The battle of the sexes game nicely complements some of the insights of first generation law and economics.[49] Consider the Coase Theorem, introduced in Chapter 1.[50]

---

[47] For a more romantic literary illustration, consider *The Gift of the Magi,* in which the wife cuts off and sells her hair to purchase a watch chain for her husband while the husband sells his watch to buy his wife a comb for her hair. O. HENRY, *The Gift of the Magi, in* THE COMPLETE WORKS OF O. HENRY 7 (Doubleday 1926) (1899). The authors thank Martin Kraus for bringing this illustration to their attention.

[48] In this case, the single mixed strategy equilibrium involves the husband going to the theater with probability 7/9 and going to the football game with probability 2/9; and the wife attaching the complementary probabilities to the two strategies (2/9 to the theater and 7/9 to the football game). The departure from (1/2,1/2) for both parties, which was the mixed strategy equilibrium for the driving game, reflects the asymmetry of payoffs in the current game when each attends her or his second best option.

[49] For a discussion of first generation law and economics scholarship, see GARY MINDA, POSTMODERN LEGAL MOVEMENTS: LAW AND JURISPRUDENCE AT CENTURY'S END 88–95 (1995).

[50] *See supra* at Chapter 1, Part II.I.

Coase posited that in a world with zero transactions costs and perfect information, resources flow to their most highly valued uses without regard to liability rules.[51] Assuming that transactions costs are low, including access to information, contract liability rules would have no bearing on how resources are finally allocated. If the legal system confers the right upon the lower valuing user, the higher valuing user will have an incentive to purchase that right, and the person holding it will have an incentive to sell. This theoretically frictionless world gives legal rules trivial status, one belied by the enormous consequence that legal rules actually have in the real world, characterized by positive transaction costs.

If we relax the assumption that all exchange is frictionless, the battle of the sexes suggests that parties will prefer clarity of legal rules to a state of contractual uncertainty. Consider a hypothetical contracting regime, for example, in which everything was literally and constantly up for grabs. One of the benefits of common law rules of contract, and also of Article II of the Uniform Commercial Code, is specifying a set of off-the-rack rules that can fill in content in the event that the parties fail to anticipate potential contingencies that might arise at the stage of contract formation.

Contract law provides innumerable examples, several of which were reviewed in Chapters 5 and 6. Here we select just a few that illustrate the essential point. Consider first a product advertisement. The legal system could treat this in one of two ways, first as an offer for the sale of goods, that once a prospective buyer accepts, forms a contract, or second, as an invitation for the buyer to make an offer. If the advertisement were treated as an offer, the advertiser's failure to comply with the terms of the ad, for example, by failing to have sufficient goods available to satisfy all acceptances, would then provide the basis for a breach of contract action. As we have seen, as a matter of formal doctrine, the legal system does not treat advertisements in this manner,[52] and instead treats them as invitations to prospective buyers to make an offer that the seller is then free to accept or reject.[53]

Imagine that a seller advertises a *loss leader*, or even engages in a *bait and switch*, meaning advertising an item attractively enough to pull people into the store in a ploy to divert their attention to other items that are less favorably priced, with the goal of never selling the advertised good at the listed price. From the perspective of a prospective buyer, the preferred rule is one that treats the advertisement as an offer and an unwillingness to

---

[51] R.H. Coase, *The Problem of Social Cost*, 3 J.L. & ECON. 1 (1960).

[52] *See supra* Chapter 5.

[53] It is hornbook law that an advertisement cannot be an offer, but the Minnesota Supreme Court in *Lefkowitz v. Great Minneapolis Surplus Store,* 86 N.W.2d 689 (Minn. 1957), found an exception where the advertisement was sufficiently specific so as to leave no room for further negotiation. Where an "offer is clear, definite, and explicit, and leaves nothing open for negotiation, it constitutes an offer, acceptance of which will complete the contract." *Id.* at 691. As Professor Jason Johnston has explained, "It is, of course, hornbook law that advertisements generally do not constitute offers," Jason Scott Johnston, *Communication and Courtship: Cheap Talk Economics and the Law of Contract Formation*, 85 VA. L. REV. 385, 399 (1999), and thus *Lefkowitz* represents one of the "exceptions to the defaults." *Id.* at 396. For an interesting argument that although the rule is consistently stated that an advertisement is not an offer, they actually function as one, see Jay M. Feinman & Stephen R. Brill, *Is an Advertisement an Offer? Why It Is and Why It Matters*, 58 HASTINGS L.J. 61, 65 (2006) (positing that "*Lefkowitz* is particularly instructive because, to use the cliché, it is the exception that proves the rule.").

sell following an acceptance as a breach. From the perspective of the seller, however, the preferred rule is to treat the advertisement as an invitation to make an offer that the seller is free to reject.

Although both sides have opposite preferences on the preferred rule, buyer and seller both benefit from clarity of the rule. If the rule favors the buyer (an ad is an offer), the seller can include language in the advertisement specifying that "nothing in this ad should be construed as an offer," and that customers are free to make offers for any goods that the seller advertises, subject to the seller's right to decline. Conversely, imagine that the legal rule provides that ads are only invitations to make an offer. This might discourage potential consumers from venturing into stores that advertise products on particularly attractive terms, for example, based upon an unusual buying opportunity or a liquidation sale. In this case, even a clear rule appearing to favor the seller would not prevent the seller from issuing a bond that ensures that buyers treat the ad as tantamount to an offer. For example, sellers could specify that the price will be available to the first one hundred customers or "while supplies last," and seller could even promise to issue rain checks in the event that the seller runs out of inventory on the day of the advertised sale.

In this example, buyer and seller hold opposite views of the preferred rule as to whether an ad should be treated as an offer, but they share a common interest in having a clear rule, which the parties are then able to negotiate around. Absent a clear rule, the seller would not be motivated to issue a disclaimer in the ad itself, anticipating that she will never honor the ad terms, and conversely will not seek to issue a bond to commit to ad terms as a device to pull consumers into the store. Conversely, absent a clear rule, buyer will not know how to construe the ad and will fear the risk of investing time and money on a fool's errand. Despite opposing views on the preferred legal rule, buyer and seller hold a common interest in clarity, even if the rule initially appears to favor the other side. Returning to Table 16.2, the same payoffs in the battle of the sexes game characterize the incentives between buyer and seller in this basic issue of contract law. Although each side most prefers her or his own rule, each side also prefers the rule favoring the other side to a state of uncertainty as to which rule governs. The states of uncertainty are captured in the outcomes where each side interprets the law either on terms favorable to him or her (the upper right solution), or alternatively on terms favorable to the other side (the lower left solution), and thus when the combined strategies do not match.

Let us now return to the dormant Commerce Clause cases described above. Are these cases better characterized in terms of the battle of the sexes or in terms of a pure coordination (driving) game? We might imagine that while one state or group of states has a substantive preference for straight mudflaps or sixty-five-foot trailers, others prefer curved mudflaps or longer single trailers. If so, then these different substantive views of highway safety would yield payoffs that more closely resemble those in Table 16:2 (depicting the battle of the sexes) than those in Table 16:1 (depicting the driving game). The worst result would arise if each state wrongly sought to anticipate the other state's laws (equivalent to the lower left solution), and an only slightly better result would arise if each state stuck to its first choice without trying to coordinate with the other states. If the states did try to coordinate, while some states might prefer a different legal regime, they would be willing to subordinate that concern in favor of the higher payoffs associated with a common regime that facilitates the flow of commerce among affected states.

Now consider the following alternative account. In both *Bibb* and *Kassel*, the out-of-sync state enacted the challenged law against a background of laws of numerous states already in place that contradicted it. Passing laws is an extremely costly process, and it is difficult to do so in one state and especially difficult to enact coordinated laws across numerous independent state jurisdictions. The surrounding states had in place a well-established set of contrary laws at the time Illinois and Iowa enacted their challenged laws.[54] If these states were playing a battle-of-the-sexes game, knowledge of the surrounding states' existing contrary laws would certainly have counseled in favor of acquiescing to receive the higher payoffs of coordination, even if Illinois and Iowa for some reason regarded those laws as inferior, rather than forging a non-pure-Nash equilibrium outcome that results in reduced payoffs for all of the states involved.

Does it seem more plausible that the challenged law was motivated by the desire for a better policy, even if contrary to that of surrounding states, or by the desire to thwart a coordinated strategy? Does it matter that Illinois did not permit both types of mudflaps, as opposed to prohibiting the more commonly used mudflap? Consider in this regard the following passage from Justice Douglas's opinion in *Bibb:*

> Such a new safety device—out of line with the requirements of the other States—may be so compelling that the innovating State need not be the one to give way. But the present showing—balanced against the clear burden on commerce—is far too inconclusive to make this mudguard meet that test.[55]

Does this passage lend support to the pure coordination or battle of the sexes account of *Bibb*? Why? Which account do you find more persuasive? Do you think *Bibb* and *Kassel* were correctly decided? Why or why not? To what extent is your answer informed by game theory? To what extent is it informed by interest group theory? What if subsequent evidence showed the nonconforming standard to have greater benefits than originally believed? Might this help to explain the default nature of the dormant Commerce Clause doctrine, meaning the power of Congress to overrule such cases?

C. The Game of Chicken (or Hawk-Dove)

1. *The Basic Game*

The chicken game, or its counterpart Hawk-Dove from evolutionary biology,[56] is different in an important respect from any of the games described thus far. Unlike the prisoners' dilemma, this game generates more than a single pure Nash equilibrium outcome. Unlike the driving game and the battle of the sexes, however, in which the pure-Nash outcomes arise when the players' combined strategies end up coordinated, in the game of chicken, the pure-Nash outcomes arise when the players each choose a different rule, thereby in some sense "failing" to coordinate strategies.

---

[54] *See* Kassel v. Consol. Freightways, 450 U.S. 662, 684 (1981) (noting that the Iowa law was out of keeping with those of surrounding states); Bibb v. Navajo Freight Lines, Inc., 359 U.S. 520, 529–30 (1959) (noting that Illinois law is out of keeping with that of almost all other states).

[55] *Bibb*, 359 U.S. at 530.

[56] These two games are identical in structure, but were developed with different vocabularies and within different disciplines. *See* MARTIN J. OSBORNE & ARIEL RUBINSTEIN, A COURSE IN GAME THEORY 30 (1994).

In the game of chicken, the players receive relatively low (and potentially deadly) payoffs if each player selects the same strategy. Whichever strategy player *A* anticipates player *B* to follow (or the reverse), it is rational to follow the opposite strategy. In its raw form, the game of chicken has the potential to result in the loss of life to one or both players.[57] Of course there are legal and other policy analogs to this game that do not result in loss of life, which we will consider. Once again, we begin with the normal form game.

Chicken is an unseemly game of nerve generally involving two drivers each seeking to outrank the other in an effort to attain status. In its traditional presentation, it is played in either of two ways. In the first illustration, Albert and Bart, drive their cars toward a cliff. The last car to stop without going over is the winner. In the second illustration, the players drive at each other at considerable speed. The first to swerve is the loser. The dangers inherent in this game are obvious. Depending upon the guts (read stupidity) of the drivers, there is a substantial risk that one or both will take their cars over the cliff (in the first game) or that they will crash head-on (in the second). Winning the game of chicken requires that the other driver become unnerved sufficiently early to prevent himself and the other player from continuing a course of play that leads to a devastating result, and potential loss of life.

Table 16:3 illustrates the payoffs in this game.

Table 16:3. The Game of Chicken

Payoffs for (Albert, Bart)	Bart Swerves	Bart does not Swerve
Albert Swerves	0, 0	**−25, 50**
Albert does not Swerve	**50, −25**	−100, −100

In this game, there are two outcomes that correspond to pure Nash equilibria: (swerve, not swerve) and (not swerve, swerve), and two outcomes that correspond to non-pure-Nash equilibria (swerve, swerve) and (not swerve, not swerve). There is a single mixed strategy equilibrium, and it can give rise to any of these four outcomes.[58] As in the prior two games in this chapter, if the players randomize over the options before them, any of the four possible outcomes might obtain.

This game differs from the preceding games in this section in that the pure-Nash equilibrium outcomes arise in the upper right and lower left boxes in which the players assume different rules, thereby not pursuing a common strategy: one goes straight and the other swerves. In this game, if both Albert and Bart swerve, neither can claim victory, and each receives a payoff of 0, meaning that each winds up with the same status ranking as before playing the game. If one player swerves while the other does not, then the one who does not swerve greatly improves his status, thus receiving the highest payoff of 50, while the one who does swerve suffers a loss of status, with a payoff of –25. Finally, if neither player swerves, then they both are badly injured, or worse, with a payoff valued at –100.

[57] The same is true for Hawk-Dove, except that birds, rather than people, risk the loss of life.

[58] In the mixed strategy equilibrium, both Albert and Bart play "swerve" with probability 3/5, and "not swerve" with probability 2/5. The strategies are symmetric because the payoffs are symmetric.

Now consider the nature of the equilibrium results. Assume that Albert anticipates that Bart is going to drive straight no matter what. In that case, given the payoffs, Albert's rational strategy is to swerve, with the resulting payoffs of 50 to Bart, and –25 to Albert. This is not a great result, of course, but it is a stable equilibrium because given Bart's strategy, Albert would reduce his payoff to –100 (and risk death) by following the alternative strategy of also driving straight. Conversely, if Bart anticipates that Albert is going to become unnerved in the game and swerve no matter what, then the rational strategy is to drive straight, again securing a payoff (in the same box) of 50, with Albert suffering a loss of –25. The same is true of the lower left box, and here we need only reverse the names in the preceding discussion, this time with Albert predictably driving straight and Bart rationally responding by swerving, or with Bart predictably swerving, and Albert responding by driving straight. These are each pure-Nash-equilibrium outcomes.

For the same reason that the upper right and lower left boxes are pure-Nash-strategy equilibria outcomes, the upper left and lower right boxes represent outcomes that are not pure-Nash equilibria. We begin with the upper left box in which both drivers swerve. Imagine that Albert anticipates that Bart will swerve no matter what. In this case, Albert receives a payoff of 0 by also swerving, but can improve that payoff to 50 by going straight, thus moving from the upper left box to the lower left box. Conversely, if Bart anticipates that Albert will swerve no matter what, Bart would receive a payoff of 0 by also swerving, and could improve that payoff to 50 by driving straight, moving this time to the upper right box.

The same analysis explains why the lower right box (–100, –100) represents an outcome that does not correspond to a pure Nash equilibrium. Imagine that Albert anticipates that Bart will drive straight no matter what, for example, if Albert demonstrates his commitment by removing the steering wheel from the car. In that case, Bart faces a certain devastating consequence by also driving straight (with a payoff of –100), but can improve his payoff (to –25) by swerving, thus placing him in the upper right box. The same result plays in reverse if instead Bart signals an absolute commitment to driving straight, this time with Albert improving his payoff from –100 to –25 by swerving, and moving from the lower right to the lower left box.

As with the driving game and the battle of the sexes, this game yields two outcomes that correspond to pure Nash equilibria and two outcomes that do not correspond to pure-Nash equilibria. Again, there is no way to know what the actual result will be in any given game. If neither player has sufficient information to form a meaningful impression as to how the other will act, it is possible that one will misread the other, and that the combined strategies will place the players in any of the four boxes.

2. Non-Myopic Equilibrium

The preceding analysis suggests that with knowledge as to the other player's bonded strategy, the drivers wind up in one of the two pure-Nash-strategy equilibria, and that without such knowledge they risk arriving at any of the four options, depending upon how well they anticipate the other player's strategy. Let us now consider a different account that rests on an alternative equilibrium concept. In the conventional analysis, the (straight, swerve) or (swerve, straight) outcomes are pure Nash because if either player commits to a strategy, the other has no alternative that improves his payoffs. Now imagine that Albert and Bart play this game in a single period without any specific knowledge concerning the strategy of the other player. How might we expect them to respond?

Professor Steven Brams has analyzed the game of chicken using a dynamic equilibrium concept known as *non-myopic equilibrium*.[59] To illustrate, we reproduce below the payoffs in Table 16:3, but this time with a series of arrows that suggest the possibility of thinking through the implications in each round of the combined strategies for each player.

Table 16:4. Non-Myopic Equilibrium in the Game of Chicken

Payoffs for (A, B)	Bart Swerves	Bart does not Swerve
Albert Swerves	*0* ↓, **0** →	*–25*, **50** ↓
Albert does not Swerve	*50*→, **–25**	*–100* ↖, **–100** ↖

To keep the exposition simple, we have italicized the payoffs for Albert and bolded the payoffs for Bart.[60] In each box, next to the relevant payoff, we have placed an arrow that signals the direction of an expected alternative strategy for a non-myopic player. Unlike the standard Nash equilibrium analysis, which inquires whether for any given strategy by the other player, there is a move that will improve the decision maker's payoffs, in this game, we ask the following additional question. Given the payoffs from each combined set of strategies, how stable is the assumption concerning the strategy of the other player? We first consider Albert's assessment of rational play given Bart's assessment of the combined strategies.

While we can begin the analysis at any strategic location, assume Albert positions himself in the lower left box hoping to drive straight while Bart swerves. Albert receives a payoff of 50 and Bart receives a payoff of −25. The problem is that while neither side knows the strategy that the other will adopt, both parties know the payoff schedule, which is reciprocal. Just as Albert pursues an initial strategy to get the favorable lower left payoffs (50, −25), Bart pursues the inverse initial strategy to get the beneficial payoffs set out on the upper right (−25, 50). With this set of combined strategies, however, the result is to have both Albert and Bart drive straight, leading each to their worst possible result (–100, –100). If they anticipate this position, however, for each player it becomes rational to change strategies to swerving to avoid the potentially deadly result, thus moving to the upper left with payoffs of (0,0). Of course, if Albert and Bart each anticipate that the other will pursue this strategy, each is then rationally motivated to drive straight once again to capture the higher payoffs associated with the lower left (for Albert) and upper right (for Bart) solutions. These combined strategies merely get the ball rolling again, as they place Albert and Bart in the lower right (−100, −100).[61]

---

[59] BRAMS, *supra* note 2, at 27–33, 127–38 (applying the concept of the chicken game to the Cuban Missile Crisis).

[60] Unlike in prior matrices, the bold in Table 16:4 is not intended to indicate a Nash equilibrium.

[61] For an amusing theatrical account in which one player continues to non-myopically (but nonetheless futilely) move back and forth in evaluating his opponent's likely placement of the poisonous goblet, see THE PRINCESS BRIDE (Act III Communications 1987).

In effect, Albert cycles from lower left to lower right to upper left, while Bart cycles from upper right to lower right to upper left. To the extent that the players are non-myopic and anticipate not just the immediate payoff from a presumed strategy from the other player, but also the other player's equally dynamic assessment of the combined strategies, it is possible that neither settles on a stable outcome except by chance.

As you read each of the illustrations below, consider which equilibrium concept, Nash or non-myopic equilibrium, better captures the underlying features of the game. What, if anything, does the concept of non-myopic equilibrium suggest about the role of the state when confronted with situations that might be characterized in terms of a game of chicken? Can you think of ways to extricate parties from the seemingly intractable difficulties that such a game creates?

3. Cultural and Historical Illustrations

The game of chicken gained popular notoriety in the 1955 movie *Rebel Without a Cause*. In the movie, a new high school student, Jim Stark (played by James Dean), and a bully named Buzz Gunderson (played by Corey Allen) play the game by driving toward a cliff, and the first to stop (or jump from the window) would lose. Buzz unsuccessfully tries to jump from his car but his shirt sleeve gets caught taking him over the cliff to his demise. While the movie demonstrates the sometimes impetuous nature of young men, this should not mask the potential real stakes involved in such a game. Within evolutionary biology, status battles among alpha male chimpanzees can be modeled using the game of chicken (or Hawk-Dove), with the real stakes being sexual access to females.[62] From an evolutionary biology perspective, gaining the status of progenitor is hardly a trivial matter on par with challenging the local bully to fit in with a high school crowd. The Hawk-Dove version of the game places two birds in a potential battle over prey. If both play Hawk, they engage in a potentially deadly mutual attack, and if both play Dove, they fail to get the prey as the price of avoiding a potentially deadly fight. If one plays Hawk while the other plays Dove, the Hawk gets the prey and the Dove flees. The payoff relationships are identical to those modeled in Table 16:3.[63] We might imagine that the alpha male chimpanzees are also playing this Hawk-Dove game with the goal of sexual access in place of prey.

The chicken game also has an historical counterpart in the famous Alexander Hamilton-Aaron Burr duel, which took place on July 11, 1804.[64] While neither contemporaneous accounts nor modern historical accounts of the duel are entirely consistent, in one version, duelists customarily missed firing or fired in a manner that imposed minimal injury, for example a shot in the leg. While the duel ended at that point, the duelists signified the requisite bravery to withstand the risk of fatal fire without having

---

[62] MARTIN A. NOWAK, EVOLUTIONARY DYNAMICS: EXPLORING THE EQUATIONS OF LIFE 61 (2006) (depicting sexual competition among primates as Hawk-Dove game and observing that "Male chimpanzees fight for dominance of a group: the alpha male has to withstand challenges from other males, and in return gets a majority of the matings").

[63] Recall that it is the payoff relationships rather than the nominal payoffs that create the game.

[64] *See generally* RON CHERNOW, ALEXANDER HAMILTON (2004). The duel, along with the biography of Alexander Hamilton more generally, has recently been popularized with *Hamilton: An American Musical*, a multi-award winning musical by Lin-Manuel Miranda based on Chernow's biography.

to kill or be killed.[65] According to some accounts, Hamilton, who shot first, shot into the air, but wide and well above Burr, with no intent to hit Burr. Burr fired the second, fatal, shot into Hamilton's lower abdomen.[66]

While the conventional account of dueling expectations appears to translate roughly into a norm of mutual swerving, it is not entirely obvious that the result would have left both duelers in the same position in which they started. Consider that by willingly subjecting oneself to a potentially life-threatening duel with a sworn enemy, even if both survive, each can claim honor among those who are most familiar with the factual circumstances that motivated the duel. In some sense, therefore, mutual swerving (throwing away both first shots) vindicates the honor of both duelists. While there was a move to end dueling prior to this most famous duel, the tragic consequence provided the major impetus to end dueling within the United States, although by some accounts the practice, while increasingly rare, continued until the Civil War.[67]

II. APPLICATIONS

A. Comparing the Driving Game and the Battle of the Sexes

The United States has the mailbox rule, which generally means that an acceptance becomes legal at the time of mailing. The rule is set out in the *Restatement (Second) of Contracts* § 63, which provides as follows:

> Unless the offer provides otherwise,
>
> (a) an acceptance made in a manner and by a medium invited by an offer is operative and completes the manifestation of mutual assent as soon as put out of the offeree's possession, without regard to whether it ever reaches the offeror; but
>
> (b) an acceptance under an option contract is not operative until received by the offeror.

By contrast, the German rule places acceptance at the time of receipt. Section 130 of the German Civil Code (BGB) states:

---

[65] For an informative account, see generally JOANNE B. FREEMAN, AFFAIRS OF HONOR: NATIONAL POLITICS IN THE NEW REPUBLIC 179 (2002) ("Leg injuries were frequent enough to cast doubt on the power and meaning of the practice [of dueling]; hinting that affairs of honor entailed more pretense than peril, a newspaper editor jeered that one combatant 'was said to have received a wound in that fashionable part, *the leg*.' ").

[66] CHERNOW, *supra* note 64, at 705–05 (describing the competing accounts of Hamilton's and Burr's seconds).

[67] *See* C.A. Harwell Wells, Note, *The End of the Affair? Anti-Dueling Laws and Social Norms in Antebellum America*, 54 VAND. L. REV. 1805, 1838 (2001) ("Clearly, the Civil War killed the duel."); *see also* EDWARD L. AYERS, VENGEANCE AND JUSTICE: CRIME AND PUNISHMENT IN THE 19TH-CENTURY AMERICAN SOUTH 271 (1984).

Effectiveness of a declaration of intent to absent parties

(1) A declaration of intent that is to be made to another becomes effective, if made in his absence, at the point of time when this declaration reaches him. It does not become effective if a revocation reaches the other previously or at the same time.

(2) The effectiveness of a declaration of intent is not affected if the person declaring dies or loses capacity to contract after making a declaration.

(3) These provisions apply even if the declaration of intent is to be made to a public authority.[68]

Is either of these rules inherently superior to the alternative? Which of the games reviewed in this chapter best fits the juxtaposition of these two rules? Why?

Based on your review of the common law, especially the contract chapters, can you identify other legal doctrines that are helpfully explained based on the driving game? Can you identify legal doctrines that are helpfully explained based on the battle of the sexes?

B. Takings Reconsidered

In this application, we revisit eminent domain, an important topic that we considered initially in Chapters 7 and 8. We now consider this doctrine through the lens of game theory, juxtaposing the holdout game, one of the models analyzed in Chapters 8 and 12, with the game of chicken, introduced in this chapter. After setting out the basic analysis, we ask that you assess how these two games, or others, apply to two cases, *Kelo v. City of New London*,[69] and *Mayor of Baltimore City v. Valsamaki*,[70] each of which are presented below. We begin with a brief analysis of the game of chicken as applied to a hypothetical private or public acquisition as part of a large-scale development scheme.

Imagine an individual homeowner in the middle of a group of adjoining properties intended for a major project, for example constructing a highway or a park, for which it is necessary to assemble a large number of contiguous parcels. Or this could be a private development, requiring the assemblage of such properties to create a theme park. Whether public or private, the individual property owner recognizes that the conversion value of the overall project, meaning the difference between the aggregate value of the existing properties and the total value of the newly deployed use of the properties, will be potentially defeated if the individual owner declines to acquiesce in the sale. For this reason, it can prove rational to decline even a seemingly generous offer, such as fair market value plus a notable premium. This rationale helps to explain the conventional understanding of eminent domain: this power, subject to just compensation, allows the government to coerce, at least in the public case, the transaction, with the result of converting the owner's property right instead into a liability rule.[71]

---

[68] BÜRGERLICHES GESETZBUCHV [BGB] [CIVIL CODE], as amended Oct. 1, 2013, § 130, *translation at* https://www.gesetze-im-internet.de/englisch_bgb/englisch_bgb.html#p0396.

[69] 545 U.S. 469 (2005).

[70] 916 A.2d 324 (Md. 2007).

[71] For a discussion of eminent domain and the use of liability rules, see *supra* Chapter 8, Part I.

Assume for a moment no eminent domain power. Because the owner recognizes that her property is essential to the development as a whole, she holds out for a higher offer. She understands that once the developer assembles the remaining parcels around her property and invests in the planned development, she has the power to prevent the developer from gaining the benefits of the planned conversion of all the acquired parcels to their higher value by exercising, in effect, the power to block.[72] As a result, she declines even an increasingly generous offer, say two to three times the property's pre-development fair market value.

Now consider how this dynamic might convert the holdout game into a game of chicken. Assume that at this point, the developer and the homeowner are locked into transacting (or declining to transact) with each other. They are effectively in a *bilateral monopoly*, the stakes of which are potentially equal to the full conversation value as described above. At this point, the developer and the property owner each have two available strategies that correlate to "drive straight" or "swerve." For the developer, swerving means acquiescing to the property owner's unreasonable demand on price as the means of acquiring the holdout lot needed for the development, and driving straight means either abandoning the development plan or continuing with the development minus the holdout's property, thereby diminishing its eventual value and appearance. In some instances, depending on the timing, the abandonment might occur after the acquisition of most or all remaining properties, including having torn them down. For the landowner, swerving means accepting a bid that, although attractive, even generous, in the absence of the planned development, fails to capture a substantially larger portion of the overall project's conversion value, and driving straight means declining such an offer, but subject to a critical risk. That risk is having the developer proceed with the overall project minus this specific property.

To the extent that the parties are "locked in," meaning forced to deal with each other, as the negotiations falter, the parties find themselves in what increasingly appears to be a game of chicken. If, from the owner's perspective, the developer fails adequately to up the ante, the financial consequences to her risk becoming severe, potentially diminishing the value of the property from its one-time fair market value to zero, as no other purchaser but the developer would have an interest. This could arise if either the developer has already torn down the surrounding properties, or if the developer proceeds to develop around the property in a manner that renders it unattractive to other purchasers. And if the owner continues to refuse even generous offers to buy, the developer confronts this difficult and costly choice as to whether to continue around the holdout. For the developer, the prospect of a theme park, golf course, or park constructed around a private residence is unappealing, and for the holdout, the prospect of a home in the middle of such a development is as well.[73]

---

[72] Recall that Disney actually employed straw purchasers to avoid this problem. *See supra* Chapter 8, Part II.E.1 and cite therein. *See also* Daniel B. Kelly, *The "Public Use" Requirement in Eminent Domain Law: A Rationale Based on Secret Purchases and Private Influence*, 92 CORNELL L. REV. 1 (2006) (discussing reliance on straw purchasers, including those involved in the Disney acquisition of property in Orlando, Florida).

[73] Of course, it is possible that through the doctrine of easement by necessity, the holdout will continue to have access to a main road, but even so, few, if any buyers, will be interested in acquiring a lot under these conditions. For a discussion of easements by necessity, see Hunter C. Carroll, *Easements by Necessity: What Level of Necessity Is Required?*, 19 AM. J. TRIAL ADVOC. 475 (1995). *See supra* Chapter 7, Part III.A.6. It is also possible,

Based on Table 16:3, the combined driving-straight strategies place the players in the lower right box (with payoffs of –100, –100). By contrast, mutual swerving, meaning compromising and accommodating the other party's demands without the benefit to the holdout of gaining a larger share of the full project conversion value, and without the benefit to the developer of acquiring the holdout lot for a price that truly reflects its original fair market value, correlates to the upper left box (payoffs at 0,0).

Remember that in the game of chicken, neither mutual swerving nor mutual driving straight is a pure-Nash equilibrium. If the homeowner believes that no matter what, the developer is committed to driving straight, she receives a higher payoff by swerving, thereby accepting the most recent reasonable offer. Conversely, if the developer believes that no matter what, the homeowner will not swerve and will insist upon a portion of the larger conversion value, then it can also receive substantially higher value by cutting its losses and acquiescing to the owner's demands for a larger share of the prize, again producing a solution that is pure Nash.[74] These combined strategies move the game toward the lower left or upper right solutions in Table 16:3, which are pure Nash.

Now consider how the juxtaposition of these two games—the holdout and the game of chicken—apply to each of the two following cases.

1. *Susette Kelo v. City of New London, Connecticut*

The question in *Kelo v. City of New London,*[75] was whether the City of New London, Connecticut could exercise its eminent domain power with respect to Susette Kelo's home to facilitate part of a large-scale private development to support a planned Pfizer plant and several related businesses. This included acquiring approximately 115 homes in the Fort Trumbull neighborhood, which would form an adjunct part of the city's larger, complex development plan. In addition to supporting the Pfizer plant, the overall project would eventually include new businesses, restaurants, and homes.

Kelo, along with several other residents, declined New London's fair market value offer, asserting that they wished to continue living in what was, for many, a lifelong community. New London instigated condemnation proceedings, and Kelo filed suit in state court, claiming that the proceedings violated her rights under the Fifth Amendment, as applied to the city under the Fourteenth Amendment due process clause. She specifically maintained that under the "public use" requirement, it was not permissible under eminent domain to take one person's private property to transfer it to another private entity simply to raise its value and the City's tax base. The trial court allowed some of the planned condemnations to proceed, and the Supreme Court of Connecticut upheld all of them as permissible public use. Kelo appealed to the U.S. Supreme Court, which sustained that ruling by a 5–4 vote. Following the litigation, Pfizer announced in 2010 that it was closing down its New London operations.

---

however, that if the surrounding development is attractive, for example a golf course or park, the holdout landowner retains marketable—or even more valuable—property.

[74] This assumes that there is no prospect for regulatory intervention, a possibility discussed below. *See infra* Part II.2.a, and accompanying text.

[75] 545 U.S. 469 (2005).

JUSTICE STEVENS delivered the opinion of the Court.

Decades of economic decline led a state agency in 1990 to designate the [City of New London, Connecticut] a "distressed municipality." . . . In 1998, the City's unemployment rate was nearly double that of the State, and its population of just under 24,000 residents was at its lowest since 1920.

These conditions prompted state and local officials to target New London, and particularly its Fort Trumbull area, for economic revitalization. To this end, respondent New London Development Corporation (NLDC), a private nonprofit entity established some years earlier to assist the City in planning economic development, was reactivated. In January 1998, the State authorized a $5.35 million bond issue to support the NLDC's planning activities and a $10 million bond issue toward the creation of a Fort Trumbull State Park. In February, the pharmaceutical company Pfizer Inc. announced that it would build a $300 million research facility on a site immediately adjacent to Fort Trumbull; local planners hoped that Pfizer would draw new business to the area, thereby serving as a catalyst to the area's rejuvenation. After receiving initial approval from the city council, the NLDC continued its planning activities . . . Upon obtaining state-level approval, the NLDC finalized an integrated development plan focused on 90 acres of the Fort Trumbull area.

The Fort Trumbull area . . . comprises approximately 115 privately owned properties, as well as the 32 acres of land formerly occupied by the naval facility . . . .

The NLDC intended the development plan to capitalize on the arrival of the Pfizer facility and the new commerce it was expected to attract. . . .

The city council approved the plan in January 2000, and designated the NLDC as its development agent in charge of implementation. The city council also authorized the NLDC to purchase property or to acquire property by exercising eminent domain in the City's name. The NLDC successfully negotiated the purchase of most of the real estate in the 90-acre area, but its negotiations with petitioners failed. As a consequence, in November 2000, the NLDC initiated the condemnation proceedings that gave rise to this case.

* * *

Two polar propositions are perfectly clear. On the one hand, it has long been accepted that the sovereign may not take the property of *A* for the sole purpose of transferring it to another private party *B*, even though *A* is paid just compensation. On the other hand, it is equally clear that a State may transfer property from one private party to another if future "use by the public" is the purpose of the taking; the condemnation of land for a railroad with common-carrier duties is a familiar example. . . .

. . .

The disposition of this case therefore turns on the question whether the City's development plan serves a "public purpose." Without exception, our cases have defined that concept broadly, reflecting our longstanding policy of deference to legislative judgments in this field.

In *Berman v. Parker* (1954), this Court upheld a redevelopment plan targeting a blighted area of Washington, D. C., in which most of the housing for the area's 5,000 inhabitants was beyond repair. Under the plan, the area would be condemned and part of it utilized for the construction of streets, schools, and other public facilities. The remainder of the land would be leased or sold to private parties for the purpose of redevelopment, including the construction of low-cost housing.... Writing for a unanimous Court, Justice Douglas refused to evaluate this claim in isolation, deferring instead to the legislative and agency judgment that the area "must be planned as a whole" for the plan to be successful....

In *Hawaii Housing Authority v. Midkiff* (1984), the Court considered a Hawaii statute whereby fee title was taken from lessors and transferred to lessees (for just compensation) in order to reduce the concentration of land ownership. We unanimously upheld the statute and rejected the Ninth Circuit's view that it was "a naked attempt on the part of the state of Hawaii to take the property of A and transfer it to B solely for B's private use and benefit." Reaffirming *Berman's* deferential approach to legislative judgments in this field, we concluded that the State's purpose of eliminating the "social and economic evils of a land oligopoly" qualified as a valid public use....

* * *

Those who govern the City were not confronted with the need to remove blight in the Fort Trumbull area, but their determination that the area was sufficiently distressed to justify a program of economic rejuvenation is entitled to our deference. The City has carefully formulated an economic development plan that it believes will provide appreciable benefits to the community, including—but by no means limited to—new jobs and increased tax revenue. As with other exercises in urban planning and development, the City is endeavoring to coordinate a variety of commercial, residential, and recreational uses of land, with the hope that they will form a whole greater than the sum of its parts. To effectuate this plan, the City has invoked a state statute that specifically authorizes the use of eminent domain to promote economic development. Given the comprehensive character of the plan, the thorough deliberation that preceded its adoption, and the limited scope of our review, it is appropriate for us, as it was in *Berman*, to resolve the challenges of the individual owners, not on a piecemeal basis, but rather in light of the entire plan. Because that plan unquestionably serves a public purpose, the takings challenged here satisfy the public use requirement of the Fifth Amendment.

* * *

In affirming the City's authority to take petitioners' properties, we do not minimize the hardship that condemnations may entail, notwithstanding the payment of just compensation. We emphasize that nothing in our opinion precludes any State from placing further restrictions on its exercise of the takings power. Indeed, many States already impose "public use" requirements that are stricter than the federal baseline.... This Court's authority, however, extends only to determining whether the City's proposed condemnations are for a "public use" within the meaning of the Fifth Amendment to the Federal Constitution. Because over a century of our case law interpreting that provision dictates an affirmative answer to that question, we may not grant petitioners the relief that they seek.

JUSTICE KENNEDY, concurring.

The determination that a rational-basis standard of review is appropriate does not, however, alter the fact that transfers intended to confer benefits on particular, favored private entities, and with only incidental or pretextual public benefits, are forbidden by the Public Use Clause.

A court applying rational-basis review under the Public Use Clause should strike down a taking that, by a clear showing, is intended to favor a particular private party, with only incidental or pretextual public benefits, just as a court applying rational-basis review under the Equal Protection Clause must strike down a government classification that is clearly intended to injure a particular class of private parties, with only incidental or pretextual public justifications.

* * *

JUSTICE O'CONNOR, with whom THE CHIEF JUSTICE, JUSTICE SCALIA, and JUSTICE THOMAS join, dissenting.

While the Takings Clause presupposes that government can take private property without the owner's consent, the just compensation requirement spreads the cost of condemnations and thus "prevents the public from loading upon one individual more than his just share of the burdens of government." . . . The public use requirement, in turn, imposes a more basic limitation, circumscribing the very scope of the eminent domain power: Government may compel an individual to forfeit her property for the *public's* use, but not for the benefit of another private person. This requirement promotes fairness as well as security. . . .

* * *

Our cases have generally identified three categories of takings that comply with the public use requirement, though it is in the nature of things that the boundaries between these categories are not always firm. Two are relatively straightforward and uncontroversial. First, the sovereign may transfer private property to public ownership—such as for a road, a hospital, or a military base. . . . Second, the sovereign may transfer private property to private parties, often common carriers, who make the property available for the public's use—such as with a railroad, a public utility, or a stadium. . . . But "public ownership" and "use-by-the-public" are sometimes too constricting and impractical ways to define the scope of the Public Use Clause. Thus we have allowed that, in certain circumstances and to meet certain exigencies, takings that serve a public purpose also satisfy the Constitution even if the property is destined for subsequent private use. See, *e.g.*, *Berman* v. *Parker* (1954); *Hawaii Housing Authority* v. *Midkiff* (1984).

. . .

The Court's holdings in *Berman* and *Midkiff* were true to the principle underlying the Public Use Clause. In both those cases, the extraordinary, precondemnation use of the targeted property inflicted affirmative harm on society—in *Berman* through blight resulting from extreme poverty and in *Midkiff* through oligopoly resulting from extreme wealth. And in both cases, the relevant legislative body had found that eliminating the existing property use was necessary to remedy the harm. . . . Thus a public purpose was realized when the harmful use was eliminated. Because each taking *directly* achieved a public benefit, it did not matter that the property was turned over to private use. Here, in contrast, New London does not claim that Susette Kelo's and Wilhelmina Dery's well-maintained homes are the source of any social harm. Indeed, it could not so claim without adopting the absurd argument that any single-family home that might be razed to make way for an apartment building, or any church that might be replaced with a retail store, or any small business that might be more lucrative if it were instead part of a national franchise, is inherently harmful to society and thus within the government's power to condemn.

In moving away from our decisions sanctioning the condemnation of harmful property use, the Court today significantly expands the meaning of public use. It holds that the sovereign may take private property currently put to ordinary private use, and give it over for new, ordinary private use, so long as the new use is predicted to generate some secondary benefit for the public—such as increased tax revenue, more jobs, maybe even aesthetic pleasure. But nearly any lawful use of real private property can be said to generate some incidental benefit to the public. Thus, if predicted (or even guaranteed) positive side-effects are enough to render transfer from one private party to another constitutional, then the words "for public use" do not realistically exclude *any* takings, and thus do not exert any constraint on the eminent domain power.

JUSTICE THOMAS, dissenting

[Justice Thomas explained that based on his assessment of original meaning, *Midkiff* and *Berman* were wrongly decided.]

Allowing the government to take property solely for public purposes is bad enough, but extending the concept of public purpose to encompass any economically beneficial goal guarantees that these losses will fall disproportionately on poor communities. Those communities are not only systematically less likely to put their lands to the highest and best social use, but are also the least politically powerful. If ever there were justification for intrusive judicial review of constitutional provisions that protect "discrete and insular minorities," *United States v. Carolene Products Co.* (1938), surely that principle would apply with great force to the powerless groups and individuals the Public Use Clause protects. The deferential standard this Court has adopted for the Public Use Clause is therefore deeply perverse. . . .

2. *Mayor of Baltimore City v. Valsamaki*

Now compare *Kelo* with a decision by the Maryland Court of Appeals. Under Maryland law, the City of Baltimore has the authority to exercise eminent domain power through an expedited process known as *quick-take condemnation.* The Maryland Constitution provides:

> [W]here such property is situated in Baltimore City and is desired by this State or by the Mayor and City Council of Baltimore, the General Assembly may provide that such property may be taken immediately upon payment therefor to the owner or owners thereof by the State or by the Mayor and City Council of Baltimore, or into court, such amount as the State or the Mayor and City Council of Baltimore, as the case may be, shall estimate to be the fair value

> of said property, provided such legislation also requires the payment of any further sum that may subsequently be added by a jury.[76]

Under Maryland Public Law, the City may employ this expedited process, taking possession within ten days of filing by persuading the court that "the public interest requires the City to have immediate possession."[77] The owner is only allowed to challenge the city's right to condemnation.[78]

This process was at issue in the case of *Mayor of Baltimore City v. Valsamaki.*[79] The city had approved a plan for "the revitalization of the Charles/North area . . . to create a unique mixed-use neighborhood with enhanced viability, stability, attractiveness, and convenience for residents of the surrounding area and of the City as a whole."[80] This included a plan to acquire Mr. Valsamaki's business, the *Magnet*, a tavern and packaged goods store. The City helped to facilitate this plan with the help of The Baltimore Development Corporation (BDC), a private not-for-profit corporation, similar to the NLDC. The Magnet served liquor on site, and also sold six-packs of beer and miniature liquor bottles, among other alcoholic beverages, for takeaway to local residents. It was situated on a site that the city hoped to combine with surrounding lots on each side to attract a grocery store and parking facility.

Although Mr. Valsamaki was nearing retirement, he was unimpressed with the BDC's $140,000 offer, and so declined to sell, prompting the city to exercise its quick-take condemnation power. He then challenged the taking in court, and after a trial judge rejected the City's attempted reliance on quick-take procedure, the ruling was ultimately affirmed in the Maryland Court of Appeals.

The *Valsamaki* court distinguished *Kelo* on two grounds: First, it questioned the need for the exercise of the quick-take process, stating: "in a quick-take action, [the City has] the burden to establish the necessity for an immediate taking."[81] Second, the court reasoned that unlike the comprehensive development plan in *Kelo*, in this case, the City lacked such a plan. The court further questioned the relationship between the city's claim to public use and the plan for eventual transfer for private development, stating: "It is virtually impossible to determine the extent of the public/private dichotomy when no one knows the who, what, and whether of the future use of the property."[82] The court ruled that the city had failed to meet its burden to demonstrate why it should not be required to acquire the land through the more onerous eminent domain procedure.[83]

---

[76] MD. CONST. art. III § 40A.

[77] Code of Public Local Laws of Baltimore City, § 21–16. 40 PLL § 21–16(a).

[78] Code of Public Local Laws of Baltimore City, § 21–16. 40 PLL § 21–16(c).

[79] *See* Mayor of Baltimore City v. Valsamaki, 916 A.2d 324 (Md. 2007).

[80] *Id.* at 328 (citing Baltimore City Ordinance No. 04–695). *See* DEP'T HOUSING & COMMUNITY DEV. BALT., URBAN RENEWAL PLAN CHARLES/NORTH REVITALIZATION AREA (Oct. 25, 1982) (amended 2007), https://planning.baltimorecity.gov/sites/default/files/Charles%20North%20URP%20a7.pdf.

[81] Mayor of Baltimore City v. Valsamaki, 916 A.2d at 354.

[82] *Id.* at 353.

[83] The court determined that for the city to take possession under the statute, it must show sufficient reasons to support immediate possession, for example, if the building or property is "immediately injurious to the health and safety of the public, or is otherwise immediately needed for public use." *Id.* at 356. The court ruled narrowly, finding that under the facts, the taking did not meet the requirements of the quick-take statute.

MAYOR AND CITY COUNCIL OF BALTIMORE CITY V. VALSAMAKI

(Maryland Court of Appeals, Feb. 8, 2007)

OPINION by CATHELL, J.,

In the case sub judice, the City did not satisfy the basic statutory mandate of § 21-16(a) of the Public Local Laws of Baltimore City. . . . The City's petitions evince a dearth of any specific evidence showing a necessity for the immediate possession of the Property via quick-take condemnation as opposed to a regular condemnation. . . . We agree with Judge Miller. . . . [T]he affidavit attached to the petition for immediate possession and title only provides that immediate possession is necessary "in order to assist in a business expansion in the area." This statement, in and of itself, while perhaps sufficient to justify regular condemnation, does not justify a quick-take condemnation. . . . Mr. Dombrowski [Director of Planning and Design for the Baltimore Development Corporation and also the Project Manager for the Baltimore North Area] testified as to what a business expansion in the area meant, stating: "It means to us, at least, the opportunity to provide for additional business expansion opportunities." When asked whether there was a specific plan for the development of the Property, he replied: "Not as yet because the procedure we follow is through a request for proposal procedure as you well know." Mr. Brodie [President of the Baltimore Development Corporation] disagreed with Mr. Dombrowski's statements to the effect that there was no specific plan for development of the property. However, when asked about what specific uses were called for in the plan for the Property, he declined to, or could not, provide a specific answer. . . . While the existence of a general urban renewal plan might, under some circumstances, justify the use of regular condemnation, it, alone, under the statute applicable in the instant case, does not suffice to provide the immediacy that needs to exist to justify quick-take condemnation with its lesser procedural due process standards. . . .

* * *

[T]he opportunities to challenge a condemnation are shortened and truncated when quick-take condemnation is used as opposed to regular condemnation. . . . The property owner was ordered out of possession of his property just six days from the time of the filing of the action and only learned that he was dispossessed when the order was served upon him. Then the time for him to respond was so short that he was not afforded time to conduct—or really to begin—discovery procedures in order to be able to address the issues of public use, necessity, or immediacy. Yet, the City did not at that time have present plans for the utilization of the Property and would only know what was to be done with the Property when private developers submitted proposals to it—which might be in an indeterminant future.

The desire for the general assemblage of properties for urban renewal might be sufficient to justify the use of regular condemnation proceedings, but absent more specific

Id. The court went on to state: "In essence, quick take procedures can be used inappropriately to destroy altogether the right of the property owner to challenge the public use prong of eminent domain." *Id.* at 347.

and compelling evidence than was presented here, does not satisfy the immediacy and necessity requirements under quick-take condemnation. . . .

* * *

. . . Justice Stevens, writing for the Supreme Court in *Kelo*, stated two general propositions regarding takings. First, "the City would no doubt be forbidden from taking petitioner's land for the purpose of conferring a private benefit on a particular private party." Second, "[n]or would the City be allowed to take property under the mere pretext of a public purpose, when its actual purpose was to bestow a private benefit." The Court, however, distinguished the situation in *Kelo*, finding that it did not fall under either of the two propositions because "[t]he takings . . . would be executed pursuant to a 'carefully considered' development plan."

The [*Kelo*] Court then proceeded to emphasize the requirement that the development plan satisfy a "public purpose," as opposed to a "public use." This is evidenced by the fact that the " 'Court long ago rejected any literal requirement that condemned property be put into use for the general public.' " The "broader and more natural interpretation of public use" is a "public purpose." Therefore, the Court found that "[t]he disposition of this case [] turns on the question whether the City's development plan serves a 'public purpose.' Without exception, our cases have defined that concept broadly, reflecting our longstanding policy of deference to legislative judgments in this field."

* * *

In *Kelo*, the Court deferred to the legislature's judgment, finding that "[t]he City has carefully formulated an economic development plan that it believes will provide appreciable benefits to the community, including—but by no means limited to—new jobs and increased tax revenue." And, that "[g]iven the comprehensive character of the plan, the thorough deliberation that preceded its adoption, and the limited scope of our review, it is appropriate for us . . . to resolve the challenges of the individual owners, not on a piecemeal basis, but rather in light of the entire plan." . . .

In the case sub judice, the necessity for immediate possession (in contrast to the public use or public purpose to be achieved) is not sufficiently shown . . . . Notwithstanding that, even had the case involved the use of regular condemnation, the evidence . . . of public use was sparse. The City has only shown that the Property is to be acquired for renewal purposes to assist in a "business expansion" in the area.

* * *

. . . [T]he only "plan" for the Property is that a private developer will possibly, at some future time, create a plan that the City might approve. . . .

Simply resting on the City's assertions in Ordinance No. 82–799 and Ordinance No. 04–695, that the Property will be taken for urban renewal or revitalization purposes is not sufficient to justify the abridgment of a property owner's rights to procedural due process by the use of the extreme power of quick-take condemnation.

In regular condemnations, however, only the public use, not the immediacy of the need, is at issue. . . .

* * *

For the aforementioned reasons, we hold that, pursuant to § 21–16 of the Public Local Laws of Baltimore City, the City failed to provide sufficient reasons for its *immediate* possession of and title to the subject Property.

QUESTIONS AND COMMENTS

The *Kelo* decision sparked strong public condemnation. Several commentators have argued against reliance on eminent domain to effectuate private-to-private transfers outside the contexts that are set out in Justice O'Connor's dissenting opinion. They argue, instead, that public use demands that the government deploy acquired land directly for such purposes as parks, schools, or roads, as opposed to allowing it to transfer acquired property to private developers who will enhance the tax revenue base by converting existing usage to one of higher financial value.[84] Our purpose here is not to resolve this important constitutional question. Instead, we ask that you evaluate the claims based on the preceding game theoretical analysis.

1. To what extent does *Kelo* reflect a conventional holdout game? To what extent does it, instead, reflect a game of chicken?

2. One argument against allowing the private-to-private transfer is that private developers can choose among a variety of locations to assemble the needed lots, as Disney illustrated with its reliance on straw purchasers to facilitate Disney World in Orlando, Florida. How, if at all, does this affect the game theoretical analysis of *Kelo?*

3. Notice that the formal purchaser in *Kelo* was the New London Development Corporation (NLDC), rather than Pfizer, or a private developer. The ultimate plan was to attract several private businesses that would purchase the assembled properties, and with the benefit of tax breaks, would build new residences and supporting business in Fort Trumbull to support the larger project. Although NLDC is formally independent, it is closely tied to the City of New London. NLDC was not charged with promoting economic development in general; rather, it was charged with promoting economic development in New London. How does this affect the game theoretical analysis of *Kelo*, and why? How do the bond referendums and the approval of tax breaks affect your analysis?

4. At the beginning of Chapter 15, we asked whether an important role of government is to encourage benign games and to discourage illicit ones. Does *Kelo* illustrate this proposition or thwart it? Why? Without resolving the underlying constitutional question of public use based on alternative considerations, such as original constitutional meaning, how, if at all, do these alternative game theoretical accounts inform the doctrinal analysis of whether private-to-private land transfers can be reconciled with the requirement of "public use," and if so, under what circumstances?[85]

---

[84] *See, e.g.*, Charles E. Cohen, *Eminent Domain After* Kelo v. City of New London: *An Argument for Banning Economic Development Takings*, 29 HARV. J.L. & PUB. POL'Y 491, 496–97, 563–64 (2006); Timothy Sandefur, *The "Backlash" So Far: Will Americans Get Meaningful Eminent Domain Reform?*, 2006 MICH. ST. L. REV. 709, 730–32; Sonya D. Jones, *That Land Is Your Land, This Land Is My Land . . . Until the Local Government Can Turn it for a Profit: A Critical Analysis of* Kelo v. City of New London, 20 BYU J. PUB. L. 139, 151–55 (2005).

[85] For a comprehensive presentation along these lines, see ILYA SOMIN, THE GRASPING HAND: "KELO V. CITY OF NEW LONDON" AND THE LIMITS OF EMINENT DOMAIN (2015).

5. If you are persuaded that *Kelo* represents a game of chicken, does the analysis require placing the City of New London and the judiciary in a paternalistic role with respect to Ms. Kelo? If so, is that normatively problematic? Why or why not?

6. Do you find the *Valsamaki* court's efforts to distinguish *Kelo* persuasive? Why or why not? Which case, *Kelo* or *Valsamaki*, better illustrates a holdout game? A chicken game? What role does the expedited procedure employed by the City of Baltimore in *Valsamaki* play in your analysis?

7. In discussing *Kelo,* the *Valsamaki* Court carefully distinguishes public use from public purpose, saying that the Supreme Court has long allowed the use of eminent domain to promote the latter. How does this insight affect the game theoretical analysis of these two cases? Does this doctrinal distinction help also to distinguish *Kelo* and *Valsamaki*?

8. The *Valsamaki* Court also distinguishes the permissibility of reliance on eminent domain from the permissibility of reliance on quick-take condemnation, as permitted in Baltimore. To what extent, if any, does the game theoretical analysis help to support the distinction that the court draws?

9. After the *Valsamaki* case concluded, Mr. Valsamaki sold his property to the Baltimore Development Corporation for $365,000, well in excess of the initial offer of $140,000.[86] Does this datum provide support for treating the case as a holdout game or as a game of chicken? Why?

10. Was *Kelo* rightly decided? Was *Valsamaki* rightly decided? Was the widespread public condemnation of *Kelo* surprising? Was it justified? Why or why not? To what extent does game theory help in answering these questions?

---

[86] Recorded Deed from George Valsamaki to Mayor & City Council of Balt., Book 9782 at 434–37 (July 31, 2007), https://mdlandrec.net/main/ (login required) (select "Baltimore City" under "Select County" drop down. Click on "Individual Search" and enter "Valsamaki" in "Last Name" field box. Click on "2007–08–01" Deed). *See* Will Skowronski, *BDC: More Mediation, Less 'Quick Take' to be Used in Property Disputes*, BALT. BUS. J. (July 11, 2007, 12:46 PM), https://www.bizjournals.com/baltimore/stories/2007/07/09/daily21.html?jst=b_ln_hl.

PART V

Institutional Applications

CHAPTER 17

The Legislature (Part 1)

Introduction

In this chapter and the next, we consider how public choice analysis, broadly defined, helps to inform our understanding of the structure and processes of legislative decision making. Our primary focus is on the United States Congress and on the judicial interpretation of statutes. This chapter, which focuses primarily on the relevant theoretical framing, proceeds in two parts. Part I presents two competing models designed to offer insights into the legislative decision-making process.[1] Part II, the Applications, introduces a case and several questions that together explore the themes of this chapter as applied to the constitutional judicial review of statutes affected by rent-seeking pressures.

We begin by reconsidering the public interest model of the legislative process, introduced in Chapter 11.[2] To better develop the implications of this model, we expound upon the influential *Legal Process School* as developed in an unpublished, yet highly influential, manuscript by Professors Henry M. Hart, Jr. and Albert M. Sacks.[3] Hart and Sacks developed a comprehensive approach to statutory construction that rests on the supposition that both legislators and courts are primarily motivated to further public interest objectives in drafting and in interpreting statutes.

We then revisit the Wilson-Hayes matrix, presented in Chapter 11, which explores the implications of interest group dynamics for each of four analytical categories of legislation. The combined matrix provides a rough sketch of the legislative process that is in tension with the supposition of public-spiritedness that informs the Legal Process School. We begin with the original, static version of the *Wilson-Hayes Matrix*. This model depicts the tendency among legislatures to oversupply or undersupply certain categories of legislation.[4] We then consider the implications of a dynamic version of this model, which highlights the important interrelationships among the identified legislative

---

1 In Chapters 23 and 24, we also introduce the specific institutional feature of bicameralism. *See infra* Chapter 8, Part II.E.

2 *See supra* Chapter 2, Part I.

3 *See* HENRY M. HART & ALBERT M. SACKS, THE LEGAL PROCESS: BASIC PROBLEMS IN THE MAKING AND APPLICATION OF LAW 1374–80 (William N. Eskridge & Philip P. Frickey eds., 1994). While a tentative edition of these materials, developed beginning in the 1940s, circulated in two bound unpublished volumes in 1958, they were posthumously published as a course book in 1994.

4 We previously considered the implicit question as to the relevant baseline in making any such normative assessment. *See supra* Chapter 12 (discussing Einer R. Elhauge thesis).

categories, and which help to explore the implications of those relationships as they might affect various proposals for the judicial construction of statutes.[5] The analysis exposes the difficulties in assuming that proposals designed to curb seemingly problematical features of the legislative process, including for example the tendency to produce private goods legislation, or to avoid contentious policy making through delegation, can be implemented without incurring other costs within the legislative process.

We can think of the Legal Process School and the Wilson-Hayes Matrix as conceptual endpoints on an analytical spectrum that depicts the extent to which observers view the legislature as furthering the public interest (the Legal Process School), or conversely, as willingly subordinating that interest to further narrow interest group objectives (the Wilson-Hayes Matrix). While most scholars, and perhaps most judges, hold views between these analytical endpoints, juxtaposing these contrasting views is helpful in two respects. First, it provides a foundation for considering calls for a more piercing scrutiny, for example taking the form of constitutional judicial review or through narrow statutory construction, for example, with respect to statutes that appear predominantly motivated by rent-seeking concerns. Second, it provides a basis for assessing a range of scholarly proposals, set out in Chapter 18, that rely upon public choice to evaluate the underlying motivation, or purpose, in the judicial construction of statutes.

I. MODELS OF LEGISLATION AND LEGISLATIVE BARGAINING

A. The Legal Process School

In the middle of the twentieth century, Professors Henry Hart and Albert Sacks developed an influential framework designed in part to describe actual judicial practices in construing statutes and in part to offer a normatively promising theory of statutory construction.[6] While the materials were written over a half century ago, the theory of statutory interpretation that Hart and Sacks devised continues to resonate with an influential group of contemporary jurisprudential scholars. In a sense, the Hart and Sacks approach gives normative content to the descriptive claims embraced by those who support a public interest understanding of legislative decision-making processes. The analysis is designed to inform courts concerning how to construe statutes, what "attitudes" to bring to this task, and how to identify the overall public-regarding design of statutes that they are called upon to apply. The Legal Process School thus provides an important normative gloss on the public interest theory of legislation that instructs courts to construe statutes so as to further the claimed underlying public interest objectives.[7]

Legal scholars routinely cite Hart and Sacks for the simple proposition that courts should "assume, unless the contrary unmistakably appears, that the legislature was made

---

[5] Portions of this discussion are based upon Maxwell L. Stearns, *The Public Choice Case Against the Item Veto*, 49 WASH. & LEE L. REV. 385 (1992).

[6] *See* HART & SACKS, *supra* note 3.

[7] The discussion that follows is largely based upon the final section of Hart and Sacks' lengthy treatise, entitled *Note on the Rudiments of Statutory Interpretation*. *See* HART & SACKS, *supra* note 3, at 1374–80.

up of reasonable persons pursuing reasonable purposes reasonably."[8] For Hart and Sacks, this premise is closely linked to the concept of legislative primacy, and thus to the role of the legislature as the "chief policy-determining agency of the society, subject only to the limitations of the constitution under which it exercises its powers."[9] The role of both the courts and agencies is to exercise "good faith and good sense" in construing statutes.

The authors summarize the proper task of legislative interpretation as follows:

> 1. Decide what purpose ought to be attributed to the statute and to any subordinate provision of it which may be involved; and then
>
> 2. Interpret the words of the statute immediately in question so as to carry out the purpose as best it can, making sure, however, that it does not give the words either—
>
> (a) a meaning they will not bear, or
>
> (b) a meaning which would violate any established policy of clear statement.[10]

Given the importance the authors ascribe to statutory language, it is perhaps not surprising that Hart and Sacks reject claims of linguistic indeterminacy in favor of the notion that language is a social construction.[11] The authors admonish courts to rely upon contemporaneous usages to inform intended statutory meaning. Hart and Sacks caution, however, that it is statutory text, and not "[u]nenacted intentions," that constitute governing law.[12] And yet, Hart and Sacks also instruct courts to avoid "linguistically permissible" constructions that produce "unusual meaning."[13] The authors identify two contexts in which courts should be cautious in ensuring that literal meaning does not produce unintended results. First, they observe that "words which mark the boundary between criminal and non-criminal conduct should speak with more than ordinary clearness." Second, they advise courts against interpreting legislation as "depart[ing] from a generally prevailing principle or policy of the law unless it does so clearly."[14]

---

8 *Id.* at 1378; *see also* Richard A. Posner, *Legal Formalism, Legal Realism, and the Interpretation of Statutes and the Constitution*, 37 CASE W. RES. L. REV. 179 (1986).

9 HART & SACKS, *supra* note 3, at 1374.

10 *Id.*

11 For a general discussion about linguistic indeterminacy and its implications for law, see Lawrence M. Solan, *The Interpretation of Legal Language*, 4 ANN. REV. LINGUISTICS 337 (2018); Jan Enberg & Dorothee Heller, *Vagueness and Indeterminacy in Law*, *in* LEGAL DISCOURSE ACROSS CULTURES AND SYSTEMS 145–68 (Vijay K. Bhatia et al. eds., 2008); Timothy A.O. Endicott, *Linguistic Indeterminacy*, 16 OXFORD J. LEGAL STUD. 667 (1996); Christian Zapf & Eben Moglen, *Linguistic Indeterminacy and the Rule of Law: On the Perils of Misunderstanding Wittgenstein*, 84 GEO. L.J. 485 (1996).

12 HART & SACKS, *supra* note 3, at 1375.

13 *Id.* at 1376.

14 *Id.* at 1376–77. Hart and Sacks trace these intuitions to Lord Blackburn's "golden rule," which they paraphrase as follows: "If Parliament means to produce an inconsistency, or absurdity, or very great inconvenience, it must be quite clear about it." *See id.* at 1209; *see also id.* at 1112 (quoting Blackburn). The authors describe their alternative formulation of the golden rule—"a statute ought always to be presumed to be the work of reasonable men pursuing reasonable purposes reasonably"—as an "even more radical suggestion." *Id.* at 1209.

Hart and Sacks link the second assertion, which they term a "golden rule," to an historically controversial canon of statutory interpretation: "statutes in derogation of the common law are to be strictly construed."[15] Without endorsing or rejecting this rule of construction, Hart and Sacks suggest that whereas legislatures can draw upon experience to change background suppositions regarding public policy, courts should not assume that a legislature has done so silently.

Against this background set of commands, the authors present the following passage, which contains the famous admonition that courts assume that legislatures comprise reasonable persons acting reasonably:

> In determining the more immediate purpose which ought to be attributed to a statute, and to any subordinate provision of it which may be involved, a court should try to put itself in imagination in the position of the legislature which enacted the measure.
>
> The court, however, should not do this in the mood of a cynical political observer, taking account of all the short-run currents of political expedience that swirl around any legislative session.
>
> *It should assume, unless the contrary unmistakably appears, that the legislature was made up of reasonable persons pursuing reasonable purposes reasonably.*
>
> It should presume conclusively that these persons, whether or not entertaining concepts of reasonableness shared by the court, were trying responsibly and in good faith to discharge their constitutional powers and duties.
>
> . . . The gist of this approach is to infer purpose by comparing the new law with the old. Why would reasonable men, confronted with the law as it was, have enacted this new law to replace it? Answering this question . . . calls for a close look at the "mischief" thought to inhere in the old law and at "the true reason of the remedy" provided by the statute for it.[16]

The authors also specifically address the questions concerning the proper role of legislative history in the judicial task of statutory interpretation:

> *First.* The history should be examined for the light it throws on *general purpose*. Evidence of specific intention with respect to particular applications is competent only to the extent that the particular applications illuminate the general purpose and are consistent with other evidence of it.
>
> *Second.* Effect should not be given to evidence from the internal legislative history if the result would be to contradict a purpose otherwise indicated and to yield an interpretation disadvantageous to private persons who had no reasonable means of access to the history.[17]

---

[15] *Id.* at 1210.

[16] *Id.* at 1378 (emphasis added).

[17] *Id.* at 1379 (emphasis in original).

While Hart and Sacks did not suggest that subsequent legislative history informs specific statutory meaning, they do claim that "judicial, administrative, and popular construction of a statute, subsequent to its enactment, are all relevant in attributing a purpose to it."[18]

1. *Discussion*

Before turning to the public choice model of legislative processes, it is worth considering some of the underlying premises of the Hart and Sacks Legal Process model. While the authors are most often cited for the proposition that legislatures comprise reasonable people acting reasonably, read in its broader context, this assertion suggests something more fundamental concerning the authors' understanding of legislation. Hart and Sacks assert that courts should presume that legislation is intended to resolve some identified "mischief" in the law or public policy. In this analysis, both judicial decisions and legislation are presumed to be principled. And yet, Hart and Sacks are not so naïve as to imagine that statutory policy has not been influenced by the rough and tumble of political maneuvering. Instead, they claim that it is the job of courts to set aside knowledge of this maneuvering in favor of treating particular statutes under review as efforts to "solve" a specific problem of law or public policy.

While Hart and Sacks do not deny that political actors sometimes behave in a self-interested fashion, they contend that this alone does not undermine larger and more public-spirited motives that courts can discern in construing statutes. Moreover, this might also require that in construing statutes, courts avoid literal objectives that threaten deeply problematical results. Part of this task, Hart and Sacks contend, includes the proper reliance upon legislative history.

Consider whether the following account provides a fair summary of the Legal Process School: The goal of statutory interpretation is to improve the prior state of the law informed by the statute that the courts are called upon to construe. If this is a fair account, how, if at all, does it differ from an understanding of statutory interpretation informed by interest group theory? How does one determine which constructions improve the state of the law? Can this be answered independently of the decision maker's normative premises concerning whatever values the law should reflect? If not, can Hart and Sacks avoid the argument that in the mind of a judge favoring a *laissez faire* philosophy, their "golden rule" admonishes construing statutes in derogation of the common law narrowly? Is that a problem? Why or why not?

B. The Wilson-Hayes Model Revisited

We will now revisit the Wilson-Hayes model of legislative procurement introduced in Chapter 11.[19] This model builds upon the insights of interest group theory to identify the conditions that are likely to give rise to various forms, or combinations, of legislation. The analysis divides legislation into four paradigms based upon whether the resulting benefits and costs are widely dispersed or narrowly concentrated. While the resulting

---

[18] *Id.*

[19] *See supra* Chapter 2, Part III.A (discussing model based on JAMES Q. WILSON, POLITICAL ORGANIZATIONS (1973); MICHAEL T. HAYES, LOBBYISTS AND LEGISLATORS: A THEORY OF POLITICAL MARKERS (1981)).

matrix is stylized and admittedly simplistic, it nonetheless offers a helpful starting point in assessing public choice intuitions that sometimes operate in tension with the public interest, or Legal Process, understanding of legislation. In addition, the dynamic version of the Wilson-Hayes model provides the basis for a more nuanced understanding of the analytical categories themselves and the relationships among those categories in procuring desired legislation.

1. *The Static Bargaining Model*

The discussion that follows builds upon the following matrix below, introduced in Chapter 11.[20]

Table 17:1. The Four Box Static Model

	Widely Distributed Benefits	**Narrowly Conferred Benefits**
Widely Distributed Costs	**Legislative Characteristics:** This desired category of legislation tends to be undersupplied as constituents exert too little pressure in support; alternatively, when pressure is brought on both sides, legislatures sometimes delegate to avoid the resulting conflict. **Illustrations:** Desired legislative responses to varied environmental crises, e.g., global climate change, national waste management, sound fiscal policy and control of national debt.	**Legislative Characteristics:** Because small organized groups exert pressure disproportionate to numbers in political processes, legislatures tend to oversupply special interest legislation. **Illustrations:** Tariffs, industry subsidies
Narrowly Conferred Costs	**Legislative Characteristics:** Given the fear that factional violence (Madison Federalist 10), or interest group logrolling (the modern phrasing), will disadvantage unpopular minorities, congressional processes include numerous veto gates that combine to enlarge	**Legislative Characteristics:** Because narrow interests directly conflict, legislators prefer to delegate to agencies, hoping to shift blame for resulting failures, while claiming credit for resulting successes; legislators can

[20] *See supra* Chapter 2, Part III.A. tbl. 2:1; *see also* Stearns, *supra* note 5, at 407.

	successful coalitions above minimum winning size.	also benefit from simply threatening regulatory delegation and can benefit from monitoring agencies.
	Illustrations: Rent control at state/local level; until ACA, efforts at national health care reform; climate change legislation	**Illustrations:** National Labor Relations Board (NLRB), Environmental Protection Agency (EPA)

The Wilson-Hayes model returns us to a central premise of interest group theory, namely that we can gain insight into the political process by analogizing the legislature to a marketplace for the procurement of various forms of legislation. The model builds upon the incentives of those who demand legislation—constituents, interest groups, and lobbyists—and those who supply it—elected members of the legislature.

a. The Demand Side

The demand side of the model focuses on the tension that public choice highlights between the sorts of legislation we expect our representatives to provide and the incentives that the relevant constituencies have in pushing for desired legislation. It is a now familiar insight that the most public-spirited legislation, for example efforts to increase police protection and national defense, to ensure the solvency of Social Security, and to guard against environmental hazards, often confront substantial difficulty in garnering the necessary vigorous demand. The difficulty is that while such legislation benefits the public broadly, this very broad support, counterintuitively, undermines the demand function as each constituency, or each voter, anticipates that others will invest the necessary resources for procurement. As each potential beneficiary free rides on the efforts of others, the overall demand function for such broad-based general interest legislation suffers.[21]

Conversely, as Mancur Olson famously observed, the demand function for governmental action is positively correlated with the ability of groups (1) to organize, and (2) to monitor and punish those who do not contribute their fair share to the group's welfare.[22] Although Olson is often presented as associating effective lobbying with a size principle, a more careful reading focuses on the susceptibility of the relevant interest groups to cohesion, organization and monitoring, and exclusion of noncontributors. Whereas large groups are often dispersed and difficult to discipline, smaller groups are often more tightly organized and have greater capacity to identify and punish those who do not contribute to collective efforts at procuring quasi-private goods benefiting group

[21] These organizational difficulties may encourage political entrepreneurship in which politicians or political activists seek to motivate an identifiable constituency to support a particular cause. JOHN W. KINGDON, AGENDAS, ALTERNATIVES, AND PUBLIC POLICIES 122–24 (2d ed. 1995) (describing "policy entrepreneurs"); RUSSELL HARDIN, COLLECTIVE ACTION 35–37 (1982); Wendy J. Schiller, *Senators as Political Entrepreneurs: Using Bill Sponsorship to Shape Legislative Agendas*, 39 AM. J. POL. SCI. 186 (1995).

[22] MANCUR OLSON, THE LOGIC OF COLLECTIVE ACTION: PUBLIC GOODS AND THE THEORY OF GROUPS (1971).

members. To the extent that groups can punish non-contributors by excluding them from continued group affiliation, or from sharing in the benefits of the group's lobbying successes, the more likely the group will avoid the free rider and collective action difficulties that plague larger constituencies that would benefit from the procurement of classic public goods.

The defining characteristics of public goods—value not diminished by consumption and the inability to exclude those who fail to contribute from receiving the benefits—are the same features that render general interest legislation difficult to procure.[23] Persons who do not contribute to national defense are equally protected as those who do contribute, and the protection of one house does not diminish the protection of its neighbor. The converse holds, however, for special interest legislation, as in the case of professional licensing or similar barriers to entry. Those who are not properly licensed or who do not anticipate the prospect of gaining such licensure are excluded from the resulting benefits. These benefits can include higher rates for member-provided services resulting from the effective elimination of competition that licensure provides.

This book's opening chapter observed that changes in legal rules only affect the conduct of those persons on the margin respecting such rules.[24] Of course most people are not on the margin with respect to the vast majority of rules at any given time. For example, changing penalties for larceny, robbery, or homicide is unlikely to motivate the vast majority to persons to commit such crimes, and likewise, such a change will not deter at least some who are predisposed to do so. Instead, the change in penalty will only affect the conduct of those on the margin with respect to such offenses.

The analysis of lobbying incentives has an important parallel feature. Interest groups work on behalf of firms, other organized groups, or individuals that share an affinity for the projects in which the interest group engages. As with legal rules, most affected persons or entities are not on the margin with respect to the vast number of legislative proposals before Congress or state legislatures. As a result, behaving rationally, interest groups will become increasingly active concerning those specific proposals that affect their members in a discernable way, meaning for which their members anticipate being on the relevant margin.

A recent study on groups lobbying for or against climate change supports this intuition.[25] The study revealed that firms most apt to benefit from, or be burdened by, increasingly stringent carbon emissions regulations are willing to invest financial resources to lobby for bills focused on climate change. Although the underlying data did not disclose which side of any given bill interests were on, the data supported what is most easily expressed as a *U-shaped lobbying-incentive curve*. The upper arms on either side intuitively correspond to the probability that affected firms are on the margin with respect to the proposed legislation, either in terms of being subject to additional compliance obligations

---

[23] Paul A. Samuelson, *The Pure Theory of Public Expenditure*, 36 REV. ECON. & STAT. 387 (1954) (defining public goods).

[24] *See supra* Chapter 1, at pp. 19–20 (discussing marginal analysis).

[25] Magali Delmas et al., *Corporate Environmental Performance and Lobbying*, 2 ACAD. MGMT. DISCOVERIES 175 (2016). *See* Magali Delmas, *Research: Who's Lobbying Congress on Climate Change*, HARV. BUS. REV. (Oct. 27, 2016), https://hbr.org/2016/10/research-whos-lobbying-congress-on-climate-change (reviewing recent studies)).

or in terms of locking in existing practices as regulatory requirements, thereby raising barriers to entry or costs to existing competitors. For firms with excellent environmental compliance, lobbying provides potential marginal benefits in raising competitor costs or excluding new competition due to the burdens associated with a stricter regulatory regime. Conversely, for firms that are likely to be burdened by compliance obligations, lobbying provides a means of either avoiding, or blunting the force of, potentially costly regulation. To be sure, environmental regulation aimed to blunt the effects of global climate change provides an enormous public benefit. What the study reveals is that lobbying incentives tend not to be motivated by such benefits *in general*, at least as compared with burdens or benefits that place affected firms on the relevant regulatory margin.

Similarly, we do not suggest that professional licensure provides benefits only to the affected professionals.[26] There are profound benefits to ensuring that those who hold themselves out as qualified to provide professional services have the requisite training and skills to do so. It is also true that the American Medical Association (AMA) and the American Bar Association (ABA), to name two prominent examples, have long been effective in pursuing the professional interests of group members. For groups whose members are far larger and whose interests are more diverse, such as National Taxpayers Union, which seeks to promote tax fairness, and the Sierra Club, which seeks to improve environmental conditions and to protect endangered species and their habitats, lobbying efforts can present greater challenges since it is more difficult to capture contributions from those who benefit and to limit the benefits of success to those who do contribute. The National Association for the Advancement of Colored People (NAACP) or the National Organization for Women (NOW) might represent intermediate cases. Both of these prominent national organizations seek to further the interests of identifiable, but rather large, groups: persons of color and women, respectively. While the potential beneficiaries of legislation that such groups seek to procure are more cohesive than the general public, consider the level of organizational difficulties that such groups nonetheless confront as a result of the size and diverse interests of potentially affected group members.

During the 2016 primary cycle and presidential election, a new loosely structured organization, Black Lives Matter (or BLM), gained prominence.[27] Can you think of a reason why this group, rather than the NAACP, gained increasing popularity and prominence during this period of time? Does the Mancur Olson theory of effective lobbying groups help to explain BLM, or does it render BLM an anomaly? Why? Which

---

[26] *See supra* Chapter 2, Part II.A.

[27] The Black Lives Matter movement was founded in 2013.During the 2016 election cycle, BLM began to expand into more policy-centered actions. *See* Jaweed Kaleem, *Black Lives Matter Has Signed onto a Platform in Time for the Presidential Election. Here's What it Says*, L.A. TIMES (Aug. 1, 2016, 3:40 PM), http://www.latimes.com/nation/la-na-pol-black-lives-platform-20160801-snap-story.html; Janell Ross & Wesley Lowery, *Black Lives Matter Shifts from Protests to Policy Under Trump*, CHI. TRIB. (May 4, 2017, 7:41 PM), http://www.chicagotribune.com/news/nationworld/ct-black-lives-matter-trump-20170504-story.html. *See also* MONICA ANDERSON & PAUL HITLIN, PEW RES. CTR., SOCIAL MEDIA CONVERSATIONS ABOUT RACE (Aug. 15, 2016), http://www.pewinternet.org/2016/08/15/the-hashtag-blacklivesmatter-emerges-social-activism-on-twitter/ (study tracking the use of #BlackLivesMatter to track growth of the Black Lives Matter Movement). *See also* Niraj Chokshi, *How #BlackLivesMatter Came to Define a Movement*, N.Y. TIMES (Aug. 23, 2016), https://www.nytimes.com/2016/08/23/us/how-blacklivesmatter-came-to-define-a-movement.html.

group, BLM or the NAACP, is likely to have greater influence in effectuating policies of particular interest to persons of color and their communities, and why?

More generally are entrepreneurial efforts on behalf of prospective members of the other listed groups consistent or in tension with insights drawn from public choice? Why? How might lawmaking efforts differ across such groupings as (1) the AMA and ABA, (2) the NAACP and NOW, and (3) Sierra Club and the National Taxpayers Union? What role, if any, might successful litigation on behalf of these interest groups play in efforts to overcome free riding? What is the relationship between litigation and lobbying strategies for such groups? To what extent do such groups employ litigation as a means to encourage membership or to raise funds? Which sets of strategies are more likely to be successful in overcoming free rider problems?

Of course it is important not to treat the Wilson-Hayes model, or any other model, as an accurate depiction of inevitably complex legislative dynamics. We do see substantial efforts, indeed often successful ones, to procure legislation that seeks to further public aims on a statewide or national scale.[28] A dynamic understanding of this model, however, helps to identify some of the processes that generate more effective demand for public interest legislation. The analysis reveals the importance of how the various legislative categories connect during any given legislative session.[29]

Consider also how presidential versus non-presidential election cycles differ in the types of legislation they motivate. To what extent do presidential candidates assume the role of political entrepreneurs, seeking to procure demand for legislative categories that are harder to obtain in off-presidential elections, the alternative two-year cycle for the House of Representatives and for one third of the Senate? How might one test the answer to this question empirically? What is the relationship between special interest legislation and legislation targeting a broad aspect of the public good? Are there identifiable mechanisms that limit the possibilities of special interest legislation while promoting other legislation that targets larger aims, however those aims are defined? To what extent are the problems exposed on the demand side reinforced by public choice dynamics on the supply side?

b. The Supply Side

While those seeking elective office certainly hold other, more laudable goals, often associated with legislation in furtherance of their conception of the public good, public choice theorists observe that politicians cannot achieve any goals unless they are

[28] While we do not dispute that others might quibble with any examples we could provide, we nonetheless offer as illustrations at the state level, laws funding programs for police and fire safety, criminal codes and highway safety regulations, and public education. At the federal level, consider the Gramm-Rudman-Hollings Act, national defense budgeting, and various environmental programs that states could not enact on their own without confronting coordination difficulties. Most recently (as of the publication of this book), consider also the Troubled Assets Relief Program (TARP) to bail out the financial sector and U.S. automobile industry. *See* Emergency Economic Stabilization Act of 2008, Pub. L. No. 110–343, §§ 101–136, 122 Stat. 3765, 3767. For a discussion of the Affordable Care Act, *see infra* at pp. 719–722.

[29] This is the focus of the next subsection, introducing the dynamic version of the Wilson-Hayes matrix. *See infra* Part I.B.

successfully elected and reelected.[30] Candidates who subordinate *the electoral goal* in favor of other objectives when the choice proves decisive to electoral success risk falling off the political radar. That is because other political actors who are more willing to engage in conduct better targeted toward electoral success stand ready to replace them.[31]

Of course, legislators do, in fact, pursue many goals apart from electoral politics. Some legislators are more safely situated than others for reelection, and as such, they have a greater degree of flexibility in focusing on larger issues related to their legislative agenda, or perhaps even the pursuit of higher elective office.[32] Those legislators who are new or otherwise vulnerable to electoral challenge, however, are most likely to pursue strategies that favor opportunities to *claim credit* with constituents for legislative successes.

Does the difference between the terms of office for the Senate (six years) versus the House of Representatives (two years) affect the ability of those in each office to pursue more public-interested legislation? What sorts of studies could you devise to test your intuitions on this question?

i. Credit Claiming

Not all strategies for claiming legislative success are equally plausible. Most legislators are more likely to convince constituents of legislative success with respect to localized items within bills than with respect to nationwide-level accomplishments.[33] For this reason, both the demand and supply functions tend to favor special interest over general interest legislation. Legislators can more convincingly claim credit for funding a highway or bridge repair, or a subsidy to local industry—benefits that are identifiable and excludable—than for laudable bills that help defense, promote fiscal soundness, or improve the environment.

---

[30] DAVID R. MAYHEW, CONGRESS: THE ELECTORAL CONNECTION 16 (2d ed. 2004); MORRIS P. FIORINA, REPRESENTATIVES, ROLL CALLS, AND CONSTITUENCIES 38–39 (1974).

[31] Of course, if one can pursue larger aims without compromising the prospect of electoral success, then the trade-off is not implicated.

[32] The 2008 election of President Barack Obama notwithstanding, conventional wisdom suggests that the Senate is a less-than-ideal stepping stone to the Presidency. *See* Barry C. Burden, *United States Senators as Presidential Candidates*, 117 POL. SCI. Q. 81, 81, 82 (2002) (noting that "it is almost unheard of for presidents to come directly from the Senate," although "the conventional wisdom holds that senators are prime presidential material."). Of course, the 2016 Trump victory might further suggest that having held a conventional political office serves as a disadvantage given that he prevailed in the Republican primary in a field of seventeen candidates, most of whom held positions as Governors or Senators, and then defeated Hillary Clinton in the general election, despite credentials that included Senator from New York, Secretary of State, and, of course, former First Lady. *See Who Is Running for President?*, N.Y. TIMES (July 26, 2016), https://www.nytimes.com/interactive/2016/us/elections/2016-presidential-candidates.html (listing candidates and the dates they dropped out of the race). It is also possible to over-read this datum given that although Trump won the Electoral College, he lost the popular vote by nearly three million votes. U.S. NAT'L ARCHIVES, *U.S. Electoral College: 2016 Electoral College Results*, https://www.archives.gov/federal-register/electoral-college/2016/election-results.html (last visited Oct. 27, 2017).

[33] *See* Janet M. Box-Steffensmeier et al., *The Effects of Political Representation on the Electoral Advantages of House Incumbents*, 56 POL. RES. Q. 259, 265 tbl.2 (2003) (quantifying the effect of various activities of legislators on constituents' perceptions and finding that sponsorship of bills with local effects was the activity that caused the greatest increase in constituents' "reason for liking incumbent" and in name recognition).

ii. Conflict Avoidance

Successful legislators also seek to avoid unnecessary conflict among constituents. Such conflict can arise when broad legislation imposes costs on those in an identifiable, and narrow, constituency. Madison's *Federalist No. 10*,[34] which concerned the threat of factional violence, evinces a concern for legislation that provides wide benefits while imposing narrow costs. To avoid what Madison termed factional violence, he sought to impose impediments to the rapid formation of majoritarian politics operating to the detriment of discrete and identifiable classes.[35] Madison's structural solution was to divide the legislature (bicameralism) and to afford the President a check (the veto) against problematic majoritarian legislation that nonetheless survives. Other mechanisms have also arisen within the Madisonian tradition that increase the needed size of governing coalitions and that thereby impose additional barriers to majoritarian politics or against Madison's feared factional violence.[36] In addition to bicameralism and presentment, such practices include calendaring rules, committee structures, seniority practices, the Senate filibuster, conference committees, and perhaps constitutional judicial review.[37] Together, these elaborate practices create the complex labyrinth—one that increases the size of governing coalitions—that bill sponsors must navigate to transform proposed bills into legislation, or in the case of the veto and constitutional judicial review, legislation that will endure post-enactment.

These institutional features also avoid Riker's theoretical prediction that in a zero-sum game, where side payments are permitted and where parties are rational and have complete information, the most stable legislative coalitions will approach minimum winning size.[38] Each of these legislative processes, also known as *veto gates*, or *negative*

---

[34] THE FEDERALIST NO. 10 (James Madison).

[35] Madison was concerned, of course, with moneyed and landed classes and with proposals that would redistribute wealth from such classes to the public at large (majoritarian violence), but the principle can be generalized to discuss other "discrete and insular" minority groups. United States v. Carolene Prods. Co., 304 U.S. 144, 152–53 n.4 (1938).

[36] Of course, as Easterbrook and others have aptly noted, these mechanisms have created their own difficulties as they have become venues for special interest bargaining, thus facilitating payoffs in the concentrated benefit, dispersed cost category. Frank H. Easterbrook, *Foreword: The Court and the Economic System*, 98 HARV. L. REV. 4, 17 (1984).

[37] While one can debate whether constitutional judicial review was anticipated at the framing, *see, e.g.*, THE FEDERALIST No. 78, as a formal matter, the doctrine was established in a later period. *See* Marbury v. Madison, 5 U.S. 137 (1803). In recent years use of the filibuster has been limited by the so-called *nuclear option* to eliminate use of the filibuster on executive branch and judiciary nominees. *See, e.g.*, RICHARD S. BETH & VALERIE HEITSHUSEN, CONG. RESEARCH SERV. RL30360, FILIBUSTERS AND CLOTURE IN THE SENATE (2014); Ted Barrett, *Trump's Judge Nominees Get a Hand from McConnell*, CNN (Oct. 26, 2017), http://www.cnn.com/2017/10/26/politics/congress-nominations-trump-judges/index.html. Until the confirmation hearing for Justice Neil Gorsuch, the Senate had retained the filibuster for Supreme Court nominees. Because of the Democratic threat of a filibuster, which some attributed to Democratic frustration over the Senate's failure to hold hearings on President Barack Obama's nomination of Merrick Garland to replace the seat left vacant after Justice Antonin Scalia died, the Republicans exercised the nuclear option, thereby eliminating the filibuster for Supreme Court nominees. *See* Matt Flegenheimer, *Senate Republicans Deploy 'Nuclear Option' to Clear Path for Gorsuch*, N.Y. TIMES (Apr. 6, 2017), https://www.nytimes.com/2017/04/06/us/politics/neil-gorsuch-supreme-court-senate.html.

[38] WILLIAM H. RIKER, THE THEORY OF POLITICAL COALITIONS (1962). For the formal statement of conditions, see *supra* Chapter 11, Part III.B, at notes 110–113.

legislative checkpoints,[39] raises the cost of procuring legislation by demanding support at various loci at which individual members of Congress are empowered to stop a bill in its tracks. By empowering sometimes even a single member of Congress in this manner,[40] these negative legislative checkpoints provide opportunities for those who might be disadvantaged by a proposed bill to bargain for favorable modifications as the price of allowing the bill to pass a particular veto gate and to move on to the next.

Because it is far easier to block than to pass proposed legislation—blocking requires only one successful veto gate, whereas successful passing requires surviving all veto gates—testing the theoretical insights of public choice can be a challenge.[41] The proof, after all, is often in what fails to make it into the pudding. The power to block, however, is real. Legislation rarely, if ever, passes in its initially proposed form, and the ultimate shape that legislation takes is largely affected by the various loci at which potentially affected interests can exert or threaten the power to block. In some instances, blocking power can result in the defeat of proposed legislation, and, in others, it can result in modifying that legislation relative to the *ideal point* of the bill sponsors.[42] As we will see in the discussion of the dynamic model, *substantive bargaining* with adversely affected groups, one of the principal means of ensuring passage of proposed legislation, has the effect of watering down bills relative to original proposals.[43] The softening of legislation from its original form moves bill sponsors off their ideal points, but, at the same time, it avoids the harsh conflicts and the potential defeat that might occur if the sponsor insisted only on voting the bill up or down in its original form.

---

[39] For a discussion of these terms, see *supra* Chapter 11, Part III.B, at p. 485 note 109, and cites therein.

[40] This can occur for example with a committee chair who refuses to schedule a matter for debate, or with a Senator threatening a filibuster absent the requisite sixty-Senator supermajority required to invoke cloture. *See* U.S. SENATE, COMM. RULES & ADMIN., STANDING RULES OF THE SENATE (specifically Rule XII, Voting Procedure, and XXII, Precedence of Motions); *see also* Gregory Koger, *Partisanship, Filibustering, and Reform in the Senate*, *in* PARTY AND PROCEDURE IN THE UNITED STATES CONGRESS (Jacob R. Straus & Matthew E. Glassman eds., 2016); Martin B. Gold & Dimple Gupta, *The Constitutional Option to Change Senate Rules and Procedures: A Majoritarian Means to Overcome the Filibuster*, 28 HARV. J.L. & PUB. POL'Y 205 (2004) (providing historical analysis of filibuster and cloture); John C. Roberts, *Majority Voting in Congress: Further Notes on the Constitutionality of the Senate Cloture Rule*, 20 J.L. & POL. 505 (2004) (providing history of the Senate's use of the filibuster and recommending modifications to filibuster and cloture rules). The current use and future of the filibuster in the Senate has recently garnered attention, with President Donald Trump suggesting the Senate should do away with the filibuster. *See* Jacob Pramuk, *Trump Needles Mitch McConnell Over the Senate's 'Horrible' Filibuster Rule*, CNBC (Sept. 28, 2017, 10:02 AM), https://www.cnbc.com/2017/09/28/donald-trump-needles-mitch-mcconnell-over-senate-filibuster-rule.html; Drew Desilver, *Trump's Nominees Have Already Faced a Large Number of Cloture Votes*, FACTTANK: PEW RES. CTR. (June 1, 2017), http://www.pewresearch.org/fact-tank/2017/06/01/trumps-nominees-have-already-faced-a-large-number-of-cloture-votes/. For a discussion of the Republicans' use of the nuclear option in connection with the nomination of Justice Neil Gorsuch, see *supra* note 37.

[41] Consider whether this helps to respond to some of the arguments that Green & Shapiro offer in their critique of public-choice based scholarship, *see supra* Chapters 12, Part V.B at note 95 (discussing critique of public choice by Professors Green and Shapiro).

[42] Ideal points are sometimes expressed along a unidimensional continuum, which can be general, for example, liberal to conservative, or specific, for example, high-to-low expenditure on a proposed project. The ideal point is the location on the relevant spectrum that represents the bill sponsor's first-choice position concerning a given policy or basket of policies. *See supra* Chapter 1, Part III.A.3.

[43] For a more detailed discussion, see Stearns, *supra* note 5, at 413–14 (describing substantive and length bargaining).

iii. Comparing State and Federal Legislative Processes

Most state constitutions provide for legislative processes that resemble the essential features of the federal legislative process. For example, with the exception of Nebraska,[44] which has a unicameral legislature, the remaining states, like Congress, have bicameral legislatures. In addition, all states have a form of presentment to the executive, although many have variations, including various forms of item veto.[45] Despite these structural similarities, it is generally believed that it is more difficult for the federal government to pass legislation than state governments. For example, although there almost invariably are winners and losers in laws respecting rent control, affecting processes for regulatory takings and historical preservation, and affecting various sorts of professional licensing, many jurisdictions have enacted such laws.[46] Proposed bills that implicate direct conflicts often falter at the federal level. One example, discussed below, involves efforts to ensure broader health insurance coverage. Why might there be a higher bar to passing federal than state legislation?

One possible explanation is that the costs of legislative bargaining are higher as a result of the larger number and greater variety of interest groups that operate at the national level. Consider the example of health care policy. For several decades, health care policy and health care reform has been a major issue at the national level with unsuccessful attempts to enact a successful policy. In 2010 the Patient Protection and Affordable Care Act (ACA) was passed with highly unusual political dynamics. These included the death of Ted Kennedy, a prominent Democratic Senator, whose vote was essential to blocking a filibuster that could derail the legislation, and his replacement with Republican Scott Brown, who had he been sworn in, could have blocked the bill's passage. Despite the fact that the House version of the ACA had been announced Dead on Arrival (DOA), this political change motivated the Senate to pass the original House bill, which President Obama then signed, with a plan for later supplemental legislation to improve the ACA without risking defeat once the formal Senate composition changed.[47] From the moment the law was proposed it was highly controversial, and it remained controversial afterward, serving as a flashpoint for major public debate, including as a major issue during the 2016 presidential election. When Donald Trump was elected President that year, "repeal and replace" of the Affordable Care Act had been a focal point of his campaign platform.

Trump's first major legislative initiative involved an effort to follow through on the repeal and replace commitment. From his earliest days in office, in January 2017 through that summer, Congress negotiated to try to enact a comprehensive repeal and replace bill. By late 2017, however, it appeared that such efforts were doomed to fail. Perhaps

---

[44] For a history of Nebraska's unicameral legislature, see *History of the Nebraska Unicameral*, NEBRASKA LEGISLATURE, http://nebraskalegislature.gov/about/history_unicameral.php (last visited Oct. 20, 2017).

[45] The item veto exists in some form in forty-four states. *See, e.g.*, Carl E. Klarner & Andrew Karch, *Why Do Governors Issue Vetoes? The Impact of Individual and Institutional Influences*, 61 POL. RES. Q. 574, 578 (2008); Thomas P. Lauth, *The Other Six: Governors Without the Line Item Veto*, 36 PUB. BUDGETING & FIN. 26 (2016).

[46] *See, e.g.*, MD. CODE ANN., STATE FIN. & PROC. § 5A–309 to 313 (West 2008) (establishing the Maryland Historical Trust for purposes of historic preservation); N.J. STAT. ANN. § 2A: 18–61.1(f) (West 2015) (preventing landlords from setting rent increases deemed unconscionable).

[47] For a more detailed history, see Leslie Meltzer Henry & Maxwell L. Stearns, *Commerce Games and the Individual Mandate*, 100 GEO. L.J. 1117 (2012).

comprehensive reform would come eventually, but in the meantime, it seemed that only piecemeal modifications, if anything, would be enacted. One major aspect of the ACA, the "individual mandate," was repealed as part of Trump's tax overhaul.[48]

What accounts for the challenges, both in enacting and in repealing the ACA? One reason may be the greater degree of difficulty of legislative negotiations at the national level, especially among interest groups. At first glance, it appears that although health care itself is immensely complicated, identifying the politics of healthcare reform is somewhat straightforward. On one hand are those who favor a more centralized, and thus more regulated system. Those favoring a single-payer system, for example, might have accepted the ACA as a necessary, if imperfect, compromise to improving the prospect of universal coverage. On the other side are interest groups that want "less regulation," and, who, fearing centralized control of various aspects of medical decision making and coverages, assume that either a single-payer system, which was not adopted, or mandated coverage, which is partly embedded in the ACA, will render the overall healthcare system less profitable and the provision of medical services more costly. As the negotiations went on, however, it became quite clear that the actual politics of the ACA were as complex as the health care delivery system itself. One reason appears to be that there is no single "health industry." Instead, there are multiple industries that form subparts within the vast medical industry complex, and the position of each industry is tied to very specific provisions of the ACA, as well as potential regulatory alternatives.

The complexity of health care reform is partly illustrated by the response of stock prices of various related industries to the Supreme Court's June 2012 decision to uphold certain key sections of the ACA in *National Federation of Independent Businesses v. Sebelius*,[49] particularly the individual mandate. Until its repeal, that provision required most Americans to either purchase health insurance or make a payment to the IRS.[50]

Economist Jonathan Hartley found that various sectors of the health industry responded differently to that news.[51] The stock of managed care companies fell an average of 6.7%, whereas biotechnology company stocks fell 1.2%. The ruling also correlated with an average increase in the stock value of hospitals of 3.2%, an average increase in health care services stocks of 1.9%, and an average increase in pharmaceutical company stocks of 0.5%. Another study of twelve healthcare industry stocks by Gang Nathan Dong found that the enactment of the ACA and the Supreme Court decision produced positive abnormal cumulative returns for the healthcare industry overall, and particularly for hospitals, medical clinics, and specialty outpatient facilities.[52] Other studies have found that some industries experienced positive cumulative abnormal returns prior to the enactment of the ACA and that those expectations changed once the law began to be

---

[48] *See* Pub. L. No. 115–97, § 11081, 131 Stat. 2054. *See also* Chapter 11 p. 468 notes 50–51, and accompanying text (discussing Trump tax reform).

[49] 567 U.S. 519 (2012).

[50] *See id.*

[51] *See* Jonathan Hartley, *Health Care Reform and Health Care Stocks: Evidence from the Affordable Care Act Supreme Court Ruling* (BFI Working Paper No. 2012–009, July 1, 2013), https://papers.ssrn.com/sol3/papers.cfm?abstract_id=2111642.

[52] Gang Nathan Dong, *Health Care Reform and the Stock Market: Economic Growth Opportunity and Private Sector Investors*, 41 J. HEALTH CARE FIN. 1 (2014).

implemented, as some predicted winners ended up gaining less than expected or actually experienced losses.[53] As these complex data suggest, there is no single "healthcare industry" in the United States, but rather, there are multiple industries that jockey for relative position to be benefited by, or to avoid bearing the cost of, various legislative initiatives.

The heterogeneity and fractionalization of interest groups potentially increases the difficulty of passing legislation in the first place and then repealing or replacing it later. Thus, when the initial efforts failed to enact a replacement to the ACA, it was reported that "Hospital Stocks Soar as Trumpcare Bill Dies."[54] Moreover, it has been reported that the stocks of health insurance companies have gained under the ACA as a result of the intersection of various complex subsidies, regulations, and regulatory exceptions.[55] The disparate positions of these various industries to the ACA and its repeal illustrates the difficulty of negotiation on a large-scale piece of legislation: some interest groups will favor reform, others will be opposed, and virtually all will be supportive of some, but not all, elements of repeal. Those opposed to reform can present themselves at various veto gates in the process and thereby head off reform. More generally, it appears that the ACA was constructed in part to encourage the buy-in of many elements of the healthcare industry, which might explain why that initiative was successful as compared to so many seemingly similar efforts in the past to increase access to the healthcare system, most notably the failed effort during the administration of Bill Clinton in the 1990s.[56]

Do you believe that the federal legislative process is more costly, and thus more difficult, to navigate? If so, is the ACA a good illustration? Why or why not?

c. Delegation

Political conflicts naturally arise when opposing interests are pitted against one another. While legislators confront particular difficulties in attempting to resolve intense and narrow constituencies pressing opposing sides on the same issue, the same conceptual difficulty arises as when the competing interests are relatively more dispersed. Within virtually every district, for example, the interests of labor conflict with those of management; the interests of landlords conflict with those of tenants; and the interests of those seeking environmental protection conflict with those of firms seeking to pursue economic development unimpeded by the resulting additional costs should such regulations pass. And indeed, political entrepreneurs working on behalf of various interests seeking large-scale reform in such areas as the environment or tax law can effectively transform a political dynamic into one that closely resembles direct and narrow

---

[53] *See* Benjamin M. Blau et al., *Key Stakeholders' Stock Returns and the Affordable Care Act*, 35 J. INS. REG. 1 (2016).

[54] Bruce Japsen, *Hospital Stocks Soar as Trumpcare Bill Dies*, FORBES (Mar. 24, 2017, 4:19 PM), https://www.forbes.com/sites/brucejapsen/2017/03/24/hospital-stocks-soar-as-trumpcare-bill-dies/#59046d9b829d.

[55] *See* Robert Lenzer, *ObamaCare Enriches Only the Health Insurance Giants and Their Shareholders*, FORBES (Oct. 1, 2013, 3:33 PM), https://www.forbes.com/sites/robertlenzner/2013/10/01/obamacare-enriches-only-the-health-insurance-giants-and-their-shareholders/#4617d0530776.

[56] *See* Jonathan Oberlander, *Learning From Failure in Health Care Reform*, 357 NEW ENG. J. MED. 1677 (2007) (discussing the failed Clinton Health Security Act).

conflict. Legislators cannot "solve" the sometimes unavoidable conflict without incurring substantial political costs with the losing side.

When the affected constituents on both sides of an issue are roughly evenly balanced, whether the constituencies are broad or narrow, an attractive option for legislators will often be to avoid the conflict through delegation. Delegation affords legislators the opportunity to claim credit for facilitating a potentially responsive solution to the issues that the constituents raise, while, at the same time, also shifting blame to the agency when the results inevitably favor one side or the other.[57] The strategy of claiming credit and shifting blame is unlikely to satisfy both sides, but it does benefit the relevant political actors.

Agency decision making also implicates the presidency since the president controls executive agency appointments and is involved in the staffing of most independent agencies.[58] Delegation thus shifts the policy focus from legislative lobbying to electoral politics, and particularly, presidential elections.[59]

An alternative analysis focuses on the implications of agency delegation for judicial decision making. In an important pair of administrative law decisions, the Supreme Court has admonished lower federal courts to exhibit deference to reasonable interpretations of ambiguous statutes,[60] but only to do so if Congress has delegated appropriate authority to the agency and the agency decision follows regularized agency procedures.[61] Thus while federal courts defer to substantive constructions of statutes that they might not have produced initially—provided agency lawmaking procedures are followed—they do not defer to the decisions of isolated agency decision makers, taking for example, the form of opinion letters.[62] While we will take up the *Chevron/Mead* doctrines in greater detail in Chapter 19,[63] consider for now whether you can reconcile these doctrines based upon insights drawn from public choice. Can you reconcile them with the Legal Process School? Which model provides a more persuasive account of these doctrines? Why?

d. The Matrix Revisited

The preceding analysis provides the basis for the static Wilson-Hayes matrix. This model suggests that important tendencies are apt to characterize the legislative process with respect to particular categories of legislation. While the analysis forecasts an oversupply of special interest legislation and an undersupply of general interest legislation, such claims necessarily rest upon a set of often-unexpressed assumptions concerning what

---

57 Peter H. Aranson, Ernest Gellhorn & Glen O. Robinson, *A Theory of Legislative Delegation*, 68 CORNELL L. REV. 1 (1982).

58 For an analysis of the role of the President in staffing executive and independent agencies, see *infra* Chapters 19 and 20.

59 For a discussion of how a president embracing a deregulatory agenda might prefer staffing agencies with like-minded bureaucrats, rather than dismantling the agencies, see *infra* Chapter 6, Part III.C.

60 Chevron U.S.A., Inc. v. Nat. Res. Def. Council, 467 U.S. 837 (1984).

61 United States v. Mead Corp., 533 U.S. 218 (2001).

62 *Id.* at 236 n.17.

63 *See infra* Chapter 19 Applications.

levels of each type of legislation we would ideally hope that the legislature might provide.[64] Any baseline or set of baselines that one might suggest for comparison—for example majoritarianism, efficiency, welfare maximization, utilitarianism, or minimizing pork—is contestable. Different commentators embrace different baselines, and assessing the merits of arguments concerning the baselines themselves rest on analyses outside any public choice model.

We now consider the assumptions that underlie the Wilson-Hayes matrix. The model presumes that the legislature is expected to provide public goods and services that private individuals or firms are unlikely to provide because of the free rider and holdout phenomena. The Wilson-Hayes model reveals the anomaly that the very tendencies that limit private incentives to provide traditional public goods limit incentives to lobby for the procurement for such goods.

The analysis thus exposes a tendency to undersupply the very category of legislation that motivated the creation of the legislature in the first instance, namely general interest legislation, characterized by widely dispersed costs and benefits.[65] Instead, the legislature is prone to mimicking private market incentives in encouraging lobbying for narrow and discrete interests, often at the expense of the larger population. As a result of various structural impediments to the rapid passage of legislation, some discrete and narrow groups are relatively well suited to protect themselves against majoritarian factions. These well organized groups are able to capture the benefits of their legislative victories. While these features of the legislative process were designed to avoid, or raise the cost of, factional politicking, they also create opportunities for special interests to procure legislative largesse at the expense of the public at large.

As you evaluate congressional bargaining processes, consider whether the system strikes the proper balance between protections against majoritarian violence on the one hand, and opportunities for special interest legislation on the other. Is it possible to maintain the protections that motivated Madison while also reducing pork barrel legislation? Why or why not? Finally, when interests directly conflict, the model predicts delegation as a solution to the political problem, even though the ultimate beneficiaries in this process might be the legislators rather than the affected constituent groups.

Let us now consider a dynamic model that builds upon the Wilson-Hayes matrix and that studies the interrelationships between and among the identified legislative categories.

2. The Dynamic Legislative Bargaining Model[66]

Beyond identifying such legislative tendencies, the Wilson-Hayes model provides a helpful starting point for considering legislation as a dynamic bargaining process. By transforming the matrix into a dynamic bargaining model, we can see how legislative bargaining forges relationships among political actors, and additionally, among various legislative paradigms.

---

[64] This point was made effectively by Einer R. Elhauge, *supra* Chapter 12, Part II.

[65] Glen O. Robinson, *Public Choice Speculations on the Item Veto*, 74 VA. L. REV. 403, 408–09 (1988).

[66] Portions of this discussion are adapted from Stearns, *supra* note 5, at 401–22.

Assume that following *Massachusetts v. EPA*,[67] a case granting the Commonwealth of Massachusetts standing to challenge the EPA's failure to regulate mobile-sourced greenhouse gas emissions, the EPA proposes a set of regulations that leading members of a Democratically controlled Congress finds inadequate to deal with the threat of global warming. Senator Green, a liberal senator from a Democratic state, proposes the "Mobile-Sourced Greenhouse Gas Emissions Reductions Act." The Act would compel the EPA to implement regulations demanding a reduction of mobile-sourced greenhouse gas emissions for new vehicles by twenty percent within six months of the statute's enactment.

Also assume that the proposed bill represents Senator Green's ideal point, meaning the precise policy that she prefers in light of her own assessment of the costs and benefits of the proposed regulation. The proposal itself falls well within the category of public interest legislation in that it addresses a problem that confronts all citizens, and indeed all persons. And because most adults drive vehicles that leave carbon footprints, the costs of the proposed reduction are also widely dispersed. Assume, however, that while the bill has general support among members of the Democratically controlled Senate, where it was proposed, that support is insufficient for passage. Several powerful interest groups will suffer from the nearly immediate compliance requirement for the initial 20% emissions reduction. Further assume that those adversely affected interests—the automobile industry, the shipping industry, and the construction industry, to name a few—exert sufficient political pressure that without some effort to appease them, the bill is destined to fail.

a. Substantive Bargaining

The negative legislative checkpoints provide opportunities for these and other affected groups to engage in *substantive bargaining*, meaning bargaining between Senator Green, the bill sponsor, and those interests who would be adversely affected if the proposed bill were passed in its initially proposed form. First, consider the suggested negotiations from Senator Green's perspective. While she would most prefer her original proposal, including the rapid 20% emissions reduction on new vehicles, Senator Green also knows that the negative legislative checkpoints afford various opposing interests the power to defeat her bill unless she engages in substantive compromise. The only way that she can achieve her larger legislative goal of imposing constraints on the EPA to motivate ambitious regulation is to water down the proposed bill, including the initial compliance requirements, in a manner that moves the bill away from her ideal point.

Table 17:2. Substantive Bargaining over Emissions Reductions Bill

6 Month Compliance	1 Year Compliance (construction industry compromise)	3 Year Compliance (automobile industry compromise)	5 Year Compromise
Green's ideal point	◄———	———►	Interest groups' ideal point

[67] 549 U.S. 497 (2007).

At the same time, however, there is a point beyond which she might no longer be willing to compromise on substance even if failing to do so means that the bill might not pass. If the adversely affected constituents insist upon the EPA's passive approach to emissions reductions (let us assume this requires a 20% reduction over a span of five years), Senator Green might prefer defeat to codifying a result so far from her preferred policy. At a minimum, this would produce a high profile campaign issue.

Assume that while the adversely affected interests prefer a five-year compliance schedule for the initial 20% reduction in mobile-sourced carbon emissions, they also realize that there is a risk that unless they agree to a compromise, some other coalitions will form that will cut them from the bargain. It is possible that the relevant interests might fracture, such that the construction industry is willing to go along if the initial compliance is extended to one year, but that the automobile industry demands a full three years. If Senator Green requires only the support of one group to avoid a veto gate, then she will form a coalition with the construction industry, extending her initial compliance deadline from six months to one year. Table 17:2 depicts both ideal points, along with the potential compromises from those points. Of course this represents only a single bargain at a single locus, and there are many other potential loci at which similar substantive bargains might take place. Assume that following this successful negotiation with the construction industry, which allowed the bill to survive one veto gate, Senator Green's bill remains short of the votes needed to ensure passage. Further assume that Senator Green is unwilling to engage in further compliance extensions and is therefore unwilling to entertain additional proposals for substantive compromise. Even at this point it remains possible for the bill to pass.

Senator Green and members of her now larger coalition can take a separate tack, which we will refer to as *length bargaining*. When confronted with other veto gates that threaten her bill's defeat, Senator Green can agree to tack on special interest items, or riders, as the precondition for support. This process will leave the substance of her bill unaffected while acquiring additional needed support for passage. These additional items might have some connection to environmental compliance, for example tax credits for the cost of acquiring new technologies that reduce mobile-sourced emissions, or they might involve something else entirely, for example funding for a highway improvement project or bridge repair.[68]

From Senator Green's perspective, even though the bargaining does not alter the overall substance of the proposed legislation, which, following the substantive bargain with the construction industry, now demands a 20% reduction in emissions from newly acquired mobile sources within one year of enactment, it nonetheless adds dead weight. These are costs that add no value beyond enlarging the coalition to secure passage. As with substantive bargaining, Senator Green is likely unwilling to add such additional weight beyond a certain point to accomplish her goal. But assuming that she is able to secure a successful coalition while still retaining the bill's larger objectives and without adding undue weight, then the combined substantive and length bargaining enable her to move from her original bill, or ideal point, to a compromise bill that successfully

[68] It is not uncommon to have riders that bear little or no relationship to the substance of the bill to which they are attached.

withstands the various Senate veto gates. The bill is now ready to be sent to the House for consideration and likely additional bargaining.

Table 17:3. Length Bargaining over Emissions Reductions Bill

No special interest riders	Low intermediate riders	High intermediate riders	Many riders
Green's ideal point	←	→	Interest groups' ideal point

Table 17:3 depicts the length bargaining process. As with substantive bargaining, we depict the preferences, or ideal points for Senator Green and for interest groups seeking to use the bill as a means of securing passage of favored riders. We also depict two intermediate positions, one favoring each side. Before exploring the model's normative implications, consider also that while Senator Green was trying to "sell" her bill and "buy" votes in this example, with respect to other statutes, she is a seller of votes that other bill sponsors seek to buy. Through *logrolling*, bill sponsors exchange support for other bills to gain support for their own. This implies that not all compromise is reflected in the text of the bill that ultimately becomes law; some compromise will involve offering support for altogether different bills, or (complicating things further) even declining to vote against another bill. And negotiations do not necessarily stop there; it is also possible to negotiate support for important committee posts, for various scheduling matters, and for decisions not to exercise such powers as the filibuster on this or some other bill.

3. Assessing the Static and Dynamic Wilson-Hayes Model

As we will see in the next chapter, scholars have relied upon intuitions drawn from the Wilson-Hayes model to offer normative proposals concerning the judicial interpretation of statutes. For now, how do you assess the Hart and Sacks model and each of the preceding variations on the Wilson-Hayes model? To what extent are these models in conflict, and to what extent are they mutually reinforcing? What are the normative implications of the Wilson-Hayes model, whether presented in its static or dynamic form? How does the Wilson-Hayes model inform the interpretive tools that Hart and Sacks develop in the Legal Process model? If you find the models inconsistent, what is the basis for your conclusion? To the extent that the models diverge, which should be preferred in the course of statutory construction and why? Is it possible to reconcile the models? If so, what assumptions must you make about the role of the judge to make the models compatible?

II. APPLICATIONS: CONSTITUTIONAL JUDICIAL REVIEW OF INTEREST-GROUP LEGISLATION

In *Powers v. Harris*,[69] the United States Court of Appeals for the Tenth Circuit considered the constitutional implications of interest-group theory for constitutional

[69] 379 F.3d 1208 (10th Cir. 2004).

judicial review of interest-group driven legislation. The various opinions in *Powers* also consider a related case from the United States Court of Appeals for the Sixth Circuit, *Craigmiles v. Giles*.[70] We will treat these together here.

The *Powers* opinions present three different approaches to the question of the appropriate judicial role when reviewing a statute that appears to be the product of special-interest group influence. Writing for a majority, Chief Judge Tacha acknowledges that the enacted statute is a protectionist measure. He concludes, however, that under established Supreme Court case law, a legislative scheme that benefits an in-state interest group at a cost imposed upon in-state consumers does not violate the Constitution.

Although Judge Tymkovich, writing in concurrence, generally shares the majority's reading of the statute as motivated by interest group pressures, he would not go so far as to describe it as having *no* other purpose than to pay off an influential interest group at the expense of consumers. Instead, he suggests that it is inappropriate for judges to "call out" the interest group influence underlying the law, especially when the court proceeds to sustain the statute against a constitutional challenge. On one reading, Judge Tymkovich encourages judges to engage in the noble lie that interest-group-driven laws nonetheless further a legitimate governmental purpose. Alternatively, Tymkovich's opinion might be construed to imply that if the court can locate no such legitimate purpose, it should then proceed to strike down the challenged law. As you read his opinion, consider why Tymkovich might urge this choice rather than allowing a frank acknowledgement of an interest group payoff while still sustaining the challenged law.

Finally, the *Powers* majority distinguished its holding from that of the United States Court of Appeals for the Sixth Circuit in *Craigmiles v. Giles*,[71] a case presenting largely indistinguishable facts. In contrast with *Powers*, however, Judge Danny Boggs, writing for the *Craigmiles* Court, struck down the challenged law as violating rational basis scrutiny.

Powers v. Harris dealt with an Oklahoma law, similar to those in other states, demanding that funeral caskets only be sold by licensed funeral directors operating a funeral home. This regulation did not apply to other related merchandise, including urns, grave markers, and monuments. The prohibition also did not apply to "pre-need" sales, meaning caskets sold in connection with funeral arrangements prior to a person's death, but only to "time-of-need" sales.

The Oklahoma State Board of Embalmers and Funeral Directors, which was empowered to enforce the legislation, limited its application to intrastate casket sales. As a result, an unlicensed Oklahoman could sell a time-of-need casket to a customer *outside* Oklahoma; an unlicensed *non-Oklahoma* salesman could sell a time-of-need casket in Oklahoma; and an unlicensed person could sell a *pre-need* casket within Oklahoma. The requirement that a salesperson possess both a funeral director's license and operate out of a licensed funeral home only applied to the intrastate sale of time-of-need caskets between an Oklahoma seller and an Oklahoma consumer.

Obtaining a funeral director's license was both time consuming and expensive, and most of the relevant training did not relate to casket sales. Applicants were required to

[70] 312 F.3d 220 (6th Cir. 2002).

[71] *Id.*

complete sixty credit hours of specified undergraduate training, to complete a one-year apprenticeship that included embalming no fewer than twenty-five bodies, and to pass both a subject-matter and an Oklahoma law exam. Finally, businesses seeking to be licensed funeral homes were required to have a fixed physical location, a preparation room that met embalming requirements, a merchandise room with an inventory of no fewer than five caskets, and suitable areas for public viewing of human remains.

Evidence introduced in *Craigmiles* demonstrates that these regulatory restrictions impose substantial costs on purchasers, and that these increased costs tend to correlate with increased cremation as a lower cost alternative to burial. Data show that lower-priced sellers of caskets are available in states that allow competition, for example, against such sellers as Costco, Walmart, and Amazon.[72] The *Powers* plaintiff was an Oklahoma corporation that sought to sell funeral merchandise, including caskets, over the Internet. Judge Tacha, writing for the majority, held that the law was not unconstitutional.[73] Tacha explained:

> Hornbook constitutional law provides that if Oklahoma wants to limit the sale of caskets to licensed funeral directors, the Equal Protection Clause does not forbid it. . . .
>
> . . . .
>
> In *United States v. Carolene Products Co.*, the Court held, pursuant to rational basis review, that when legislative judgment is called into question on equal protection grounds and the issue is debatable, the decision of the legislature must be upheld if "any state of facts either known or which could reasonably be assumed affords support for it." Second-guessing by a court is not allowed.
>
> Further, rational-basis review does not give courts the option to speculate as to whether some other scheme could have better regulated the evils in question. In fact, we will not strike down a law as irrational simply because it may not succeed in bringing about the result it seeks to accomplish, or because the statute's classifications lack razor-sharp precision. Nor can we overturn a statute on the basis that no empirical evidence supports the assumptions underlying the legislative choice.
>
> Finally, "because we never require a legislature to articulate its reasons for enacting a statute, it is entirely irrelevant for constitutional purposes whether the conceived reason for the challenged distinction actually motivated the legislature." "[T]hose attacking the rationality of the legislative classification have the burden 'to negative every conceivable basis which might support it[ ]' " As such, we are not bound by the parties' arguments as to what legitimate state interests the statute seeks to further. In fact, "this Court is *obligated* to seek out other conceivable reasons for validating [a state statute.]" Indeed, that the

---

[72] Jacob Passy, *Costco and Amazon Even Have Deals on Caskets*, MARKETWATCH.COM (June 25, 2017), http://www.marketwatch.com/story/even-if-you-buy-a-cheap-casket-at-costco-or-amazon-it-could-cost-you-in-the-end-2017-06-19.

[73] 379 F.3d 1208 (10th Cir. 2004).

purpose the court relies on to uphold a state statute "was not the reason provided by [the state] is irrelevant to an equal protection inquiry."

These admonitions are more than legal catchphrases dutifully recited each time we confront an equal protection challenge to state regulation—they make sense. First, in practical terms, we would paralyze state governments if we undertook a probing review of each of their actions, constantly asking them to "try again." Second, even if we assumed such an exalted role, it would be nothing more than substituting our view of the public good or the general welfare for that chosen by the states. As a creature of politics, the definition of the public good changes with the political winds. There simply is no constitutional or Platonic form against which we can (or could) judge the wisdom of economic regulation. Third, these admonitions ring especially true when we are reviewing the regulatory actions of states, who, in our federal system, merit great respect as separate sovereigns.

Thus, we are obliged to consider every plausible legitimate state interest that might support the [Funeral Service Licensing Act] FSLA—not just the consumer-protection interest forwarded by the parties. Hence, we consider whether protecting the intrastate funeral home industry, absent a violation of a specific constitutional provision or a valid federal statute, constitutes a legitimate state interest. If it does, there can be little doubt that the FSLA's regulatory scheme is rationally related to that goal.[74]

After reviewing various justifications offered for the law, the court turned to the key proffered justification, which was whether the desire to transfer wealth from in-state consumers to an in-state interest group (in this case, licensed funeral home directors) was a legitimate state interest. Judge Tacha observed that it was:

Implicit in Plaintiffs' argument is the contention that intrastate economic protectionism, even without violating a specific constitutional provision or a valid federal statute, is an illegitimate state interest. Indeed, Plaintiffs describe Oklahoma's licensure scheme as "a classic piece of special interest legislation designed to extract monopoly rents from consumers' pockets and funnel them into the coffers of a small but politically influential group of businesspeople—namely, Oklahoma funeral directors." Amici are not so coy. In their view, Oklahoma's licensure scheme "is simply. . . protectionist legislation[,]" and "[u]nder the Constitution, . . . economic protectionism is not a legitimate state interest."[75]

Judge Tacha rejected the *Craigmiles* court's reliance on commerce clause case law in that case, which also raised an equal protection and substantive due process challenge to a regulation that involved intra-state protectionism. Judge Tacha stated:

. . . As such, these passages do not support the contention espoused in *Craigmiles* . . . that intrastate economic protectionism, absent a violation of a specific federal statutory or constitutional provision, represents an illegitimate

[74] *Id.* at 1211, 1216–18 (citations and footnotes omitted).

[75] *Id.* at 1218 (citations omitted).

> state interest. Our country's constitutionally enshrined policy favoring a national marketplace is simply irrelevant as to whether a state may legitimately protect one intrastate industry as against another when the challenge to the statute is purely one of equal protection. . . .
>
> In contrast, the Supreme Court has consistently held that protecting or favoring one particular intrastate industry, absent a specific federal constitutional or statutory violation, is a legitimate state interest. . . .

Judge Tacha further disagreed with Judge Boggs' reliance on a line of cases involving equal protection challenges to laws affecting politically unpopular groups:

> [I]n focusing on the actual motivation of the state legislature and the state's proffered justifications for the law, the *Craigmiles* court relied heavily on *Cleburne v. Cleburne Living Center, Inc.* We find this emphasis misplaced. . . .
>
> [No] majority of the Court has stated that the rational-basis review found in *Cleburne* and *Romer v. Evans* differs from the traditional variety applied above. . . . But "[e]ven if we were to read *Cleburne* to require that laws discriminating against historically unpopular groups meet an exacting rational-basis standard," which we do not, "we do not believe the class in which [plaintiffs] assert they are a member merits such scrutiny."
>
> On the other hand, *Romer* and *Cleburne* may not signal the birth of a new category of equal protection review. Perhaps, after considering all other conceivable purposes, the *Romer* and *Cleburne* Courts found that "a bare . . . desire to harm a politically unpopular group," constituted the only conceivable state interest in those cases. Under this reading, *Cleburne* would also not apply here because we have conceived of a legitimate state interest other than a "bare desire to harm" non-licensed, time-of-need, retail, casket salespersons.
>
> Finally, perhaps *Cleburne* and *Romer* are merely exceptions to traditional rational basis review fashioned by the Court to correct perceived inequities unique to those cases. If so, the Court has "fail[ed] to articulate [when this exception applies, thus] provid[ing] no principled foundation for determining when more searching inquiry is to be invoked." Regardless, the Court itself has never applied *Cleburne*-style rational-basis review to economic issues. Following the Court's lead, neither will we.[76]

Judge Tacha concluded:

> We do not doubt that the FSLA "may exact a needless, wasteful requirement in many cases. But it is for the legislature, not the courts, to balance the advantages and disadvantages of the [FSLA's] requirement[s]." Under our system of government, Plaintiffs " 'must resort to the polls, not to the courts' " for protection against the FSLA's perceived abuses.
>
> As Winston Churchill eloquently stated: "[D]emocracy is the worst form of government except for all those other forms that have been tried." Perhaps the facts here prove this maxim. A bill to amend the FSLA to favor persons in

[76] *Id.* at 1223–24.

the Plaintiffs' situation has been introduced in the Oklahoma House three times, only to languish in committee. While these failures may lead Plaintiffs to believe that the legislature is ignoring their voices of reason, the Constitution simply does not guarantee political success.

> Because we hold that intrastate economic protectionism, absent a violation of a specific federal statutory or constitutional provision, is a legitimate state interest and that the FSLA is rationally related to this legitimate end, we AFFIRM.[77]

Judge Tymkovich offered a concurring opinion.[78] While he agreed with the holding, he was troubled by the majority's candid acknowledgement of a protectionist purpose. Tymkovich explained:

> . . . I write separately because I believe the majority overstates the application of "intrastate economic protectionism" as a legitimate state interest furthered by Oklahoma's funeral licensing scheme.
>
> The majority opinion usefully sets forth an overview of the rational basis test. Under the traditional test, judicial review is limited to determining whether the challenged state classification is rationally related to a legitimate state interest. As the majority explains, and I agree, courts should not (1) second-guess the "wisdom, fairness, or logic" of legislative choices; (2) insist on "razor-sharp" legislative classifications; or (3) inquire into legislative motivations. I also agree that the burden rests with the challenger to a legislative classification "to negative every conceivable basis" supporting the law. Courts should credit "every plausible legitimate state interest" as a part of their judicial review under this deferential standard.
>
> Where I part company with the majority is its unconstrained view of economic protectionism as a "legitimate state interest." The majority is correct that courts have upheld regulatory schemes that favor some economic interests over others. Many state classifications subsidize or promote particular industries or discrete economic actors. And it is significant here that Oklahoma's licensing scheme only covered intrastate sales of caskets. But all of the cases rest on a fundamental foundation: the discriminatory legislation arguably advances either the general welfare or a public interest.
>
> The Supreme Court has consistently grounded the "legitimacy" of state interests in terms of a public interest. The Court has searched, and rooted out, even in the rational basis context, "invidious" state interests in evaluating legislative classifications. Thus, for example, in the paradigmatic case of *Williamson v. Lee Optical, Inc.*, the Supreme Court invoked consumer safety and health interests over a claim of pure economic parochialism. Rather than hold that a government may always favor one economic actor over another, the Court, if anything, insisted that the legislation advance some public good.

---

77 *Id.* at 1225 (citations omitted).

78 *Id.* at 1225 (Tymkovich, J., concurring).

While relying on these time-tested authorities, the majority goes well beyond them to confer legitimacy to a broad concept not argued by the Board—unvarnished economic protectionism. Contrary to the majority, however, whenever courts have upheld legislation that might otherwise appear protectionist, as shown above, courts have always found that they could also rationally advance a *non-protectionist* public good. The majority, in contrast to these precedents, effectively imports a standard that could even credit legislative classifications that advance no general state interest.

The end result of the majority's reasoning is an almost per se rule upholding intrastate protectionist legislation. I, for one, can imagine a different set of facts where the legislative classification is so lopsided in favor of personal interests at the expense of the public good, or so far removed from plausibly advancing a public interest that a rationale of "protectionism" would fail. No case holds that the bare preference of one economic actor while furthering no greater public interest advances a "legitimate state interest."

We need not go so far in this case for two reasons. First of all, the record below and the district court's findings of fact support a conclusion that the funeral licensing scheme here furthers, however imperfectly, an element of consumer protection. The district court found that the Board had in fact brought enforcement actions under the Act to combat consumer abuse by funeral directors. The licensing scheme thus provides a legal club to attack sharp practices by a major segment of casket retailers. Secondly, the history of the licensing scheme here shows that it predates the FCC's deregulation of third-party casket sales or internet competition, and, at least in the first instance, was not enacted solely to protect funeral directors facing increased intrastate competition. I would therefore conclude that the district court did not err in crediting the consumer protection rationale advanced by the Board.

The licensing scheme at issue here leaves much to be desired. The record makes it clear that limitations on the free market of casket sales have outlived whatever usefulness they may have had. Consumer interests appear to be harmed rather than protected by the limitation of choice and price encouraged by the licensing restrictions on intrastate casket sales. Oklahoma's general consumer protection laws appear to be a more than adequate vehicle to allow consumer redress of abusive marketing practices. But the majority is surely right that the battle over this issue must be fought in the Oklahoma legislature, the ultimate arbiter of state regulatory policy.

I therefore conclude that the legislative scheme here meets the rational basis test and join in the judgment of the majority.[79]

Finally, consider the following brief excerpt from Judge Danny Boggs's opinion in *Craigmiles v. Giles*. Unlike the Sixth Circuit, Judge Danny Boggs determined that

[79] *Id.* at 1225–27 (citations and footnote omitted).

"[P]rotecting a discrete interest group from economic competition is not a legitimate governmental purpose."[80] The Sixth Circuit concluded:

> Finding no rational relationship to any of the articulated purposes of the state, we are left with the more obvious illegitimate purpose to which licensure provision is very well tailored. The licensure requirement imposes a significant barrier to competition in the casket market. By protecting licensed funeral directors from competition on caskets, the FDEA harms consumers in their pocketbooks. If consumer protection were the aim of the 1972 amendment, the General Assembly had several direct means of achieving that end. None of the justifications offered by the state satisfies the slight review required by rational basis review under the Due Process and Equal Protection clauses of the Fourteenth Amendment. As this court has said, "rational basis review, while deferential, is not toothless."
>
> Judicial invalidation of economic regulation under the Fourteenth Amendment has been rare in the modern era. Our decision today is not a return to *Lochner*, by which this court would elevate its economic theory over that of legislative bodies. No sophisticated economic analysis is required to see the pretextual nature of the state's proffered explanations for the 1972 amendment. We are not imposing our view of a well-functioning market on the people of Tennessee. Instead, we invalidate only the General Assembly's naked attempt to raise a fortress protecting the monopoly rents that funeral directors extract from consumers. This measure to privilege certain businessmen over others at the expense of consumers is not animated by a legitimate governmental purpose and cannot survive even rational basis review.[81]

Subsequent cases have amplified the emerging circuit split as to whether economic protectionism favoring an in-state interest group constitutes a legitimate state interest under rational basis scrutiny. In *Sensational Smiles v. Mullen*, the Second Circuit agreed with the Tenth Circuit's ruling in *Powers*, reaching the conclusion "that economic favoritism is rational for purposes of our review of state action under the Fourteenth Amendment."[82] Judge Droney authored a concurring opinion stating that the law must be rationally related to some legitimate public purpose separate from protectionism, and he rested his analysis on the state's legitimate interest in protecting public health.[83]

By contrast, both the Fifth and Ninth Circuits followed the Sixth Circuit's *Craigmiles* decision and required more than simple protectionism as a rational justification under rational basis review. In *St. Joseph Abbey v. Castille*, the Fifth Circuit wrote, "[N]either precedent nor broader principles suggest that mere economic protection of a particular industry is a legitimate governmental purpose."[84] The Ninth Circuit stated in *Merrifield v.*

---

[80] 312 F.3d 220, 224 (6th Cir. 2002).

[81] *Id.* at 228–29 (citations omitted).

[82] Sensational Smiles v. Mullen, 793 F.3d 281, 286 (2d Cir. 2015), *cert. denied* 136 S. Ct. 1160 (2016).

[83] *Sensational Smiles*, 793 F.3d at 288 (Droney J., concurring in part and concurring in the judgment).

[84] St. Joseph Abbey v. Castille, 712 F.3d 215, 222 (5th Cir. 2013).

Lockyer, "[M]ere economic protectionism for the sake of economic protectionism is irrational with respect to determining if a classification survives rational basis review."[85]

DISCUSSION QUESTIONS

1. Together, *Powers* and *Craigmiles* suggest three possible approaches to judicial review of rent-seeking legislation: (1) Determining that the judiciary has no role in policing rent-seeking legislation; (2) Deferring generally to legislative rent seeking unless the court cannot identify any other legitimate purpose (however implausible) that is independent of payoffs to a special interest group; or (3) Engaging in a less deferential and more searching inquiry to determine the actual purposes of the statute, including rent seeking, and invalidating the statute if that appears to be the sole motivation. Which approach is most consistent with the insights of public choice theory? Is it possible to select among these options without first having accepted a normative baseline concerning the appropriate (or at least tolerable) extent of interest group involvement in legislative processes? Is it possible to select among these options without first embracing an independent theory concerning the role that interest groups play in the process of legislative procurement? For example, will you reach a different result if you view interest groups as necessary facilitators of overall legislative processes that help to procure general interest legislation, on the one hand, or if you instead view interest groups solely as securing rents, without providing any corresponding benefits to the legislative process, on the other? How does this characterization relate to the three models reviewed in this chapter: the legal process school, the static public choice model, and the dynamic public choice model? Do your answers more generally to the questions presented here depend on which of these models you find most suitable in characterizing the legislative process?

2. In *Powers* the court observed that legislation to repeal the restriction on casket sales had been introduced into the state legislature three times, only to "languish in committee" each time. Does this result reflect a lack of public support for repeal of the regulation? Does the majority opinion assume that the legislature will repeal the restriction if it fails to advance the public interest or becomes obsolete? Does the concurring opinion? Is such an assumption sound? Why or why not?

Consider also some of the political dynamics affecting these regulations. On one side are licensed funeral home directors, who benefit from those laws. On the other side are consumers who pay higher prices when paying for funerals and related expenses, along with such large companies as Costco and Amazon, who sell directly to consumers. Funerals are unlike other purchases in that most consumers are not experienced or repeat customers. Are there reasons to think that these large interstate retailers are ineffective at standing in for the consumers? Why or why not? Might your answer differ in states like Oklahoma and Mississippi, where the excerpted cases were litigated, as compared with larger states, such as California or New York? Why or why not?

3. Consider Judge Tacha's analysis of whether *Cleburne* and *Romer* demand a more exacting rational basis scrutiny test. In *Cleburne v. Cleburne Living Center*,[86] the Supreme Court invalidated a decision to deny a permit to construct a home for adults with intellectual disabilities. The Court rejected various alternative justifications offered in support of the law, and instead homed in on a single justification deemed illicit: the desire to harm persons with

[85] Merrifield v. Lockyer, 547 F.3d 978, 991 n.15 (9th Cir. 2008).

[86] 473 U.S. 432 (1985).

intellectual disabilities, deemed a politically unpopular group. In *Romer v. Evans*,[87] the Supreme Court struck down Amendment 2 to the Colorado Constitution, which excluded various forms of minority sexuality or sexual orientation as a basis for inclusion within the state or local antidiscrimination laws. Once more, the Court determined that the law could only be explained in terms of animus against a politically unpopular group.

In reviewing these cases, Judge Tacha concludes that the Supreme Court has never applied the test derived from those cases, disallowing laws motivated by a "bare . . . desire to harm," or animus against, "a politically unpopular group," to strike down an economic regulation. How does this assertion relate to the suggestion in Chapters 11 and 12 by Bruce Ackerman and Geoffrey Miller that insularity is sometimes a strength, rather than a limitation, in the context of legislative participation?[88] Does Tacha's analysis of when the *Cleburne* and *Romer* test does and does not apply support the claim that these scholars might be committing a category error within the framework of the Wilson-Hayes model? Why or why not?

4. Consider Judge Boggs's assertion in *Craigmiles* that the Court has never expressly permitted rent seeking, or a simple wealth transfer from one group to another, to constitute a rational justification in support of a law. Judge Boggs further claims that striking down the licensure law for in-state casket sales, when there is no apparent alternative justification to support it, does not signal a reversion to the regime associated with *Lochner v. New York*. Judge Droney supported the same view in his concurring opinion in *Sensational Smiles*.[89] We previously reviewed *Lochner* and related cases in Chapters 11 and 12. Are Judge Boggs and Judge Droney correct in claiming that striking down these challenged laws on the ground that they insulate an in state industry from competition is distinguishable from *Lochner*? Do the models reviewed in this chapter help in answering that question. Why or why not?

5. In none of the cases discussed in this set of Applications was the original complaint for violation of the state law filed by consumers. Instead, in most cases, the complaints were brought by the state's funeral home regulatory board. Typically, these boards are dominated by members of the funeral home industry. As an example, in *St. Joseph Abbey*, the nine-member board was required by law to have four licensed funeral directors, four licensed embalmers, and one independent representative. The complaint was filed by the chair of the Louisiana Funeral Directors Association Legislative Committee, a licensed funeral home director, and the owner of several funeral homes. He competed with monks of St. Joseph's Abbey who also sought to sell caskets to the public. Does the fact that complaints in these cases are brought by competitors, rather than consumers, help to explain the underlying political dynamics of these cases? If so, how, if at all, does this affect the legal or economic analysis?

---

[87] 517 U.S. 620 (1996).

[88] *See supra* Chapter 11 pp. 496–498 notes 142–147 (discussing Ackerman and Miller).

[89] *See* Sensational Smiles v. Mullen, 793 F.3d 281, 288–91 (2d. Cir. 2015) (Droney, J., concurring).

CHAPTER 18

The Legislature (Part 2)

Introduction

In this chapter, we present an array of normative theories concerning the judicial construction of statutes informed by public choice. These theories are advanced by prominent judges, legal scholars, and political scientists. The underlying literature is rich and varied, offering a range of perspectives, often drawn from the same underlying economic insights. We can divide these scholars in various ways, including a reference to particular public choice traditions, with the first group adhering more closely to the Chicago tradition, and a corresponding concern for legislative market failure, and the second group following more closely the Virginia tradition, with a stronger institutional focus and a somewhat more positive assessment of legislative bargaining processes. One might also view this from an ideological perspective, with the first group coming to public choice from the right and the latter coming to it from the left. If this characterization seems apt, consider the extent to which the authors rely upon public choice to reinforce preexisting ideological views.

The first group of scholars relies upon public choice to advance claims seeking to limit the reach of statutes, often with the effect of raising the costs of legislative bargaining. These scholars include Judge Frank Easterbrook and former Judge Richard Posner, of the United States Court of Appeals for the Seventh Circuit and members of the University of Chicago Law School faculty; Kenneth Shepsle, a political scientist at the Department of Government at Harvard University; and Jonathan Macey, a professor at the Yale Law School.[1] In our presentation, we will uncover important differences and similarities in the approaches that these scholars take. Each tends to hold the common law in high regard and to emphasize the normative implications of public choice models for legislative processes that alter background common law rules. These scholars question whether in construing statutes, courts should be skeptical of claims that the legislature is generally motivated by the desire to further the public interest. This question has implications for whether statutory construction should be sparing, perhaps limited to the text, or expansive, seeking to further identified legislative objectives.

---

[1] We could group Professor Macey with the latter camp, given his willingness to infer a broad legislative purpose and to align payoffs accordingly. We instead grouped him with the conservatives based on the specific legislative ends he presumes courts should seek to advance.

The second group of scholars generally offers a more optimistic view of both legislative processes and of the role of courts in furthering benign statutory objectives in the course of statutory interpretation.[2] These scholars include Professor Daniel Farber and the late Professor Philip Frickey, both of the University of California at Berkeley, Boalt Hall School of Law; Professor William Eskridge, of the Yale Law School; Professor Einer Elhauge, of the Harvard Law School; and McNollgast, an acronym for two political scientists at Stanford, Mathew D. *Mc*Cubbins and Roger *Noll*, and one at the California Institute of Technology, Barry Wein*gast*. Although these scholars also hold varied and conflicting views concerning the proper role of courts in statutory interpretation, in a certain respect each can be viewed, at least in part, as heir to tradition associated with the Hart and Sacks Legal Process School, described in Chapter 17.[3] These scholars tend to take a more sanguine view of the legislative process and of the capacity of judges to discern public interest objectives in assessing statutes that courts are called upon to interpret. Each of these scholars claims support for this view in the public choice literature.

The varied perspectives that these scholars represent, including conflicting normative claims, raise important questions concerning the nature of public choice scholarship as it relates to statutory construction. Is it possible to separate the ideological perspectives, or attitudes, of scholars relying on public choice from the normative claims they advance? Can we separate the normative claims presented in this chapter from the often implicit attitudinal baselines of the scholars advancing them?[4] If not, and if public choice does not provide its own normative baselines against which to assess these proposals, how can we meaningfully assess competing claims of scholars relying on public choice?

In Chapter 17, we presented the Legal Process School and the Wilson-Hayes models as analytical endpoints. In this chapter, we will see that legal scholars influenced by these traditions generally rest somewhere in between the endpoints of a broader spectrum. The first group of scholars described above tend to express a greater distrust of the legislative process, and a corresponding willingness to raise barriers to the cost of interest group bargaining. The second group is generally more accepting of legislative bargaining and therefore willing to lower the cost of legislative procurement through the exercise of judicial construction of statutes.

After reviewing contributions of the first group of scholars in Part, I, and of the second group in Part II, we present other considerations in Part III. We conclude Part IV with a case study. This includes two detailed case excerpts, a panel and an en banc decision,[5] from the same case, which help in evaluating these competing normative proposals.

---

[2] These scholars can also be described as heirs to the Virginia public choice tradition.

[3] It should not be surprising, therefore, that two of these scholars, Professors Eskridge and Frickey, are the editors of the Hart and Sacks eventual published work, HENRY M. HART & ALBERT M. SACKS, THE LEGAL PROCESS: BASIC PROBLEMS IN THE MAKING AND APPLICATION OF LAW 1374–80 (William N. Eskridge & Philip P. Frickey eds., 1994).

[4] *Cf.* Einer R. Elhauge, *Does Interest Group Theory Justify More Intrusive Judicial Review?*, 101 YALE L.J. 31 (1991).

[5] Although the en banc decision vacates the panel decision, the juxtaposition helps to evaluate the competing arguments in the case.

As you review the judicial opinions in Part IV, consider the following questions: Which of the various scholarly approaches presented in Part I are most helpful in assessing the case under review? To what extent are the intuitions respecting the case developed in the larger course of your legal training consistent or in tension with insights that you have gained from your study of public choice? In the event these intuitions conflict, which should prevail?

We will now examine the varying perspectives of the legal scholars.

I. SCHOLARS EXPRESSING SKEPTICISM ABOUT THE LEGISLATIVE PROCESS

A. Textual Minimalists

We begin with a group of scholars who contend that insights from public choice demonstrate the inability of courts to infer meaning beyond what is expressed in the written terms of the statute. As a result, these scholars tend to advocate that courts construe statutes narrowly. They are also generally distrustful of extraneous sources of information—those that go beyond the text or historical context of the statute—although they are generally open to extrinsic sources of contemporaneous meaning.

We can roughly place this group of scholars into three subgroups: (1) Those who interpret public choice as suggesting the impossibility of ascribing collective meaning beyond the literal text of statutes and who thus impose a very strict form of judicial minimalism in judicial interpretation. In this camp, we place Kenneth Shepsle and Judge Frank Easterbrook. (2) Those who are skeptical of the notion of legislative intent, but who accept collective meaning beyond the literal text and who are willing to entertain some contemporaneous sources supporting broader constructions. In this camp, we place Judge Richard Posner and McNollgast. And (3) those willing to engage in an admitted legal fiction in which courts focus on the legislature's stated intent to further benign statutory objectives, even when doing so might discount payoffs to groups that negotiated their procurement during the complex processes of legislative bargaining. Here we place Jonathan Macey.

Overall, these scholars share a general distrust of legislative processes and therefore seek to raise the cost of obtaining interest group payoffs through the judicial process. And yet, these scholars offer quite different perspectives on how judges should go about this task.

1. *Kenneth Shepsle*

In his aptly titled essay, *Congress Is a "They" not an "It": Legislative Intent as an Oxymoron*,[6] Professor Kenneth Shepsle offers a broadside attack against those who ascribe legislative intent to federal statutes. Shepsle's essential insight, which develops from his application of Arrow's Theorem to the question of legislative intent, is that it is mistaken to

[6] Kenneth A. Shepsle, *Congress Is a "They," Not an "It": Legislative Intent as an Oxymoron*, 12 INT'L REV. L. & ECON. 239 (1992).

anthropomorphize an institution, and that this is especially true for a highly complex institution like the United States Congress. Because Congress comprises 535 individual actors, each with her or his separate set of intents, and because congressional processes include agenda setting, strategic manipulation of voting procedures, and voting for reasons often separate from the merits of proposed bills or other legislative matters, legislative outcomes cannot be interpreted to have meaning beyond the statute's specific language.

Consider the following:

> It is evident that Congress is composed of *many* majorities. . . . And each majority is composed of many individuals. . . . When some point . . . defeats the status quo, we only know two things for certain. First, one majority prevailed, but there were clearly others that could have, except for "other factors" (unknown, and possibly unknowable). Second, the winning majority consists of many legislators; their respective reasons for voting against the status quo may well be as varied as their number.
>
> The first claim should raise some doubts about the normative status of any particular victor. For unspecified reasons a particular majority was assembled around a particular replacement for the status quo. Why that particular majority? Hard to say. It could be for Chicago School interest group reasons. But then again it could be because some particular majority had procedural advantages. . . .
>
> The second claim adds an independent indictment to reading much, either substantively or normatively, into winning policy. With $(n+1)/2$ or more individuals in the winning coalition, there is not a single legislative intent, but rather many *legislators'* intents. *Congress is a 'they,' not an 'it.'*[7]

Shepsle compares statutory interpretation to filling in incomplete contracts, and he considers the implications for several specific tools of statutory interpretation, none of which he fully endorses:

> Perhaps the most extreme is the "plain meaning" doctrine, according to which . . . neither intention nor prediction play a role. In the circumstances of cases apparently falling in the interstices of a statute, the Court must resist bringing the case under the statute's rubric. It may neither generalize the language of a statute, read intent into its words other than what is explicitly stated, nor forecast what the enacting majority (or some other majority for that matter) might have ruled. If the plain meaning of the statute's language does not cover a circumstance, then the statute is inapplicable. In a sense, this position, a minimalist one for courts, asserts that the *legislature* must complete otherwise incomplete statutes, not the courts. In either the interstitial case or the circumstance in which different statutes, with different dispositional implications for the case at hand, apply, it is the Court's obligation to seek further legislative guidance.[8]

---

7 *Id.* at 244 (third emphasis added).

8 *Id.* at 252–53 (footnote omitted).

While Shepsle concedes that some might regard his view as extreme and possibly impractical, he claims that if adopted, it will motivate rational legislators to "make their statutes plainer and more meaningful."[9]

2. *Judge Frank Easterbrook*

Judge Frank Easterbrook expresses similar sentiments in his famous essay, *Statutes' Domains.*[10] Easterbrook begins with the question "When does a court construe a statute, treaty, or constitutional provision and when hold it inapplicable instead?"[11] Easterbrook contends that this is an overlooked question and that the general presumption that when parties rely upon a statute for relief a court is duty-bound to "construe" it is incorrect. He explains:

> Yet to construe a statute at all is to resolve an important question in favor of the party invoking it. The interesting questions in litigation involve statutes that are ambiguous when applied to a particular set of facts. The construction of an ambiguous document is a work of judicial creation or re-creation. Using the available hints and tools—the words and structure of the statute, the subject matter and general policy of the enactment, the legislative history, the lobbying positions of interest groups, and the temper of the times—judges try to determine how the Congress that enacted the statute either actually resolved or would have resolved a particular issue if it had faced and settled it explicitly at the time. Judges have substantial leeway in construction. Inferences almost always conflict, and the enacting Congress is unlikely to come back to life and "prove" the court's construction wrong. The older the statute the more the inferences will be in conflict, and the greater the judges' freedom.
>
> If, however, the court finds the statute inapplicable to the subject of the litigation, it never begins this task of creative construction. Even if the judge *knows* how Congress would have handled the question presented, the court will do nothing. It will say to the litigant: "Too bad, but legislative intentions are not legal rules." Whoever relies on the statute loses. . . .
>
> The choice between construction and a declaration of inapplicability thus may make all the difference to the case.[12]

Easterbrook concedes that some readers might be troubled by his claimed distinction and conclude that "to declare a statute inapplicable to a dispute *is* an act of construction, and that [he is] therefore talking nonsense."[13] To support his claimed distinction, Easterbrook offers the following illustration:

> Consider, for example, whether a statute providing for the leashing of "dogs" also requires the leashing of cats (because the statute really covers the category "animals") or wolves (because the statute really covers the category

---

[9] *Id.* at 253.

[10] Frank H. Easterbrook, *Statutes' Domains*, 50 U. CHI. L. REV. 533 (1983).

[11] *Id.* at 533.

[12] *Id.* at 553–34 (footnote omitted).

[13] *Id.* at 534–35.

> "canines") or lions ("dangerous animals"). Most people would say that the statute does not go beyond dogs, because after all the verbal torturing of the words has been completed it is still too plain for argument what the statute means. Perhaps it is a quibble, but in my terminology this becomes a decision that the statute "applies" only to dogs. For rules about the rest of the animal kingdom we must look elsewhere.[14]

Easterbrook's larger argument is that judges should presume against construing statutes in those cases in which the statutes, properly read, do not appear to apply to the case before them. Like Shepsle, based upon such problems as cycling, agenda control, and procedural obstacles affecting statutory outcomes, Easterbrook claims that legislative outcomes cannot be presumed rational attempts to further some larger objective that extends beyond the actual statutory language.

Easterbrook therefore proposes that Congress can ensure that courts provide the proper "domain" to statutes in either of two ways. First, they can identify specific policy goals and instruct courts precisely how to pursue those goals in the text of the statute such as the precise rules governing tender offers under the national securities laws.[15] Alternatively, they can set out the statutory goals and instruct courts to develop the necessary rules in furtherance of those goals. This is more akin to delegating a form of rule-making power to courts. The Sherman Act has largely been interpreted as falling into this latter category.[16]

Easterbrook contends that if the statute in a case falls into the first category, then courts should enforce the statute as written but do no more than that. Easterbrook holds to this position whether the underlying statute is more properly classified as special or public interest legislation. If it is special interest legislation, the court serves societal interests in limiting interest group payoffs to those expressly set out in the statute itself. If instead it is public benefiting legislation, the court errs if it fails to recognize that from the perspective of the enacting legislature, more of a good thing can at some point become a bad thing. Easterbrook explains:

> Legislators seeking only to further the public interest may conclude that the provision of public rules should reach so far and no farther, whether because of deliberate compromise, because of respect for private orderings, or because of uncertainty coupled with concern that to regulate in the face of the unknown is to risk loss for little gain. No matter how good the end in view, achievement

---

[14] *Id.* at 535 (footnote omitted).

[15] *See* Williams Act, 15 U.S.C. §§ 78m(d)–(e), 78n(d)–(f) (2012); and accompanying regulations at 17 C.F.R. §§ 240.14d–1 to –10 (2017); 17 C.F.R. §§ 240.14e–1 to –8 (2017).

[16] *See* Sherman Act, 15 U.S.C. §§ 1–38 (2012). *See* Nat'l Soc'y of Prof'l Eng'rs v. United States, 435 U.S. 679, 688 (1978) ("Congress, however, did not intend the text of the Sherman Act to delineate the full meaning of the statute or its application in concrete situations. The legislative history makes it perfectly clear that it expected the courts to give shape to the statute's broad mandate by drawing on common-law tradition."); United States v. Assoc. Press, 52 F. Supp. 362, 370 (S.D.N.Y. 1943) (Hand, J.) ("Congress has incorporated into the Anti-Trust Acts the changing standards of the common law, and by so doing has delegated to the courts the duty of fixing the standard for each case."). *But see* ROBERT H. BORK, THE ANTITRUST PARADOX: A POLICY AT WAR WITH ITSELF 53 (1978) ("Congress, by its use of common law terminology in the Sherman Act, most certainly did not delegate any such free value-choosing role to the courts. And if it had attempted to do so, the courts should have refused the commission.").

of the end will have some cost, and at some point the cost will begin to exceed the benefits.[17]

Easterbrook instructs courts to apply a very different mode of reasoning when statutes fall into the second category involving delegating to courts the authority to construct the means of effectuating Congress's specified objectives. In those instances, courts should instead fill in the statute with its own rules that are based upon the contemporary (the time of decision), rather than contemporaneous (the time of statutory enactment), wisdom. That is because the fact of delegation to courts legitimates the value added from the new judicial construction of the legislation by a body "long prorogued."[18]

Easterbrook rejects arguments that in the event of a seeming "blank" or interstitial gap, it is the job of courts to fill in based upon construction. Easterbrook claims that the courts have no authority to fill in the blank by trying to figure out how the legislature *would have* filled the blank if it had done so. Easterbrook instead proposes that courts should leave the blank and not try to construe it because the only legitimate basis for doing so would be to further legislative intent. As a result of agenda control, logrolling, or *ad hoc* special interest influence, Easterbrook claims that it is not possible to identify a coherent majority will and that the notion of a public purpose that a statute seeks to serve is incoherent.

Easterbrook maintains that logrolling makes legislative majorities seem more coherent (since the practice provides broader support for enacted bills), but, at the same time, he cautions that the process makes the notion of legislative intent less coherent (since the apparent support is very likely motivated by non-merits considerations). In a regime typified by logrolling, attempts to fill in statutory gaps become little more than "wild guesses" as to how the legislature *would* have wanted to decide questions that it did not actually decide.[19]

Finally, consider the following related passage:[20]

> Because legislatures comprise many members, they do not have "intents" or "designs," hidden yet discoverable. Each member may or may not have a design. The body as a whole, however, has only outcomes. It is not only impossible to reason from one statute to another, but also impossible to reason from one or more sections of a statute to a problem not resolved.
>
> This follows from the discoveries of public choice theory. Although legislators have individual lists of desires, priorities, and preferences, it turns out to be difficult, sometimes impossible, to aggregate these lists into a coherent collective choice. Every system of voting has flaws. The one used by legislatures is particularly dependent on the order in which decisions are made. Legislatures customarily consider proposals one at a time and then vote them up or down. This method disregards third or fourth options and the intensity with which legislators prefer one option over another. Additional options can

[17] Easterbrook, *supra* note 10, at 541.

[18] *Id.* at 545.

[19] *Id.* at 548.

[20] *Id.* at 547–48.

be considered only in sequence, and this makes the order of decision vital. It is fairly easy to show that someone with control of the agenda can manipulate the choice so that the legislature adopts proposals that only a minority support. The existence of agenda control makes it impossible for a court—even one that knows each legislator's complete table of preferences—to say what the whole body would have done with a proposal it did not consider in fact.

> One countervailing force is logrolling, in which legislators express the intensity of their preferences by voting against their views on some proposals in order to obtain votes for other proposals about which their views are stronger. Yet when logrolling is at work the legislative process is submerged and courts lose the information they need to divine the body's design. A successful logrolling process yields unanimity on every recorded vote and indeterminacy on all issues for which there is no recorded vote.
>
> In practice, the order of decisions and logrolling are not total bars to judicial understanding. But they are so integral to the legislative process that judicial predictions about how the legislature would have decided issues it did not in fact decide are bound to be little more than wild guesses. . . .[21]

Easterbrook further contends that these seemingly arbitrary practices render reliance upon legislative history illegitimate. Consider the following passage from *Statutes' Domains* discussing whether the Federal Communications Act, which authorizes the Federal Communications Commission to regulate television and radio broadcasts, also authorizes it to regulate cable television:

> Suppose that within a month after Congress passed the Communications Act a court declares the statute inapplicable to cable television. The FCC consequently lacks regulatory jurisdiction. Immediately thereafter, during the same session of Congress that passed the Communications Act, the pertinent committee in each house of Congress reports out a short amendment giving the FCC jurisdiction. The texts of the amendment are identical, and the unanimous committee reports state that the amendment is necessary to correct a terrible oversight. Each report states that the committee originally intended to confer on the FCC jurisdiction over cable systems, but that during the session members of the staff charged with drafting the language to implement the design resigned, and their successors, unaware of the original plan, had not carried it out. As a result the legislation did not implement the agreed-upon plan, and this technical amendment would perfect the statute.
>
> Suppose further that the leaders of both parties endorse the amendment, and the President expresses willingness to sign it when it reaches his desk. Yet although the amendment encounters no opposition, it also does not pass. Perhaps it never is scheduled for time on the floor because other, more pressing legislation consumes the remainder of the session. Perhaps members who support the amendment hold it hostage in an effort to secure enactment of some other bill over which there is vigorous debate. Perhaps the bill is *so* popular that it becomes the vehicle for a school prayer amendment or some

[21] *Id.*

other factious legislation, in the hope that it will carry the disputed legislation with it, but the strategy succeeds only in killing both proposals. There are a hundred ways in which a bill can die even though there is no opposition to it.[22]

Easterbrook maintains that judicial gap-filling fails to appreciate that specific legislative sessions expire. Because no legislature has time to decide every issue, Easterbrook claims that judicial gap-filling improperly reduces the cost of passing legislation.[23] If each legislature possessed unlimited time and foresight, then it is just as possible that subsequent legislatures would repeal earlier legislation as it is that the original legislature would have enacted more legislation or filled in more blanks. In effect, Easterbrook argues, judicial blank-filling based on vague "legislative intent" improperly empowers a legislature to legislate beyond its actual term and to avoid submitting this "new" legislation to consideration by the executive veto.

QUESTIONS AND COMMENTS[24]

Do you agree with Shepsle that minimalist judicial construction of statutes will force Congress to legislate with greater precision? Why? Whether it will or will not, should present litigants be subject to narrow interpretations due to the inability of the enacting Congress to specifically include textual language resolving their dispute? Why or why not?

Consider Easterbrook's distinction between construction and non-construction, including his opening illustration concerning the dog leash law. Assume that you are clerking for a judge who is called upon to resolve a case involving a claim that the statute demanded the leashing of an animal other than a dog, perhaps a Vietnamese Pig, and that leashing the animal would have avoided a bite, thus constituting negligence per se. If you were clerking for Judge Easterbrook, how would you draft the opinion in a manner that successfully avoided statutory construction? If you were clerking for a judge who instructed you to interpret the statute against the claimant, how would you draft the opinion in a manner that properly construed the statute? Would both opinions maintain as the basis for denying relief, at least with respect to the claim that failing to abide by the dog leash law in the case of the pig was negligence per se, that the statute demands the leashing of dogs, not pigs? If so, how do these two approaches differ? Perhaps Easterbrook's argument suggests that absent the statute, the court is called upon to apply the common law in assessing the underlying legal claim. If so, however, does this avoid the implicit construction in setting aside the statutory basis for relief as a prelude to reaching the underlying common law issue? If not, are the approaches two ways of saying the same thing? Why or why not? If so, is Easterbrook "talking nonsense"?

Consider Easterbrook's argument against reliance upon legislative history. To focus the analysis, let us generalize Easterbrook's Communications Act hypothetical as follows. In Time Period 1 (T1), Congress enacts Statute *A*. In T2, the Supreme Court determines that on a given set of facts, Facts *X*, Statute *A* produces a particular result, Result *Y*. In T3, the same

---

22 *Id.* at 537–38 (footnotes omitted).

23 For a very different normative understanding of this observation about legislative sessions, consider EINER ELHAUGE, STATUTORY DEFAULT RULES: HOW TO INTERPRET UNCLEAR LEGISLATION 9–10 (2008) (proposing that courts should generally construe ambiguous statutory provisions based upon contemporary enactable legislative preferences).

24 This discussion is adapted from MAXWELL STEARNS, PUBLIC CHOICE AND PUBLIC LAW: READINGS AND COMMENTARY 631–35 (1997).

Congress seeks to amend Statute *A* to correct the Supreme Court's error to instead say the following: On Facts *X*, Statute *A* produces the opposite result from that announced by the Supreme Court, or Result *not-Y*. Despite otherwise sufficient consensus, and the willingness of the President to sign the relevant legislation into law, due to any number of procedural problems, the proposed amendment in T3 fails to pass. In T4, the Supreme Court once again gets a case presenting Facts *X*, and must decide whether to rely upon the subsequent legislative history from T3 as a means of avoiding the problematical precedent in T2.

Judge Easterbrook explains that there is a nearly universal judicial consensus *against* reliance on subsequent legislative history and uses this to bolster his claim against legislative history. Consider his argument:

> If such powerful evidence of the intent of Congress about the domain of its statutes is not dispositive in matters of construction versus inapplicability, the usual kind of evidence is even less helpful. To delve into the structure, purpose, and legislative history of the original statute is to engage in a sort of creation. It is to fill in blanks. And without some warrant—other than the existence of the blank—for a court to fill it in, the court has no authority to decide in favor of the party invoking the blank-containing statute.[25]

Consider the following response. The subsequent legislative history that Easterbrook describes is extremely "helpful" in discerning legislative intent respecting Statute *A*. The problem is that it is inadmissible for independent reasons. The fact that the evidence of legislative intent, as revealed in P3, is not "dispositive" in case 2, therefore, says very little about whether other evidence of legislative intent—evidence that does not suffer from the same evidentiary defect associated with legislative history—is or is not helpful. The real difficulty with subsequent legislative history is that bills frequently die for procedural reasons that have little or nothing to do with support (or lack thereof) on the merits. Moreover, some sections within bills are attached in the amending process to gain support for the overall bill even though those sections, if freestanding, would not garner independent majority support.[26] Ultimately, Easterbrook's analysis might counsel against admitting evidence of the shadow history concerning bills not passed, or of provisions that passed as part of a larger legislative bargain, as evidence of legislative intent. Can you identify reasons for the general understanding that evidence of this sort is generally impermissible? How, if at all, does this vary from the sorts of evidence of legislative intent that, for example, Hart and Sacks are likely to find admissible and useful to statutory interpretation? If you conclude that they are different, can you articulate a rule that would draw out the distinction?

Returning to Judge Easterbrook's hypothetical, imagine instead that well documented evidence of legislative intent for Statute *A* demonstrated a substantial likelihood that on Facts *X*, Congress intended Result *not-Y*, but that the statute itself was not precise on the question. Assume for example, that this position was clearly expressed without opposition on the floor of the Congress and was recorded, also without opposition, in the committee report. Assume once again that Case 1 arises before the Supreme Court. Does Judge Easterbrook's argument against the subsequent legislative history shed light on the potential value of relying upon the actual legislative history in this case? Assuming that Judge Easterbrook is correct that it is extremely difficult for Congress to overturn a judicial decision even with broad Congressional

[25] Easterbrook, *supra* note 10, at 539.

[26] Maxwell L. Stearns, *The Public Choice Case Against the Item Veto*, 49 WASH. & LEE L. REV. 385, 397 (1992).

consent to do so, does this counsel in favor of or against using available evidence of legislative history as a means of approximating legislative preferences?[27]

Also consider Judge Easterbrook's argument that as a result of the procedural and other complexities in Congress that public choice exposes in the legislative process, it is not possible to assess intensities of preference. Might efforts to include misleading assertions in the legislative record prompt other counter-statements that would signal credibility problems to courts? Easterbrook also claims that legislative decision making is particularly agenda prone. Does this mean that prior to the formal implementation of a voting path by a committee chair, those who might be adversely affected are not able to negotiate a more favorable path? If they are able to negotiate the voting path, what does that suggest about Easterbrook's argument concerning the inability of legislators to register intensities of preferences concerning legislative proposals? What about logrolling? Does this process limit or further the power of litigants to register intensities of preference? Why?

B. Legislative Skeptics Influenced by the Legal Process School

We now consider the approaches to statutory interpretation offered by Judge Richard Posner, Professor Jonathan Macey, and McNollgast. These scholars also express a distrust of legislative processes, especially when compared to the process of common law decision making. And yet, based in part on intuitions from the Legal Process School, these scholars propose methods of teasing out public-regarding purposes in the judicial construction of statutes. As you read their proposals, consider how their views of the judicial task differ from those advanced by Professor Shepsle or Judge Easterbrook.

1. Judge Richard Posner

Judge Posner's normative analysis of statutory interpretation rests in part on his premise about the differences between the common law, which he regards as a logical system, and statutory law, which he regards as a strictly textual system. Posner claims that because the common law is conceptual, unlike authoritative written legal texts, it exists independently of particular verbal formulations:

> The concepts of negligence, of consideration, of reliance, are not tied to a particular verbal formulation, but can be restated in whatever words seem clearest in light of current linguistic conventions. Common law is thus unwritten law in a profound sense. There are more or less influential statements of every doctrine but none is authoritative in the sense that the decision of a new case must be tied to the statement, rather than to the concept of which the statement is one of an indefinite number of possible formulations.[28]

By contrast, Posner maintains that statutory and constitutional law cannot be understood separately from the relevant text:

---

[27] Consider these questions also when we discuss Einer Elhauge's analysis of enactable preferences, *infra* pp. 762–766.

[28] Richard A. Posner, *Legal Formalism, Legal Realism, and the Interpretation of Statutes and the Constitution*, 37 CASE W. RES. L. REV. 179, 186 (1986).

> Statutory and constitutional law differs fundamentally from common law in that every statutory and constitutional text—the starting point for decision, and in that respect (but that respect only) corresponding to judicial opinions in common law decision-making—is in some important sense not to be revised by the judges. They cannot treat the statute as a stab at formulating a concept which they are free to rewrite in their own words. . . . [T]here is no such thing as deduction from a text. No matter how clear the text seems, it must be interpreted (or decoded) like any other communication, and interpretation is neither logical deduction nor policy analysis.[29]

While Posner describes the common law as a logical system separate from any specific verbal formulation contained in a judicial opinion, as you read the following passage, consider the extent to which this analysis depends upon Judge Posner's normative conception of the common law.

> The modern exemplar of formalism in common law is the positivist economic analysis of that law which Professor Landes and I and others have expounded. Taking as our premise the claim that the common law seeks to promote efficiency in the sense of wealth maximization (that is, abstracting from distributive considerations), and adding some data and assumptions about technology and human behavior, we deduce a set of optimal common law doctrines and institutions and then compare them with the actual common law. I use "deduction" in a literal sense. Microeconomic theory is a logical system like calculus or geometry (hence economic theory can be and often is expressed mathematically); more precisely a family of such systems.[30]

Do you agree with Posner's distinction between the common law as a logical system and statutes as purely text based? Judge Posner implicitly concedes that at least some common law rules depart from normative assertions concerning optimal, or efficient, common law rules. That is why he states that "optimal common law doctrines" can be compared with "actual common law." What does this observation suggest about whether the common law itself is "unwritten in a profound sense?" Does Judge Posner mean that the actual common law, or an efficient body of common law rules, exist independent of its written form? Are there other potential benchmarks for evaluating common law rules that are similarly "unwritten," and that can be used in evaluating actual common law rules, as distinguished from efficient common law rules?

What about statutes as pure text-based systems? When a statute effectively delegates specific policy goals to the judiciary, does it remain true that judges cannot "rewrite [statutory objectives] in their own words"? Is it possible that some statutes not taking the form of broad delegations nonetheless contain articulable premises independent of their literal wording?

By casting legislation as a purely textual system, Judge Posner implies that trying to discern a "purpose" in legislation wrongly ascribes common-law-like reasoning to the process of statutory construction. Nonetheless, Posner balks at dismissing altogether the notion of legislative purpose. Posner claims that the purpose of the law, broadly defined,

---

29 *Id.* at 187 (footnote omitted).

30 *Id.* at 185 (footnote omitted).

provides helpful context in interpreting ambiguous legislative communications. Consider, for example, Judge Posner's response to those who flatly reject judicial reliance on legislative history based upon insights drawn from public choice:

> Then there is the growing skepticism about the traditional props of statutory interpretation, such as reference to purpose, to legislative history, and to rules of interpretation. Public-choice theory makes the attribution of unified purpose to a collective body increasingly difficult to accept—though I think it is possible to overdo one's skepticism in this regard. Institutions act purposively, therefore they have purposes. A document can manifest a single purpose even though those who drafted and approved it have a variety of private motives and expectations.[31]

Now consider McNollgast's complementary analysis:[32]

> [A]s social choice theorists have known since Condorcet, majority-rule decisionmaking in the absence of agenda control can be unstable. But these observations do not imply that the concept of statutory intent lacks content. In the first place, that legislators all have different intentions does not imply that they do not or cannot strike bargains in order to construct a common understanding of the intention of a particular statute. . . . The number of legislators does not change the basic dynamic of policymaking: in the U.S., it is Congress as a whole that makes laws, not individual members of Congress. The fact that a particular agreement about intention might be defeated by another intention in a majority rule process with no agenda control does not mean that an enacted bill lacks meaning, just as a collective bargaining agreement does not lack meaning because a majority of union members might vote for an alternative that was not presented to them. To deny that a single, common intention for a statute is possible is to deny as well that Congress can legislate or that private parties can contract, a claim that is patently false.[33]

Judge Posner supports his argument concerning legislative intent using an analogy involving a platoon commander seeking to decode an ambiguous command:[34]

> [The] military analogy . . . may help make clear that in arguing that judges have a duty to interpret, even when the legislative text is unclear, I am not arguing for judicial activism. The relationship between a military officer and his superiors and their doctrines, preferences, and values is, after all, the very model of obedience and deference. But the relationship does not entail inaction when orders are unclear. On the contrary, it requires "interpretation" of the most creative kind. And nothing less will discharge the judicial duty, even for those who believe, as I do, that self-restraint is, at least in our day, the proper

---

[31] *Id.* at 195–96.

[32] McNollgast, *Legislative Intent: The Use of Positive Political Theory in Statutory Interpretation*, LAW & CONTEMP. PROBS., Spring 1994, at 3.

[33] *Id.* at 19.

[34] For a movie that explores the theme of a garbled communication in the context of a military operation, with potentially devastating consequences if not properly deciphered, see CRIMSON TIDE (Hollywood Pictures 1995).

> judicial attitude. Creative and willful are not synonyms. You can be creative in imagining how someone else would have acted knowing what you know as well as what he knows. That is the creativity of the great statutory judge.[35]

Judge Posner also criticizes Easterbrook's suggested division between statutes that delegate policy making to courts and those that create their own underlying policies:

> If adopted, this proposal might well reduce the effective power of the legislative branch. In the class of statutes that judges classified as authorizing common law, the legislature would have little or no effect on policy; policy would be made by the courts. In the residual class the legislature would have little power also, for its statutes would be given no effect beyond the applications "expressly addressed" by the legislators.[36]

Although Judge Posner rejects the Hart and Sacks premise that "courts deem the enacting legislators reasonable persons intending reasonable results in the public interest,"[37] he nonetheless considers himself at least partially heir to the Legal Process tradition:

> Far from thinking interpretation irrelevant, [Hart and Sacks] devote most of their discussion of statutory interpretation to techniques for "decoding" the statutory communication. It is only when all else fails that a court is to assume that the legislators were trying to do the same thing that courts do; it is only the most difficult, the indeterminate, issues of statutory interpretation that are to be subjected to common law formalist-realist reasoning. The fact that the court is to decode first, and reason in common law fashion only if the effort to decode fails, suggests that Hart and Sacks were well aware that not all legislation is reasonable in a common law sense.[38]

2. McNollgast

McNollgast go one step further than Posner, positing that a nuanced understanding of congressional bargaining processes allows judges to gain insights into legislative intent:

> In general, an observer (a jurist) who is informed (for example, about legislative intent) can learn from a signal of an informed party (a legislator) in either of two circumstances. First, the observer can learn whether the informed party bore some cost to communicate the signal. Although the content of the signal may be meaningless to the observer, the fact that the informed party bore a cost to communicate it nonetheless tells the observer that the informed party believed that the benefit of communicating would likely outweigh the cost incurred to do so. Second, if the informed party can be punished for

[35] Posner, *supra* note 28, at 200.

[36] *Id.* at 198.

[37] *Id.* at 192.

[38] *Id.* at 193. Posner goes on to explain that the authors' "discussion implies a more comfortable and confident view of 'interpretation' (broadly conceived) than is likely to gain many adherents today." *Id.* at 193–94. Posner ascribes this to a variety of challenges to traditional interpretive claims, including the assumption that statutes are generally welfare enhancing, the problem of understanding intent, and the problem of reliance on evidence of legislative intent described more fully in the text.

> sending false signals, the observer can conclude that some lies are unprofitable for the informed party (those for which the expected benefit for lying is less than the expected penalty). This reasoning allows the observer to conclude that certain signals are more likely to reflect the truth than others.[39]

For McNollgast, this intuition follows from the fact that there are reliable, or pivotal, members of Congress who play a key role in transforming proposals into law. Ironically, perhaps, this is due to the very veto gates that public choice reveals as essential to congressional bargaining. In effect, their analysis of the proper reliance upon legislative history is tied to the intuitions underlying the dynamic legislative bargaining model.[40] McNollgast explain:

> We use the term "pivotal" in a broader sense than simply the "swing" voters in Congress who must be induced to vote for a bill if it is to be enacted. As we use the term, anyone who occupies a "veto gate" in the institutional structure of legislative decisionmaking is also pivotal. Think of the legislative process as a decision tree, in which different members of the legislature are assigned different responsibilities at various nodes. A pivotal member is one whose action at a particular node can determine which branch of the tree the process will subsequently follow.[41]

The authors add that "The single most important feature of the legislative process in the House and Senate is that, to succeed, a bill must survive the gauntlet of veto gates in each chamber, each of which is supervised by members chosen by their peers to exercise gatekeeping authority."[42] According to McNollgast, identifying pivotal nodes and the actors who control them can provide valuable information concerning which sources of legislative history are more or less worthy of credit.

QUESTIONS

To what extent do you read the Posner and McNollgast analyses as critiques of the Easterbrook and Shepsle approaches to statutory interpretation? How might Easterbrook and Shepsle respond? Which set of positions do you find more persuasive and why? Which do you find more consistent with the lessons of public choice theory? Which do you find more consistent with the lessons of the Legal Process School? Why?

C. Professor Jonathan Macey: An Integration[43]

Professor Jonathan Macey relies upon public choice to take up the Hart and Sacks challenge directly.[44] Macey's project is to encourage courts to construe statutes so as to further whatever public interest objects they appear to contain while at the same time

---

[39] McNollgast, *supra* note 32, at 8.

[40] *See supra* Chapter 17, at 20–24.

[41] McNollgast, *supra* note 32, at 7.

[42] *Id.* at 18.

[43] Portions of this discussion are adapted from STEARNS, *supra* note 24, at 637–39.

[44] Jonathan R. Macey, *Promoting Public-Regarding Legislation Through Statutory Interpretation: An Interest Group Model*, 86 COLUM. L. REV. 223 (1986).

limiting some of the more egregious payoffs necessary to secure the legislative deal. Macey argues that the enterprise of statutory interpretation by the judiciary requires judges to reconcile what he presents as two competing goals under the Constitution: (1) honoring the primary authority of the legislature to create policy, and (2) checking against legislative excesses, including reducing interest group influence, thus making legislation more public-regarding. Macey claims that those advocating what he terms the "legislation-as-contract" approach, including Easterbrook,[45] seek to vindicate the terms of the statutory bargain struck between the legislature and interest groups and, if necessary, are willing to delve into the statutory history to uncover the full terms of the bargain. Macey argues that this approach honors the first principle (legislative supremacy) but violates the second (checking interest-group activity). Conversely, Macey claims that those who urge greater judicial activism in striking down special-interest legislation on constitutional grounds, as occurred during the *Lochner* era, vindicate the second principle but fail to properly weigh the first.

Macey claims that between these two extremes lies the "traditional" approach to statutory interpretation which "refers to the classic, time-honored methods of statutory interpretation that judges actually employ to decide cases."[46] Under this approach, which is informed by the Legal Process School, Macey claims that judges should apply the statute as written but should not try to vindicate interest-group purposes that lie beyond the statutory language. Macey argues that this approach promotes the public interest by seeking out the public-regarding features of statutes that were motivated in part to benefit narrow interest groups, and that, therefore, it properly balances his two identified goals.

Macey divides statutes into three categories: (1) public interest statutes; (2) "open-explicit" statutes that make clear and direct payoffs to interest groups; and (3) "hidden-implicit" statutes that embed more obscure payoffs to interest groups that courts might or might not choose to enforce. Where the terms and intent of the statute advance the public interest, Macey claims that judges should simply enforce the statute as written since the two competing goals are not in conflict. Each of the two remaining subcategories present a more difficult judicial task.

Macey argues that where the statute is unambiguous and the terms, including the payoffs, of a special-interest bargain are clear, making the bargain "open-explicit," judges are duty bound to honor the terms of the bargain consistent with legislative primacy in policymaking. Where instead the terms of the special interest bargain are more obscure, and thus the bargain is "hidden-implicit," Macey argues that judges should construe the statute consistently with its stated public-regarding purpose even if that frustrates the terms of the embedded special interest bargain.

Macey maintains that this approach furthers the public interest because open-explicit bargains are much more costly for interest groups to acquire than hidden-implicit bargains since the former are more likely to generate public opposition. Macey observes:

> When the legislature has passed a statute that claims to be in the public interest but in fact benefits an interest group, that interest group may meet with

[45] Macey uses this term to characterize the argument in Easterbrook, *supra* note 10. *See* Macey, *supra* note 44, at 226.

[46] Macey, *supra* note 44, at 227.

frustration in the courts when it tries to enforce the statute. The statute is unlikely to serve the ends it claims to serve and at the same time enrich a particular group. When the court interprets the statute so as to serve the public, the court may . . . inadvertently invalidate a legislative bargain. But when this happens it is all to the common good.[47]

Professor Macey claims support for his analysis and for his assertion about the proper judicial role in policing—or at least raising costs respecting—special interest legislation in the following passage from the *Federalist* No. 78[48]:

> But it is not with a view to infractions of the Constitution only that the independence of the judges may be an essential safeguard against the effects of occasional ill humors in the society. . . . [T]he firmness of the judicial magistracy is of vast importance in mitigating the severity and confining the operation of such laws. It not only serves to moderate the immediate mischiefs of those which may have been passed but it operates as a check upon the legislative body in passing them; who, perceiving that obstacles to the success of an iniquitous intention are to be expected from the scruples of the courts, are in a manner compelled, by the very motives of the injustice they mediate, to qualify their attempts.

In evaluating Macey's claim respecting this passage, it will be helpful to compare the following alternative analysis offered Judge Posner:

> Another general problem of interpretation is that no one knows for sure whether the framers of the Constitution intended federal courts merely to translate (so far as they were able) the specific commands of Congress into particular case outcomes, or instead, as suggested by Alexander Hamilton [in the passage quoted above], to exert a civilizing influence—to act as a buffer between the legislators and the citizenry even when no constitutional issue was raised. The role of the judge in "civilizing" statutes was not problematic for Hart and Sacks because they were willing to assume in all doubtful cases that the statute was intended to achieve the civilized result. On such an assumption there is no difference between being a translator and being a buffer, so Hamilton could be left in peace.[49]

DISCUSSION QUESTIONS

What are the fundamental differences between Posner and Macey concerning the proper judicial task in statutory interpretation? Which is closer to the position advanced by Easterbrook and Shepsle? Which is closer to the position advanced by the Legal Process School? Which of the approaches among these groups of scholars is best informed by public choice analysis? Which is more persuasive as a matter of legal policy? How do these questions relate to Judge Posner's assertion in the final quoted passage that Hart and Sacks "were willing to assume in all doubtful cases that the statute was intended to achieve the civilized result"?

---

[47] *Id.* at 254.

[48] THE FEDERALIST NO. 78, at 438 (Alexander Hamilton) (Clinton Rossiter ed., 1961).

[49] Posner, *supra* note 28, at 195 (footnote omitted).

Has Macey adequately supported his conclusion that it is the role of courts to provide an additional check against interest group payoffs secured in the political process? Is Macey correct that this is an accepted constitutional goal? If not, should it be? Can you identify any potential adverse consequences that might flow from Macey's regime? How, if at all, is Macey's proposed regime different from the constitutional regime associated with *Lochner v. New York*? Is Macey's willingness to allow interest group payoffs when the terms are open/explicit, but not when they are hidden/implicit, sufficient to distinguish *Lochner*? How, if at all, is Macey's proposal different from the common law canon demanding that statutes in derogation of the common law be narrowly construed? Does the answer to this question inform whether Macey is operating in the Legal Process tradition? Why or why not?

II. SCHOLARS EMBRACING A MORE OPTIMISTIC VIEW OF THE LEGISLATIVE PROCESS

We now turn to a group of scholars who generally embrace a more optimistic view of the legislature and a greater willingness to allow courts to further legislative objectives through the interpretation of statutes. We begin with Professors Daniel Farber and Philip Frickey, who we can describe as falling within the Legal Process tradition or alternatively within the tradition of small "r" republicanism.[50] These scholars criticize the Chicago public choice school and claim that a broader reading of public choice supports a more substantial judicial role using statutory construction to further active political participation. In addition, we consider the work of William Eskridge, who more transparently than other scholars relies upon the Wilson-Hayes model to advance a comprehensive theory designed to carve out particular rules of judicial construction of statutes depending upon the analytical category into which the underlying legislation falls. Finally, we consider an analysis of statutory interpretation by Professor Einer Elhauge. Elhauge challenges the foundational assumption among most scholars that statutory construction is dependent on preferences of the enacting, or contemporaneous, legislature. He claims instead that the relevant question is how construction furthers the preferences of today's legislature, or a suitable proxy, which he terms "enactable preferences."

A. Farber and Frickey

Professor Daniel Farber and the late Professor Philip Frickey advance several claims that are intended to dispel the conclusion that public choice compels ascribing no more to statutes than literal meaning strictly based upon the written text. For both theoretical and pragmatic reasons, the authors claim that public choice is consistent with a more active judicial role in construing statutes, one that is consistent with common judicial practices, including reliance upon legislative history. The authors summarize their position as follows:

> We believe . . . that public choice theory is compatible with a more respectful attitude toward legislative intent. In our view, public choice theory

[50] Not to be confused with large "R" Republican politics.

> is consistent with a flexible, pragmatic approach to statutory construction, in which legislative intent plays an important role.[51]

Consider the authors' challenge to Chicago public choice arguments respecting legislative coherence and the possibility of discerning legislative intent beyond a statute's literal meaning. The authors reject the claim that the possibility of cycling preferences, or other difficulties revealed by social choice, undermine the concept of legislative intent. Farber and Frickey partly base their analysis upon a body of literature that describes three related concepts: the uncovered set, the yolk, and the strong point. The authors explain:

> [T]he uncovered set consists of outcomes that could survive sophisticated voting procedures by "dominating" other outcomes. The yolk is the smallest sphere that intersects all of the median planes, where a median plane is one that divides the voters' ideal points (each voter's most preferred outcome) into groups of equal size. In a rough sense, the center of the yolk is the median of the various voters' ideal outcomes. The strong point is the one that beats the most alternatives in pairwise voting.
>
> Remarkably these very different definitions turn out to describe very similar outcomes.[52]

The authors add: "We do not suggest that courts perform the elaborate calculations involved in these mathematical models. We believe that many judges will, however, have a good intuitive sense of the legislative center of gravity."[53]

How, if at all, does this framing relate to the McNollgast decision-node analysis? Does the concept of a decision node suggest that bargains might reflect outcomes not captured in such concepts as the uncovered set, strong point, or yolk? In a regime of active legislative bargaining, is it possible to determine whether specific interest group payoffs reflect outcomes that rest on some notion of a legislative center of gravity? Why or why not? Which of these approaches is more likely to be intuitive to a judge called upon to construe a statute? Why?

In addition, as discussed in Chapters 13, Farber and Frickey maintain that the fairness norm is conducive to stability despite the theoretical possibility of constructing preferences that cycle. By fairness, the authors claim that when confronted with various empty core bargaining games, participants are quite likely to split any resulting super-additive gains evenly,[54] rather than introducing continual options that hold temporary majority support, but that will inevitably be superseded by a series of additional introduced options that combine to create a cycle. The authors explain:

> The incentive to move away from these "natural" equilibria [meaning equal division as a fairness solution] is small because the ensuing cycling is likely to

---

[51] Daniel A. Farber & Philip P. Frickey, *Legislative Intent and Public Choice*, 74 VA. L. REV. 423, 424 (1988).

[52] *Id.* at 433. *See also* William Panning, *Formal Models of Legislative Processes*, *in* HANDBOOK OF LEGISLATIVE RESEARCH (Gerhard Loewenberg et al. eds., 1985).

[53] Farber & Frickey, *supra* note 51, at 437.

[54] Super-additivities mean the gains that arise from various superior coalition strategies that are available to replace existing coalition strategies in an empty core game. *See* Maxwell L. Stearns, *The Misguided Renaissance of Social Choice*, 103 YALE L.J. 1219, 1236–40 (1994).

send the outcome back into the equilibrium area anyway. Rational behavior calls for quickly finding and sticking with the equilibrium area.[55]

Farber and Frickey maintain that this intuition is closely tied to appreciating institutional rationality and to the processes through which institutions select decision-making rules. The authors maintain that " 'natural selection' would eliminate any legislature that failed to develop defenses to cycling and instability,"[56] and ask "What purpose is served by a legislature the outcomes of which are entirely unpredictable and fortuitous?"[57]

QUESTIONS AND COMMENTS

Does social choice support the authors' claim that legislative decision-making is likely to evolve in a manner that thwarts cycling? Are fairness norms likely to limit cycling? How, if at all, does the authors' social choice analysis inform the proper judicial construction of ambiguous statutory provisions? Consider Professor Shepsle's response to the Farber and Frickey cycling analysis, presented more fully in Chapters 13 and 14.[58] Recall that Shepsle contends that Arrow's result "does not entail constant flux and indeterminacy,"[59] but that it might call into question the normative merit of particular outcomes that embed cycling preferences.

Which positive account of the relative infrequency of cycling, that offered by Farber and Frickey or the response by Shepsle, do you find more persuasive? Which is more consistent with insights from public choice? Shepsle argues that the method through which institutions avoid cycles is influenced by factors that render outcomes "arbitrary or otherwise morally indefensible."[60] Is it possible that the processes through which those outcomes are achieved nonetheless legitimate those outcomes? Might the "manner in which majority cycling is resolved" give outcomes a "compelling" or at least adequate "normative justification"? Is it helpful to cast a non-Condorcet winner as, nonetheless, a legislative center of gravity, for example, as reflected in such concepts as uncovered sets, strong points, or yolks? Is it helpful to distinguish the merits of particular outcomes that are the product of cycling and voting paths from the merits of processes that generate those outcomes? How might Farber and Frickey, or Shepsle, respond? Can the legislative bargaining processes themselves—either length bargaining or substantive bargaining—lend normative legitimacy to outcomes that would not arise independently of those decision-making processes? Why or why not? Do group outcomes ever exist independently of the processes that generate them? Why or why not?

---

[55] Farber & Frickey, *supra* note 51, at 434–35. *See also* WILLIAM N. ESKRIDGE, JR., DYNAMIC STATUTORY INTERPRETATION (1994).

[56] Farber & Frickey, *supra* note 51, at 435. Professor William Eskridge advances a similar argument in his book, *Dynamic Statutory Interpretation. See* Maxwell L. Stearns, *Book Review*, 86 PUB. CHOICE 379 (1996) (reviewing ESKRIDGE, *supra* note 55).

[57] Farber & Frickey, *supra* note 51, at 435.

[58] *See supra* Chapter 3, Part II.E.

[59] Shepsle, *supra* note 6, at 242 n.6.

[60] *Id.*

B. William Eskridge

We will now turn to Professor William Eskridge's arguments advocating a more active judicial role in furthering objectives contained in statutes. Eskridge initially developed his thesis in an article, *Politics Without Romance: Implications of Public Choice Theory for Statutory Interpretation*,[61] and later extended his thesis in a book-length treatment, *Dynamic Statutory Interpretation*.[62] For our purposes, the article is particularly important as it sets out an ambitious normative assessment of the Wilson-Hayes model for statutory interpretation.[63]

Eskridge maintains that presumptive judicial deference to Congress is inappropriate given that unlike courts, Congress has the capacity, and frequently the tendency, to remain inert. He explains:

> Perhaps the most important lesson of public choice theory for statutory interpretation is that it deepens our understanding of the court–legislature dialogue. A court is often tempted to finesse a hard interpretational choice by "leaving it to the legislature." This is frequently the worst place to leave the choice. Before doing that, the court ought to consider the legislature's incentives to act (and to act constructively) or not to act.[64]

Eskridge continues:

> [T]he mandatory jurisdiction of federal cases makes it difficult for judges—unlike legislators—to avoid the task of updating statutory policy. Litigants before a court are entitled to a decision, and devices to avoid the merits (such as questions of standing) are invoked only in exceptional cases.
>
> . . . [C]ourts behaving in a common law manner have a comparative advantage over Congress in updating symmetrical, public goods laws. . . .[65]

Eskridge maintains that the political insularity of federal judges provides a further benefit in encouraging courts to update statutory policy. He explains:

> The very nonaccountability of judges gives them—unlike legislators—the freedom to make hard policy choices without falling athwart the dilemma of the ungrateful electorate. Their relative nonaccountability also leaves them with few incentives to cozy up to interest groups, who can in most instances do them no good. In short, precisely because they are not subject to reelection pressures, judges avoid a major force skewing legislators' views.[66]

---

[61] William N. Eskridge, Jr., *Politics Without Romance: Implications of Public Choice Theory for Statutory Interpretation*, 74 VA. L. REV. 275 (1988).

[62] ESKRIDGE, *supra* note 55.

[63] For a discussion of Eskridge's analysis of how majority voting in a legislature can produce a social welfare loss, see *supra* Chapter 13, Part II.F.

[64] Eskridge, *supra* note 61, at 279.

[65] *Id.* at 303.

[66] *Id.* at 305 (footnote omitted).

Eskridge also claims that the different nature of interest group involvement within each institution favors judicial, as opposed to legislative, updating of statutes:

> Although interest groups play a role in the judicial process, it appears that the incidence and influence of group behavior are different in the judicial (in comparison to the legislative) arena. To begin with, there is less likely to be the same high degree of asymmetry of viewpoints in litigation that there routinely is in legislation. Courts generally have at least two parties representing opposing interests in a litigated case, and a court will refuse to hear a case that does not reflect a truly adversarial controversy.[67]

Finally, Eskridge offers a comprehensive synthesis of various scholarly works resting upon public choice, which takes the form of an updated Wilson-Hayes matrix.[68] As you review this matrix, consider its relationship to the approaches to statutory interpretation offered by Hart and Sacks. Consider its relationship to prior presentation of the static and dynamic Wilson-Hayes models. Finally, compare the approach depicted in the matrix with those of the various other scholars relying upon public choice. Notice that Eskridge claims to integrate the approaches of various scholars within his larger framework. Does he succeed? Why or why not? Which of these approaches is more consistent with your own assessment of the teachings of public choice? Why? Which approach is most sound as a matter of policy? Why?

---

[67] *Id.* at 303–04.

[68] The following is adapted from *id.* at 299 and 325. Eskridge presents this in two forms, and for ease of comparison, we have marked the original as such, and the other entries are from the version that appears later in the same article. We have reoriented the matrix, reversing the upper right and lower left corner to match our earlier presentation, but we have not altered its content.

Table 18:1. Dynamic Statutory Interpretation

Distributed benefit/distributed cost	Concentrated benefit/distributed cost
Original: Interpret in a common law fashion, limited by the statutory language, updating to reflect changed circumstances (similar to Posner's theory). **Danger:** The legislature's failure to update the law as society and the underlying problem change. **Response:** Courts can help maintain a statute's usefulness by expanding it to new situations and by developing the statute in common law fashion. **Caveat:** Courts should be reluctant to create special exceptions for organized groups.	**Original:** Interpret narrowly and refuse to provide special benefits unless clearly required by statute (similar to Easterbrook's view). **Danger:** Rent seeking by special interest groups at the expense of the general public. **Response:** Courts can narrowly construe the statute to minimize the benefits. Court should err in favor of stinginess with public largesse.
Distributed benefit/concentrated cost	**Concentrated benefit/concentrated cost**
Original: Interpret to effectuate stated public purposes and to reflect changing legal or constitutional values, within the frame of ongoing agency implementation (similar to Macey's theory). **Danger:** Regulated groups' evasion of duties; as agencies are "captured" by groups, regulation becomes a means to exclude competition. **Response:** Courts can monitor agency enforcement and private compliance, and can open up procedures to allow excluded groups to be heard. Courts should seek to make the original public goal work.	**Original:** Interpret to effectuating original deal among interest groups effectuating the stated purposes of the statute within the frame of ongoing agency interpretation (similar to Macey's theory). **Danger:** The statutory "deal" often grows unexpectedly lopsided over time. **Response:** Err against very much judicial updating, unless affected groups are systematically unable to get legislative attention.

C. Einer Elhauge

Professor Einer Elhauge has offered a novel theory of statutory interpretation that in some respects builds upon intuitions drawn from Professor Eskridge. Whereas Professor Eskridge seeks to update statutory policy to overcome perceived legislative bargaining problems that public choice helps to identify, Professor Elhauge offers a two-part prescription for legislative interpretation.[69] In the first part, he maintains that overall legislative satisfaction is enhanced when the judiciary does not seek to further the interests of the enacting, or contemporaneous, legislature in the construction of ambiguous statutory provisions, but rather when courts construe such provisions with reference to what he terms the "enactable preferences" of the sitting legislature at the time of the judicial decision. In the second, he argues that when it is not possible to identify enactable legislative preferences, courts sometimes optimize satisfaction by announcing rules that are "preference eliciting," meaning that the judicial decision motivates a legislative response with the effect of formally enacting present legislative preferences into law.

---

[69] *See* ELHAUGE, *supra* note 23, at 9–10.

We begin with Elhauge's thesis concerning enactable preferences:

> My first major point will be that the default rules that overall best maximize the political preferences of the *enacting* legislative polity turn out to track the preferences of the *current* legislative polity when the latter can be reliably ascertained from official action. By "official action," I mean either agency decisions interpreting the statute or subsequent legislative statutes that help reveal current enactable preferences even though they do not amend the relevant provision.
>
> This argument for current preferences default rules may be the most counterintuitive of my claims. Why wouldn't the enacting legislative polity want its *own* political preferences followed? The key to the answer is that the question here is not what result the enacting legislative polity would most likely want for the *particular* statute; if that were the question then it would be true that the legislature would want its own preferences followed. However, the question here is instead what *general* rules for resolving uncertainties about statutory meaning—including uncertainties in older statutes that are being interpreted and applied during the time that the enacting legislative polity holds office—would most maximize the political satisfaction of the enacting legislative polity? In choosing such general statutory default rules, the enacting legislative polity would prefer *present* influence (while it exists) over *all* the statutes being interpreted, rather than *future* influence (when it no longer exists) over the *subset* of statutes it enacted.[70]

Elhauge further contends that when neither current nor enactable preferences are clearly discernible, political satisfaction is sometimes maximized when the judiciary rules contrary to anticipated and strongly held legislative preferences with the result of eliciting a contrary legislative response. Elhauge recognizes the potential risk associated with this proposed default rule, and counsels a narrow set of applications:

> Preference-eliciting default rules will . . . enhance political satisfaction only when the chosen interpretation is more likely to elicit a legislative response, by a margin sufficient to outweigh a weak estimate that another interpretation is more likely to match enactable preferences. In other words, a necessary condition for applying a preference-eliciting default rule is the existence of a significant differential likelihood of legislative correction. Where that and other conditions are met, a preference-eliciting default rule can create statutory results that reflect enactable preferences more accurately than any judicial estimate of current or enactor preferences possibly could.[71]

Consider one prominent illustration of each of Elhauge's default rules: first, the enactable preference rule, and then the preference-eliciting rule. Elhauge contends that absent statutory guidance on the sitting legislature's preferred interpretation of an existing statute, agency interpretation offers a useful proxy for enactable preferences because

[70] *Id.* at 9–10 (italics in original).

[71] *Id.* at 12.

agency policy is generally made by political appointees who are therefore at least indirectly subject to some degree of political accountability.

Elhauge discusses two major Supreme Court decisions that relate to when federal courts should defer to agency interpretations of statutes. In *Chevron U.S.A. Inc. v. Natural Resources Defense Council, Inc.*,[72] the Court announced a general policy of deferring to agency construction of ambiguous statutory provisions even if the agency construction differs from that which the federal court would have produced as an initial matter.

Elhauge explains the intuition underlying *Chevron* as follows:

> *Chevron* deference depends on agencies being fairly accurate barometers of current enactable preferences, or at least more accurate than judicial estimates would be. Although the phrase "legislative preferences" is often used as a shorthand for enactable preferences, in systems like the United States' the set of preferences that are actually enactable is strongly influenced not just by legislators but also by the executive, who has the powers to veto legislation and put issues on the public agenda. Each is in turn influenced by outside political forces, which lobby, organize, contribute, and otherwise constrain the actions of both legislators and executives. In such a system, agencies must be responsive to executive, legislative, and general political influences for their actions to be likely to minimize the dissatisfaction of enactable political preferences in a way that merits *Chevron* deference.[73]

In *United States v. Mead Corp.*,[74] the Supreme Court announced a major exception to the *Chevron* agency deference rule, holding that when the agency policy is not adopted through formal processes, the announced policy is not subject to *Chevron* deference.[75] The *Mead* Court ruled that *Chevron* deference does not apply to "agency letter rulings, opinion letters, policy statements, manuals, and enforcement guidelines."[76]

Elhauge reconciles the two cases as follows:

> This distinction—between individualized determinations and rulemaking for a general class of persons—may not make much sense if we focus on the coercive effect of the decision, but is entirely understandable if we instead understand this doctrine as a current preferences default rule. Individualized determinations cannot be said to reflect the current enactable preferences of any general set of interested parties. One-shot individualized interpretations are also unlikely to provoke any legislative oversight. They thus do not suffice to justify judicial application of a current preferences default rule, especially since

---

[72] 467 U.S. 837 (1984).

[73] ELHAUGE, *supra* note 23, at 99.

[74] 533 U.S. 218 (2001).

[75] We will set out a more thorough examination of *Chevron* and *Mead*, *infra* Chapters 18 and 19.

[76] ELHAUGE, *supra* note 23, at 91. The *Mead* Court stated: "Interpretations such as those in opinion letters—like interpretations contained in policy statements, agency manuals, and enforcement guidelines, all of which lack the force of law—do not warrant *Chevron*-style deference." United States v. Mead Corp., 533 U.S. at 236 n.17 (quoting Christensen v. Harris County, 529 U.S. 576, 587 (2000)).

adopting that default rule would create an interpretation that would be binding on the general class of affected persons.[77]

In addition to analyzing the enactable preferences default rule, Elhauge evaluates those limited circumstances in which he encourages courts to rule in a manner that elicits an intended legislative response, even though the elicited legislative response contradicts the initial judicial ruling.[78] Professor Elhauge explains his intuition as follows:

> Suppose a statute has two plausible meanings: option *A* is 60% likely to reflect enactable preferences, and option *B* is 40% likely to do so. Suppose also that, if option *A* turned out not to conform to enactable preferences, the odds are 0% that the legislature might correct it. In contrast, if option *B* did not match enactable preferences, the odds are 100% that the legislature would correct it. If the court chooses option *A*, then the expected political satisfaction will be 60%, because in the 40% of cases where this interpretation did not match enactable preferences, the legislature would not correct it. However, if the court chooses option *B*, then the expected political satisfaction will be 100%, because in the 40% of cases where the default rule does turn out to match enactable preferences, the legislature will leave it in place, whereas in the 60% of cases where the default rule does not match enactable preferences, the legislature will replace it with option *A*. Choosing preference-eliciting option *B* will thus ultimately increase the expected satisfaction of enactable preferences, even though option *B* itself is less likely to reflect enactable preferences than *A*.[79]

Elhauge goes on to explain:

> The existence of preference-eliciting default rules means that an ex post statutory override does not prove that the judicial interpretation was mistaken, as is often supposed. To the contrary, such statutory overrides mean that the preference-eliciting default rule achieved its purpose: forcing explicit decision making by the political process.[80]

Professor Elhauge distinguishes this analysis from Professor Macey's interpretive rule encouraging courts to further the claimed public-regarding purpose of statutes containing hidden implicit bargains. The critical difference, Elhauge explains, is that whereas Macey places the burden of clarification on the parties seeking the benefit of the interest group bargain, Elhauge would place the burden on those challenging the unpopular payoff as a means of encouraging legislative overruling.[81]

Elhauge claims that his analysis helps to explain the rule of lenity. The purpose of the rule is not the relief afforded to an unpopular criminal offender. Instead, it is the

---

77 ELHAUGE, *supra* note 23, at 94.

78 As an illustration, Elhauge discusses the decision to grant relief to the Guantanamo detainees in the *Hamdan* case, a result that elicited a rather immediate Congressional response. *Id.* at 163–64.

79 *Id.* at 153.

80 *Id.* at 154 (footnote omitted).

81 *See id.* at 163.

motivation that the ruling creates in the sitting legislature to enact a contrary rule by statute. Elhauge explains:

> [P]reference-eliciting analysis provides a ready justification for this counterintuitive canon. By providing the most lenient reading in unclear cases, the rule of lenity forces legislatures to define just how anti-criminal they wish to be, and how far to go with the interest in punishing crime when it runs up against other societal interests. If instead courts broadly (or even neutrally) interpreted criminal statutes in cases of unclarity, this would often produce an overly broad interpretation that would likely stick, because there is no effective lobby for narrowing criminal statutes. In contrast, an overly narrow interpretation is far more likely to be corrected by statutory interpretation, because prosecutors and other members of anti-criminal lobbying groups are heavily involved in legislative drafting and can more readily get on the legislative agenda to procure any needed overrides.[82]

QUESTIONS AND COMMENTS[83]

Let us now compare the approaches to statutory interpretation offered by Farber and Frickey, Eskridge, and Elhauge. Recall that Professors Eskridge and Frickey ultimately published the Hart and Sacks Legal Process course materials. It is not surprising, therefore, that these authors view themselves as heirs, at least in part, to the Hart and Sacks scholarly tradition. We will begin with Farber and Frickey. To what extent are their assumptions about the legislative process informed by public choice and to what extent by other sources of political theory? Consider, for example, their claim that political actors will be motivated to produce fairness solutions rather than forcing empty core games back into the throes of cycling. Are the Farber and Frickey intuitions about the institutional implications of fairness grounded in social choice theory? Is their understanding of fairness consistent with Arrow's specified fairness criteria, and their linkage to democratic norms, or is it instead linked to some other set of normative considerations? If the latter, what are those normative considerations?

Consider also their argument concerning the evolution of institutions away from procedural devices that conduce to cycling. As previewed in Chapter 13 and 14, some institutional decision-making rules can be explained as mechanisms to avoid cycling. In elections, for example, rules that would produce cycling would risk failing to select a candidate when voter preferences cycled. As we will see in Chapter 22, within appellate courts, outcome voting and stare decisis formalize case resolutions in a manner that limits the appearance of cycling and thus that promotes stable doctrine. Still other institutions employ rules that exhibit a strong status quo preference. As we have seen in the study of parliamentary rules, even motion-and-amendment procedures that formally limit votes relative to options can permit the requisite number of binary comparisons to disclose cycles when we consider the possibility of informal practices that allow actors to identify their preferences in advance of formal agenda setting or voting.

How, if at all, does the Farber and Frickey analysis distinguish the evolutionary paths of courts and legislatures? Do you agree with Farber and Frickey that institutional evolution

[82] *See id.* at 169.

[83] Portions of the discussion that follows are based upon STEARNS, *supra* note 24, at 712–24.

would yield legislatures that avoid cycling even when the underlying preference structures do not demonstrate support for any single outcome representing a change from the status quo? Are there, instead, reasons why legislative practices might evolve to favor a status quo bias under these conditions? Is Shepsle's response to Farber and Frickey helpful in answering these questions?[84] Why or why not?

Is it possible to find appealing the Farber and Frickey normative intuitions concerning the role of courts in construing statutes even while disagreeing that they have accurately described the evolutionary paths of legislatures? To what extent does their assertion favoring a more respectful role for the use of legislative history turn on their public choice analysis of the legislature? Are courts well suited to locate intuitively the center of legislative gravity, whether characterized in terms of the uncovered set, yolk, or strong point? How do these concepts relate to the locating a Condorcet winner? Notice that Farber and Frickey do not claim that these outcomes are preferred to all available alternatives in binary comparisons, and thus those concepts can apply even when preferences cycle. As a result, such outcomes are necessarily disfavored to some alternative option, but within the relevant models are treated as stable. Must such regimes relax range to effectuate outcomes?[85] If so, what are the mechanisms for imposing the range restriction? Are those mechanisms likely present in Congress? Why or why not?

Now consider Professor Eskridge's arguments for dynamic statutory interpretation. Eskridge offers an ambitious analysis that requires identifying the analytical category into which each statute, or relevant statutory provision, falls using the Wilson-Hayes analysis.

Eskridge maintains that public choice reveals a considerable basis for caution in ascribing benign motives to at least some categories of legislation.[86] Recall from Chapter 14 Eskridge's hypothetical in which *A* and *B* succeed in securing Decision 1, with a shared payoff of 100, to the detriment of *C* and a corresponding societal welfare loss of 20, as compared with Decision 3.[87] In a robust legislature with a tradition of vote trading, this welfare-reducing outcome might not arise. Instead, if we assume a vote on Decision 1 at a given decision node, *C* could then promise a reciprocal commitment to repay a value up to the value *C* obtains, equal to 40, with a preferable outcome in some future vote trade.

If so, is it possible (if somewhat ironic) that Eskridge's dynamic statutory analysis rests upon an unduly static conception of congressional bargaining? In effect, Eskridge's analysis is premised upon a political market failure. But consider whether his analysis successfully captures political market dynamics. As previously explained, for this danger to manifest itself, a successful coalition must willingly leave money on the table, forgoing potentially greater gains from trade, and potentially improving social welfare for all participants. By pursuing their own self-interest, *A* and *B* also improve the outcome for *C*.

This suggests a danger in evaluating truncated legislative enactments in isolation from other legislative components. Consider how this further relates to Eskridge's larger project, captured in his now-combined analytical matrices. We can approach this analysis at both a micro- and macro-level. We will begin, for example, by inquiring about the same premises that underlie the related political market failure analyses suggested by Judge Easterbrook and

---

[84] Shepsle, *supra* note 6, at 242 n.6.

[85] *See supra* Chapters 13 and 14, Part II.B. (discussing range).

[86] It is for this reason that Eskridge borrows from Buchanan and Tullock the title "Politics without Romance." Eskridge, *supra* note 61.

[87] *See supra* Chapter 14, Part II.F.

Professor Macey. Specifically, within each of the four boxes of Eskridge's modified Wilson-Hayes matrix, we could inquire about the possibility of market failure and how the proposed rule of statutory construction might improve upon the claimed defect. We might also consider Eskridge's overall project with the benefit of a wider lens.

Specifically, consider the nature of relying upon the Wilson-Hayes matrix to demarcate specific analytical categories and the appropriate judicial response. The Wilson-Hayes matrix is a helpful heuristic in considering possible endpoints along two combined analytical spectrums: narrowly or broadly spread costs and narrowly or widely spread benefits. Does this combined set of analytical devices correspond to helpful judicial approaches in evaluating isolated categories of legislation? Consider, once more, substantive and length bargaining and the McNollgast decision node analysis. Assume that bargaining at a particular decision node results in negotiations to support or decline more than a single bill. Is it possible in such a dynamic bargaining regime to know whether a given piece of legislation pits narrow or broad beneficiaries against narrow or broad cost bearers? Why or why not? How does the answer to this question inform Eskridge's larger project of tailoring judicial responses to the nature of the legislation under review? How does it inform the analysis within each of the four micro-categories for Eskridge and for those upon whom Eskridge relies?

Consider also Eskridge's evolutionary analysis of courts and legislatures. Whereas Farber and Frickey suggest that legislative adaptation favors cycle-avoiding decisional rules, Eskridge appears to suggest the opposite. Legislatures, unlike courts, have a built-in status quo bias as a result of which, Eskridge maintains, courts have a comparative advantage in updating statutes. This is because unlike legislatures, courts usually have mandatory jurisdiction in cases they are called upon to decide. In addition, Eskridge maintains that the judiciary guarantees a broader range of perspectives—at a minimum two parties are generally represented in any given case—than legislatures. Is this persuasive? Does social choice analysis give any guidance as to why courts, unlike legislatures, are generally required to resolve cases and issues within properly docketed cases? Does it give any guidance as to why legislatures, unlike courts, are empowered to avoid collective decisions on bills absent a majority or Condorcet winner, or absent a set of vote trades that achieve majority support over a larger number of formally separate bills? How, if at all, does this analysis inform Eskridge's proposal to rely upon the judicial obligation to resolve cases as the basis for encouraging courts to update statutes? How does this relate to the earlier analysis comparing the merits of substantive outcomes with the legitimacy of the processes generating them?

Finally, consider Eskridge's analysis in light of the Legal Process School. Does his analysis rest upon the Hart and Sacks presumption that legislators are reasonable persons acting reasonably? Would Hart and Sacks endorse Eskridge's dynamic statutory interpretive regime? Why or why not?

Now consider Professor Elhauge's enactable preferences and preference-eliciting default rules. In his earlier article, *Does Interest Group Theory Justify More Intrusive Judicial Review?*,[88] Elhauge inquired whether those who rely upon interest group theory to advocate more stringent judicial review of statutes are resting upon a typically unstated normative baseline about the appropriate extent of interest group influence in the political process. What baseline is Elhauge employing in advancing his two suggested statutory default rules? Is present political satisfaction necessarily the proper normative baseline against which to gauge default rules for statutory interpretation? Why or why not?

---

[88] Elhauge, *supra* note 4.

Professor Elhauge suggests that most legislators would prefer temporary influence over all ambiguous statutory provisions subject to judicial resolution during the period of time that they are in office to an indefinite, or at least prolonged, influence on ambiguous statutory provisions that they enacted, after their terms expire. Is that a testable hypothesis? If so, what is an appropriate test? Is it possible that legislators would prefer a longer influence respecting those policy issues that they chose to address in the statutes that they had a role in passing, rather than a shorter lived influence over statutes that were the object of their predecessors' attention but that were subject to litigation during their terms in office?

Can you identify institutional mechanisms that improve the likelihood that courts construe ambiguous statutory provisions consistently with enactable preferences? Can you identify institutional mechanisms that have the opposite effect, encouraging courts to weigh the preferences of the enacting legislature to the extent that they can discern those preferences? Is the presence or absence of these possible institutional mechanisms relevant to testing whether Elhauge's suggested default rule rests upon sound premises?

In considering these questions, consider a famous article on the federal judiciary by Professor William Landes and Judge Richard Posner. Landes and Posner posit that one of the principal benefits of an independent federal judiciary is that it prolongs the payoffs of bargains made—including interest group bargains—in the political process.[89] The analysis is fairly straightforward. While no one imagines that judges are altogether immune from political influence, Article III tenure provides as effective a means as practicable of political insulation since Congress has no truly effective means of punishing federal judges for decisions that Congress objects to politically.[90] As a result, Article III tenure increases the probability that in enforcing statutes, federal judges will be more likely to weigh the intentions of those who drafted them, as opposed to those of present legislators, as compared with a regime that does not afford such political insulation. If Elhauge has identified an appropriate normative baseline with which to evaluate the meaning of ambiguous statutory provisions, would the framers have created a judiciary that was relatively more removed from, or relatively closer to, present (or contemporary) legislative processes? Is the answer to this question helpful in assessing whether Professor Elhauge's normative baseline is testable?

Elhauge responds to the Landes and Posner model as follows: "[i]n the cases at issue in [Elhauge's] book, the statutory meaning is uncertain, and thus a particular resolution of that uncertainty was never bid for, nor resolved, by the original bargaining."[91] Is that an adequate response? Is it likely that the framers only intended to prolong the original meaning with respect to the narrow class of expressly articulated interest group bargains or more generally with respect to the application of policies embedded in federal statutes? Is the intuition that underlies the Landes and Posner thesis limited to interest group payoffs, or does it suggest something more general about the judicial incentives to vindicate the preferences of the enacting, rather than today's, Congress?

---

[89] We will revisit this question in Chapters 23 and 24. For now it is sufficient to observe that the longer payoff might motivate political involvement that helps facilitate the procurement of desired general interest legislation.

[90] Impeachment has proved largely ineffective in disciplining judges based upon the substance of their decisions. Punishing judges more generally with a diminution of permissible benefits (salaries are protected under Article III) would require imposing sanctions on the entire judiciary, not simply those judges with whom a congressional majority disagrees.

[91] ELHAUGE, *supra* note 23, at 53.

As a purely descriptive matter, Elhauge's asserted baseline has an intuitive appeal. Past Congresses lack present political power. While Article III courts are substantially removed from present political processes, it would be naïve to suggest that they are therefore immune from present political influence. And yet, present political preferences will rarely point in a single direction. As Professor Matthew Stevenson has observed, *Chevron* deference advantages the executive branch's interpretation of ambiguous statutory provisions, rather than present political preferences more generally.[92] In the event that the executive and legislative branches are controlled by the same party, this might not be problematical to Elhauge's thesis. What does Stevenson's analysis suggest, however, when the two political branches are controlled by different parties?[93] Would an unelected judiciary with *Chevron* deference or an elected judiciary without *Chevron* deference be more likely to infuse ambiguous statutory provision with present *enactable* legislative preferences? Why?

Now consider Elhauge's preference-eliciting statutory default rule. Are the courts well equipped to gauge the conditions under which their decisions are likely to prompt subsequent corrective legislative action? If there is strong support for a pro-criminalizing measure, is the rule of lenity a good means of triggering that political force into legislation? Is there a risk that such a rule might lead to legislative over-compensation given that resulting legislative action will be motivated by a politically unpopular judicial ruling, for example releasing a convicted criminal for an egregious crime based upon the failure of the statute in question to cover with sufficient precision and notice each element of the offense? Is there a risk that such rulings might instead motivate another form of political market failure, for example, a cascade effect favoring over-criminalization, or excessive relaxation of protections against civil liberties, than would be the case if such policies were announced under more dispassionate circumstances?

Consider also whether the rule of lenity is compelled by considerations disconnected from the desire to maximize present political satisfaction.[94] Might the rule of lenity instead be compelled by the *Ex Post Facto* Clause,[95] which prevents retroactively criminalizing conduct? To what extent is it motivated by the Due Process Clause?[96] Might courts employ the rule of lenity in spite of their own preferences as a means of furthering these independent constitutional considerations, rather than to trigger a corrective legislative response? Professor Elhauge provides probabilistic estimates designed to show that such rulings potentially produce legislative overrides in a high percentage of cases.[97] Is this argument sufficient to

---

[92] Matthew Stephenson, *Legislative Allocation of Delegated Power: Uncertainty, Risk, and the Choice Between Agencies and the Courts*, 119 HARV. L. REV. 1035, 1065–68 (2006).

[93] For a discussion of the tensions between conventional understandings of separation of powers and the reality of divisions dominated by party politics, see *infra* Chapter 23 (discussing Daryl J. Levinson & Richard H. Pildes, *Separation of Parties, Not Powers*, 119 HARV. L. REV. 2312 (2006)).

[94] *See, e.g.*, Keeler v. Superior Court, 470 P.2d 617 (Cal. 1970) (finding due process violation in prosecution of man charged with murder of fetus, since the statutory definition of murder did not include fetuses as victims); 1970 Cal. Stat. ch. 1311 § 1 (codified at CAL. PENAL CODE § 187) (expanding the definition of murder to include the killing of a fetus).

[95] U.S. CONST. art. I, § 10, cl. 1 ("No State shall . . . pass any . . . ex post facto law. . . .").

[96] In *Bouie v. City of Columbia*, 378 U.S. 347 (1964), the Supreme Court infused the ex post facto principle into the Fourteenth Amendment Due Process Clause to prevent the retroactive judicial relaxation of a prosecutorial standard. In *Marks v. United States*, 430 U.S. 188 (1977), the Supreme Court applied *Bouie* to reverse a conviction where the prosecutor retroactively lowered the standard for an obscenity prosecution based upon a rejection of a narrowest grounds plurality ruling established in *Memoirs v. Massachusetts*, 383 U.S. 413 (1966).

[97] Einer Elhauge, *Preference-Eliciting Statutory Default Rules*, 102 COLUM. L. REV. 2162, 2176 (2002) (specifying conditions such that "a preference-eliciting default rule that only provoked ex post legislative

support Elhauge's broader thesis? Are the data equally consistent with the claim that the rule of lenity is motivated by independent constitutional considerations?

Finally, consider the relationship between this statutory default rule and default constitutional doctrines, such as the dormant Commerce Clause doctrine. In this area, the federal courts announce rules that Congress has the constitutional authority to override with ordinary legislation. Congress rarely does so. Does this suggest that the Court has correctly identified enactable legislative preferences, or alternatively, does it suggest that these cases are not politically salient and that most of the time inertia will favor whatever results obtain in federal courts? Is there a way to test which of these accounts provides a better explanation for the results? Overall, do you find Elhauge's suggested default rules of statutory construction persuasive? Why or why not?

III. OTHER CONNECTIONS

A. Hart and Sacks Revisited

Consider also the analytical connection between the theses advanced by Farber and Frickey, Eskridge, and Elhauge, on the one hand, and the Legal Process School, on the other. Which set of proposals is more consistent with the suggestions advanced by Hart and Sacks? Why? Do these scholars works provide a theoretical basis grounded in public choice for the normative prescriptions of the Legal Process School? Why or why not?

B. Coase Revisited[98]

Finally, let us return to the Coase theorem, introduced in Chapter 1 and discussed in several preceding chapters. Coase observed that in a world without transactions costs and perfect information, resources will flow to their most highly valued uses regardless of which party bears the property right. Is it helpful to analogize Congress and the federal judiciary to actors in a low or high transactions cost world respecting the rules of statutory construction? Easterbrook and Shepsle suggest that the optimal interpretive rules are quite narrow, and that Congress must specifically delegate to the courts policy-making powers if it wishes to have the courts engage in "construction" beyond literal wording. Macey would afford courts flexibility provided that Congress makes plain (or open-explicit) its payoffs to interest groups. Otherwise, however, he would suppress such payoffs to the extent that they are in tension with the statute's larger stated objectives.

Now consider the Coasian implications of these proposals. Even assuming that a proposed alternative respecting statutory interpretation is normatively superior, if only a small number of courts adopt it, does the change make it more difficult for Congress to legislate against a known set of judicial practices? Consider for example the extent to which members of Congress who are dissatisfied with the present regime, which looks to a host of sources to inform statutory meaning (including what Judge Posner identifies as the "traditional props of statutory interpretation"[99]), can minimize the impact of such

---

correction 20% of the time would actually be 92% successful at provoking legislative reconsideration of all kinds").

[98] Portions of the discussion that follows is adapted from STEARNS, *supra* note 24, at 719–23.

[99] Posner, *supra* note 28, at 195.

sources within the framework of existing rules. While Congress and the federal judiciary do not bargain as such over indicia of legislative intent, individual congressmen routinely include statements in the legislative record, either on the floor of the relevant house or in the relevant committee reports. If particular assertions included in the record are dubious, other members of Congress can include opposing statements. Does this suggest that a default rule permitting or excluding reliance on legislative history is more effective in lowering the relevant transactions costs? Why or why not?

Consider also the more ambitious legislative proposals that would allow courts to update statutes without regard to the preferences of the enacting legislators. Are there comparable mechanisms that would allow members of Congress to insist that they do not want the statutes they enact updated? For instance, consider the following unusual admonition in this note in the Civil Rights Act of 1991:

> No statements other than the interpretive memorandum appearing at Vol. 137 Congressional Record § 15276 (daily ed. Oct. 25, 1991) shall be considered legislative history of, or relied upon in any way as legislative history in construing or applying, any provision of this Act that relates to Wards Cove—Business necessity/cumulation/alternative business practice.[100]

Does this example help in identifying the preferred default rule? From a Coasian perspective, which of the various sets of approaches to statutory interpretation offered in this chapter seems optimal? Why? Is your answer to this question consistent with the teachings of public choice? Is it consistent with the legal process school? Can the two be reconciled? Why or why not?

IV. APPLICATION

A. Statutory Interpretation and Interest-Group Dynamics

We now present two opinions, the original (and vacated) panel opinion and the *en banc* opinion, in *Mississippi Poultry Ass'n, Inc. v. Madigan*.[101] *Mississippi Poultry* raised the issue of how a judge should deal with a question of statutory interpretation where there was substantial reason to believe that interest-group politics were at work. Applying the *Chevron* doctrine, the Court was required to determine whether the United States Department of Agriculture's regulation providing that foreign poultry inspection rules must be "at least equal to" the American regime was a reasonable interpretation of federal law requiring foreign poultry inspection regimes to be "the same as" those under domestic law. The Mississippi Poultry Association challenged the USDA's regulation, claiming that it was inconsistent with the plain language of the statute, and that the phrase "the same as" required the inspection regime to be identical to the domestic regime. In response to this claim, the USDA characterized such an interpretation as "absurd" because it would bar poultry inspected under rules superior to the American system. As we will see, answering this challenge required the Court to determine the law's underlying purpose. We then present an excerpt from the Fifth Circuit's *en banc* opinion in the case, which

---

[100] Civil Rights Act of 1991, Pub. L. No. 102–166, Sec. 105(b), 105 Stat. 1071, 1075.

[101] 992 F.2d 1359 (5th Cir. 1993); 31 F.3d 293 (5th Cir. 1994) (en banc).

achieved the same result as the panel court albeit with an alternative analysis. As you read these opinions, consider how the various theorists we have described in this chapter would go about construing "the same as" clause and which approach is most persuasive.

MISSISSIPPI POULTRY ASS'N, INC. V. MADIGAN[102]

WEINER, CIRCUIT JUDGE.

This is an appeal from the district court's grant of summary judgment rejecting the Secretary of Agriculture's interpretation of a critical inspection standard contained in the Poultry Products Inspection Act (PPIA). Like Pertelote, we heed Chanticleer's clarion call to resolve the central issue of this most recent in a long and illustrious line of gallinaceous litigation: whether the interpretation of poultry importation standards by the Defendant-Appellant Secretary of Agriculture (the Secretary) is entitled to deference under *Chevron USA v. Natural Resources Defense Council.* Finding the language employed by Congress both clear and unambiguous, we conclude not only that we owe no such deference to the Secretary's interpretation, but also that his interpretation is unsupportable under the plain language of the statute.

At issue in this appeal is the interpretation of § 17(d) of the PPIA and the implementing regulation promulgated jointly by the Secretary and the Food Safety and Inspection Services (FSIS) (collectively, "the Agency"). Section 466(d) provides that all imported poultry products

shall . . . be subject to *the same* inspection, sanitary, quality, species verification, and the residue standards applied to products produced in the United States; and . . . have been processed in facilities and under conditions that are *the same as* those under which similar products are processed in the United States.

The Agency promulgated a regulation interpreting the foregoing statutory language as requiring that "[t]he foreign inspection system must maintain a program to assure that the requirements referred to in this section, *at least equal to* those applicable to the Federal System in the United States, are being met."

During the required notice and comment period, the FSIS received thirty-one comments on the proposed rule, more than 75% of which opposed the "at least equal to" language. Nonetheless, in the preamble to the final rule, the FSIS stated that it did not believe that a literal application of the term "the same as" was the intent of Congress, although the FSIS acknowledged that "there are certain features that any system must have to be considered 'the same as' the American system."

Congress reacted to the effrontery of the "at least equal to" language in the regulation by enacting § 2507 of the Food, Agriculture, Conservation, and Trade Act of 1990 (1990 Farm Bill). In that section, Congress addressed the Agency's interpretation, stating that "the regulation promulgated by the Secretary of Agriculture, through the [FSIS], with respect to poultry products offered for importation into the United States does not reflect the intention of

[102] 992 F.2d 1359 (5th Cir. 1993).

the Congress." It then "urge[s]" the Secretary, through the FSIS, to amend the regulation to reflect the true legislative intent. Further, in the House Conference Report accompanying the 1990 Farm Bill, Congress declares that although certain technical deviations from United States standards, such as dye color and materials used for knives, may be acceptable, the "fundamental inspection system, intensity, procedures, and food safety standards, . . . should be *the same as* those prevalent in the United States for any such country to be certified for export to the United States." The Agency resisted Congress' expressed wishes, however, and the regulation remained unchanged.[103]

In addition, § 2507(b)(2) of the Farm Bill "urge[d] the secretary . . . to repeal the October 30, 1989 regulation and promulgate a new regulation reflecting the intention of the Congress." The USDA issued its final regulation despite Congress's "urging" and continued opposition of the American poultry industry.

Two nonprofit trade associations representing domestic poultry producers, the Mississippi Poultry Association, Inc., and the National Broiler Council (the "Associations"), challenged the USDA regulation as arbitrary and capricious under the Administrative Procedure Act. The Associations argued that the statutory language requiring that foreign poultry inspection regimes be "the same as" those in the United States meant that foreign poultry regimes must be *identical* to that in the United States, thus barring the USDA standard which only demanded that the foreign scheme be "at least equal to" the domestic scheme. The district court had agreed with the Associations' argument and held that USDA's regulation violated the plain language of the statute and that therefore no *Chevron* deference was owed.

Writing for the Fifth Circuit, Judge Weiner agreed that the statutory language was unambiguous and barred the USDA's regulation. After discussing various dictionary definitions of "the same," Weiner concluded that, in context, it could be construed to mean "identical." Judge Weiner also pointed to Congress's rebuke of the USDA in the 1990 Farm Bill as corroborating his interpretation:

> In that Act, Congress stated emphatically and unequivocally that the Agency has misinterpreted the "same as" standard. The Agency's efforts to make much of Congress' failure actually to amend the statute is a red herring. There simply was no need for Congress to amend the statute; it already stated precisely what Congress wanted it to state. Congress desired the "same as" language, and that is the language it placed in the statute. It is not required to respond to the Agency's disregard of unequivocally expressed congressional intent by amending a statute that is both clear and unambiguous on its face.

In response, the agency argued that this literalist interpretation would produce absurd results, such as barring the importation of poultry products processed under superior inspection systems. Judge Weiner responded that this would be the case only if the purpose of the law was believed to be the advancement of health and safety goals. Weiner stated:

[103] *Id.* at 1360–62 (footnotes omitted).

Even if the Agency is correct, however, we cannot agree that the result is absurd. Had the Agency labeled the actions of Congress *protectionism*, we would not necessarily disagree. But, while that may be deemed in some quarters to be unwise or undesirable, it cannot be labeled "absurd" in the context of divining the *result intended by Congress*. The Agency's complaint, therefore, is one implicating the clear policy choice of Congress—a choice made, undoubtedly, in response to effective lobbying by domestic poultry producers. It is not within the purview of the Agency, however—or of the courts for that matter—to alter, frustrate, or subvert congressional policy. Our "third branch" role under the constitutional scheme of separation of powers is limited—as is the role of the Agency—to determining whether that policy is clearly expressed. We conclude that it is in this instance.

. . . .

This final argument exposes the true nature of this case as a dispute between the Executive and Legislative branches over the propriety of Congress' policy choices. Although the Agency makes a compelling argument that the "at least equal to" language is the better standard, it simply is not the court's role to judge which branch has proposed the preferable rule. Congress has made clear that "the same as" requires *identical* inspection and processing procedures, and the fact remains that it is Congress that has the right to make the choice, even if it proves to be the wrong choice.[104]

Weiner concluded:

. . . After application of the traditional tools of statutory construction, we conclude that the plain language of § 466(d) of the PPIA clearly demonstrates that Congress intended "the same as" to be a synonym for "identical." Any lingering doubt as to Congress' intent is dispelled by its subsequent passage of the 1990 Farm Bill in which it expressly rejected the Agency's unilateral mutation of "the same as" standard to the "at least equal to" language in its regulation.

The Agency's attempts to conjure up ambiguity are unavailing. As we find under the first step of the *Chevron* methodology that the language of the statute is unambiguous, there is neither need nor authority for us to proceed further. We therefore owe no deference to the Agency's interpretation and grant none.

For the foregoing reasons, the district court's summary judgment is AFFIRMED.[105]

Judge Reavley issued a dissenting opinion in which he argued that as a matter of plain language, the phrase "the same as" was ambiguous and that Congress had not actually chosen "identicality over equivalence."[106] Reavley argued:

In describing the statutory structure in which Congress placed "same" in section 466(d), the majority ignores an argument that contravenes its decision.

---

104 *Id.* at 1365, 1367–68 (footnotes omitted).

105 *Id.* at 1368 (footnote omitted).

106 *Id.* (Reavley, J., dissenting).

> In 21 U.S.C. § 451, Congress bases the entire PPIA on its finding that "[u]nwholesome, adulterated, or misbranded poultry products" hurt people and destroy markets for poultry. . . . [T]he Secretary's interpretation of "same" to mean "equivalent" results in wholesomeness, absence-of-adulteration, and proper-marking qualities which *meet* or *better* the results of an identicality standard. In fact, the *only* result of substituting an identicality standard for the Secretary's equivalence standard is to erect a trade barrier, as the majority recognizes.
>
> While the majority claims to strictly adhere to the principle that words "take their purport from the setting in which they are used," it ignores the fact that section 466(d) appears in a poultry-inspection act which is expressly based upon Congress' exclusive finding that *unwholesome, adulterated, and misbranded* poultry must be eliminated to protect people and poultry markets. Where is the majority's explanation of how an identicality standard is consistent with section 451?
>
> My analysis of the extant structural arguments shows that the ones relied upon by the majority are inconclusive, and the section 451 argument indicates that Congress did not choose identicality. Thus, even under the majority's understanding of "make[s] some sense," the Secretary's interpretation of "same" is entitled to deference. . . .[107]

Judge Reavley also examined the legislative history and policy of the statute and concluded that it supported his argument that Congress had not foreclosed the USDA's regulation through the plain language of the statute. In particular, Reavley argued that the legislative history reveals no evidence that Congress intended this measure to serve as a form of backdoor trade protectionism for the benefit of the domestic poultry industry.

> Legislative history and policy together affirmatively establish that Congress has *not* "directly spoken to the precise question" of whether "same" means "identical" or "equivalent" in section 466(d). The *only* rational policy effect of choosing identicality over equivalence is that fewer foreign birds will enter the United States under an identicality standard than would enter under an equivalence standard. By definition, the Secretary's equivalence standard results in poultry that is *at least* as safe and correctly-packaged as that produced under federal standards. If Congress chose between identicality and equivalence in enacting section 466(d) as the majority holds, it must have done so because of the trade implications of an identicality standard. No one suggests another reason. But there is no record anywhere of any congressional consideration of the trade implications of an identicality standard before Congress passed section 466(d). This wholesale lack of attention to the *only* rational policy difference between identicality and equivalence establishes that Congress never chose between identicality and equivalence.
>
> The majority evades this critical point with the truism that neither courts nor agencies can alter policy choices made by Congress. This truism does not alter the fact that we sit to determine *whether* Congress has in fact made a policy

[107] *Id.* at 1374–75 (citations and footnotes omitted).

> choice, regardless of the merit of that choice. I would decide this case according to the simple logic that if Congress wanted to erect a trade barrier, someone, somewhere, would have said something about why a barrier was justified, what it was supposed to accomplish, or how its effectiveness would be monitored.

Judge Reavley noted that from 1972 to 1984, the Secretary applied an equivalence standard to foreign poultry. Reavley explains:

> While the 1985 Farm Bill was under consideration on the Senate floor, Senator Helms offered an amendment which substituted "the same as" for "at least equal to" in the portion of the 1985 Farm Bill that became section 466(d). Senator Helms explained that his amendment was "purely technical" and intended to "clarif[y] the provision to reflect the original intent of the provision as adopted by the committee in markup." Without any debate, further explanation, or recorded vote, the Senate adopted Senator Helms's amendment. . . .
>
> . . . Senator Helms . . . did not affirmatively indicate that he desired an identicality standard or that he wanted to change the substance of the Agriculture Committee's equivalence standard. Nor did he mention the trade consequences of a substantive change. Instead, he said that he wanted the provision to reflect the Agriculture Committee's "original intent," which it expressed in an equivalence standard. These points indicate that Senator Helms did not subjectively desire an identicality standard.
>
> But even if Senator Helms harbored this subjective intent, are we to attribute it to Congress *as an institution* when Senator Helms indicated that his amendment was of minimal importance, failed to call Congress' attention to the major trade consequences of such an interpretation of the amendment, and most importantly, *used equivocal language* to institute an identicality standard? . . .

Finally, Judge Reavley addressed the 1990 "sense of Congress" resolution:

> Predictably, the majority turns to section 2507 of the 1990 Farm Bill, where Congress declares that its "sense" is to "urge" the Secretary to substitute "same" for the equivalence standard challenged in this case. But a careful study of section 2507 and its background teaches that section 2507 better explains why the Secretary clings to an equivalence standard rather than adopting the position that the majority would have him take.
>
> Section 2507 undeniably has the force of federal law. But by its own terms, this "law" only states a fact that the 101st Congress believes to be true and makes a suggestion to the Secretary. The plaintiffs do not contend that Congress established an identicality standard in section 2507; in their complaint, they only seek a declaratory judgment that 9 C.F.R. § 381.196 is inconsistent with the *PPIA*, which includes section 466(d) and does not include section 2507.
>
> The plaintiffs contend that the intent of the 101st Congress as expressed in the 1990 Farm Bill is relevant to determine what the intent of the 99th Congress was in drafting the 1985 Farm Bill. I am aware of no case where any

court has held that subsequent legislative history is at all relevant to cases like this one, where, rather than determine what a statute means, we must determine "whether Congress has directly spoken to the precise question at issue." Even the most unambiguous intent in 1990 cannot establish the intent of a different group of people five years earlier. Section 2507 has no bearing on our present inquiry. . . .

Nowhere in section 2507 or its history does Congress suggest that the Secretary adopt an identicality standard, even though the Secretary publicly explained in 1989 that he understood his choices to be between identicality and equivalence. Instead of helping the Secretary interpret "same," Section 2507 and its history simply "urge" the Secretary to adopt a "same" standard, and to ignore technical deviations from this standard. But the Secretary understood his equivalence standard to operate just like a "same" standard that permits various technical deviations. If Congress demands something different, it has yet to say so.[108]

Judge Reavley concluded his dissent by stating:

The decision of what "same" means should remain with the Secretary until Congress says otherwise, and no one contends that the Secretary's choice has an unreasonable effect. I would reverse the district court's decision and render judgment for the Secretary.[109]

The Fifth Circuit reheard *Mississippi Poultry en banc*. Although the *en banc* decision vacated the panel decision, in this case, it achieved the same result. More notably, while Judge Weiner, who authored both the majority panel decision and the majority decision for the *en banc* court, applied different reasoning. The Court reiterated the panel decision's argument concerning Congress's power to enact a protectionist measure, but added a second rationale: Congress demanded identicality to reduce the administrative costs associated with reviewing different inspection regimes.

MISSISSIPPI POULTRY ASS'N V. MADIGAN (EN BANC)[110]

WEINER, CIRCUIT JUDGE:

. . . Reduced to the simplest terms, Congress . . . subjected all domestic poultry production sold in *inter*state commerce to a single, federal program with uniform standards.

Congress also addressed the issue of foreign standards. Under § 17(d) of the PPIA, Congress directed the Secretary to require imported poultry products to be "subject to *the same* . . . standards applied to products produced in the United States." Were that congressional mandate to be enforced strictly, all poultry sold in *inter* state commerce—whether produced in this country or anywhere else in the world—would be inspected pursuant to the uniform federal standards. Despite this congressional command, however, the Secretary promulgated the challenged regulation allowing foreign—but not domestic—

[108] *Id.* at 1377–80 (citations and footnotes omitted).

[109] *Id.* at 1380.

[110] 31 F.3d 293 (5th Cir. 1994).

poultry products to be imported and sold in interstate commerce, even though such poultry is inspected under *different* standards, as long as the foreign standards are determined by the Secretary to be "at least equal to" the federal standards. Given the plain language and structure of the PPIA, we conclude that this regulation cannot withstand the instant challenge. Because the phrase "at least equal to," as used in the PPIA, inescapably infers the existence of a *difference*—and the phrase "the same as," as used in the PPIA, eschews any possibility of more than a technical or de minimis difference, neither phrase can ever be synonymous with the other in the PPIA.

. . . In 1957 Congress enacted the PPIA, thereby establishing a comprehensive federal program for the regulation of poultry products. The PPIA was enacted to serve a two-fold purpose: To protect consumers from misbranded, unwholesome, or adulterated products, and to protect the domestic poultry market from unfair competition.

Typically, the safety and unfair competition goals are closely related. Of significance here, however, was Congress' concern with more than differences in *product* when it addressed unfair competition. Specifically, Congress also recognized that differences in *regulation* could also cause unfair competition. Indeed, in its original form, § 2 of the PPIA justified regulation of poultry sold in "large centers of population" on the belief that uninspected poultry products—regardless of whether such products were unsafe—adversely affected the national market for inspected poultry products.[111]

Judge Weiner reiterated, as in his vacated panel opinion, that the plain language of "the same as" prohibited the USDA's proffered reading as "at least equal to."

He further maintained that the 1990 Farm Bill confirmed his reading that with respect to foreign poultry imports, the 1989 "same as" requirement demanded identicality rather than equivalency:

The [1990 Farm Bill was enacted,] not surprisingly, within one year following the Secretary's promulgation of the "at least equal to" regulation. In § 2507 of the 1990 Farm Bill Congress first reiterated the facts of this inter-branch dispute: In 1985 Congress had enacted a statute requiring imported poultry to meet "the same" standards as domestic interstate poultry, and in 1989 the Secretary had promulgated a regulation imposing merely "at least equal to" standards. Congress then stated in plain, direct, and unequivocal language that the Secretary's regulation "does not reflect the intention of the Congress."

Congress' store of "institutional knowledge" is important. Accordingly, courts have long held that subsequent legislation is relevant to ascertaining the intent of Congress. Although subsequent legislation has been characterized as being anything from of "great weight" or having "persuasive value," to being of "little assistance" to the interpretative process, resolution of the proper weight to be accorded such legislation depends on the facts of each case. Here,

---

[111] *Id.* at 295–96 (footnotes omitted).

given: 1) the substantial overlap in membership between the Congress that passed the 1985 Farm Bill and the Congress that passed § 2507;[112] 2) the close temporal proximity between the passage of the 1985 Farm Bill and of § 2507; 3) the unmistakable specificity and directness with which § 2507 addressed the Secretary's interpretation; and 4) the alacrity with which Congress through § 2507 responded to the Secretary's interpretation, we find § 2507 to be highly persuasive, albeit not per se binding. Further, given the structure and history of the PPIA discussed earlier, we also conclude that § 2507 merely states the obvious: That the Secretary's adoption of the "at least equal to" standard "does not reflect" the intent of Congress as plainly expressed in § 17(d) of the PPIA.[113]

Finally, Judge Weiner rejected what he regarded as the USDA's attempt to rewrite the statute to bring about a more desirable policy:

> The Secretary strenuously argues that an "at least equal to" standard protects American consumers from "unhealthful, unwholesome, or adulterated" products while allowing foreign poultry products to be imported at reasonable costs. In contrast, the Secretary asserts that imposition of "the same" standards with accompanying "jot for jot" identicality would raise these costs to a prohibitive, protectionist level without any concomitant increase in the safety and quality of the imported product. According to the Secretary, holding foreign poultry producers to "the same" standards even contains the seed of an absurdity: That such a practice would prohibit the importation of poultry products produced under *superior* foreign standards!
>
> . . . .
>
> As a parting comment, we also observe that the Secretary's arguments fail to account for the various legitimate reasons why Congress might want to hold imported poultry to the federal standards. For example, requiring such congruity between foreign and federal standards means that *all* poultry—domestic and foreign—sold *inter* state must be produced and inspected according to *one* set of rules. Accordingly, such an approach maintains uniformity in the national market, thereby presumably engendering the lowered information costs and enhanced consumer confidence commonly associated with such uniformity.
>
> In addition, adopting such an approach offers the traditional advantage associated with "bright line" rules—agency personnel would no longer be required to make subjective, fact-specific judgments as to whether one country's standards are somehow in globo "at least equal to" federal standards. If we operate from the uncontested assumption that the Secretary has devised a federal program that ensures safety, then lessening of subjectivity here also reduces the risk that unsafe products might be imported—i.e., that agency personnel might err, even once, in concluding that a foreign program which

[112] Four hundred and thirty-five members of the Congress that passed § 2507 [in 1990] were members of the Congress that added 'the same' language to § 17(d) as part of the 1985 Farm Bill.

[113] *Id.* at 302–03 (footnotes omitted).

> differs substantially from our own nevertheless offers safety standards "at least equal to" the federal program.
>
> These points place the foregoing policy discussion in proper perspective. Although such a discussion is helpful to our understanding of the PPIA and § 17(d)—and is necessary as a check for any "absurdities"—these policy concerns cannot control the disposition of this case. Policy choices are for Congress—not the courts. And here Congress has chosen—twice.[114]

Judge Higginbotham issued a dissenting opinion in which he determined that the language of the statute was ambiguous and that the USDA's interpretation, and promulgated regulation, was reasonable. Even though the *en banc* opinion downplayed the protectionism rationale for insisting upon an identicality standard, Judge Higginbotham argued that protectionism was a foreseeable consequence of such a reading and that absent explicit congressional guidance, the court should not lightly infer an intent to produce this result. Higginbotham explained:

> This case is simple. Congress has insisted that foreign poultry meet the "same" standards as domestic poultry. It did so in a statute addressed to "unwholesome, adulterated or misbranded poultry products." Our court today holds that under this statute, the Department of Agriculture must forbid the importation of all foreign poultry produced by quality standards higher and lower than those in the United States. It reads "same" standards to mean identical processes and identical plants. Make no mistake about it: as the majority interprets the statute, virtually all importation of poultry is illegal. The majority insists on this literalism despite the common sense reading of "same" in the context of standards of quality to mean the same minimum level of wholesomeness, that is, "at least equal to." This absurdity is a lion in the street for the majority, and it never deals with it. It does not because it cannot. The Department of Agriculture has implemented the statute by regulations that allow importation of poultry produced by standards "at least equal to" our own. Dictionaries of the English language permit not "different in relevant essentials," or "equivalent" as meanings of the word "same." This reference to dictionary meanings is quite different from a game-like use of "modify." Rather, these are meanings as old as the republic. The choice of meanings is found in context.

Higginbotham considered the political implications of the majority ruling:

> Deny, deny, explain, explain—the inescapable reality is that under the majority's view, we must tell France and Israel, for example, that they may not import poultry into the United States because their standards for cleanliness and wholesomeness are higher or lower than those in the United States. The standards are not, and it is doubtful if they could be, implemented in identical "facilities" and under identical "conditions," as the majority insists they must be. Further, by the majority opinion, we allow Canada and Mexico [under the North American Free Trade Agreement (NAFTA)] to meet some undefined, but lesser standard. First the panel opinion, and now the en banc opinion, hints

[114] *Id.* at 308–10 (footnotes omitted).

> at a latent congressional purpose of trade protectionism. It is indeed a curious blend of protectionism that would protect American poultry interests from the threat of foreign poultry that is superior because it is healthier for the consumer. This insistence that a foreign producer lower its standards of health to meet the statutory command of sameness may be a form of trade protectionism, but it remains an absurdity.[115]

Judge Higginbotham then argued that the statutory language does not recognize the majority's distinction between state and federal standards. The only policy purpose expressly recognized in the legislative history was the protection of consumers from unsafe poultry products. By contrast, there was no "sign or signal" in the legislative history that the law was intended to have a protectionist purpose.

> The majority's . . . argument, as I understand it, is that by using alternative processes to ensure the quality of poultry, a foreign nation might gain some strategic advantage. That the statute does not say same processes, but same standards, does not slow the majority. Congress might indeed be unhappy if it unwittingly deprived domestic poultry producers of processes for ensuring the quality of chickens that were less expensive than, and as effective as, those required by federal law. If foreign poultry producers adopted these processes of poultry production, and thereby increased their sales in the United States, Congress might well respond. It could do so by banning the less expensive foreign poultry, the approach the majority opinion takes, or by allowing American poultry producers to adopt the foreign process, the approach I myself would think preferable. It is crucial to point out, however, that Congress has not as of yet done either. The majority has simply grafted onto the PPIA its own policy concern, reading it into the word "same," and never, I repeat, confronting the question—same as what?[116]

Judge Higginbotham concluded his dissent by questioning the majority's use of subsequent legislative enactments:

> The majority relies on legislation passed subsequent to the PPIA to support an identicality standard. Congress responded to the Secretary's regulation in section 2507 of the Food, Agriculture, Conservation, and Trade Act of 1990 by stating that the regulation "does not reflect the intention of Congress" and "urg[ing] the Secretary . . . to repeal the October 30, 1989 regulation and promulgate a new regulation reflecting the intention of Congress." Congress did not purport to amend the PPIA nor did it make a finding as to its intentions at the time it passed the PPIA. The Secretary did not change the regulation in response to Congress' admonition.
>
> The Supreme Court has made clear how to approach this legislation. "If th[e] language [of the 1990 Act] is to be controlling upon us, it must be either (1) an authoritative interpretation of what the [1985] statute meant, or (2) an authoritative expression of what the [1990] Congress intended. It cannot, of course, be the former, since it is the function of the courts and not the

---

[115] *Id.* at 310–11 (Higginbotham, J., dissenting) (footnotes omitted).

[116] *Id.* at 313–14 (footnotes omitted).

> Legislature . . . to say what an enacted statute means." Nor can it be the latter because the 1990 Act made no claim to enact a new or to alter an old law. The language of the Act is clear: Congress urged the Secretary of Agriculture to repeal the October 30, 1989 regulation and to promulgate a new one. If, as I believe, the language of the PPIA permitted the Secretary's interpretation, Congress's later urging did not alter that fact.[117]

DISCUSSION QUESTIONS

1. How would the various commentators whose works are described in this chapter have interpreted the statute at issue in this case? Consider the following possibilities. Judge Easterbrook would follow the majority panel opinion and read the statute as having a protectionist purpose. On this reading, "same" means "identical." Judge Posner would instead agree with the reasoning of the *en banc* majority, acknowledging the dual purposes of the law (consumer protection and economic protectionism), while also recognizing that Congress could elect a bright-line rule for administrative convenience. It is less clear whether Posner would find the law to be ambiguous, and thus subject to administrative interpretation. Professor Macey would agree with the holding of the dissent from the *en banc* opinion. He would stress that if Congress had a protectionist intent, that intent was "hidden-implicit." The court therefore should enforce law's stated purpose of consumer protection, or perhaps the USDA interpretation, which advances the public interest. Finally, Hart and Sachs, and perhaps those scholars who consider themselves heir to the Legal Process tradition, would side with the dissenting opinion, reading the law to advance the public interest goals of consumer welfare and to prevent "unfair" competition (rather than competition *per se*). Do you agree or disagree with these characterizations? Why or why not? Assuming you do agree, can any of these approaches be said to be "correct"?

2. The Fifth Circuit ultimately concluded that the Secretary of Agriculture had misinterpreted the relevant statutory language. The court also noted that after the USDA proposed its initial rule, it received thirty-one comments, of which 75% were opposed to the proposed interpretation. After the rule was finalized, the Mississippi Poultry trade association filed suit, and it ultimately prevailed. Consider this dynamic in light of Elhauge's distinction between enactable preferences and preference-eliciting default rules. Had the USDA interpreted the law so as to require "identicality" in the first instance, how likely is it that those opposed to that interpretation would have organized to file regulatory comments or to sue? Assuming that the costs of the identicality standard would have been spread broadly over all poultry purchasers, including private purchasers and the food service industry, the additional costs per purchase would have been too small to garner intense political opposition. By contrast, the beneficiaries of the identicality standard were a well-organized interest group with much at stake. By interpreting the statute in a manner that disadvantaged the well-organized interest group, the USDA effectively invited a contrary congressional response, regulatory response, or a lawsuit. Within the framework of Elhauge's analysis, is the USDA interpretation of identicality a preference-eliciting rule? Why or why not?

3. In the panel opinion, Judge Weiner observes that the definition of "same" as "identical" is not absurd if the judge recognizes that one purpose of the law was protectionism. In his dissent, Judge Reavley observes that the claimed protectionist purpose is nowhere

[117] *Id.* at 314 (footnotes omitted).

expressly stated, a view that Judge Higginbotham reiterates. To what extent, if any, should courts try to infer interest-group motivations that underlie legislation when the legislature is silent? To what extent should a Court try to infer implicit public-interest purposes of legislation? Does failing to discern legislative motivation risk inviting courts to rule based on their own intuitions concerning likely motivations underlying a challenged law? If so which approach is preferable? Why?

4. Following the initial promulgation of the USDA's regulation, Congress announced a "Sense of Congress" resolution that criticized the USDA's interpretation. Congress did not, however, amend the statute or take other corrective action. If Congress intended "the same as" to mean "identical," why did it express this through a "sense of Congress" resolution that "urged" the Secretary to follow its interpretation, rather than by amending the statute so as to define "the same as" to mean "identical"? Had Congress done the latter, would it also have had to clarify that the amendment enacted a trade restriction? Could it have rested on another ground? Did it need any expressly stated ground to mandate identicality?

Because the Secretary of Agriculture is a member of the President's cabinet, we can infer that the agency's interpretation was consistent with the wishes of the executive branch. If Congress had passed a bill overriding the Secretary's interpretation, is it likely that the President would have signed that bill into law, or is it more likely he would have vetoed the bill? The answer might imply that when Congress delegates to an agency, it is sometimes costly to overturn the agency interpretation when the President or his advisors are apt to block those efforts. Consider these dynamics as you read the materials on delegation by Congress to agencies in Chapters 20 and 21.

5. The *en banc* opinion notes that the Congress that enacted the "Sense of Congress" resolution was very close in composition to the Congress that enacted the initial legislation (with 435 members of the 1985 Congress who supported the original legislation also supporting the "Sense of Congress" resolution as active members of both houses in 1990). What weight might Easterbrook attach to the "sense of Congress" resolution? How might this datum influence Professor Eskridge's construction of "the same as"? How might it influence Farber and Frickey? How does this relate to Shepsle's observation that Congress is a "they," not an "it"?

What relevance, if any, should a subsequent statement of Congress have in interpreting legislation? Should the degree of continuity in the composition of the Congress matter to whether a later-enacted sense of Congress resolution is controlling? Should the length of time passed since the initial law was enacted matter? Why or why not?

6. In the majority panel opinion, Judge Weiner justifies his reading of the law by emphasizing its implicit protectionist purposes. In his *en banc* opinion, which reaches the same result, however, he instead emphasizes a claimed public interest justification for the law, namely that it will serve to minimize administrative costs in monitoring different poultry inspection regimes. Why might Weiner, on further consideration, have based his opinion on a public interest justification for the law? Might this have been necessary to forge a majority coalition on the *en banc* court, but not for a majority panel decision? How, if at all, does this affect your analysis of the case, and why?

CHAPTER 19

The Executive Branch and Agencies (Part 1)

Introduction

Under the United States Constitution, the President is afforded broad powers through which to influence the creation, interpretation, and execution of federal laws. Article I, § 7, which sets out the processes through which Congress enacts statutes, provides the President veto power over bills approved in both Houses of Congress, thus making the President a de facto third legislative house. Article II, § 2 empowers the President, with the advice and consent of the Senate, to appoint Officers of the United States. While the Senate holds the power of advice and consent respecting cabinet level appointments (although not with respect to "inferior officers") the President alone is charged with the power to remove cabinet officers who report to him unless the cabinet official is impeached. Finally, the Constitution provides the President the power, once more with the advice and consent of the Senate, to appoint Article III judges, who serve for a period of "Good Behaviour."[1] Among the most important practical consequences of this constitutional structure for modern analysis of government is the twentieth century growth of the vast administrative state. This includes the creation of myriad so-called independent agencies whose members are protected from removal by the President and whose internal decision making is to a considerable extent insulated from outside review. This chapter focuses on the internal operations of the executive branch, especially department and agency decision making and regulatory policy making within bureaucracies.

In terms of their influence on law and public policy, administrative agencies have become the functional equivalent of a fourth branch of the federal government. For instance, the 113th Congress enacted a total of 296 laws (of which 212 were substantive and 84 were ceremonial) and the 112th Congress passed 283 laws (of which 208 were substantive and 75 were ceremonial).[2] The Supreme Court now decides fewer than 100

---

[1] U.S. CONST. art. III, § 1. Relationships and interactions among the branches, including the executive veto, are discussed in Chapter 23.

[2] Drew DeSilver, *In Late Spurt of Activity, Congress Avoids 'Least Productive' Title*, PEW RESEARCH CTR.: FACTTANK (Dec. 29, 2014), http://www.pewresearch.org/fact-tank/2014/12/29/in-late-spurt-of-activity-congress-avoids-least-productive-title/. The 114th Congress was slightly more productive. *See* Kevin King,

cases per year. According to a 2012 report by the Administrative Conference of the United States, there is "no authoritative list of government agencies," and thus there is no comprehensive count of the total number of independent agencies and "components" of the executive branch; at that time, estimates ranged from about 250 to over 400.[3] In 2016, there were 95,894 published pages in the *Federal Register*, which lists proposed agency regulations, rulings, and other activities.[4] Of those, 38,652 were devoted to the publication of final rules. Administrative agencies obviously play an enormous role in the modern legal ecosystem.

The modern administrative state has largely developed based on the premise that to effectively address problems in the complex modern world, we must have disinterested experts insulated both from the rough and tumble of electoral politics and from market incentives. The civil service system, which insulates bureaucrats from political pressures and from using government resources for partisan political purposes, grows out of this tradition. This principle reached its apex within the United States in the first half of the twentieth century with the establishment of "independent agencies." These include the Federal Trade Commission and the Securities and Exchange Commission. The Commissioners are appointed for terms of years, sometimes with rules that require partisan political balance. Unlike executive branch appointments, officers of independent agencies are substantially insulated from pressures associated with the prospect of presidential removal power. As you read the materials that follow, consider the extent to which the intuition that agencies facilitate expert government, removed from political influence, is affected by Supreme Court doctrines, involving judicial deference to agency rulemaking. Also consider whether the intuition concerning agency insulation is consistent, or in tension, with the models presented in this chapter. Does economic analysis, and specifically the tools of public choice, help to test the underlying assumptions that motivated the rise and continuity of the modern administrative state? Why or why not? If you conclude that such analysis is not consistent with the original development of the administrative state, does it nevertheless provide the basis for an alternative justification?

Given the central role that presidential politics plays in directing regulatory policy, our analysis begins by considering the nature of presidential politics itself. We begin with a simple spatial model that grows out of the median voter analysis presented in Chapter 13.[5] We then modify the simplifying assumptions to consider how the temporal staging of presidential elections into primaries and general elections changes the predictions of the basic median voter analysis, and we further consider the implications of the more nuanced analysis for the formation of federal policy, both at the agency level and through judicial construction of statutes. Unlike the basic median voter model, which predicts policy convergence by the two candidates, a two-staged election with established parties

Congressional Productivity Increases in 114th Congress, But Lags Behind Historical Averages, QUORUM (Dec. 20, 2016), https://www.quorum.us/data-driven-insights/114th-congressional-productivity-numbers-2016/215/.

[3] DAVID E. LEWIS & JENNIFER L. SELIN, ADMINISTRATIVE CONFERENCE OF THE UNITED STATES SOURCEBOOK OF UNITED STATES EXECUTIVE AGENCIES 14–15 (2012), https://www.vanderbilt.edu/csdi/Sourcebook12.pdf.

[4] CLYDE WAYNE CREWS, JR., TEN THOUSAND COMMANDMENTS: AN ANNUAL SNAPSHOT OF THE FEDERAL REGULATORY STATE (2017 ed.).

[5] *See supra* Chapter 13.

predicts some degree of policy divergence between the two major party candidates. This analysis proves important in assessing the normative foundations, and implications, of agency deference rules that largely insulate both executive and independent agencies in their interpretation and implementation of federal statutes. Finally, in the aftermath of the 2016 election, we consider a further refinement to the model. This refinement questions whether the conventional left-right political axis used to describe presidential elections is undergoing a modification. We further inquire as to the possible implications of such a modification.

Against that background, this chapter presents several positive theories of agency delegation. These include models that assess congressional decisions to delegate, the form such delegations take, and judicial review both of the delegations themselves and of resulting agency regulations. We close with several case studies designed to test some of the implications of these models.

Beginning with a series of cases concerning Congress's power to limit the President's ability to terminate officers, the Supreme Court has drawn a distinction between executive and independent agencies. Executive agencies are those in which the agency head (often a cabinet official) serves at the pleasure of the President. Given the direct political accountability of executive agencies, those who head them are obviously expected to pursue the President's policy initiatives. Although executive agency heads are subject to congressional oversight, as a general matter, the primary incentives of such officials arise as a consequence of their political accountability to the President. Despite direct political accountability, the President risks some degree of what economists refer to *agency-cost slippage*. This means that the cabinet officials hold some degree of authority to depart from strict presidential preferences. A President would not be effective if he removed a cabinet member for each and every perceived transgression. Even so, the boundaries for pursuing objectives contrary to presidential preferences are generally more constrained for heads of executive agencies than for heads of independent agencies.

Independent agencies are those in which the senior officials are protected by statute from unilateral executive removal power. The Chairs and Commissioners on independent agencies—such as the Federal Trade Commission (FTC), Securities and Exchange Commission (SEC), and Federal Communications Commission (FCC)[6]—are typically appointed for a term of years and are otherwise removable "for cause" or some similar standard. By statute, many independent agencies are required to have partisan balance or representation, thereby giving the out-of-power party some degree of policy influence. The greater degree of political insulation, as compared with executive officials, coupled with generally weak regulatory oversight, renders more challenging the task of modeling incentives of independent agency heads. Historically, the consequences of agency scrutiny have varied considerably. The Civil Aeronautics Board (CAB) and the Interstate Commerce Commission (ICC), both of which were subject to intense media and political criticism, were eventually terminated. Other agencies that have been subject to similar scrutiny, such as the FTC, were dramatically reformed in the face of heavy political and public pressure. Still others, such as the SEC and the FCC, whose performance has been long criticized, have been subject to only modest reforms and remain a frequent target of criticism. What do these varied results suggest about the likely differences in agency slack

[6] For a list and descriptions of executive and independent agencies, see LEWIS & SELIN, *supra* note 3.

as between executive and independent agencies? To whom are independent agencies accountable? What motivates or constrains those who head them? How, if at all, does accountability differ as between independent agency heads and civil servants working within the agencies?

I. THE MEDIAN VOTER THEOREM MEETS NON-MEDIAN PRESIDENTIAL CANDIDATES

In Chapter 13, we introduced the *median voter theorem.* That simple spatial model demonstrates that in a system in which the head of state is selected through a direct election, the pure Nash equilibrium is a stable two-party system. The model also predicts considerable, if not complete, policy convergence among the leading candidates, each of whom is motivated to capture a majority of the electorate, represented along a single dimensional, typically cast as left-right, ideological spectrum. A major difficulty that theorists confront is that within the United States, where the President is elected by the citizenry, rather than, for example, a minimum winning parliamentary coalition,[7] there is often substantial policy divergence between the leading candidates. This difference between the predictions of the median voter model and observed political behavior is important not only for revisiting assumptions about how the President is elected, but also for considering the President's role in influencing the formation of regulatory policy.

The median voter theorem predicts that the policy platforms of presidential nominees of two major parties will tend to converge toward the preferences of the median voter, leaving only narrow policy differences. In practice, however, the Democratic and Republican presidential nominees typically hold sharp policy disagreements. This divergence between the predictions of the median voter model and observed electoral politics can be explained in substantial part by the two-staged electoral system by which presidential candidates are selected. This system combines primaries (or caucuses)[8] with a general election among each party's primary winners.[9] The two-stage election process creates countervailing pressures that pull the major party candidates toward, and away

---

[7] For a discussion of the differing implications of parliamentary designation of the head of state, see *infra* Chapter 23. This description leaves aside of course, the formality of the Electoral College.

[8] *See* WILLIAM G. MAYER & ANDREW E. BUSCH, THE FRONT-LOADING PROBLEM IN PRESIDENTIAL PRIMARIES 19 (2004). The authors note, "[U]nlike presidential primaries, which occur on a single, definite date, caucuses are multistage affairs, in which meaningful delegate selection decisions are made over a period of several months. . . ." (footnote omitted). What are the implications of the larger investment required to participate in a caucus versus a primary for whether the outcomes are likely to reflect the preferences of the median party voter?

[9] For related works that consider the impact of two-stage elections on candidate locations using the general framework of the median voter theorem, see Donald Wittman, *Candidate Motivation: A Synthesis of Alternative Theories*, 77 AM. POL. SCI. REV. 142 (1983); James Adams et al., Move to the Center or Mobilize the Base? (Aug. 31, 2006), http://citation.allacademic.com/meta/p_mla_apa_research_citation/1/5/2/3/0/pages152307/p152307-1.php; Gilles Serra, Primary Divergence: The Effects of Primary Elections on Candidate Strategies in the Downsian Model (Apr. 2, 2007) (unpublished manuscript) (on file with authors) (paper was presented at the 2006 Annual Meeting of the American Political Science Association).

from, the competing ideal points of their respective party base and of the general election's median voter.

The analysis explains why the prediction of the median voter model of candidate convergence does not hold in practice and why elections do not witness complete ideological fluidity of candidates moving as far in the direction of the party base as needed to secure the nomination and then all the way back to the general election's median voter to secure victory in the general election. After reviewing the basic two-staged model, which identifies factors that encourage just these sorts of identifiable ideological shifts, we set out a more detailed analysis that identifies factors that temper such fluidity at each election stage. While the precise equilibrium—in both primaries and in the general election—will of course vary for each election cycle, as demonstrated below, the net effect of the combined processes is substantially greater candidate policy divergence than the single-period median voter hypothesis predicts.

The sometimes sharp divergence between the policy positions of the major party presidential candidates has the potential to produce wide policy swings when the party of presidential administration changes hands. One might assume that the life-tenured federal judiciary would temper broad agency-driven policy swings. And yet, important administrative law doctrines related to agency deference have just the opposite effect. These doctrines reinforce the control of agencies over regulatory policy, thereby tending to amplify, rather than dampen, policy swings when the presidency changes parties.

An important pair of administrative law cases holds that when an agency uses proper procedures to provide a reasonable construction of an ambiguous federal statute, a federal court is obligated to defer to the agency's interpretation even if the result that the agency obtains contradicts what a federal court would have ruled as a matter of first impression.[10] In a more recent case, the Supreme Court has gone further and held that even if the Supreme Court had previously construed an ambiguous federal statute in a manner that a federal agency later interprets differently, the agency interpretation, rather than the Court's, controls.[11] The combination of three factors—(1) potentially substantial policy divergence between leading presidential candidates, (2) significant presidential influence over the direction of agency policy, and (3) presumptive judicial deference to agency policy affecting the construction of federal statutes—demonstrates the importance of properly modeling the presidential selection process in an effort to better understand agency incentives.

A. The Median Voter Theorem Revisited

1. *Predicting Complete Convergence in a Single-Staged Election*

We begin with a single-stage presidential election and then introduce a two-stage election, including a primary and general election. The analysis begins with figure 19:1, reproduced from Chapter 13, which depicts the median voter theorem in a single period

---

[10] *See* United States v. Mead Corp., 533 U.S. 218 (2001); Chevron U.S.A. Inc. v. Nat. Res. Def. Council, Inc., 467 U.S. 837 (1984).

[11] *See* Nat'l Cable & Telecomms. Ass'n v. Brand X Internet Servs., 545 U.S. 967, 980–86 (2005).

election. The model rests on the following premises: (1) a single dimensional liberal-to-conservative continuum; (2) two candidates whose ideal points (meaning their preferred set of packaged policy positions) occupy opposing ends of the ideological spectrum; and (3) presidential candidates who behave rationally in pursuit of winning the election.[12] The Democratic candidate (*D*) occupies the liberal (*L*) end of the spectrum (to the left), and the Republican candidate (*R*) occupies the conservative (*C*) end of the spectrum (to the right).

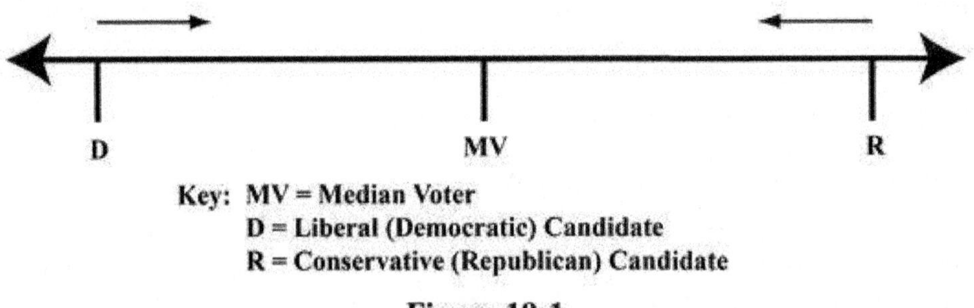

Key: MV = Median Voter
D = Liberal (Democratic) Candidate
R = Conservative (Republican) Candidate

Figure 19:1

Based upon these assumptions, the model predicts that as each candidate seeks to capture larger segments of the electorate, he or she will move toward the position embraced by the general election's median voter (*MV*). The model further assumes that as each candidate takes on more moderate views relative to her or his ideal point (with *R* moving left and *D* moving right), those voters who prefer a more extreme candidate (or one whose ideal point occupies the relevant endpoint of the ideological spectrum) will continue to support a candidate who remains ideologically less distant, rather than vote for the opposite candidate (or not vote at all) as a result of the preferred candidate's decision to moderate her or his views.

The median voter model helps to explain the persistence of the two-party system within the United States, as the major party candidates effectively squeeze out the necessary policy space that would allow a stable third party candidacy to flourish.[13] And

---

12 *See supra* Chapter 13, at p. 543.

13 Duverger's law predicts that direct elections generally yield two party systems, a phenomenon that is closely linked to the insights of the median voter theorem. *See* MAURICE DUVERGER, POLITICAL PARTIES: THEIR ORGANIZATION AND ACTIVITY IN THE MODERN STATE 216–28 (Barbara & Robert North trans., Methuen & Co. 2d ed. 1959) (setting out thesis later referred to as Duverger's law); *see also* William H. Riker, *Political Science and Rational Choice*, *in* PERSPECTIVES ON POSITIVE POLITICAL ECONOMY 163, 177–81 (James E. Alt & Kenneth A. Shepsle eds., 1990) (describing Duverger's law). This does not imply that a third party candidate can never prevail in a system of direct election, as occurred, for example, in the election of former professional wrestler, Jesse Ventura, in the Minnesota gubernatorial race as a member of the Reform Party in 1998. In that election, however, Ventura won a plurality of the votes, and he might well not have been a Condorcet winner had the election produced a runoff between the two leading contenders. *See, e.g.*, Jodi Wilgoren, *Gov. Ventura Says He Won't Seek Re-election*, N.Y. TIMES, June 19, 2002, at A14. A start-up party also might replace one of the two existing parties if the larger party fails to converge sufficiently toward the electoral median. One example is the supplanting of the Whig party by the Republican Party in the United States. In the end, however, the system returned to a stable, but reformulated, two-party system. In Great Britain, a parliamentary system, and thus one not characterized by direct election of the prime minister, despite some periods of two-party dominance, consistent with Duverger's law, the history of party fluctuations does not suggest a stable two-party equilibrium. For background, see Michael Barone, *In the U.K., the Two-Party System*

yet, as Donald Wittman has observed, the model fails to explain the frequently observed divergence in party platforms in actual presidential elections.[14]

2. *Predicting Policy Divergence in a Two-Staged Election*

Let us now adapt figure 19:1 to account for two-staged elections. Professor Gilles Serra has extended Professor Donald Wittman's intuition that the median voter theorem fails adequately to capture the ideological distance observed between major party platforms by developing a two-staged election model operating along a single dimension.[15] We begin with a simple adaptation of the Serra model that accounts for ideological candidate location. In the discussion that follows, we start with a simple two-staged model and then consider the implications of relaxing some of the underlying assumptions for the eventual ideological placement of the major party candidates in any given presidential election.

Figure 19:2 depicts a truncated ideological spectrum for each of the two major parties that emerge in the United States system of direct presidential election, and relates the primary spectrum for each party to the larger spectrum for the general presidential election, depicted in Figure 19:1.

In this model, the Republican spectrum begins at the far right of the larger spectrum depicted in figure 19:1 and continues slightly to the left of *MV*, and the Democratic spectrum begins at the far left of the large spectrum and continues slightly to the right of *MV*. Notice that in this model, each primary spectrum includes at least some voters who are on the side opposite the party's base constituency. As a result, the generally liberal Democratic Party includes some moderate to conservative Democratic voters, and the generally conservative Republican Party includes some moderate to liberal Republican voters. One benefit of this assumption, as shown in the next part, is that it allows for an observed phenomenon in actual elections, namely the ability of major party candidates to appeal to *crossover voters*, meaning those who in a given election might vote either for a Republican or Democratic candidate.[16]

Has Become a Thing of the Past, NAT'L REV. (May 1, 2015, 12:00 AM), http://www.nationalreview.com/article/417744/uk-two-party-system-has-become-thing-past-michael-barone.

[14] *See* Wittman, *supra* note 9, at 143 (positing that rational major party candidates who are motivated to win the general election will take positions during primaries to secure the party nomination that "maximize[ ] the expected utility of the party's median voter.").

[15] *See* Serra, *supra* note 9, at 6–8. Serra predicts that in a highly competitive primary race, the result is a commitment to the position of the party median voter, which can change in cases of incumbency. *See id.* at 13–18. Serra further explains that because incumbency limits primary competition, this poses a threat to the preferred ideological positioning of the party base. The essential difference between Serra's model and the model developed here is that Serra assumes full voter participation and presents the spatial dimension of each party as starting at the extreme right or left and ending at the precise location of the general election median voter. Our analysis instead treats voter turnout as dependent on candidate location along the ideological dimension and further assumes that there are some crossover voters, which allows for some left of center Republican voters and some right of center Democratic voters. The authors thank Gilles Serra for helping to develop portions of this discussion.

[16] At various points in history, the degree of distance on the side opposite the party base has varied considerably. Southern Democrats, for example, potentially occupied positions quite far to the right of the general electoral median voter, whereas Rockefeller Republicans occupied positions substantially to the left of

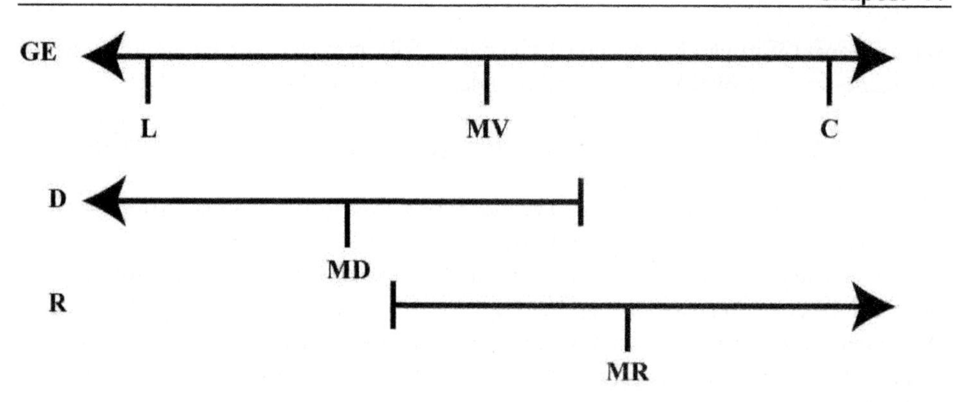

Key: GE = General Electorate
D = Registered Democratic Voters (as compared with General Electorate)
R = Registered Republican Voters (as compared with General Electorate)
MV = Median Voter
MD = Median Democratic Voter
MR = Median Republican Voter

Figure 19:2

In this simple model, the predictable result appears to be some degree of candidate divergence as each candidate positions herself or himself at or near the relevant party's median voter along the truncated ideological spectrum to secure the nomination. The distance between the median Democratic and median Republican voter is considerably greater than the complete policy convergence that the single-stage application of the median voter theorem depicted in figure 19:1 predicts. If we continue to assume full electoral participation, this time within each party, then, ultimately, successful primary candidates will rationally move toward the median party voter as they compete with other primary candidates for the nomination. As in the single-staged median voter analysis, those voters within each party who prefer a more ideologically extreme candidate—generally thought of as the *party base*—will nonetheless vote for those candidates who have moderated their positions by moving toward the party's median voter, rather than by declining to vote or by voting for a primary candidate whose views are on the opposite side of the party's median voter.

Assuming that this analysis captures the dynamics of presidential primaries, it highlights a substantial difficulty for the nominated candidate. Once each major party candidate secures the nomination, the same analysis would suggest that he or she is rationally motivated to converge back toward *MV* in an effort to win the general election. If the candidate is assumed to act rationally at each stage, then the model implies complete candidate fluidity as candidates will move along the single-dimensional ideological

the general electoral median voter, at least over some issues. For an informative book that touches on these themes, see JAMES L. SUNDQUIST, DYNAMICS OF THE PARTY SYSTEM: ALIGNMENT AND REALIGNMENT OF POLITICAL PARTIES IN THE UNITED STATES (rev. ed. 1983). The empirical incidence of such voters is less important than is realizing that neither party cuts off at the precise point that represents the general election's theoretical median voter. As a consequence, in any general election, crossover voters have the potential to support either major party candidate, based on any number of variables, including but not limited to ideological distance from her or his ideal point.

spectrum toward the party's median voter (or perhaps even further if, as suggested below, the party's base turns out to vote in disproportionate numbers), as needed to secure the nomination, and then back toward *MV* as needed to win the general election. In this analysis, the two-staged model does no better at explaining major candidate divergence than the one-staged model.

3. *Complexities in the Two-Stage Model*

We now modify the two assumptions that undergird both the single-staged and two-staged electoral models to restore the intuition that introducing a primary (or caucus) stage produces a more stable policy distance between major party candidates than a single-stage election. The analysis demonstrates that although the precise issue locations of each candidate will vary from election to election, there are predictable forces that simultaneously pull toward the general electoral median voter and toward the extreme positions of each party's base. The net effect of the two-staged system limits the probability of complete policy convergence by the major party candidates, thus reinforcing the basic intuition underlying the two-staged model.

a. The Voter Probability Distribution Function

The preceding analysis assumes an even distribution of voters across the ideological spectrum for the general election and also for the truncated spectra for the primary elections. Consider the possibility, however, that a larger number of voters occupy a relatively moderate ideological position than occupy the ends of the ideological spectrum in the general election. If so, we can depict the general electorate in the form of a probability distribution function (PDF), which assumes a bell-shaped or Gaussian, form.[17] The PDF is shown in figure 19:3.

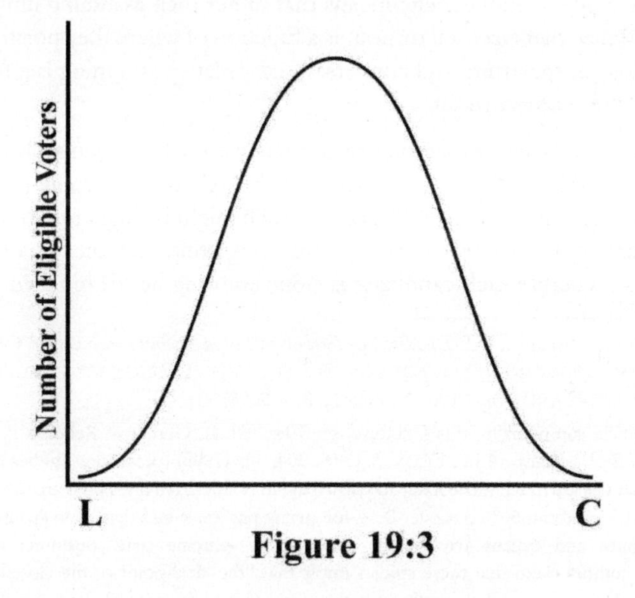

Figure 19:3

[17] Aidan Lyon, *Why Are Normal Distributions Normal?*, 65 BRIT. J. PHIL. SCI. 621 (2014).

If we continue the assumption of full voter participation, this standard distribution would enhance the tendency of the candidates, after having secured the relevant party nomination, to move toward *MV*. Such moves would improve their efforts to capture a larger and larger number of general electoral voters. Moreover, as Professor William Niskanen has demonstrated, it would give a potentially enhanced payoff because a *flipped crossover voter* is the equivalent of two votes—one vote gained plus one taken from the other side—whereas a voter lost due to diminished enthusiasm is simply one vote lost.[18]

Niskanen's intuition is strengthened to the extent that there are voters in each party whose positions are distant from the party base in a moderate direction, which enhances the possibility of appealing to voters registered to the other party as one moves in the direction of *MV* in the general election. If we continue to assume full voter participation, an assumption we relax below, these factors encourage moves toward *MV* as each candidate rationally seeks to capture potential moderate voters. Obviously, the result would thwart the interests of those who sought to secure a candidate committed to their party's core values. The question thus arises as to how voter turnout might temper the candidate's motivation to move toward the position of *MV*.

b. Non-Uniform Electoral Turnout (or Challenging the Assumptions of a Single Dimensional Scale)

A competing consideration for candidates seeking a major party nomination is that while ideologically extreme voters might be fewer in number, as demonstrated in the bell-shaped PDF, studies demonstrate that the party base participates in politics in a manner disproportionate to its numbers.[19] Assuming that this higher incidence of general political participation translates into disproportionate turnout in general elections, then each candidate's rational ideological placement might be endogenous to anticipated voter turnout. In this context, endogeneity means that rather than assuming universal turnout, candidates recognize that electoral turnout is a function of where they position themselves along the ideological spectrum, and conversely, candidate positioning is a function of the expected impact on voter turnout.

This analysis provides an alternative perspective on Niskanen's observation about the two-to-one payoff for flipping a moderate voter relative to turning out a voter from the candidate's core constituency.[20] The cost of each might be higher than that of securing two base voters; both major candidates are competing for the general electorate's moderate voters, whereas each candidate is alone courting her or his own base. It is also

---

[18] *See* William A. Niskanen, *U.S. Elections Are Increasingly Biased Against Moderates*, 23 CATO J. 463 (2004), *reprinted in* WILLIAM A. NISKANEN, REFLECTIONS OF A POLITICAL ECONOMIST: SELECTED ARTICLES ON GOVERNMENT POLICIES AND POLITICAL PROCESSES 237 (2008).

[19] For an article summarizing this literature, see Elisabeth R. Gerber & Rebecca B. Morton, *Primary Election Systems and Representation*, 14 J.L. ECON. & ORG. 304, 309 (1998) (presenting studies that show "voters with strong partisan ties are much more likely to participate in political activities than are other voters"; that in 1988, voter turnout was about 50% but over 80% for strong partisans; and that "one group of party elites—convention delegates and caucus participants—have more extreme issue positions than the general electorate."). The authors claim that these studies imply that "the ideal point of the closed primary election median voter is likely to diverge substantially from the ideal point of the general election median voter." *Id.* at 310.

[20] *See supra* note 18 and accompanying text.

likely easier to appeal to the relatively more homogenous base voters with targeted campaigning. Courting moderates also risks diminishing enthusiasm among the party base.

Assuming that voters holding more extreme ideological views tend to be more politically engaged, candidates also confront the risk that moving toward the center of the ideological spectrum during the general electoral cycle will have a disproportionate dampening effect on those *eligible voters* most likely to become *actual voters* in the general election. Political candidates ultimately are concerned with capturing a majority of actual voters as needed to win the general election, rather than with appealing to a majority of eligible or potential voters, only some of whom turn out at the polls. The trade-off is reflected in figure 19:4 below.

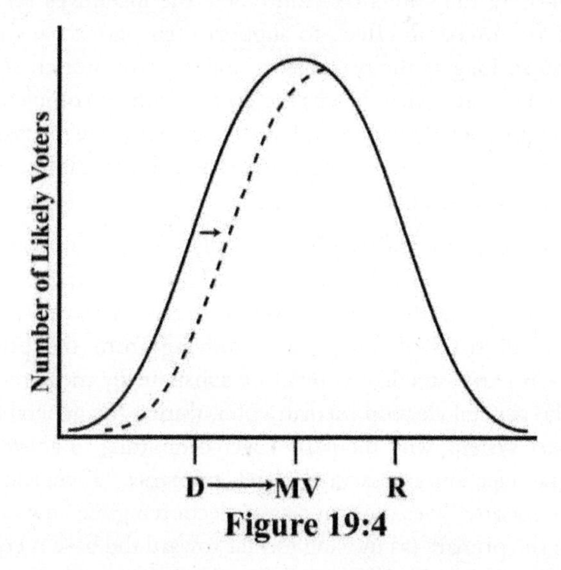

Figure 19:4

Figure 19:4, which focuses on the Democratic candidate, reveals the disproportionate tempering effect on more ideologically liberal voters as the candidate moves toward the ideal point of the general election's median voter. Together, figures 19:3 and 19:4 reveal that whereas general election candidates seek to capture the larger percentage of eligible voters bunched toward the middle of the bell-shaped PDF (and the two-for-one arithmetic of flipped voters), they have to rationally weigh this incentive against the corresponding risk of sacrificing support among the *party base* or *party faithful*, that smaller percentage of the electorate likely to become actual voters.[21] The question

[21] For an interesting, related study on the 2002 congressional elections, see Niskanen, *supra* note 18. Niskanen observes that in that election, candidates most "at risk" were those reputed to be moderates, a result that he claims is in tension with the median voter hypothesis. Niskanen attributes the failure of the median voter theory to explain the 2002 election results, which displaced some moderate incumbents, to the assumption underlying the median voter theorem that voter turnout is exogenous to a candidate's ideological placement. Niskanen explains that if instead "the decision of *whether* to vote is [dependent] of the issue positions of the candidates," then "candidates have an incentive to choose an issue position closer to the median of their party base than to the median of the total electorate (in the relevant constituency)." *See id.* at 239–40. Are there reasons why moderate congressional candidates might be more vulnerable in general elections than moderate presidential candidates, assuming such a candidate secures her or his party nomination? One interesting consequence of the Niskanen study is that it suggests that Congress as an institution is more politically polarized

remains whether the party faithful retain control over the party nominee past the point of nomination.

c. Two-Staged Presidential Elections as a Multi-Period Game

Assume that each two-staged election is equivalent to two separate single-period games. This means that after each election cycle, voters experience a sort of collective amnesia and confront the next election cycle uninformed by what happened in the past. With this sort of electoral myopia, we might well imagine that the two-party system provides the party faithful no meaningful power to rein in their party's nominee. Once the candidate is chosen, the voters confront anew the incentives set out in the single period model and are forced, in effect, to support their party's candidate regardless of policy convergence, so long as the two major candidates do not cross ideological paths with each other. The question then is why we do not witness complete convergence (or even flipping) along the relevant ideological spectrum? Are there mechanisms that reward candidates who adhere to commitments made in the primary campaign and that punish defections during the general election?

Consider the extent to which primaries allow a set of commitment-bonding strategies played out over multiple elections. If we view each individual election as a round of play in a multi-period game, this has the potential to raise the cost—although it certainly does not eliminate all risk—of a candidate moving from the primary ideal point (associated with each party's median voter) to a substantially more moderated position, closer to that of the general election median voter, during the general election. To what extent is the primary system, with the party base committing to active participation not only in the general election but also in later primaries, a vehicle for encouraging enforceable commitments? Does the two-staged election regime limit complete candidate fluidity not only in the primary (as moving too far toward the base is costly given the risk of having to renege in the general election), but also in the general election (as moving toward *MV* threatens diminished turnout among the base)?

Does treating the election as a multi-period game help to restore the intuition that the two-staged election system promotes meaningful policy distance between the leading presidential candidates? Can you identify particular devices at the primary stage that operate to bind presidential candidates from straying too far from positions taken to secure the party nomination?

d. Turnout and Dimensionality

The preceding discussion raises several empirical issues, including the ideological incidence of voters along the conventional left-right political spectrum, candidate fluidity from the primary to the general election cycle, and the willingness of base voters to abstain or vote third party (the functional equivalent) as a response to what they view as excessive moderation in the general election cycle. Despite these concerns, in general, the net effect

than the general electorate. Does this help to answer the preceding question? Why or why not? Might it matter that 2002 was an *off-year* congressional election with no presidential election, when overall turnout tends to be lower?

of the factors identified above is likely closer to the observed divergence between major party candidates in most recent presidential election cycles than the simpler median voter hypothesis predicts.

The analysis also depends in large part on the extent to which the voting spectrum is accurately captured in left-right terms. Might some base voters be more willing to "punish" a seemingly moderate candidate with a greater chance of winning the general election by instead supporting a less electable candidate who stands closer to their ideal point?[22] Alternatively, might such voters be willing to abstain or vote third party in the general election if the moderate candidate wins the party nomination? How plausible is it that base voters care more about party control than success in a given election cycle? Are single issue voters, meaning those who will refuse to support their party's nominee if she or he strays on such core issues as "right to life," "freedom of choice," and "pro-gun control" or "pro-Second Amendment rights" behaving irrationally? Are such voters elevating the concern for party control over the concern for party victory?

What other factors affect turnout? Available data demonstrate that during the 2008 Obama-McCain election, voter turnout was the most diverse in history, with African American voters setting a "historic first" by having the "highest turnout rate" among "young eligible voters."[23] The African American community had long been considered a core constituency of the Democratic Party. Does the differential turnout in the 2008 general election as compared with prior elections demonstrate that African American voters can be turned out in higher numbers than they have been historically—and to that extent are not captured—based upon the enthusiasm for the selected candidate and his or her policies? Why or why not? How might this relate to the broader question of dimensionality and party control?

Consider also state laws governing the nature of party candidate selection. States have adopted a variety of approaches to selecting candidates for general elections, including primaries, caucuses, conventions, or a combination. Some of these processes are closed, meaning that only registered party members can participate, whereas others are open, meaning that voters registered to other parties or as independent can also participate.[24] What are the tradeoffs involved in selecting between open and closed primaries? Caucuses versus primaries? Do closed primaries help the base retain control of the party even at the risk of defeat in general elections, or do they ensure higher levels of turnout by the party base? More generally, does the existence of a variety of mechanisms suggest that none of these options is necessarily "superior" to others? Should states be

---

[22] *New York Times* columnist David Brooks offered this thesis to explain the decision of some Republican party leaders to support Mitt Romney over John McCain in the 2008 primary cycle despite knowing Romney had a lower likelihood of winning the general election, positing that "some would rather remain in control of a party that loses than lose control of a party that wins." *See* David Brooks, Opinion, *Road to Nowhere*, N.Y. TIMES, Jan 2, 2008, at A17.

[23] MARK HUGO LOPEZ & PAUL TAYLOR, PEW RESEARCH CTR., DISSECTING THE 2008 ELECTORATE: MOST DIVERSE IN U.S. HISTORY 6 (2009). According to this study, which is based on Census Bureau data, "[v]oter turnout rates among black, Latino and Asian eligible voters were higher in 2008 than in 2004. . . . The voter turnout rate among black eligible voters was 5 percentage points higher in 2008 than in 2004. . . ." *Id.* at 4.

[24] *See, e.g.*, Karen M. Kaufmann et al., *A Promise Fulfilled? Open Primaries and Representation*, 65 J. POL. 457, 459 (2003).

allowed to compel political parties to hold open primaries in which those registered to another party, or as independents, can participate? Why or why not?

e. Did Election 2016 Affect the Dimensionality of Presidential Politics?

The 2016 Presidential pitted Republican Party nominee, Donald Trump, a businessman and reality television personality with no prior political experience, against Democratic Party nominee, Hillary Clinton, the first woman to secure a major party nomination, and former Secretary of State, Senator from New York, and first lady to President Bill Clinton. Trump won the nomination despite facing sixteen opponents, most of whom had significant governmental experience, and despite his having been strongly disfavored by nearly the entire Republican Party establishment.[25] Hillary Clinton, a consummate insider, struggled with popularity throughout her long primary campaign, principally against Bernie Sanders, a candidate who was a self-declared Democratic Socialist, and who joined the Democratic Party to run for its presidential nomination.[26] Neither Trump nor Sanders were longstanding members of the parties whose nominations they sought, although Sanders, a United States Senator from Vermont, has caucused with the Senate Democrats. Despite being outsiders, during the primary season, Trump and Sanders together secured forty-four percent of the popular votes cast.[27] Although both Clinton and Trump were widely viewed as unusually unpopular candidates, in the lead-up to the general election between Clinton and Trump, pollsters overwhelmingly, yet mistakenly, predicted a Clinton victory.[28]

In a comprehensive study, *Political Divisions in 2016 and Beyond: Tensions Between and Within the Two Parties,* political scientist Lee Drutman, of the *Democracy Fund Voter Study Group*, gathered survey data on twelve sets of topic-specific questions to actual voters to

---

[25] Trump appears to have benefitted substantially by open primary voting, especially in early states. *See* Mark Fahey & Eric Chemi, *Trump's Big Advantage: Open Primaries* (Mar. 22, 2016), https://www.cnbc.com/2016/03/22/trumps-big-advantage-open-primaries.html.

[26] Despite struggling with popularity, Clinton secured 2842 delegates to Bernie Sanders' 1865 delegates to win the Democratic nomination. *Delegate Tracker*, ASSOC. PRESS (July 25, 2016, 9:32 PM), https://interactives.ap.org/2016/delegate-tracker/; Patrick Healy & Jonathan Martin, *Democrats Make Hillary Clinton a Historic Nominee*, N.Y. TIMES (July 26, 2016), https://www.nytimes.com/2016/07/27/us/politics/dnc-speakers-sanders-clinton.html. Clinton won a majority of state primaries (thirty-four state primaries and taking 54% of the total pledged delegates), but her substantial lead in the superdelegate count was seen by many as making her nomination a foregone conclusion from early in the primary race. Clinton carried 571 superdelegates to second-place Bernie Sanders' forty-four superdelegates. *2016 Presidential Primaries Results*, POLITICO (Dec. 13, 2016, 1:57 PM), https://www.politico.com/mapdata-2016/2016-election/primary/results/map/president/; Hope Yen et al., *AP: Count: Clinton Has Delegates to Win Democratic Nomination*, ASSOC. PRESS (June 7, 2016), https://www.apnews.com/4c9c850385c84b12ad5b85fda49743f9.

[27] Maxwell L. Stearns, *Election 2016 and the Structural Constitution: A Preliminary Framing*, 76 MD. L. REV. ENDNOTES 4 (2016) [hereinafter Stearns, *Election 2016*].

[28] *See* Heather Long, *Key Model Predicts Big Election Win for Clinton*, CNN (Nov. 1, 2016, 9:32 AM), http://money.cnn.com/2016/11/01/news/economy/hillary-clinton-win-forecast-moodys-analytics/index.html (citing the Moody's Analytics model predicting a win for Clinton); *see also* Nicholas A. Valentino, John Leslie King & Walter W. Hill, *Polling and Prediction in the 2016 Presidential Election*, 50 COMPUTER 110 (2017), http://ieeexplore.ieee.org/document/7924268/ (examining potential reasons for inaccurate predictions of Clinton winning the 2016 presidential election).

test what drove the election results. The study revealed that although most issues aligned voters along a conventional left-right dimension, one notable issue revealed a possible dimensionality split. The finding is depicted in the following graphic[29]:

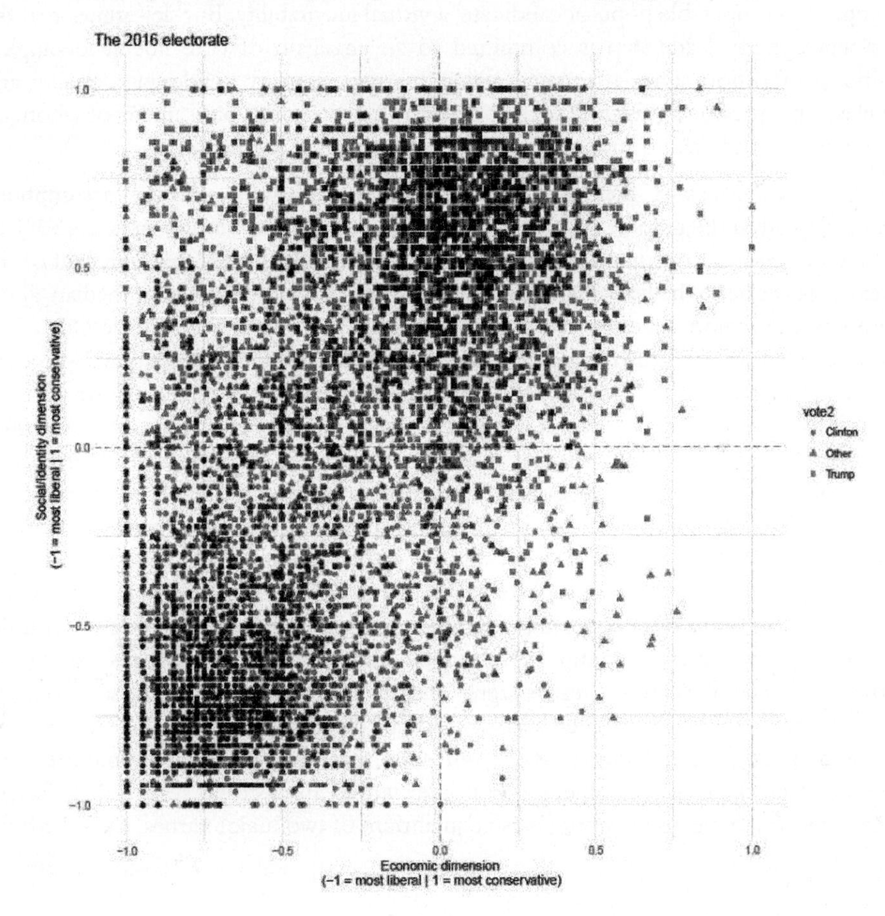

The graphic divides voters based on whether they identify as economic liberals (left) or economic conservatives (right), and based upon whether they identify as social liberals (bottom) or as social conservatives (top). The resulting four quadrants—traditional Democrats (lower left); populists (upper left); traditional Republicans (upper right); and libertarians (lower right)—suggest a possible split from the conventional left-right political axis. The lower left quadrant represents economic and social liberals, the traditional Democratic base, and the upper right represents economic and social conservatives, the traditional Republican base. The anomaly involves the 73% of voters who identify as economic liberals, split between social liberals and social conservatives. The latter subgroup, comprising the populist quadrant, typically form part of the Democratic base, and yet, about half voted for Trump.

---

[29] Lee Drutman, *Political Divisions in 2016 and Beyond: Tensions Between and Within the Two Parties*, DEMOCRACY FUND VOTER STUDY GROUP Fig. 2 (June 2017), https://www.voterstudygroup.org/publications/2016-elections/political-divisions-in-2016-and-beyond (The 2016 Electorate) (presenting original graphic in color).

In a *Wall Street Journal* op-ed, titled *How Trump Won, in Two Dimensions,*[30] George Mason Scalia Law Professor Frank Buckley posited that the populist voters pose an insurmountable problem for the future of the Democratic party and render Donald Trump, or a comparable populist candidate, a virtual inevitability. Buckley argues that the Democratic party leadership is committed to an amalgam of core liberal ideological positions—abortion rights, affirmative action, marriage equality, gender pay equality, and the like—that preclude attracting socially conservative populist voters, many of whom, as economic liberals, used to support Democratic presidential candidates.

Professor Maxwell Stearns criticized Buckley's analysis and the assumptions embedded within the graphic.[31] Stearns argues that the graphic wrongly presents 73% of actual voters as left of center on economic issues. Stearns maintains that only half of the voters can ever be to the left or right of center, whether defined as mean or median, along any policy dimension, revealing the problem of self-reporting as voters have little sense of the actual mean or median along such dimensions. Recalibrating the graphic to account for the actual midpoint along the economic axis moves a large percentage of populist voters into the upper-right quadrant, the traditional Republican party base. Stearns argues that given the remaining incidence of voters in the graphic after this adjustment, these two apparent dimensions collapse into the conventional left-right axis.[32] He nonetheless maintains that the 2016 election might have thwarted such conventional political assumptions.[33] Stearns argues that several indicators suggest a possible *insider-outsider dimension*, including the percentage of Republicans supporting Clinton, and the percentage of Sanders primary voters supporting Trump, in the general election,[34] coupled with the general antipathy toward Trump expressed by many leading Republicans during the primary and general election. Stearns argues that given the closeness of the election, this added dimension might have been sufficient to tip the Electoral College result, although not the popular vote, in Trump's favor. Ultimately, Stearns observes, if Trump prevailed as an outsider, over time he emerges an insider within an electoral system that, for the reasons shown above, yields a pure Nash equilibrium of two major parties, albeit with the

---

30 F.H. Buckley, *How Trump Won in Two Dimensions*, WALL ST. J. (Aug. 9, 2017), https://www.wsj.com/articles/how-trump-won-in-two-dimensions-1502320256; *see* Max Stearns, *The False Inevitability of Donald Trump*, BLINDSPOT BLOG (Aug. 15, 2017), https://www.blindspotblog.us/single-post/2017/08/15/The-False-Inevitability-of-Donald-Trump [hereinafter Stearns, *The False Inevitability of Donald Trump*].

31 *See* Stearns, *The False Inevitability of Donald Trump*, *supra* note 30.

32 *Id.* Stearns further observes that although Trump prevailed in the Electoral College, he lost the popular vote by approximately 3 million votes out of approximately 137 million votes cast, suggesting that along the left-right policy dimension, the median voter supported Hillary Clinton. *See id.*

33 Stearns, *Election 2016*, *supra* note 27. Stearns further explored this theme in Maxwell L. Stearns, *Reflections on the Aftermath of Election 2016*, 77 MD. L. REV. 271 (2017) and Maxwell L. Stearns, *Ideological Blindspots (part IV): The Dimensionality of Trumpism*, BLINDSPOT BLOG (Apr. 14, 2017), https://www.blindspotblog.us/single-post/2017/04/14/Ideological-Blindspots-part-IV-The-Dimensionality-of-Trumpism [hereinafter Stearns, *Dimensionality of Trumpism*].

34 Approximately 8% of Republicans voted for Clinton compared to the same percentage of Democrats who voted for Trump in the 2016 presidential election. *Exit Polls: National President*, CNN POLITICS (Nov. 23, 2016, 11:58 AM), http://www.cnn.com/election/results/exit-polls. *See* Danielle Kurtzleben, *Here's How Many Bernie Sanders Supporters Ultimately Voted For Trump*, NPR POLITICS (Aug. 24, 2017), https://www.npr.org/2017/08/24/545812242/1-in-10-sanders-primary-voters-ended-up-supporting-trump-survey-finds.

possible effect of recalibrating who comprises the Democratic and Republican coalitions.[35]

Based on these models, do you believe that the conventional unidimensional left-right spectrum used to evaluate presidential politics was disrupted in the 2016 election? Do any of the multidimensional models better explain that election and outcome than the traditional unidimensional model?[36] What additional data, if any, would you want to have in order to test these competing hypotheses? To what extent might any crossover voters be explained by idiosyncratic features of this election, such as the polarizing personalities of the major party candidates, rather than a fundamental change in the dimensionality of the electorate?

If you conclude that the 2016 election did result in a dimensional shift, do you find the analyses offered by Drutman, Buckley, Stearns, or some other explanation, such as candidate popularity, a more persuasive account? Why? Does the 2016 election cycle suggest that any particular system of selecting candidates might be superior to others in identifying either more electable or higher-quality candidates who will ultimately gain the support of the public at large? Does the foregoing analysis provide any guidance to a judge considering a constitutional challenge to a law requiring open, or blanket, primaries?[37]

More generally, if the 2016 election represents a fundamental shift in the electoral process, would you expect those changes to affect the model of regulation and delegation presented below? For example, at least one commentator has claimed that notwithstanding Donald Trump's populist campaign rhetoric and "outsider" posture, his cabinet and agency appointments have largely held conventional Republican views and have generally produced regulatory policies that are generally indistinguishable from conventional conservative policy views.[38] Of course the ideological valence of cabinet officials does not disprove that during the election itself, Trump might have effected a dimensional shift. Moreover, other commentators have observed that some of Trump's cabinet, advisory appointees, and policies do not fit past patterns of modern Republican

---

35 *See* Stearns, *Dimensionality of Trumpism*, *supra* note 33.

36 Exit polls reveal that despite the record unpopularity of the two major party nominees, in the end, 89% of self-reported Democrats stated that they voted for Hillary Clinton and 89% of Republicans voted for Donald Trump. *See Exit Polls: National President*, CNN POLITICS (Nov. 23, 2016, 11:58 AM), http://www.cnn.com/election/results/exit-polls.

37 Some state political parties have challenged state laws regulating the conduct of primary elections, including "open" primaries, which allow voters registered to one party to vote in the primary of the other party, or "blanket" primaries, which allow states to treat primaries of different parties uniformly for purposes of deciding who runs in the general election. In *Wash. State Grange v. Wash. State Republican Party*, 552 U.S. 442 (2008), the Supreme Court upheld Washington State's requirement of a blanket primary system. That system demands that the two top vote-getters in the primaries run off in the general election without regard to their party affiliation. In Justice Thomas's majority opinion, he rejected the argument that the rule prevented parties from selecting their own candidates, allegedly in violation of the rule established in *Cal. Democratic Party v. Jones*, 530 U.S. 567 (2000), and instead reasoned that the parties remain free to select their candidates outside the primary system but remain subject to the top vote-getting rule in the general election. *Grange*, 552 U.S. at 452–57.

38 *See, e.g.*, Steve Collinson, *Donald Trump's Cabinet a Boon for Conservatives*, CNN.COM (Dec. 20, 2017), http://www.cnn.com/2016/12/20/politics/donald-trump-cabinet-conservatives/index.html (arguing that Donald Trump's cabinet is a "boon" for conservatives, not populists).

Presidents.[39] How do you relate Trump's appointees to the preceding theories? Please consider the implications of the preceding analysis for the models of agency behavior, the power of executive termination, and judicial deference rules in this chapter and in Chapter 20.

B. Presidential Politics and Regulatory Policy Revisited

The various policy commitment strategies made during the primary stage—and specifically the predicted divergence between the policy positions of the major party candidates—has a potentially significant effect on the likely regulatory policies that the President and her or his appointees will pursue. Securing the support of one side or the other among such conventionally opposed groups as industry or environmentalists, labor or management, and the drug industry or consumers, raises the political cost of departing from these positions when enacting policy. Although there is some observed policy convergence in the general election cycle, the two-staged electoral system inhibits complete policy convergence. Agency deference doctrines render such policy distancing in elections all the more important.

Under the doctrine established in *Chevron U.S.A. Inc. v. Natural Res. Def. Council, Inc.*,[40] the federal judiciary is obligated to give deference to a reasonable agency interpretation of an ambiguous federal statutory provision. *Chevron* deference applies even if the interpretation differs from the construction that the federal court would provide in the first instance. Under *United States v. Mead Corp.*,[41] *Chevron* deference does not apply when an agency uses an insufficiently formal instrument to announce its interpretation; instead, an attenuated degree of deference (known as *Skidmore* deference)[42] nonetheless may be applicable. And under *National Cable & Telecommunications Ass'n v. Brand X Internet Services*,[43] the Supreme Court will even disregard its own prior interpretation of an ambiguous federal statute if an agency, acting within the scope of its proper jurisdiction, subsequently provides a different, yet reasonable, interpretation. The Court has recently suggested that

---

[39] *See* Editorial, *No Experience, No Problem*, N.Y. TIMES (Nov. 24, 2016), https://www.nytimes.com/2016/11/24/opinion/no-experience-no-problem.html; Paul Waldman, Opinion, *Donald Trump Has Assembled the Worst Cabinet in American History*, WASH. POST (Jan. 19, 2017), https://www.washingtonpost.com/blogs/plum-line/wp/2017/01/19/donald-trump-has-assembled-the-worst-cabinet-in-american-history/?utm_term=.6b33732d8142; Alyson Shontell, *How to Lose Friends and 'Exfoliate' People—Trump's Son-in-Law, Jared Kushner, Is Caught Between 2 Worlds, and His Friends are Cutting Ties*, BUS. INSIDER (Mar. 29, 2017, 8:31 AM), http://www.businessinsider.com/jared-kushner-trump-white-house-2017-3; Sonam Sheth, *Ivanka Trump's New White House Position Could Be an Ethical Minefield*, BUS. INSIDER (Mar. 25, 2017, 9:29 AM), http://www.businessinsider.com/ivanka-trump-white-house-west-wing-donald-trump-ethics-legal-2017-3. Erica Werner, *GOP Senators Recoil as Trump Tariffs Mark Major Break with His Party*, WASH. POST (Mar. 1, 2018), https://www.washingtonpost.com/news/business/wp/2018/03/01/gop-senators-recoil-as-trumps-tariffs-mark-major-break-with-his-party/?utm_term=.78e8bac78597.

[40] 467 U.S. 837 (1984).

[41] 533 U.S. 218 (2001).

[42] *See* Skidmore v. Swift & Co., 323 U.S. 134 (1944).

[43] 545 U.S. 967 (2005).

Chevron deference might be inappropriate when an implicit delegation carries potentially major policy consequences.[44]

As you read the materials that follow, consider the impact of presidential elections in affecting the "meaning" of federal statutes given the President's central role in staffing agencies. On one account of the preceding model, the primary system has the effect of preserving substantial policy distance between the two major parties, which predictably produces considerable policy swings when the party controlling the White House changes hands. Judicial deference rules enhance the effect of such policy swings by removing final interpretive authority over ambiguous statutory provisions from Article III courts and conferring it, instead, upon executive and independent agencies. Because the President has a more immediate effect in staffing agencies than in staffing the judiciary (given the life tenure of judges and thus the reduced incidence of replacements), the President has a greater likelihood of affecting administrative interpretations than judicial constructions of statutes.[45]

Of course, the President does appoint federal judges (with Senate approval), but the effect of such appointments on the construction of statutes is likely to be felt over a longer period of time and often with the result of a considerable lag between presidential administrations.[46] Within the federal judiciary, setting the context in which agency deference rules apply, the Supreme Court's interpretation of statutes is otherwise final (barring congressional override), and presidential appointments to that Court are sporadic and sometimes unpredictable.

Why might the Supreme Court have articulated a set of doctrines that effectively vests construction of statutes in the very agencies whose interpretations are subject to judicial review? Under the model developed by Professors Landes and Posner, the independent judiciary prolongs the meaning of statutes as envisioned by the drafters, at

---

[44] *See* King v. Burwell, 135 S. Ct. 2480 (2015). For a more detailed presentation of this case, see *infra*, at 35.

[45] For an analysis that considers the implications of presidential policy swings from the ideal point of the general election's median voter, see Matthew C. Stephenson, *Optimal Political Control of the Bureaucracy*, 107 MICH. L. REV. 53 (2008). Professor Stephenson is not concerned with the causes of predictable presidential policy divergence from the preferences of the median voter. *Id.* at 83 n.81 and cites therein. Instead, he is concerned with the consequence of that divergence for the claim that tighter presidential control over agency policies promotes majoritarian bureaucratic accountability. Stephenson maintains that under specified assumptions, some degree of insulation from presidential control is more likely, counterintuitively, to increase bureaucratic tracking of majoritarian policy preferences. Stephenson claims that those advocating a unitary executive, or what he terms strong presidentialism, commit the analytical error of equating "the *expected value of the distance* between two variables" with "the *distance between the expected value* of these two variables." *Id.* at 73. Because Presidents tend to represent ideal points, perhaps for reasons set out in the text, that are closer to the median party voter and thus some distance to one side or the other of the general election's median voter, an insulated bureaucracy is more likely over time to track the true median voter's ideal point than is an agency increasingly subject to the control of changing presidential administrations. Stephenson's largely positive account rests on the premise that bureaucratic action is intended to reflect the preferences of the median voter, rather than, for example, that of the successful political coalition as one of the several means of encouraging democratic engagement.

[46] The interaction between the judiciary and agencies does seem to matter, however, as there is some empirical evidence that judges act more deferentially toward regulations issues by a President of their own party, which might further exacerbate policy swings. *See* discussion *infra* notes 83–91 and accompanying text.

least when compared with the alternative of a *dependent* judiciary.[47] Recall that in Professor Elhauge's model, *Chevron* deference promotes political satisfaction as gauged against what he terms "enactable preferences."[48] Which, if either, of these models does the preceding analysis of the role of two-staged presidential elections in affecting policy change better support? Bear this question in mind as you read the rest of this chapter and consider the incentives of the bureaucrats in construing statutes.

More generally, does the preceding analysis help to explain the nature of bureaucratic behavior? Does the answer to this question depend on whether we are discussing executive or independent agencies? Why or why not? We now turn to the second inquiry, namely, what motivates the agencies themselves.

II. DELEGATION

We now hold aside bureaucratic incentives and consider the congressional motivations to delegate rulemaking authority to agencies. Congress might delegate for benign reasons: to benefit from agency-policy expertise, to minimize costly legislative processes, or to focus limited congressional resources on higher priority policies.[49] Congress might also delegate for reasons that seem problematic: to avoid hard choices, to disclaim responsibility for unpopular policies, or to facilitate agency rent extraction from particular constituencies or interest groups. Even if motivated by benign purposes, delegation inevitably raises legislative agency costs, as agencies risk departing from Congress's expected or preferred outcomes.

A. Congressional Control of Delegated Authority

Congress can reduce the problem of agency costs by making narrow and tightly circumscribed delegations, thus spelling out the scope of the delegation in precise detail. Narrowly defined delegations rein in the discretion of both current and future bureaucrats. Restricting agency discretion, however, risks reducing the intended benefits to Congress of the initial delegation. Such delegations substitute congressional mandates for agency expertise, forcing Congress to expend more time and resources articulating and enforcing limits on agency discretion. This both reduces the anticipated workload savings from delegation and reduces agency flexibility to respond to changing circumstances. Congress thus confronts a delegation trade-off: it must confer sufficient authority to be able to capture the benefits of delegation, but it must also limit excessive agency costs. Terry Moe summarizes the resulting trade-off as follows:

> The most direct way [to control agencies] is for today's authorities to specify, in excruciating detail, precisely what the agency is to do and how it is to do it, leaving as little as possible to the discretionary judgment of bureaucrats—and

---

[47] *See supra* Chapter 18. *See infra* Chapter 24 (providing more detailed discussion of Landes and Posner model).

[48] For discussion, see *supra* Chapter 18, Part II.B.3.

[49] *See* David Epstein & Sharyn O'Halloran, *Administrative Procedures, Information, and Agency Discretion*, 38 AM. J. POL. SCI. 697, 698 (1994) (summarizing rationales for delegation).

> thus as little as possible for future authorities to exercise control over, short of passing new legislation. . . .
>
> Obviously, this is not a formula for creating effective organizations. In the interests of political protection, agencies are knowingly burdened with cumbersome, complicated, technically inappropriate structures that undermine their capacity to perform their jobs well.[50]

Once Congress has delegated authority to an agency, it can control agency discretion to deviate from Congress's preferred policy either through ex ante controls or ex post ongoing oversight. Ex ante controls involve "issues of agency design," such as reporting and consultation procedures that an agency must follow in making policy.[51] Congress may also exert control over the establishment of new departments, the location of new agencies within the executive branch, and how far down the organizational hierarchy political appointments will reach. As with using narrow delegations to control agency discretion, ex ante controls are not costless. For example, greater constraints limit agencies from adapting to new situations.

Ex post controls include those institutional features that check agency actions on a regular basis, such as congressional oversight and annual budget appropriations. The federal judiciary also exerts ongoing control through the enforcement of administrative law requirements, and the President exerts control through his power of appointment (subject, where applicable, to the confirmation process).

Because exercising control (whether ex ante or ex post) is costly, Congress must anticipate some agency slack. Thus Congress's willingness to delegate is inversely correlated to the expected cost of ensuring bureaucratic compliance. Congress also will be less willing to confer regulatory discretion when faced with a substantial information asymmetry as between Congress and the agency, as this further raises monitoring costs. Thus, the value to Congress of ex post oversight controls will increase as the anticipated disparity in policy preferences between Congress and the agency rises and as information asymmetries between Congress and the agency decrease.[52] Where it is difficult to monitor and control agency discretion, Congress will delegate less and stipulate its objectives more precisely. When delegation occurs despite information asymmetries, such as where reliance on technical expertise is necessary, Congress tends to hold more oversight hearings to monitor agency behavior.[53]

Tighter ex ante controls, such as statutory precision or more stringent appointments requirements, reduce agency costs by allowing Congress more input over agency policies. Conversely, narrow delegations raise the risk of *legislative drift* (sometimes called *coalition drift*). Legislative drift is a change over time in regulatory policy from changes in the ideological composition of Congress or of the relevant oversight committees. Thus, if the median member of Congress or the applicable oversight committee changes, the desired scope of agency delegations and the preferred approach to agency oversight will change

---

[50] Terry M. Moe, *Political Institutions: The Neglected Side of the Story*, 6 J.L. ECON. & ORG. 213, 228 (1990).

[51] Epstein & O'Halloran, *supra* note 49, at 698–99.

[52] *Id.* at 708.

[53] *See* DAVID EPSTEIN & SHARYN O'HALLORAN, DELEGATING POWERS: A TRANSACTION COST POLITICS APPROACH TO POLICY MAKING UNDER SEPARATE POWERS 207–11 (1999).

as well. In addition, as discussed in Chapter 11, one element of the willingness of interest groups to lobby for favorable legislation is the legislation's expected durability, i.e., the duration of the resulting stream of benefits.[54] Thus, interest groups will provide greater support for legislation with a relatively longer expected life. The fear that a future Congress will reverse the decision of the current Congress reduces the expected value of the legislation and hence the support that interest groups will provide. Rational members of Congress, therefore, are likely to prefer policies that reduce the threat of legislative drift, thereby increasing the expected value of their delegations.

Legislative drift should be distinguished from *bureaucratic drift.* Bureaucratic drift occurs when Congress delegates authority but the agency subsequently pursues policies at odds with the enacting Congress's expectations. Broader delegations reduce the risk of legislative drift by insulating the agency from subsequent changes in congressional preferences, but, at the same time, such delegations increase the risk of bureaucratic drift. Congress can mitigate bureaucratic drift through monitoring and oversight. Doing so, however, is costly and difficult, especially with respect to complex and rapidly changing areas of regulation, and thus where delegation is considered most appropriate. Where delegations are not carefully constrained and specified at the outset, the risk of bureaucratic drift is most acute.

Legislative and bureaucratic drift are thus mirror images of each other.[55] Professors David Epstein and Sharyn O'Halloran explain:

> In order to check runaway bureaucracies, *legislatures must structure agency decision-making to be responsive to congressional demands.* However, this ensures that future Congresses will be able to influence policy outcomes, thereby exacerbating the consequences of coalitional drift. [Thus], ex ante decisions about bureaucratic structure are intimately linked with issues of ongoing oversight.[56]

There is a sharp difference between the two sets of monitoring tools. Tight ex ante controls can be reversed only by subsequent legislation, an expensive and time-consuming process. As a result, such controls risk becoming entrenched. Conversely, broader delegation with intensive ex post oversight requires discretion on the part of contemporary members of Congress, which might produce policy that departs from that preferred by the enacting legislature.[57]

B. Positive Theories of Delegation

Epstein and O'Halloran conclude that these trade-offs describe many observed patterns of delegation. They find that "Congress delegates less and constrains more under divided government" (when Congress and the Presidency are controlled by different parties) and thus when the risk of bureaucratic drift is high.[58] Congress also tends to

---

[54] *See supra* Chapter 11.

[55] Kenneth A. Shepsle, *Bureaucratic Drift, Coalitional Drift, and Time Consistency: A Comment on Macey*, 8 J.L. ECON. & ORG. 111 (1992).

[56] Epstein & O'Halloran, *supra* note 49, at 712 (emphasis added).

[57] *Id.* at 713.

[58] *See* EPSTEIN & O'HALLORAN, *supra* note 53, at 11, 121–62.

delegate less discretion when legislation is passed over a presidential veto or in the face of a presidential veto threat because that threat signals presidential hostility to the act and a high risk that the executive branch will use its discretion in opposition to the enacting Congress's wishes. Finally, divided government also affects the structure of delegation. Under divided government, Congress is less likely to delegate to executive branch departments and is more likely to delegate to independent agencies or even state governments. Thus, Epstein and O'Halloran conclude that Congress's decision to delegate is not explained primarily by a desire to rely on technical agency expertise or constraints on Congress's time. Instead, it is strategic: Congress is aware that agencies make political decisions and, therefore, Congress's willingness to delegate depends on the degree of policy agreement between Congress and the President.

Congress might sometimes be forced to delegate more discretionary authority than it would prefer as the price for implementing a policy that it seeks to pursue but that the President at least initially disfavors. Epstein and O'Halloran illustrate with agriculture subsidies.[59] Farm subsidies as they exist today are widely viewed as a distributional *pork barrel* program that confers significant financial benefits upon farmers with little, if any, corresponding public benefits. Congress often supports distributive programs that allow members to *claim credit* with their constituencies for conferring the legislative benefits while imposing dispersed costs that incur relatively minor political opposition. Farm subsidies require minimal expertise or discretion by the President, and thus, would seem to require little discretionary delegation. According to Epstein and O'Halloran, however, the President has unexpectedly broad discretion over program implementation, which, the authors contend, is the President's price for acquiescing in the congressional bargain. They further contend that the President, who is elected by the nation as a whole, will generally be reluctant to endorse pork barrel projects that favor narrow regional interests. The authors conclude, "The untold story of agricultural policy, then, is that it relies heavily on executive discretion for implementation, this authority being supplied as a bribe for presidential support of agricultural programs."[60]

Professors Aranson, Gellhorn, and Robinson (AGR) maintain that the private goods nature of electoral processes also applies equally to the President and to members of Congress, and thus they challenge the conclusion that the President will generally exhibit hostility toward pork barrel legislation.[61] How might AGR explain the broad presidential discretion in implementing the farm subsidy program? Historically, Presidents have tended to be more supportive of free trade policies than Congress, although Donald Trump appears to be a notable exception. Can you explain these phenomena? Professors McCubbins, Noll, and Weingast (McNollgast) argue that "because of the importance, visibility, historical significance and clear accountability of the office, the President's personal reputation hinges much more on the broad performance of the government than

---

[59] *Id.* at 220–21.

[60] *Id.* at 221.

[61] *See* Peter H. Aranson, Ernest Gellhorn & Glen O. Robinson, *A Theory of Legislative Delegation*, 68 CORNELL L. REV. 1, 41–43 (1982).

is the case for legislators."[62] Does that help to explain the historical trend respecting international trade, even if it does not account for Trump? Why or why not?

Would a legislature specifically concerned about agency capture be more likely to prefer ex ante or ex post controls on agency decision making? Professor Terry Moe has argued that in setting up the EPA, Congress spelled out voluminous and detailed ex ante procedural regulations that create a complicated and lengthy process for regulatory approval. The EPA gave environmental interest groups a substantial voice in the regulatory process through a variety of mechanisms for public participation.[63] Complex regulatory procedures enable Congress to achieve substantive goals indirectly, while also affording favored interest groups a de facto veto over adverse agency action.[64] Can you explain why Congress facilitated this result? Is it relevant that EPA was created in the early-1970s, when policy makers were highly concerned with the risk of industry capture of the regulatory process? To what extent does this analysis assume minimal agency costs as between environmental interest groups and the public?

C. Congressional Responses to Agency Drift

In theory, Congress can rectify any agency deviation from its preferences with ex post oversight. McNollgast have argued, however, that reliance on ex post monitoring might not allow Congress fully to rectify bureaucratic drift because Congress frequently will be unable to "reproduce the policy outcome that was sought by the [original] winning coalition."[65] As a result of congressional turnover, some members of the initially successful legislative coalition might no longer be in Congress, and the new members who replaced them might hold different preferences, leading to a shift in location for the median member of Congress on the issue. The agency's regulatory policy might have mobilized a previously unorganized or dormant constituency that prefers the agency's selected policy. Some members of the original coalition might have changed their views to favor the new regulatory policy and thus oppose efforts to rein in the agency. As a result of congressional bargaining processes, including the veto gates described in Chapter 11, a successful exercise of blocking power by a member of Congress, or a presidential veto, is sufficient to protect agency policy against congressional override. Does this explain the popularity of the one-house veto? Does it call into question the soundness of the Supreme Court decision invalidating this practice in *INS v. Chadha*?[66] Why or why not?

---

[62] McNollgast, *The Political Economy of Law*, *in* 2 HANDBOOK OF LAW AND ECONOMICS 1651, 1689–90 (A. Mitchell Polinsky & Steven Shavell eds., 2007).

[63] *See* Terry M. Moe, *The Politics of Bureaucratic Structure*, *in* CAN THE GOVERNMENT GOVERN? 267, 310–20 (John E. Chubb & Paul E. Peterson eds., 1989).

[64] *See* McNollgast, *supra* note 62, at 1710–13.

[65] Matthew D. McCubbins, Roger G. Noll & Barry R. Weingast, *Structure and Process, Politics and Policy: Administrative Arrangements and the Political Control of Agencies*, 75 VA. L. REV. 431, 433 (1989).

[66] 462 U.S. 919 (1983). For a more detailed presentation of *Chadha* and the one-house veto, *see infra* Chapter 23. For a related analysis of how the one-house veto allows Congress to move the scope of delegation closer to its ideal point rather than that of the President, as compared with the post-*Chadha* regime, see William N. Eskridge, Jr. & John Ferejohn, *The Article I, Section 7 Game*, 80 GEO. L.J. 523 (1992).

Consider McNollgast's analysis in the context of *Mississippi Poultry Ass'n, Inc. v. Madigan*, presented in Chapter 18.[67] Recall that the United States Department of Agriculture (USDA) promulgated regulations governing poultry inspections that defined the legislative term "the same as" to mean "at least equal to." The initial statute was adopted with strong support, and some members of Congress criticized the USDA's regulatory interpretation as deviating from Congress's original intent. Despite this, Congress did not enact legislation overruling the agency interpretation. The USDA adopted Congress's apparent preferred meaning only when ordered to do so by the United States Court of Appeals for the Fifth Circuit. Does this case support McNollgast's intuition that it is more difficult for Congress to police departures from intended policy positions ex post than to constrain agency discretion ex ante? Why or why not?

Given the difficulty of reversing agency action, McNollgast argue that one purpose of administrative procedures may be to "erect a barrier against an agency carrying out such a *fait accompli* by forcing the agency to move slowly and publicly, giving politicians (informed by their constituents) time to act before the status quo is changed."[68] Administrative rulemaking requires cumbersome, but public and deliberative, processes. Before an agency can enact a new policy, it must engage in *notice and comment rulemaking*. This means it must first announce that it is considering a new rule and then solicit the views of interested parties. In some instances, the agency must hold public hearings. The agency must also produce a record that sets forth the reasons for its decision and explains why it rejected proposed alternatives. Legislation often mandates consultation with designated stakeholders elsewhere in the government, or with affected private interests, thereby entrenching interests that were part of the initial legislative coalition. The authors explain:

> These procedures allow politicians to prevent deviations before they occur. The members of the coalition enacting the policy can adopt a blanket agreement to inhibit all possible deviations while the nature of the deviation is still in doubt and the coalition has not yet formed that might support the deviation. Delay gives the old coalition time to mobilize its constituents before the agency undermines it by enunciating a noncomplying policy that changes the status quo.[69]

Much bureaucratic delay is ascribed to the pursuit of other objectives, for example due process concerns, or to bureaucratic incentives or agency costs. McNollgast argue, however, that this delay and inefficiency might intentionally slow the pace of agency action, thereby providing Congress and interest groups with the time and means to block planned departures from preferred policy outcomes.

McNollgast argue that Congress's reliance on the *fire alarm theory* of monitoring agency behavior and preventing agency drift explains, among other things, the origins of the Administrative Procedure Act (APA) of 1946.[70] McNollgast note that the APA was

---

[67] *See supra* Chapter 18.

[68] McCubbins, Noll & Weingast, *supra* note 65, at 442 (emphasis added).

[69] *Id.* (footnote omitted).

[70] Matthew McCubbins, Roger G. Noll & Barry R. Weingast, *The Political Origins of the Administrative Procedure Act*, 15 J.L. ECON. & ORG.180 (1999).

not enacted until the end of the New Deal, and attribute those earlier deferential positions to the political reality that when Democrats controlled the White House and both houses of Congress, they had little desire to erect procedural hurdles to new regulations. In addition, at the beginning of the New Deal, the federal courts were still dominated by Republican appointees who were perceived as hostile to the New Deal. As a result, Washington Democrats were reluctant to create judicially enforceable rights for parties to challenge New Deal policies.

By 1946, however, the landscape had changed. Roosevelt had died, and Democrats risked losing control of Congress in the 1946 midterm elections (as actually occurred) and losing the White House in 1948, as Harry Truman was not then considered a particularly strong candidate. In addition, by 1946, Roosevelt had substantially shifted the federal judiciary in favor of supporting the New Deal. These combined factors encouraged Democrats to reverse their earlier position and to support enacting the APA. McNollgast argue that the Democrats sought to erect procedural hurdles facing the threat of a new Republican President and to make those rules enforceable in the federal courts, thereby entrenching New Deal regulatory policies. In this analysis, the APA allowed a Democratically controlled Congress to assert greater control over agency behavior, thereby keeping the agencies more accountable and in line with intent of previously enacted legislative policies.

Finally, Professor Jonathan Macey has argued that through the use of agency structure, an enacting Congress can simultaneously address the problems of both agency and legislative drift.[71] Macey argues that Congress can intentionally structure agency jurisdiction and operations so as to increase the likelihood that it will be captured by preferred special-interest groups. A favorably inclined group that is essentially hard-wired into the agency's architecture will help keep the agency on mission.

Macey argues that the most effective vehicle for aligning an agency mission with effective interest group monitoring is to define the agency's mission narrowly. One example is giving an agency jurisdiction over one identifiable industry, as happened with the Securities Exchange Commission (SEC), Commodities Futures Trading Commission (CFTC), and Office of the Comptroller of the Currency (The Comptroller), rather than defining the agency's scope by function, for example, the Federal Trade Commission (FTC). Macey explains:

> The ability to structure an administrative agency as a single-interest or a multi-interest organization enables Congress to exert greater ex ante control over the outcomes generated by the agency. Congress accomplishes this by controlling the ability of outside interest groups to exert political pressure on the agency, and by reducing the incentive of new interest groups to form to protest the agency's actions.
>
> In general, then, where a single interest group dominates the original decision-making process in Congress that leads to a particular legislative enactment, the resulting administrative agency will be a single-interest-group agency. Where the original decision-making process in Congress involves a

[71] Jonathan R. Macey, *Organizational Design and Political Control of Administrative Agencies*, 8 J.L. ECON. & ORG. 93, 100–04 (1992).

> compromise among a large number of interest groups, the resulting administrative agency will provide access to all of these groups. This is an as-yet-unrecognized manifestation of the well-known congressional tendency to create regulatory structures that "mirror" the political environment existing at the time of the initial statutory enactment.[72]

Macey further explains:

> The initial jurisdictional design of an agency will determine which interest groups will have ready access to the agency, and on what terms. In this way, the enacting legislators can, to a large degree, determine in advance the extent to which, and the terms on which, the agency will be "captured" by the groups it regulates. The enacting coalition therefore can minimize the amount of bureaucratic drift and legislative drift likely to occur.[73]

Macey identifies several tools that the legislature has at its disposal when setting up an agency. First is the initial hardwiring of the agency to determine its degree of responsiveness to different interest groups. Macey offers as an example the establishment of a central bank. In general, there is an inverse correlation between the independence of a central bank from political pressure and the inflation rate: independent central banks tend to have lower inflation rates. Macey notes that this has significant implications for the expected degree of influence debtors are likely to exert over monetary policy. Macey argues that if creditor interest groups have higher influence relative to debtor interest groups at the bank's inception, then the bank is more likely to be structured as independent; conversely, if debtor interest groups are more influential, then the bank is less likely to be independent. The influence of interest groups through this initial agency hardwiring can then be reinforced, as desired, through agency procedural rules that either enfranchise or disenfranchise interest groups seeking to influence agency decision making.

Macey argues that more specialized agencies are prone to interest group capture. An agency whose scope is defined by the industry it regulates, rather than the functions it performs, is more likely to be staffed by relevant industry experts, who are also insiders. Thus, the Comptroller is likely to be staffed by employees drawn from, or anticipating post-governmental employment within, the banking industry. Such persons are likely to hold particular biases about the importance of the national banking industry and to draw on industry professionals and trade publications for information about the industry. Conversely, defining the agency's jurisdiction to regulate a number of competing industries will predictably reduce the likelihood that the agency will be dominated by the representatives of a single industry.

A final factor affecting Congress's choice of agency scope is the effect on inter-agency competition. Macey argues that affected industries under single-industry agencies tend to become agency partisans, meaning interest groups that support the agency in intra-governmental battles. Macey illustrates this with the conflict among the SEC, the CFTC, and the Comptroller concerning whether futures contracts for securities deliveries should be treated as futures (subject to CFTC oversight) or as securities contracts (subject to SEC oversight). As might be expected, securities dealers argued that they were securities

---

72 *Id.* at 99–100.

73 *Id.* at 100.

contracts, advocating SEC jurisdiction, whereas interests regulated by the CFTC (such as the Chicago Board of Trade) advocated CFTC jurisdiction. Congress could have avoided the conflict by combining regulatory authority over options, futures, and securities into a single agency. It elected otherwise.[74] Macey suggests that structuring these agencies with a single-industry jurisdiction allowed Congress simultaneously to reduce agency and legislative drift, thereby increasing the expected durability of the legislation and the present value of the resulting rents it was expected to produce. On the other hand, this form of agency hardwiring reduces agency discretion, with the attendant costs of diminished regulatory flexibility and subsequent opportunities for rent-extraction from affected industries.

Congress also chooses whether to establish agency responsibilities based on "function-specific" or "industry-specific" regulations. Function-specific regulation is defined with reference to the regulatory body's scope and function rather than a particular industry. Thus, the authority of agencies such as the EPA, the Occupational Safety and Health Administration (OSHA), Equal Employment Opportunity Commission (EEOC), and the FTC is defined by function and thus cuts across industry boundaries. Agencies engaged in industry-specific regulation define their jurisdiction by the industries they regulate, as illustrated by the SEC, CFTC, FCC, or the Comptroller.

Function-based versus industry-based regulation presents important trade-offs. An industry-specific agency might have more expertise regarding the industry's particular structure and idiosyncrasies, but it might also have a greater propensity to industry capture. By contrast, a general-jurisdiction agency might have a greater expertise in generally applicable principles and policies, but it might have less detailed industry-specific knowledge.[75]

Consider, for example, the formulation of competition policy. Under federal law, there are a variety of agencies that regulate mergers for compliance with antitrust laws. The FTC and the Antitrust Division of the Department of Justice hold concurrent jurisdiction over mergers, a jurisdiction also shared with other industry-specific agencies. For instance, the FCC reviews mergers in the telecommunications industry, the Department of Transportation (DOT) reviews mergers in the airline industry, and the Federal Reserve Board reviews mergers in the banking industry. The FTC and Antitrust Division might have greater general expertise in applying antitrust law and policy, and the industry-based regulator might have greater industry specific expertise, coupled with a greater likelihood of industry capture.

From a public interest perspective, what factors should Congress consider when deciding whether to regulate a given industry through a specific sector-based agency or through a multi-industry, function-based agency? Do the same considerations concerning capture apply in the choice of whether to establish specialized courts, such as the Federal

---

[74] The Seventh Circuit finally held that the CFTC had exclusive jurisdiction over trading in investment vehicles that could be characterized both as securities and investment contracts. Chi. Mercantile Exch. v. SEC, 883 F.2d 537 (7th Cir. 1989).

[75] Todd J. Zywicki, Director, Off. Pol'y Planning, Fed. Trade Comm'n, Address at the Competition Policy Research Center, Fair Trade Commission of Japan, Inaugural Symposium: Competition Policy and Regulatory Reform: Means and Ends, How Should Competition Policy Transform Itself? Designing the New Competition Policy (Nov. 20, 2003).

Circuit (to hear patent appeals) or Bankruptcy Courts, versus allowing more cases to be resolved in the first instance in federal district courts, which have more general jurisdiction.[76]

III. JUDICIAL REVIEW OF AGENCY ACTION

The analysis of regulation has gone through three basic phases over the past century: (1) the "public interest era" of the post-New Deal period, (2) the "capture era" of the 1960s and 1970s, and (3) the modern "public choice era" since the 1980s. What implication have these changes in intellectual framing had for law?

A. Influence of Regulatory Theories on Courts

Professor Thomas Merrill has argued that the intellectual development of these three theories of governmental regulation helps to explain the evolution of legal doctrine concerning judicial oversight of agencies in the twentieth century.[77] Even if judges did not consciously apply these theories in their decision making, Merrill suggests, judicial doctrines implicitly reflect the prominence of these underlying theories in different historical periods.

Merrill argues that at the dawn of the administrative state during the New Deal, courts were imbued with the ethic of the public interest model of government. As a result, they tended to exhibit substantial deference to agency decision making and congressional delegation, based upon the Progressive Era presumption that regulatory policy should be made by disinterested experts. This mindset is reflected in the *Legal Process School*, described in Chapter 17.[78] As a matter of judicial doctrine, this school stressed the need for transparency and procedural regularity in agency decision making and exhibited great deference to resulting regulatory policies. Although Hart and Sacks did not imagine that regulatory experts were immune to special interest pressures, they encouraged judicial constructions that brought out the public interest elements of enacted regulatory policies. Otherwise, they favored a minimal role for judicial oversight of agency decision making that emphasized the centrality of policy making by regulators and deference by judges.

Beginning in the 1960s, however, judges and scholars increasingly realized that in practice, regulatory results often diverged from public interest objectives. This development led to a questioning of *public interest theory* and a shift toward *capture theory*.[79] The capture critique of the administrative state corresponded with the *consumer protection movement* led by Ralph Nader, who bemoaned the capture of regulatory agencies by the

---

[76] For arguments that the Federal Circuit is prone to capture by the interests of the patent bar, see Stuart Minor Benjamin & Arti K. Rai, *Fixing Innovation Policy: A Structural Perspective*, 77 GEO. WASH. L. REV. 1, 17–18 (2008); Arti K. Rai, *Engaging Facts and Policy: A Multi-Institutional Approach to Patent System Reform*, 103 COLUM. L. REV. 1035, 1110 (2003); John R. Thomas, *Formalism at the Federal Circuit*, 52 AM. U. L. REV. 771, 792–94 (2003); *see also* G. Marcus Cole & Todd J. Zywicki, The New Forum-Shopping Problem in Bankruptcy (working paper, June 10, 2009), http://papers.ssrn.com/sol3/papers.cfm?abstract_id=1417621) (discussing bankruptcy courts).

[77] Thomas W. Merrill, *Capture Theory and the Courts: 1967–1983*, 72 CHI.-KENT L. REV. 1039 (1997).

[78] *See supra* Chapter 17.

[79] Capture theory is discussed in Chapter 11.

business interests that they were established to regulate. Merrill argues that many of the judges of the D.C. Circuit during the 1960s and 1970s, who were themselves veterans of the New Deal and sympathetic to Nader's goals, were distressed by the apparent evolution of regulation away from New Deal and Progressive objectives. Some of these judges, including perhaps most notably J. Skelly Wright, came to implicitly embrace capture theory. A natural consequence of this reconceived understanding of agency dynamics, Merrill claims, was heightened judicial oversight of agency processes to try to prevent interest group capture of regulation. Judges influenced by capture theory, however, tended not to abandon their earlier intuitions informed by public interest theory as to the proper *ends* of government; instead, they were increasingly vigilant in ensuring that bureaucrats were not distracted from their regulatory missions by what they regarded as excessive interest group influence.

Merrill describes the intellectual transition from public interest to capture theory as follows:

> [Capture] theory . . . contains a theory of comparative institutional advantage. Implicit in capture theory is the understanding that the central problem of the administrative state is a relatively limited one. Only administrative agencies are subject to the unique pathologies of bureaucracy such as interest group capture. Rival institutions, like the legislature and the courts, were implicitly regarded as being immune from these pathologies or at least as suffering from them to a significantly diminished degree. Moreover, in terms of interest group influence, the problematic actor was seen to be the business lobby. Other groups, such as labor unions or advocates for civil rights or the environment, were tacitly assumed to be champions of the public interest.
>
> [This intuition] created an ideal atmosphere for vigorous reform efforts. For example, one solution might be for Congress to enact more detailed legislation, thereby helping to ensure that policy is made by a healthy democratic institution (the legislature), and leaving comparatively little room for the corrupted institution (the agency) to undermine that policy. And in fact, there was a decisive move in the early 1970s toward enacting longer and more detailed regulatory statutes, in order to constrain the discretion of agencies. These statutes typically provided for policy to be made by informal rulemaking open to all, and included strict deadlines for the adoption of rules that could be enforced by citizen suits in court.
>
> More importantly for present purposes, capture theory also suggests that aggressive judicial oversight and control of agencies is needed in order to counteract the distortions of the administrative process introduced by interest group capture and other pathologies. Specifically, by forcing agencies to adopt an administrative process that is more open and to give greater consideration to underrepresented viewpoints in that process, courts may be able to counteract the distortions emphasized by the theory.[80]

[80] Merrill, *supra* note 77, at 1051–52 (footnotes omitted).

Merrill maintains that the *public choice era* began in the mid-1980s. During this time (which presumably continues today), there was a retreat from the capture-theory-inspired position that had prompted robust judicial review of agency action. Merrill posits that the *economic theory of regulation*, also sometimes referred to as the *public choice theory of regulation*, differs from capture theory in two significant ways. First, capture theory is narrowly focused on the dysfunctions of administrative agencies alone, whereas the economic theory of regulation applies its tools to governmental action generally, including the actions of legislatures and courts. Thus, capture theory accepts the public interest premises on which Congress establishes regulatory agencies in the first instance, but seeks to avoid what it regards as excessive interest group influence affecting the ends of agency regulation. Public choice theory, by contrast, questions the motivating goals of regulation, focusing on forms of regulation that ultimately benefit the very industries that agencies are called upon to regulate. Second, capture theory is concerned with the undue influence of one particular group—producers—whereas public choice considers the influence of all organized groups, "including not just business and producer groups, but also environmental groups, labor unions, civil rights groups, and rent control activists."[81]

Merrill asserts that the interest group theory of regulation has motivated a judicial retrenchment from the activist agency oversight that typified the capture era. This followed from judicial and academic commentary expressing skepticism of all organs of government, including the judiciary. This retrenchment was not marked, however, by a return to the earlier era of deference to legislatures and bureaucrats that characterized those influenced by the public interest model. Merrill explains:

> The decline of judicial assertiveness in the recent period, and the partial return of authority and autonomy to agencies . . . cannot be considered in any sense a revival of the public interest conception of the administrative state, or a rehabilitation of administrative agencies as institutions in the eyes of the judiciary. Rather, it is a product of a deeper and more generalized pessimism about the administrative state, and in particular, of a spreading disenchantment with all forms of activist government. I . . . refer to this shift in attitudes as a movement toward a "public choice" conception of the administrative state, although I hasten to add that I do not mean to imply that (most) judges have either studied or become practitioners of formal public choice theory. . . . I simply mean a conception that is skeptical about the capacity of *any* governmental institution to serve the public interest, primarily because all governmental institutions—agencies, legislatures, the White House, and even the courts—are subject to manipulation by organized groups, and hence cannot be regarded as dispassionate guardians of the public interest.[82]

"In effect," Merrill concludes, "capture theory's pessimism about the performance of administrative agencies has been generalized to include all political institutions."[83] Merrill further concludes that just as the pessimism of the "capture era" brought about recommendations to relocate some decision-making authority from agencies to courts,

---

[81] *Id.* at 1069.

[82] *Id.* at 1044.

[83] *Id.* at 1053.

the "public choice era" brought about support for a more general reallocation of authority from government to private market actors and institutions.

If public choice identifies difficulties in the decision-making processes of agencies, Congress, and courts, might the theory counsel in favor of clear rules concerning which institution holds primary lawmaking responsibility? Does the *Chevron* doctrine, for example, improve political accountability by designating the agency as the central focus of administrative lawmaking within its scope, or does it reduce accountability by permitting Congress to shift responsibility for controversial decisions? Merrill maintains that if there is no basis for preferring one institution over another, then there is also no justification for reviving the nondelegation doctrine, which would shift decision-making authority from one flawed decision maker (agencies) to another (legislatures). Do you agree with this conclusion? Does this necessarily follow from the teachings of public choice?

Does public choice, properly understood, imply a universal condemnation of all organs of government? Or might public choice, instead, imply that although no institution, including any governmental organ or entities that emerge within private markets, is perfect, each nonetheless has the potential to improve the human condition when its relative, or comparative, advantages are recognized and harnessed, often in combination with other, also imperfect, institutions? Does social choice help to provide a means of comparing institutions that avoids the claim that all institutions are inherently or equivalently defective?[84] Which reading of public choice do you find more persuasive? Why?

As a descriptive claim about judicial perceptions of institutional competence, whose analysis is more persuasive? Given that courts are not steeped in public choice, as Merrill concedes, is there reason to believe that courts might regard themselves as above the sort of interest group influences that some public choice theorists ascribe to agencies and Congress? Why or why not? If you conclude that judges are likely to view themselves in this way, why do they remain largely reticent to continue to insist upon stringent rulemaking processes? Are judges concerned that policing rent-seeking activity might motivate interest groups to direct their efforts toward courts to the extent they failed to further their objectives within legislative or administrative processes?

B. Courts and Administrative Rulemaking

Courts are also important players in the production of regulation as they interact with Congress and the executive branch. Thus, judicial attitudes toward regulation have a major impact on the formation of regulatory policy. Professor Richard Revesz has examined the role of ideology in the judicial review of administrative decision making. Analyzing rulings of the United States Court of Appeals for the District of Columbia Circuit on the validity of regulations issued by the EPA, Revesz concludes that judges' ideologies significantly influence that court's decision making on administrative law issues.[85] Revesz finds that during periods in which Republican-appointed judges

---

[84] *See generally* Chapter 13. For an article that addresses this question, see Maxwell L. Stearns, *The Misguided Renaissance of Social Choice*, 103 YALE L.J. 1219 (1994).

[85] Richard L. Revesz, *Environmental Regulation, Ideology, and the D.C. Circuit*, 83 VA. L. REV. 1717 (1997).

controlled it, that court was more likely to reverse an EPA rule when the challenger represented industrial interests. He further finds that when Democratic-appointed judges controlled it, that court was more likely to reverse when the challenger represented environmental interests. Revesz finds no evidence of a consistent pattern of deference to the EPA by judges of either party, as he claims would be the case if judicial behavior were motivated by a general theory concerning the relationships among the branches of government. If, for example, Republican judges were generally more deferential to the executive branch, then it should not matter who the challenging party is. Instead, for judges of either party, Revesz concludes that deference largely turns on the identity of the challenging party.

Revesz also finds ideological voting to be more prevalent in cases raising procedural rather than substantive challenges. Judges can impose their ideological views through either substantive interpretation of enabling acts or by the degree of deference courts afford agencies on procedural grounds. By basing deference on procedural rules, courts can affect administrative outcomes without having to take responsibility for substantive rulings. Revesz hypothesizes that judges will prefer such procedural rulings to substantive rulings as the former are less apt to be reviewed by the United States Supreme Court. Revesz argues that the use of procedural gambits to resolve controversial cases supports the intuition that judges not only vote based upon ideological considerations but also that they craft opinions based on strategic considerations, including sometimes packaging decisions in a manner that reduces the probability of further appellate review.

Revesz finds that individual judges are more likely to vote ideologically when there are other like-minded judges on the panel. For instance, in the cases that Revesz reviewed, a Republican judge was much more likely to reverse in a case involving an industry challenge to an EPA regulation when there was at least one other Republican on the panel, and a Democratic judge was significantly less likely to reverse in such a case when there was at least one other Democrat on the panel. A Democratic-appointed judge sitting with two Republican-appointed judges tends to vote more conservatively than the reverse configuration. From this evidence, Revesz concludes that while both individual ideology and panel composition have important effects on judicial behavior, the ideology of colleagues proves more significant than personal ideology in predicting actual voting patterns.

Revesz concludes that because judges appear to take the likelihood of Supreme Court reversal into account before deciding whether to allow ideology to affect voting behavior, his findings support the hypothesis that "D.C. Circuit judges employ a strategically ideological approach to judging, versus either a nonideological or a naively ideological approach."[86] Revesz concludes that the different behavior exhibited in procedural versus non-procedural cases indicates that D.C. Circuit judges "regard the Supreme Court as the primary reviewer of their decisions, rather than Congress."[87]

In a subsequent article, Professors Frank Cross and Emerson Tiller found further support for the claim that D.C. Circuit judges vote ideologically in cases reviewing

---

[86] *Id.* at 1766–67.

[87] *Id.* at 1768. Supreme Court review of circuit court decisions is rare, however, suggesting that the constraining effect of even this review is attenuated.

administrative agency decisions.[88] They conclude that the willingness of judges on the D.C. Circuit to grant deference to administrative agencies depends to a significant extent on whether the agency action is consistent with the ideological preferences of the reviewing judge. But the authors also find that judges on panels with others appointed by Presidents of the same party are twice as likely to vote ideologically as are judges on divided panels, meaning those in which judges are appointed by Presidents of different parties. The authors label this the "whistleblower" phenomenon, meaning that the presence of a potential dissenting judge on a panel who will signal that other panelists are following their ideological preferences rather than the law has the potential to inhibit ideological judicial behavior.

Research has confirmed the basic empirical findings of these studies. In *Are Judges Political? An Empirical Analysis of the Federal Judiciary*,[89] Professors Cass R. Sunstein, David Schkade, Lisa M. Ellman and Andres Sawicki (SSES) examine judicial decisions across a number of subject areas and confirm the basic findings that for most areas of law (including administrative law) judicial ideological preferences influence outcomes. SSES find that judges also are influenced by the ideological preferences of *other* judges on their panel, in some cases even more so than by their personal preferences. When three judges of the same party sit together, for example, they tend to vote more ideologically, a phenomenon that SSES refer to as "ideological amplification."[90] Where a judge of one party sits with two judges of another party, the minority judge tends to vote more like the majority judges. The authors label this effect "ideological dampening."[91] In addition, SSES find that judges are more likely to uphold the agency interpretations of administrations headed by members of the same political party as the President who appointed the judge to the bench (i.e., judges appointed by Republican Presidents are more likely to uphold agency interpretations by Republican administrations, and Democratic-appointed judges are more likely to uphold agency interpretations by Democratic administrations).

In a spirited response to the articles by Revesz, and by Cross and Tiller (and anticipating the later findings by SSES), then-Chief Judge Harry T. Edwards of the D.C. Circuit challenged the conclusions finding strategic and ideologically based judging.[92] Edwards argued that the claimed "panel composition effects" might reflect deliberative judicial processes rather than ideologically motivated decision making. Edwards writes:

> My own view is that if panel composition turns out to have a "moderating" effect on judges' voting behavior, this is a sign that panel members are behaving collegially: that is, they are discussing the case with each other and reaching a mutually acceptable judgment based on their shared sense of the proper outcome. In such a collegial deliberative process, we would expect to find that the presumed political views of different judges push the outcome towards the center of the spectrum (where there is a spectrum). The

88 Frank B. Cross & Emerson H. Tiller, *Judicial Partisanship and Obedience to Legal Doctrine: Whistleblowing on the Federal Courts of Appeals*, 107 YALE L.J. 2155 (1998).

89 CASS R. SUNSTEIN, DAVID SCHKADE, LISA M. ELLMAN & ANDRES SAWICKI, ARE JUDGES POLITICAL? AN EMPIRICAL ANALYSIS OF THE FEDERAL JUDICIARY (2006).

90 *Id.* at 9.

91 *Id.* at 8–9.

92 Harry T. Edwards, *Collegiality and Decision-Making on the D.C. Circuit*, 84 VA. L. REV. 1335 (1998).

Revesz and the Cross and Tiller studies are both consistent with the phenomenon of collegiality.

In explaining my view of collegiality I start with three observations drawn from many years of working and talking with my colleagues on the D.C. Circuit. First, judges on my court who are convinced that the law requires a certain result in a case do not decline to take a position simply to avoid registering a dissent. Second, judges who are in the majority and convinced that the law requires a certain result do not moderate their views because they fear that a dissent will somehow draw attention to flaws in the majority opinion. Finally, the judges on a panel usually agree on the correct result in a case. And when there is initially no clear view as to what the judgment should be in a particular case, we normally work hard in our deliberations to find the correct result.[93]

Are you more persuaded by the explanation that judges vote strategically and ideologically or by Judge Edwards's response that the statistical findings demonstrate collegiality and compromise? Is there any empirical test that might distinguish Judge Edwards's theory of collegiality, on one hand, and the ideological and strategic-voting theories offered by Revesz and Cross and Tiller, on the other?

IV. APPLICATIONS

A. Deference to Agency Decision Making

Perhaps the most crucial and contested legal issue respecting agency decision making involves the degree of deference owed by courts to agency interpretations of enabling statutes. Two general approaches have been offered, the "*Chevron* standard" and the "*Skidmore* standard," although as we will also see, there are a variety of nuances and exceptions to the doctrines that these cases announce. As you read the following two cases, consider the extent to which public choice theory provides support for one standard over the other and the extent to which public choice insights inform, or should inform, the Supreme Court's decision.

CHEVRON U.S.A. INC. V. NATURAL RESOURCES DEFENSE COUNCIL[94]

Chevron U.S.A. Inc. v. Natural Resources Defense Council, Inc. is one of the most important Supreme Court cases of recent decades. *Chevron* arose in response to new regulations established by the EPA interpreting the Clean Air Act. The specific issue in *Chevron* was review of the decision by the EPA to amend its earlier regulatory definition of a "stationary source" of air pollution, which had defined each individual source of pollution in a plant (e.g., each smokestack) as a "stationary source," to instead allow a state to treat the entire plant as a "stationary source." The new regulation produced a figurative "bubble" over the entire plant. As a result, an existing plant that contained several pollution-emitting devices could install or modify one piece of equipment without

---

[93] *Id.* at 1358–59 (footnote omitted).

[94] 467 U.S. 837 (1984).

meeting the permit conditions if the alteration would not increase the total emissions from the plant. The Court held that the change in the definition was permissible. Justice Stevens, writing for a unanimous Supreme Court, wrote:

> When a court reviews an agency's construction of the statute which it administers, it is confronted with two questions. First, always, is the question whether Congress has directly spoken to the precise question at issue. If the intent of Congress is clear, that is the end of the matter; for the court, as well as the agency, must give effect to the unambiguously expressed intent of Congress. If, however, the court determines Congress has not directly addressed the precise question at issue, the court does not simply impose its own construction on the statute, as would be necessary in the absence of an administrative interpretation. Rather, if the statute is silent or ambiguous with respect to the specific issue, the question for the court is whether the agency's answer is based on a permissible construction of the statute.
>
> "The power of an administrative agency to administer a congressionally created . . . program necessarily requires the formulation of policy and the making of rules to fill any gap left, implicitly or explicitly, by Congress." If Congress has explicitly left a gap for the agency to fill, there is an express delegation of authority to the agency to elucidate a specific provision of the statute by regulation. Such legislative regulations are given controlling weight unless they are arbitrary, capricious, or manifestly contrary to the statute. Sometimes the legislative delegation to an agency on a particular question is implicit rather than explicit. In such a case, a court may not substitute its own construction of a statutory provision for a reasonable interpretation made by the administrator of an agency.[95]

After concluding that the regulation was not inconsistent with the statutory language or legislative history of the Clean Air Act, the Court also specifically noted that it would not second-guess the policy conclusions of the EPA:

> The arguments over policy that are advanced in the parties' briefs create the impression that respondents are now waging in a judicial forum a specific policy battle which they ultimately lost in the agency and in the 32 jurisdictions opting for the "bubble concept," but one which was never waged in the Congress. Such policy arguments are more properly addressed to legislators or administrators, not to judges.
>
> In these cases, the Administrator's interpretation represents a reasonable accommodation of manifestly competing interests and is entitled to deference: the regulatory scheme is technical and complex, the agency considered the matter in a detailed and reasoned fashion, and the decision involves reconciling conflicting policies. Congress intended to accommodate both interests, but did not do so itself on the level of specificity presented by these cases. Perhaps that body consciously desired the Administrator to strike the balance at this level, thinking that those with great expertise and charged with responsibility for administering the provision would be in a better position to do so; perhaps it

[95] *Id.* at 842–44 (citation and footnotes omitted).

simply did not consider the question at this level; and perhaps Congress was unable to forge a coalition on either side of the question, and those on each side decided to take their chances with the scheme devised by the agency. For judicial purposes, it matters not which of these things occurred.

Judges are not experts in the field, and are not part of either political branch of the Government. Courts must, in some cases, reconcile competing political interests, but not on the basis of the judges' personal policy preferences. In contrast, an agency to which Congress has delegated policymaking responsibilities may, within the limits of that delegation, properly rely upon the incumbent administration's views of wise policy to inform its judgments. While agencies are not directly accountable to the people, the Chief Executive is, and it is entirely appropriate for this political branch of the Government to make such policy choices—resolving the competing interests which Congress itself either inadvertently did not resolve, or intentionally left to be resolved by the agency charged with the administration of the statute in light of everyday realities.

When a challenge to an agency construction of a statutory provision, fairly conceptualized, really centers on the wisdom of the agency's policy, rather than whether it is a reasonable choice within a gap left open by Congress, the challenge must fail. In such a case, federal judges—who have no constituency—have a duty to respect legitimate policy choices made by those who do. The responsibilities for assessing the wisdom of such policy choices and resolving the struggle between competing views of the public interest are not judicial ones: "Our Constitution vests such responsibilities in the political branches."

We hold that the EPA's definition of the term "source" is a permissible construction of the statute which seeks to accommodate progress in reducing air pollution with economic growth.[96]

UNITED STATES V. MEAD CORP.[97]

In *United States v. Mead Corp.*, the Supreme Court addressed the scope of *Chevron*. The issue in *Mead* was whether a tariff classification ruling by the United States Customs Service should be afforded *Chevron* deference. Justice Souter, writing for the *Mead* majority, concluded that under the facts as presented in *Mead*, *Chevron* deference would not apply. Instead, the Court applied the doctrine of *Skidmore v. Swift & Co.*,[98] that "the ruling is eligible to claim respect according to its persuasiveness."[99] The Court drew the distinction as follows:

> We granted certiorari in order to consider the limits of *Chevron* deference owed to administrative practice in applying a statute. We hold that administrative implementation of a particular statutory provision qualifies for *Chevron*

[96] *Id.* at 864–66 (citation and footnotes omitted).

[97] 533 U.S. 218 (2001).

[98] 323 U.S. 134 (1944).

[99] 533 U.S. at 221.

deference when it appears that Congress delegated authority to the agency generally to make rules carrying the force of law, and that the agency interpretation claiming deference was promulgated in the exercise of that authority. Delegation of such authority may be shown in a variety of ways, as by an agency's power to engage in adjudication or notice-and-comment rulemaking, or by some other indication of a comparable congressional intent. The Customs ruling at issue here fails to qualify, although the possibility that it deserves some deference under *Skidmore* leads us to vacate and remand.

When Congress has "explicitly left a gap for an agency to fill, there is an express delegation of authority to the agency to elucidate a specific provision of the statute by regulation," and any ensuing regulation is binding in the courts unless procedurally defective, arbitrary or capricious in substance, or manifestly contrary to the statute. But whether or not they enjoy any express delegation of authority on a particular question, agencies charged with applying a statute necessarily make all sorts of interpretive choices, and while not all of those choices bind judges to follow them, they certainly may influence courts facing questions the agencies have already answered. "[T]he well-reasoned views of the agencies implementing a statute 'constitute a body of experience and informed judgment to which courts and litigants may properly resort for guidance,' " and "[w]e have long recognized that considerable weight should be accorded to an executive department's construction of a statutory scheme it is entrusted to administer. . . ." The fair measure of deference to an agency administering its own statute has been understood to vary with circumstances, and courts have looked to the degree of the agency's care, its consistency, formality, and relative expertness, and to the persuasiveness of the agency's position. The approach has produced a spectrum of judicial responses, from great respect at one end, to near indifference at the other. Justice Jackson summed things up in *Skidmore* v. *Swift & Co.*:

> "The weight [accorded to an administrative] judgment in a particular case will depend upon the thoroughness evident in its consideration, the validity of its reasoning, its consistency with earlier and later pronouncements, and all those factors which give it power to persuade, if lacking power to control."[100]

The Court concluded:

Underlying the position we take here, like the position expressed by Justice Scalia in dissent, is a choice about the best way to deal with an inescapable feature of the body of congressional legislation authorizing administrative action. That feature is the great variety of ways in which the laws invest the Government's administrative arms with discretion, and with procedures for exercising it, in giving meaning to Acts of Congress. Implementation of a statute may occur in formal adjudication or the choice to defend against judicial challenge; it may occur in a central board or office or in dozens of enforcement agencies dotted across the country; its institutional lawmaking may be confined

[100] *Id.* at 226–28 (citations and footnotes omitted).

> to the resolution of minute detail or extend to legislative rulemaking on matters intentionally left by Congress to be worked out at the agency level.
>
> Although we all accept the position that the Judiciary should defer to at least some of this multifarious administrative action, we have to decide how to take account of the great range of its variety. If the primary objective is to simplify the judicial process of giving or withholding deference, then the diversity of statutes authorizing discretionary administrative action must be declared irrelevant or minimized. If, on the other hand, it is simply implausible that Congress intended such a broad range of statutory authority to produce only two varieties of administrative action, demanding either *Chevron* deference or none at all, then the breadth of the spectrum of possible agency action must be taken into account. Justice Scalia's first priority over the years has been to limit and simplify. The Court's choice has been to tailor deference to variety. This acceptance of the range of statutory variation has led the Court to recognize more than one variety of judicial deference, just as the Court has recognized a variety of indicators that Congress would expect *Chevron* deference.[101]

Writing in dissent, Justice Scalia argued that *Skidmore* deference to agency action was, among other things, inconsistent with the purposes of permitting delegation in the first place, namely to allow Congress to rely on agency expertise in crafting regulations. Scalia expressed the further concern that the *Mead* rule would motivate strategic timing and styling of agency decision making. As shown in the next case excerpt, this concern was largely ameliorated by *National Cable and Telecommunications Ass'n v. Brand X Internet Services*.[102] Scalia stated that a "practical effect of today's opinion will be an artificially induced increase in informal rulemaking," given that "formal adjudication is not an option but must be mandated by statute or constitutional command." Scalia further stated:

> [The] majority's approach will lead to the ossification of large portions of our statutory law. Where *Chevron* applies, statutory ambiguities remain ambiguities subject to the agency's ongoing clarification. They create a space, so to speak, for the exercise of continuing agency discretion. As *Chevron* itself held, the Environmental Protection Agency can interpret "stationary source" to mean a single smokestack, can later replace that interpretation with the "bubble concept" embracing an entire plant, and if that proves undesirable can return again to the original interpretation. For the indeterminately large number of statutes taken out of *Chevron* by today's decision, however, ambiguity (and hence flexibility) will cease with the first judicial resolution. *Skidmore* deference gives the agency's current position some vague and uncertain amount of respect, but it does not, like *Chevron*, *leave* the matter within the control of the Executive Branch for the future. Once the court has spoken, it becomes *unlawful* for the agency to take a contradictory position; the statute now *says* what the court has prescribed. . . .

---

[101] *Id.* at 235–37 (footnotes omitted).

[102] 545 U.S. 967 (2005).

> One might respond that such ossification would not result if the agency were simply to readopt its interpretation, after a court reviewing it under *Skidmore* had rejected it, by repromulgating it through one of the *Chevron*-eligible procedural formats approved by the Court today. Approving this procedure would be a landmark abdication of judicial power. It is worlds apart from *Chevron* proper, where the court does not *purport* to give the statute a judicial interpretation—except in identifying the scope of the statutory ambiguity, as to which the court's judgment is final and irreversible. . . . By contrast, under this view, the reviewing court will not be holding the agency's authoritative interpretation within the scope of the ambiguity; but will be holding that the agency has not used the "delegation-conferring" procedures, and that the court must therefore *interpret the statute on its own*—but subject to reversal if and when the agency uses the proper procedures.
>
> . . . I know of no case, in the entire history of the federal courts, in which we have allowed a judicial interpretation of a statute to be set aside by an agency—or have allowed a lower court to render an interpretation of a statute subject to correction by an agency. . . .

Scalia concluded:

> It was possible to live with the indeterminacy of *Skidmore* deference in earlier times. But in an era when federal statutory law administered by federal agencies is pervasive, and when the ambiguities (intended or unintended) that those statutes contain are innumerable, totality-of-the-circumstances *Skidmore* deference is a recipe for uncertainty, unpredictability, and endless litigation. To condemn a vast body of agency action to that regime (all except rulemaking, formal (and informal?) adjudication, and whatever else might now and then be included within today's intentionally vague formulation of affirmative congressional intent to "delegate") is irresponsible.[103]

At the time of *Mead,* Scalia was almost certainly correct in asserting that "no case in the entire history of the federal courts . . . allowed a judicial interpretation of a statute to be set aside by an agency." And yet, this is precisely the effect of *Brand X*, which follows.

NATIONAL CABLE AND TELECOMMUNICATIONS ASS'N V. BRAND X INTERNET SERVICES[104]

In his majority opinion, Justice Thomas described the case issue as follows:

> Title II of the Communications Act of 1934, 48 Stat. 1064, as amended, 47 U.S.C. § 151 *et seq.*, subjects all providers of "telecommunications servic[e]" to mandatory common-carrier regulation, § 153(44). In the order under review, the Federal Communications Commission concluded that cable companies that sell broadband Internet service do not provide "telecommunications servic[e]" as the Communications Act defines that term, and hence are exempt from mandatory common-carrier regulation under Title II. We must decide

---

[103] 533 U.S. at 246–50 (Scalia, J., dissenting) (citations omitted).

[104] 545 U.S. 967 (2005).

whether that conclusion is a lawful construction of the Communications Act under *Chevron U.S.A. Inc.* v. *Natural Resources Defense Council, Inc.*, and the Administrative Procedure Act, 5 U.S.C. § 555 *et seq.* We hold that it is.

Resolving the issue implicated an open question that Justice Scalia addressed in his *Mead* dissent. Justice Scalia claimed that *Mead* posed two important risks. First, it risked disallowing Congress to rely on delegation for the primary reason of benefiting from expertise. Second, and more relevant to *Brand* X, *Mead* risked ossifying judicial statutory construction on the ground that if the judiciary resolved an issue contrary to a subsequent agency interpretation, "no case, in the entire history of the federal courts, [has] allowed a judicial interpretation of a statute to be set aside by an agency—or . . . allowed a lower court to render an interpretation of a statute subject to correction by an agency. . . . There is, in short, no way to avoid the ossification of federal law that today's opinion sets in motion." The *Brand X* case squarely addressed this issue and in doing so, avoided the second problem Scalia ascribed to *Mead.*

In *Brand X,* the United States Court of Appeals for the Ninth Circuit had issued a contrary interpretation on the substantive meaning of the relevant provision of the Communications Act as compared with a later, contrary ruling by the FCC. The Ninth Circuit then reasoned that its interpretation was necessarily binding against the later agency interpretation. Justice Thomas explained the basis for disallowing the Ninth Circuit to deny *Chevron* deference as follows, and also for applying deference despite agency inconsistency:

> We first consider whether we should apply *Chevron*'s framework to the Commission's interpretation of the term "telecommunications service." We conclude that we should. We also conclude that the Court of Appeals should have done the same, instead of following the contrary construction it adopted in [*AT&T Corp.* v.] *Portland.*
>
> . . . .
>
> . . . Agency inconsistency is not a basis for declining to analyze the agency's interpretation under the *Chevron* framework. Unexplained inconsistency is, at most, a reason for holding an interpretation to be an arbitrary and capricious change from agency practice under the Administrative Procedure Act. . . . For if the agency adequately explains the reasons for a reversal of policy, "change is not invalidating, since the whole point of *Chevron* is to leave the discretion provided by the ambiguities of a statute with the implementing agency." . . . That is no doubt why in *Chevron* itself, this Court deferred to an agency interpretation that was a recent reversal of agency policy. . . We therefore have no difficulty concluding that *Chevron* applies.
>
> B
>
> The Court of Appeals declined to apply *Chevron* because it thought the Commission's interpretation of the Communications Act foreclosed by the conflicting construction of the Act it had adopted in *Portland.* . . . It based that holding on the assumption that *Portland*'s construction overrode the Commission's, regardless of whether *Portland* had held the statute to be unambiguous. . . . That reasoning was incorrect.

A court's prior judicial construction of a statute trumps an agency construction otherwise entitled to *Chevron* deference only if the prior court decision holds that its construction follows from the unambiguous terms of the statute and thus leaves no room for agency discretion. This principle follows from *Chevron* itself. *Chevron* established a "presumption that Congress, when it left ambiguity in a statute meant for implementation by an agency, understood that the ambiguity would be resolved, first and foremost, by the agency, and desired the agency (rather than the courts) to possess whatever degree of discretion the ambiguity allows." *Smiley [v. Citibank]*. Yet allowing a judicial precedent to foreclose an agency from interpreting an ambiguous statute, as the Court of Appeals assumed it could, would allow a court's interpretation to override an agency's. *Chevron*'s premise is that it is for agencies, not courts, to fill statutory gaps. . . . The better rule is to hold judicial interpretations contained in precedents to the same demanding *Chevron* step one standard that applies if the court is reviewing the agency's construction on a blank slate: Only a judicial precedent holding that the statute unambiguously forecloses the agency's interpretation, and therefore contains no gap for the agency to fill, displaces a conflicting agency construction.

A contrary rule would produce anomalous results. It would mean that whether an agency's interpretation of an ambiguous statute is entitled to *Chevron* deference would turn on the order in which the interpretations issue: If the court's construction came first, its construction would prevail, whereas if the agency's came first, the agency's construction would command *Chevron* deference. Yet whether Congress has delegated to an agency the authority to interpret a statute does not depend on the order in which the judicial and administrative constructions occur. The Court of Appeals' rule, moreover, would "lead to the ossification of large portions of our statutory law," *Mead* (Scalia, J., dissenting), by precluding agencies from revising unwise judicial constructions of ambiguous statutes. Neither *Chevron* nor the doctrine of *stare decisis* requires these haphazard results.[105]

KING V. BURWELL[106]

The tenuous balance between *Chevron* and *Mead/Skidmore* deference was further affected by two additional cases issued during the Obama administration. Unlike *Brand X*, however, these cases scaled back the deference that judges pay to administrative agencies, at least in some cases. In general, these cases suggest that where an administrative regulation touches on a matter of particularly large public or social import, the Supreme Court will infer that Congress was less likely to defer to agency decision making. The contours of this relatively new doctrine remain unclear. It is also unclear whether these cases mark a more general trend away from judicial deference to administrative agencies or are, instead, isolated exceptions that rest on their own idiosyncratic facts.

---

[105] 545 U.S. 980–83.

[106] 135 S. Ct. 2480 (2015).

King v. Burwell involved a challenge to the Patient Protection and Affordable Care Act (variously referred to as the "Affordable Care Act," the "ACA," or "Obamacare"), a flagship piece of legislation passed into law during the early years of the Obama Administration. The law survived a constitutional challenge in 2012 when the court held in *National Federation of Independent Businesses v. Sebelius* that the so-called individual mandate, which required individuals who were not otherwise covered by insurance to purchase it or to make a payment to the IRS, was a valid exercise of Congress's taxing power.[107]

The ACA also required that each state establish an "Exchange" where people could shop for insurance. The Exchange could be created in either of two ways. First, a state could establish an exchange for itself (a "State Exchange"). And second, "if a State nevertheless chooses not to establish its own Exchange, the Act provides that the Secretary of Health and Human Services 'shall . . . establish and operate such Exchange within the State" (a "Federal Exchange").[108] To make health insurance policies more affordable, the ACA provided for refundable tax for individuals with household income within 100 to 400 percent of the federally defined poverty line for individuals who purchased an insurance plan through "an Exchange established by the State."

The issue in *King v. Burwell* was whether the ACA's tax credits are available in states that chose not to establish a State exchange, but rather relied upon the establishment of the Federal exchange. The question arose from the following provision of the ACA: "the amount of the tax credit depends in part on whether the taxpayer has enrolled in an insurance plan through "an Exchange established by the State under section 1311 of the Patient Protection and Affordable Care Act."[109]

By the time of *King v. Burwell*, only sixteen states and the District of Columbia had established State Exchanges; the other thirty-four states elected to rely on the Federal Exchange operating within them created by HHS.[110] The case issue was whether individuals who purchased insurance policies on the Federal Exchange were eligible for the tax credits under the ACA given that the Exchange in which they purchased insurance was not "an Exchange established by the State."

The IRS answered in the affirmative, ruling that the tax credits remained available for insurance purchased on either a State or Federal exchange. "As relevant here, the IRS Rule provides that a taxpayer is eligible for a tax credit if he enrolled in an insurance plan through 'an Exchange,' which is defined as "an Exchange serving the individual market . . . regardless of whether the Exchange is established and operated by a State . . . or by HHS.' "[111]

Four residents of Virginia, which relied upon the Federal Exchange, sued. They claimed that Virginia's Federal Exchange did not qualify as "an Exchange established by

---

[107] 567 U.S. 519 (2012).

[108] 135 S. Ct. at 2487.

[109] *Id.*

[110] For Plan Year 2018, there are twelve state-based exchanges and five state-based exchanges on the federal platform; the remaining states fully rely on the Federally-facilitated Exchange. *State-Based Exchanges*, CTRS. FOR MEDICARE & MEDICAID SERVS. (Sept. 15, 2017), https://www.cms.gov/CCIIO/Resources/Fact-Sheets-and-FAQs/state-marketplaces.html.

[111] 135 S. Ct. at 2487.

the State" and that, as a result, they are not eligible for the tax credit. Moreover, if they were not eligible for the tax credit, then the cost of buying insurance would exceed eight percent of their annual income, thereby exempting them from the ACA's individual mandate requirement.

The threshold issue in the case was whether under the *Chevron* doctrine the Supreme Court should defer to the IRS's interpretation of the ACA. Chief Justice Roberts held that it should not:

> When analyzing an agency's interpretation of a statute, we often apply the two-step framework announced in *Chevron*. Under that framework, we ask whether the statute is ambiguous and, if so, whether the agency's interpretation is reasonable. This approach "is premised on the theory that a statute's ambiguity constitutes an implicit delegation from Congress to the agency to fill in the statutory gaps." *FDA v. Brown & Williamson Tobacco Corp.* "In extraordinary cases, however, there may be reason to hesitate before concluding that Congress has intended such an implicit delegation."
>
> This is one of those cases. The tax credits are among the Act's key reforms, involving billions of dollars in spending each year and affecting the price of health insurance for millions of people. Whether those credits are available on Federal Exchanges is thus a question of deep "economic and political significance" that is central to this statutory scheme; had Congress wished to assign that question to an agency, it surely would have done so expressly. *Utility Air Regulatory Group v. EPA* (quoting *Brown & Williamson*). It is especially unlikely that Congress would have delegated this decision to the IRS, which has no expertise in crafting health insurance policy of this sort. This is not a case for the IRS.[112]

The court went on to hold that even though the language in question seemingly limited the tax credits to policies purchased on a State Exchange, the overall purposes of the law made it clear that Congress intended the tax credits to apply to policies purchased on Federal Exchanges as well. According to Chief Justice Roberts, the universal application of the tax credits was necessary to effectuate the overall design of the law.[113] First, the ACA sought to provide for "guaranteed issue" (meaning coverage for preexisting conditions) and "community rating" requirements (creating a system of cross-subsidies from healthier to less healthy individuals to stabilize the risk pool and keep down premiums for higher risk individuals). Second, the Act required individuals to maintain health insurance coverage or to make a payment to the IRS, the so-called individual mandate.[114]

Chief Justice Roberts reasoned that the requirement to purchase coverage or make a payment to the IRS was necessary to offset the adverse selection problem that would otherwise arise from ensuring coverage for preexisting conditions by forcing healthier

---

[112] *Id.* at 2489. Both *Brown & Williamson*, 529 U.S. 120 (2000), and *Utility Air Regulatory Group*, 134 S. Ct. 2427 (2014), are discussed *infra* in Chapter 20.

[113] 135 S. Ct. at 2486–87.

[114] This aspect was repealed in the Tax Cut and Jobs Act of 2017, Pub. L. No. 115–97, § 11081, 131 Stat. 2054.

individuals into the risk pool. Finally, the tax credit system was designed to encourage individuals to actually purchase insurance. The Chief Justice maintained that disallowing the extension of the tax credits to Federal Exchanges would undermine the system in two ways: First, it would necessarily raise premiums; and second, it would increase the cost of purchasing insurance to greater than eight percent of income for many people and, counterintuitively, relieve those individuals of the obligation to comply with the individual mandate, thereby risking a "death spiral" for the overall system. According to Chief Justice Roberts, the tax credits were so central to the overall scheme that the statute should be construed to make the credits available to insurance purchased on Federal Exchanges.

Chief Justice Roberts closed by stating:

> In a democracy, the power to make the law rests with those chosen by the people. Our role is more confined—"to say what the law is." *Marbury v. Madison*. That is easier in some cases than in others. But in every case we must respect the role of the Legislature, and take care not to undo what it has done. A fair reading of legislation demands a fair understanding of the legislative plan.
>
> Congress passed the Affordable Care Act to improve health insurance markets, not to destroy them. If at all possible, we must interpret the Act in a way that is consistent with the former, and avoids the latter. Section 36B can fairly be read consistent with what we see as Congress's plan, and that is the reading we adopt.[115]

Justice Scalia authored a dissent, joined by Justices Thomas and Alito. According to Justice Scalia, the language of the statute was unambiguous:

> The Court holds that when the Patient Protection and Affordable Care Act says "Exchange established by the State" it means "Exchange established by the State or the Federal Government." That is of course quite absurd, and the Court's 21 pages of explanation make it no less so.[116]

He continued:

> Words no longer have meaning if an Exchange that is not established by a State is "established by the State." It is hard to come up with a clearer way to limit tax credits to state Exchanges than to use the words "established by the State." And it is hard to come up with a reason to include the words "by the State" other than the purpose of limiting credits to state Exchanges. "[T]he plain, obvious, and rational meaning of a statute is always to be preferred to any curious, narrow, hidden sense that nothing but the exigency of a hard case and the ingenuity and study of an acute and powerful intellect would discover." . . . Under all the usual rules of interpretation, in short, the Government should lose this case. But normal rules of interpretation seem always to yield to the overriding principle of the present Court: The Affordable Care Act must be saved.[117]

---

[115] *Id.* at 2496.

[116] *Id.* at 2496 (Scalia, J., dissenting).

[117] *Id.* at 2497.

Justice Scalia further discussed the majority's policy argument that the ACA sought to further three interrelated purposes for which eligibility for the tax credit on both State and Federal Exchanges was necessary. Justice Scalia argued that Congress also intended a *fourth* purpose: A preference that the exchanges be set up and run by the states, rather than the federal government. Justice Scalia noted that establishing and operating an insurance exchange is expensive and complicated, and thus Congress might have thought it necessary to provide incentives to states to establish an Exchange:

> A State would have much less reason to take on these burdens if its citizens could receive tax credits no matter who establishes its Exchange. (Now that the Internal Revenue Service has interpreted § 36B to authorize tax credits everywhere, by the way, 34 States have failed to set up their own Exchanges.) So even if making credits available on all Exchanges advances the goal of improving healthcare markets, it frustrates the goal of encouraging state involvement in the implementation of the Act. This is what justifies going out of our way to read "established by the State" to mean "established by the State or not established by the State"?[118]

Justice Scalia also took issue with Chief Justice Roberts's claim that in interpreting certain statutes that the Court deems of particular public import, the Court should provide less deference than for general statutes:

> Today's opinion changes the usual rules of statutory interpretation for the sake of the Affordable Care Act. That, alas, is not a novelty. In *National Federation of Independent Business v. Sebelius*, this Court revised major components of the statute in order to save them from unconstitutionality. The Act that Congress passed provides that every individual "shall" maintain insurance or else pay a "penalty." This Court, however, saw that the Commerce Clause does not authorize a federal mandate to buy health insurance. So it rewrote the mandate-cum-penalty as a tax. The Act that Congress passed also requires every State to accept an expansion of its Medicaid program, or else risk losing all Medicaid funding. This Court, however, saw that the Spending Clause does not authorize this coercive condition. So it rewrote the law to withhold only the incremental funds associated with the Medicaid expansion. Having transformed two major parts of the law, the Court today has turned its attention to a third. The Act that Congress passed makes tax credits available only on an "Exchange established by the State." This Court, however, concludes that this limitation would prevent the rest of the Act from working as well as hoped. So it rewrites the law to make tax credits available everywhere. We should start calling this law SCOTUScare.
>
> Perhaps the Patient Protection and Affordable Care Act will attain the enduring status of the Social Security Act or the Taft-Hartley Act; perhaps not. But this Court's two decisions on the Act will surely be remembered through the years. The somersaults of statutory interpretation they have performed ("penalty" means tax, "further [Medicaid] payments to the State" means only incremental Medicaid payments to the State, "established by the State" means

[118] *Id.* at 2504.

> not established by the State) will be cited by litigants endlessly, to the confusion of honest jurisprudence. And the cases will publish forever the discouraging truth that the Supreme Court of the United States favors some laws over others, and is prepared to do whatever it takes to uphold and assist its favorites.[119]

DISCUSSION QUESTIONS

1. From a public choice perspective, as a general rule, which form of deference, *Chevron* or *Skidmore*, makes the most sense? Does the *Chevron* Court assume that when Congress delegates it does so based on the traditional model of delegation, meaning to benefit from agency expertise, rather than the strategic models of delegation, implying an effort to take credit for desired outcomes and pass blame for problematic ones, as some public choice theorists suggest? In determining the deference owed to an agency interpretation, should it matter why Congress delegates? If it should, how would a court determine congressional motive?

2. The *Chevron* Court concludes that, on the case facts, the reasons for the Congressional delegation of rulemaking authority is unknown: Congress might have done so to benefit from the EPA's expertise, without having considered the policy question ultimately resolved by EPA and called into question in the *Chevron* case, or after failing to resolve competing interest-group pressures, with the result of having interests "on each side . . . take their chances with the scheme devised by the agency," a sort of regulatory "lottery."[120] More importantly, the *Chevron* Court concludes that the reason why Congress chose to delegate is irrelevant: "For judicial purposes, it matters not which of these things occurred." Do you agree? If you think that the reasons for the delegation should matter, do you also think that judges are capable of determining congressional motivations? Assuming that Courts can distinguish delegations for "good" reasons (such as reliance on agency expertise) from "bad" reasons (following interest-group capture or to allow interest groups to play the "delegation lottery") should the degree of judicial deference to agency decision making turn on the quality of the reasons for the delegation? Why or why not? If Congress delegates in order to avoid blame for enacting controversial policies, should that have any implications for the appropriate degree of deference owed to an agency? Should judges try to prevent Congress from delegating if the reason for doing so is to avoid political accountability? If not, should judges try to articulate rules that heighten agency accountability?

3. Prior to becoming a Judge (and later Justice), Justice Scalia edited the journal *Regulation*, a public-choice-influenced academic journal that studies regulation and the regulatory process, suggesting at least some formal familiarity with public choice scholarship. Before joining the judiciary, Justice Breyer also had considerable scholarly familiarity with regulation and public choice scholarship. Yet as illustrated in *Mead*—where Breyer joined the majority opinion, while Scalia, writing alone, dissented—these Justices disagree on fundamental questions of judicial deference to agency decision making. To what extent, if at all, does their disagreement arise from differences in their understanding of the regulatory

---

[119] *Id.* at 2506–07 (citations omitted).

[120] For an analysis of delegation as a form of "regulatory lottery" favored by interest groups and Congress when Congress is unable to assemble a successful political coalition, see Aranson, Gellhorn & Robinson, *supra* note 61.

process and the ability of the judiciary to improve it? Can either of their views be said to be more compatible with the insights of public choice theory? Do either of their views tend to confirm Merrill's hypothesis about the influence of public choice theory on judicial doctrine? Might a judge's views on the wisdom of *Chevron* deference versus *Mead/Skidmore* deference depend upon whether that judge is most persuaded by the public interest, capture theory, or the economic theory of regulation? In this context, consider that one of Justice Breyer's first jobs out of law school was as special counsel and then chief counsel of the U.S. Senate Committee on the Judiciary, where he worked closely with liberal committee chairman Senator Edward M. Kennedy to pass the Airline Deregulation Act that closed the Civil Aeronautics Board.[121] Other supporters of deregulation at the time included consumer advocate Ralph Nader. Although there is little Democratic political support for deregulation, can you see why capture theory might lead Democrats to support a deregulatory agenda?

4. Justice Scalia argues that the *Skidmore* doctrine provides agencies with an incentive to "rush out barebones, ambiguous rules construing statutory ambiguities, which they can then in turn further clarify through informal rulings entitled to judicial respect." Scalia's concern implicitly assumes that agencies act strategically in the manner and timing of issuance of regulations. Is this statement consistent with public interest theories of delegation? Public choice theories? If agencies do act strategically in the issuance of regulations, should that affect whether, or the degree to which, judicial deference should be granted?

5. Which of the various agency delegation theories is most consistent with *Mead*? Do you agree with Elhauge that the combined *Chevron/Mead* regime promotes enactable preferences by allowing rules to develop consistently with the best available proxy for contemporary (but not necessarily contemporaneous) congressional intent[122]? Why or why not? Do you agree that it is an appropriate normative benchmark? Why or why not?

6. Do any of the theories of delegation discussed here shed any light on Chief Justice Roberts's view that judges should be less deferential to the decisions of administrative agencies with respect to statutory schemes that are seen as holding particular public importance?

7. One implication of the Supreme Court's decision in *King* is that by refusing to defer to the regulation issued by the IRS, the Court essentially freezes into the statutory language the requirement that tax credits be made available for policies purchased on either a State or Federal Exchange. In 2016, Republican Donald Trump was elected President. During his campaign, Trump expressed substantial criticism of the ACA and further expressed a desire to repeal and replace it. Repealing and replacing a major piece of legislation can take years, if it is successful at all. Note that because of the Court's ruling in *King*, President Trump's discretion to revoke the tax credit is limited. Had the Supreme Court deferred to the IRS's rule, by contrast, the Trump Administration would have been able to unilaterally revoke the tax credit, and if Chief Justice Roberts is correct, that would have started a "death spiral" for the ACA. Given these dynamics, does limiting judicial deference to administrative agencies have either a pro- or anti-regulatory bias, at least as applied to *King*? Note in this context McNollgast's argument that Democrats supported the APA in 1946 in order to block or slow a feared *deregulatory* agenda by a Republican President and Congress. As part of a major tax overhaul, the Trump administration repealed the "individual mandate," a key conceptual piece of the ACA. How, if at all, does that relate to the proper scope of agency-deference rules?

---

[121] *See* Adam Thierer, *Who'll Really Benefit from Net Neutrality Regulation?*, CBS NEWS (Dec. 21, 2010), https://www.cbsnews.com/news/opinion-wholl-really-benefit-from-net-neutrality-regulation/.

[122] *See supra* Chapter 18.

8. Soon after being inaugurated, President Donald Trump appointed Neil Gorsuch to the Supreme Court. Gorsuch is widely perceived as being skeptical of the *Chevron* doctrine.[123] Justice Clarence Thomas has also been critical of *Chevron* deference, arguing that, as the doctrine has evolved, it has come to empower administrative agencies to make fundamental policy decisions, which he sees as a task properly for Congress. In his concurring opinion in the case of *Michigan v. EPA*, addressing a challenge to an EPA rulemaking, Justice Thomas wrote:

> These cases bring into bold relief the scope of the potentially unconstitutional delegations we have come to countenance in the name of *Chevron* deference. What EPA claims for itself here is not the power to make political judgments in implementing Congress' policies, nor even the power to make tradeoffs between competing policy goals set by Congress. It is the power to decide—without any particular fidelity to the text—which policy goals EPA wishes to pursue. Should EPA wield its vast powers over electric utilities to protect public health? A pristine environment? Economic security?[124]

Do the theories of delegation discussed in this chapter provide any help in answering the normative question as to how much deference courts should provide to agency decision making?

9. In Justice Thomas's opinion in *Brand X*, he argues that the ruling is essential to avoid the anomaly that an administrative interpretation of an ambiguous provision within its scope, followed by a judicial ruling, could lead to opposite policy as compared with the reverse sequence. This dynamic resembles the problem of path dependence described in Chapter 13. Are these the same analytical problem, or despite the surface similarities, do they operate differently? Consider that in this context, the agency interpretation controls regardless of ordering as a consequence of *Chevron* deference. Does that break the cycle that otherwise would appear in the path-dependent outcome? Why or why not?

---

[123] *See* Gutierrez-Brizuela v. Lynch, 834 F.3d 1142, 1149 (10th Cir. 2016) (Gorsuch, J., concurring) ("[T]he fact is *Chevron* and *Brand X* permit executive bureaucracies to swallow huge amounts of core judicial and legislative power and concentrate federal power in a way that seems more than a little difficult to square with the Constitution of the framers' design."); Ilya Somin, Opinion, *Gorsuch Is Right About* Chevron *Deference*, WASH. POST: VOLOKH CONSPIRACY (Mar. 25, 2017), https://www.washingtonpost.com/news/volokh-conspiracy/wp/2017/03/25/gorsuch-is-right-about-chevron-deference/?utm_term=.57ad63d37588.

[124] Michigan v. EPA, 135 S. Ct. 2699, 2713 (2015) (Thomas, J., concurring) (citation omitted). *See supra* Chapter 18.

CHAPTER 20

The Executive Branch and Agencies (Part 2)

Introduction

Chapter 19 discussed the external constraints on agency action, focusing on the political context in which agencies operate and the decision by Congress to delegate to the agencies. This chapter turns to the internal dynamics of agency behavior and considers how bureaucrats behave. The chapter focuses on two specific questions. First, what goals do rational bureaucrats pursue? Second, how are bureaucratic preferences translated into agency action? As you read the chapter, consider the implications of these models of bureaucratic behavior developed below for how courts should approach issues of delegation, including its the judicial deference doctrines reviewed in Chapter 19.

I. WHAT DO BUREAUCRATS MAXIMIZE?

In Chapter 17, we began with the premise that the overarching incentive of legislators is to be elected and re-elected. While legislators undoubtedly hold other, more lofty, objectives, in a competitive political system, those politicians unwilling to behave *as if* they are primarily motivated to be elected and re-elected will eventually fall off the radar of electoral politics. In this sense, the assumption that legislators act as if they are motivated by the goal of re-election is analogous to the assumption in the study of private markets that the most robust models assume firms are primarily motivated to maximize profits even though, once more, we know that those running them hold other, more lofty objectives.[1]

Unlike legislators, bureaucrats do not face direct electoral constraints, and unlike firms, they do not face external market pressures. The vast majority of governmental employees are non-political and are protected by civil service regulations from direct partisan political pressure.[2] Senior governmental officials and agency heads typically serve at the discretion of those who appoint them (usually the President) or for a set term of years. But civil service protections limit the power of senior officials to hire and fire

[1] *See* Armen A. Alchian, *Uncertainty, Evolution, and Economic Theory*, 58 J. POL. ECON. 211 (1950).

[2] It is estimated that about ninety percent of civilian federal government employees are protected by the Civil Service Act. Herbert Kaufman, *Major Players: Bureaucracies in American Government*, 61 PUB. ADMIN. REV. 18, 20–21 (2001).

subordinates beyond their immediate staff members. In addition, within the United States, as in most countries, professional bureaucrats are relatively constrained in their ability to earn income beyond their fixed salary. Compensation is often seniority-based, and bureaucrats have limited opportunities for financial reward resulting from exemplary performance, just as they do not typically risk financial punishment for substandard performance. In general, therefore, bureaucrats are largely immune from the direct electoral or financial incentives that motivate either elected officials or private market actors.

The American administrative state dates back to the Progressive Era of the early twentieth century as embodied in the intellectual and political influence of Woodrow Wilson. Before entering politics, Wilson was a leading academic who urged the study of the "science of administration" and the implementation of policy by a trained corps of unbiased and disinterested experts, a model inspired by the German administrative state.[3] The model of bureaucracy advanced during the Progressive Era implicitly assumed that unbiased experts, insulated from political and market pressures and guided by proper procedures and rules, would best discern and pursue the public interest. The civil service reforms and the creation of independent agencies, such as the Interstate Commerce Commission (1887), the Federal Trade Commission (1914), and later the multiple "alphabet soup" agencies created during the New Deal, were designed to produce the benefits of insulation from political pressure and to rest government employment on merit-based criteria, such as competitive examinations, rather than through political party affiliation (the "spoils" system). Once insulated from improper influences, bureaucrats were expected to identify and pursue the public interest in a relatively selfless and disinterested manner.

These assumptions about bureaucratic motivations came to dominate analyses of agency decision-making during the first half of the twentieth century and the paradigm approached its apex in the proliferation of new expert agencies during the New Deal, while continuing (and even accelerating) during the Johnson and Nixon Administrations.[4] Some recent commentators have applied insights of public choice theory and from "positive political theory" to suggest that even though the naïve model of delegation may not be robust, continued delegation to agency specialists is consistent with public preferences.[5]

Public choice theory rejects the premise that governmental actors are selfless, disinterested actors motivated purely by the pursuit of the public interest, even assuming

---

[3] Woodrow Wilson, *The Study of Administration*, 2 POL. SCI. Q. 197 (1887); *see also* JAMES M. LANDIS, THE ADMINISTRATIVE PROCESS 46 (1938) ("The administrative process is, in essence, our generation's answer to the inadequacy of the judicial and the legislative processes.").

[4] For an informative discussion that claims the scope of regulatory expansions during the late Johnson and Nixon administrations eclipsed that of the New Deal, see Theodore J. Lowi, *Two Roads to Serfdom: Liberalism, Conservatism and Administrative Power*, 36 AM. U. L. REV. 295, 298–99 (1987) ("Depending on who is doing the counting, an argument can be made that Congress enacted more regulatory programs in the five years between 1969 and 1974 than during any other comparable period in our history, including the first five years of the New Deal.").

[5] *See* David B. Spence & Frank Cross, *A Public Choice Case for the Administrative State*, 89 GEO. L.J. 97 (2000); *see also* Jonathan Bendor & Adam Meirowitz, *Spatial Models of Delegation*, 98 AM. POL. SCI. REV. 293 (2004).

we could agree as to how to define such terms. And yet, it is true that bureaucrats are not primarily motivated by the desire to maximize income and are not subject to electoral pressures. What then do bureaucrats maximize? Observers have proposed three main hypotheses concerning bureaucratic motivations: (1) agency expansion, (2) autonomy maximization, and (3) congressional control. We review each model and then consider the extent to which the views of the general public influence agency decision-making.

A. The Agency-Expansion Hypothesis

Writing in the late nineteenth century, the German political economist Max Weber posited that, in general, bureaucrats seek to maximize power.[6] Modern public choice theorists have essentially adopted, and elaborated on, Weber's intuition, offering a number of specific corroborating studies.[7]

In his 1971 book *Bureaucracy and Representative Government*,[8] William Niskanen provided the first systematic effort to study bureaucracies within a public choice framework. Niskanen began by specifying the likely variables that influence a bureaucrat's utility function: "salary, perquisites of the office, public reputation, power, patronage, output of the bureau, ease of making changes, and ease of managing the bureau."[9] Niskanen linked many of these factors to agency size. James Q. Wilson summarized Niskanen's view, stating, "The utility of a business person is assumed to be profits; that of a bureaucrat is assumed to be something akin to profits: salary, rank, or power."[10] Wilson added: "Since both bureaucrats and business executives are people, it makes sense to assume that they prefer more of whatever they like to less."[11] Niskanen relied upon this utility function to model how a rational individual would behave within a bureaucratic environment. Niskanen's model predicts that bureaucrats are primarily engaged in "empire building," meaning that they seek to maximize the size of their budgets and the scope of their agency's jurisdictional domain.

Within Niskanen's model, rational bureaucrats seek to maximize the bureau's budget during their tenure in office. With the exception of two variables in the bureaucrat's utility function—the ease of making policy changes and the ease of bureau management, which also depends on the actions of others—the remaining variables are positively correlated to the "total budget of the bureau during the bureaucrat's tenure in office."[12] As with public choice models more generally, it is not necessary that every bureaucrat share the

---

6 Max Weber, *Bureaucracy*, *in* FROM MAX WEBER: ESSAYS IN SOCIOLOGY 196, 233–34 (H.H. Gerth & C. Wright Mills eds., trans., 1946); *see also* DENNIS C. MUELLER, PUBLIC CHOICE III, at 360 (2003).

7 Portions of the discussion that follows, and the use of the term *empire building* to summarize Niskanen's views, are adapted from Todd J. Zywicki, *Institutional Review Boards as Academic Bureaucracies: An Economic and Experiential Analysis*, 101 NW. U. L. REV. 861 (2007).

8 WILLIAM A. NISKANEN, JR., BUREAUCRACY AND REPRESENTATIVE GOVERNMENT (1971).

9 *Id.* at 38.

10 JAMES Q. WILSON, BUREAUCRACY: WHAT GOVERNMENT AGENCIES DO AND WHY THEY DO IT, at xviii (1989).

11 *Id.*

12 NISKANEN, *supra* note 8, at 38 (emphasis omitted). Niskanen further observes that while the exceptional elements of the utility function are not primarily furthered by budgetary concerns, larger budgets ameliorate these concerns as well.

same motivation. Some bureaucrats, for example, might seek higher salaries, others more power. Regardless of individual motives, Niskanen maintains that budget-maximization tends to advance such goals. After all, bureaus with larger budgets are able to undertake more activities than those with smaller budgets. Even public-interested bureaucrats will tend to favor budgetary expansion.

Niskanen suggests that, in an important respect, bureaucratic management is subject to the same sorts of "survivor" biases witnessed in electoral politics or market competition. Even if bureaucrats do not consciously seek to maximize agency budgets, only those bureaucrats willing to "play the game" of competing for larger budgets and power will survive in the sharp-elbowed world of political conflict.

There is some empirical support for Niskanen's model. For instance, there is "ample evidence that bureaucrats systematically request larger budgets" and that they often succeed in having budgets set at the maximum politically feasible level.[13] Bureaucrats also have a "substantial impact on budgetary outcomes,"[14] generally producing larger budgets.

Because of their independence, bureaucrats are largely insulated from direct public pressure. As a result, the two primary constituencies with whom bureaucrats interact are agency employees and members of Congress, who confirm nominations and provide administrative oversight. Niskanen contends that those constituencies also tend to support enhanced agency budgets. Agency employees will prefer agency expansions, especially into novel areas, to enhance their prospects for internal promotion as part of a growing enterprise, along with their post-government career prospects in the private sector. For example, attorneys who participate in regulatory drafting will be in high demand by law firms involved in advising clients respecting regulatory compliance.[15]

Congressional overseers also will tend to support larger budgets. Most regulatory oversight is performed at the committee level.[16] Committee membership typically is self-selected and, not surprisingly, legislators generally serve on committees that are considered most important to their constituencies. For instance, representatives of agricultural districts typically serve on agriculture committees; representatives from western districts serve on committees related to public lands; representatives of districts with military bases or large military contractors generally serve on military committees; and representatives of urban districts generally serve on committees dedicated to banking, housing, and welfare policy. Niskanen argues that self-selection means that oversight committee members tend to support the missions of the agencies under their jurisdiction, and thus to support larger budgets relative to the median legislator. Niskanen further

---

[13] André Blais & Stéphane Dion, *Conclusion: Are Bureaucrats Budget Maximizers?*, *in* THE BUDGET-MAXIMIZING BUREAUCRAT: APPRAISALS AND EVIDENCE 355, 355 (André Blais & Stéphane Dion eds., 1991) [hereinafter BUDGET-MAXIMIZING BUREAUCRAT] (emphasis omitted).

[14] *Id.* at 358 (emphasis omitted).

[15] The precise manner in which "revolving door" incentives might influence policy will vary among agencies. *See* PAUL J. QUIRK, INDUSTRY INFLUENCE IN FEDERAL REGULATORY AGENCIES 143–74 (1981); *see also* Robert A. Katzmann, *Federal Trade Commission*, *in* THE POLITICS OF REGULATION 152 (James Q. Wilson ed., 1980); Suzanne Weaver, *Antitrust Division of the Department of Justice*, *in* THE POLITICS OF REGULATION, *supra*, at 123.

[16] William A. Niskanen, Jr., *Bureaucrats and Politicians*, 18 J.L. & ECON. 617 (1975), *reprinted in* WILLIAM A. NISKANEN, JR., BUREAUCRACY AND PUBLIC ECONOMICS 243 (1994).

observes that even the process of consolidating previously dispersed agency functions into a single department tends to result in increased expenditures rather than improved administrative efficiency.

Professor Tim Muris, who worked in the senior staff at the FTC in the 1980s and then served as Chairman of the FTC from 2001 to 2004, has offered an alternative explanation of increased regulatory expenditures that is linked to changes in the federal budget process.[17] Muris observes that "For most of our nation's first century, a single committee in each house controlled almost all spending authority." After reviewing the history of shifts between decentralization and centralized congressional spending power, Muris turned to the relevant modern history:

> Unfortunately, the process of spreading spending jurisdiction among committees began anew in 1932 when the Reconstruction Finance Corporation was created and financed outside normal appropriations channels. Decentralization accelerated during the next four decades, particularly between 1965 and 1975. By the mid 1970s, most substantive congressional committees had authority to report legislation to the floor committing funds from the U.S. Treasury. In 1932, the Appropriations Committees controlled 89 percent of outlays through the annual federal budget process. By 1992, fewer than 40 percent of federal outlays resulted from decisions under the Appropriators' control.
>
> This balkanization of spending authority creates a "common pool" problem. When no one owns a common resource, such as the fish in a lake, there is an incentive for too much fishing, depleting the population. With the budget, the common resource is general-fund revenue. As the Appropriations Committee controls less and less spending, and, correspondingly, other congressional committees control more and more, no one committee has the incentive to restrain spending because the total level of spending is no longer the responsibility of any one committee. To the contrary, the resulting competition among committees to spend results in more spending than would otherwise occur, increasing deficit spending.[18]

Does this history counsel in favor of a renewed call for tightened central control of congressional budgeting processes, such as restoring all spending authority to a single committee? Would such a change have the potential to improve both fiscal and regulatory discipline by reducing potential mismatches between chosen regulatory policies and their implementation? Why or why not?

Whatever the root cause, the process of agency expansion also provides congressional overseers with opportunities for rent extraction.[19] Agencies can threaten regulatory activity, thus encouraging members of Congress to offer their constituents

---

[17] *Budget Process Reform: Hearing Before the H. Comm. on Rules*, 106th Cong., 1st Sess. 120 (1999) (prepared statement of Timothy J. Muris, Foundation Professor, George Mason Univ. School of Law); *see also* W. Mark Crain & Timothy J. Muris, *Legislative Organization of Fiscal Policy*, 38 J.L. & ECON. 311 (1995).

[18] *Budget Process Reform: Hearing Before the H. Comm. on Rules*, *supra* note 17, at 121; *see also* Crain & Muris, *supra* note 17, at 311.

[19] For a related discussion, see *supra* Chapter 11 (discussing rent extraction).

benign intervention by holding the agency at bay. Morris Fiorina notes that Congress can even initiate this rent-extraction process by enacting vague legislation, knowing in advance that the regulators will inevitably make mistakes, at which point Congress can intervene to "piously [denounce] the evils of bureaucracy" and set matters right: Fiorina claims that this process allows Congressmen to "take credit coming and going."[20] Once again, this process also provides oversight officials with regulatory expertise that proves of value in the private market.

Over time, Niskanen modified his model, claiming that bureaucrats seek to maximize their *discretionary* budget, rather than their overall budget. Thus, for instance, agencies would not necessarily seek to acquire large budgetary responsibilities connected to ministerial activities such as processing food stamps or Social Security checks, as these mechanical functions do not have a substantial discretionary component that will augment the agency's power or prestige. Niskanen defines discretionary budget as "the difference between . . . total budget and the minimum cost of producing the expected output."[21] In effect, this is equivalent to the agency-cost slack between the legislature and the regulatory agency. The discretionary budget permits the bureaucrat to enlarge his perquisites and otherwise improve the status of the agency. In general, enhanced agency budgets correlate with enhanced discretion since effective monitoring becomes more difficult as a function of agency growth. Niskanen argues:

> Some part of this discretionary budget will be spent in ways that serve the bureau, such as additional staff, capital, and perquisites. The remainder will be spent in ways that serve the interests of the political review authorities. The distribution of this surplus between spending that serves the interests of the bureaus and that which serves the interests of the review authorities, as in any bilateral bargaining, will depend on the relevant information, alternatives, and bargaining strategies available to the two parties.[22]

Niskanen's model has been criticized on several grounds. Bureaucrats themselves do not obtain obvious direct benefits from increased agency budgets, thus raising questions about their incentives to seek larger budgets. Although growing budgets might offer greater opportunities for promotion for rank-and-file employees, salaries of governmental employees vary little based on agency size.[23] Those who work in larger agencies are unlikely to earn higher salaries (or have opportunities for more non-pecuniary income, such as leisure) as compared with those who work in smaller agencies. Moreover, federal bureaucrats do not have particularly generous perquisites, such as ornate offices or cushy travel arrangements. As compared with the private sector, working conditions in governmental agencies are relatively spare. And yet, large and growing agencies might be intrinsically more prestigious thus providing greater opportunities for lucrative post-

---

[20] MORRIS P. FIORINA, CONGRESS: KEYSTONE OF THE WASHINGTON ESTABLISHMENT 46–47 (2d ed. 1989).

[21] NISKANEN, *supra* note 8, at 245.

[22] William A. Niskanen, *A Reflection on* Bureaucracy and Representative Government, *in* BUDGET-MAXIMIZING BUREAUCRAT, *supra* note 13, at 19.

[23] *See* Ronald N. Johnson & Gary D. Libecap, *Agency Growth, Salaries and the Protected Bureaucrat*, 27 ECON. INQUIRY 431 (1989); Robert A. Young, *Budget Size and Bureaucratic Careers*, *in* BUDGET-MAXIMIZING BUREAUCRAT, *supra* note 13, at 33.

governmental employment. But even here there are exceptions. Comparatively small agencies such as the SEC are quite powerful and prestigious and provide substantial opportunities for lucrative post-governmental employment.

B. The Agency-Autonomy Hypothesis

James Q. Wilson challenged Niskanen's assumption that bureaucrats are primarily motivated to maximize budgets. He writes, "[B]ureaucrats have a variety of preferences; only part of their behavior can be explained by assuming they are struggling to get bigger salaries or fancier offices or larger budgets."[24] Bureaucrats might instead be motivated by ideological views or professional norms.[25] Indeed, contrary to Niskanen's predictions, agencies sometimes resist expansions to their authority and scope.[26]

Wilson argues that rather than being imperialistic, bureaucrats tend to be averse to risk and to conflict with other agencies. Bureaucrats thus tend to avoid pursuing larger budgets and responsibilities if the result generates conflict. Wilson claims that a more accurate model of agency behavior rests on "autonomy" or "independence," rather than jurisdictional or budgetary expansion.[27] Wilson defines autonomy as:

> [A] "condition of independence sufficient to permit a group to work out and maintain a distinctive identity." There are two parts to [this] definition, an external and an internal one. The external aspect of autonomy, independence, is equivalent to "jurisdiction" or "domain." Agencies ranking high in autonomy have a monopoly jurisdiction (that is, they have few or no bureaucratic rivals and a minimum of political constraints imposed on them by superiors). The internal aspect of autonomy is identity or mission—a widely shared and approved understanding of the central tasks of the agency.[28]

Autonomy takes many forms, such as independence from oversight, external constituencies, or rivalry from other agencies. According to Wilson, successful bureaucracies resist incursions onto their turf and avoid taking on tasks that are not at the heart of their institutional mission or that "will produce divided or hostile constituencies."[29] Rational bureaucrats will resist proposals to expand agency budgets or jurisdiction that risk creating conflict with rival agencies, undertaking new and difficult tasks, or producing problematic constituency relations.[30]

Agency expansions thus have costs as well as benefits. A relatively small agency, for example, might have effective "monopoly" power in a given regulatory field, a satisfied clientele, and considerable policy expertise. Specialization allows the regulators to navigate congressional oversight procedures and to better manage potential jurisdictional conflict

---

[24] WILSON, *supra* note 10, at xviii.

[25] Spence & Cross, *supra* note 5, at 117.

[26] *See infra* notes 35–37 and accompanying text.

[27] WILSON, *supra* note 10, at 182.

[28] *Id.* (quoting PHILIP SELZNICK, LEADERSHIP IN ADMINISTRATION 121 (1957)).

[29] *Id.* at 191.

[30] For a largely complementary analysis, see MORTON H. HALPERIN, BUREAUCRATIC POLITICS AND FOREIGN POLICY 51 (1974) (positing that bureaucracies "are often prepared to accept less money with greater control than more money with less control").

with other agencies. Agency expansion might provoke interagency conflict by forcing the agency into regulatory areas in which it lacks both expertise and clientele support. Wilson observes, for example, that when the United States Department of Agriculture (USDA) began to administer the Food Stamp program, it encountered new conflicts with various congressional oversight committees, interest groups, and clientele concerned with welfare programs for lower-income groups, as opposed to its previous clientele, who were focused on farming and agricultural products. Agency expansions also threaten a less satisfactory and less cost-effective administration of assigned regulatory functions, thus inviting heightened public and congressional scrutiny. The combined effects might also harm the agency's public reputation and bring its leaders under scrutiny, a foreseeable result that bureaucrats would prefer to avoid.

Wilson observes that these complications might lead agencies to resist expansion of their budget and authority if expansion compromises their autonomy or other beneficial aspects of agency culture. In contrast with Niskanen, Wilson contends that "[g]overnment agencies are more risk averse than imperialistic. They prefer security to rapid growth, autonomy to competition, stability to change."[31] Agencies pursuing expansion, he argues, are characterized by especially "benign environments—strong public support and popular leadership."[32] The typical bureaucracy is "defensive, threat-avoiding, scandal-minimizing," not " 'imperialistic' or expansionist."[33] "In short," Wilson writes, "agencies quickly learn what forces in their environment are capable of using catastrophe or absurdity as effective political weapons, and they work hard to minimize the chances that they will be vulnerable to such attacks."[34]

Contrary to Niskanen's hypothesis, Wilson argues that the typical bureaucracy will be reluctant to take on activities that embrace seemingly intractable problems and that are fraught with the danger of unintended consequences including regulatory failure and criticism. Wilson notes, for example, that the Federal Bureau of Investigation (FBI) originally resisted investigating narcotics and organized crime because the potential costs (broadly understood) exceeded the benefits to the agency. According to Wilson, the FBI feared that narcotics trafficking could not be "solved" in the same way as kidnappings and bank robberies, thus risking public criticism. The Bureau also feared the potential for corruption associated with drug and Mafia investigations and the complex new demands that undertaking such responsibilities would pose, including undercover operations, which "make the internal management of the organization more difficult or even threaten the existence of its shared sense of mission."[35] The result of the FBI's resistance to agency expansion was the creation of the Drug Enforcement Agency ("DEA"). Thus, while Wilson agrees that "[a]ll else being equal, big budgets are better than small," his model is premised on the intuition that "all else is not equal"[36] and that "[a]utonomy is valued at least as much as resources, because autonomy determines the degree to which it is costly

---

[31] James Q. Wilson, *The Politics of Regulation*, *in* THE POLITICS OF REGULATION, *supra* note 15, at 357, 376 (footnote omitted).

[32] *Id.*

[33] *Id.* at 378.

[34] *Id.* at 377.

[35] WILSON, *supra* note 10, at 182–83.

[36] *Id.* at 182.

to acquire and use resources."[37] As a result, the agency is unlikely to sacrifice its autonomy to secure more resources or an enlarged jurisdiction.

The bureaucratic preference for autonomy over empire-building is also consistent with the greater opportunities of governmental employees to consume leisure or to shirk in performing one's duties, as compared with comparable workers in the private sector. Civil service protections not only insulate governmental employees from improper political and market pressures but they also weaken incentives for productivity and reduce accountability for rank-and-file bureaucrats. At a minimum, civil service protections reduce incentives to expend greater than average effort. In fact, government employees may self-select for positions that provide security and reduced accountability in place of the higher potential remuneration, greater accountability, and reduced job security that characterize comparable employment in the private sector.

Studies of government-owned corporations indicate that as compared with otherwise similar private market actors, government employees tend to work less and at lower efficiency, while drawing higher salaries for any given level of professional responsibility.[38] Professor Dennis Mueller reviewed seventy-one academic studies comparing work incentives in private firms and government bureaucracies. Mueller located only five studies finding that public firms operated with a greater level of cost effectiveness than comparable private firms and only ten studies that found no difference in cost effectiveness.[39] In each of the remaining fifty-six studies, "state-owned companies were found to be significantly less efficient than privately owned firms supplying the same good or service."[40] Mueller concludes, "The provision of a good or service by a state bureaucracy or by a state-owned company generally leads to lower residual profits, and/or higher costs and lower productivity."[41] Scholars have claimed that workers in firms in regulated industries protected from competition exhibit similar inefficiencies.[42]

Do you find these claims persuasive? Are there contexts in which a governmental employee's output should be gauged against criteria other than efficiency? If so, what are those criteria? To what extent are the claimed findings of comparative bureaucratic or government inefficiencies generalizable? Would you expect to find similar results in other areas of employment in which the incentives for productivity are attenuated, at least as compared with traditional firm settings, including, for example, university professors

---

37 *Id.* at 195.

38 For a general discussion of government-owned corporations, see FROM BUREAUCRACY TO BUSINESS ENTERPRISE: LEGAL AND POLICY ISSUES IN THE TRANSFORMATION OF GOVERNMENT SERVICES (Michael J. Whincop ed., 2003).

39 MUELLER, *supra* note 6, at 373.

40 *Id.*

41 *Id.* Mueller observes, for example, that the public school system in the United States has been criticized as "fai[ling] its citizens not by educating too many students, but educating them poorly" as compared with what he claims are "more efficiently organized private schools." *Id.* at 384 (citing JOHN E. CHUBB & TERRY M. MOE, POLITICS, MARKETS, AND AMERICA'S SCHOOLS (1990)). *But see* CHRISTOPHER A. LUBIENSKI & SARAH THEULE LUBIENSKI, THE PUBLIC SCHOOL ADVANTAGE: WHY PUBLIC SCHOOLS OUTPERFORM PRIVATE SCHOOLS (2013).

42 For summaries of this literature, see Sandra E. Black & Philip E. Strahan, *The Division of Spoils: Rent-Sharing and Discrimination in a Regulated Industry*, 91 AM. ECON. REV. 814 (2001); James Peoples, *Deregulation and the Labor Market*, J. ECON. PERSP., Spring 1998, at 111.

(especially those with tenure)? What about unionized work forces that provide relatively higher degrees of job seniority? How, if at all, might these analyses relate to the behavior of life-tenured judges?

C. Congressional Control Model

Models of budget-maximizing, autonomy-maximizing, or leisure-maximizing bureaucrats assume that congressional oversight of agency activity is lax and passive, enabling bureaucrats to pursue their own agendas rather than those of Congress or the public at large.[43] Congress holds relatively few and generally perfunctory oversight hearings that focus primarily on such matters as budgets and confirmations of agency heads. This ineffective and ad hoc oversight is said to result from three factors:

> First, agencies control information from their policy area. Second, access to clientele fosters agency-clientele alliances to protect agencies from their nominal overseers in Congress. And third, the high cost of passing new legislation to redirect agency policy limits congressional action in all but the most important cases. The resulting bureaucratic insulation affords bureaucrats a degree of discretion which, in turn, is used to pursue their own private goals rather than the public purposes for which they were originally created.[44]

Thus, it is argued that lax and ineffective congressional oversight enables inefficient agency expansion or deviation from preferred congressional policies.

Other scholars have questioned this model of congressional passivity, arguing that Congress, behaving rationally, will seek to limit agency departures from its preferred policies. Because bureaucrats and members of Congress are repeat players, it is unlikely that Congress would tolerate ongoing deception and inefficiency, as would be required to maintain continuous regulatory expansion or shirking.[45] Moreover, when Congress decides to delegate authority to an agency, it should take into account any agency biases toward inefficient regulatory expansion.[46]

In a case study of the FTC, Weingast and Moran argued that focusing on the absence of active formal oversight overlooks important informal dynamics in the relationship between agencies and Congress. Instead, the authors propose a "[c]ongressional dominance" model that focuses on the informal relationships between congressional committees and agencies.[47] The authors describe the model as follows:

> [C]ongressmen—or, more specifically, particular congressmen on the relevant committees—possess sufficient rewards and sanctions to create an incentive system for agencies. Agency mandate notwithstanding, rewards go to those

---

[43] *See* THEODORE J. LOWI, THE END OF LIBERALISM: THE SECOND REPUBLIC OF THE UNITED STATES (2d ed. 1979).

[44] Barry R. Weingast & Mark J. Moran, *Bureaucratic Discretion or Congressional Control? Regulatory Policymaking by the Federal Trade Commission*, 91 J. POL. ECON. 765, 767 (1983).

[45] *See* Gary J. Miller & Terry M. Moe, *Bureaucrats, Legislators, and the Size of Government*, 77 AM. POL. SCI. REV. 297 (1983).

[46] *See* Spence & Cross, *supra* note 5, at 117–18.

[47] *See* Weingast & Moran, *supra* note 44, at 768.

> agencies that pursue policies of interest to the current committee members; those agencies that fail to do so are confronted with sanctions. It follows that if the incentive system worked effectively, then agencies would pursue congressional goals even though they received little direct public guidance from their overseers. Congressmen on the relevant committees may appear ignorant of agency proceedings because they gauge the success of programs through their constituents' reactions rather than through detailed study. Public hearings and investigations are resource-intensive activities, so they will hardly be used by congressmen for those policy areas that are operating smoothly (i.e., benefiting congressional clientele). Their real purpose is to police those areas functioning poorly. The threat of ex post sanctions creates ex ante incentives for the bureau to serve a congressional clientele.[48]

The authors claim that their view carries the following "striking implication: the more effective the incentive system, the less often we should observe sanctions in the form of congressional attention through hearings and investigations."[49] Stated differently, "direct and continuous monitoring of inputs rather than of results is an inefficient mechanism by which a principal constrains the action of his agent."[50] In the Weingast and Moran analysis, the absence of visible congressional monitoring counterintuitively suggests that the agency is abiding congressional priorities. Only when informal constraints break down must Congress rely upon formal oversight mechanisms. Thus, Weingast and Moran challenge the inference that the absence of aggressive, public, congressional oversight reflects agency independence from congressional control.

Weingast and Moran argue that congressional control over independent agencies actually is pervasive, albeit not always visible. They identify several mechanisms through which Congress influences agency behavior. First, agencies are subject to a competitive budgetary process. Few agencies stand in the position of a bilateral monopoly with Congress; instead, the various agencies compete with each other for budgetary allocations, and Congress should favor those that perform their duties in a relatively more cost-effective manner. The resulting competition constrains individual agencies seeking to increase their size and budgets and also reduces the information asymmetries between Congress and the agency by forcing the agency to explain its operations in order to justify its budget request.[51] Second, Congress can and does exert formal oversight control when necessary through hearings and investigations. Third, Congress can "make life miserable for an agency by endless hearings and questionnaires."[52] The best way to avoid this harassment is "to further congressional interests."[53] Finally, Congress can use its power to confirm appointments to negotiate with the President over nominations. Thus, even

---

48 *Id.* at 768–69.

49 *Id.* at 769.

50 *Id.*

51 *See* DONALD A. WITTMAN, THE MYTH OF DEMOCRATIC FAILURE: WHY POLITICAL INSTITUTIONS ARE EFFICIENT 95 (1995).

52 McNollgast, *The Political Economy of Law*, *in* 2 HANDBOOK OF LAW AND ECONOMICS 1651, 1705 (A. Mitchell Polinsky & Steven Shavell eds., 2007).

53 *Id.*

though confirmation hearings often appear perfunctory, the formal hearings do not necessarily reflect the extensive private negotiations that precede the hearings.

Although bureaus compete for congressional resources, members of Congress are motivated to reduce agency conflict and can use the committee process to do so. The congressional committee system allows individual members of Congress to create what amounts to a system of congressional mini-monopolies that oversee particular agencies and departments with minimal interjurisdiction conflict. As previously noted, self-selecting on committees gives members of Congress disproportionate influence over issues that matter most for electoral support. The committee system also reduces the information asymmetries between Congress and agencies by allowing committee overseers to develop the requisite expertise with which to effectively monitor agency performance.[54]

Because oversight committees exert disproportionate influence over agency policy as compared with Congress more generally, Weingast and Moran predict that changes in committee preferences should translate into changes in agency policy. Conversely, stable committee membership promotes stable agency policy, even if agency leadership changes. The agency independence model would predict that agency leadership should matter more.

Weingast and Moran test their model with evidence of the FTC's behavior in the late 1970s and early 1980s. During the late 1970s, the FTC aggressively asserted authority over broad segments of the American economy. The Commission launched investigations of "advertising aimed at children . . ., the used car market, the insurance industry," and professional licensing organizations, as well as launching major antitrust suits against the nation's largest oil companies and breakfast cereal manufacturers.[55] After encouraging these efforts for many years, congressional overseers reversed course, publicly lambasting the FTC for overreaching and passing targeted legislation to halt several FTC investigations. At one point, Congress even refused to authorize the FTC's budget, temporarily suspending the agency's activities (the funding was later reauthorized). The FTC responded to this pressure by closing nearly all of its controversial rulemaking investigations and suspending what many considered its most ambitious and controversial antitrust prosecutions.

Weingast and Moran argue that the FTC's behavior during this period contradicts the predictions of the agency independence model.[56] Under the agency independence view, Congress intervened only after the FTC had operated independently for a decade, by which time it had severely strayed from preferred congressional policy. In this analysis,

---

[54] *See* DAVID EPSTEIN & SHARYN O'HALLORAN, DELEGATING POWERS: A TRANSACTION COST POLITICS APPROACH TO POLICY MAKING UNDER SEPARATE POWERS 166–67 (1999); Albert Breton & Ronald Wintrobe, *The Equilibrium Size of a Budget Maximizing Bureau: A Note on Niskanen's Theory of Bureaucracy*, 83 J. POL. ECON. 195 (1975); Rui J.P. de Figueiredo, Jr., Pablo T. Spiller & Santiago Urbiztondo, *An Informational Perspective on Administrative Procedures*, 15 J.L. ECON. & ORG. 283 (1999).

[55] Weingast & Moran, *supra* note 44, at 776.

[56] Weingast and Moran's critique is specifically targeted against KENNETH W. CLARKSON & TIMOTHY J. MURIS, THE FEDERAL TRADE COMMISSION SINCE 1970: ECONOMIC REGULATION AND BUREAUCRATIC BEHAVIOR (1981) and ROBERT A. KATZMANN, REGULATORY BUREAUCRACY: THE FEDERAL TRADE COMMISSION AND ANTITRUST POLICY (1980). Weingast & Moran, *supra* note 44, at 776.

the FTC was the exception that proved the rule: Had it been more restrained in its activities, it could have continued to act indefinitely unimpeded by congressional interference. Most agencies, by contrast, operate unchecked by avoiding extreme positions that alienate important constituencies and congressional overseers.

Weingast and Moran instead claim that the FTC's behavior is better captured by the congressional dominance model. In their analysis, the agency's behavior in both the earlier activist and later retrenchment periods reflect congressional preferences or, more specifically, those of the relevant oversight committee members. Weingast and Moran demonstrate that the preferences of the oversight committee changed from supporting to opposing FTC activism, thus changing agency policies. Whereas in 1977, Congress "consistently criticized the FTC for lack of progress on their many investigations," the authors observe that these were the "very investigations that drew so much criticism [two] years later."[57] The change in the FTC's behavior reflected the rapid change in Congress during this period:

> Between 1976 and 1979, the dominant coalition on the relevant congressional committees changed from favoring to opposing an activist FTC. This resulted from the nearly complete turnover of those on and in control of the relevant Senate oversight subcommittee. None of the senior members of the subcommittee responsible for major FTC legislation and direction for the previous decade returned after 1976. Those previously in the minority took control of the subcommittee and began reversing the policies initiated by their predecessors. The 1979 and 1980 hearings were simply the most visible culmination of this process.
>
> The congressional choice explanation suggests that the FTC initiated controversial policies because it got strong signals to do so from Congress. Far from roaming beyond its congressional mandate as an exercise in bureaucratic discretion, the FTC aggressively implemented its new authority in concert with its congressional sponsors. With the turnover in 1977, however, the FTC lost its congressional support and thus was vulnerable to the subsequent reversals.[58]

In fact, Weingast and Moran observe that many of those on the FTC oversight committee during the 1970s were champions of consumer protection legislation who sponsored major pieces of pro-consumer legislation that characterized the era of regulatory expansion. Indeed, those members urged the FTC to be more active, as was reflected in the agency's consumer protection agenda.

From 1977 to 1979, however, there was a dramatic turnover of membership on the Senate Commerce Committee and Subcommittee on Consumer Affairs that included a rapid replacement of liberals with conservatives. From 1966 to 1976, members of the subcommittee were substantially more liberal than the Senate as a whole. By 1979, however, the pendulum had swung in the opposite direction with the result that subcommittee members were substantially more conservative than the Senate as a whole. Weingast and Moran conclude that the FTC's crisis resulted from changes in

---

[57] Weingast & Moran, *supra* note 44, at 777.

[58] *Id.* at 777–78.

congressional preferences rather than the agency's activities, a finding that is consistent with the congressional control model but not the agency independence model.

Other studies have corroborated substantial congressional influence over the FTC. Roger Faith, Donald Leavens, and Robert Tollison found that congressional influence helps to explain the pattern of FTC merger enforcement.[59] Unlike Weingast and Moran, however, Faith, Leavens, and Tollison concluded that constituent politics played a larger role than ideology. The authors found that an FTC merger challenge was significantly more likely to be dismissed if the headquarters of a merging firm was located within the district of one of the congressional oversight subcommittee members than if it was not.[60] They conclude that this finding is potentially consistent with either the budget-maximizing or congressional oversight models, but is inconsistent with the autonomy model. They further conclude that their analysis supports Richard Posner's observation that Congress often spurred FTC antitrust investigations at the behest of firms located in their district in order to gain a competitive advantage.[61]

Professor Timothy Muris, who chaired the FTC from 2001 through 2004, has challenged the congressional control model, claiming that it overstates congressional influence on FTC policymaking.[62] Muris argues that agency outputs reflect the interaction of several internal and external constituencies: Congress, courts, the President, and the internal staff itself. Muris further notes that Congress itself does not speak with a unified voice. Indeed, its members represent different, and conflicting, constituent interests. In addition, the FTC responds to two other principals: the President (who appoints the Chairman), and the judiciary, which in proper cases ensures that FTC actions fall within the agency's statutory mandate. Moreover, agencies have their own independent bureaucratic culture:

> What Weingast and Moran miss in explaining the FTC, however, is the importance of the agency's staff, both in its ideological character and in its career goals. During the early 1970s, for example, numerous liberal employees were drawn to the "revitalized" commission. . . . [T]his new blood [made the agency more liberal], paralleling the increased [liberalism] of both the Senate and House subcommittees overseeing the FTC. While the composition of these subcommittees became more conservative in the late 1970s, the composition of the FTC staff remained liberal. Thus, contrary to the approach of Weingast and Moran, we would expect to find a more dramatic shift in FTC caseload in the early 1970s, when *both* Congress and the FTC staff changed politically, than we would find in the late 1970s, when only Congress changed. The evidence available supports this prediction.[63]

---

[59] Roger L. Faith, Donald R. Leavens & Robert D. Tollison, *Antitrust Pork Barrel*, 25 J.L. & ECON. 329 (1982).

[60] *Id.* at 335–42.

[61] Richard A. Posner, *The Federal Trade Commission*, 37 U. CHI. L. REV. 47 (1969). Subsequent research has further illuminated the political constraints on the FTC as well as the agency's internal conflicts. *See* Malcolm B. Coate et al., *Bureaucracy and Politics in FTC Merger Challenges*, 33 J.L. & ECON. 463 (1990).

[62] Timothy J. Muris, *Regulatory Policymaking at the Federal Trade Commission: The Extent of Congressional Control*, 94 J. POL. ECON. 884 (1986).

[63] *Id.* at 888–89.

Muris thus argues that the agency bureaucracy has an internal dynamic of its own that is at least partially independent of congressional incentives. Sometimes congressional and agency preferences push in the same direction, thereby amplifying policy swings. Other times, however, they push against each other so that even if agency policy moves in the same general direction as Congress, the bureaucracy may moderate the extent of the swing.

Niskanen also has challenged the assumptions that underlie the congressional control model. From the perspective of individual members of Congress, monitoring is a public good because any resulting savings inure to the benefit of Congress or the nation as a whole.[64] Like other public goods, monitoring is subject to collective action and free-riding problems. Thus, although Congress as a whole might have incentives to monitor agency waste and inefficiency, individual members of Congress do not, or at least do not to the same extent.[65] Agency monitoring is costly and requires allocation of time and staffing resources that could be rationally dedicated to other tasks that promote legislators' interests more directly, such as constituent service or legislative activity. Niskanen contends that members of Congress will rationally monitor agency behavior only up to the point where a member's private marginal costs exceed the member's private marginal benefits. As compared with activities that produce discrete and excludable benefits for which members of Congress can claim credit with constituents, monitoring activities tend to be undersupplied. Rational legislators are likely to prefer responding to constituent complaints as a low cost source of information from which to sort potential targets of abusive or inefficient exercises of agency powers, often referred to as a *fire alarm theory* of oversight, discussed in Chapter 19.[66]

Which model best explains the behavior of agencies and bureaucrats: the budget-maximization hypothesis, the autonomy hypothesis, or the congressional control hypothesis? To what extent are these models mutually exclusive and to what extent are they complementary? Are there conditions, or periods of time, when one of the models is likely to be more robust in explaining agency behavior than another? How, if at all, is your answer related to presidential versus non-presidential election cycles? Why? How might these various models apply in other contexts, such as managerial incentives in large, nonprofit organizations such as charities or universities?

Should these models, individually or in combination, influence the judicial response to agency activities? Should they affect, for example, agency deference rules under the *Chevron* and *Mead* doctrines? Should they affect the attitude of courts toward the so-called nondelegation doctrine? Why or why not? Does the selection among these models help to frame the inquiry as to which types of policy domains Congress is more prone to delegate to agencies and under which circumstances? Why? How might the selection affect whether particular regulatory policies are, or should be, vested in executive or independent agencies? Why?

---

[64] *See also* Gordon Tullock, *Public Decisions as Public Goods*, 79 J. POL. ECON. 913 (1971).

[65] *See* NISKANEN, *supra* note 8, at 249–54.

[66] *See supra* Chapter 19, Part IV.C.

D. Monitoring by the Public

Bureaucrats are structurally further insulated from effective monitoring by the public than are elected officials; as a result, agencies are also potentially subject to a corresponding increase in interest group influence. Citizens do not vote directly for bureaucrats, and, as a result, bureaucrats lack direct electoral accountability for their decisions. In general, federal agencies receive less popular attention than Congress, and the complex regulatory labyrinth often makes the processes and outcomes of regulatory activity difficult for most people to comprehend. Moreover, the processes of agency rulemaking are more opaque than elections, and agency responsiveness to the general public is therefore all the more attenuated. Former Administrators of the Office of Information and Regulatory Affairs (OIRA) Christopher DeMuth and Douglas Ginsburg have observed that, as a practical matter, "public" participation in administrative rulemaking process "is limited to those organized groups with the largest and most immediate stakes in the results."[67] They observe:

> Although presidents and legislatures are themselves vulnerable to pressure from politically influential groups, the rulemaking process—operating in relative obscurity from public view but lavishly attended by interest groups—is even more vulnerable. A substantial number of agency rules could not survive public scrutiny and gain two legislative majorities and the signature of the president.[68]

Judge Ralph Winter also has commented on the divergence of agency rulemaking from public preferences:

> Much has been made of the consumer's inability to affect his market destinies and his lack of product information. Yet surely these criticisms are even more cogent where government is involved. A product which does not satisfy consumers is far more likely to disappear than a government ruling. When the [Interstate Commerce Commission I.C.C.)] prohibits new truckers from entering the market, consumers rarely know of the ruling—much less why it was made—and, of course, can do nothing to change it.[69]

Moreover, even if citizens were able to acquire meaningful information regarding regulatory policy, the agencies themselves would still have minimal incentive to seek input from average citizens on regulatory matters. As Steven Croley has observed:

> Direct citizen participation in regulatory decisionmaking is thus both rare—taking place only as often as elections for political representatives—and very crude—citizens vote for political candidates with very little information about

---

[67] Christopher C. DeMuth & Douglas H. Ginsburg, *White House Review of Agency Rulemaking*, 99 HARV. L. REV. 1075, 1081 (1986).

[68] *Id.*

[69] Ralph K. Winter, Jr., *Economic Regulation vs. Competition: Ralph Nader and Creeping Capitalism*, 82 YALE L.J. 890, 894 (1973).

> those candidates' positions on regulatory issues, and must moreover vote for a mixed bundle of such policies at once.[70]

Croley concludes:

> Because most citizens are largely uninformed about most regulatory decisions, and because they moreover lack incentives to become sufficiently informed to reward legislators who do not shirk, legislators do not—cannot—protect the broad regulatory interests of their constituencies. This is true because organized interest groups—industry groups, occupational groups, and trade associations—who *are* informed because they have an especially high demand for regulatory goods do monitor legislators, punishing those who consistently fail to provide such goods and rewarding those who provide favorable regulation. Thus interest groups capitalize on the opportunities created by principal-agent slack, made worse by most voters' collective action problems, in order to buy regulatory goods that advantage them.[71]

David Spence and Frank Cross have challenged this description of agency indifference to public preferences.[72] They acknowledge that the public itself is rationally ignorant about agency activities; nonetheless, they contend that the public might support delegation on the belief that expert decision makers have more expertise on a given issue than Congress and that, as a result, the agency is more likely to get the "correct" answer. The median voter in the electorate often will have no particular substantive preference on a given issue, but instead will prefer that government experts select the policy that they determine to be best. Spence and Cross further argue that voters will prefer to rely upon skilled experts rather than generalist elected representatives to make these policy decisions. If so, voters will support broad discretion for agency decision making even if congressional oversight is limited and bureaucratic control attenuated.

Consider Winter's claim that citizens cannot move agency behavior. To what extent, if any, is this in tension with the history of the AIDS-activist lobby on the issue of speeding up access to the AIDS cocktail through fast-track FDA approval during the 1980s and early 1990s?[73] The result was to speed up approval of the AIDS cocktail relative to the ordinary regulatory processes, which are extremely expensive and can take years or even decades to accomplish. Does this example run counter to or confirm Winter's thesis? Is the AIDS-activist lobby the type of group that Winter was describing? If not, what characteristics might distinguish this group politically and account for its success?

To what extent do the insights from these models help to explain opportunities for citizen watchdog groups? Do these groups emerge as political entrepreneurs who are able to capitalize on the inability of private citizens to effectively monitor agency conduct? Are

---

[70] Steven P. Croley, *Theories of Regulation: Incorporating the Administrative Process*, 98 COLUM. L. REV. 1, 38 (1998).

[71] *Id.* (footnote omitted).

[72] Spence & Cross, *supra* note 5; *see also* Bendor & Meirowitz, *supra* note 5.

[73] Wendy K. Mariner, *Activists and the AIDS Business*, 257 SCIENCE 1975 (1992) (reviewing PETER S. ARNO & KARYN L. FEIDEN, AGAINST THE ODDS: THE STORY OF AIDS DRUG DEVELOPMENT, POLITICS AND PROFITS (1992)) (observing that AIDS activists, such as ACT UP, successfully pushed FDA to change trial and approval processes in the late 1980s to allow fast track approval of AIDS cocktail).

such groups effective at harnessing citizen demand for regulatory reform? Why or why not? To what extent do activist monitoring groups have their own institutional interests in maximizing their influence or budgets affecting them in ways that risk departing from the interests of the public more generally?[74] Would you anticipate that such groups are effective in securing promises during presidential primaries that subsequently affect the direction of regulatory policy? If so, does this counsel in favor or against agency deference rules? Why?

II. CHARACTERISTICS OF AGENCY BEHAVIOR

Public choice theorists generally claim that observed features of bureaucratic behavior are at odds with the public interest model of politics. Specifically, the motivation and opportunity to shirk, and incentives to pursue other goals, produces incentives that depart from majoritarian or efficiency objectives. In this part, we address these claims.

A. Systematic Bias in Decision Making

Economists have predicted that the incentive structure faced by bureaucrats will lead to unduly risk-averse decision-making, producing an inefficiently high level of regulation.[75] The concepts of Type I and Type II error help to explain the precise nature of the competing risks that regulators seek to avoid.

Type I errors, also referred to as "false positives," arise when a regulatory burden is sub-optimally high, and, as a result, certain safe goods or services are classified by the regulator as unreasonably dangerous. Type II error, or false negatives, arises when the regulatory burden is suboptimally low, and, as a result, dangerous goods are classified by the regulator as safe. Both types of errors—Type I and Type II—impose costs on consumers either by prohibiting the sale of safe goods or by permitting the sale of dangerous goods. The total economic cost of a regulatory regime will include the sum of these two types of error multiplied by the harm to consumers that the errors produce plus the administrative costs of making the decisions.

These error costs need not be symmetrical. For instance, for criminal law enforcement, the American legal system accepts as a foundational premise that the cost of false positives (the erroneous conviction of innocent defendants) exceeds the cost of false negatives (the erroneous acquittal of guilty defendants). This assumption is reflected in the aphorism that it is better to allow ten (or one hundred) guilty men to go free than to wrongly convict one innocent man.[76] As a result of the asymmetrical assessment of these competing costs, the American legal system imposes a substantially higher standard

---

[74] Todd J. Zywicki, *Baptists? The Political Economy of Environmental Interest Groups*, 53 CASE W. RES. L. REV. 315 (2002).

[75] *See* Sam Peltzman, *An Evaluation of Consumer Protection Legislation: The 1962 Drug Amendments*, 81 J. POL. ECON. 1049 (1973); *see also* MUELLER, *supra* note 6, at 370–71 (summarizing literature).

[76] *See* 4 WILLIAM BLACKSTONE, COMMENTARIES *352; *see also* Alexander Volokh, *n Guilty Men*, 146 U. PA. L. REV. 173 (1997) (reviewing different articulations of the phrase over time).

of proof for convictions in criminal cases (beyond a reasonable doubt) than in civil cases (preponderance of the evidence).[77]

Strict cost-benefit analysis suggests that social welfare is maximized when regulators act in a risk-neutral manner. This means that regulators are expected to weigh the opportunity costs of delayed approval in preventing suffering or saving lives equally with the costs to those who might be injured by premature approval of a drug. From the perspective of individual bureaucrats, however, private cost may not align with public costs; instead a bureaucrat might be systematically risk-averse. From that perspective, erroneously approving a harmful drug by setting the regulatory bar too low threatens public condemnation, regulatory oversight, and potentially severe career consequences. By contrast, the delay of a useful drug for further testing, while also producing potentially significant social costs, might be harder to identify and thus be less likely to invite criticism. For instance, the Food and Drug Administration might be overly cautious in approving valuable new medications, requiring extensive testing and limiting the treatments for which the new drugs may be approved. Such bureaucrats might exert considerable caution even though the resulting delays or disapprovals of potentially life-saving medicines can produce significant harms to patients who would benefit by approval (taking the form of Type I error). These harms are of potentially comparable magnitude to harms resulting from setting the regulatory bar too low, and thus wrongly approving unsafe medicines (taking the form of Type II error).

Empirical studies tend to support the theoretical claim that regulators are unlikely to be risk neutral as between these two kinds of error. Instead, studies demonstrate that regulation is systematically biased in favor of avoiding the more tangible harm associated with Type II error than the abstract and generally unobservable harm from Type I error.[78] As an example, the Department of Housing and Urban Development (HUD) tends to allocate funds to cities with less risky investment projects to avoid the criticism that funded projects have failed, notwithstanding the claimed goal of using program funding to help "distressed" cities. Not surprisingly, housing projects in cities that are distressed are far more likely to be characterized as high risk.[79]

John Allison, Chairman of the BB&T Bank Corporation provides another example that illustrates how bureaucratic risk aversion can produce agency costs with the effect of undermining preferred Executive Branch policy.[80] In September 2008, in response to the American financial crisis at the time, the government enacted the Trouble Asset Relief Program (TARP), which was intended to stabilize the financial sector and avert bank

[77] *See supra* Chapter 10, at Part I.G.1.

[78] *See* MUELLER, *supra* note 6, at 370–71.

[79] John R. Gist & R. Carter Hill, *The Economics of Choice in the Allocation of Federal Grants: An Empirical Test*, 36 PUB. CHOICE 63 (1981).

[80] John Allison, Chairman, BB&T Corporation, Keynote Address, The Competitive Enterprise Institute's 25th Anniversary Gala (June 11, 2009) (transcript on file with authors); *see also* Judith Burns, *BB&T Chair Blasts TARP as a "Huge Rip-Off"*, WALL ST. J., June 12, 2009, https://www.wsj.com/articles/SB124482152282410185 (summarizing Allison's remarks).

failures.[81] The administrations of both President George W. Bush[82] and Barack Obama[83] stated that an additional justification for infusing capital into the financial sector was to encourage banks to make new loans. Allison, however, notes that the private incentives of ground-level bank examiners directly contradicted this goal. Whereas each President sought to encourage greater lending as a means of jump-starting the economy, individual bank examiners were primarily motivated to ensure that the banks that they oversaw avoided unnecessary risks that could lead to failure, thereby jeopardizing their individual stature. As a result, local examiners forced banks to tighten lending standards and to curtail lending. Allison maintains that one effect was to inhibit his bank from making loans that it would have made absent TARP, possibly causing some businesses to fail that otherwise might not have.

Does the assumption that risk neutrality is welfare-enhancing always hold? Are there circumstances in which social welfare is enhanced by discounting one form of error in favor of another? Does the different standard of proof in the criminal and civil context illustrate this proposition? Why or why not? Are there other regulatory contexts in which the danger of false positives is greater than of false negatives? Or the reverse? Why or why not?

Political actors hold other biases that affect policy making. Senior political officials and legislators, for example, are predicted to exhibit a short-term bias, selecting policies with benefits that materialize during the expected office tenure (or before an election cycle), with substantial discounting for costs that are incurred beyond her term of office. Professor Todd Zywicki has observed that "Politicians and regulators . . . have an incentive to maximize their political and financial support in the next electoral cycle, whether two, four, or six years."[84] Consider two examples that run in potentially opposite ideological directions, first, persistent budget deficits, which result from providing benefits today at the expense of voters in the future, and second, delayed action (or, more to the point, inaction) on global climate change, which delays potentially costly regulatory interventions that benefit future generations at a cost to present economic activity.[85] Other policy decisions also reflect this tendency toward short-run vote maximization. Thus, for instance, the federal government historically has a poor record of managing federal lands for long-term benefit. Grazing, logging, and mining rights on federal lands traditionally have been sold for below-market prices to win political support from extractive business interests, leading to overuse of those resources. As a result of these

---

[81] Emergency Economic Stabilization Act of 2008, Pub. L. No. 110–343, §§ 101–136, 122 Stat. 3765–800.

[82] *See* Press Release, Remarks by Secretary Henry M. Paulson, Jr. on Financial Rescue Package and Economic Update (Nov. 12, 2008), https://www.treasury.gov/press-center/press-releases/Pages/hp1265.aspx.

[83] *See* Press Release, Secretary Geithner Introduces Financial Stability Plan (Feb. 10, 2009), https://www.treasury.gov/press-center/press-releases/Pages/tg18.aspx.

[84] Todd J. Zywicki, *Environmental Externalities and Political Externalities: The Political Economy of Environmental Regulation and Reform*, 73 TUL. L. REV. 845, 900 (1999); *see also* John A. Baden & Richard L. Stroup, *The Environmental Costs of Government Action*, POL'Y REV., Spring 1978, at 23.

[85] For a related discussion, see Max Stearns, *Ideological Blindspots (Part III): The Grandchildren*, BLINDSPOT BLOG (Mar. 29, 2017), https://www.blindspotblog.us/single-post/2017/03/29/Ideological-Blindspots-part-II-The-Grandchildren.

subsidies, the direct costs of running those federal programs exceed the revenues generated. Although these subsidies are difficult to justify from an environmental or financial perspective, they appear to generate political benefits to regulators and their political overseers. As with the tendency for the government to accrue budget deficits and to delay meaningful regulatory interventions to address global climate change, federal resource policy thus tends toward the promotion of short-term political goals at the expense of long-term environmental and economic goals.

B. Marginality and Cost Externalization

Commentators have also observed that bureaucrats tend to exhibit an imperfect understanding of marginal costs and benefits of regulation.[86] Justice Stephen Breyer has argued, for example, that policy makers select issues for their regulatory agenda based upon such random factors as news cycles and media attention, rather than based upon a systematic cost-benefit analysis.[87] One barrier to effective cost-benefit analysis of regulation is the absence of a price signal to convey to regulators the relative benefits and costs. In addition, many regulatory costs are borne by private market actors, rather than by the agency, further inhibiting helpful feedback signals concerning the optimal scope and form of regulation.

Numerous efforts have been made to identify substitutes for market valuation in the regulatory context. These include proxies for marginal costs and benefits of regulations, as seen, for example, in the Paperwork Reduction Act, which aims to measure the administrative costs of regulations on private actors. While these methods improve such cost estimates, they are crude measures at best. Cost-benefit analysis is often inconsistently applied, thus producing unpredictable results. While commentators have identified some life-saving regulations implemented at low cost, they have also identified regulations that fail cost-benefit analysis.[88]

Regulatory compliance also has distributional effects. For instance, certain types of regulation (such as command-and-control environmental regulation) impose compliance costs largely without regard to the scale of the regulated firm.[89] Regulatory compliance requirements that demand fixed capital investments, for example, tend to place disproportionate burdens on small businesses that must amortize those costs over a smaller production schedule as compared with larger competitors.[90] Paperwork and other

---

86 *See* W. Kip Viscusi, *The Dangers of Unbounded Commitments to Regulate Risk*, *in* RISKS, COSTS, AND LIVES SAVED: GETTING BETTER RESULTS FROM REGULATION (Robert W. Hahn ed., 1996); Christopher C. Demuth, *The Regulatory Budget*, REGULATION, Mar.–Apr. 1980, at 29, 34–36.

87 *See* STEPHEN BREYER, BREAKING THE VICIOUS CIRCLE: TOWARD EFFECTIVE RISK REGULATION 19–29 (1993).

88 *See* W. Kip Viscusi et al., *Measures of Mortality Risk*, 14 J. RISK & UNCERTAINTY 213, 228 tbl.9 (1997).

89 Zywicki, *supra* note 84, at 864–66.

90 A 2010 report from the Small Business Administration Office of Advocacy assessed the regulatory burden on American businesses at $8,086 on average, but noted that small businesses (defined as employing fewer than 20 employees) bore regulatory costs of $10,585 per employee, whereas firms with over 500 employees bore regulatory costs of $7,755 per employee, a 36 percent difference. *See* NICOLE V. CRAIN & W. MARK CRAIN, THE IMPACT OF REGULATORY COSTS ON SMALL FIRMS (Sept. 2010), https://www.sba.gov/sites/default/files/The%20Impact%20of%20Regulatory%20Costs%20on%20Small%20Firms%20(Full).pdf.

regulatory compliance measures also impose many fixed costs, and studies have found that larger companies spend proportionately less on legal services (as a percentage of sales) than do small companies.[91] By contrast, other forms of regulation deliberately take account of firm size, such as taxes on the volume of pollution emitted as a by-product of a factory's production. Taxes based on production tend to have less severe distributional consequences than those that impose burdens independent of output.

The focus on governmental regulation also might ignore alternative market-based means of accomplishing regulatory goals, such as investments in name brands and third-party rating agencies, such as Consumers Union.[92] Providing unsafe products or services, or simply products of low quality, can result in effective financial penalties from diminished demand for those goods or services and a corresponding decline in the value of the firm's stock. The resulting financial losses often greatly exceed expected civil liability, including government penalties and fines.[93] Although regulatory oversight undoubtedly provides important benefits in terms of consumer safety in a broad range of areas, regulators sometimes risk overlooking or discounting non-governmental alternatives that serve similar functions, thereby leading to inefficient levels or types of regulation.

C. Selection Bias and Commitment to Regulatory Mission

Bureaucrats also risk a tendency toward "tunnel vision." This means too narrow a focus on their particular regulatory agenda at the expense of alternative policy goals.[94] Over forty years ago, Anthony Downs posited that bureaucrats' "views are based upon a 'biased' or exaggerated view of the importance of their own positions 'in the cosmic scheme of things.' "[95] If so, this sense of regulatory mission might be reinforced by a selection bias in the types of matters and persons with whom regulators routinely interact respecting related policy questions.

Consider, for example, how government makes agriculture policy.[96] The FTC has focused its efforts on improving consumer economic welfare and, as a result, has tended to favor increased competition and lower prices for agricultural products. In contrast with the FTC, the United States Department of Agriculture (USDA) is highly concerned with the welfare of farmers, its primary constituency, even if the resulting policies raise average consumer prices. Rather than pursuing policies designed to lower prices for all consumers, as the FTC does, the USDA might prefer reduced competition and higher agricultural prices with a food stamp program that maintains demand among low income consumers.

---

[91] B. Peter Pashigian, *A Theory of Prevention and Legal Defense with an Application to the Legal Costs of Companies*, 25 J.L. & ECON. 247 (1982).

[92] *See generally* REPUTATION: STUDIES IN THE VOLUNTARY ELICITATION OF GOOD CONDUCT (Daniel B. Klein ed., 1997); Benjamin Klein & Keith B. Leffler, *The Role of Market Forces in Assuring Contractual Performance*, 89 J. POL. ECON. 615 (1981).

[93] *See* Mark L. Mitchell, *The Impact of External Parties on Brand-Name Capital: The 1982 Tylenol Poisonings and Subsequent Cases*, 27 ECON. INQUIRY 601 (1989); Mark L. Mitchell & Michael T. Maloney, *Crisis in the Cockpit? The Role of Market Forces in Promoting Air Travel Safety*, 32 J.L. & ECON. 329 (1989).

[94] *See* BREYER, *supra* note 87, at 10–19; *see also* Zywicki, *supra* note 7.

[95] ANTHONY DOWNS, INSIDE BUREAUCRACY 107 (1967).

[96] This paragraph is based on Zywicki's personal experience at the FTC.

Each agency tends to emphasize its particular regulatory mission and constituencies, even if those objectives sometimes conflict with the missions of other agencies.

Economic theory predicts that organizations will tend to attract individuals with a comparative advantage at—and a considerable interest in and commitment to—the tasks that they are called upon to perform. Employment generally provides two types of remuneration: monetary income and non-monetary, or psychic, income, such as intrinsic satisfaction or a sense of "doing good." As Spence and Cross observe, "That agencies are systematically more loyal to their basic mission seems persuasive, even obvious. People who are sympathetic to that mission are more likely to be attracted to work at the agency."[97] A principled commitment to the value of an agency's mission also might reconcile the apparent anomaly that bureaucrats seek increased budgets even if they do not personally benefit.[98] Larger budgets and a broader scope of authority will give the agency greater ability to pursue their desired regulatory objectives and, to that extent, reinforce a bureaucrat's sense of beneficial accomplishment.

Bureaucrats also pursue ideological and political objectives.[99] One study of public employees in eleven countries found them to be more politically left of center than the general population and to generally support a larger government role in the economy.[100] A study by Donald Blake also found a general tendency of government employees to lean ideologically left of center.[101] This orientation might result from either self-interest (within various governmental systems, political parties to the left of center generally tend to support larger public sectors) or ideology. The direction of causation is largely irrelevant, however, as the ideological orientation of employees might both reflect and cause a preference for larger and more activist government. For instance, Tim Muris has argued that one possible explanation for what he characterizes as the FTC's extreme activist tilt during the late-1970s was the influx of many new "Naderite," ideologically motivated consumer-activist lawyers into the agency.[102]

Regulators can also structure regulation so as to create ongoing demand for their services. As Richard Harris and Sidney Milkis have observed, "Because the lifeblood of bureaucratic entities is administrative programs, bureaucrats enhance their position by helping to develop new programs and protect their current position by opposing the destruction of existing programs."[103] Todd Zywicki has observed that by writing highly complex, detailed, and specific regulations, bureaucrats can build "obsolescence" into

---

[97] Spence & Cross, *supra* note 5, at 120 (emphasis omitted); *see also id.* at 115 n.76 (providing examples).

[98] Blaise & Dion, *supra* note 13, at 356–57.

[99] *See, e.g.*, William W. Buzbee, *Remember Repose: Voluntary Contamination Cleanup Approvals, Incentives, and the Costs of Interminable Liability*, 80 MINN. L. REV. 35, 82–96 (1995).

[100] André Blais, Donald E. Blake & Stéphane Dion, *The Voting Behavior of Bureaucrats*, *in* BUDGET-MAXIMIZING BUREAUCRAT, *supra* note 13, at 205.

[101] Donald E. Blake, *Policy Attitudes and Political Ideology in the Public Sector*, *in* BUDGET-MAXIMIZING BUREAUCRAT, *supra* note 13, at 231.

[102] *See* Muris, *supra* note 62 (referring to policy positions associated with Ralph Nader); *see also* RICHARD A. HARRIS & SIDNEY M. MILKIS, THE POLITICS OF REGULATORY CHANGE: A TALE OF TWO AGENCIES 154–80 (2d ed. 1996).

[103] HARRIS & MILKIS, *supra* note 102, at 47.

regulations, thereby requiring their ongoing services to update them.[104] This might explain the historical preference among environmental regulators for economically inefficient, technology-based, command-and-control regulation rather than more cost-effective decentralized market-based schemes. Technology-based standards place an ongoing demand for regulatory services given the pace of technological change. Thus, Zywicki notes that each technological development will initiate a new round of conflict among competing interest groups, with some urging the required adoption of the new technology and others supporting the status quo.

If these characterizations are sound, what do they suggest about the nature of those prone to pursuing careers as agency bureaucrats? Are agencies generally biased in favor of regulatory expansion? What about those who joined the ranks of federal bureaucracy during such conservative administrations as Ronald Reagan, George W. Bush, or Donald Trump?[105] Did those administrations attract bureaucrats who enjoyed psychic income from pursuing deregulatory agendas? Consider also why the Reagan, Bush II, and Trump administrations did not dismantle agencies whose earlier, more liberal, policies they sought to reverse, instead staffing those agencies with bureaucrats favoring a deregulatory agenda. Is this consistent with the theories advanced by Harris and Milkis, and Zywicki, that bureaucrats pursue policies that promote continued demands for their services? Dismantling an agency as a means of deregulation makes it more difficult for another administration to sharply reverse the direction of regulatory policy.[106] By retaining the agencies, yet staffing with deregulators, however, these administrations were able to demand ongoing support to maintain deregulatory policies over time. Do you find this analysis persuasive? Why or why not?

Do the same arguments concerning the absence of pricing mechanisms in affecting the level of governmental regulation and services apply to those bureaucrats who are inclined to pursue either regulatory or deregulatory agendas? Is it possible that the zeal for deregulation will be applied without adequate consideration of the costs of removing regulatory protections already in place? Why or why not? Which of the preceding models, if any, is most helpful in answering these questions? Why?

D. Executive Branch Response to Agency Costs

The growth of the administrative state since the New Deal has created special challenges for the President in seeking to coordinate the various regulatory initiatives throughout the executive branch.[107] Although it is difficult for the President to closely supervise the thousands of ongoing regulatory, adjudicatory, and other processes within the executive branch, in the end it is the President who bears political responsibility for those activities. This is all the more complicated as several departments and agencies may

[104] Zywicki, *supra* note 84, at 894.

[105] *See* HARRIS & MILKIS, *supra* note 102, at 181–224.

[106] Does this help to explain the phenomenon of "midnight regulations"? *See* Elizabeth Kolbert, Comment, *Midnight Hour*, NEW YORKER (Nov. 24, 2008), http://www.newyorker.com/talk/comment/2008/11/24/081124taco_talk_kolbert (discussing the history of midnight regulations since Jimmy Carter).

[107] *See* DeMuth & Ginsburg, *supra* note 67, at 1079–80.

share overlapping jurisdiction respecting an issue, reviewing the same activity from a variety of perspectives and with different objectives and preferences.

This problem of creating coherent regulatory policy has been chronic, and Presidents have given this responsibility to different offices over time, including the Vice President.[108] In recent decades, the primary office performing this duty has been the OIRA. Growing out of an informal regulatory review process in Richard Nixon's Office of Management and Budget, OIRA was established as part of the 1980 Paperwork Reduction Act. OIRA reviews all economically significant regulations proposed by executive branch agencies, and its central tasks have been supported by Presidents of both parties for the past thirty years.[109] Sally Katzen, OIRA Administrator during the Clinton Administration, described the importance of its oversight process as follows:

> The agencies focus like a laser, as they should, on their statutory missions—in the case of EPA, protecting the environment. The White House and OIRA take a broader view and consider how, for example, an environmental proposal will affect energy resources, tax revenues, health policy, etc. Stated another way, EPA is pursuing a parochial interest; OIRA is tempering that with the national interest, as it should.[110]

Assuming this is correct, the analysis raises an important question: What does the head of OIRA rationally seek to maximize? To what extent does the preceding analysis imply that a given Administration's regulatory priorities are likely to affect any seemingly independent analysis of the relative costs and benefits of various agency activities that have the potential to produce regulatory conflict? In the event that two or more agency programs conflict, how is that conflict likely to be resolved? To what extent is public choice analysis helpful in answering this question? To what extent is the spatial model of presidential selection that opened Chapter 19 helpful in answering this question? Given the potential conflicts among agencies respecting overlapping areas, is it possible that the agency deference rules announced in *Chevron* and *Mead* promote a race to regulate first? Does this raise analytical difficulties for judicial deference? Why or why not? Keep these questions in mind as you review the application, which follows.

Law professor Cass Sunstein, who served as the Administrator of OIRA from 2009 to 2012, refers to the office as "the cockpit of the regulatory state."[111] In addition to playing the role of coordinating regulatory policy across the executive branch, Sunstein identifies three additional functions that OIRA performs. First, he argues that OIRA plays a role in improving the substance of regulations by serving as a central regulatory clearinghouse among different regulatory agencies, enabling the President to draw upon "specialized information held by diverse people (often career officials) within the

---

[108] *See* Keith Werhan, *Delegalizing Administrative Law*, 1996 U. ILL. L. REV. 423, 425–31.

[109] *See* Exec. Order No. 12,866, 3 C.F.R. 638 (1993), *reprinted as amended in* 5 U.S.C. § 601 (2006); *see also* Lisa Schultz Bressman & Michael P. Vandenbergh, *Inside the Administrative State: A Critical Look at the Practice of Presidential Control*, 105 MICH. L. REV. 47 (2006); Steven Croley, *White House Review of Agency Rulemaking: An Empirical Investigation*, 70 U. CHI. L. REV. 821 (2003); Sally Katzen, *A Reality Check on an Empirical Study: Comments on "Inside the Administrative State,"* 105 MICH. L. REV. 1497 (2007).

[110] Katzen, *supra* note 109, at 1505.

[111] *See* CASS R. SUNSTEIN, SIMPLER: THE FUTURE OF GOVERNMENT 3–4 (2013).

executive branch.[112] Second, OIRA serves as "a guardian of a well-functioning administrative process" by promoting the integrity and transparency of the public comment system so as to encourage thorough decision making and public confidence in regulatory outputs.[113] Finally, Sunstein notes that in addition to reactively refereeing disputes among various agencies, OIRA also plays a proactive role of "establishing the regulatory priorities of the executive branch.[114] Thus, through OIRA, the President can push out regulatory initiatives to federal agencies and departments. Sunstein offers the example of OIRA's role in overseeing the execution of President Obama's "call for a government-wide regulatory lookback designed to reassess rules [then] on the books."[115]

III. APPLICATIONS: DEFERENCE TO AGENCY DECISIONS WHETHER TO REGULATE

Public choice insights have influenced judicial deference to agency decision making in contexts implicating agency self-interest, as it arises in various settings.[116] For instance, some cases directly involve an agency's financial self-interest, such as the interpretation of a contract entered into between an agency and a private party or the interpretation of a statute potentially implicating the agency's contractual obligations. Sometimes statutory construction can affect an agency's competitive position against private entities within the marketplace.[117]

Another potentially far-reaching context that holds considerable implications for the preceding models involves an agency's interpretation of its own jurisdiction, even before reaching the substance of its regulation. Based upon insights from public choice, the analysis likely varies depending on whether the agency seeks to expand or, instead, to protect its autonomy and independence. As you read the cases that follow, consider which of the theories of agency incentives, by Niskanen, Wilson, or the others that we have reviewed, best explains the agencies' decisions whether to assert or withhold jurisdiction. Consider also the normative question as to whether public choice theory suggests a need for a different degree of deference depending on whether an agency is seeking to expand or to contract its jurisdiction.

---

[112] *Id.* at 30–31.

[113] *Id.* at 31.

[114] *Id.* at 31–32.

[115] *Id.* at 32.

[116] *See* Timothy K. Armstrong, Chevron *Deference and Agency Self-Interest*, 13 CORNELL J.L. & PUB. POL'Y 203 (2004); *see also* Nathan Alexander Sales & Jonathan H. Adler, *The Rest Is Silence:* Chevron *Deference, Agency Jurisdiction, and Statutory Silences*, 2009 U. ILL. L. REV. 1497.

[117] For an example, consider *Air Courier Conf. of Am. v. Am. Postal Workers Union AFL-CIO*, 498 U.S. 517 (1991), where the Supreme Court declined to confer standing to postal workers contesting the relaxation of part of the postal monopoly based on claimed harm to their future employment, and holding that the postal monopoly was created to serve low service areas rather than to benefit postal employees or their union.

We present three cases: *FDA v. Brown & Williamson Tobacco Corp.*,[118] *Massachusetts v. EPA*,[119] and *Utility Air Regulatory Group v. Environmental Protection Agency (UARG)*.[120]

FDA v. Brown & Williamson Tobacco Corp.[121]

Brown & Williamson addressed the question of whether the FDA had the authority to regulate tobacco and, specifically, to regulate cigarettes and smokeless tobacco as "devices" that deliver nicotine to the human body. The FDA asserted the authority to do so, a position that the United States Supreme Court ultimately rejected.

Under the Food and Drug Act, the FDA must ensure that any product regulated by it must be "safe" and "effective" for its intended use. Thus, the Act generally requires the FDA to prevent the marketing of any drug or device where the potential for inflicting death or physical injury is not offset by the potential therapeutic benefit. In its rulemaking proceeding, the FDA determined that " 'tobacco products are unsafe,' 'dangerous,' and 'cause great pain and suffering from illness.' "[122] It further found that the consumption of tobacco products presents " 'extraordinary health risks,' and that 'tobacco use is the single leading cause of preventable death in the United States.' "[123]

Writing for the Court in *FDA v. Brown & Williamson Tobacco Corp.*, Justice O'Connor determined that given FDA's statutory mandate and its factual findings respecting cigarettes and smokeless tobacco products, if those products were classified as "devices" under the statute, the "FDA would be required to remove them from the market."[124] However, she noted, Congress has made clear its intent that tobacco products not be removed from the market and, in fact, had enacted several pieces of legislation since 1965 related to the problem of tobacco and health, legislation that was predicated on the assumption that tobacco products would remain legal.

Justice O'Connor wrote:

> In determining whether Congress has spoken directly to the FDA's authority to regulate tobacco, we must also consider in greater detail the tobacco-specific legislation that Congress has enacted over the past 35 years. At the time a statute is enacted, it may have a range of plausible meanings. Over time, however, subsequent acts can shape or focus those meanings. The "classic judicial task of reconciling many laws enacted over time, and getting them to 'make sense' in combination, necessarily assumes that the implications of a statute may be altered by the implications of a later statute." This is particularly so where the scope of the earlier statute is broad but the subsequent statutes more specifically address the topic at hand. "[A] specific policy

118 529 U.S. 120 (2000).

119 549 U.S. 497 (2007).

120 134 S. Ct. 2427 (2014).

121 529 U.S. 120 (2000).

122 *Id.* at 134.

123 *Id.*

124 *Id.* at 135.

> embodied in a later federal statute should control our construction of the [earlier] statute, even though it [has] not been expressly amended."
>
> Congress has enacted six separate pieces of legislation since 1965 addressing the problem of tobacco use and human health. . . .
>
> In adopting each statute, Congress has acted against the backdrop of the FDA's consistent and repeated statements that it lacked authority under the FDCA ["Food Drug and Cosmetics Act"] to regulate tobacco absent claims of therapeutic benefit by the manufacturer. In fact, on several occasions over this period, and after the health consequences of tobacco use and nicotine's pharmacological effects had become well known, Congress considered and rejected bills that would have granted the FDA such jurisdiction. Under these circumstances, it is evident that Congress' tobacco-specific statutes have effectively ratified the FDA's long-held position that it lacks jurisdiction under the FDCA to regulate tobacco products. Congress has created a distinct regulatory scheme to address the problem of tobacco and health, and that scheme, as presently constructed, precludes any role for the FDA.[125]

Justice O'Connor further observed that until this case, the FDA consistently and expressly disavowed jurisdiction to regulate tobacco. In fact, Congress's actions over time made clear "Congress' intent to preclude *any* administrative agency from exercising significant policymaking authority on the subject of smoking and health."[126] For instance, when the Federal Trade Commission at one point moved to regulate cigarette labeling and advertising, "Congress enacted a statute reserving exclusive control over both subjects to itself."[127] The Court notes:

> Taken together, these actions by Congress over the past 35 years preclude an interpretation of the FDCA that grants the FDA jurisdiction to regulate tobacco products. We do not rely on Congress' failure to act—its consideration and rejection of bills that would have given the FDA this authority—in reaching this conclusion. Indeed, this is not a case of simple inaction by Congress that purportedly represents its acquiescence in an agency's position. To the contrary, Congress has enacted several statutes addressing the particular subject of tobacco and health, creating a distinct regulatory scheme for cigarettes and smokeless tobacco. In doing so, Congress has been aware of tobacco's health hazards and its pharmacological effects. It has also enacted this legislation against the background of the FDA repeatedly and consistently asserting that it lacks jurisdiction under the FDCA to regulate tobacco products as customarily marketed. Further, Congress has persistently acted to preclude a meaningful role for *any* administrative agency in making policy on the subject of tobacco and health. Moreover, the substance of Congress' regulatory scheme is, in an important respect, incompatible with FDA jurisdiction. Although the supervision of product labeling to protect consumer health is a substantial component of the FDA's regulation of drugs and devices, the

---

[125] *Id.* at 143–44 (citations omitted).

[126] *Id.* at 149.

[127] *Id.*

> FCLAA ["Federal Cigarette Labeling and Advertising Act"] and the CSTHEA ["Comprehensive Smokeless Tobacco Health Education Act of 1986"] explicitly prohibit any federal agency from imposing any health-related labeling requirements on cigarettes or smokeless tobacco products.
>
> Under these circumstances, it is clear that Congress' tobacco-specific legislation has effectively ratified the FDA's previous position that it lacks jurisdiction to regulate tobacco.[128]

In addition to criticizing the FDA for this sudden reversal of position, the Court questioned whether Congress would have delegated to the FDA the authority to regulate or even to ban tobacco. The Court concluded that it was highly implausible that Congress would have impliedly delegated such a far-reaching authority to the FDA, especially in such a cryptic manner:

> Finally, our inquiry into whether Congress has directly spoken to the precise question at issue is shaped, at least in some measure, by the nature of the question presented. Deference under *Chevron* to an agency's construction of a statute that it administers is premised on the theory that a statute's ambiguity constitutes an implicit delegation from Congress to the agency to fill in the statutory gaps. In extraordinary cases, however, there may be reason to hesitate before concluding that Congress has intended such an implicit delegation.
>
> This is hardly an ordinary case. Contrary to its representations to Congress since 1914, the FDA has now asserted jurisdiction to regulate an industry constituting a significant portion of the American economy. In fact, the FDA contends that, were it to determine that tobacco products provide no "reasonable assurance of safety," it would have the authority to ban cigarettes and smokeless tobacco entirely. Owing to its unique place in American history and society, tobacco has its own unique political history. Congress, for better or for worse, has created a distinct regulatory scheme for tobacco products, squarely rejected proposals to give the FDA jurisdiction over tobacco, and repeatedly acted to preclude any agency from exercising significant policymaking authority in the area. Given this history and the breadth of the authority that the FDA has asserted, we are obliged to defer not to the agency's expansive construction of the statute, but to Congress' consistent judgment to deny the FDA this power.
>
> . . . .
>
> [W]e are confident that Congress could not have intended to delegate a decision of such economic and political significance to an agency in so cryptic a fashion. To find that the FDA has the authority to regulate tobacco products, one must not only adopt an extremely strained understanding of "safety" as it is used throughout the Act—a concept central to the FDCA's regulatory scheme—but also ignore the plain implication of Congress' subsequent tobacco-specific legislation. It is therefore clear, based on the FDCA's overall

128 *Id.* at 155–56 (citations omitted).

regulatory scheme and the subsequent tobacco legislation, that Congress has directly spoken to the question at issue and precluded the FDA from regulating tobacco products.

By no means do we question the seriousness of the problem that the FDA has sought to address. The agency has amply demonstrated that tobacco use, particularly among children and adolescents, poses perhaps the single most significant threat to public health in the United States. Nonetheless, no matter how "important, conspicuous, and controversial" the issue, and regardless of how likely the public is to hold the Executive Branch politically accountable, an administrative agency's power to regulate in the public interest must always be grounded in a valid grant of authority from Congress. And " '[i]n our anxiety to effectuate the congressional purpose of protecting the public, we must take care not to extend the scope of the statute beyond the point where Congress indicated it would stop.' "[129]

MASSACHUSETTS V. EPA[130]

A few years later, in *Massachusetts v. EPA* the Supreme Court revisited the question of an agency's authority to determine its jurisdiction, but in the context of an agency's *refusal* to assert jurisdiction. The case arose when Massachusetts and several other states sued the EPA, requesting that it be ordered to regulate certain "greenhouse gases," including carbon dioxide, that were alleged to cause global climate change that harmed the party states. Section 202(a)(1) of the Clean Air Act requires that the EPA "shall by regulation prescribe . . . standards applicable to the emission of any air pollutant from any class . . . of new motor vehicles . . . which in [the EPA Administrator's] judgment causes[s], or contribute[s] to, air pollution . . . reasonably . . . anticipated to endanger public health or welfare."[131] The EPA refused to regulate on the basis that is was not authorized to do so under the Clean Air Act and that even if it had such power, it was a reasonable exercise of its discretion to refuse action in light of what it viewed as the uncertainty of climate change science as well as the practical difficulties associated with various proposed regulatory solutions.

Writing for the majority of the *Massachusetts* Court, Justice Stevens held that EPA did have authority to regulate under the statute and that its refusal to do so was not based on specific findings about the lack of scientific evidence. The Court opened by noting the high importance of the issue:

A well-documented rise in global temperatures has coincided with a significant increase in the concentration of carbon dioxide in the atmosphere. Respected scientists believe the two trends are related. For when carbon dioxide is released into the atmosphere, it acts like the ceiling of a greenhouse, trapping solar energy and retarding the escape of reflected heat. It is therefore a species—the most important species—of a "greenhouse gas."

---

129 *Id.* at 159–61 (citations omitted).

130 549 U.S. 497 (2007).

131 42 U.S.C. § 7521(a)(1) (2012).

> Calling global warming "the most pressing environmental challenge of our time," a group of States, local governments, and private organizations, alleged in a petition for certiorari that the Environmental Protection Agency (EPA) has abdicated its responsibility under the Clean Air Act to regulate the emissions of four greenhouse gases, including carbon dioxide. Specifically, petitioners asked us to answer two questions concerning the meaning of § 202(a)(1) of the Act: whether EPA has the statutory authority to regulate greenhouse gas emissions from new motor vehicles; and if so, whether its stated reasons for refusing to do so are consistent with the statute.[132]

Justice Stevens first determined that the Commonwealth of Massachusetts had standing to present the challenge in its sovereign capacity and as owner of coastal property allegedly subject to erosion as a consequence of global warming. The Court also noted that it was taking the case despite reservations more generally about whether specific plaintiffs had standing because of the "unusual importance of the underlying issue."[133] The Court noted the immense international debate on the issue and ongoing efforts to address it through legislative and international action. The majority opinion continued:

> Congress . . . addressed the issue in 1987, when it enacted the Global Climate Protection Act. Finding that "manmade pollution—the release of carbon dioxide, chlorofluorocarbons, methane, and other trace gases into the atmosphere—may be producing a long-term and substantial increase in the average temperature on Earth," Congress directed EPA to propose to Congress a "coordinated national policy on global climate change," and ordered the Secretary of State to work "through the channels of multilateral diplomacy" and coordinate diplomatic efforts to combat global warming. Congress emphasized that "ongoing pollution and deforestation may be contributing now to an irreversible process" and that "[n]ecessary actions must be identified and implemented in time to protect the climate."
>
> Meanwhile, the scientific understanding of climate change progressed. In 1990, the Intergovernmental Panel on Climate Change (IPCC), a multinational scientific body organized under the auspices of the United Nations, published its first comprehensive report on the topic. Drawing on expert opinions from across the globe, the IPCC concluded that "emissions resulting from human activities are substantially increasing the atmospheric concentrations of . . . greenhouse gases [which] will enhance the greenhouse effect, resulting on average in an additional warming of the Earth's surface."
>
> Responding to the IPCC report, the United Nations convened the "Earth Summit" in 1992 in Rio de Janeiro. The first President Bush attended and signed the United Nations Framework Convention on Climate Change (UNFCCC), a nonbinding agreement among 154 nations to reduce atmospheric concentrations of carbon dioxide and other greenhouse gases for the purpose of "prevent[ing] dangerous anthropogenic [*i.e.*, human-induced]

---

[132] Massachusetts v. EPA, 549 U.S. 497, 504–05 (2007) (footnotes omitted).

[133] *Id.* at 506.

> interference with the [Earth's] climate system." The Senate unanimously ratified the treaty.
>
> Some five years later—after the IPCC issued a second comprehensive report in 1995 concluding that "[t]he balance of evidence suggests there is a discernible human influence on global climate"—the UNFCCC signatories met in Kyoto, Japan, and adopted a protocol that assigned mandatory targets for industrialized nations to reduce greenhouse gas emissions. Because those targets did not apply to developing and heavily polluting nations such as China and India, the Senate unanimously passed a resolution expressing its sense that the United States should not enter into the Kyoto Protocol. President Clinton did not submit the protocol to the Senate for ratification.[134]

After disposing of several questions involving standing, the Court turned to the merits of the case:

> On the merits, the first question is whether § 202(a)(1) of the Clean Air Act authorizes EPA to regulate greenhouse gas emissions from new motor vehicles in the event that it forms a "judgment" that such emissions contribute to climate change. We have little trouble concluding that it does. In relevant part, § 202(a)(1) provides that EPA "shall by regulation prescribe . . . standards applicable to the emission of any air pollutant from any class or classes of new motor vehicles or new motor vehicle engines, which in [the Administrator's] judgment cause, or contribute to, air pollution which may reasonably be anticipated to endanger public health or welfare." Because EPA believes that Congress did not intend it to regulate substances that contribute to climate change, the agency maintains that carbon dioxide is not an "air pollutant" within the meaning of the provision.
>
> The statutory text forecloses EPA's reading. The Clean Air Act's sweeping definition of "air pollutant" includes "*any* air pollution agent or combination of such agents, including *any* physical, chemical . . . substance or matter which is emitted into or otherwise enters the ambient air. . . ." On its face, the definition embraces all airborne compounds of whatever stripe, and underscores that intent through the repeated use of the word "any." Carbon dioxide, methane, nitrous oxide, and hydrofluorocarbons are without a doubt "physical [and] chemical . . . substance[s] which [are] emitted into . . . the ambient air." The statute is unambiguous.
>
> Rather than relying on statutory text, EPA invokes post-enactment congressional actions and deliberations it views as tantamount to a congressional command to refrain from regulating greenhouse gas emissions. Even if such post-enactment legislative history could shed light on the meaning of an otherwise-unambiguous statute, EPA never identifies any action remotely suggesting that Congress meant to curtail its power to treat greenhouse gases as air pollutants. That subsequent Congresses have eschewed enacting binding emissions limitations to combat global warming tells us nothing about what Congress meant when it amended § 202(a)(1) in 1970 and 1977. And unlike

[134] *Id.* at 508–09 (citations and footnotes omitted).

> EPA, we have no difficulty reconciling Congress' various efforts to promote interagency collaboration and research to better understand climate change with the agency's pre-existing mandate to regulate "any air pollutant" that may endanger the public welfare. Collaboration and research do not conflict with any thoughtful regulatory effort; they complement it.[135]

The Court then addressed the apparent inconsistency with *FDA v. Brown & Williamson Tobacco Corp.*:

> EPA's reliance on *Brown & Williamson Tobacco Corp.*, is . . . misplaced. In holding that tobacco products are not "drugs" or "devices" subject to Food and Drug Administration (FDA) regulation pursuant to the Food, Drug and Cosmetic Act (FDCA), we found critical at least two considerations that have no counterpart in this case.
>
> First, we thought it unlikely that Congress meant to ban tobacco products, which the FDCA would have required had such products been classified as "drugs" or "devices." Here, in contrast, EPA jurisdiction would lead to no such extreme measures. EPA would only *regulate* emissions, and even then, it would have to delay any action "to permit the development and application of the requisite technology, giving appropriate consideration to the cost of compliance." However much a ban on tobacco products clashed with the "common sense" intuition that Congress never meant to remove those products from circulation, there is nothing counterintuitive to the notion that EPA can curtail the emission of substances that are putting the global climate out of kilter.
>
> Second, in *Brown & Williamson* we pointed to an unbroken series of congressional enactments that made sense only if adopted "against the backdrop of the FDA's consistent and repeated statements that it lacked authority under the FDCA to regulate tobacco." We can point to no such enactments here: EPA has not identified any congressional action that conflicts in any way with the regulation of greenhouse gases from new motor vehicles. Even if it had, Congress could not have acted against a regulatory "backdrop" of disclaimers of regulatory authority. Prior to the order that provoked this litigation, EPA had never disavowed the authority to regulate greenhouse gases, and in 1998 it in fact affirmed that it *had* such authority. There is no reason, much less a compelling reason, to accept EPA's invitation to read ambiguity into a clear statute.
>
> EPA finally argues that it cannot regulate carbon dioxide emissions from motor vehicles because doing so would require it to tighten mileage standards, a job (according to EPA) that Congress has assigned to DOT. But that DOT sets mileage standards in no way licenses EPA to shirk its environmental responsibilities. EPA has been charged with protecting the public's "health" and "welfare," a statutory obligation wholly independent of DOT's mandate to promote energy efficiency. The two obligations may overlap, but there is no

[135] *Id.* at 528–30 (citations and footnotes omitted).

> reason to think the two agencies cannot both administer their obligations and yet avoid inconsistency.
>
> While the Congresses that drafted § 202(a)(1) might not have appreciated the possibility that burning fossil fuels could lead to global warming, they did understand that without regulatory flexibility, changing circumstances and scientific developments would soon render the Clean Air Act obsolete. The broad language of § 202(a)(1) reflects an intentional effort to confer the flexibility necessary to forestall such obsolescence. Because greenhouse gases fit well within the Clean Air Act's capacious definition of "air pollutant," we hold that EPA has the statutory authority to regulate the emission of such gases from new motor vehicles.[136]

The EPA further argued that even if it had legal authority to regulate greenhouse gases, it was a reasonable exercise of its discretion to decline to act. The Court rejected this claim, writing:

> Nor can EPA avoid its statutory obligation by noting the uncertainty surrounding various features of climate change and concluding that it would therefore be better not to regulate at this time. If the scientific uncertainty is so profound that it precludes EPA from making a reasoned judgment as to whether greenhouse gases contribute to global warming, EPA must say so. That EPA would prefer not to regulate greenhouse gases because of some residual uncertainty—which, contrary to Justice Scalia's apparent belief, is in fact all that it said—is irrelevant. The statutory question is whether sufficient information exists to make an endangerment finding.
>
> In short, EPA has offered no reasoned explanation for its refusal to decide whether greenhouse gases cause or contribute to climate change. Its action was therefore "arbitrary, capricious, . . . or otherwise not in accordance with law." We need not and do not reach the question whether on remand EPA must make an endangerment finding, or whether policy concerns can inform EPA's actions in the event that it makes such a finding. We hold only that EPA must ground its reasons for action or inaction in the statute.[137]

In one of two dissenting opinions in the case, Justice Scalia argued that nothing in the statute compels the EPA Administrator to determine whether a given substance creates a public health risk, only that the EPA must act if such a judgment is made. Thus, Scalia maintained, the EPA Administrator has discretion whether to make any such judgment in the first place, especially given the contentious nature of the underlying scientific claims about global climate change and the difficulties of identifying a workable regulatory solution to the problem. Scalia explained:

> The provision of law at the heart of this case is § 202(a)(1) of the Clean Air Act (CAA), which provides that the Administrator of the Environmental Protection Agency (EPA) "shall by regulation prescribe . . . standards applicable to the emission of any air pollutant from any class or classes of new

[136] *Id.* at 530–32 (citations omitted).

[137] *Id.* at 534–35 (citations omitted).

> motor vehicles or new motor vehicle engines, which *in his judgment* cause, or contribute to, air pollution which may reasonably be anticipated to endanger public health or welfare." As the Court recognizes, the statute "condition[s] the exercise of EPA's authority on its formation of a 'judgment.' " There is no dispute that the Administrator has made no such judgment in this case.
>
> The question thus arises: Does anything *require* the Administrator to make a "judgment" whenever a petition for rulemaking is filed? Without citation of the statute or any other authority, the Court says yes. Why is that so? When Congress wishes to make private action force an agency's hand, it knows how to do so. Where does the CAA say that the EPA Administrator is required to come to a decision on this question whenever a rulemaking petition is filed? The Court points to no such provision because none exists.[138]

Scalia continues, "I am willing to assume, for the sake of argument, that the Administrator's discretion in this regard is not entirely unbounded—that if he has no reasonable basis for deferring judgment he must grasp the nettle at once."[139] But, he continued:

> The Court dismisses this analysis as "rest[ing] on reasoning divorced from the statutory text." "While the statute does condition the exercise of EPA's authority on its formation of a 'judgment,' . . . that judgment must relate to whether an air pollutant 'cause[s], or contribute[s] to, air pollution which may reasonably be anticipated to endanger public health or welfare.' " True but irrelevant. When the Administrator *makes* a judgment whether to regulate greenhouse gases, that judgment must relate to whether they are air pollutants that "cause, or contribute to, air pollution which may reasonably be anticipated to endanger public health or welfare." But the statute says *nothing at all* about the reasons for which the Administrator may *defer* making a judgment—the permissible reasons for deciding not to grapple with the issue at the present time. Thus, the various "policy" rationales that the Court criticizes are not "divorced from the statutory text," except in the sense that the statutory text is silent, as texts are often silent about permissible reasons for the exercise of agency discretion. The reasons EPA gave are surely considerations executive agencies *regularly* take into account (and *ought* to take into account) when deciding whether to consider entering a new field: the impact such entry would have on other Executive Branch programs and on foreign policy. There is no basis in law for the Court's imposed limitation.
>
> EPA's interpretation of the discretion conferred by the statutory reference to "its judgment" is not only reasonable, it is the most natural reading of the text. The Court nowhere explains why this interpretation is incorrect, let alone why it is not entitled to deference under *Chevron U. S. A. Inc.* v. *Natural Resources Defense Council, Inc.* As the Administrator acted within the law in

---

[138] *Id.* at 549–50 (Scalia, J., dissenting) (citations omitted).

[139] *Id.* at 550.

declining to make a "judgment" for the policy reasons above set forth, I would uphold the decision to deny the rulemaking petition on that ground alone.[140]

On remand to the EPA, the EPA issued a Notice of Proposed Rulemaking in July 2008 that solicited comments on the possible health effects of greenhouse gases but refused to make any conclusions or findings on the issue.[141] The Notice was prefaced with the following statement by the EPA Administrator:

> EPA's analyses leading up to this ANPR [Advance Notice of Proposed Rulemaking] have increasingly raised questions of such importance that the scope of the agency's task has continued to expand. For instance, it has become clear that if EPA were to regulate greenhouse gas emissions from motor vehicles under the Clean Air Act, then regulation of smaller stationary sources that also emit GHGs [greenhouse gases]—such as apartment buildings, large homes, schools, and hospitals—could also be triggered. One point is clear: the potential regulation of greenhouse gases under any portion of the Clean Air Act could result in an unprecedented expansion of EPA authority that would have a profound effect on virtually every sector of the economy and touch every household in the land.
>
> This ANPR reflects the complexity and magnitude of the question of whether and how greenhouse gases could be effectively controlled under the Clean Air Act. This document summarizes much of EPA's work and lays out concerns raised by other federal agencies during their review of this work. EPA is publishing this notice today because it is impossible to simultaneously address all the agencies' issues and respond to our legal obligations in a timely manner.
>
> I believe the ANPR demonstrates the Clean Air Act, an outdated law originally enacted to control regional pollutants that cause direct health effects, is ill-suited for the task of regulating global greenhouse gases. Based on the analysis to date, pursuing this course of action would inevitably result in a very complicated, time-consuming and, likely, convoluted set of regulations. These rules would largely pre-empt or overlay existing programs that help control greenhouse gas emissions and would be relatively ineffective at reducing greenhouse gas concentrations given the potentially damaging effect on jobs and the U.S. economy.[142]

That Notice was followed in April 2009 by a Proposed Rule, issued after the intervening change in presidential administrations. The new Proposed Rule differed significantly from the previous Notice. It stated:

> Today the Administrator is proposing to find that greenhouse gases in the atmosphere endanger the public health and welfare of current and future generations. Concentrations of greenhouse gases are at unprecedented levels compared to the recent and distant past. These high atmospheric levels are the

---

[140] *Id.* at 552–53 (citations omitted).

[141] Regulating Greenhouse Gas Emissions Under the Clean Air Act, 73 Fed. Reg. 44,354 (July 30, 2008).

[142] *Id.* at 44,354–55.

> unambiguous result of human emissions, and are very likely the cause of the observed increase in average temperatures and other climatic changes. The effects of the climate change observed to date and projected to occur in the future—including but not limited to the increased likelihood of more frequent and intense heat waves, more wildfires, degraded air quality, more heavy downpours and flooding, increased drought, greater sea level rise, more intense storms, harm to water resources, harm to agriculture, and harm to wildlife and ecosystems—are effects on public health and welfare within the meaning of the Clean Air Act. In light of the likelihood that greenhouse gases cause these effects, and the magnitude of the effects that are occurring and are very likely to occur in the future, the Administrator proposes to find that atmospheric concentrations of greenhouse gases endanger public health and welfare within the meaning of Section 202(a) of the Clean Air Act.[143]

UTILITY AIR REGULATORY GROUP V. EPA[144]

In December 2009, the EPA under the Obama Administration made a formal finding that the emission of certain greenhouse gases might reasonably be anticipated to "endanger" public health and welfare.[145] The Administrator's "endangerment" finding provided the predicate for a number of regulatory actions taken by the EPA during the Obama Administration to regulate emissions of various greenhouse gases from both mobile and stationary sources under the Clean Air Act.

Among its new regulations, the EPA made stationary sources subject to the EPA's "Prevention of Significant Deterioration" (PSD) requirements and permitting requirements. In particular, the new EPA rules provided for the first time that relatively small sources of emissions would be required to obtain permits to operate. The extension of these requirements potentially would have swept into the coverage of the rule "numerous small sources not previously regulated under the" Clean Air Act, including " 'smaller industrial sources,' 'large office and residential buildings, hotels, large retail establishments, and similar facilities."[146] To limit the reach of its rule, the EPA further provided a "Tailoring Rule" that excluded many smaller sources of greenhouse gases.

The combined rules were challenged by several parties, including several states. The cases eventually found their way to the Supreme Court, which in *Utility Air Regulatory Group v. Environmental Protection Agency* (*UARG*) rejected the EPA's rule as an unreasonable application of its regulatory authority.

Under the Clean Air Act, EPA is required to formulate national ambient air quality standards (NAAQS) for air pollutants. Prior to its greenhouse gases rulemaking, the EPA had issued NAAQS for six pollutants: sulfur dioxide, particulate matter, nitrogen dioxide,

---

[143] Proposed Endangerment and Cause or Contribute Findings for Greenhouse Gases Under Section 202(a) of the Clean Air Act, 74 Fed. Reg. 18,886, 18,886 (proposed Apr. 24, 2009).

[144] 134 S. Ct. 2427, 2436 (2014).

[145] Endangerment and Cause or Contribute Findings for Greenhouse Gases Under Section 202(a) of the Clean Air Act, 74 Fed. Reg. 66,496–66,546 (Dec. 15, 2009).

[146] 134 S. Ct. at 2436.

carbon monoxide, ozone, and lead.[147] "States have primary responsibility for implementing the NAAQS by developing 'State implementation plans[,]' under which they "must designate every area within [their respective] borders as 'attainment,' 'nonattainment,' or 'unclassifiable,' with respect to each NAAQS."[148] For stationary sources the State's implementation plan must also include permitting programs whose requirements vary according to the classification of the area in which the source is located or is proposed to be located. Stationary sources located in areas designated attainment or unclassifiable are also subject to the Clean Air Act's PSD provisions, which require a firm to obtain a permit before it is authorized to construct or modify any " 'major emitting facility' " in " 'any area to which the PSD [program] applies.' "[149] Because of the EPA's expansive interpretation of the PSD program, every area of the country has been designated attainment or unclassifiable for purposes of the PSD rules; thus, "on EPA's view, all stationary sources are potentially subject to PSD review."[150]

The Clean Air Act defines a "major emitting facility" as "any stationary source with the potential to emit 250 tons per year of 'any air pollutant' (or 100 tons per year for certain types of sources)."[151] To qualify for a permit, the facility "must not cause or contribute to the violation of any applicable air-quality standards . . . and it must comply with emissions limitations that reflect the 'best available control technology' (or BACT) for 'each pollutant subject to regulation under' the Act."[152] In addition, under Title V of the Clean Air Act, it is unlawful to operate any "major source" without a comprehensive operating permit.[153]

After reviewing the preceding history, Justice Scalia, writing for the Court, stated:

> This litigation presents two distinct challenges to EPA's stance on greenhouse-gas permitting for stationary sources. First, we must decide whether EPA permissibly determined that a source may be subject to the PSD and Title V permitting requirements on the sole basis of the source's potential to emit greenhouse gases. Second, we must decide whether EPA permissibly determined that a source already subject to the PSD program because of its emission of conventional pollutants (an "anyway" source) may be required to limit its greenhouse-gas emissions by employing the "best available control technology" for greenhouse gases.[154]

The Court then considered the applicability of the PSD and Title V requirements:

> EPA thought its conclusion that a source's greenhouse-gas emissions may necessitate a PSD or Title V permit followed from the Act's unambiguous language. The Court of Appeals agreed and held that the statute "compelled" EPA's interpretation. . . . We disagree. The statute compelled EPA's

---

[147] *Id.* at 2435.

[148] *Id.*

[149] *Id.* (citations omitted).

[150] *Id.*

[151] *Id.*

[152] *Id.* (citations omitted).

[153] *Id.* 2435–36.

[154] *Id.* at 2438.

> greenhouse-gas inclusive interpretation with respect to neither the PSD program nor Title V.
>
> The Court of Appeals reasoned by way of a flawed syllogism: Under [*Massachusetts v. EPA*], the general, Act-wide definition of "air pollutant" includes greenhouse gases; the Act requires permits for major emitters of "any air pollutant"; therefore, the Act requires permits for major emitters of greenhouse gases. The conclusion follows from the premises only if the air pollutants referred to in the permit-requiring provisions (the minor premise) are the same air pollutants encompassed by the Act-wide definition as interpreted in *Massachusetts* (the major premise). Yet no one—least of all EPA—endorses that proposition, and it is obviously untenable.[155]

Scalia concluded that the EPA conflated two distinct concepts under the Clean Air Act, first its mandate to require permitting for major emitters of "any air pollutant," and second, its broader discretion, but not requirement, to regulate "all airborne compounds of whatever stripe." Scalia observed:

> Those interpretations were appropriate: It is plain as day that the Act does not envision an elaborate, burdensome permitting process for major emitters of steam, oxygen, or other harmless airborne substances. It takes some cheek for EPA to insist that it cannot possibly give "air pollutant" a reasonable, context-appropriate meaning in the PSD and Title V contexts when it has been doing precisely that for decades.[156]

Scalia added that in many other contexts, the EPA itself distinguishes between the narrower category of regulated "air pollutants" and the larger category of "airborne compounds." He wrote: "Although these limitations are nowhere to be found in the Act-wide definition, in each instance EPA has concluded—as it has in the PSD and Title V context—that the statute is not using "air pollutant" in *Massachusetts*' broad sense to mean any airborne substance whatsoever."[157]

He continued, "*Massachusetts* did not invalidate all these longstanding constructions. That case did not hold that EPA must always regulate greenhouse gases as an 'air pollutant' everywhere that term appears in the statute, but only that EPA must 'ground its reasons for action or inaction in the statute,' rather than on 'reasoning divorced from the statutory text.' "[158] Thus:

> *Massachusetts* does not strip EPA of authority to exclude greenhouse gases from the class of regulable air pollutants under other parts of the Act where their inclusion would be inconsistent with the statutory scheme. The Act-wide definition to which the Court gave a "sweeping" and "capacious" interpretation, is not a command to regulate, but a description of the universe of substances EPA may consider regulating under the Act's operative provisions. *Massachusetts* does not foreclose the Agency's use of statutory

---

155 *Id.* at 2439.

156 *Id.* at 2440.

157 *Id.*

158 *Id.* at 2440–41 (internal citations omitted).

> context to infer that certain of the Act's provisions use "air pollutant" to denote not every conceivable airborne substance, but only those that may sensibly be encompassed within the particular regulatory program. As certain amici felicitously put it, while *Massachusetts* "rejected EPA's categorical contention that greenhouse gases could not be 'air pollutants' for any purposes of the Act," it did not "embrace EPA's current, equally categorical position that greenhouse gases must be air pollutants for all purposes" regardless of the statutory context.

Having concluded that the EPA was not compelled to apply PSD and Title V requirements to greenhouse gases, the Court went on to reject the EPA's claim that it had discretion to impose the requirements, concluding that the EPA's position was not a reasonable interpretation of the statute:

> EPA itself has repeatedly acknowledged that applying the PSD and Title V permitting requirements to greenhouse gases would be inconsistent with—in fact, would overthrow—the Act's structure and design. . . . EPA described the calamitous consequences of interpreting the Act in that way. Under the PSD program, annual permit applications would jump from about 800 to nearly 82,000; annual administrative costs would swell from $12 million to over $1.5 billion; and decade-long delays in issuing permits would become common, causing construction projects to grind to a halt nationwide. The picture under Title V was equally bleak: The number of sources required to have permits would jump from fewer than 15,000 to about 6.1 million; annual administrative costs would balloon from $62 million to $21 billion; and collectively the newly covered sources would face permitting costs of $147 billion. Moreover, "the great majority of additional sources brought into the PSD and title V programs would be small sources that Congress did not expect would need to undergo permitting." EPA stated that these results would be so "contrary to congressional intent," and would so "severely undermine what Congress sought to accomplish," that they necessitated as much as a 1,000-fold increase in the permitting thresholds set forth in the statute.
>
> Like EPA, we think it beyond reasonable debate that requiring permits for sources based solely on their emission of greenhouse gases at the 100- and 250-tons-per-year levels set forth in the statute would be "incompatible" with "the substance of Congress' regulatory scheme." A brief review of the relevant statutory provisions leaves no doubt that the PSD program and Title V are designed to apply to, and cannot rationally be extended beyond, a relative handful of large sources capable of shouldering heavy substantive and procedural burdens.[159]

The Court concluded that such a massive enlargement of the EPA's authority was contrary to any reasonable construction of the reach of EPA's jurisdiction:

> EPA's interpretation is also unreasonable because it would bring about an enormous and transformative expansion in EPA's regulatory authority without clear congressional authorization. When an agency claims to discover

[159] *Id.* at 2442–43 (citations omitted).

> in a long-extant statute an unheralded power to regulate "a significant portion of the American economy," . . . we typically greet its announcement with a measure of skepticism. We expect Congress to speak clearly if it wishes to assign to an agency decisions of vast "economic and political significance." The power to require permits for the construction and modification of tens of thousands, and the operation of millions, of small sources nationwide falls comfortably within the class of authorizations that we have been reluctant to read into ambiguous statutory text. Moreover, in EPA's assertion of that authority, we confront a singular situation: an agency laying claim to extravagant statutory power over the national economy while at the same time strenuously asserting that the authority claimed would render the statute "unrecognizable to the Congress that designed" it. Since, as we hold above, the statute does not compel EPA's interpretation, it would be patently unreasonable—not to say outrageous—for EPA to insist on seizing expansive power that it admits the statute is not designed to grant.[160]

The Court concluded that the EPA's decision to "tailor" the reach of the rule to exclude many smaller sources lacked a statutory foundation and thus exceeded the agency's authority:

> In the Tailoring Rule, EPA asserts newfound authority to regulate millions of small sources—including retail stores, offices, apartment buildings, shopping centers, schools, and churches—and to decide, on an ongoing basis and without regard for the thresholds prescribed by Congress, how many of those sources to regulate. . . . We reaffirm the core administrative law principle that an agency may not rewrite clear statutory terms to suit its own sense of how the statute should operate. . . . Agencies are not free to "adopt . . . unreasonable interpretations of statutory provisions and then edit other statutory provisions to mitigate the unreasonableness." Because the Tailoring Rule cannot save EPA's interpretation of the triggers, that interpretation was impermissible under *Chevron*.[161]

The Court went on to uphold the EPA's imposition of the BACT for "anyway" sources as a valid exercise of its authority.

In an opinion concurring in part and dissenting in part, Justice Breyer agreed with the majority that the BACT rules were valid but disagreed with the majority conclusion that the PSD, Title V, and Tailoring Rules were not.[162] Breyer argued that the Clean Air Act vested the EPA with broad discretion to pursue the overall purposes of the Clean Air Act and maintained that the Act did not limit the EPA within the strict linguistic boundaries that the majority imposed. Breyer maintained his reading was more sensible, stating:

> For one thing, my reading is consistent with the specific purpose underlying the 250 tpy threshold specified by the statute. The purpose of that number was

---

[160] *Id.* at 2444 (citation omitted).

[161] *Id.* at 2446 (citations omitted).

[162] *Id.* at 2449–55 (Breyer, J., concurring in part and dissenting in part). Breyer's opinion was joined by Justices Ginsburg, Sotomayor, and Kagan.

> not to prevent the regulation of dangerous air pollutants that cannot be sensibly regulated at that particular threshold, though that is the effect that the Court's reading gives the threshold. Rather, the purpose was to limit the PSD program's obligations to larger sources while exempting the many small sources whose emissions are low enough that imposing burdensome regulatory requirements on them would be senseless.[163]

Justice Breyer reasoned that Congress intended to empower administrative agencies to make precisely the sorts of judgments made by EPA in crafting its rules in this case. Breyer stated:

> Last, but by no means least, a source related exception advances the Act's overall purpose. That broad purpose, as set forth at the beginning of the statute, is "to protect and enhance the quality of the Nation's air resources so as to promote the public health and welfare and the productive capacity of its population." The expert agency charged with administering the Act has determined in its Endangerment Finding that greenhouse gases endanger human health and welfare, and so sensible regulation of industrial emissions of those pollutants is at the core of the purpose behind the Act. The broad "no greenhouse gases" exception that the Court reads into the statute unnecessarily undercuts that purpose, while my narrow source-related exception would leave the Agency with the tools it needs to further it.[164]

Justice Alito, joined by Justice Thomas, also wrote a partial concurrence and partial dissent. Alito agreed with the majority's conclusion on the PSD, Title V, and Tailoring Rules, and he dissented from the majority's upholding of the applicability of the BACT rules for "anyway" sources, arguing that Congress intended the Clean Air Act to apply only to "the emissions of conventional pollutants and is simply not suited for use with respect to greenhouse gases."[165]

DISCUSSION QUESTIONS

1. In *FDA v. Brown & Williamson Tobacco Corp.*, the FDA asserted jurisdiction that the Court concluded it lacked. In *Massachusetts v. EPA*, the EPA refused to assert jurisdiction that the Court determined it had. Following *Massachusetts v. EPA*, on remand, the Bush Administration's EPA Administrator initially continued to refuse asserting its jurisdiction. By contrast, when the Obama Administration came into power, the EPA reversed course and pursued a more aggressive regulatory policy. In *UARG*, the EPA asserted authority simultaneously to regulate, and to exempt from regulation, sources of pollution that the Court later said that it lacked the authority to regulate. Do the models discussed in this chapter offer the basis for a consistent account of the combined decisions of the Court and of the agencies in these cases?

2. In *Brown & Williamson*, the extreme public importance of the issue, and the dramatic consequences that would flow from a contrary ruling, led the Court to infer that

---

[163] *Id.* at 2453.

[164] *Id.* at 2454–55.

[165] *Id.* at 2458 (Alito, J., concurring in part and dissenting in part).

Congress did not intend for the FDA to regulate tobacco. In *Massachusetts v. EPA*, the Court noted the extreme importance of the underlying regulatory issue and suggested that this might indicate Congress's intent to have the EPA regulate greenhouse gas emissions. Can the two cases—and the premises upon which they rest—be reconciled? What does public choice, or other theories of delegation, suggest about whether Congress generally should be presumed to have delegated authority respecting particularly important and controversial issues?

3. In *Massachusetts v. EPA*, Justice Scalia argued that if Congress wanted EPA to regulate greenhouse gases, it could simply mandate that the Administrator make a judgment as required by the statute or alternatively simply order EPA to regulate. Scalia suggested that given the high-profile nature of the issue, Congress's failure to take such steps implied that Congress did not intend for the EPA to regulate greenhouse gases. Do any of the models discussed in this chapter explain why the EPA Administrator refused to make this judgment? Or why Congress did not order EPA to make that judgment?

4. In *UARG*, Justice Scalia claimed that the Court typically "expect[s] Congress to speak clearly if it wishes to assign to an agency authority to regulate respecting an area of vast "economic and political significance.' " Do the models of legislative discussed in Chapter 19 provide any insight into Scalia's premise that Congress's refusal to order the EPA to regulate on such a controversial and high-profile issue suggests that Congress did not intend the EPA to do so? Based on the theories developed in this chapter, or more generally in this book, can you surmise why Congress might have wanted EPA to regulate in this highly controversial area yet chose not to provide a clear statement of its intent when doing so?

5. On remand, the Bush Administration's EPA Administrator originally expressed the opinion that regulation of greenhouse gases is an issue that should be left to Congress and not undertaken by the EPA. The Administrator's position might be read to anticipate the Supreme Court's later holding in *UARG* that Congress could not plausibly be assumed to vest such broad authority in the hands of the EPA without some clearer indication. Based on the models set out in this chapter, why might the EPA Administrator have embraced this position? Why might Congress be willing to allow the EPA to issue regulations on greenhouse gases rather than enacting related legislation as requested by the EPA Administrator?

6. Is it relevant to the determination of whether Congress intended EPA to act that the Senate declined to ratify the Kyoto Treaty? Why or why not?

7. In *Brown & Williamson*, Justice O'Connor noted that on an issue as important and high-profile as the possible banning of tobacco, it would be illogical to assume that Congress would permit an agency to act without a clear expression of congressional intent. This approach was echoed, and perhaps amplified, in Justice Scalia's opinion for the Court in *UARG*. In *Massachusetts v. EPA*, by contrast, Justice Stevens stressed the public and economic importance of regulating greenhouse gases while also maintaining that at the time the Clean Air Act was enacted, given the available scientific knowledge, Congress could not have anticipated that greenhouse gases, including carbon dioxide, might later be considered a pollutant. Justice Stevens further posited that a central reason for congressional delegation is to allow agencies to respond to changing conditions. Justice Breyer's dissenting opinion in *UARG* echoes Justice Stevens's argument and speculates that Congress might have wanted to delegate the "expert agency charged with administering the Act" to apply its expertise in effectuating the law's purposes. Based on the models discussed in this chapter, which of the underlying assumptions—those expressed by Justice O'Connor (echoed by Scalia) or by

Justice Stevens (echoed by Breyer)—concerning congressional behavior is more persuasive, and why?

8. As noted at the outset of this chapter, the foundation of the modern administrative state is often traced to the ideas of Woodrow Wilson, writing at the end of the nineteenth century. In *The Study of Administration*,[166] Wilson argued that the rise of the administrative state was inevitable in light of the growing complexity of society and the economy, and that it is thus necessary to develop a system of more formal training for government officials who could competently operate the emerging administrative state. As Wilson framed the issue, administrative expertise is seen largely as scientific decision making through expert management of administrative *processes*, and is thus independent of the substantive area to be regulated. In a sense, Wilson viewed administrative expertise as the public policy equivalent to the expertise one acquires in a Masters of Business Administration (MBA) program. In each instance, the core expertise involves generally applicable managerial skills that are largely fungible and that apply independently of the particular industry in which one is operating. Thus, an MBA degree rests on the idea that there is a core set of technical tools that apply to management of a bank, a furniture manufacturer, or an airline. Wilson's intuition concerning bureaucratic expertise is parallel inasmuch as he envisions a science of administration. Compare this with Justice Breyer's opinion in *UARG*. Breyer views agency expertise in terms of subject-matter, and relies on intuitions about in-depth knowledge as applied to the challenges of regulating particular industries.

Which, if either, of these characterizations seem more appropriate in the setting of judicial deference to regulatory policy making? Why? Might these approaches be reconciled if those with appropriate general training later specialize in a particular field of expertise? Why or why not?

9. Professor Lisa Heinzerling has given the name "power canons" to the Supreme Court's requirement that Congress provide a "clear statement" when it intends for an agency to regulate on matters that are particularly controversial or of particular public import.[167] She notes that the power canons are "directed as much to Congress as to the agencies."[168] Heinzerling notes that the power canons "require clear congressional language to enable an ambitious regulatory agenda but not to disable one."[169] She asserts that because of the asymmetric effect of this implicit clear-statement rule, it is ultimately a fig leaf for the anti-regulatory ideological agenda of the current Supreme Court: "This asymmetry is the power canons' tell; it is a sign that they mask a judicial agenda hostile to a robust regulatory state."[170] Do you think Heinzerling is correct that the clear-statement rule is merely cover for a conservative deregulatory agenda? Does a fair application of the clear-statement rule necessarily compel results that are hostile to regulation? Is the outcome in *King v. Burwell* consistent or in tension with Professor Heinzerling's power canons hypothesis? Why? Must outcomes uniformly apply in the same direction for Heinzerling's thesis behold? Why or why not?

---

[166] Wilson, *supra* note 3.

[167] Lisa Heinzerling, *The Power Canons*, 58 WM. & MARY L. REV. 1933, 1937 (2017).

[168] *Id.* at 1938. This applies, for example, to *UARG* and *King v. Burwell*, both discussed in Chapter 19.

[169] *Id.*

[170] *Id.*

To what extent can the three cases reviewed here be explained by the models of ideological judging discussed in Chapter 19? Please keep this question in mind as you read the "attitudinal model" of judicial behavior in Chapter 21.

10. As noted in Chapter 19, Justice Thomas has expressed skepticism of the *Chevron* doctrine. One reason is that providing deference to administrative agencies encourages those agencies to act strategically by trying to push the boundaries of their jurisdiction so as to enlarge the agency's power and discretion.[171] Do the theories of bureaucratic behavior discussed in this chapter provide help to address this concern?

11. In *Whitman v. American Trucking Associations, Inc.*,[172] the Supreme Court addressed a nondelegation challenge to certain rules issued by the EPA under the Clean Air Act. Under the Act, the Administrator of the EPA is required to set national ambient air quality standards (NAAQS) for each air pollutant for which "air quality criteria" have been issued. Once NAAQS have been promulgated, the Administrator must review the standard and the criteria on which it is based every five years. In 1997, EPA revised the NAAQS for particulate matter and ozone. The American Trucking Associations challenged the EPA action on the ground that the delegation of this authority to the EPA was made without an "intelligible principle" and therefore was an improper delegation under the Supreme Court's precedent in *J.W. Hampton, Jr., & Co. v. United States*.[173]

Several states joined the American Trucking Association (ATA) in challenging the rules. In *Massachusetts v. EPA*, the named plaintiff and several other states joined in bringing the action to try to force the EPA to regulate greenhouse gases (several other states filed an *amicus* brief supporting the EPA). In *American Trucking*, Michigan, Ohio, and West Virginia opposed the EPA's regulation. In *Massachusetts*, the states bringing the action included California, Connecticut, Illinois, Maine, Massachusetts, New Jersey, New Mexico, New York, Oregon, Rhode Island, Vermont, and Washington. Those who filed *amicus* briefs opposing the action in *Massachusetts* included Alaska, Idaho, Kansas, Michigan, Nebraska, North Dakota, Ohio, South Dakota, Texas, and Utah. Does public choice help to provide an explanation of the various states' positions in these two cases?

Professor Todd Zywicki has offered the following hypothesis: Environmental regulation can be very costly. States that adopt stricter environmental regulations such as regulation of greenhouse gases, whether for practical or ideological reasons, thereby create a competitive disadvantage for in-state businesses.[174] Other states, notably rural states with low population densities, will be less concerned about issues of ambient air quality and greenhouse gases and will thus oppose strict environmental regulations for economic or ideological reasons. Producers of raw materials (such as coal) or other products (such as automobiles or auto parts) that are likely to be adversely affected by such regulations also will oppose stricter regulation.

---

[171] *See* Michigan v. EPA, 135 S. Ct. 2699, 2713 (2015) (Thomas, J., concurring) ("Although we hold today that EPA exceeded even the extremely permissive limits on agency power set by our precedents, we should be alarmed that it felt sufficiently emboldened by those precedents to make the bid for deference that it did here.").

[172] 531 U.S. 457 (2001).

[173] 276 U.S. 394, 409 (1928).

[174] *See* Zywicki, *supra* note 84; Jason Scott Johnston, *Climate Change Hysteria and the Supreme Court: The Economic Impact of Global Warming on the U.S. and the Misguided Regulation of Greenhouse Gas Emissions Under the Clean Air Act*, 84 NOTRE DAME L. REV. 1 (2008); Henry N. Butler & Todd J. Zywicki, *Expansion of Liability Under Public Nuisance*, 20 SUP. CT. ECON. REV. 1 (2010).

On this account, states that unilaterally enact strict environmental regulations will support federal action that enables them to export the cost of their regulations onto states with different policy preferences, which Zywicki calls "political externalities." Does this breakdown of state economic interests provide the basis for a persuasive account of the lineup of states in *Massachusetts* and *American Trucking*? If so, does Zywicki's thesis provide any normative insight with respect to the nondelegation doctrine and the allocation of decision-making authority among Congress, agencies, and the courts? Which body is in the best position to respond to the inevitable distributional consequences of any proposed regulation? Why? How does this analysis relate to the distinction between *Pareto* and Kaldor-Hicks efficiency?

In *American Trucking*, Justice Breyer wrote a concurring opinion upholding the delegation. Breyer reasoned that the statute affords the EPA Administrator wide latitude to update the requirements of the Clean Air Act and to weigh those standards that " 'protect the public health' with 'an adequate margin of safety' " against other values such as economic effects and feasibility.[175] Can those trade-offs be resolved as a matter of "technical expertise"? Does the EPA's technical expertise include assessing the economic effects of its regulatory policies? Breyer also argues that given the substantial effect of ambient air quality standards on "States, cities, industries, and their suppliers and customers, Congress will hear from those whom compliance deadlines affect adversely, and Congress can consider whether legislative change is warranted." Should this "fire alarm" theory of delegation, meaning that in the event of a significant and unintended result, affected parties will notify Congress, be relevant to the question of whether a court should uphold a delegation? Why or why not?

---

175 531 U.S. at 494.

CHAPTER 21

The Judiciary (Part 1)

Introduction

The next two chapters focus on the judiciary. In this chapter, we apply the various tools of public choice to study the behavior of judges and to explain several prominent features of hierarchical common law judicial systems. Although there is considerable variation among judicial systems, we focus on several shared features of common law systems, while also noting relevant differences among systems where appropriate.

This chapter has four parts. Part I considers how to apply the economist's understanding of rationality to judges. Within the United States, Article III tenure substantially removes judges from many pressures that correspond with electoral political processes along with competitive pressures that correspond with market actors. Not all judicial systems afford judges the lifelong tenure and protection against salary reduction, as is the case under Article III.[1] Term-limited or elected judges are subject to codes of professional conduct that are designed, in part, to limit the influence of partisan political pressures, although life tenure provides more secure protections.[2] To the extent that judges are successfully removed from such pressures, the question arises how to construct economic models designed to capture judicial motivations and then translate those into identifiable maximands.

Part II presents various models designed to explain stare decisis or precedent. Not all judicial systems have precedent, at least as a formal constraint. Even in civil law regimes, however, which formally eschew precedent, commentators have observed that judges treat the decisions of prior courts on similar questions of law as important and influential sources of authority, with the effect of affording such decisions a hybrid status not unlike precedent.[3] Of course even common law systems, which are largely defined by

---

[1] U.S. CONST. art. III, § 1 ("The judges, both of the Supreme and inferior courts, shall hold their offices during good behavior. . . .").

[2] *See* MODEL CODE OF JUDICIAL CONDUCT (2007). *See also* Matthew J. Streb & Brian Frederick, *Judicial Reform and the Future of Judicial Elections*, *in* RUNNING FOR JUDGE 204 (Matthew J. Streb ed., 2007) (detailing the efforts of states to maintain an impartial elected judiciary); Mary L. Volcansek, *Appointing Judges the European Way*, 34 FORDHAM URB. L.J. 363 (2007) (describing the approaches used in several European countries to protect judicial selection from partisan influence).

[3] For a general discussion, see FRANCESCO PARISI, LIABILITY FOR NEGLIGENCE AND JUDICIAL DISCRETION 381–95 (2d ed. 1992); JOHN HENRY MERRYMAN & ROGELIO PÉREZ-PERDOMO, THE CIVIL

adherence to precedent,[4] vary considerably in the presumptive strength that they attach to the doctrine. Given the pervasive nature of some form of precedent within most judicial systems, legal scholars and economists have developed a variety of explanations, sometimes taking the form of models, to account for this persistent judicial norm. These include: (1) that judges have developed the doctrine on their own to enhance their individual ideological imprimatur on developing doctrine; (2) that society has imposed the obligation on courts to gain the benefit of stable legal doctrine; and (3) that the doctrine emerged historically within English practice as a result of intra-jurisdictional competition favoring those courts that offered more stable doctrine.[5] We will consider these sometimes competing, and sometimes complementary, accounts. The stare decisis analysis will also provide important insights into the pyramidal nature of judicial hierarchies and into the legal concept of materiality.

Part III introduces the longstanding jurisprudential distinction between holding and dictum. This includes both traditional and newly developed approaches to an age-old doctrinal challenge. Part IV presents three applications, each involving a Supreme Court decision.

In Chapter 22, we then continue the study of the judiciary, focusing on the tools of social choice. That chapter considers three important aspects of judicial decision making: first, decision-making processes that govern individual cases, including outcome voting and the narrowest grounds rule; second, the decision-making processes that govern groups of cases over time, including horizontal stare decisis and standing; and third, the tiers of scrutiny doctrines, which allow the Supreme Court to manage broad categories of cases through information signaling across a large number of judicial hierarchies. Each chapter concludes with applications.

I. MODELS OF JUDICIAL DECISION MAKING

A. Judicial Rationality

We begin with the following inquiry: What does rationality mean in the context of judicial decision making? Jurists, legal scholars, political scientists, and economists have expressed sharp disagreement on this question. In large part, this is due to the difficulty of identifying an acceptable proxy for rationality that can then be translated into a plausible maximand for judicial behavior. Although economic models are reductionist, simplifying assumptions are necessary to explain or emphasize notable features of the processes under review, whether in markets or governmental institutions. Thus far we have explored models that rest on one or more of the following simplifying assumptions:

(1) Firms seek to maximize profits,

LAW TRADITION: AN INTRODUCTION TO THE LEGAL SYSTEMS OF EUROPE AND LATIN AMERICA 39–47 (3d ed. 2007).

[4] Jonathan R. Macey, *The Internal and External Costs and Benefits of Stare Decisis*, 65 CHI.-KENT L. REV. 93 (1989).

[5] In Chapter 22, we introduce a social choice model that explains horizontal stare decisis as a partial solution to the problem of cycling judicial preferences over multiple cases. *See* Chapter 22 Part II.

(2) Individuals seek to produce and enjoy wealth,

(3) Legislators seek to be elected and re-elected, and

(4) Bureaucrats seek to expand the scope of their agency's budgets or their autonomy.

Most observers would likely agree that these admittedly general claims have explanatory power respecting large numbers of actors. And yet, with respect to specific firms or individuals, each generalization is contestable. The underlying assumptions are best understood as stylized, or heuristic, devices that allow economists to model and test hypotheses related to the probable efficacy of particular policy proposals. Although individual persons and firms are motivated by myriad objectives, identifying a plausible set of simplifying maximands allows for models that render the resulting analyses more manageable.

1. *What Do Judges Maximize?*[6]

How does rationality-based modeling help to inform our understanding of judges, especially those with Article III, or comparable, tenure?[7] Is it possible to identify credible proxies or maximands for those for whom the usual carrots and sticks that motivate other private or governmental actors have been effectively removed? With rare exceptions, Article III judges have practically no meaningful prospect of career advancement as a result of excellent job performance, have a vanishingly small likelihood of losing their jobs or job benefits as a result of substandard performance, and are unlikely to enhance their salaries other than by longevity of service.[8] Given the important role that judges play within our lawmaking system,[9] is it possible to identify a sufficiently plausible proxy or set

[6] Richard A. Posner, *What Do Judges and Justices Maximize? (The Same Thing Everybody Else Does)*, 3 SUP. CT. ECON. REV. 1 (1993). Judge Posner announced his retirement at the age of seventy-eight, on August 28, 2017. Sam Charles, *Judge Posner, One of World's "Leading Public Intellectuals," Retires*, CHI. SUN-TIMES (Sept. 1, 2017), https://chicago.suntimes.com/news/federal-appellate-judge-richard-posner-legal-giant-set-to-retire/.

[7] *See supra* note 1, and cite therein. *See also* Denise Dancy, *Judicial Selection, in* NAT'L CENTER FOR STATE COURTS, FUTURE TRENDS IN STATE COURTS: 20TH ANNIVERSARY PERSPECTIVE 12–13 (2008), https://cdm16501.contentdm.oclc.org/digital/api/collection/ctadmin/id/1258/download (listing the various methods other countries use to choose their judges); Roy A. Schotland, *New Challenges to States' Judicial Selection*, 95 GEO. L.J. 1077, 1084–85 (2007) (noting that judges are appointed in eleven states, face retention elections in nineteen states, and face contested elections—some partisan, some nonpartisan—in nineteen states).

[8] The salaries of Article III judges are fixed by Congress based upon duration on the level court on which the judge serves. *See* 28 U.S.C. § 5 (2012) (Supreme Court Justices); § 44 (circuit court judges); § 135 (district court judges). In 2007, Chief Justice Roberts pushed for a 50% salary increase for Article III judges. *See* CHIEF JUSTICE JOHN G. ROBERTS, 2007 YEAR-END REPORT ON THE FEDERAL JUDICIARY 6–8 (2008), http://www.supremecourtus.gov/publicinfo/year-end/2007year-endreport.pdf. CHIEF JUSTICE JOHN G. ROBERTS, 2008 YEAR-END REPORT ON THE FEDERAL JUDICIARY 7 (2008), https://www.supremecourt.gov/publicinfo/year-end/2008year-endreport.pdf ("I must make this plea again—Congress must provide judicial compensation that keeps pace with inflation."). He did not succeed in securing that increase, yet he has not continued to press for it.

[9] One interesting question is whether judges in other systems, in particular civilian regimes, and regimes with separate constitutional courts, are subject to different maximands than those that we might apply in modeling common law judges.

of proxies for rationality that provides the basis for constructing meaningful economic models designed to study judicial behavior?

In an intriguing article, *What do Judges and Justices Maximize? (The Same Thing as Everybody Else)*, Judge Richard Posner describes the underlying puzzle as follows:

> At the heart of economic analysis of law is a mystery that is also an embarrassment: how to explain judicial behavior in economic terms, when almost the whole thrust of the rules governing compensation and other terms and conditions of judicial employment is to divorce judicial action . . .—to take away the carrots and sticks. . . . The economic analyst has a model of how criminals and contract parties, injurers and accident victims, parents and spouses—even legislators, and executive officials such as prosecutors—act, but falters when asked to produce a model of how judges act.[10]

Posner compares judges to actors who are generally understood to work within contexts removed from ordinary private market incentives or from incentives associated with most political actors. These actors include directors of nonprofits, electoral voters, and spectators at sporting events.

Posner begins by considering the theory of nonprofits offered by Professor Henry Hansmann of the Yale Law School. Hansmann claims that for benefactors who are unable to monitor the distribution of their contributions to the ultimate beneficiaries, the nonprofit form improves the likelihood of the intended distribution because it prevents directors from profiting from residual income.[11] At one level, the nonprofit form provides a compelling analogy to judging, given that the public, like the charitable benefactor, has little practical means of effectively monitoring the dispensation of justice. At the same time however, removing incentives that motivate other governmental actors, for example the political accountability of elected officials, invites the risk of judicial slack. Posner suggests that to some extent, this concern can be ameliorated through careful judicial screening.

Posner emphasizes that in constructing a judicial utility function, he seeks to explain the motives of those he describes as "ordinary," rather than "extraordinary," judges.[12] For this more common group, Posner claims, the relevant factors include popularity, prestige,

---

10 Posner, *supra* note 6, at 2.

11 *See* Henry B. Hansmann, *The Role of Nonprofit Enterprise*, 89 YALE L.J. 835 (1980).

12 Although his focus in this article is United State Circuit Court judges, toward the end of his judicial career, Judge Posner made plain that he regarded most then-sitting Supreme Court Justices as rather ordinary. Despite the extraordinary position that they hold, Posner stated that only two of the then-sitting justices, Ruth Bader Ginsburg and Stephen Breyer, are truly qualified to be on that court, and that the last great Supreme Court justice was Robert Jackson. *See* David Lat, *Judge Richard Posner on SCOTUS: "The Supreme Court is Awful,"* ABOVE THE LAW (Oct. 24, 2016), https://abovethelaw.com/2016/10/judge-richard-posner-on-scotus-the-supreme-court-is-awful/; *see also* David Lat, *Judge Richard Posner Corrects the Record Regarding His Supreme Court Comments*, ABOVE THE LAW (Oct. 28, 2016), https://abovethelaw.com/2016/10/judge-richard-posner-corrects-the-record-regarding-his-supreme-court-comments/.

pursuit of the public interest, the desire to avoid being overruled (more pronounced for district court than appeals court judges at the federal level),[13] reputation, and leisure.[14]

Posner also compares judges to those who vote in political elections. Posner observes that this is "a valued consumption activity of many people," and explains that judges "are constantly voting."[15] Posner suggests that for most judges, even those on the Supreme Court, the joy of voting comes not from the often supposed power play associated with resolving disputes, but rather from the sense of "satisfaction from casting votes that are not merely symbolic expressions, but count."[16] Posner adds that for judges who craft their own opinions, as Posner was known to do,[17] judging provides the additional satisfaction of being a published author. Posner further explains why appeals court judges sometimes defer to one member who holds particularly strong views on a case. "Going-along" or "live and let live" voting is different from legislative logrolling, Posner claims, because the former is "leisure-serving" while the latter is "power-maximizing."[18]

Posner contends that an important characteristic of judging, much like serious sports fandom or attendance at the theater, rests on ensuring compliance with the rules of the game or on suspending disbelief as needed to appreciate the tensions and nuances in a presented work of fiction.[19] Posner goes on to explain that: "The pleasure of judging is bound up with compliance with certain self-limiting rules that define the 'game' of judging," and claims:

> It is a source of satisfaction to a judge to vote for the litigant who irritates him, the lawyer who fails to exhibit proper deference to him, the side that represents a different social class from his own; for it is by doing such things that you

---

[13] Posner explains:

> Judges don't like to be reversed (I speak from experience), but aversion to reversal does not figure largely in the judicial utility function. It is nonexistent in the case of Supreme Court Justices, and fairly unimportant in the case of court of appeals judges because reversals of appellate decisions by the Supreme Court have become rare and most reflect differences in judicial philosophy or legal policy rather than mistake or incompetence by the appellate judges. Hence they are not perceived as criticism. [One study] found that reversal rates do not affect district judges' chances of promotion.

Posner, *supra* note 6, at 14–15 (citing Richard S. Higgins & Paul H. Rubin, *Judicial Discretion*, 9 J. LEGAL STUD. 129 (1980) (additional citations omitted)). Would appellate judges view en banc reversal in the same manner? Why or why not? *Compare* Richard S. Higgins & Paul H. Rubin, *Judicial Discretion*, 9 J. LEGAL STUD. 129 (1980), *with* Stephen J. Choi, Mitu Gulati & Eric A. Posner, *What Do Federal Judges Want? An Analysis of Publication, Citations, and Reversal*, 28 J. L. ECON. & ORG. 518, 524 (2012).

[14] *Id.* at 13–15, 20–23. Article III salary protection breaks away from historical practice among English common law judges whose salaries often depended litigant filing fees. *See* discussion Chapter 10, *supra* Part I.H.2.b.2.

[15] Posner, *supra* note 6, at 16.

[16] *Id.* at 18.

[17] Cass R. Sunstein, *Richard Posner, Leader of a Legal Revolution*, BLOOMBERG VIEW (Sept. 3, 2017), https://www.bloomberg.com/view/articles/2017-09-03/richard-posner-leader-of-a-legal-revolution.

[18] Posner, *supra* note 6, at 22.

[19] *Id.* at 25–26. Posner asserts that legal academics fail to recognize this analogy given their excessive focus on judicial opinions, which form a relatively smaller slice of the overall drama for judges for whom, "as for Hamlet, 'the play's the thing.' " *Id.* at 26 (quoting WILLIAM SHAKESPEARE, HAMLET act 2, sc. 2).

> know that you are playing the judge role, . . . and judges for the most part are people who want to be—judges.[20]

Do you find the various analogies that Posner identifies—directors of nonprofits, electoral voters, and fans of sports or the arts—persuasive in considering likely judicial motivations? Why or why not? Can you identify significant considerations that enter a judicial utility function that are absent in these contexts? If so, can you think of reasons why Posner might have omitted them from his model?

Consider Judge Posner's identification of particular characteristics he associates with judging, coupled with his claim that judges enjoy "playing the judge role." Does this analysis rest on a circular argument about the nature of judges and judicial behavior? If so, is that a problem? Is there a way to avoid the circularity?

2. *The Attitudinal Model: Sincere Versus Strategic Voting on the Supreme Court*

In Posner's judicial utility function, the desire to influence legal policy through case decision making plays a subordinate role.[21] In the works of other scholars, this is often treated, instead, as the overriding judicial maximand. An influential body of political science scholarship studies *judicial politics*.[22] These scholars, whose early work focused predominantly on the United States Supreme Court, tend to view judging as a quasi-political activity primarily motivated by the desire to affect legal policy in cases jurists are called upon to decide. And yet, while many political scientists accept the premise that Supreme Court Justices seek to affect legal policy, such scholars are split on whether the justices vote sincerely based on ideological predilections or vote strategically in their efforts to move doctrine in their preferred direction.

Adherents to the *Attitudinal Model*[23] posit that in the United States Supreme Court, the most robust predictor of case votes and outcomes rests on the ideological predilections—or "attitudes"—of the deciding justices, whose primary motivation is assumed to be infusing their normative policy preferences into legal doctrine.[24] The model

---

[20] *Id.* at 28. Posner's judicial utility function also includes income, reputation, popularity, prestige, and avoiding reversal. *See id* at 31.

[21] While Posner does not ignore ideology, observing that ideologues are more likely than others to be appointed at a young age with the understanding that their views will proceed to the bench, see, e.g., *id.* at 27, he does not incorporate it as a specific element in his utility function.

[22] LAWRENCE BAUM, AMERICAN COURTS: PROCESS AND POLICY (6th ed. 2008); LEE EPSTEIN & JACK KNIGHT, THE CHOICES JUSTICES MAKE (1998).

[23] JEFFREY A. SEGAL & HAROLD J. SPAETH, THE SUPREME COURT AND THE ATTITUDINAL MODEL REVISITED (2002).

[24] Attitudinalists and other judicial politics scholars often pit their supposition against what they describe as the *Legal Model.* They claim that the legal model holds that judges neutrally apply governing law based upon the dispassionate application of legal authority, statutes, regulations, or precedents. *See* Tracey E. George, *Developing a Positive Theory of Decisionmaking on U.S. Courts of Appeals*, 58 OHIO ST. L.J. 1635 (1998); Tracey E. George & Lee Epstein, *On the Nature of Supreme Court Decision Making*, 83 AM. POL. SCI. REV. 323 (1992). To be clear, attitudinal scholars do not claim that the left-right ideological axis captures all votes or outcomes, but rather they contend that particular case facts that implicate identifiable political attitudes are more robust than alternative predictors of Supreme Court votes and case outcomes. *See* Lee Epstein et al., *The Political (Science) Context of Judging*, 47 ST. LOUIS U. L.J. 783, 794–95 n.46 (2003). *See* Theodore W. Ruger et al., *The Supreme Court*

generally assumes that Supreme Court decisions, and the justices that participate in them, are almost uniformly susceptible of measurement along a single normative liberal-to-conservative ideological dimension, or spectrum. Based upon this premise, attitudinal scholars contend that if each justice votes honestly with respect to her or his preferred ideological view in each case, the outcome will reflect the preferences of a majority, based upon the coalition members' attitudinal predilections.

The Attitudinal model raises a difficult methodological question of measurement.[25] Judges are defined as "liberal" or "conservative" because they author or join decisions that are coded as liberal or conservative in the relevant database.[26] And outcomes are coded based upon whether liberal or conservative Justices comprise the majority coalition. As a way out of this seeming loop, Attitudinal scholars have sought external corroborating data when coding judicial ideology. These include past voting behavior (prior to joining the Supreme Court) and newspaper editorials.[27] The *Segal-Cover scoring system* seeks external confirmation of ideological coding in pre-confirmation newspaper editorials respecting Supreme Court nominees.[28] In addition, the *Martin-Quinn scoring index*[29] relies upon *Bayesian statistical analysis*[30] to track each Justice's *ideal point*, or preferred policy position, over time relative to those of other members of the Court for each year she or he is a member.[31] The Martin-Quinn system is notable in exposing the degree to which the ideal points of specific members of the Court "drift" over time, as compared with those of other Court members. Corroborating data that informs the Segal-Cover system, which relies upon information that is complete, or frozen in time, once a jurist ascends to the Supreme Court, is unlikely to account for observed *ideological drift*.[32]

Forecasting Project: Legal and Political Science Approaches to Predicting Supreme Court Decisionmaking, 104 COLUM. L. REV. 1150, 1157–59 (2004).

[25] *See* SEGAL & SPAETH, *supra* note 23, at 320–21 (discussing circularity criticism and responses).

[26] *See* ICPSR UNITED STATES SUPREME COURT JUDICIAL DATABASE TERM SERIES, https://www.icpsr.umich.edu/icpsrweb/ICPSR/series/86 (last visited Oct. 25, 2017) (providing searchable data collection compiled by Harold J. Spaeth and James L. Gibson of "all aspects of United States Supreme Court decision-making from the beginning of the Warren Court in 1953 up to the completion of the 1995 term of the Rehnquist Court."); Washington University of Law, The Supreme Court Database, http://scdb.wustl.edu/about.php (last visited Oct. 25, 2017) (providing searchable "Case Centered and Justice Centered data" for the 1946 through 2016 terms of the United States Supreme Court).

[27] SEGAL & SPAETH, *supra* note 23, at 320–24; Jeffrey A. Segal & Albert D. Cover, *Ideological Values and the Votes of U.S. Supreme Court Justices*, 83 AM. POL. SCI. REV. 557 (1989); Saul Brenner & Theodore S. Arrington, *Ideological Voting on the Supreme Court: Comparing the Conference Vote and the Final Vote with the Segal-Cover Scores*, 41 JURIMETRICS J. 505 (2001).

[28] Segal & Cover, *supra* note 27, at 559.

[29] Andrew D. Martin et al., *The Median Justice on the United States Supreme Court*, 83 N.C. L. REV. 1275 (2005).

[30] For a discussion of Bayesian analysis, see *supra* Chapter 15, at 636.

[31] Martin et al., *supra* note 29, at 1296–98.

[32] *Id.* at 1301–02. Felix Frankfurter, Byron White, Harry Blackmun, John Paul Stevens, and David Souter experienced notable ideological drift during their tenures on the Court. For a general discussion of ideological drift, see Maxwell L. Stearns, *Standing at the Crossroads: The Roberts Court in Historical Perspective*, 83 NOTRE DAME L. REV. 875, 922–37, 950–54 (2008); Lee Epstein et al., *Ideological Drift Among Supreme Court Justices: Who, When, and How Important?*, 101 NW. U. L. REV. 1483 (2007).

Political scientists have also called into question the attitudinal assumption that the Justices further their preferred policy views by voting consistently with their attitudes and thus without engaging in strategic voting behavior. In an early landmark work, *Elements of Judicial Strategy*,[33] Professor Walter F. Murphy likened Supreme Court Justices to other policy-minded officials who engage in strategic voting behaviors to further desired policy objectives. More recently, a group of political scientists has sought to demonstrate similar strategic interactions among members of the Supreme Court. The papers of various former Justices, including Brennan, Marshall, and Powell,[34] have provided rich data to use in the pursuit of this important research project.

Professors Lee Epstein and Jack Knight claim that Justices sometimes press insincere views in their effort to pursue an acceptable outcome more likely to gain majority support even when that position diverges from their ideal point.[35] Professors Forrest Maltzman, Paul Wahlbeck, and James Spriggs draw somewhat different implications from the same data, which they claim supports their "collective decision-making postulate."[36] The postulate holds that individual justices will seek to further their own policy preferences based upon a careful consideration of the policy preferences and strategies of other members on the Court. The authors demonstrate the importance of careful timing given the limited opportunities to influence opinion drafts. Such opportunities disappear once an opinion gains majority support.

An important feature of both works is the nature of the judicial interactions these political scientists rely upon to illustrate judicial strategy. Epstein and Knight rely upon *Craig v. Boren*,[37] a case presenting an equal protection challenge to a state law that imposed different gender-based age restrictions on access to so-called nonintoxicating or 3.2% beer.[38] The authors show that Brennan's papers reveal that he originally advanced an intermediate scrutiny test in the hope of forging a successful majority coalition, rather than insisting upon his sincerely held view, which favored strict scrutiny.[39] Maltzman, Spriggs, and Wahlberg offer a similar account of Brennan's voting behavior that draws upon *Pennsylvania v. Muniz*.[40] In that case, Justice Brennan successfully formed a majority coalition that recognized but limited a routine booking exception to the requirement of

---

[33] WALTER F. MURPHY, ELEMENTS OF JUDICIAL STRATEGY (1964).

[34] CONNIE L. CARTLEDGE, THURGOOD MARSHALL: A REGISTER OF HIS PAPERS IN THE LIBRARY OF CONGRESS (2001), http://lcweb2.loc.gov/service/mss/eadxmlmss/eadpdfmss/2001/ms001047.pdf; *Powell Papers*, WASHINGTON & LEE UNIVERSITY SCHOOL OF LAW, http://law.wlu.edu/powellarchives/page.asp?pageid=236 (last visited Oct. 25, 2017); AUDREY WALKER & MICHAEL SPANGLER, WILLIAM J. BRENNAN JR.: A REGISTER OF HIS PAPERS IN THE LIBRARY OF CONGRESS (2001), http://lcweb2.loc.gov/service/mss/eadxmlmss/eadpdfmss/2002/ms002010.pdf. *See also* ONLINE ARCHIVE OF CALIFORNIA, REGISTER OF THE WILLIAM H. REHNQUIST PAPERS (2008), http://pdf.oac.cdlib.org/pdf/hoover/rehnquis.pdf.

[35] *See* EPSTEIN & KNIGHT, *supra* note 22.

[36] *See* FORREST MALTZMAN, JAMES F. SPRIGGS II, & PAUL J. WAHLBECK, CRAFTING LAW ON THE SUPREME COURT: THE COLLEGIAL GAME 17 (2000).

[37] 429 U.S. 190 (1976).

[38] *Id.* at 192.

[39] MALTZMAN, SPRIGGS, & WAHLBECK, *supra* note 36, at 6–9.

[40] 496 U.S. 582 (1990).

Miranda warnings,[41] even though the position he claimed to prefer, expressed in Marshall's dissent, disallowed the exception altogether.[42]

Legal scholars have questioned the foundations of such political science accounts of Supreme Court voting behavior, including the assumption that jurists are primarily motivated to influence legal policy.[43] Is it possible to reconcile the common supposition among lawyers that judges are expected to behave "judicially" with the premise that they are first and foremost policy makers for whom preexisting attitudinal views are the most robust predictor of case outcomes? If the primary motivation of judges is to influence legal policy, what does this suggest about traditional understandings of constrained decision making, judicial modesty, abiding by precedent, and respect for separation of powers? Is it possible to reconcile the political scientists' understanding of judicial motivation with widely shared intuitions within the legal community concerning a properly limited judicial role? Are the political scientists unduly "cynical" or are the lawyers excessively "naïve"? Or is this a false dichotomy?

As noted above, attitudinalists, and other judicial politics scholars, generally pit their accounts of judicial behavior against what they label the *Legal Model*.[44] This alternative presents law as a kind of scientific or deductive process such that in any given case, the neutral application of shared legal principles is expected to produce a correct, or at least preferred, result. In our post-Realist legal culture,[45] very few legal scholars would subscribe to such a view. Indeed, this view appears to be something of a caricature of actual legal processes, which are more aptly characterized by contentious claims about the meaning of often ambiguous legal sources. Is it possible to reject the Attitudinal Model without reverting to an unrealistic, or hopelessly naïve, vision of the judicial process, for example, the Legal Model? Is it possible to identify a plausible judicial maximand that does not require assuming that judges are primarily motivated to affect legal policy?

One possible escape valve is to assume that some judges' ideological predilections, or attitudes, equate to a modest, non-policy-making, role in resolving cases. If so, one can accept the notion that judges seek to advance their own attitudes in resolving cases with

---

41 Miranda v. Arizona, 384 U.S. 436 (1966).

42 *See* MALTZMAN, SPRIGG & WAHLBECK, *supra* note 36, at 3–4. An interesting question is whether Brennan's sincere position was actually the one expressed in correspondence to Marshall, which might have been cheap talk, as opposed to his eventual opinion.

43 It is of course important to distinguish arguments that the attitudinal assumption is normatively problematic—judges should not seek to infuse their preferences into the law—from arguments that it is not descriptive—judges do not in fact seek to infuse their preferences into the law. *See* Frank B. Cross, *Political Science and the New Legal Realism: A Case of Unfortunate Interdisciplinary Ignorance*, 92 NW. U. L. REV. 251 (1997) (arguing that the attitudinal approach is incomplete without considering the effects of legal rules); Charles Gardner Geyh, *The Endless Judicial Selection Debate and Why It Matters for Judicial Independence*, 21 GEO. J. LEGAL ETHICS 1259, 1272 (noting that a judge who decides cases solely on attitudinal or political considerations would be violating the *Model Code of Judicial Conduct*).

44 George & Epstein, *supra* note 24, at 326–28.

45 For an informative history of the legal realism movement, see LAURA KALMAN, LEGAL REALISM AT YALE 1927–1960 (1986). Some maintain that we are all realists, or post realists, now. *Id.* at 229 (" 'We are all realists now.' The statement has been made so frequently that it has become a truism to refer to it as a truism."). *See also* Patrick McKinley Brennan, *Locating Authority in Law, and Avoiding the Authoritarianism of "Textualism"*, 83 NOTRE DAME L. REV. 761, 762 (2008); Mark A. Hall & Ronald F. Wright, *Systematic Content Analysis of Judicial Opinions*, 96 CALIF. L. REV. 63, 77 (2008).

the notion that for some, and perhaps many, judges, judicial attitudes incorporate important notions of judicial restraint. Might judges who hold such a view be the "ordinary" judges Posner seeks to describe? Might this explain his omission of the desire to influence legal policy as an independent factor in his judicial utility function? Whether this account explains the attitudes of a small number of judges, the vast majority of judges, or somewhere in between, is of course an empirical question.[46] In addition, it is important to consider whether the notion of constraint-as-attitude is more likely to explain judges on particular kinds of courts.

Attitudinal scholars limit their formal claim that the most robust predictor of case outcomes is judicial attitudes to the Supreme Court.[47] To the extent that this limitation is appropriate, is it because only judges sitting on the highest level court are interested in imbuing the law with their preferred ideological cast, or is it instead because such judges have the most meaningful opportunities to do so? Unlike federal district court rulings, which can be overruled by the circuit court of appeals, or circuit court rulings, which can be overruled by the circuit en banc or in the Supreme Court, Supreme Court decisions are subject to fewer constrains. Such cases can only be overruled only by a subsequent reconsideration of the issue in a later Supreme Court case, by Congress for cases of statutory interpretation, or via constitutional amendment for an exercise of constitutional judicial review.[48]

Consider federal circuit court judges. Given the relative rarity of Supreme Court review,[49] is there any reason to think that they are less prone than Supreme Court Justices to infusing decisions with their preferred understandings of legal policy? Is en banc review within a circuit an effective means of disciplining appeals court judges who seek to embed preferred policy preferences into case law?

The attitudinal model's assumption that the primary motivation affecting judicial decision making is to affect legal policy has a significant counterpart within more than

---

[46] Can you think of a way to test this empirical question?

[47] Specifically, attitudinal scholars limit the model to judges who satisfy the following conditions: (1) complete docket control; (2) judges with life tenure; (3) judges without further career ambition; and (4) judges who sit atop the judicial hierarchy and thus who cannot be overturned by a higher court. Within the United States, and possibly the world, this might limit the model to the Supreme Court. The authors thank Lee Epstein for this clarification. *See* SEGAL & SPAETH, *supra* note 23, at 92–93.

[48] Overruling via constitutional amendment has occurred only four times in the entire history of the Supreme Court. These include the Eleventh Amendment (limiting federal court jurisdiction in suits against states); the Fourteenth Amendment (rendering all persons born or naturalized in the United States citizens of the United States and of the state in which they reside); the Sixteenth Amendment (enhancing Congressional taxation power); and the Twenty-Sixth Amendment (lowering voting age to eighteen years). *See* Symposium, *Original Ideas in Originalism: Does the Constitution Prescribe Rules for its Own Interpretation?*, 103 NW. U. L. REV. 857 (2009); *see also* Michael Stokes Paulson, *Can a Constitutional Amendment Overrule a Supreme Court Decision?*, 24 CONST. COMMENT. 285 (2007).

[49] *See* JAMES C. DUFF, ADMINISTRATIVE OFFICE OF THE U.S. COURTS, 2006 JUDICIAL BUSINESS OF THE UNITED STATES COURTS 101 tbl.A–1, 102 tbl.B (2006), http://www.uscourts.gov/file/document/judicial-business-2006 (noting that the Supreme Court heard ninety cases in the 2005 October term, compared to more than 66,000 cases filed in the Courts of Appeal in the year ending Sept. 2006). Since 2010 when Justice Kagan was confirmed, the Supreme Court heard on average seventy-eight cases per term. As of the beginning of January 2017, right before Donald Trump's inauguration, the Supreme Court granted certiorari in only fifty-eight cases. Josh Blackman, *SCOTUS After Scalia*, 11 NYU J.L. & LIBERTY 48, 59–60 (2017).

one legal scholarly tradition. Consider, for example, how this assumption relates to the claim within Critical Legal Studies that "law is politics."[50] Is it possible to embrace the assumption that jurists seek to influence legal policy based upon their ideological predilections without equating the normative legitimacy of judicial and legislative policymaking? If so, what are the bases for distinguishing these two lawmaking functions?

As we will see in the materials that follow, some scholars writing within the law and economics tradition also claim that judges are largely motivated to influence legal policy. And yet, such scholars often hold normative disagreements concerning legal policy with those who embrace a critical legal perspective. What accounts for these differences? Is it simply a function of the different ideological perspectives—or attitudes—of the legal scholars themselves?

II. ECONOMIC MODELS OF STARE DECISIS

We begin by briefly revisiting the game theoretical models of stare decisis, introduced in Chapter 15 to describe the single-period and iterated prisoners' dilemmas. These models are designed to explain an apparent anomaly operating within common law based judicial systems.[51] Assuming that judges are motivated to embed their preferred legal policy preferences into case outcomes, why then do judges adhere to a regime of stare decisis, which prevents them from doing so in those cases in which a contrary precedent prevents a preferred outcome?

A. Internal Foundations Revisited: The Game Theoretical Origins of Stare Decisis

Professors Erin O'Hara and Eric Rasmusen suggest that each judge on a multi-member court prefers to constrain her colleagues to her precedents without being reciprocally constrained by her colleagues' contrary precedents.[52] The resulting incentives likely thwart a regime of precedent in favor of one in which each judge decides cases on her or his own, unconstrained by precedent.[53] This provides each jurist a temporary imprimatur on a larger number of cases, rather than a more lasting imprint—one adhered to by other judges in the form of precedent—over the relatively smaller number of cases in which the issue presented has not yet been resolved as a matter of stare decisis.

---

[50] For simplicity, we are grouping together schools that employ a critical perspective, including critical race theory and certain strands of feminist theory. While these schools are by no means equivalent, they do share certain important characteristics related to the normative foundations of legislative and judicial lawmaking. For a helpful overview of the critical legal studies movement, see MARK KELMAN, GUIDE TO CRITICAL LEGAL STUDIES (1990).

[51] *See supra* Chapter 15, at 627–641.

[52] Although we used a two-judge court for expositional purposes, see *supra* Chapter 15, the analysis can be generalized to larger appellate courts.

[53] To be clear, the judges might adhere to each others' decisions when they agree to them on the merits, but that is different than adhering to precedent because it is precedent. The obligation of stare decisis assumes that judges will apply precedents with which they disagree in cases that are materially indistinguishable. Erin O'Hara, *Social Constraint or Implicit Collusion?: Toward a Game Theoretic Analysis of Stare Decisis*, 24 SETON HALL L. REV. 736, 737–38 (1993).

The resulting regime of mutual defection (from mutual adherence to precedent) creates a problem for supporting stare decisis with a game theoretical foundation. Even if we include multiple iterations, provided they are not endless, the game threatens to unravel to a single-period prisoners' dilemma, restoring mutual defection as the dominant outcome.[54]

As we have also seen, however, game theoretical analysis does not force a simple binary choice between a single-period prisoners' dilemma or a game in which players anticipate endless iterations. More sophisticated models assess the implications of *probabilistic end periods* and *trigger strategy equilibria*.[55] If we assume that the players receive some benefit from appearing cooperative, these models suggest the possibility that discounting the payoffs of defection in future rounds of play allows the players to avoid the low payoffs associated with mutual defection equilibrium outcomes. If so, these models imply that such players will yield a positive set of cooperative behaviors in at least some circumstances.

Several commentators have suggested that jurists observe precedent in part because doing so is consistent with collegiality and is thus properly judicial.[56] While such accounts possess an admittedly circular quality (judges observe stare decisis because they prefer collegiality and collegiality includes observing stare decisis), in our view it would be mistaken to entirely dismiss such claims. Certainly it is the case that judges are generally the sorts of professionals who enjoy engaging in those behaviors that are most likely to be considered judicial, and all that implies. Consistent with Posner's model of judging, adhering to precedent might be one of the "rules of the game" the adherence to which enhances judicial satisfaction. But even accepting this premise begs the question why such norms emerge as "judicial" behaviors in the first instance.

B. A Comment on the Scope of Opinions and the Importance of Legal Materiality

Before discussing alternative accounts of stare decisis, it is important to consider a related anomaly that Professors Erin O'Hara and Eric Rasmusen address. O'Hara and Rasmusen inquire why rational judges, when deciding cases subject to precedent, generally decline to overreach—or at least to do so dramatically—when articulating their holdings.[57] To take an extreme example, imagine a case involving whether a promise to repay a previously forgiven debt provides consideration in a newly formed contract, rendering the promise enforceable. Imagine that Judge A, to whom this case is assigned, uses the case also to resolve the separate policy question whether the governing jurisdiction's rule in cases involving mutual fault is comparative fault or contributory negligence.

Professor O'Hara suggests that rational jurists might decline to overreach in such cases if they anticipate some difficulty in predicting how the present case might influence

---

[54] *See supra* Chapter 15, at 640.

[55] *See supra* Chapter 15, at 632–641.

[56] RICHARD A. POSNER, THE FEDERAL COURTS: CHALLENGE AND REFORM 381–82 (1996); Harry T. Edwards, *The Effects of Collegiality on Judicial Decision Making*, 151 U. PA. L. REV. 1639 (2003).

[57] O'Hara, *supra* note 53, at 741–42; Eric Rasmusen, *Judicial Legitimacy as a Repeated Game*, 10 J.L. ECON. & ORG. 63, 67 (1994).

future doctrinal development. In our hypothetical, we might imagine that Judge A selects a rule of contributory negligence, perhaps thinking the rule lowers administration costs, without fully considering the implications for a future tort victim whose negligence, fairly assessed, accounts for only a small percentage of a very large personal loss that was overwhelmingly the fault of the tortfeasor.[58] In Professor Rasmusen's alternative account, individual judges limit the scope of their opinions to leave sufficient legal policy space open for all jurists so that each judge has the potential to meaningfully influence developing doctrine. In effect, Rasmusen argues that judicial self-restraint promotes a benign mutual accommodation that allows all jurists to make law within the confines of those cases that they are called upon to decide.

Does game theory help to assess these accounts? Might some jurists elect to fill legal policy voids when other jurists are reticent due to a perceived inability to forecast future legal developments? Alternatively might some jurists exhibit more confidence than others in claiming to hold a comprehensive normative framework for assessing broad bodies of caselaw, including myriad open questions of legal policy? If so, would this undermine the equal opportunity to influence law that the O'Hara and Rasmusen models anticipate? In Rasmusen's analysis, what would prevent judges who do not share the concern about leaving sufficient legal policy space open for future judging from producing opinions that dramatically overreach? How does this relate to the single period or iterated prisoners' dilemma games? Which, if either, of these games better captures the stakes for rational jurists? Does your answer differ depending on whether we are considering Judge Posner's ordinary judge or, or instead, a judge who is more intellectually ambitious, such as (before his retirement) Posner himself?

Now consider the following alternative account as to why judges might not systematically overreach in crafting opinions.[59] Judges tend not to overreach because were they to do so, they would risk encouraging other judges not only to avoid their opinions that do overreach, but also, and more importantly, to decline giving their legitimate holdings proper stare decisis effect. Consider, once more, the prior hypothetical involving Judge A's announcement of the contributory negligence rule in a contract case. We might imagine Judge B in a subsequent case that squarely presents the issue, for example, one in which plaintiff's contributory negligence of 10% entirely wipes out plaintiff's recovery, declining to give Judge A's tort holding stare decisis effect. Judge B might include the following passage in her opinion: "Nothing in Case 1 compelled Judge A to pronounce on tort law because that case turned on a question of contract law. We therefore decline to treat any assertions about the choice of negligence regime as part of the holding in that earlier case."

---

[58] Todd Zywicki and Anthony Sanders suggest an analogous justification for precedent relying upon information costs confronting judges attempting to determine whether a proposed legal innovation will actually improve the law overall given the co-evolution of legal rules in disparate settings. Given the complex interactions between legal rules and the manner in which they feed back into individual expectations and planning, the authors claim that judges apply stare decisis to avoid the uncertainty associated with potential welfare-reducing consequences that might otherwise arise elsewhere in the legal system. *See* Todd J. Zywicki & Anthony B. Sanders, *Posner, Hayek, and the Economic Analysis of Law*, 93 IOWA L. REV. 559 (2008).

[59] Portions of this discussion are based upon Michael Abramowicz & Maxwell Stearns, *Defining Dicta*, 57 STAN. L. REV. 953 (2005); MAXWELL L. STEARNS, PUBLIC CHOICE AND PUBLIC LAW: READINGS AND COMMENTARY 540–47 (1997).

Judge A might rightly fear that if she routinely overreaches, Judge B will not only fail to provide stare decisis effect to those holdings that are excessively broad, but also that Judge B will distrust her opinions in general. As a result, Judge A is rationally motivated to defend the scope of her legitimate holdings. To do so, she will explain why announcing each holding is necessary in light of the material facts of the case that she is called upon to decide. In this analysis, each judge fears that absent a clear exposition of material facts demonstrating the need to announce the specific holding in each case, her colleagues will not afford her holdings stare decisis effect. As a result, each judge is rationally motivated not only to limit overreaching, but also to articulate justifications for each holding, grounded in material case facts set out in written opinions.

Do you find the materiality account of the scope of opinions persuasive? Why or why not? Does it help to explain the nature of written judicial opinions? How does it differ from the account that O'Hara and Rasmusen offer? Which is more consistent with observed judicial practice? Which provides the basis for a more persuasive normative justification for stare decisis?

C. The Game Theoretical Origins of Pyramidal Courts

We now examine the prisoners' dilemma among judges on the same level court. The following analysis helps to explain pyramidal judicial hierarchies. It begins with the observation that within the federal court system, district court judges do not routinely abide each other's precedents, although they abide precedents from higher courts, and appellate court panels abide precedent, both horizontally, adhering to their own earlier decisions, and vertically, also adhering to precedents of higher courts.

Professors William Landes and Richard Posner considered the prisoners' dilemma that confronts judges in the construction of precedent.[60] The authors suggested a separate mechanism that helps judges avoid what O'Hara described as non-productive competition.[61] Landes and Posner suggest that the resulting competition encourages the formation of pyramidal judicial hierarchies.

To illustrate, imagine a group of mediators who implicitly recognize the prisoners' dilemma that confronts them respecting horizontal precedent. They realize that each jurist will continue in the role of mediator, resolving specific disputes but without transforming their rulings into precedents that govern similar future cases.

Imagine the mediators discuss their frustration over the temporary impact each has in resolving specific disputes without the more lasting impact of making law. The mediators wish to elevate themselves from dispute resolution to actual judging, and so they consider various strategies. This includes an admonition to take more seriously the legal bases of prior rulings when deciding present cases. Realizing that this is unlikely to produce the desired result of transforming individual decisions into precedents, they try an alternative. The mediators will take turns meeting as an appellate tribunal, in randomly

---

60 William M. Landes & Richard A. Posner, *Legal Precedent: A Theoretical and Empirical Analysis*, 19 J.L. & ECON. 249 (1976).

61 *Id.* at 273 (arguing that "the free-rider problem" of judges who do not wish to follow precedent "is held in check by the structure of appellate review [and that] decision according to precedent will often constitute rational self-interested behavior of judges who personally disagree with the precedent in question.").

drawn groups of three to avoid the appearance of arbitrariness and the risk of ties, and in that capacity, they will resolve disagreements among the mediators over legal policy when individual mediators express disagreement in the resolution of particular disputes. The appellate resolutions will form binding precedents for the individual mediators as those who fail to abide the rulings are subject to reversal on appeal, but the precedents will only apply vertically, meaning top-down, rather than horizontally based on rulings among individual mediators.[62]

We might also imagine that as the regime becomes more sophisticated, different appellate panels will themselves express occasional disagreements over legal policy, and seek to impose constraints on future panels that depart from earlier panel decisions as precedent. As we will discuss in Chapter 22, horizontal stare decisis—adhering to the precedents of the same appellate court—helps to avoid potential intransitivities among multimember courts, thereby stabilizing legal doctrine.[63] For now, assume that vertical stare decisis does not ensure doctrinal consistency among differently constituted appellate tribunals, as for example, among differing circuit courts of appeal. A partial solution is adding one more step to the judicial hierarchy. By adding a single larger panel supreme court, presumably of at least five members,[64] the judicial system can enforce stare decisis from the supreme court to the appellate courts and from the appellate courts to the trial courts. And notably the regime emerges as stable with only these three steps in the judicial hierarchy. This is a pervasive judicial structure, not merely within the United States, but throughout western democracies.[65]

Once this regime is established, the intermediate appellate court and the supreme court are likely to assume a more professional and specialized form. Judges, or justices, will be appointed to their specific positions within the judicial hierarchy, rather than occupying them on a temporary or randomly drawn basis from a lower rung on the ladder. The skills associated with adjudicating trials and appeals are notably different and it is not surprising therefore that judges will experience significant career specialization—and even some degree of jealous professional rivalry—regarding their respective spheres of influence in the resolution of disputes, on the one hand, and in the creation of binding precedents, on the other.

The resulting institutional arrangements also have the important effect of enhancing the stability, and thus the value, of individual adjudications. Rather than simply resolving disputes between the parties, the regime creates a vehicle for the anticipated development and application of an emerging body of precedent. This allows the parties to better

---

[62] In a regime in which courts are engaged in competition, based for example on filing fees, jurisdiction, or other incentives, see Chapter 10, at 426, we might also imagine mimicking behavior to the extent that those judiciaries structured pyramidally do better, and thus increase the scope of their court's dockets or jurisdiction, as a result of providing more stable doctrine.

[63] *See infra* Chapter 22, Part II. This problem can arise within en banc supreme courts; en banc appeals courts; and among differently constituted appellate tribunals, for example, randomly drawn panels of three within larger courts of appeals.

[64] If drawn from the ranks of the courts of appeals, at least as an interim measure, a minimum of five reduces the risk that the Supreme Court will be controlled by a single appellate tribunal as it can overrule, for example, a two-to-one majority decision with a larger majority.

[65] Michele Taruffo, *Institutional Factors Influencing Precedents*, *in* INTERPRETING PRECEDENTS: A COMPARATIVE STUDY 437 (D. Neil MacCormick & Robert S. Summers eds., 1997).

ascertain the probable outcomes of potential legal disputes, and thus to make better assessments concerning how to conduct their personal and business affairs and also whether to take a cases to trial or to settle.[66] A major benefit of the resulting judicial hierarchy, therefore, is in enhancing the overall value of the judicial outputs relative to the mediation regime, thereby moving the regime from mediation to judging.

QUESTIONS AND COMMENTS

Does game theory help to explain stare decisis within our judicial system? Why or why not? If it is helpful, which of the models do you find more persuasive, and why? Can you identify benefits to the absence of precedent at the trial level within judicial hierarchies? Is consistency more valuable at the appellate than the trial level? Why or why not? Why do separate circuits operating in the United States Courts of Appeals fail to adhere to each other's precedents? Is stare decisis more valuable at the Supreme Court level than across differing courts of appeals? Do different circuit courts decline to follow each others' precedents for the same reasons that district court judges on the same court fail to abide each other's precedents? If so, what are those reasons?

D. External Foundations of Stare Decisis

The preceding discussion centered on the internal origins of a regime of stare decisis,[67] and specifically, on how the regime of precedent, whether operating in horizontal or vertical form, benefits the judges themselves. The question was why judges are motivated to *supply* a precedent-driven legal regime. In the discussion that follows, we consider the external benefits, or policy justifications, for stare decisis. Here we focus instead on why society might *demand*, or at least prefer, a judicial system that includes precedent as a substantial component.

In an exchange of articles, Professors Lewis Kornhauser and Jonathan Macey relied upon game theoretical and traditional law and economics analyses to assess the normative merit of stare decisis within common law systems. While Professor Kornhauser maintains that stare decisis has the potential to provide stability when the legal regime confronts more than one pure-strategy Nash equilibrium as a solution to a game that we can characterize in terms of a battle of the sexes, he also identifies conditions under which stare decisis threatens the paradoxical result of locking in regimes favoring inferior technologies. We begin with Kornhauser's positive account of the doctrine, which tracks two of the games introduced in Chapter 16: (1) the pure coordination Nash equilibrium game, and (2) the battle of the sexes.

---

[66] *See* Bruce H. Kobayashi, *Case Selection, External Effects, and the Trial/Settlement Decision*, *in* DISPUTE RESOLUTION: BRIDGING THE SETTLEMENT GAP 17 (David A. Anderson ed., 1996); Leandra Lederman, *Precedent Lost: Why Encourage Settlement, and Why Permit Non-Party Involvement in Settlements?*, 75 NOTRE DAME L. REV. 221 (1999); George L. Priest & Benjamin Klein, *The Selection of Disputes for Litigation*, 13 J. LEGAL STUD. 1 (1984).

[67] This includes the discussion of stare decisis in Chapter 15.

1. *Stare Decisis and the Pure-Strategy Nash Equilibrium Game*

Recall that in Chapter 16, we reviewed several games that presented two pure Nash equilibria, and two non-pure Nash outcomes. The simplest of these games, reproduced below, involves two drivers each deciding whether to drive on the right or left hand side of the road.

Table 21:1. The Driving Game

Payoffs for (A, B)	B drives left	B drives right
A drives left	**10, 10**	0, 0
A drives right	0, 0	**10, 10**

In this game, the two pure-strategy Nash equilibria are depicted in the upper left and lower right boxes, with payoffs of (10,10). The game is assumed to be one of simple coordination, meaning that each player is indifferent to the choice of right or left driving, but does hold a strong preference (indicated by the dramatic differences in the payoffs between the Nash equilibrium outcomes and the non-equilibrium outcomes) for coordinated versus non-coordinated driving regimes.[68] In contexts in which the driving game will be played sequentially, a stare decisis regime can induce stability around one of the pure-strategy Nash equilibrium results by demanding consistency with that outcome in future rounds.[69] As Kornhauser recognizes, however, the narrow range of legal contexts involving simple coordination problems highlights the limited nature of this normative account of stare decisis.[70]

2. *Stare Decisis as a Means of Stabilizing Battle of the Sexes Games*

Kornhauser also suggests a game justifying stare decisis that can readily be expressed in terms of a battle of the sexes. The game involves the judicial selection of two presumptive, or off-the-rack, contract liability rules governing the purchase of goods: caveat emptor (buyer beware) or caveat venditor (seller beware).[71] In its simplest form, caveat emptor means that the buyer assumes all risk of defects following point of sale. This can be expressed in terms of an "as is" contract that places all duties to inspect on the buyer prior to execution of the contract. By contrast, caveat venditor can be viewed as a form of strict products liability, coupled with a full set of warranties for

[68] For a general discussion, see Lewis A. Kornhauser, *An Economic Perspective on Stare Decisis*, 65 CHI.-KENT L. REV. 63, 79–80 (1989).

[69] If decisions are simultaneous, then it is possible that each party will attempt to anticipate the other party's strategy, but will do so incorrectly, thus risking a non-pure-Nash equilibrium. *See also supra* Chapter 16 (discussing relevant games).

[70] *See* Kornhauser, *supra* note 68, at 80.

[71] While Kornhauser does not present it in these terms, as explained in the text, it equates to a battle of the sexes game.

nonconformities.[72] These two rules represent endpoints on a spectrum of potential off-the-rack contracting rules that could include an intermediate set of solutions, including for example, a buyer's right of inspection and a seller's liability for concealed defects or a set of limited warranties depending upon the use to which the goods are put, with the burden on the buyer for risks associated with nonconforming uses.

For expositional purposes, Kornhauser assumes that these more extreme regimes, caveat emptor and caveat venditor, are the only available off-the-rack contract rules for the sale of goods that provide clearly identifiable and predictable outcomes for buyers and sellers.[73] The following table illustrates the game[74]:

Table 21:2. Caveat Emptor Versus Caveat Venditor

Payoffs are (Row, Column)	a	b	c
A	**5,3**	7,1	1,2
B	3,2	4,6	0,4
C	4,3	3,2	**2,5**

Kornhauser explains that the upper left and lower right corner solutions, presented in bold, are the only pure-strategy Nash equilibria:

> In [Table 7:2], (A,a) is an equilibrium because Row cannot improve upon her payoff of 5, conditional on Column's choice of strategy a. If Row chooses B rather than A she would receive 3; if she chooses C rather than A she would receive 4. Similarly, Column cannot improve his payoff of 3, conditional on Row's choice of strategy A. If Column chooses b rather than a, he receives 1 rather than 3; if he chooses c rather than a, he receives 2 rather than 3. A parallel argument reveals that (C,c) is also an equilibrium.
>
> No other pair of choices meets this criterion of each actor's choice being her best response to her opponent's chosen strategy. Consider for example the strategy pair (B,b) which makes Column best off. This pair is not an equilibrium because, conditional on Column's choice of b, Row does best to choose A, which gives her a payoff of 7 rather than 4.[75]

This game, and its corresponding justification for stare decisis, differs in an important way from the driving game. Whereas that game involved a pure coordination game, in this game, the players care very much about, and indeed hold opposite views concerning, the chosen legal regime. And yet, once the legal regime is selected, stare decisis locks that regime in place as a Nash equilibrium, at least absent either legislative or judicial overruling, because any unilateral move would make the moving party worse off.

---

72 *See* DAVID G. OWEN, PRODUCTS LIABILITY LAW § 1.2, at 17–18 (2005).

73 This assumption is important because it is not otherwise obvious that potential intermediate outcomes necessarily disadvantage both buyer and seller, relative to each of their preferred endpoints.

74 Table 7:2 is reproduced from Kornhauser, *supra* note 68, at 81.

75 *See id.* at 81 n.29.

The battle of the sexes game has potentially broader application in the context of common law litigation than the driving game because of the greater opportunity for gains from seeking to displace the disfavored rule. In the driving game, claimants seek the benefit of ex post gains when the selected rule is one they did not happen to choose even though ex ante, they were indifferent to the choice of rule. By contrast, in a battle of the sexes game, claimants prefer the rule that they did select to the one they wish to displace. As a result, litigation involving the driving game only provides the basis for ex post gains, whereas litigation involving the battle of the sexes provides the basis for both ex ante and ex post gains.

As seen in Chapters 5 and 6, contract rules favoring one side nonetheless can be potentially welfare enhancing to the extent that the resulting certainty reduces the cost of contracting even for parties who prefer an alternative rule. The battle of the sexes game can be generalized to cases in which each party prefers her or his own off-the-rack rule but would prefer the other side's off-the-rack rule to a state of uncertainty respecting future contract negotiations.

3. Stare Decisis and the Risk of Entrenching Inferior Technologies

Let us now consider the case that Kornhauser claims is more difficult for stare decisis. Kornhauser begins with the premise that the legal regime seeks to optimize social welfare and must select among two competing legal regimes that affect the relative values of driving and walking during an era of technological change. Kornhauser first considers a regime in which driving is uncommon, for example, in the advent of cars at the beginning of the twentieth century, or in a remote location with unpaved roads. When walking is the more highly valued activity, the optimal rule is presumed to be strict liability with dual contributory negligence, and when driving is more highly valued, the optimal rule is presumed to be negligence with contributory negligence. We can depict the two regimes in a single matrix that embraces all four negligence/non-negligence combinations and that identifies potential driver liability in each category under each set of rules.[76]

Table 21:3

Alternative Tort Regimes: Negligence with Contributory Negligence (Rule 1) and **Strict Liability with Dual Contributory Negligence (Rule 2)**		
(Rule 1; **Rule 2**)	Driver Negligent	Driver non-negligent
Pedestrian negligent	no liability; **liability**	no liability; **no liability**
Pedestrian non-negligent	liability; **liability**	no liability; **liability**

Because either driver or pedestrian can be negligent or nonnegligent, there are four resulting combinations for either legal regime. The liability as between the two parties only changes in two of the four categories as a result of a change in these two liability rules. The table lists only driver's liability (the inverse liability is that of pedestrian) in the

[76] This table is taken from STEARNS, *supra* note 59, at 548 tbl.3.

event of an accident with pedestrian, with the result for the first rule set out in Roman typeface and for the second rule set out in bold. In the upper right and lower left boxes, where only one of the two parties is negligent, the choice of rule does not affect the outcome. In either case, the negligent party bears the full risk of the accident. By contrast, when neither or both parties to the accident are negligent, the selection of liability rule determines which party bears the risk.

When walking is the more highly valued activity, the operative regime is strict liability with dual contributory negligence. In this regime, when both the driver and pedestrian are negligent, or when neither is negligent, the driver bears the burden of the accident, with the liability rule set out in bold. Conversely, when driving becomes the more highly valued activity, the operative regime is negligence with contributory negligence. In this regime, when neither or both are negligent, the pedestrian bears the risk of accidents, with the results set out in Roman typeface.

Kornhauser explains the resulting anomaly as follows:

> Suppose the court announces a rule of negligence. Then, if the value of driving is high, the statically (second-)best rule will prevail. If, on the other hand, the value of driving is low, negligence will be far from the statically (second-)best rule. The higher the probability that driving will have a high value, the more preferable will negligence (with stare decisis) be to strict liability (with stare decisis).
>
> Whether stare decisis should be adopted however will depend on the nature of the first-best optimum. Suppose the valuations of activities are such that both injurer and victim should adopt moderate (or low) levels of the activity. Under stare decisis, the actor who escapes liability will always adopt a high level of activity. Under a practice of no stare decisis, however, each actor will be uncertain whether she will bear the cost of an accident. . . . For certain relative values of activities, then, the uncertainty over the legal rule induces the actors to adopt activity levels closer to the social optimum.[77]

In effect, Kornhauser argues that although stare decisis can sometimes be welfare enhancing in driving and battle of the sexes games, stare-decisis-induced stability can also be welfare reducing during eras of technological change. This seemingly paradoxical result arises from the problem of adverse reliance upon an inferior—or outdated—legal regime that continues to elevate the legal status of the lesser valued activity.[78] Counterintuitively, perhaps, a regime without legal certainty would encourage the parties to consider on their

---

[77] *See* Kornhauser, *supra* note 68, at 85–86 (footnote omitted).

[78] For an early case demonstrating the relative undervaluation of vehicular traffic, and of the need to impose safety measures, such as gates at railroad crossings, to protect drivers and passengers, see Baltimore & Ohio R.R. v. Goodman, 275 U.S. 66 (1927). Writing for the majority, Justice Holmes rejected the negligence claim of a surviving spouse of a man killed by an oncoming train at a railroad crossing, stating:

> In such circumstances it seems to us that if a driver cannot be sure otherwise whether a train is dangerously near he must stop and get out of his vehicle, although obviously he will not often be required to do more than to stop and look. It seems to us that if he relies upon not hearing the train or any signal and takes no further precaution he does so at his own risk.

Id. at 70. Do you believe that Holmes correctly identified the driver as the party best suited to avoiding the accident? Why or why not?

own the relative values of the activities in which they are engaged, without regard to which activity the legal system, strengthened by stare decisis, had selected as more highly valued some time in the past. Kornhauser suggests that such a regime is likely to be social welfare enhancing in periods of technological transition.

4. *Macey's Critique and the Use of Stare Decisis in Promoting Judicial Specialization*

In a responsive essay, Professor Jonathan Macey rejects Kornhauser's claim that stare decisis risks entrenching an inferior legal regime following an era of technological change. The difficulty that Kornhauser identifies, Macey posits, arises only if stare decisis operates rigidly, favoring specific activities like driving or walking. Instead, legal rules are frequently expressed at a higher level of generality.[79] Imagine, for example, that the underlying substantive rule to which stare decisis applies is construed as protecting the more highly valued activity. If so, stare decisis itself allows a change in the specific liability rule as between two competing activities depending upon their relative value in a period of technological progress. With such flexibility in the stare decisis regime, the pedestrian will alter her conduct at the very least in the period in which driving is clearly more highly valued, and quite likely also in periods of uncertainty as to which activity is more highly valued.

Translating this into common law doctrine, we might imagine that the duty to use reasonable care in tort includes an assessment of the relative value of the two competing activities that pose reciprocal risk.[80] A regime that in one period places presumptive liability on vehicles (strict liability with dual contributory negligence) would not necessarily induce excessive pedestrian reliance in a period of technological progress that later places a higher value on driving, and a correspondingly greater duty on pedestrians to avoid unnecessary risks (negligence with contributory negligence). Undue reliance is avoided if pedestrians realize that the increased prevalence of vehicular traffic imposes greater duties on the pedestrians themselves to avoid careless strolls (for example, in the street at night with dark clothing) that might result in avoidable accidents.

Professor Macey goes further and identifies four important functions that stare decisis serves: (1) minimizing error costs; (2) increasing the public goods aspects of decisions; (3) minimizing the costs of judicial review; and (4) increasing the power of courts relative to that of the legislature. Although each argument is important in assessing stare decisis, given the chapter's focus on judicial behavior, Macey's error cost justification is particularly relevant to our analysis.

Macey explains:

> [J]udges apply two sorts of legal skills when deciding a case. One sort of legal skill is the skill involved in formulating, articulating, and applying substantive legal doctrine to a particular legal dispute. The second set of legal skills allows

---

[79] Macey, *supra* note 4, at 104. The following discussion is based in part on STEARNS, *supra* note 59, at 549–50.

[80] *See* Macey, *supra* note 4, at 103–04.

the judge to determine what sorts of cases are alike, in order to "check" his result in the first case.

. . . It is easy to see that stare decisis can be extremely valuable to a legal system. In developed legal systems judges will be checking their opinions against several, perhaps hundreds of similar cases that have evolved in the common-law process over hundreds of years. If we retain our assumption that other judges usually are correct when they reach legal decisions, then the prevailing substantive legal rule on a particular issue is very likely to be correct.

. . . Clearly, not even the best judges go about formulating what they believe to be the substantively correct legal result in every case, and then checking that result with the relevant precedents. Instead, judges generally employ stare decisis precisely because it enables them to *avoid* having to rethink the merits of particular legal doctrine. Instead of rethinking, the judges can "free-ride" on the opinions of previous judges.

At the same time, however, judges are likely to feel more confident about their abilities and instincts when deciding certain sorts of cases than when deciding others. For those classes of cases about which judges feel they have a particular expertise, the idealized checking process described above is a valid portrayal of the judging process. Thus a practice of stare decisis not only permits judges to conserve judicial resources, it allows them to specialize in particular areas of the law.

Judges can free-ride on the expertise of other judges in those areas in which they do not specialize, and create new law in those areas in which they feel they have expertise. This phenomenon is particularly obvious in multi-judge panels such as those that exist on federal circuit courts of appeals. . . . Stare decisis may be viewed as a legal innovation that allows judges to expand the process of trading experience and expertise over time and across jurisdictions.[81]

5. *A Comment on the Condorcet Jury Theorem and the Nature of Judicial Reliance*

Professor Macey's analysis rests upon an important intuition about how individual judges generate reliable information and convey it to their colleagues. Although Macey does not couch his analysis in terms of the *Condorcet Jury Theorem*, the theorem is helpful in assessing Macey's claim. Condorcet posited that in the context of a decision admitting of two answers, one of which is correct, when members of a jury are at least 50% likely to select the correct answer, the probability that the jury selects the right answer increases as the size of the jury increases.[82]

---

[81] Macey, *supra* note 4, at 102–03 (footnote omitted).

[82] Saul Levmore, *Ruling Majorities and Reasoning Pluralities*, 3 THEORETICAL INQUIRIES L. 87 (2002); Maxwell L. Stearns, *The Condorcet Jury Theorem and Judicial Decisionmaking: A Reply to Saul Levmore*, 3 THEORETICAL INQUIRIES L. 125 (2002).

The intuition is fairly easy to explain. Imagine that there are two options, A and B, and that each juror is at least 50% likely to know that the correct answer is A. The jurors who know A to be correct will select it. The jurors who do not know will split approximately evenly over A and B. As the size of the jury is enlarged, the risk that random error will result in the jury preferring the wrong answer is reduced. The "bump" that distinguishes those who know the right answer from those who do not is more pronounced as a result of the increasing likelihood, with larger numbers, that those guessing sort their answers randomly.[83] Two critical assumptions underlie the jury theorem: first, the question admits of a correct answer; and second, each juror, expected to be at least 50% likely to know the right answer, derives that answer independently, meaning that she or he is not influenced by the potentially erroneous decisions of other jurors. Otherwise, *information cascades* risk a wave favoring a wrong answer.[84]

Macey suggests that stare decisis allows judges to employ analogical reasoning, rather than analysis from first principles, as they progress from case facts to outcomes. Assume that common law judges confront groups of similar fact patterns over time and that they make independent assessments concerning how to resolve these cases. Over time, a large corpus of case decisions on related questions of common law rules will develop, providing highly valuable information to jurists concerning how to resolve particular disputes. This will hold even if many such jurists lack the technical competence to reason from first principles from case facts to outcomes.

---

[83] This can be generalized to more than two answers, as illustrated in the once-popular American game show, *Who Wants to Be a Millionaire?* The Indian version of the game inspired the Academy Award winning *Slumdog Millionaire*. The game involved trivia questions in which the players were given three "lifelines": phone a friend, eliminate two responses, and ask the audience. Ask the audience was often the best choice. The questions were accompanied by four multiple choice answers of which one was correct. Assume that the studio audience members are 25% likely to know the answer. As you increase the audience size, you increase the probability that those who do not evenly distribute their votes over all answers, thereby ensuring that the correct answer receives a distinguishing bump. There are two notable limitations: first a credible decoy could misdirect a sufficiently large segment of participants to throw off the signaling effect of the bump associated with the correct answer; and second, a very obscure question that few audience members know the answer to and for which an expert is required might have an inadequate bump. For the first problem, elimination could prove more helpful, provided the decoy response is removed. For the second problem, phone a friend could prove more helpful if that friend holds the relevant obscure expertise. For academic literature on the Condorcet Jury Theorem as applied to law, see Nicholas Quinn Rosenkranz, *Condorcet and the Constitution: A Response to the Law of Other States*, 59 STAN. L. REV. 1281, 1308 (2007); John O. McGinnis & Michael Rappaport, *The Condorcet Case for Supermajority Rules*, 16 SUP. CT. ECON. REV. 67 (2008); Eric A. Posner & Cass R. Sunstein, *The Law of Other States*, 59 STAN. L. REV. 131 (2006); Adrian Vermeule, *Common Law Constitutionalism and the Limits of Reason*, 107 COLUM. L. REV. 1482 (2007). For a popular study that explores conditions under which groups produce more accurate data than individuals, see JAMES SUROWIECKI, THE WISDOM OF CROWDS 10 (2004) (identifying the following as necessary conditions to the wisdom of crowds: diversity of opinion, independence, decentralization, and aggregation); *see also id.* at 3–4 (discussing *Who Wants to Be a Millionaire*).

[84] Lisa R. Anderson & Charles A. Holt, *Information Cascades in the Laboratory*, 87 AM. ECON. REV. 847 (1997); Sushil Bikhchandani et al., *Learning from the Behavior of Others: Conformity, Fads, and Informational Cascades*, J. ECON. PERSP., Summer 1998, at 151; Timur Kuran & Cass R. Sunstein, *Availability Cascades and Risk Regulation*, 51 STAN. L. REV. 683 (1999); Beth Z. Shaw, *Judging Juries: Evaluating Renewed Proposals for Specialized Juries from a Public Choice Perspective*, 2006 UCLA J.L. & TECH. 3.

QUESTIONS AND COMMENTS

Can you identify the differing assumptions concerning judicial rationality that inform the stare decisis analyses that O'Hara, Rasmusen, Kornhauser, and Macey offer? Are their analyses consistent or in tension with your own assessment of the concept of judicial rationality? Why? Do you believe it more helpful to describe the judicial obligation of stare decisis as internally constructed or externally imposed? Why? Are these two perspectives mutually exclusive? Why or why not? If not, how might these views be reconciled? Which of the specific justifications for stare decisis do you find most persuasive?

Do you find the various games that Kornhauser relies upon helpful in explaining stare decisis? In policy contexts that implicate the driving game, do courts or the legislatures typically select the governing policy? If legislatures provide policy in such contexts, how does this relate more generally to Kornhauser's stare decisis analysis? When legislatures fail to create needed policy, does this suggest that something other than pure coordination is likely to be at stake? Now consider the battle of the sexes game. Does the common law process of selecting default contract rules help illustrate the benefits of stare decisis in this context?

Do you find Macey's error cost justification for stare decisis persuasive? Does the Condorcet Jury Theorem support or undermine Macey's analysis of the benefits that stare decisis provides in promoting judicial specialization? Why? Can the Condorcet Jury Theorem explain the relative size of appellate court and supreme court panels? Why or why not?

E. An Interest-Group Perspective on Precedent

Professor Todd Zywicki relies upon interest group theory to respond to the conventional law and economics account of stare decisis. Zywicki maintains that such accounts might fail adequately to consider the incentives that stare decisis creates for parties seeking to manipulate favorable legal doctrine through investments in strategic litigation.[85] Zywicki analogizes common law rule generation to legislative rulemaking. In both contexts, the value of the stream of rents an interest group obtains is a function of two variables: (1) the value of the rent in each period, multiplied by (2) the number of periods over which the rents are expected to accrue. The present value of a wealth transfer to an interest group can be enlarged by increasing either the per-period payout or the payout duration. Zywicki further notes that the same collective action problems that affect legislative rent seeking are likely to apply in the litigation context as discrete, well-organized interest groups are better suited to organize, and thus manipulate, the favorable development of preferred doctrine than more dispersed heterogeneous groups.[86]

One implication of Zywicki's model is that strict adherence to stare decisis has the potential to increase the stability of both efficient and inefficient precedents, including those that result from rent-seeking litigation. Moreover, although a stronger stare decisis doctrine increases the societal costs of rent-producing precedents by making overruling more difficult, it simultaneously increases the value of the "prize" by increasing the precedent's lifespan. Zywicki contends that to the extent that rent-seeking litigation dynamics approximate those in legislatures by rewarding well-organized groups, the result

[85] Todd J. Zywicki, *The Rise and Fall of Efficiency in the Common Law: A Supply-Side Analysis*, 97 NW. U. L. REV. 1551 (2003).

[86] *See also* MANCUR OLSON, THE LOGIC OF COLLECTIVE ACTION (1965).

is to increase the production and maintenance of inefficient precedents relative to efficient precedents. Zywicki posits, therefore, that interest groups might prefer a more costly common law ex ante that produces more stable rules, with longer payouts, ex post, and that this likely holds for groups that are better suited than their competitors to engage in judicial rent-seeking.

Zywicki maintains that strict stare decisis might not be an optimal rule, preferring instead a relatively weak form of precedent. He envisions, for example, a regime in which legal rules do not gain precedential status until they are reaffirmed by several independent judges considering the issue, and in which individual precedents can be revisited.

As an historical matter, Zywicki observes, during the formative centuries of common law development, precedent was relatively weak, whereas a stricter form of stare decisis emerged in the late-nineteenth century and persists today. It was during the earlier period, Zywicki claims, that most of the economically efficient common law doctrines developed. By contrast, Zywicki claims, rent-seeking litigation and inefficient legal rules have become increasingly prevalent in the United States over the past century.

Do you find Zywicki's account of stare decisis persuasive? Zywicki claims that the past century has produced increasingly inefficient precedent, raising the question, as compared with what? For example, is it possible to determine whether the common law is more or less efficient than statutory law? Is it possible to assess whether the relative efficiencies of these two general categories of law has changed over the relevant historical periods that Zywicki has studied? Why or why not?

F. Attitudinal Accounts of Stare Decisis

Before leaving the stare decisis analysis, it is worth considering the Attitudinal account of precedent on the Supreme Court. While Attitudinal scholars have leveled numerous challenges, both theoretical and empirical, to the constraining influence of precedent,[87] we consider two. Professors Jeffrey Segal and Harold Spaeth have argued that precedent is not a meaningful constraint on judicial behavior because robust data suggest that both sides of any dispute are able to locate and cite to available precedents to support preferred case positions. The authors explain:

> Though precedent, like plain meaning and intent, looks backward, it does not appreciably restrict judicial discretion for a number of reasons. First, and most basic, precedents lie on both sides of most every controversy, at least at the appellate level. If losing litigants at trial did not have authority to support their contentions, no basis for appeal would exist. . . .
>
> As further evidence that precedents exist to support the contentions of both parties, merely consult any appellate court case containing a dissenting opinion. This, as well as the majority opinion, will likely contain a substantial number of references to previously decided cases. Reference to these cases will

[87] *See, e.g.*, SAUL BRENNER & HAROLD J. SPAETH, STARE INDECISIS: THE ALTERATION OF PRECEDENT ON THE SUPREME COURT, 1946–1992 (1995).

undoubtedly show that those cited by the majority support its decision, whereas those specifically cited by the dissent bolster its contrary position.[88]

In a later edition of the same work, the same authors modify this argument, observing: "Since there are always some cases supporting both sides in virtually every conflict decided by the Court, [a definition of precedent that rests on a jurist's citation to consistent case authority] turns stare decisis into a trivial concept, at least for explanatory purposes."[89] The authors then suggest the following analysis:

> Rather, the best evidence for the influence of precedent [established in a case] must come from those who dissented from the majority opinion in the case under question, for we *know* that these justices disagree with the precedent. If the precedent established in the case influences them, that influence should be felt in that case's progeny, through their votes and opinion writing. Thus, determining the influence of precedent requires examining the extent to which justices who disagree with a precedent move toward that position in subsequent cases.[90]

Based upon these arguments, and statistical inferences from the Supreme Court Database, the authors maintain that ideological predilection, rather than precedent, is the overriding determinant of Supreme Court decision making.

Consider the following response to the first argument. Jurists tend to provide extensive citation respecting divisive issues or respecting issues most subject to ambiguity within cases they are deciding. In the context of a constitutional challenge to a state statute restricting access to abortion procedures, for example, there are a large number of issues over which legal propositions are well settled. These include, as illustrations, the Supreme Court's power of constitutional judicial review, the incorporation of many provisions of the Bill of Rights against the states, the existence of a right of privacy, the inclusion of the abortion right as part of the right of privacy, and many others. In most cases, precedent operates as a set of agreed-upon background principles that help frame those issues that ultimately prove decisive. In many cases, most or all issues are well settled, but not surprisingly, in the Supreme Court, the number of cases presenting important unsettled issues is larger.

Will citation counting give a reasonable proxy for whether arguments for or against the challenged abortion statute are supported by precedent? Why or why not? Even in divisive Supreme Court cases, precedent plays a significant role that the citation count methodology cannot take into account.

With respect to the second argument, is the fact that the Justices, acting individually, seek to preserve the opportunity to limit a precedent by continuing to distinguish cases that they disagreed with initially, or even by advocating overruling, sufficient to claim the precedent is not a constraint? Is inquiring whether dissenting Justices move to embrace contrary majority decisions the correct test of the doctrine of stare decisis? Why or why

---

[88] *See* JEFFREY A. SEGAL & HAROLD J. SPAETH, THE SUPREME COURT AND THE ATTITUDINAL MODEL 45–46 (1993).

[89] *See* JEFFREY A. SEGAL & HAROLD J. SPAETH, THE SUPREME COURT AND THE ATTITUDINAL MODEL REVISITED 294 (2002).

[90] *Id.* at 292.

not? Is the Supreme Court itself the best institution for assessing the constraining effect of stare decisis within the judiciary? Why or why not?

After *Gregg v. Georgia*,[91] which overruled *Furman v. Georgia*,[92] upheld the death penalty against a constitutional challenge, Justices Brennan and Marshall alternately produced dissenting opinions that insisted, consistent with their votes in each of these cases, that the death penalty violated the Eighth Amendment prohibition against cruel and unusual punishment as applied to the states via the Fourteenth Amendment.[93] What does this practice suggest about stare decisis? Should justices adhere to their own personal "precedents" or to the majority precedents of the Supreme Court? As a normative matter, should Justices operate consistently in this regard, either always following their initially articulated views or always changing their votes to reflect contrary majority views? Why? Please keep these questions in mind as you evaluate the social choice analysis of Supreme Court decision-making rules in Chapter 22.

III. HOLDING AND DICTUM

In an article titled *Dicta and Article III*,[94] Professor Michael Dorf engaged in a thoughtful critique of the Supreme Court's approach to defining holdings. One of the central concerns expressed in the article is the tendency of the Supreme Court to reevaluate, and redefine, past holdings as needed to accommodate new caselaw without the need to formally overrule.

As a helpful example, Professor Dorf discusses *Morrison v. Olson*.[95] The case involved a challenge to the Ethics in Government Act,[96] a now-lapsed statute that created a basis for appointing an independent counsel, with a defined jurisdictional mandate, including a process for terminating the office. Most notably, the Act imposed restrictions on the President's power to remove the independent counsel. Under then-governing Supreme Court caselaw, the President had unlimited authority to remove subordinates engaged in core executive functions, whereas Congress was empowered to insulate from the President's removal powers those engaged in quasi-judicial or quasi-legislative functions, as such agencies were deemed "independent" of the executive branch.

In his majority opinion in *Morrison*, Chief Justice Rehnquist sustained the Ethics in Government Act against a constitutional challenge, and in so doing, recast the earlier removal decisions based on what he identified as his "present considered view."[97] Rather than endorsing the formalist separation of powers analysis articulated in those earlier

---

91 428 U.S. 153 (1976).

92 408 U.S. 238 (1972).

93 *See, e.g.*, McCleskey v. Bowers, 501 U.S. 1281, 1281–82 (1991) (Marshall, J., dissenting from denial of certiorari); Clemons v. Mississippi, 494 U.S. 738, 755–56 (1990) (Brennan, J., dissenting); Saffle v. Parks, 494 U.S. 484, 515 (1990) (Brennan, J., dissenting); Hildwin v. Florida, 490 U.S. 638, 641 (Brennan, J., dissenting) (Marshall, J., dissenting).

94 Michael Dorf, *Dicta and Article III*, 142 U. PA. L. REV. 1997 (1994).

95 487 U.S. 654 (1988).

96 Ethics in Government Act of 1978, Pub. L. No. 95–521, 92 Stat. 1824.

97 Morrison v. Olson, 487 U.S. 654, 689–90 (1988).

cases,[98] Rehnquist employed a balancing test, inquiring instead as to whether the removal restriction for this particular office infringed upon the President's ability to exercise core executive powers, to which he answered no.

The purpose here is not to review the substantive merits of this *Morrison* or of the Ethics in Government Act, but rather it to relate this to Professor Dorf's larger project of defining holding and dictum. Dorf maintains that the traditional understanding of holding as "facts plus outcome" is thwarted when the Court willingly recasts past facts-plus-outcome-based holdings in a manner that is designed to justify new holdings without the need to overrule past case decisions.

Dorf's analysis builds upon the work of, among others, Professor Arthur Goodhart, who provided a variation of a *facts-plus-outcome analysis* as the basis for distinguishing *holding* from *dictum*. Goodhart maintained that: "It is by his choice of the material facts that the judge creates law."[99] A holding, in Goodhart's view, is a proposition that for a given set of facts that the court deems material then generates the case result. For Goodhart, an important question becomes how material facts are determined. One of Professor Dorf's central points is that however this is determined in a given case in the past should operate as a constraint on the attempt of later courts to redefine those facts as the basis of avoiding harder questions associated with the question whether to overrule.

Now consider some alternative approaches to this important distinction: *Black's Law Dictionary* offers the following definition of dictum: "[a] judicial comment made while delivering a judicial opinion, but one that is unnecessary to the decision in the case and therefore not precedential."[100]

Karl Llewelyn distinguishes "holding" from *ratio decidendi* as follows: "The actual *holding* must be stated quite narrowly . . . [encompassing the] precise point at issue . . . that the case decided."[101] "The actual *holding* must be stated quite narrowly . . . [encompassing the] precise point at issue . . . that the case decided." By contrast, Llewelyn states the *ratio decidendi* embraces "the generally applicable rule of law on which the opinion says the holding rested."[102]

Llewelyn further distinguishes the *ratio decidendi* from the *rule of the case*, which means "the principle for which a case stands," as may be developed in later case law.[103] Llewelyn further distinguishes *dictum* and *obiter dictum*, maintaining that dictum may have "second-order precedential value," whereas obiter dictum is "merely a remark in passing," equivalent in weight to the view expressed by a legal scholar.[104]

---

[98] *See* Humphrey's Executor v. United States, 295 U.S. 602 (1935); Weiner v. United States, 357 U.S. 349 (1958); Myers v. United States, 272 U.S. 52 (1926).

[99] Arthur L. Goodhart, *The Ratio Decidendi of a Case*, 22 MOD. L. REV. 117, 119 (1959).

[100] BLACK'S LAW DICTIONARY 1102 (10th ed. 2014).

[101] KARL LLEWELLYN, THE CASE LAW SYSTEM IN AMERICA 14 (1989).

[102] *Id.*

[103] *Id.* at 15.

[104] *Id.* at 14.

Professor Larry Alexander maintains that a compelling approach to defining a holding borrows from Ronald Dworkin.[105] This approach would inquire as to the moral or political theory that best captures the overall body of relevant cases.

Finally, in an article titled *Defining Dicta*, Professors Michael Abramowicz and Maxwell Stearns criticize the *Black's Law Dictionary* definition of dictum, among others described here. They observe, for example, that in cases involving alternative holdings, the necessity test cannot be effectively applied.

To illustrate, imagine that a federal district court judge dismisses a case on summary judgment based on two alternative grounds: (1) the plaintiff failed to satisfy the statute of limitations because her claimed justification for tolling the statute is unsuccessful; and (2) if the statute of limitations should be tolled, the plaintiff has nonetheless failed to demonstrate a genuine issue of material fact with respect to one of the elements in the prima facie case. In this situation, with two alternative holdings, either of which is sufficient to grant defendant's motion for summary judgment, we cannot say that either factual predicate is "necessary" to the court's resolution. And yet, it seems problematic to maintain that the case was dismissed on summary judgment with no holding.

After reviewing several plausible definitions, Abramowicz and Stearns offer their own:

> A holding consists of those propositions along the chosen decisional path of paths of reasoning that (1) are actually decided, (2) are based upon the facts of the case, and (3) lead to the judgment. If not a holding, a proposition stated in a case counts as dicta.[106]

Based on your review of the problem of holding, dicta, and materiality as set out in this chapter, which, if any, of these competing approaches is most appropriate? Are any complete, or must they be combined in different contexts? If the latter, what are those contexts? To what extent are your answers informed by game theory or other law and economics tools?

As you read the materials in the next chapter on individual case decision making, consider whether the Abramowicz and Stearns definition is excessively general as applied to cases without alternative holdings. In those contexts are the other tests more helpful? Is the problem of embedded cycles within fractured panel cases analogous to the problem of alternative holdings? How does this relate to the problem of multicriterial decision making?

Consider also Professor Dorf's concern about revising holdings from the past to avoid overruling. Is it better for the Supreme Court to adopt a stricter understanding of holding if the price is more frequent overruling? What if, instead, the price is failing to achieve present desired holdings? How do these questions relate to the game theoretical approaches to judicial decision making set out in this chapter? Consider also how they relates to the social choice approach to judicial decision making set out in Chapter 22.

---

[105] Larry Alexander, *Striking Back at the Empire: A Brief Survey of Problems in Dworkin's Theory of Law*, 6 LAW & PHIL. 419 (1987).

[106] Abramowicz & Stearns, *supra* note 59, at 1065.

Professor Alexander's analysis borrows from Ronald Dworkin. Does this combined analysis avoid some of the difficulties in defining holding or dictum? Does it risk sometimes exacerbating those difficulties?

Finally, consider some of the earlier definitions described above, including those by Goodhart and Llewelyn. Are the distinctions these scholars devise intended to avoid some of the difficulties that Dorf identifies with reframing past holdings? Are they designed to avoid some of the problems that Abramowicz and Stearns identify with alternative holdings? If so, do they succeed?

IV. APPLICATIONS

We present three applications, each involving a major Supreme Court decision. The first two involve the various models of stare decisis presented in Part II, and the third involves the distinction between holding and dictum discussed in Part III.

A. Planned Parenthood of Southeastern Pennsylvania v. Casey, 505 U.S. 833 (1992)

In this application we consider two prominent Supreme Court decisions that turned on an analysis of the stare decisis doctrine. In the first, *Planned Parenthood of Southeastern Pennsylvania v. Casey*, a plurality of three members of the Supreme Court, Justices O'Connor, Kennedy, and Souter, articulated the criteria that it determined were necessary when deciding whether to adhere to or abandon precedent as applied to its decision not to overturn the landmark case, *Roe v. Wade* (1973). In the second, Justice Kennedy, writing for a majority, emphasized one criterion, reliance, in applying the stare decisis doctrine to overturn the landmark decision, *Bowers v. Hardwick* (1986). After presenting the relevant summaries and excerpts, we ask you to compare the various approaches to stare decisis applied in these cases to the various models set out in this chapter.

PLANNED PARENTHOOD OF SOUTHEASTERN PENNSYLVANIA V. CASEY

Casey involved a challenge to the following provisions of a Pennsylvania abortion statute: (1) informed consent; (2) parental notification for minors; (3) spousal notification for married women; (4) an exemption from the first three provisions in the event of a medical emergency; and (5) specified reporting requirements. The *Casey* Court fractured, and one majority, the liberals and moderates, struck down the spousal notification provision, and a different majority, the conservatives and moderates, sustained each of the remaining provisions. In Chapter 22, we will revisit *Casey* to consider its social choice implications for Supreme Court decision making. In this application, we focus on the Court's analysis of stare decisis. The principal effect of the Casey ruling was to revise the framework for assessing the challenged abortion statute under *Roe v. Wade.*

In *Roe v. Wade* (1973), the Supreme Court held that abortion was a fundamental right, protected under its privacy doctrine articulated in *Griswold v. Connecticut* (1965). In Casey, the controlling plurality instead treated a woman's interest in terminating her pregnancy as a liberty interest, thereby reducing the governing standard for reviewing state laws limiting access to abortion from strict scrutiny to its newly constructed undue burden test. The plurality also revisited the *Roe v. Wade* trimester framework under which the state's identified interests in regulating abortion became compelling at specific points in the pregnancy. Under *Roe*, because the medical risks to the woman of aborting were determined to be lower early in a pregnancy than carrying the fetus to term, the state's power to limit abortion access to further its interest in maternal health did not become compelling until the end of the first trimester. In addition, because the *Roe* Court determined that the state's interest in the potentiality of human life did not become compelling until the fetus was capable of meaningful existence outside the mother's womb, it further determined that the state could not regulate abortion to promote that interest until viability, which coincides with the end of the second trimester.

In their jointly authored plurality opinion, which also issued the Court's judgment, Justices O'Connor, Kennedy, and Souter considered whether to adhere to *Roe v. Wade* as a matter of precedent, and they rejected various arguments for declining to honor what they labeled *Roe*'s "essential holding," albeit without embracing the entire holding. In declining to overrule *Roe*, the plurality further noted important differences between the judicial decisions to overrule *Lochner v. New York* (1905) in *Parrish v. West Coast Hotel* (1937), and to overrule *Plessy v. Ferguson* (1896) in *Brown v. Board of Education* (1954). Although the *Casey* plurality did not overrule *Roe*, it declined to embrace *Roe*'s trimester framework; it downgraded abortion from a fundamental right to a liberty interest; and it elevated the state's interest in the potentiality of human life. Applying its undue burden test, the plurality struck down the spousal notification provision while upholding each of the remaining provisions of the Pennsylvania statute.

JUSTICE O'CONNOR, JUSTICE KENNEDY, and JUSTICE SOUTER announced the judgment of the Court.

> I
>
> Liberty finds no refuge in a jurisprudence of doubt. Yet 19 years after our holding that the Constitution protects a woman's right to terminate her pregnancy in its early stages, *Roe v. Wade*, that definition of liberty is still questioned . . . .
>
> At issue in these cases are five provisions of the Pennsylvania Abortion Control Act of 1982, as amended in 1988 and 1989. 18 Pa. Cons. Stat. §§ 3203–3220 (1990) . . . . The Act requires that a woman seeking an abortion give her informed consent prior to the abortion procedure, and specifies that she be provided with certain information at least 24 hours before the abortion is performed. § 3205. For a minor to obtain an abortion, the Act requires the informed consent of one of her parents, but provides for a judicial bypass option if the minor does not wish to or cannot obtain a parent's consent. § 3206. Another provision of the Act requires that, unless certain exceptions apply, a married woman seeking an abortion must sign a statement indicating that she has notified her husband of her intended abortion. § 3209. The Act exempts compliance with these three requirements in the event of a "medical emergency," which is defined in § 3203 of the Act. See §§ 3203, 3205(a), 3206(a), 3209(c). In addition to the above provisions regulating the

performance of abortions, the Act imposes certain reporting requirements on facilities that provide abortion services. §§ 3207(b), 3214(a), 3214(f).

* * *

The obligation to follow precedent begins with necessity, and a contrary necessity marks its outer limit. With Cardozo, we recognize that no judicial system could do society's work if it eyed each issue afresh in every case that raised it. See B. Cardozo, The Nature of the Judicial Process 149 (1921). Indeed, the very concept of the rule of law underlying our own Constitution requires such continuity over time that a respect for precedent is, by definition, indispensable. See Powell, Stare Decisis and Judicial Restraint, 1991 Journal of Supreme Court History 13, 16. At the other extreme, a different necessity would make itself felt if a prior judicial ruling should come to be seen so clearly as error that its enforcement was for that very reason doomed.

Even when the decision to overrule a prior case is not, as in the rare, latter instance, virtually foreordained, it is common wisdom that the rule of *stare decisis* is not an "inexorable command," and certainly it is not such in every constitutional case . . . . Rather, when this Court reexamines a prior holding, its judgment is customarily informed by a series of prudential and pragmatic considerations designed to test the consistency of overruling a prior decision with the ideal of the rule of law, and to gauge the respective costs of reaffirming and overruling a prior case. Thus, for example, we may ask whether the rule has proven to be intolerable simply in defying practical workability, . . .; whether the rule is subject to a kind of reliance that would lend a special hardship to the consequences of overruling and add inequity to the cost of repudiation . . .; whether related principles of law have so far developed as to have left the old rule no more than a remnant of abandoned doctrine . . .; or whether facts have so changed, or come to be seen so differently, as to have robbed the old rule of significant application or justification . . . .

So in this case we may enquire whether *Roe*'s central rule has been found unworkable; whether the rule's limitation on state power could be removed without serious inequity to those who have relied upon it or significant damage to the stability of the society governed by it; whether the law's growth in the intervening years has left *Roe*'s central rule a doctrinal anachronism discounted by society; and whether *Roe*'s premises of fact have so far changed in the ensuing two decades as to render its central holding somehow irrelevant or unjustifiable in dealing with the issue it addressed.

1

Although *Roe* has engendered opposition, it has in no sense proven "unworkable," . . . representing as it does a simple limitation beyond which a state law is unenforceable . . . .

2

* * *

While neither respondents nor their *amici* in so many words deny that the abortion right invites some reliance prior to its actual exercise, one can readily imagine an argument stressing the dissimilarity of this case to one involving property or contract. Abortion is customarily chosen as an unplanned response to the consequence of unplanned activity or to the failure of conventional birth control, and except on the assumption that no intercourse would have occurred but for *Roe*'s holding, such behavior may appear to justify no reliance claim. Even if reliance could be claimed on that unrealistic assumption, the argument might run, any reliance interest would be *de minimis*. This argument would be premised on the hypothesis that reproductive planning could take virtually immediate account of any sudden restoration of state authority to ban abortions.

To eliminate the issue of reliance that easily, however, one would need to limit cognizable reliance to specific instances of sexual activity. But to do this would be simply to refuse to face the fact that for two decades of economic and social developments, people have organized intimate relationships and made choices that define their views of themselves and their places in society, in reliance on the availability of abortion in the event that contraception should fail. The ability of women to participate equally in the economic and social life of the Nation has been facilitated by their ability to control their reproductive lives. . . .

No evolution of legal principle has left *Roe*'s doctrinal footings weaker than they were in 1973. No development of constitutional law since the case was decided has implicitly or explicitly left *Roe* behind as a mere survivor of obsolete constitutional thinking.

It will be recognized, of course, that *Roe* stands at an intersection of two lines of decisions, but in whichever doctrinal category one reads the case, the result for present purposes will be the same. The *Roe* Court itself placed its holding in the succession of cases most prominently exemplified by *Griswold v. Connecticut*, ... When it is so seen, *Roe* is clearly in no jeopardy, since subsequent constitutional developments have neither disturbed, nor do they threaten to diminish, the scope of recognized protection accorded to the liberty relating to intimate relationships, the family, and decisions about whether or not to beget or bear a child . . . .

Roe, however, may be seen not only as an exemplar of *Griswold* liberty but as a rule (whether or not mistaken) of personal autonomy and bodily integrity, with doctrinal affinity to cases recognizing limits on governmental power to mandate medical treatment or to bar its rejection. If so, our cases since *Roe* accord with *Roe*'s view that a State's interest in the protection of life falls short of justifying any plenary override of individual liberty claims. *Cruzan v. Director, Mo. Dep't of Health* . . . .

Finally, one could classify *Roe* as *sui generis*. If the case is so viewed, then there clearly has been no erosion of its central determination . . . .

Even on the assumption that the central holding of *Roe* was in error, that error would go only to the strength of the state interest in fetal protection, not to the recognition afforded by the Constitution to the woman's liberty . . . . As we described in *Carey v. Population Services International,* the liberty which encompasses those decisions

> "includes 'the interest in independence in making certain kinds of important decisions.' While the outer limits of this aspect of [protected liberty] have not been marked by the Court, it is clear that among the decisions that an individual may make without unjustified government interference are personal decisions 'relating to marriage, procreation, contraception, family relationships, and child rearing and education.' " (citations omitted).

* * *

In a less significant case, *stare decisis* analysis could, and would, stop at the point we have reached. But the sustained and widespread debate *Roe* has provoked calls for some comparison between that case and others of comparable dimension that have responded to national controversies and taken on the impress of the controversies addressed. Only two such decisional lines from the past century present themselves for examination, and in each instance the result reached by the Court accorded with the principles we apply today.

The first example is that line of cases identified with *Lochner v. New York*, which imposed substantive limitations on legislation limiting economic autonomy in favor of health and welfare regulation, adopting, in Justice Holmes's view, the theory of laissez-faire. (dissenting opinion). The *Lochner* decisions were exemplified by *Adkins v. Children's Hospital of District of Columbia*, in which this Court held it to be an infringement of constitutionally protected liberty of contract to require the employers of adult women to satisfy minimum wage standards. Fourteen years later, *West Coast Hotel Co. v. Parrish*, signaled the demise of *Lochner* by overruling *Adkins*. In the meantime, the Depression had come and, with it, the lesson that seemed unmistakable to most people by 1937, that the interpretation of contractual freedom protected in *Adkins* rested on fundamentally false factual assumptions about the capacity of a relatively unregulated market to satisfy minimal levels of human welfare. As Justice Jackson wrote of the constitutional crisis of 1937 shortly before he came on the bench: "The older world of *laissez faire* was recognized everywhere outside the Court to be dead."

* * *

The second comparison that 20th century history invites is with the cases employing the separate-but-equal rule for applying the Fourteenth Amendment's equal protection guarantee. They began with *Plessy v. Ferguson*, holding that legislatively mandated racial segregation in public transportation works no denial of equal protection, rejecting the argument that racial separation enforced by the legal machinery of American society treats the black race as inferior. The *Plessy* Court considered "the underlying fallacy of the plaintiff's argument to consist in the assumption that the enforced separation of the two races stamps the colored race with a badge of inferiority. If this be so, it is not by reason of anything found in the act, but solely because the colored race chooses to put that construction upon it." Whether, as a matter of historical fact, the Justices in the *Plessy* majority believed this or not . . ., this understanding of the implication of segregation was the stated justification for the Court's opinion. But this understanding of the facts and the rule it was stated to justify were repudiated in *Brown v. Board of Education (Brown I)*.

* * *

The Court in *Brown* addressed these facts of life by observing that whatever may have been the understanding in *Plessy*'s time of the power of segregation to stigmatize those who were segregated with a "badge of inferiority," it was clear by 1954 that legally sanctioned segregation had just such an effect, to the point that racially separate public educational facilities were deemed inherently unequal. Society's understanding of the facts upon which a constitutional ruling was sought in 1954 was thus fundamentally different from the basis claimed for the decision in 1896. While we think *Plessy* was wrong the day it was decided, we must also recognize that the *Plessy* Court's explanation for its decision was so clearly at odds with the facts apparent to the Court in 1954 that the decision to reexamine *Plessy* was on this ground alone not only justified but required.

West Coast Hotel and *Brown* each rested on facts, or an understanding of facts, changed from those which furnished the claimed justifications for the earlier constitutional resolutions . . . . In constitutional adjudication as elsewhere in life, changed circumstances may impose new obligations, and the thoughtful part of the Nation could accept each decision to overrule a prior case as a response to the Court's constitutional duty.

Because the cases before us present no such occasion it could be seen as no such response. Because neither the factual underpinnings of *Roe*'s central holding nor our understanding of it has changed (and because no other indication of weakened precedent has been shown), the Court could not pretend to be reexamining the prior law with any justification beyond a present doctrinal disposition to come out differently from the Court of 1973. To overrule prior law for no other reason than that would run counter to the view repeated in our cases, that a decision to overrule should rest on some special reason over and above the belief that a prior case was wrongly decided . . . .

* * *

IV

From what we have said so far it follows that it is a constitutional liberty of the woman to have some freedom to terminate her pregnancy. We conclude that the basic decision in *Roe* was based on a constitutional analysis which we cannot now repudiate. The woman's liberty is not so unlimited, however, that from the outset the State cannot show its concern for the life of the unborn, and at a later point in fetal development the State's interest in life has sufficient force so that the right of the woman to terminate the pregnancy can be restricted.

* * *

Liberty must not be extinguished for want of a line that is clear. And it falls to us to give some real substance to the woman's liberty to determine whether to carry her pregnancy to full term.

We conclude the line should be drawn at viability . . . We adhere to this principle for two reasons. First, as we have said, is the doctrine of *stare decisis*. Any judicial act of line-drawing may seem somewhat arbitrary, but *Roe [v. Wade]* was a reasoned statement, elaborated with great care. We have twice reaffirmed it in the face of great opposition. Although we must overrule those parts of *Thornburgh* [*v. American College of Obstetricians and Gynecologists*] and *Akron* [*v. Akron Center for Reproductive Health, Inc.*] which, in our view, are inconsistent with *Roe*'s statement that the State has a legitimate interest in promoting the life or potential life of the unborn, . . . the central premise of those cases represents an unbroken commitment by this Court to the essential holding of *Roe*. It is that premise which we reaffirm today.

The second reason is that the concept of viability, as we noted in *Roe*, is the time at which there is a realistic possibility of maintaining and nourishing a life outside the womb, so that the independent existence of the second life can in reason and all fairness be the object of state protection that now overrides the rights of the woman . . . . Consistent with other constitutional norms, legislatures may draw lines which appear arbitrary without the necessity of offering a justification. But courts may not. We must justify the lines we draw. And there is no line other than viability which is more workable . . . . The viability line also has, as a practical matter, an element of fairness. In some broad sense it might be said that a woman who fails to act before viability has consented to the State's intervention on behalf of the developing child.

The woman's right to terminate her pregnancy before viability is the most central principle of *Roe v. Wade*. It is a rule of law and a component of liberty we cannot renounce.

On the other side of the equation is the interest of the State in the protection of potential life. The *Roe* Court recognized the State's "important and legitimate interest in protecting the potentiality of human life." . . . . That portion of the decision in *Roe* has been given too little acknowledgment and implementation by the Court in its subsequent cases. Those cases decided that any regulation touching upon the abortion decision must survive strict scrutiny, to be sustained only if drawn in narrow terms to further a compelling state interest. . . . Not all of the cases decided under that formulation can be reconciled with the holding in *Roe* itself that the State has legitimate interests in the health of the woman and in protecting the potential life within her. In resolving this tension, we choose to rely upon *Roe*, as against the later cases.

Roe established a trimester framework to govern abortion regulations. Under this elaborate but rigid construct, almost no regulation at all is permitted during the first trimester of pregnancy; regulations designed to protect the woman's health, but not to further the State's interest in potential life, are permitted during the second trimester; and during the third trimester, when the fetus is viable, prohibitions are permitted provided the life or health of the mother is not at stake. . . . Most of our cases since *Roe* have involved the application of rules derived from the trimester framework.

* * *

A framework of this rigidity was unnecessary and in its later interpretation sometimes contradicted the State's permissible exercise of its powers.

Though the woman has a right to choose to terminate or continue her pregnancy before viability, it does not at all follow that the State is prohibited from taking steps to ensure that this choice is thoughtful and informed. Even in the earliest stages of pregnancy, the State may enact rules and regulations designed to encourage her to know that there are philosophic and social arguments of great weight that can be brought to bear in favor of continuing the pregnancy to full term and that there are procedures and institutions to allow adoption of unwanted children as well as a certain degree of state assistance if the mother chooses to raise the child herself. " '[T]he Constitution does not forbid a State or city, pursuant to democratic processes, from expressing a preference for normal childbirth.' " *Webster v. Reproductive Health Services*. . . It follows that States are free to enact laws to provide a reasonable framework for a woman to make a decision that has such profound and lasting meaning . . . .

We reject the trimester framework, which we do not consider to be part of the essential holding of *Roe* . . . . A logical reading of the central holding in *Roe* itself, and a necessary reconciliation of the liberty of the woman and the interest of the State in promoting prenatal life, require, in our view, that we abandon the trimester framework as a rigid prohibition on all previability regulation aimed at the protection of fetal life . . . .

* * *

All abortion regulations interfere to some degree with a woman's ability to decide whether to terminate her pregnancy. It is, as a consequence, not surprising that despite the protestations contained in the original *Roe* opinion to the effect that the Court was not recognizing an absolute right, . . . the Court's experience applying the trimester framework has led to the striking down of some abortion regulations which in no real sense deprived women of the ultimate decision. Those decisions went too far . . . . Not all governmental intrusion is of necessity unwarranted . . . .

Roe v. Wade was express in its recognition of the State's "important and legitimate interest[s] in preserving and protecting the health of the pregnant woman [and] in protecting the potentiality of human life." The trimester framework, however, does not fulfill *Roe*'s own promise that the State has an interest in protecting fetal life or potential life . . . . Before viability, *Roe* and subsequent cases treat all governmental attempts to influence a woman's decision on behalf of the potential life within her as unwarranted. This treatment is, in our judgment, incompatible with the recognition that there is a substantial state interest in potential life throughout pregnancy . . . .

The very notion that the State has a substantial interest in potential life leads to the conclusion that not all regulations must be deemed unwarranted . . . . In our view, the undue burden standard is the appropriate means of reconciling the State's interest with the woman's constitutionally protected liberty.

A finding of an undue burden is a shorthand for the conclusion that a state regulation has the purpose or effect of placing a substantial obstacle in the path of a woman seeking an abortion of a nonviable fetus. A statute with this purpose is invalid because the means chosen by the State to further the interest in potential life must be calculated to inform the woman's free choice, not hinder it . . . .

Some guiding principles should emerge. What is at stake is the woman's right to make the ultimate decision, not a right to be insulated from all others in doing so. Regulations which do no more than create a structural mechanism by which the State, or the parent or guardian of a minor, may express profound respect for the life of the unborn are permitted, if they are not a substantial obstacle to the woman's exercise of the right to choose . . . .

Unless it has that effect on her right of choice, a state measure designed to persuade her to choose childbirth over abortion will be upheld if reasonably related to that goal. Regulations designed to foster the health of a woman seeking an abortion are valid if they do not constitute an undue burden.

* * *

[After applying this test to strike the spousal notification provision, and to retain the remaining provisions, of the Pennsylvania statute, the plurality concluded:]

* * *

Our Constitution is a covenant running from the first generation of Americans to us and then to future generations. It is a coherent succession. Each generation must learn anew that the Constitution's written terms embody ideas and aspirations that must survive more ages than one. We accept our responsibility not to retreat from interpreting the full meaning of the covenant in light of all of our precedents. We invoke it once again to define the freedom guaranteed by the Constitution's own promise, the promise of liberty.

B. Lawrence v. Texas, 539 U.S. 558 (2003)

In response to a criminal complaint about possible gunfire, Houston police entered John Lawrence's apartment, whereupon some of the officers claimed to witness Lawrence and Tyron Garner engaging in a sex act, although the specific reports concerning what the officers observed were in conflict. The men were arrested and eventually convicted and fined $200 for violating a Texas statute that criminalized "deviate sexual intercourse with another individual of the same sex." Lawrence and Garner appealed their convictions, which had been affirmed in the state court of appeals, to the United States Supreme Court.

In a six-to-three vote, the Supreme Court struck down the challenged Texas statute as violating the Due Process Clause. In the majority opinion, Justice Kennedy held that due process prohibited states from criminalizing consensual intimacy between consenting adults, including members of the same sex. In doing so, the Lawrence Court overruled *Bowers v. Hardwick* (1986), which had rejected a constitutional challenge to neutrally worded consensual sodomy statute as applied to same-sex intimacy.

JUSTICE KENNEDY delivered the opinion of the Court.

> Liberty protects the person from unwarranted government intrusions into a dwelling or other private places. In our tradition the State is not omnipresent in the home. And there are other spheres of our lives and existence, outside the home, where the State should not be a dominant presence. Freedom extends beyond spatial bounds. Liberty presumes an autonomy of self that includes freedom of thought, belief, expression, and certain intimate conduct. The instant case involves liberty of the person both in its spatial and more transcendent dimensions.
>
> * * *
>
> The Court began its substantive discussion in *Bowers v. Hardwick* (1986) as follows: "The issue presented is whether the Federal Constitution confers a fundamental right upon homosexuals to engage in sodomy and hence invalidates the laws of the many States that still make such conduct illegal and have done so for a very long time." . . . That statement, we now conclude, discloses the Court's own failure to appreciate the extent of the liberty at stake. To say that the issue in *Bowers* was simply the right to engage in certain sexual conduct demeans the claim the individual put forward, just as it would demean a married couple were it to be said marriage is simply about the right to have sexual intercourse. . . . The statutes [at issue] seek to control a personal relationship that, whether or not entitled to formal recognition in the law, is within the liberty of persons to choose without being punished as criminals.
>
> * * *

It suffices for us to acknowledge that adults may choose to enter upon this relationship in the confines of their homes and their own private lives and still retain their dignity as free persons. When sexuality finds overt expression in intimate conduct with another person, the conduct can be but one element in a personal bond that is more enduring. The liberty protected by the Constitution allows homosexual persons the right to make this choice.

* * *

At the outset it should be noted that there is no longstanding history in this country of laws directed at homosexual conduct as a distinct matter. . . . Thus early American sodomy laws were not directed at homosexuals as such but instead sought to prohibit nonprocreative sexual activity more generally.

* * *

[The] historical grounds relied upon in *Bowers* are more complex than the majority opinion [by Justice White] and the concurring opinion by Chief Justice Burger indicate. Their historical premises are not without doubt and, at the very least, are overstated.

It must be acknowledged, of course, that the Court in *Bowers* was making the broader point that for centuries there have been powerful voices to condemn homosexual conduct as immoral. The condemnation has been shaped by religious beliefs, conceptions of right and acceptable behavior, and respect for the traditional family. For many persons these are not trivial concerns but profound and deep convictions accepted as ethical and moral principles to which they aspire and which thus determine the course of their lives. These considerations do not answer the question before us, however. The issue is whether the majority may use the power of the State to enforce these views on the whole society through operation of the criminal law. "Our obligation is to define the liberty of all, not to mandate our own moral code." *Planned Parenthood of Southeastern Pa. v. Casey.*

Chief Justice Burger . . . further explained his views as follows: "Decisions of individuals relating to homosexual conduct have been subject to state intervention throughout the history of Western civilization. Condemnation of those practices is firmly rooted in Judeao-Christian moral and ethical standards." . . . As with Justice White's assumptions [expressed in the majority opinion] about history, scholarship casts some doubt on the sweeping nature of [this] statement . . . as it pertains to private homosexual conduct between consenting adults. See, *e.g.*, Eskridge, *Hardwick and Historiography.* [We] think that our laws and traditions in the past half century are of most relevance here [and] show an emerging awareness that liberty gives substantial protection to adult persons in deciding how to conduct their private lives in matters pertaining to sex. "[H]istory and tradition are the starting point but not in all cases the ending point of the substantive due process inquiry."

* * *

This emerging recognition should have been apparent when *Bowers* was decided. In 1955 the American Law Institute promulgated the Model Penal Code and made clear that it did not recommend or provide for "criminal penalties for consensual sexual relations conducted in private."

* * *

In *Bowers* the Court referred to the fact that before 1961 all 50 States had outlawed sodomy, and that at the time of the Court's decision 24 States and the District of Columbia had sodomy laws . . . . Justice Powell pointed out that these prohibitions often were being ignored, however . . . .

The sweeping references by Chief Justice Burger to the history of Western civilization and to Judeo-Christian moral and ethical standards did not take account of other authorities pointing in an opposite direction . . . .

[Almost] five years before *Bowers* was decided the European Court of Human Rights considered a case with parallels to *Bowers* and to today's case. An adult male resident in Northern Ireland alleged he was a practicing homosexual who desired to engage in consensual homosexual conduct. The laws of Northern Ireland forbade him that right . . . . The court held that the laws proscribing the conduct were invalid under the European Convention on Human Rights . . . . Authoritative in all countries that are members of the Council of Europe (21 nations then, 45 nations now), the decision is at odds with the premise in *Bowers* that the claim put forward was insubstantial in our Western civilization.

In our own constitutional system the deficiencies in *Bowers* became even more apparent in the years following its announcement. The 25 States with laws prohibiting the relevant conduct referenced in the *Bowers* decision are reduced now to 13, of which 4 enforce their laws only against homosexual conduct. In those States where sodomy is still proscribed, whether for same-sex or heterosexual conduct, there is a pattern of nonenforcement with respect to consenting adults acting in private. The State of Texas admitted in 1994 that as of that date it had not prosecuted anyone under those circumstances . . . .

Two principal cases decided after *Bowers* cast its holding into even more doubt. In *Planned Parenthood of Southeastern Pa. v. Casey*, the Court reaffirmed the substantive force of the liberty protected by the Due Process Clause. The *Casey* decision again confirmed that our laws and tradition afford constitutional protection to personal decisions relating to marriage, procreation, contraception, family relationships, child rearing, and education. In explaining the respect the Constitution demands for the autonomy of the person in making these choices, we stated as follows: "These matters, involving the most intimate and personal choices a person may make in a lifetime, choices central to personal dignity and autonomy, are central to the liberty protected by the Fourteenth Amendment. At the heart of liberty is the right to define one's own concept of existence, of meaning, of the universe, and of the mystery of human life. Beliefs about these matters could not define the attributes of personhood were they formed under compulsion of the State."

Persons in a homosexual relationship may seek autonomy for these purposes, just as heterosexual persons do. The decision in *Bowers* would deny them this right.

The second post-*Bowers* case of principal relevance is *Romer v. Evans*. There the Court struck down class-based legislation directed at homosexuals as a violation of the Equal Protection Clause. *Romer* invalidated an amendment to Colorado's constitution which named as a solitary class persons who were homosexuals, lesbians, or bisexual either by "orientation, conduct, practices or relationships," and deprived them of protection under state antidiscrimination laws. We concluded that the provision was "born of animosity toward the class of persons affected" and further that it had no rational relation to a legitimate governmental purpose.

* * *

Equality of treatment and the due process right to demand respect for conduct protected by the substantive guarantee of liberty are linked in important respects, and a decision on the latter point advances both interests .... When homosexual conduct is made criminal by the law of the State, that declaration in and of itself is an invitation to subject homosexual persons to discrimination both in the public and in the private spheres. The central holding of *Bowers* has been brought in question by this case, and it should be addressed. Its continuance as precedent demeans the lives of homosexual persons.

The stigma this criminal statute imposes, moreover, is not trivial. The offense, to be sure, is but a class C misdemeanor, a minor offense in the Texas legal system. Still, it remains a criminal offense with all that imports for the dignity of the persons charged ....

The foundations of *Bowers* have sustained serious erosion from our recent decisions in *Casey* and *Romer*. When our precedent has been thus weakened, criticism from other sources is of greater significance. In the United States criticism of *Bowers* has been substantial and continuing, disapproving of its reasoning in all respects, not just as to its historical assumptions ....

* * *

The doctrine of *stare decisis* is essential to the respect accorded to the judgments of the Court and to the stability of the law. It is not, however, an inexorable command .... In *Casey* we noted that when a Court is asked to overrule a precedent recognizing a constitutional liberty interest, individual or societal reliance on the existence of that liberty cautions with particular strength against reversing course. ("Liberty finds no refuge in a jurisprudence of doubt").

The holding in *Bowers*, however, has not induced detrimental reliance comparable to some instances where recognized individual rights are involved. Indeed, there has been no individual or societal reliance on *Bowers* of the sort that could counsel against overturning its holding once there are compelling reasons to do so. *Bowers* itself causes uncertainty, for the precedents before and after its issuance contradict its central holding.

The rationale of *Bowers* does not withstand careful analysis. In his dissenting opinion in *Bowers* JUSTICE STEVENS came to these conclusions:

"Our prior cases make two propositions abundantly clear. First, the fact that the governing majority in a State has traditionally viewed a particular practice as immoral is not a sufficient reason for upholding a law prohibiting the practice; neither history nor tradition could save a law prohibiting miscegenation from constitutional attack. Second, individual decisions by married persons, concerning the intimacies of their physical relationship, even when not intended to produce offspring, are a form of "liberty" protected by the Due Process Clause of the Fourteenth Amendment. Moreover, this protection extends to intimate choices by unmarried as well as married persons." (footnotes and citations omitted).

JUSTICE STEVENS' analysis, in our view, should have been controlling in *Bowers* and should control here. *Bowers* was not correct when it was decided, and it is not correct today. It ought not to remain binding precedent. *Bowers* v. *Hardwick* should be and now is overruled.

The present case does not involve minors. It does not involve persons who might be injured or coerced or who are situated in relationships where consent might not easily be refused. It does not involve public conduct or prostitution. It does not involve whether the government must give formal recognition to any relationship that homosexual persons seek to enter. The case does involve two adults who, with full and mutual consent from each other, engaged in sexual practices common to a homosexual lifestyle. The petitioners are entitled to respect for their private lives . . . .

* * *

The judgment of the Court of Appeals for the Texas Fourteenth District is reversed, and the case is remanded for further proceedings not inconsistent with this opinion.

It is so ordered.

JUSTICE O'CONNOR, concurring in the judgment.

The Court today overrules *Bowers v. Hardwick*. I joined *Bowers,* and do not join the Court in overruling it. Nevertheless, I agree with the Court that Texas' statute banning same-sex sodomy is unconstitutional . . . . Rather than relying on the substantive component of the Fourteenth Amendment's Due Process Clause, as the Court does, I base my conclusion on the Fourteenth Amendment's Equal Protection Clause.

This case raises a different issue than *Bowers:* whether, under the Equal Protection Clause, moral disapproval is a legitimate state interest to justify by itself a statute that bans homosexual sodomy, but not heterosexual sodomy. It is not. Moral disapproval of this group, like a bare desire to harm the group, is an interest that is insufficient to satisfy rational basis review under the Equal Protection Clause . . . . Indeed, we have never held that moral disapproval, without any other asserted state interest, is a sufficient rationale under the Equal Protection Clause to justify a law that discriminates among groups of persons.

Whether a sodomy law that is neutral both in effect and application, . . . would violate the substantive component of the Due Process Clause is an issue that need not be decided today. I am confident, however, that so long as the Equal Protection Clause requires a sodomy law to apply equally to the private consensual conduct of homosexuals and heterosexuals alike, such a law would not long stand in our democratic society . . . .

JUSTICE SCALIA, with whom THE CHIEF JUSTICE and JUSTICE THOMAS join, dissenting:

"Liberty finds no refuge in a jurisprudence of doubt." *Planned Parenthood of Southeastern Pa. v. Casey*. That was the Court's sententious response, barely more than a decade ago, to those seeking to overrule *Roe v. Wade*. The Court's response today, to those who have engaged in a 17-year crusade to overrule *Bowers v. Hardwick*, is very different. The need for stability and certainty presents no barrier.

It seems to me that the "societal reliance" on the principles confirmed in *Bowers* and discarded today has been overwhelming. Countless judicial decisions and legislative enactments have relied on the ancient proposition that a governing majority's belief that certain sexual behavior is "immoral and unacceptable" constitutes a rational basis for regulation. . . . State laws against bigamy, same-sex marriage, adult incest, prostitution, masturbation, adultery, fornication, bestiality, and obscenity are likewise sustainable only in light of *Bowers'* validation of laws based on moral choices. Every single one of these laws is called into question by today's decision; the Court makes no effort to cabin the scope of its decision to exclude them from its holding . . . .

The Court today does not . . . describe homosexual sodomy as a "fundamental right" or a "fundamental liberty interest," nor does it subject the Texas statute to strict scrutiny. Instead, having failed to establish that the right to homosexual sodomy is " 'deeply rooted in this Nation's history and tradition,' " the Court concludes that the application of Texas's statute to petitioners' conduct fails the rational-basis test, and overrules *Bowers'* holding to the contrary. . . .

It is (as *Bowers* recognized) entirely irrelevant whether the laws in our long national tradition criminalizing homosexual sodomy were "directed at homosexual conduct as a distinct matter." . . . Whether homosexual sodomy was prohibited by a law targeted at same-sex sexual relations or by a more general law prohibiting both homosexual and heterosexual sodomy, the only relevant point is that it *was* criminalized—which suffices to establish that homosexual sodomy is not a right "deeply rooted in our Nation's history and tradition." The Court today agrees that homosexual sodomy was criminalized and thus does not dispute the facts on which *Bowers actually* relied . . .

[T]he Court says: "[W]e think that our laws and traditions in the past half century are of most relevance here. These references show *an emerging awareness* that liberty gives substantial protection to adult persons in deciding how to conduct their private lives *in matters pertaining to sex*." . . . Apart from the fact that such an "emerging awareness" does not establish a "fundamental right," the statement is factually false. States continue to prosecute all sorts of crimes by adults "in matters pertaining to sex": prostitution, adult incest, adultery, obscenity, and child pornography. Sodomy laws, too, have been enforced "in the past half century," in which there have been 134 reported cases involving prosecutions for consensual, adult, homosexual sodomy . . . .

In any event, an "emerging awareness" is by definition not "deeply rooted in this Nation's history and tradition[s]," as we have said "fundamental right" status requires. Constitutional entitlements do not spring into existence because some States choose to lessen or eliminate criminal sanctions on certain behavior. Much less do they spring into existence, as the Court seems to believe, because *foreign nations* decriminalize conduct . . . .

Today's opinion is the product of a Court, which is the product of a law-profession culture, that has largely signed on to the so-called homosexual agenda, by which I mean the agenda promoted by some homosexual activists directed at eliminating the moral opprobrium that has traditionally attached to homosexual conduct . . . .

* * *

It is clear . . . that the Court has taken sides in the culture war, departing from its role of assuring, as neutral observer, that the democratic rules of engagement are observed. Many Americans do not want persons who openly engage in homosexual conduct as partners in their business, as scoutmasters for their children, as teachers in their children's schools, or as boarders in their home. They view this as protecting themselves and their families from a lifestyle that they believe to be immoral and destructive. The Court views it as "discrimination" which it is the function of our judgments to deter. So imbued is the Court with the law profession's anti-anti-homosexual culture, that it is seemingly unaware that the attitudes of that culture are not obviously "mainstream"; that in most States what the Court calls "discrimination" against those who engage in homosexual acts is perfectly legal; that proposals to ban such "discrimination" under Title VII have repeatedly been rejected by Congress, . . . that in some cases such "discrimination" is *mandated* by federal statute . . .; and that in some cases such "discrimination" is a constitutional right, see *Boy Scouts of America v. Dale*. Let me be clear that I have nothing against homosexuals, or any other group, promoting their agenda through normal democratic means . . . . I would no more *require* a State to criminalize homosexual acts—or, for that matter, display *any* moral disapprobation of them—than I would *forbid* it to do so. What Texas has chosen to do is well within the range of traditional democratic action, and its hand should not be stayed through the invention of a brand-new "constitutional right" by a Court that is impatient of democratic change . . . . [I]t is the premise of our system that those judgments are to be made by the people, and not imposed by a governing caste that knows best.

C. Sessions v. Morales-Santana, 137 S. Ct. 1678 (2017)[107]

In a series of cases, the Supreme Court has vacillated as to how to apply the intermediate scrutiny test to gender-based claims arising under the Fourteenth Amendment Equal Protection Clause (for state law claims) or under the Fifth Amendment Due Process clause (for federal law claims). Intermediate scrutiny demands (1) an important governmental interest, and (2) means substantially in furtherance of that interest. The test is designed to fall between two other equal protection tiers of scrutiny. Strict scrutiny, applied paradigmatically in race cases, demands: (1) a compelling governmental interest, and (2) narrow tailoring. That test places the burden to satisfy both criteria on the government defending the challenged classification. Rational basis scrutiny, the default rule, which applies in the absence of a suspect or quasi-suspect class, or a fundamental right, demands (1) a legitimate governmental interest, and (2) means rationally in furtherance of that interest. That test places the burden on the challenger, who may succeed by proving the absence of either of the two prongs.

The recent gender-classification volley is ambiguous as to which party bears the burden of proof. In *United States v. Virginia*,[108] a case involving an equal protection challenge to the exclusion of women from the Virginia Military Institute, a state institution of higher learning, coupled with an alternative program for women housed at Mary Baldwin College, Justice Ginsburg, writing for a majority, ratcheted the intermediate scrutiny test upward. She demanded (1) an exceedingly persuasive justification; (2) that the justification be contemporaneous with the enacted law or policy, rather than constructed after the fact; and (3) that the burden of proof fall entirely on the government. This functionally elevated intermediate scrutiny to strict scrutiny, and the result was to strike the challenged restriction down despite the necessary program modifications required to admit women.

In *Tuan Anh Nguyen v. INS*,[109] Justice Kennedy applied a more relaxed intermediate scrutiny test to sustain a provision of the Immigration and Nationality Act that that automatically conferred citizenship status on foreign-born illegitimate children of U.S. citizen mothers, but that required affirmative steps prior to maturity before similarly situated children of U.S. citizen fathers could acquire citizenship. Justice Kennedy rejected the argument that DNA

---

[107] The discussion that follows is based on Maxwell L. Stearns, Obergefell, Fisher *and the Inversion of Tiers*, 19 U. PA. J. CONST. L. 1043 (2017); *see also infra* Chapter 22 at 973–975 (presenting thesis set out in the article).

[108] 518 U.S. 515 (1996).

[109] 533 U.S. 53 (2001).

evidence rendered the presumption of parenthood for mothers, but not fathers, obsolete, claiming that real differences between the sexes nonetheless permitted a stronger presumption of parental bonding in the case of mothers, who were invariably aware of the child's birth, as compared with fathers, who might not have been aware even of the child's conception, let alone birth. Justice Kennedy did not mention the additional criteria that Justice Ginsburg added in *United States v. Virginia*, and he appeared to impose the burden on the party challenging the law, who was not awarded citizenship, and was thus subject to deportation.

In *Sessions v. Morales-Santana*,[110] Justice Ginsburg, writing for a majority of six that included Justice Kennedy, applied intermediate scrutiny to evaluate a Fifth Amendment Due Process Clause challenge to § 1401(a)(7) of the Immigration and Nationality Act. That provision imposed a longer, ten-year, durational residency requirement on U.S. citizen fathers, of which five must be post-age fourteen, as compared to a one-year durational residency requirement for U.S. citizen mothers, who are the parents, along with a non-U.S. citizen, of an illegitimate child who was born outside the United States, and who later seeks to become a U.S. citizen.

The child of a deceased U.S. citizen father fell short of the post-age-fourteen five-year durational residency requirement by twenty days, and was thus subject to deportation due to his criminal record. He brought suit,[111] claiming that because he would have been granted citizenship status, thereby preventing deportation, had his mother been the U.S. citizen parent, the challenged statutory provision violated his Fifth Amendment Due Process Clause right.

Justice Ginsburg distinguished *Nguyen,* stating that unlike the presumption of parental bonding, which relates to connectedness to the United States, differences in durational residency based on the parent's gender have no such justification. Ginsburg also ratcheted back upward the demands of intermediate scrutiny consistent with *United States v. Virginia*, albeit by distinguishing, rather than overruling, *Nguyen*. Although Ginsburg determined that the statutory distinction drawn in § 1401(a)(7) violated due process, she nonetheless denied petition's demand for relief. She reasoned that the Supreme Court lacked the power to level-up a remedy respecting naturalization, as the Constitution confers exclusive authority to set conditions for naturalization on Congress.[112]

QUESTIONS

1. The *Casey* opinion offers a four-part test for stare decisis, derived from the following factors: (1) practical workability; (2) reliance; (3) whether the past rule has been

[110] 137 S. Ct. 1678 (2017) (Gorsuch, J., recused).

[111] *Id.* at 1686.

[112] *Id.* at 1698.

abandoned; and (4) changed facts. Do these factors, individually or in combination, better support the internally developed or externally imposed theories of stare decisis? If they fit the internal theory, what motivates the Court to develop them? If they fit the external theory, has the Court accurately captured the relevant considerations?

2. The *Casey* opinion further applies these considerations to the overrulings of *Plessey* and *Lochner*? Do you find the application of the four factors to those cases persuasive? Why or why not?

3. How does your answer to question 2 relate to the Attitudinal Model? Does that model offer an alternative account for the decision in *Casey* not to abandon *Roe*? If so, how does the fact that seven of the nine deciding justices were appointed by Republican presidents affect your analysis?

4. Is the relationship between *Lawrence* and *Bowers* closer to that between *Casey* and *Roe,* or to the description in *Casey* of the decisions to overrule *Plessey* in *Brown* and *Lochner* in *West Coast Hotel*? In his *Lawrence* dissent, Justice Scalia rejects the comparison of the decision to retain *Roe*'s essential holding to the latter overrulings, and he determines that reliance interests respecting *Bowers* were afforded inadequate consideration. With respect to reliance, whose analysis is more persuasive, Justice Kennedy's majority opinion or Justice Scalia's dissent? How, if at all, does your answer inform which of the stare decisis models is most persuasive? Why?

5. In his *Lawrence* dissent, Justice Scalia states: "At the end of its opinion—after having laid waste the foundations of our rational-basis jurisprudence—the Court says that the present case 'does not involve whether the government must give formal recognition to any relationship that homosexual persons seek to enter.' . . . Do not believe it."

Assuming that Justice Scalia believes that having found a fundamental right to consensual same-sex sodomy mandates finding a fundamental right to same-sex marriage, should Justice Scalia have joined the majority, rather than dissent, in *Obergefell v. Hodges*, 135 S. Ct. 2584 (2015), which found a right to same-sex marriage? Why or why not? If you conclude that Scalia should have joined the *Obergefell* majority, why do you believe he instead dissented? How does your answer relate to the decisions by Justices Brennan and Marshall to routinely dissent from decisions to decline review of death penalty cases in which they claimed the penalty violated the Fourteenth Amendment despite contrary Supreme Court precedent?[113] How does this relate to the Attitudinal analysis of stare decisis?

6. Do *Casey* and *Lawrence* support or undermine the efforts to use economic reasoning to justify stare decisis? Why or why not? How do these cases relate to the O'Hara and Rasmusen analyses of stare decisis? Do you find their models helpful in evaluating these two cases? Why or why not?

7. The *Morales-Santana* Court found a violation of due process yet denied the claimant relief. In doing so, Justice Ginsburg ratcheted back upward the criteria for evaluating a gender-based equal protection claim against a challenged law. Based on the various models of holding and dictum set out in part IV, or based on your own intuitions about the distinction, what was the Court's holding? What is the present status of the Supreme Court's equal protection

[113] *See* MICHAEL MELLO, AGAINST THE DEATH PENALTY: THE RELENTLESS DISSENTS OF JUSTICE BRENNAN AND MARSHALL (1996); Michael Mello, *Adhering to Our Views: Justices Brennan and Marshall and the Relentless Dissent to Death as Punishment*, 22 FLA. ST. U.L. REV. 591 (1995).

doctrine concerning intermediate scrutiny, including most notably, which party bears the burden of proof?

8. If you conclude in response to Question 7 that the Court's conclusion regarding due process was dictum because the Court failed to award Mr. Morales-Santana relief, does this imply that any equal protection case in which the result is to level down rather than to level up relief, the substantive legal resolution, as opposed to resolution on the remedy, is necessarily dictum? Why or why not? If you conclude that all such substantive resolutions are dictum, how does that relate to the various analyses distinguishing holding and dictum presented in part IV? How does this relate more generally to distinguishing holding and dictum in cases in which after finding a constitutional violation, a court denies relief on a separate procedural ground?

9. Do any of your answers to Questions 7 and 8 help to explain why Justice Kennedy, who authored *Nguyen*, joined *Morales-Santana* despite the apparent doctrinal tension between those two cases? Why or why not?

CHAPTER 22

The Judiciary (Part 2)

Introduction

This chapter continues the economic analysis of judicial decision making, with a particular focus on social choice. Social choice is helpful in analyzing the unique features of multimember courts and also in assessing persistent doctrines that arise as a function of multicriterial decision making. We adopt the general framing of Professor Maxwell Stearns in constructing three sets of models, each of which explores an anomalous, yet persistent aspect of decision making or doctrine in the United States Supreme Court. The analysis also carries important implications for other courts within the federal judiciary and for alternative judicial systems.

The chapter is divided into three main parts, each of which centers on a specific model or set of doctrines. Part I considers the processes of deciding individual cases, including outcome voting and the narrowest grounds doctrine. Part II evaluates the much-criticized standing doctrine and further explores stare decisis, a doctrine that we also considered from various perspectives in Chapter 21. Part III evaluates the frequently contested set of doctrines associated with tiers of scrutiny, which the Supreme Court relies upon to classify and resolve important equal protection and individual rights cases. Professor Stearns's general approach is positive, explaining these decision-making rules and doctrines as they presently exist, although the analysis also contains normative elements, identifying areas in which doctrines could be improved. We will also consider alternative framings and normative proposals advanced by several prominent scholars and jurists to change existing protocols and rules. The chapter concludes with applications.

I. A SOCIAL CHOICE ANALYSIS OF INDIVIDUAL CASE DECISION-MAKING RULES[1]

In this part we will consider the implications of social choice for voting protocols that affect how the Supreme Court decides individual cases. Several of the insights apply

[1] Portions of the analysis in this part and in Part II are based upon MAXWELL L. STEARNS, CONSTITUTIONAL PROCESS: A SOCIAL CHOICE ANALYSIS OF SUPREME COURT DECISION-MAKING (2000); *see id.* at 97–156 (describing static constitutional process involving resolution of individual cases); *see also id.* 157–211 (describing dynamic constitutional process involving how groups of cases are decided over time).

to other levels of the judicial hierarchy and to courts operating within alternative judicial systems. In addition to considering a social choice model developed by Maxwell Stearns, we consider alternative framings of existing protocols, and normative proposals to change them, advanced by Judge (then-Professor) Frank Easterbrook, Judge (then-Professor) John Rogers, Professors David Post and Steven Salop, Professors Lewis Kornhauser and Lawrence Sager, and Professor Jonathan Remy Nash.

The analysis set out in this part, which explains the Court's decision-making processes in individual cases, operates in parallel with the analysis in Part II, explaining how the Court resolves larger numbers of cases over time. As a result, the analysis in this part is more detailed, and much of the later analysis borrows from the concepts developed here. The analysis to follow explains the Supreme Court's reliance upon outcome voting, rather than issue voting, and the narrowest grounds doctrine, articulated in *Marks v. United States*.[2]

A. Social Choice Revisited

In Chapters 13 and 14, we saw that under certain conditions, groups of individuals who hold internally consistent, or transitive preferences, will discover that their combined preferences are intransitive, or cycle, when aggregated through voting procedures commonly associated with majority rule. The Condorcet paradox shows that with persons holding the following ordinal preferences over options ABC (P1: ABC; P2: BCA; and P3: CAB), the group as a whole cycles such that ApBpCpA, where p means preferred by simple majority rule. By contrast, with the following more well-behaved preferences, shifting only P3's second and third ordinal ranking (P1: ABC; P2: BCA; and P3: CBA), B emerges as a Condorcet winner, defeating A and C in direct binary comparisons.

Arrow's Theorem generalizes the paradox of voting in the following sense: Any rule designed to ensure that the members' preferences do not cycle will inevitably run up against some other important norm associated with fair or democratic decision making. A group of three or more persons selecting among three or more options cannot ensure transitive (or noncyclical) outputs without violating at least one, and possibly more than one, of the following conditions:[3] (1) *Range*: The collective decision-making rule must select its outcome in a manner consistent with the members' selection from among all conceivable ordinal rankings over three available alternatives; (2) *Independence of irrelevant alternatives*: In choosing among paired alternatives, participants are assumed to decide solely based upon the merits of those options and without regard to how they would rank options that might be introduced later; (3) *Unanimity*: If a change from the status quo to an alternate state will improve the position of at least a single participant without harming anyone else, the decision-making body must so move; and (4) *Nondictatorship*: The group

[2] 430 U.S. 188, 193 (1977). During the late stages of this book's production, the Supreme Court heard *Hughes v. United States*, No. 17–155 (argued Mar. 27, 2018), which, among other issues, raised a challenge to the narrowest grounds rule. Professor Stearns filed an amicus brief, Brief of Law Professors as Amici Curiae in Support of Neither Party, *Hughes*, No. 17–155 (filed Jan. 26, 2018), 2018 WL 637338, that responded to additional scholarship, including separate works by Professors Richard Re and Ryan C. Williams. The opinion in *Hughes v. United States* ultimately avoided addressing the narrowest grounds doctrine and is now available at 2018 WL 2465187 (June 4, 2018).

[3] This presentation is reproduced from Chapters 13 and 14, Parts I.E and III.A.

cannot consistently vindicate the preferences of one member against the contrary will of the group as a whole.[4]

Maxwell Stearns has argued that whereas legislatures routinely avoid *Independence* in their decision-making processes—consider the discussion of vote trading or logrolling in Chapter 19 and 20[5]—appellate courts, including the United States Supreme Court, have important institutional norms that encourage compliance with *Independence* but that relax *Range*. Stearns's analysis reveals that this operates at the level of individual cases and groups of cases over time.

Before reviewing the relevant cases, it is helpful to consider the larger framing of potential categories for case resolution on the nine-member Supreme Court. The Court can issue unanimous, majority, and fractured panel opinions.[6] It can also issue three-judgment cases in which there is no majority for a single judgment. Within individual cases, a social choice problem only arises when there is no first-choice majority candidate. As a result, Stearns argues, the difficulties associated with aggregating collective preferences do not arise in either unanimous or majority opinion cases. The Court has developed an informal norm that has effectively solved the potential difficulty in three-judgment cases.

As a general matter, within the fractured panel category, the Court will issue a combination of opinions that includes the following: a plurality opinion, one or more concurrences in the judgment,[7] and one or more dissents. Individual opinions sometimes combine elements from more than a single category, such as concurrences in part, concurrences in the judgment in part, and dissents in part. To simplify, we focus on the basic categories.[8]

The problem of aggregating collective preferences into a meaningful social outcome arises in the context of cases that: (1) lack a majority winner, (2) offer at least two alternative justifications for reaching the judgment, and (3) offer a logical pathway to an opposite judgment. The simplest case involves a plurality, a concurrence in the judgment, and a dissent, and a subset of these cases includes features from which it is possible to infer an embedded cycle. To be clear, most cases in this category do not possess these features. When that is the case, the opinions line up neatly along a single dimension and

---

[4] *See id.*; STEARNS, *supra* note 1, at 41–94 (providing more detailed presentation, and comparison with Arrow's original presentation).

[5] *See supra* Chapter 5, Part I.B.2.A.

[6] By fractured panel opinions, we mean opinions that have a majority for one judgment, but lack a majority opinion consistent with that judgment.

[7] The Justice concurring in the judgment agrees with the judgment issued by the plurality opinion or other opinion issuing the judgment, but provides an independent rationale, whereas a concurring Justice joins the opinion issuing the judgment, and separately offers additional analysis.

[8] Other combinations are possible. For example, a non-plurality opinion will sometimes issue the judgment, and there can be concurrences, partial concurrences, and partial dissents, and even partial concurrences, partial concurrences in the judgment, and partial dissents. It is also possible that all jurists agree to the same outcome such that there is either a majority opinion or a plurality opinion, along with several concurrences or concurrences in the judgment, but no dissents. *See, e.g.*, Washington v. Glucksberg, 521 U.S. 702 (1997). In addition, it is possible to have multiple opinions of equal size coalitions, and thus no plurality opinion. *See, e.g.*, Miller v. Albright, 523 U.S. 420 (1998) (presenting three opinions for two Justices each consistent with the judgment, and two dissenting opinions written or joined by the remaining three Justices).

one of the opinions emerges as a Condorcet winner. Stearns explains why, in the more problematic subset of fractured panel cases, it is plausible to identify conditions that expose the absence of a Condorcet winner, and thus an embedded cycle. The analysis is helpful in assessing Supreme Court decision-making rules.

To illustrate, consider three somewhat stylized Supreme Court decisions. The first case, based upon *Kassel v. Consolidated Freightways Corp.*,[9] demonstrates how the separate opinions in a fractured panel case combine to reveal a possible embedded cycle.[10] The second case, based upon *Planned Parenthood of Southeastern Pennsylvania v. Casey*,[11] demonstrates the conditions under which a fractured panel case can nonetheless yield a Condorcet winner. *Casey* represents the "normal" fractured-panel case, and *Kassel* represents an important anomalous case. As we will see, the Supreme Court's narrowest grounds rule succeeds in the normal cases in selecting those non-majority opinions that nonetheless express the Court's dominant, or Condorcet-winning, holding. The final case, *Arizona v. Fulminante*,[12] represents a subset of the anomalous cases that illustrate an alternative approach. In these cases, one or more justices avoids the apparent anomaly by altering his or her vote. These vote-switching efforts produce their own difficulties, and also some controversy as to how the justices should vote more generally when resolving cases.

Following the analysis, we consider several alternative normative assessments that other scholars have advanced. We then assess the implications, more generally, for Supreme Court decision making.

1. *Kassel v. Consolidated Freightways*

Kassel involved a challenge arising under the Dormant Commerce Clause Doctrine to an Iowa law that prevented sixty-five-foot twin trailers from traveling through the state, with exceptions that benefited various in-state interests.[13] The law imposed substantial burdens on interstate truckers because the rigs Iowa prohibited were permitted in the surrounding states. As a result, truckers traveling with nonconforming rigs from one side of Iowa to the other had to either go around the state or make separate runs with each trailer. Either alternative substantially raised the cost of shipping goods in commerce.

Consolidated Freightways, an international shipping company, challenged the Iowa law as violating the Dormant Commerce Clause Doctrine. The difficulty was that under

---

[9] 450 U.S. 662 (1981).

[10] Each of the case discussions is simplified to highlight the preference aggregation features associated with the relevant social choice phenomenon. For more detailed treatments of the cases, see STEARNS, *supra* note 1, at 99–106 (discussing *Kassel*); *id.* at 16–23, 129–30 (discussing *Planned Parenthood of Southeastern Pa. v. Casey*); *id.* at 146–47, 149–52 (discussing *Arizona v. Fulminante*).

[11] 505 U.S. 833 (1992).

[12] 499 U.S. 279 (1991).

[13] The exceptions allowed such vehicles to serve border cities, allowed Iowa shippers a possible exemption for vehicles up to seventy feet long, and allowed intrastate transit of mobile homes to Iowa residents. *Kassel*, 450 U.S. at 665–67. The statutory history is somewhat unusual in that the challenge rested in part on legislative history concerning the governor's decision not to sign into law a bill that would have repealed the challenged statute. For a more detailed discussion, see Maxwell Stearns, *The Misguided Renaissance of Social Choice*, 103 YALE L.J. 1219, 1256–57, 1267–70 (1994).

traditional dormant Commerce Clause analysis, state highway safety laws were subject to low level rational basis scrutiny. After the Iowa Supreme Court sustained the state law against the dormant Commerce Clause challenge, Consolidated Freightways successfully petitioned for writ of certiorari in the United States Supreme Court. The Supreme Court ultimately issued three separate opinions, none commanding majority support.

Writing for a plurality of four, Justice Powell voted to strike down the challenged law as violating the dormant Commerce Clause Doctrine. Powell rejected low level rational basis scrutiny in favor of the somewhat stricter balancing test, which permitted the Court to weigh the claimed safety benefits of the law against the burdens that the law posed for commerce. Powell further determined that in applying that test, the Court was permitted to weigh arguments that were not raised in the legislature when the law passed, but rather that were presented initially by trial counsel. Based upon his independent balancing assessment, Powell rejected the state's proffered justification for the challenged law, thus voting to strike the law down.

In an opinion concurring in the judgment, Justice Brennan, writing for two, disagreed with Powell's resolution of both dispositive issues. Brennan concluded that it was not the Court's job to independently weigh safety benefits against burdens on commerce, instead reasoning that the issue was whether the enacting legislature had a rational basis in support of the law. Brennan also rejected Powell's willingness to entertain newly constructed arguments of trial counsel that were not offered as a contemporaneous justification at the time that the truck ban was enacted. Because Brennan found that the actual arguments in support of the law evinced a protectionist motivation, he concluded that even under low level rational basis scrutiny, the law was virtually per se unconstitutional.

Finally, writing for three Justices, then-Associate Justice Rehnquist dissented. Rehnquist agreed with Justice Brennan that the Court should not independently weigh safety benefits against burdens on commerce, thus concluding that the appropriate test was rational basis scrutiny. Rehnquist agreed with Powell, however, that in seeking to determine whether the state satisfied the selected test, the Court was free to consider not only contemporaneous legislative justifications, but also newly constructed arguments submitted by trial counsel. Based upon newly introduced safety justifications, Rehnquist determined that the legislature had a rational justification in support of the challenged law, and thus, he voted to sustain the law against the dormant Commerce Clause Doctrine challenge.

Stearns maintains that with reasonable assumptions, the *Kassel* case plausibly embeds a cycle. The analysis begins with a proposition that is consistent with all three *Kassel* opinions: If (1) the Court applied low level rational basis scrutiny (the more lenient of the two available substantive tests) *and* (2) if the Court willingly entertained novel safety justifications not presented to the legislature (the more lenient of the two available evidentiary rules), *then* (3) the Court should sustain the challenged law. Conversely, applying either of the two less lenient rules, rational basis or admitting novel evidence, suffices to strike the law down.

Accepting this premise, although Powell and Brennan each struck the law down on the ground that one of the two conditions for sustaining it was not met (with Powell applying the more stringent substantive test and Brennan applying the more stringent evidentiary rule), separate majorities supported the necessary preconditions for sustaining the law. Brennan plus Rehnquist, for a total of five Justices, supported the laxer rational basis scrutiny test, and Powell plus Rehnquist, for a total of seven Justices, supported the laxer evidentiary rule, allowing consideration of newly presented evidence. Justice Rehnquist implicitly recognized the resulting anomaly.[14] The Court's judgment was nonetheless in tension with the separate majority resolutions of each of the two issues that the three opinions deemed dispositive and that, in combination, supported the dissent.

Stearns explains the voting anomaly by treating the three opinions as packages of resolved issues, each leading to a preferred case judgment, as set out in Table 22:1[15]:

Table 22:1. *Kassel* in Two Dimensions

	Rational Basis	Balancing Test
Allow Novel Evidence	C. Rehnquist (for 3)	A. Powell (for 4)
Exclude Novel Evidence	B. Brennan (for 2)	

The Powell analysis (package A: lenient evidentiary rule, strict substantive rule), leads to striking the challenged law down; the Brennan analysis (package B: strict evidentiary rule, lenient substantive rule) leads to striking the challenged law down; and the Rehnquist analysis (package C: lenient evidentiary rule, lenient substantive rule), leads to sustaining the challenged law. Based upon the previously stated proposition that is consistent with all three opinions,[16] Stearns demonstrates that although each opinion is internally consistent, the combined logic of the opinions reveals separate majority preferences for a lenient evidentiary rule (Powell plus Rehnquist) and for a lenient substantive rule (Brennan plus Rehnquist). An individual Justice, such as Justice Rehnquist, who expressed these combined issue resolutions, would logically dissent.

Stearns further demonstrates alternate ways of constructing the embedded cycle across the *Kassel* opinions. Imagine that each opinion-writing Justice must ordinally rank his second and third choices over the remaining alternatives. If Powell cares more about the outcome than about the reasoning to achieve that outcome, his ordinal preferences are (ABC). If Brennan is more concerned with selecting the preferred substantive standard (rational basis scrutiny) than with the outcome, his ordinal preferences are (BCA). Finally, if Rehnquist, who is inevitably forced to choose opinions leading to a contrary result, is more concerned about the evidentiary issue than the choice of substantive standard, his ordinal preferences are (CAB). These preferences combine into a forward cycle:

[14] Thus, Justice Rehnquist stated:

> It should not escape notice that a majority of the Court goes on record today as agreeing that courts in Commerce Clause cases do not sit to weigh safety benefits against burdens on commerce when the safety benefits are not illusory. . . . I do not agree with my Brother Brennan, however, that only those safety benefits somehow articulated by the legislature as *the* motivation for the challenged statute can be considered in supporting the state law.

450 U.S. at 692 n.4 (emphasis in original).

[15] STEARNS, *supra* note 1, at 101 tbl.3.1 (presenting table).

[16] See *id.* at 100.

ApBpCpA. It is also possible to posit assumptions that yield a reverse cycle: Powell (ACB), Brennan (BAC), Rehnquist (CBA), thus generating the (reverse) cycle ApCpBpA. Each combination rests upon equally plausible assumptions concerning how the Justices would rank order their preferences over the packaged alternatives.[17]

We now consider each of the two remaining case paradigms. We then consider why the Supreme Court employs voting rules susceptible to generating this anomaly.

2. *Planned Parenthood v. Casey*

We will now revisit *Planned Parenthood of Southeastern Pennsylvania v. Casey*,[18] a case that we reviewed for its stare decisis implications in Chapter 21. Here we consider why this fractured panel case, unlike *Kassel*, yields a Condorcet winner.[19] In *Casey*, the Supreme Court was invited to overrule the landmark 1973 abortion decision, *Roe v. Wade*.[20] Instead, *Casey* produced five separate opinions, none containing majority support, the combined effect of which was to modify *Roe* without overturning it. To simplify the analysis, Professor Stearns combines those joining the various *Casey* opinions into three camps: liberal (Blackmun and Stevens); moderate (O'Connor, Kennedy, and Souter); and conservative (Rehnquist, Scalia, Thomas, and White).[21]

Recall that *Casey* presented a challenge to five provisions of the Pennsylvania abortion statute: (1) informed consent; (2) parental notification for minors; (3) spousal notification for married women; (4) an exemption from the first three provisions in the event of a medical emergency; and (5) reporting requirements. A majority comprising the moderate and liberal camps voted to strike down the spousal notification provision, and a majority comprising the moderate and conservative camps voted to sustain the remaining provisions. For our purposes, the specific holdings are less important than the role of the Court's voting protocols in effecting a transformation in the substantive analysis of challenged abortion laws under *Roe v. Wade*.

The *Roe* Court held abortion to be a fundamental right, protected within the constitutional zone of privacy first articulated in *Griswold v. Connecticut*.[22] Applying strict scrutiny, the *Roe* Court determined that the state's identified interests in regulating abortion did not become compelling, and thus sufficient to overcome a woman's right to abort, until specific points in the pregnancy. Because the risks associated with abortion

---

17 The apparent voting anomaly in *Kassel* illustrates the problem of multidimensionality and asymmetry, introduced in Chapters 13 and 14. *See also* STEARNS, *supra* note 1, at 67–77; Maxwell L. Stearns, *Should Justices Ever Switch Votes?:* Miller v. Albright *in Social Choice Perspective*, 7 SUP. CT. ECON. REV. 87 (1999).

18 505 U.S. 833 (1992).

19 *See* STEARNS, *supra* note 1, at 129–30 (presenting *Casey* as a unidimensional case).

20 410 U.S. 113 (1973). Ruth Marcus, *Preelection Ruling Likely on Abortion: Pennsylvania Asks High Court Review*, WASH. POST, Dec. 10, 1991, at A1 ("At least four justices are believed to be ready to overrule *Roe*, an outcome that [the ACLU's] Kolbert predicted yesterday is 'highly likely' in the Pennsylvania case"); David G. Savage, *The Rescue of* Roe vs. Wade*: How a Dramatic Change of Heart by a Supreme Court Justice Saved Abortion—Just When the Issue Seemed Headed for Certain Defeat*, L.A. TIMES, Dec. 13, 1992, at A1 (expressing surprise at *Casey* holding).

21 The categorization, which necessarily oversimplifies complex nuances in each Justice's jurisprudence, helps to explain the relationships among the various camps in the *Casey* opinions.

22 381 U.S. 479 (1965).

are lower early on in a pregnancy as compared with carrying the fetus to term, the state was not permitted to regulate abortion based on its interest in maternal health until the end of the first trimester. The Court further determined that the state's interest in the potential life represented by the fetus did not become compelling until the fetus is capable of meaningful existence outside the mother's womb, or the point of viability, coinciding with the end of the second trimester.

In *Casey*, Justices O'Connor, Kennedy, and Souter issued a joint opinion that considered first whether to adhere to *Roe v. Wade* as a matter of precedent. The joint opinion rejected various arguments for declining to adhere to *Roe*, but did not retain *Roe* in its entirety. Instead, the Court retained only what it characterized as *Roe*'s "essential holding."[23] Most notably, this did not include the trimester framework or the characterization of abortion as a fundamental right. Instead, the joint authors found that because technology rendered late abortions safer and also rendered viability earlier, the trimester framework proved increasingly unworkable.[24] In addition, the joint authors reasoned that the *Roe* Court had given inadequate weight to the state's interest in the potentiality of human life. Because the joint authors determined that abortion was a liberty interest rather than a fundamental right, they applied the newly formulated undue burden test, rather than strict scrutiny, to assess the challenged law. Under this test, the Court found that only the spousal notification provision posed an undue burden, thus striking that provision, while sustaining the remaining challenged provisions of the Pennsylvania statute.

Justices Stevens and Blackmun, by contrast, wrote a partial concurrence and partial dissent, in which they rejected the joint authors' revision of *Roe* in favor of the original doctrinal formulation. That formulation included the trimester framework and the viability test for evaluating whether the state's interest in potential life becomes compelling. Finally, Rehnquist, Scalia, Thomas, and White rejected the joint authors' stare decisis analysis, preferring to overturn *Roe* outright. Because they viewed abortion as a mere liberty interest, subject to low level scrutiny, the conservatives would have sustained the challenged Pennsylvania law in its entirety. Stearns depicts the *Casey* opinions, along a single dimension, in the following table.[25]

---

23 Planned Parenthood of Se. Pa. v. Casey, 505 U.S. 833, 846 (1992).

24 *Id.* at 860.

25 *See* STEARNS, *supra* note 1, at 129.

Table 22:2. The *Casey* Decision in One Dimension

A Blackmun, Stevens (Liberal)	B. O'Connor, Kennedy, Souter (Moderate)	C. Rehnquist, Scalia, White, Thomas (Conservative)
Strike down all restrictive provisions based upon either stare decisis or analysis of merits of original *Roe* decision	Strike down only spousal notification provision, based upon stare decisis revision of *Roe*	Uphold all provisions based upon critical analysis of original *Roe* decision
Broad abortion right	⟵⟶	Narrow abortion right

Table 22:2, which depicts *Casey*, is notably different from Table 22:1, which depicts *Kassel.* Like *Kassel*, *Casey* presented more than one controlling case issue. At a minimum, it presented the following issues: (1) Does stare decisis require adhering to *Roe*?; (2) What is the relevant test for evaluating the abortion right?; and (3) Under the selected test, how do each of the challenged provisions fare? And yet, it is intuitive to present the resolutions of these issues by each camp along a single normative dimension capturing the breadth or narrowness of the protected abortion right.[26] Although both the Liberal and Conservative camps were critical of the Moderate camp's stare decisis analysis and decision to revise *Roe*, consistent with the prior analysis, the fundamental issue is how each of those camps would choose, if forced to rank the remaining opinions ordinally. The answer is intuitive. The liberals, A, would almost certainly prefer the partial relief afforded in the revised *Roe* formulation that the moderates provide, B, to overturning *Roe* as embraced by C. Conversely, the conservatives would almost certainly prefer the moderates' revision of *Roe*, and its demotion of abortion to a liberty interest protected by the lesser undue burden standard, B, to the original *Roe* formulation advocated by the liberals, A. The second and third ordinal rankings of the moderates are irrelevant; either way, B is the Condorcet winner.

Stearns argues that the same intuition used to analyze *Casey* helps explain the Supreme Court's reliance on the narrowest ground rule, set out in *Marks v. United States.*[27] While the details of *Marks* are unnecessary for our purposes, suffice to say that the Court evaluated an opinion that possessed the characteristic features of *Casey.* The separate opinions could be cast along a single dimension. The issue in the case was whether a criminal defendant could rely upon the narrowest grounds holding in a Supreme Court plurality opinion, which had afforded a relatively higher level of protection than a later majority decision, which retroactively lowered the relevant prosecutorial standard.[28] The

[26] Recall that in Chapters 13 or 14, we presented a stylized version of *Casey* that illustrated the median voter theorem. *See supra* Chapters 13 or 14, Parts I.B. and I.G.1.

[27] 430 U.S. 188 (1977). For a more detailed analysis of this case, see Maxwell L. Stearns, *The Case for Including* Marks v. United States *in the Canon of Constitutional Law*, 17 CONST. COMMENT. 321 (2000).

[28] In 1957, the Supreme Court held that the government could prosecute materials as obscene that violated "contemporary community standards." *See* Roth v. United States, 354 U.S. 476, 489, 492 (1957). In 1966, a controlling plurality of the Supreme Court elevated the prosecutorial standard to demand that the

prosecutor maintained that only majority decisions produced binding precedents, but the Court, with Justice Powell writing, instead stated:

> When a fragmented Court decides a case and no single rationale explaining the result enjoys the assent of five Justices, "the holding of the Court may be viewed as that position taken by those Members who concurred in the judgments on the narrowest grounds. . . ."[29]

Stearns translates the narrowest grounds doctrine as follows: In a case that sustains a law against a constitutional challenge, the controlling opinion is the one consistent with that result that would sustain the fewest laws, and in a case that strikes down a law on constitutional grounds, the controlling opinion is the one consistent with that result that would strike down the fewest laws. In effect, the opinion consistent with the judgment that would have the smallest effect in changing the law resolves the case on the narrowest grounds. In a case like *Casey*, with multiple judgments, apply the test separately to each judgment.

In *Casey*, applying the doctrine is straightforward. Of the opinions sustaining the challenged provisions of Pennsylvania law, the plurality would apply a stricter test and thus sustain fewer such laws than the conservatives. Of the opinions striking down the spousal notification provision, the plurality would apply a more deferential standard than the liberals' preferred strict scrutiny test and thus would strike down the fewest laws. Notice that the joint opinion, which represents the Condorcet winner, states the holding for each judgment on the narrowest grounds.

Now consider whether *Marks* can be applied in *Kassel*. The Court resolved two issues in *Kassel*: (1) which of two substantive standards to apply, the more lenient rational basis test or the stricter balancing test; and (2) which of two evidentiary rules to apply, the more lenient rule, allowing novel evidence, or the stricter rule, excluding such evidence. Under *Marks*, the opinion consistent with the outcome that resolves the case on the narrowest grounds states the holding. The two opinions consistent with the outcome of striking down the challenged Iowa statute are those of Powell and Brennan. But each is narrower on one issue yet broader on the other. The Powell opinion is narrower on the question of the evidentiary rule: the more relaxed test would sustain more challenged laws. The Brennan opinion is narrower on the question of the substantive rule: the more relaxed evidentiary rule would sustain more challenged laws.

Stearns explains that the *Marks* doctrine does not apply in cases like *Kassel* because of the problem of dimensionality and asymmetry. The two opinions consistent with the outcome resolve the two issues in opposite fashion, yet achieve the same result. Neither of the opinions resolves the case on narrower grounds; rather each resolves it on opposite grounds. Although we might say that Rehnquist would resolve the case on narrower grounds, applying the more relaxed substantive and evidentiary rules, under the *Marks* doctrine, his dissenting opinion is ineligible to state the holding.

---

materials alleged to be obscene be "utterly without redeeming social value." Memoirs v. Massachusetts, 383 U.S. 413, 418 (1966). And in 1973, the Supreme Court, in a majority opinion, reverted to a modified version of the *Roth* contemporary community standards test, a laxer prosecutorial standard. Miller v. California, 413 U.S. 15, 24 (1973).

[29] 430 U.S. at 193 (quoting Gregg v. Georgia, 428 U.S. 153, 169 n.15 (1976)).

Stearns thus shows that while the *Marks* rule succeeds in cases in which the opinions can be cast along a single dimension, it fails in the smaller subset of cases that present multidimensionality and asymmetry. As a result of the problematic results that such cases potentially produce, individual jurists have, on rare occasion, avoided such results by engaging in vote-switching. This strategic maneuver invites its own difficulties, as the next case illustrates.

3. *Arizona v. Fulminante*

In *Arizona v. Fulminante*,[30] a man was convicted of capital murder and sentenced to death following a trial in which the prosecution admitted two confessions. Fulminante maintained that the first confession was coerced and that the second was fruit of the poisonous tree.[31] The question before the Supreme Court was whether admitting an allegedly coerced confession provides the basis for reversing his capital murder conviction.

The three Justices who produced opinions, Chief Justice Rehnquist, Justice Kennedy, and Justice White, distilled the case to three issues: (1) Was the first confession coerced?; (2) If so, does harmless error analysis apply?; and (3) If so, on these facts is the admission harmless error? Once more, Stearns explains that all three opinions are consistent with the following proposition: If (1) the confession was coerced, *and* (2.a) if harmless error analysis did not apply (rendering its admission reversible error) *or* (2.b) if harmless error analysis applied but the confession's admission into evidence was not harmless error, then (3) the conviction should be reversed. Conversely, if (1) the confession was not coerced, (2) if harmless error analysis did apply, and if the admission was harmless error, then (3) the result should be to affirm.

Writing in part for a majority of five that did not include Justice Kennedy, Justice White determined that the confession was coerced. Justice Kennedy, writing separately, concluded that the confession was not coerced. Consistent with that conclusion, Justice Kennedy should have voted to affirm because harmless error analysis is irrelevant to the admission of a voluntary confession. In part of his opinion for a majority of five, the Chief Justice determined that if the confession is coerced, harmless error analysis applies. In part of his opinion for a differently constituted majority of five, which included Justice Kennedy, Justice White further determined that admitting the coerced confession was not harmless error. In his separate opinion, Justice Kennedy stated the following:

> My own view that the confession was not coerced does not command a majority.
>
> In the interests of providing a clear mandate to the Arizona Supreme Court in this capital case, I deem it proper to accept in the case now before us the holding of five Justices that the confession was coerced and inadmissible. I agree with a majority of the Court that admission of the confession could not

---

[30] 499 U.S. 279 (1991). For a more detailed discussion, see STEARNS, *supra* note 1, at 146–47, 149–52; Stearns, *supra* note 17, at 136–39.

[31] 499 U.S. at 284.

be harmless error when viewed in light of all the other evidence; and so I concur in the judgment. . . .[32]

Table 22:3 is helpful to the discussion that follows:[33]

Table 22:3. *Arizona v. Fulminante*

	Confession coerced	Confession not coerced
Admission not Harmless	B. Marshall, Brennan, Stevens, White, *[Kennedy]*	A. *Kennedy* (moves left)
Admission Harmless	C. Scalia	D. Rehnquist, O'Connor, Souter

Had Kennedy stuck to his original position and not reached the admissibility question, or had he expressed it strictly as dictum, the *Fulminante* decision would have presented the same voting paradox as in *Kassel*. Whereas separate majorities determined that the confession was coerced (camps B and C) and the admission of the confession was not harmless (camps B and A), only four Justices would have embraced both positions as required to reverse the conviction. As in *Kassel*, camps A and C would have reached the same outcome, affirm, based upon opposite resolutions of the each of the two dispositive case issues. Scalia determined that despite the coerced confession, the admission is harmless. Kennedy would have determined that the confession is not coerced, thus avoiding the harmlessness question altogether. Instead, Kennedy switched his vote to join the Brennan camp, based upon the contrary majority determination on coercion (camps B and C), with the result that he joined a majority finding that admitting the now-coerced confession could not be harmless error. Thus, rather than affirming, the Court reversed the conviction based upon Justice Kennedy's vote switch.

B. Normative Implications of Supreme Court Voting Anomalies

Legal scholars have drawn differing implications from these and similar voting anomaly cases. Judge (then-Professor) John Rogers criticized Justice White for a similar vote switch in *Pennsylvania v. Union Gas Co.*,[34] claiming that the decision to acquiesce in a contrary majority's resolution of an underlying issue is an abdication of the judicial obligation to resolve cases in a principled fashion.[35] Professors David Post and Steven Salop, by contrast, defended Justice White's vote switch and suggested that in cases producing such voting anomalies, an alternative voting protocol, which they term "issue voting," is normatively preferable to outcome voting.[36] Professors Lewis Kornhauser and

---

[32] *Id.* at 313 (Kennedy, J., concurring in the judgment).

[33] Table 22:3 is reproduced from Stearns, *supra* note 17, at 139.

[34] 491 U.S. 1 (1989).

[35] John M. Rogers, *"I Vote this Way Because I'm Wrong": The Supreme Court Justice as Epimenides*, 79 KY. L.J. 439, 442 (1990) ("[A] Supreme Court justice should not vote contrary to his own stated analysis, because such action is harmful and destabilizing to the determinacy of the law.").

[36] David Post & Steven C. Salop, *Rowing Against the Tidewater: A Theory of Voting by Multijudge Panels*, 80 GEO. L.J. 743, 752 (1992) ("[B]y voting to affirm the court of appeals, Justice White allowed the Court to

Lawrence Sager suggested a metavote in cases that present the voting anomaly as a means of deciding whether to apply an outcome-voting or issue-voting rule. And Professor Jonathan Nash suggested a "context specific voting protocol" that automatically facilitates a switch to an issue-voting regime under specified conditions. We now consider these scholars' alternative voting protocols:

Professors David Post and Steven Salop advance the following approach:

> An alternative approach [to resolving voting anomaly cases] would have the court as a whole . . . assess each of the legal issues raised in the case and reach collective decisions on each of those issues, again by majority vote. The court's judgment then would be determined by the result it reached on each of the underlying issues. We call this "issue voting" in our analysis.[37]

The authors further state:

> [O]utcome-voting by appellate courts is deeply flawed. It is arguably no fairer than issue-voting to the individual litigants before the court. More importantly, it is fundamentally inconsistent with an appellate court's role of providing guidance to lower courts and the community as a whole as to the legal consequences of specific actions.[38]

By contrast,[39] Professors Lewis Kornhauser and Lawrence Sager prefer avoiding a fixed rule on the voting protocol. Instead, in those cases that the authors characterized as presenting the "doctrinal paradox," the authors propose the following metavote regime:

> In a paradoxical case . . . the question of collegial agency is open and problematic. In such a case, a multi-judge court ought to make that question and its resolution an explicit, reflective, articulated, and formal part of its decision of the case. The judges should deliberate about the appropriate collegial action to take in the case before them, given their convictions about all those matters that they would be called on to determine were they deciding the case as individuals rather than as a group. They should vote on the question of collegial action as they would any other question, and they should proffer an opinion or several opinions justifying their metavote.[40]

In a detailed critique of these alternative normative proposals on voting protocols,[41] John Rogers argues:

---

preserve the outward appearance of outcome-voting. Given the Court's apparent predisposition toward outcome-voting, Justice White was forced to vote against his own analysis of the case in order to reach the result the Court would have reached under an issue-voting rule.").

[37] *Id.* at 744. The authors refer to such cases as presenting "paradoxical holdings." *Id.* at 766.

[38] *Id.* at 745. The authors add that in such cases incoherence arises from "path dependence, precedent inconsistency, and paradoxical holdings," with the result that "it is obvious that outcome-voting should be disfavored." *Id.* at 770.

[39] Lewis A. Kornhauser & Lawrence G. Sager, *The One and the Many: Adjudication in Collegial Courts*, 81 CALIF. L. REV. 1 (1993).

[40] *Id.* at 30.

[41] John M. Rogers, "Issue Voting" by Multimember Appellate Courts: A Response to Some Radical Proposals, 49 Vand. L. Rev. 997 (1996). For a separate comprehensive article in which Professor Rogers

> [F]or Professors Post and Salop to advocate issue voting in all cases, they must accept some results that will deeply embarrass the judicial system. If, for instance, there are three constitutional challenges to a criminal defendant's capital conviction and different groups of only three justices agree with each challenge, the criminal could be executed although all justices independently find the conviction unconstitutional. Post and Salop basically say, why not? One answer is that the polity that ultimately must accept judicial decisions will have a hard time accepting such a result. The only way to defend headlines like "JONES EXECUTED; ALL JUSTICES AGREE CONVICTION UNCONSTITUTIONAL" would be to explain that the justices voted issue-by-issue on what the law is, and the application of this law requires execution. But who made the decision? Who did the applying? Each justice can say that if the court had agreed with him or her, the defendant would not have been executed. But this is not how the public thinks judges should act. Judges should not be voting on the law like legislators but should be applying the law and bearing responsibility for the proper application of the law. It would fundamentally undermine the responsibility of the judiciary to permit, or require, judges to vote for results that they oppose.[42]

Rogers also criticizes the Kornhauser and Sager proposed meta-voting regime:

> How should the metavote be taken if there are different majorities on determinative issues in the metavote? Should there be issue voting or outcome voting on the metavote? Neither answer is fully satisfactory. Outcome voting on the metavote could lead to the very sort of path dependence that Kornhauser and Sager are trying to address. But deciding whether to have issue voting might require a meta-metavote. Nightmares of infinite regression are conceivable.[43]

Professors Post and Salop respond to an argument that issue voting is indeterminate because issues can be divided and subdivided at multiple levels. The authors claim that courts can avoid this problem if they adhere to their proposed "issue decomposition rule":

> A *primary* issue on which multimember courts should vote is a question of law presented by a case that (a) is logically independent of any other questions presented by the case, in the sense that the question can be resolved as a logical matter without reference to any other accompanying questions, (b) is potentially dispositive of the outcome of the case, in the sense that resolution of the question can uniquely determine the outcome of the case, and (c) cannot be further decomposed into separate subquestions that fulfill criteria (a) and (b).[44]

---

criticizes individual vote switches by Justices seeking to avoid anomalous results in voting paradox cases, see Rogers, *supra* note 35, at 439.

[42] Rogers, *supra* note 41, at 1022 (footnotes omitted).

[43] *Id.* at 1025.

[44] David G. Post & Steven C. Salop, *Issues and Outcomes, Guidance, and Indeterminacy: A Reply to Professor John Rogers and Others*, 49 VAND. L. REV. 1069, 1078 (1996).

The authors concede that this rule is only a partial solution to the indeterminacy objection, stating:

> This issue decomposition rule will produce a unique set of primary issues defined vertically. That is, it provides a manageable "stopping rule" for the vertical issue decomposition process. However, cases may present alternative primary issues at any level of decomposition defined horizontally.[45]

Professor Jonathan Remy Nash has proposed a "context-sensitive voting protocol," that he maintains avoids some of the difficulties with prior issue-voting proposals while presenting what he maintains is a preferred alternative to outcome voting.[46] Nash explains:

> Pure questions of law (once isolated in respect of separate causes of action or charges) should be treated without decomposition—that is, under outcome-based voting with respect to each question of law. [Such questions] present a setting where the risk of an intractable guidance problem flowing from the use of outcome-based voting is relatively low (though not . . . nonexistent).
>
> After outcome-based voting has been used to establish the proper (pure) legal standard governing a particular cause of action or charge, every application of law to fact under that standard should be determined separately, using issue-based voting. These situations are the counterpoint to pure questions of law: Application of issue-based voting is more likely to be fair, while outcome-based voting is more likely to generate guidance problems, especially for courts on remand and future courts.[47]

Professor Stearns offers a different approach to the seemingly anomalous results represented in both the voting paradox and vote-switch cases. The analysis, which relies upon social choice theory, is intended as a positive, or explanatory, account of existing Supreme Court voting protocols. Stearns explains appellate court reliance upon the combined regime of outcome and the narrowest grounds doctrine, rather than issue voting,[48] along with other anomalies that arise over larger groups of cases over time.

In this analysis, the Court's rules are best understood as staged responses to specific collective decision-making anomalies. Each incremental improvement presents another difficulty that becomes the target of the next staged judicial response. The net result of the staged rules is to increasingly narrow—without entirely eliminating—the inherent difficulties in transforming aggregate judicial preferences in specific cases into outcomes, while honoring, as much as feasible, the rationality and fairness conditions reflected in Arrow's Theorem.

---

45 *Id.* at 1083.

46 Jonathan Remy Nash, *A Context-Sensitive Voting Protocol Paradigm for Multimember Courts*, 56 STAN. L. REV. 75 (2003).

47 *Id.* at 147–48 (footnotes omitted). For a critique of the Nash proposal and others, see Michael I. Meyerson, *The Irrational Supreme Court*, 84 NEB. L. REV. 895, 949–51 (2006).

48 *See, e.g.*, 430 U.S. 188 (1977).

C. A Social Choice Account of Supreme Court Voting Rules

Stearns's analysis returns us to the paradox of voting. Recall that when individuals hold the following preferences (P1: ABC, P2: BCA; P3: CAB), there is an intransitivity such that ApBpCpA. In contrast, with a change in P3's preferences to CBA, option B emerges the Condorcet winner, defeating both A and C in direct binary comparisons. Neither of these two preference sets—containing or lacking a Condorcet winner—has a first-choice majority candidate. And yet, in the second case, majority rule favors B, the first choice for P2 and second choice for P1 and P3, as the Condorcet winner.

When the Supreme Court issues unanimous or majority decisions, there is no social choice problem. In either instance, a majority of the Court agrees with a single rationale justifying the case judgment. The social choice difficulty arises in a smaller subset of cases lacking a majority opinion. Within that category, there are two paradigmatic cases. In the first, the Court typically issues a plurality opinion and one or more concurrences in the judgment that together form the majority favoring the judgment. In the second, the Court fractures not merely on the rationale, but also on the judgment itself.

In practice, the three-judgment case has not proved a serious problem.[49] In each case that has split the Court over three judgments—affirm, remand, reverse—none with majority support, one or more Justices embracing a more extreme position (affirm or reverse) has opted to vote for the intermediate remand outcome. This problem has tended to arise in criminal cases, and the jurist who has exhibited a willingness to depart from his preferred judgment, or ideal point, has stated that it would not be acceptable in such a case for the Court to decline to give clear guidance to the lower court as to how to dispose of the case.[50]

This informal solution in three-judgment cases might have much to commend it. On the specific question as to which judgment to apply, especially in a criminal case, most jurists are apt to view the choice among judgments as resting along a single normative dimension. This is best captured along a pro-defendant (reverse conviction) to pro-government (affirm conviction) spectrum. Those who would embrace an extreme position along that spectrum are apt to prefer a middle ground (affirm unless . . . or reverse unless . . .) to a position that embraces the opposite judgment (affirm outright or reverse outright). On these assumptions, remanding emerges the Condorcet winner.

Jurists might sometimes prefer one extreme (affirm or reverse) to the opposite extreme (reverse or affirm), rather than to a seeming middle ground (remand). For example, a Justice might prefer to have a broad constitutional protection in a given area of constitutional law, but if not successful, prefer to cut off litigation rather than invite a complex body of constitutional common law. Or conversely, a Justice might hold the opposite view, preferring to close off a body of constitutional doctrine, but preferring a

---

[49] *See* STEARNS, *supra* note 1, at 153–54; Stearns, *supra* note 17, at 109.

[50] Although the formal rule articulated in *Marks* only applies when a majority agrees to a single judgment, would a lower court be justified in applying the logic of the narrowest grounds rule in a three-judgment case in which no Justice favoring a more extreme position solved the problem by opting for the remand? Why or why not?

clear set of protections to a complex body of constitutional law. Although such situations are plausible, they have not manifested themselves in the form of avoiding a single judgment in any actual Supreme Court decision. Instead, through informal accommodation, the Justices have effectively "solved" this theoretical difficulty. The social choice problem is more significant in the context of a subset of fractured panel decision cases.

As previously shown, this subgroup of cases divides into two categories. The more common category comprises cases resting along a single issue dimension. In such cases, it is most plausible to intuit preferences across the opinions that generate a stable outcome, or Condorcet winner. To illustrate, imagine that one group of Justices seeks to affirm a murder conviction finding that the claimed Fourth Amendment violation does not apply to state courts; a second group of Justices seeks to reverse the conviction on the ground that it rested on the admission of evidence obtained without a warrant, in violation of the Fourteenth Amendment, which applies the Bill of Rights to the states; and a third group, which would also reverse, accepts incorporation doctrine, but would allow the state to avoid a warrant in exigent circumstances, although it concludes such circumstances are absent in the case. For simplicity, we can label the first group as Liberal, the second as Conservative, and the third as Moderate. In such cases, it is intuitive that the first group would rank its preferences Liberal, Moderate, Conservative, and the second group would rank its preferences Conservative, Moderate, Liberal. The ordinal rankings of the middle group do not matter; either way, the moderate position emerges the Condorcet winner. This holds even though there are two controlling issues.[51]

Supreme Court decision-making rules easily resolve these types of cases, but they create an ongoing difficulty within a narrow subset of fractured panel cases. Aggregation problems do not arise in unanimous, majority, or three-judgment cases (this last one for practical, rather than theoretical, reasons), or in the common fractured-panel cases that yield a Condorcet winner. They arise only in a narrow class fractured panel cases that implicate more than a single dimension. To be clear, the issue is not the number of case issues; rather it is the number of dimensions that the case issues implicate.

As seen in *Casey* and in the Fourth Amendment hypothetical, it is not hard to cast cases with multiple issues along a single dimension and to surmise the dominant outcome absent a majority opinion. In these situations the extreme positions are symmetrical around the median. Even without complete information, it is reasonable to assume that those taking a strong view on one issue favoring a given side would likely take an opposing view of a separate controlling issue favoring the other side. In *Casey* this involves the merits of *Roe* and stare decisis; in the Fourth Amendment hypothetical, it involves the substantive Fourth Amendment doctrine and incorporation. The problem of multidimensionality and asymmetry only arises in the narrower class of cases in which Justices who hold opposite preferences concerning the resolution of each of two dispositive case issues nonetheless concur in the case judgment, and in which the Justices

[51] In his article on vote switching, Professor Stearns formalized this as presenting a case of multidimensionality and symmetry, meaning that opposite issue resolutions produce opposite judgments. Stearns, *supra* note 17, at 117–21.

in dissent resolve one issue in favor of each camp favoring an opposite judgment.[52] This is the situation in *Kassel.*

Recall that in that case, Justice Brennan determined that the relevant substantive test in evaluating the challenged Iowa statute was the less strict rational basis test, and that the relevant evidentiary rule was strict, disallowing newly developed trial evidence not considered by the enacting legislature. By contrast, Justice Powell determined that the relevant test was the stricter balancing test and that the relevant evidentiary rule was lax, allowing newly presented trial evidence. Justice Rehnquist, writing in dissent, applied the less strict version of both tests. Whereas Justices Brennan and Powell resolved both issues in opposite fashion, their opposite resolutions nonetheless led them to the same judgment. Justice Rehnquist resolved one issue in favor of Brennan (the relaxed substantive test) and one issue in favor of Powell (the relaxed evidentiary rule), yet voted for the opposite judgment.

The voting anomaly manifests itself in *Kassel* for an important reason. To determine the logical ordinal rankings over these opinions, we would need to know whether Justices Powell and Brennan are more concerned with having one of the two substantive issues resolved in their preferred manner (ranking Rehnquist's opinion second and each other's opinion third), or instead are more concerned with the case judgment (ranking each other's opinion second, and Rehnquist's opinion third). Of course it is possible that one cares more about one of the substantive issues, whereas the other cares more about the case judgment. For this reason, with reasonable assumptions, it is possible to construct a forward or a backward cycle.

This analysis does not rest upon the validity of any specific assumptions. Because Supreme Court decision-making rules limit the information concerning judicial preference rankings, we cannot know with certainty. Instead, the analysis demonstrates the conditions under which one can reasonably infer intransitive judicial preferences. The combination of multidimensionality and asymmetry produces the voting anomaly. No single justice in *Kassel* would logically apply the lax substantive test (rational basis) and the lax evidentiary rule (allowing in new evidence) yet strike down the challenged Iowa statute. And yet, that is the consequence for the Court as a whole when we aggregate the majority issue and outcome resolutions. Stearns posits that this social choice problem is also an inevitable consequence of the Court's sequential decision-making rules. He further maintains that seeking to avoid the problem in the relatively small subset of cases in which it arises would create substantially greater problems in the larger run of cases.

Consider once more issue versus outcome voting. Assume the two identified issues in *Kassel*—the substantive test and the evidentiary rule—are controlling. This invites the following alternative voting protocols. First, as actually occurs, we can have a controlling vote on the outcome—affirm or reverse—and then assess the various rationales at the opinion stage. Second, we could have the justices vote on these controlling issues and allow the separate resolutions to control the case outcome, avoiding a separate outcome vote. Third, we could define categories in which each voting protocol applies. Those favoring issue voting prefer the second or third option. The proposed regimes include a general issue-voting rule (Post and Salop), a metavote on issue or outcome voting

[52] For a discussion of dimensionality and symmetry, see *supra* Chapter 14, at 586.

(Kornhauser and Sager), or a context-specific protocol (Nash). In cases like *Kassel*, the choice of protocol controls the ultimate case disposition. Under outcome voting, the result is to strike down the challenged Iowa statute. Assuming that the metavote favors issue voting, the various issue-voting regimes would instead sustain the challenged law.

While the outcome- and issue-voting rules lead to opposite case outcomes, it is important to recognize an important feature that these rules hold in common. Social choice reveals that to determine if an outcome is a socially significant choice or the arbitrary product of a voting regime, we must allow as many binary comparisons as options. Rules that satisfy the Condorcet criterion or, in Arrow's terminology, that satisfy range, meet this condition. Range requires that the decision-making rule select an outcome that is consistent with each person's ordinal rankings over three or more options.[53] *Kassel* presents no fewer than the following three questions that control the case outcome:

(1) Should the Court apply the more lenient substantive test (rational basis)? **Yes**.

(2) Should the Court apply the more relaxed evidentiary rule (admitting novel evidence)? **Yes**.

(3) Should the Court sustain the challenged Iowa statute? **No**.

With all three questions permitted, we see that separate majorities answer yes to questions (1) (Brennan and Rehnquist) and (2) (Powell and Rehnquist), which logically leads to sustaining the challenged statute, as occurs under issue-voting. By contrast, the third vote produces the opposite outcome (Brennan and Powell), which is the actual *Kassel* result.

Stearns demonstrates that both voting regimes provide stable outcomes by preventing the requisite number of binary comparisons to reveal a cycle. Why, then, has the Supreme Court, like all appellate courts, opted for outcome voting? Stearns maintains that the answer rests with an analytical flaw that affects issue-voting, which economists refer to as *endogeneity*.[54]

Endogeneity implies that outcomes are a function of the rules that generate them. Conversely, an outcome is exogenous when it arises consistently and independently of the choice of rule. The selection of issue-voting has the potential to motivate the Justices to identify issues differently than they would under outcome-voting.[55] Justices who are more concerned with a case judgment than with how specific issues should be resolved will attempt to forge a voting path leading to their preferred case judgment. The selection of issues might differ from those selected under the outcome-voting regime. That regime effectively encourages jurists to identify a preferred *outcome* and then to construct the most persuasive opinion to encourage a majority to join it.[56] Stearns contends that issue-voting advocates fail to appreciate that the issues identified in cases subject to the voting paradox are endogenous to the voting protocol. If the voting protocol changes, so too might the formulation of case issues.

---

[53] *See supra* Chapter 14, at 597.

[54] *See* Maxwell L. Stearns, *How Outcome Voting Promotes Principled Issue Identification: A Reply to Professor John Rogers and Others*, 49 VAND. L. REV. 1045 (1996).

[55] *See id.*

[56] For a study of coalition formation in the Supreme Court, see FORREST MALTZMAN, JAMES F. SPRIGGS & PAUL J. WAHLBECK, CRAFTING LAW ON THE SUPREME COURT (2000).

This relates to the acknowledgment by Professors Post and Salop that their issue decomposition rule works for issues defined *vertically*, not *horizontally*.[57] Consider which level of division is more likely to match cases in which cycling is apt to occur.

Stearns further maintains that the selection of voting regime will affect resolutions beyond the narrow class of voting paradox cases. More broadly, issue voting would create opportunities for strategic identification of governing issues, thereby affecting a larger corpus of cases. This includes fractured panel cases resting along a single-issue dimension, majority cases, and even unanimous cases. By, instead, divorcing the selection of case outcome from the identification of a voting path, outcome voting encourages principled identification of dispositive issues. Under this regime, Justices select issues based on the desire to construct an analysis supporting the outcome that is sufficiently persuasive to encourage a majority to join.

This returns us to the narrowest grounds rule. The Supreme Court occasionally fractures, and a subset of the resulting cases—those characterized by multidimensionality and asymmetry—produce a voting anomaly. When the Supreme Court issues a fractured panel decision, the *Marks* rule identifies the Condorcet-winning opinion, if there is one, as expressing the holding. The combined effect of outcome voting and the narrowest grounds rule therefore encourages case resolutions (relaxing range and the Condorcet criterion) by disallowing all possible votes over issues and outcomes. At the same time, it promotes principled decision making. It thus adheres to independence of irrelevant alternatives by encouraging the identification of issues for non-strategic reasons.[58] The voting paradox arises only in the narrow class of fractured panel cases in which the opinions cannot be cast along a common normative dimension and in which preferences are asymmetrical.

COMMENTS AND QUESTIONS

In a 2015 decision by the United States Court of Appeals for the Third Circuit, *Hanover Realty v. Village Supermarkets, Inc.*,[59] Judge Ambro engaged in a vote switch, affecting the case outcome, and Judge Greenberg produced a dissent critical of the vote switch. In their separate opinions, the judges carefully debated the merits of the various scholarly works described above. Among the issues debated is whether vote switching risks strategic issue identification, with Judge Greenberg raising the concern, and Judge Ambro arguing otherwise. The case nicely demonstrates that these scholarly debates are not purely academic and that their relevance goes beyond the Supreme Court to any multi-member appellate panel. Although Judge Ambro engaged in a vote switch, Judge Greenberg criticized him for it, and the practice remains rare. The rarity helps to explain the detailed analysis within the opinions of the relevant scholarly works.

---

[57] *See supra* pp. 959–960. For a discussion demonstrating the ability to use creative issue definitions in *National Mutual Insurance Co. v. Tidewater Transfer Co.*, 337 U.S. 582 (1949), a case presenting a voting paradox, so as to forge an unintended outcome under the proposed issue-voting regime, see Stearns, *supra* note 54, at 1059–61.

[58] *See supra* Chapter 14, at p. 599.

[59] 806 F.3d 162 (3d Cir. 2015).

Does the social choice analysis help to explain the rarity of the vote-switch practice in the Supreme Court and elsewhere? Does it effectively respond to the various proposals for issue voting? Are the concerns raised by those advocating issue voting sufficient to outweigh the stability of outcome voting and its effect in limiting opportunities for strategic identification of controlling issues? Why or why not?

Do you agree with Judge Rogers that the Justices should not defer to contrary majorities when resolving controlling case issues? Why or why not? Do you agree with him that individual Justices who engage in vote switching are behaving in an unprincipled or non-judicial way? What does Rogers mean by unprincipled? Are there circumstances in which you would defend switching votes? Is there a principled way to narrow the class of eligible cases?

Are Supreme Court Justices or other appellate judges generally likely to be more concerned with case outcomes or with the resolution of controlling issues within cases? How does your answer affect your preferences respecting issue versus outcome voting or respecting vote switching?

Is the narrowest grounds rule normatively defensible? Do cases like *Kassel* and *Fulminante*, in which the doctrine's underlying logic fails, undermine the rule's validity? If you conclude that it is not defensible, what rule would you replace it with?[60] Is plurality rule better than the narrowest grounds rule for fractured panel Supreme Court cases? Why or why not?

II. MACRO-ANALYSIS OF SUPREME COURT VOTING RULES: A SOCIAL CHOICE ACCOUNT OF HORIZONTAL STARE DECISIS AND STANDING

Judge (then-Professor) Frank Easterbrook has relied upon social choice to challenge, among other things, the logical foundations of stare decisis in the Supreme Court.[61] His analysis rests on a dynamic account of developing doctrine and provides the basis for an important comparison with the Stearns's social choice analysis of Supreme Court decision-making rules.

Judge Easterbrook and Professor Stearns differ in their descriptive account of which Arrovian criteria are adhered to or relaxed in Supreme Court decision making, and in appellate decision making more generally. Easterbrook maintains that the Supreme Court relaxes rationality (transitivity), but that it generally adheres to each Arrovian fairness condition:[62] range, unanimity, independence of irrelevant alternatives (IIA), and nondictatorship. By contrast, Stearns claims, consistent with his preceding analysis, that the Supreme Court relaxes range, but generally adheres to the remaining fairness conditions, unanimity, independence, nondictatorship, along with rationality (transitivity). Easterbrook's analysis is intended to explain pervasive doctrinal inconsistencies and to revisit the question of how to treat stare decisis. Stearns's analysis is intended to explain the path-dependent nature of Supreme Court doctrine as it relates to both stare decisis

---

[60] As previously noted, *supra* note 2, the Court recently avoided resolving this question, thus leaving the narrowest ground doctrine in place.

[61] *See* Frank H. Easterbrook, *Ways of Criticizing the Court*, 95 HARV. L. REV. 802 (1982).

[62] For consistency, we are employing the Arrow's Theorem conventions presented throughout the book.

and standing doctrine. As you read the discussion that follows, consider which framing is more robust in accounting for not only the extant bodies of Supreme Court case law, but also for Supreme Court decision making processes.

A. Ways of Criticizing the Court: The Social Choice Case Against Strict Stare Decisis

Easterbrook maintains that all of Arrow's fairness conditions—range, independence of irrelevant alternatives, unanimity, and nondictatorship—are applicable in Supreme Court decision making. Based on this assumption, Easterbrook further posits that it is not possible for the Court to ensure transitive, or rational, doctrine. Instead, over time, the Court might develop a stock of precedent that will "allow[ ] the Justices to 'prove' anything they like, without fear of contradiction."[63]

As a normative matter, Easterbrook criticizes the value of adhering to stare decisis in those cases in which, as a result, doctrine is affected by the order of precedent. Easterbrook states:

> The upshot of stare decisis is that the meaning of . . . [some] constitutional [doctrines] . . . [is] uncertain; everything depends on the fortuitous order of decision. Yet this is plainly unsatisfactory; no sensible theory of constitutional adjudication, interpretive or noninterpretive, allows such happenstance to determine the course of the law. The order of decisions has nothing to do with the intent of the framers or any of the other things that might inform constitutional interpretation.[64]

Easterbrook argues that the "best way out of the trap of path dependence (but not out of the problem of cycling) is to relax or abandon stare decisis when there are three or more competing positions."[65] Easterbrook observes that the Justices sometimes express views in separate opinions—leading to fractured decisions for the Court as a whole—that do not accord with existing precedent. Easterbrook states:

> This is essentially what the Court has done, and the result is exactly what the critics decry: plurality decisions with each of three (or more) positions expressed; Justices who adhere to their views despite intervening cases' apparently inconsistent decisions; the revisiting of rules adopted and abandoned in the past. . . . For all the objections to this outcome, it seems preferable to an aggravated form of path dependence, under which the Court adopts and adheres to positions that a majority of the Justices find constitutionally untenable.[66]

Are you persuaded by Easterbrook's positive account of Supreme Court decision making? Why or why not? Are you persuaded by his suggestion that the Court should relax precedent to avoid path dependence?

---

[63] Easterbrook, *supra* note 61, at 831.

[64] *Id.* at 819–20.

[65] *Id.* at 820.

[66] *Id.* at 820–21.

B. Constitutional Process: A Positive Social Choice Account of Stare Decisis and Standing

In his dynamic model of Supreme Court decision making, Stearns demonstrates that the problem of intransitive judicial preferences can arise not only within individual cases, as shown above, but also across groups of cases over time. Stearns offers a social choice assessment of Supreme Court voting rules affecting the larger development of constitutional doctrine, with a particular emphasis on horizontal stare decisis and standing. The analysis is analytically parallel to the prior social choice account of outcome voting and the narrowest grounds rule.

Stearns demonstrates that even in cases in which the Supreme Court issues majority decisions, the Court's members sometimes manifest intransitive preferences over groups of cases. To illustrate, consider two actual cases that the Court decided on the same day in 1982, Washington v. Seattle School District No. 1[67] and Crawford v. Board of Education.[68] Both cases involved the question whether a state that was not previously subject to de jure segregation, but which had taken affirmative steps to integrate its public schools, could be prevented by a state constitutional amendment or a statewide initiative from taking further integrative steps beyond that which is constitutionally required without running afoul of the requirements of equal protection set out in the Fourteenth Amendment or, in the case of Washington State, that plus the parallel state equal protection requirement.

In Crawford, California had passed a constitutional amendment that prevented state courts from ordering integrative busing unless the court determined that a federal court would find that the order was necessary to remedy a violation of the Fourteenth Amendment Equal Protection Clause. Writing for a majority of six, Justice Powell sustained the amendment against a federal equal protection challenge. Brennan wrote a concurrence for two, and Marshall dissented alone. In Seattle, Washington State passed a referendum that prevented local school boards from ordering integrative busing unless necessary to avoid a violation of either the state or federal equal protection requirements. Writing for a majority of five, Justice Blackmun struck down the referendum. Powell wrote a dissent for four. To explore the voting anomaly, consider the voting line-ups in the two cases:[69]

In Table 22:4, asterisks appear next to the names of five Justices, Chief Justice Burger and Justices Powell, Rehnquist, and O'Connor, who joined the majority opinion in *Crawford* and the *Seattle* dissent, and Justice Marshall, who joined the majority in *Seattle*, and who alone dissented in *Crawford*. In his dissenting opinion in *Crawford*, Marshall maintained that although the Court had decided *Crawford* and *Seattle* in opposite fashion, the cases were constitutionally indistinguishable. In his dissenting opinion in *Seattle*, Justice Powell rejected several arguments offered to distinguish the two cases. As a matter of substantive equal protection law, one can debate whether the two cases are indistinguishable, but for purposes of the social choice analysis, resolving this debate is

[67] 458 U.S. 457 (1982).

[68] 458 U.S. 527 (1982).

[69] STEARNS, *supra* note 1, at 28 tbl.1.2.

unnecessary.[70] Whatever the merits of relevant arguments, a majority of the Court—Powell, Burger, Rehnquist, O'Connor, and Marshall—rejects any basis for distinction, implying that the cases should be decided in the same manner. And yet, the Court as a whole, in two separate majority opinions issued on the same day, resolved them in opposite fashion.

Table 22:4. Supreme Court Voting Line-up in *Seattle* and *Crawford*

Seattle

Majority	*Dissent*
Blackmun	**Powell***
Marshall*	**Burger***
Brennan	**Rehnquist***
White	**O'Connor***
Stevens	

Crawford

Majority	*Concurrence*	*Dissent*
Powell*	**Brennan**	**Marshall***
Burger*	**Blackmun**	
Rehnquist*		
O'Connor*		
Stevens		
White		

At this point, the social choice implications should be intuitive. Stearns identifies three separate and overlapping majorities. One majority seeks to sustain the *Crawford* amendment against the equal protection challenge. A second majority seeks to strike down the *Seattle* initiative based upon equal protection. And a third majority seeks to resolve these cases in a consistent fashion such that both should either be upheld or struck down. Obviously it is not possible to simultaneously satisfy all three majorities.

To highlight the anomaly, imagine that the two cases were issued sequentially, one year apart, rather than on the same day. If we assume that the Justices vote consistently with their preferences as expressed in the opinions that they drafted or joined, the case ordering would have controlled both outcomes. If *Crawford* arose first, the Court would have sustained the challenged law. If *Seattle* came up one year later, the five Justices with asterisks next to their names would not resolve the case as a matter of first impression,

[70] For a discussion distinguishing the cases, albeit on grounds not discussed in the opinions, see Julian N. Eule, *Judicial Review of Direct Democracy*, 99 YALE L.J. 1503, 1566 (1990) ("In marked contrast to Initiative 350, Proposition 1 was a complementary plebiscite. . . . Admittedly, none of this is explicit in the two opinions."); *see also* Maxwell L. Stearns, *Direct (Anti-) Democracy*, 80 GEO. WASH. L. REV. 311, 370–73 (2012) (relating Professor Eule's case distinction to the social choice analysis of direct democracy). For a more detailed discussion of direct democracy, including the social choice analysis, see *infra* Chapter 24.

but rather, would have asked whether *Crawford* controlled *Seattle*. If we assume that the Justices resolved this sincerely, based on their expressed views in the actual cases and thus consistently with the independence criterion, they would answer yes, and based upon stare decisis, would vote to sustain the *Seattle* initiative, thereby sustaining both challenged laws. Conversely, if *Seattle* were decided first, a majority would have voted to strike down the challenged initiative. One year later, when *Crawford* is presented, the same five Justices would ask if *Seattle* governs *Crawford*, and on the same reasoning, would strike down the *Crawford* amendment as well, with the result that both laws are struck down. The actual cases were presented simultaneously, such that neither controlled the other as precedent. Instead, the *Crawford* amendment was sustained and the *Seattle* initiative struck down, thwarting the crossover majority who determined that the cases should have been decided in like manner.

Now consider the implications of this analysis for the doctrine of stare decisis. As we have already seen, social choice demonstrates the need for the same number of binary comparisons as options if we seek to determine the social significance of the eventual outcome or set of outcomes. Within legislatures, for example, it is commonplace to limit the number of votes relative to options through any number of formal rules, for example, a limit on amendments, or a prohibition on reconsideration of defeated alternatives.[71] If there are more options than permitted amendments, or if defeated options cannot be reconsidered and pitted against the one poised to be selected, it is not possible to know whether the outcome is a Condorcet winner or the product of a voting path. The common practice of preventing reconsideration of defeated alternatives thus ensures an outcome, but does so at the cost of uncertainty as to that outcome's social significance. Stearns maintains that stare decisis as the judicial equivalent of this time-honored cycle-breaking rule, and that it ensures that an option defeated in a prior case is not be brought back to undermine the validity of a subsequent judicial outcome.

Crawford and *Seattle* illustrate the analysis. These two cases presented three binary choices: (1) uphold or strike the California amendment (*Crawford*); (2) uphold or strike the Washington referendum (*Seattle*); and (3) decide the cases consistently or inconsistently (stare decisis). In the hypothetical sequential presentations, the rule of stare decisis effectively takes one of the options off the table, thereby limiting range. It does so by removing the choice to decide the second case—the one subject to prior precedent—on its independent merits without regard to the obligation of precedent. Stare decisis thus has the potential to ground substantive case outcomes in the order in which the cases are presented and decided. *Crawford* followed by *Seattle* produces opposite doctrine in both cases as compared with *Seattle* followed by *Crawford*.

In contrast with Judge Easterbrook, Professor Stearns thus maintains that the Supreme Court decision-making rules relax range, and he further argues that Supreme Court Justices generally adhere to Arrovian Independence. Stearns contends that this latter feature of judicial decision making is reinforced by the practice of writing or joining published opinions that accompany case judgments. Fellow jurists and academics are thus able to identify inconsistencies in judicial voting behaviors, and this encourages sincere

[71] William H. Riker, *The Paradox of Voting and Congressional Rules for Voting on Amendments*, 52 AM. POL. SCI. REV. 349 (1958) (discussing Congressional rule limiting votes relative to options); *see also supra* Chapter 14, at Part I.A.2.

voting, albeit imperfectly. By contrast, Stearns maintains that the social choice profile of legislatures is opposite: adhering to range but relaxing independence. Legislators do not defend their votes with written opinions, and through vote trading and other customary practices, effective legislators allow factors beyond the merits of specific proposed bills to influence voting behaviors. Although formal rules sometimes limit the number of votes relative to legislative options, informal practices allow legislators to gain additional information beyond what formal voting reflects, thereby adhering to range.[72]

The preceding analysis reveals that stare decisis renders the substantive evolution of doctrine path dependent, meaning that substantive outcomes are a function of how cases are ordered. Stearns posits that the real problem is not the fortuitous effect of timing on doctrine, which was the normative basis for Easterbrook's claim that social choice justifies relaxing stare decisis.[73] Instead, Stearns maintains that as a normative matter, some degree of doctrinal arbitrariness dictated by the fortuitous case orderings is acceptable. What matters is whether the process through which case orders are determined is accepted as legitimate.

In this analysis, the primary difficulty that stare decisis creates is not path dependence, but rather, it is the resulting incentive among interest groups to time cases for maximal doctrinal effect. Stearns posits that litigants intuitively grasp the significance of case orderings as a consequence of stare decisis in formulating test cases and in seeking to present more favorable cases first. He notes that stare decisis is a presumptive rule that stabilizes substantive doctrine over the short to moderate term and that the Court sometimes relaxes it (formally overruling in only a small number of cases) when, over time, cycles eventually manifest themselves doctrinally.

Stearns further maintains that when the Court was particularly prone to possessing cyclical preferences, it had an incentive to erect defenses to potential litigant path manipulation. In that context, the Supreme Court's standing rules improved the likelihood that fortuitous historical events—an act *producing an injury* that is *caused by* someone else and that is susceptible of *meaningful judicial redress*—rather than the desire to favorably affect doctrine, presumptively controlled case orderings. In this analysis, the standing rules do not prevent doctrinal path dependence. That is an inevitable consequence of stare decisis. Instead, standing raises the cost of deliberate path manipulation.[74]

This analysis, once more, suggests that staged rules improve the combined fairness and rationality of judicial decision making. The first rule breaks down cyclical preferences: outcome voting in individual cases and stare decisis in groups of cases over time. And the

---

[72] *See* Riker, *supra* note 71.

[73] *See* Easterbrook, *supra* note 61, at 818.

[74] Stearns further demonstrates that applying stare decisis within, but not across, circuit courts is consistent with the social choice analysis. *See* STEARNS, *supra* note 1, at 197–98. Stearns explains:

> Because the evolution of legal doctrine within the circuit will sometimes be the arbitrary product of path dependence, the Supreme Court has [an incentive] . . . to ensure that . . . stare decisis is adhered to *within* but not *among* the circuits. *Intra-* but not *inter*-circuit stare decisis avoids the indeterminacy that would result from cyclical preferences within each circuit. At the same time, the regime ensures that path-dependent iterations, which produce arbitrary bodies of law within a given circuit, are not automatically replicated across the circuits.

Id. at 197.

second improves overall fairness: the narrowest grounds rule in selecting an available Condorcet-winning opinion, and standing in promoting fortuity as the presumptive driver of case orderings.[75]

QUESTIONS AND COMMENTS

Standing is among the most contentious Supreme Court doctrines. Legal scholars fault the doctrine for inconsistent applications and claim that the results are often the product of ideological, or strategic, rather than principled, concerns. Does Stearns's social choice analysis avoid these criticisms? Does social choice provide a means of reconciling the seeming inconsistencies of standing with a principled set of normative justifications?

Does the social choice analysis of stare decisis help to explain the doctrine's evolution within pyramidal courts? Does it help to explain why the doctrine applies within appellate panels—either of three or en banc—when it does not apply among individual jurists acting as trial courts? Can you explain why federal circuit courts do not give stare decisis effect to each other's opinions, whereas they do so internally?

Easterbrook claims that the Supreme Court adheres to all Arrovian fairness conditions, but relaxes transitivity, while Stearns claims that the Supreme Court generally relaxes range, but adheres to the other Arrovian conditions. Which account provides a stronger positive account of Supreme Court doctrines affecting individual cases? Which provides a stronger positive account of Supreme Court doctrines over groups of cases over time? Which offers the basis for a stronger normative argument concerning the role of stare decisis and standing? Why?

III. A SOCIAL CHOICE ANALYSIS OF TIERS OF SCRUTINY

In an article titled *Obergefell, Fisher, and the Inversion of Tiers*,[76] Professor Stearns provides a comprehensive framework designed to explain pervasive doctrinal anomalies associated with the Supreme Court tiers of scrutiny doctrines. Stearns claims that his analysis offers a simpler way of framing the doctrines, which, if followed, would provide the basis for more consistent and predictable applications. The article does not propose abandoning the tiers' doctrines, replacing them with a single tier, or substituting a more finely grained menu of tiers. Instead, Stearns demonstrates why a system of tiers approximating the one we have is an inevitable feature of our constitutional jurisprudence, and he explains how to avoid the doctrinal anomalies that have generated critical commentary.

---

[75] Stearns further explains the complementary nature of certiorari and standing doctrine in minimizing the most egregious effects of litigant path manipulation. *See* STEARNS, *supra* note 1, at 197 (demonstrating that with only certiorari but no standing, ideologically motivated litigants could effectively time circuit splits in a manner that would render Supreme Court docket control illusory).

[76] This discussion is based on Maxwell L. Stearns, Obergefell, Fisher, *and the Inversion of Tiers*, 19 U. PA. J. CONST. L. 1043 (2017), and is adapted from the summary discussion in Maxwell L. Stearns, Obergefell, Fisher, *and the Inversion of Tiers*, BALKINIZATION (Apr. 24, 2016), https://balkin.blogspot.com/2016/04/obergefell-fisher-and-inversion-of-tiers.html.

The tiers doctrine historically began with a binary division, rational-basis scrutiny or strict scrutiny. The former, more relaxed standard, is the baseline, and the latter, more stringent standard, requires a justificatory trigger, typically a suspect class or a fundamental right. The later-introduced third tier, intermediate scrutiny, was principally developed for cases involving gender-based distinctions, and it too has not been applied in a consistent manner. The most significant anomalies in the system of tiers involve applying strict scrutiny to sustain race-based affirmative action, and applying rational basis scrutiny to strike laws adversely affecting non-suspect (or quasi-suspect), yet politically vulnerable groups. The result has been to transform the once-binary scheme into a system with the following five categories:

Table 22:5. Tiers of Scrutiny in One Dimension

(1) Rational Basis	(2) Rational Basis Plus	(3) Intermediate	(4) Strict Scrutiny Lite	(5) Strict Scrutiny
Lax review				Stringent review

As a matter of black letter law, it is commonplace to express the tiers along a simple linear scale, as shown in Table 22:5, ranking the tiers from lax to stringent. Stearns explains that in predicting case outcomes, however, the Table 22:5 presentation fails. When the Court applies *rational basis plus*, it strikes the challenged law, and when it employs *strict scrutiny lite*, it sustains the challenged laws. In terms of prediction, therefore, strict scrutiny lite abuts traditional rational basis, with both tiers used to sustain the challenged classification, and rational basis plus abuts strict scrutiny, with both tiers used to strike down the challenged classification. On first principles, it is hard to imagine that anyone would devise our present inverted system of tiers, which generates the sequence 1**4**3**2**5, as reflected in Table 22:6. Stearns demonstrates that the analytical difficulty involves the failure to match the scheme of tiers with the underlying dimensionality of the case law.

Table 22:6. Tiers of Scrutiny Recast

(1) Rational Basis	**(4) Strict Scrutiny Lite**	(3) Intermediate	**(2) Rational Basis Plus**	(5) Strict Scrutiny
More likely to sustain				More likely to strike

Stearns explains that dimensions are normative scales of measurement used to evaluate virtually anything being compared. Some dimensions involve simple binaries—black versus white, male versus female—although such binaries oversimplify as applied to some individuals. Other dimensions present more nuanced scales of measurement, for example, continuous gradations of height or weight. Single dimensions often combine multiple criteria. Stearns illustrates as follows: Larger objects tend to be heavier, allowing us to rank modes of transportation—a scooter, a bicycle, a car—in a manner that captures both size and weight. And yet, such alignments sometimes break down. Adding an aloft hot air balloon—larger than a car yet lighter than a scooter—forces the need to split the dimensions of size (scooter, bicycle, car, *then* hot air balloon) and weight (hot air balloon *then* scooter, bicycle, car).

Stearns maintains that advocates of an array of tiers, including former Justice Thurgood Marshall,[77] fail to recognize that even a single dimension is capable of sorting infinite data provided the dimension captures the relevant normative stakes. And yet, even a small number of data will thwart a single dimension if that dimension fails to capture those stakes. Conversely, Stearns demonstrates that advocates of a single tier, such as retired Justice John Paul Stevens,[78] fail to recognize that new descriptors along a single dimension, marking which laws are or are not permissible, will necessarily emerge to fill the need for doctrinal guidance. Because lower courts will come to associate those articulated characteristics as bases for striking or sustaining challenged laws, the new terminology will, over time, replicate the system of tiers, albeit with less guidance, at least until the system sorts itself out.

Stearns offers the following example, illustrated in Table 22:7. We can sort infinite integers along the odd/even dimension or along the prime/non-prime dimension. And yet, we need both dimensions—*odd/even* and *prime/non-prime*—to sort the deceptively simple bolded sequence, 2,3,4, when the two sets of criteria are combined. The number 2, the sole even prime, forces a split of these two dimensions, just as the hot air balloon forced a split over the dimensions of size and weight. Stearns claims that by analogy, the inversion of tiers has arisen because the category of benign racial classifications is the hot air balloon (or number 2) in our equal protection jurisprudence.

Table 22:7: Dimensionality in Categorizing Integers

	Odds	Evens
Primes	**3**, 5, 7, 11, 13, 17, 19 . . .	**2**
Nonprimes	9, 15, 21 . . .	**4**, 6, 8 . . .

Benign racial preferences force a split in the dimensionality of tiers that the Supreme Court has refused to allow. The result has been to contort strict scrutiny to sustain the narrow set of relevant challenged laws, as seen in *Regents of the University of California v. Bakke*,[79] and *Grutter v. Bollinger*.[80] Justice Kennedy expressed this concern following *Fisher v. University of Texas at Austin*,[81] when he criticized Justice O'Connor's relaxed version of strict scrutiny as applied in *Grutter*, stating that although strict scrutiny need not be fatal, neither should it be feeble.[82] And yet, Justice Kennedy himself applied strict scrutiny in a similarly deferential manner to Justice O'Connor in *Fisher I*, when the case returned to the Supreme Court post-remand in *Fisher II*.[83] In that case, writing for a majority, Justice

[77] *See* Stearns, *Obergefell*, *supra* note 76.

[78] *See id.*

[79] 438 U.S. 265 (1978).

[80] 539 U.S. 306 (2003).

[81] 133 S. Ct. 2411 (2013).

[82] 133 U.S. at 2421.

[83] Fisher v. Univ. of Texas at Austin *(Fisher II)*, 136 S. Ct. 2198 (2016).

Kennedy upheld the complex affirmative action program that coupled race-based preferences with guaranteed admission to any state university for those graduating in the top ten percent of their class.

Table 22:8, which presents the jurisprudence of race in two dimensions, illustrates the analytical difficulty:

Table 22:8. Race and Dimensionality

	Condoning benign use of race	Not condoning benign use of race
Condoning adverse use of race		Jim Crow
Not condoning adverse use of race	Modern liberal	Color-blind

Consider what the two intuitively opposite extreme positions concerning race nonetheless hold in common: Although modern liberals condone benign racial classifications, and Jim Crow condones adverse racial classifications, both groups permit some express reliance on race. By contrast, the color-blind position rejects any express reliance on race. Stearns posits that the valence of color-blindness, a once-liberal position (as shown in Justice Harlan's dissent in *Plessy v. Ferguson*[84]) that is now a core element of conservative race jurisprudence, arises as a unique consequence of this country's tragic historical treatment of race. He further observes that both modern liberals and modern conservatives claim that their competing normative views are a necessary consequence of the tragic lessons of Jim Crow.

Until the modern era, reliance on race was almost invariably coupled with the intent and effect of disadvantaging oppressed minorities, most notably African Americans. Whereas in the era of Jim Crow, the categories of *antidiscrimination* and *anti-subordination* went hand in hand, benign racial classifications now force a dimensionality split in which modern conservatives insist upon antidiscrimination, and modern liberals insist instead upon anti-subordination. The dimensionality of race is demonstrated by the peculiar fact that although modern liberals and Jim Crow resolve each of the two core inquiries reflected in Table 22:8 in opposite fashion, both allow some use of race. By contrast, the color-blind position resolves one issue in favor of each camp (failing to condone adverse reliance on race, along with modern liberals, and failing to condone benign reliance on race, along with Jim Crow), yet insists upon an opposite outcome respecting the constitutional permissibility of employing race.

Stearns maintains that dimensionality complicates tiers analysis because by insisting upon classifying benign race cases (discriminating, but not subordinating) under strict scrutiny, the Court has inevitably contorted its strict scrutiny test to make the cases fit. By contrast, if the Court allowed a separate test (intermediate scrutiny), or if it split the dimensions across the two sets of cases—benign and adverse reliance on race, each along

[84] 163 U.S. 537 (1896).

its own permissibility spectrum—for separate treatment, the cases would naturally align within the existing framework of tiers.

Stearns claims that the problem of dimensionality is endemic to race. It does not arise in other equal protection settings. For example, cases implicating gender generally sort neatly along a single dimension of anti-subordination. This does not mean that hard cases do not arise, that the line of permissibility is unwavering, or that the Supreme Court has always gotten it right. It simply means that as a general proposition, we lack a principled normative commitment to sex-blind jurisprudence akin to that associated with race. Modern liberals and modern conservatives sometimes disagree on where to draw the line of constitutional permissibility in gender cases, but they implicitly agree that the normative inquiry in such cases involves the single dimension scale of anti-subordination. For the binary division along a single dimension scale, the traditional two-tier scheme, strict or rational basis scrutiny, is adequate to the task. Indeed, reliance on intermediate scrutiny to do the work of the more traditional tests is manifest in such cases as *United States v. Virginia*,[85] (intermediate scrutiny as de facto strict scrutiny) versus *Tuan Anh Nguyen v. INS*,[86] (intermediate scrutiny as de facto rational basis review).

Stearns claims that ironically, the Court has removed intermediate scrutiny where this alternative test has work to do, and it has imposed intermediate scrutiny where it does not. This insight helps to explain yet another tiers' anomaly: the Equal Protection Clause, adopted to combat the historical treatment of race, now permits greater legislative flexibility respecting benign gender-based than benign race-based classifications.

Stearns further explains the animus cases as providing one-time passes to strike laws adversely affecting vulnerable groups for whom legislative classifications might sometimes be appropriate, and thus without calling into question the presumptive validity of laws more generally affecting such groups. The analysis also offers insights into Justice Kennedy's principal reliance in *Obergefell v. Hodges*[87] on due process, rather than equal protection, to strike the ban on same-sex marriage. While the ruling appears to avoid tiers altogether, Stearns maintains that the strategy is destined to fail in the long term. We know that bans on same-sex marriage fall on the prohibited side of a binary divide, one implicating the dimension of anti-subordination. We will eventually learn if there are any permissible bases for relying on sexual orientation in legislative classifications (for example sexual orientation *preferences* to eradicate past discriminatory practices), and thus where, if at all, the permissibility line along that dimension will be drawn.

Stearns concludes by observing that ignoring the problem of sorting cases over existing tiers cannot eliminate the need for tiers. Recognizing the role of dimensionality in the application of tiers, however, provides the basis for a simpler path forward, one that will improve the clarity of case presentations and analyses in this important body of case law.

Commentators, and law students, are often critical of the Supreme Court's treatment of tiers of scrutiny. Does the social choice account make the analysis more

---

[85] 518 U.S. 515, 533 (1996).

[86] 533 U.S. 53 (2001).

[87] 135 S. Ct. 2071 (2015).

comprehensible? If so, why do you think that the Court continues with the existing complex tiers scheme?

IV. CASE ILLUSTRATIONS

In this part, we consider the implications of several models of judicial behavior set out in this chapter for three high profile Supreme Court decisions: *Bush v. Gore*,[88] *Adarand Constructors, Inc. v. Pena*,[89] and *Gonzales v. Carhart*.[90] The first two cases involve equal protection doctrine. Beyond that surface similarity, however, these opinions apply equal protection in disparate contexts and with substantially different precedential implications. They also hold potentially divergent implications for the nature and role of judicial strategy in the context of Supreme Court decision making. The third case involves partial birth abortion, although the part of the opinion that we are concerned with involves abortion more generally.

These cases present complex issues and analyses, and our focus is limited to specific aspects that invite the possibility of elements of strategy among the deciding Justices. We will present a summary of the background cases as needed to focus attention on targeted issues within or across the relevant opinions. We begin with the 2000 decision, *Bush v. Gore*, a case that is less influential as a matter of equal protection doctrine than it was in determining the outcome of the 2000 presidential election in favor of Republican nominee George W. Bush over Democratic nominee Al Gore.[91] We then consider the 1995 decision, *Adarand Constructors, Inc. v. Pena*, a case that remains a centerpiece of modern equal protection jurisprudence, especially in the sensitive area of race and benign race-based preference. Finally, we present a brief discussion based on a concurring opinion in *Gonzales v. Carhart*, an abortion case that upheld a federal ban on partial birth abortion just seven years following a contrary decision involving a similar state law restriction in *Stenberg v. Carhart*.[92]

As you read the discussions of the cases that follow, it will be helpful to bear the following questions in mind: Do these cases support or undermine the assumption that Supreme Court Justices vote sincerely or strategically? Do these cases help to identify judicial practices that inhibit strategic judicial decision making, whether or not those structures succeeded in doing so in the cases themselves? Do these cases support or detract from the Attitudinal Model, introduced in Chapter 21? More generally, do these cases—or at least the features of the cases that are the focus of the presentations that follow—represent norms of judicial behavior on the Supreme Court, or exceptions to those norms, and why? Do they capture judicial behavior on other appellate courts? Why or why not? Do they support or undermine any preceding social choice models of Supreme Court decision making?

---

88 531 U.S. 98 (2000).

89 515 U.S. 200 (1995).

90 550 U.S. 124 (2007).

91 The analysis is based on STEARNS, *supra* note 1, at 315–23 (Afterword on *Bush v. Gore*). For a more detailed presentation, see Michael Abramowicz & Maxwell L. Stearns, *Beyond Counting Votes: The Political Economy of* Bush v. Gore, 54 VAND. L. REV. 1849 (2001).

92 530 U.S. 914 (2000).

A. Bush v. Gore[93]

In *Bush v. Gore*,[94] the Supreme Court intervened for the second time in the controversial 2000 presidential election and for the first time played a decisive role in choosing the President of the United States. The discussion and graphic that follow will establish a time line that will help to explain the relationship between the two cases and to offer the background for the case analysis, which draws upon various models presented in this chapter.

1. *The Bush v. Gore Timeline*

Following the historically close November 7, 2000 election, it was clear that the assignment of the twenty-five Electoral College seats from Florida would control whether Al Gore or George Bush would become President. Bush led the Florida election by a mere 1784 votes, less than one half of one percent of the ballots cast. Under Florida law, a result within that margin produced an automatic machine recount.

In Florida, along with other states, the post-election period was divided into two phases. The protest period allowed challenges before Secretary of State Katherine Harris to alleged voting improprieties prior to the official certification of Electoral Votes. The contest period allowed time for a judicial challenge to the certification of results prior to sending the slate of electors to the Electoral College.[95] The timing of these two phases was zero sum for states like Florida that sought the benefit of the so-called safe harbor provision of 3 U.S.C. § 5.[96] That statute, enacted in the aftermath of the contested Tilden-Hayes Election of 1876, provided that any slate of electors submitted six days prior to the meeting of the Electoral College that was selected in a manner consistent with state law in effect prior to the election is presumed conclusive. The original protest period in Florida ran from November 7, 2000 through November 14, 2000, and the original contest period ran from November 14, 2000 until December 12, 2000.

On November 14, 2000, Katherine Harris announced that Bush remained in the lead by the narrower margin of 300 votes. The first Supreme Court decision followed a decision of the Florida Supreme Court issued on November 21, 2000. In *Palm Beach Canvassing Board v. Harris*,[97] the Florida Supreme Court had determined that to accommodate the manual recounts needed to resolve the alleged voting improprieties raised by Gore in his protest, it was necessary to extend the protest period from November 14 through November 26, 2000, with the effect of correspondingly shortening the contest period. The United States Supreme Court granted certiorari and heard oral

---

[93] Portions of the discussion that follow are based upon Abramowicz & Stearns, *supra* note 91; MAXWELL L. STEARNS, CONSTITUTIONAL PROCESS: A SOCIAL CHOICE ANALYSIS OF SUPREME COURT DECISION MAKING 315–23 (paperback ed. 2002) (Afterword on *Bush v. Gore*).

[94] 531 U.S. 98 (2000).

[95] *See* FLA. STAT. ANN. § 102.166 (2000) (protest phase); *id.* § 102.168 (contest phase).

[96] 3 U.S.C. § 5 (2000).

[97] 772 So. 2d 1220 (Fla. 2000).

argument on December 1, issuing a unanimous remand to the Florida Supreme Court in *Bush v. Palm Beach County Canvassing Board*,[98] on December 4.

The *Palm Beach County Canvassing Board* remand inquired whether the Florida Supreme Court decision to extend Florida's statutory protest period at the expense of the statutory contest period was based upon an application of the relevant state statute or some other source of law, most notably the state constitution's requirement of equal protection. This question was important in assessing whether the Florida Supreme Court's revised state election procedure had been implemented consistently with Article II of the U.S. Constitution. Article II confers upon state legislatures the power to make laws governing the state's selection of Electors to the Electoral College for the President and Vice President of the United States. By the time the Supreme Court decision in *Palm Beach County Canvassing Board* was issued, however, that question was essentially moot. Even under the extended protest period, Katherine Harris declared Bush the winner. The *Palm Beach County Canvassing Board* Court nonetheless issued a minimalist unanimous decision that appeared to remain above the partisan fray while providing a check against a potentially problematical state court intervention into a presidential election in a manner that might have run afoul of Article II.

After Katherine Harris certified George W. Bush the winner of Florida's twenty-five electoral votes on November 26, 2000, Al Gore, along with other affected voters, contested the election outcome by filing four legal challenges. *Bush v. Gore* grew out of one of those challenges, filed on November 27, 2000, in Leon County seeking a manual recount of undervotes.[99] Undervotes are ballots that failed to properly register a vote for a President and Vice President and thus were not counted toward the final election result. Gore appealed an order by the Leon County Circuit Court denying his request to the Florida Supreme Court. Although Gore had only requested manual recounts of undervotes in specified counties, the Florida Supreme Court ordered a recount of undervotes in all counties throughout the state in which such a recount had not yet taken place, and mandated an intent-of-the-voter standard.

Immediately thereafter, George W. Bush successfully petitioned the United States Supreme Court for certiorari and for a stay.[100] In addition to claiming that the Florida court ruling ran afoul of a federal statute that provides a safe harbor if the electors were certified by December 12, 2000,[101] Bush raised two constitutional claims. First, because Article II expressly grants the power to state legislatures to establish by statute the rules governing elections for the selection of electors of the president and vice president, the Florida Supreme Court order, which altered the state's legislated election process, violated Article II. Second, because the order failed to provide a mechanism to ensure that the recount would be consistently applied within and across counties, and instead applied a problematic intent-of-the-voter standard, the order violated the Fourteenth Amendment Equal Protection and Due Process Clauses.

---

[98] 531 U.S. 70 (2000).

[99] 531 U.S. at 101.

[100] Bush v. Gore, 531 U.S. 1048 (2000).

[101] 531 U.S. at 103.

The Supreme Court granted certiorari and stayed the recount, which was scheduled to begin on December 9, 2000. Following oral argument on December 11, 2000, the Supreme Court issued its ruling on December 12, the final day of the certification period and six days prior to the scheduled meeting of the Electors. Table 22.A.1 summarizes the time line.

In contrast with *Palm Beach County Canvassing Board*, the *Bush v. Gore* Court was badly fractured, producing a complex set of opinions. Ultimately the combined opinions produced a victory for Bush. In a *per curiam* for five justices, *Bush v. Gore* overturned the Florida Supreme Court's statewide recount of undervotes. That opinion held that the Florida Supreme Court violated equal protection by failing to ensure consistent standards for the recount and that the timeline under the 3 U.S.C. § 5 safe harbor provision disallowed a timely cure. As a consequence, the Court effectively mandated that the Secretary of State's certified slate for George W. Bush was final.

The *Bush v. Gore* Court divided into four major camps. The *per curiam* opinion, which found an equal protection violation, was joined by Chief Justice Rehnquist and Justices Kennedy, O'Connor, Scalia, and Thomas. In theory, the equal protection problem resulting from a lack of a uniform standards could have been cured on remand with more specific standards, also including perhaps ballots beyond those classified as undervotes. The *per curiam* opinion foreclosed that possibility because the date for certification was upon the Court. The opinion itself was issued on December 12, 2000, the same date as was required for the benefit of the safe harbor provision. And because one day earlier, in response to the *Palm Beach County Canvassing Board* remand, the Florida Supreme Court had clarified that the state intended to benefit from the federal safe harbor provision,[102] the *per curiam* authors determined that timing prevented a recount.

Chief Justice Rehnquist, joined by Justices Scalia and Thomas, who joined the *Bush v. Gore per curiam* opinion, also produced a separate concurrence. The concurring opinion rested on Article II, concluding that the Florida recount order was inconsistent with the constitutional delegation to state legislatures to enact rules governing the selection of electors for the President and Vice President. Justice Souter dissented. Justice Breyer joined Souter's dissent and also produced his own. Souter and Breyer both agreed to an equal protection violation but determined it could be cured with a clearer standard if on remand the Florida Supreme Court were permitted to assess the risk of sacrificing the benefit of the safe harbor to allow additional time for a recount. Justices Stevens and Ginsburg joined Souter's dissent except with respect to the portion expressing partial support for the *per curiam*'s equal protection analysis. Ginsburg and Stevens filed separate dissents in which they found no violation of either equal protection or of Article II.

---

[102] *See* Palm Beach County Canvassing Bd. v. Harris, 772 So. 2d 1273 (Fla. 2000).

Table 22:9: *Bush v. Gore* Timeline (2000)

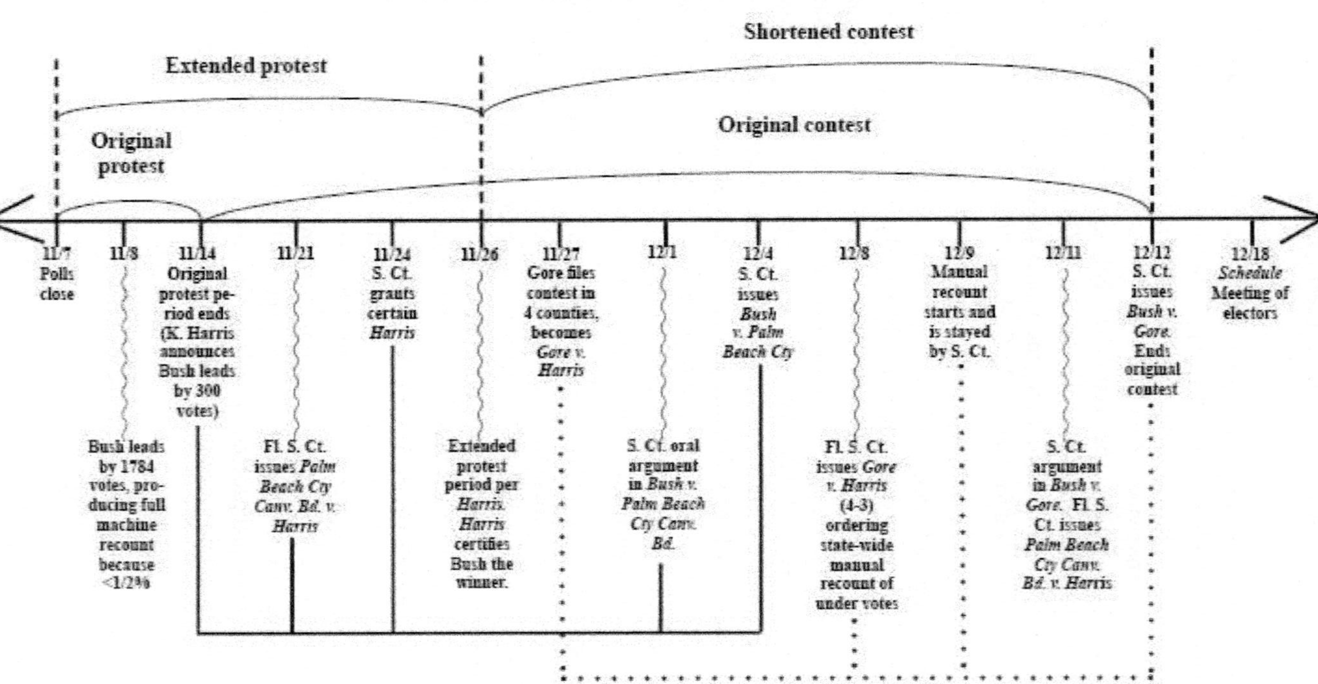

The *per curiam* reasoned as follows:

> Upon due consideration of the difficulties identified to this point, it is obvious that the recount cannot be conducted in compliance with the requirements of equal protection and due process without substantial additional work. It would require not only the adoption . . . of adequate statewide standards for determining what is a legal vote, and practicable procedures to implement them, but also orderly judicial review . . . . In addition, the . . . recount . . . requires that the vote tabulation equipment be used to screen out undervotes, a function for which the machines were not designed. . . . [Perhaps] even a second screening would [therefore] be necessary. Use of the equipment for this purpose, and any new software developed for it, would have to be evaluated for accuracy by the Secretary [of State], as required by Fla. Stat. Ann. § 101.015 (Supp. 2001).
>
> The Supreme Court of Florida has said that the legislature intended the State's electors to "participat[e] fully in the federal electoral process," as provided in 3 U.S.C. § 5. 772 So.2d, at 1289; see also *Palm Beach Canvassing Bd.* v. *Harris*, 772 So.2d 1220, 1237 (Fla. 2000). That statute, in turn, requires that any controversy or contest that is designed to lead to a conclusive selection of electors be completed by December 12. That date is upon us, and there is no recount procedure in place under the State Supreme Court's order that comports with minimal constitutional standards. Because it is evident that any recount seeking to meet the December 12 date will be unconstitutional for the reasons we have discussed, we reverse the judgment of the Supreme Court of Florida ordering a recount to proceed.[103]

The separate concurrence began by stating: "We join the per curiam opinion."[104] The concurring Justices then offered an alternative analysis that rested on Article II. The opinion explained:

> In Florida, the legislature has chosen to hold statewide elections to appoint the State's 25 electors. Importantly, the legislature has delegated the authority to run the elections and to oversee election disputes to the Secretary of State (Secretary) . . . and to state circuit courts . . . . Isolated sections of the code may well admit of more than one interpretation, but the general coherence of the legislative scheme may not be altered by judicial interpretation so as to wholly change the statutorily provided apportionment of responsibility among these various bodies. In any election but a Presidential election, the Florida Supreme Court can give as little or as much deference to Florida's executives as it chooses, so far as Article II is concerned, and this Court will have no cause to question the court's actions. But, with respect to a Presidential election, the court must be both mindful of the legislature's role under Article II in choosing the manner of appointing electors and deferential to those bodies expressly empowered by the legislature to carry out its constitutional mandate.[105]

---

[103] 531 U.S. at 110.

[104] *Id.* at 111 (Rehnquist, C.J., Scalia, J., &Thomas, J., concurring).

[105] *Id.* at 113–14.

Two dissenting Justices, Souter and Breyer, conceded an equal protection problem, but contended it could be cured on remand. Justice Breyer explained:

> Nonetheless, there is no justification for the majority's remedy, which is simply to reverse the lower court and halt the recount entirely. An appropriate remedy would be, instead, to remand this case with instructions that, even at this late date, would permit the Florida Supreme Court to require recounting *all* undercounted votes in Florida, including those from Broward, Volusia, Palm Beach, and Miami-Dade Counties, whether or not previously recounted prior to the end of the protest period, and to do so in accordance with a single uniform substandard.[106]

Justice Stevens, joined by Justice Ginsburg, altogether rejected the majority's equal protection analysis:

> Admittedly, the use of differing substandards for determining voter intent in different counties employing similar voting systems may raise serious concerns. Those concerns are alleviated—if not eliminated—by the fact that a single impartial magistrate will ultimately adjudicate all objections arising from the recount process. Of course, as a general matter, "[t]he interpretation of constitutional principles must not be too literal. We must remember that the machinery of government would not work if it were not allowed a little play in its joints." If it were otherwise, Florida's decision to leave to each county the determination of what balloting system to employ—despite enormous differences in accuracy—might run afoul of equal protection. So, too, might the similar decisions of the vast majority of state legislatures to delegate to local authorities certain decisions with respect to voting systems and ballot design.
>
> Even assuming that aspects of the remedial scheme might ultimately be found to violate the Equal Protection Clause, I could not subscribe to the majority's disposition of the case. As the majority explicitly holds, once a state legislature determines to select electors through a popular vote, the right to have one's vote counted is of constitutional stature. As the majority further acknowledges, Florida law holds that all ballots that reveal the intent of the voter constitute valid votes. Recognizing these principles, the majority nonetheless orders the termination of the contest proceeding before all such votes have been tabulated. Under their own reasoning, the appropriate course of action would be to remand to allow more specific procedures for implementing the legislature's uniform general standard to be established.[107]

In his separate dissent, Stevens criticized what he viewed as the Court's remarkable intervention:

> What must underlie petitioners' entire federal assault on the Florida election procedures is an unstated lack of confidence in the impartiality and capacity of the state judges who would make the critical decisions if the vote count were to proceed. Otherwise, their position is wholly without merit. The

[106] *Id.* at 146 (Breyer, J., dissenting).

[107] *Id.* at 126–27 (Stevens, J., dissenting) (quoting Bain Peanut Co. of Tex. v. Pinson, 282 U.S. 499, 501 (1931) (Holmes, J.) (alteration in original)) (footnote omitted).

> endorsement of that position by the majority of this Court can only lend credence to the most cynical appraisal of the work of judges throughout the land. It is confidence in the men and women who administer the judicial system that is the true backbone of the rule of law. Time will one day heal the wound to that confidence that will be inflicted by today's decision. One thing, however, is certain. Although we may never know with complete certainty the identity of the winner of this year's Presidential election, the identity of the loser is perfectly clear. It is the Nation's confidence in the judge as an impartial guardian of the rule of law.[108]

2. *A Social Choice Analysis of Bush v. Gore*

Professors Michael Abramowicz and Maxwell Stearns have analyzed the *Bush v. Gore* case using social choice analysis. The authors claim that the combined opinions exposed a series of fault lines that not only split the five-Justice conservative majority from a four-Justice liberal dissent, but that also divided the conservative majority itself over two potentially conflicting rationales.

Abramowicz and Stearns argue that beneath the surface of the apparent controlling majority in *Bush v. Gore* rested a likely set of divisions as to how to define and resolve controlling case issues that threatened to destabilize the Court's ruling, or at least the appearance of consensus supporting the doctrinal justification for ending the Florida recount. These divisions were of potentially sufficient magnitude and importance that had the Justices voted consistently with what appears to have represented their initial preferred positions—or ideal points—the result might well have been to decide the first Supreme Court case controlling the outcome of a presidential election with a set of opinions that revealed the basis for cyclical preferences, thus calling into question the stability—and legitimacy—of the Court's opinion.

The authors identify a possible underlying cycle, but claim that the case is more notable in demonstrating significant limitations on the power of Justices to vote strategically. In effect, the authors contend that *Bush v. Gore* represents the exception proving (or at least supporting) the rule that Supreme Court decision-making processes substantially limit the incentives of the Justices to vote other than sincerely in resolving logically controlling case issues. The authors claim that based upon reasonable assumptions, it is plausible to demonstrate that at least one group of justices, those who joined a separate concurring opinion, pursued what can be described as a strategic course.

The *per curiam* opinion hinted that whereas a majority of five supported the equal protection rationale, not all did so enthusiastically. Beyond the opening sentence of the separate concurrence, which read "We join the per curiam opinion,"[109] the concurring Justices ignored equal protection in their separate opinion, resting on Article II. In addition, the *per curiam* contained the following unusual disclaimer: "Our consideration is limited to the present circumstances, for the problem of equal protection in election processes generally presents many complexities."[110] In effect, the *per curiam* immediately

---

108 *Id.* at 128–29.

109 *Id.* at 111 (Rehnquist, C.J., Scalia, J., & Thomas, J., concurring).

110 *Id.* at 109 (per curiam).

disclaimed the case's precedential significance beyond the case facts. Finally, Abramowicz and Stearns observe, along with other commentators, an apparent doctrinal inversion in which the conservative majority applied equal protection over the objection of their liberal colleagues. With the limited exception of affirmative action, judicial conservatives generally take a less expansive equal protection analysis, whereas judicial liberals generally embrace a more expansive approach.[111]

The *per curiam*'s equal protection analysis was sufficiently contentious that almost all conservative commentators who supported the result preferred the concurrence's alternative Article II framing.[112] If the Supreme Court had rested on Article II, and if the Florida Supreme Court's statewide manual recount violated the constitutional grant of authority to the state legislature, then there would have been nothing to cure upon remand and no need to worry about whether December 12, 2000 imposed a fixed deadline under 3 U.S.C. § 5.

Based upon this analysis, Abramowicz and Stearns claim that the most plausible scenario for strategic voting in *Bush v. Gore* did not affect the case outcome. Instead, it provided the appearance of majority support for a rationale supporting an outcome that would nonetheless have obtained had each just voted sincerely.

The analysis proceeds in two steps. First the authors consider the implications of casting the Justices' preferences along a single normative dimension, such that a consensus position (or Condorcet winner) emerges. They then relax this assumption to consider a more nuanced presentation that better accounts for the decision's peculiar features.

Table 22.A.2 provides a stylized breakdown of the *Bush v. Gore* opinions. The opinions are cast along a normative issue dimension based on the breadth or narrowness of the Supreme Court's power to scrutinize state court decisions that interfere with presidential elections.

Chief Justice Rehnquist, joined by Justices Scalia and Thomas, a group considered the most reliable conservatives at the time of decision, provided the broadest bases for overturning the Florida Supreme Court. These justices rested their analysis both on equal protection (joining the *per curiam*) and on Article II (the separate opinion analysis). The *per curiam* opinion, also joined by the more moderate conservatives, Justices O'Connor and Kennedy, relied solely upon equal protection. It found a violation based upon the subjective recount standard, which focused on the voter's intent, and the decision to limit the recount to undervotes. The *per curiam* determined that the equal protection defect could not be cured given the timing of the safe harbor provision. Justices Souter and Breyer, the leftmost dissenting justices in this presentation—immediately to the right of the bolded vertical line separating those who did and did not support the judgment—in Table 22:A.2, found a potential equal protection problem, but would have allowed a cure on remand. Finally, the rightmost dissenting justices, Stevens and Ginsburg, found no violation of Article II or equal protection.

---

111 Abramowicz & Stearns, *supra* note 91, at 1867–73.

112 For a notable exception, see Nelson Lund, *The Unbearable Rightness of* Bush v. Gore, 23 CARDOZO L. REV. 1219 (2002).

Table 22:10. A Unidimensional Social Choice Model of Bush v. Gore

(A) Rehnquist, Scalia, Thomas (concurring)	(B) O'Connor, Kennedy (per curiam)	(C) Souter, Breyer (dissenting)	(D) Stevens, Ginsburg (dissenting)
Florida Supreme Court decision violates Article II and equal protection	Florida Supreme Court decisions violates equal protection only; Florida Supreme Court's expressed desire to receive benefit of safe harbor prevents timely remand for corrective remedy satisfying equal protection	Florida Supreme Court decision violates equal protection only; safe harbor provision is not mandatory, thus permitting timely remand for corrective remedy satisfying equal protection	Florida Supreme Court decision does not violate Article II or equal protection

Broad Mandate to correct state judicial intervention in elections ⟷ Narrow Mandate to correct state judicial intervention in elections

Table 22.A.2 treats the case as the functional equivalent of a fractured panel case in which the opinions can be cast along a single issue dimension. In this framing, the concurring justices provide two independent bases for overturning the Florida Supreme Court decision: Article II and equal protection. The analysis assumes that whereas Justices O'Connor and Kennedy favored ruling for Bush, they were disinclined to issue a ruling that rested on overturning a state court construction of state law, specifically one that construed the state statute to benefit from the safe harbor even at the expense of failing to remedy a meritorious challenge to voting irregularities. As a result, they also were disinclined to support the concurring Justices' Article II analysis but were willing to accept a basis for overruling that was at least not inconsistent with the Florida court's prior interpretation of Florida law, which construed the state election law to permit such a remedial order. The analysis further assumes that Justices O'Connor and Kennedy were unwilling to join the liberal Breyer/Souter opinions that would have invited the possibility of a further recount, which, based upon available information at the time of decision, created the possibility of a victory for Gore. By necessary implication, O'Connor and Kennedy would also not have been willing to go farther, as did Stevens and Ginsburg, and find against any constitutional defect in the Florida court ruling.

In this scenario, if Justices O'Connor and Kennedy were seeking to produce a judgment overruling the Florida Supreme Court decision without resting that decision on Article II, then the positions of the remaining Justices provided these centrist jurists with little room to maneuver. They were bounded on the left by the concurring jurists' Article II analysis, and they were bounded on the right by an equal protection analysis that admitted of a potential cure upon remand. Only by grounding their opinion in the much-criticized equal protection analysis, but finding that the factual peculiarities associated with the timing of the decision preclude an actual (rather than nominal) remand, could they produce the desired narrowest-grounds result.

Although the *per curiam* analysis has been roundly criticized, even by those favoring the result, on these assumptions, the opinion represents a stable outcome. And yet this analysis leaves some of the most anomalous features of *Bush v. Gore* unexplained, including why the concurring Justices joined in what became the *per curiam* opinion.

Abramowicz and Stearns claim that a seemingly obvious answer—to ensure a majority as needed to produce a governing precedent—is refuted by the limiting language disclaiming any pretense of meaningful precedential status. Thus, although the analysis might explain why Justices O'Connor and Kennedy found the equal protection analysis attractive, it does not explain why the concurring Justices joined the *per curiam*. This is especially counterintuitive given those jurists' general predisposition against expansive equal protection analysis in the area of voting rights, and given that they could have achieved the same judgment by resting exclusively on Article II.

By relaxing the assumptions needed to create a unidimensional presentation of *Bush v. Gore*, Abramowicz and Stearns are able to evaluate the implications of a more nuanced presentation. Whereas the prior analysis assumed that Chief Justice Rehnquist and Justices Scalia and Thomas sincerely held their views on Article II and on equal protection, and considered the options available to Justices O'Connor and Kennedy on the assumption that they sought to produce a result for Bush, in this analysis, the authors instead assume that Chief Justice Rehnquist and Justices Scalia and Thomas signed on to the *per curiam* analysis on the basis of alternative strategic considerations. The authors defend this intuition based on the previously identified anomalies: first, the nominal support for equal protection among the concurring justices; the general equal protection inversion in voting rights jurisprudence; and the *per curiam*'s fact-specific precedential disclaimer.

Reflecting these considerations, Table 22.A.3 depicts the initial positions, or ideal points, of the various camps in *Bush v. Gore*. In this analysis, the concurring Justices embraced only the Article II analysis and Justices O'Connor and Kennedy embraced only the equal protection analysis grounds for reversing the Florida Supreme Court. Within the dissent box, the names Souter and Breyer appear in italics to reflect the fact that while they preferred to affirm, they did find an equal protection problem, albeit one that they determined could be cured on remand. Unlike table 22.A.2, table 22.A.3 presents the issues in *Bush v. Gore* along two dimensions, with asymmetrical preferences.

One majority—the *per curiam* Justices (excluding the concurring Justices who joined only for strategic reasons) and the dissenters—determined that the Florida Supreme Court decision could not be reversed on the basis of a violation of Article II. Another majority—the concurring Justices and the dissenters (totaling five if we include Souter and Breyer)—determined that the Florida Supreme Court could not be reversed on the basis of a violation of equal protection. Presumably, all nine deciding Justices agreed that absent a violation of either Article II or equal protection, there was no basis upon which to reverse the Florida Supreme Court. And yet, a third majority—those in concurrence plus O'Connor and Kennedy—voted to reverse and (nominally) to remand.

Table 22:11. *Bush v. Gore* in Two Dimensions with Asymmetrical Preferences

	Florida Supreme Court ruling should be reversed on the basis of equal protection	Florida Supreme Court ruling should not be reversed on the basis of equal protection
Florida Supreme Court ruling should be reversed on the basis of Article II		(A) Rehnquist, Scalia, Thomas
Florida Supreme Court ruling should not be reversed on the basis of Article II	(C) O'Connor, Kennedy	(B) *Souter, Breyer,* Stevens, Ginsburg

The authors maintain that this more nuanced presentation better accounts for the likely strategic accommodations in *Bush v. Gore.* Even if every camp ruled strictly in accordance with its ideal point, under outcome voting the result would have been to rule for Bush. This holds even though separate and overlapping majorities prefer resolving each of the two identified dispositive issues in a manner that favors Gore.

If the authors' underlying assumptions hold, the analysis reveals the exceedingly narrow possibilities for strategic behavior in *Bush v. Gore.* The analysis reveals that outcome voting inhibits not only strategic issue identification but also strategic voting on the resolution of issues the justices ultimately identified as controlling. Thus, in an issue-voting regime, the result of this case would have been for Gore, given that separate majorities would have found no violation either of equal protection or of Article II. Under issue voting, the Rehnquist camp would not have been motivated to join in the equal protection analysis to produce a precedent on equal protection, but rather would have done so to create an outcome for Bush. Of course, the outcome-voting regime makes that strategy unnecessary. By instead sticking to their respective ideal points, thereby voting sincerely, outcome-voting allowed the Rehnquist and O'Connor camps to combine for a majority (albeit a split one) ruling for Bush.

Abramowicz and Stearns conclude that the Rehnquist camp might have joined the *per curiam* equal protection analysis not to alter the Court's judgment and not to create an equal protection precedent. Instead, the analysis supports an alternative instrumental justification for a limited instance of strategic behavior, one motivated by political rather than doctrinal concerns. Abramowicz and Stearns contend that it is one thing to decide a case controlling the choice of President by a one-vote margin. It is quite another to control the outcome of a presidential election by one vote through a set of published opinions that reveal separate majority issue resolutions favoring the candidate who lost. Whereas *Bush v. Gore* reveals the limits on the power of individual Justices to vote strategically, it also explains why in that case, which revealed multidimensional and asymmetrical preferences, the concurring Justices likely joined the *per curiam* opinion even without necessarily embracing its reasoning. They did so, the authors claim, to create the appearance of a united front in resolving a case that would inevitably be subject to intense, perhaps unprecedented, media and public scrutiny.

DISCUSSION QUESTIONS

1. Does the attitudinal model described in Chapter 21 provide an adequate account of *Bush v. Gore*? What does the social choice account add to an attitudinal analysis of the case? Can the attitudinal model account for the potential strategic judicial behavior described in the preceding analysis? Why or why not?

2. Is there any theory of precedent discussed in Chapters 21 or 22 that can explain the attitude toward precedent articulated in *Bush v. Gore*, namely, that the case was not intended to have precedential effect? What, if anything, does the *per curiam*'s disclaiming precedential status imply about that case or about judicial precedent more generally? Why do we not see justices more regularly limiting the precedential scope of their opinions? Would allowing justices to designate particular Supreme Court opinions as non-precedential be sound policy? Why or why not?

3. How, if at all, might the outcome and analysis of *Bush v. Gore* change under the approaches offered by Rogers, Post and Salop, Kornhauser and Sager, and Nash? Would any of these authors' alternative voting protocols have produced a more preferable outcome in the case? Why or why not?

4. Does the application of outcome voting in *Bush v. Gore* help to produce an outcome that legitimates the decision? Why or why not? Would an alternative voting protocol have affected the decision's legitimacy? Do you think the case is legitimate? Why or why not?

B. Adarand v. Pena[113]

The next case illustrates another aspect of strategic voting on the Supreme Court, this time in a case that created an enormously influential precedent affecting race-based set-asides and tiers of scrutiny. This case was decided against the backdrop of a series of equal protection cases involving race-based preferences. After briefly summarizing those cases, we will highlight the particular features of *Adarand* that involve possible strategic voting behavior.

The analysis begins with a longstanding debate among members of the Supreme Court concerning whether to apply the traditional strict scrutiny standard in cases that involve race when the purpose for using race is to benefit that affected minority group. Justice Brennan, joined by other liberal members of the Court, long took the position that although the use of race requires a more exacting standard than rational basis scrutiny, under which most racial classifications would survive judicial challenge, because the use of race in these cases is benign, it is not appropriate to employ strict scrutiny. Chief Justice Rehnquist and other conservative members generally preferred strict scrutiny in all race cases, which would likely disallow benign racial preferences.

[113] Portions of this discussion are adapted from Stearns, *supra* note 27.

In *Fullilove v. Klutznick*,[114] Justice Brennan, writing for a plurality of four, sustained a federal racial set-aside program in a case involving a minority preference program in the context of construction contracting, applying the intermediate scrutiny standard. That standard, associated most notably with sex- or gender-based classifications, requires an important governmental interest and means that substantially further that interest. In *City of Richmond v. J.A. Croson Co.*,[115] a majority rejected the application of the *Fullilove* standard to a program adopted by the city of Richmond, Virginia. The program was designed to mirror the federal program sustained under intermediate scrutiny in *Fullilove. Croson* instead applied strict scrutiny, holding that the states and municipalities held less regulatory power respecting race than Congress, which was expressly given enforcement power under § 5 of the Fourteenth Amendment.

In *Metro Broadcasting, Inc. v. FCC*,[116] Justice Brennan for the first time succeeded in securing majority support for the application of intermediate scrutiny in the context of a racial preference for broadcast licensing as implemented by the Federal Communications Commission (FCC). In sustaining the FCC order under the intermediate scrutiny test, the *Metro Broadcasting* Court was able to distinguishing *Croson* and to afford precedential status to the intermediate scrutiny test previously announced in the *Fullilove* plurality decision, at least for benign racial classifications enacted at the federal level.

Against this background, the Supreme Court once more confronted the question of what standard to apply in the context of race-based set-asides in the landmark 1995 decision, *Adarand Constructors, Inc. v. Pena*.[117] In *Adarand*, the Central Federal Lands Highway Division (CFLHD), part of the United States Department of Transportation (DOT), included a federal racial set-aside incentive for highway contracting. Adarand had submitted a lower bid than the successful bidder, Gonzales, a covered minority under the incentive scheme. The general contractor stated that but for the incentive program, he would have accepted Adarand's lower bid.

Although Justice O'Connor wrote a majority opinion for the *Adarand* Court, the decision contained an important anomaly. In this instance, the relevant text *precedes* the formal majority opinion. The reporter's entry reads as follows:

> O'Connor, J., announced the judgment of the Court and delivered an opinion with respect to Parts I, II, III-A, III-B, III-D, and IV, which was for the Court except insofar as it might be inconsistent with the views expressed in the concurrence of Scalia, J., and an opinion with respect to Part III-C. Parts I, II, III-A, III-B, III-D, and IV of that opinion were joined by Rehnquist, C.J., and Kennedy and Thomas, JJ., and by Scalia, J., to the extent heretofore indicated; and Part III-C was joined by Kennedy, J. Scalia, J., and Thomas, J., filed opinions concurring in part and concurring in the judgment. Stevens, J., filed a dissenting opinion, in which Ginsburg, J., joined. Souter, J., filed a dissenting

[114] 448 U.S. 448 (1980).

[115] 488 U.S. 469 (1989).

[116] 497 U.S. 547 (1990).

[117] 515 U.S. 200 (1995).

opinion, in which Ginsburg and Breyer, JJ., joined. Ginsburg, J., filed a dissenting opinion, in which Breyer, J., joined.[118]

The *Adarand* Court produced a total of five separate opinions. These included Justice O'Connor's opinion, in part for a majority and in part for herself and Justice Kennedy; Justice Scalia's partial concurrence and partial concurrence in the judgment; and three dissents, authored by Justices Stevens, Souter, and Ginsburg. In its simplest form, the *Adarand* case represents a five-to-four split on the question whether to apply strict or intermediate scrutiny to this racial preference, with the conservative members of the Court applying strict scrutiny, thereby striking the challenged program down. As in *Bush v. Gore*, however, beneath this surface-level agreement rested a set of fault lines that involved considerable disagreement not only between the majority and dissent but also among members of the apparent majority coalition. Also, as in *Bush v. Gore*, an interesting question arises as to why at least one member of that coalition joined despite significant differences between the two relevant ideal points.

The primary question in *Adarand* centered on which tier of scrutiny to apply when assessing a benign race-based classification. In her opinion for the Court, Justice O'Connor reviewed the doctrinal history and then stated:

> A year [after *Croson*, a case applying strict scrutiny to a municipal race-based set-aside], however, the Court took a surprising turn. *Metro Broadcasting, Inc.* v. *FCC* involved a Fifth Amendment challenge to two race-based policies of the Federal Communications Commission (FCC). In *Metro Broadcasting*, the Court repudiated the long-held notion that "it would be unthinkable that the same Constitution would impose a lesser duty on the Federal Government" than it does on a State to afford equal protection of the laws. It did so by holding that "benign" federal racial classifications need only satisfy intermediate scrutiny, even though *Croson* had recently concluded that such classifications enacted by a State must satisfy strict scrutiny. "[B]enign" federal racial classifications, the Court said, "—even if those measures are not 'remedial' in the sense of being designed to compensate victims of past governmental or societal discrimination—are constitutionally permissible to the extent that they serve *important* governmental objectives within the power of Congress and are *substantially related* to achievement of those objectives." The Court did not explain how to tell whether a racial classification should be deemed "benign," other than to express "confiden[ce] that an 'examination of the legislative scheme and its history' will separate benign measures from other types of racial classifications."
>
> Applying this test, the Court first noted that the FCC policies at issue did not serve as a remedy for past discrimination. Proceeding on the assumption that the policies were nonetheless "benign," it concluded that they served the "important governmental objective" of "enhancing broadcast diversity," and that they were "substantially related" to that objective. It therefore upheld the policies.

---

[118] 515 U.S. at 202–03 (internal citations omitted).

By adopting intermediate scrutiny as the standard of review for congressionally mandated "benign" racial classifications, *Metro Broadcasting* departed from prior cases in two significant respects. First, it turned its back on *Croson*'s explanation of why strict scrutiny of all governmental racial classifications is essential:

> Absent searching judicial inquiry into the justification for such race based measures, there is simply no way of determining what classifications are 'benign' or 'remedial' and what classifications are in fact motivated by illegitimate notions of racial inferiority or simple racial politics. Indeed, the purpose of strict scrutiny is to 'smoke out' illegitimate uses of race by assuring that the legislative body is pursuing a goal important enough to warrant use of a highly suspect tool. The test also ensures that the means chosen 'fit' this compelling goal so closely that there is little or no possibility that the motive for the classification was illegitimate racial prejudice or stereotype.

We adhere to that view today, despite the surface appeal of holding "benign" racial classifications to a lower standard, because "it may not always be clear that a so-called preference is in fact benign." "[M]ore than good motives should be required when government seeks to allocate its resources by way of an explicit racial classification system."

Second, *Metro Broadcasting* squarely rejected one of the three propositions established by the Court's earlier equal protection cases, namely, congruence between the standards applicable to federal and state racial classifications, and in so doing also undermined the other two—skepticism of all racial classifications and consistency of treatment irrespective of the race of the burdened or benefited group. Under *Metro Broadcasting*, certain racial classifications ("benign" ones enacted by the Federal Government) should be treated less skeptically than others; and the race of the benefited group is critical to the determination of which standard of review to apply. *Metro Broadcasting* was thus a significant departure from much of what had come before it.

The three propositions undermined by *Metro Broadcasting* all derive from the basic principle that the Fifth and Fourteenth Amendments to the Constitution protect *persons*, not *groups*. It follows from that principle that all governmental action based on race—a *group* classification long recognized as "in most circumstances irrelevant and therefore prohibited,"—should be subjected to detailed judicial inquiry to ensure that the *personal* right to equal protection of the laws has not been infringed. These ideas have long been central to this Court's understanding of equal protection, and holding "benign" state and federal racial classifications to different standards does not square with them. "[A] free people whose institutions are founded upon the doctrine of equality," should tolerate no retreat from the principle that government may treat people differently because of their race only for the most compelling reasons. Accordingly, we hold today that all racial classifications, imposed by whatever federal, state, or local governmental actor, must be analyzed by a reviewing court under strict scrutiny. In other words, such classifications are

> constitutional only if they are narrowly tailored measures that further compelling governmental interests. To the extent that *Metro Broadcasting* is inconsistent with that holding, it is overruled.[119]

In Part III.D of her opinion for the Court, Justice O'Connor responded to concerns that by raising the standard to strict scrutiny, the result would be to imperil any potentially benign use of race. Specifically, Justice O'Connor raised the possibility that even under the chosen standard, some challenged statutes might survive. O'Connor explained:

> Finally, we wish to dispel the notion that strict scrutiny is "strict in theory, but fatal in fact." The unhappy persistence of both the practice and the lingering effects of racial discrimination against minority groups in this country is an unfortunate reality, and government is not disqualified from acting in response to it. As recently as 1987, for example, every Justice of this Court agreed that the Alabama Department of Public Safety's "pervasive, systematic, and obstinate discriminatory conduct" justified a narrowly tailored race-based remedy. When race-based action is necessary to further a compelling interest, such action is within constitutional constraints if it satisfies the "narrow tailoring" test this Court has set out in previous cases.[120]

Justice Scalia produced a short concurring opinion, which we reproduce in full:

> I join the opinion of the Court, except Part III-C, and except insofar as it may be inconsistent with the following: In my view, government can never have a "compelling interest" in discriminating on the basis of race in order to "make up" for past racial discrimination in the opposite direction. Individuals who have been wronged by unlawful racial discrimination should be made whole; but under our Constitution there can be no such thing as either a creditor or a debtor race. That concept is alien to the Constitution's focus upon the individual, see Amdt. 14, § 1 ("[N]or shall any State . . . deny *to any person*" the equal protection of the laws) (emphasis added), and its rejection of dispositions based on race, see Amdt. 15, § 1 (prohibiting abridgment of the right to vote "on account of race"), or based on blood, see Art. III, § 3 ("[N]o Attainder of Treason shall work Corruption of Blood"); Art. I, § 9 ("No Title of Nobility shall be granted by the United States"). To pursue the concept of racial entitlement—even for the most admirable and benign of purposes—is to reinforce and preserve for future mischief the way of thinking that produced race slavery, race privilege and race hatred. In the eyes of government, we are just one race here. It is American.
>
> It is unlikely, if not impossible, that the challenged program would survive under this understanding of strict scrutiny, but I am content to leave that to be decided on remand.[121]

---

119 *Id.* at 225–27 (citations omitted).

120 *Id.* at 237 (citations omitted).

121 *Id.* at 239 (Scalia, J., concurring in part and concurring in the judgment) (citations omitted).

The dissenters rejected the application of strict scrutiny altogether. Justice Souter's opinion provided a detailed analysis,[122] which reviewed some of the themes discussed in connection with *Metro Broadcasting*.

Consider why Justice Scalia, who expressly rejected Justice O'Connor's strict scrutiny analysis as not being "strict in theory, but fatal in fact," nonetheless joined this portion of her opinion, and did so subject the caveat that: "In my view, government can never have a 'compelling interest' in discriminating on the basis of race in order to 'make up' for past racial discrimination in the opposite direction."[123] In Scalia's analysis, therefore, strict scrutiny in race cases is always fatal since there is never a sufficiently compelling governmental interest to justify the use of race. And yet, Justice Scalia did join Part III.D of O'Connor's opinion, subject to the unusual caveat described above, which created the possibility that strict scrutiny might be less than fatal.

DISCUSSION QUESTIONS

1. In a more ordinary course of events, we might have expected Justice Scalia to issue a concurrence in the judgment. This would have allowed him to vote consistently with the outcome—striking down the federal race-based preference—while also explaining that the application of strict scrutiny should invariably be fatal to such laws. Can you explain why, instead, Scalia elected to join the O'Connor opinion even though he disagreed on the fundamental question whether strict scrutiny is fatal? Is *Metro Broadcasting* relevant in answering this question? Why or why not?

2. What motivated the differing views on whether strict scrutiny should or not should not be fatal? Is *Grutter v. Bollinger*[124] the Supreme Court decision that sustained the affirmative action program at the University of Michigan Law School, relevant in answering this question? Why or why not? If you think that *Grutter* is relevant, do you also think that anticipating this future case makes Scalia's position strategic? Does it make O'Connor's inclusion of a caveat—strict in theory is not fatal in fact—strategic? Can both positions be strategic? Why or why not?

3. Is *Adarand* consistent or in tension with the attitudinal model? While that model can certainly account for the five-to-four conservative majority, can it also account for Justice Scalia's decision to join the majority opinion, rather than to write a concurrence in the judgment based upon his preferred view that strict scrutiny should be fatal in fact? Why or why not?

4. How does *Adarand* relate to the social analysis of tiers of scrutiny presented in Part III of this chapter? Which approach, that of Brennan in *Metro Broadcasting* or that of O'Connor in *Adarand* makes the presentation of tiers simpler? Which is normatively preferable? Are those the same question? Why or why not?

---

[122] *Id.* at 267–71 (Souter, J., dissenting).

[123] *Id.* at 239 (Scalia, J. concurring).

[124] 539 U.S. 306 (2003).

C. Gonzales v. Carhart

In closing we briefly consider one final case, *Gonzales v. Carhart*,[125] which upheld a federal Partial-Birth Abortion Ban Act. Just seven years earlier, in *Stenberg v. Carhart*,[126] the Supreme Court struck down Nebraska's partial birth abortion ban on the ground that it lacked an exception for the mother's health. The *Gonzales* Court reached a contrary conclusion even though that statute also lacked such a health exception, based upon Congressional findings that such a health exception was not necessary. While the constitutional issues surrounding this issue are interesting in their own right, for our purposes, the more notable point is the breakdown of the Justices and the separate opinion of Justice Thomas. Justice Kennedy wrote for a majority of five to uphold the federal ban. The majority also included Chief Justice Roberts and Justices Scalia, Thomas, and Alito. Justice Thomas filed a separate concurrence that Justice Scalia also joined. Justice Ginsburg wrote a dissent, joined by Justices Stevens, Souter, and Breyer.

Justice Thomas's concurrence was short, and we reproduce it in full:

> I join the Court's opinion because it accurately applies current jurisprudence, including *Planned Parenthood of Southeastern Pa.* v. *Casey*. I write separately to reiterate my view that the Court's abortion jurisprudence, including *Casey* and *Roe* v. *Wade*, has no basis in the Constitution. I also note that whether the Partial-Birth Abortion Ban Act of 2003 constitutes a permissible exercise of Congress' power under the Commerce Clause is not before the Court. The parties did not raise or brief that issue; it is outside the question presented; and the lower courts did not address it.[127]

DISCUSSION QUESTIONS

1. Justice Kennedy formed part of the jointly authored plurality opinion in *Planned Parenthood v. Casey*,[128] which in 1992 revised the 1973 framework set out in *Roe v. Wade*,[129] but which declined to overturn *Roe*'s "essential holding." The *Casey* revision included abandoning the trimester framework and asserting that *Roe* had given inadequate weight to the state's interest in the potentiality of human life represented in the fetus. Based upon *Casey*, it appears likely that Justice Kennedy disagrees with Thomas on the merits of overturning *Roe*. That is certainly less obvious, however, for Chief Justice Roberts and Justice Alito. If, in fact, these two members of the Court agreed that *Roe* should not be retained, should they have joined Justice Thomas's *Gonzales* dissent? Can we infer from their decision not to join that they disagree on the merits? If they agree but did not join, was this decision "strategic"? Why or why not? Are decisions not to join separate opinions, concurrences or dissents, different from decisions not to join controlling opinions? If so, how? Do any of the models set out in Chapter 21 or this chapter help to answer this question? Why or why not?

---

125 550 U.S. 124 (2007).

126 530 U.S. 914 (2000).

127 550 U.S. at 168–69 (Thomas, J., concurring).

128 505 U.S. 833 (1992).

129 410 U.S. 113 (1973).

2. Does the attitudinal model provide insight into the voting patterns in *Gonzales* and the Court's treatment of precedent? Easterbrook argues that when confronted with a case in which following precedent would lead judges to a non-preferred result, the Court prefers to sacrifice transitivity (treating like cases similarly) rather than range (ruling consistently with member selections over all options). Stearns argues that Supreme Court voting rules sacrifice range, but promote adherence to independence. Which view more accurately describes the outcomes and positions of various Justices in *Gonzales* and other abortion cases?

CHAPTER 23

Constitutions (Part 1)

Introduction

Each of the preceding chapters in this part applied public choice to specific governmental institutions: legislatures, the executive branch (including agencies), and the judiciary. This final set of institutional applications explores the implications of public choice for constitutional design and implementation. Constitutions are themselves institutions that result from a series of collective decision-making processes and that motivate other forms of collective action. These include initial drafting, pre-adoption modifications, debates over ratification, voting on ratification, amendments, and implementation and interpretation by various organs of government. Among the primary objectives of constitutions is to establish the legitimate foundations of governmental powers,[1] to allocate those powers among the specific organs of government that the constitution creates or recognizes,[2] and to provide a road map for the development of positive law and policy, including instructions for constitutional change.

Constitutions perform these complex functions in a variety of ways. First, as a *horizontal* matter, constitutions determine within a given level of government, for example, national or state, which institutional bodies possess particular powers. This sometimes includes the power of a given branch of government to establish its internal decision-making procedures. In the United States, this implicates such decision-making processes as bicameralism, presentment, and even constitutional judicial review. Second, as a *vertical* matter, constitutions divide powers among different levels of government: national, state, or local. This analysis implicates questions of federalism and the scope of federal and state governmental powers. Although the precise terminology for these levels of decision-making authority varies among nations, western democracies generally operate in a

[1] Within the United States, this constitutional feature takes a different form in the federal and state contexts. Whereas state constitutions operate on a plenary powers model in which, most notably, legislative power is presumed to exist unless restricted by the state or federal constitutions, the federal Constitution demands a specific or implied delegation of power, usually taken from the preexisting collective powers of the states, as a precondition to its exercise, and also includes express limitations on federal governmental powers. *See, e.g.*, Gibbons v. Ogden, 22 U.S. (9 Wheat.) 1, 233–34 (1824) (Johnson, J., concurring); Maxwell L. Stearns, *The Misguided Renaissance of Social Choice*, 103 YALE L.J. 1219, 1258 (1994).

[2] The United States Constitution, for example, does not create state governments, but recognizes their pre-existing powers. *See, e.g.*, U.S. CONST. amend. X ("The powers not delegated to the United States by the Constitution, nor prohibited by it to the States, are reserved to the States respectively, or to the people.").

manner that includes some important similar structural characteristics. Third, constitutions typically set out enumerated protections of individual liberties. In the United States, this takes expression, most notably, in the Bill of Rights. The enumerated powers are generally not exhaustive, and through various interpretive mechanisms, including most notably judicial review, constitutions also provide a means for recognizing unenumerated rights. Finally, constitutions generally establish mechanisms for internal change, taking the form of amending provisions. In this chapter, we are primarily concerned with structural constitutionalism, rather than with the proper jurisprudential methodologies for constitutional judicial review.[3]

In *Federalist No. 51*, James Madison described a fundamental problem that confronts constitutional architects:

> It may be a reflection on human nature that such devices [taking the form of various structural limitations on governmental institutions] should be necessary to control the abuses of government. But what is government itself but the greatest of all reflections on human nature? If men were angels, no government would be necessary. If angels were to govern men, neither external nor internal controls on government would be necessary. In framing a government which is to be administered by men over men, the great difficulty lies in this: you must first enable the government to control the governed; and in the next place oblige it to control itself. A dependence on the people is, no doubt, the primary control on the government; but experience has taught mankind the necessity of auxiliary precautions.[4]

As Madison observes, the government must be made strong enough "to control the governed," for example by protecting property rights, enforcing contracts, preventing crime, and securing national defense. In the framing of the United States Constitution, these functions would sometimes be performed by the federal government, and other times by the states. Madison further recognized that once the government is established with the necessary powers to promote the general welfare and to preserve the social order, it becomes necessary to restrain the government itself from unduly infringing on individual liberty. Madison's "auxiliary precautions" can be understood as an effort by the Framers of the United States Constitution to strike an appropriate balance that simultaneously ensures that the government is sufficiently strong to secure the legitimate ends of governance but not so strong as to threaten individual liberty.

As with our analysis of other institutions, we do not suggest that public choice, or economics more generally, provides the sole or dominant method of understanding the institutions under review. We do believe, however, that public choice helps to explain several important features about constitutional structure and decision making that remain anomalous when viewed exclusively with more traditional methodologies. As you read the following materials, consider the extent to which those concerns expressed by public choice theorists about developing appropriate mechanisms that limit opportunities for rent seeking by special interests, and that avoid excessive agency costs by governmental

---

[3] For a discussion of that question as it relates to tiers of scrutiny, see *supra* Chapter 22, Part III.

[4] THE FEDERALIST NO. 51, at 322 (James Madison) (Clinton Rossiter ed., 1961).

actors, help to frame the various tradeoffs that confront constitutional architects and those operating within constitutional systems.

Part I recasts Madison's *Federalist No. 51* framing based on the landmark book, *The Calculus of Consent: Logical Foundations of Constitutional Democracy*,[5] by Nobel Laureate James Buchanan and Professor Gordon Tullock,[6] the first work systematically to apply insights from public choice to the specific features of the United States Constitution. Part II assesses three specific features of constitutional governance, each designed to curb excessive governmental powers: supermajority rules, fundamental rights, and exit. Part III reviews the constitutional establishment of, and limits on, executive powers. Part IV discusses an important article by Daryl Levinson and Richard Pildes, titled *Separation of Parties, Not Powers*, which argues that modern constitutional jurisprudence is confounded by the Framers' historically mistaken premise that jealousies would derive primarily from institutionalism rather than from party affiliation.[7]

Chapter 24 continues the analysis of Constitutions. It reviews special attributes of the judiciary, federalism, direct democracy, and the amending process. Each of these chapters closes with applications.

I. BUCHANAN AND TULLOCK, THE CALCULUS OF CONSENT

As previously stated, Buchanan and Tullock were the first scholars to take basic insights from public choice and apply them systematically to the United States Constitution. This work focuses on two important aspects of constitutional design: first, pre-commitment strategies that limit governmental powers and that channel decision making through specified procedures, and second, mechanisms that reduce agency costs by limiting opportunities for government officials to benefit from pursuing objectives that depart from those for whom they are expected to serve and for whose benefit they derive their power.

First, constitutions can be understood as pre-commitment devices that specify that the government will only exercise powers that are properly delegated and in a particular manner, following procedures specified in advance. Although not all such rules are specified in the constitutional text itself, these include rules for enacting legislation, rules for ratifying treaties, rules for impeachment, rules that limit police and prosecutorial authority, rules specifying the scope and limits of governmental powers, rules governing constitutional amendment processes, and rules establishing and limiting constitutional judicial review. These rules can change over time, either based on constitutional amending, or based on new interpretations of the constitutional text. For example, although this was

---

[5] JAMES M. BUCHANAN & GORDON TULLOCK, THE CALCULUS OF CONSENT: LOGICAL FOUNDATIONS OF CONSTITUTIONAL DEMOCRACY (1962).

[6] For an accessible introduction that distinguishes the economic approach to constitutions from alternative perspectives, see James M. Buchanan, *The Constitutional Way of Thinking*, 10 SUP. CT. ECON. REV. 143 (2003). *See also* A.C. Pritchard & Todd J. Zywicki, *Finding the Constitution: An Economic Analysis of Tradition's Role in Constitutional Interpretation*, 77 N.C. L. REV. 409 (1999) (defining "efficiency" purposes of constitutions as creating enforceable supermajoritarian precommitments and reducing agency costs by governmental actors).

[7] Daryl J. Levinson & Richard H. Pildes, *Separation of Parties, Not Powers*, 119 HARV. L. REV. 2311 (2006).

not true originally, since the Warren Court era, the Supreme Court has applied the Bill of Rights both to the federal government and to the states. And although the Equal Protection Clause of the Fourteenth Amendment applies only to the states, the Supreme Court has interpreted the Fifth Amendment, which applies to the federal government, to include the commands of equal protection.

Second, constitutions seek to mitigate the problem of agency costs. In this context, agency costs arise when government actors pursue their own objectives at the expense of those for whom they have been entrusted with delegated powers. Judicial independence, for example, has the potential to reduce agency costs by limiting political pressures on judges not to enforce sometimes unpopular constitutional pre-commitments that limit immediately desired exercise of governmental powers. Alternatively, however, the very same political insulation potentially provides judges with the opportunity to pursue their own private objectives, including leisure or case decisions that infuse ideological predilections or attitudes.[8]

A. The Logical Foundations of Constitutional Democracy

In applying public choice intuitions to the specific context of the United States Constitution, Buchanan and Tullock introduced a novel analytical approach. Legal analysts customarily begin by positing the *ends* of government and then deducing those constitutional rules that will bring about those ends. Buchanan and Tullock, by contrast, first considered the *means* that individuals would agree to use in setting up a constitution for self-governance and then relied upon such means to deduce agreeable ends.

1. Stages of Constitutional Decision Making

Buchanan and Tullock rely upon an exchange model of politics as the fundamental underpinning in understanding constitutional design. A foundational aspect of their analysis involves distinguishing two periods in governmental decision making: first, the "constitutional" stage, and second, the "post-constitutional," or positive law, stage.[9] The constitutional stage establishes the rules for how decisions will be made at the post-constitutional stage. For instance, the constitutional stage determines whether the legislature will take unicameral or bicameral form, whether the head of state will be selected through a Parliamentary (legislatively determined) or Presidential (electorally determined) system, and which substantive regulatory areas will be controlled at the national or state and local levels. Although refinements will continue through such means as practical accommodations, judicial decision making, or even amendment, in general,

---

[8] We explored this theme in Chapters 21 and 22.

[9] While Buchanan and Tullock imagine these stages as forming a chronological sequence, a more nuanced understanding recognizes that constitutional interpretation informs constitutional framing (stage 1) by refining foundational rules that affect those mechanisms governing the creation of positive law (stage 2). This process continues *even though* constitutional interpretation operates concurrently with positive law decision making in stage 2. For an analysis that posits a risk of unifying these stages and of entrenching power elites at one stage to form a preferred constitution in a later stage, see Tom Ginsburg, *Public Choice and Constitutional Design*, *in* ELGAR HANDBOOK ON PUBLIC CHOICE AND PUBLIC LAW 261 (Daniel Farber & Anne Joseph O'Connell eds., 2010).

the structures established in the constitutional stage frame ordinary or positive lawmaking in the post-constitutional stage.

Buchanan and Tullock argue that for some issues, it is likely easier to achieve consensus during the constitutional stage, because at that point individuals are considering general rules intended to govern post-constitutional interactions. In the post-constitutional stage, individuals will be aware of their place in society and thus are apt to be concerned about how proposed policies will likely benefit or harm them. At the constitutional stage, by contrast, policy issues tend to be presented at a higher level of generality. Thus, at the stage of constitutional formation, there is likely to be greater agreement on fair and neutral rules.[10] The authors liken the selection of constitutional rules to the adoption of rules at the outset of playing a game, where none of the players can anticipate which specific rules might benefit her or him during a particular round of play. As a result, as compared with rulemaking in the post-constitutional stage, this reduces conflicts of interest that will inevitably arise. As Buchanan and Tullock observe:

> This is not to suggest that he will act contrary to his own interest; but the individual will not find it advantageous to vote for rules that may promote sectional, class, or group interests because, by presupposition, he is unable to predict the role that he will be playing in the actual collective decision-making process at any particular time in the future. He cannot predict with any degree of certainty whether he is more likely to be in a winning or a losing coalition on any specific issue. Therefore, he will assume that occasionally he will be in one group and occasionally in the other. His own self-interest will lead him to choose rules that will maximize the utility of an individual in a series of collective decisions with his own preferences on the separate issues being more or less randomly distributed.[11]

Are Buchanan and Tullock correct in their assumption that at the constitutional stage of inquiry individuals will be largely unable to anticipate what the likely impact of the rules will be on their individual circumstances? Consider, for example, the very different statuses envisioned during the post-constitutional stage based on race and sex at the time of the Constitution's framing. If persons cannot fully anticipate their status at the time of constitutional formation, will this remain true when the Constitution is subsequently amended? Will it be true when the federal judiciary interprets the Constitution through the process of judicial review? Bear these questions in mind as you read the discussion of the constitutional amendments in Chapter 24.

2. *Normative Foundations of Constitutional Decision-Making Rules: The Primacy of Unanimity*

In the context of collective decision making, Buchanan and Tullock posit that unanimity holds conceptual primacy. Like Pareto superiority, its counterpart in the private sphere, as a theoretical matter unanimity appears to avoid the problem of "externalities."[12]

---

[10] *See* BUCHANAN & TULLOCK, *supra* note 5, at 78.

[11] *Id.*

[12] As we will later see, this assertion creates potential difficulty in the context of constitutional choice. *See infra* pp. 1015–1017.

As a consequence, this decision-making rule uniquely ensures that collective action will be accomplished in a manner likely to further social welfare.[13]

To appreciate the authors' argument, let us briefly return to the context of private exchange. In assessing whether a given exchange is welfare enhancing, meaning that it benefits society by producing wealth, it is insufficient to rest upon the claimed benefits to the actual parties to the exchange. We must also consider any external costs (or benefits) to third parties. For example, while *A* might employ *B* to provide a service on mutually beneficial terms, in performing the contract terms, *B* might cause pollution to *C*'s detriment. Because *A* and *B* consent to the transaction, we can infer from their revealed preferences that both are thereby better off. Unless *A* and *B* compensate *C* for any resulting externality, however, we cannot know if the transaction is social welfare enhancing or, instead, if it risks negative social costs. If those suffering externalities are fully compensated and thus voluntarily consent to the transaction, then we can infer that exchange improves social welfare by making at least one party better off and leaving no one worse off. If, instead, the potential gains to *A* and *B* are insufficient to compensate *C*, then proceeding with the transaction risks reducing social welfare.

Although the Pareto criterion (exchange benefiting at least one person without harming others) represents a normatively appealing measure of social welfare, it poses intractable difficulties in implementation. The difficulties include identifying and bargaining with all individuals who might suffer from a given collective action. In addition, to ensure the optimal allocation of resources (meaning not only that individual transactions are Pareto superior, but also that all such transactions take place with the overall result of Pareto optimality), it is not sufficient to avoid *negative* externalities. It becomes necessary to identify and seek contributions from persons who benefit from *positive* externalities. Given the insuperable practical hurdles associated with locating and compensating potential losers (or seeking contributions from potential winners) from collective action, economists typically substitute Kaldor-Hicks efficiency (allowing gains sufficient for winners to compensate losers, but without actual compensation) as an imperfect proxy.[14]

As the following example illustrates, collective decision making raises social welfare concerns parallel to those that arise in the context of market exchange. Assume that *A* and *B* wish to build a road costing $60, allowing each to benefit by an amount of $25, but providing *C* no benefit.[15] Assume that *A* and *B* vote to fund the road by imposing a tax on all three constituents in equal amounts of $20. If *A* and *B* can force *C* to share this tax burden equally, *C* will suffer a net loss of $20.[16] Under a regime that demands the unanimous consent of all participants, by contrast, *C* would simply veto the project. In this example, under a unanimity rule, only if *A* and *B* gained sufficient social surplus from building the road to compensate *C* for the resulting tax burden would the project proceed.

---

[13] Assuming no mistakes, the unanimity rule would invariably enhance social welfare, but as with any rule, it remains possible that individuals will erroneously proceed with transactions that prove mistaken, and thus reduce, social welfare.

[14] RICHARD A. POSNER, ECONOMIC ANALYSIS OF LAW § 1.2, at 13 (6th ed. 2003).

[15] In this illustration, *A*, *B* and *C* can represent individuals or, more plausibly, neighborhoods within a particular city.

[16] *See supra* Chapter 13.

In fact, however, the total social benefit of the project, $50, is lower than the total social cost of $60. Only by imposing a negative external cost on *C* of $20, effectively forcing a non-beneficiary of the road to subsidize it, do *A* and *B* perceive a net gain of $10 (contributing $40 in taxes toward the road but receiving a combined benefit worth $50).[17]

Buchanan and Tullock argue that in the context of collective choice, unanimity serves the same function as does Pareto superiority in private exchange because it forces the necessary side payments from winners to losers that ensure that resulting transactions improve social welfare.[18] In an important passage, Buchanan and Tullock explain that while welfare economists have traditionally focused on private exchange externalities as a normative justification for market regulation, the political process itself is susceptible of generating its own externalities:

> [I]t is especially surprising that the discussion about externality in the literature of welfare economics has been centered on the external costs expected to result from *private* action of individuals or firms. To our knowledge little or nothing has been said about the *external* costs imposed on the individual by *collective* action. Yet the existence of such external costs is inherent in the operation of any collective decision-making rule other than that of unanimity. Indeed, the essence of the collective-choice process under majority voting rules is the fact that the minority of voters are forced to accede to actions which they cannot prevent and for which they cannot claim compensation for [resulting damages]. Note that this is precisely the definition previously given for externality.
>
> [T]he rule of unanimity makes collective decision-making voluntary in [the] sense [that potentially disadvantaged persons possess effective veto power]. Therefore, in the absence of costs of organizing decision-making, voluntary arrangements would tend to be worked out which would effectively remove all relevant externalities. Collectivization, insofar as this is taken to imply some coercion, would never be chosen by the rational individual. As previously emphasized, the individual will choose collectivization only because of its relatively greater efficiency in the organization of decision-making. The existence of external costs (or the existence of any externality) creates opportunities for mutually advantageous "trades" or "bargains" to be made among individuals affected and also profit possibilities for individuals who are acute enough to recognize such situations. Furthermore, if we disregard the costs of making the required arrangements, voluntary action would more or less automatically take place that would be sufficient to "internalize" all [externalities], that is, to reduce expected external costs to zero. As implied earlier, all ordinary market exchange is, in a real sense, directed toward this end. Moreover, if there were no costs of organizing such exchanges, we could expect marketlike arrangements to expand to the point where all conceivable relevant externalities would be eliminated.[19]

---

[17] This example is drawn from the discussion in Chapter 18, at 33 (discussing example by Bill Eskridge). For a discussion of the related concept of forced riding, see *supra* Chapter 1, at 18–19.

[18] BUCHANAN & TULLOCK, *supra* note 5, at 92.

[19] *Id.* at 89–90.

Buchanan and Tullock treat two different costs as externalities: first, those costs posed by activities that arise from adverse, or downstream, effects on third parties; and second, the tax burdens imposed on those forced to fund projects that provide them (as with *C* in our road hypothetical) with no corresponding benefit. Thus, Buchanan and Tullock state:

> The private operation of the neighborhood plant with the smoking chimney may impose external costs on the individual by soiling his laundry, but this cost is no more external to the individual's own private calculus than the tax cost imposed on him unwillingly in order to finance the provision of public services to his fellow citizen in another area.[20]

Whatever difficulties the Pareto criterion poses for private market exchange are potentially exacerbated in the context of collective decision making. We can frame the difficulty in terms of two kinds of transactions costs. First, a unanimity standard for collective action would pose considerable costs associated with identifying and negotiating with everyone who potentially suffers adverse consequences from a proposed collective decision. Second, unanimity invites a separate problem of strategic bargaining. By affording each individual full veto power over any proposed collective choice, unanimity would invite strategic behavior in which rational individuals would seek to secure a disproportionate share of the surplus resulting from welfare-enhancing collective action—perhaps even a complete bargaining breakdown—*whether or not* that action adversely affects them.[21]

DISCUSSION QUESTIONS

To what extent does the road hypothetical require assuming a single period of play? Would anticipating multiple rounds of play reduce the likelihood that *A* and *B*, who want the road, would support the welfare reducing result of spending $60 for a project with a social value of $50 by placing *C*, who receives no benefit, in the position of a forced rider?[22] Why or why not?

Consider the argument that the Buchanan and Tullock analysis of the unanimity baseline as a precondition to collective action implicitly limits social welfare considerations to payoffs and losses among private market participants. How, if at all, might the analysis change if the

---

[20] *Id.* at 65–66. The authors further suggest that when collective action is not constrained by institutions such as private property, government externalities might loom larger than private market externalities. One way to frame the Buchanan and Tullock analysis is to distinguish between "political" externalities (those identified by Buchanan and Tullock as created by collective action, which includes what we have previously introduced as forced riding) and "economic" externalities (those created by private market actors). *See* Todd J. Zywicki, *Environmental Externalities and Political Externalities: The Political Economy of Environmental Regulation and Reform*, 73 TUL. L. REV. 845 (1999).

[21] Some evidence from experimental economics indicates that the strategic bargaining problem might not be as important in practice as in theory and that the threat of strategic bargaining does not increase as group size increases and may actually fall. *See* DENNIS C. MUELLER, PUBLIC CHOICE III, at 73 (2003) (citing the experimental results of Vernon L. Smith and specifically the results of Elizabeth Hoffman & Matthew L. Spitzer, *Experimental Tests of the Coase Theorem with Large Bargaining Groups*, 15 J. LEGAL STUD. 149, 151 (1986), for the finding that "efficiency improved with larger groups").

[22] For a related discussion, see *supra* Chapter 14 (discussing vote-trading hypothetical) and Chapter 18 (same).

authors were to extend the sphere of inquiry to include the potential payoffs or losses among legislators? Do such cases as *Lochner v. New York*,[23] recognizing a right of economic substantive due process, on the one hand, and *West Coast Hotel Co. v. Parrish*,[24] applying rational basis scrutiny to economic regulations of working conditions, on the other, demonstrate the inevitability at some point within a constitutional democracy of choosing whether to adhere to the unanimity norm in either the market or the legislative spheres?[25] If so, does public choice analysis provide the framework for choosing which normative baseline to apply? Why or why not?

B. Specific Features of Constitutional Design

Buchanan and Tullock afford unanimity a privileged analytical position when assessing the efficiency of collective choice. But as previously noted, unanimity, like Pareto efficiency, proves unworkable in practice as a feature of constitutional design. With respect to the Pareto standard for private action, because of the insuperable practical hurdles associated with locating and compensating potential losers (or seeking contributions from potential winners) from collective action, economists use Kaldor-Hicks as an alternative efficiency measure.

Buchanan and Tullock claim that once we abandon the unanimity benchmark, no obvious normatively superior decision-making rule emerges. Each alternative presents its own set of conceptual difficulties. Buchanan and Tullock approach the choice of imperfect alternatives to unanimity by focusing on two problems that are inherent in collective choice—*external costs* and *decision costs*—and they propose that the optimal decision-making rule minimizes the sum of these costs.[26]

The *External-Costs Function* describes "for the single individual with respect to a single activity, the costs that he expects to endure as a result of the actions of others [as a function of] the number of individuals who are required to agree before a final political decision is taken for the group."[27] As noted above, collective decision making can impose externalities where certain individuals are forced to bear greater costs than benefits from a particular collective decision. As a result, the expected *external* costs of a given collective decision (measured in present value terms) will be downward-sloping as the number of individuals needed to secure agreement increases. Thus, where the consent of only one or a few are needed for collective action, the expected external costs for all citizens in the polity will be relatively high, whereas if the consent of many members is needed, then expected external costs will be relatively low.

---

[23] 198 U.S. 45 (1905).

[24] 300 U.S. 379 (1937).

[25] For a related discussion, see *supra* Chapter 13 (discussing the tradeoff between honoring the unanimity norm in the market and legislative spheres). For a discussion demonstrating the possibility that in a direct democracy in which Coasian assumptions apply, unanimous consent to democratic action has the potential to produce the same results as private market unanimity since winners and losers could be fully compensated in both spheres, see James M. Buchanan, *The Coase Theorem and the Theory of the State*, 13 NAT. RESOURCES J. 579, 583–84 (1973).

[26] Portions of the discussion that follow are adapted from MAXWELL L. STEARNS, PUBLIC CHOICE AND PUBLIC LAW: READINGS AND COMMENTARY 409–17 (1997).

[27] BUCHANAN & TULLOCK, *supra* note 5, at 64.

The *Decision-Making Costs* function is the private costs that each member of the group must incur to participate in making a decision. As an initial matter, these costs include those private costs required to simply inform oneself about the decision to be made and to make up one's mind concerning, for example, such matters as whether to support a higher level of government expenditures or lower taxes. But such costs also include the time and effort to secure agreement with other group members. The costs of securing agreement take two forms. First, they include the costs of negotiation among the parties to reach agreement. As the size of the relevant group increases, thereby increasing the number of people who must consent, the negotiation costs of reaching agreement also rises. Second, such costs include the costs of dealing with strategic holdouts. As the percentage of the group needed to reach agreement rises, so too do holdouts' incentives and opportunities. Buchanan and Tullock explain:

> [Our] bargaining-cost function operates in two ranges: in the lower reaches it represents mainly the problems of making up an agreed bargain among a group of people, any one of whom can readily be replaced. Here, as a consequence, there is little incentive to invest resources in strategic bargaining. Near unanimity, investments in strategic bargaining are apt to be great, and the expected costs very high.[28]

With respect to the decision-making costs function, therefore, the costs of reaching agreement will increase at an increasing rate as the number of individuals required to agree to a proposed collective action increases.

The cost functions are depicted on the graph below:[29]

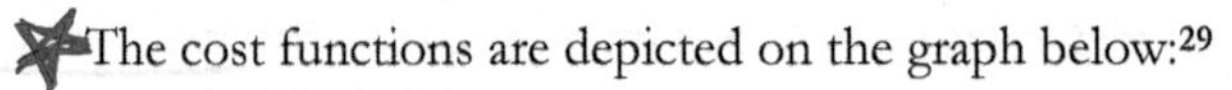

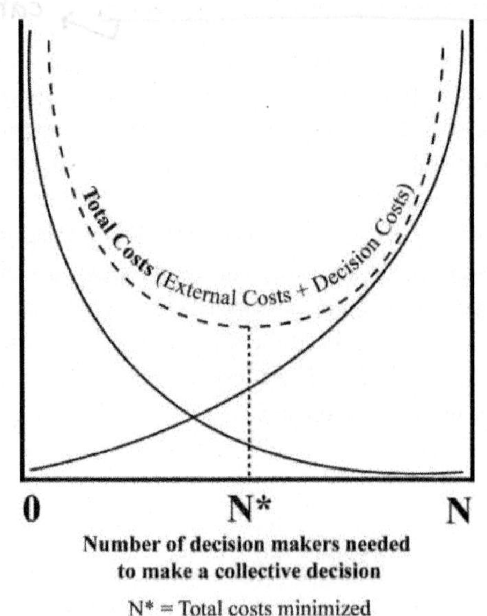

Figure 23:1

28 *Id.* at 69.

29 STEARNS, *supra* note 26, at 410.

Buchanan and Tullock argue that decision makers would choose the decision-making rule that minimizes the sum of external and decision-making costs.[30]

C. Limitations to the Buchanan and Tullock Decision-Making Model

The preceding Buchanan and Tullock model of collective decision making describes the dynamics of achieving consensus within a direct democracy.[31] Most political decisions, however, are made, instead, by representative government. In *Federalist No. 10*, James Madison likewise demonstrated that direct democracy is impractical as a consequence of the decision costs associated with direct public participation, in addition to inviting problems associated with the "violence of factions." As a result, Madison maintained that representative democracy is not only necessary to reduce decision-making costs, but also that it is an important means of reducing the probability of laws that are the product of factional violence.

Madison recognized that *factions*, what we call interest groups, are inevitable in a free society. People who inevitably hold rival economic interest (such as debtors versus creditors), behaving rationally, will seek to influence governmental policy to their advantage. A central function of the Constitution, Madison suggests, is to allow meaningful democratic participation among such interests without falling victim to destructive factional violence.

Madison identified two principal devices that help to achieve this goal: (1) the removal of the government in a large republic from local prejudices through the institution of representative democracy; and (2) the division of Congress into two chambers, meaning bicameralism. Not surprisingly, each solution raises problems of its own.

1. *Representative Democracy*

Madison argued first for the superiority of representative democracy to direct democracy:

> The two great points of difference between a democracy and a republic are: first, the delegation of the government. . . .
>
> The effect of the first difference is, on the one hand, to refine and enlarge the public views by passing them through the medium of a chosen body of citizens, whose wisdom may best discern the true interest of their country and whose patriotism and love of justice will be least likely to sacrifice it to temporary or partial considerations. Under such a regulation it may well happen that the public voice, pronounced by the representatives of the people, will be more consonant to the public good than if pronounced by the people themselves, convened for the purpose. On the other hand, the effect may be

[30] The cost-minimization point might be to the left or right of the intersection of the two separate cost curves depending upon their slopes.

[31] Of course, the same tradeoff between decision and external costs can be used to assess dynamics within representative legislatures.

> inverted. Men of factious tempers, of local prejudices, or of sinister designs, may, by intrigue, by corruption, or by other means, first obtain the suffrages, and then betray the interests of the people.[32]

Madison further analyzed the optimal size of government as follows:

> In the first place it is to be remarked that however small the republic may be the representatives must be raised to a certain number in order to guard against the cabals of a few; and that however large it may be they must be limited to a certain number in order to guard against the confusion of a multitude. Hence, the number of representatives in the two cases not being in proportion to that of the constituents, and being proportionally greatest in the small republic, it follows that if the proportion of fit characters be not less in the large than in the small republic, the former will present a greater option, and consequently a greater probability of a fit choice.
>
> . . . .
>
> . . . Extend the sphere and you take in a greater variety of parties and interests; you make it less probable that a majority of the whole will have a common motive to invade the rights of other citizens; or if such a common motive exists, it will be more difficult for all who feel it to discover their own strength and to act in unison with each other. Besides other impediments, it may be remarked that, where there is a consciousness of unjust or dishonorable purposes, communication is always checked by distrust in proportion to the number whose concurrence is necessary.[33]

Although not framed in terms of external and decision costs, Madison's analysis resembles the tradeoffs that Buchanan and Tullock identify, as reflected Figure 23:1. Madison considers representative democracy, with large districts that combine multiple interests, superior to direct democracy in frustrating majority factions and promoting public-benefiting legislation.

At the same time, representative government raises a new problem of agency costs as elected representatives might hold preferences that diverge from those of their constituencies. Madison acknowledges the potential for disloyal agents, "Men of factious tempers, of local prejudices, or of sinister designs, may, by intrigue, by corruption, or by other means, first obtain the suffrages, and then betray the interests, of the people."[34] Agency costs represent the divergence between the preferences of the voter, or principal, and the policy chosen by the legislator, or agent. Agency costs are distinct from costs imposed by majorities on minorities. Recall that Madison posited that the latter costs will be reduced by representative government. Agency costs are imposed by government officials on the public at large when legislators pursue personal interests contrary to constituent interests. Agency costs are an inevitable feature of representative government. If all voters participated in the creation of public policy, as in the idealized New England

---

32 The Federalist No. 10, at 50 (James Madison) (Clinton Rossiter ed., 1961).

33 *Id.* at 50–51.

34 *Id.* at 50.

town meeting, agency costs would, in theory, be eliminated, although that benefit would likely be overwhelmed by other costs.

There is thus an inherent tradeoff between direct and representative democracy: reducing decision costs raises agency costs, and the reverse also holds. Reducing agency costs raises decision-making costs by requiring greater public participation and less delegation of authority to elected officials. Similarly, reducing the size of the constituency of elected officials will tend to reduce agency costs by making constituent monitoring more effective. As district sizes are reduced, however, the size of the legislature must increase. Enlarging the size of the legislature reduces the likelihood of a sharp divergence between the views of those who govern and the views of those whom they represent (agency costs) but, at the same time, increases the costs of reaching a collective decision (decision costs). Conversely, reducing the size of the legislature makes collective decisions easier to reach (reducing decision costs) but increases the risk that the enacted policies will diverge from those that the electorate prefers (increasing agency costs).

2. *Bicameralism*

Madison's second protection against majority faction is bicameralism. This requires that legislation pass through two Houses rather than one, thereby slowing its pace and raising the effective level of consent for legislative action. In explaining the need to divide the legislature into two chambers, Madison stated:

> In republican government, the legislative authority necessarily predominates. The remedy for this inconveniency is to divide the legislature into different branches; and to render them, by different modes of election and different principles of action, as little connected with each other as the nature of their common functions and their common dependence on the society will admit.[35]

Consistent with Madison's insights, Buchanan and Tullock rely upon public choice to explain the normative foundations for bicameralism, a prevalent feature among western democracies.[36] To do so, the authors distinguished two categories of legislative proposals, one involving equal preference intensities among the electorate and the other involving varying preference intensities. As suggested in Chapter 1,[37] logrolling has the potential to enhance welfare when participants (or those they represent) hold varying intensities of preferences. In this sense, logrolling is analogous to voluntary market exchange: It is only because "people place different *marginal* valuations on *scarce* goods"[38] that opportunities for mutually beneficial trades arise. If everyone placed the same marginal valuation on all goods then there would be no reason to expend effort on trading. With equal intensities, those harmed cannot induce those benefiting to trade.[39] Buchanan and Tullock

---

[35] THE FEDERALIST NO. 51, at 322 (James Madison) (Clinton Rossiter ed., 1961).

[36] BUCHANAN & TULLOCK, *supra* note 5, at 233.

[37] For a related discussion, see *supra* Chapter 1 Part III.C.

[38] ARMEN ALCHIAN & WILLIAM R. ALLEN, EXCHANGE & PRODUCTION: COMPETITION, COORDINATION, & CONTROL 45 (3d ed. 1983).

[39] This insight is by no means limited to legislative vote trading. Of the two principle mediums for creating wealth in private markets, production and exchange, the latter rests upon disparate intensities of preference. Professors Alchian and Allen explain:

demonstrate that with equal preference intensities, the requisite consensus level among the electorate to create public policy through the legislature is roughly the same in both a bicameral and unicameral legislature.[40] In the more common case, however, in which intensities are not uniform, Buchanan and Tullock demonstrate that bicameralism substantially—and favorably—alters the calculus of consent.

a. The Theory of Minimum Winning Coalitions Revisited

The analysis of bicameralism returns us to William Riker's theory of minimum winning coalitions.[41] Buchanan and Tullock demonstrate that if we assume enacting legislation is a zero-sum game in which side payments are permitted,[42] then just over one-half of the voters within each district would be a successful voting coalition in electing a representative from that district. In addition, just over one-half of the representatives in the legislature as a whole would be a successful coalition in enacting legislation. The result is that just over one-half of the voters in just over one-half the districts could effectively control legislative policy in a unicameral legislature. In a unicameral legislature with simple majority rule, therefore, just over one-quarter of the population has the potential to become a successful governing coalition, with the result of imposing high external costs, potentially burdening as much as three-fourths of the electorate. Buchanan and Tullock posit that during constitutional formation, a rational populace is likely to adopt either of two devices to increase the size of successful legislative coalitions. The electorate could implement supermajority rule with a unicameral legislature or, alternatively, it could implement simple majority rule in a bicameral legislature.[43] The authors demonstrate that simple majority rule with a bicameral legislature—assuming differing electoral requirements within each chamber[44]—raises the size of successful electoral coalitions from just over one quarter to just over seven-sixteenths.[45] The latter figure, while still less

---

> Trade is commonly believed to occur because people have too much of some goods—that is, they supposedly have a **surplus** of those goods. But this is not so. Trade goes on all the time, but virtually never do we think we have "too much" of things. In fact, trade occurs because participants find it mutually attractive, because people place different *marginal* valuations on *scarce* goods. If my marginal personal value of something you own exceeds your marginal personal value, we would both find it attractive to engage in a sale of some of that good to me, at a price below my marginal personal value and above yours.

ALCHIAN & ALLEN, *supra* note 38, at 45. Stated differently, exchange creates wealth to the extent that the participants procure surpluses, and those surpluses arise only if the participants' intensities of preference are not uniform for the goods or services that are subject to exchange. The same holds true in legislative markets for vote trading.

[40] BUCHANAN & TULLOCK, *supra* note 5, at 243.

[41] *See supra* Chapter 17, at 715–717.

[42] WILLIAM H. RIKER, THE THEORY OF POLITICAL COALITIONS 32 (1962) (positing that "[i]n n-person, zero-sum games, where side-payments are permitted, where players are rational, and where they have perfect information, only minimum winning coalitions occur" (emphasis omitted)).

[43] *See* BUCHANAN & TULLOCK, *supra* note 5, at 242.

[44] The electoral composition will differ, for example, if in the Senate, each member is elected on a state-wide basis and in the House, each member is elected on a smaller district-wide basis. The consensus requirement is broadened because no majority within each House answers to precisely the same electorate.

[45] *See* BUCHANAN & TULLOCK, *supra* note 5, at 244.

than half the population, more closely accords with traditional understandings of majority rule.

To achieve the same consensus requirement in a unicameral legislature, we would need to impose a seven-eighths supermajority voting requirement. That alternative, however, would substantially raise the decisional costs of legislation by allowing legislative minorities of one-eighth of the legislature to block legislation. Moreover, applying the above analysis, a voting minority of one-sixteenth in the population at large could block legislation by electing one-eighth of the legislature. Thus, although supermajority rules reduce external costs, they dramatically increase decision-making costs. In the bicameral legislature, the requisite consensus is raised without affording such a narrow minority within a single chamber—or within the population at large—effective veto power. With simple majority rule in a bicameral legislature (assuming no other impediments to the passage of legislation), blocking legislation requires the consent of a majority within one of the two chambers, each elected from the population as a whole. Based upon this analysis, Buchanan and Tullock posit that bicameralism is preferable to unicameralism because although each mechanism reduces external costs, bicameralism does so with a smaller marginal increase in decision-making costs.

For bicameralism to be effective in raising the effective level of support for a decision, the members of the two houses should respond to different constituencies. The value of bicameralism is diminished to the extent that the constituencies, and hence preferences, of the two houses of a bicameral legislature are similar. With similarly composed constituencies, it becomes possible to replicate the same winning coalition in both houses of the legislature. Distinct constituencies improve the functioning of bicameralism by enhancing effective electoral support for resulting legislation. Two other prominent constitutional features significantly affect the calculus of consent. Whereas bicameralism raises the consensus threshold to just under one half of the population, the presidential veto, discussed more fully below,[46] raises the effective size of minimum winning coalitions to just over one half. If we assume that the President represents the entire electorate, then the veto power, at least in theory, affords a simple majority of the population at large with the power to block legislation.[47] In addition, constitutional judicial review further raises the requisite consensus level for certain categories of legislation in which simple majority rule in a bicameral legislature (and the potential capture by seven sixteenths of the electorate) has the potential to produce significant adverse consequences for affected minorities or with respect to certain fundamental rights.

b. Levmore's Alternative Account of Bicameralism[48]

Now consider Professor Saul Levmore's response to the foregoing Buchanan and Tullock thesis. Levmore questions whether the congressional model of bicameralism provides a good testing ground for the Buchanan and Tullock thesis given that there is considerable overlap among the relevant constituencies in both the Senate and House of Representatives. Within the Senate, the two senators from each state answer to the same

---

[46] *See infra* pp. 1023–1025.

[47] BUCHANAN & TULLOCK, *supra* note 5, at 248.

[48] Portions of the discussion that follow are adapted from STEARNS, *supra* note 26, at 414–16.

electorate, and as an extreme case, members of both the House and Senate elected in Wyoming answer to the very same state-wide electorate. In fact, Levmore suggests, one would achieve more diversity in Congress by simply dividing each state in half and having the separate halves of each state choose one Senator, so long as Senate districts were drawn differently from House districts.[49]

Levmore suggests that a better explanation for bicameralism is that it increases the size of the governing electoral coalition while allowing what he terms "strong-Condorcet winners," meaning those Condorcet winners that will prevail in each house on a given issue on matters of national legislative policy, to survive. In addition, Levmore suggests that bicameralism raises costs to agenda setters in each house given that for any bill to pass it must be approved in both houses in the same form.[50] While 26% of the electorate might govern in a bicameral regime, this does not mean that the same minority coalition will remain a stable governing coalition. Instead, with defections and newly formed coalitions, the effective governing coalition might give rise to something that closely resembles a cycling or empty core bargaining game, as coalitions are repeatedly made and broken.[51]

Levmore's larger insight is that solving the consensus problem in a unicameral legislature would require a stringent supermajority rule. The Condorcet criterion is of course grounded in the majoritarian norm,[52] and thus the difficulty with a supermajority voting rule is that it thwarts, rather than furthers, the legislature's ability to ensure that strong Condorcet winners prevail in the legislative process.

How might Buchanan and Tullock respond? Which explanation do you find more persuasive? Why? To what extent is the historical development of bicameralism in the United States consistent or in tension with the models developed by Buchanan and Tullock, on the one hand, and by Levmore, on the other?

c. Bicameralism in Historical Perspective: The Seventeenth Amendment

The theory of bicameralism highlights one frequently overlooked component of the United States Senate as created in the original Constitution. Prior to the enactment of the Seventeenth Amendment in 1913, United States Senators were elected indirectly, selected instead by state legislatures. In practice, some states permitted elections, although formal state legislative ratification was required.[53] By contrast, members of the House of

---

[49] Saul Levmore, *Bicameralism: When Are Two Decisions Better Than One?*, 12 INT'L REV. L. & ECON. 145, 154 (1992). For instance, if we imagine House districts being drawn horizontally across a state, Senate districts could be drawn vertically so as to maximize the diversity between the two Houses.

[50] *Id.* at 147–49, 155–59. Levmore acknowledges that the conference committee, which carries messages between the chambers to a substantial extent, might mitigate this benefit. *Id.* at 148–49.

[51] *See id.* at 151–53. *See also supra* Chapter 13.

[52] For a discussion of the Condorcet criterion, see *supra* Chapter 13.

[53] *17th Amendment to the U.S. Constitution: Direct Election of Senators*, NAT'L ARCHIVES CTR. FOR LEGIS. ARCHIVES (Aug. 15, 2016), https://www.archives.gov/legislative/features/17th-amendment; Jay S. Bybee, *Ulysses at the Mast: Democracy, Federalism, and the Sirens' Song of the Seventeenth Amendment*, 91 NW. U. L. REV. 500 (1996); Ralph Rossum, *Popular Election of Senators*, HERITAGE GUIDE TO THE CONSTITUTION, http://www.

Representatives were always elected directly by the people based on geographic districting. A primary motivation for this arrangement was to place the House and Senate on the basis of different constituencies, in order to slow the process of legislation and to raise the level of consensus necessary for congressional action. Following the earlier quote from *Federalist No. 51*,[54] Madison maintained that relying upon different constituencies would limit factional (or interest group) manipulation of the legislative process:

> Another advantage accruing from this ingredient in the constitution of the Senate is the additional impediment it must prove against improper acts of legislation. No law or resolution can now be passed without the concurrence, first, of a majority of the people, and then of a majority of the States. It must be acknowledged that this complicated check on legislation may in some instances be injurious as well as beneficial; and that the peculiar defense which it involves in favor of the smaller States would be more rational if any interests common to them and distinct from those of the other States would otherwise be exposed to peculiar danger. But as the larger States will always be able, by their power over the supplies, to defeat unreasonable exertions of this prerogative of the lesser States, and as the facility and excess of law-making seem to be the diseases to which our governments are most liable, it is not impossible that this part of the Constitution may be more convenient in practice than it appears to many in contemplation.[55]

Passage of the Seventeenth Amendment in 1913 reduced the "diversity of constituencies" between the House of Representatives and the Senate by placing both houses on more similar constituency bases. One apparent effect of this has been to decrease the costs of federal legislation and thereby increase its volume. To what extent has the reduction in bicameralism corroborated Madison's intuition concerning the importance of dividing Congress and rendering each house accountable to different constituencies as a means of reducing the overall scope of legislation that is "injurious as well as beneficial"?

Todd Zywicki argues that the overall effect of the Seventeenth Amendment might in fact have been biased in favor of increasingly eroding the original bicameral protection of different electoral accountability between the houses, and along with that, exacerbating the ratio of special-interest to general-interest legislation.[56] Zywicki argues that this result was a foreseeable and perhaps even intended consequence of the amendment.

Zywicki also argues that the history of the Seventeenth Amendment illustrates the theory of "Baptists and Bootleggers" described in Chapter 11. On the one hand, the amendment was motivated by the "good government" progressive movement, which was largely premised upon an ideology of spreading democratic forms of governance, and which associated the then-existing system with corruption taking the form of alleged

---

heritage.org/constitution/#!/amendments/17/essays/178/popular-election-of-senators (last visited Oct. 20, 2017).

[54] [].

[55] THE FEDERALIST NO. 62, at 346 (James Madison) (Clinton Rossiter ed., 1961).

[56] *See* Todd J. Zywicki, *Beyond the Shell and Husk of History: The History of the Seventeenth Amendment and Its Implications for Current Reform Proposals*, 45 CLEV. ST. L. REV. 165 (1997); Todd J. Zywicki, *Senators and Special Interests: A Public Choice Analysis of the Seventeenth Amendment*, 73 OR. L. REV. 1007 (1994).

bribes that were claimed to influence the selection of particular Senators. On the other hand, the amendment also received support from the less high-minded desire of special interests that hoped to gain influence over federal legislation and of urban political machines that sought to exert greater influence over electoral politics.

Assuming the accuracy of this historical account, to what extent does it suggest that twentieth-century growth of the federal government was not merely foreseeable, but possibly intended? If so, does public choice theory provide a basis for explaining the result? Can you identify any methods of determining whether in fact the Seventeenth Amendment has caused an increase in special-interest legislation or in the ratio of special to general interest legislation? Is it possible to isolate other factors contributing to the increase in national legislation as compared with the Seventeenth Amendment? If so, how?

II. SUPERMAJORITY RULES, FUNDAMENTAL RIGHTS, AND EXIT

In this part, we consider three separate mechanisms that help to discipline legislatures operating within constitutional systems, including the United States and the several states. These include supermajority rules, which make enacting particular types of legislation, or approving other specified policies falling within the domain of one or both branches of the legislature, more difficult to accomplish; the judicial identification of fundamental rights, typically based on equal protection or due process, which thereby precludes infringing on those rights through the means of ordinary legislation; and jurisdictional competition, often manifested through exit, a disciplining mechanism that operates with greater effect at the local and state levels, than at the national level, given the relative cost differences in relocation across these settings.[57]

A. Supermajority Rules in the U.S. Constitution

Despite concerns about the efficiency of supermajority rules in terms of appropriately balancing decision-making and external costs, the United States Constitution nonetheless includes several specific provisions that demand higher levels of consensus than simple majorities. As an illustration, consider the Constitution's amendment provision, set out in Article V, which provides that proposed amendments will become effective only upon the consent of two-thirds of the United States House of Representatives and Senate as well as three-fourths of the states.[58] Article V imposes greater consensus restrictions on certain possible amendments, including a provision that "no State, without its Consent, shall be deprived of its equal Suffrage in the Senate."[59] The approval of two-thirds of the Senate is required for treaty ratification.[60] While an executive officer can be impeached by a simple majority of the House of Representatives,

---

[57] We do not specifically address capital mobility, a form of exit that affects interjurisdictional competition in attracting business, although it operates on similar principles.

[58] U.S. CONST. art. V.

[59] *Id.*

[60] *Id.* art. II, § 2, cl. 2.

a minimum of two-thirds consent in the Senate is required for conviction.[61] In addition, to override a presidential veto, a two-thirds vote is required in each House of Congress.[62]

1. An Economic Model of Supermajority Rules

Building on the analysis of Buchanan and Tullock, Professors John McGinnis and Michael Rappaport have proposed a general positive and normative theory of supermajority rules under the Constitution.[63] Recall that Buchanan and Tullock premised their argument on the unique normative value of the unanimity benchmark for collective decision making, analogous to the unique status provided to Pareto optimality in standard welfare economics. McGinnis and Rappaport suggest that the argument about the normative value of unanimity should be extended to actions taken by supermajorities as well.

McGinnis and Rappaport maintain that as applied to supermajority rules, the Buchanan and Tullock framing fails to account for the opportunity cost of the forgone social benefits that result from supermajority rules in blocking harmful legislation and for the costs associated with having many different voting rules governing different collective decisions. McGinnis and Rappaport refer to the former as *substitution costs* and to the latter as *administrative costs*.

Substitution costs are defined as those costs that arise when those blocked by a supermajority rule in one legislative arena try to achieve similar results in another arena governed by a less stringent rule. Administrative costs are "the costs of identifying and applying the correct rule governing the legislative action and the costs from mistakenly applying the wrong rule."[64] For example, if a given end can be achieved either through taxation or regulation, and spending laws are subject to a supermajority rule but regulatory laws are not, interest groups will try to gain by regulation what they are unable to gain by appropriation.

McGinnis and Rappaport posit that supermajority voting rules are apt to be efficient when used to inhibit special interests trying to enact legislation and are apt to be inefficient when used to inhibit special interests seeking to block legislation. Based on this premise, the authors advance the following normative proposal:

> On these assumptions, one possible solution is to apply supermajority rule to regulatory legislation and majority rule to deregulatory legislation. This strategy has the advantage of applying the voting rule most appropriate to the array of special interests. . . . [T]he possible disadvantage is an increase in administrative costs.[65]

---

61 *Id.* art. I, § 3, cl. 6.

62 *Id.* art. I, § 7, cl. 3.

63 *See* John O. McGinnis & Michael B. Rappaport, *Majority and Supermajority Rules: Three Views of the Capitol*, 85 TEX. L. REV. 1115 (2007). While the authors present several independent arguments to justify supermajority rules, we focus here only on the argument that builds on the Buchanan and Tullock analysis.

64 *Id.* at 1126.

65 *Id.* at 1139.

McGinnis and Rappaport further claim that decisions made by supermajority rules have a particularly strong normative justification. They maintain that supermajority rules generally reflect a deep, reflective consensus of views among members of society, and are thus particularly worthy of respect when rules enacted through this more demanding process later conflict with other rules adopted by simple majority vote.[66] In addition, the authors maintain, the Constitution, adopted through majoritarian processes, including the original Constitution and the Bill of Rights, reflects deep societal consensus, which created highly effective institutions for self-governance.

McGinnis and Rappaport also argue that the normative weight to be afforded rules adopted by supermajorities implies that in interpreting the Constitution, judges should be guided by the document's original meaning, as the Constitution's express terms were adopted through such demanding processes. By contrast, decisions of the Supreme Court that infuse new meaning to constitutional text are not approved by electoral supermajorities, but rather reflect the view of a majority of the Supreme Court.

QUESTIONS AND COMMENTS

Do you find the McGinnis and Rappaport extension and critique of the Buchanan and Tullock analysis persuasive? Is it feasible to determine what is or is not a "special interest" for purposes of determining when a supermajority rule should or should not be required? Can you identify problems with implementing such a proposal? More generally, what are the costs of increasing the range of regulatory policies subject to supermajority rule?

Might the McGinnis and Rappaport proposal, which counsels for higher levels of deference for laws enacted by supermajorities, itself fall victim to the authors' problem of administrative costs? Consider whether the proposal would create a non-binary status as to the validity of enacted laws. How might that work in practice? What problems might this create for judicial review? For societal reliance on enacted laws? For interest group incentives respecting laws they deem problematic?

Is the extension of the Buchanan and Tullock unanimity analysis to the context of supermajority rules persuasive? How does this relate to the implications of the Condorcet criterion in evaluating voting rules? Does demanding a supermajority rule thwart the Condorcet criterion? If so, should that criterion be thwarted some of the time? All of the time? Only for laws we disfavor? Does the selection of specific contexts for which supermajority rules should or should not apply, for example demanding supermajorities when seeking to enact special interest legislation and abandoning the requirement when seeking to repeal such legislation, suggest that the analysis might be driven by substantive views concerning favored or disfavored laws? How does this relate to Professor Elhauge's observation that public choice analysis often rests upon unstated premises concerning the appropriate extent of interest group involvement? Does the fact that the Constitution was adopted through supermajoritarian processes support the McGinnis and Rappaport argument that these processes further imply that judges should look to the original meaning of the Constitution when engaging in constitutional interpretation? Or would insisting upon original meaning have to be defended on other grounds?

---

[66] *See* JOHN O. MCGINNIS & MICHAEL B. RAPPAPORT, ORIGINALISM AND THE GOOD CONSTITUTION (2013).

B. Fundamental Rights as Effectively Restoring Constitutional Unanimity

A corollary to Buchanan and Tullock's analysis of the optimal level of agreement necessary to take collective action is that failure to attain the required level of agreement results in collective inaction. One implication is that citizens will seek to remove from the public sector authority over decisions when they rationally conclude that regulatory intervention should not be permitted absent a very high level of consensus, perhaps approaching unanimity, a level that might be practically unattainable.[67]

Consider the role of fundamental rights analysis in effectively restoring a rule of unanimity over specified subject areas. Some rights or interests are viewed as so important to the individual that the fear of external costs looms large even in a regime characterized by bicameralism. Many of the provisions of the Bill of Rights reflect this intuition. Consider, for instance, the First Amendment's prohibition on the establishment of religion, at least as it has been interpreted by the Supreme Court.[68] Throughout history, governments have established official religions, and the historical record suggests that this was possibly contemplated at the state level by the Framers of the Bill of Rights, which originally applied only to the federal government.[69] In America today, however, few individuals would consent to the establishment of a particular state-sponsored religion except at extraordinarily high levels of consent, approaching unanimity. Attaining such a high level of agreement is practically impossible, however, although it is possible that a lower level of consensus might be obtainable for generic expressions of belief in respect of a universal deity as is reflected, for example, in the motto "In God We Trust" on coinage or in the general consensus that the inclusion of "one nation under God" in the Pledge of Allegiance does not offend the Establishment Clause.[70] The Constitution's prohibition on the establishment of religion effectively relegates questions of conscience to the sphere of private, non-collective action.

Another area in which constitutions might provide an effective unanimity check on the political process involves rights of the criminally accused. Ordinary political processes might systematically undervalue the rights of the accused in criminal proceedings because most citizens and legislators are apt to be more sympathetic to victims of crime than to

---

[67] Thus, Professor Ginsburg has noted that protecting rights through constitutions reduces the stakes of politics by putting certain important substantive issues off-limits to the political process. *See* Ginsburg, *supra* note 9, at 23–24.

[68] *See, e.g.*, Edwards v. Aguillard, 482 U.S. 578 (1987) (invalidating Louisiana's "Creationism Act" under the Establishment Clause).

[69] *See* Barron v. Baltimore, 32 U.S. (7 Pet.) 243 (1833) (holding that bill of rights does not apply to state governments). For leading historical works, see PHILIP A. HAMBURGER, SEPARATION OF CHURCH AND STATE (2005); LEONARD LEVY, THE ESTABLISHMENT CLAUSE: RELIGION AND THE FIRST AMENDMENT (1994).

[70] As an example of a suit, dismissed for want of standing, that claimed otherwise, see Elk Grove Unified Sch. Dist. v. Newdow, 542 U.S. 1, 4–5 (2004) (denying standing to raise Establishment Clause challenge to inclusion of "under God" in the Pledge of Allegiance).

the criminally accused.[71] This might explain why criminal procedure is a particular focus of constitutional design.[72]

Other constitutional protections can also be explained as limitations on the power of groups to impose external costs on certain individuals. For instance, the requirement that "just compensation" be paid for any taking of private property might reflect the intuition that individuals are generally unwilling to permit collective action that transforms private lands to public use, unless the burdened party is appropriately compensated.[73]

The insight that individuals are unlikely to agree to collective action except at very high levels of consent for some regulatory interventions extends as well to intimate questions of internal family decision making, certain familial relationships (including spousal privilege), and the choice of where to live and raise a family. As Buchanan has observed, an advantage of coupling a sphere of individual liberty with market exchange is allowing individuals and transacting parties to undertake actions that move them from lower to higher levels of social welfare without requiring universal consent.[74]

C. Exit as an Alternative to Unanimity

As an alternative to demanding very high levels of consensus as a means of reducing external costs, individuals can elect to exit the group, thereby extricating themselves from disadvantageous collective decisions. The right of exit implicates federalism, which we explore more fully below. For now, consider that exit enables individuals to effectively truncate the tail of the distribution concerning the Buchanan and Tullock external-cost function. Those who occupy the tail end of this distribution for particular regulatory activity, including for example those who strongly oppose (or support) such policies as the death penalty or abortion regulations have the ability to locate to other jurisdictions whose laws better match their views on these issues. The converse is also true. Exit increases the homogeneity of preferences among those who remain, thereby reducing the slope of the decision costs curve and improving the prospects for collective agreement.

Consider in this context Justice Scalia's partial dissenting opinion in *Planned Parenthood of Southeastern Pennsylvania v. Casey*.[75] Scalia argued that highly contentious constitutional issues are more divisive on a national scale, where persons are likely to embrace very different belief systems, than at a more local level, where similarities in socioeconomic status, education, and religious views tend to produce greater

---

[71] *Cf.* Craig S. Lerner, *Legislators as the "American Criminal Class": Why Congress (Sometimes) Protects the Rights of Defendants*, 2004 U. ILL. L. REV. 599.

[72] Professor Craig Lerner has observed that this might be less true respecting white collar crime. Lerner claims that a sufficient number of elected officials at one time or another might themselves be criminal defendants, or be friends with elected officials accused of crimes, that they will seek to ensure protections of rights specifically in the white collar context, although not necessarily in other criminal law contexts. *Id.* at 628.

[73] *See* Armstrong v. United States, 364 U.S. 40, 49 (1960) ("The Fifth Amendment's guarantee that private property shall not be taken for a public use without just compensation was designed to bar Government from forcing some people alone to bear public burdens which, in all fairness and justice, should be borne by the public as a whole.").

[74] *See* James M. Buchanan, *Social Choice, Democracy, and Free Markets*, 62 J. POL. ECON. 114, 121–22 (1954).

[75] 505 U.S. 833 (1992).

commonality of philosophical views. Scalia maintained that *Roe v. Wade*,[76] which identified a fundamental right to abortion, effectively undercut the possibility of state level resolutions that he believed would provide most people with more satisfying results:

> Profound disagreement existed among our citizens over the issue—as it does over other issues, such as the death penalty—but that disagreement was being worked out at the state level. As with many other issues, the division of sentiment within each State was not as closely balanced as it was among the population of the Nation as a whole, meaning not only that more people would be satisfied with the results of state-by-state resolution, but also that those results would be more stable.[77]

Assuming that Scalia is correct that there is likely a higher degree of agreement on controversial social issues, such as abortion and the death penalty, at the state and local level, as opposed to the national level, is the variance of preference on constitutional issues based on geography an appropriate basis for resting the final policy choice at the state level? Remember the argument about fundamental rights as effectively restoring a rule of unanimity. By labeling abortion a fundamental right, did the *Roe v. Wade* Court effectively categorize abortion as an area in which women seeking to terminate unwanted pregnancies would not agree to allow anything less than unanimity as a precondition to restrictions on this claimed right, at least at certain stages of the pregnancy? Is Scalia's analysis more consistent with an exit model, and is the fundamental rights analysis more consistent with a unanimity model? If so, can the two approaches be reconciled? How? If not, how does one choose which model is more appropriate to the issue of abortion, or for that matter, any claimed constitutional right?

QUESTIONS AND COMMENTS

How does the choice of voting rule change based upon whether the decision is being made by one body acting independently or whether it requires the agreement of more than one body? For instance, treaty approval requires two-thirds support only in the U.S. Senate. Why would the Constitution require unicameralism with a supermajority rule in that context rather than bicameralism with simple majority rule? Does the economic analysis of constitutions provide a compelling explanation? Does the Buchanan and Tullock model help to explain why this power vested with the Senate, rather than House?

In November 2013, the United States Senate changed its internal operating rules to eliminate the filibuster of nominees to the lower federal courts.[78] In April 2017, during the proceedings over Donald Trump's Supreme Court nominee Neil Gorsuch, most Democratic

---

[76] 410 U.S. 113 (1973).

[77] 505 U.S. at 995 (Scalia, J., concurring in the judgment in part and dissenting in part).

[78] Earlier that year, in July 2013, Senate Majority Leader Harry Reid had threatened to eliminate the filibuster for Executive Branch nominees (the so-called nuclear option). That showdown was averted when Republicans and Democrats struck a bargain to allow certain nominees to go forward to a vote. *See* Paul Kane & Ed O'Keefe, *Senate Reaches Tentative Deal on Filibuster Rules*, WASH. POST (July 16, 2013), https://www.washingtonpost.com/politics/senate-poised-to-take-up-key-rule-changes/2013/07/16/167045da-ee1d-11e2-9008-61e94a7ea20d_story.html?hpid=z1&utm_term=.377dd5dc032a. The truce lasted only until November, however, when the Senate voted to formally change their rules to eliminate the filibuster for all nominees except for the Supreme Court.

Senators filibustered Gorsuch's nomination, resulting in the Republicans taking the so-called nuclear option, thereby eliminating the filibuster for Supreme Court confirmations.[79] Under the prior filibuster rule, to invoke cloture and end debate required a supermajority of sixty votes, thus raising the de facto nomination threshold for judicial nominees from 50% to 60%.

Should it make a difference in determining the optimal voting rule (simple majority versus supermajority rule) whether both the President and the Senate are controlled by the same party? Consider the following argument. Appointment of judges potentially imposes external costs on those who disagree with the selection, especially for those judges who are more "extreme" than most in the sense that their preferences differ more substantially from the preferences of the median voter than other judges. When the President and a majority of the Senate are controlled by the same party, the likelihood that judicial nominations will be extreme predictably rises. This heightened risk might suggest the propriety of requiring a higher degree of consensus for decision making when the same party controls the White House and Senate. Is that argument persuasive? Is there a rejoinder to this analysis? If you were empowered to amend the Constitution, would you impose differential consensus requirements for judicial nominees in this circumstance? Why or why not? Should the same analysis apply in other settings involving the Senate's power of advice and consent, such as for cabinet officers?

Consider other contexts in which this model might apply. Might the general requirement of jury unanimity in criminal cases explain the right of litigants to exercise peremptory challenges, thereby allowing the removal of potential "outliers" who might not objectively weigh the evidence and who might thwart unanimity for improper reasons? If so, how does this relate to doctrines that disallow the exercise of peremptory challenges based on such criteria as race or sex?[80]

---

[79] For an account of the Senators who filibustered Gorsuch's nomination and Senators who voted for the nuclear option, see *How Senators Voted on the Gorsuch Filibuster and the Nuclear Option*, N.Y. TIMES (Apr. 6, 2017), https://www.nytimes.com/interactive/2017/04/06/us/politics/gorsuch-supreme-court-vote.html; *see also* Scott Detrow & Nina Totenberg, *Democrats Have the Votes to Filibuster Gorsuch and Force 'Nuclear' Senate Showdown*, NPR (Apr. 3, 2017, 1:19 PM), http://www.npr.org/2017/04/03/522458682/democrats-have-the-votes-to-filibuster-gorsuch-and-force-nuclear-senate-showdown. Among the reasons motivating strong Democratic opposition was the failure of the Republican-controlled Senate to hold hearings on President Barack Obama's nominee, Merrick Garland, to replace Justice Antonin Scalia, who passed away during the final year of Obama's second term. *See* Mike DeBonis, *Judge Dashes Merrick Garland's Final, Faint Hope for a Supreme Court Seat*, WASH. POST (Nov. 18, 2016), https://www.washingtonpost.com/news/powerpost/wp/2016/11/18/judge-dashes-merrick-garlands-final-faint-hope-for-a-supreme-court-seat/?utm_term=.0717d961f42b; Ariane de Vogue & Ashley Killough, *Gorsuch Touts Family, Roots While Democrats Revisit Garland Snub*, CNN (Mar. 20, 2017, 11:48 PM), http://www.cnn.com/2017/03/20/politics/neil-gorsuch-confirmation-hearing/index.html; *Senator Mitch McConnell on Merrick Garland Supreme Court Nomination*, C-SPAN (Mar. 16, 2016), https://www.c-span.org/video/?c4585255/senator-mitch-mcconnell-merrick-garland-supreme-court-nomination.

[80] Batson v. Kentucky, 476 U.S. 79 (1986) (demanding prosecution make neutral proffer when challenged for pattern of race-based peremptories); Powers v. Ohio, 499 U.S. 400 (1991) (extending *Batson* rule to apply to defense based on third-party standing); J.E.B. v. Alabama *ex rel.* T.B., 511 U.S. 127 (1994) (extending *Batson* rule to gender context).

III. EXECUTIVE POWERS

A. Executive Veto as "Tricameralism"

While a simplified constitutional analysis might suggest that the President is empowered to execute laws created by Congress, the reality is more complex. The United States Constitution carves out a large role for the President in the enactment of congressional policy. Article I, § 7 provides that for a bill to become law, it must pass both Houses of Congress in identical form and be presented to the President, who then has the power to sign it into law or to veto it.

As an initial approximation, we can model the President's veto power as creating a "tricameral" legislature with the President serving as the "third house," whose approval is required for proposed legislation to become law. The analogy is, of course, imperfect in that unlike the two Houses of Congress, the President is presented with a binary choice to accept or to veto proposed bills. Nonetheless, applying the Buchanan and Tullock framework, the presidential veto enhances the diversity of constituencies required to enact legislation. Whereas members of the House of Representatives represent geographic districts, and Senators represent states as a whole, the President represents the entire nation. At the same time, requiring consent of a third House raises decision-making costs.

At one level, the veto might suggest an additional safeguard against interest-group driven, or otherwise undesirable, legislation. Alternatively, it might be viewed as a means of ensuring that only those legislative bargains approved by a majority of the voters are likely to become law, thereby increasing the effective size of governing coalitions.[81] If so, the veto helps control the external costs that arise when discrete groups form successful legislative coalitions that impose such costs on the electorate. On the other hand, the President might be responsive to well-organized interest groups, albeit different ones, perhaps, than those influencing Congress. If so, the system might exacerbate special-interest influence over lawmaking.[82]

In *Federalist No. 73*, Alexander Hamilton argues that the veto would help frustrate majority faction and special-interest influence on legislation.[83] Hamilton argues:

> [I]t furnishes an additional security against the enaction of improper laws. It establishes a salutary check upon the legislative body, calculated to guard the community against the effects of faction, precipitancy, or of any impulse unfriendly to the public good, which may happen to influence a majority of that body.
>
> The propriety of a negative has, upon some occasions, been combated by an observation that it was not to be presumed a single man would possess more virtue and wisdom than a number of men; and that unless this presumption

[81] *See* W. Mark Crain & Robert D. Tollison, *The Executive Branch in the Interest-Group Theory of Government*, 8 J. LEGAL STUD. 555, 556–57 (1979).

[82] Peter H. Aranson, Ernest Gellhorn & Glen O. Robinson, *A Theory of Legislative Delegation*, 68 CORNELL L. REV. 1, 41 (1982).

[83] We do not discuss here Hamilton's separate argument that the veto is necessary for the Executive to prevent encroachments on his power by the legislature.

> should be entertained, it would be improper to give the executive magistrate any species of control over the legislative body.
>
> But this observation, when examined, will appear rather specious than solid. The propriety of the thing does not turn upon the supposition of superior wisdom or virtue in the executive, but upon the supposition that the legislature will not be infallible; that the love of power may sometimes betray it into a disposition to encroach upon the rights of other members of the government; that a spirit of faction may sometimes pervert its deliberations; that impressions of the moment may sometimes hurry it into measures which itself, on maturer reflection, would condemn. The primary inducement to conferring the power in question upon the executive is to enable him to defend himself; the secondary one is to increase the chances in favor of the community against the passing of bad laws, through haste, inadvertence, or design. The oftener the measure is brought under examination, the greater the diversity in the situations of those who are to examine it, the less must be the danger of those errors which flow from want of due deliberation, or of those missteps which proceed from the contagion of some common passion or interest. It is far less probable that culpable views of any kind should infect all the parts of the government at the same moment and in relation to the same object than that they should by turns govern and mislead every one of them.[84]

Hamilton further observes that the effect of this tricameral system is to frustrate the enactment of good laws as well as bad, but that by raising the effective level of consent for the proposed legislation, the veto will proportionately block more bad than good laws:

> It may perhaps be said that the power of preventing bad laws includes that of preventing good ones; and may be used to the one purpose as well as to the other. But this objection will have little weight with those who can properly estimate the mischiefs of that inconstancy and mutability in the laws, which form the greatest blemish in the character and genius of our governments. They will consider every institution calculated to restrain the excess of lawmaking, and to keep things in the same state in which they happen to be at any given period as much more likely to do good than harm; because it is favorable to greater stability in the system of legislation. The injury which may possibly be done by defeating a few good laws will be amply compensated by the advantage of preventing a number of bad ones.
>
> . . . .
>
> It is evident that there would be greater danger of his not using his power when necessary, than of his using it too often, or too much.[85]

The United States Constitution gives the President a qualified, rather than absolute, veto. Congress has the power to override the President's veto with a two-thirds vote of both Houses. The Constitution thus creates two alternative pathways to enacting

[84] THE FEDERALIST NO. 73, at 411 (Alexander Hamilton) (Clinton Rossiter ed., 1961).

[85] *Id.* at 411–13.

legislation: approval by a tricameral process with simple majorities in both Houses plus the Presidents' signature, or approval by a two-thirds supermajority in both Houses alone.

B. The Executive Veto in Practice

Professors Mark Crain and Robert Tollison have argued that the presidential veto exacerbates interest group influence by giving such groups an additional bite at the legislative apple, allowing them to enhance the durability of interest group bargains.[86] Recall from Chapter 11 that in the basic interest group model of government, politicians act as "brokers" among interest groups who help facilitate bargains that are then embedded in resulting legislation. Crain and Tollison argue that "the veto power raises the costs of reneging on previous legislative contracts, and, as such, we should observe more vetoes when proposed bills seek to renege or to alter the terms of past legislative procurements by special interests."[87] Specifically, Crain and Tollison maintain that the veto provides the President with a tool to prevent future sessions of Congress from reneging on past interest group bargains.

The authors' model predicts more vetoes when legislative majorities are relatively larger, whether or not the White House and Congress are controlled by the same party. Larger majorities, who are more secure politically and thus less dependent upon particular special interests, are better positioned to repeal prior interest group bargains and to strike new ones. Crain and Tollison argue that if the traditional model of the veto power were sound—i.e., the veto serves to frustrate special-interest legislation—vetoes would be more likely with narrow majorities, and thus when legislation is more likely to contain payoffs to special interests.

Examining state-level data, Crain and Tollison corroborated their thesis, rather than Hamilton's. Veto rates increase when legislative consensus is high, not low, such as when a single party holds a supermajority in the legislature. Vetoes are also less common when legislative turnover is low (and thus when legislative tenure is high), which they interpret as providing alternative means for ensuring the durability of interest group legislative bargains. By contrast, party correspondence between the executive and legislative branches makes no difference in the exercise of veto power, which, the authors contend, further contradicts Hamilton's account.

Do you find the Crain and Tollison theory persuasive? Can you reconcile this theory with the Buchanan and Tullock analysis that the veto is designed to raise the calculus of consent? Why, or why not?

C. Executive Veto and Legislative Bargaining[88]

While the President's veto power is formally binary—he must accept or reject bills in their entirety—it is mistaken to assume that this gives the President no role in the

---

[86] Crain & Tollison, *supra* note 81, at 557.

[87] *Id.*

[88] This discussion draws upon Maxwell L. Stearns, *The Public Choice Case Against the Item Veto*, 49 WASH. & LEE L. REV. 385 (1992), and Glen O. Robinson, *Public Choice Speculations on the Item Veto*, 74 VA. L. REV. 403 (1988).

course of legislative bargaining. The President's veto power gives him substantial bargaining leverage during the process of legislative drafting. Studies of the item veto have centered on the nature of bargaining between the President and Congress, and they offer important insights not only into the proposed modification of the veto, but also into its present use as a means of inter-branch bargaining.[89]

The item veto would provide the President with the power to excise specific items contained in larger bills approved by both Houses of Congress. Item veto advocates claim that this power would allow the President to respond effectively to what they regard as strategic congressional behavior that takes the form of bundling special-interest items in otherwise desired legislation and forcing a binary choice upon the President to accept or reject the overall package. In theory, the item veto would allow the President to strike the special-interest riders while retaining the larger pieces of public interest legislation to which those riders are attached.

Professor Glen Robinson analogizes the relationship between Congress and the President respecting the veto power to a "bilateral monopoly," in which the President buys the legislation that Congress sells.[90] Without the item veto, Congress has substantial leverage because the President is given a binary choice respecting each bill such that vetoing a bill to defeat a special-interest item it contains is rarely palatable politically. The item veto would provide the President additional power, and as a result, would raise costs to Congress of enacting private interest legislation.

problem: rent seeking

Robinson does not contend that the item veto will pose intractable problems for congressional bargaining, and he offers hypothetical inter-branch bargains in which Congress either threatens to hold larger, public interest bills hostage unless the President commits not to separately veto attached special-interest legislation, or in a less certain case, in which Congress disaggregates the package, forcing the President to approve the special-interest legislation separately as a condition of forwarding the desired public interest bill.[91] Robinson also envisions the possibility that the President might threaten to veto a desired item to secure, for example, the support by the Senate Armed Services Committee Chair on a desired defense initiative, but cautions that the "[t]he President's threat is only as menacing as his bargaining position allows."[92]

---

[89] The item veto exists in some form in forty-four states. *See, e.g.*, Carl E. Klarner & Andrew Karch, *Why Do Governors Issue Vetoes? The Impact of Individual and Institutional Influences*, 61 POL. RES. Q. 574, 578 (2008); Thomas P. Lauth, *The Other Six: Governors Without the Line Item Veto*, 36 PUB. BUDGETING & FIN. 26 (2016). The line-item veto originated in the Constitution of the Confederate States of America, and in 1876, the first legislative proposal for presidential item veto authority was introduced and has been introduced into Congress more than 150 times since then. *See, e.g.*, John R. Carter & David Schap, *Line-Item Veto: Where Is Thy Sting?*, J. ECON. PERSP., Spring 1990, at 103, 103–04; Roger H. Wells, *The Item Veto and State Budget Reform*, 18 AM. POL. SCI. REV. 782, 782 (1924). Although the Supreme Court struck the Line Item Veto Act of 1996 in *Clinton v. City of New York*, 524 U.S. 417 (1998), the Trump Administration recently proposed conferring such power upon the President. *See* Salvador Rizzo, *Trump Administration Botches Basic Civics While Calling for Line-Item Veto*, WASH. POST (Mar. 27, 2018), https://www.washingtonpost.com/news/fact-checker/wp/2018/03/27/trump-administration-botches-basic-civics-while-calling-for-line-item-veto/?utm_term=.4a64278a15c0.

[90] *See* Robinson, *supra* note 88, at 410–12.

[91] *Id.* at 417–19 (illustrating with two negotiations over grants to smokestack industries as a precondition to passing air pollution regulation).

[92] *Id.* at 418.

Robinson concludes that by demanding that Congress pursue such complex bargaining strategies, the item veto raises the cost to the procurement of special-interest legislation. As a result, Robinson claims, the item veto is likely to have an overall positive effect, albeit perhaps a modest one, in favorably altering the ratio of special to general interest legislation.

Professor Maxwell Stearns has offered an alternative and more skeptical public choice analysis of the item veto, which returns us to the dynamic variation of the Wilson-Hayes legislative bargaining model presented in Chapter 17.[93] Recall that the Wilson-Hayes matrix can be recast to introduce two kinds of bargains, substantive bargaining and length bargaining, each with the effect of increasing the likelihood that desired general interest legislation will pass.[94] Although bill sponsors can be expected to engage in both forms of bargaining, they will do so only to a point, as each form reduces the value of the bill to its sponsor as compared with its original proposed form (corresponding to the sponsor's ideal point). These forms of bargaining allow the bill sponsor to navigate the bill through the various veto gates, or negative legislative checkpoints, as needed to secure a successful legislative coalition, which in Congress is generally well above minimum winning size.[95] Through substantive bargaining, the sponsor seeks to buy support by compromising the bill's terms (thus departing from her ideal policy position) to appease those interests most likely adversely affected by the bill in its original form. Although such bargaining will increase the size of the legislative coalition, it still might prove insufficient for passage, or at least the sponsor might be unwilling to further weaken the bill sufficiently to gain the necessary support for passage. To gain additional needed support, the bill sponsor can also negotiate adding special-interest riders that benefit vote sellers, which adds overall deadweight to the bill (albeit without affecting the bill's substance).

Stearns recasts the debate over the item veto as follows: Those supporting the item veto contend that the proposal would allow Congress to continue substantive bargaining, which falls within the Madisonian tradition of imposing barriers to factional legislative violence, but would limit length bargaining, which only produces undesirable special-interest legislation. It would do so, advocates claim, by either allowing the President to excise resulting bargains or by limiting the incentives to secure special-interest items in the first place. In this analysis, the item veto would allow the President to excise special-interest legislation but would have little or no effect on legislative policy.

Relying upon interest group theory, Stearns demonstrates that if members of Congress and the President behave rationally, the item veto is instead likely to have the opposite effect, namely allowing the President to influence the direction of legislative policy, while tying the President's hands respecting the most egregious special-interest legislation. The analysis rests on the observation that the President has greater control in selecting which bills to support than with whom he must bargain in Congress (who controls the various veto gates or negative legislative checkpoints) to get those bills passed. Rather than diminishing length bargaining, Stearns demonstrates that the item veto will simply change the locus of such bargaining to the President or his allies in Congress. The President will offer to decline to exercise the item veto as needed to ensure

[93] *See supra* Chapter 17.

[94] *See supra* Chapter 17.

[95] *See supra* Chapter 17; *see* RIKER, 42, at 32–46.

that his preferred legislation gains the necessary support for passage. Because the President cannot control with whom he must bargain in Congress to secure passage, however, those in control of the various negative legislative checkpoints will serve as brokers for the most valuable special-interest legislation, which will provide the basis for the most valuable reciprocal commitments by those who directly benefit from the resulting special-interest legislation.

Stearns concludes that the overall effect of the item veto is ultimately not captured by the overall amount of general interest or special-interest legislation, but rather by the effect of the item veto on who controls the overall direction of legislative policy. Empirical studies generally have corroborated Stearns's hypothesis that at the state level, the item veto has been used more to affect policy than to excise special-interest legislation.[96]

Which model of the item veto do you find more persuasive? How does the analysis of the item veto inform the Buchanan and Tullock analysis of the actual veto as a consensus-raising measure? How does it inform the Crain and Tollison analysis of the actual veto as a special-interest-bargain preservation device? Do you believe that the item veto is a sound policy? Why or why not? Do you think that the answer to this policy question is the same at the state and federal levels? Why or why not?

D. A Comment on Coalition Formation in Parliamentary Versus Presidential Voting Regimes

Another important variable that affects coalition building in passing legislation involves the manner through which the head of state is chosen. This marks a fundamental difference between the presidential system, operating within the United States, and parliamentary systems, operating in many other democratic nations throughout the world. While voters in the United States select the President (albeit subject to the peculiarity of the Electoral College) through a direct election process, in parliamentary regimes, a successful legislative coalition elects the Prime Minster who then forms the government.

In the parliamentary regime, a market for relatively small parties emerges as these parties hope to become tipping points in the formation of successful governing coalitions. In a parliament of sixty persons with three parties, *A*, *B*, *C*, of equal size, we might imagine that any of the following three coalitions of forty would form: *AB*, *BC*, or *CA*. But following the theory of minimum winning coalitions, we know that each of these coalitions is over weighted. If we start with *AB*, a subgroup comprising seventeen members of *C*—which we will refer to as *C'*—can splinter off and propose to *B* that forming a new *BC'* coalition will improve the payoffs to the new members. The overall benefit of being in the governing coalition is now divided by thirty-seven, rather than by forty. Applying Riker's theory, this too is over weighted, and so we might imagine a

[96] For studies that are consistent with the Stearns hypothesis, see Carter & Schap, *supra* note 89, at 112 (summarizing studies and concluding that "[t]he empirical studies to date . . . provide little or no evidence that total spending, budget outcomes, or executive power are substantially affected in general by item-veto authority"); Douglas Holtz-Eakin, *The Line Item Veto and Public Sector Budgets: Evidence from the States*, 36 J. PUB. ECON. 269, 291 (1988) (concluding that "long-run budgetary behavior is not significantly affected by the power of an item veto [but that] in particular political circumstances the item veto may permit increased control over the budget").

subgroup of A, A', with sixteen members splinting off and proposing to B' yet another iteration, with a now smaller governing coalition CA' thirty-three members. With each round of forming, breaking, and reforming coalitions, newer and smaller parties will form that allow for a mix of strategies in the creation of governing coalitions. In a regime that takes this form of bargaining, we might imagine that much of the bargaining over policy occurs at the stage of forming the governing coalition.

How might this differ from the nature of coalition building over legislation in the United States Congress? Which system appears more likely to be conducive to special-interest politicking? Which is more likely conducive to providing public interest legislation? Why? How might one resolve these questions empirically?

As one interesting example, consider the Israeli Knesset. Studies have shown that while the majority coalitions vary, successful coalitions invariably include within them a group of minority religious parties. Until recently, one consequence has been to ensure a continuation of exemption from military service for ultra-orthodox Jews.[97] Does social choice analysis help to explain why in the United States, by contrast, the religious right has generally formed a coalition with the Republican Party? How does the difference between forming coalitions during the primary stage, and thus prior to general elections, in the United States, versus in the post-election stage, in the Knesset, affect the formation of public policy affecting minority religious groups? More generally, is either a parliamentary or direct electoral system less likely to be subject to interest group influence? Or are the two systems equally subject to the same pressures manifested in different ways?

IV. SEPARATION OF PARTIES, NOT POWERS

In a prominent article, Professors Darryl Levinson and Richard Pildes set out a fundamental challenge to the Madisonian concept of separation of powers as expressed most notably in the *Federalist No. 51*.[98] Within that framing for Congress to act collectively to maintain the system of checks and balances and to safeguard that body's power from incursion by the President, it is necessary that the self-interest of Congress be aligned with the overall mission of the institution. For example, the U.S. Senate originally was appointed by state legislatures. The Framers envisioned that Senators would jealously protect the interests of their states. In this conception, it was essential that the election and reelection of U.S. Senators depended in large part on the state legislative monitoring.[99]

---

[97] *See* NORMAN SCHOFIELD & ITAI SENED, MULTIPARTY DEMOCRACY: ELECTIONS AND LEGISLATIVE POLITICS 92–95 (2006); Marissa Newman, *Knesset Approves Ultra-Orthodox Draft Exemptions Until 2023; Yesh Atid to Appeal*, TIMES OF ISR. (Nov. 24, 2015, 5:06 AM), https://www.timesofisrael.com/knesset-set-to-approve-ultra-orthodox-draft-exemptions-until-2023/ (discussing military exemption for Haredi). On September 12, 2017, the Israeli High Court of Justice ruled the military exemption for ultra-orthodox Jews was unconstitutional. The court gave the Israeli government a year to develop new legislation. Isabel Kershner, *Israel's Military Exemption for Ultra-Orthodox Is Ruled Unconstitutional*, N.Y. TIMES (Sept. 12, 2017), https://www.nytimes.com/2017/09/12/world/middleeast/israel-ultra-orthodox-military.html; Yonah Jeremy Bob, *Court Orders Gov't Pass New Law or Draft All Haredim*, JERUSALEM POST (Sept. 12, 2017), http://www.jpost.com/israel-news/politics-and-diplomacy/court-orders-govt-to-pass-new-law-or-draft-all-haredim-504901.

[98] *See supra* text accompanying note 35. Daryl J. Levinson & Richard H. Pildes, *Separation of Parties, Not Powers*, 119 HARV. L. REV. 2311 (2006); THE FEDERALIST NO. 51 (James Madison).

[99] *See* sources cited *supra* note 56.

Madisonian checks and balances rests on a similar premise:

> But the great security against a gradual concentration of the several powers in the same department, consists in giving to those who administer each department the necessary constitutional means and personal motives to resist encroachments of the others. The provision for defense must in this, as in all other cases, be made commensurate to the danger of attack. Ambition must be made to counteract ambition. The interest of the man must be connected with the constitutional rights of the place. . . .
>
> This policy of supplying, by opposite and rival interests, the defect of better motives, might be traced through the whole system of human affairs, private as well as public. We see it particularly displayed in all the subordinate distributions of power, where the constant aim is to divide and arrange the several offices in such a manner as that each may be a check on the other—that the private interest of every individual may be a sentinel over the public rights. These inventions of prudence cannot be less requisite in the distribution of the supreme powers of the State.[100]

In *Separation of Parties, Not Powers*, Professors Darryl Levinson and Richard Pildes question the ongoing validity of this theoretical constitutional foundation.[101] Levinson and Pildes argue that almost from the beginning, and certainly as the Constitution has evolved, the defining characteristic of the American political system has been the dominance of political parties and the conflicts between them, rather than theoretical conflicts between or among the various branches of the federal government. They write:

> To this day, the idea of self-sustaining political competition built into the structure of government is frequently portrayed as the unique genius of the U.S. Constitution, the very basis for the success of American democracy. Yet the truth is closer to the opposite. The success of American democracy overwhelmed the Madisonian conception of separation of powers almost from the outset, preempting the political dynamics that were supposed to provide each branch with a "will of its own" that would propel departmental "[a]mbition . . . to counteract ambition." The Framers had not anticipated the nature of the democratic competition that would emerge in government and in the electorate. Political competition and cooperation along relatively stable lines of policy and ideological disagreement quickly came to be channeled not through the branches of government, but rather through an institution the Framers could imagine only dimly but nevertheless despised: political parties. As competition between the legislative and executive branches was displaced by competition between two major parties, the machine that was supposed to go of itself stopped running.
>
> Few aspects of the founding generation's political theory are now more clearly anachronistic than their vision of legislative-executive separation of powers. Nevertheless, few of the Framers' ideas continue to be taken as literally or sanctified as deeply by courts and constitutional scholars as the passages

[100] THE FEDERALIST NO. 51, at 290 (James Madison) (Clinton Rossiter ed., 1961).

[101] Levinson & Pildes, *supra* note 98.

> about interbranch relations in Madison's *Federalist 51*. To this day, Madison's account of rivalrous, self-interested branches is embraced as an accurate depiction of political reality and a firm foundation for the constitutional law of separation of powers. In the Madisonian simulacrum of democratic politics embraced by constitutional doctrine and theory, the branches of government are personified as political actors with interests and wills of their own, entirely disconnected from the interests and wills of the officials who populate them or the citizens who elect those officials. Acting on these interests, the branches purportedly are locked in a perpetual struggle to aggrandize their own power and encroach upon their rivals. The kinds of partisan political competition that structure real-world democracy and dominate political discourse, however, are almost entirely missing from this picture.
>
> [The] invisibility of political parties has left constitutional discourse about separation of powers with no conceptual resources to understand basic features of the American political system. It has also generated judicial decisions and theoretical rationalizations that float entirely free of any functional justification grounded in the actual workings of separation of powers. Ignoring the reality of parties and fixating on the paper partitions between the branches, the law and theory of separation of powers are a perfect fit for the government the Framers designed. Unfortunately, they miss much of the government we actually have.[102]

Levinson and Pildes argue that particularly during periods where the political parties are cohesive and polarized, the "degree and kind of competition between the legislative and executive branches will vary significantly and may all but disappear, depending on whether party control of the House, Senate, and presidency is divided or unified."[103] They add that the distinction of party-unified and party-divided government "thus rivals, and often dominates, the constitutional distinction between the branches in predicting and explaining interbranch political dynamics."[104]

Starting from the foundation that political parties matter more than formal institutional structures, Levinson and Pildes go on to offer a number of reforms that benefit from recognizing this important reality. For example, they argue for the increased use of supermajority rules (such as the now-abandoned availability of the filibuster for judicial nominations[105]) during periods of unified government. They suggest that it might be appropriate to increase the political independence of the bureaucracy, stating: "One way to ensure that government is never fully unified is to protect this branch from falling into the hands of the majority party—by keeping it independent of *both* parties."[106] They also suggest several novel structural reforms that would be designed to increase the ability of minority parties to serve a checking function on unified government, such as reducing the use of "safe districting" for elections (i.e., "gerrymandering"), reforms to primary

---

[102] *Id.* at 2312–14.

[103] *Id.* at 2312 (Abstract).

[104] *Id.*

[105] Matt Flegenheimer, *Senate Republicans Deploy "Nuclear Option" to Clear Path for Gorsuch*, N.Y. TIMES (Apr. 6, 2017), https://www.nytimes.com/2017/04/06/us/politics/neil-gorsuch-supreme-court-senate.html.

[106] Levinson & Pildes, *supra* note 98, at 2375.

election rules, changes to legislative rules that enhance the power of minority parties during periods of unified government, and other reforms that would encourage divided government. They also acknowledge that in pushing for greater power for minority parties they are confronting a tradeoff with other political values, namely the encouragement of political accountability and decisive action by the governing party. Nevertheless, they conclude that the need to attenuate the excesses during periods of unified government outweighs the overall loss in accountability and decisiveness that their reforms could bring about. Levinson and Pildes conclude:

> From nearly the start of the American republic, the separation of powers as the Framers understood it, and as contemporary constitutional law continues to understand it, had ceased to exist. The enduring institutional form of democratic political competition has turned out to be not branches but political parties. Absorbing that insight [is] essential, not just for descriptive and historical analyses of the practice of democracy in America, but also for normative thought about constitutional law and the design of democratic institutions today. If inter-branch checks and balances remain a vital aspiration, the failure of the Framers' understanding of political competition raises the risk of mismatch between constitutional structures and constitutional aims. Recognizing that failure and replacing it with an understanding of the actual mechanisms of political competition suggests new approaches to constitutional law and institutional design that would more effectively realize the aims of the separation of powers.
>
> Such a project is all the more urgent as we come to terms with an emerging equilibrium of ideologically coherent and polarized political parties. Strong parties will accentuate the differences between unified and divided government, making constitutional law's conceptualization of a singular, static system of separation of powers all the more problematic. And when strong parties combine with extended periods of unified government, the challenge to the Madisonian picture separation of powers, and to the values it is meant to protect, is stark. If the goal is a system of separation of powers that resembles the one Madison and subsequent generations of constitutional theorists imagined, it will have to be built not around branches but around the institutions through which political competition is in fact organized modern democracies: political parties.[107]

In a related analysis, Professor Todd Zywicki has argued that unexpected developments since the ratification of the original Constitution, particularly the decisive influence of partisan political parties, have confounded certain elements of the original constitutional structure.[108] Zywicki focuses on the particular functions provided specifically to the Senate under the Constitution. For example, many of those responsibilities were provided to the Senate specifically because Senators were to be elected by state legislatures, which the Framers believed would insulate Senators from political pressures and conduce to the election of individuals of high character and

---

[107] *Id.* at 2385–86.

[108] *See* Todd Zywicki, *The Senate and Hyper-Partisanship: Would the Constitution Look Different if the Framers Had Known that Senators Would be Elected in Partisan Elections?*, 10 GEO. J. L. & PUB POL'Y 375 (2012).

judgment. The Seventeenth Amendment changed the selection of Senators to one of direct, and partisan, elections.

Consider also the Constitution's process for impeaching a government officer: First, the House must "impeach" by majority vote and then the Senate shall have the power to try the case but may convict only upon two-thirds vote of those present. Zywicki writes, "It is plausible to envision an indirectly-elected, non-partisan Senate sitting as a sort of trial jury to weigh the evidence of an impeachment trial. On the other hand, it is equally implausible to envision a partisan-elected Senate doing the same, especially in our current era of hyper-partisanship."[109] Zywicki points to the spectacle of the impeachment of President Bill Clinton, where there was little doubt that virtually all members of Congress would vote along party lines, as an example of the poor fit between the impeachment process established by the Constitution and modern partisan elections.

Zywicki notes that several other key features of the constitutional structure, such as the Senate's "advice and consent" role for nominations, were tied to the assumption that the Senate would be less partisan and political in nature than the House. The advice and consent method of selection is consistent with the views of the Framers that Senate confirmation would focus on the nominee's character and sound judgment, and independence from the President, rather than the nominee's partisan political views. It is not clear, however, that Framers would have changed the process by which judges and other government officials are selected had they known that the Senate would be elected in partisan direct elections, especially given the equally, or more, partisan nature of politics in the House.

The arguments by Levinson and Pildes, and Zywicki, suggest that as history has developed, the importance of political parties has come to dominate many of the formal structures of the Constitution. Do you agree? Are United States Senators, for example, more likely to respond to the political demands of their party than to the institutional powers of the Senate? Should judges take these developments into account in interpreting the Constitution? Should the Constitution be amended to adjust to the large role played by political parties today? Might the Framers have allocated powers, and designed some constitutional features, differently had they anticipated these changes?

Consider also the following: Although the Framers did not anticipate the emergence of formal parties in their present form, the structures that they created, including direct presidential election, rather than Congressional selection of our head of state, made a two-party system all but inevitable. This follows from the median voter theorem. Indeed, the party system was eventually baked into the formal constitutional structure in the Twelfth Amendment, which for the first time recognized the importance of having the candidates for President select their own running mates and having the candidates for President and Vice President of the same party run as a ticket.[110] This ended the dysfunction of early political shotgun weddings that forced former rivals for the oval office to serve together as President and Vice President.

---

[109] *Id.* at 377.

[110] U.S. CONST. amend. XII; Paul R. Abramson et al., *Third-Party and Independent Candidates in American Politics: Wallace, Anderson, and Perot*, 110 POL. SCI. Q. 349 (1995).

Given that the original constitutional design rendered the two-party system inevitable, might the Madisonian commitment to institutional structure instead serve as a set of mechanisms designed to blunt the worst effects of the potential factional violence that might emerge? Might the Framers have thought the formal separation of powers more aspirational than descriptive? Is this a fair reading of *The Federalist*? Or this reading too optimistic, even Pollyannaish? How might Levinson and Pildes respond?

Finally, although the Constitution's original framers did not envision the Seventeenth Amendment, is that necessarily the benchmark for evaluating present policy respecting the constitutional allocations of power as it relates to the Senate? The drafters of the Seventeenth Amendment, and the ratifying states, are the framers of these aspects of the post-Seventeenth Amendment Constitution. They insisted upon direct senatorial elections with full knowledge of the prior constitutional structures that allocated specific powers to that body. Had they wished to do so, they could have altered such structures as well, but they chose not to. Is this an appropriate rejoinder to the concerns that Professor Zywicki's raises? Why or why not?

V. APPLICATIONS

In this part we present two cases, *INS v. Chadha*,[111] and *National Labor Relations Board v. Noel Canning*.[112] Both cases explore issues related to separation of powers, bicameralism, and the relationship between the various branches of the federal government. Consider the extent to which the approaches that the separate Justices take in the various opinions, and the outcomes of each case, reflect insights from the materials in this chapter or the earlier chapters in this volume.

A. INS v. Chadha

INS v. Chadha addressed the constitutionality of the "one-House veto," a procedure through which, after Congress delegates decision-making authority to an agency, one House of Congress retains the power to reverse an agency policy by unilateral action, notwithstanding the constitutional requirements of bicameralism and presentment. This summary procedure allows Congress to retain a modicum of control by reducing the burdens of checking agency decision-making. As you will see, the Court invalidated the one-House veto, and in later cases extended this holding to the context of two House vetoes. More notably, in the three main opinions that we discuss, the majority opinion written by Chief Justice Burger, a concurrence by Justice Powell, and a dissent by Justice White,[113] each Justice takes a different view of and propriety of the one-House veto and of its relationship more generally to the functions of agency delegation and separation of powers.

Chadha was an East Indian born in Kenya who held a British passport. He came to the United States in 1966 on a nonimmigrant student visa that expired in 1972. The

---

[111] 462 U.S. 919 (1983).

[112] 134 S. Ct. 2550 (2014).

[113] Then-Associate Justice Rehnquist also produced a dissent, which we do not include in the discussion below. INS v. Chadha, 462 U.S. 919, 1013 (1983) (Rehnquist, J., dissenting).

following year, the District Director of the Immigration and Naturalization Service ordered that Chadha "show cause" why he should not be deported. Chadha applied for a suspension of deportation, which the immigration judge granted on the ground that Chadha had satisfied the statutory criteria, including most notably the "extreme hardship"[114] requirement. The Attorney General then transmitted the immigration judge's order to Congress as a recommendation to suspend deportation, which Congress had the power to accept or to override via the so-called one-House veto of either the House or Senate. If either House executed the one-House veto, the Attorney General was then required to carry out the deportation order.[115] Based upon a review of 340 suspension cases, Representative Eilberg, the Chairman of the Judiciary Subcommittee on Immigration, Citizenship, and International Law, successfully introduced a resolution that ultimately won the approval of the House of Representatives. It reversed the suspension order for six aliens, including Chadha, who had overstayed their visas but who the immigration judge had determined met the eligibility requirements for suspending their deportation, "particularly as it relates to hardship.' "[116]

Chief Justice Burger, writing for the Court, explained:

> The resolution was passed without debate or recorded vote. Since the House action was pursuant to § 244(c)(2), the resolution was not treated as an Art. I legislative act; it was not submitted to the Senate or presented to the President for his action.[117]

Chadha challenged the constitutionality of the proceedings under which he was ordered to be deported.

For the *Chadha* majority, the issue turned entirely on the constitutionality of the one-House veto, a procedure that the Court implicitly conceded had the benefit of allowing Congress to reduce the cost of monitoring agency action. Burger explained:

> [T]he fact that a given law or procedure is efficient, convenient, and useful in facilitating functions of government, standing alone, will not save it if it is contrary to the Constitution. Convenience and efficiency are not the primary objectives—or the hallmarks—of democratic government and our inquiry is sharpened rather than blunted by the fact that congressional veto provisions are appearing with increasing frequency in statutes which delegate authority to executive and independent agencies. . . .[118]

Burger responded to Justice White, who, writing in dissent, defended the one-House veto on grounds of administrative practicality:

---

114 The law required him to demonstrate that "he had resided continuously in the United States for over seven years, was of good moral character, and would suffer 'extreme hardship' if deported." *Id.* at 924 (majority opinion).

115 Section 244(c)(2) of the Immigration and Nationality Act (codified at 8 U.S.C. § 1254(c) repealed 1996)) authorized either house to veto the Attorney General's decision to suspend deportation of an individual.

116 *Chadha*, 462 U.S. at 926.

117 *Id.* at 927–28 (footnote omitted).

118 *Id.* at 944.

JUSTICE WHITE undertakes to make a case for the proposition that the one-House veto is a useful "political invention," and we need not challenge that assertion. . . . But policy arguments supporting even useful "political inventions" are subject to the demands of the Constitution which defines powers and, with respect to this subject, sets out just how those powers are to be exercised.[119]

The Court then discussed the bicameralism and presentment requirements as they related to the one-House veto:

The Presentment Clauses

The records of the Constitutional Convention reveal that the requirement that all legislation be presented to the President before becoming law was uniformly accepted by the Framers. Presentment to the President and the Presidential veto were considered so imperative that the draftsmen took special pains to assure that these requirements could not be circumvented. During the final debate on Art. I, § 7, cl. 2, James Madison expressed concern that it might easily be evaded by the simple expedient of calling a proposed law a "resolution" or "vote" rather than a "bill." As a consequence, Art. I, § 7, cl. 3, was added.

The decision to provide the President with a limited and qualified power to nullify proposed legislation by veto was based on the profound conviction of the Framers that the powers conferred on Congress were the powers to be most carefully circumscribed. It is beyond doubt that lawmaking was a power to be shared by both Houses and the President. . . .

. . . .

The President's role in the lawmaking process also reflects the Framers' careful efforts to check whatever propensity a particular Congress might have to enact oppressive, improvident, or ill-considered measures. The President's veto role in the legislative process was described later during public debate on ratification:

"It establishes a salutary check upon the legislative body, calculated to guard the community against the effects of faction, precipitancy, or of any impulse unfriendly to the public good which may happen to influence a majority of that body.

". . . The primary inducement to conferring the power in question upon the Executive is, to enable him to defend himself; the secondary one is to increase the chances in favor of the community against the passing of bad laws, through haste, inadvertence, or design."

The Court also has observed that the Presentment Clauses serve the important purpose of assuring that a "national" perspective is grafted on the legislative process:

---

[119] *Id.* at 945 (citation omitted).

> "The President is a representative of the people just as the members of the Senate and of the House are, and it may be, at some times, on some subjects, that the President elected by all the people is rather more representative of them all than are the members of either body of the Legislature whose constituencies are local and not countrywide. . . ."[120]

Chief Justice Burger further considered the implications of the one-House veto for the constitutional requirement of bicameralism:

> By providing that no law could take effect without the concurrence of the prescribed majority of the Members of both Houses, the Framers reemphasized their belief . . . that legislation should not be enacted unless it has been carefully and fully considered by the Nation's elected officials. . . .
>
> [After reviewing the views of several Framers on bicameralism, Burger stated:]
>
> These observations are consistent with what many of the Framers expressed, none more cogently than Madison in pointing up the need to divide and disperse power in order to protect liberty [quoting the previously excerpted language from the Federalist 51]:[121]

Burger then summarized the combined effect of bicameralism and presentment as follows:

> We see therefore that the Framers were acutely conscious that the bicameral requirement and the Presentment Clauses would serve essential constitutional functions. The President's participation in the legislative process was to protect the Executive Branch from Congress and to protect the whole people from improvident laws. The division of the Congress into two distinctive bodies assures that the legislative power would be exercised only after opportunity for full study and debate in separate settings. The President's unilateral veto power, in turn, was limited by the power of two-thirds of both Houses of Congress to overrule a veto thereby precluding final arbitrary action of one person. It emerges clearly that the prescription for legislative action in Art. I, §§ 1, 7, represents the Framers' decision that the legislative power of the Federal government be exercised in accord with a single, finely wrought and exhaustively considered, procedure.[122]

Burger then considered whether the one-House veto was "legislative" in nature and therefore subject to the requirements of bicameralism and presentment. Burger explained that while the spheres of legislative, executive, and judicial functions are not hermetically sealed, and while the Constitution itself identifies specific circumstances when a single House of Congress can act, the requirements of bicameralism and presentment apply to those actions that are " 'legislative in . . . character and effect."[123] Burger explained:

> Examination of the action taken here by one House pursuant to § 244(c)(2) reveals that it was essentially legislative in purpose and effect. In

---

[120] *Id.* at 946–48 (citations and footnote omitted).

[121] *Id.* at 948–50 (citations omitted).

[122] *Id.* at 951 (citation omitted).

[123] *Id.* at 952.

purporting to exercise power defined in Art. I, § 8, cl. 4, to "establish an uniform Rule of Naturalization," the House took action that had the purpose and effect of altering the legal rights, duties, and relations of persons, including the Attorney General, Executive Branch officials and Chadha, all outside the Legislative Branch. Section 244(c)(2) purports to authorize one House of Congress to require the Attorney General to deport an individual alien whose deportation otherwise would be canceled under § 244. The one-House veto operated in these cases to overrule the Attorney General and mandate Chadha's deportation; absent the House action, Chadha would remain in the United States. Congress has *acted* and its action has altered Chadha's status. . . .

Finally, we see that when the Framers intended to authorize either House of Congress to act alone and outside of its prescribed bicameral legislative role, they narrowly and precisely defined the procedure for such action. There are four provisions in the Constitution, explicit and unambiguous, by which one House may act alone with the unreviewable force of law, not subject to the President's veto [including initiating (by the House of Representatives) and trying (by the Senate) impeachments, the Senate's power of advice and consent for Presidential appointments, and the Senate's power to ratify treaties.]

Clearly, when the Draftsmen sought to confer special powers on one House, independent of the other House, or of the President, they did so in explicit, unambiguous terms. . . .

The Court concluded:

The veto authorized by § 244(c)(2) doubtless has been in many respects a convenient shortcut; the "sharing" with the Executive by Congress of its authority over aliens in this manner is, on its face, an appealing compromise. In purely practical terms, it is obviously easier for action to be taken by one House without submission to the President; but it is crystal clear from the records of the Convention, contemporaneous writings and debates, that the Framers ranked other values higher than efficiency. . . .

The choices we discern as having been made in the Constitutional Convention impose burdens on governmental processes that often seem clumsy, inefficient, even unworkable, but those hard choices were consciously made by men who had lived under a form of government that permitted arbitrary governmental acts to go unchecked. There is no support in the Constitution or decisions of this Court for the proposition that the cumbersomeness and delays often encountered in complying with explicit constitutional standards may be avoided, either by the Congress or by the President. With all the obvious flaws of delay, untidiness, and potential for abuse, we have not yet found a better way to preserve freedom than by making the exercise of power subject to the carefully crafted restraints spelled out in the Constitution.[124]

---

[124] *Id.* at 952–55, 958–59 (citation and footnotes omitted).

Burger concluded that "the congressional veto provision in § 244(c)(2) is severable from the Act and that it is unconstitutional."[125]

In a concurrence in the judgment, Justice Powell took a very different view concerning the nature of the actions that the one-House veto represents:

> On its face, the House's action appears clearly adjudicatory. The House did not enact a general rule; rather, it made its own determination that six specific persons did not comply with certain statutory criteria. It thus undertook the type of decision that traditionally has been left to other branches. . . . Where, as here, Congress has exercised a power "that cannot possibly be regarded as merely in aid of the legislative function of Congress," the decisions of this Court have held that Congress impermissibly assumed a function that the Constitution entrusted to another branch.
>
> The impropriety of the House's assumption of this function is confirmed by the fact that its action raises the very danger the Framers sought to avoid—the exercise of unchecked power. In deciding whether Chadha deserves to be deported, Congress is not subject to any internal constraints that prevent it from arbitrarily depriving him of the right to remain in this country. Unlike the judiciary or an administrative agency, Congress is not bound by established substantive rules. Nor is it subject to the procedural safeguards, such as the right to counsel and a hearing before an impartial tribunal, that are present when a court or an agency adjudicates individual rights. The only effective constraint on Congress' power is political, but Congress is most accountable politically when it prescribes rules of general applicability. When it decides rights of specific persons, those rights are subject to "the tyranny of a shifting majority."[126]

Responding to this argument, Chief Justice Burger observed:

> JUSTICE POWELL'S position is that the one-House veto in this case is a *judicial* act and therefore unconstitutional as beyond the authority vested in Congress by the Constitution. . . . But the attempted analogy between judicial action and the one-House veto is less than perfect. Federal courts do not enjoy a roving mandate to correct alleged excesses of administrative agencies; we are limited by Art. III to hearing cases and controversies and no justiciable case or controversy was presented by the Attorney General's decision to allow Chadha to remain in this country. . . . Thus, JUSTICE POWELL'S statement that the one-House veto in this case is "clearly adjudicatory" simply is not supported by his accompanying assertion that the House has "assumed a function ordinarily [entrusted] to the federal courts." We are satisfied that the one-House veto is legislative in purpose and effect and subject to the procedures set out in Art. I.[127]

---

[125] *Id.* at 959.

[126] *Id.* at 964–66 (Powell, J., concurring) (citations and footnotes omitted).

[127] *Id.* at 957 n.22 (majority opinion) (citations omitted).

Writing in dissent, Justice White focused on what he regarded as the administrative benefits of the one-House veto. White began by noting the broad reach of the Court's ruling:

> Today the Court not only invalidates § 244(c)(2) of the Immigration and Nationality Act, but also sounds the death knell for nearly 200 other statutory provisions in which Congress has reserved a "legislative veto." For this reason, the Court's decision is of surpassing importance. And it is for this reason that the Court would have been well advised to decide the cases, if possible, on the narrower grounds of separation of powers, leaving for full consideration the constitutionality of other congressional review statutes operating on such varied matters as war powers and agency rulemaking, some of which concern the independent regulatory agencies.
>
> The prominence of the legislative veto mechanism in our contemporary political system and its importance to Congress can hardly be overstated. It has become a central means by which Congress secures the accountability of executive and independent agencies. Without the legislative veto, Congress is faced with a Hobson's choice: either to refrain from delegating the necessary authority, leaving itself with a hopeless task of writing laws with the requisite specificity to cover endless special circumstances across the entire policy landscape, or in the alternative, to abdicate its law-making function to the Executive Branch and independent agencies. To choose the former leaves major national problems unresolved; to opt for the latter risks unaccountable policymaking by those not elected to fill that role. . . . The device is known in every field of governmental concern: reorganization, budgets, foreign affairs, war powers, and regulation of trade, safety, energy, the environment, and the economy.[128]

Justice White linked the increased use of the one-House veto to the growth of the administrative state:

> The legislative veto developed initially in response to the problems of reorganizing the sprawling Government structure created in response to the Depression. The Reorganization Acts established the chief model for the legislative veto. When President Hoover requested authority to reorganize the government in 1929, he coupled his request that the "Congress be willing to delegate its authority over the problem (subject to defined principles) to the Executive" with a proposal for legislative review. He proposed that the Executive "should act upon approval of a joint committee of Congress or with the reservation of power of revision by Congress within some limited period adequate for its consideration." Congress followed President Hoover's suggestion and authorized reorganization subject to legislative review. Although the reorganization authority reenacted in 1933 did not contain a legislative veto provision, the provision returned during the Roosevelt administration and has since been renewed numerous times. Over the years, the provision was used extensively. Presidents submitted 115 Reorganization

[128] *Id.* at 967–68 (White, J., dissenting) (footnote omitted).

Plans to Congress of which 23 were disapproved by Congress pursuant to legislative veto provisions.

. . . .

Over the quarter century following World War II, Presidents continued to accept legislative vetoes by one or both Houses as constitutional, while regularly denouncing provisions by which congressional Committees reviewed Executive activity . . . . .

. . . .

Even this brief review suffices to demonstrate that the legislative veto is more than "efficient, convenient, and useful." It is an important if not indispensable political invention that allows the President and Congress to resolve major constitutional and policy differences, assures the accountability of independent regulatory agencies, and preserves Congress' control over lawmaking. Perhaps there are other means of accommodation and accountability, but the increasing reliance of Congress upon the legislative veto suggests that the alternatives . . . are not entirely satisfactory.[129]

Turning to the constitutional issue, White explained:

The Constitution does not directly authorize or prohibit the legislative veto. Thus, our task should be to determine whether the legislative veto is consistent with the purposes of Art. I and the principles of separation of powers which are reflected in that Article and throughout the Constitution. We should not find the lack of a specific constitutional authorization for the legislative veto surprising, and I would not infer disapproval of the mechanism from its absence. From the summer of 1787 to the present the Government of the United States has become an endeavor far beyond the contemplation of the Framers. Only within the last half century has the complexity and size of the Federal Government's responsibilities grown so greatly that the Congress must rely on the legislative veto as the most effective if not the only means to insure its role as the Nation's lawmakers. But the wisdom of the Framers was to anticipate that the Nation would grow and new problems of governance would require different solutions. Accordingly, our Federal Government was intentionally chartered with the flexibility to respond to contemporary needs without losing sight of fundamental democratic principles. . . .

. . . In my view, neither Art. I of the Constitution nor the doctrine of separation of powers is violated by this mechanism by which our elected Representatives preserve their voice in the governance of the Nation.[130]

Justice White further explained how, as a practical matter, the interests of the President and both Houses are preserved in the one-House veto regime:

The President's approval is found in the Attorney General's action in recommending to Congress that the deportation order for a given alien be

[129] *Id.* at 968–69, 972–73 (citations omitted).

[130] *Id.* at 977–79 (footnote omitted).

suspended. The House and the Senate indicate their approval of the Executive's action by not passing a resolution of disapproval within the statutory period. Thus, a change in the legal status quo—the deportability of the alien—is consummated only with the approval of each of the three relevant actors. The disagreement of any one of the three maintains the alien's pre-existing status: the Executive may choose not to recommend suspension; the House and Senate may each veto the recommendation. The effect on the rights and obligations of the affected individuals and upon the legislative system is precisely the same as if a private bill were introduced but failed to receive the necessary approval. "The President and the two Houses enjoy exactly the same say in what the law is to be as would have been true for each without the presence of the one-House veto, and nothing in the law is changed absent the concurrence of the President and a majority in each House."

Thus understood, § 244(c)(2) fully effectuates the purposes of the bicameralism and presentation requirements. . . .[131]

Turning to the question of separation of powers, White explained:

[T]he history of the separation-of-powers doctrine is also a history of accommodation and practicality. Apprehensions of an overly powerful branch have not led to undue prophylactic measures that handicap the effective working of the National Government as a whole. The Constitution does not contemplate total separation of the three branches of Government. "[A] hermetic sealing off of the three branches of Government from one another would preclude the establishment of a Nation capable of governing itself effectively."

Our decisions reflect this judgment. . . .[132]

Justice White concluded:

I regret the destructive scope of the Court's holding. . . . Today's decision strikes down in one fell swoop provisions in more laws enacted by Congress than the Court has cumulatively invalidated in its history. I fear it will now be more difficult "to insur[e] that the fundamental policy decisions in our society will be made not by an appointed official but by the body immediately responsible to the people." I must dissent.[133]

DISCUSSION QUESTIONS

1. In the case of Mr. Chadha, what is the actual harm that arises from the deviation from formal bicameralism and presentment? Applying the insights of public choice theory, is

[131] *Id.* at 994–96.

[132] *Id.* at 999 (citations and footnote omitted).

[133] *Id.* at 1002–03 (citation omitted).

it possible that as a constitutional matter we might want to categorically permit or disallow the one-House veto even if the benefits and costs are not readily apparent in a given case?

2. In his dissent, Justice White writes, "But the history of the separation of powers doctrine is also a history of accommodation and practicality." White is referring to a long line of cases that includes most notably *Youngstown Sheet & Tube Co. v. Sawyer (Steel Seizure)*, 343 U.S. 579 (1952), in which Justices Black and Frankfurter debated in separate opinions the role of longstanding political accommodations between the President and Congress in informing constitutional separation of powers. So viewed, to what extent does this sort of accommodation inform our understanding of the external costs and decision costs in the Buchanan and Tullock framework? For example, does the prevalence of the one House veto suggest that the decision costs of passing full blown legislation to check against agency activity are too high? If so, is this a relevant factor in assessing the constitutionality of the one-House veto? Why or why not?

3. Levinson and Pildes suggest that the structure of interactions between the President and Congress differ between periods of unified and divided government and that Congress is much more deferential to the President during periods of unified government. In examining the history of accommodation between the President and Congress, should it be relevant whether the particular practice under consideration arose during a period of unified or divided government? Should it matter if the time when the act in question is being challenged is a period of unified or divided government? Does this asymmetrical response to Executive action by Congress provide any insight as to whether Courts in general should defer to historical precedents of struggles between Congress and the President?

4. Building on Buchanan and Tullock's distinction between the "constitutional" and "legislative" levels of analysis what should be the relationship between the original constitutional text on one hand, and post-constitution practices and norms on the other? Consider the following analysis. Justice White sees the constitutional level of analysis as embodying two sometimes competing goals: on one hand is the protections provided by the separation of powers, and on the other, is the need for government operational efficiency. Chief Justice Burger, by contrast, sees the separation of powers, and the values it furthers, as having been accepted at the constitutional stage of analysis as a means of precommitting future government officials from short-circuiting those structures and the protections they provide. Subsequent history, by contrast, can be seen as operating at the level of legislative processes. If the Levinson and Pildes analysis is sound, and if separation of powers waxes and wanes between periods of unified and divided government, which doctrinal framing does that analysis most strongly support? Does it support the Buchanan and Tullock framework? Why or why not?

5. Chief Justice Burger's opinion, in marked contrast with that of Justice White, embraces a rigid separation of powers formalism that refuses to permit action by a single House other than in the circumstances precisely identified in the Constitution itself. Do the materials in this chapter suggest support for constitutional formalism in this context? Consider the argument that the one-House veto is not constitutionally problematic because contrary to Chief Justice Burger's argument, the underlying law that created it went through the "finely wrought and exhaustively considered, procedure" set out in Article I, § 7. In this analysis, because the statute creating the one-House veto was enacted by constitutional means, the vehicle it created to check against agency action lies outside the scope of Article I, § 7. Conversely, one might argue, given the high costs of securing constitutionally established

lawmaking procedures, it is important to insist upon rigid adherence to formalism. Which of these arguments is more persuasive? Which finds stronger support in public choice? Why?

6. Justice Powell views Congress's action as akin to judicial decision making. Chief Justice Burger replies by claiming that unlike Congress, a court does not have a "roving mandate to correct alleged excesses of administrative agencies; we are limited by Art. III to hearing cases and controversies." Does this argument undermine or strengthen Powell's position that the one-House veto is unconstitutional? Why? Does the analysis help to inform the understanding developed in this chapter and elsewhere in this book concerning the differences between adjudicatory and legislative lawmaking? Why or why not?

7. In Chapter 19, we examined the question of delegation by Congress to agencies from the perspective of public choice theory. Based upon your review of *Chadha*, how does that analysis relate to the question of the propriety of the one-House veto?

B. National Labor Relations Board v. Noel Canning

In *National Labor Relations Board v. Noel Canning*, the Supreme Court addressed the scope of the President's Recess Appointment power under the Constitution. The Constitution provides that as a general matter the President has the power to nominate "Office[rs] of the United States" but that those nominees can take office only if the President obtains "the Advice and Consent of the Senate" to the nomination.[134] The Recess Appointments Clause provides an exception, permitting the President, acting alone, "to fill up all Vacancies that may happen during the Recess of the Senate, by granting Commissions which shall expire at the End of their next Session."[135]

NLRB v. Noel Canning arose from the effort of President Barack Obama to use the Recess Appointment Clause to appoint three individuals to fill vacancies on the five-member National Labor Relations Board (NLRB).[136] In 2011 President Obama nominated three individuals to these open seats: Sharon Block, Richard Griffin, and Terrence Flynn.[137] As of January 2012, Flynn's nomination had been pending in the Senate awaiting confirmation for approximately one year; the Block and Griffin nominations had been pending for a few weeks. "On January 4, 2012, the President, invoking the Recess Appointment Clause, appointed all three to the Board."[138] As constituted with the three new members, the NLRB brought an action against Noel Canning for alleged violations of federal labor law.

From seperation of powers POV, we would want to narrowly construe the recess appointments power → recess appointments allows a unilateral action by one branch - the executive

Noel Canning challenged the NLRB's action on the basis that the Senate had not been in "recess" for purposes of the Recess Appointment clause. Under federal law, the NLRB could not operate without a quorum, which, by statute, required at least three

[134] U.S. CONST. art. II, § 2, cl. 2.

[135] U.S. CONST. art. II, § 2, cl. 3.

[136] Nat'l Lab. Relations Bd. v. Noel Canning, 134 S. Ct. 2550, 2557 (2014). A separate case challenged the appointment of Richard Cordray, which made it to the United States Court of Appeals for the District of Columbia Circuit. State Nat'l Bank of Big Spring v. CFPB, 795 F.3d 48 (D.C. Cir. 2015) (deciding that the bank had standing to challenge the recess appointment of Cordray, and remanding case to district court for consideration of Cordray in light of *NLRB v. Noel Canning*, among other things); *see also* PHH Corp. v. CFPB, 881 F.3d 75 (D.C. Cir. 2018) (en banc) (deciding that the structure of CFPB was not unconstitutional).

[137] 134 S. Ct. at 2557.

[138] *Id.*

members. If the appointments were struck down, the NLRB would lack a quorum, and the action against the company was invalid. The United States Court of Appeals for the DC Circuit agreed with Noel Canning's claim that the appointments failed to comply with the requirements of the Recess Appointments clause. In a unanimous decision, the Supreme Court affirmed, striking down the recess appointments and thus invalidating the action against Noel Canning.

Justice Breyer's opinion for the Court considered three issues. First, the Court examined the phrase "recess of the Senate." The Court asked whether it referred to only an "inter-session recess," meaning "a break between formal sessions of Congress," or instead, whether it also included "an intra-session recess, such as a summer recess in the midst of a session"?[139] Second, the Court considered the phrase "vacancies that may happen," and asked whether that phrase "refer[s] only to vacancies that first come into existence during a recess, or [whether] it also include[s] vacancies that arise prior to a recess but continue to exist during the recess?"[140] Finally, having determined that the clause can apply to intra-session recesses, the Court addressed how to calculate the duration of a recess.[141] Specifically, the Court asked whether so-called *pro forma* sessions of the Senate were sufficient to interrupt the calculation of time necessary to qualify as a "recess" under the Constitution.

Justice Breyer began by recognizing competing concepts that needed to be balanced in interpreting the Recess Appointments Clause. These included recognizing, first, that appointing judges and senior government officials required agreement between the President and the Senate, and second, that the President needs to be able to make recess appointments to ensure the smooth operation of the government during periods when the Senate is unavailable to act on presidential nominees. Breyer stressed the need to protect the President's staffing requirements, while, at the same time, seeking to ensure that the Recess Appointment Clause is not used to end-run the Senate's "advice and consent" function.

Breyer writes:

> Before turning to the specific questions presented, we shall mention two background considerations that we find relevant to all three. First, the Recess Appointments Clause sets forth a subsidiary, not a primary, method for appointing officers of the United States. The immediately preceding Clause—Article II, Section 2, Clause 2—provides the primary method of appointment. It says that the President "shall nominate, and by and with the Advice and Consent of the Senate, shall appoint Ambassadors, other public Ministers and Consuls, Judges of the supreme Court, and all other Officers of the United States" (emphasis added).

Quoting Alexander Hamilton's *Federalist No. 67*, Breyer noted that the Appointments Clause was intended as an exception to the general rule:

---

[139] *Id.* at 2556.

[140] *Id.*

[141] *Id.*

Hamilton further explained that the

> "ordinary power of appointment is confided to the President and Senate *jointly*, and can therefore only be exercised during the session of the Senate; but as it would have been improper to oblige this body to be continually in session for the appointment of officers; and as vacancies might happen *in their recess*, which it might be necessary for the public service to fill without delay, the succeeding clause is evidently intended to authorise the President *singly* to make temporary appointments."
>
> Thus the Recess Appointments Clause reflects the tension between, on the one hand, the President's continuous need for "the assistance of subordinates," and, on the other, the Senate's practice, particularly during the Republic's early years, of meeting for a single brief session each year. We seek to interpret the Clause as granting the President the power to make appointments during a recess but not offering the President the authority routinely to avoid the need for Senate confirmation.[142]

Justice Breyer emphasized the importance of placing "significant weight upon historical practice," especially in interpreting provisions that regulate "the relationship between Congress and the President."[143]

The Court held first that the Recess Appointments clause could apply to both inter and intra-session recess appointments, provided that the latter are "of substantial length,"[144] given the importance of ensuring "the continued functioning of the Federal Government when the Senate is away,"[145] which arises in both contexts. Breyer noted that the Senate's "capacity to participate in the appointments process has nothing to do with the words it uses to signal its departure,"[146] a conclusion that he claimed was supported by extensive historical evidence.

Given this conclusion, Breyer had to resolve "how long a recess must be in order to fall within the clause."[147] Justice Breyer concluded that "a 3-day recess would be too short" and that a recess "of more than 3 days but less than 10 days is presumptively too short to fall within the Clause."[148] He continued:

> We add the word "presumptively" to leave open the possibility that some very unusual circumstance—a national catastrophe, for instance, that renders the Senate unavailable but calls for an urgent response—could demand the exercise of the recess-appointment power during a shorter break. (It should go without saying—except that JUSTICE SCALIA compels us to say it—that

---

142 *Id.* at 2559 (citations omitted).

143 *Id.* at 2559.

144 *Id.* at 2560–61.

145 *Id.* at 2559.

146 *Id.* at 2559.

147 *Id.* at 2565–56.

148 *Id.* at 2567.

political opposition in the Senate would not qualify as an unusual circumstance.)[149]

Justice Breyer then turned to the second question, whether the clause applied only to vacancies that "initially occur during a recess," or whether it also applied to "vacancies that initially occur before a recess and continue to exist during the recess?"[150] He held that it applied to both. But he also acknowledged the potential difficulty with this interpretation:

> A broad interpretation might permit a President to avoid Senate confirmations as a matter of course. If the Clause gives the President the power to "fill up all vacancies" that occur before, and continue to exist during, the Senate's recess, a President might not submit any nominations to the Senate. He might simply wait for a recess and then provide all potential nominees with recess appointments. He might thereby routinely avoid the constitutional need to obtain the Senate's "advice and consent."[151]

Despite this concern, Justice Breyer concluded the Senate was well-equipped to prevent this occurrence by simply remaining in session, thereby "preventing recess appointments by refusing to take a recess."[152] In addition, the President faces built-in incentives to continue to use the ordinary nomination and confirmation processes as a norm, as recess appointees can serve for only a limited term and lacking the political legitimacy, and clout, associated with a full confirmation process.

Finally, Justice Breyer turned to the third question of determining the "calculation of the Senate's 'recess.' "[153] Justice Breyer asked whether *pro forma* sessions of the Senate were sufficient to interrupt a recess and thereby restart the recess clock. Justice Breyer held that they were. He writes,

> In our view, however, the *pro forma* sessions count as sessions, not as periods of recess. We hold that, for purposes of the Recess Appointments Clause, the Senate is in session when it says it is, provided that, under its own rules, it retains the capacity to transact Senate business. The Senate met that standard here.[154]

Breyer offered two justifications. First, during *pro forma* sessions, the Senate *said* it was in session, not in recess. And second, although the Senate resolved that it would not actually conduct substantive business during the *pro forma* sessions, it retained the power to do so.

After reviewing some of the dynamics that might arise as a consequence of the decision between the Presidency and the Senate respecting recess appointments, Breyer continues:

> [T]he Recess Appointments Clause is not designed to overcome serious institutional friction. It simply provides a subsidiary method for appointing

---

[149] *Id.*

[150] *Id.*

[151] *Id.* at 2569.

[152] *Id.*

[153] *Id.* at 2573.

[154] *Id.* at 2574.

officials when the Senate is away during a recess. Here, as in other contexts, friction between the branches is an inevitable consequence of our constitutional structure. That structure foresees resolution not only through judicial interpretation and compromise among the branches but also by the ballot box.[155]

He concludes his opinion by defending his resolution as striking the proper balance between the competing goals of the "advice and consent" and Recess Appointments clause:

> The Recess Appointments Clause responds to a structural difference between the Executive and Legislative Branches: The Executive Branch is perpetually in operation, while the Legislature only acts in intervals separated by recesses. The purpose of the Clause is to allow the Executive to continue operating while the Senate is unavailable. We believe that the Clause's text, standing alone, is ambiguous. It does not resolve whether the President may make appointments during intra-session recesses, or whether he may fill pre-recess vacancies. But the broader reading better serves the Clause's structural function. Moreover, that broader reading is reinforced by centuries of history, which we are hesitant to disturb. We thus hold that the Constitution empowers the President to fill any existing vacancy during any recess—intra-session or intersession—of sufficient length.
>
> JUSTICE SCALIA would render illegitimate thousands of recess appointments reaching all the way back to the founding era. More than that: Calling the Clause an "anachronism," he would basically read it out of the Constitution. . . . He performs this act of judicial excision in the name of liberty. We fail to see how excising the Recess Appointments Clause preserves freedom. In fact, Alexander Hamilton observed in the very first Federalist Paper that "the vigour of government is essential to the security of liberty." The Federalist No. 1, at 5. And the Framers included the Recess Appointments Clause to preserve the "vigour of government" at times when an important organ of Government, the United States Senate, is in recess. JUSTICE SCALIA's interpretation of the Clause would defeat the power of the Clause to achieve that objective.
>
> The foregoing discussion should refute JUSTICE SCALIA's claim that we have "embrace[d]" an "adverse-possession theory of executive power." . . . Instead, as in all cases, we interpret the Constitution in light of its text, purposes, and "our whole experience" as a Nation. And we look to the actual practice of Government to inform our interpretation.
>
> Given our answer to the last question before us, we conclude that the Recess Appointments Clause does not give the President the constitutional authority to make the appointments here at issue.[156]

[155] *Id.* at 2576–77 (citations omitted).

[156] *Id.* at 2577–78.

Justice Scalia filed an opinion concurring in the judgment, joined by Justices Roberts, Thomas, and Alito.[157] He agreed with the majority that the appointments in this case were improper but he disagreed with Justice Breyer on the applicability of the clause to intra-session recesses and for vacancies that did not arise during inter-session recesses, based on his reading of the plain language of the clause. Moreover, he disagreed with the majority opinion's heavy reliance on the history of the use of the recess appointments clause, arguing that the history of accommodation between the President and Senate did not give the Court authority to ignore the Constitution's clear commands. He writes:

> To prevent the President's recess-appointment power from nullifying the Senate's role in the appointment process, the Constitution cabins that power in two significant ways. First, it may be exercised only in "the Recess of the Senate," that is, the intermission between two formal legislative sessions. Second, it may be used to fill only those vacancies that "happen during the Recess," that is, offices that become vacant during that intermission. Both conditions are clear from the Constitution's text and structure, and both were well understood at the founding. The Court of Appeals correctly held that the appointments here at issue are invalid because they did not meet either condition.
>
> Today's Court agrees that the appointments were invalid, but for the far narrower reason that they were made during a 3-day break in the Senate's session. On its way to that result, the majority sweeps away the key textual limitations on the recess-appointment power. It holds, first, that the President can make appointments without the Senate's participation even during short breaks in the middle of the Senate's session, and second, that those appointments can fill offices that became vacant long before the break in which they were filled. The majority justifies those atextual results on an adverse-possession theory of executive authority: Presidents have long claimed the powers in question, and the Senate has not disputed those claims with sufficient vigor, so the Court should not "upset the compromises and working arrangements that the elected branches of Government themselves have reached." . . .
>
> The Court's decision transforms the recess-appointment power from a tool carefully designed to fill a narrow and specific need into a weapon to be wielded by future Presidents against future Senates. To reach that result, the majority casts aside the plain, original meaning of the constitutional text in deference to late-arising historical practices that are ambiguous at best. The majority's insistence on deferring to the Executive's untenably broad interpretation of the power is in clear conflict with our precedent and forebodes a diminution of this Court's role in controversies involving the separation of powers and the structure of government. I concur in the judgment only.

not based on text, but AP based on history

[157] *Id.*at 2592 (Scalia, J., concurring in the judgment).

Justice Scalia began by criticizing the majority's view that a historical practice of accommodation between the branches should be permitted to override the Constitution's text and the structures that the text defines.[158] He writes:

> Today's majority disregards two overarching principles that ought to guide our consideration of the questions presented here. First, the Constitution's core, government-structuring provisions are no less critical to preserving liberty than are the later adopted provisions of the Bill of Rights. Indeed, "[s]o convinced were the Framers that liberty of the person inheres in structure that at first they did not consider a Bill of Rights necessary."
>
> Second and relatedly, when questions involving the Constitution's government structuring provisions are presented in a justiciable case, it is the solemn responsibility of the Judicial Branch " 'to say what the law is.' " This Court does not defer to the other branches' resolution of such controversies; as JUSTICE KENNEDY has previously written, our role is in no way "lessened" because it might be said that "the two political branches are adjusting their own powers between themselves." Since the separation of powers exists for the protection of individual liberty, its vitality "does not depend" on "whether 'the encroached-upon branch approves the encroachment.' " . . .
>
> Our decision in *Chadha* illustrates that principle. There, we held that a statutory provision authorizing one House of Congress to cancel an executive action taken pursuant to statutory authority—a so-called "legislative veto"—exceeded the bounds of Congress's authority under the Constitution. We did not hesitate to hold the legislative veto unconstitutional even though Congress had enacted, and the President had signed, nearly 300 similar provisions over the course of 50 years. Just the opposite: We said the other branches' enthusiasm for the legislative veto "sharpened rather than blunted" our review. Likewise, when the charge is made that a practice "enhances the President's powers beyond" what the Constitution permits, "[i]t is no answer . . . to say that Congress surrendered its authority by its own hand." "[O]ne Congress cannot yield up its own powers, much less those of other Congresses to follow. Abdication of responsibility is not part of the constitutional design."
>
> Of course, where a governmental practice has been open, widespread, and unchallenged since the early days of the Republic, the practice should guide our interpretation of an ambiguous constitutional provision. But " '[p]ast practice does not, by itself, create power.' " That is a necessary corollary of the principle that the political branches cannot by agreement alter the constitutional structure. Plainly, then, a self-aggrandizing practice adopted by one branch well after the founding, often challenged, and never before blessed by this Court—in other words, the sort of practice on which the majority relies in this case—does not relieve us of our duty to interpret the Constitution in light of its text, structure, and original understanding.[159]

---

[158] *Id.* at 2593 (Scalia, J., concurring in the judgment).

[159] *Id.* at 2592–93 (Scalia, J. concurring in the judgment).

Although disagreeing that recess appointments could be made during intra-session recesses or that they could be made for vacancies that occur during a congressional session, Scalia concurred in the judgment. He concluded:

> What the majority needs to sustain its judgment is an ambiguous text and a clear historical practice. What it has is a clear text and an at-best-ambiguous historical practice. . . . There is thus no ground for the majority's deference to the unconstitutional recess-appointment practices of the Executive Branch.
>
> . . . Henceforth, the Senate can avoid triggering the President's now-vast recess-appointment power by the odd contrivance of never adjourning for more than three days without holding a *pro forma* session at which it is understood that no business will be conducted. How this new regime will work in practice remains to be seen. . . . In any event, the limitation upon the President's appointment power is there not for the benefit of the Senate, but for the protection of the people; it should not be dependent on Senate action for its existence.
>
> The real tragedy of today's decision is not simply the abolition of the Constitution's limits on the recess-appointment power and the substitution of a novel framework invented by this Court. It is the damage done to our separation-of-powers jurisprudence more generally. It is not every day that we encounter a proper case or controversy requiring interpretation of the Constitution's structural provisions. Most of the time, the interpretation of those provisions is left to the political branches—which, in deciding how much respect to afford the constitutional text, often take their cues from this Court. We should therefore take every opportunity to affirm the primacy of the Constitution's enduring principles over the politics of the moment. Our failure to do so today will resonate well beyond the particular dispute at hand. Sad, but true: The Court's embrace of the adverse-possession theory of executive power (a characterization the majority resists but does not refute) will be cited in diverse contexts, including those presently unimagined, and will have the effect of aggrandizing the Presidency beyond its constitutional bounds and undermining respect for the separation of powers.

DISCUSSION QUESTIONS

1. Justice Breyer's opinion for the court places substantial weight on historical practice regarding the interaction between the President and the Senate, particularly with respect to whether the Recess Appointments Clause applies to intra-session recesses. Justice Scalia challenges that line of reasoning, arguing that historical practice cannot override what he construes as clear, and contrary, constitutional text. Scalia suggests that by focusing only on the question of the interaction between the President and Senate, Breyer misses the overarching purpose of those structures, namely, preserving individual liberty, as opposed to construing the stated requirements as ends in themselves. Breyer responds that historical practice reflects balanced practical considerations that will not be undermined by the Court's ruling. Which approach do you find more persuasive, and why?

2. How does the question whether to defer to historic practice as between the President and Senate relate to the problem of agency cost? In studying agency delegation, we saw that Congress often delegates strategically, sometimes seeking to claim credit for certain actions and resist blame. In some instances, Congress appears willing to yield some of its powers, and to allow the Executive to increase its powers, in ways that serve the interests of individual members. To what extend does this imply that the Madisonian premise that the Executive and Legislative branches will regard themselves in an institutionally driven set of checks and balances fail to capture actual separation of powers dynamics? How does this relate to the Levinson and Pildes thesis?

Professor Neomi Rao, the present Administrator of the Office of Information and Regulatory Affairs ("OIRA"),[160] has argued that whereas delegation to the Executive branch diminishes congressional power as whole, it might actually *increase* the power of individual members of Congress.[161] This dichotomy arises because when Congress legislates, it does so collectively. When Congress delegates, however, individual members of Congress can exercise power through personal influence over agency decisions through informal measures of oversight and influence as discussed in Chapter 19. This incentive structure potentially fragments the collective Congress into individual actors, undermining the assumption that Congress will jealously guard its powers from encroachment by the President. Rao argues that in such instances, individual members of Congress might sometimes prefer to collude and share administrative power with the Executive, which can simultaneously increase the power of the President and of *individual* members of Congress, even as it diminishes the power of the *collective* Congress. Rao argues that these incentives lead to a tendency by Congress to "overdelegate" to the Executive branch and that more vigilant judicial monitoring of delegation is appropriate.

To what extent does Justice Breyer's argument depend on the assumption that Congress will jealously guard its powers from encroachment by the President? Does Rao's argument concerning a divergence between the interests of individual members of Congress and the "collective Congress" challenge Justice Breyer's willingness to defer to the historical practice as between the President and Senate in this context? About Justice White's deference to tradition in *Chadha*? To what extent does Rao's argument reflect Professor Shepsle's observation, discussed in Chapter 17, that Congress is a "they, not an it"? What implications does this hold for the Madisonian separation-of-powers model? What implications does it hold for the Levinson and Pildes alternative separation-of-parties framing?

3. From a game theoretical perspective, does the Madisonian vision of checks and balances assume that power allocations among the branches, and as between the federal and state governments, are necessarily zero sum? If so, is the assumption sound? Why or why not? Assuming any accretion of power to one branch or level of government comes at the expense of power originally vested elsewhere, does that necessarily imply that rebalancing powers based on practical accommodations over time is mistaken? Does it matter that in some contexts, both sides in a rebalancing acquiesce? When this occurs, does it imply that the game might instead be positive sum? Or is insisting on the original power allocation, as Justice Scalia

---

[160] Steve Eder, Neomi Rao, The Scholar Who Will Help Lead Trump's Regulatory Overhaul: Trump Rules, N.Y. Times (July 9, 2017), https://www.nytimes.com/2017/07/09/business/the-scholar-who-will-help-lead-trumps-assault-on-rules.html.

[161] *See* Neomi Rao, *Administrative Collusion: How Delegation Diminishes the Collective Congress*, 90 N.Y.U. L. REV. 1463 (2015).

suggests, essential to preserving individual liberty? Can you think of a way to test empirically whether such power allocation games are likely to be zero- or positive-sum?

In Chapter 15, we saw that in a prisoners' dilemma game, although mutual defection is the pure Nash equilibrium solution in a single period, mutual cooperation can emerge the pure Nash equilibrium when the parties anticipate unlimited iterations. Is it fair to assume that Congress and the Presidency, unlike individuals, reasonably anticipate continuous future rounds of play? If so, does this suggest that these institutions have identified circumstances resulting in mutual accommodations over time with payoffs that are positive sum? Or does it instead imply that the political branches are prone to collude to augment federal powers at the expense of individual liberty? How does the separation of parties thesis affect this analysis?

As Adam Pritchard and Todd Zywicki support the collusion view, stating:

> But those locked in this zero-sum game inevitably will try to change the rules to make it a positive-sum game for themselves. Thus, state and federal government actors seek to collude over the allocation of authority and revenues, maximizing each level's ability to distribute rent-seeking opportunities. The federal courts have insufficient incentive to enforce violations of federalism and separation of powers, especially when those violations further policies favored by individual judges. Over time, the separation of powers deteriorates into a system of collusion of powers, with the individual elements conspiring to increase their collective powers. While the eventual distribution of the spoils of increased government power are uncertain, substantial gains from trade, coupled with a sufficiently small number of actors, ensure that the collective action necessary to create this surplus usually will be feasible.
>
> While there are gains to trade among the actors involved, their collective action imposes external costs on the public at-large. The public is largely powerless to stop this collusion, and individual citizens will generally lack the incentive to police these structural protections. The costs to any individual of fighting this collusion of powers will far outweigh any potential individual benefits. As a result, federal and state actors will gain at the expense of the general public. A close analogy exists to sellers' gains from agreeing to cartelize a market to extract higher prices from buyers.[162]

Professors Pritchard and Zywicki posit that many of the traditional accommodations between the branches of the federal government can be seen as consistent with the "collusion of powers" model to increase the power of *both* the Executive and Legislative branches simultaneously, rather than as consistent with broad, consensus-grounded traditions. As a result, they call into question the soundness of the historical analysis that informs the opinions of Justice Breyer for the *Noel Canning* majority and of Justice White dissenting in *Chadha*. They contrast the types of traditions upon which these jurists rely with traditions that develop from broader, consensus-generating processes, which they see as a potentially valuable source of constitutional values.[163]

---

[162] A.C. Pritchard & Todd J. Zywicki, *Constitutions and Spontaneous Orders: A Response to Professor McGinnis*, 77 N.C. L. REV. 537, 539 (1999).

[163] *See* A.C. Pritchard & Todd J. Zywicki, *Finding the Constitution: An Economic Analysis of Tradition's Role in Constitutional Interpretation*, 77 N.C. L. REV. 409 (1999). For a related discussion arising in a federalism context, see *infra* Chapter 24 (discussing Michael Greve thesis concerning "collusive federalism").

Do you agree with the Pritchard and Zywicki analysis? Why or why not? Is it possible that rather than reflecting an aggrandizement of power through mutual collusion, the historical practices upon which Justices Breyer and White rely reflect the very different reality of a Constitution drafted ratified in the late 1780s, that provides only a bare bones framing of separation of powers and checks and balances, and that, as a result, demands genuine play in the joints to render the system functional over very extended periods of time? Is the relative challenge of amending the Constitution consistent or in tension with this understanding? Why or why not? Which framing do you find more persuasive? Why?

4. In *NLRB v. Noel Canning*, *amicus* briefs were filed on behalf of Noel Canning's challenge by the Republican Speaker of the House John Boehner, by Senate Republican Leader Mitch McConnell, and 44 other members of the United States Senate. Every member of the Senate represented in McConnell's brief was a Republican. No Democratic member of Congress or of the Senate filed any brief in opposition to the Obama administration's reliance upon the Recess Appointments power. Senate Majority Leader Harry M. Reid, a Democrat, supported President Obama's reliance on the Recess Appointment power and criticized the Supreme Court ruling, stating: "President Obama did the right thing when he made these appointments on behalf of American workers."[164] What does this history suggest about the separation of power, and separation of parties, models of constitutionalism?

5. In *Noel Canning*, Justices Breyer and Scalia express very different understandings of the role of formal versus informal institutional checks in safeguarding against potential abuses of executive powers. Justice Breyer's analysis is reminiscent of the "congressional control model" of Barry Weingast and Mark Moran discussed in Chapter 20. Recall that Weingast and Moran posited that the relatively rare use of formal oversight tools (such as hearings and contested confirmation battles) does not imply that Congress has failed to engage in active control of independent agencies. Is a similar analysis appropriate in this context? Does Justice Breyer's analysis suggest that judicial enforcement of formal text-based limits on separation of powers should be avoided? Why or why not?

6. Justice Scalia notes that one implication of deferring to historical practice is that a compromise between the President and the Senate today can eventually be used as "a weapon" by future Presidents against future Senates. Consider Levinson and Pildes's argument that the degree of accommodation that the Legislature makes to the President will differ depending on whether it is a period of unified or divided party government. If they are correct, that would suggest that the Senate might make accommodations to the President during periods of unified government that might later be asserted as a precedent during a period of divided government. What implications does this analysis hold for Justice Breyer's reliance on historical practice? If historical practice is considered relevant to deciding such cases, should judges attempt to discern whether any particular practice arose during a period of unified or divided government? Do you see any administrability problems with this approach?

7. The separation of parties' model invites a kind of chicken-and-egg problem. On the one hand, the Levinson and Pildes analysis might imply that existing constitutional rules should be interpreted to vary in their application depending on whether a challenged separation of powers accommodation arises during a period of unified or divided government. On the other hand, it might imply that the Constitution should be amended or otherwise

---

[164] *See* Robert Barnes, *Supreme Court Rebukes Obama on Recess Appointments*, WASH. POST (June 26, 2014), https://www.washingtonpost.com/politics/supreme-court-rebukes-obama-on-recess-appointments/2014/06/26/e5e4fefa-e831-11e3-a86b-362fd5443d19_story.html?utm_term=.27609809a6e4.

altered—could this be accomplished through constitutional judicial review?—to embrace formal but prospective rules that recognize these changed governance circumstances and that instruct the judiciary to respond accordingly.

Which of these possible readings do you find more compelling? If you find the former approach more compelling, how would you reconcile that with the language of the Constitution, which only in the most limited way, such as in the Twelfth Amendment, recognizes the existence of political parties, and even then, does not acknowledge the very real problem of divided government? If you find the latter approach more compelling, how would you accommodate the enormous challenge—bordering on impossibility—of amending the Constitution to reflect such a profound change in the premises of our constitutional democracy? If you held the power to amend the Constitution to reflect the separation of parties' model, what amendment or amendments would you enact?

Consider these questions in the context of a longer historical framing. In superseding the Articles of Confederation with the Constitution, the Framers avoided the Articles' amending process, which required the unanimous consent of all states. Consider Article 2: "Each state retains its sovereignty, freedom, and independence, and every power, jurisdiction, and right, which is not by this Confederation expressly delegated to the United States, in Congress assembled."[165] Although the Articles envisioned amending, and despite the challenges under the Articles—a single branch, the lack a head of state, the lack of a general federal judiciary, the inability of direct taxation, and the like—the decision not to use the Articles amending process might have resulted from the foundational question of sovereignty. Amending would have implied accepting the Articles' premise that the States, rather than the People, were the ultimate sovereign. By avoiding the Articles' amending process, and instead sending the proposed Constitution to popularly elected State ratifying conventions, as opposed to preexisting state general assemblies, the Framers signaled a change in the foundational premise of the new governing document.

Would superseding the Constitution with a system that recognized the foundational role of parties require a similar abandonment of constitutional premises that would make the task of amending to accomplish the goal problematic, and perhaps impossible? Why or why not? If it would, does this risk opening a Pandora's Box respecting a host of other historical features of the existing Constitution that would justify abandonment? Do these problems help to explain the continued reliance upon a formal system of separation of powers that does not align with the reality of separation of parties? Why or why not?

---

[165] ARTICLES OF CONFEDERATION of 1781, art. II.

CHAPTER 24

Constitutions (Part 2)

Introduction

Chapter 23 relied upon various tools of public choice to assess structural aspects of the legislature and separation of powers within constitutional systems. Our particular emphasis involved the United States Constitution. This chapter considers other aspects of constitutional systems.

Part I provides a detailed focus of the judiciary, including the role of life-tenured judges and the power of judicial review—topics of particular interest to law students. Part II considers various aspects of federalism, a critical feature that has been described as an invention of those who framed the United States Constitution.[1] Part III evaluates direct democracy, an increasingly prevalent, if criticized, alternative to conventional legislative lawmaking. Part IV considers the amending process, one that in the U.S. Constitution has been widely criticized for its relative difficulty. The chapter concludes, in part V, with an Application.

I. THE JUDICIARY AND JUDICIAL REVIEW

A. The Basic Framing

Among other objectives, the independent judiciary has been justified as furthering two goals associated with bicameralism and the executive veto: first, frustrating special-interest groups, or factions; and, second, enforcing individual rights. As Alexander Hamilton states in *Federalist No. 78*:

> This independence of the judges is equally requisite to guard the Constitution and the rights of individuals from the effects of those ill humors which the arts of designing men, or the influence of particular conjunctures, sometimes disseminate among the people themselves, and which, though they speedily give place to better information, and more deliberate reflection, have a tendency, in the meantime, to occasion dangerous innovations in the government, and serious oppressions of the minor party in the community. [Although the people have the right to government grounded in their consent]

1 United States v. Lopez, 514 U.S. 549, 575–76 (1995) (Kennedy, J., concurring).

> yet it is not to be inferred from this principle that the representatives of the people, whenever a momentary inclination happens to lay hold of a majority of their constituents incompatible with the provisions in the existing Constitution would, on that account, be justifiable in a violation of those provisions; or that the courts would be under a greater obligation to connive at infractions in this shape than when they had proceeded wholly from the cabals of the representative body. Until the people have, by some solemn and authoritative act, annulled or changed the established form, it is binding upon themselves collectively, as well as individually; and no presumption, or even knowledge of their sentiments, can warrant their representatives in a departure from it prior to such an act. But it is easy to see that it would require an uncommon portion of fortitude in the judges to do their duty as faithful guardians of the Constitution, where legislative invasions of it had been instigated by the major voice of the community.[2]

Scholars working in the public choice tradition have modeled the role of the independent judiciary in a manner consistent with Hamilton's account. Professors A.C. Pritchard and Todd Zywicki, for instance, argue that judicial review furthers the goals of precommitment and reduction of agency costs. As they define the terms, "Precommitment allows a super-majority to put certain actions beyond the power of government in order to preclude potentially rash actions by future majority coalitions that are inconsistent with society's long-term interest."[3] By placing the authority to enforce these constitutional precommitments in an independent body, society can "bind itself to the mast" to limit the choices of future majorities.

Following Buchanan and Tullock, Pritchard and Zywicki note that, ideally, constitutional rights would be amendable only by unanimous vote.[4] As previously discussed, however, the unanimity standard is impracticable, thus leading to the adoption of supermajority precommitments as a proxy for unanimity. Recall also that agency costs arise when public officials pursue their own personal interests at the expense of their principals, here their constituents. Pritchard and Zywicki summarize the forms that these agency costs might take:

> Actors in all three branches of government may impose agency costs on the citizenry (the "principal"): legislators, who will garner votes and money by extracting wealth from the public at large and transferring that wealth to concentrated interest groups; enforcement authorities, who may exploit a lack of monitoring by legislatures and voters to act in their own interests; and

[2] THE FEDERALIST NO. 78, at 469–70 (Alexander Hamilton) (Clinton Rossiter ed., 1961). In addition, as discussed in Chapter 17, Hamilton advanced the view that beyond policing unconstitutional laws, the independent judiciary could interpret statutes to further public interest goals, thus making special-interest payoffs from enacted statutes more difficult to secure, although this function generally has not been translated into constitutional doctrine.

[3] A.C. Pritchard & Todd J. Zywicki, *Finding the Constitution: An Economic Analysis of Tradition's Role in Constitutional Interpretation*, 77 N.C. L. REV. 409, 446–67 (1999).

[4] For a discussion of the Buchanan and Tullock analysis of the importance of unanimity norm and the need to relax it based upon impracticability, see *supra* Chapter 23.

judges, who may use their positions and independence to impose their personal policy preferences on society and to increase their status.[5]

Pritchard and Zywicki describe as "constitutionally efficient" those policies that reduce agency costs or that are supported by a high degree of consensus, for example, as indicated by supermajorities, thus rendering them fit to be the subject of a precommitment. Judicial review in this model works to enforce precommitments and to limit agency costs. The authors acknowledge, however, that an independent judiciary potentially creates or enhances agency costs with respect to those judges who might use their powers inappropriately to define new rights that lack the necessary grounding in supermajority support.

Does public choice theory justify an independent judiciary that plays such a precommitment role in interpreting the Constitution? Consider, for instance, that the President has only a qualified veto of legislation, which can be overridden by two-thirds vote in both Houses of Congress. By contrast, Article V of the Constitution is highly cumbersome, and, as discussed below, is subject to several of its own agency-cost problems, thereby making the threat of constitutional amendment an extremely weak check on judicial agency costs. Is the amending process a sufficient check against unpopular Supreme Court decisions that interpret the Constitution?

Over the years, there have been several legislative proposals to allow Congress, by a supermajority vote, to overturn unpopular Supreme Court rulings.[6] Leaving aside the constitutional questions of such a practice, would this proposal be wise or unwise as a matter of public policy? Does your answer depend on the level of congressional consensus required for such legislative overrides? Why or why not?

Is it possible that the system is functioning as intended without legislative overrides, and that the Supreme Court has responded to the changing perceptions as to what rights are, or should be, deemed fundamental over time? Is it possible to answer this question based on tools of public choice? Or does the answer, instead, depend on holding a commitment to a particular jurisprudential philosophy, such as original meaning or living constitutionalism?

---

[5] Pritchard & Zywicki, *supra* note 3, at 447–48.

[6] For one example, see Congressional Accountability for Judicial Activism Act, H.R. 3920, 108th Cong. (2004), introduced by Representative Ron Lewis (R. Kan.), which would have permitted Congress to overrule Supreme Court decisions striking down acts of Congress on constitutional grounds. This Bill and a similar bill sponsored again by Representative Lewis did not pass. *See also* ROBERT BORK, COERCING VIRTUE: THE WORLDWIDE RULE OF JUDGES 80 (2003) (discussing related proposal). *See also* Private Property Rights Protection Act, H.R. 1443, 112th Cong. (2012). This bill was introduced to overturn *Kelo v. City of New London*, 545 U.S. 469 (2005). The bill, titled the Private Property Rights Protection Act, introduced from the 109th through the 115th Congress, would have prohibited states from using eminent domain over property to be used for economic development and would have established a private right of action for affected property owners for alleged violations by a state or local government.

B. The Independent Judiciary in Practice

In an important study of the federal judiciary,[7] Professor William Landes and then-Professor Richard Posner claimed that judicial independence is likely to prolong the durability of special-interest bargains secured in the legislature.[8] As compared with elected judges, who are more likely to be responsive to the sitting legislature when construing statutes, Article III judges, who are politically insulated, are freer to interpret statutes with reference to the "intent of the enacting legislature."[9] As a result, the authors claim, to the extent that such legislation included bargains among interest groups to secure the deal, the independent judiciary is more likely than a dependent judiciary to seek evidence of, and to ensure and prolong the payoffs from, the resulting bargain. Article III judges are thus apt to extend the reach of legislation beyond the life of the enacting legislature, increasing the expected value of the resulting economic rents.

Some scholars have criticized the Landes and Posner thesis on various normative grounds. Jonathan Macey has argued that, to the contrary, part of the judiciary's role is to minimize or avoid interest group payoffs.[10] Einer Elhauge maintains that political satisfaction is optimized when the judiciary resolves statutory ambiguities with reference to contemporary enactable preferences rather than with reference to those of prorogued legislative sessions.[11] Donald Boudreaux and Adam Pritchard argue that if, in fact, judicial independence prolongs the duration of interest group bargains, then, as a result of the higher present value of the interest groups payoffs, the procurement costs will predictably rise as legislators will rationally demand higher payment for more durable benefits. As a result, the authors maintain, the independent judiciary should inhibit, rather than promote, related legislative bargaining.[12] Boudreaux and Pritchard conclude that the purpose of judicial independence is to limit enforcement of interest group payoffs, which, conversely, will facilitate legislative bargaining.

Robert Tollison has claimed a partial corroboration of the Landes and Posner thesis. Tollison posits that if judicial independence prolongs the life of ordinary legislation, the frequency of state constitutional amending should negatively correlate to the degree of state judicial independence.[13] In states that have dependent judiciaries, there is a greater

---

7 William M. Landes & Richard A. Posner, *The Independent Judiciary in an Interest-Group Perspective*, 18 J.L. & ECON. 875 (1975).

8 Recall from Chapter 11 that increasing the durability of legislation increases the present value of the resulting economic rents, thereby also increasing the willingness of interest groups to invest in securing the legislation.

9 Landes & Posner, *supra* note 7, at 883.

10 Jonathan R. Macey, *Promoting Public-Regarding Legislation Through Statutory Interpretation: An Interest Group Model*, 86 COLUM. L. REV. 223 (1986).

11 EINER ELHAUGE, STATUTORY DEFAULT RULES: HOW TO INTERPRET UNCLEAR LEGISLATION 9–10 (2008).

12 *See* Donald J. Boudreaux & A.C. Pritchard, *Reassessing the Role of the Independent Judiciary in Enforcing Interest-Group Bargains*, 5 CONST. POL. ECON. 1, 9–11 (1994).

13 *See* Robert D. Tollison, *Public Choice and Legislation*, 74 VA. L. REV. 339, 347 (1988); *see also* Gary M. Anderson, William F. Shughart II & Robert D. Tollison, *On the Incentives of Judges to Enforce Legislative Wealth Transfers*, 32 J.L. & ECON. 215, 220–27 (1989) (demonstrating that judges with a higher degree of independence—as measured by enforcement of original contracts—receive higher salaries); *but see* Jonathan R. Macey, *Transactions Costs and the Normative Elements of the Public Choice Model: An Application to Constitutional Theory*,

benefit from state constitutional amending since amending, the more difficult procedure, becomes necessary to extend the life of interest group bargains as compared with states that have independent judiciaries, which are more solicitous of the views of the enacting legislature. Tollison claims support for his thesis in his empirical study of state constitutions.

Although the Landes and Posner analysis has been criticized, to what extent do the criticisms fail properly to capture the normative implications of the thesis? Consider the following argument. Assuming that the independent judiciary has the claimed effect of prolonging the life of special-interest bargains, it does not necessarily do so for the sake of advancing interest group payoffs themselves. Rather, given the difficulty of securing federal legislation, including special-interest payoffs secured in the course of legislative bargaining,[14] the promise of an extended payoff from successful legislative procurements increases the motivation of interest groups to participate in legislative bargaining. The overall goal for the system, in this analysis, is not to provide payoffs to special interests for their own sake. Instead, motivating active participation by special interests is the necessary grease in the complex legislative machine that facilitates the passage of desired *general interest* legislation. In this analysis, by prolonging the life of special-interest legislation, the independent judiciary helps to motivate active political participation by interest groups as needed to facilitate the passage of desired general interest legislation.

To what extent does this suggested normative justification for judicial independence, which is consistent with the Landes and Posner thesis, run parallel to the normative argument for declining to adopt the item veto, as discussed in Chapter 23? Both arguments presume that existing constitutional mechanisms (the independent judiciary and the actual presidential veto) can be viewed as benefiting special interests, but that the overriding normative justification for conferring the benefit is to encourage desired public interest legislation. Do you find this argument persuasive in the context of the independent judiciary? Why or why not?

II. FEDERALISM

Public choice theory also has important implications for the study of federalism, meaning the division of power between two or more levels of government. While it is common to view federalism as operating within nations, the increasing interdependency of the global economy has also invited the development of new governance institutions with federalism-style structures operating internationally. Interdependencies created by the challenges of global trade, terrorism, environmental impacts, and migration have all contributed to the growth of such novel governance regimes. Many matters previously governed at the national or sub-national level are increasingly subject to the jurisdiction of regional, international, or global entities. Such institutions as the European Union, World Trade Organization, and United Nations, relatively modern innovations, are now taking an increasingly larger role with respect to a broad domain of human activity. This

---

74 VA. L. REV. 471, 496–97 (1988) (criticizing the Anderson, Shughart and Tollison thesis on the ground that, ironically, compensatory rewards for enforcing original agreements demonstrates dependence on the sitting legislature).

[14] *See supra* Chapter 17.

invites the challenge of knitting together diverse national economic, political, and cultural practices into novel governance structures and of allocating decision-making authority among spheres of government in a manner that sometimes challenges traditional notions of sovereignty, but that also implicates the theoretical foundations of federalism.

Whether the challenges of federalism are old (such as the knitting together of the United States into a nation in the late Eighteenth Century) or new (such as constructing a global environmental policy), the underlying analytical structure—and challenges—remain the same: What is the appropriate level of governance for particular regulatory powers, and should such power be exclusive or shared with other levels of government? The overriding normative goal should be to allocate governmental powers where they can be exercised most effectively.

Accomplishing this objective requires balancing two offsetting policy goals, each of which gives rise to a distinct model of federalism. The first model presents federalism in static form. As a formal matter, how does the federalism regime "assign" or "match" a given power to the appropriate level of governance? The second model focuses on the dynamic relationships that emerge after such formal assignments of power are complete. As a dynamic matter, how does "competitive federalism" affect the allocation of power among different jurisdictions within a nation, or other sovereign entity, for citizens, firms, and tax revenues?

In theory, jurisdictional authority should be neither over- nor under-inclusive with respect to the problem for which power has been assigned. Because political jurisdictions are constrained by geographic, historical, cultural, and strategic considerations, to name a few, they do not operate within a robust competitive environment. Instead, they tend by nature to be "lumpy." There is rarely, if ever, a perfect match that renders the organ or level of governance to which power is assigned perfectly suited to resolving the problems motivating the assignment.[15]

A. Static Federalism: The Matching Problem

We begin with the *assignment problem* or the *matching problem*, which relate to spillovers or externalities. Solving these problems involves balancing the competing dynamics of free riding and forced riding.[16] We begin with a stylized example involving the proper level of governance for regulating bodies of water internal to a state, running through contiguous states, and abutting contiguous and noncontiguous states.

The Commonwealth of Virginia contains or abuts three different types of bodies of water: (1) lakes that are entirely self-contained within the state; (2) rivers that flow from points in Virginia to points within, or through, neighboring states; and (3) the Atlantic Ocean, which abuts not only Virginia and other states along the eastern shore, but also Canada and Mexico, and countries on altogether different continents. To simplify the analysis, assume that the full impact of any regulations affecting each body of water affects

---

[15] Once again, it is helpful to remember the nirvana fallacy. The issue is not whether an assignment is perfect, but rather whether it is better than available alternatives. *See supra* Chapter 13.

[16] For discussions of these terms, *see* Chapter 1.

only those states or nations with direct physical contact to the water, meaning that there are no additional inter-jurisdictional spillover effects.

Based upon this premise, the formal theory of federalism suggests that the assigned regulatory powers respecting each of these three types of bodies of water will vary according to the governance level that represents the best fit based strictly upon the geographical consideration of physical contact with the relevant body of water. If, for example, an assignment is under-inclusive—giving Virginia exclusive regulatory powers respecting a river that also runs through North Carolina—this creates the risk that the regulators will fail to give adequate consideration to the concerns of affected interests of the neighboring state. For example, the governing body might permit Virginians to dump waste in a manner that adversely affects out-of-state downstream users.

The matching problem can also result from an over-inclusive assignment of decision-making authority. In the case of the lake contained within Virginia, for example, consider whether residents of North Carolina or Maryland would have the proper incentives regarding its usage if afforded regulatory power. One might, for example, imagine residents of North Carolina—who may be competing for tourism dollars—seeking to restrict the use of the lake in Virginia in connection with a resort.

Todd Zywicki has presented empirical support to establish that politicians in industrial northern states have historically exerted pressure to enact federal environmental regulations that operate to the economic detriment of states in the developing regions elsewhere in the United States. Doing so has protected unionized manufacturing jobs from competition in the Sunbelt.[17]

Does this illustrate failing properly to match regulatory powers with affected interests? Why or why not? Does it illustrate the Buchanan and Tullock thesis that externalities necessarily include being forced to contribute to public activity benefiting others? Which governing institution(s) should have the power to regulate activity affecting the Atlantic Ocean, given that it touches upon multiple continents? How is your answer affected by the fact that global climate change resulting from, among other sources, mobile-sourced carbon emissions, threatens hurricanes and other environmental harms at a greater rate in countries that are not the primary contributors to those threats?[18]

B. Dynamic Federalism: Jurisdictional Competition

One model of competitive federalism suggests that states compete to attract residents and resources, and that rational individuals, acting like consumers, will select those jurisdictions that best match their preferences for publicly provided goods and

---

[17] *See* Todd J. Zywicki, *Environmental Externalities and Political Externalities: The Political Economy of Environmental Regulation and Reform*, 73 TUL. L. REV. 845, 866–68 (1999).

[18] *See, e.g.*, Andrew C. Revkin, *Poor Nations to Bear Brunt as World Warms*, N.Y. TIMES (Apr. 1, 2007), http://www.nytimes.com/2007/04/01/science/earth/01climate.html (noting implications of Intergovernmental Panel on Climate Change report finding that poor countries, who have traditionally not been the largest polluters, are likely to bear most of the burden of climate change and be less capable of dealing with its effects.).

taxes.[19] In this model, developed by Charles Tiebout, public goods will be efficiently provided according to voter preferences where "(1) people and resources are mobile; (2) the number of jurisdictions is large; (3) jurisdictions are free to select any set of laws they desire; and (4) there are no spillovers" onto other jurisdictions.[20]

Although Tiebout was concerned with identifying mechanisms for providing an optimal mix of taxes with the provision of public goods, his model can be extended to assess mechanisms that facilitate an optimal match of individual preferences respecting governmental policies in general, including economic or social policies.[21] Even so, individuals choose where to live based upon countless variables beside particular public goods or social policies. These typically include employment opportunities, family, and quality of education. Although the Tiebout model predicts some degree of competition among political jurisdictions, consider the extent to which people might be inframarginal with respect to the decision where to live. In this context, inframarginal implies that the provision of particular governmental goods or services, or decisions on specific economic or social policies, might not have a substantial effect on the location decisions of many constituents whose choices are dominated by other considerations.

Assuming that most people are inframarginal with respect to where they live, what are the implications for constraining government regulatory burdens? Economists have identified *agglomeration economies*, meaning the clustering of firms in a particular industry within a given metropolitan area, such as the financial sector in New York City.[22] Although for persons seeking employment in that sector, the industry location is apt to dominate the general geographical choice, does meaningful competition nonetheless prevail at the municipal level respecting the decision as to where to live?[23]

A second model of competitive federalism focuses on the power of individuals to "exit" one jurisdiction and to relocate to another.[24] The "exit" model is closely related to the Tiebout model, but rather than focusing on the ability of consumers to move into those jurisdictions that offer a preferred mix of policies, it instead focuses on the role of exit as a means of checking state governmental powers to tax and regulate. The massive migration of African-Americans from the American South to northern cities to escape

---

[19] *See* Charles M. Tiebout, *A Pure Theory of Local Expenditures*, 64 J. POL. ECON. 416 (1956), *reprinted in* 1 ECONOMICS OF FEDERALISM 5 (Bruce H. Kobayashi & Larry E. Ribstein eds., 2007). Tiebout's approach was to some extent anticipated in Friedrich A. Hayek, *The Economic Conditions of Interstate Federalism*, NEW COMMONWEALTH Q., Sept. 1939, at 131, *reprinted in* FRIEDRICH A. HAYEK, INDIVIDUALISM AND ECONOMIC ORDER 255 (1948); F.A. HAYEK, THE CONSTITUTION OF LIBERTY (1960).

[20] Bruce H. Kobayashi & Larry E. Ribstein, *Introduction* to 1 ECONOMICS OF FEDERALISM, *supra* note 19, at xi. This is an idealized model of perfect competition among jurisdictions. Slight deviations from the conditions described would reduce the efficiency of inter-jurisdictional competition on the margin, but would not entirely undermine the model.

[21] Tiebout himself recognized that the principle extended to non-economic variables such as the desire "to associate with 'nice' people." Tiebout, *supra* note 19, at 418 n.12.

[22] *See* David Schleicher, Why Are There Cities? Local Government Law and the Economics of Agglomeration 64–65 (April 2009) (unpublished manuscript) (on file with George Mason University Library system).

[23] Tax incentives on commuting costs could potentially affect municipal exit. For an examination of tax policy and commuting expenses, see Tsilly Dagan, *Commuting*, 26 VA. TAX REV. 185 (2006).

[24] *See* Richard A. Epstein, *Exit Rights Under Federalism*, LAW & CONTEMP. PROBS., Winter 1992, at 147.

institutionalized discrimination during the Jim Crow era provides an example of the use of "exit" rights under federalism.

Federalism provides helpful insights into other constitutionally established institutions. The opportunity for exit rights under federalism helps to explain the seeming anomaly that Congress and state legislatures tend toward bicameralism, whereas local governments tend toward unicameralism.[25] Professor Saul Levmore suggests that relatively fierce jurisdictional competition at the county and municipal level, unlike at the state and federal levels, is effective at disciplining regulatory waste. Certainly, local governments can be wasteful. The Tiebout model suggests, however, that local jurisdictional competition is likely to produce a better match between the desired provision of goods and services and constituent preferences than takes place at higher levels of government. In addition, one empirical study finds that local governments above a certain minimum size that face substantial competition from surrounding municipalities tend to have proportionally lower spending levels.[26] This suggests that jurisdictional competition promotes a more efficient provision of public goods and services. These findings corroborate an important insight generally attributed to Albert Hirschman. Hirschman posited that individuals unable to exit a particular jurisdiction can more meaningfully affect policy through electoral "voice" at local than at higher levels of governance.[27]

The ability of adversely affected parties to exit a given jurisdiction places a substantially greater constraint on the power of winning coalitions to impose external costs on political losers. The threat, and even the actuality, of exit permits those most likely to be harmed by regulatory waste to truncate the external costs function (in the Buchanan and Tullock model), and the enhanced power of voice at the local level further checks against potentially excessive agency costs. Saul Levmore posits that the combined strategies of exit, per Tiebout, and voice, per Hirschman, provide an effective substitute for either a supermajority requirement in a unicameral legislature or simple majority rule in a bicameral legislature. This helps to explain the persistence of unicameralism, typically with simple majority rule, at the county and municipal level.[28]

C. Competitive Federalism and Choice of Law

The relationship between federalism and exit also has important implications for the permissibility of contractual choice of law. In theory, contractual choice of law promotes

---

[25] Saul Levmore, *Bicameralism: When Are Two Decisions Better Than One?*, 12 INT'L REV. L. & ECON. 145, 159–62 (1992).

[26] Robert P. Inman & Daniel L. Rubinfeld, *The Political Economy of Federalism*, *in* PERSPECTIVES ON PUBLIC CHOICE 73, 80–86 (Dennis C. Mueller ed., 1997).

[27] ALBERT O. HIRSCHMAN, EXIT, VOICE, AND LOYALTY: RESPONSES TO DECLINE IN FIRMS, ORGANIZATIONS, AND STATES (1970).

[28] Levmore also inquires why juries are unicameral bodies of twelve, rather than, say, bicameral bodies of six. Levmore, *supra* note 25, at 145–46. Can you think of advantages or disadvantages to each of these regimes? Would bicameral juries be more likely to benefit the prosecutor or defendant? For a social choice analysis of juries, see Edward P. Schwartz & Warren F. Schwartz, *Deciding Who Decides Who Dies: Capital Punishment as a Social Choice Problem,* 1 LEGAL THEORY 113 (1995); Edward P. Schwartz & Warren F. Schwartz, *Decisionmaking by Juries Under Unanimity and Supermajority Voting Rules*, 80 GEO. L.J. 775 (1992).

private ordering by allowing those who prefer the law of another jurisdiction, as compared with the law governing their immediate transactions, to effectively exit, thereby gaining the benefit of that preferred legal regime, without incurring the ordinary costs of physical exit. Some scholars have argued that legal systems optimize preferences when they broadly permit contractual choice of law.[29] Doctrinally, this would allow contracting parties in a given jurisdiction to designate an alternative jurisdiction's legal regime without requiring that either party demonstrate a traditionally required nexus to the governing law's jurisdiction. While these proposals nominally implicate private law, they nonetheless hold significant implications for state sovereignty and federalism and for the relative efficacy of exit versus voice in affecting the direction of legal policy for contracting parties.

Consider the following argument. Given the information costs associated with contracting out of a particular jurisdiction's legal regime, proposals to allow, or to broaden, contractual choice of law are most likely to benefit relatively wealthy and sophisticated actors. The choice of law argument presents the following choice: We can either allow jurisdictions to continue to "capture" those individuals and businesses who would most benefit from contractual choice of law, or we can allow such persons and firms to effectively exit through the low cost means of contract. The cost is low because the parties need not physically relocate to gain the benefit of another jurisdiction's laws. The alternative approach, corresponding to capture, carries two potential costs: (1) the welfare reduction associated with insisting that parties operate against a set of background rules that they prefer to avoid; and (2) in cases in which the regulatory burden becomes unduly costly, the possibility that some of the disadvantaged parties might eventually physically exit to gain the benefit of another jurisdiction's law. Conversely, the capture regime encourages those who are most likely to be effective in doing so to work toward liberalizing the legal regime that they find immediately disadvantageous, rather than allowing them to contract away from the jurisdiction's law with the effect of truncating the decision cost curve for those who remain affected by the problematic law. How should these competing considerations be weighed?

Edward Peter Stringham and Todd J. Zywicki observe that for a choice of law regime to promote effective matching of individual preferences with the selected legal regime, the process must require that the parties make the choice voluntarily *ex ante*, and thus before any legal dispute arises, rather than *ex post*, or after potential litigation arises.[30] As a basic tenet of contract law, we can assume that relatively sophisticated and well-informed parties will reasonably predict which jurisdiction's law best suits their needs and preferences. When the parties enter into their contractual relationship, neither party

---

[29] For a law and economics analysis of choice of law, see ERIN A. O'HARA & LARRY E. RIBSTEIN, THE LAW MARKET (2009). The authors review the literature on contractual choice of law, discuss various contexts in which broadening choice of law might be beneficial, and suggest a legal rule to facilitate expansive choice of law. The authors suggest two limits in their proposed choice of law regime: (1) those contracting for another jurisdiction's choice of law must take that jurisdiction's law in its entirety for the specific contract, rather than picking and choosing among various jurisdictions' laws; and (2) state jurisdictions can prevent parties from engaging in contractual choice of law by designating certain contract rules as super-mandatory. *See id.* at 218–22. Assuming you find the proposal to expand contractual choice of law rules attractive, do you further agree with these proposed restrictions? Can you think of a reason to disallow cherry-picking particular legal rules rather than forcing the Hobson's choice of taking various legal regimes in their entirety?

[30] *See* Edward Peter Stringham & Todd J. Zywicki, *Rivalry and Superior Dispatch: An Analysis of Competing Courts in Medieval and Early Modern England*, 147 PUB. CHOICE 497 (2011).

expects the contractual relationship to fail, and should it fail for unforeseen reasons, neither can predict on which side of the dispute, the alleged breaching party or the claimed victim of breach, she or he will be. To maximize the joint surplus, which can then be shared, the parties will have an incentive to select the legal regime that minimizes transaction costs. By contrast, where either party has an opportunity to select the forum *after* the relationship sours, each party is motivated to select the jurisdiction that favors her or his side, even if that selection is not the best choice ex ante. Thus, systems of jurisdictional competition and choice of law promote beneficial forum-shopping when they encourage cost-saving legal rules that enlarge the contractual surplus, as opposed to strategic forum-shopping, which instead condones efforts by one side or the other to select a regime that, although not conducive to promoting shared gains ex ante, provides the selecting party a greater benefit ex post. Zywicki contends that in some contexts, including bankruptcy law, it might prove difficult to ascertain *a priori* whether a particular system of interjurisdictional competition is structured so as to promote beneficial or harmful forum-shopping in light of all relevant incentives and constraints.[31]

Two factors have raised the stakes for international choice of law: first, the increasing integration of the global economy; and second, the increased importance of production involving such intangibles as intellectual property and financial instruments. For example, some jurisdictions, such as the Cayman Islands and Switzerland, have held themselves out as providing particularly capital-friendly legal regimes for sophisticated financial transactions. Critics of resulting transactions have expressed concern that parties have relied upon the law of such jurisdictions to evade legitimate national laws and regulations, thereby promoting illegal activity.[32] Some scholars claim that the evolution of the Cayman Islands as a global financial center, and the development of other specialized legal regimes, have also had benign effects, including serving as vehicles for economic development in undeveloped countries, perhaps contributing to stability, democracy, and the rule of law.[33]

Do you believe that choice of law should be liberalized? Why or why not? Does your answer depend on whether the context is domestic or international? Why or why not? In this area of law, there is at least a potential conflict between conventional law and economics analysis, which tends to focus on efficiency at the level of the individual transaction, and public choice analysis, which tends to focus on broader institutional implications of proposed changes in public policy. At the transactional level, broadened choice of law allows the parties to benefit from a more efficient legal regime, and then to share in the resulting gains. At the institutional level, however, this very feature might

---

[31] *See* Todd J. Zywicki, *Is Forum-Shopping Corrupting America's Bankruptcy Courts?*, 94 GEO. L. REV. 1141 (2006).

[32] *See, e.g.*, Juliette Garside et al., *The Panama Papers: How the World's Rich and Famous Hide Their Money Offshore*, THE GUARDIAN (Apr. 3, 2016), https://www.theguardian.com/news/2016/apr/03/the-panama-papers-how-the-worlds-rich-and-famous-hide-their-money-offshore (reporting that numerous national leaders such as Vladimir Putin and others had relied on offshore bank accounts located in Panama to allegedly hide illegal money and to illegally avoid taxes); U.S. DEP'T OF JUST., SWISS BANK PROGRAM (Feb. 16, 2017), https://www.justice.gov/tax/swiss-bank-program (reporting non-prosecution agreements and civil settlements with seventy-eight Swiss banks that included admissions that "they had reason to believe that [those involved] had committed tax-related criminal offenses in connection with undeclared U.S.-related accounts.").

[33] *See* Tony Freyer & Andrew P. Morriss, *Creating Cayman as an Offshore Financial Center: Structure and Strategy Since 1960*, 45 ARIZ. ST. L.J. 1297 (2013).

work toward entrenching inferior laws, thereby burdening those least able to work toward having those laws changed. Similarly, at the international transactional level, expansive choice of law might allow sophisticated parties to share in resulting gains from less restrictive substantive rules in jurisdictions seeking to attract capital. At the same time, however, a consequence is to undermine often important national and international regulatory policies, including particular forms of prohibited financial transactions.

D. The Franchise Theory of Federalism[34]

In a study of federal deference to local regulation, Professor Jonathan Macey advanced what he terms the "franchise theory of federalism."[35] Macey explains:

> In an ordinary business franchise, the owner of a product, service, or technology, rather than market its own goods, often will choose to sell another firm the rights to market them under a franchise arrangement. Under certain circumstances firms find it in their interests to employ this sort of contractual arrangement. [We can identify] three general situations in which Congress [by analogy to franchisors] will "franchise" the right to regulate in a particular area to the states [by analogy to franchisees]: (1) when a particular state has developed a body of regulation that comprises a valuable capital asset and federal regulation would dissipate the value of that asset; (2) when the political-support-maximizing outcome varies markedly from area to area due to the existence of spatial monopolies, variegated local political optima, and variations in voter preferences across regions; and (3) where Congress can avoid potentially damaging political opposition from special-interest groups by putting the responsibility for a particularly controversial issue on state and local governments.[36]

Macey's franchise theory of federalism suggests that even with no constitutional or societal rule requiring that members of Congress defer to local decision makers, rational members of Congress would still sometimes find such deference in its best interest. In this analysis, federalism is not a doctrine with independent political content, but rather, it is a handy label that politicians attach to outcomes that they reach for independent reasons. Among the forces that Macey contends conduce to local, rather than national, decision making in those instances when the Constitution permits regulation at either level are the following: (1) the desire to appease constituents with intense and competing preferences on given issues that are more likely to be consistent within, than across, specific geographic regions; (2) the desire to allow local legislators to claim credit with their constituents for political victories; and (3) the desire to protect or reward investments that produce local political capital. Allowing local regulation enables politicians at the local level (those who create the political benefit) and at the national level (those who facilitated the local provision of the benefit) to claim credit with their constituents for the favorable

---

[34] Portions of the discussions that follow are adapted from MAXWELL L. STEARNS, PUBLIC CHOICE AND PUBLIC LAW: READINGS AND COMMENTARY 895–96 (1997).

[35] *See* Jonathan R. Macey, *Federal Deference to Local Regulators and the Economic Theory of Regulation: Toward a Public-Choice Explanation of Federalism*, 76 VA. L. REV. 265, 268 (1990).

[36] *Id.* at 268–69 (footnote omitted).

results that are achieved. This model resembles the public choice account of agency delegation, which suggests that decisions to defer to agencies (like decisions to defer to state or local governmental units) provide a benefit to members of Congress because if the other decision-making unit performs well, they can take the credit, and if it performs poorly, they can seize a new political opportunity for correction (and once accomplished, still take credit).[37]

Perhaps the most interesting illustration of the franchise theory of federalism involves allowing states to continue to regulate corporate chartering. Building upon the work of Professor Roberta Romano, who explained the persistence of Delaware's dominance of corporate chartering, Macey explains the mutual benefit to federal and state politicians from this regime. In her famous study of Delaware corporate law,[38] Roberta Romano posited that Delaware's longstanding dominance in corporate law chartering does not result from the superiority of Delaware's substantive law—laws that virtually any other state could quickly replicate[39]—but rather from the state's unique ability to issue a credible bond. Summarizing Romano's thesis, Macey explains:

> Delaware is a small state. It obtains an extremely high proportion of its budget (sixteen percent) from franchise taxes on corporate chartering. Delaware relies on these revenues more than other states because for other states, revenues from corporate chartering represent only a small portion of their total budget. In other words, the high percentage of Delaware's budget that is derived from chartering revenues represents a credible (bonded) promise that the state will not renege on its earlier promise to respond in consistent ways to new phenomena. Delaware has been able to retain its dominance because it is able to offer a reliable promise that its corporation law will remain highly attractive to managers in the future. Competing states are unable to match Delaware's promise of future performance because they cannot offer the same credible bond.[40]

Macey's franchise theory extends the Romano thesis to account for the general practice of federal lawmakers facilitating this corporate chartering, thus allowing Delaware, a tiny state, to assume a place of national prominence in this specialized area of law. The overall arrangement benefits both federal lawmakers (who benefit from facilitating successful local lawmaking) and state lawmakers (who get credit for providing managers valuable opportunities to incorporate in a state whose law remains predictable).

Professor Mark Roe has refined the model of Delaware's dominance in corporate law as the outcome of a complex interaction between Delaware and the national government.[41] Because of its prominence, Delaware essentially makes corporate law for the entire country, a task that typically would be thought to be allocated to the federal

---

[37] *See supra* Chapter 17, at pp. 720–722. This also draws upon the theory of rent extraction, as discussed in Chapter 17.

[38] *See* Roberta Romano, *Law as a Product: Some Pieces of the Incorporation Puzzle*, 1 J.L. ECON. & ORG. 225 (1985).

[39] Macey, *supra* note 35, at 277.

[40] *Id.* at 278 (footnotes omitted).

[41] Mark J. Roe, *Delaware's Politics*, 118 HARV. L. REV. 2491 (2005).

government. In fact, the federal government could at any time preempt all or much of the field of corporate law. Through its authority over the regulation of the sale of securities, Congress has in fact made major incursions from time to time on the scope of Delaware's authority.

Roe explains that Delaware typically has the opportunity to move first in creating new law governing corporations. Where managers and investors agree on the shape of the law, Delaware's primacy is generally assured. Even if these constituencies have an incentive to create lopsided laws in their favor, they restrain themselves from going too far out of a fear that Congress will intervene to strike a different balance. In this analysis, when Delaware law breaks down, such as in a flurry of corporate scandals, Congress risks implicit public blame and is more likely to intervene and displace Delaware law.

Roe analogizes the relationship between Delaware and the federal government to that between Congress and regulatory agencies (as described in Chapter 19). Congress will implicitly delegate to Delaware so long as the benefits to Congress of doing so exceed the costs of relinquishing control over national, corporate legal policy. Where, however, the costs become large—such as in high-profile corporate scandals that create a media and public outcry for federal action, Congress is more apt to intervene. Roe argues that the Sarbanes-Oxley law illustrates this dynamic.[42] The law was enacted in response to perceived failures in Delaware's corporate law, and it provides federal rules for several areas of corporate governance that traditionally were governed by state law. These include new disclosure rules designed to increase transparency, to provide stricter limits on conflicts of interest, and to impose stiffer criminal penalties for corporate malfeasance.[43]

E. Application of Constitutional Federalism to Legal Doctrine

The preceding discussion of federalism has implications for understanding several constitutional law doctrines. Here we briefly examine two doctrines: the *anti-commandeering doctrine* and the *dormant Commerce Clause doctrine*.

1. The Anti-Commandeering Doctrine[44]

An interesting contrast case for Macey's franchise theory of federalism involves the anti-commandeering doctrine. In *New York v. United States*,[45] the Supreme Court struck down a statute that effectively required states to legislate on Congress's behalf. The Court held that under Article I, § 8 of the United States Constitution, or alternatively under the Tenth Amendment (which Justice O'Connor described in her *New York* majority opinion as "mirror images" of each other), Congress lacks the power to commandeer state legislatures.

---

[42] *Id.* at 2495 (citing Sarbanes-Oxley Act of 2002, Pub. L. No. 107–204, 116 Stat. 745).

[43] *See id.* at 2521–22, 2528–29.

[44] Portions of the discussions that follow are adapted from STEARNS, *supra* note 34, at 896–97.

[45] 505 U.S. 144 (1992).

The *New York* Court struck down the take-title provision of the Low-Level Radioactive Waste Policy Amendments Act of 1985.[46] Under the challenged law, states were required over a period of years to meet a series of progressive deadlines for self-sufficiency with respect to disposing of low-level radioactive waste. The controversial take-title provision required that states failing to become self-sufficient by the specified deadlines, either by joining a regional pact with other states or by placing a waste disposal facility in state, take title of low-level radioactive waste generated within their borders or compensate producers of such waste for the failure to do so. New York, which challenged the provision, was the only state that had failed to comply with the statute's deadlines for self-sufficiency, and thus it was the only state subject to the take-title provision's draconian sanction.

In striking down the challenged provision and holding that neither Article I, § 8, nor the Tenth Amendment, permit Congress to commandeer states into legislating on its behalf, Justice O'Connor underscored yet another dimension of federalism, one closely tied to the economic theory of delegation. O'Connor explained:

> [W]here the Federal Government compels States to regulate, the accountability of both state and federal officials is diminished. If the citizens of New York, for example, do not consider that making provision for the disposal of radioactive waste is in their best interest, they may elect state officials who share their view. That view can always be pre-empted under the Supremacy Clause if it is contrary to the national view, but in such a case it is the Federal Government that makes the decision in full view of the public, and it will be federal officials that suffer the consequences if the decision turns out to be detrimental or unpopular. But where the Federal Government directs the States to regulate, it may be state officials who will bear the brunt of public disapproval, while the federal officials who devised the regulatory program may remain insulated from the electoral ramifications of their decision. Accountability is thus diminished when, due to federal coercion, elected state officials cannot regulate in accordance with the views of the local electorate in matters not pre-empted by federal regulation.[47]

In this analysis, the same credit-taking/blame-shifting that public choice theorists have associated with agency delegations also comes into play with congressional commandeering of state legislatures. If the regulatory program succeeds, members of Congress and of the state legislature can each take credit for its success. If the regulatory program fails, members of Congress can blame their state counterparts for creating the unsatisfactory result, and state legislatures can blame Congress for requiring them to regulate in the first instance.

Do you find this analysis persuasive? Why or why not? Do you believe that the Supreme Court decided the *New York* case correctly? Why or why not? To what extent is your answer informed by public choice? How would you analyze this case under Macey's franchise theory of federalism? How do these approaches differ?

---

[46] Pub. L. No. 99–240, 99 Stat. 1842.

[47] 505 U.S. at 168–69.

2. *The Dormant Commerce Clause Doctrine*

Whereas the prior discussions focused on the benefits of federalism, either as a matter of policy or as a matter of political accountability, the Supreme Court's dormant Commerce Clause doctrine is helpful in considering some of the resulting costs. In a game theoretical study of the dormant Commerce Clause doctrine,[48] Professor Maxwell Stearns has argued that under some circumstances, individual states can obstruct benign pro-commerce regimes. Stearns's larger analysis rests on combining the prisoners' dilemma game and games that are conducive to multiple pure Nash equilibria to explain the dormant Commerce Clause and related doctrines. For our immediate purposes, the latter games are most relevant.[49] The analysis reveals the conditions under which individual states have the capacity, and sometimes the tendency, to interfere with political union in a manner that justifies federal intervention, even when Congress has declined to reach the underlying issue by statute.

To illustrate, imagine a desired regulatory policy that will allow certain trucks to travel through states as needed to ensure the cost-effective delivery of goods. As seen in the presentation of *Bibb v. Navajo Freight Lines, Inc.*,[50] when most or all states agree upon a common truck feature—in this instance, straight mudflaps—a single state, like Illinois, can disrupt the flow of commerce by instead insisting upon curved mudflaps. If we assume that neither policy is superior as a safety measure, then this rule invites a game that conduces to more than a single pure-Nash strategy equilibrium. Either cooperative result—all straight or all curved mudflaps (or permitting either mudflap)—provides participating states a relatively high payoff. Conversely, when a single state selects a contrary rule, the result is to force the states outside the pure Nash equilibrium outcome, thereby limiting the ability of the states to facilitate commerce in a cost-effective manner. In this analysis, the election by Illinois of a contrary rule implies that it sought to reduce its share of the cost of facilitating interstate commerce, a result in tension with the constitutional objective of promoting national political union.[51]

Do you find this explanation of *Bibb* persuasive? How does it relate to the franchise theory of federalism? How does it relate to the preceding analysis of the anti-commandeering doctrine? Can you explain why Congress tends not to interfere with Supreme Court decisions under the dormant Commerce Clause doctrine even though as a matter of blackletter law, Congress has the authority to reverse those decisions by ordinary legislation? Does public choice help in answering this question?[52]

---

[48] *See* Maxwell L. Stearns, *A Beautiful Mend: A Game Theoretical Analysis of the Dormant Commerce Clause Doctrine*, 45 WM. & MARY L. REV. 1 (2003). For earlier works studying the problem of interstate coordination in promoting multistate commercial activity, see RICHARD A. EPSTEIN, BARGAINING WITH THE STATE 127–44 (1993); Dan L. Burk, *Federalism in Cyberspace*, 28 CONN. L. REV. 1095 (1996); and Saul Levmore, *Interstate Exploitation and Judicial Intervention*, 69 VA. L. REV. 563 (1983).

[49] *See supra* Chapter 15, Part II.A.

[50] 359 U.S. 520 (1959). *See supra* Chapter 15, Part II.A.

[51] For a similar account of *Kassel v. Consolidated Freightways*, 450 U.S. 662 (1981), see Stearns, *supra* note 48, at 49–55, 130–33.

[52] For an analysis claiming that dormant Commerce Clause rulings should be mandatory and thus not subject to overruling by Congress, see Norman R. Williams, *Why Congress May Not "Overrule" the Dormant Commerce Clause*, 53 UCLA L. REV. 153 (2005). For a contrary analysis using game theory to explain the default

F. Preserving Federalism

After society agrees on a set of constitutional principles to promote the general welfare, some may find it in their interest to deviate from those rules to advance specific goals, including partisan objectives. This can include efforts to relax, or avoid, rules that arise from federalism, raising the question how to preserve this important feature of constitutional design. One immediate challenge in a system of vertical federalism involves jurisdictional supremacy. In the United States, for example, the federal government holds a trump card over state and local governments when acting within its sphere of authority. This can create a centrifugal force toward greater centralization of political power, as lobbyists and members of Congress increasingly preempt state and local regulation. This pressure might arise from either interest groups or legislators who perceive a corresponding political benefit.

Professor Michael Greve distinguishes between two varieties of federalism: "competitive federalism" and "cartel federalism."[53] Greve maintains that the United States Constitution is designed to promote "competitive federalism." The goal is to encourage states to compete to attract people and resources through the provision of beneficial government services and policies. Competitive federalism mimics competitive market processes in disciplining jurisdictions, as opposed to firms, to satisfy citizen, as opposed to consumer, demand by enacting policies that threaten other jurisdictions with exit as through better matching of constituent preferences.

Greve defines cartel federalism in opposite terms: the effort by political elites across jurisdictions to suppress economic and political competition among states (hence "cartel") with the federal government serving as the cartel enforcement institution. Greve maintains that the federal government serves this function primarily through an intricate network of transfer payments from the federal government to the states, a process that on the margin tends to dampen interstate competition and, along with it, political accountability. The process further increases the influence of interest groups, favoring a uniform policy. Greve argues that elites benefit by both the diminution of political accountability and dampening of interstate competition in a manner analogous to private market cartels, which benefit firms at the expense of consumers.

Greve explains:

> ***The Citizens' Choice: Competitive Federalism.*** "The great difficulty" in forming "a government which is to be administered by men over men," James Madison wrote in *The Federalist*, is that "you must first enable the government to control the governed; and in the next place oblige it to control itself." This calculus applies to federalism as to all institutional choices. For the purpose of controlling the governed, a single central government will do. Thus, from the prospective citizens' vantage, the point of entrusting a second set of junior governments with authority over the same citizens and territory is to oblige government to control itself.

---

nature of dormant Commerce Clause rulings, see Maxwell L. Stearns, *The New Commerce Clause Doctrine in Game Theoretical Perspective*, 60 VAND. L. REV. 1, 48 n.211 (2007).

[53] MICHAEL GREVE, THE UPSIDE-DOWN CONSTITUTION (2012).

. . . .

> ***State Choice: Cartels.*** Now invert the perspective, and think of federalism as a bargain among states—that is to say, state officials or political elites. What is their constitutional choice? Prospective citizens . . . will embrace competitive federalism because it promises to reduce government abuse and exploitation [at] all levels. States, in diametrical contrast, will embrace union only if, and to the extent that, it promises to enhance the "power, emolument and consequence of the[ir] offices," in Alexander Hamilton's words. Much like private producers in economic markets, states "as states" will seek to obtain more revenue for their product—government services—than they could generate under competitive conditions. . . . That requires various cartelizing noncompete agreements, and the enforcement of those agreements against free-riding states in turn requires a central government. At the same time, a central government that is sufficiently strong to protect the states' surplus may also be sufficiently strong to confiscate it, and states will want to guard against that eventuality.[54]

According to Greve, competitive federalism was the dominant constitutional model in the United States in the nineteenth and early twentieth centuries. That model gave way during the New Deal to a model of cartel federalism, which limited interstate cooperation and which allowed a larger role for the federal government to adopt policies that suppressed competition. Greve argues that theorists of constitutional federalism today focus on the proper "balance" between the state and federal governments. He maintains, instead, that we should be concerned with preventing the natural tendencies among competitors—including political elites—to want to protect themselves from competition and the resulting political accountability when enacted policies fail.

Do you find this analysis persuasive? Why or why not? What counterarguments might one raise as to Greve's concerns about cartel federalism, both with respect to the incentives of elites to cooperate and the overall effect of federal programs that tend to suppress interstate competition?

To what extent does Greve's argument mirror that of Pritchard and Zywicki, discussed in Chapter 23, regarding the separation of powers? Recall that Pritchard and Zywicki noted that the Madisonian separation of powers rested on the assumption that each branch of government will consider itself locked in a competitive, prisoners'-dilemma-style game with the other branches. Despite this, Pritchard and Zywicki note that in an iterated prisoners' dilemma game, the result might give rise to cooperative strategies that can prove beneficial in some instances, yet harmful in others. If, as a result of cooperation, *all* branches of government can simultaneously increase their power, this might turn what had been a zero-sum conflict into a positive-sum game for the players, but not necessarily for the public. Greve suggests that the "game" of competitive federalism gives rise to a similar dynamic in which political elites are repeat players who cooperate in ways that enhance their power at the public expense.

---

[54] MICHAEL S. GREVE, FEDERALISM AND THE CONSTITUTION: COMPETITION VERSUS CARTELS 8–9, 11 (2015), https://www.mercatus.org/system/files/Greve-web-6-3-15.pdf.

Do you find this analogy persuasive? Why or why not? What evidence might support, or undermine, Greve's argument? Is the "federalism game" structurally similar to the "separation of powers game" in terms of the application of an iterated prisoners' dilemma? Why or why not?

How do these analyses relate to Stearns's model of the dormant Commerce Clause doctrine, which identifies other games, aside from the Prisoners' Dilemma, that states sometimes play with the effect of undermining beneficial cooperative strategies among states? Is it fair to say that Stearns takes a more optimistic view of federal intervention with state regulatory powers than Pritchard and Zywicki, and Greve? Are the theories reconcilable? If so, do you believe that federal courts have the tools with which to ascertain the circumstances under which states are likely to engage in beneficial competition, one the one hand, or in problematic strategies that undermine political union, on the other? Why or why not? Does your answer depend upon judicial familiarity with game theory? Or are there other methods of identifying beneficial or problematic state strategies?

Consider the case of agriculture price subsidies. Because agricultural products are sold in national and international markets, efforts to subsidize the price of certain crops (such as corn) will be largely ineffective if done on a state-by-state basis. Iowa, for instance, could not effectively unilaterally raise the market price of corn above the prevailing market price because its corn farmers would be undersold by farmers in other states. As a result, effective agriculture subsidies must operate at a national level.[55] In such situations, the elevation of decision-making authority to a higher jurisdiction acts as sort of a cartel enforcement mechanism to protect the favored interest from competition. How can constitutions be designed to preserve the structure of constitutional federalism (or other constitutional limitations) given the incentives to depart from that structure?

To what extent does the preceding analysis suggest that although the United States Constitution creates a regime of federalism, the ultimate protections for preserving federalism are political? Consider for example the following passage from Justice Blackmun's majority opinion in *Garcia v. San Antonio Metropolitan Transit Authority*,[56] which overruled *National League of Cities v. Usery*.[57] In *National League of Cities*, the Court relied upon a "traditional governmental functions" test to invalidate congressional power to apply the Fair Labor Standards Act's minimum wage and overtime provisions to state employees. By contrast, the *Garcia* Court sustained the application of such provisions to municipal employees, declaring the traditional governmental functions test "unworkable." Writing for the *Garcia* majority, Justice Blackmun explained:

> [The States retain their sovereign powers only] to the extent that the Constitution has not divested them of their original powers and transferred those powers to the Federal Government. . . .
>
> . . . .

[55] For a consistent analysis that presents *Wickard v. Filburn*, 317 U.S. 111 (1942), as a proper result under the Commerce Clause, see Stearns, *supra* note 52, at 28–40.

[56] 469 U.S. 528 (1985).

[57] 426 U.S. 833 (1976).

> . . . [T]he principal means chosen by the Framers to ensure the role of States in the federal system lies in the structure of the Federal Government itself. . . .
>
> . . . State sovereign interests, then, are more properly protected by procedural safeguards inherent in the structure of the federal system than by judicially created limitations on federal power.[58]

In his separate opinion, Justice Powell referred to the "rise of numerous special interest groups that engage in sophisticated lobbying, and make substantial campaign contributions to some Members of Congress."[59] He added, "These groups are thought to have significant influence in the shaping and enactment of certain types of legislation. Contrary to the Court's view, a 'political process' that functions in this way is unlikely to safeguard the sovereign rights of States and localities."[60]

Finally, Justice O'Connor, who later drafted the majority opinion in *New York v. United States*, responded in her *Garcia* dissent as follows:

> The central issue of federalism . . . is whether any realm *is* left open to the States by the Constitution—whether any area remains in which a State may act free of federal interference. "The issue . . . is whether the federal system has any *legal* substance, any core of constitutional right that courts will enforce." The true "essence" of federalism is that the States *as States* have legitimate interests which the National Government is bound to respect even though its laws are supreme. . . .
>
> . . . .
>
> . . . With the abandonment of *National League of Cities*, all that stands between the remaining essentials of state sovereignty and Congress is the latter's underdeveloped capacity for self-restraint.[61]

Which if any of these views of federalism—those of Blackmun, Powell, or O'Connor—finds stronger support in the theory of public choice? Why? O'Connor suggests the possibility that absent judicial protection of federalism, Congress inevitably tends in the direction of increasing federal control over areas that were traditionally subject to state and local regulation. If this is true, is it owing to the problem of special interests that Powell recognizes in his opinion? How would Macey analyze *Garcia* under the franchise theory of federalism? How would Mark Roe analyze this case? Notice that the analyses of Macey and Roe are consistent with the claim that special interests might prefer in some instances to retain regulatory powers at the state or local levels. Is this insight inconsistent with O'Connor's analysis? With Powell's? Which analysis is more persuasive? Why?

Professor Barry Weingast describes "self-enforcing federalism," meaning a scheme in which all actors find it in their individual self-interest to adhere to the constitutional

---

[58] 469 U.S. at 549–50, 552.

[59] *Id.* at 575 n.18 (Powell, J., dissenting).

[60] *Id.*

[61] *Id.* at 580–81, 588 (O'Connor, J., dissenting) (citation omitted).

rules, thereby stabilizing the overall constitutional order.[62] Weingast posits that the primary explanation for the stability of the system of *vertical federalism* (meaning the protection of state authority from the federal government) in the United States until the 1930s was not constitutional structure, but political reality.[63] He argues that the majority of the American public supported federalism, in large part because debates over slavery and civil rights made the various regions of the country wary of ceding too much power to the national government that could later be turned against their own region.[64] As Weingast writes:

> Most citizens were deeply suspicious of the national government because of its potential to impose policies favored by other regions or interests. Early in the 19th century, before the rise of an integrated, interregional economy, the solution was simply for both North and South to agree to limit the federal government's authority, thus limiting the ability of either region to impose its will on the other. Although the partisan debate involved the role of the federal government in the economy, the range of involvement was relatively circumscribed, limited to such issues as tariffs and internal improvements.
>
> The "balance rule" or the equal representation of the North and the South in the Senate, served as the principal institution providing durability to the agreement between the regions. The balance rule afforded each region a veto over national policymaking. . . . [This] institution had a profound effect on national politics. The main implication for present purposes is that the set of concurrent vetoes prevented national policies that were considered especially inimical by either region. The balance rule's double veto thus provided the political foundations for the preservation of a slave economy in the South, a free one in the North, and a limited national government.[65]

Consider also the relationship between the Seventeenth Amendment, discussed in Chapter 23, and federalism. In the original Constitution, state legislatures elected each state's United States Senators. As Madison wrote, the appointment of Senators by the state legislatures would "giv[e] to the State governments such an agency in the formation

---

[62] *See* Barry R. Weingast, *The Constitutional Dilemma of Economic Liberty*, J. ECON. PERSP., Summer 2005, at 89, 102–05, The concept of self-enforcing constitutional rules can be found in James Madison's writings as well as those of the Nineteenth Century Swedish economist Knut Wicksell. *See* Richard E. Wagner & James D. Gwartney, *Public Choice and Constitutional Order*, *in* PUBLIC CHOICE AND CONSTITUTIONAL ECONOMICS 29, 44–49 (James D. Gwartney & Richard E. Wagner eds., 1988). John C. Calhoun's proposal that a "concurrent majority" be required for certain important political decisions is also grounded in the idea of self-enforcing constitutionalism. *See* JOHN C. CALHOUN, A DISQUISITION ON GOVERNMENT AND A DISCOURSE ON THE CONSTITUTION AND GOVERNMENT OF THE UNITED STATES (Richard K. Cralle ed., Charleston, Walker & James 1851).

[63] *See* Barry R. Weingast, *The Economic Role of Political Institutions: Market-Preserving Federalism and Economic Development*, 11 J.L. ECON. & ORG. 1 (1995). Regarding the relative importance of the Constitution versus politics in preserving federalism, Weingast asserts, "The immediate answer—that the Constitution prevented it—begs the question, for it ignores the issues of constitutional interpretation and constitutional adherence." *Id.* at 19. Is that correct? To what extent might the causal relationship run in the opposite direction—i.e., to what extent might the Constitution shape public opinion as to the proper balance between the federal and state governments?

[64] *See id.* at 19.

[65] *Id.* at 19.

of the federal government as must secure the authority of the former."[66] The Seventeenth Amendment replaced this scheme with direct election, thereby removing this protection of federalism from ordinary political processes operating at the level of Congress.

Todd Zywicki maintains that when state legislatures were the natural constituency of U.S. Senators, Senators rationally sought to advance the interests of their principals, the state legislators who elected them, by protecting state governments from incursion by the federal government. This arrangement, Zywicki maintains, embodied Madison's insight set out in *The Federalist 51* that the "interests of the man" should be "connected with the constitutional rights of the place."[67] By this comment, Madison meant to emphasize that the most effective way to preserve the Constitution's structure was to provide incentives that would harness the forces of individual self-interest to promote the overall goals of the Constitution. The preservation of constitutional structure, therefore, was largely a by-product of political actors pursuing their self-interest. Thus, as originally designed, one purpose of the U.S. Senate was to address the fear by the states that they would be unduly burdened by the new national government. The original Constitution thus provided that Senators would be elected by state legislatures. Following Madison's dictum, that mode of election was intended to align the self-interest of the individual Senator in being re-elected with the demands of his constituents, i.e., the state legislatures. As such, it was assumed that the composition of the Senate would provide a political check on actions of the federal government that unduly infringed upon the powers of the states.

With respect to a wide range of fiscal and regulatory matters, Zywicki argues that this arrangement safeguarded state interests throughout most of the nineteenth century, by imposing limits on the reach of the federal government. In this period, the federal government remained relatively limited in scope and tended to focus its regulatory powers on those areas most obviously within its delegated spheres of authority, including the military and interstate transportation, such as building canals and roads. Even though the federal government naturally expanded in size during periods of crisis such as wars, Zywicki observes that it generally restored itself to a more modest size when the crisis abated. Correspondingly, state governments then reasserted the scope of their regulatory powers to earlier levels. Zywicki further claims that state legislators generally retained control over many issues that implicated special-interest politics, thus allowing state level politicians to reap the rewards of interacting with interest groups.

Consistent with the exit theory of federalism, Zywicki concludes that the practice of engaging in special-interest politics at the state level might also improve overall social welfare by reducing the overall level of rent-seeking activity in the economy as compared with a regime of increased centralized regulatory powers that resulted from adopting the Seventeenth Amendment. By contrast, Zywicki claims, under the present regime, the interests of the Senators are much closer to those of the members of the House of

---

[66] THE FEDERALIST NO. 62, at 345 (James Madison) (Clinton Rossiter ed., 1961). Hamilton referred to this provision of election of U.S. Senators by state legislatures as the "absolute safeguard" to the states to preserve their authority from federal incursion. THE FEDERALIST NO. 59, at 332 (Alexander Hamilton) (Clinton Rossiter ed., 1961).

[67] THE FEDERALIST NO. 51, at 290 (James Madison) (Clinton Rossiter ed., 1961).

Representatives, and thus Senators have less incentive to protect the authority of the states as such or to preserve the constitutional principle of federalism.

Do you find this analysis persuasive? Can you identify other mechanisms beside the manner of senatorial selection that motivate federal political sensitivity to concerns of states? If so, what are they, and how might they be implemented? If not, what does that suggest about the proper role of federal judicial power in enforcing federalism? Does partisan gerrymandering, which generally allows state legislatures to control the political party composition of the state delegations to the House of Representatives, have the effect of switching the relationships between the Houses of Congress in terms of their incentives to protect state legislative interests? Specifically, does partisan gerrymandering encourage members of the House to fulfill the function of protecting state interests that Senators served prior to the Seventh Amendment? Why or why not? Is Macey correct that federalism is ultimately a function of the political interests of federal actors? If so, is this necessarily a bad result? Why or why not?

Consider David Schleicher's response to Zywicki.[68] Schleicher suggests that although the Framers sought, in theory, to promote self-enforcing constitutional constraints for federalism through direct election of Senators, the early development of political parties soon overwhelmed that institutional design. Schleicher argues that the rise of national political parties, especially beginning with the Presidency of Andrew Jackson, corresponded to national elections dominating state elections and issues. As a result, early on, national Senate elections dominated state legislative elections for reasons of party politics, more so than due to the nature of senatorial selection. Prior to the Seventeenth Amendment, more citizens had been voting for state legislators based in large part on who they supported for the U.S. Senate, rather than for their substantive views on state and local issues. As a result, Schleicher argues, the adoption of the Seventeenth Amendment might have had the ironic effect of *increasing* the vibrancy of federalism by restoring the elections for local officials to local matters, rather than being overwhelmed by the higher-profile Senate elections.

How does Schleicher's argument about the relationship between political parties and institutional design relate to the arguments by Levinson and Pildes in Chapter 23 regarding "Separation of Parties, Not Powers"? Which account of the Seventeenth Amendment, Zywicki's or Schleicher's, seems more persuasive? Why? How does Schleicher's argument relate to Weingast's idea of self-enforcing constitutional federalism and his argument that political realities were more important than constitutional structure in preserving federalism? Which do you think is more important in preserving federalism, constitutional structure (as suggested by Madison and Zywicki) or partisan beliefs (as suggested by Weingast and Schleicher)?

---

[68] David Schleicher, *The Seventeenth Amendment and Federalism in an Age of National Political Parties*, 65 HASTINGS L.J. 1043 (2014).

III. DIRECT DEMOCRACY

Direct democracy provides an important case study of the interplay between constitutional economics and federalism at the state level.[69] First appearing in 1898 in South Dakota, direct democracy is now commonplace at the state and local levels.[70] Twenty-seven states, and the U.S. Virgin Islands, provide for state-wide initiatives, popular referendums, or both, although such activity has generally been concentrated in about a half-dozen states.[71] A legislative referendum for state constitutional amendments is required in every state except Delaware. Moreover, about half the nation's cities also provide for some form of direct democracy.[72]

A commonly expressed justification for direct democracy is that it helps to overcome the problem of agency costs between elected officials and the public. In this framing, well-organized special interest groups influence legislative processes in ways that benefit them yet thwart the will of popular majorities. Direct democracy is seen as a means for the public to "polic[e] their wayward legislative agents"[73] and to reassert majoritarian policy preferences against special-interest generated political outcomes. Direct democracy helps achieve this desired result in two ways, first as a direct effect of voters overriding the decisions of elected officials, and second, as an indirect effect of inducing elected officials to adopt policies closer to those preferred by the median electoral voter under the threat of being reversed by the voters in a referendum.[74]

Empirical evidence suggests that direct democracy helps align governmental policy with the preferences of the median electoral voter, especially when agency costs of elected officials are high, and on highly contested social issues.[75] This outcome requires that

---

[69] For a recent overview and analysis, see Elizabeth Garrett, *Direct Democracy*, *in* RESEARCH HANDBOOK ON PUBLIC CHOICE AND PUBLIC LAW 137 (Daniel Farber & Anne Joseph O'Connell eds., 2010).

[70] *Id.* at 137–38.

[71] *Id.* at 138. *See also Initiative and Referendum States*, NAT'L CONFERENCE ST. LEGISLATURES (Dec. 2015), http://www.ncsl.org/research/elections-and-campaigns/chart-of-the-initiative-states.aspx.

[72] Garrett, *supra* note 69, at 138.

[73] *Id.*

[74] John G. Matsusaka, *Direct Democracy Works*, J. ECON. PERSP., Spring 2005, at 185, 192; Elisabeth R. Gerber, *Legislative Response to the Threat of Popular Initiatives*, 40 AM. J. POL. SCI. 99 (1996).

[75] JOHN G. MATSUSAKA, FOR THE MANY OR THE FEW: THE INITIATIVE, PUBLIC POLICY, AND AMERICAN DEMOCRACY (2004). *See* Garrett, *supra* note 69, at 140. Thad Kousser and Mathew D. McCubbins reach a contrary result, claiming that initiatives might produce results that the public disfavors relative to the status quo as a result of proposals that are piecemeal components over larger issues of public policy and for which electoral preferences are prone to cycle; that are based upon incomplete information, for example, with respect to how enacted measures will be financed; and that are motivated by non-policy goals such as turning out voters to affect elections rather than to enact the specific initiative, which the authors label crypto-initiatives. *See* Thad Kousser & Mathew D. McCubbins, *Social Choice, Crypto-Initiatives, and Policymaking by Direct Democracy* 78 S. CAL. L. REV. 949 (2004). Kousser and McCubbins discuss two sets of sequential initiatives, in Oregon and in Massachusetts, that they contend illustrate voting cycles, the first involving related tax and education-funding measures, and the second involving a ban on radioactive waste disposal followed by a decision not to ban nuclear waste producing electrical power plants. *Id.* at 965–66. In each instance, a later plebiscite cut back on the more expansive plebiscite that preceded it, resulting in a more moderate policy. For an empirical analysis of some of claims set out in the Kousser and McCubbins article, see Matsusaka, *supra*, at 202.

certain basic criteria be met including, most notably, sufficient turnout to ensure that voting preferences are meaningfully representative of the electorate as a whole.[76] Where concerns about agency costs and interest group influence are high, such as on issues of taxation and spending, direct democracy has the potential to constrain the decisions of elected officials. States with an initiative process are more likely to adopt institutional reforms that impose tax and expenditure limits on the government and to require supermajority vote for tax increases. States permitting initiatives also tend to fund more specific governmental services with user fees, rather than with broad-based taxes that facilitate wealth redistribution, as compared to states without initiatives. Referendums operate as a check against certain progressive, or redistributive, tax policies. Taxing and spending, along with the salaries of senior executive officials, are generally lower overall in states with than without initiatives.[77]

Access to the initiative process has been especially instrumental in states that have enacted term limits, an issue on which agency costs arising from legislator self-interest are likely to be high: "[Twenty-two] of 24 initiative states adopted term limits for their congressmen or state legislatures, compared to two of 26 noninitiative states."[78] Professor Ilya Somin has found that states with the initiative have been more likely to adopt laws that place strong limits on the power of the government to take private property for public

---

Maxwell Stearns responds that these examples instead illustrate a shift in voting preferences along a single normative dimension, with the latter plebiscite in each instance reflecting a collective sense of initially having taken the policy direction too far. *See* Maxwell L. Stearns, *Direct (Anti-) Democracy*, 80 GEO. WASH. L. REV. 311 (2012). Stearns nonetheless agrees with the authors that a form of cycling, which he labels "plebiscycles," are prone to be suppressed in plebiscite voting. These cycles potentially arise when the policy dimension implicated by the voter initiative or referendum is combined with the alternative dimension, one generally disallowed formal consideration in the ballot measure, involving whether voters would have preferred to leave the matter to legislative resolution and compromise, along with a host of other issues, rather than insisting that it be resolved by them via plebiscite. *See id.* at 362–69.

[76] *See* Garrett, *supra* note 69, at 140.

[77] Matsusaka, *supra* note 74, at 195–96.

[78] *Id.* at 195. According to the National Conference of State Legislatures' (NCSL), there are twenty-six initiative and referendum states and fifteen term-limited states. Comparing the lists reveals that thirteen of the twenty-six initiative and referendum states are also term-limited states. The NCSL data was last updated in December 2015. *See Initiative and Referendum States*, NAT'L CONF. ST. LEGISLATURES (DEC. 2015), http://www.ncsl.org/research/elections-and-campaigns/chart-of-the-initiative-states.aspx. Only fifteen states have term limits for state legislators. *See The Term-Limited States*, NAT'L CONF. ST. LEGISLATURES (Mar. 3, 2013), http://www.ncsl.org/research/about-state-legislatures/chart-of-term-limits-states.aspx; Niraj Chockshi, *Are Term Limits for State Lawmakers a Good Idea?*, WASH. POST (Mar. 21, 2014), https://www.washingtonpost.com/blogs/govbeat/wp/2014/03/21/are-term-limits-for-state-lawmakers-a-good-idea/?utm_term=.e15e30ad9a80.

By mid-1995, voters or legislatures in twenty-three states had approved Congressional term limits. Reformers during the early 1990s used initiative and referendum to put Congressional term limits on the ballot in twenty-four states. Voters in eight of those states approved the Congressional term limits. *See* Dana Priest & William Claiborne, *Voters in Several States, D.C. Adopt Limits for Legislators*, WASH. POST, Nov. 9, 1994, at A25, https://www.washingtonpost.com/wp-srv/politics/special/termlimits/stories/110994.htm. However, in May 1995, the U.S. Supreme Court ruled 5–4 in *U.S. Term Limits, Inc. v. Thornton*, 514 U.S. 779 (1995), that states cannot impose term limits upon their federal representatives or senators. *See* SULA P. RICHARDSON, CONG. RESEARCH SERV. 96–152, TERM LIMITS FOR MEMBERS OF CONGRESS: STATE ACTIVITY (updated Apr. 26, 2000). This ruling halted the federal term limit campaign; however, term limits upon state legislatures remain in force in fifteen states. *See State Legislative Term Limits*, U.S. TERM LIMITS, https://termlimits.org/term-limits/state-term-limits/state-legislative-term-limits/ (last visited Oct. 27, 2017).

development following the Supreme Court decision, *Kelo v. City of New London*,[79] another issue on which agency costs and special interest activity might be high, whereas he claims that non-initiative states have adopted largely symbolic reforms.[80]

Direct democracy appears to be effective for grassroots citizen groups seeking to end-run traditional political processes in which well-funded and sophisticated interest groups tend to hold a comparative advantage in influencing policy.[81] John Matsusaka claims empirical support for a correlation between direct democracy institutions (including its use in Switzerland) and various measures of governance quality, such as the efficient provision of governmental services.[82] Some scholars argue that direct democracy is effective in enacting laws that manifest community values, such as those related to the death penalty, parental consent for abortions, same-sex marriage, and prohibitions against employment discrimination.[83]

Direct democracy facilitates a closer matching of policies to preferences of the median electoral voter along particular policy dimensions by disaggregating political issues into more discrete choices. Professor Elizabeth Garrett explains that political candidates hold views that represent " 'bundles' of issues, so a voter might decide to support a candidate because, on balance, her positions more closely track the voter's preferences even though the lawmaker's position on a particular issue is far from the voter's."[84] The initiative process, by contrast, enables citizens to separate out these bundles into discrete policy choices and invites an up or down vote on each separate issue. Some authors thus contend that this process produces a closer match between citizen preferences and policy outcomes.[85]

In a study titled *Direct (Anti-)Democracy*, Professor Maxwell Stearns employed social choice theory to assess whether plebiscites, including voter initiatives and referendums, further democratic values. As the title suggests, Stearns concludes, counterintuitively, that plebiscites bear features that are correlated with anti-democratic institutions.[86] Rather than accept general statements about plebiscites and whether they are normatively sound or unsound in establishing policy, Stearns reasoned that an objective measure of such claims involves identifying the social choice profile of plebiscites, using the Arrow's Theorem criteria, and then comparing the resulting profile with the social choice profile of legislatures, our most democratic institution, and with appellate courts, our least democratic institution. Stearns demonstrates that the social choice profile of plebiscites matches that of appellate courts, and is opposite that of legislatures, thereby rendering direct democracy anti-democratic.

---

[79] 545 U.S. 469 (2005).

[80] Ilya Somin, *The Limits of Backlash: Assessing the Political Response to* Kelo, 93 MINN. L. REV. 2100 (2009).

[81] ELISABETH R. GERBER, THE POPULIST PARADOX: INTEREST GROUP INFLUENCE AND THE PROMISE OF DIRECT LEGISLATION (1999).

[82] *See* Matsusaka, *supra* note 74, at 201 (summarizing studies).

[83] *See id.* at 195 (summarizing studies).

[84] Garrett, *supra* note 69, at 140.

[85] Timothy Besley & Stephen Coate, *Issue Unbundling via Citizens' Initiatives* (Nat'l Bureau of Econ. Research, Working Paper No. 8036, 2000); ROBERT D. COOTER, THE STRATEGIC CONSTITUTION 143–48 (2000).

[86] Stearns, *supra* note 75.

Recall that the social choice profile reveals that legislatures relax independence but adhere to range. Legislative bodies, through formal or informal practices, generally allow members to assess all conceivable ordinal rankings over available legislative options.[87] Legislatures relax independence through a variety of institutions that allow for the commodification of legislative preferences, rather than merely permitting ordinal preference rankings. Such practices include logrolling, which allows members of the legislature to register intensities of preference, not merely the binary choice to support or oppose a bill. By contrast, through a variety of rules such as outcome voting and the presumptive adherence to precedent, appellate courts relax range, thereby ensuring outcomes even when member preferences are intransitive in individual cases or in groups of cases over time.[88] As a result of these rules, combined with the narrowest grounds doctrine, and standing and other justiciability rules, appellate courts generally adhere to independence. With narrow exceptions,[89] appellate jurists are almost invariably motivated to vote sincerely on their preferred resolution of case outcomes and on the issues embedded within those cases.

Stearns contends that because of the large number of electoral voters, vote trading, or other forms of strategic voting, are almost invariably impractical. Those who vote in plebiscites are motivated to vote sincerely to move policy in their preferred direction. In addition, at the point at which a plebiscite is balloted, barring the highly unlikely event of a tie, as a result of the large number of voters, there is almost always a guaranteed outcome. This holds true even if the voters might have preferred to avoid resolving the substantive issue by throwing it, along with many other issues, into the legislative hopper, where legislators can negotiate based not only on ordinal, but also cardinal, preferences. The resulting social choice profile of plebiscites, like that of appellate courts, adheres to independence but relaxes range. Although this might seem counterintuitive in that plebiscite voters are directly involved in the policy decision, on closer reflection, Stearns maintains, it becomes less so. Unlike legislators, referendum voters lack the means to commodify preferences, and like judicial review, the plebiscites remove issues for legislative consideration, where intensities of preference affect outcomes. Although plebiscites move policy closer to the median voter along particular issue dimensions, Stearns contends that this is not necessarily a democratic virtue; instead, over a larger bundle of issues, the electorate often eschews median positions on various specific policy issue dimensions to allow larger packages of resolved issues that account for both ordinal and cardinal preferences.

Stearns further describes a political anomaly concerning direct democracy. Although this characterization is necessarily overgeneralized, many conservatives tend to favor direct democracy and express skepticism over judicial review, whereas many liberals tend to hold the opposite predilections. And yet, these institutions share a common social choice profile with the dynamic of removing discrete issues from legislative consideration. Stearns posits that the principle of removal is not motivating ideologies respecting judicial review versus plebiscites; rather, the ideological divergence is motivated by the differing substantive results that voters believe each institution is more likely to produce. Stearns

---

87 *See supra* Chapter 21 (discussing social choice profile of legislatures).

88 *See supra* Chapter 21 (discussing social choice profile of appellate courts).

89 *See supra* Chapter 21 (discussing limited opportunities for strategic Supreme Court voting).

contends that institutional preferences are more likely based on partisan ideology than based on a core commitment to democratic values. Stearns is not entirely opposed to direct democracy, which he claims is beneficial in some limited contexts, but he is concerned about its use to thwart substantive policies over which, for example, identifiable minority groups, likely to be outnumbered in such process, hold intense preferences that are more capable of being expressed in the legislative process.[90]

Which account of direct democracy do you find most persuasive? Does voter satisfaction with particular results demonstrate that direct democracy is sound policy? That it is democratic? Is the relevant criterion for analysis the median voter along a single issue dimension for each issue? Or is it instead satisfaction respecting the aggregate bundle of issues? Should policy be assessed based on ordinal preferences, cardinal preferences, or a combination? Does it matter which policy is being assessed? Is there a way to test empirically which regime is preferred? How does this relate to the problem of assessing voter mobility given that people locate in jurisdictions based on bundled goods and services, rather than based on any one of them? Is it possible that dissatisfaction with direct democracy would motivate those who reside in affected jurisdictions to relocate? Why or why not?

IV. CONSTITUTIONAL AMENDMENT

While constitutional architects seek to embed durable values into the constitutions they craft,[91] they also are concerned about the danger of obsolescence. Invariably, constitutions include amending provisions.[92] These include provisions that seek to strike the appropriate balance in promoting electoral accountability (reducing agency costs) and ensuring proper functioning (reducing decision or external costs). Whether or not constitutions are ever truly drafted behind a veil of ignorance, the process of amending certainly takes place with affected persons well aware of their respective positions in society. Not surprisingly, therefore, the process of constitutional amendment necessarily embraces many of the same interest-group and agency-cost dynamics that characterize ordinary legislative processes.

Building upon these assumptions, Donald Boudreaux and Adam Pritchard have proposed a public choice model of the constitutional amendment process.[93] Their analysis suggests the irony that interest groups that are sufficiently powerful to be the object of constitutional constraint are likely also to be best poised to exert sufficient influence to amend the very constitutions that constrain them. The authors observe that an interest

---

[90] Stearns, *supra* note 75, at 380–83. For empirical studies calling into question claims that direct democracy is conducive to majority tyranny, thus allowing laws that are discriminatory against unpopular minorities to pass, see Todd Donovan & Shaun Bowler, *Direct Democracy and Minority Rights: An Extension*, 42 AM. J. POL. SCI. 1020 (1998); Zoltan L. Hajnal, Elisabeth R. Gerber & Hugh Louch, *Minorities and Direct Legislation: Evidence from California Ballot Proposition Elections*, 64 J. POL. 154 (2002).

[91] *See* William A. Niskanen, *Conditions Affecting the Survival of Constitutional Rules*, CONST. POL. ECON., Spring/Summer 1990, at 53.

[92] For a formal model of the optimal decision-making rule for constitutional amendments, see Thomas F. Schaller, *Consent for Change: Article V and the Constitutional Amendment Process*, 8 CONST. POL. ECON. 195 (1997).

[93] Donald J. Boudreaux & A.C. Pritchard, *Rewriting the Constitution: An Economic Analysis of the Constitutional Amendment Process*, 62 FORDHAM L. REV. 111 (1993).

group seeking favorable governmental action can pursue that result through either of two means, ordinary legislation or a constitutional amendment. A constitutional amendment is more costly to secure because amending demands a greater number of successful successive supermajority coalitions. For that very reason, however, constitutional amendments are more durable once procured.[94] As a result, interest groups will pursue a constitutional amendment where the benefits of enhanced durability exceed the marginal costs of amending as compared with legislating.

Boudreaux and Pritchard claim that the incentives of interest groups to pursue a constitutional amendment rather than ordinary legislation is a function of two variables, first, "maintenance costs," and second, the strength and timing of opposition. Maintenance costs are "the costs an interest group incurs over time in order to continue to lobby effectively for privileges conferred by the government."[95] The authors posit that "interest groups with high maintenance costs have a greater demand for constitutional protection of their privileges than do groups with low maintenance costs."[96]

The authors cast this theory as an intertemporal or dynamic extension of Mancur Olson's theory of collective action.[97] Whereas Olson focused primarily on the costs associated with initial organization, Boudreaux and Pritchard focus on the costs of maintaining group organization over time and on the rational response of other interest groups likely to be affected by such maintenance costs. For instance, an interest group that expects to become larger and more diffuse over time might fear a risk of a future decline in political influence as its organization and maintenance costs predictably rise. Such a group will rationally find more value in the possibility of a constitutional amendment than a group that predicts a continued similar composition over time and thus no discernible change in its ability to exert beneficial political influence in the future. As examples, the authors suggest that such ideologically motivated interest groups as advocates for temperance in the early twentieth century might have anticipated higher maintenance costs over time than groups characterized by narrowly defined self-interest, including labor unions or industry trade groups. As a result, the authors predict that interest groups that coalesce around ideological goals will be more likely to lobby for a constitutional amendment, whereas interest groups defined around a particular set of financial concerns might find legislative lobbying more cost effective.

The authors contend that a second factor affecting the choice between pursuing an amendment and pursuing legislation is the expectation over time of well-organized political opposition. Presently weak opposition that is expected to grow might make it more attractive to pursue a constitutional amendment. Conversely, when future opposition is expected to be weak, interest groups are apt to prefer investing in the legislative process.

---

[94] Recall that the present value of the stream of economic rents to be transferred through a given law will be a function of both the value transferred each period as well as the expected durability of the law. *See supra* Chapter 11.

[95] *See* Boudreaux & Pritchard, *supra* note 93, at 118.

[96] *Id.*

[97] For a discussion of Olson's theory, see *supra* Chapter 11.

Do you find the Boudreaux and Pritchard model persuasive? To what extent does it help to explain specific amendments to the United States Constitution? Does it help to explain the enactment of the Bill of Rights? Does it help to explain unsuccessful efforts to pursue amendments to secure an item veto, a balanced budget, or term limits? Why or why not? The authors also observe that although the Constitution has been amended to limit presidential terms, proposals to limit congressional terms have failed. They attribute this result to the fact that the President has no role under Article V in the amending process. Do you find this argument persuasive? Why or why not?

Mark Crain and Robert Tollison have also argued that interest groups will seek a constitutional amendment where it is an efficient way to increase the expected durability of a desired policy.[98] The authors claim that where other governmental mechanisms, including case decisions by an independent judiciary, prolong the durability of a legislatively procured benefit (and therefore the expected value to the interest group), this will temper demand for pursuing more costly constitutional amendments, a prediction that they corroborate empirically.

Subsequent studies corroborate that constitutional amendments are more common when other means of increasing the expected duration of interest group bargains are weaker.[99] For example, states with dependent judiciaries are likely to have longer and more frequently amended constitutions, indicating a substitution between the two mechanisms for increasing durability. The relatively small number of amendments to the federal constitution might therefore reflect the effectiveness of the federal judiciary in securing interest group deals, consistent with the Landes and Posner analysis.[100]

An alternative account for the infrequency of federal constitutional amendments focuses on the role of the Supreme Court in effectively amending the Constitution through judicial decisions. In this account, the infrequency of amendments is not due to the ability of interest groups to secure long term deals in legislation enforced by the independent judiciary, but rather it is due to the ability of interest groups to secure changes to the Constitution through judicial interpretation in independent courts. Consider, for example, Justice Ginsburg's explanation that the Equal Rights Amendment, which failed ratification, proved unnecessary since the Supreme Court itself basically accomplished the same result doctrinally through its gender-based equal protection jurisprudence.[101] In turn, interest groups would be expected to pursue in any given case the strategy—formal

---

[98] W. Mark Crain & Robert D. Tollison, *Constitutional Change in an Interest-Group Perspective*, 8 J. LEGAL STUD. 165 (1979).

[99] Gary M. Anderson, Delores T. Martin, William F. Shughart II & Robert D. Tollison, *Behind the Veil: The Political Economy of Constitutional Change*, *in* PREDICTING POLITICS: ESSAYS IN EMPIRICAL PUBLIC CHOICE 89 (W. Mark Crain & Robert D. Tollison eds., 1990). Other structures such as the executive veto would presumably be relevant as well.

[100] *See supra* part I.B.

[101] *See, e.g.*, Jeffrey Rosen, *The New Look of Liberalism on the Court*, N.Y. TIMES MAG. (Oct. 5, 1997), http://www.nytimes.com/1997/10/05/magazine/the-new-look-of-liberalism-on-the-court.html (discussing speech by Justice Ginsburg in which she stated: "There is no practical difference between what has evolved and the E.R.A.," and that "I would still like it as a symbol to see the E.R.A. in the Constitution for my granddaughter.").

amendment versus judicial interpretation—that provides the greatest likelihood of success.[102] Can you reconcile these two accounts? If not, which is more persuasive? Why?

Adam Pritchard and Todd Zywicki have further drawn on public choice insights to inform the process of informal amendment through the judicial construction of constitutional provisions. The authors focus specifically on the use of tradition to inform constitutional interpretation.[103] In theory, they argue, tradition can be a valuable source of constitutional change. The authors maintain that properly understood, the development of tradition is a consensual, bottom-up process for developing new, widely shared supermajoritarian norms that can subsequently serve as a basis for new constitutional precommitments. Moreover, because of the spontaneous, consensual roots of tradition, it is resistant to interest group manipulation.

In fact, the authors claim, the Supreme Court has long looked to tradition as a source of constitutional values. But Pritchard and Zywicki criticize the sources of tradition used in practice by the Supreme Court. They focus on the two dominant approaches: first, that of Justice Scalia, which looked to the historical practices of state regulation of a given activity as a source of tradition, and second, that of Justice Souter, which relied upon constitutional common law as developed by the Supreme Court.

The authors reject Scalia's approach on the ground that it allows state legislatures, which are subject to interest group pressures, to inform the permissible scope of constitutional limits on the scope of their own exercise of regulatory powers. In addition, they note, Scalia's approach would create a one-way "ratchet" in terms of limiting recognized constitutional rights since any example of a contrary state law would be a datum against recognizing the claimed constitutional tradition. Pritchard and Zywicki also reject Souter's approach because it merely substitutes different agency costs (by judges rather than legislators) and different special interests (those with a comparative advantage in litigation rather than in legislation). Moreover, the authors claim that rather than producing new norms through a decentralized, consensus-building process shaped by feedback, the articulation of new rules by the Supreme Court is a highly centralized process made by a handful of Justices with minimal feedback from the populace.

Pritchard and Zywicki tentatively propose an alternative judicial "finding" model of tradition. In this model, the best source for identifying tradition returns the Justices to state constitutions, which are a bottom up source arising through a sufficiently complex set of processes so as to avoid the most obvious manifestations of interest group influence. The authors suggest, for example, that if three-quarters of the states came to recognize a new constitutional right (such as a right to privacy) or a new constitutional remedy (such as the exclusionary rule), the Supreme Court could claim that these rights have a root source in a legitimate American set of constitutional traditions.

Do you find this analysis persuasive? Does it set too high a standard for articulating constitutional rights? Why or why not? Does it set too low a standard? To what extent is it consistent with the framework set out by Buchanan and Tullock? Does this approach avoid the difficulties associated with formal amending under Article V? Why or why not?

---

[102] *See* Pritchard & Zywicki, *supra* note 3.

[103] *Id.*

V. APPLICATION

In *Romer v. Evans*,[104] the Supreme Court addressed the constitutionality of Colorado Amendment 2, a 1992 statewide referendum affecting access by gays, lesbians, and other sexual minorities to various protections under state and municipal law. Prior to adopting the amendment, several Colorado municipalities had "banned discrimination in many transactions and activities, including housing, employment, education, public accommodations, and health and welfare services"[105] on a variety of bases including sexual orientation. Amendment 2 effectively repealed these ordinances by proclaiming that no state or municipal law shall give protected status on the basis of sexual orientation.

The amendment, which Justice Kennedy, writing for the *Romer* majority, reproduced in its entirety, provides as follows:

> No Protected Status Based on Homosexual, Lesbian or Bisexual Orientation. Neither the State of Colorado, through any of its branches or departments, nor any of its agencies, political subdivisions, municipalities or school districts, shall enact, adopt or enforce any statute, regulation, ordinance or policy whereby homosexual, lesbian or bisexual orientation, conduct, practices or relationships shall constitute or otherwise be the basis of or entitle any person or class of persons to have or claim any minority status, quota preferences, protected status or claim of discrimination. This Section of the Constitution shall be in all respects self-executing.[106]

Justice Kennedy began his opinion by explaining how the amendment does more than simply repeal specific protections on the basis of "homosexual, lesbian or bisexual orientation, conduct, practices or relationships." Kennedy explained:

> Yet Amendment 2, in explicit terms, does more than repeal or rescind these provisions. It prohibits all legislative, executive or judicial action at any level of state or local government designed to protect the named class, a class we shall refer to as homosexual persons or gays and lesbians. . . .[107]

While Justice Kennedy agreed with the Colorado Supreme Court that the amendment violated the Constitution, he disagreed that the relevant test was strict scrutiny. Justice Kennedy began his analysis by considering the argument the state advanced in support of the amendment:

> The State's principal argument in defense of Amendment 2 is that it puts gays and lesbians in the same position as all other persons. So, the State says, the measure does no more than deny homosexuals special rights. This reading of the amendment's language is implausible. We rely not upon our own interpretation of the amendment but upon the authoritative construction of Colorado's Supreme Court. The state court, deeming it unnecessary to determine the full extent of the amendment's reach, found it invalid even on a

---

[104] 517 U.S. 620 (1996).

[105] *Id.* at 624.

[106] *Id.* (quoting Colorado Amendment 2).

[107] *Id.*

modest reading of its implications. The critical discussion of the amendment, set out in *Evans I*, is as follows:

> The immediate objective of Amendment 2 is, at a minimum, to repeal existing statutes, regulations, ordinances, and policies of state and local entities that barred discrimination based on sexual orientation. . . .
>
> Sweeping and comprehensive is the change in legal status effected by this law. So much is evident from the ordinances the Colorado Supreme Court declared would be void by operation of Amendment 2. Homosexuals, by state decree, are put in a solitary class with respect to transactions and relations in both the private and governmental spheres. The amendment withdraws from homosexuals, but no others, specific legal protection from the injuries caused by discrimination, and it forbids reinstatement of these laws and policies.
>
> The change Amendment 2 works in the legal status of gays and lesbians in the private sphere is far reaching, both on its own terms and when considered in light of the structure and operation of modern antidiscrimination laws. That structure is well illustrated by contemporary statutes and ordinances prohibiting discrimination by providers of public accommodations. "At common law, innkeepers, smiths, and others who 'made profession of a public employment,' were prohibited from refusing, without good reason, to serve a customer." The duty was a general one and did not specify protection for particular groups. The common-law rules, however, proved insufficient in many instances, and it was settled early that the Fourteenth Amendment did not give Congress a general power to prohibit discrimination in public accommodations. In consequence, most States have chosen to counter discrimination by enacting detailed statutory schemes.[108]

After explaining that "Colorado's state and municipal laws"[109] specify a broader class of covered businesses than was customary under the common law, Kennedy described the class of persons "within [the] ambit of [the laws'] protection," as follows:[110]

> Enumeration [of groups of persons] is the essential device used to make the duty not to discriminate concrete and to provide guidance for those who must comply. In following this approach, Colorado's state and local governments have not limited antidiscrimination laws to groups that have so far been given the protection of heightened equal protection scrutiny under our cases. Rather, they set forth an extensive catalog of traits which cannot be the basis for discrimination, including age, military status, marital status, pregnancy, parenthood, custody of a minor child, political affiliation, physical or mental disability of an individual or of his or her associates—and, in recent times, sexual orientation.
>
> Amendment 2 bars homosexuals from securing protection against the injuries that these public-accommodations laws address. That in itself is a

108 *Id.* at 626–28 (citations omitted).

109 *Id.* at 628.

110 *Id.*

severe consequence, but there is more. Amendment 2, in addition, nullifies specific legal protections for this targeted class in all transactions in housing, sale of real estate, insurance, health and welfare services, private education, and employment.

Not confined to the private sphere, Amendment 2 also operates to repeal and forbid all laws or policies providing specific protection for gays or lesbians from discrimination by every level of Colorado government. . . .

. . . .

. . . [E]ven if, as we doubt, homosexuals could find some safe harbor in laws of general application, we cannot accept the view that Amendment 2's prohibition on specific legal protections does no more than deprive homosexuals of special rights. To the contrary, the amendment imposes a special disability upon those persons alone. Homosexuals are forbidden the safeguards that others enjoy or may seek without constraint. They can obtain specific protection against discrimination only by enlisting the citizenry of Colorado to amend the State Constitution or perhaps, on the State's view, by trying to pass helpful laws of general applicability. This is so no matter how local or discrete the harm, no matter how public and widespread the injury. We find nothing special in the protections Amendment 2 withholds. These are protections taken for granted by most people either because they already have them or do not need them; these are protections against exclusion from an almost limitless number of transactions and endeavors that constitute ordinary civic life in a free society.[111]

After describing the reach of Amendment 2, Justice Kennedy explained why it violates the Constitution even under rational basis scrutiny:

The Fourteenth Amendment's promise that no person shall be denied the equal protection of the laws must coexist with the practical necessity that most legislation classifies for one purpose or another, with resulting disadvantage to various groups or persons. We have attempted to reconcile the principle with the reality by stating that, if a law neither burdens a fundamental right nor targets a suspect class, we will uphold the legislative classification so long as it bears a rational relation to some legitimate end.

Amendment 2 fails, indeed defies, even this conventional inquiry. First, the amendment has the peculiar property of imposing a broad and undifferentiated disability on a single named group, an exceptional and, as we shall explain, invalid form of legislation. Second, its sheer breadth is so discontinuous with the reasons offered for it that the amendment seems inexplicable by anything but animus toward the class it affects; it lacks a rational relationship to legitimate state interests.

. . . By requiring that the classification bear a rational relationship to an independent and legitimate legislative end, we ensure that classifications are not drawn for the purpose of disadvantaging the group burdened by the law.

---

[111] *Id.* at 628–29, 631 (citations omitted).

Amendment 2 confounds this normal process of judicial review. It is at once too narrow and too broad. It identifies persons by a single trait and then denies them protection across the board. The resulting disqualification of a class of persons from the right to seek specific protection from the law is unprecedented in our jurisprudence. The absence of precedent for Amendment 2 is itself instructive. . . .

It is not within our constitutional tradition to enact laws of this sort. . . . A law declaring that in general it shall be more difficult for one group of citizens than for all others to seek aid from the government is itself a denial of equal protection of the laws in the most literal sense. . . .

. . . .

A . . . related point is that laws of the kind now before us raise the inevitable inference that the disadvantage imposed is born of animosity toward the class of persons affected. "[I]f the constitutional conception of 'equal protection of the laws' means anything, it must at the very least mean that a bare . . . desire to harm a politically unpopular group cannot constitute a *legitimate* governmental interest." . . . Amendment 2, however, in making a general announcement that gays and lesbians shall not have any particular protections from the law, inflicts on them immediate, continuing, and real injuries that outrun and belie any legitimate justifications that may be claimed for it. We conclude that, in addition to the far-reaching deficiencies of Amendment 2 that we have noted, the principles it offends, in another sense, are conventional and venerable; a law must bear a rational relationship to a legitimate governmental purpose, and Amendment 2 does not.

. . . .

. . . Amendment 2 violates the Equal Protection Clause, and the judgment of the Supreme Court of Colorado is affirmed.[112]

Justice Scalia, with whom the Chief Justice and Justice Thomas joined, dissented:

The Court has mistaken a Kulturkampf for a fit of spite. The constitutional amendment before us here is not the manifestation of a "bare . . . desire to harm" homosexuals, but is rather a modest attempt by seemingly tolerant Coloradans to preserve traditional sexual mores against the efforts of a politically powerful minority to revise those mores through use of the laws. That objective, and the means chosen to achieve it, are not only unimpeachable under any constitutional doctrine hitherto pronounced (hence the opinion's heavy reliance upon principles of righteousness rather than judicial holdings); they have been specifically approved by the Congress of the United States and by this Court.

In holding that homosexuality cannot be singled out for disfavorable treatment, the Court contradicts a decision, unchallenged here, pronounced only 10 years ago, and places the prestige of this institution behind the proposition that opposition to homosexuality is as reprehensible as racial or

---

[112] *Id.* at 631–36 (citations omitted).

> religious bias. Whether it is or not is *precisely* the cultural debate that gave rise to the Colorado constitutional amendment (and to the preferential laws against which the amendment was directed). Since the Constitution of the United States says nothing about this subject, it is left to be resolved by normal democratic means, including the democratic adoption of provisions in state constitutions. This Court has no business imposing upon all Americans the resolution favored by the elite class from which the Members of this institution are selected, pronouncing that "animosity" toward homosexuality, is evil. I vigorously dissent.[113]

Justice Scalia began his equal protection analysis by claiming that "[t]he amendment prohibits *special treatment* of homosexuals, and nothing more."[114] Scalia explained:

> [The Amendment] would not affect, for example, a requirement of state law that pensions be paid to all retiring state employees with a certain length of service; homosexual employees, as well as others, would be entitled to that benefit. But it would [for example] prevent the State or any municipality from making death-benefit payments to the "life partner" of a homosexual when it does not make such payments to the long-time roommate of a nonhomosexual employee. . . .
>
> . . . .
>
> . . . The only denial of equal treatment it contends homosexuals have suffered is this: They may not obtain *preferential* treatment without amending the State Constitution. That is to say, the principle underlying the Court's opinion is that one who is accorded equal treatment under the laws, but cannot as readily as others obtain *preferential* treatment under the laws, has been denied equal protection of the laws. If merely stating this alleged "equal protection" violation does not suffice to refute it, our constitutional jurisprudence has achieved terminal silliness.[115]

Justice Scalia then set out an analysis that turns on the nature of lawmaking in a multilevel democracy:

> The central thesis of the Court's reasoning is that any group is denied equal protection when, to obtain advantage (or, presumably, to avoid disadvantage), it must have recourse to a more general and hence more difficult level of political decisionmaking than others. The world has never heard of such a principle, which is why the Court's opinion is so long on emotive utterance and so short on relevant legal citation. And it seems to me most unlikely that any multilevel democracy can function under such a principle. For *whenever* a disadvantage is imposed, or conferral of a benefit is prohibited, at one of the higher levels of democratic decisionmaking (*i.e.*, by the state legislature rather than local government, or by the people at large in the state

---

[113] *Id.* at 636 (Scalia, J., dissenting) (citations omitted).

[114] *Id.* at 638.

[115] *Id.* at 638–39.

constitution rather than the legislature), the affected group has (under this theory) been denied equal protection. . . . [T]he Court's theory is unheard of.

. . . The Court's entire novel theory rests upon the proposition that there is something *special*—something that cannot be justified by normal "rational basis" analysis—in making a disadvantaged group (or a nonpreferred group) resort to a higher decisionmaking level. That proposition finds no support in law or logic.[116]

Justice Scalia then described what he viewed as a rational justification for the enacted law:

I turn next to whether there was a legitimate rational basis for the substance of the constitutional amendment—for the prohibition of special protection for homosexuals. It is unsurprising that the Court avoids discussion of this question, since the answer is so obviously yes. The case most relevant to the issue before us today is not even mentioned in the Court's opinion: In *Bowers* v. *Hardwick*, we held that the Constitution does not prohibit what virtually all States had done from the founding of the Republic until very recent years—making homosexual conduct a crime. . . . If it is constitutionally permissible for a State to make homosexual conduct criminal, surely it is constitutionally permissible for a State to enact other laws merely *disfavoring* homosexual conduct. . . . And *a fortiori* it is constitutionally permissible for a State to adopt a provision *not even* disfavoring homosexual conduct, but merely prohibiting all levels of state government from bestowing *special protections* upon homosexual conduct. . . .

. . . If it is rational to criminalize the conduct, surely it is rational to deny special favor and protection to those with a self-avowed tendency or desire to engage in the conduct. . . .[117]

Justice Scalia then described why he regarded the amendment as a reasonable exercise of regulatory power:

First, as to its eminent reasonableness. The Court's opinion contains grim, disapproving hints that Coloradans have been guilty of "animus" or "animosity" toward homosexuality, as though that has been established as un-American. Of course it is our moral heritage that one should not hate any human being or class of human beings. But I had thought that one could consider certain conduct reprehensible—murder, for example, or polygamy, or cruelty to animals—and could exhibit even "animus" toward such conduct. Surely that is the only sort of "animus" at issue here: moral disapproval of homosexual conduct, the same sort of moral disapproval that produced the centuries-old criminal laws that we held constitutional in *Bowers*. The Colorado amendment does not, to speak entirely precisely, prohibit giving favored status to people who are *homosexuals*; they can be favored for many reasons—for example, because they are senior citizens or members of racial minorities. But

---

[116] *Id.* at 639–40.

[117] *Id.* at 640–42 (citation and footnote omitted).

it prohibits giving them favored status *because of their homosexual conduct*—that is, it prohibits favored status for *homosexuality*.

But though Coloradans are, as I say, *entitled* to be hostile toward homosexual conduct, the fact is that the degree of hostility reflected by Amendment 2 is the smallest conceivable. . . . Colorado not only is one of the 25 States that have repealed their antisodomy laws, but was among the first to do so. But the society that eliminates criminal punishment for homosexual acts does not necessarily abandon the view that homosexuality is morally wrong and socially harmful; often, abolition simply reflects the view that enforcement of such criminal laws involves unseemly intrusion into the intimate lives of citizens.

There is a problem, however, which arises when criminal sanction of homosexuality is eliminated but moral and social disapprobation of homosexuality is meant to be retained. The Court cannot be unaware of that problem; it is evident in many cities of the country, and occasionally bubbles to the surface of the news, in heated political disputes over such matters as the introduction into local schools of books teaching that homosexuality is an optional and fully acceptable "alternative life style." The problem (a problem, that is, for those who wish to retain social disapprobation of homosexuality) is that, because those who engage in homosexual conduct tend to reside in disproportionate numbers in certain communities, and, of course, care about homosexual-rights issues much more ardently than the public at large, they possess political power much greater than their numbers, both locally and statewide. Quite understandably, they devote this political power to achieving not merely a grudging social toleration, but full social acceptance, of homosexuality.

By the time Coloradans were asked to vote on Amendment 2, their exposure to homosexuals' quest for social endorsement was not limited to newspaper accounts of happenings in places such as New York, Los Angeles, San Francisco, and Key West. Three Colorado cities—Aspen, Boulder, and Denver—had enacted ordinances that listed "sexual orientation" as an impermissible ground for discrimination, equating the moral disapproval of homosexual conduct with racial and religious bigotry. The phenomenon had even appeared statewide: The Governor of Colorado had signed an executive order pronouncing that "in the State of Colorado we recognize the diversity in our pluralistic society and strive to bring an end to discrimination in any form," and directing state agency-heads to "ensure non-discrimination" in hiring and promotion based on, among other things, "sexual orientation." I do not mean to be critical of these legislative successes; homosexuals are as entitled to use the legal system for reinforcement of their moral sentiments as is the rest of society. But they are subject to being countered by lawful, democratic countermeasures as well.

That is where Amendment 2 came in. It sought to counter both the geographic concentration and the disproportionate political power of homosexuals by (1) resolving the controversy at the statewide level, and (2)

> making the election a single-issue contest for both sides. It put directly, to all the citizens of the State, the question: Should homosexuality be given special protection? They answered no. The Court today asserts that this most democratic of procedures is unconstitutional. Lacking any cases to establish that facially absurd proposition, it simply asserts that it *must* be unconstitutional, because it has never happened before.[118]

Justice Scalia then responded to Justice Kennedy's argument that included in the " '[c]onstitution's guarantee of equal protection is the principle that government and each of its parts remain open on impartial terms to all who seek its assistance.' "[119]

> [This proposition] is proved false every time a state law prohibiting or disfavoring certain conduct is passed, because such a law prevents the adversely affected group . . . from changing the policy thus established in "each of [the] parts" of the State. . . .
>
> . . . The Constitutions of the States of Arizona, Idaho, New Mexico, Oklahoma, and Utah *to this day* contain provisions stating that polygamy is "forever prohibited." Polygamists, and those who have a polygamous "orientation," have been "singled out" by these provisions for much more severe treatment than merely denial of favored status; and that treatment can only be changed by achieving amendment of the state constitutions. The Court's disposition today suggests that these provisions are unconstitutional, and that polygamy must be permitted in these States on a state-legislated, or perhaps even local-option, basis—unless, of course, polygamists for some reason have fewer constitutional rights than homosexuals.
>
> . . . .
>
> Has the Court concluded that the perceived social harm of polygamy is a "legitimate concern of government," and the perceived social harm of homosexuality is not?
>
> I strongly suspect that the answer to the last question is yes, which leads me to the last point I wish to make: . . . The Court's stern disapproval of "animosity" towards homosexuality might be compared with what an earlier Court (including the revered Justices Harlan and Bradley) said in *Murphy* v. *Ramsey*, rejecting a constitutional challenge to a United States statute that denied the franchise in federal territories to those who engaged in polygamous cohabitation:
>
> "[C]ertainly no legislation can be supposed more wholesome and necessary in the founding of a free, self-governing commonwealth, fit to take rank as one of the co-ordinate States of the Union, than that which seeks to establish it on the basis of the idea of the family, as consisting in and springing from the union for life of one man and one woman in the holy estate of matrimony; the sure foundation of all that is stable and noble in our civilization; the best guaranty of that reverent morality which

[118] *Id.* at 644–47 (citations omitted).

[119] *Id.* at 647.

> is the source of all beneficent progress in social and political improvement."

I would not myself indulge in such official praise for heterosexual monogamy, because I think it no business of the courts (as opposed to the political branches) to take sides in this culture war.

But the Court today has done so, not only by inventing a novel and extravagant constitutional doctrine to take the victory away from traditional forces, but even by verbally disparaging as bigotry adherence to traditional attitudes. To suggest, for example, that this constitutional amendment springs from nothing more than " 'a bare . . . desire to harm a politically unpopular group,' " is nothing short of insulting. (It is also nothing short of preposterous to call "politically unpopular" a group which enjoys enormous influence in American media and politics, and which, as the trial court here noted, though composing no more than 4% of the population had the support of 46% of the voters on Amendment 2.)

When the Court takes sides in the culture wars, it tends to be with the knights rather than the villains—and more specifically with the Templars, reflecting the views and values of the lawyer class from which the Court's Members are drawn. How that class feels about homosexuality will be evident to anyone who wishes to interview job applicants at virtually any of the Nation's law schools. The interviewer may refuse to offer a job because the applicant is a Republican; because he is an adulterer; because he went to the wrong prep school or belongs to the wrong country club; because he eats snails; because he is a womanizer; because she wears real-animal fur; or even because he hates the Chicago Cubs. But if the interviewer should wish not to be an associate or partner of an applicant because he disapproves of the applicant's homosexuality, *then* he will have violated the pledge which the Association of American Law Schools requires all its member schools to exact from job interviewers: "assurance of the employer's willingness" to hire homosexuals. This law-school view of what "prejudices" must be stamped out may be contrasted with the more plebeian attitudes that apparently still prevail in the United States Congress, which has been unresponsive to repeated attempts to extend to homosexuals the protections of federal civil rights laws.

Today's opinion has no foundation in American constitutional law, and barely pretends to. The people of Colorado have adopted an entirely reasonable provision which does not even disfavor homosexuals in any substantive sense, but merely denies them preferential treatment. Amendment 2 is designed to prevent piecemeal deterioration of the sexual morality favored by a majority of Coloradans, and is not only an appropriate means to that legitimate end, but a means that Americans have employed before. Striking it down is an act, not of judicial judgment, but of political will. I dissent.[120]

---

[120] *Id.* at 647–48, 651–53 (citations omitted).

DISCUSSION QUESTIONS

1. Compare the ruling and logic in *Romer v. Evans* with the Court's holding in *Powers v. Harris*,[121] discussed in Chapter 17. Both cases purport to apply the same level of scrutiny to the law in question, rational basis, and yet they achieve seemingly contrary results in terms of actual deference afforded to the state lawmakers. Can you identify reasons for this seeming divergence in the application of this judicial standard? To what extent is public choice helpful in answering that question? Powers doesnt implicate an insular minority?

(Handwritten margin note: there were available methods for individuals to avoid application of the law in Powers, but not in Romer)

2. Writing for the *Romer* majority, Justice Kennedy suggests that there is a preferred level at which the relevant political decisions concerning antidiscrimination policies in various settings should be made, and in this case it is local rather than state. Writing in dissent, Justice Scalia observes that, traditionally, higher levels of governmental authority retain the power to trump lower levels of governmental authority when their regulatory authority is concurrent. Does public choice provide any guidance as to the preferred level at which such policies should be made? Does Madison's "size" principle say anything about this question? Does Tiebout's exit model? Does Levmore's analysis explaining why local governments tend toward unicameralism, whereas state and federal governments tend toward bicameralism? Does it matter that the challenged law was not secured through ordinary legislation, but rather through a statewide referendum? Why or why not?

3. *Romer* also raises an important issue concerning how to identify operative constitutional baselines. The majority frames Amendment 2 as manifesting hostility toward gays and lesbians by denying them the benefit of statutory protections afforded others. By contrast, the dissent frames the amendment as denying the same group special treatment. Can either framing be said to be "correct"? Can this question be answered without first answering whether gays and lesbians are a suspect or quasi suspect class? Can you identify reasons why Justice Kennedy did not resolve this preliminary issue? Is it possible to know whether this is an example of majority vindication or minority suppression? To what extent, if any, does public choice help in answering these questions?

4. The majority opinion in *Romer* suggests that gays and lesbians might be uniquely subject to political animus or bias because of traditional societal hostility. Justice Scalia's dissent, by contrast, claims that this group holds disproportionate political influence due to such factors as geographic concentration and group cohesion. In other words, the majority suggests that the lawmaking process may be prone to a political market failure at the state level that disproportionately disadvantages gays and lesbians, thus requiring federal judicial correction, whereas the dissent suggests a political market failure at the local level disproportionately benefiting gays and lesbians, thus justifying statewide correction in the form of a referendum. Is it possible to know which of the two claimed (and opposite) forms of political market failure better characterizes the underlying facts? Why or why not?

5. Justice Scalia states: "[Amendment 2] sought to counter both the geographic concentration and the disproportionate political power of homosexuals by (1) resolving the controversy at the statewide level, and (2) making the election a single-issue contest for both sides. It put directly, to all the citizens of the State, the question: Should homosexuality be given special protection?" Consider this argument in light of the discussion of referendums. Does Amendment 2 relate to a subject matter that is well suited to the referendum process? Is this an area in which it is normatively preferable to locate the preference of the median

---

[121] 379 F.3d 1208 (10th Cir. 2004).

electoral voter state-wide on this single issue, or, instead, is it preferable to allow those most affected by the proposed law to register their intensities of preference over this, and a larger basket of issues, within the state legislature? Are the public choice tools developed in this chapter and more broadly in this book helpful in answering this question? Why or why not?

6. Justice Scalia notes that Colorado was one of twenty-five states (at that time) that had repealed prior laws criminalizing homosexual behavior. Does that observation shed any light on the question of whether the *Romer* majority properly relied upon an animus analysis in striking the Colorado initiative down under rational basis scrutiny? Why or why not?

7. After *Romer*, in 2003, the Supreme Court struck down *Bowers v. Hardwick*, in the case of *Lawrence v. Texas*, 539 U.S. 558 (2003). Justice Scalia relies upon *Bowers* in his dissenting opinion in *Romer* as reflecting social norms consistent with Amendment 2. Does the rejection by the Supreme Court of *Bowers* affect the analysis? If so, how? In *Obergefell v. Hodges*,[122] the Supreme Court found a fundamental right under the Due Process Clause to same sex marriage. In its ruling, it also stated that equal protection provides an alternative rationale for its ruling. Kennedy stated:

> The right of same-sex couples to marry that is part of the liberty promised by the Fourteenth Amendment is derived, too, from that Amendment's guarantee of the equal protection of the laws. The Due Process Clause and the Equal Protection Clause are connected in a profound way, though they set forth independent principles. Rights implicit in liberty and rights secured by equal protection may rest on different precepts and are not always co-extensive, yet in some instances each may be instructive as to the meaning and reach of the other. In any particular case one Clause may be thought to capture the essence of the right in a more accurate and comprehensive way, even as the two Clauses may converge in the identification and definition of the right. See *M. L. B.*, 519 U. S., at 120 121; *id.*, at 128 129 (Kennedy, J., concurring in judgment); *Bearden v. Georgia*, 461 U.S. 660, 665 (1983). This interrelation of the two principles furthers our understanding of what freedom is and must become.[123]

Does this discussion help to explain the *Romer* Court's decision not to define sexual minorities as a suspect or quasi-suspect class? Do the tools of public choice help to explain the Court's doctrinal approach in these cases? Why or why not?

122 135 S. Ct. 2584 (2015).

123 135 S. Ct. at 2602–03.

Index